Literature
of Developing
Nations
for Students

National Advisory Board

Literature of Developing Nations
for Students

Presenting Analysis, Context, and Criticism on
Literature of Developing Nations

Volume 1

Elizabeth Bellalouna, Michael L. LaBlanc, and Ira Mark Milne, Editors

GALE GROUP

Detroit
New York
San Francisco
London
Boston
Woodbridge, CT

Literature of Developing Nations for Students

Staff

Series Editors: Elizabeth Bellalouna, Michael L. LaBlanc, and Ira Mark Milne.

Contributing Editors: Elizabeth Bodenmiller, Reginald Carlton, Anne Marie Hacht, Jennifer Smith.

Managing Editor: Dwayne Hayes.

Research: Victoria B. Cariappa, *Research Team Manager.* Maureen Eremic, Barb McNeil, Cheryl Warnock, *Research Specialists.* Andy Malonis, *Technical Training Specialist.* Barbara Leevy, Tamara Nott, Tracie A. Richardson, Robert Whaley, *Research Associates.* Scott Floyd, Nicodemus Ford, Sarah Genik, Timothy Lehnerer, *Research Assistants.*

Permissions: Maria Franklin, *Permissions Manager.* Margaret A. Chamberlain, Edna Hedblad, *Permissions Specialists.* Erin Bealmear, Shalice Shah-Caldwell, Sarah Tomasek, *Permissions Associates.* Debra Freitas, Julie Juengling, Mark Plaza, *Permissions Assistants.*

Manufacturing: Mary Beth Trimper, *Manager, Composition and Electronic Prepress.* Evi Seoud, *Assistant Manager, Composition Purchasing and Electronic Prepress.* Stacy Melson, *Buyer.*

Imaging and Multimedia Content Team: Randy Bassett, *Image Database Supervisor.* Robert Duncan, Dan Newell, *Imaging Specialists.* Pamela A. Reed, *Imaging Coordinator.* Dean Dauphinais, Robyn V. Young, *Senior Image Editors.* Kelly A. Quin, *Image Editor.*

Product Design Team: Kenn Zorn, *Product Design Manager.* Pamela A. E. Galbreath, *Senior Art Director.* Michael Logusz, *Graphic Artist.*

Library of Congress Cataloging-in-Publication Data

Literature of developing nations for students / Michael L. LaBlanc, Elizabeth Bellalouna, Ira Mark Milne, editors.
    v.; cm.
    Includes bibliographical references and index.
    Contents: v. 1. A-L — v. 2. M-Z.
    ISBN 0-7876-4928-7 (set: alk. paper) — ISBN 0-7876-4929-5 (vol. 1) — ISBN 0-7876-4930-9 (vol. 2)
    1. Fiction—Stories, plots, etc. 2. Fiction—History and criticism. 3. Developing countries—Literatures—History and criticism. [1. Fiction—Stories, plots, etc. 2. Fiction—History and criticism. 3. Developing countries—Literatures—History and criticism.] I. LaBlanc, Michael L. II. Bellalouna, Elizabeth. III. Milne, Ira Mark. IV.Title.
    PN3326 .L58 2000
    809'.891724—dc21

                00-056023

Table of Contents

Introduction

Purpose of the Book

The purpose of *Literature of Developing Nations for Students* (*LDNfS*) is to provide readers with a guide to understanding, enjoying, and studying novels by giving them easy access to information about the work. Part of Gale's "For Students" Literature line, *LDNfS* is specifically designed to meet the curricular needs of high school and undergraduate college students and their teachers, as well as the interests of general readers and researchers considering specific literary works. Each volume has entries on literary works by international authors (both men and women) of developing nations.

The information covered in each entry includes an introduction to the literary work and the author of the literary work; a plot summary, to help readers unravel and understand the events in a literary work; descriptions of important characters, including explanation of a given character's role in the literary work as well as discussion about that character's relationship to other characters in the literary work (please note that entries dealing with poems do not have descriptions of characters); analysis of important themes in the literary work; and an explanation of important literary techniques and movements as they are demonstrated in the literary work.

In addition to this material, which helps the readers analyze the literary work itself, students are also provided with important information on the literary and historical background informing each work. This includes a historical context essay, a box comparing the time or place the literary work was written to modern Western culture, a critical overview essay, and excerpts from critical essays on the literary work. A unique feature of *LDNfS* is a specially commissioned overview essay on each literary work, targeted toward the student reader.

To further aid the student in studying and enjoying each literary work, information on media adaptations is provided, as well as reading suggestions for works of fiction and nonfiction on similar themes and topics. Classroom aids include ideas for research papers and lists of critical sources that provide additional material on the literary work.

Selection Criteria

The titles for each volume of *LDNfS* were selected by surveying numerous sources on teaching literature and analyzing course curricula for various school districts. Some of the sources surveyed included: literature anthologies; *Reading Lists for College-Bound Students: The Books Most Recommended by America's Top Colleges;* textbooks on teaching dramas, novels, poems, and short stories; College Board surveys of dramas, novels, and poems commonly studied in high schools; National Council of Teachers of English (NCTE) surveys of dramas, novels, and poems commonly studied in high schools; and the Young Adult Library Services Association (YALSA) list of best books for young adults of the past twenty-five years.

Input was also solicited from our expert advisory board, as well as educators from various areas. Because of the interest in expanding the canon of literature, an emphasis was placed on including as wide a range of international, multicultural, and women authors of developing natiuons as possible. Our advisory board members—current high school and college teachers—helped pare down the list for each volume. If a work was not selected for the present volume, it was often noted as a possibility for a future volume. As always, the editors welcome suggestions for titles to be included in future volumes.

How Each Entry Is Organized

Each entry, or chapter, in *LDNfS* focuses on one literary work. Each entry heading lists the full name of the literary work, the author's name, and the date of publication of the literary work. The following elements are contained in each entry:

- **Introduction:** a brief overview of the literary work which provides information about its first appearance, its literary standing, any controversies surrounding the work, and major conflicts or themes within the work.

- **Author Biography:** this section includes basic facts about the author's life, and focuses on events and times in the author's life that inspired the literary work in question.

- **Plot Summary:** a description of the major events in the literary work. Lengthy summaries are broken down with subheads.

- **Characters:** an alphabetical listing of major characters in the literary work (except poems). Each character name is followed by a brief to an extensive description of the character's role in the literary work, as well as discussion of the character's actions, relationships, and possible motivation.

   Characters are listed alphabetically by last name. If a character is unnamed—for instance, the narrator in *Invisible Man*–the character is listed as ''The Narrator'' and alphabetized as ''Narrator.'' If a character's first name is the only one given, the name will appear alphabetically by that name.

   Variant names are also included for each character. Thus, the full name ''Jean Louise Finch'' would head the listing for the narrator of *To Kill a Mockingbird,* but listed in a separate cross-reference would be the nickname ''Scout Finch.''

- **Themes:** a thorough overview of how the major topics, themes, and issues are addressed within the literary work. Each theme discussed appears in a separate subhead, and is easily accessed through the boldface entries in the Subject/Theme Index.

- **Style:** this section addresses important style elements of the literary work, such as setting, point of view, and narration; important literary devices used, such as imagery, foreshadowing, symbolism; and, if applicable, genres to which the work might have belonged, such as Gothicism or Romanticism. Literary terms are explained within the entry, but can also be found in the Glossary.

- **Literary Heritage:** this section gives a brief overview of the literary tradition (or oral tradition, if a literary tradition is lacking) that lies behind and provides a context for a given work.

- **Historical Context:** This section outlines the social, political, and cultural climate *in which the author lived and the literary work was created.* This section may include descriptions of related historical events, pertinent aspects of daily life in the culture, and the artistic and literary sensibilities of the time in which the work was written. If the literary work is a historical work, information regarding the time in which the literary work is set is also included. Each section is broken down with helpful subheads.

- **Critical Overview:** this section provides background on the critical reputation of the literary work, including bannings or any other public controversies surrounding the work. For older works, this section includes a history of how the literary work was first received and how perceptions of it may have changed over the years; for more recent literary works, direct quotes from early reviews may also be included.

- **Criticism:** an essay commissioned by *LDNfS* which specifically deals with the literary work and is written specifically for the student audience, as well as excerpts from previously published criticism on the work (if available).

- **Sources:** an alphabetical list of critical material quoted in the entry, with full bibliographical information.

- **Further Reading:** an alphabetical list of other critical sources which may prove useful for the student. Includes full bibliographical information and a brief annotation.

In addition, each entry contains the following highlighted sections, set apart from the main text as sidebars:

- **Media Adaptations:** a list of important film and television adaptations of the literary work, including source information. The list also includes stage adaptations, audio recordings, musical adaptations, etc.

- **Topics for Further Study:** a list of potential study questions or research topics dealing with the literary work. This section includes questions related to other disciplines the student may be studying, such as American history, world history, science, math, government, business, geography, economics, psychology, etc.

- **Compare and Contrast Box:** an "at-a-glance" comparison of the cultural and historical differences between the author's time and culture and late twentieth-century Western culture. This box includes pertinent parallels between the major scientific, political, and cultural movements of the time or place the literary work was written, the time or place the literary work was set (if a historical work), and modern Western culture. Works written after the mid-1970s may not have this box.

- **What Do I Read Next?:** a list of works that might complement the featured literary work or serve as a contrast to it. This includes works by the same author and others, works of fiction and nonfiction, and works from various genres, cultures, and eras.

Other Features

A Cumulative Author/Title Index lists the authors and titles covered in each volume of the *LDNfS* series.

A Cumulative Nationality/Ethnicity Index breaks down the authors and titles covered in each volume of the *LDNfS* series by nationality and ethnicity.

A Subject/Theme Index, specific to each volume, provides easy reference for users who may be studying a particular subject or theme rather than a single work. Significant subjects from events to broad themes are included, and the entries pointing to the specific theme discussions in each entry are indicated in **boldface.**

Each entry has several illustrations, including photos of the author, stills from film adaptations (if available), maps, and/or photos of key historical events.

Citing Literature of Developing Nations for Students

When writing papers, students who quote directly from any volume of *Literature of Developing Nations for Students* may use the following general forms. These examples are based on MLA style; teachers may request that students adhere to a different style, so the following examples may be adapted as needed.

When citing text from *LDNfS* that is not attributed to a particular author (i.e., the Themes, Style, Historical Context sections, etc.), the following format should be used in the bibliography section:

> "Anowa." *Literature of Developing Nations for Students.* Eds. Elizabeth Bellalouna, Michael L. LaBlanc, and Ira Mark Milne. Vol. 1. Detroit: Gale, 2000. 72–4.

When quoting the specially commissioned essay from *LDNfS* (usually the first piece under the "Criticism" subhead), the following format should be used:

> Petrusso, Annette. Essay on "Anowa," *Literature of Developing Nations for Students.* Eds. Elizabeth Bellalouna, Michael L. LaBlanc, and Ira Mark Milne. Vol. 1. Detroit: Gale, 2000. 75–8.

When quoting a journal or newspaper essay that is reprinted in a volume of *LDNfS,* the following form may be used:

> Cohen, Derek. "Athol Fugard's 'Boesman and Lena,'" in *The Journal of Commonwealth Literature*, Vol. XII, No. 3 April, 1978, 78–83; excerpted and reprinted in *Literature of Developing Nations for Students*, Vol. 1, eds. Elizabeth Bellalouna, Michael L. LaBlanc, and Ira Mark Milne (Detroit: Gale, 2000), pp. 177–80.

When quoting material reprinted from a book that appears in a volume of *NfS,* the following form may be used:

> Myriam J. A. Chancy, "Lespoua fe viv: Female Identity and the Politics of Textual Sexuality in Nadine Magloire's 'Le Mal de Vivre' and Edwidge Danticat's 'Breath, Eyes, Memory,'" in *Framing Silence: Revolutionary Novels by Haitian Women* (Rutgers University Press, 1997), pp. 120–33; excerpted and reprinted in *Literature of Developing Nations for Students*, Vol. 1, eds. Elizabeth Bellalouna, Michael L. LaBlanc, and Ira Mark Milne (Detroit: Gale, 2000), pp. 195–201.

We Welcome Your Suggestions

The editors of *Literature of Developing Nations for Students* welcome your comments and ideas. Readers who wish to suggest novels to appear in future volumes, or who have other suggestions, are cordially invited to contact the editors. You may contact the editors via e-mail at:

mark.milne@galegroup.com. Or write to the editors at:

Editors, *Literature of Developing Nations for Students*
Gale Group
27500 Drake Road
Farmington Hills, MI 48331–3535

Literary Chronology

1889: Gabriela Mistral is born Lucia Goday Alcayaga in Vicuna, in the Elqui valley in northern Chile on April 7.

1890: Jean Rhys is born Ella Gwendolyn Rees Williams in 1890 in Dominica.

1896: Manuel Rojas is born in Buenos Aires, Argentina, on January 8.

1899: Jorge Luis Borges is born into an old, wealthy, Argentinean family in Buenos Aires on August 24.

1904: Pablo Neruda is born Neftalí Ricardo Reyes Basoalto in the town of Parral in southern Chile.

1906: Leopold Sedar Senghor is born in Joal, a village in Central Senegal.

1907: Rasipuram Krishnaswami Narayan is born in Madras (now known as Chennai), South India, on October 10.

1914: Octavio Paz is born Octavio Paz Lozano in Mexico City in the middle of the Mexican Revolution.

1918: Juan José Arreola is born on September 12 in Ciudad Guzman, in Jalisco, Mexico.

1920: Clarice Lispector, the youngest of three daughters, is born in Tchetchelnik, Ukraine, to Ukrainian parents on December 10.

1920: Amos Tutuola is born in Abeokuta, Western Nigeria, in 1920.

1924: Gabriela Mistral's poem about motherhood, "Fear," is published in her second collection of poetry.

1925: Rosa (Cuthbert) Guy is born in Diego Martin, Trinidad, on September 1.

1927: Manuel Rojas publishes one of his best known and most widely anthologized tales, "The Glass of Milk."

1928: Gabriel García Márquez is born March 6 in Aracataca, Colombia.

1928: Carlos Fuentes is born on November 11 in Panama City.

1929: Miriam Bâ is born.

1930: Chinua Achebe is born in eastern Nigeria on November 16.

1930: Derek Walcott is born January 23 in the capital city of Castries on the eastern Caribbean island of St. Lucia.

1932: Athol Harold Lannigan Fugard is born June 11 in Middelburg, a small village in the semi-desert Karoo region of South Africa.

1932: Manuel Puig is born on December 28 in General Villegas, in the pampas of Argentina.

1934: Austin C. Clarke is born on July 26 in St. James, Barbados.

1936: Mario Vargas Llosa is born in Arequipa, Peru.

1937: Anita Desai is born Anita Mazumdar on June 24 in Mussoorie, India.

1938: Ngugi wa Thiong'o is born James Thiong'o Ngugi, in Limuru, Kenya, on January 5.

1938: José Raúl Bernardo is born on October 3 in Havana, Cuba.

1939: ''Pierre Menard, Author of Quixote'' is first published.

1940: Ama Ata Aidoo is born Christina Ama Aidoo on March 23 in Abeadzi Kyiakor, Gold Coast (now known as Ghana).

1940: Bharati Mukherjee is born into an elite caste level of Calcutta society on July 27.

1941: Jorge Luis Borges establishes his reputation as a writer of fiction with the publication of his short story "The Garden of Forking Paths."

1942: Isabel Angelica Allende is born on August 2 in Lima, Peru.

1943: Gita Mehta is born in New Delhi, India.

1945: Gabriela Mistral receives the Nobel Prize for Literature.

1945: "Prayer to the Masks" is published in Senghor's first collection, *Songs of the Shadow*.

1947: First published in India in the newspaper *The Hindu*, R.K. Narayan's short story ''An Astrologers Day'' becomes the title story of a collection of short stories.

1949: Jamaica Kincaid is born in Antigua on May 25 as Elaine Potter Richardson.

1949: Victor Hernández Cruz is born in the barrio El Guanabano in the town of Aguas Buenas, Puerto Rico.

1951: Laura Esquivel is born in Mexico.

1952: Judith Ortiz Cofer is born February 24 in Hormigueros, Puerto Rico.

1952: "The Switchman" is published in the collection *Confabulario*.

1953: Ana Castillo, a leading voice in the Chicana/o movement, is born.

1954: Omar Sigfrido Castaneda is born on September 6 in Guatemala City, Guatemala, but grows up in Michigan and Indiana after his family moves to the United States.

1954: Octavio Paz publishes "Fable" after returning to Mexico from Paris.

1956: "Ode to My Socks" ("Oda a los calcetines") is published.

1957: Gabriela Mistral dies in Rosalyn Bay, Long Island, in January.

1958: Christina Garcia is born in Havana, Cuba, on July 4. Garcia moves to the U.S. with her parents when she is two years old.

1958: *Where the Air Is Clear* is published.

1959: Rigoberta Menchu is born to poor Native Indian parents in Guatemala.

1960: Clarice Lispector's story about personal relationships, "Family Ties," is published.

1962: Derek Walcott's poem about the Mau Mau Uprising in Kenya, "A Far Cry from Africa," is published.

1962: *The Time of the Hero*, Mario Vargas Llosa's first novel, is published in 1962.

1967: Nobel Prize-winning poet Derek Walcott publishes the play *Dream on Monkey Mountain*.

1967: *One Hundred Years of Solitude* is published.

1968: Gabriel García Márquez publishes "The Handsomest Drowned Man."

1969: Edwidge Danticat is born January 19 in Port-au-Prince, Haiti.

1969: Athol Fugard's *Boesman and Lena* premieres at the Rhodes University Little Theatre in Grahamstown, South Africa, on July 10.

1969: Joanne Hyppolite is born in Les Cayes, Haiti. Her family moves to the United States when she is four years old.

1970: Ama Ata Aidoo's *Anowa* is first published (although Aidoo had begun writing the play in the late 1960s), and later makes its British premiere in London in 1991.

1970: Aidoo's first collection of short stories, *No Sweetness Here*, is published.

1971: Pablo Neruda is awarded the Nobel Prize for Literature.

1973: Manuel Rojas dies in his adopted homeland of Chile on March 11.

1973: "Business" is one of a suite of five poems published in Victor Hernández Cruz's collection *Mainland*.

1973: Rosa Guy publishes the first of her trilogy of young adult novels, *The Friends*.

1973: Pablo Neruda dies of cancer in Santiago on September 23.

1974: The short story "The Martyr" by Kenyan novelist Ngugi wa Thiong'o, East Africa's leading writer, is first published in his collection *Secret Lives and Other Stories*.

1976: Manuel Puig publishes his best known novel, *Kiss of the Spider Woman*.

1977: Clarice Lispector dies on December 9.

1977: After six years of work, Ngugi wa Thiong'o publishes *Petals of Blood*.

1978: Jamaica Kincaid's short story "Girl" is first published in the June 26 issue of *The New Yorker*.

1978: Anita Desai's short story "Studies in the Park" is first published, in her collection *Games at Twilight*.

1979: Manuel Puig is awarded the American Library Association Notable Book Award for *Kiss of the Spider Woman*.

1979: Jean Rhys dies at the age of 88.

1980: Miriam Bâ publishes *So Long a Letter*.

1981: Miriam Bâ dies after a long illness.

1982: Isabelle Allende establishes her literary reputation with the publication of *The House of the Spirits*.

1982: Gabriel García Márquez wins the Nobel Prize for Literature.

1984: Rigoberta Menchú stirs international debate over the treatment of Native Indians with the publication of her autobiography *I, Rigoberta Menchú: An Indian Woman in Guatemala*.

1985: Jamaica Kincaid's second book, *Annie John*—comprised of short stories that first appeared in *The New Yorker*, is published.

1986: Jorge Luis Borges dies of liver cancer in Geneva, Switzerland.

1987: After a twenty-one-year hiatus from writing, Chinua Achebe publishes *Anthills of the Savannah* in Great Britain.

1988: Bharati Mukherjee's short story "The Middleman" is originally included in her second collection of short fiction, *The Middleman and Other Stories*, which won the 1988 Book Critics Circle Award for best fiction.

1989: Bharati Mukherjee's *Jasmine*, the story of a widowed Punjabi peasant reinventing herself in America, is published.

1989: Laura Esquivel publishes her first novel, *Like Water for Chocolate: A Novel in Monthly Installments, with Recipes, Romances and Home Remedies*, which becomes a bestseller in Mexico and is successful in the United States.

1990: Manuel Puig dies from complications following a gallbladder operation.

1990: Austin C. Clarke's short story "Leaving This Island Place" is published in the short story collection *From Ink Lake: Canadian Stories*.

1990: Octavio Paz is awarded the Nobel Prize in Literature.

1990: Amos Tutuola publishes *The Village Witch Doctor and Other Stories*.

1991: Omar S. Castaneda's *Among the Volcanoes*, a coming-of-age story written for young adults and set in a place far removed from the environments familiar to American readers, is published.

1992: Rigoberta Menchu is awarded the Nobel Peace Prize.

1992: Judith Ortiz Cofer first publishes "The Latin Deli: An Ars Poetica" in *Americas Review*.

1992: Derek Walcott is awarded the Nobel Prize in Literature for his poetry.

1993: Gita Mehta publishes *A River Sutra*.

1993: "Pierre Menard, Author of the Quixote" is published.

1993: *So Far From God* is published.

1994: Edwidge Danticat's *Breath, Eyes, Memory* is published. Danticat is hailed by *Publishers Weekly* as "a distinctive new voice with a sensitive insight into Haitian culture."

1995: Judith Ortiz Cofer publishes "Bad Influence" in *Stories of the Barrio: An Island Like You*.

1995: *Seth and Samona* is published in 1995.

1996: Laura Esquivel publishes her second novel, *The Law of Love*.

1996: *Valley Song* is published.

1966: *Wide Sargasso Sea* is published.

1997: Omar S. Castaneda dies of a heroin overdose in January.

1997: Cristina Garcia's *The Aguero Sisters* is published.

1997: Tutuola dies of diabetes and hypertension on June 8 in poverty and obscurity, having been unable to afford adequate medical attention for his ailments.

1998: Isabel Allende's literary celebration of sex and food, *Aphrodite: A Memoir of the Senses*, makes its way onto the *New York Times* best-seller list.

1998: *The Farming of the Bones* is published.

1998: Octavio Paz dies on April 19.

1998: José Raúl Bernardo publishes his historical novel *Silent Wing*.

Acknowledgments

The editors wish to thank the copyright holders of the excerpted criticism included in this volume and the permissions managers of many book and magazine publishing companies for assisting us in securing reproduction rights. We are also grateful to the staffs of the Detroit Public Library, the Library of Congress, the University of Detroit Mercy Library, Wayne State University Purdy/Kresge Library Complex, and the University of Michigan Libraries for making their resources available to us. Following is a list of the copyright holders who have granted us permission to reproduce material in this volume of *Literature of Developing Nations for Students (LDNfS)*. Every effort has been made to trace copyright, but if omissions have been made, please let us know.

COPYRIGHTED MATERIALS IN *LDNfS*, VOLUMES 1 & 2, WERE REPRODUCED FROM THE FOLLOWING PERIODICALS:

Américas, v. 45, July-August, 1993; v. 48, November-December, 1996. © 1993, 1996 Américas. Both reprinted by permission of Américas, a bimonthly magazine published by the General Secretariat of the Organization of American States in English and Spanish.—*ARIEL: A Review of International English Literature*, v.29, October, 1998 for "Fables of the Plague Years: Postcolonialism, Postmodernism, and Magical Realism in 'Cien anos de soledad'" by Dean J. Irvine. Copyright © 1998 The Board of Governors, The University of Calgary. Reproduced by permission of the publisher and the author./ v. 24, April, 1993 for "Jean Rhys's Construction of Blackness as Escape from White Femininity in 'Wide Sargasso Sea'" by Maria Olaussen. Copyright © 1993 The Board of Governors, The University of Calgary. Reproduced by permission of the publisher.—*Belles Lettres: A Review of Books by Women*, v. 10, Fall, 1994. Reproduced by permission.—*Booklist*, v. 94, February 1, 1998; v. 94, July, 1998. Copyright © 1998 by the American Library Association. Both reproduced by permission.—*Christian Century*, v. 116, September 22, 1999. Copyright 1999 Christian Century Foundation. Reproduced by permission from The Christian Century.—*CLA Journal*, v. xxxvii, September, 1993. Copyright, 1993 by The College Language Association. Used by permission of The College Language Association.—*College Literature*, v. 19, October-February, 1992; v. 22, February, 1995. Copyright © 1992, 1995 by West Chester University. Both reproduced by permission.—*Commonweal*, v. 121, January 14, 1994. Copyright © 1994 Commonweal Publishing Co., Inc. Reproduced by permission of Commonweal Foundation.—*Comparative Literature*, v. 43, Fall, 1991 for "Myth, Contingency, and Revolution in Carlos Fuentes's La region mas transparente" by Maarten Van Delden. Reproduced by permission of the author.—*Confluencia*, v. 1, Fall, 1985. Reproduced by permission.—*Dallas Morning News*, October 20, 1996. © 1996 The Dallas Morning News. Reproduced by permission..—*Explicator*, v. 55, Winter, 1997. Copyright © 1997 Helen Dwight Reid Educational Foundation. Reproduced with permission of the Helen Dwight Reid Educational Foundation, published by Heldref Publications, 1319 18th Street, NW, Washington, DC 20036-1802.—*French Review*, v. 6, October, 1990. Copyright 1990 by the American Association of Teachers of French. Reproduced by permission.—*Hispania*, May, 1970 for "Aristotle and Vargas Llosa: Literature, History and the Interpretation of Reality" by Frank Dauster; v. 71, December, 1988 for "This is No Way to Run a Railroad: Arreola's Allegorical Railroad and Possible Source" by John R. Burt. © 1988 The American Association of Teachers of Spanish and Portuese, Inc. Reproduced by permission of the publisher and the author. © 1970, 1988 The American Association of Teachers of Spanish and Portuese, Inc. Both reproduced by permission of the publisher and the authors.—*Humanist*, v. 53, March-April, 1993 for "Nagugi wa Thiong'o and the Politics of Language" by Theodore Pelton. Copyright 1993 by the American Humanist Association. Reproduced by permission of the author.—*International Fiction Review*, v. 21, 1994. © copyright 1994 International Fiction Association. Reproduced by permission.—*Journal of Commonwealth Literature*, n. 5, July, 1968; v. xii, April, 1978; v. xvii, 1982. All reproduced with the kind permission of Bowker-Saur.—*Latin American Literary Review*, v. vi, Fall-Winter, 1977; v. xiv, January-June, 1986. Reproduced by permission.—*Latin American Perspectives*, v. 26, November, 1999. Reproduced by permission of Sage Publications, Inc.—*Literary Criterion*, v. xxvii, 1991. v. xxix, 1994. Both reproduced by permission.—*London Times*, September 18, 1997. Reproduced by permission.—*Los Angeles Times*, July 29, 1998; October 10, 1999. Copyright, 1998, 1999, Los Angeles Times. Both reproduced by permission.—*Maclean's Magazine*, v. 102, October 23, 1989 for "Jasmine" by Eleanor Wachtel. © 1989 by Maclean's Magazine. Reproduced by permission of the author.—*MELUS*, v. 22, 1997; v. 23, Spring, 1998. Copyright, MELUS: The Society for the Study of Multi-Ethnic Literature of the United States, 1997 Reproduced by permission.—*Modern Fiction Studies*, v. 26, Summer, 1980; v. 44, Winter, 1998. Copyright © 1980, 1998 by Purdue Research Foundation, West Lafayette, IN 47907. All rights reserved. Both reproduced by permission of The Johns Hopkins University.—*Multicultural Review*, v. 5, June, 1996. Reproduced by permission of Greenwood Publishing Group, Inc., Westport, CT.—

NACLA Report on the Americas, v. 32, March-April, 1999; v. 32, May-June, 1999. Copyright 1999 by the North American Congress on Latin America. Both reproduced by permission.—*Nation*, (New York), v. 246, April 16, 1988; v. 254, January 27, 1992; v. 262, January 29, 1996; New York, v. 264, May 19, 1997. © 1988; 1992; 1996; 1997 The Nation magazine/ The Nation Company, Inc. All reproduced by permission.—*New Literary History*, v. 24, Spring, 1993. Copyright © 1993 by New Literary History. Reproduced by permission of The Johns Hopkins University Press.—*New Statesman & Society*, v. 6, June 18, 1993. © 1993 Statesman & Nation Publishing Company Limited. Reproduced by permission.—*North American Review*, v. 281, March-April, 1996. Reproduced by permission.—*NWSA Journal*, v. 11, March 22, 1999. Reproduced by permission.—*Publisher's Weekly*, v. 237, December 21, 1990; v. 240, March 29, 1993; v. 241, January 24, 1994; v. 242, June 19, 1995; v. 245, January 19, 1998; v. 245, June 1, 1998. Copyright 1990, 1993, 1994, 1995, 1998 by Reed Publishing USA. All reproduced from Publishers Weekly, published by the Bowker Magazine Group of Cahners Publishing Co., a division of Reed Publishing USA., by permission.—*Research in African Literatures*, v. 23, Spring, 1992; v. 25, Summer, 1994. Copyright © 1992, 1994 Indiana University Press. Both reproduced by permission.—*Review of Contemporary Fiction*, v. 13, Summer, 1993. Copyright, 1993, by John O'Brien. Reproduced by permission.—*Romance Notes*, v. xxiv, Winter, 1983. Reproduced by permission.—*Romantic Review*, v. 86, January, 1995. Reproduced by permission.—*Studies in Short Fiction*, v. 29, Winter, 1992; v. 31, Summer, 1994; v. 32, Spring, 1995 Copyright 1992, 1994, 1995 by Newberry College. All reproduced by permission.—*Texas Studies in Literature and Language*, v. xix, Winter, 1977. Reproduced by permission.—*Times* (London), August 21, 1997; April 30, 1998. © Times Newspapers Limited 1998. All reproduced from The Times, London by permission.—*Times Literary Supplement*, July 4, 1986; May 18-24, 1990. © The Times Supplements Limited 1986, 1990. Both reproduced from The Times Literary Supplement by permission.—*Twentieth Century Literature*, v. 39, Winter, 1993. Copyright 1993, Hofstra University Press. Reproduced by permission.—*UNESCO Courier*, November, 1989. Reproduced by permission.—*Washington Times*, May 15, 1997. Copyright © 1997 News World Communications, Inc. Reprinted with permission of The Washington Times.—*Women's Studies*, v. 22, March, 1993. © Gordon and Breach Science Publishers. Reproduce by permission.—*World Literature Today*, v. 52, Winter, 1978; v. 64, Summer, 1991; v. 69, Winter, 1995; v. 72, Winter, 1998; v. 73, Spring, 1999. Copyright 1978, 1991, 1995, 1998, 1999 by the University of Oklahoma Press. All reproduced by permission of the publisher.—*World Literature Written in English*, November, 1974; v. 28, Spring, 1988 © Copyright 1974 WLWE-World Literature Written in English. Reproduced by permission of the publisher.

COPYRIGHTED MATERIALS IN *LDNfS*, VOLUMES 1 & 2, WERE REPRODUCED FROM THE FOLLOWING BOOKS:

Chancy, Myriam J. A. From *Framing Silence: A Revolutionary Novels by Haitian Women*. Rutgers University Press, 1997. Copyright (c) 1997 by Myriam J. A. Chancy. All rights reserved. Reproduced by permission of Rutgers, The State University.— Cruz, Victor Hernandez. From *Mainland*. Random House, 1973. Reproduced by permission of Random House, Inc.—Evans, Jennifer. From *Annual Selected Papers of the ALA*. Edited by Stephen H. Arnold. Three Continents Press, 1983. Reproduced by permission.—Fulks, Barbara P. From *Reference Guide to World Literature, 2nd ed.* Edited by Lesley Henderson. St. James Press, 1995. Reproduced by permission.—Nagel, James. From *Traditions, Voices, and Dreams*. Edited by Melvin J. Friedman and Ben Siegel. University of Delaware Press, 1995. Reproduced by permission.—Neruda, Pablo. From *Neruda and Vallejo: Selected Poems*. Edited by Robert Bly. Beacon Press, 1971. Copyright © 1971 by Robert Bly. Reproduced by permission.—Ojo-Ade, Femi. From *Africana Literature Today*. Africana Publishing Company, 1982. Reproduced by permission in the U.S. by Holmes & Meier Publishers, Inc. In the world market by Heinemann Educational Books Ltd.—Paz, Octavio. From *Octavio Paz: Selected Poems*. Edited by Eliot Weinberger. A New Directions Book, 1984. Reproduced by permission.—Peters, Jonathan. From *A Dance of Masks*. Three Continents Press, 1978. Copyright © 1978 by Three Continents Press, copyright © 1996 by Three Continents Press/Lynne Rienner Publishers. Reproduced by permission of Lynne Publishers, Inc.—Reeve, Richard M. From *Carlos Fuentes, A Critical View*. Edited by Robert Broday and Charles Rossman. University of Texas Press, 1982. Copyright © 1982 by the University of Texas Press. All rights reserved. Reproduced by permission.—Tittler, Jonathan. From *Twyane's World Authors Series Online*. G. K. Hall & Co., 1999. Reproduced by permission.—Walcott, Derek.

From *Poetry for Students*. Edited by Mary Ruby. The Gale Group, 1999. Reproduced by permission of the author.—Willis, Robert J. From *Staging the Impossible: The Fantastic Mode in Modern Drama*. Edited by Patrick D. Murphy. Greenwood Press, 1992. Reproduced by permission of Greenwood Publishing Group, Inc., Westport, CT.

PHOTOGRAPHS AND ILLUSTRATIONS APPEARING IN *LDNFS,* VOLUMES 1 & 2, WERE RECEIVED FROM THE FOLLOWING SOURCES:

Achebe, Chinua, photograph. AP/Wide World Photos. Reproduced by permission.— Allende, Isabel, photograph. AP/Wide World Photos. Reproduced by permission.—Allende, Isabel, photograph. Archive Photos. Reproduced by permission.— Allende, Salvador (riding in car), photograph. UPI/Bettmann. Reproduced by permission.—Bernardo, Jose-Raul, photograph by Jerry Bauer. © Jerry Bauer. Reproduced by permission.—Borges, Jorge Luis (on couch, painting behind), photograph by Harold Mantell. Reproduced by permission.— Borges, Jorge Luis, photograph. The Library of Congress.—Bronte, Charlotte (engraved according to an act of Congress), 1873, engraving. Archive Photos/Kean. Reproduced by permission.—Castillo, Ana, portrait. Photograph by Barbara Seyda.— Cavazos, Lumi, (holding baby in arms), starring in Alfonso Arau's film ''Like Water for Chocolate'', photograph. The Kobal Collection. Reproduced by permission.—Clarke, Austin, photograph by John Reeves. Reproduced by permission.—Colombian Troops (line up on lawn), Bogota, Colombia, 1949, photograph. CORBIS/Bettmann. Reproduced by permission.—Colombian Troops (wearing various styles of military uniforms), Colon, Panama, 1902, photograph. CORBIS. Reproduced by permission.—Cortes, Hernan (approaching Aztec emperor Montezuma), Tenochtitlan, Mexico, engraving. The Library of Congress.—Cruz, Victor Hernandez (reading poetry outdoors), photograph. Arte Publico Press Archives, University of Houston. Reproduced by permission.—Danticat, Edwidge (hand on forehead), New York City, 1998, photograph by Doug Kanter. AP/Wide World Photos. Reproduced by permission.—Danticat, Edwidge, Ixel Cervera (Danticat singing her book for Cervera), New York City, 1998, photograph by Bebeto Matthews. AP/Wide World Photos. Reproduced by permission.—de Cervantes, Miguel, photograph.—Desai, Anita. Photograph courtesy of William Heinemann.—Eighth Street, Little Havana, Miami, Florida, c. 1981, photograph. Russell

Thompson/Archive Photos. Reproduced by permission.—Esquivel, Laura, photograph by Jerry Bauer. © Jerry Bauer. Reproduced by permission.—Esquivel, Laura, sitting wearing a flower print dews, photograph. © Jerry Bauer. Reproduced by permission.—Family near mealtime, Central Africa, photograph. United Nations. Reproduced by permission.—Fuentes, Carlos, photograph by Hugh Peralta. Archive Photos, Inc./Reuters. Reproduced by permission.—Fugard, Athol, photograph. AP/Wide World Photos. Reproduced by permission.—Fugard, Athol (seated on couch with Amy Irving), 1988, photograph. AP/Wide World Photos. Reproduced by permission.—Garcia, Cristina, photograph. AP/Wide World Photos. Reproduced by permission.—Garcia Marquez, Gabriel (looking right, in dark shirt), 1982, photograph. AP/Wide World Photos. Reproduced by permission.—Group of slaves disembarking (three-masted ship in distance), engraving. The Library of Congress.—Guy, Rosa, photograph by Jerry Bauer. © Jerry Bauer. Reproduced by permission.—Hurt, William and Raul Julia. From a scene from ''Kiss of the Spider Woman,'' photograph. The Kobal Collection. Reproduced by permission.—Mandela, Nelson and F.W. de Klerk, 1994, photograph. Reuters/Bettmann. Reproduced by permission.—Marti, Jose (arms folded across chest), photograph. The Library of Congress.—Menchu, Rigoberta, (hand raised, speaking), Tokyo, Japan, 1993, photograph. Reuters/Bettmann. Reproduced by permission.—Mistral, Gabriela, photograph. The Library of Congress.—Mukherjee, Bharati. © Jerry Bauer. Reproduced by permission.—Mukherjee, Bharati, photograph. AP/Wide World Photos. Reproduced by permission.—Muslim woman on beach, Senegal, 1978, photograph by Owen Franken. © Owen Franken/CORBIS. Reproduced by permission.—Narayan, R.K., photograph by Jerry Bauer. Reproduced with permission.—Neruda, Pablo, photograph by Jerry Bauer. © Jerry Bauer. Reproduced by permission.—Open boats along shore of Gold Coast, British West Africa, c. 1890-1910, photograph. © Corbis. Reproduced by permission.—Ortiz Cofer, Judith (seated), photograph. Arte Publico Press Archives, University of Houston. Reproduced by permission.—Paz, Octavio, photograph. AP/Wide World Photos. Reproduced by permission.—People being held in stadium (armed soldier standing guard), Santiago, Chile, 1973, photograph. CORBIS/Bettmann. Reproduced by permission.—Pinochet, Augusto (speaking into microphones, his right hand lifted, in uniform), 1978, photograph. AP/Wide World Photos. Reproduced by permission.—Puig, Manuel (wearing banned collar jacket), photograph by Jerry Bauer. © Jerry Bauer. Reproduced by permission.—Quiche/Mayan Indian woman weaving on backstrap loom, c. 1980, Guatemala, photograph. CORBIS/ Jack Fields. Reproduced by permission.—Rhys, Jean, photograph by Jerry Bauer. © Jerry Bauer. Reproduced by permission.—Schoolchildren, Dakar, Senegal, 1978, photograph by Owen Franken. © Owen Franken/ Corbis. Reproduced by permission.—Senghor, Leopold, photograph. AP/Wide World Photos. Reproduced by permission.—The July, 1970, Playbill for Athol Fugard's ''Boesman and Lena,'' Directed by John Berry, with James Earl Jones as Boesman, Ruby Dee as Lena and Zakes Mokae as Old African, at the Circle in the Square Theater, NY, Credit page, photograph. PLAYBILL (r) is a registered trademark of Playbill Incorporated, N.Y.C. All rights reserved. Reproduced by permission.—Vargas, Llosa (Jorge) Mario (Pedro), photograph. Jerry Bauer. Reproduced by permission.—Walcott, Derek, photographs by Jerry Bauer. © Jerry Bauer. Reproduced by permission.—Woman standing in ocean, watching ship in distance, a scene from the film version of Jean Rhys' novel ''Wide Sargasso Sea.'' The Kobal Collection. Reproduced by permission.

Contributors

Diane Andrews Henningfeld: Andrews Henningfeld is associate professor of English at Adrian College in Michigan; she has written extensively for a variety of educational and academic publishers. Entry on "The Garden of Forking Paths." Original essay on "The Garden of Forking Paths."

Cynthia Bily: Bily teaches writing and literature at Adrian College in Adrian, MI, and writes for various educational publishers. Entry on "Girl." Original essays on *Anthills of the Savannah*, and "Girl."

Adrian Blevins: Blevins, a poet and essayist who has taught at Hollins University, Sweet Briar College, and in the Virginia Community College System, is the author of *The Man Who Went Out for Cigarettes*, a chapbook of poems, and has published poems, stories, and essays in many magazines, journals, and anthologies. Original essay on "Girl."

Liz Brent: Brent has a Ph.D. in American Culture, specializing in cinema studies, from the University of Michigan; she is a freelance writer and teaches courses in American cinema. Entries on *Kiss of the Spider Woman*, "Leaving This Island Place," "The Martyr," "The Middleman," "No Sweetness Here," "Studies in the Park," and "The Village Witch Doctor." Original essays on *Anowa*, "Bad Influence," "Family Ties," "The Garden of Forking Paths," "Girl," "The Glass of Milk," "The Handsomest Drowned Man in the World," *Kiss of the Spider Woman*, "Leaving This Island Place," "Management of Grief," "The Martyr," "The Middleman," "No Sweetness Here," "Studies in the Park," and "The Village Witch Doctor."

Jennifer Bussey: Bussey holds a bachelor's degree in English literature and a master's degree in interdisciplinary studies; she is an independent writer specializing in literature. Entries on *Among the Volcanoes* and *Anthills of the Savannah*. Original essays on *Among the Volcanoes*, *Anthills of the Savannah*, "Management of Grief," and "Studies in the Park."

David Donnell: Donnell teaches at the University of Toronto, and has published seven books of poetry. His work is included in the *Norton Anthology of Modern Poetry*, and his volume *Settlement* has received Canada's prestigious Governor General's Award. Original essay on "A Far Cry from Africa."

Donald G. Evans: Evans is an adjunct professor at Hamilton College in Cedar Rapids, IA, as well as a free-lance writer for *Advertising Age* and editor for *Story Quarterly* . Entry on *Jasmine*. Original essay on *Jasmine*.

Darren Felty: Felty is visiting instructor at the College of Charleston, SC, and has a Ph.D. in literature from the University of Georgia. Entry on *Annie John*. Original essay on *Annie John*.

James Frazier: Frazier has an M.A. with a major in English literature from the University of Texas at Austin; he also teaches English and speech at Lytle High School, Lytle, TX. Entry on "The Management of Grief." Original essay on "The Management of Grief."

Lane A. Glenn: Glenn is an author, educator, director, and actor, located in Lansing, MI. Entries on *Boesman and Lena* and *Valley Song*. Original essays on *Boesman and Lena* and *Valley Song*.

Carole Hamilton: Hamilton is a freelance writer and an instructor at Cary Academy, Cary, NC. Entries on "Family Ties," *One Hundred Years of Solitude*, and "Pierre Menard, Author of Quixote." Original essays on "Family Ties," *One Hundred Years of Solitude*, and "Pierre Menard, Author of Quixote."

Jhan Hochman: Hochman holds a Ph.D. in English and an M.A. in cinema studies; his articles have appeared in *Democracy and Nature*, *Genre*, *ISLE*, and *Mosaic*. Entry on "A Far Cry from Africa." Original essay on "A Far Cry from Africa."

Jeremy W. Hubbell: Hubbell is a freelance writer, holds an M.Litt. from the University of Aberdeen, and is pursuing a Ph.D. in history at the State University of New York at Stony Brook. Entries on *Aphrodite: A Memoir of the Senses*, *The Time of the Hero*, and *Where the Air is Clear*. Original essays on *Aphrodite: A Memoir of the Senses*, *The Time of the Hero*, and *Where the Air is Clear*.

Elizabeth Judd: Judd is a freelance writer and book reviewer with an M.F.A. in English from the University of Michigan and a B.A. from Yale. Entry on *The Aguero Sisters*. Original essay on *The Aguero Sisters*.

Chelva Kanaganayakam: Kanaganayakam is an associate professor in the Department of English at the University of Toronto; his writings include *Structures of Negation: The Writings of Zulfikar Ghose*, *South Asian Writers and their Worlds*, and *Dark Antonyms and Paradise: The Poetry of Rienzi Crusz*. Entry on "An Astrologer's Day." Original essay on "An Astrologer's Day."

David J. Kelly: Kelly is a professor of English at College of Lake County, IL. Entries on "Fear" and "Seth and Samona." Original essays on "Fear" and "Seth and Samona."

Lydia S. Kim: Kim holds an M.S. Ed. from the University of Pennsylvania in Philadelphia, and teaches language arts and social studies at Cary Academy, Cary, NC. Entry on *I, Rigoberta Menchu*. Original essay on *I, Rigoberta Menchu*.

Rena Korb: Korb has a master's degree in English literature and creative writing, and has written for a wide variety of educational publishers. Original essays on "Family Ties," "The Friends," and "The Middleman."

Uma Kukathas: Kukathas is a freelance writer and a student in the Ph.D. program in philosophy at the University of Washington, specializing in social, political, and moral philosophy. Entries on "Fable," "Ode to My Socks," and *Petals of Blood*. Original essays on "Fable," "Ode to My Socks," and *Petals of Blood*.

Aviya Kushner: Aviya Kushner is the Contributing Editor in Poetry at *BarnesandNoble.com* and the Poetry Editor of *Neworld Magazine*. She is a graduate of the acclaimed creative writing program in poetry at Boston University, where she received the Fitzgerald Award in Translation. Her writing on poetry has appeared in *Harvard Review* and *The Boston Phoenix*, and she has served as Poetry Coordinator for *AGNI Magazine*. She has given readings of her own work throughout the United States, and she teaches at Massachusetts Communications College in Boston. Original essay on "A Far Cry from Africa."

Kimberly Lutz: Lutz is an instructor at New York University, and has written for a wide variety of educational publishers. Entries on *A River Sutra*, *So Long A Letter*, and *Wide Sargasso Sea*. Original essays on *A River Sutra*, *So Long A Letter*, and *Wide Sargasso Sea*.

Jennifer Lynch: Lynch teaches at the Potrero Hill After School Program and the Taos Literacy Program; she also contributes to *Geronimo*, a journal of politics and culture. Entries on "Bad Influence" and "The Switchman." Original essays on "Bad Influence" and "The Switchman."

Sarah Madsen Hardy: Madsen Hardy has a doctorate in English literature, and is a freelance writer and editor. Original Essay on "Girl."

Mary Mahony: Mahony has an M.A. in English from the University of Detroit and an M.L.S. from Wayne State University; she is an instructor of English at Wayne County Community

College in Detroit, MI. Entry on *The Friends*. Original essay on *The Friends*.

Sheri Metzger: Metzger is a freelance writer, has a Ph.D., and is an adjunct professor in the Department of English at the University of New Mexico in Albuquerque, NM. Entries on "The Handsomest Drowned Man in the World" and *House of the Spirits*. Original essays on "Bad Influence," "The Glass of Milk," "The Handsomest Drowned Man in the World," and *House of the Spirits*.

Tyrus Miller: Miller is an assistant professor of comparative literature and English at Yale University, where he teaches twentieth-century literature and visual culture; he has published a book entitled *Late Modernism: Politics, Fiction, and the Arts between the World Wars*. Entry on "Prayer to the Masks." Original essay on "Prayer to the Masks."

Carl Mowrey: Mowery has a Ph.D. in writing and literature from Southern Illinois University, Carbondale, IL. Entry on "The Glass of Milk." Original essays on "Fear" and "The Glass of Milk."

Wendy Perkins: Perkins is an assistant professor of English at Prince George's Community College, MD; she has a Ph.D. in English from the University of Delaware. Entries on "The Latin Deli," *The Law of Love*, and *Like Water for Chocolate*. Original essays on "The Latin Deli," *The Law of Love*, and *Like Water for Chocolate*.

Annette Petrusso: Petrusso is a freelance author and screenwriter, located in Austin, TX. Entries on *Anowa* and *Dream on Monkey Mountain*. Original essays on *Anowa* and *Dream on Monkey Mountain*.

Dean Rader: Rader has published widely in the field of American and Latin American art and literature. Original essays on "The Handsomest Drowned Man in the Wolrd," "Ode to My Socks," and "Pierre Menard, Author of Quixote."

Michael Rex: Rex is an adjunct professor at the University of Detroit-Mercy, MI. Entry on *So Far From God: A Novel*. Original essay on *So Far From God: A Novel*.

Chris Semansky: Semansky holds a Ph.D. in English from Stony Brook University, and teaches writing and literature at Portland Community College in Portland, OR. His collection of poems *Death, But at a Good Price* received the Nicholas Roerich Poetry Prize for 1991 and was published by Story Line Press and the Nicholas Roerich Museum. Semansky's most recent collection, *Blindsided*, has been published by 26 Books of Portland, OR. Entry on "Business." Original essays on "Business," "The Latin Deli," and "Prayer to the Masks."

Emily Smith Riser: Smith Riser has a master's degree in English literature, and teaches high school English. Original essay on *Among the Volcanoes*.

Christine Thompson: Thompson has an M.A., and is a part-time English instructor at Jefferson Community College, Watertown, NY. Entry on *Silent Wing: A Novel*. Original essay on *Silent Wing: A Novel*.

Karen D. Thompson: Thompson has done graduate work at the University of North Carolina, Greensboro, and has taught English at Asheboro High School (NC), Manor High School, Dripping Springs High School, and Dripping Springs Middle School (TX). Original essays on "The Friends" and "Studies in the Park."

Kelly Winters: Winters is a freelance writer, and has written for a wide variety of academic and educational publishers. Entries on *Breath, Eyes, Memory* and "The Farming of Bones." Original essays on *Breath, Eyes, Memory*, "A Far Cry from Africa," "The Farming of Bones," and *House of the Spirits*.

Paul Witcover: Witcover is a novelist and editor in New York City with an M.A. in creative writing and literature from the City University of New York. Original essay on "A Far Cry from Africa."

The Agüero Sisters

Cristina Garcia

1997

In 1997, when *The Agüero Sisters* was published, Cristina Garcia confirmed that her literary subject was multigenerational Cuban-American families with all their conflicts, emotional complexity, and belief in magic and miracles. By the time this novel was published, Garcia was already well known for her first novel, *Dreaming in Cuban*, which received outstanding reviews when it was published in 1992.

The Agüero Sisters is clearly the work of the same author as *Dreaming in Cuban*. Not only do the two share a preoccupation with family dynamics, but both novels have justifiably been praised for their unusual and poetic use of language. Garcia wrote poetry before she began her first novel. In an interview in *Newsday*, Garcia said: "Language is what drives a narrative. If I'm reading a novel and it doesn't engage me sentence by sentence, I won't finish it." She said that she stopped being a journalist because of her love of poetry: "I first started reading poetry in a serious way when I was about thirty. After that, there was no turning back. It was just this explosion of language and possibility that I hadn't known existed." Throughout *The Agüero Sisters* her love of language comes through in unforgettable images. Reina recalls her dead mother's throat as "an estuary of color and disorder." She describes a "sky collapsing with stars," a refrigerator that coughs "like a four-pack-a-day smoker," and rain that's "hard, linear and relentless, like self-important men."

Author Biography

The challenges and opportunities of exile are a subject that Garcia explores in *The Agüero Sisters* and one that has played an ongoing role in her own life. Born in Havana, Cuba, on July 4th, 1958, Garcia moved to the U.S. with her parents when she was two years old. Growing up in New York with a younger sister and brother, she recalls having been raised in mostly Jewish neighborhoods, where few Latinos lived. Her parents worked in a drug store and a card shop, and later owned a restaurant in Brooklyn, where Garcia herself sometimes worked. Garcia spoke ''kitchen Spanish'' at home and told an interviewer for *Newsday* that even now her Spanish vocabulary isn't broad and probably makes her ''sound like a twelve-year-old.'' As a teenager, Garcia and her younger sister were sent to Switzerland to study French during summer vacations. She attended Barnard College in New York City and received her master's degree from Johns Hopkins School of Advanced International Studies in 1981. Garcia then became a cultural and political reporter for *Time* magazine, where she worked from 1983 until 1988.

Garcia did not return to Cuba until 1984, when she was an adult. After the trip, she told an interviewer at *Newsday* that she ''became incorrigibly Cuban. . . . It sort of hit me retroactively, this identity thing.'' She did not, however, feel comfortable among the Cuban immigrants in Florida. Recalling her stint at the Miami bureau of *Time,* she told a writer for the *Chicago Sun-Times,* ''I expected to feel at home there, but I never felt more alienated.'' In that same article, Garcia discussed the difficulty that she and other first-generation Americans encounter when it comes to claiming the freedom to write fiction: ''It's like a friend of mine, Victor Suarez (author of the novel *Latin Jazz*), said— children of immigrants have a hard time with the idea of becoming an artist or poet because it is still threatening and ephemeral to our parents.''

In 1992, Garcia's first novel, *Dreaming in Cuban,* was published to much acclaim and was nominated for a National Book Award. Garcia's second novel, *The Agüero Sisters*, was published in 1997 and was also well-received. Garcia now lives with her daughter, Pilar, in Los Angeles.

Plot Summary

Prologue

Set in the Zapata Swamp in Cuba, more than three decades before the main drama of Garcia's *The Agüero Sisters* unfolds, the prologue lets the reader in on the family secret that informs the main action of the novel. Ignacio and Blanca Agüero, husband-and-wife naturalists, are on the first collecting trip they've undertaken together in nine years. They're hunting ruddy ducks for a new museum collection in Boston. The trip takes on a slightly unreal aspect because of the unsparing sunlight: ''*On cloudless days like this*, the light in the Zapata was so fierce that even the most experienced travelers were deceived, made to consider all manner of ruinous delusions.'' When Blanca spots a rare type of bee hummingbird, she turns to alert her husband only to find he's pointing a double-barreled gun at her. With no explanation, he shoots her and then carries her body seventeen miles to the nearest village, and lies about the deed.

Part I: Tropical Disturbances

Garcia tells the intertwined stories of the Agüero family, and although each person's individual story is intricately connected to the stories of all the other characters, they are also essentially separate. This section opens with Reina Agüero climbing a telephone pole as she repairs a high-voltage cable outside El Cobre, a town in eastern Cuba. While fixing a water pump there, Reina is in a freak accident and is pinioned in the highest branches of a large tree that's hit by lightning. She receives skin grafts from loved ones and her scars become a symbol of family solidarity. Her daughter, Dulce, now has a missing strip of thigh and her scar ''reminds Reina of the purplish burns on her own mother's forearms. Blanca Mestre Agüero had started as a chemist and bore the telltale signs of her profession's serious demands.'' After Reina recovers, she decides to visit Constancia in Miami and make peace with her own history.

Constancia is also undergoing changes. Her husband, Heberto Cruz, is determined to leave his successful tobacco business in New York and has purchased a condominium on Key Biscayne, Florida, where they'll retire together. Once the couple arrives in Florida, Heberto begins spending time with his brother, Gonzalo, and soon goes off on a counterrevolutionary mission, against Constancia's

Cristina Garcia

wishes. One night, Constancia dreams that her face is being operated upon by a plastic surgeon, and the next day she wakes to find that her face has been replaced by that of her mother. Around the same time, she goes into business for herself, marketing creams and lotions to women with a nostalgia for Cuba.

Interspersed throughout the present-day story are excerpts from Ignacio's diary. He tells of his own father, Reinaldo Agüero, whose job it was to read to the cigar workers in their factory, and of his own birth, which is brought on by his mother's sighting of a siguapa stygian owl, a bird that brings

bad luck and that carries away his mother's placenta and rains blood on the town's parade. Constancia and Reina both muse on their pasts; when Constancia was a baby, her mother left home and returned years later nearly eight months pregnant. Although neither know that their father killed their mother, both are uncomfortable with the version of events they've been told.

Part II: A Common Affliction

Ignacio's own story continues, with his being appointed a full professor of general science and biology at the University of Havana. He falls in love and marries the beautiful and mysterious Blanca Mestre.

Constancia's business, Cuerpo de Cuba, takes off, and she spends her days listening to a radio program called "La Hora de los Milagros," or "The Miracle Hour." She is wildly successful: "Each item in her Cuerpo de Cuba line will embody the exalted image Cuban women have of themselves: as passionate, self-sacrificing, and deserving of every luxury." As Heberto fights his counterrevolutionary battle in the Florida Everglades, his brother Gonzalo, Constancia's first husband, lies dying in the hospital.

Reina's arrival in Florida is soon followed by the appearance of Constancia's two children and her own daughter, Dulce. Reina gets a job restoring vintage cars. Isabel, nearly nine months pregnant and abandoned by her longtime boyfriend, gives birth to a son whom she names Raku. Silvestre returns to see his father, Gonzalo, and upon seeing him for the first time, smothers the dying man with a pillow. When Constancia is told by a santero (a religious man) that the sisters must go to Cuba, the two set off in a boat. On the trip, Reina tells Constancia that Papá killed their mother: "He shot her like one of his birds, and then he watched her die." The two fight at sea, and each comes to her own peace with what happened in their youth.

Coda: A Root in the Dark

Constancia learns that Heberto is dead, and she continues on her voyage to Cuba by boat. She wants to pick up Heberto's body, have him cremated, and then carry the ashes with her as she goes to Camagüey, where her father's papers are buried. In the meantime, Dulce returns to Miami, where she reunites with her mother and gets a job in a sandwich shop. In the final scenes, Reina becomes pregnant, creating a link to the future. And Constancia plumbs the past, returning to her mother's family farmhouse and finding her father's diary. There, she reads his story. The novel ends with the last installment of Ignacio's diary. He says that the murder of his wife was unplanned, and that after her death, he held her body and heard "Blanca's voice in the stirring of grasses and reeds, in the crisscrossing cranes overhead, in the swaying clumps of cowlily leaves."

Characters

Constancia Agüero Cruz

One of the sisters of the title, Constancia is petite, feminine, and proper, and these traits stand in stark contrast to her sister Reina, whose Amazonian figure suits her larger-than-life personality. When the novel opens, Constancia is fifty-one years old and living in New York with her husband, Heberto Cruz. She's a successful businesswoman who sells makeup out of a deep conviction of its importance. She's "motivated not by commissions, only by the satisfaction of staving off women's little everyday deaths." The way Constancia sees herself is shaped by and reflected in her external appearance. Rejecting "the modern ethos of comfort before style," she wears high-heeled shoes and color-coordinated outfits to perform the routine tasks of her work day. Constancia sees her own appearance as a selling tool. She's "partial to Adolfo suits, which set off her petite figure, and she completes every ensemble with a short strand of pearls. Her foreign accent and precise manner intimidate clients into buying whatever she suggests." When the couple retire to Key Biscayne, Florida, Constancia opens her own business—Cuerpo de Cuba—and creates a line of natural body and face creams. She's a brilliant marketer and soon becomes a very successful entrepreneur. One morning, Constancia wakes to find her face has been replaced by that of her long-dead mother, Blanca Mestre Agüero, who abandoned her as a young child. In many ways, Constancia has resolutely put her family history behind her. Yet of all the characters she's the most susceptible to superstition and magic. Constancia's favorite radio show is *La Hora de Los Milagros,* or "the miracle hour," and she "knows in her heart that miracles arrive every day from the succulent edge of disaster, defying nature, impossible to resist."

Ignacio Agüero

Ignacio is the patriarch of the Agüero family, but his character isn't well understood by either Reina or Constancia, who don't know that he has committed a shocking act. He shot and killed Blanca Mestre Agüero, his wife and the mother of both sisters, in the Zapata Swamp many years before the main action of the novel occurs. After this terrible deed, he leaves the swamp and "began to tell his lies." Two years later, he commits suicide. As the novel progresses, Ignacio is seen as an increasingly sympathetic character, thanks to his first-person diary account of his life. Ignacio writes his own story, and in doing so, he provides a partial history of Cuba. Born in 1904, two years after Cuba got its independence, Ignacio becomes a renowned naturalist who publishes many books, the most famous of which is entitled *Cuba: Flora and Fauna.* In his youth, Ignacio read to the workers in his father's cigar factory and he pursued the beautiful chemist Blanca Mestre, who later became his wife. It was the explicit goal of his career to catalog "every one of Cuba's nearly extinct birds." His diary staves off his own extinction by letting his daughters learn the truth about him long after his death. This novel is so concerned with what things mean that the family name Agüero is translated as "omen" or "augury."

Reina Agüero

Reina, one of the two sisters in the title of the novel, is tall (5'11''), voluptuous, romantic, and irresistible to men. Reina's daughter, Dulce, describes her mother as a woman who "puts her faith in electricity and sex." In many ways, Reina is the opposite of her practical and petite older sister. When the novel opens, Reina is forty-eight and is living in Havana, Cuba, in the apartment where she was raised. She's suffering from a bad case of insomnia and in her sleeplessness she endlessly wrestles with the family's past. Reina is a skilled, traveling electrician—a profession that suits her. It allows her to meet and make love to men from all over the country. "The most daring of her colleagues call her Compañera Amazona, a moniker she secretly relishes." Both Constancia and Reina undergo physical transformations. Constancia wakes up to find she has taken her mother's face, and Reina is hit by lightning when she's working as an electrician in El Cobre, a town in eastern Cuba. Reina's skin is so badly burned that it's stitched back together with donations from friends, family members, and lovers. "Most of Reina's nutmeg color is gone, replaced by a confusion of shades and textures. A few patches of her skin are so pink and elastic, so perfectly hairless, they look like a newborn pig's." Reina is emotional—she cherishes the memory of her mother's having breast-fed her until she was five, and she lives among the papers and debris of Ignacio's past—but she has trouble connecting to Constancia. In the years after their mother's death, Reina "wishes her sister could have given her something vital then, something to ease her grief. But all that was essential collapsed between them in those years, collapsed but did not die."

Pepín Beltrán

Reina's lover of twenty-four years, Beltrán is married, wears orthopedic shoes, and is an official in the Ministry of Agriculture. When Reina is hit by lightning, he is one of the people who contributes some of his own skin for her skin graft. He is loyal to the ideals of the revolution and remains in Cuba after Reina departs for Miami.

Gonzalo Cruz

Gonzalo Cruz was Constancia's first husband and her love for him stays with her, despite her marriage to his brother, Heberto. Gonzalo and Constancia were only married for four months; Gonzalo left her when he found out that she was pregnant and he never made any effort to meet their son, Silvestre. Gonzalo seems legendary. He marries six times, is known for being an unforgettable lover, and has a war wound—a shortened leg—from the Bay of Pigs. Gonzalo takes pride in his own outrageousness and in his injury: "Gonzalo could have fixed his leg years ago, but he prefers it damaged, the pretext it gives him to boast of his valor." Throughout most of the novel, Gonzalo is in the hospital, sick and dying.

Heberto Cruz

Constancia's husband, Heberto, is a stable, successful businessperson, a man with a "steady mercantile drive" who owns a tobacco shop on Sixth Avenue in Manhattan and then undergoes a dramatic personality change in retirement. After urging Constancia to move to Key Biscayne, Florida, Heberto is convinced by his older brother, Gonzalo, to become a counterrevolutionary. He becomes involved in a plot to overthrow the Cuban government. "Years ago, Heberto had wanted to join his father and exiled brothers in the Bay of Pigs invasion, longed to commandeer one of the Cruzes' secretly donated ships. But Constancia threatened to leave him and move to Spain." Heberto departs for the Florida Everglades and is killed in action.

Isabel Cruz

The artist in the family, Constancia's daughter, Isabel, has received some family traits that link her to her mother, her aunt, and her grandmother. When the novel opens, Isabel is a potter, living in Oahu and pregnant with her first child. Isabel's work is free-form—"odd shards of clay and other materials combined to suggest something recycled, something tampered with or incomplete." Isabel is described as having a "quiet defiance." After she gives birth to her son, Raku, her former boyfriend Austin sends a money order for two hundred dollars, but Isabel tears up the check and Constancia is frightened by her "daughter's resoluteness."

Silvestre Cruz

When most of the action of the novel takes place, Silvestre is thirty-three, a homosexual, and working at a library clipping articles for a news magazine. Silvestre is Constancia's son by her first husband, Gonzalo Cruz. When Silvestre was a child, Constancia sent him to an orphanage in Colorado because she was frightened by rumors that Cuban children would be rounded up and sent to boarding school in the Ukraine. At the orphanage, he contracted a 107-degree fever that left him permanently deaf. "Silvestre desperately attempted to conquer the damage, to discipline his other senses to make up for the unyielding silence. He strengthened his eyesight, his senses of smell and touch and taste, to fatiguing degrees."

Dulce Fuerte

Reina's daughter represents the younger generation in Cuba. She's the daughter of a well-known revolutionary, José Luís Fuerte, and she worked as a volleyball coach at José Martí High School before she became a prostitute. For Dulce, her personal history is a burden and she is very bitter. She says, "I spent practically my whole childhood in boarding schools, wearing navy-blue uniforms, picking lettuce or lemons or yams and reciting useless facts." She used to joke with Che Guevara's son about their "respective revolutionary burdens." In order to leave Cuba, she marries an older man and flees to Madrid.

Blanca Mestre Agüero

Murdered in the opening pages of the novel, Blanca is a compelling but enigmatic character, one who's seen almost exclusively through the memories of her daughters and her husband. She's important because it is her face that Constancia later assumes in one of the novel's strange touches, and it is the memory of her nurturing (she breast-fed Reina until her younger daughter was five years old) that haunts Reina throughout her life. Slight in stature, Blanca is described as being a beauty, "delicately boned as certain birds." Like her husband, Blanca was a famous naturalist. She's also characterized by her fierce independence. Blanca abandons her five-month-old daughter, Constancia, and when she returns to her husband and child, she is pregnant with another man's child. As befits a character who haunts the living, Blanca seems spooky and slightly unreal. She has strange eating habits, drinking milk all day and eating her sole meal of steak, fried eggs over rice, and a ripe mango each day at four a.m. This is how Ignacio describes his first impressions of his future wife: "*Her gifts had nothing to do with intelligence, which she displayed in impressive abundance, but were born of qualities much less tangible. Instinct. Intuition. An uncanny sense for the aberrational.*"

Themes

American Dream

Constancia represents the American Dream. Her success selling lotions and creams to Cuban-American women shows how well she understands the market she's pursuing. Her fervor for selling products is so intense that she even paints Heberto's motorboat in a floral motif to promote her new perfume—Flower of Exile. Reina is uncomfortable with Constancia's preoccupation with making money and sees the boat as a "gliding advertisement for her sister." By the time Constancia returns to Cuba, she is so thoroughly Americanized that she sees the rough skin of her countrywomen as an entrepreneurial opportunity. "When El Commandant kicks the bucket, Constancia speculates, just imagine all the lotions and creams she could sell!" In this novel, the comforts of the American Dream can come at the cost of exploiting the culture of one's childhood and one's family members.

Change and Transformation

Throughout this novel, the characters go through physical changes that reflect their spiritual states of being. Reina's accident is one example. After she's struck by lightning, she receives skin grafts from various lovers and relatives, and she becomes a walking symbol of the different people in her life. Perhaps the most dramatic instance of transformation is Constancia's face turning into that of her mother. Before her face changes, Constancia dreams that she's undergone plastic surgery and then awakens to find her face appears to have been "rearranged in the night.... Then it hits her with the force of a slap. This is her mother's face." Her changed appearance has various consequences. It connects Constancia to a woman and a past she sometimes despises and it makes her business a wild

Topics for Further Study

- Reina writes Constancia of deprivation in Cuba, telling her of brain surgeons who bake birthday cakes on the weekend for extra cash. Constancia thinks to herself that she never would have been happy in Cuba after 1959. Research the economic situation in Cuba today and examine what role economics play in Reina and Dulce's lives.

- Garcia told an interviewer for the *Chicago Sun-Times* that while living in Hawaii, at the edge of a bird sanctuary, she became obsessed with ostracized ducks and began reading up on naturalism. Birds play an important role in this novel. Research some of the birds that Garcia refers to and consider their significance in the story that Garcia is telling. Remember that birds migrate and that they can become extinct.

- The custody battle over Elian Gonzalez was prominent in the news in early 2000. Many Cubans immigrated to the U.S. after Fidel Castro took power. What have been the different U.S. immigration policies toward Cubans and how have these policies changed between 1959 and the present day?

- Toward the end of the novel, Constancia consults a santero. Research the Afro-Cuban religion Santeria and discuss its influence on the actions of Constancia and the other characters in this novel.

---

success because her youthful appearance helps her sell products.

Memory and Reminiscence

In *The Agüero Sisters*, family history must be faced up to—literally and figuratively. Silvestre, who never knew his father, and Constancia, who hates her mother, are doomed to remember their parents because their own faces manifest their connection to the previous generation. Reina, on the other hand, willingly accepts the role of guardian of her parents' personal histories. She is grateful to have insomnia because it gives her the chance to sort through her father's books, papers, and bird remains. "The past she combs through is long dead, sloughed off from Papá's life like the desiccated skin of a snake." As long as an individual is remembered in this novel, he or she has not really died. "To be forgotten," Reina decides, "is the final death."

Sex

Reina expresses herself through her sexuality. Her lovemaking is a gift she bestows on men all over Cuba. "Often, Reina selects the smallest, shyest electrician in a given town for her special favors, leaving him weak and inconsolable for months." She enjoys a healthy sense of self-esteem; she argues that the signs of aging never harmed a man's desire—a belief that runs directly counter to Constancia's professional commitment to supplying women with creams to help them make themselves more youthful and attractive. At one point, Reina says to Constancia, "*Oye, chica*, since when did cellulite ever deter passion?" At another moment, she says, "Por favor, mere creams and lotions won't make a woman desirable. The confidence in her walk is what gives birth to lust." Although Reina's self-confidence is appealing, she finds that same strutting sexuality unattractive in the men she encounters. "They are all much too sure of their allure. This is a problem in Cuba. Even the most gnarled, toothless, scabrous, sclerotic, pigeon-toed, dyspeptic, pestilential men on the island believe themselves irresistible to women. Reina has pondered this incongruity. Too much mother coddling is her theory. After the love and embraces of a Cuban *mami*, what man wouldn't think he was the center of the universe?"

Truth and Falsehood

In the opening scene at the Zapata Swamp, Ignacio Agüero shoots his wife, carries her body seventeen miles to the nearest village, then "began to tell his lies." For his daughters, who are told that their mother has drowned, Ignacio's deception will be a disaster, one that literally fractures their sense of how they look at all aspects of the world. Constancia later believes another lie: that her mother has killed herself. The lies result in violence between the sisters. Reina "lifts her sister by the throat. To choke out the final lies. Papá's lies. Constancia's willful, stone-blind lies." It is only after that confrontation, which takes place in a boat hovering between the U.S. and Cuban coasts, that both women can move forward in their lives.

Style

Setting

The Cubans in this novel live side by side with the past. In Havana, Reina lives in the apartment where she was raised. Dangling from the chandelier in her father's study is a bird's nest; Reina lives "amidst the debris of her childhood." To Ignacio and Blanca Agüero, the natural world of Cuba is like the Garden of Eden. "The Agüeros often imagined what Cuba must have been like before the arrival of the Spaniards, whose dogs, cats, and rats multiplied prodigiously and ultimately wreaked havoc with the island's indigenous creatures. Long ago, Cuba had been a naturalist's dream." In an interview in the *Santa Fe New Mexican* in 1997, Garcia said, "Cuba has always lived in my imagination. I have only spent a half of a month in Cuba since I was 2 1/2, so I don't have much to go on in that sense . . . to me, Cuba is on the page. In an odd sense, it is what I create for myself. I don't think I fit in Cuba, I don't fit in the exile community in Miami. So in many ways, it is the search for home. The search for Cuba begins on the page."

The settings in the United States reflect the longings of the Cuban-American community for home. Little Havana in Miami is like a museum of the Cuban past. In the U.S., at "the best *bodega* in Little Havana, two dozen varieties of bananas are sold. There are pyramids of juicy mangoes, soursops, custard apples, and papayas. In a flash, they'll make her a milk shake that tastes of her past. Every Friday, Constancia loads up her pink Cadillac convertible with fresh fruit to purée and cries all the way home." But the Cuban-Americans living in Miami and Key Biscayne are replicating a Cuba that no longer exists. Reina and the other Cubans in this novel live modestly and are accustomed to food shortages. Reina's longtime lover, Pepín, believes that it's the gusanos (a derogatory name for those Cubans who left for the U.S., which literally means "worm") who undid the accomplishments of the revolution. The wealth they brought back—even extra-strength aspirin—made citizens start skipping the May Day parade and begin refusing to cut their quota of sugarcane. Reina writes Constancia "with news of successive deprivations. Reina says it's sad to see the near-empty baskets and shelves of the markets in Cuba, the withered vegetables, the chickens too scraggly even for soup." In Garcia's world, each culture is longing for the perceived comforts of the other.

Point of View

One of the most complicated and intriguing aspects of Garcia's novel is its shifting perspectives. Although Reina and Constancia are at the heart of the novel, these two protagonists (the central characters who serve as a focus for the themes and incidents of the novel) don't tell their stories in their own voices. Ignacio Agüero has left behind a diary, in which he narrates the events of his life in the first person, telling his own story and offering opinions about the various actions and characters. Presumably, this story is the true one, the one he knows in his heart and not the one he tells his daughters after he began lying. Reina's daughter, Dulce, also tells her own story in the first person. In this way, Garcia brackets the main action of the sisters' stories with the highly personal opinions of both the older and younger generations. The first-person sections allow us to view the main events with distance. For someone like Reina's daughter, Dulce, the revolution feels different than it does for the older generation. Dulce says: "I used to be friends with Che Guevara's son in high school. We used to joke about our respective revolutionary burdens. Last I heard, he was a heavy-metal musician, pierced everywhere and trying to leave the country."

By interspersing different points of view, Garcia gives the reader information that her characters don't possess. For instance, the reader knows from the opening pages that Ignacio murdered his wife, but neither Constancia nor Reina knows this until the very end of the novel.

Literary Heritage

The influence of magical realism, a literary style common in Latin America in which fantastic or dreamlike events happen alongside more conventionally realistic ones, is clearly felt in *The Agüero Sisters*. Garcia mentions a man who was hit by lightning and reads everything backward, and a woman who swallows silver dust to stop hallucinating. Fantastic events are, as Michiko Kakutani said in a 1997 *New York Times* review, "a symptom both of the natural world's surpassing strangeness and the bizarre predicaments the human species likes to invent for itself." Some of the events Kakutani cited are the man who's saved from his angry workers by a flock of tree ducks, the man who's killed in a hurricane by "a high velocity avocado," and the fact that Reina and Constancia's grandmother dies in a pig stampede.

Garcia herself believes that second-generation Cuban immigrants are in a particularly good position to transform their experiences into art. "They're very close to these roots but not scarred by them, or at least not directly scarred," Garcia said in an interview published in the *Phoenix Gazette*. "They had a chance to be educated in this country. It's the best of both worlds." She continued, "I think another point is that a couple of generations ago, assimilation was considered a key to success and parents didn't speak to their kids in their native language. . . . Now, being bilingual or multilingual is looked at as an asset, not something you have to bury."

Historical Context

The Revolution of Fidel Castro

Although *The Agüero Sisters* takes place more than thirty years after Fidel Castro came to power in Cuba, many of the economic and social situations that the characters wrestle with date back to the revolution. For instance, it is for primarily political reasons that huge numbers of Cubans like Heberto Cruz and Constancia Agüero Cruz left Cuba once Castro was in power.

Castro, then a young lawyer, took control of Cuba in February 1959 by initiating guerrilla warfare against Fulgencio Batista, the dictator who had seized power in 1952 and who was known for his arrogance and corruption. Although Batista enjoyed the support of the United States for much of his rule, by the time that Castro defeated him Batista had begun to alienate his American supporters, so Castro's takeover was not met with too much resistance by the U.S. government. Although at first Castro was very popular in Cuba, American officials during the administration of Dwight D. Eisenhower soon realized that the new government was not going to allow the U.S. to dictate terms as it had for many years. (The U.S. had established strong economic ties in Cuba in the early 1900s and played a significant role in developing Cuba's economy.) Castro also pushed for a radical restructuring of the economy, and the Soviet Union supported him.

Cuban-American Migration

Although *The Agüero Sisters* takes place in the early '90s, many of the events were shaped by Cuban-American migration patterns. Between 1959 and 1962, more than 155,000 Cubans left the island. Of the close to one million Cubans living in the United States today, more than half arrived here after 1959. Between December 1965 and December 1972, 257,000 Cubans came to the United States. The American policy of welcoming refugees was a strategy for destabilizing the Castro government because it deprived Cuba of many of its merchants and professionals. The U.S. saw the flight of refugees as harmful to Cuba's economic future and as a symbolic victory against Communism. Most of these immigrants were fiercely opposed to Castro and his regime, but they were also proud of their Cuban identity and had a strong desire to return to their homelands.

The majority of the first wave of Cuban immigrants after the Castro revolution went to Miami, where they were close to Cuba and could enjoy a climate very similar to that at home. This is clearly seen in *The Agüero Sisters*; those who live in Miami have created a Little Havana to replicate the foods of their homeland. When Constancia moves to Florida, she is both thrilled and disturbed by the similarities to her childhood: "Everywhere, there is a mass of disquieting details. The deep-fried croquettes for sale on the corner. The accent of the valet who parks her car. Her seamstress's old-fashioned stitching. And the songs, slow as regret, on the afternoon radio."

When Constancia sends Silvestre to an orphanage in Colorado, the motivation also dates back to the revolution. Like other parents at the time, she fears that her child will be shipped off to boarding school in the Ukraine, so she voluntarily sends him away instead. Wild rumors circulated in Cuba—rumors that were fanned by U.S. officials—that children would be forcibly taken from their homes and sent to the Soviet Union and educated as Communists. Within three years' time, 14,048 children, mostly males, left Cuba and were cared for by various groups, including the Catholic Church. Today, there are many well-educated, middle-class Cuban Americans who did not rejoin their families until they were adults, if they ever went home again at all.

The Agüero family also reflects some demographic trends in Cuban immigrants. Unlike other Hispanic groups in the U.S., professionals and semiprofessionals are overrepresented in the Cuban population here. In addition, Cuban Americans tend to be older than other Hispanic groups. Currently, ten percent of Cubans in the United States are over sixty-five years of age.

Critical Overview

The Agüero Sisters received far less critical attention than Garcia's universally praised first novel, *Dreaming in Cuban*. Some seemed to prefer the early novel, although almost all felt that her second novel confirmed Garcia's place as an important talent. In the *New York Times*, Michiko Kakutani said, "Although *The Agüero Sisters* lacks the compelling organic unity of Ms. Garcia's remarkable debut novel, *Dreaming in Cuban* (1992), it should ratify Ms. Garcia's reputation as a highly original, highly gifted young writer. It also attests, like that earlier book, to Ms. Garcia's intuitive understanding of families and the fierce, enduring connections that bind one generation to another."

The reviews for her second novel were, with a few exceptions, favorable. Pico Iyer, writing in *Time*, called *The Agüero Sisters* a "beautifully rounded work of art, as warm and wry and sensuous as the island [Garcia] so clearly loves." Lloyd Sachs, writing in the *Chicago Sun-Times*, praised her for her "storyteller's love of irony and the unexpected with a modern poet's love of oblique language and heated logic. On the surface, she deals with the splintering of generations of Cuban families by Castro's revolution and the inseparability of the personal from the political. Deep down, she deals in strange destiny and the blackest magic." And Dan Cryer of *Newsday* was convinced that *The Agüero Sisters* is the better novel of the two, de-

scribing it as "a deeper, more profound plunge into the mysteries of loyalty, love and identity (national, familial and otherwise)."

Garcia earned praise for her oblique approach to storytelling. In her *New York Times* review, Deirdre McNamer said, "Ms. Garcia is a strikingly deft and supple writer, both in her sensibilities and her language. She has a talent for the oblique that allows her to write what amounts to a family saga by focusing not on the strict beat that constitutes conventional plot development but on seemingly off-hand memories and exchanges. The large events in the book—a lightning strike, a patricide, a guerrilla attack on Cuba—occur in the wings, so to speak. They are not what Ms. Garcia's characters choose to tell us much about. The important stories occur in the interstices between these dramatic events."

Other reviewers pointed out that Garcia has been somewhat misclassified and her ties to the magical realists exaggerated. Dan Cryer noted: "Some critics have mistakenly labeled Garcia as a magical realist in the Gabriel García Márquez mode. This characterization is silly and misleading. She does not make characters fly, birds talk or time twist backward. Still, hers is a prose, like the Colombian Nobel Prize winner's, rich with the delights of the senses. Her essentially realist vision overflows with warmth and brio."

Critics were quick to notice and speculate about the similarities between *The Agüero Sisters* and *Dreaming in Cuban*. A few critics faulted Garcia for revisiting old material in her second novel. Ilan Stavans, writing in the *Nation*, said *The Agüero Sisters* reads "like a hand-me-down," and lamented that "with only a slight difference in approach, Garcia already gave her readers this material." Although he praised her writing, he concluded that "Garcia has written, in many ways, the same book twice." And yet even after leveling this serious criticism, Stavans emphasized: "Don't get me wrong: Garcia is an immensely talented writer whose work, like that of Jessica Hagedorn, Sherman Alexie and David Foster Wallace, is renewing American fiction."

Others noted the family resemblance but, like Cryer, felt that *The Agüero Sisters* was the better book. Nina King, writing in the *Washington Post*, said, "The many parallels in theme and technique between Garcia's two novels might suggest a failure of authorial imagination. But *The Agüero Sisters* is undoubtedly the better novel of the two: denser, more focused, with a greater richness of language and of comic invention. To my mind, it's a case of practice making perfect." And in discussing the two books, Ruth Behar wrote in the *Chicago Tribune* that *The Agüero Sisters* is "an even more gorgeously written, even more flamboyantly feminist vision of Cuban and Cuban-American history, women's lives, memory and desire."

Criticism

Elizabeth Judd,

Elizabeth Judd is a freelance writer and book reviewer with an M.F.A. in English from the University of Michigan and a B.A. from Yale. In this essay, she discusses Garcia's exploration of how personal and national histories shape the characters' destinies in The Agüero Sisters.

For Constancia and Reina Agüero, two sisters struggling to come to terms with the histories of their countries and their families, the truth is slippery, something that's been fractured by lies. History is in the eye of the teller, and facts are far from stable. Like other Cuban Americans, Garcia herself is used to radically different interpretations of the same event. In the *Los Angeles Times*, she said, "All of my mother's family stayed in Cuba by choice. My mother was the only one who came. All of my father's family decided to come to the United States. My mother joined my father's camp. So we were politically polarized. My mother's family was very pro-Castro, pro-revolution—many of them still are. My father's side is virulently anti-Castro, anti-Communist. I grew up in the middle of this black-and-white extreme situation." And in an interview in *Newsweek*, Garcia enlarged upon this point: "in my family, and I see it in other Cuban families as well, there's this fierce struggle over family myth and history. People have political agendas and axes to grind. Everyone's version is competing with everybody else's, and who can tell where the truth really is?"

One aspect of Cuban history is, of course, politics. Garcia points out that for many, politics is an excuse for posturing. When Reina arrives in Miami, she knows that revolutionary rhetoric will no longer fly, and she usually remembers to play her role perfectly. When she forgets, trouble breaks out:

Little Havana, Miami.

"The other day, Reina's vernacular slipped, and she called the Winn-Dixie cashier *campañera* by mistake. Well, all hell broke loose on the checkout line, and a dozen people nearly came to blows!" Here, political talk is a prelude to a slapstick brawl and is tinged with farce. While the Winn-Dixie customers overreact, thirty-one-year-old Dulce is so worn out by politics that her opinion of the revolution is comically understated: "At minimum, it can make a person permanently irritable."

What makes politics comical is the human dimension, the warring personalities involved. When Constancia's mild-mannered husband, Heberto Cruz, joins his brother Gonzalo's underground exile group, La Brigada Caimán, for him, the goal of the enterprise is personal, "to break free from his leashed life." Not only is he absolutely clear-sighted on this point, but so is Constancia. She sees that what attracts Heberto to "a quasi-historical calling" is the grandeur of it, the opportunities for fulfilling his own inner possibilities. "'Men always confuse patriotism with self-love!' Constancia hisses between bites of fried plantains. It's a perverse form of idealism. Why else all the primping and medals, all the oiled and spit-shined leathers? In her opinion, war should be strictly personal, like philosophy or sexual preference." Politics is akin to sexual attrac-

What Do I Read Next?

- In Garcia's first novel, *Dreaming in Cuban*, three generations of a Cuban-American family are divided over their conflicting feelings about everything from the Cuban revolution and Fidel Castro to their new life in Brooklyn.

- Like Garcia, Julia Alvarez is concerned with how families are bound together in their adopted culture and what divides them as they look back on their lives in their birth countries. In *How the Garcia Girls Lost Their Accents*, four young sisters leave the Dominican Republic with their parents and are sent to prep school before forging new-world lives.

- Gabriel García Márquez's classic *One Hundred Years of Solitude* is a family history in which the most fantastic wonders happen alongside far more ordinary events in the fictional village of Macondo. A master of magical realism, Márquez tells of an entire town plagued with insomnia and a woman who ascends to heaven while hanging her laundry out to dry.

- Cuban-American writer Oscar Hijuelos made music his theme in his exploration of the immigrant experience. In *The Mambo Kings Play Songs of Love*, the novel for which Hijuelos won a Pulitzer Prize, two young Cuban musicians go from Havana to New York in 1949, determined to be mambo stars in the U.S. Both Hijuelos and Garcia share an interest in music, showing how songs can evoke mood and emotions like longing and nostalgia.

---

tion in this novel. Heberto tacks the Cuban flag to his and Constancia's bedroom wall, and Gonzalo woos Heberto to his cause much as he romantically won Constancia in their youth. Constancia "knows firsthand how persuasive a salesman her ex-husband can be. Thirty-five years ago, Gonzalo came courting her, ferocious with dreams. He cut open a vein in his leg to impress her, brought her a wreath of dead bees. . . . Constancia considered him a hazard, like languor or sunstroke. . . ."

One's relationship to one's country is similar to the relationships in a family. Dulce makes this explicit when she compares Cuba to "an evil stepmother, abusive and unrewarding of effort. More, more, and more for more nothing." However, one's role in history can also be a way of escaping one's family responsibilities. When Dulce thinks of her father, a well-known revolutionary, his exalted reputation makes his personal shortcomings that much harder to bear.

> Reina knows that Dulcita resents her father, the veneration he still receives as a Hero of the Revolution. As her daughter grew older, his picture stared back at her from her history books, his slogans were extolled while she endlessly harvested lemons or yams. All Dulcita's life, it was José Luís Fuerte this, José Luís Fuerte that, until it made her ill.
>
> *If he was so great, why didn't he ever see me?*

Dulcita was six years old when she asked Reina this.

One counterbalance to political pain is humor. Garcia mocks revolutionary fervor: "In recent years, small propeller planes buzzed over Havana like persistent insects, dropping leaflets urging a mass uprising. If these pilots were truly interested in building solidarity with their *hermanos* in Cuba (who, incidentally, were already gagging on propaganda), they would have dropped more useful items: sewing kits or instant soup, bars of soap, even decent novels, for that matter. The leaflets, Reina remembers, were barely suitable for toilet paper. They left tenacious exclamation points on her buttocks, which, despite vigorous scrubbing, took many days to fade." The exclamation points on Reina's flesh give an absurd twist to what otherwise would be a serious message. Throughout, a sense of practicality deflates the romanticism of the revolutionary cause. If the revolutionaries are play-acting, driven by their own personal needs to generate propaganda, then the proper response is a reality check, someone asking for instant soup instead of yet another pamphlet.

Subjectivity can be a balm, too. It's Constancia's unique talent to invent products that elicit nostalgia in a generic enough way so that each user will take from the product what she needs. "Already, Constancia has received dozens of letters from women who confess that they feel more *cubana* after using her products, that they recall long-forgotten details of their childhoods in Sagua la Grande, Remedios, Media Luna, or Santa Cruz del Sur. . . . Politics may have betrayed Constancia's customers, geography overlooked them, but Cuerpo de Cuba products still manage to touch the pink roots of their sadness." Here, the same object is rich in meaning for many different women, but what the creams and lotions mean depends upon the individual and her own unique situation and set of memories.

Subjectivity becomes harmful when the same object is interpreted so differently that it drives a wedge between family members or lovers. Ignacio Agüero's lies about his wife's death rob his daughters of their ability to perceive reality and communicate about it meaningfully. Constancia and Reina are so divided that little common ground remains. "Reina remembers how, after her mother's death, everyone's vision splintered. There was a bird that hovered over Mami's burial plot at the Colón Cemetery. Her father pronounced it a common crow. Constancia, fresh from the farm in Camagüey, insisted it was electric blue. Reina wanted to believe her sister, but *she* saw a bird on fire, tiny and bathed in violent light. It broke the air around them, invited an early dusk. Reina recalls how the emptiness seemed to surround them then, a sad bewilderment that has never lifted." This is a poetic evocation of how small differences can be magnified until nothing is perceived the same way. Although Reina wants to believe her sister's version of events, she can't. She literally sees a different reality, a bird on fire where her sister sees electric blue. Those differences persist, keeping them apart.

Humor isn't Garcia's only solution to the various rifts Cuban Americans experience. For the greater differences—such as the family feud between the sisters—much more than humor is required. Here, Garcia turns to magic and religion. "When logic fails, when reason betrays, there is only the tenuous solace of magic, of ritual and

> "The history that counts is that one that's lived on a daily basis. 'There's no substitute,' wrote Garcia, 'for the quiet culture of a life together, the endless days commemorating nothing, amassing history bit by bit.'"

lamentation." The book's final scene, in which the two sisters fight with one another and Reina nearly drowns before they reach some sort of unspoken resolution, is propelled by Constancia's visit to the santero. In a 1997 *Chicago Tribune* article, Ruth Behar wrote: "In the midst of such confusion and moral crisis, Santeria, the Afro-Cuban religion that survived slavery and the revolution, offers perhaps the only source of spiritual solace for Cubans here and there, or so at least suggests Garcia, whose novel is anchored in the clairvoyance of this enduring faith."

In Garcia's world, magic and religion are manifestations of the deep connections people share, those connections that reach well beyond language. The members of the Agüero family, no matter where they live, no matter who's alive and who's dead, share a physical bond that keeps recurring in mysterious ways. Blanca Agüero is left with a mark on her heel while swimming on her honeymoon; Constancia marks Isabel on the foot while trying to revive her from heatstroke; and Isabel's son, Raku, is born with a red birthmark on his foot. Nina King, writing in the *Washington Post Book World,* commented: "Though they have been separated for 30 years, the two sisters' experiences sometimes involve a mysterious parallelism." The example she gives is Constancia's having woken up with her mother's face and Reina's having been struck by lightning and given skin grafts from family and friends. In Garcia's world, people are an amalgamation of their loved ones. Even emotional memories are handed down from generation to generation. Ignacio recalls that his mother's out-of-wedlock daughter was drowned in September, and even though that sad event occurred before his birth, each year, in September, he feels sad.

In the end, history is an illusion, or, in Reina's words, ''It's all a mock history.'' Magic and religion help point us in the right direction, but what seems to matter most is simple things, such as the shrimp-and-watercress omelet that the sisters share in a boat halfway between Florida and Cuba. The history that counts is that one that's lived on a daily basis. ''There's no substitute,'' wrote Garcia, ''for the quiet culture of a life together, the endless days commemorating nothing, amassing history bit by bit.''

Source: Elizabeth Judd, in an essay for *Literature of Developing Nations for Students*, Gale, 2000.

Ana Maria Hernandez

In the following brief essay, Ana Maria Hernandez describes The Agüero Sisters, *Garcia's second novel, as a ''whydunit'' using satire, metaphor, and a variety of character narrations (the Aguero sisters, their daughters, and a third person narrator) to unfold the mystery of a family murder/suicide.*

Cristina Garcia's second novel opens in the mystical Zapata Swamp on the southern coast of Cuba, a place long imbued with mystery and magic in Cuban folklore and Afro-Cuban ritual. It is there that Ignacio Aguero, a renowned naturalist, murders the mysterious Blanca, his wife and research associate. Two years later, he commits suicide, leaving no explanatory note. The novel thus becomes a whydunit, as in the case of Garcia Marquez's *Cronica de una muerte anunciada*. The reader approaches the story from multiple points of view, attempting to elucidate the reasons for the murder/suicide and its effect on the surviving Aguero daughters and their own progeny.

The novel is masterfully structured with a mosaic of narrations from the Aguero sisters, their daughters Dulce and Isabel, Ignacio Aguero, and a third-person narrator who localizes each sister alternately. The diminutive Constancia, unwanted by her mother and virtually abandoned by the latter after the birth of her half-sister Reina, relies on appearance (she is a cosmetologist), social connections, and the conventional trappings of success: a sizable income, a well-placed condo, a boat, a (pink!) Cadillac. Reina, resembling her mother's mulatto lover, basks in her mother's love and solicitous attention (she is breastfed until she is five), and grows up self-assured, androgynous, and libidinous—perhaps excessively so. The forty-eight-year-old Reina's animal magnetism and endless conquests seem a bit hyperbolic even by the standards of magic realism, to which Garcia subscribes in a subdued manner. Constancia embodies the traditional values of Cuban middle-class exiles, whereas Reina, a master electrician by training and profession and a solid supporter of the revolution until the job-related accident that results in her defection to Miami, represents the blue-collar outlook of the supposedly classless society in which she grew up and the survival skills of the last wave of exiles.

Garcia meticulously researches every aspect of her novel—from ornithology to cosmetology by way of electrical engineering and antique-car repair—and conveys her findings with an admirable command of language and a gift for metaphor. Her careful reconstructions of habitats long destroyed and traditions long abandoned inspire Cubans to remember and non-Cubans to discover; especially noteworthy is her evocation of the lectores, cigar-factory employees whose function it was to entertain cigar rollers with readings from the classics, hoping to improve the quality of their product by improving the minds of its makers. The descriptions of the Cuban landscape around the beginning of this century provided by the naturalist Aguero are particularly lyrical and almost mystical, even though we suspect that some of the species described are figments of the author's imagination. At one point she places a leatherback turtle—whose usual habitat excludes the Caribbean—in the waters around the (former) Isle of Pines to the south of Cuba. Aguero spots the gigantic turtle as she digs her nest on the black volcanic sands of the isle and lays her eggs at midnight. He then watches in dread as predatory seagulls and stray dogs threaten the nest: ''What choice did I have? I sat on the leatherback's nest all that day and all the next night, guarding her eggs from predators, guarding the eggs for her.'' Immediately following an episode in which Ignacio's first love goes sour after his beloved asks him to exterminate a colony of bats that had infested her attic, the landscape and its creatures become a metaphor for the subjectivity of the character and an affirmation of the eternal laws of nature over the vicissitudes of human life and love. Such juxtapositions abound throughout the novel.

Satire is an important element in *The Aguero Sisters*—specifically about the exile community in

Miami, with the usual planned invasions of Cuba and the sacralization of everything pre-Castro. Most amusing is the mushrooming of Constancia's line of cosmetics, ''Cuerpo de Cuba,'' which caters to aging Cuban baby-boomers by offering a special emollient for every sagging part of their anatomy (''Cuello de Cuba,'' ''Rodillas de Cuba,'' ''Muslos de Cuba''). This is a humorous, well-written, most enjoyable work from the author of *Dreaming in Cuban*.

Source: Ana Maria Hernandez, ''The Aguero Sisters,'' (Book review) in *World Literature Today,* Vol. 72, No. 1, Winter, 1998, p. 134.

Rachel Campbell-Johnston

In her brief essay on Garcia's The Agüero Sisters, *Rachel Campbell-Johnston describes a loose, sometimes even nebulous, emotionally based plotline driven by the lives of the Aguero sisters and using Cuban political and cultural history as its bedrock.*

Cuba, the outpost of a decayed ideal, nurtures a distinctive temperament. The giddy hedonism of an island which surely senses it cannot barricade itself much longer against the modern world mingles with disappointment of a shattered dream. This novel by Cuban emigree Cristina Garcia captures both these moods, distilling them into the twinned themes of sex and death.

The Aguero Sisters is the interleaving narrative of two daughters, Reina and Constancia. Reina, the younger, works as an electrician in Cuba. Statuesque and sensual, with thighs strengthened by shinning up telegraph poles, her body is an open invitation to pleasure. ''If she could grasp nothing in its entirety then why not celebrate what she could grasp with her own senses.'' She luxuriates in a power to reduce men to a state of helplessness. But when she is struck by lightning (the improbable becomes the norm in this novel) she begins to think it would be better if she were dead. Her grafted skin, mismatched and scratchy, smells to her of blood and sour milk. It ruins her familiar pleasures—''her rapture and her hot black scent.'' Until suddenly, at precisely 5:13 one morning, she suddenly knows one thing for certain: that she can no longer stay in Cuba. She illicitly escapes to join her sister Constancia in Miami.

Constancia, her elder sister, is petite with lacquered nails, carnelian lips and a firm belief that

> Garcia meticulously researches every aspect of her novel—from ornithology to cosmetology by way of electrical engineering and antique-car repair—and conveys her findings with an admirable command of language and a gift for metaphor."

comfort should never be placed before style. Owner of a successful company manufacturing beauty products, her chief concern is to stave off women's ''little everyday deaths.'' ''If politics have betrayed the Cubans and geography overlooked them, her Cuerpo de Cuba products still manage to touch the pink roots of their sadness.''

Though the two sisters seem so different, they are rooted in a Cuban past which draws them together. The voices of their parents—two biologists whose life of shared passion ended in sudden and violent death—provides a context for their daughters' voices. Together they shape a mesmerising—if bewildering—portrait of a family whose lives reflect the mood and history of Cuba.

This is a loose, drifting novel. Curiously, and often irritatingly, nebulous, the plot hinges on memories and emotions, magic and impossible turns of fate. To try to pin it down is to lose it. ''You don't know how much of what you see, mi hija, you never see at all,'' Reina's mother says. But always a stringent sense of reality twists through the dreams. History forms a harsh bedrock to this tale.

Source: Rachel Campbell-Johnston, ''The Familial Crises of Two Cuban Misses,'' in *The Times,* August 21, 1997, p. 34.

Deidre McNamer

In the following essay, Deidre McNamer describes Garcia's The Agüero Sisters *as a meditation on the juxtaposition of past and present Cuba through the personal lives of the Aguero sisters. McNamer stresses Garcia's ability to highlight the*

"" Cuba, the outpost of a decayed ideal, nurtures a distinctive temperament. The giddy hedonism of an island which surely senses it cannot barricade itself much longer against the modern world mingles with disappointment of a shattered dream."

critical elements of "evolution, exile and extinction" within the confines of personal relationships and reflection.

In a certain way, extinction and augury are intertwined. The lineaments of the future can be divined by what the present refuses to support—an idea that is at the heart of *The Aguero Sisters,* Cristina Garcia's exhilarating meditation on Cubans and Cuba in the early 1990s.

As she did five years ago in her acclaimed first novel, *Dreaming in Cuban,* Ms. Garcia uses a divided family—some of the members remained in Cuba after the revolution, others made lives in America—as a way to talk about larger issues like patriotism, exile and the psychological costs of cultural fragmentation. However, there's an important difference between the two books. *Dreaming in Cuban* was set in the 1970s, when Fidel Castro's island still shimmered as a fierce and outsized symbol of all that was at stake in the cold war, and when the ruptures between those who stayed and those who left were still raw. Since then, the world has been vastly reconfigured. Now Castro is an old man, flogging a tired experiment. A skeptical new generation of Cubans and Cuban-Americans has come of age, and their parents—who lived through the revolution as children or young adults—are a disappearing species.

The Aguero sisters—their family name means "omen" or "augury"—belong to that species and are the focus of Ms. Garcia's exuberant attention. (It should be said right off that she is a very funny writer, one who uses her wit not to trivialize her characters but to encourage greater access to the conditions of their lives.)

Reina Aguero, when we first meet her, is a 48-year-old master electrician who lives in one room of a Havana apartment that once belonged to her parents and now houses seven other families She is regal, competent and enthusiastically promiscuous, though her grand passion is a married bureaucrat with orthopedic shoes who has been her lover for 24 years. Her parents were naturalists who catalogued Cuban flora and fauna on the verge of extinction, and Reina lives rather contentedly among the remains of their work—stuffed bats, old field notes—until December of 1990, when a literal bolt of lightning prompts her to take a closer look at her life.

Her half sister, Constancia, 51, has lived in America for nearly 30 years and is a paragon of capitalist enterprise. For many years, her husband, Heberto, owned a Manhattan tobacco store that sold the world's finest hand-rolled cigars, including illegal Cuban imports. Constancia herself is a genius at selling cosmetics, her motivation the sheer "satisfaction of staving off women's little everyday deaths." The couple move to Miami, where Constancia sets up her own cosmetics line, Cuerpo de Cuba, and Heberto becomes involved in the heady enterprise of anti-revolutionary politics. Off he goes with a submachine gun to crash around in the Everglades with La Brigada Caiman, a bunch of old crocodiles who still think they're going to liberate Cuba. In his waning years, he has finally discovered the sharp thrill, "the promising grandeur of a quasi-historical calling."

But Miami's exile community has become aged and brittle, an invalid with a fever. Even Constancia finds the air "thickly charged with expiring dreams." And in that respect it's not so different from Cuba itself. Seen through the distinctly unrosy gaze of Dulce Fuerte, Reina's aimless 32-year-old daughter, Cuba in the 1990s is beset by a virulent combination of deprivation and boredom; it is a place where "the future is frozen" and everything from sex to a santeria initiation is sold for tourist dollars. Dulce wonders idly what her revolutionary father would think of her today. "I used to be friends with Che Guevara's son in high school," she says. "We used to joke about our respective revolutionary burdens. Last I heard, he was a heavy-metal musician, pierced everywhere and trying to leave the country."

Ms. Garcia is a strikingly deft and supple writer, both in her sensibilities and her language.

She has a talent for the oblique that allows her to write what amounts to a family saga by focusing not on the strict beat that constitutes conventional plot development but on seemingly offhand memories and exchanges. The large events in the book—a lightning strike, a patricide, a guerrilla attack on Cuba—occur in the wings, so to speak. They are not what Ms. Garcia's characters choose to tell us much about. The important stories occur in the interstices between these dramatic events.

In a slight misstep at the beginning of the novel, however, Ms. Garcia seems to suggest otherwise. The prologue describes an apparent murder: the mother of the Aguero sisters is shot by her husband, Ignacio, while the two naturalists are on a collecting trip in 1948. Ignacio's motive is deeply unclear, so the reader is encouraged at the outset to expect the working out of that mystery during the course of the novel. Why did he do it? And furthermore, why was each of the daughters given a different version of her mother's death? Why was each version a lie?

Ignacio's voice is present in the form of nine dispatches that survived his death. But only in the very last one does he talk about the shooting of his wife. There is no gradual illumination of that shocking incident, as there would be in a conventional mystery. Instead, what Ignacio chooses to address is the Cuba of his childhood and the creatures that lived in abundance then, including men like his father, whose job was to read to hushed factory workers while they rolled cigars by hand. He remembers his growing obsession with birds and the day his parents gave him the voluminous, magnificently illustrated *Birds of the World*. He describes the day he saw an eight-foot leatherback turtle drag herself onto a beach and lay her eggs, and the day he and his future wife, Blanca, stalked a mauve frog a quarter-inch long. With exactness and insight, he offers a record of his own existence: what he yearned for, what he noticed, what disappeared as he watched. The mysterious shooting soon takes its place among the many large mysteries of a single human existence.

All credit to Ms. Garcia, Ignacio's creator. The novelist's geomancy might consist, as much as anything, in the ability to illuminate what is crucial while seeming not to. By letting Ignacio speak to us in his naturalist's voice about many things that don't appear to pertain to the story, she eloquently highlights the novel's major themes: evolution, exile, extinction—and the last days of some very rare birds.

Source: Deidre McNamer, ''World of Portents,'' in *The New York Times Book Review,* June 15, 1997, sec. 7, p. 38, col. 2.

> " The large events in the book—a lightning strike, a patricide, a guerrilla attack on Cuba—occur in the wings, so to speak. They are not what Ms. Garcia's characters choose to tell us much about. The important stories occur in the interstices between these dramatic events."

Ilan Stavans

In the following essay, Ilan Stavans ambivalently describes Garcia's The Agüero Sisters *as a well-written telenovel, a tangled and melodramatic path of well-written characters capturing, through the flow of their lives, the essence of the Cuban Diaspora. His criticism of the novel, however, is that Garcia utilizes a style too similar to her first novel,* Dreaming in Cuban, *in structure and plot, which diminishes both works.*

Cristina Garcia's second novel, *The Aguero Sisters,* is a magisterial melodrama. Its plot wends through fraternal rivalries, pregnant daughters at odds with their mothers, unexplained murders, illegitimate children seeking to unravel their obscure origins—a family feud of epic proportion, traversing generations. One could easily confuse it with the latest prime-time telenovela on Univision, save for its lack of orchestral music and commercial interruption. Then, too, there is Garcia's astonishing literary style and dazzling attention to the telling detail, so alien to the world of soap operas. But her universe is ruled by primal emotions just the same, bordering on the ersatz.

At the heart of *The Aguero Sisters* is a Cuban lineage that spans the twentieth century and globetrots from Europe to the United States and back to the Caribbean basin. Ignacio Aguero, the family patriarch, is a renowned biologist. The novel opens as he kills his estranged wife, Blanca, while on a trip collecting fauna in the Zapata Swamp, on the banks of the Rio Hanabana. Pretending it was either a suicide or an accident, he carries her seventeen

> " *The Agüero Sisters* is indeed impressive, a book about revenge and love and hatred but especially about courage, in all its forms: courage to antagonize a regime, courage to be reconciled with one's own past courage to find the truth."

miles to the nearest village and, as related by the novel's too-lucid omniscient narrator (whose sections are interleaved with the characters' own narrations, not always well differentiated), he begins to tell his lies.

To illuminate the spectra of emotions thrown off by such an event, Garcia resorts to a narrative marked by counterpoint: In a Faulknerian approach (think of *As I Lay Dying*), she shifts scenes and subplots from this character to the next, from one viewpoint to another— from Constancia, the oldest Aguero sister, to her second husband, Heberto Cruz, a counterrevolutionary plotting another Bay of Pigs-style invasion of Cuba; from Reina's, Constancia's younger sister, to Reina's estranged daughter, Dulce Fuerte, and Constancia's first husband, Gonzalo, himself Heberto's brother. . . and so on. As the various storylines unfold, each crashes against and redeems the others. This allows Garcia, in a fashion reminiscent of Fernando Ortiz's *Cuban Counterpoint: Tobacco and Sugar*, to play a fascinating game of light and shadow, using one character to explain another and vice versa. A quote from early on:

> Constancia pulls her husband to the dance floor. He is diminutive, like her, and she is dressed in white, like him. Together they look like a first communion date. Heberto is a good dancer, but often reluctant. Constancia is not, but excessively enthusiastic. She lurches too far to the right on a turn, but Heberto reels her in with a practiced air. Then he steadies her with a palm to the small of her back and leads her across the room.

The chorus of voices in this novel echo off a single sounding board, though: Ignacio Aguero. His reflective journal, in fact, functions as a palimpsest of sorts: The family secret—the murder—lies hid-

den within it, and to bring the truth to light, characters variously hide it and unearth it. This, of course, is a technique as old as the novel itself, but in the baroque world of Hispanic America it has become the artifice of first resort, probably because of the collective urge to return, time and again, to the wound that lies at the origin of everything: the shock of birth. Borges's masterpieces are all palimpsests, and *One Hundred Years of Solitude* is cast as a modern rendering of an ancient Gypsy scroll.

Not that in Cristina Garcia's hands this feels artificial. So what if it is derivative, a reader might ask—how much in art and literature isn't? Furthermore, isn't it in the nature of melodrama to deploy stock characters in archetypal situations? Sure, and Garcia brilliantly captures the cultural temperament of the Cuban diaspora. Always in search of something new, Constancia opens Cuerpo de Cuba, a beauty factory in Miami, and becomes a millionaire. As the novel progresses, she leaves the United States for Cuba, where her father's diary lies buried. Her sister Reina has migrated in the opposite direction. Fed up with Cuban socialism, she moves to the United States and becomes Constancia's confidante. Itinerancy, indeed, is the only constant: New Yorkers move to Florida, Cubans to Spain and the United States, Miamians to Cuba—a never-ending Gulf Stream whose flow symbolizes the real cycle of personal revolution.

Yet it is unfortunate that, with only a slight difference in approach, Garcia already gave her readers this material. The bulk of *The Aguero Sisters* takes place in 1991, as a group of Cuban counterrevolutionaries plan to overthrow Havana, unfolding in the same time frame and fashion, give or take a few years, as her debut novel, *Dreaming in Cuban*. The first book was also about—what else?— sibling rivalries and counterrevolutionaries and the crossroads of passion and politics. *The Aguero Sisters* reads, then, like a hand-me-down: Sisters swap partners, santeros unite the spiritual and the earthly, and Cuba is portrayed not as one nation but two: Fidel's and everyone else's.

Both novels are populated with a similar cast of characters and rotate around the search for clues to family identity. And as the genealogy in each is unscrambled, truth becomes more tangled. "It's all a mock history," Reina whispers at one point in *The Aguero Sisters*, and a bit later Constancia concludes, "Knowledge is a kind of mirage"—a statement [that] could pointedly apply to her precursors, the protagonists of *Dreaming in Cuban*.

Don't get me wrong: Garcia is an immensely talented writer whose work, like that of Jessica Hagedorn, Sherman Alexie and David Foster Wallace, is renewing American fiction. *Dreaming in Cuban* was original and endearing when it was published in 1992, and while some accused Garcia of misrepresenting the Afro-Cuban tradition, I embraced the book for addressing admirably what Jose Marti once called las dos Cubas, both from within and from without. Melodrama it was, sure, but it had much more to it than laughter and Kleenex. Five years later, Garcia does write with more assurance, and her themes bear a certain Jewish flavor—memory and endurance, tradition and modernity. Not accidentally are Cubans sometimes called the Jews of the Caribbean.

Still, my feelings about *The Aguero Sisters* are ambivalent. Garcia has written, in many ways, the same book twice. Not word by word, like a Pierre Menard redrafting *Don Quixote* in the style of French symbolism. But she has become her own imitator, however deftly. *The Aguero Sisters* is indeed a wonderful book, but not a wonderful second book. It treads the same ground as its predecessor without taking new risks, without expanding into new horizons. Its prose is stupendous, its characters well rounded. But it is also predictable, simply because Garcia has prepared us for the same structure and plot—so much so that the excellence of *Dreaming in Cuban* seems retrospectively diminished by its author showing us the props and strings of its melodramatic structure. Not that I would rank her alongside Corin Tellado, the father of all Spanish-speaking melodramatists: Garcia's imagination is a treasure box of possibilities. So I feel disappointed that she has not dared to explore new structures and techniques, to reinvent herself as an artist. This puts me in mind of a memorable drama teacher I once had, whose motto was, "Don't give your audience only what it wants! Teach it to want more."

Melodrama has the habit of infiltrating serious literature everywhere, of course. One need only invoke Rosario Ferre's *The House on the Lagoon*, Julia Alvarez's *How the Garcia Girls Lost Their Accents* and *Yo!*, Denise Chavez's *Face of an Angel* and Ana Castillo's *So Far From God* to see the extent to which this is true, especially among Latinas. The reason, perhaps, is the emphasis Hispanic culture places on emotions and the signal influence soap operas have played in it since the fifties. Garcia's is a universe in which passion reigns and everyone is vulnerable and peevish and a bit insin-

cere. Garcia surely isn't the sole explorer of the telenovela qua literary form—though she is one of the most gifted. Should we expect to be surprised in a writer's second act, or is being impressed enough?

In the end, *The Aguero Sisters* is indeed impressive, a book about revenge and love and hatred but especially about courage, in all its forms: courage to antagonize a regime, courage to be reconciled with one's own past courage to find the truth. As Ignacio Aguero, the family patriarch, tells his daughters, "The quest for truth is far more glorious than the quest for power."

Source: Ilan Stavans, "The Aguero Sisters," (Book review) in *The Nation,* Vol. 264, No. 19, May 19, 1997, p. 32.

Sources

Behar, Ruth, review, in *Chicago Tribune*, June 8, 1997, p. 1.

Cryer, Dan, review, in *Newsday*, May 5, 1997, p. B02.

Iyer, Pico, review, in *Time*, May 12, 1997, p. 88.

Kakutani, Michiko, review, in *New York Times*, May 27, 1997, p. C16.

King, Nina, review, in *Washington Post*, July 13, 1997, p. X01.

Kirkwood, Cynthia Adina, "A Cuban Odyssey: It Took a Trip to Havana to Piece Together Cristina Garcia's History and Literary Quest," in *Los Angeles Times*, August 30, 1992, p. E7.

Lopez, Ruth, "Five Questions" (interview with Cristina Garcia), in *Santa Fe New Mexican*, June 8, 1997, p. E3.

McNamer, Deirdre, "World of Portents," in *New York Times*, June 15, 1997, sec. 7, p. 38.

Miller, Susan, "Caught between Two Cultures," in *Newsweek*, April 20, 1992.

Porter, William, "Worlds Apart: *Dreaming in Cuban* Novelist to Read from her Works in Valley," in *Phoenix Gazette*, March 31, 1993, p. D3.

Sachs, Lloyd, review, in *Chicago Sun-Times*, June 10, 1997, p. 35.

Stavans, Ilan, review, in *Nation*, Vol. 264, No. 19, May 19, 1997, p. 32.

Vourvoulias, Bill, "Talking with Cristina Garcia," in *Newsday*, May 4, 1997.

Further Reading

Burkett, Elinor, "Author Focuses on Cuban Nostalgia," in *Chicago Tribune*, April 9, 1992, p. 11I.

In this interview, Garcia describes how it feels to be a Cuban-American writer and discusses her childhood and literary beginnings.

Davila, Florangela, ''Cristina Garcia Identifies with Her Characters,'' in *Seattle Times*, June 17, 1997, p. C1.
An interview with Garcia in which she discusses how a flock of ducks was the inspiration for her second novel.

Garcia, Cristina, ''Star-Spangled,'' in *Washington Post*, July 18, 1999, p. W21.
Garcia writes of her own childhood and how it felt to celebrate her birthday on the Fourth of July, the birthday of her adopted country.

Italie, Hillel, ''Imagining Cuba,'' in the *Associated Press*, March 30, 1992.
Garcia discusses the beginnings of her first novel.

Stephenson, Anne, ''*Dreaming in Cuban* Has Happy Ending: First-Time Novelist Hailed as Major Voice for Latinos,'' in *Arizona Republic*, March 31, 1993.
In this interview, Garcia discusses what it feels like to be called ''a major new voice in an emerging chorus of Latino writers'' and how her family reacted to her first novel.

Among the Volcanoes

Omar S. Castañeda

1991

Among the Volcanoes is a coming-of-age story written for young adults and set in a place far removed from the environments familiar to American readers. Castañeda was able to write the novel in part due to funding from a Fulbright Fellowship for research in Central America that allowed him to study more closely the culture and people of his heritage. Published in 1991 in the United States, the novel is intended for readers between the ages of twelve and eighteen. It is set in the author's native Guatemala and tells the story of a teenager, Isabel Pacay, who experiences the same feelings and uncertainties as any adolescent, but in a very difficult place and time. The political climate is hostile and very dangerous, her mother is afflicted with a debilitating illness, she must stop attending school in order to care for her family, and she is having problems with her fiancé. To make matters worse, Isabel does not always think like the other members of her community. They are very tradition-minded, while she has dreams of taking a different path with her life than the one she is expected to follow.

Although critical response was scant, those who reviewed the novel praised it for its compelling and realistic portrayal of Mayan culture in Guatemala. At the same time, critics felt that the universal themes would appeal to Castañeda's young audience. The book addresses betrayal, love, the difficulties of making decisions as teenagers approach adulthood, the discomfort of not quite fitting in with the rest of the community, discovering one's identi-

ty, and the nature of family relationships. The story is about Isabel's responsibility, not just to her family and her fiancé, but ultimately to herself.

Author Biography

Omar Sigfrido Castañeda was born on September 6, 1954, in Guatemala City, Guatemala, but grew up in Michigan and Indiana after his family moved to the United States. Although he became an American citizen in 1986, he returned to Guatemala on numerous occasions to study Mayan life and culture for his novels, short stories, and picture book.

Before becoming a respected novelist and English professor, Castañeda joined the military, where he served for four years in avionics (electronics used in airplanes) communications maintenance. After his service in the military, he attended Indiana University in Bloomington, where he earned a B.A. in 1980 and an M.F.A. in 1983. When he later became an educator, his work took him to Florida, Washington, and China. His wife's work as an anthropologist allowed the couple to travel to foreign countries such as Mexico and China, as well as to return to Guatemala.

Castañeda was an award-winning writer, earning such prestigious honors as an Ernest Hemingway fellowship, a Critchfield Research Award, a Fulbright Central American Research Grant (during which he wrote *Among the Volcanoes*), and a Pulitzer Prize nomination. Some of his work reflects the magic realism style so popular in Central America. His primary literary influences were Gabriel Garcia Marquez and Miguel Angel Asturias.

Castañeda's work is characteristic of the new Latin American style of literature that combines emotions and aesthetics with strong ethnic and political viewpoints. In a *Booklist* article, Rosemary Brosnan quotes Castañeda: ''You cannot separate politics from art. One can only ignore or obfuscate the politics in art. Those who try to separate the two are really sanctioning the dominant view.'' This sentiment accounts for the fact that he often used his writing to express his concern for peace and justice in Guatemala.

Castañeda died of a heroin overdose in January 1997. He was a professor of writing at Western Washington University at the time, and his death came as a shock to the campus. He is survived by his wife and two children.

Plot Summary

Chapters One through Five

Isabel Pacay, the oldest of four children, is a teenage girl taking care of the family because her mother, Manuela, is very ill. She realizes that ''by being the first, she was now the last,'' because she must now put everyone else's needs before her own. One morning her father leaves without breakfast, and Isabel follows him under the guise of going to get the water. She watches him as he sacrifices a chicken to both the native and Christian gods, while praying specifically for Isabel. She returns home and prepares breakfast. After the younger children leave for school, Isabel's mother goes to the altar and performs the healing rituals as instructed by Eziquel Coxol, the town healer. Isabel worries that her mother will never get better, and that she will be forever stuck as the woman of the house. Her dream is to become a teacher, and even though she knows it seems impossible, she is unwilling to give up hope.

When Manuela has another attack, Isabel heads into town to find Eziquel. There she finds many of the villagers gathered around an American imploring the mayor to allow him to do his medical work in their village. Because of the hostile political climate, however, the natives are suspicious of strangers. Isabel, who loves learning, is intrigued by this man who has come from so far away. As the crowd breaks up, Isabel sees her fiancé, Lucas. He is distant and cold to her, leaving her confused as she goes to find Eziquel. Isabel returns home with the healer, and for the first time, Manuela admits how sick she is. When Isabel's father, Alfredo, comes home, the family talks about the strange American. After dinner, Alfredo drinks his rum and tells stories to the children.

The next day, Isabel talks to her best friend, Teresa, about Lucas' strange behavior. Teresa and Lucas were engaged; he broke off the engagement because he was in love with Isabel. Isabel marvels at how Teresa is able to remain friends with her. Teresa agrees to talk to Lucas about his aloof manner.

Chapters Six through Ten

The American approaches Isabel. Nobody will talk to him, and he hopes Isabel will be different. She learns that his name is Allan Waters and that he is a medical student working on an illustrated book of symptoms that will allow patients to communicate with doctors who do not speak their languages.

Isabel talks to him briefly, until Manuela calls her away.

On her way into town, Isabel encounters Lucas, and their exchange is cold and formal. When Isabel returns home, she finds many of the women in the village talking to Manuela about Isabel's indiscretion in talking to the American. That night, Alfredo warns her about the dangers of trusting strangers and about the importance of resisting change. Isabel disagrees. Their discussion is interrupted by the sound of a rock hitting the house. When they investigate, they find a red candle in a circle of pine with a burnt tuft of hair. It is a bad sign, and Alfredo remains watchful all night.

One day, Isabel wanders off by herself, and as she is crouched in a group of rocks in a cave, she sees a small group of guerrillas butcher a local man's steer. She is terrified and stays completely still, but one of the men sees her. He looks right at her but does nothing. After they leave, Isabel stays still for a while longer before going back home.

On Sunday, everyone gathers for Mass, and Isabel goes to confession before the service. She admits to feeling resentful at being forced to stay home and take care of the house instead of going to school as she would prefer. The priest assures her that her feelings are normal and tells her that she has committed no sin.

The whole village turns out for a celebration of the newly installed waterline that will give the village a constant and reliable source of water. The festival includes music and a soccer game in which Lucas, one of Isabel's brothers, and many of the other boys will play. Isabel's family leaves the house to go to the festival, and Manuela sees how badly Isabel wants to go. In a tender moment, she insists that her daughter go. During the soccer game, Lucas makes an incredible but dangerous play, and Isabel rushes out to him. Without thinking about the fact that they are in front of the whole town, they kiss. Isabel's father takes her by the arm and escorts her home.

Chapters Eleven through Fifteen

As Manuela's condition worsens, Isabel grieves the loss of the person her mother once was. She was so vibrant and full of life, and now she can barely walk by herself. Isabel suggests to Eziquel that they should take Manuela to Sololá to the Western hospital. He considers it. Alfredo tells Eziquel of the red candle and the other signs that have been left at their house. Isabel's brother runs in to tell them that

the army is in town with another proclamation, and the children go to hear it. Isabel recognizes one of the military men as the guerrilla who saw her when she was hiding in the rocks. She wonders why the same man would be on both "sides," and what it could mean.

Alfredo, Isabel, Allan, and Isabel's siblings all accompany Manuela on her trip to the hospital. It is a trip that takes most of the day, and they see strange people along the way. In the hospital, the doctor conducts a basic examination but wants to draw blood and take X-rays to confirm his diagnosis. Manuela refuses, and Allan persuades the doctor to give him the medication for her anyway. Allan asks Isabel to meet him at the soccer field the next day.

When Isabel meets Allan, Lucas sees them together, and his jealousies mount. He wants to fight Allan, but Isabel stops him. Lucas storms away, leaving Isabel emotionally wrecked as Allan explains to her how to use the medication for her mother. Feeling alone, Isabel visits her wise teacher for advice. He tells her how much teaching means to him and that she must find a way to pursue her dream. She feels lost, and he tells her that it is important that she ask herself what it is she really wants and not be afraid of the answer. Later that day, Manuela has another attack, and Isabel encourages Alfredo and Eziquel to use the Western medicine. They agree. While they take care of Manuela, Isabel goes to find Lucas. They talk, and she discovers that Teresa has been telling Lucas lies, exploiting his insecurities and jealousies about the American. Teresa has told Lucas that Isabel does not want to marry him, and Isabel comes to realize why Lucas has been so cold. She also concludes that Teresa is the one responsible for all the bad signs at the house. Isabel tells Lucas that she wants to marry him, but that she also wants to be a teacher. She only asks that he promise that they will try to find a way for her to be both wife and teacher. He cannot see a way, but he agrees they will try. She is thrilled.

Lucas Choy

Lucas is Isabel's handsome and athletic fiancé. Because he was in love with Isabel, Lucas broke off his previous engagement to Teresa, Isabel's best friend. Isabel accepted his proposal, and he began planning for their future.

Lucas' belief system is very traditional and reflects the attitudes of the village. He is a hard worker, finding work wherever he can. For a while, he works with the men who are digging the water-line channel that will provide running water to the village. He loves Isabel, and also needs to know that she loves him. When he sees how curious she is about Allan, the American visitor, and sees her interact with him, he becomes very jealous and begins to doubt their relationship. When Lucas is hurt, he becomes stubborn and unwilling to talk.

Lucas' hesitance to work out personal problems almost leads to the breakup of his relationship with Isabel. Confused by jealousy, Lucas allows Teresa, who secretly wants him back, to fill his head with doubts about Isabel. Ultimately, the truth emerges, and Lucas and Isabel realize they are meant for each other. In fact, he loves her enough to agree that they will try to make her dream of becoming a teacher come true, although he cannot see how.

Eziquel Coxol

Eziquel is the sanjorin, or town healer. He is an older man, in his sixties, with as much energy and vigor as an adolescent. His medicine is based on the principles of appeasing the traditional gods, casting spells, and performing rituals. Isabel describes him as ''mystical'' and imagines him as ''someone who spoke directly to the gods and who had power over the bric-a-brac of nature.''

Not until he has exhausted every treatment he knows does he agree that perhaps Manuela, Isabel's mother, should visit the Western doctors in Sololá. Due to a fight with Isabel's father, Alfredo, however, Eziquel does not accompany the family and Allan on their trip to the hospital. When the family returns and Manuela has another fit, Isabel implores the men to give her mother the medicine Allan has gotten from the doctor in Sololá. Both Alfredo and Eziquel agree.

Alfredo Pacay

Isabel's father, Alfredo, is a hard-working man who earns just enough to provide for his family while at the same time making himself emotionally available to them. He makes a special effort on behalf of Isabel, as she fills the role of the woman of the house. One morning, Alfredo even sneaks out of the house and sacrifices a chicken to the gods (both native and Christian) while praying specifically for Isabel. Alfredo knows Isabel would rather be going to school, but also respects her as a maturing woman capable of handling life's difficulties.

Alfredo enjoys telling legends and stories to his children. He also teaches them that there is danger in accepting new things. Even when Isabel expresses her disagreement with him on this point, he explains that he once believed he could enable his children to become educated and to better their lives, but now he sees that there is no use in trying to change the way things are.

Diego Pacay

Diego is the younger of Isabel's two brothers. He is a typical young boy who plays with tops, likes to be with his friends, and admires his older brother.

Isabel Pacay

Isabel is the novel's main character. She is a Mayan teenager who is forced to stay home from school and take care of the family because her mother is ill. Isabel handles all of her usual errands in addition to the work that her mother would normally do. Isabel loves school and misses going every day, but her responsibilities at home prevent her from continuing her education. Already, many of Isabel's friends have left school to get married, as is expected of girls their age. Isabel's dream is to be a teacher, a position that would allow her to fuel her own love of learning while educating and inspiring children. In her village, however, it is unlikely that her dream will ever come true, as she is expected to marry soon and take on the full-time role of wife and mother. As Isabel comes to terms with her own identity, she grapples with the conflict between the tradition of her village and her desire to follow her dream.

Isabel is miserable with her additional responsibilities to the family, and she feels selfish because she is not more willing to make sacrifices. She sees how her mother suffers physically and wonders what gives her the right to feel that she, in perfect health, is really suffering at all. At confession, she is told that her feelings are perfectly normal and that she is doing nothing wrong. Still, she cannot shake the feeling that she is somehow deficient as a woman because of her private resentment.

Isabel is engaged to handsome Lucas Choy, who broke his previous engagement with her best friend, Teresa, because he was in love with Isabel. She is amazed at Teresa's willingness to be her friend despite what happened with Lucas. While Isabel loves Lucas and wants to marry him, she is not ready to give up her dream of being a teacher. She is very sensitive to Lucas' moods and feelings, and when he is upset with her, she is determined to talk to him and resolve their problems.

When the American Allan Waters comes to town, Isabel seems to be the only one who is not afraid of him. She is fascinated by what she can learn from this foreigner and senses that he is harmless and can be trusted. Unlike the others in her village, Isabel is not afraid of change and seeks ways to combine the old traditions and beliefs with new ways of thinking and doing things. In the end, after a talk with her teacher, Isabel finds a way to make peace with Lucas without losing him, and even does so without agreeing to sacrifice the dream that means so much to her.

José Pacay

At twelve, José is the older of the two brothers. He is among the last of his peers to remain in school and is eager to be finished. José dislikes school as much as Isabel loves it. He much prefers working in the fields, cutting wood, and fishing. José is also very athletic and enjoys showing off his soccer skills.

Manuela Pacay

Manuela is Isabel's very ill mother. Her illness is incapacitating, causing her to suffer weakness, fatigue, swollen limbs, severe chest pains, and fits. Her infrequent walks are extremely difficult and taxing. During the course of the novel, the reader only sees Manuela in her weakened state, although Isabel's memories provide occasional flashbacks to the vibrant and joyful woman she once was. Manuela is a very devout woman, carefully performing all the rituals as instructed by the village healer. Not wanting to cause undue trouble, she often says she is fine when it is clear that she is not. Only twice does she admit in front of Isabel how bad her condition really is.

Although Manuela agrees to go to Sololá to the Western hospital, she refuses any tests beyond a basic examination. Isabel stays with her while the doctor listens to her chest and heart, but Manuela refuses to allow the doctor to draw a blood sample or take X-rays. She is stubborn and resolute. Isabel later explains that taking Western medicine is unthinkable to Manuela because it is like something from another world entering her body and staying there forever.

One scene allows the reader to see Manuela's soft and maternal side. Seeing how badly her daughter wants to go with the rest of the village to see the soccer game, she insists that Isabel go. She understands that her daughter spends most of her time in the house or running errands and knows that a young girl needs to have fun, and, moreover, that Isabel deserves it. She squeezes Isabel's hand and says of her daughter's domestic duties, "I know this is hard for you." In this moment, Isabel realizes that her mother is still a loving and understanding person, despite the illness from which she suffers.

Marcelina Pacay

Isabel's much younger sister, Marcelina, helps Isabel as best she can by carrying small bundles, taking food to their brothers in the fields, and flattening dough into tortillas. Marcelina is a playful and spirited child who loves Isabel like a mother.

Teresa

Isabel's best friend, Teresa, keeps her informed of what is going on at school in her absence. Isabel feels she can confide in her good friend Teresa, and when she begins to have problems with Lucas, it is Teresa to whom she turns. Teresa promises to talk to Lucas to try to help resolve matters.

Teresa, however, secretly has feelings for Lucas and tells him lies about Isabel to try to win him back. She says that Isabel does not want to marry him and that she wants an American to take her away from their village. Teresa exploits Lucas' insecurities about Allan, but in the end her schemes do not work. Once Isabel and Lucas talk out their problems, their relationship is stronger than ever.

Allan Waters

Allan is an American medical student visiting Guatemala as part of his studies. His father was a doctor who traveled through Central America on medical projects, and Allan hopes to follow in his footsteps. Isabel is struck by Allan's appearance the first time she sees him: He has long, wavy blond hair and blue eyes that initially make Isabel believe he is blind. Allan gestures broadly to make his points, while the natives keep their arms close to their bodies. His clothes are unusual, and later, when Isabel talks to him, she is aghast at how much he has spent on items like his backpack, camera, and ticket to fly to Guatemala.

Allan hopes to create a book of symptoms that will enable Guatemalan people of all languages to communicate with any doctor to get the medical care they need. The book is to contain pictures of symptoms, so all the patient has to do is point. To create this book, Allan needs to observe and interact with natives to better understand what symbols and artistic styles are most meaningful to them. Unfortunately, Allan is greeted with mistrust and suspicion because he is a foreigner; the political climate is such that trusting strangers can bring disaster.

When Isabel persuades Alfredo and Manuela to go to the Western hospital in Sololá, Allan accompanies them. He hopes to gain their trust while at the same time finding the elusive cure for Manuela's worsening condition. When Manuela refuses to submit to tests, Allan convinces the doctor to give him the medication for her anyway.

Although Allan initially feels that he is doing the Mayans a favor by trying to help them, he learns that he must be patient among people who do not feel they need help. Instead of being arrogant and patronizing, he learns to be respectful and observant.

Maestro Andrés Xiloj

Maestro Andrés is the teacher at the village school. Isabel is very fond of him, and he appreciates her desire to learn. To Isabel, he is a wise and understanding man who can advise without judging. When Isabel feels most lost and uncertain about what action to take, it is Maestro Andrés who tells her she does not have to sacrifice all of her dreams for the sake of pleasing everyone else. He tells her that he was once jailed for a teachers' strike and how he suffered in jail. Isabel learns that there can be consequences for making unpopular decisions, but that if she is true to herself, she can handle the outcome. Maestro Andrés also tells her that she should ask herself what she really wants and not be afraid if the answer is unconventional. His advice helps her to see what she must do, thus leading her to make a decision that will bring her fulfillment and personal growth.

Themes

Freedom and Responsibility

Although Isabel understands that as the oldest daughter her duty is to take care of the family when her mother is sick, she cannot help but resent the new demands placed on her. In the first chapter, Castañeda writes, "She was the oldest child. She had duties. She was already at an age where marriage was expected, not idle desires to become a teacher. Sometimes, however, the duties were too

much for her. She didn't feel smart enough or old enough to handle everything. Not yet, anyway." As Manuela's condition worsens, Isabel feels ashamed, because rather than being concerned only for her mother, she is filled with feelings of resentment and despair. When Eziquel, the healer, tells Manuela how lucky she is to have a daughter such as Isabel to take care of things, Isabel reels: "His words opened for Isabel the floodgate of her dread of never returning to school. . . . She would be doomed to care for her family until they all moved away or died. Even marriage would be postponed."

Torn between guilt and personal misery, Isabel declares her selfishness at confession. The priest, however, assures her that her feelings are completely normal and tells her not to be so hard on herself. She is fulfilling her responsibilities like a good daughter, so she has no reason to feel shame, he says. Still, the priest's words do not ease her guilt.

Isabel often notices the birds around her and wishes "she could be a bird with the power to fly up and away from the problems not only of her village, but those within her own family." Although she longs to be carefree and unfettered, she realizes that she is growing into adulthood, and that with age come responsibilities. By the end of the story, she has learned that freedom and responsibility are not necessarily opposites. When she takes responsibility for herself and talks to Lucas honestly about her seemingly impossible desires to be a teacher, she gains a sense of liberation. In the final words of the novel, all Isabel and Lucas "cared about was that, nestled among the volcanoes of Guatemala, there existed a hope with a secret pair of wings." In embracing her duties as a mature woman, Isabel finds her wings at last.

Making Choices

Throughout the novel, Castañeda portrays people in different situations faced with difficult choices. Isabel chooses to carry out her duties without complaining, even though inside she feels desperate. Through Isabel's memories of her mother, the reader understands that Manuela made choices out of love for her family. She made personal sacrifices, suffered the loss of two children, and never expected any reward. Isabel realizes that motherhood is "a path without detours, without places to rest. And though there were sister travelers, no one praised those who made the difficult and isolated journey." Manuela's resolve in her decision-making is seen first-hand when she refuses to allow the doctor in

Topics for Further Study

- Research guerrillas to determine the main reasons why they emerge in unstable political climates. Whose interests do they represent? Think about the scene in which Isabel recognizes one of the military men as the guerrilla who saw her the day she was hidden in the rocks. Propose two possible reasons why this man is "on both sides."

- Look through books featuring Latin American art, and find at least three works that complement *Among the Volcanoes*. What do the similarities between the book and the artwork reveal about the culture or lifestyle? How do the colors, faces, landscapes, or other features of the artwork enhance your ability to understand the novel?

- Read about shamanism in Native American cultures. Consider shamans' practices, belief systems, medicines, and roles within their tribes. Compare and contrast your findings with what you know about the character Eziquel Coxol. What conclusions can you draw about human nature and communities?

- Castañeda includes bird imagery in *Among the Volcanoes* because birds are an integral feature of the jungle environment in which the novel takes place. Isabel speaks of having wings, and to her birds represent freedom from responsibilities, problems, and fear. Imagine that Isabel lived in another part of the world. What might symbolize freedom if she lived in Australia? Japan? Europe? the United States?

- In Western medicine, there is a trend toward considering the roles of both body and mind in the healing of physical disease. In other words, a growing number of doctors believe that our thoughts and attitudes can affect our bodies. Assuming that Manuela's disease is not fatal, what would a modern-day doctor, who advises patients based on the body-mind model, say about her chances for recovery?

Sololá to run any tests on her. She makes a choice that she would rather suffer from the illness than submit to the full course of Western medicine. Certainly, there are consequences for such a decision, but at the end of the novel Alfredo and Eziquel also make a choice—that they will not sit idly by and let Manuela die when they have the Western medicine available.

Allan makes choices from a different viewpoint than that of the Mayan villagers. He is part of the Western world, and he has made a choice to travel to Guatemala (like his father) and help people get better medical care. He does not understand enough about their culture to consider whether or not his efforts will be welcomed, so he is alarmed when his presence is met with suspicion and hostility. His most daring choice, however, is to give Isabel the medicine for Manuela, when he knows it may not be the cure. Worse, if it is the wrong treatment (Manuela

would not allow tests to confirm the doctor's diagnosis), the medicine could harm her and thus end any hope of the Mayans accepting Allan or Western medicine. Castañeda does not reveal exactly why Allan makes this choice. Perhaps Allan feels it is his best (or only) chance to prove his worth to the Mayans. Perhaps he simply feels it is Manuela's best chance to be well again.

Castañeda shows that people make poor choices when they are filled with insecurity and doubt. Because Teresa wants Lucas back, she lies to him about Isabel's feelings. Lucas is plagued with jealousy, so he believes her. In both cases, these characters make choices based on personal insecurity rather than good sense, trust, and loyalty. As a result, Lucas temporarily creates distance between himself and Isabel when he really loves her very much, and Teresa ruins her friendships with both Isabel and Lucas.

Old Ways and New Ways

Among the Volcanoes portrays simple village life in the contemporary world. While modern conveniences are readily available all over the world, the village of Chuuí Chopaló is celebrating the installation of a single faucet in town. Castañeda contrasts the old ways with the new in various instances throughout the book to demonstrate the beauty and value of each in its own way. With regard to religion, villagers maintain their devotion to the gods of their indigenous religions, but also participate in Roman Catholic practices. Manuela's illness brings the blending of religious practices into sharp focus. One woman, for example, suggests that Manuela ''pass a fresh egg over her body and say three Our Fathers.'' At Eziquel's altar, Isabel notices a row of Catholic icons and saints over a row of stone idols, incense, and pine twigs. Similarly, Manuela performs the daily rituals of feeding her altar's stone mouth, but the family also attends Mass on Sunday.

As a parent, Alfredo teaches the children that ''anything new is very dangerous.'' Not until Manuela's condition is serious does he consider going to the Western hospital to try modern medicine. For Alfredo, change on a large scale must be approached with caution, whereas change on a small scale is less frightening. He routinely drinks rum and smokes cigars, even though he admits that traditionally, these were practices reserved for ceremonies. When it comes to interacting with strangers or adopting their ways, however, he is very suspicious, because the political climate in which he has lived has taught him that trusting the wrong people can have grave consequences.

Style

Point of View

Among the Volcanoes is narrated from the third-person point of view. The novel is Isabel's story, however, and the narration is from her perspective. The reader is allowed into her thoughts and feelings, which makes her realizations and transformations understandable and credible to the reader. The story is told in the present tense, so Isabel's reactions and feelings are fresh. By telling the story in the present tense, Isabel's decision-making and growth are more interesting because neither the reader nor Isabel knows what will happen next. By staying in the present moment,

Castañeda is also able to describe details of Isabel's surroundings in a way that would not be as authentic if the story were being told from memory. The colors of the birds, the music of the village festival, the excitement of the crowd watching soccer, and the rush of feeling when Isabel sees Lucas are more realistic because they are told as they are experienced.

Setting

Set in Guatemala in the rural village of Chuuí Chopaló, *Among the Volcanoes* offers a portrait of daily life among the Mayans. The people of the village are poor; men support their families by laboring in the fields or by fishing. Isabel's family owns chickens and one pig, but they eat mostly beans, eggs, tortillas, and peppers.

Political unrest is a major force in the village's life. There is guerrilla activity combating the military government, and there are horrible stories of local men being taken away and killed. The people of Chuuí Chopaló live in fear and are accustomed to living that way. Periodically, the military enters the village with a proclamation, which everyone is required to hear. After they make announcements, soldiers leave their proclamations posted for all to see. The villagers are equally afraid of the military and the guerrillas.

Village life is characterized by a strong sense of tradition. There are time-honored ways of doing things, and those ways are rarely challenged from within. Women are expected to leave school and marry in their middle to late teens. Men generally attend school a bit longer, but ultimately leave to work for their families in the fields. Families occupy the same houses for many generations. Castañeda writes, ''In Chuuí Chopaló, change always had something of fear housed within its bright skin.''

Symbolism

Castañeda writes about birds throughout the story. By describing many different types of birds—eagles, hummingbirds, chickens, vultures, blackbirds, and others—he introduces them into a variety of scenes without being heavy-handed with the symbolism. At the core of the novel is Isabel's desire to leave her cares and responsibilities behind and to follow her dreams. To her, birds represent all the freedom and flight she desires but cannot have because she must face her responsibilities. She is growing up and becoming a woman, not a hummingbird or an eagle. She speaks of her wish that she had wings, so at the end of the novel when she confronts her difficult decisions with maturity, she has given wings to her hope. In an unexpected way, she feels what she imagines birds feel.

Water is another important element in the story. As Isabel explains, water is a profound symbol of life in her culture. In fact, it is so basic and critical that the Mayans pray to it. The installation of the faucet in the town is a cause for celebration. The village holds a soccer game complete with music to commemorate the day. The fact that Allan's last name is Waters reinforces the idea that it is not the word ''water'' that holds meaning in the Mayan culture; it is the actual substance that is revered.

Literary Heritage

Before the twentieth century, Guatemala's literary heritage was defined primarily by a sixteenth-century work, *Popol Vuh*, a Mayan creation narrative and account of world history. The twentieth century, however, expanded the literary base of Guatemalan culture with the work of such writers as Enrique Gomez Carrillo, Rafael Arévalo Martinez, Mario Monteforte Toledo, Omar Castañeda, and 1967 Nobel Prize winner Miguel Angel Asturias.

Central and South American literature has been deeply influenced by magic realism, a style of writing that incorporates magic, myth, dreams, and the supernatural into otherwise conventional and realistic fiction. Magic realism became popular after World War II, and its Latin American roots are most closely associated with the work of Argentine Jorge Luis Borges and Colombian Gabriel Garcia Marquez. Many contemporary Latin American authors, including Chilean Isabel Allende and Guatemalan Omar Castañeda, utilize elements of magic realism in their fiction. Some scholars suggest that the use of magic realism in Latin American literature is a way of reconciling two distinct realities in postcolonial times—the traditional ways and the new ways of the colonialists.

Historical Context

Political Instability

Since Guatemala's independence in 1839, it has been subjected to extreme political instability and terror. Guatemala's leaders have been dictators,

military presidents, and elected officials, many of whom have been overthrown by coups. The hostility between the military and guerrilla forces has resulted in violence, bloodshed, and panic. In some cases, military regimes were so intent on ending guerrilla tactics that they massacred entire villages. The combined tasks of leading the country, controlling guerrilla activity, and addressing human rights seem overwhelming. This political climate provides the backdrop for *Among the Volcanoes*, where the villagers' daily lives are affected by the harsh realities of danger and violence. Just before the novel's 1991 publication, elections were held in Guatemala. The January 1991 inauguration of Jorge Serrano marked the first time one elected official was replaced by another. Serrano expressed his intention to bring peace to the land by negotiating with guerrillas, holding corrupt officials responsible, and putting an end to human rights violations. Unfortunately, Serrano was removed from office only two years later.

Conflicting Ways of Life

Guatemala is defined by three historical stages—Mayan indigenous, Spanish colonial, and modern republican—although some scholars note that the distinct lifestyles of each are slowly merging into a cohesive contemporary culture.

As missionary efforts expanded into Central America, religion became a problematic cultural issue for many Guatemalans. Roman Catholicism became increasingly popular beginning in the sixteenth century, and Protestantism reached Guatemala in the mid-1800s, although there were few converts until the growth of Pentecostal sects in the 1960s. While Guatemalans were receptive to the new religious ideologies, they were hesitant to abandon the religious belief systems of their ancestors. Castañeda depicts the ways in which people incorporate the new beliefs and symbols with the traditional ones, a melding that continues today.

Tradition remains a powerful force, particularly among people who live in small rural villages. They prefer to keep to themselves, living a lifestyle similar to that of their ancestors. Modern conveniences are slow to be introduced in this context. As recently as the 1990s, only 54 percent of Guatemalans had access to health care. Further, only 60 percent of Guatemalans had access to a source of pure drinking water and sanitation, which explains why the village of Chuuí Chopaló responded with such excitement to the installation of the water-line channel.

Compare & Contrast

- **Guatemala:** Illiteracy rates are among the highest in Central America in 1998: 44 percent of all Guatemalans over the age of fifteen are illiterate (51.4 percent of women and 37.5 percent of men).

  United States: Illiteracy has been widely eliminated by 1998. Still, 2.4 percent of Americans over the age of twenty-five are functionally illiterate. This means they cannot read or write well enough to perform daily tasks.

- **Guatemala:** Only 58 percent of primary-school-aged children in 1998 attend school, despite the fact that it is free and mandatory. At the secondary level, this number drops to 16 percent.

  United States: Education is more available than ever in 1995: 82 percent of Americans over the age of twenty-five have completed high school, and 23 percent of the population has finished at least four years of college.

- **Guatemala:** In 1990 girls are expected to marry as early as their middle to late teens.

  United States: The median age for women to marry in 1990 is twenty-four.

- **Guatemala:** Because girls do not work in the fields, their ''usefulness'' to the family is limited. They are valued more when they marry and take care of their own families.

  United States: American girls have more opportunities than ever. Within the family, children are not generally expected to contribute substantially to the family's income, so girls and boys are regarded equally. While there are still areas in which women are limited in the workplace, these situations are constantly being challenged.

- **Guatemala:** In 1990, eighty percent of Guatemalans live below the poverty level. The gap between the lower class and the upper class is wide, causing tension and resentment.

  United States: Fewer than 14 percent of American households have income below the poverty level in 1996. The top 20 percent of households earned 49 percent of the nation's income, while the bottom 20 percent earned 3.7 percent. This indicates a gap between the upper and lower classes, but it is not as severe as the one in Guatemala.

- **Guatemala:** In 1998, 60 percent of the people live in rural areas, and 40 percent live in urban areas, primarily Guatemala City.

  United States: In 1998, 25 percent of the people live in rural areas, and 75 percent live in urban areas.

Ethnic Composition and Class Structure

Guatemala's population is composed of indigenous Mayans and ladinos, who are people of mixed native and European heritage. Guatemala is unique among Latin American countries in that it still has a large native population that has preserved its ethnic identity.

There is a wide class gap in Guatemalan social structure, and most of the elite members of society are those who have more European blood, which fuels tensions between the classes. Statistics in 1987 revealed that, in earnings, the top 10 percent of the population held 44 percent of the income while the bottom 10 percent held only nine-tenths of one percent. In the twentieth century, the class gap widened as the population continued to grow and resources were exported rather than kept within the country's borders for its own people.

Education

In Guatemala, public education is free and mandatory, but soft enforcement and lack of resources results in inadequate education for most

Guatemalans. At the elementary school level, 58 percent of children attend school, and at the high school level, only 16 percent attend. In rural areas, such as the village described in *Among the Volcanoes*, these figures are lower. In fact, it is not uncommon for a rural school to offer education only through the third grade.

Critical Overview

When *Among the Volcanoes* was published in 1991, it did not attract widespread critical attention, although it was well-received by the critics who reviewed it. The novel appears on educational reading lists for its sensitive portrayal of teenaged Isabel and its vibrant and realistic depiction of rural Mayan life. The critical consensus is clearly that Castañeda made excellent use of the Fulbright research fellowship that enabled him to travel to his native Central America to study the Mayan people and their culture. One critic found the characters and their lives as realistic and informative as educational programming. Critics universally praised Castañeda's reverent treatment of the Mayan culture, acknowledging that the compelling presentation makes it interesting to American teenagers who know very little about Guatemala. Diane Roback and Richard Donahue of *Publishers Weekly* commended Castañeda for his "quietly realistic portrait of life" in Guatemala that includes political upheaval, poverty, and cultural elements. Lucinda Snyder Whitehurst of *School Library Journal* praised Castañeda for not sensationalizing the fact that the Pacays live in times of political danger, but rather showing how their constant fear has become a part of their daily lives.

According to Roback and Donahue, Isabel's life is "both simpler and harder" than the life of a typical American teenager. American culture accepts and welcomes change, making transitions less traumatic to the community. In Isabel's Mayan village, however, change is met with extreme resistance and suspicion. At the same time, the people of the village understand that they must accommodate changes they cannot stop. Whitehurst made special note that the Pacays find ways to reconcile traditional beliefs with contemporary Catholicism, education, and new ideas about women. Impressed with the multidimensional character of Isabel, Whitehurst

A small village nestled on the shore of Lake Atitlan, Guatemala. A volcano rises on the opposite bank.

wrote that she is a "smart girl who respects and cares for her family, but also one who wants more for herself." The critic added that Castañeda's teenage readers will "readily relate to the universal feeling of not fitting in."

Among the Volcanoes is respected among Castañeda's work, although he garnered the most attention for his only picture book, *Abuela's Weave*. All of his writing relates to his Central American heritage, and many of his short stories are solidly in the tradition of magic realism so popular among Latin American authors.

Criticism

Jennifer Bussey

Bussey holds a bachelor's degree in English literature and a master's degree in interdisciplinary studies. She is an independent writer specializing in literature. In the following essay, she discusses the central theme of Isabel's complicated journey of self-discovery in Among the Volcanoes.

What Do I Read Next?

- Castañeda's *Imagining Isabel* is the sequel to *Among the Volcanoes*. In this book, Isabel has married Lucas and has an opportunity to accept a teaching position, but doing so will involve her in guerrilla activities.

- *Across the Great River*, a novel by Irene Beltran Hernandez, tells the story of a young girl who must help care for her family when they are separated while illegally crossing the Mexican-American border.

- E. Jean Langdon and Gerhard Baer published *Portals of Power: Shamanism in South America* to introduce Western readers to the roles and

practices of healers in twelve different South American societies.

- *I, Rigoberta Menchu: An Indian Woman in Guatemala* is Menchu's personal account of her experiences in Guatemala. This book was published in 1987, before she was awarded the 1992 Nobel Peace Prize for her efforts at publicizing her country's human rights violations.

- *The Forty-Third War* is Louise Moeri's novel about a twelve-year-old Central American boy who is sent for military training at a guerrilla camp. His experiences teach him about death, fear, and conflict.

At the center of Omar S. Castañeda's intriguing and richly detailed book *Among the Volcanoes* is Isabel, a teenaged girl who finds herself shouldering responsibilities she is uncertain she can handle. Her mother is extremely ill, so Isabel, as the oldest daughter, must take on the duties of running the household. She loves school and thrives on learning, but her responsibilities at home simply will not allow her to continue attending. While Isabel performs all the tasks expected of her, she resents this burden and fears that she will never be able to return to the life she once knew. Worse, she is terrified that she will be forced to give up her dream of becoming a teacher. She is engaged to Lucas Choy, a handsome young man who loves her very much. He knows she loves school, but expects that once they are married, she will focus all of her attention on being the woman of his house. Isabel is in the difficult position of desiring a path for herself that her village does not accept for her.

In many ways, Isabel is a typical teenager, which allows Castañeda's young American readers to identify with her even though her reality is far removed from their own. Isabel struggles with questions of her identity. Is she destined to be exactly like her mother? Must she conform to the expectations of her community? If she looks within and

discovers what she really wants, can she have it? Isabel is very clear about what she wants—to be a teacher—but she is very uncertain about how to achieve this. The only supportive person is her own teacher, who is introduced in only one scene as a wise advisor who genuinely cares about Isabel's feelings and the difficult decisions she must make. Isabel is also typical in her lack of enthusiasm for adult responsibilities that prevent her from leading a social and carefree life. She enjoys talking to her best friend, Teresa, and seeing her fiancé, Lucas. While she performs the tasks around the house, in her heart she longs to be free. Isabel's tendency to trust people and question her father's cynicism is another typical adolescent trait. She feels that she has lived long enough in the world that she knows things her father does not. She perceives his skepticism as unwarranted in some cases and resolves to do things her own way.

As Isabel matures during the course of the story, she comes to better understand her relationship to the family and the village. When her mother, Manuela, is rendered unable to help at all around the house, Isabel must step in to take her place. As a result, Isabel comes to understand her mother better. Castañeda wrote, "Then she understood that it was the insignificant events that spoke more strongly of what parenthood meant. Like leaving school, to some. These small sacrifices told her that motherhood was not a grand landscape dotted with large and poignant markers, but was mostly a simple, everyday road with no real beginning and no end in sight.'' Still, Isabel's insights into her mother's world do not change the fact that her own future is closely tied to Manuela's ability to take care of the family. When Manuela refuses to submit to additional tests by the doctor at the Western hospital, Isabel is secretly devastated. She thinks, ''If she would simply submit, then she would live. But her mother's decision was final. At the base of this refusal, Isabel's own future, her vision of teaching, lay broken. Also shut out was Alfredo's dream for his children, his family. All of them lay besieged by the calamity and by her mother's refusal to consider possibilities. But this refusal was one demanded by the forces of the village itself.'' This moment shows the reader that the village is an integral part of each family. The strong sense of community and tradition affects even the most personal and important decisions. For Isabel, she is not struggling just with her family's expectations and rules, but also with those of the entire village. The theme of balancing the community and family with the self is central to Isabel's journey. In order to decide for herself what her path should be, she must take the larger context into account. Perhaps in the United States a teenager could ultimately decide to cast off concerns for the whole in favor of the individual, but in Isabel's culture, this is not an option.

Although critics generally credit the arrival of Allan Waters in the village for Isabel's ultimate ability to take a stand for her dreams, the teacher seems to be the real catalyst for her decision. Allan reinforces what Isabel already believes—that it is important to keep an open mind about possibilities outside of one's familiar context. He is fascinating to her simply by virtue of the fact that he comes from a foreign land. In the first chapter, Castañeda tells readers that Isabel loves learning about faraway places ''with names like Orlando, New York, or the tongue-twisting Indianapolis.'' Although the political atmosphere fosters deep distrust of strangers, Isabel feels that Allan is harmless and truly wants to help. She is right about him, and so his presence reinforces her faith in her intuition about people. Her eventual refusal to abandon her dream, however, comes from her conversation with her teacher, Maestro Andrés Xiloj. Desperate and confused, she goes to talk to her teacher about what she should do with her life. Her mother refuses to take

> In many ways, Isabel is a typical teenager, which allows Castañeda's young American readers to identify with her even though her reality is far removed from their own."

the medicine, her fiancé is angry, and she feels trapped in her own life. She knows that she can talk to Maestro Andrés without his judging her. He explains that when he was a child, he wanted nothing else but to teach. He wanted to help his country in this way, and even though it has been an extremely difficult way of life, he continues to do it. He tells her about a teacher's strike that landed him in jail, where he suffered until his release. His path has been challenging, but he is satisfied with the choices he has made. He tells Isabel, ''It was something like finding a new way to be what I wanted to be. And understanding the danger of being different. . .And not trying to be more than I had a right to be, not trying to be superhuman. It was compromising, I suppose.'' Maestro Andrés advises Isabel to talk to Lucas about their troubles, but first she must ask herself what she really wants. Once she knows herself well enough to understand what she wants, she will be able to explain it to him. Maestro Andrés's parting words are, ''Understand it with your bones, Isabel. Understand it with your blood. What matters most is the strength to accept myself. . .I mean you. Each of us—accepting ourselves. Each of us. You and me. . .And then holding on no matter how hard it gets.''

After talking with Maestro Andrés, Isabel is able to tell Lucas that she loves him, which are words he desperately needs to hear. She is also able to tell him that while she wants to marry him, she wants him to promise her that they will at least try to find a way for her to become a teacher. He is resistant because he does not see any possible way, but she assures him that she will also be a wife and mother, and that all she is asking is that they try. He agrees, and Isabel finally feels all the freedom she had longed for throughout the story. She learns that, for her, freedom does not come from casting off all her responsibilities, but from embracing them as long as she is also true to herself. In the end, she finds courage to give words to her desires without apology. She also learns that she is capable of imagining something different for herself beyond what is expected of her according to tradition.

Throughout the novel, Castañeda uses bird imagery. Everywhere Isabel goes, there are birds of all shapes and sizes. Birds are meaningful to Isabel because they represent freedom from worry and duty. She wishes she could be a bird and fly away from her difficult life. Living in the lush environment of Central America, Isabel would encounter a variety of birds on a daily basis, so their inclusion in the story is realistic. Castañeda refers to them subtly throughout the book as a constant reminder of Isabel's longing to be free. The scene in which her father sacrifices a chicken is very significant because his prayer is for Isabel, which frightens her deeply. As she watches him sacrifice a bird, her personal symbol of freedom, he prays for his daughter, indicating that she will be shouldering the household responsibilities indefinitely. Much later in the book, she goes to visit her teacher in a state of panic and despair. Castañeda writes of ''her heart battered inside its cage.'' As Maestro Andrés talks to Isabel, he reveals that he always wanted to be a roadrunner. This surprises Isabel, as the roadrunner is regarded with contempt in their village, but Maestro Andrés explains that the roadrunner is smart because it chooses not to fly most of the time. If it flew, people would likely shoot it, so instead it runs very fast. It is also a bird that has not been domesticated like chickens and turkeys, waiting to be eaten. He remarks, ''It has chosen neither to fly too high nor to always grovel on the ground in fear.'' This analogy helps Isabel see that in order to find happiness, she will have to find a way to compromise. At the end of the novel, when Lucas has agreed that they will try to find a way for her to teach, Isabel is thrilled. A group of boys passes by Lucas and Isabel, and their ''movement past them was like the blur of hummingbirds, their shouts the cawing of crows.'' Castañeda then closes the story by writing that ''all they cared about was that, nestled among the volcanoes of Guatemala, there existed a hope with a secret pair of wings.'' As Isabel's journey of self-discovery is fulfilled, the liberated feelings she associates with birds move from the external world to her internal world, leaving the reader with a great sense of hope.

Source: Jennifer Bussey, in an essay for *Literature of Developing Nations for Students*, Gale, 2000.

Emily Smith Riser

Riser has a master's degree in English literature and teaches high school English. In the following essay, she discusses themes and historical context in Among the Volcanoes.

In Omar Castañeda's *Among the Volcanoes*, the main character, Isabel Pacay, is a typical adolescent girl, faced with issues similar to those of many teenagers the world over: She has boy problems, family pressures, a deceitful best friend, dreams and fears for the future. However, she also is placed in a setting where she experiences a variety of conflicts, some of which she is conscious of and some of which she is too isolated or too young to see. These can be seen through the historical context, the themes, and the imagery Castañeda employs.

It is useful to put the novel in its historical context in order to better understand Isabel's situation. While knowing the history is not necessary to understanding the basic storyline, it helps to deepen one's understanding of the novel's setting and themes. Isabel's family lives in a Quiche village in central Guatemala. The Quiche are descendants of the Mayans, whose complex and extremely advanced civilization collapsed around 900 A.D. In the sixteenth century, Spanish conquerors arrived in Guatemala, bringing their religion and customs, which to some extent have been incorporated into the Quiche lifestyle (remarkably, however, the Quiche have retained their language and many of their traditional religious practices). The twentieth century in Guatemala was characterized by civil war, military coups, revolutions, and violence. At the same time, the gulf between the very rich and the very poor increased dramatically. As the population increased, a large amount of resources were committed to producing exports rather than to helping the poor, mostly rural, citizens. In the 1990s, the majority of Guatemalans lived on less than one U.S. dollar per day. Isabel Pacay lives in this world—an impoverished Quiche village, with the backdrop of guerilla warfare and government unrest—while at the same time enjoying a pride in her culture's rich history and spiritual beliefs.

The author of the novel, Omar Castañeda, was born in Guatemala but grew up and lived his adult life in the United States. Much of his work, including *Among the Volcanoes*, reveals his position on Guatemalan politics. In fact, Castañeda told Jonathan Harrington that ''you cannot separate politics from art. . .Those who try to separate the two are really sanctioning the dominant view.'' It is clear that Castañeda has strong opinions on the Guatemalan government's treatment of the impoverished Quiche villagers and the government's catering to European and American interests. This is most clear in the trip the Pacay family takes with Allan Waters, an American medical student, to the city, where Isabel's father and Waters discuss the scenes of villagers forced to sell items that do not reflect the true national heritage but rather are what the tourists think look like native crafts. Additionally, Castañeda implies that the guerillas whose shadows are constantly present in the lives of the villagers are really agents of the Guatemalan government, and are there to keep the villagers in fear and submission to the government.

In the novel, it becomes clear that Isabel is being pulled between two worlds: the western or American world in which a girl can become an independent woman with a career, but often sacrifices close family ties and traditions, and the native Guatemalan world in which a girl gets married at a young age and is expected to take care of her family. Isabel's story presents several other serious, seemingly unresolvable conflicts: Allan Waters' insistence on modern medicine versus Isabel's mother's reliance on the medicine man; the struggle between Isabel's desire to be a teacher and her desire to marry Lucas Choy; the dichotomy between male roles and female roles. Addressing these sorts of ambiguous conflicts, in an interview with Jonathan Harrington, Castañeda said, ''Because I am Guatemalan, but have always lived in non-Hispanic communities in the U.S., I have had to deal with conflicting views of the world. I've always been concerned with biculturality.'' In *Among the Volcanoes*, this notion of biculturality is dealt with through Isabel's quest to reconcile all of these competing worldviews. The miracle of the story is that she does appear to resolve many of these seemingly irreconcilable conflicts.

The title *Among the Volcanoes* is literal and figurative: The village is placed geographically on the slopes of volcanoes; at the same time, Isabel is placed among many forces that threaten her in the same way a volcano does—with the promise of eventual catastrophic eruption. She fears that she is being selfish when she becomes ''convinced that she could be an exception to the volcanic forces that smelted people into acceptable molds,'' and yet she desires more than anything to defeat those forces. She does not want to be like all of the other girls in her village. She has her own dreams, but these conflict directly with what is expected of her.

> ''Isabel's story presents several other serious, seemingly unresolvable conflicts: Allan Waters' insistence on modern medicine versus Isabel's mother's reliance on the medicine man; the struggle between Isabel's desire to be a teacher and her desire to marry Lucas Choy; the dichotomy between male roles and female roles.''

Through nature imagery, especially imagery of birds, Isabel is shown learning to deal with her situation. In the first chapter, Isabel furtively follows her father to the inlet of the lake and spies on him as he makes a prayer and sacrifices one of their family's hens. As he kills the chicken, he frightens Isabel by praying for her, his eldest daughter: She realizes then that her mother's illness is worse than she thought, and that her father fears for Isabel for some reason. She is not surprised that her father prays not only to the Christian god, but to the ''old gods,'' the gods of the Mayans, since even the Catholic priest mixes the two religions during Mass (a reconciliation that she might find reassuring, since she is struggling so much with the incongruities between the old traditions and the western ways). The death of the hen is contrasted with Isabel's perception of the name of her village, Chuuí Chopaló, which sounds to Isabel like ''birdsong on her own tongue,'' and

> echoe[s] the call of some unknown bird—the bird she might become...The chirping of the name Chuuí Chopaló gave her the sensation of a bird that flew high above the waters, soaring free above any danger, any misfortune.

She imagines herself as this bird, with wings growing out of her shoulders and soaring above the lake.

Much later in the novel, Isabel's teacher, Andrés Xiloj, tells her that when he was a child, he dreamed of being like a roadrunner. This surprises Isabel, because "usually he said the students should be like quetzales, flying high and free. She had never heard him or anyone else mention the [roadrunner] with anything but disdain." Xiloj explains that he believes the roadrunner is the smartest bird because people would try to kill it if it flew, so instead "it stays low, hidden secretive. And it isn't like other birds—turkeys or chickens—who give themselves up to people and peck around the house until they are eaten. Those birds have become slaves." Isabel thinks that Xiloj means that as a child he wanted to be like the guerrillas; however, he explains that he did not want to cause trouble:

> It was something like finding a new way to be what I wanted to be. And understanding the danger of being different. . .Knowing that there is danger, but not cowering like everyone else because of it. . .It was compromising, I suppose. Like the roadrunner: It chooses to be different, but not so different that it gets attacked.

This is the image that Isabel needs to understand how to compromise and still stay true to herself. Until this point, she has wanted to be the quetzal, with no responsibilities and flying free above the lake-sea. Now she realizes that she does not have to be the quetzal; instead, she can be the roadrunner, taking part in the world and compromising with the forces that surround her, rather than giving in to them, to get what she needs to be fulfilled and happy.

References to the *Popol Vuh*, a Maya-Quiche book of history, religion, and mythology, can be found in *Among the Volcanoes*. The *Popol Vuh*, written secretly in the sixteenth century to record sacred Mayan myths, also reflects the clash of cultures between the Spanish conquerors and the native Mayans in Guatemala. Just like Castañeda's novel, the Mayan text shows a suspicion of the foreign influence, but at the same time acknowledges that change in the culture is inevitable. The challenge is to reconcile these two forces in a satisfactory way; this is Isabel Pacay's personal struggle as well. In an interview with T. L. Kelly, Castañeda said that his female characters "have allegiance to some of the traditions they have been raised with and they realize that those same traditions are hurting them, damaging them, and they try to invent some new possibilities for themselves. They fight against the easy acceptance of foreign views." Isabel creates this new possibility for herself through deciding to follow her heart and the traditions she knows by marrying Lucas Choy, but at the same time asserting that she will pursue her dream of becoming a teacher. Because of the strength

of her character, there is no doubt left at the end of the novel that she will be successful. Indeed, in *Imagining Isabel*, a sequel to the novel written in 1994, Isabel does succeed in her quest.

Source: Emily Smith Riser, in an essay for *Literature of Developing Nations for Students*, Gale, 2000.

Diane Donahue

In their very brief review of Castañeda's Among the Volcanoes, *Diane Roback and Richard Donahue describe a novel that offers the reader a "quietly realistic portrait" of a girl struggling to make a life for herself in contemporary Central America.*

In Guatemala, life is both simpler and harder for teenagers than in the U.S. Isabel Pacay wants to go to school and become a teacher, but not only is her family very poor, no one in the village, not even her boyfriend, seems to see beyond tradition. When her mother becomes ill, Isabel is expected to stay home, take care of the family and give up her dreams. With the help of an American medical researcher, however, Isabel finds the courage within herself to do what she believes is right. More than anything, the novel offers a quietly realistic portrait of life in Central America: the poverty, ever-present political unrest and proud cultural background make Isabel's dilemma compelling.

Source: Diane Donahue, "Among the Volcanoes," (book review) in *Publisher's Weekly*, Vol. 237, No. 51, December 21, 1990, p. 57.

Sources

Brosnan, Rosemary, "Lyll Becerra de Jenkins," in *Booklist*, September 1, 1997, Vol. 94, No. 1, pp. 110-11.

Harrington, Jonathan, "A Truly Immense Journey: Profile of Omar S. Castañeda," in *The Americas Review*, Vol. 23, Nos. 3-4, 1995, pp. 204-16.

Kelly, T. L., "Straddling the Volcanoes: An Interview with Omar Castañeda," in *Literary Nonfiction by T. L. Kelly* (online), April 12, 2000, http://www.randomviolins.org/~dwap/literati/interv1.htm.

Roback, Diane, and Richard Donahue, "Among the Volcanoes," in *Publishers Weekly*, Vol. 237, No. 51, Fall, 1993, p. 57.

Snyder Whitehurst, Lucinda, "Among the Volcanoes," in *School Library Journal*, Vol. 37, No. 3, March, 1991, pp. 21.

Further Reading

Ashabranner, Brent, *Children of the Maya, A Guatemalan Indian Odyssey*, Dodd, 1986.
This is an illustrated nonfiction book about a group of Guatemalan Mayans who flee their native land to escape the political situation. They come to the United States and settle in southern Florida.

Carlson, Lori M., *Where Angels Glide at Dawn: New Stories from Latin America*, Econo-Clad Books, 1999.
A collection of ten short stories, this book provides insights into a variety of people's lives and their situations.

Castañeda, Omar S., *Naranjo the Muse: A Collection of Stories*, Arte Publico Press, 1997.
Castañeda's use of magical realism brings intrigue to this collection of interrelated stories.

———, *Remembering to Say ''Mouth'' or ''Face''*, Black Ice Books, 1993.
This award-winning collection of short fiction includes magical realism, social harshness, and surrealistic elements in stories about often-uprooted characters.

Jenness, Aylette, *A Life of Their Own: An Indian Family in Latin America*, Crowell, 1975.
This nonfiction book describes the daily life and rituals of a Latin American family. It focuses on Guatemalan Indians and is written for adolescents.

Tadlock, Dennis, trans.,*Popol Vuh: The Mayan Book of the Dawn of Life*, Touchstone Books, 1996.
This book provides a respected translation of the ancient Mayan text that relates the creation narrative and an account of world history.

Annie John

Jamaica Kincaid

1985

Ever since Jamaica Kincaid's work began appearing in *The New Yorker* magazine, it has excited critics and enthralled readers. Kincaid has been praised for her ability to tell the story of a girl attaining womanhood with all the emotion and beauty it deserves. Simultaneously, Kincaid expresses the significance and politics involved in that transition. Her second book, *Annie John* (1985), is comprised of short stories that first appeared in *The New Yorker*. Some critics consider *Annie John* a novel because the compilation of interwoven stories uncover the moral and psychological growth of the title character. This bildungsroman (coming-of-age story) has become Kincaid's best-known work to date.

Through Annie, Kincaid has brilliantly brought girlhood in the West Indies to literature as a masterful work of art. That art is a prose blend of European, American, and Caribbean folk forms of expression. The result is an effective rendering of a girl's struggle to discover her own identity. Annie is a girl growing up in an idyllic garden setting. At first she is the sole figure in that Eden—she has only her parents and Miss Maynard to interact with—and she maintains her sense of singularity when she finally begins mixing with others. Her omnipotent mother keeps the powers of the world and of death at a distance. Gradually, however, her mother introduces death and separation in order to mature Annie and prepare her for the world. The story of the mother creating the daughter is not unlike the works of Mary Shelley (*Frankenstein*) or John Milton

(*Paradise Lost*) in the sense that the created becomes more than the creator intended.

Author Biography

Jamaica Kincaid once said in an interview that her history began on ships and continues as corruption. By this she meant that the ideal human morality—which the Europeans tried to disseminate with empire—had instead become political, cultural, and moral corruption. That was the gift left behind as independence. Her island of Antigua is a microcosm of all newly independent colonies and the ensuing corruption. And Kincaid, like other West Indian people, is an amalgam of all who arrived at these islands by boat—Carib Indian, African, and Scottish. Kincaid explained this to Allan Vorda, for *The Mississippi Review,* by telling how the library (from which she stole books as a girl) that was ruined by an earthquake in 1974 would have been rebuilt by the colonial administrator. "Antigua used to be a place of standards. There was a sort of decency that it just doesn't have anymore. I think the tragedy of Antigua for me, when I began to see it again, was the loss of the library."

At the time of the earthquake, Kincaid was living in New York and she had recently taken up her new name. She was born in Antigua on May 25, 1949 as Elaine Potter Richardson, daughter of Annie Richardson and a father of whom she will not speak. When her family's economic situation made a turn for the worse, Kincaid dropped out of the university. At seventeen, she was sent to Westchester, New York, to work as an *au pair,* or nanny. Kincaid continued to pursue her education, however, and studied photography at the New School and later attended Franconia College in New Hampshire. In her early twenties, the desire to write became urgent but she did not think serious writing was being done anymore.

Dreading to be exposed, should her attempt to write fail, she fished about for a new name. She was not familiar with the black power movement or other African-American political groups and so did not choose an African name. Besides, she has often said, the only thing she has in common with Africa is her skin color. Her consciousness is a construct of the western hemisphere. Reflecting this consciousness, along with her view of her history as a blend of corruption and boats, she chose the name Jamaica. Jamaica is derived from *Xaymaca,* the translation

Columbus made of the Carib Indian word for that island, translated again into English. She chose Kincaid because, as she told Allan Vorda, "it just seemed to go together with Jamaica."

Soon after becoming Jamaica Kincaid, her writing came to the attention of William Shawn, editor of the *The New Yorker.* She became a staff writer there in 1976 and married the editor's son, Allen Shawn. In 1983, her collection of stories titled *At the Bottom of the River* won an American Academy Zabel award. Kincaid followed up *At the Bottom of the River* with *Annie John* in 1985. In addition to writing fiction, Kincaid has published *A Small Place,* about colonialism and tourism in Antigua. She also continues to write a gardening column.

Plot Summary

Jamaica Kincaid's *Annie John* tells the story of a girl's painful growth into young womanhood. Annie Victoria John, the narrator, progresses from a blissful childhood in Antigua, when she is the center of her mother's attention, to a trying adolescence filled with fierce maternal conflict, to her departure from Antigua for England at the age of seventeen.

Figures in the Distance

At ten, Annie does not know that children die until a young girl dies in Annie's mother's arms. Annie's mother (also named Annie John) must prepare the child for burial while Annie's father, Alexander, builds her coffin. Annie begins to see her mother's hands differently after this experience and, for a time, does not want to be touched by or look at them. Soon, after two more of her acquaintances die, Annie secretly begins to sneak to strangers' funerals. Then a humpbacked girl her own age dies. Annie runs to the girl's funeral after school, forgetting to pick up fish for dinner. She is caught lying to her mother about her mistake and must eat dinner alone and go to bed without a kiss. However, when in bed, her mother comes and kisses her anyway.

The Circling Hand

In the chapter's early pages, Annie describes her idyllic holidays when she and her mother bathe together and share her mother's activities. She describes her mother's trunk, in which she has kept all of Annie's possessions since birth. She sometimes tells Annie stories about each of the trunk's objects,

Jamaica Kincaid

delighting Annie, who revels in her mother's love. This life of "paradise" begins to falter, though, when Annie's body begins to change. Annie's mother now forces her to stop wearing dresses made from her mother's fabric and sends Annie to learn both manners and the piano, at which Annie fails through misbehavior. Then Annie accidentally catches her parents making love and stares at her mother's hand making circular motions on her father's back. That night, Annie behaves defiantly toward her mother for the first time and is silently sure she will never let her mother touch or kiss her again. The next day, though, she allows her mother to kiss her when she returns from her first day at her new school.

Gwen

When Annie first arrives at her new school, she is friendless and unsure of herself. After her teacher assigns them autobiographical essays to write, however, Annie shows she is the smartest girl in her class. She writes of a day she spent with her mother bathing nude in the sea. She lost sight of her mother and, afraid of the water, could not swim to find her. When her mother returned, she comforted Annie, telling her she would never leave her. Annie later dreamt of this event, only her mother does not return in the dream. She told her mother of the dream and received comfort again. Annie moves many of the

girls to tears with this story. She does not tell them, however, that the story's ending is fiction. In actuality, her mother responded to the nightmare by warning Annie against eating unripe fruit before bed. Later that day, Annie makes friends with Gweneth Joseph, and they become inseparable companions. Annie soon becomes the first of her friends to menstruate. At school recess, in a nook of old tombstones, she exhibits her menstruation to them and they comfort her. Annie returns home to her mother, whom she feels she no longer loves.

The Red Girl

In her continuing rebellion against her mother, Annie strikes up a secret friendship with the Red Girl, an unkempt girl with red hair who loves to play marbles, a game forbidden by Annie's mother. Annie begins to see the Red Girl secretly, to play marbles, and to steal, hiding her treasures underneath the house. When caught with a marble, Annie lies that she does not play marbles. Her mother, not believing her, searches under the house for Annie's marble collection but cannot find it. After days of futile searching, she tells Annie a terrifying story of her own girlhood. Annie, moved by the story, almost tells the truth until she recognizes her mother's attempt to manipulate her. The Red Girl soon moves away, and Annie dreams of living with her on a deserted island, where they joyfully send misdirected ships crashing into rocks.

Columbus in Chains

During history class, Annie reads ahead to a picture of Columbus chained in the bottom of a ship. Annie loves this picture of the colonizer brought low, and she relates it to a story about her grandfather, Pa Chess, who was rendered immobile by an illness. Annie writes her mother's laughing response to Pa Chess's plight under Columbus's picture: "The Great Man Can No Longer Just Get Up and Go." She is caught by her teacher and must copy Books I and II of John Milton's *Paradise Lost*. At home, Annie's misery is compounded when her mother disguises breadfruit, which Annie hates, as rice and then laughs about it.

Somewhere, Belgium

When fifteen, Annie feels an inexplicable misery that sits inside her like a "thimble that weighed worlds." She and her mother are constantly at odds, though they hide their conflicts from others. Annie has a recurring dream in which she thinks, "'My mother would kill me if she got the chance. I would kill my mother if I had the courage.'" Since she has always been taught that dreams are the same as real life, the dream's words haunt her. Annie daydreams of living alone in Belgium like Charlotte Brontë, the author of *Jane Eyre*, her favorite novel. One day, while studying her reflection in a shop window, Annie is taunted by four boys. She recognizes one of them as a childhood playmate who once almost hanged himself accidentally while she just stood by watching and who made her sit naked on a red ants' nest. When she returns home, her mother scolds her for talking to the boys, saying she acted like a slut. Annie retorts in kind, then goes to her room. She thinks about the trunk under her bed, which makes her both long for her mother and wish her dead. When her father offers to build her some new furniture, Annie requests her own trunk.

The Long Rain

Despite a lack of clear symptoms, Annie falls ill for three and a half months and cannot leave her bed. Corresponding with her illness is an unusual period of heavy rains. Her illness distorts her perceptions, one time causing her to try to wash clean the imperfections in her framed photographs, ruining them. Annie's grandmother Ma Chess arrives and assures Annie's mother that the girl's sickness is not like her uncle Johnnie's, who died from a curse after laying two years in bed. Ma Chess, an obeah (or voodoo) woman, becomes Annie's primary caregiver. On the day the rains stop, Annie's illness disappears. During her illness, Annie has grown taller than her mother, and she now feels repulsed by the world in which she lives.

A Walk to the Jetty

Now seventeen and willing to go anywhere to escape Antigua, Annie is scheduled to leave for England to study nursing. She mentally sums up her life, concentrating on her relationship with her parents. She says a polite goodbye to Gwen, who will soon be married, something which Annie vows never to be. She then walks between her parents to the docks and surveys the world she is leaving, feeling both gladness and sharp pain. At her ship, she bids farewell to her parents, both crying with her mother and feeling suspicious of her. The novel ends with her in her cabin listening to the waves making "an unexpected sound, as if a vessel filled with liquid had been placed on its side and now was slowly emptying out."

Characters

Ma Chess

Annie John's grandmother embodies the traditions of the West Indies that Annie's mother abandoned when she left Dominica. Annie John's father's preference for Dr. Stephens indicates his desire to also leave these traditions behind. However, one day, Grandmother arrives and does not leave until Annie recovers.

Father

See Mr. Alexander John

Grandmother

See Ma Chess

Mr. Alexander John

Mr. Alexander John, Annie's father, is thirty-five years older than his wife and has many unacknowledged heirs. He is a carpenter who brings humorous tales about Mr. Oatie, his partner in the construction business, back to the lunch table. These daily reports have the effect of emphasizing the growing tension between mother and daughter. During the lunch routine, they behave properly toward each other and Mother rarely fails to be amused by his stories. Mr. John represents the world of masculinity for which Annie's mother is preparing her. Until Annie is ushered into that world, however, it remains as distant as the haunting idea of boys playing marbles.

Mr. John built the family's house and made the furniture within. He protests against allowing the obeah woman to tend to Annie and he does not like Ma Chess. However, there is one moment of closeness between Annie and her father when he tells her of his own mother. Given the fears and obsession Annie has with her mother, this apparent empathy with Mr. John is actually a moment when Annie vicariously experiences the fantasy of being like her father—sleeping with mother until the age of eighteen when mother, then, conveniently dies.

Miss Annie Victoria John

The title character is a precocious young girl growing up in an Edenic garden governed by her loving mother. This changes with the onset of puberty and the declaration of independence her mother imposes on her. A civil war breaks out between them not unlike the Angelic war of *Paradise Lost*. The more Annie struggles to be distant

Media Adaptations

- An audiocassette was made of *Annie John* in 1994 by Airplay Inc.

---

and different from her mother the more alike they become. In the end, Annie leaves the island with her own trunk, calling to mind the exodus her mother made from Dominca years before.

As the narrator of the story, Annie is at liberty to fabricate reality as she sees fit. Consequently, the line between myth or dream and reality is thin. She actively imitates her favorite literary personae, Satan and Jane Eyre, who moved into their own adult identities through rebellion and flight and recreated, in some ways, the exact world from which they fled.

Annie also allows the traditional culture to exist with the present. She loves her grandmother and the magic her grandmother has. She is not afraid to give that as much importance as the magic of the school-teacher and the doctor.

Finally, Annie dies to her childish self—the self that ruled the girls who gathered among the tomb-stones during recess and the child who hid marbles and stolen books beneath the house. This occurs during a three-month rain while she is ill. Recovery comes with the help of her grandmother and the realization that she is too large for her home—she is now literally taller than both her parents. Not only does she want to leave, she must leave as a necessary step in her formation as a woman. She must take her trunk and go to a new place and build her world there.

Mrs. Annie Victoria John

Having fallen out with her father at age sixteen, Mrs. John packed her yellow-and-green trunk and left Dominica for Antigua. The boat she left in was hit by a hurricane and was lost at sea for five days. The boat was a ruin but Mrs. John and her trunk were fine. Annie's baby clothes and memories are kept in this same trunk beneath her bed. It is fitting

that the mother's trunk comes to be used in this way because, as she says to Annie, "I loved you best."

Mrs. John is the benevolent goddess governing the garden from which little Annie observes death. The paradise cannot remain such forever and gradually the mother introduces death and separation. She has formed Annie and she sends Annie away.

Mother's position is typical of Caribbean women. The women run the households and the men are sent out to work. Consequently, the children are indistinguishable from the mother while she goes about her tasks until it is appropriate to give the children their own identities. But in *Annie John* this situation becomes abnormally tense because there is only one identity. Furthermore, there is only one name. The mother fights to give it away while Annie struggles to take it.

Ma Jolie

A local obeah woman reccomended by Ma Chess. Mother calls her to come minister to Annie. Ma Jolie does not know as much as Ma Chess, however, and can do little. She prescribes tradition-al medicines, places appropriate candles in the room, and pins a foul-smelling sachet to Annie's nightgown. The obeah concoctions are set behind Dr. Stephens's on the shelf above Annie's bed.

Gweneth Joseph

She is the first girl at the new school to notice Annie. It is not long before the two girls fall in love and become inseparable. But, eventually, Annie becomes bored with Gwen and in the end comes to see Gwen as a silly, giggling schoolgirl when she comes to bid Annie farewell. She tells Annie of her engagement and receives a humored blessing. Annie stands inwardly amazed that she ever loved Gwen.

Little Miss

See Miss Annie Victoria John

Mineu

Mineu is a playmate of Annie's and the only boy close to her age in the narrative. When together, Annie and Mineu like to reenact local events. This play leads Mineu to fake his own hanging in order to imitate an actual hanging. Annie watches as it goes wrong. She is unable to move. Luckily a neighbor comes and saves the boy. Years later she meets him in the street. They simply say "hello." Meanwhile, his friends snicker and poke each other while Annie's mother catches sight of the scene. Later, her mother calls her a slut for talking to him.

Mother

See Mrs. Annie Victoria John

Red Girl

The Red Girl embodies the very antithesis of what Annie has been taught to be proper. They meet when the Red Girl climbs a tree to collect a guava in a manner normally reserved to boys. She is dirty and smelly, and she plays marbles with the boys. Annie embraces and kisses her, as the ultimate rebellion against her mother's notions. It is the temptation of the Red Girl that leads Annie into a ''series of betrayals of people and things.''

Ruth

The daughter of the Anglican minister doesn't fare well in Antigua. Ruth is one of the few English children in the community. She is an embarrassed blonde who is frequently the class dunce. Annie thinks that Ruth would rather be home in England ''where no one would remind her constantly of the terrible things her ancestors had done.''

Dr. Stephens

The family doctor is an Englishman named Dr. Stephens. He represents modern science and has served the family through Annie's other illnesses—like hookworm. Mother agrees with his theory that germs need to be rooted out and destroyed. He represents modern science and is approved of by Mr. John, but his medicinal prescriptions prove ineffectual against Annie's debilitating depression.

Themes

Death

Death enters the frame of *Annie John* at the outset and never leaves. As a distant event observed by Annie, death serves as a counter reality to Annie's position as the beloved of her mother. Consequently, Annie's obsession with this other reality keeps the possibility of separation as the end of her blissful girlhood absolutely hidden. Death also serves to exaggerate the distance of the story and, thus, hide the narrator. In the first sentence, therefore, the adult narrator transforms into a girl fascinated by the apparently abstract concept of death.

There is a literal graveyard in the distance that Annie sees figures, not people per se, enter and leave. Death comes closer when Nalda, Sonia's mother, and then Miss Charlotte die. Annie is attentive to this facet of life and watches it. She observes funerals. She notes where death is. Yet she does not grieve. Annie wants to touch death by touching the hunched back of a dead girl whose funeral she attends for the purpose of observation. Disturbing Annie's peace, however, death nears her twice through the person of her mother, who was holding Nalda and talking to Miss Charlotte when they died. These two events foreshadow the discovery of imperfection in Annie's universe.

Death does not come to Annie but she dies to three things: her girlhood, her mother, and her home. The first two take place through inevitable growth events. There is much that marks Annie as becoming a woman and, therefore, rivaling her mother for ownership of their shared name. The two primary events are her first menstruation and her illness. Her first menstruation is full of death images beyond the obvious significance of biological change—she faints because, she says, ''I brought to my mind a clear picture of myself sitting at my desk in my own blood.'' Her illness is a mock death. When she comes forth from her sick bed she is taller and no longer seems to be of the Antiguan world.

Identity

The central struggle, or agon, in Annie's story is her struggle to bring forth her own identity. That identity is fulfilled through the scripted story of the trunk—she will have her identity when she leaves bearing her trunk. This struggle involves mood swings, rebellious adventures, the awakening of sexuality, and a coming to terms with historical reality. However, the person on whom this struggle is focused, and who has some responsibility in its instigation, is her mother. The mother-daughter tension dominates the work. The tension is not eased, though Annie's struggle meets with success. She gains an identity despite her adult telling of her story, in which she clearly becomes a woman in her mother's image, but actual reconciliation is absent. Annie's trunk-carrying identity, then, is a death to her self and loss of her mother.

Life as a child is set up as Edenic. Annie is indistinguishable from her mother and happiness reigns. That is, until the day her mother says they are now separate. The demand for Annie to suddenly be independent, to have her own subjectivity, is the high point of the book. It arrives in Chapter 2, in the central image of her parents having sex and particularly ''The Circling Hand'' of her mother on her father's back. At that point, Annie says, ''To say that I felt the earth swept away from under me would not be going too far.'' Her model of the universe—a dual universe with two beings in one dress fabric—had suddenly become a universe of independent bodies all doing their own things to their own ends. The rest of the work details the way in which Annie puts herself back together and finds her own reflection. She had been seeing herself as a smaller version of her mother but gradually she sees her own reflection in a shop window. She reminds herself of ''Satan just recently cast out of heaven.'' Eventually, identity formation leads her to a figurative death. Her recovery from her illness is also her arrival at her identity as a woman. Recovered, she is taller, conscious of her power as a woman who knows herself, and with her new wisdom she sees she has outgrown the island of Antigua.

Annie uses several tools to form her identity. The first is her body. Her prowess and strength afford her respect from her classmates and captainship of the volleyball team. The other tool is her intellect. Being above average, she is not delinquent in opportunities to boost her confidence. But this does not prove as important as knowledge gained by observing people at home and hearing stories. One such story is of her mother's departure from Dominica. Annie knows the story well and, therefore, always has an example of strong womanhood before her. She also knows the story of her father, but she rejects his narrative although she empathizes with his tragedy. There are other narratives she rejects. Uncle John was a promising young man who died young. Annie notes that his belongings are kept in a trunk. Annie's things are in a trunk, too, but she decides to follow her mother's narrative and leave Antigua with a trunk—a new one—rather than follow the other narratives which both involve death. Reinforcing her choice is Charlotte Brontë's story of *Jane Eyre,* whose heroine also strikes out on her own.

Post-Colonialism

Post-colonialism is a literary theory developed in response to the literature being written by people in countries previously governed by the British crown. In the years since the granting of independence, the people of these nations have had to reconcile their identity as educated British subjects with their awareness of their own subjugation by that government. This resonates directly with Annie's identification with *Jane Eyre* as well as references to Milton and Shakespeare. Annie has been taught English literature—stories from the land of the former colonial administration. However, the postcolonial writer does not reject this literature; instead, she embraces it as her own. She also embraces the English tongue as her language, but now she will use it to tell her own story.

There are many references to the history of colonialism in *Annie John*, but two key moments involve a classmate named Ruth and Christopher Columbus. Both occur in Chapter 5, ''Columbus in Chains,'' but resonate throughout the entire work. Being a good student with aspirations, Annie has trouble remembering the reality of her heritage or discerning whether she fits in ''with the masters or the slaves—for it was all history, it was all in the past, and everybody behaved differently now.'' Still, there is some remembering and hard feelings over the past. Annie says of Ruth, ''Perhaps she wanted to be in England, where no one would remind her [what] her ancestors had done.''

Crucial to Annie's understanding of herself as a postcolonial subject is her crime against history. She is caught not paying attention to a history lesson, but she is punished for defacing her schoolbook in a way that was blasphemous. ''I had gone too far this time,'' she says, ''defaming one of the great men in history, Christopher Columbus, discoverer of the island that was my home.'' Annie is aware of how tenuous is the idea that this island is her home. She is here only as the curious result of Empire. Still, it is her home, just as English culture is hers but with a little obeah thrown in.

Style

Point of View

The first-person (''I'') retrospective narrative is constructed with episodes. The main character in *Annie John* is, of course, Annie. Therefore, the reader sees Annie's Antigua. There are eight episodes highlighted in the chapter headings. During each episode more information is given about Annie. The timeline jumps but there is a steady progression from Annie as a young girl to her departure from home as a young woman.

This narrative, however, is ironic because the adult Annie establishes the reality of the story as if it were the perspective of little Annie. In other words,

Annie knows her own story's outcome but tries not to reveal this. The novel opens by literally noticing figures in a distance and also by placing the story at a distance, "during the year I was ten." Thus the effort on the part of the young Annie to show her mother as an Old Testament deity is offset by the adult attempt to reconcile. The mother remains beautiful and loved, though the literal narrative might say she is simply left behind.

Symbolism

The most important symbol of the work is the trunk. Each of the characters has a trunk—a place where their identity formation blocks are kept. In the case of Uncle John, it is all that is left. For Annie, the trunk with all of her baby things is a fun thing to clean out because she then hears stories about herself. When she leaves Antigua, Annie—like her mother when she left Dominica—takes a new trunk to build a new life. Father has a trunk but it is not solid. Father's trunk is ubiquitous. It is made up of all the women and illegitimate children that Annie and her mother run into. It is made up of the house and furniture he built. He adds to this trunk daily with stories about work because there is no one who wants to tell his story—Mother is busy with Annie's story.

Irony

Irony is akin to an "inside joke." It occurs when the intended meaning is the opposite of what is actually said. Kincaid offers many wonderful moments of irony. One example is in Chapter 5, when Annie says that colonialism is past and now "all of us celebrate Queen Victoria's birthday." It is a rather sudden cultural reference in the midst of a paragraph about the past. Many things happen in the phrase. Annie has been saying that the past is behind them, yet they still celebrate a past queen's birthday. She is also noting that the personification of colonialism (the reign of Queen Victoria was the heyday of the Empire) is celebrated with a national holiday.

More of these ironic moments involve works of literature. For example, on the desk of Miss Nelson, an Englishwoman, is an elaborate edition of Shakespeare's play *The Tempest*. She is reading this work while the girls are writing their autobiographical essays. The irony is that on the one hand, the teacher is simply reading one of the great plays of English literature. The deeper implication is very complex because that play has become a grand touchstone for all postcolonial writers, especially those of the Caribbean. The reason is this: many intellectuals of

those islands read that play as the moment of conquest, as if Shakespeare was writing the reality of colonialism into effect with his play. Further, the figure of Caliban—a native of the island forced into labor—mixes his identity with the spirit of the island, Sycorax. Caliban is a slave who has learned English so that he can curse his master. The children writing their essays are a result of the same process—brought to the island and now expected to peacefully get along with their former masters. Particularly, Annie's narrative involves her being stranded on a little island—like the characters in the play—but unable to call to her mother. She, like Caliban, yells at her master but there can be no understanding.

Dream Vision

Unlike the culture whose literature she adores (in *Jane Eyre,* for example, mythology has been banished from England), Annie does not divide the mythical from reality. Kincaid uses this in the narrative itself, so that dreams and myth are written in and make up her characters. The result of this is the legitimating of oral tradition. The first instance of this appears early in the novel and concerns the dead. Annie reports that "sometimes they showed up in a dream, but that wasn't so bad, because they usually only brought a warning." Another example of this technique comes when Kincaid has Annie recite her autobiographical essay. This essay is atypical because in some sense it is a very mature psychological metaphor, but it also mythologizes the mother-daughter relationship. A final example is the event of Annie's and Mother's "black things," subjective demons, wrestling on the lunch table only to return—never to grapple again—to their rightful owners. This blending of realities validates dreaming as a way of thinking; it carries on the traditions represented by the obeah woman and Ma Chess.

Literary Heritage

Because Kincaid was born and raised in Antigua, an island in the West Indies, and emigrated to New York as a young adult, her fiction may be categorized as emerging from both Caribbean and American literary traditions. The virtual genocide of indigenous peoples of the West Indies by European colonizers in the sixteenth century explains why there is no surviving indigenous oral or literary tradition of the islands of the West Indies. Until the

1900s, literature emerging from the region was derived from the literary traditions of the conquering nations, including Spain, France, Great Britain, and the Netherlands. In the 1920s, however, a movement of writers influenced by Spanish-American Modernism began to develop a distinctive West Indian literature identified with the segment of the region's population largely of African descent. Distinguishing themselves from European literary aesthetics, these poets drew from oral folkloric traditions to strive for "the construction into poetic forms of the rhythmic and tonal elements of the islands' rituals and speech patterns, using Symbolist and Surrealist techniques" (*Encyclopaedia Britannica*). Kincaid's writing style, which utilizes a non-standard form of written English, follows this tradition in its success at capturing both the speech patterns and folkloric elements of West Indian culture.

Historical Context

Contact, Colonialism, and Independence

Originally inhabited by the Siboney people, the island of Antigua, the setting for Kincaid's *Annie John*, was populated by Arawak and Carib Indians when Christopher Columbus arrived there during his second voyage in 1493. He named the island after a church in Sevilla, Spain, named Santa Maria de la Antigua. Thirty years later it became an outpost of the Spanish Conquistadors. In 1629, the French made a base there as Spanish power descended and the British had not yet taken control. French control was brief, however, and the English arrived in 1632. The Treaty of Breda formalized this situation in 1667.

From 1674 to 1834, the island was one large sugar plantation. Slaves were imported from Africa because the indigenous peoples fled or had been killed. The end of slavery brought freedom but no opportunity to be free. For the next hundred years, Antigua and surrounding islands were under the jurisdiction of one and then another federation. Greater independence was achieved in 1967, with statehood within the British Commonwealth granted in 1981. Finally the seven islands of the East Caribbean formed a merger. The single nation of the Organization of Eastern Caribbean States (OECS) came into being in 1987 and included the former British colonies: Antigua, Barbados, Dominica, Grenada, Jamaica, Montserrat, St. Kitts-Nevis-Anguilla, St. Vincent, Tobago, and Trinidad.

Latin America and the Caribbean

The 1980s was a troubled decade for the nations of Latin America and the Caribbean. Warily, they attempted to cease being the playground and raw material supplier of Europe and America. In doing so, they strengthened old trading alliances and forged new ones. Meanwhile, the United States began to create NAFTA with Canada and Mexico, while Europe moved closer to unionization. In addition to economic competition, the United States practiced active interventionism.

Acting out of the Monroe Doctrine—that the United States will not tolerate interference by any European power (including Russia) in the affairs of the Western Hemisphere—and the precedent set by President Theodore Roosevelt, the United States intervened everywhere to both good and bad effect. The United States still enforces a trade embargo against Cuba that has been in effect since 1959. It may never be known just how involved the United States was in the turmoil that disrupted life in El Salvador and Nicaragua throughout the 1980s. Nor will the full story of Haiti's troubles be known. Less mysterious, however, were the invasions of Grenada in 1983 and Panama in 1989. In the first case, the Reagan administration acted in reaction to a coup, the potential endangerment of U.S. medical students, and the fear of even closer ties between Grenada and Cuba. The leader of Panama, on the other hand, was accused of laundering drug money. He was arrested in the invasion and is currently serving a sentence of forty years in the United States.

The 1980s in the United States

In the decade of the eighties, culture in the United States sought to blend its past into the now. It was marked by pastiche, superficiality, recreations of old movie serials, nostalgia for a golden age that only ever existed on television, and "culture wars." The economy hummed at the surface with any sort of lifestyle and time available for consumption. Meanwhile, corporate mergers, downsizing, and an abrupt shift toward a service economy left industrial America partially unemployed and the labor movement—beginning with the air-traffic controllers's strike of 1981—drastically weakened. To offset this industrial downsizing, the government embarked on an immense weapons program. The result was a staggering national debt and a huge arsenal of nuclear warheads that most hope will never be used.

Race Relations

The Civil Rights movement encountered a backlash in the 1980s for which it was unprepared. Leaders of the movement knew the highpoints and victories of the 1960s were past, but they could hardly believe that the Miami riots of 1980 announced a decade of violence. Membership in neo-Nazi and Ku Klux Klan groups rose while racially motivated hate-crimes increased in frequency. Normally tolerant environments, like college campuses, reflected this trend.

Elections in the 1980s reflected the drastic change. Reverend Jesse Jackson, considered by many to be the successor to Martin Luther King Jr., ran twice for president in 1984 and 1988 as a Democrat. But the 1980s instead saw Republican President Ronald Reagan complete two terms of office that were succeeded by George Bush. Reagan won in a landslide because the populace felt that change might have occurred too fast. The brakes were applied and civil rights victories began to be overturned. In 1987, the legendary civil rights activist and the first black to serve on the U.S. Supreme Court, Justice Thurgood Marshall, expressed his opinion that President Reagan was ranked at the bottom in terms of civil rights for all Americans black or white. In a symbolic capping off of the decade, the elections of 1989 brought Republican David Duke, a former Ku Klux Klan grand wizard, to the Louisiana legislature. Much to the relief of the embarrassed Republican Party, Duke's later bid for the U.S. Senate was unsuccessful.

Critical Overview

Response to *Annie John* has been unanimous in its praise. Reviewers focus on Kincaid's successful writing of a girl's coming of age as well as the wonder and excitement of a historic epicenter—the Caribbean. More serious views of the work simply explore this theme further by investigating the family as represented in the story and as existing in the West Indies. Critics have also noticed aspects of the novel which break new ground, for example, the harmony with which Kincaid treats the blending of obeah and modern medicine.

First reviews of the work in 1985 were excited, glowing, and attentive to Kincaid's prose ability. Paula Bonnell wrote in *The Boston Herald* that the publication of Kincaid's first two books were "eagerly awaited events." Both, she continued, "are recreations of the self in that emotional country where dreams and what might have happened are part of the truest story of one's life." Jacqueline Austin agreed. She wrote a review in *VLS* months later saying, "Kincaid does write what she knows, what she knows is rare: pure passion, a past filled with curious events, a voice, and above all a craft." Austin also commented in passing about heritage. She names other writers from the West Indies to say that Kincaid is in a group trying to "encompass two traditions." John Bemrose is more particular in his review for *Maclean's Magazine*. He says, "The instrument of Kincaid's success is a prose style whose subtly varied cadences suggest the slow, dignified pace of life in colonial Antigua. She also knows her way around the human heart." In the *Times Literary Supplement* in the fall of 1985, Ike Onwordi noted that Kincaid's work is an "episodic" autobiography using "language that is poetic without affectation."

More scholarly analysis of *Annie John* followed slowly. In 1990, H. Adlai Murdoch wrote an article for *Callaloo*, entitled "Severing the (M)other Connection: The Representation of Cultural Identity in Jamaica Kincaid's *Annie John*" where he attempted to reconfigure the Oedipal tools of Freud for an utterly matriarchal order. Murdoch argued that as Caribbean writers began to create their own literature free of the aegis of empire, they confronted the Oedipal tensions of identity formation. Such a reading assumes that the only route to the child's, or the newly independent nation's, subjectivity is by confrontation and overthrow of the father, or ruling power. Only then can the child own his culture, or mother. "The issue of subjectivity, beset with problems such as recognition of self and other and oedipal conflict under the most conventional circumstances, is complicated further here given the additional factors of colonialism and pluralism which continue to mark Caribbean society and culture." Murdoch adds Lacan's notion of mirror as well as the notion of phallic signifier. Together they enable a reading in which Annie's mother is the main power broker against whom

Antigua serves as the setting for Kincaid's Annie John.

Annie struggles, as would the son against the father in traditional Freudian readings, to attain her independent subjectivity.

More recent criticism reflects postcolonial theory and views Kincaid as a postcolonial writer. Bill Ahscroft, Gareth Griffiths, and Helen Tiffin wrote the book on postcolonialism in 1989—*The Empire Writes Back: Theory and Practice in Post-Colonial Literatures.* The theory arises out of the historical fact that English literature as a discipline arose concurrently with the pressures of Empire. Consequently, previously colonized people found themselves independent but speaking English after the British left. They were not returned to pre-colonialism. They had to create a new cultural identity at peace with the unpleasantness of colonialism and their new sovereignty. With the realization of this phenomenon, critics like James Nagel reread Kincaid's *Annie John* as more than a bildungsroman or coming-of-age story. Thus in his 1995 article "Desperate Hopes, Desperate Lives: Depression and Self-Realization in Jamaica Kincaid's *Annie John* and *Lucy*," he builds upon Murdoch's insight. The mother becomes blended with the greater powers and the Oedipal constructs fracture beneath the pressure. The family's dynamics are now linked to the greater historical event that is Antigua.

Nagel notes the traditional bildungsroman aspects of the novel and then includes the background: "a legacy of slavery and deprivation and the rich texture of Annie's family life . . . as well as the English cultural overlay on the social patterns of Antigua . . . the eminence of the Anglican Church . . . European Christianity . . . folk rituals of potions and curses. . . . Everything in this society has a dual foundation, even the local dialect." The novel is seen here for its complexity and applauded for its ability to express the multiplicity of Antigua through the charm of a little girl. But that is art—to show how people live in their own circumstances. Allen Vorda quotes Henry Louis Gates saying this about Kincaid: "she never feels the necessity of claiming the existence of a black world or a female susceptibility. She assumes them both. I think its a distinct departure that she's making, and I think that more and more black American writers will assume their world the way that she does. So that we can get beyond the large theme of racism and get to the deeper themes of how black people love and cry and live and die. Which, after all, is what art is all about."

Beyond the areas where Kincaid subtly breaks new ground—as in her casual blending of traditional and modern medicine through the meeting of the obeah and pharmaceutical medicines—there is the serious craft that Gates describes. Kincaid's writing is wonderful and her story captivatingly emotional because, while she is expressing a political transformation, she focuses on the human effect—the effect on the little girl.

Criticism

Darren Felty

Darren Felty is a visiting instructor at the College of Charleston. In the following essay, he examines the struggles of Annie John, Jamaica Kincaid's protagonist, to define her own character in relation to her family and culture.

Critics often characterize Jamaica Kincaid's *Annie John* as a bildungsroman, or a coming-of-age narrative that traces the protagonist's quest for both self-knowledge and a distinct place in the world.

Such a description proves apt for Kincaid's largely autobiographical novel, since her work revolves around a series of conflicts related to her young protagonist's search for emotional stability and self-definition. Growing up worshiping her mother and living in a nurturing, almost blissful environment, Annie loses a secure sense of herself with the advent of puberty and her mother's insistence on emotional separation.

In addition to Annie's familial life, Kincaid also explores the cultural dynamics of Antigua through Annie's confrontations with the island's colonial legacy and her depictions of persistent African belief systems.

By focusing the work through Annie's eyes, Kincaid allows the reader intimate access to Annie's attempts to define herself in relation to others and to her culture. Yet despite this point of view and the lyrical, evocative style of Annie's narration, Kincaid does not romanticize Annie's conflicts or strain for reader sympathy. Instead, Kincaid insists on honestly portraying Annie's multiple reactions to her dilemmas, whether they evoke the reader's compassion or reproach. By doing so, she invites the reader to share her main character's negotiation of her turbulent adolescence and to witness the slow, painful development of inner resources that allow her to embark on a journey into the unknown.

Throughout the novel, Annie's relationship with her mother remains at the heart of her most pressing conflicts. The older Annie who narrates the book describes her early years as Edenic, with only fleeting doubts to interfere with her intense love for her mother. In fact, basking in her mother's attention, Annie recognizes the "paradise" of her existence and pities those people who lack such love.

Soon, however, Annie becomes one of these people herself when she enters puberty. Recognizing the end of her daughter's childhood, Annie's mother forces her to move beyond their close relationship, to begin the process of becoming independent. Yet Annie is not prepared for such a sudden transition and what it implies about her future. Confused over her bodily changes and in need of reassurance, she instead finds, in her eyes, betrayal.

Her most troubling and significant moment of transition comes when she unwittingly discovers her mother's sexuality. Returning early from Sunday school, Annie finds her parents making love and focuses her feelings of betrayal on her mother's hand. Horrified, Annie sees the hand as "white and bony, as if it had been left out in the elements. It seemed not to be her hand, and yet it could only be her hand, so well did I know it. It went around and around in the same circular motion [on Annie's father's back], and I looked at it as if I would never see anything else in my life again."

For Annie, the hand that had nurtured her and was always full of life and strength now appears dead as she recognizes her exclusion from her parents' lives. She no longer resides within the comforting "circle" of her mother's hand and is figuratively expelled from her Eden.

After this time, Annie's feelings for her mother remain intense, but they are twisted toward anger, hatred, and mistrust. Annie never stops loving her mother, despite her youthful assertions to the contrary, but she cannot recover the purity of the love she felt in her early youth, and she remains ever cognizant of this loss.

Annie soon finds a partial means of filling this emotional void: friendships with girls her own age. While Annie enjoys being a leader among her peers, she saves her most intense feelings for her private relationships.

With Gwen Joseph and, later, the Red Girl, she often keeps herself apart from the other girls. Such

What Do I Read Next?

- A story similar to that of Annie's is Kincaid's more recent *Lucy* (1990). This novel tells the story of a young woman (17-19) as she struggles to form herself in her new life in America. Many of the themes developed in *Annie John* are further explored here. Especially evident is the affinity of the young girl with the biblical and Miltonic Lucifer, whence Kincaid took the character's name.

- Written twenty–four years earlier than *Annie John*, *Miguel Street*, by V. S. Naipaul, is set in similar surroundings and with a similar plot. The author wrote in absentia, as did Kincaid, but his story was that of a boy growing up in the pseudo-Victorian society of Trinidad.

- Derek Walcott, poet of the Caribbean and Nobel prize winner in 1992, has two collections dealing directly with the themes in Kincaid's work—writing in absentia, in America, and being estranged from home. The two works are *The Fortunate Traveller* (1981) and *MidSummer* (1984).

- Annie refers to her favorite writers throughout her narration. One writer referred to is Charlotte Brontë and her novel *Jane Eyre*. The comparison is revealing as Jane must also struggle to form her identity but against dead parents and an overbearing, cruel step-family. Curiously, Jane becomes the governess for Mr. Rochester's little girl whose West Indian step-mother is kept in the attic—she is insane.

- Linking again with the same themes of the Caribbean and colonialism is Jean Rhys' *Wide Sargasso Sea* (1966). Born in Dominica, Rhys moved to Europe and took part in the writing circles of pre-WWI. She then disappeared in Cornwall to emerge with an answer to Charlotte Brontë's *Jane Eyre*. Rhys writes directly back to the center of empire by explaining the circumstances of the insane woman in Rochester's attic.

---

isolation emulates, however incompletely, her childhood feelings of being a privileged extension of her mother. Her ardent friendship with Gwen, for instance, clearly functions as a substitute for Annie's lost maternal relationship. Like Annie's mother, Gwen is neat and self-controlled, and she also makes Annie the center of her world, which Annie craves. Yet, like Lucifer expelled from Heaven (to whom Annie refers later in the book), Annie ultimately embraces rebellion as the means to reconcile herself to her exile from her mother's affections.

Hence her attraction toward the Red Girl, who represents the opposite of what Annie's mother values. She bathes and changes clothes only once a week, does not attend Sunday school, and plays the forbidden game of marbles. Free from rigid parental dictates and constraints, which Annie wants to be, the Red Girl becomes the embodiment of Annie's resistance to parental authority. By playing marbles with the Red Girl and then lying about it to her mother, Annie asserts an independence won through deception, which she sees as the only means open to her.

Yet Annie's open rebellions against her mother, while they help define her independence, also highlight Annie's continuing reliance on her mother for guidance. Ironically, to assert her own break with (and to hurt) her mother, she models her behavior on what she has learned from her mother. In the contest of wills over the marbles, for instance, Annie adopts negative characteristics like subterfuge and manipulation, which she believes her mother uses against her.

Kincaid further portrays this element of their relationship through her use of the trunk. For Annie as a child, her mother's trunk was a symbol of familial intimacy and her own significance, since her mother would recount Annie's youth by describing the history of its contents. It also betokened strength and independence, since her mother used it when escaping her childhood home. After a caustic argument, Annie requests her own trunk, a gesture that stresses her desire to overthrow her mother's influence. What Annie does not acknowledge, however, is her evident desire to emulate her mother. By requesting a trunk, she chooses her mother's method of rebellion against unwanted parental control and places herself on the path to independence that her mother has walked before her.

While familial conflicts are central to Annie's maturation and self-discovery, they alone do not shape her character. Kincaid also emphasizes the impact of cultural forms and attitudes on Annie, and Annie's reaction to them helps the reader understand the sense of self she is developing.

Running throughout the book are features of English influence, such as the Anglican church, English holidays, Annie's British textbooks, and even her middle name, Victoria. Annie recognizes her colonial status, but such knowledge does not lead her to feel inferior. In fact, she considers her slave heritage as a moral strength in comparison to the English colonizers, upon whose graves she and her friends daily walk.

Indeed, Annie is overtly contemptuous of the European colonizing mentality that enabled the Spanish and English to enslave others for their own aggrandizement. Contrary to her teachers, she does not revere Columbus and particularly relishes the picture of him as a captive in a ship. She underscores her enjoyment at his humbling by writing ''The Great Man Can No Longer Just Get Up and Go'' under the picture, drawing the words and sentiment from her mother's statement about her own father's debilitating illness.

Such a renunciation of colonial power parallels, in part, her attempts to reject parental authority. As with her familial relationships, she chafes at the implied cultural constraints that European institutions and attitudes have placed upon her. She cannot, however, completely escape them, as revealed by her love for the British novel *Jane Eyre*, her writing in Old English script under Columbus's picture, and her ultimate voyage to England itself. In fact, while her insolence toward colonial symbols reflects her desire for autonomy, it also reveals her need to combat the continuing hold of the colonizers' views on her own self-definitions.

A more substantial form of resistance to European influence seems to come from the African cultural traditions still thriving in Antigua. Kincaid shows that the colonial figures in the work justify to themselves the degradation of others by privileging rationality and science over emotion and mystery.

In direct opposition to this philosophy is obeah, the West Indian descendant of African voodoo practiced by female figures in the book. Obeah involves a belief in transformation, especially of spiritual forms, and embraces the flux of the natural world rather than trying to control it. These elements of obeah prove particularly relevant to *Annie John*, since the novel addresses the inescapability of both change and the impulses of nature.

Like the colonial elements of Antigua, obeah beliefs help shape Annie's life and her sense of herself. She makes no distinction, for instance, between the waking world and the dream world, and her mother works to protect their home from outside curses and bad spirits. Annie herself, while she never outwardly embraces obeah practices like her mother and grandmother, never mocks or rejects them. Indeed, they offer her a compelling alternative to colonial belief systems and, perhaps more importantly, form a link to her maternal heritage that helps her through the darkest period in her life.

Annie's extended illness marks her most important transition in the book. The world's treacheries and corruptions seem to force her to retreat into a womb-like existence in which her perception of reality becomes warped. Kincaid accentuates the potency and mysteriousness of this illness by coupling it with a period of continuous rain, as if nature itself were in sympathy with Annie, providing her with the water for her womb environment.

Conventional medicine fails to relieve her condition, and her grandmother, Ma Chess, soon arrives, fearing that Annie has been cursed. Not bound by the strictures of Western rationality and attuned to life's emotional chords, Ma Chess immediately recognizes the true nature of Annie's distress and encourages Annie's return to virtual infancy while tending to her like a mother.

Thus, if only for a short time, Annie finally restores the undivided, nurturing existence she formerly shared with her mother and escapes the pain that has been plaguing her. These experiences seem to prepare her for the next stages in her journey, in which she will strive not to restore previous bonds, but to rend them.

Though she re-creates a sense of her former intimacy with her mother, Annie's illness does not relieve her resentment and suspicion. In fact, when she emerges from this state, she feels an even stronger separation from her family and environment and is ready to leave her home.

Her final day on Antigua reflects both her desire to escape and her remorse over another loss in her life. She contemplates her past and her home, and she measures the changes in herself by the stasis she believes she witnesses in others' lives, like her parents and Gwen.

The final lines in the book, while Annie waits to embark for England, underscore her sense of the fundamental alterations in her life and character: ''I could hear the small waves lap-lapping around the ship. They made an unexpected sound, as if a vessel filled with liquid had been placed on its side and now was slowly emptying out.'' Such imagery proves telling, for Annie, too, is ''emptying out'' in order to become a vessel for new experiences.

Like the vessel placed on its side, this transformation proves disorienting as well as liberating. She is trying to move beyond her past and beyond her mother's influence in order to redefine (or ''refill'') herself, but is unsure of what may result. She cannot see who she will become, but she can see who and what she does not want to be.

Like her language and imagery, Annie's character has grown richer and more complex throughout the book, and her journey vividly portrays Kincaid's vision of the necessary and excruciating search for selfhood that, like Annie's quest, is never complete.

Source: Darren Felty, in an essay for *Literature of Developing Nations for Students*, Gale, 2000.

Diane Simmons

Diane Simmons, in her essay on Jamaica Kincaid's novels Annie John *and* Lucy, *focuses on how canonical literature of the West, most notably John Milton's* Paradise Lost *and Charlotte Bronte's* Jane Eyre, *has influenced not only the plotline of Kincaid's novels but also Kincaid herself.*

As a child schooled in the British colonial system, West Indian writer Jamaica Kincaid was nourished on a diet of English classics, reading from Shakespeare and Milton by the age of five. Sometimes the canonical works of English literature were administered as punishment; for her schoolgirl crimes Kincaid

was forced to copy large chunks of John Milton's *Paradise Lost*. Other works, such as Charlotte Bronte's *Jane Eyre*, were Kincaid's best friends and she read them over and over.

In her relation to the English language and the English literature with which colonial children were so assiduously inculcated, Kincaid presents a paradox. The emphasis on England, Kincaid has said, the constant inference that England was the center of the universe, robbed colonial children of a sense of their own worth. Further, the rigorous study of English only enhanced the power of what Kincaid has called ''the language of the criminal.'' This language, she writes in her long essay, ''A Small Place,'' is inherently biased in favor of those who enslaved and continue to dominate her people:

> For the language of the criminal can contain only the goodness of the criminal's deed. The language of the criminal can explain and express the deed only from the criminal's point of view. It cannot contain the horror of the deed, the injustice of the deed, the agony, the humiliation inflicted on me.

It is no accident that Kincaid's reading in English literature served to diminish, even to ''erase'' her while it enhanced the beauty and power of everything British. English studies emerged as a discipline out of the ''same historical moment'' which ''produced the nineteenth century colonial form of imperialism,'' writes Bill Ashcroft et. al. Both English studies and colonialism

> proceeded from a single ideological clime and . . . the development of the one is intrinsically bound up with the development of the other, both at the level of simple utility (as propaganda for instance) and at the unconscious level, where it leads to the naturalizing of constructed value (e.g. civilization, humanity, etc.) which conversely, established ''savagery,'' ''native,'' ''primitive,'' as their antitheses and as the object a reforming zeal.

One result of making literature ''central to the cultural enterprise of Empire'' was to cause ''those from the periphery to immerse themselves in the imported culture, denying their origins in an attempt to become 'more English than the English.'''

For Kincaid, immersed in the English classics, in a world where, she has said, ''everything seemed divine and good only if it was English,'' the requirement was to be as English as possible: ''. . . my whole upbringing was something I was not; it was English. It was sort of a middle-class English upbringing—I mean, I had the best table manners you ever saw.'' But table manners would prove not to be enough: ''Of course there was the final hurdle that you could never pass, you could never be English. You could never be a real person.''

Kincaid has shown how the English classics invited her to ''erase'' herself. This was accomplished not only by a focus on the geography of England, her wars, and her kings and queens, but also through depictions of English life as if it were the only real life. The ''softer views,'' Kincaid says:

> were the ones that made the most lasting impression on me, the ones that made me really feel like nothing. ''When morning touched the sky'' was one phrase, for no morning touched the sky where I lived. The morning where I lived came on abruptly with a shock of heat and loud noise.

But while Kincaid has explored the negative impact of colonial education, she has also made positive use of the English classics. Milton's *Paradise Lost,* she says, taught her that questions of justice and injustice could be considered and articulated, inspiring her to express her own sense of wrong. Though this was undoubtedly not the intention of the colonial educators, the young Kincaid found a hero with whom she could identify in *Paradise Lost*: the defiant outcast Lucifer. Given several books of *Paradise Lost* to copy out as punishment, Kincaid was especially sensitive to Milton's study of Satan's crime and punishment:

> My feeling of how wrong my own punishment was, was very much in my small mind as I was [copying out pages of *Paradise Lost*]. So . . . this story about the powerless and the powerful is very much connected with my feelings of powerlessness. And I think it is very connected to justice and injustice, whatever Milton intended. . . . My version [of *Paradise Lost*] had a painting of Lucifer. His hair was snakes, all striking. Oh it was fabulous! I was the wrong person to give it to. Milton's work. . . . left me with this feeling of articulating your own pain, as Lucifer did, that it seemed too that if you couldn't say what was wrong with you then you couldn't act. . . . I felt quite aggrieved as a child. . . . I did feel that I was cast out of only own paradise.

Not only is Kincaid able to identify with Milton's great anti-hero, and to use *Paradise Lost* in her own examination of domination, but she also sees her education in the English classics as an undeniable part of who she is:

> I'm very much against people denying their history. There was an attempt, successful, by English colonization to make a certain kind of person out me and it was a success, it worked, it really worked. My history of domination culturally in all the ways it had existed is true . . . I do not spend my present time trying to undo it. I do not for instance spend my life now attempting to have some true African heritage. My

> **" Kincaid, in her reinscription of the paradise lost theme found in Milton, as well as in her rewriting of the story of a young woman's struggle for autonomy in *Jane Eyre,* seems to do precisely this: to take these great works of English literature, to read them in her own terms, and to turn them to her own use."**

history is that I came from African people who were enslaved and dominated by European British people and that is it. And there is no attempt to erase it.

In her decision to make use of, rather than repress, her colonial education, Kincaid is part of a new wave of post-colonial writers. In the past, writes Francoise Lionnet, (herself a native of the former British crown colony, Mauritius), writers have tried to ignore the colonial language and literary traditions in their efforts to get at their own authentic story and language. But often they have been paralyzed by their inability to find an alternative method of communication. Lionnet dramatizes this point by retelling Henry Louis Gates, Jr.'s anecdote about a little known Haitian writer, Edmond Laforest, who, trapped between official French and his mother tongue of Haitian Creole, tied a fat Larousse dictionary around his neck and jumped to his death from atop a high bridge. More recently, Lionnet says, writers ''have succeed[ed] in giving voice to their repressed traditions'' through a ''dialogue with the dominant discourses they hope to transform.'' To refuse to use the dominant language and to be thereby silenced, she argues, is to continue to grant the power structure its own terms. Rather Lionnet calls for a mixing, allowing those who were subjected to the rule of a culture very different from their own—and she includes herself in this group—to

> nurture our differences without encouraging us to withdraw into new dead ends, without enclosing us within facile oppositional practices or sterile denunciations and disavowals. . . . On a textual level, we can choose authors across time and space and read them together for new insights.

Kincaid, in her reinscription of the paradise lost theme found in Milton, as well as in her rewriting of the story of a young woman's struggle for autonomy in *Jane Eyre*, seems to do precisely this: to take these great works of English literature, to read them in her own terms, and to turn them to her own use.

Kincaid's relation to the paradise lost theme and Milton's work in particular is complex. In her short story collection *At the Bottom of the River,* and in her autobiographical novels *Annie John* and *Lucy,* she both uses and subverts the European creation story to explore her own predicament, identifying her protagonists with both the hapless Eve and the bold, raging Satan, then countering Milton's story by creating her own, different version of paradise.

The paradise which Kincaid's young protagonists lose is, first, their mother's love. The preoccupation with this loss, which is seen as the withdrawal of love by a once adoring mother, is a theme running throughout Kincaid's fiction. This loss is spelled out most clearly in *Annie John.* Here and in the other works, this paradise becomes a hell as the mother's love turns to obsessive control and mocking contempt.

But Kincaid's protagonists have lost another heaven, knowing themselves to be the descendants of slaves in a still racist colonial society, people who have been cast out from a place where their existence was right and natural, compatible with the beauty of creation, to a place where they would ''never be a real person,'' where they would be eternally criminalized though the crime can never be fully explained. These, like Lucifer, find themselves in a place of eternal loss, very much ''unlike the place from whence they fell!'' (Milton 1.75).

The two forms of loss—the lost mother love, the lost home and freedom—are clearly linked for Kincaid: There is, she says,

> an ease with which people abandon their children . . . I trace that to slavery . . . even affection in [West Indian] societies is shown through cruelty. The legacy of these people, my people, is that everything is expressed through cruelty and pain. . . . Society is like that, the cruelty gets passed on to the weak, the weaker you are the more you suffer.

Finally there is a third paradise for Kincaid's protagonists to lose, the beautiful English ''fairy tale of how we met you, your right to do the things you did, how beautiful you were, are and always will be.'' Kincaid has written in ''On Seeing Eng-land for the First Time'' of how she felt when the ''fairy tale'' of England that she had been taught was finally killed by the reality of England:

> The space between the idea of something and its reality is always wide and deep and dark. . . . This space starts out empty, there is nothing in it, but it rapidly becomes filled up with obsession or desire or hatred or love—sometimes all of these things, sometimes some of these things. [I finally saw] England, the real England, not a picture, not a painting, not through a story in a book, but England, for the first time. In me the space between the idea of it and its reality had become filled with hatred, and so when at last I saw it I wanted to take it into my hands and tear it into little pieces and then crumble it up as if it were clay, child's clay.

Thus Lucy, taught at the age of ten to memorize a long poem in tribute to the daffodil, an English flower she will not see until she is nineteen, must refuse the flower's beauty when she finally encounters it, knowing how it has been used to betray her, seducing her away from love of her own flora, her own land. Like Eve she must turn her back on the garden; it is beautiful but it is not really hers. Where Lucy's employer, Mariah, sees ''beautiful flowers'' which she wants Lucy to love as much as she does, Lucy sees ''sorrow and bitterness.'' (The poem, not identified by Kincaid, is probably Wordsworth's ''I Wandered Lonely as a Cloud,'' in which the speaker sees ''A host, of golden daffodils; / Beside the lake, beneath the trees / Fluttering and dancing in the breeze''.)

Thus paradise, for Kincaid's protagonists, as for Lucifer and Eve, is shown to be a cruel trick, a sadistic lure. In whatever form it presents itself— mother love, the lost Africa, the English fairy tale— it seems designed to make one love it with all one's heart before one is cast out forever. In Milton's story a cold, power-mad God does the casting out; in Kincaid's work this role is assigned to the betraying mother, and also to imperial British authority, past and present.

Kincaid appears to subvert Milton's attempt to justify God's actions by identifying her protagonists with Satan. But doing so, Kincaid points up the seeds of subversion planted by Milton himself. While Milton saw his work as upholding the legitimacy of divine power, as ''justifying the ways of God to men,'' *Paradise Lost* at the same time offers an unavoidably subversive reading of that power. With his yearning, bravely striving Lucifer and his insensitive God, Milton tells a story of cold establishment rectitude and the criminalization of anyone who would do other than reflect that establishment glory back to itself. As Kincaid says, Lucifer is fabulous; "the images of dynamism and magnitude heaped upon Satan carry far more conviction than those applied to any other character." And surely we cannot help admiring him for his stubborn refusal to "repent or change" though he fully understands the overwhelming power of his adversary. Milton's Satan, Percy Bysshe Shelley wrote, as

> a moral being is as far superior to his God, as One who perseveres in some purpose which he has conceived to be excellent in spite of adversity and torture, is to One who in the cold security of undoubted triumph inflicts the most horrible revenge upon his enemy, not from any mistaken notion of inducing him to repent of a perseverance in enmity, but with the alleged design of exasperating him to deserve new torments.

Kincaid then not only uses Milton for her purposes, but also holds a mirror up to Milton. The injustice and suffering Kincaid experiences at the hands of the British in the West Indies can be seen as a continuation of the injustice found at the very heart of British culture which, as Milton paints it, worships cold omnipotence.

It is in Kincaid's first novel, *Annie John,* the story of a West Indian childhood, that paradise is most clearly seen as cruel trick, as the joy and security of enveloping mother's love is abruptly withdrawn. When Annie is very young she feels herself to be the beloved center of her mother's world: "Sometimes when I gave her [something she had asked me to fetch] she might stoop down and kiss me on my lips and then on my neck. It was in such a paradise that I lived." But as Annie approaches maturity, her mother changes. When Annie asks her mother if they can look through a trunk of keepsakes, one of their former shared pleasures, "A person I did not recognize answered in a voice I did not recognize, 'Absolutely not! You and I don't have time for that anymore.'" The mother's love is apparently withdrawn because Annie has begun, however inadvertently, to mature. Annie's sin is similar to Eve's the first, slight, near-unconscious step toward a mature sensibility is cause for violent expulsion by a power which will brook nothing but utter childlike innocence and ignorance. Annie's response, though, is similar to Lucifer's. She has lost a paradise but does not submit; rather she retains, like Lucifer, "the unconquerable will, / And study of revenge, immortal hate, / And courage never to submit or yield." Thus Annie teaches herself to scorn her once-adored mother, to steal and lie, and to do anything she knows her mother would hate. She takes up with the dirty and uncivilized Red Girl and like Lucifer, who declares that "The mind

is its own place, and in itself/ Can made a Heaven of Hell, a Hell of Heaven," Annie now tries to make a heaven out of her outcast state. The "paradise" of the mother's world lost, she now declares the Red Girl's wild, dirty life a paradise: the Red Girl

> didn't like to go to Sunday school, and her mother didn't force her. She didn't like to brush her teeth, but occasionally her mother said it was necessary. She loved to play marbles, and was so good that only Skerritt boys now played against her. Oh, what an angel she was, and what a heaven she lived in!

But Annie's claim to make a heaven of her hell is mostly bravado; she finds she cannot sustain herself on revenge, and the joy goes out of her rebellions.

As Annie reaches her fifteenth birthday, the awkwardness and confusion of adolescence is so like a punishment that it seems to bear out the mother's attitude that Annie's new maturity is a kind of sin or perversion. In part, she is Eve, suddenly ashamed of her body:

> My whole head was so big, and my eyes, which were big too, sat in my big head wide open, as if I had just had a sudden fright. My skin was black in a way I had not noticed before, . . . On my forehead, on my cheeks were little bumps, each with a perfect, round white point. My plaits stuck out in every direction from under my hat; my long, thin neck stuck out from the blouse of my uniform.

Like Eve, Annie is, in part, still the innocent child, mysteriously taken over by evil. Annie is also still Lucifer but no longer the proud, rebellious Lucifer. Rather she has become the degraded Lucifer of Milton's later books for whom "Revenge, at first though sweet, / Bitter ere long back on itself recoils." Now Annie sees herself as

> old and miserable. Not long before, I had seen a picture of a painting entitled The Young Lucifer. It showed Satan just recently cast out of heaven for all his bad deeds, and he was standing on a black rock all alone and naked. Everything around him was charred and black, as if a great fire had just roared through. His skin was coarse, and so were all his features. His hair was made up of live snakes, and they were in a position to strike. Satan was wearing a smile, but it was one of those smiles that you could see through, one of those smiles that makes you know the person is just putting up a good front. At heart, you could see, he was really lonely and miserable at the way things had turned out.

At the book's conclusion Annie, identified with Eve once again, sadly departs the failed paradise of her mother's love for a new world, one that is unknown but which, she knows, can never replace the lost dream.

In a chapter of *Annie John* entitled "Somewhere, Belgium," the protagonist begins to escape her increasingly oppressive surroundings by imagining herself living alone in Belgium, "a place I had picked when I read in one of my books that Charlotte Bronte, the author of my favorite novel, *Jane Eyre,* had spent a year or so there." In this daydream Annie was far from her mother, who could only communicate by sending letters to "Somewhere, Belgium." Here Annie would be alone, adult, and wise, "walking down a street in Belgium, wearing a skirt that came down to my ankles and carrying a bag filled with books that at last I could understand."

Like Milton, Bronte seems to have offered a way of thinking about the questions of power and powerlessness, just and injustice that concerned Kincaid from an early age. By nine she was refusing to stand up at the refrain "God Save Our King," and hated "Rule, Britannia," with its refrain, "Britons never ever shall be slaves," reasoning that "we weren't Britons and that we were slaves." For the young Kincaid, as for others, Bronte's work was "an epic of self-determination, the painful acquisition of identity, of independence"; indeed, Bronte's heroine views herself as a "rebel slave" as she struggles against the class system that oppresses an orphaned and penniless female. Even in its own day Bronte's work was seen as rebellious; when *Jane Eyre* was published in 1847 reviewers found it shockingly radical, and Bronte was described as "soured, coarse and grumbling, an alien from society and amenable to none of its laws." Her heroine was seen as "proud and ungrateful," and Victorian critics were horrified by her anger.

But, also like Milton, Bronte has been seen as subverting her own apparent intent. Milton's project of "justifying the ways of God to man" is undercut by the identification which both contemporary and modern readers have felt with the courageous, doomed Satan. Similarly, Bronte's "epic of self-determination" for a young Victorian Englishwoman is undercut by the figure of Bertha, who introduces another story of domination into the text.

Bertha is Rochester's first wife, the dark, West Indian woman whom he, the impoverished younger son of English gentry, married for her money. Once the advantageous match is made, Rochester finds his wife to be guilty of unspecified crimes that show her to be "intemperate and unchaste." She is pronounced insane and shipped to England to be imprisoned forever in his attic. Here she will be the secret cause of Rochester's dissipations, his self-loathing, and his inability to find true happiness. Further, it is Bertha who botches Rochester's romance with his young governess, Jane. Even stripped, vilified, and imprisoned, Bertha is still a critical force, the "'dark' secret, maddening burden of imperialism concealed in the heart of every English gentleman's house of the time."

The presence of Bertha also undermines our belief in Jane's devotion to the principles of equality which she espouses so urgently for herself. Events in the novel turn, as Boumelha points out, on questions of wealth and inheritance, as all of the wealth comes from the fruits of imperialism, reaped in the West Indies. Rochester's fortune is really Bertha's. Jane's eventual inheritance, which frees her to marry Rochester as an equal, comes from a long lost uncle with business interests in the West Indies. Jane's view of herself as a "rebel slave," therefore, and her devotion to the principle of self-determination, is severely compromised by her acceptance of—indeed her profound desire to be accepted by—a society whose wealth and sense of superiority rests almost entirely on the backs of slaves and other subjugated people. Further, Jane herself profits richly and directly from the oppression of others. Finally, Judith Weissman argues, Jane's rage is not that of a "radical who wants justice, but the rage of the outsider who wants to win."

Like Satan, Bertha loses in the end, but like Satan she is not without her moment of glorious defiance. Bertha starts the fire that will destroy Rochester's manor house and that will maim and blind her husband. Then Bertha climbs to the roof of the house where she stands "waving her arms above the battlements, and shouting out till they could hear her a mile off. . . . She was a big woman, and had long black hair . . . streaming against the flames as she stood." Rochester tries to reach her but as he nears she "yelled and gave a spring and the next minute she lay smashed on the pavement." Jane, who once desired freedom and broad horizons, will become wife and nurse to a diminished Rochester; Bertha, it might be said, is the one who flies free.

Bronte then, like Milton, offers Kincaid the paradoxical opportunity both to identify with and to subvert the classic texts of English literature and by extension the English world view which they represent. If we look at Kincaid's novels *Annie John* and *Lucy* as a two-part bildungsroman, we may see many similarities in the predicament and progress of Bronte's heroine, Jane, and of Kincaid's protagonists, Annie and Lucy. Foremost among these is the sense of being constantly and unfairly put in the wrong by those whose interest is power not justice. At the same time, an examination of these three works together points out the difference, at least as seen by these two writers, between class oppression, and oppression that stems from the ruptures of slavery and from colonialism. At the end of *Jane Eyre*, Jane not only triumphs utterly over her former oppressors, the Reeds, but also regains her lost birthright so that she can re-enter the class which once persecuted her. Jane's loss of her birthright is a mistake that can be repaired; once this is done there is a comfortable place for her within the social organization. For Annie and Lucy, by contrast, the wrong can never be completely righted. Their birthright was not mistakenly mislaid, as was Jane's, but purposely obliterated; their rightful place can never be found.

Jane's struggle with an oppressive class system in nineteenth-century England has many parallels to the struggle of Annie and Lucy with an oppressive system based on class and race in twentieth-century Antigua and America. In both cases the social and political structure is echoed in the home lives of the young girls. In Annie's case, the mother's refusal to accept the girl's impending maturity mirrors the colonial society's refusal to recognize the mature humanity of those descended from slaves. In Jane's case, her persecution by the Reed family, rich relatives with whom the orphaned and impoverished girl lives, reflects nineteenth-century English society's castigation of those who cannot be placed within a rigid class system, and who therefore, however inadvertently, are seen as challenging the system. Jane, as one of the maids points out, does not even have the status of a servant who would, at least, have a secure place in the social organization:

> "For shame, for shame!" cried the lady's maid. "What shocking conduct, Miss Eyre, to strike a young gentleman, your benefactress' son! Your young master." "Master! How is he my master? Am I a servant?" "No; you are less than a servant, for you do nothing for your keep. There, sit down, and think over your wickedness."

While both Jane Eyre and Annie John are portrayed as virtually blameless, both are criminalized, Annie for her impending maturity in a racist society, Jane for her very existence outside clear class boundaries. In both works, the theme of rebellion is linked to that of enslavement. Kincaid gives Annie an awareness of her slave heritage, an awareness that is in itself something of a rebellion,

since the colonial school system seeks to bury the horror of slavery under a glossy historical pageant. And Bronte, writing in 1847, likens Jane to a desperate slave who has dared to fight back against her master. Jane muses, "I was conscious that a moment's mutiny had already rendered me liable to strange penalties, and, like any other rebel slave, I felt resolved, in my desperation, to go all lengths." To both Jane and Annie, it is clear that the system in which they live is committed to their continued, psychic "enslavement."

In *Jane Eyre* and *Annie John,* the young girls are criminalized and scapegoated by those who are clearly inferior to them. In both books the girls's tormentors are painted in distinctly unflattering terms; those who would dehumanize are seen as less than human. In *Jane Eyre,* Bronte does not allow us to imagine any innate aristocracy in the Reeds. They are dishonest, bullying, self-pitying, utterly unable to grasp that Jane, too, is a human being. Fourteen year-old John Reed, Jane's chief tormentor, is, moreover, ugly:

> large and stout for his age, with a dingy and unwholesome skin; thick lineaments in a spacious visage, heavy limbs and large extremities. He gorged himself habitually at table, which made him bilious, and gave him dim and bleared eye with flabby cheeks.

Similarly, Annie's teachers, the representatives of colonial power, are painted as petty and ridiculous. Like the Reeds they have no redeeming features; they appear to be as soulless as they are physically unattractive. Annie's headmistress

> looked like a prune left out of its jar a long time and she sounded as if she had borrowed her voice from an owl. The way she said, "Now girls. . . ." When she was just standing still there, listening to some of the other activities, her gray eyes going all around the room hoping to see something wrong, her throat would beat up and down as if a fish fresh out of water were caught inside.

Both Jane and Annie are aware that they are being treated with injustice and hypocrisy, and both have a sense of self that does not allow them to submit, even though they understand that they will never, in their present circumstances have the power to prevail. For both, the attempt to rebel brings on a crisis, as they are overwhelmed by the enormity of the forces allied against them. Jane defends herself against John Reed's unprovoked attack, and when she refuses to apologize, she is locked into the majestically ghostly Red Room where she goes into a fit of terror and falls unconscious. Similarly Annie, struggling to rebel against forces both at home and at school which would deny her true identity, is finally crushed by the weight of her opposition and falls into a long illness.

For both Jane and Annie it is this collapse that opens the way for escape. After Jane is revived, a kindly chemist is called, and hearing how she has been treated, suggests that she be sent away to school, to which the cold and bitter Mrs. Reed agrees. Though Jane is not yet freed of class oppression, she has made a step; her rebellion has, at least freed her of the Reeds's intimate brand of subjugation. When Annie falls ill, it is her maternal grandmother, Ma Chess, who arrives and who, like the chemist in Jane Eyre, recognizes that the illness is one of the spirit. Though the chemist's intercession is mild compared to Ma Chess's act of rebirthing, the two healers bring about similar results. In both cases a kindly, healing presence, which acknowledges the girl's pain, provides just enough help to allow the girl to survive and escape. Both young women, it seems, have threatened the forces aligned against them through the only means available to them; they are prepared to die of their ill-treatment, and under this threat relief has been provided.

Jane goes away to school, Lowood, and nurtured there by the kind, noble and intellectual Miss Temple, finds serenity. Miss Temple, like Ma Chess, re-mothers Jane, whose only previous experience with maternal nurture has been the harsh and grudging care of her aunt, Mrs. Reed, and the flippant attentions of the maid, Bessie. But eventually Miss Temple marries and goes away and in the absence of her calming presence Jane grows restless as some inner self demands definition. She begins to yearn for experience of the "wide" world and a "varied field of hopes and fears, of sensations and excitement" which awaited those who sought "real knowledge of life amidst its perils." Jane then goes to the great estate, Thornwood Hall, where she becomes governess for Mr. Rochester's charge, Adele, and where she is soon loved for her own virtuous and original self by the jaded Edward Rochester.

In *Annie John,* Kincaid's young protagonist also leaves for school. When next seen in *Lucy,* however, she has skipped school and gone directly to a position in a well-to-do family, taking care of the children. Here, like Jane at Thornwood Hall, Lucy is appreciated for her own deep and interesting self by her wealthy employer, Mariah, and the two, like Jane and Rochester, come to resemble loving companions more than master and servant.

Although both Jane and Lucy are treated kindly, and to a great extent as equals by their employers, they are still seen as mere servants by their employers's friends, and as such not quite fully human. At a party, Mr. Rochester's guests do not hesitate to denigrate the entire governess class in tones loud enough for Jane to hear, and when one of the group warns that Jane can hear the conversation, the woman speaking replies, "'I hope it may do her good!' Then, in lower tone, but still loud enough for [Jane] to hear, 'I noticed her; I am a judge of physiognomy, and in hers I see all the faults of her class.'"

Kincaid's interest in *Jane Eyre,* the similarity of themes in Bronte's work and in Kincaid's, then the sudden divergence as Bronte veers off into a happy ending unavailable to Kincaid, seems to demonstrate, among other things, the difference between class oppression and oppression that springs from abduction, slavery and imperial exploitation. In Bronte's world wrongs can conceivably be righted; in Kincaid's they cannot. As *Lucy* draws to a close, Kincaid's protagonist comes less and less to resemble the Cinderella-like Jane Eyre, more and more to resemble Bertha Mason.

As Bertha is the secret that explains Jane and shows up who she really is, Lucy, exploder of fairy tales, can be read as the secret self of the early, yearning Annie, a girl who still hoped for magical solutions to her problems through a Bronte-esque escape to "Somewhere, Belgium." Further, Kincaid presents Lucy, as, like Bertha, a "burden of imperialism" who cannot be gotten rid of. Lucy destroys Mariah's pleasure in daffodils by demonstrating how the seemingly innocent flowers were used as a tool of colonial oppression. Further, Lucy grasps, even if the supposedly environmentally correct Mariah doesn't, the connection between the comforts of privilege and "the decline of the world that lay before them." And Lucy sees through the desire to rinse history in romance, to see ruin as exotic. She understands that her lover, Paul, is fascinated by her in part because, "He loved ruins; he loved the past but only if it ended on a sad note, from a lofty beginning to a gradual, rotten decline...." She dashes Mariah by not being gratified when Mariah confides that she has some Indian blood, "as if she were announcing her possession of a trophy." Rather than being pleased, Lucy sees that the privileged Mariah, whose Great Lakes summer home was probably once the home of those with rather more Indian blood, has so thoroughly internalized her right to have what she wants that she feels perfectly innocent, and so can easily afford the exotic luxury of identifying with those at whose expense her privilege has been bought. Like Bertha, who always manages to escape her attic prison just in time to upset Rochester's plans to proceed as if she doesn't exist, Lucy is always there, refusing to allow her history to be ignored or romanticized.

Kincaid's two autobiographical novels, in their very similarity to Bronte's bildungsroman and to Milton's creation myth, involve these canonical works in a dialogue on power and oppression. Rather than ignoring the part of her heritage that includes Charlotte Bronte and John Milton, rather than allowing her own story to be misshaped by literary traditions of a culture that was never her own, Kincaid has, to use Lionnet's phrase, "interact[ed] on an equal footing with . . . the traditions that determine [her] present predicament." If we read *Annie John* and *Lucy* as re-writings of *Jane Eyre,* we can see Kincaid setting out the difference between the kind of oppression Jane suffers and that experienced by Annie and Lucy. As Kincaid's Lucy asks her friend Mariah, "How do you get to be the sort of victor who can claim to be the vanquished also?", we can imagine Kincaid asking Bronte: How can your imagination of justice, your vision of resistance, be at once so inflamed and so limited?

Source: Diane Simmons, "Jamaica Kincaid and the Canon: In Dialogue with 'Paradise Lost,' and 'Jane Eyre,'" *MELUS,* Vol. 23, Issue 2, Summer, 1998, p. 65.

James Nagel

In this essay on Jamaica Kincaid's novel Annie John, *James Nagel explores the plot and narrative strategy of the novel—a West Indian, feminine "coming of age" tale told from the point of view of the maturing Annie John—to discuss how the life of the character of Annie John is built from, struggles against, and echoes the British colonial system in which she was raised.*

On the surface, everything about *Annie John* suggests the traditional *Bildungsroman:* it traces the central episodes in the life of a young girl from prepubescent familial bliss to her ambivalent turmoil about her mother and a permanent departure from home at seventeen. Along the way she struggles through alternate moods of embracing and rejecting her parents, the satisfying and troubling subterfuge of social expectations, the awakening of an uneasy sexuality, and the gradual formulation of an internal life that seeks release from the strictures of home and the culture of Antigua. . . .

It is an exciting but painful journey. Essentially, it proves a tragic "coming of age in Antigua," despite the overlay of humor and charm throughout the narrative. The central issue from start to finish is Annie's relationship with her mother. The central image is that of the trunk, one that contained mementos of the mother's youth in Dominica and then comes to hold the treasured reminiscences of every stage of Annie's childhood. It is appropriate that Annie brings a similar trunk with her when she leaves Antigua at seventeen. In the matter of the trunk, as in so much else, Annie's life recalls that of her mother and brings them as close together in their separation as they were on their island. This is an awareness the adult narrator would have that the child would not. It is buttressed by the special irony that although the child Annie sees the mother as a heartless despot, the Annie who narrates portrays "no tyrant but a beautiful, loving woman who adores her only child and is wise enough to wish her daughter independent" [as Charlotte H. Bruner states in *World Literature Today* 59, 1985]. The act of telling a story of rebellion with such a loving portrait of a mother is, in effect, an act of psychological reconciliation that never achieves material fulfillment. For there is no indication that Annie ever returns home. On one level, she need not, for what her story reveals is the process by which, in striving for independence, she recapitulates the life of her mother. It is no small point that both the child and the mother share the same name, "Annie John."

The book begins with ten-year-old Annie's childhood fascination with death, a subject with somber values set off against the sunny and carefree world of her everyday life. Her conflicts are with the world of the supernatural, with the imponderable causal forces that live in shadow and sign and that wrest a comforting meaning from random events. Her preoccupation with death is a normative fixation and an attempt to understand the most profound developments around her. Beyond the charm of innocent grotesquerie, her fixation offers the revelation of Annie's character and of a lively and creative mind. It reveals also a love for storytelling, an unsentimental confrontation with the most unpleasant realities, and a child's faulty logic that accepts folklore as transcendent reality.

In a sense Annie must reach outward for conflict. The world she lives in, at least on her level of engagement, is prelapsarian, an antediluvian feast of family love and lore. Her mother is not so much long suffering as long rejoicing. She is so in love with her daughter and life as to celebrate even its most minute details, from routine household tasks to the bark she uses to scent Annie's bath water. Indeed, the artifacts of the young girl's existence speak of adoration: Her father built the house she lives in with his own hands. He even lovingly crafts the furniture in her room, the spoon she eats with, the entire household. It is a brilliant context in which to begin the story: For this caring household is the world that Annie will come to resent and rebel against in her final departure.

Although as narrator she stresses these details, at the time of the action Annie is oblivious to them. She is obsessed instead with her immediate concern for a progression of expirations—from Nalda to Sonia's mother to Miss Charlotte and the humpback girl, whose passing inspires in Annie not compassion but a desire to rap on the hump to see if it is hollow. Even these episodes bring her back under the sway of her mother, however. For it is the latter who tells the stories of death in the family, and it is she who is holding Nalda in her arms when she dies. This tragedy is given cruel interpretation by Annie:

> I then began to look at my mother's hands differently. They had stroked the dead girl's forehead; they had bathed and dressed her and laid her in the coffin my father had made. . . . For a while, though not for very long, I could not bear to have my mother caress me or touch my food or help me with my bath. I especially couldn't bear the sight of her hands lying still in her lap.

It is the first negative transformation in Annie's attitude toward her mother. Annie begins to visit funeral parlors, an obsession that brings her home late one evening without the fish she was supposed to deliver. She lies about the incident: "That night, as a punishment, I ate my supper outside, alone, under the breadfruit tree, and my mother said that she would not be kissing me good night later, but when I climbed into bed she came and kissed me anyway.". . .

When Annie turns twelve everything changes. She enters the first stages of the love-hate relationship with her mother that informs the central plot of the narrative [according to Bruner]. Ironically, it is not the terrors of death that lead to the schism but the act that brought her life: she discovers her parents making love and is revolted. To provide a context for this event, the narrator sketches a background of familial closeness, how mother and daughter would bathe together in water scented with flowers and oils. Annie tells of her mother's departure from Dominica with the trunk and of the many times the mother later removed Annie's things from it, caressing each item as an emblem of her daughter's previous growth: "As she held each thing in her hand she would tell me a story about myself." In contrast, the father's background is rich in love of a more perverse and complex variety. He has loved and abandoned a series of women, leaving several with children he does not now acknowledge. This is a fact that hangs over their lives, seeking expiation. Abandoned as a small child, he grew up with his grandmother, sleeping with her until he was eighteen, when she died. The father weeps when he relates this story, and Annie experiences a sudden growth of sensibility in her compassion for him.

The turning point for Annie comes when her mother informs her that it is time for her to have her own clothes, not simply imitations of her mother's dresses. Annie is shocked at this demand for her discrete identity: "To say that I felt the earth swept away from under me would not be going too far." Here Annie would seem to be confronting the classic confusion of a girl in her relationship with her mother: She desires the closest possible identification and shows distress when the mother suggests any degree of separation. . . . Her mother exhibits disgust at Annie's many lies, but the event from which their relationship never recovers is the parental sex scene, particularly the image of her mother's hand, making a circular motion, on her husband's back. It proves an imagistic referent that lends the title "The Circling Hand," indicating that it is the preeminent event. This image is invested with Annie's confrontation with adult sexuality, a development that will prove more difficult for her than the discovery of death. In the absence of siblings, Annie must share love with the "other" parent, a fact that inspires not rivalry toward her father but a bitter resentment of her mother: "I was sure I could never let those hands touch me again; I was sure I could never let her kiss me again. All that was finished." In her place Annie proclaims her love for a schoolmate, Gwen, and this and other surrogate loves sustain her through the break with her mother.

Annie's ambivalence toward her mother intensifies in the second chapter devoted to Annie at twelve; the implication is that the year was pivotal in her development. Annie is in a new school, and much of the chapter is a description of a typical school day. Yet the salient dimensions of the episode deal with Annie's growing maturity. There is here a nostalgic look back at the unconditional love she has received throughout her childhood from her mother, as well as her compelling need to move beyond the family to the larger social world around her. The key document is an autobiographical essay she writes in school. In it she describes swimming with her mother and the profound sense of isolation and abandonment she feels when her mother momentarily slips from view. Annie is not simply puzzled or startled; she experiences a momentary crisis of being: "A huge black space then opened up in front of me and I fell inside it. . . . I couldn't think of anything except that my mother was no longer near me." When her mother sees her crying, she hugs her closely and promises never to leave her again, but Annie is left with the sensation of abandonment.

The depth of Annie's dependence and antipathy here adumbrates the more exaggerated passage she will make through her dark night of the soul in the penultimate chapter. Yet even now there are pathological implications to the depth of her emotion. That these events are juxtaposed with an account of her first menstruation is also important in that Annie's struggle toward emotional maturity is linked to her biological coming of age. Similarly, the intensification of Annie's love for Gwen is set against the diminution of her love for her mother, a diminution that continues until Annie reflects that "I could not understand how she could be so beautiful even though I no longer loved her."

From this point on every episode contains another expression of Annie's continuing rebellion and of her substitution of other emotional alliances for the close bond she formerly shared with her mother. Soon these ideas take the form of Annie's stealing and lying and playing marbles, all forbidden activities. There is also her infatuation with the Red Girl, who is the personification of familial anarchy in that she refuses to bathe more than once a week. Gwen, the socially correct young lady who has Annie's mother's full approval, is replaced by the Red Girl, who is free from convention and discipline: "Oh, what an angel she was, and what a heaven she lived in!" That this expression of betrayal contains portions of both pain and pleasure is expressed in Annie's relationship with the Red Girl. The latter pinches Annie and then kisses the injured spots: "Oh, the sensation was delicious—the combination of pinches and kisses." That all of this activity takes place at a time commensurate with the previous chapter becomes clear when Annie starts to menstruate, the second rendering of that event in the book. Once again it is a transitional event in that it coincides with the departure of the Red Girl and the cessation of playing marbles. But through this episode Annie has expanded the terrain of her rebellion. Embracing forbidden friends, and violating the most sacred shibboleths of social behavior, she masks her true nature behind a conventional facade. This double life will come to exact its bounty. . . .

In "Somewhere, Belgium," a title derived from an escape fantasy, Annie has turned fifteen and has entered into a deep depression, the etiology of which would seem to be an emotional schism. Many aspects of her life are warm and protective. These include the stories of her father's youth and the many objects around her crafted by his own hands, as well as the familiar story of Annie's mother leaving home at her age. But on another level Annie's already tenuous circumstances have grown worse. Promoted two grades, she is no longer in the same class with Gwen. Their relationship falters while at the same time the younger Annie suffers in the company of older girls well into adolescence. Her own hesitant steps toward courtship all end badly, even the games she plays with neighborhood boys; in each instance her mother expresses not so much outrage as disgust. When she stops on the way home to flirt with one of the boys from her youth, her mother observes the event and later accuses her of behaving like a slut. Her words move Annie to say "like mother like daughter" and the mother to respond that "until this moment, in my whole life I knew without a doubt that, without an exception, I loved you best."

Annie becomes deeply torn: she is filled with a sense of her mother's love for her, which moves her to tears; at the same time she wishes the older woman were dead. Their duplicitous relationship—outward harmony concealing a deep inner antipathy—is now an obstacle to any integration of self for Annie: "I could not be sure whether for the rest of my life I would be able to tell when it was really my mother and when it was really her shadow standing between me and the rest of the world." Annie needs desperately to be part of the rest of the world, hence the fantasy about escaping to Belgium.

These unresolved conflicts lead to Annie's dark night of the soul at fifteen, a sleep that continues throughout a long rain of more than three months. Caused by no discoverable physical illness, Annie's sleep is a mechanism to escape emotional irresolution. It is also an episode that allows for one last family summation, even the mysterious appearance of the maternal grandmother, who comes, still dressed in black since the death of her son decades before, with ritual cures and potions. It is clear, however, that the causative factor does not lend itself to these cures nor to those of Western medicine: ''I looked inside my head. A black thing was lying down there, and it shut out all my memory of the things that had happened to me.'' This illness resembles in many respects the archetypal pathology in the female *Bildungsroman:* ''Sleep and quiescence in female narratives represent a progressive withdrawal into the symbolic landscapes of the innermost self.... Excluded from active participation in culture, the fictional heroine is thrown back on herself'' [according to Marianne Hirsch in *The Voyage In: Fictions of Female Development*, 1983]. In this case, however, Annie's conflict results less from the problems of acculturation than from the more fundamental issue of growing up in her family.

Annie's illness takes her back through the progression of her life, with her parents' tender solicitations; they treat her like an infant, seeing to her every need. The complexity of her feelings toward her parents is omnipresent, as when Ma Jolie suggests that the cause of the illness may be the curses of the women Annie's father abandoned. Other familial objects also possess a negative resonance for her, as does the photograph of her in her communion dress, wearing shoes her mother had forbidden. It was another confrontation that had led Annie to wish her mother dead. Annie's need to break free of the constraints of this heritage is exemplified by her washing the images off the family photographs, except for her own portrait and that of the forbidden shoes. All of this is consistent with the theories of Nancy Chodorow, who postulates [in *Reproduction of Mothering: Psychoanalysis and the Sociology of Gender*, 1978] that

> mothers feel ambivalent toward their daughters, and react to their daughters' ambivalence toward them. They desire both to keep daughters close and push them into adulthood. This ambivalence in turn creates more anxiety in their daughters and provokes attempts by these daughters to break away.

The illness does not abate, however, until Annie begins to realize that she never wants to see her mother again, that her world has become an ''unbearable burden.'' As soon as she is able to articulate this awareness, she quickly recovers. It has been a transforming respite, one that leads to the resolution of the book in the last chapter.

Source: James Nagel, ''Desperate Hopes, Desperate Lives: Depression and Self-Realization in Jamaica Kincaid's *Annie John* and *Lucy*,'' in *Traditions, Voices, and Dreams: The American Novel Since the 1960s,* edited by Melvin J. Friedman and Ben Siegel, University of Delaware Press, 1995, pp. 237–53.

Jacqueline Austin

In the following excerpt, reviewer Austin compares Jamaica Kincaid's first novel, Annie John, *with her collection of short stories. Austin states that Kincaid writes well-crafted, passionate accounts of a past filled with curious events.*

''Write what you know,'' says the experienced author to the younger one. Hence the critic's 10-mile bookshelf of breathless first novels about growing up normal: meager accounts, bitter, adoring, or pompous, of parents and school; death and love; television, baseball, dry or wet dreams. Jamaica Kincaid's first novel is not, thank the Muse, one of these: instead, it is one of those perfectly balanced wanderings through time which seem to spring direct from Nature. The parents and school, death and love are there, but oh, with what a difference, and 148 pages become 300 when you read a book twice. In her collection of stories, *At the Bottom of the River*, and here, in *Annie John*, Kincaid does write what she knows. What she knows is rare: pure passion, a past filled with curious events, a voice, humor, and above all a craft.

Ten-year-old Annie John lives in a paradise: a back yard in Antigua overseen by a benevolent goddess—her mother. ''That summer, we had a pig that had just had piglets; some guinea fowl; and some ducks that laid enormous eggs that my mother said were big even for ducks. I hated to eat any food except for the enormous duck eggs, hard-boiled. I had nothing to do every day except to feed the birds and the pig in the morning and in the evening. I spoke to no one other than my parents . . .'' Into this Eden come twin serpents: death and separation from the mother. At first they seem innocent. From the yard, Annie observes, with curiosity, ''various small, sticklike figures, some dressed in black, some dressed in white, bobbing up and down in the distance'': mourners at a child's funeral. Gradually, death comes closer. One day, an acquaintance dies, a deformed girl. ''On hearing that she was dead, I wished I had tapped the hump to see if it was hollow.'' Annie surreptitiously views the corpse and then lies about it to her mother. This is the first in a series of evasions for which she is punished.

Until now, Annie and her mother were almost one. They wore dresses cut from the same cloth; they went shopping together; they even bathed together. ''Sometimes it was just a plain bath. . . . Other times, it was a special bath in which the barks and flowers of many different trees, together with all sorts of oils, were boiled in the same large caldron . . . my mother would bathe different parts of my body; then she would do the same to herself.'' They took these baths after her mother and an obeah woman had interpreted the world's signals: "the way a dog she knew, and a friendly dog at that, suddenly turned and bit her; how a porcelain bowl she had carried from one eternity and hoped to carry into the next suddenly slipped out of her capable hands and broke into pieces the size of grains of sand . . . one of the many women my father had loved, had never married, but with whom he had had children was trying to harm my mother and me by setting bad spirits on us.'' Occasionally the pair would spend a gorgeous afternoon lingering over the objects in Annie's trunk—objects redolent of a shared past which seemed to promise to continue always.

But one day the mother cuts Annie a dress of fabric different from her own; this shock precipitates a slow decline in their relationship. They still keep the appearance of unity, but it's hypocritical: their smiles are false, and mask the most intimate kinds of treachery. The full break comes when Annie reaches puberty. She is now a stranger even to herself. Everything about her, from her nose to her habit of lying, is a mostly unpleasant surprise. This alienation worsens into disease, and ultimately into a total break with Antigua.

Derek Walcott has a poem, "Love After Love," in which he prophesies to himself, and we listen in: "The time will come / when, with elation, / you will greet yourself arriving / at your own door, in your own mirror, / and each will smile at the other's welcome . . .'' The poem closes with a command. "Peel your own image from the mirror. / Sit. Feast on your life.'' Though Annie John replaces her mother with different objects of desire, first with the conventional schoolgirl Gwen and then with the wild Red Girl, she never does realize that both are reflections of herself, never experiences elation, except at her impending escape, and never feasts on her life—though Jamaica Kincaid does.

At the end of the book, Annie has just gone through a long illness. Having been treated by both doctors and obeah women, she rises from her sickbed several inches taller than her mother—that many inches farther from Eden. She decides to leave Antigua and become a nurse. As Annie embarks for England, the mother hugs her fiercely and declares, "in a voice that raked across my skin, 'It doesn't matter what you do or where you go, I'll always be your mother and this will always be your

home.''' Annie hides her revulsion and goes to lie down in her berth, where "everything trembled as if it had a spring at its very center. I could hear the small waves lap-lapping around the ship. They made an unexpected sound, as if a vessel filled with liquid had been placed on its side and now was slowly emptying out.''

The past always threatens to contain the future; it's impossible for the future to break free while still embraced by the past. The daughter must tell her mother, "No, I am not you; I am not what you made me," and this, whether truth or a lie, precipitates sexuality, originality, an honest relationship to personal truth. Annie is clearly an autobiographical figure, not perhaps in specific detail, but certainly in her internal development, her emotions, the tempering of her mind, the changes in her image from within the skin. How has Kincaid broken free? How has she acknowledged her past?

First novelists usually try to cope with their heritage: Kincaid has had to encompass two traditions. This has been the plaint, and the strength, of writers from the West Indies—both black, like George Lamming, and white, like Jean Rhys. In her two books, Kincaid makes an impressive start, fusing folk tale with novel, poetry with fiction, West Indian locutions and rhythms with "European" ones. She has proven herself to be a big, exotic fish in a small, brightly colored pond—the personal interior narrative. It will be interesting to see what happens once she throws herself into the ocean.

Politics, colonial history, the theme of expatriation: these would be natural extensions for Kincaid. Like an old-time cartographer, she seems to avoid some territory. "There be dragons here." In one scene, Annie defaces a picture of Christopher Columbus by scrawling an inscription in Old English-style lettering. She is caught by her prunes-and-persimmons teacher. Her punishment? To copy out part of John Milton's *Paradise Lost*. The white teacher, who equates Columbus practically with God, the old English lettering, Annie's hatred of Columbus and his so-called "discovery"—all these are literary plums ripe for the plucking.

There are many ways in which Kincaid could arrange the plums in her particular literary dish. She could walk farther down her folkways or, like George Lamming in his 1953 *In the Castle of My Skin*, further relate her experience to "universal" mythic history:

The scent of the air . . . filled the nostrils and the ears and the eyes so that everything smelt and looked and felt like iodine and raw fish and the liquid of the grape leaf ... Bob arched his back and we heard the syllables stumbing past his lips. ''Sea Come No Further, Sea Come No Further.'' His voice went out like the squeak of an insect to meet the roar of the wave ...

What the waves erase here, other than the boys' toeprints, are the imaginary footprints of King Canute.

Kincaid could also give up her Eden. *At the Bottom of the River* and *Annie John* are wonderful books, but they are, in subject, very much alike. These books epitomize elegy to a particular place and state of being, an impulse which can only sustain itself so long before it becomes redundant. For most writers, personal interior vision is not enough to precipitate a full break from the past. It is significant that the happiest moments in *Annie John* are moments of stasis:

> Soon after, I started to menstruate, and I stopped playing marbles. I never saw the Red Girl again. For a reason not having to do with me, she had been sent to Anguilla to live with her grandparents and finish her schooling. The night of the day I heard about it, I dreamed of her ... I took her to an island, where we lived together forever, I suppose, and fed on wild pigs and sea grapes. At night, we would sit on the sand and watch ships filled with people on a cruise steam by. We sent confusing signals to the ships, causing them to crash on some nearby rocks. How we laughed as their cries of joy turned to cries of sorrow.. . .

With *Annie John*, Kincaid has completed the themes begun in *River*. The two are companion volumes: an object lesson in showing how far a writer's technique can stretch. *River* seemed to be dictated straight from heart to hand, almost bypassing the mind. The voice in *''Girl,''* for example, quoted first mother, then daughter, in a rhythm so strong it seemed to be hypnosis, aimed at magically chanting out bits of the subconscious. Now *Annie John* fills in between the bits; it gives the passions of *River* a rationale. The surreality, imagination, internal and external detail are still there, but they now flow in a single narrative wave.

Kincaid's subject matter ... is so interesting that her style, sumptuous as it is, becomes transparent. She is a consummate balancer of feeling and craft. She takes no short or long cuts, breathes no windy pomposities: she contents herself with being direct. The reader feels that even if this writer had had the bad luck to be born elsewhere, she would have made it as wonderful as ''her'' Antigua.

Cynthia Ozick, Mary Gordon, and Susan Sontag have sighed over Kincaid's virtuosity with language, and they were right. Her language recalls Henri Rousseau's painting: seemingly natural, but in reality sophisticated and precise. So lush, composed, direct, odd, sharp, and brilliantly lit are Kincaid's word paintings that the reader's presuppositions are cut in two by her seemingly soft edges. Her wisdom, measured craft, and reticence will carry her on to more complicated and wider canvases, to larger geographies of the mind.

Source: Jacqueline Austin, ''Up from Eden,'' in *Voice Literary Supplement,* Vol. 34, April, 1985, pp. 6–7.

Sources

Ashcroft, Bill, Gareth Griffiths, and Helen Tiffin, *The Empire Writes Back: Theory and Practice in Post-colonial Literatures*, Routledge, 1989.

Austin, Jacqueline, ''Up from Eden,'' in *VLS*, No. 34, April, 1985, pp. 6-7.

Bemrose, John, ''Growing Pains of Girlhood,'' in *Macleans Magazine*, Vol. 98, No. 20, May 20, 1985, p. 61.

Bonnel, Paula, '''Annie's Travels to Second Childhood,'' in *The Boston Herald*, March 31, 1985, p. 126.

Murdoch, H. Adlai, ''Severing The (M)other Connection: The Representation of Cultural Identity in Jamaica Kincaid's *Annie John*,'' in *Callaloo*, Vol. 13, No. 2, Spring, 1990, pp. 325-40.

Nagel, James, ''Desperate Hopes, Desperate Lives Depression and Self-Realization in Jamaica Kincaid's *Annie John* and *Lucy*,'' in *Traditions, Voices, and Dreams: The American Novel since the 1960s*, edited by Melvin J. Friedman and Ben Siegal, University of Delaware Press, 1995.

Onwordi, Ike, ''Wising Up,'' in *The Times Literary Supplement*, No. 4313, November 29, 1985, p. 1374.

Vorda, Allan, ''Interview with Jamaica Kincaid,'' in *Mississippi Review Web Edition*, http://sushi. St.usm.edu/mrw/9604/kincaid.html, 1996.

Further Reading

Bemrose, John, ''Growing Pains of Girlhood,'' in *Maclean's Magazine*, Vol. 98, No. 20, May 20, 1985, p. 61.
> In this complimentary review, Bemrose praises Kincaid's graceful style and her depiction of Annie John's resistance to the constraints of her environment.

Bonnell, Paula, '''Annie's Travels to Second Childhood,'' in *The Boston Herald*, March 31, 1985, p. 126.
> Bonnell commends Kincaid's rich rendering of life in Antigua and her ability to communicate the emotional reality of Annie John's struggles.

Cudjoe, Selwyn R., ''Jamaica Kincaid and the Modernist Project: An Interview,'' in *Caribbean Women Writers: Essays from the First International Conference*, edited by Selwyn R. Cudjoe, Calaloux Publications, 1990, pp. 215-32.

In this interview, Kincaid discusses her career, her familial relationships, Caribbean culture, and critical responses to her work. She specifically addresses the ending of *Annie John*.

Dutton, Wendy, ''Merge and Separate: Jamaica Kincaid's Fiction,'' in *World Literature Today*, Vol. 63, No. 3, Summer, 1989, pp. 406-10.

Dutton explores the connections between *At the Bottom of the River* and *Annie John*, seeing them as complementary texts that together develop one cohesive story.

Ferguson, Moira, *Colonialism and Gender Relations from Mary Wollstonecraft to Jamaica Kincaid: East Caribbean Connections*, Columbia University Press, 1994.

Taking a grand historical view, Ferguson links Kincaid's work to the struggle over gender in English literature.

———, *Jamaica Kincaid: Where the Land Meets the Body*, University Press of Virginia, 1994.

Ferguson's book-length study investigates Kincaid's connections between motherhood and colonialism, the harsh tone these connections produce, and her protagonists' struggles for self-determination.

Gaspar, David Barry, *Bondmen and Rebels: A Study of Master-Slave Relations in Antigua*, Duke University Press, 1993.

Gaspar details the legacy of the colonial power dynamic in which Annie grows up.

Ismond, Patricia, ''Jamaica Kincaid: 'First They Must Be Children,''' in *World Literature Written in English*, Vol. 28, No. 2, Autumn, 1988, pp. 336-41.

Comparing *Annie John* to various stories in *At the Bottom of the River*, Ismond explores relationships between mothers and daughters in Kincaid's work, as well as Kincaid's reliance on childhood perception and fantasy.

Kincaid, Jamaica, *A Small Place*, Plume, 1989.

Kincaid reflects on the place where she grew up and asks Western tourists to join her. In doing so, she reveals the Antigua tourists never see—the one without hospital and library.

Murdoch, H. Adlai, ''Severing the (M)other Connection: The Representation of Cultural Identity in Jamaica Kincaid's *Annie John*, in *Callaloo,* Vol. 13, No. 2, Spring, 1990, pp. 325-40.

Murdoch employs psychoanalytic concepts and Antiguan cultural conflicts to illuminate Annie John's rebellion against authority and her search for identity.

Natov, Roni, ''Mothers and Daughters: Jamaica Kincaid's Pre-Oedipal Narrative,'' in *Children's Literature: Annual of the Modern Language Association Division of Children's Literature and The Children's Literature Association*, Vol. 18, 1990, pp. 1-16.

Natov explores Kincaid's use of imagery, particularly associated with Annie John's mother and with water, to illustrate Annie's changing relationships and perceptions.

Perry, Donna, ''Initiation in Jamaica Kincaid's *Annie John*,'' in *Caribbean Women Writers: Essays from the First International Conference*, edited by Selwyn R. Cudjoe, Calaloux Publications, 1990, pp. 245-53.

Connecting Kincaid's novel with other works by women of color and Third World women, Perry relates the traditions of female storytelling, obeah, and intergenerational blood ties to Annie John's development.

Simmons, Diane, *Jamaica Kincaid*, Twayne Publishers, 1994.

Simmons' book-length study focuses on Kincaid's treatment of loss and betrayal in her works, as well as her use of obeah (the magical power of transformation) and the rhythm and repetition in her prose. Her chapter on *Annie John* includes a comparison to J. D. Salinger's *Catcher in the Rye*.

Snell, Marilyn, ''jamaica kincaid hates happy endings,'' an interview in *Mother Jones*, September/October, 1997, pp. 28-31.

Kincaid explains to Snell that she feels it is her duty to bring people down a bit from their oblivious happiness.

Timothy, Helen Pyne, ''Adolescent Rebellion and Gender Relations in *At the Bottom of the River* and *Annie John*,'' in *Caribbean Women Writers: Essays from the First International Conference*, edited by Selwyn R. Cudjoe, Calaloux, 1990, pp. 233-42.

Timothy examines the links between Caribbean cultural practices and beliefs and Kincaid's treatment of mother-daughter conflicts.

White, Evelyn C., ''Growing Up Black,'' in *The Women's Review of Books*, Vol. III, No. 2, November, 1985, p. 11.

White praises Kincaid's ability to evoke both life in Antigua and the painful struggles of adolescence. She contends that while Kincaid addresses colonialism, she foregrounds her young protagonist's internal dilemmas.

Anowa

Ama Ata Aidoo

1970

Anowa is the second, last, and most accomplished play written by Ghanaian playwright, poet, short-story writer, and novelist Ama Ata Aidoo. Anowa was first published in 1970 and had its British premiere in London in 1991; Aidoo had begun writing *Anowa* in the late 1960s. Aidoo based the play on regional legends and folktales, some of which were about the "disobedient daughter." In such stories, a young woman refuses to marry a suitor, resulting in disaster. Aidoo gave such stories her own twist, incorporating a more complicated portrayal of gender and drawing parallels with contemporary Ghanaian history. At the center of the play is the title character, Anowa, who finds her own husband and remains true to her own ideals, resulting in an unhappy marriage and conflict that leads to death.

Set in the 1870s, many critics believe that *Anowa* underscores the similarities between the slave trade occurring in the Gold Coast (as Ghana was then known) in that time period and the treatment of women in contemporary society. Some believe *Anowa* is feminist, while others focus on the economic aspects. Most agree that it is thoroughly modern in the dilemmas it presents. As Mildred A. Hill-Lubin writes in her essay "Ama Ata Aidoo and the African Diaspora: Things 'All Good Men and Women Try to Forget,' but I Will Not Let Them" (included in *Emerging Perspectives on Ama Ata Aidoo*, 1999), "Anowa . . . combines the political and the personal and demonstrates the

interconnectedness of race, gender, and economic oppressions. It reveals the complicity of Africans in the slaves trade, notes the cover-up in terms of silence.''

Author Biography

Aidoo was born Christina Ama Aidoo on March 23, 1940, in Abeadzi Kyiakor, what was then called the Gold Coast (later known as Ghana). She was the daughter of Nana Yaw Fama and his wife Maame Abba Abasema. Her father was a chief of Abeadzi Kyiakor (located in south central Ghana) and raised as royalty. Though women were not often educated at the time, Aidoo's father believed that for the good of Africa, both women and men should be well-educated. She attended Wesley Girls High School in Cape Coast, Ghana. By the age of fifteen, Aidoo wanted to be a writer. Aidoo later entered the University of Ghana in Legon. Before graduating in 1964, Aidoo took classes with Efua Sutherland, a famous Ghanian dramatist with an interest in folklore. Aidoo began writing in English, though her first language is Fanti, using traditional forms.

After graduation, Aidoo spent two years (1964-66) as a junior research fellow at her alma mater. It was here that she wrote her first drama, *The Dilemma of a Ghost*. Focusing on an African-American woman who has come to her new husband's homeland and the cultural problems that ensue, the play was performed at the University of Ghana in 1964 and published in 1965 to mixed reviews. Aidoo left Ghana for two years, 1967 to 1969, to go to the United States for a creative writing fellowship at Stanford University. While there, Aidoo began work on another play, *Anowa* (1970). This play also focused on the problems of a woman, the title character.

When Aidoo returned to Ghana, she began to teach English at the University of Cape Coast, beginning in 1970. While focusing on teaching, Aidoo also continued to write. That year she published a short story collection, *No Sweetness Here*. The collection included stories she had written as early as her days as a student. Aidoo published her first novel in 1977, *Our Sister Killjoy: or, Reflections from a Black-Eye Squint*. Combining verse with prose, the novel was regarded as innovative. Aidoo would not publish anything major for eight years. One reason for this break in her writing career was politics. From 1982 to 1983, Aidoo took a post

in the Ghanaian government headed by Jerry Rawlings. She was the minister of education. However, because of her radical views, Aidoo was forced out of the position and her native country. With her daughter Kinni Likimani, Aidoo moved to Zimbabwe, which became her primary residence.

Soon after the move, Aidoo resumed publishing. In 1985, she published her first collection of poems, *Someone Talking to Sometime*. She would publish other collections of short stories, poems, and children's literature throughout the 1990s. Her second major novel, *Changes: A Love Story* (1991), shared thematic concerns with *Anowa*, though it was set in contemporary times. While Aidoo continued to write, she also occasionally was a writer-in-residence and held visiting professorships in the United States while lecturing and making other appearances throughout the world.

Plot Summary

Prologue

Anowa opens with the entrance of the Old Man and Old Woman (collectively known as The-Mouth-That-Eats-Salt-and-Pepper). They set up the action of the play, focusing on the oddness of a girl called Anowa. Anowa has refused to marry any of the men who asked for her hand for several years. They say that many believe Badua has spoiled her daughter, which would account for her behavior. The Old Woman thinks that Anowa is a born priestess, and Badua has denied her daughter's destiny.

Phase 1

In the village of Yebi in Ghana, some time in the 1870s, Anowa is fetching water for her mother when she sees Kofi Ako. They smile at each other. Their moment together is witnessed by a woman and her husband. As the woman stares at them, she drops her tray. Anowa and Kofi laugh.

Inside the cottage of Anowa's parents, Badua is cooking, worrying aloud about her daughter's refusal to get married. Her husband, Osam, enters, and tells her she complains too much. He is not concerned about Anowa's situation, and reminds his wife that he wanted to apprentice her to a priestess. Badua is horrified at the suggestion. She will not let her only surviving child become a priestess because they are not people. Osam points out that Anowa is not a normal person, so that might not be such a bad thing.

Anowa returns and informs them that she has agreed to be married to Kofi Ako. Badua becomes angry. She believes that Kofi Ako is a good-for-nothing man, though admittedly handsome. Badua tries to draw Osam into the conversation, but he will not take sides.

Sometime later, Anowa is packing her belongings. She and her mother argue about her marriage. Anowa insists she likes him, while Badua insults the family he comes from. Osam contradicts his wife, insisting that they have made good husbands. Anowa pledges not to return to Yebi for a long time, and that she will help her husband make something of his life. Badua points out Kofi Ako's every failure, and she and her daughter almost come to blows.

At the end of the phase, the Old Man and Old Woman return. The Old Woman believes children have become more disobedient, while the Old Man says that Badua should be happy that Anowa has married at all.

Phase 2

A few years later, Kofi and Anowa are on the highway to the coast, carrying skins to sell. They seek shelter from the rain in a thicket. Kofi Ako worries that the work might be too harsh for her. She insists that she is strong. Anowa suggests that he marry another wife who could help them out. Kofi Ako is upset by this suggestion. As the conversation continues, it becomes clear that the two have not yet had a child, a distressing fact for both of them. They do not know why. Anowa nods off to sleep, and Kofi Ako reveals that his wife is often mistaken for his sister because she works so hard with him. He believes she will settle down and act more like a proper wife.

The next day, the pair dry their skins in the sun. Kofi Ako still does not understand why his wife likes to work, and suggests they buy slaves to make their life easier. Anowa is horrified by the idea, and will not allow him to consider it. Kofi Ako does not understand his wife's position. He insists that they will do it because everyone else does it, among other reasons.

Back at the cottage of Anowa's parents, Badua and Osam discuss their daughter. Osam admits he always feared Anowa and her strangeness. He is worried that she will never come back, and that they will never know her children. Badua tells him that Anowa has not had children. They speculate on the reasons why. Badua wants to go and find her, but Osam tells her Anowa is not lost. Badua and Osam

reveal that Anowa and Kofi Ako are rich because their trade has increased due to their growing number of slaves. While Osam also knows that Anowa is unhappy about their owning slaves, Badua thinks her problems with it are foolish.

Back on the highway some time later, a better-dressed Kofi Ako leads several slaves carrying loads of skins. Anowa calls for him. She has no load to carry, yet is angry that she cannot keep up. He pays more attention to his slaves than her. Anowa tells him that she is unhappy not working and does not want to look after the house. She again suggests that Kofi Ako marry another wife, which upsets him. This leads to a discussion about their lack of children, which Anowa assumes is her fault. Her restlessness frightens him, and he wants to buy some female slaves to be her companions. Kofi Ako gets angry with her and wishes that she were different and had children. Anowa can only laugh.

The Old Man returns. He does not like the idea of slavery. The Old Woman enters. She believes Anowa is a witch, and has come from evil.

Phase 3

Several years later, Kofi Ako is a prosperous man with many slaves and a big house in Oguaa. Anowa enters, wearing old clothes without shoes. She looks old as she relates a disturbing incident from his childhood.

The scene changes slightly and two young slaves, a boy and a girl, talk about Anowa and Kofi Ako, whom they are to call Mother and Father. The girl says that others claim Anowa is a witch, but she is sympathetic to her mistress's growing unhappiness. Kofi Ako has told Anowa to leave, but will not tell her why. The girl envies the life Anowa could have, full of jewels and no work.

Anowa enters the room quietly and overhears part of their conversation. The girl says that Kofi Ako is afraid of women. The boy chases the girl out of the room. Wearing much gold, Kofi Ako enters and sits on his throne-like chair. He still wants Anowa to be like other women, while she does not like owning slaves and not working. Her habits of dressing in poor clothes and creeping around the house upset him. Because they are still without children, Anowa wants to find him another wife. Kofi Ako tells her that she has destroyed him and wants her to leave. Though Anowa presses, Kofi Ako will not tell her why. She refuses to leave because she has nowhere to go. She wants to live separately from him in the house as they have for years.

As Anowa speculates on the reasons, she has a revelation. She has the boy slave gather some elders. She asks them if they ever heard of a situation where a husband wants to divorce his wife without giving her a reason. None have, and Anowa sends them to consult with others on this question. Kofi Ako threatens to brand her a witch if she continues in this matter. He promises to give her half their wealth if she will leave. Kofi Ako calls the boy and tells him to help her pack.

Anowa will not allow him to send her away. She says she has not slept with him for years and that he has not shown interest in other women. Anowa accuses him of being like a woman, that is, impotent, in front of the boy and several other slaves. She decides to leave, as he exits. As Anowa pauses, Kofi Ako shoots himself offstage. At the end of the play, the Old Woman reports that Anowa killed herself by drowning as well. She blames Anowa for the deaths, while the Old Man believes Anowa was true to herself.

Characters

Kofi Ako

Kofi Ako is Anowa's husband. Anowa's mother believes he is a fool and comes from a bad family, while Osam is content that his daughter is finally getting married. Anowa wants to help him make something of himself. Together, the couple builds a business trading skins. At first, Kofi Ako seems willing to accept his wife's help, though he wishes that she were more like other wives. To make this possible and improve their lives, Kofi Ako decides to buy slaves to help in the business. Anowa is vehemently opposed to owning slaves, but Kofi Ako rationalizes that because everyone else does it, it must be okay. Kofi Ako's strategy pays off in some ways. They do become very rich with a big house in Oguaa, but their marriage becomes strained. Anowa wants to work and is lost when forced to do nothing. The couple drifts apart while living under the same roof. A bigger issue between them is their lack of children, which Anowa initially blames on herself. When Kofi Ako asks her to leave without giving a reason in phase three, Anowa comes to question Kofi Ako's manhood. When she accuses him of being like a woman and implying that he is impotent in front of several slaves, Kofi Ako kills

Media Adaptations

- *Anowa* was produced for radio by BBC Radio 3 in September, 1995.

himself. Kofi Ako never really understood his wife, only what society expected a wife to be.

Anowa

As the title character, Anowa is the center of the play. She is a young Ghanaian woman who is regarded as unusual and wild by others in her village, including her parents. Before meeting Kofi Ako in phase one, Anowa has refused to marry anyone who asked her. Her parents, especially her mother Badua, worry about her and her future. Her desire to marry Kofi Ako, whom her mother regards as less-than-perfect husband material, is another unexpected twist in her life. Osam, and others in the play, believe that Anowa would have been better off being a priestess.

After marrying Kofi Ako, Anowa is happy to help him in his work and build their business. Their only problem is their lack of children, which Anowa blames on herself in the form of some unknown shortcoming. While Kofi Ako appreciates Anowa's work to some degree, he would like it better if she would act more like a traditional wife. Anowa has no desire to live a life of leisure. Over her protests, Kofi Ako buys slaves which builds their business further. As Kofi Ako's wealth grows, Anowa becomes more alienated from him. By the end of the play, Anowa is still barren and Kofi Ako wants her to leave. Anowa has a revelation that Kofi Ako is less than a man, and him impotency has made them childless. Like her husband, Anowa kills herself by the end of the play. Her free-spirited ways were never appreciated by anyone in *Anowa*.

Abena Badua

Badua is the mother of Anowa and wife of Osam. She is bewildered by her only surviving child and her attitudes. Like Kofi Ako, Badua wants

Anowa to be normal. For Badua, this means to have married at an appropriate age. She rejects Osam's suggestion that Anowa would have been better off training to be a priestess. Such a woman would not have been a person. Badua is appalled when Anowa announces that she will marry Kofi Ako. This is the worst man Anowa could have married. In Badua's opinion, he is a fool. Badua and Anowa's disagreement comes to blows. When Anowa leaves, she vows not to return and says that her mother is driving her away. Despite their differences, in phase two, Badua expresses a desire to go and look for her. Badua does not understand her daughter, nor, in many ways, her husband. Badua is very set in her beliefs and has no desire to compromise them. Some villagers believe that Anowa is different because her mother spoiled her as a child.

Being-The-Mouth-That-Eats-Salt-And-Pepper

This couple set up and comment on the action of the play. The Old Woman is very critical of Anowa and the choices she makes, while the Old Man is more sympathetic.

Boy

Boy is one of the slaves owned by Kofi Ako. He is very interested in Girl, and with her discusses Kofi Ako and Anowa in phase three. The Boy follows orders given to him, and does not gossip like Girl does.

Girl

Girl is a slave in the household of Kofi Ako and Anowa. She gossips to Boy about the couple's problems. She tells him how many believe there is something wrong with Anowa, but is also sympathetic to her mistress's lack of children. Girl can imagine what she would do in Anowa's position. She also believes that Kofi Ako is afraid of women.

Old Man

See Being-The-Mouth-That-Eats-Salt-And-Pepper

Old Woman

See Being-The-Mouth-That-Eats-Salt-And-Pepper

Osam

Osam is the father of Anowa and the husband of Badua. Though local custom dictates that he does not play much of a role in finding a husband for his daughter, Osam does not have a big problem with her marrying Kofi Ako. He admits that she is wild, but his wife has previously shot down his suggestion that Anowa be apprenticed to a priestess. Unlike Badua, Osam has some understanding of his daughter and her beliefs. Osam comprehends Anowa's problem with slavery. Yet he also acknowledges in phase two that he has always feared Anowa and thought her strange. Osam gets along with his wife, though he believes that she complains too much. They often disagree, but stay together.

Panyin-Na-Kakra

Panyin-Na-Kakra are a set of eight-year-old twin boys who are slaves in the house of Kofi Ako and Anowa. In phase three, the boys fan the gilded chair of Kofi Ako before his arrival. When Anowa sees them doing this task, she sends them away.

Themes

Custom and Tradition

Much of the plot of *Anowa* turns on the power of custom and tradition, and the consequences of not following such tenets of society. Anowa does not subscribe to most customs. She has refused to marry after reaching puberty, as is tradition in her area. Further, she has turned down every man who has asked for her hand for six years. Her attitude befuddles her anxious mother as well as her father to a lesser degree. Anowa has always been different—described variously as wild and strange—but her nontraditional attitudes alienate those around her.

This character trait becomes more problematic after she is finally married to Kofi Ako. She helps him start a skin-trading business and does much work for it. Traditionally women keep the home and do not do work. While Kofi Ako appreciates her support at first, he longs for a more custom-following wife. To that end, he expresses a desire to buy slaves for their business. Anowa is appalled by the prospect of owning other people, though Kofi Ako points out that it is a common practice. Despite her feelings on the matter, he does buy them and grows rich with a big house and many slaves. Anowa refuses to take on her traditional role. She will not wear rich clothes or use people as slaves. Her defiance of tradition and custom leads to an empty marriage and to her own suicide and that of Kofi Ako. While Anowa has remained true to her beliefs, her attitude has harmed those around her.

Pride

The driving force behind Anowa's actions is pride. Though her attitudes and behavior might seem wild, strange, or just bizarre to those around her, she gives *Anowa* a moral, self-respecting center. Anowa does not care much what people think. She follows her beliefs, not sharing the others characters' overriding concern with custom and tradition. She does not want to marry anyone who has asked for her hand, so she does not. When she meets someone she does want to marry, Kofi Ako, she does, despite her parents' protests. Work is important to Anowa. She wants her husband to succeed and personally contributes to his business. Kofi Ako does not understand why she wants to work so hard, but it gives Anowa pride in herself.

Anowa's pride is not just in herself, but extends to her treatment of others. When Kofi Ako proposes that they buy slaves to make their lives easier and improve their business, Anowa is dismayed. Her pride is tempered by respect for other human beings. She tells him in phase two, "Kofi, no man made a slave of his friend and came to much himself. It is wrong. It is evil." Kofi Ako ignores her insights and buys the slaves anyway. The richer they become the more unhappy Anowa becomes and the more their marriage is strained. Anowa is left with less to do, and while she retains her pride, she is increasing alienated from the world. In some ways, her pride is her downfall. That she sticks to her beliefs shows her strength, but it also dooms her in the end as both she and her husband take their own lives.

Choices and Consequences

Many of the choices made in *Anowa* have extreme consequences. Badua's attitude towards Anowa leads directly to Anowa's declaration that she will not return to Yebi. Anowa never returns. More implicitly, choices Kofi Ako and Anowa make seem to lead to their lack of children. At first, Anowa chooses to blame this situation on herself. She tries to remedy it by encouraging him on more than one occasion to marry another wife or two. Kofi Ako will not make this choice. Instead, slaves are his answer to this problem, which will solve it by

Topics for Further Study

- Research folk stories in Ghana and/or West Africa, particularly those on "disobedient daughters." Compare them with *Anowa*, discussing how they influenced Aidoo's dramatic choices.

- Compare and contrast *Anowa* with William Shakespeare's *Macbeth* (performed c. 1606; published c. 1623). Focus on the differences and similarities between Anowa in phase three and Lady Macbeth.

- Discuss *Anowa* in terms of feminism. Make an argument about whether the play is feminist.

- Research the history of slavery in nineteenth-century Ghana. Is the depiction of slavery accurate in *Anowa*? How does it underscore the play's themes?

creating wealth. Kofi Ako's choice to buy slaves has the consequence of straining his marriage to the point of breaking. Anowa ends up interpreting his choices and concluding that he is impotent, less than a man. Her public declaration leads to their double (though separate) suicide. *Anowa* shows the consequences of making hard choices and how they deeply affect lives like Anowa's.

Style

Setting

Anowa is a drama set in the 1870s in Ghana. The action of the play takes place in three distinct places. In phase one, *Anowa*'s action is confined to the village of Yebi, primarily to the cottage of Badua and Osam. There is a brief return to the cottage in phase two, which mostly takes place on a highway near the coast several years after phase one. The final phase of *Anowa* is set a few years later in Oguaa at Kofi Ako's big house built with the riches of his trade. All of the settings of *Anowa* have a domestic edge, underscoring the importance of the marital and familial relationships.

Greek Chorus

The prologue as well as the beginning and the end of nearly every phase consists of commentary given by The-Mouth-That-Eats-Salt-And-Pepper, a sort of Greek Chorus. The Old Man and Old Woman who comprise The-Mouth-That-Eats-Salt-And-Pepper (a regional expression for society's opinion) set the scene for the play, giving a little background about the main characters and conflicts. As the story unfolds, the pair gives their opinions on the action. The Old Man is somewhat sympathetic to Anowa and her ways, while the Old Woman is highly critical. She believes Anowa is a witch, among other things. They are not particularly well-developed as characters, but more of a moral compass for the play. The pair shows contrasting views of society—between men and women, perhaps—towards Anowa and the decisions she and others make.

Monologue

Many characters give long monologues in *Anowa*. These monologues reveal motivations and develop characters. The Old Man opens the play with a monologue that describes the local geography, gods, and conflicts. He also introduces the names of Kofi and Anowa and hints at their basic characteristics. At the end of phase two, he comments on the situations that have developed, sympathizing with Anowa's anti-slavery stance. In the same section, the Old Woman has a monologue in which she expresses hope that Kofi Ako will put Anowa in her place. Earlier in phase two, after Anowa falls asleep and Kofi Ako puts her in a leafy bed, he expresses his conflicted feelings for Anowa. He does not understand her, commenting that many mistake Anowa for his sister instead of his wife. A sister would work as hard as Anowa does for her brother, but not a wife. He resolves to change the situation and make her more like a wife and he like a husband. Anowa has several monologues in phase three in which she relates an incident from her childhood and reflects on her childless state. Monologues add depth to the characterizations in *Anowa*.

Lighting/Transitions

Within each of the three phases that comprise *Anowa*, Aidoo has transitions between smaller scenes that make up the phase. These transitions consist of

the lighting going down, then rising again. The transitions denote passage of time. In phase one, the time passage is rather short, though unspecified. After Anowa announces that she will marry Kofi Ako and there is tension within the family, there is a transition and the next scene begins. In it, Anowa is packing to leave with Kofi Ako.

The transitions in phase two denote longer periods of time and different places. The phase begins by the side of the highway, with a discussion about buying slaves. After the transition, the phase shifts back to the cottage of Badua and Osam. They talk about the new wealth of Kofi Ako and the number of slaves he owns. Of more concern to them is the barrenness of their daughter. After another lighting-driven transition, the phase returns to Kofi Ako, Anowa, and their new slaves. Again, some time has passed, though how much is not clear.

There are only two transitions in phase three, placed after the main action has ended. After the confrontation between Kofi Ako and Anowa, the lights go down, and there is a funeral for the couple. After the lights go down again, the Old Man and Woman return to give their final comments. These transitions make the action of the play more continuous and make its staging simpler.

Literary Heritage

Like many African countries and cultures, each ethnic group in Ghana has a tradition of oral storytelling, including myths and legends about their religious figures and the beginning of the universe. Folktales, like one Aidoo based *Anowa* on, are particularly important ways of both entertaining and imparting values. One type of folkstory is the "dilemma tale," which presents social and moral issues in a way which provokes discussion of the topics raised. In many ways, *Anowa* is a dramatized dilemma tale that Aidoo modified in a modern way.

While there is an emphasis on performance in the oral transmission of folktales, Ghana has a more modern theatrical tradition. Beginning in the late nineteenth centuries, commercial theater shows and troupes traveled throughout Ghana, coming into their own after World War II. Part of so-called "concert parties," three or more comedic actors in a troupe used stock characters to comment on social and familial problems while entertaining audiences. Primarily a nonurban phenomenon, these concert parties as a whole were rather like vaudeville in the United States in the late nineteenth and early twentieth century in form, and, to some degree, content.

Historical Context

A country in Western Africa, Ghana is made up of different ethnic groups. While almost forty percent are Akin peoples, other ethnic groups include Ewe, Ga-Adangme, Hausa, and Mole-Dagbani. Each has their own language, customs, and traditions, though some overlap. There are more than fifty native languages in the area, though about a quarter of the population speaks English, the official language of the government.

By 1970, Ghana was politically unstable, in part because of the diverse interests of these groups. The second half of the twentieth century was marked by many political problems. Until 1957, Ghana (then known as the Gold Coast) was a colony of Great Britain. The country obtained its independence partially because of the efforts of Kwame Nkrumah.

A native of the Gold Coast, Nkrumah received a university education in the United States. Beginning in 1947, he began fighting for his native country's independence. He promoted self-rule for the Gold Coast through the political party he helped form, the Convention People's Party (CPP). When independence was gained, Nkrumah was named prime minister (later president when Ghana became a republic) and CPP, the ruling party. Ghana became the first African country south of the Sahara desert to become independent in this manner.

As a leader, Nkrumah developed Ghana's health and educational systems to some degree. But he also used money to build expensive things like a stadium, instead of building up the country's economic infrastructure. Nkrumah was essentially a dictator by the time a combination of army and police officers staged a coup d'etat in early 1966. At the time, Nkrumah was in China, and he died in exile in 1972.

Those who staged the coup formed the National Liberation Council, which drew up a new constitu-tion for Ghana. The Council was dissolved in October 1969 when new elections were held and democracy returned. The Progress Party was put into power, led by prime minister Kofi Busai. In 1970, Edward Akufo-Addo was elected president. The tenure of the Progress Party was short-lived because of continued political instability. The Progress Party did not include all of Ghana's ethnic groups. In 1972, another coup d'etat was staged by a military leader, an army officer named Igantius K. Acheampong.

Thus, by 1970, Ghana had suffered from long-term economic instability as it tried to become more modern. The country's biggest export (seventy percent of the total) crop was cacao—the basic ingredient in chocolate. Under the Progress Party regime, the price dropped significantly, greatly affecting Ghana's rural population. While Ghana was becoming increasingly urban, only about a third of the population lived in cities. Those who lived in rural areas were mostly employed as farmers in some capacity. A significant part of the population lived in poverty. Though wealth was no longer tied to lineage, and education and better jobs were available in cities, the lack of a strong economy affected everyone.

The position of women was also undergoing a slow process of change. Women still were seen primarily as childbearers. It was important for women in both urban and rural areas to have children, though those in rural areas generally had more children than their urban counterparts. Women who were better educated and economically independent generally had fewer children. Education had become more common and available. A 1960 law required that everyone attend elementary school until the age of twelve. Still some parents were reluctant to give their daughters any education, believing it might hurt their prospects for marriage. Though many dropped out, there were those who came to teach on the university level, like Aidoo. In 1970, Ghana was most definitely a country in transition.

Critical Overview

In one of the few public performances of *Anowa*—a 1991 production in London, some twenty-one years

Compare & Contrast

- **1870s:** A significant part of what is now Ghana is ruled as a colony by Great Britain, with minimal input from local people. There are attacks to keep trade routes open in the interior of the future country.

  1970: Ghana is politically unstable, just three years after a coup replaced President Nkrumah.

  Today: Ghana is more politically stable under the long-term leadership of Jerry Rawlings. While there are accusations of governmental corruption, Rawlings remains above the fray.

- **1870s:** The coastal areas of what would become Ghana are the most developed because they are the focus of trade. Urban areas are just developing.

  1970: About twenty-eight percent of the country lives in an urban environment, with most urban areas found along the coast.

  Today: More than a third of Ghanaians live in an urban environment.

- **1870s:** Women are primarily childbearers, though they also work as farmers and sell fish and produce.

  1970: As educational opportunities increase for women, the number of occupational opportunities also increase, though primarily in urban areas. Many in rural areas still work as farmers and sellers of farm-related products.

  Today: More women continue to become educated and hold jobs in urban areas, which continue to attract newcomers looking for better economic opportunities.

- **1870s:** Though missionaries convert some to Christianity, most Ghanaians follow local traditional religious beliefs.

  1970: More than half the population follows a Christian faith.

  Today: About 64.1 percent of Ghanaians are Christian, while 17.6 percent continue to follow traditional beliefs.

---

after its publication—many critics praised the play, drawing parallels between it and contemporary society. Comparing *Anowa* to a work by William Shakespeare, Malcolm Rutherford of the *Financial Times* writes, ''do not go to see *Anowa* looking for something exotic. What will strike you is not how different it is from developed western culture, but how similar.'' Louise Kingsley of *The Independent* makes an analogous statement. She argues that ''though the intimate bickerings of husband and wife are common to males and females the world over, Anowa's decline is, to European eyes at least, as much a consequence of her uncompromising nature as of her moral stance.''

One London critic echoes the sentiments of many scholars who have commented on *Anowa*. Anne Karpf in *The Guardian* writes, ''Lyrical and eloquent . . . *Anowa* brings us a typical Aidoo

heroine, strong and nonconformist, but ultimately felled by conservative forces.'' Many scholars compare *Anowa* with Aidoo's previous play, *The Dilemma of a Ghost*, as well as her novels, looking at how she has handled certain themes and her development of characters.

For example, Eldred Durosimi Jones in *African Literature Today* writes, ''Like the earlier play, it [*Anowa*] preserves something of the representative nature of the folk-tale. It keeps in touch with social reality but does not become totally absorbed in realistic detail. The impact of particularities is dulled. . . . This eschewing of too much inconsequential realism gives the play its archetypal quality.'' Vincent O. Odamtten makes a similar point in his book *The Art of Ama Ata Aidoo*. He believes Aidoo's second play is more honest in its confrontation of history. He argues, ''*Anowa* enables us to better see how, as social beings, as both producers and products, we are implicated in the transmission and perpetuation of our past in our present and possible futures.''

Several scholars have found the dream that Anowa describes near the beginning of phase three particularly important. Comparing Aidoo's writing with several other African women authors, Maggi Phillips in *Research in African Literatures* believes ''Anowa's bleak tones present the breakdown of human relationships, a breakdown that may not be salvaged unless we listen, as the Old Man advises, to the cries and dreams of the embattled heart.'' In Maureen N. Eke's essay in *Emerging Perspectives on Ama Ata Aidoo,* ''Diasporic Ruptures and (Re)membering History: Africa as Home and Exile in *Anowa* and *Dilemma of a Ghost,*'' she also analyzes the dream. Eke believes the dream accounts for Anowa's oddness and also that it raised questions she has needed to be answered her whole life. Anowa is on a quest for the truth. However, Eke writes, ''Like her community, Anowa is encouraged to sleep the sleep of silence and forgetfulness'' over slavery.

Other critical scholars look at *Anowa* in terms of motherhood. Naana Banyiwa Horne, in ''The Politics of Mothering: Multiple Subjectivity and Gendered Discourse in Aidoo's Plays'' (also included in *Emerging Perspectives on Ama Ata Aidoo*), focuses on the Anowa's failed quest to become a mother. She the examines motives of each of the female characters in the play, focusing on Anowa, as well as matrilineal kinship in Ghanaian society. Horne blames Kofi Ako for the situation at the end of the play.

Horne writes, ''through *Anowa* , Aidoo pays tribute to the industry and ingenuity of our foremothers. In fact, the story of Anowa, symbolically, mirrors patriarchy's maneuvers to erode women's effective participation in the global economy. . . . Even though Anowa is the brains behind the business, Kofi Ako eventually runs her out, vetoing her participation so that he can freely exploit slave labor to build an economic empire.''

In his *The Art of Ama Ata Aidoo*, Odamtten makes a similar point. He argues, ''What comes through in Aidoo's play is that the issues of gender oppression are materially based, that the dominant social relations that arise and are part of the economic production relations of a given society, at a particular historical moment, produce specific modes of behavior or cultural practices. These practices

Aidoo's novel explores conflicting attitudes and ethical implications of colonialism and slavery.

may not be the result of deliberate or malicious intent by individuals in that society. But neither is it one's destiny to accept cultural practices that one finds abhorrent or counterproductive.''

Criticism

Annette Petrusso

In this essay, Petrusso analyzes how Aidoo depicts male-female relationships of different generations in Anowa.

Many critics have commented on the fact that though *Anowa* is set in what later became Ghana in the 1870s, some of the issues and ideas Aidoo has woven into the story are thoroughly modern. Anowa's individuality and complex, often problematic relationship with both her parents and husband are often mentioned. Another is the depiction of several generations and how they handle conflict in different ways. The play is built around male-female relationships, implicitly contrasting different generations.

What Do I Read Next?

- *Efuru*, a work by Flora Nwapa published in 1966, also focuses on choices an African woman makes concerning marriage and children and the societal pressures placed on her.

- *Changes* is a novel by Aidoo published in 1991. Like *Anowa*, *Changes* focuses on the societal pressure placed on a woman over marriage, though in a modern setting.

- *The Joys of Motherhood*, a work by Buchi Emercheta published in 1980, also focuses on values in African life and how they directly affect women.

- *The Dilemma of a Ghost* , a play by Aidoo first performed in 1964, focuses on how an African-American woman handles familial pressure placed on her when she comes to Ghana with her husband, a native Ghanaian.

- *Boesman and Lena*, a play by South African playwright Athol Fugard first performed in 1969, also focuses on the tense relationship between a couple.

In *Anowa* there are three main couplings: The Old Man and Old Woman (also known as Being-The-Mouth-That-Eats-Salt-And-Pepper), the elder generation; Badua and Osam, the parental generation; and Anowa and Kofi Ako, the younger generation. This essay discusses these relationships and how they form the core of the play.

The oldest couple in *Anowa* are the Old Man and the Old Woman. They are not part of the main action of the play, but more of a chorus commenting on the choices and attitudes displayed by the "real" characters. The name "Being-The-Mouth-That-Eats-Salt-And-Pepper" is a local euphemism for a gossip, further underlining how they represent society's opinion. While it is unclear from the play whether the Old Man and Old Woman are married, they represent their genders in their age group. Aidoo presents them as a couple, implying they function as a unit.

The Old Man and Old Woman are supposed to live in the village of Yebi, where Anowa lives with her parents until the end of phase one. Thus, it is a specific segment of a society close to Anowa that is providing what should be knowledgeable commentary. From the beginning, Aidoo sets up a contrast with the pair. In the stage descriptions at the beginning of the prologue, Aidoo writes, "She is never

still and very often speaks with agitation, waving her stick. . . . He is serene and everything about him is more orderly." The Old Man and Old Woman rarely agree.

The Old Man is more sympathetic to Anowa and her troubles than the Old Woman from the first. The Old Woman disagrees with his every opinion. At the end of phase two, for example, the Old Man shares Anowa's horror at Kofi Ako's acquisition of slaves. He states, "there must be something unwholesome about making slaves of other men, something that is against the natural state of man and the purity of his worship of the gods." The Old Woman is only concerned that Anowa has not had any children and will not act as a proper wife to Kofi Ako. Her only indirect comment on the slavery matter is "she would rather be poor than prospering."

At the end of *Anowa*, the Old Woman blames Anowa for Kofi Ako's demise. She shows no compassion towards Anowa or her situation. The Old Man does. He gets the final lines of the play, which include one insightful statement: "She [Anowa] was true to herself." The Old Man seems to understand Anowa's motivations better than the Old Woman. She is more concerned with Anowa's every transgression. The Old Woman is quick to blame Anowa's mother, Badua, for bringing up her daughter in an incorrect manner. The Old Man examines how the action reflects changes in social trends, while the Old Woman is only concerned with judging the wrongs of individuals, with no thought to the big picture.

Badua and Osam, Anowa's parents, share many characteristics with the Old Man and Old Woman. Badua is as quick to judge as the Old Woman, while her husband is depicted as more thoughtful, like the Old Man. Badua and Osam are definitely a longtime married couple, as their more personal troubles and manner of fighting indicate. Underneath the disagreements, however, is a partnered core. Both Osam and Badua stay within their defined roles as man and woman, husband and wife.

In phase one, where Osam and Badua are the primary characters, Osam tries to offer solutions to their problem with Anowa, but Badua does not want to hear them. Osam has wanted to apprentice their daughter to a priestess, but Badua wants her to be married in the socially accepted fashion and "normal." Indeed most of Badua's mental energy is spent on wanting her daughter to be a different kind of person, one that accepts her societal role and lives the kind of life her mother wants her to live.

On page twelve in phase one, for example, Badua lists all she wants for her daughter, some of which she does not even have for herself. Osam is more realistic. He tells Badua, "My wife, people with better vision than yours or mine have seen that Anowa is not like you or me." Later in the phase, Badua cannot accept that Anowa, against all social norms, has found her own husband and will live a different kind of life. Osam stays out of the manner, accepting that his daughter has made a decision. He only becomes critical when the bickering between Badua and Anowa turns nasty, and Anowa is mean to her mother's face.

After Anowa leaves with Kofi Ako, there is a scene in phase two which shows Osam and Badua's reactions to their married daughter's choices. Badua still only thinks in terms of what she wants Anowa to be and the socially acceptable role in her village. For a moment, Badua expresses a desire to look for her, while Osam realizes that Anowa probably does not want to be found. Later in the scene, Osam, like the Old Man, expresses understanding about Anowa's opinions on slavery. Badua can only see that her daughter, though barren, is living a wealthy life that many women would envy. Badua cannot see beyond her own life and values. Osam is not particularly worldly either, but he is more understanding of

> Aidoo portrays male-female relationships in a complex, thought-provoking manner. . . .Anowa remains true to herself but pays a harsh price. The many possible interpretations of Anowa make it a very interesting play."

opinions that are different than his own. This duality has much in common with the Old Man and Old Woman.

The bulk of *Anowa* concerns the relationship between Anowa and Kofi Ako. In many ways, it is the exact opposite of the previous couples discussed. While Anowa is outspoken in her opinions, as Badua and the Old Woman are, she has a certain strength and independence that they do not. Anowa does not have regard for social norms, as she shows over and over again. She did not marry when most girls in her culture did, and turned down many suitors. Anowa chose to marry Kofi Ako, over her mother's protests. Anowa also enjoys working and helping her husband with his trade in direct fashion. Indeed one of her goals upon marrying him was to make him a success. Early in phase two, Anowa is carrying skins like her husband.

Kofi Ako, on the other hand, shares more of the values of Badua and the Old Woman. While these older women do not exactly respect him, at least in the first part of *Anowa*, they change their opinions when he becomes very rich from his trade. When Kofi Ako marries Anowa, he knows she is different from other women, and appreciates this to some degree. However, as the play goes, he wants her to become a more socially acceptable wife who keeps house and does not do the kind of hard labor Anowa favors. As Kofi Ako becomes more wealthy, his tolerance for Anowa's "strange" ways lessens.

One major difference between Kofi Ako and Anowa as a couple and Anowa's parents is how they argue and treat each other. The bulk of Badua and Osam's problems are discussed between them. While they disagree, they seem basically supportive of the other. No one leaves or throws the other out. Kofi Ako and Anowa never compromise on their beliefs. Kofi Ako never accepts that his wife is different and will remain that way. Anowa never accepts what Kofi Ako wants for her. The biggest argument between them is over slaves. Anowa is appalled that Kofi Ako wants to build their wealth by buying men and women. She never accepts this, even when they grow wealthy on slave labor. Anowa wants to work herself. Kofi Ako never understands her problem with slavery. When she first learns of his plan and vehemently protests, Kofi Ako replies, ''Everyone does it . . . does not everyone do it? And things would be easier for us.''

Because the couple's communication is so poor and they are so unhappy with each other by phase three, Kofi Ako wants Anowa to leave, though he will not give her a specific reason. This is the point of contention for Anowa. By this time, the couple is wealthy with a big house in Oguaa. While Kofi Ako dresses well, Anowa wears what she has worn from the beginning of the play. The couple has never been able to produce a child, a fact that Anowa blames on herself until the end of the play. When Kofi Ako and Anowa have their final argument over the reason why Kofi wants her to leave, it is bitter and drawn out. The couple has lived in separate parts of the house and slept in separate beds for some time. Their verbal tug of war is mean and bitter. It ends with Anowa accusing Kofi Ako of being less than a man. She blames him for their lack of children because he must be impotent, with some slaves present. He kills himself moments later, though Anowa finally agrees to leave. She never finds out his reason and kills herself by drowning later on.

Aidoo portrays male-female relationships in a complex, thought-provoking manner. Each of these three couples has a different kind of relationship, in part because of their different ages, experiences, and life expectations. The only true failure among the three, Kofi Ako and Anowa's relationship falters when their duality grows unbalanced. Neither will let go of their fundamental beliefs in any manner, constructive or otherwise. Aidoo could also be interpreted as condemning the inverted roles Kofi Ako and Anowa take versus the Old Man and Old Woman and Osam and Badua. Anowa remains true to herself but pays a harsh price. The many possible interpretations of *Anowa* make it a very interesting play.

Source: Annette Petrusso, in an essay for *Literature of Developing Nations for Students,* Gale, 2000.

Liz Brent

Brent has a Ph.D. in American culture with a specialization in film studies from the University of Michigan. She is a freelance writer and teaches courses in the history of American cinema. In the following essay, Brent discusses folk proverbs in Aidoo's play Anowa *.*

Aidoo's play *Anowa* concerns a young woman, Anowa, who marries a young man, Kofi Ako, against her parents' wishes. The young couple leave their home village of Yebi in order to strike out on their own, making their own way in the world. At first, Anowa works along with her husband, but he soon purchases slaves to do their work for them, and the couple prospers. From the beginning, Anowa is against the purchase of slaves, but Kofi acts against her wishes. As the years go on, their material wealth increases with the increasing number of slaves Kofi buys, but their marriage deteriorates. Throughout the play, scenes between Anowa and her husband are interspersed with conversations between Badua and Osam, Anowa's parents, and an Old Woman and Old Man. In much of the dialogue, characters refer to traditional proverbs and folk sayings in order to argue their point or convince another person of their opinion. Although these proverbs and sayings are probably not familiar to the non-African reader, one may figure out their meaning by the context in which they are used. In the following essay, I quote several of the proverbs uttered by these characters, and discuss their meaning in the context of the play.

> The sapling breaks with the bending that will not grow straight.

This proverb is spoken by the Old Woman about Anowa's refusal to obey her parents' wishes to marry. In this context, it means that the child (''sapling'') who deviates (''bends'') from her parents' rules will not grow to be an upstanding (''straight'') adult.

> A prophet with a locked mouth is neither a prophet nor a man.

This statement is made by Osam, Anowa's father, to Badua, Anowa's mother. Osam is arguing that their daughter was meant to be a priestess (or ''prophet''), and that not allowing her to express her spiritual calling (''with a locked mouth'') will prevent her from becoming a priestess, but will not make it possible for her to lead a normal life as a woman (to be ''a man'').

> The yam that will burn, shall burn, boiled or roasted.

Osam also evokes this proverb in arguing with his wife that Anowa is meant to be a priestess (''a yam that will burn''), and so no matter what she is made to do by her parents (be ''boiled or roasted''), she will still fulfill her destiny in the end. Another interpretation may be that a child who is destined to turn out bad (''burn'') will do so no matter how her parents rear (''cook'') her.

> Marriage is like a piece of cloth. . . . And like cloth, its beauty passes with wear and tear.

Anowa's mother, Badua, says this to Anowa in attempting to convince her not to marry Kofi. Badua feels that Anowa is taken in by Kofi's physical beauty, and is trying to explain to her that a marriage based on physical beauty, or attraction, will not last in the long run.

> Some of us feel that the best way to sharpen a knife is not to whet one side of it only.

This is spoken by the Old Man to the Old Woman. He is arguing that she must consider both ''sides'' of the situation between Anowa and her parents in order to make a clear judgment (''sharpen a knife'') on it.

> Is she the best potter who knows her clay and how it breathes?

The Old Man continues to point out that, just because a man and woman have given birth to a child, that does not necessarily mean that they know what is best for her. He is suggesting that perhaps Anowa knows herself (''her clay'') and what she needs from life (''how it breathes'') better than her parents do.

> Some people babble as though they borrowed their grey hairs and did not grow them on their own heads.

The Old Woman says this to the Old Man, implying that what he is saying is without wisdom, and so he sounds as if he were really a young man (without grey hair) who has only put on the guise of an old man (''borrowed their grey hairs''), rather than gaining the true wisdom which comes with age.

> The infant which tries its milk teeth on every bone and stone, grows up with nothing to eat dried meat with.

The Old Woman says this to the Old Man, in arguing that Anowa should be made to behave her parents' wishes, as she is too young to make wise decisions. The saying means that a baby who is teething and tries to chew the most difficult items (''tries its milk teeth on every bone and stone'') will ruin its teeth by the time it is an adult (''with nothing to eat dried meat with''). In other words, allowing a young girl, such as Anowa, to make her own—

> " Part of Aidoo's project in writing this play was to record in writing, and reproduce on stage, elements from the oral tradition of African culture. . . . At the same time, however, Aidoo plants a seed of doubt in the reader's mind as to the value of relying solely on traditional wisdom in making life decisions."

unwise—decisions about her life will only leave her without wisdom or resources as an adult.

> The man who hates you does not care if you wait in the sun for your clothes to dry before you can go and join the dance.

Kofi makes this statement to Anowa, as, early in their marriage, they are discussing their attempt to support themselves on their own, without the help of their families, and away from their home village. The expression means that a person who does not care about you (''hates you'') will take no interest in your personal problems, large or small. Kofi is suggesting to Anowa that they are truly on their own in the world, and cannot expect sympathy or aid from the families and community whom they left on a negative note.

> A shrine has to be worshipped however small its size. And a kind god angered is a thousand times more evil than a mean god unknown.

Anowa says this to Kofi as they are arguing about the value of using ''medicines and taboos'' to solve their problems. Kofi thinks that there is no harm in such remedies, but Anowa feels that one cannot resort to such measures lightly. Her point is that using ''medicines and taboos'' requires a commitment on their part to the cure; in other words, they must ''worship'' the ''shrine'' of these ''medicines and taboos,'' even if they only wish to use them in a ''small'' way. Furthermore, Anowa argues that the positive benefits of these cures (''a kind god'') can be overshadowed by the possible negative consequences (''a kind god angered is a thousand times more evil. . .'').

The Gold Coast during the late nineteenth century.

A crab never fathers a bird.

Badua says this to Osam during one of their arguments about Anowa. Osam is trying to point out to Badua that Anowa has always been an unusual child, and that the fact that she left her home and family with her husband should come as no surprise. In explaining that Anowa has always been different, Osam mentions that others in their village "fear her," and that he himself "has always feared her." Badua retorts that "a crab never fathers a bird," meaning that, if Anowa is different and to be feared, and she is Osam's daughter, then Osam, too, must be different and feared by others. In other words, the child is a reflection on the parent, since the child can only be so different from her parents (one species cannot "father" another). Badua is trying to argue that Anowa is really not so strange and different from anyone else, just as Osam is not strange or different.

One stops wearing a hat only when the head has fallen off.

Or:

Our elders said that one never stops wearing hats on a head which still stands on its shoulders.

Anowa makes these statements at two different points in arguing with Kofi that she wishes to continue working, even though they have slaves to do their work for them. Anowa's point is that she was meant to work, and that doing work (like "wearing a hat") will continue to suit her until the day she dies ("only when the head has fallen off").

Aidoo's play consists primarily of pairs of couples—Badua and Osam, Anowa and Kofi, the Old Woman and the Old Man—arguing with one another over how Anowa has chosen to conduct her life. During the course of these arguments, each character refers to traditional sayings and proverbs in order to support her or his side of the argument. Part of Aidoo's project in writing this play was to record in writing, and reproduce on stage, elements from the oral tradition of African culture. These traditional proverbs are demonstrated to contain many universal wisdoms. At the same time, however, Aidoo plants a seed of doubt in the reader's mind as to the value of relying solely on traditional wisdom in making life decisions. At one point during an argument between Anowa and Kofi, Kofi suggests that such traditional wisdom is not always the best; he states that "proverbs do not always describe the truth of reality." This statement is important to the broader implications of the play, and the role of traditional proverbs in the dialogue. A central theme is that of tradition, and breaking with tradition. Anowa has broken with her family tradition in marrying a man of whom her mother does not approve, Kofi, and leaving their village with him, never to return. Just as tradition does not necessarily account for "the truth of reality" in Anowa's life, so, this line suggests, traditional wisdom, as expressed in these proverbs, is not always the best wisdom.

Source: Liz Brent, in an essay for *Literature of Developing Nations for Students*, Gale, 2000.

Sources

Aidoo, Ama Ata, *Anowa*, Longman Group, 1970.

Eke, Maureen N., "Diasporic Ruptures and (Re)Membering History: Africa as Home and Exile in *Anowa* and *The Dilemma of a Ghost*," in *Emerging Perspectives on Ama Ata Aidoo*, Africa World Press, 1999, p. 654.

Hill-Lubin, Mildre A., "Ama Ata Aidoo and the African Diaspora: Things 'All Good Men and Women Try to Forget,' but I Will Not Let Them," in *Emerging Perspectives on Ama Ata Aidoo*, Africa World Press, 1999, p. 49.

Horne, Naana Banyiwa, "The Politics of Mothering: Multiple Subjectivity and Gendered Discourse in Aidoo's Plays," in *Emerging Perspectives on Ama Ata Aidoo*, Africa World Press, 1999, p. 319.

Jones, Eldred Durosimi, review of *Anowa*, in *African Literature Today*, 1976, p. 143.

Karpf, Anne, "The Arrival of Aidoo," in *The Guardian*, September 8, 1995, p. T21.

Kingsley, Louise, review of *Anowa*, in *The Independent*, April 6, 1991, p. 24.

Odamtten, Vincent O., *The Art of Ama Ata Aidoo: Polylectics and Reading against Neocolonialism*, University Press of Florida, 1994, pp. 43, 46.

Phillips, Maggi, "Engaging Dreams: Alternative Perspectives on Flora Nwapa, Buchi Emecheta, Ama Ata Aidoo, Bessie Head, and Tsitsi Dangarembga's Writing," in *Research in African Literatures*, Winter, 1994, p. 89.

Rutherford, Malcolm, review of *Anowa*, in *Financial Times*, April 9, 1991, p. 23.

Further Reading

Hemming, Sarah, "Word of Mouth," in *The Independent*, April 3, 1991, p. 14.
    This article, in part an interview with Aidoo, compares *Anowa* with Aidoo's 1991 novel *Changes*.

McGregor, Maxine, "Ama Ata Aidoo," in *African Writers Talking: A Collection of Radio Interviews*, Cosmo Pieterse and Dennis Duerden, editors, Africana Publishing Corp., 1972, pp. 18-27.
    In this interview, Aidoo discusses her plays, theater in Ghana, and other writing-related issues.

Needham, Anuradha Dingwaney, "An Interview with Ama Ata Aidoo," in *The Massachusetts Review*, Spring, 1995.
    In this interview, Aidoo discusses feminism, nationalism, and her writing.

Uzoamaka, Ada, and Wilentz Azodo, Gay, eds., *Emerging Perspectives on Ama Ata Aidoo*, African World Press, 1999.
    This collection of critical essays covers the whole of Aidoo's canon, including several focusing on *Anowa*.

Anthills of the Savannah

Chinua Achebe

1987

After a twenty-one-year hiatus from writing, Chinua Achebe published *Anthills of the Savannah* in Great Britain in 1987. It was published in the United States the following year. The novel just prior to *Anthills of the Savannah* was *A Man of the People*, a book that foreshadows the military coups that would figure largely in Nigerian politics in the coming years. To many of Achebe's readers, *Anthills of the Savannah* is the logical extension of this novel as it depicts the inner workings and consequences of such a coup.

Critical reception was overwhelmingly positive, and many critics regard this novel as Achebe's best to date. Achebe was already respected as one of the founding fathers of Nigeria's literary coming-of-age, so the success of *Anthills of the Savannah* only confirmed his place among Nigeria's leading intellectuals. In 1987 *Anthills of the Savannah* was a finalist for the Booker Prize, Britain's most prestigious literary award.

Anthills of the Savannah tells the story of three schoolmates who become major figures in a new regime in the fictional West African land of Kangan. Achebe addresses the course unbridled power often takes and demonstrates how the fierce pursuit of self-interest comes at tremendous cost to the community as a whole. Critics note that this novel is a departure for the author in that he creates fully developed female characters and suggests that the

women are sources of moral strength, tradition, and hope in the face of violence and deception.

Author Biography

Born in eastern Nigeria on November 16, 1930, Chinua Achebe was deeply influenced by the Ibo (one of the three major ethnic groups in Nigeria) and by the British colonial and post-colonial elements of contemporary African society. His father, one of the first Christian converts in the village, was a member of the Church Missionary Society and strongly discouraged his son from accepting native, non-Christian belief systems. Still, Achebe was drawn to the traditional beliefs and mythology of the Ibo. He began to learn English at the age of eight, and at fourteen he was selected to attend the Government College at Unuahia, one of West Africa's best schools. In 1948, he became a student in the first class at University College in Ibadan. Although intending to study medicine, he soon changed in favor of English coursework.

One year after graduating with honors in 1953, Achebe went to work for the Nigerian Broadcasting Company. His radio career ended, however, in 1966, when he left his position as Director of External Broadcasting in Nigeria during the political and religious unrest leading to the Biafran War, a civil war that lasted from 1967 to 1970. Achebe joined the Biafran Ministry of Information and became involved in fundraising and diplomatic endeavors, a role similar to that of Chris Osodi in *Anthills of the Savannah*. In 1971, Achebe became the editor of *Nigerian Journal of New Writing*. Achebe is also a respected lecturer and teacher. From 1972 to 1975, he was Professor of English at University of Massachusetts at Amherst, and in 1987 he accepted a year-long position as Professor of African Studies at University of Connecticut at Storrs. In addition, he has been Professor Emeritus at University of Nigeria at Nsukka since 1984.

Achebe began to exercise his writing ability while still working in radio, but it was not until he left broadcasting that he began to pursue writing seriously. His work includes poetry, short stories, children's writing, and novels. Achebe was one of the first to write in English about the contours and complexities of African culture. His first novel, *Things Fall Apart*, published in 1958, remains his best-known. Upon its publication, Achebe earned a reputation as a writer with a uniquely African point of view who could write honestly about British colonialism in Nigeria. Achebe published *No Longer at Ease*, *The Sacrificial Egg and Other Stories*, *Arrow of God*, and *A Man of the People*, then waited twenty-one years to publish *Anthills of the Savannah* in 1987. His work since then includes *Hopes and Impediments: Selected Essays 1965-1987* and *Beyond Hunger in Africa*.

Regarded as one of the founders of Nigeria's literary development, Achebe uses his work to call for an end to oppression and a return to order, integrity, and beauty. He continues to combine his role as a storyteller with a sense of responsibility to write with purpose and to instruct his readers.

Plot Summary

Part I

Set in the fictitious West African country of Kangan, *Anthills of the Savannah* opens with a meeting of the regime's president and his Cabinet. The government has been in place for two years, since a coup overthrew the former dictator. Three men, friends since childhood, have assumed important positions in the new system. Sam is the president, Chris Oriko is the Commissioner of Information, and Ikem Osodi is the editor of the government-controlled newspaper, the *National Gazette*. Ikem is an intellectual and a poet who is very outspoken about the need to reform the government. Chris acts as a mediator between Ikem and Sam.

Sam has become a leader without regard for his people, seeking only to acquire more power for himself by any means necessary. Chris and Ikem realize that Sam is rapidly becoming a dictator. They helped get him appointed to the position, even encouraging him when he felt that his military background was inadequate preparation for a position of such importance. Now, Chris and Ikem regret their previous support of their friend and seek to control Sam in their own ways. Meanwhile, Sam's obsession with power has made him paranoid and temperamental. When Sam decides he wants to be elected "President-for-Life," a national referendum is called but the region of Abazon refuses to participate. Sam in turn denies the region access to water despite a drought, expecting that without water or food the people will give in. When delegates from Abazon arrive at the capital on a mission for mercy, Sam suspects that they are actually planning an insurrection. In fact, his paranoia leads

Chinua Achebe

him to believe that the insurrection is being assisted by someone close to him.

Although Chris is aware of how dangerous Sam is becoming, he believes that by staying in his government position he can serve his country. Meanwhile, Ikem's editorials are becoming more radical, and Chris tries to convince him to tone them down.

Ikem has a girlfriend, Elewa, who is semi-literate and works in a shop. She is pregnant with his child. Chris's fiancee, Beatrice, is a well-educated woman who holds a position as administrator for one of the state offices. She has known Ikem since youth and works for Sam, so she has connections to all of the major characters. She observes the government's activities and Chris's and Ikem's reactions, and feels that she is the only one sensitive enough to truly understand the situation. She expresses to Chris and Ikem that they are approaching the problem incorrectly because they are not really connecting to the people and the land.

Part II

Sam commands Chris to fire Ikem from his position as editor, at which point Chris responds in a highly unusual way—he refuses to obey Sam's order. Sam believes that Ikem is involved in the "protest" staged by the delegates of Abazon, but

Chris knows better. Still, Ikem is fired and soon after addresses a student group at a university. Never one to hold his tongue, he is very vocal about his criticism of the government. He makes a joke about the regime minting coins with Sam's head on them, which is turned into propaganda claiming that Ikem has called for the beheading of the president. Ikem is taken from his home in the middle of the night and shot and killed by the state police.

Part III

Chris realizes just how dangerous Sam has become and goes into hiding after using his contacts within the international press to publicize the truth about Ikem's murder. With the help of Emmanuel, a student leader who greatly admires Chris; Abdul, a sympathetic cab driver; and a small covert network of supporters, Chris is able to escape the capital city of Bassa by bus and head for Abazon. Meanwhile, the government orders Chris's arrest and threatens anyone found to be withholding information about him.

On the bus trip, Chris begins to feel reconnected to his native land and Emmanuel meets a beautiful student named Adamma. The bus is stopped by a mob caught up in a drunken frenzy. They are celebrating the news that Sam has been killed and his regime overthrown in another coup. As Chris and the other bus passengers make their way through the crowd, gathering bits of information, Chris sees Adamma being dragged off by a soldier to be raped. Chris rushes to her rescue, and the soldier shoots and kills him.

Part IV

Emmanuel, Abdul, and Adamma return to Bassa to tell Beatrice and the others what has happened. Although grief-stricken, Beatrice hosts a naming ceremony for Ikem's baby girl, born after his murder. Men traditionally perform the ceremony, but Beatrice fulfills this role, naming the child Amaechina, a boy's name that means "May the Path Never Close."

Characters

Abdul

A cab driver and family man sympathetic to Chris's plight, he uses his cab to help Chris get out of the city and works with Emmanuel to make the plans to get Chris up north.

Adamma

One of the passengers on the bus taken by Chris, Emmanuel, and Abdul as they leave Bassa and head north to safety, Adamma is about to be raped when Chris steps in to save her. As a result, Chris is shot and killed, and Adamma returns to Kangan with Emmanuel.

Agatha

Agatha is Beatrice's flighty, religious, and judgmental house girl. She is a devout Christian who attends services regularly and does not hide her disapproval of Beatrice's allowing Chris into her bed. Beatrice is often impatient and short with Agatha, but as the novel progresses, she begins to feel more compassion for her.

Elewa

Ikem's pregnant girlfriend, Elewa represents the common people. Unlike Chris, Ikem, and Beatrice, she is semiliterate and works in a shop. She is highly emotional and expressive. Through Elewa, Beatrice comes to understand that coming from humble origins does not necessarily make a person frail or insecure. On the contrary, Elewa's emotional displays belie her resilience and self-confidence.

General Ahmed Lango

General Lango is a duplicitous man who works his way into Sam's inner circle, only to lead the coup that will overthrow and kill him.

Emmanuel Obote

Emmanuel is a student who is a leader at his university and a great admirer of Chris. When Chris flees for his life, Emmanuel accompanies him and helps make the complex plans involved in trying to get Chris out of danger. He is also with Chris when he is killed and returns to tell Beatrice of his dignity even at the moment of death. Emmanuel stands in contrast to the typical students described by Ikem during his speech at the university, in which he referred to students and workers as the most derelict in their civic duties. Achebe seems to suggest that Emmanuel will continue Chris's work in encouraging people to think for themselves regardless of environmental hardship.

Beatrice Okoh

Chris's fiancee, Beatrice is one of Achebe's most fully developed female characters. She works for Sam and is an old friend of Ikem's, so, through her connections to Chris, Ikem, and Sam, she plays a significant role in the action of the novel. She was born the fifth daughter to her parents (one sister has died). Her father had been hoping for a son, so she was named Nwanyibuife, which means "A Woman Is Also Something" As an adult, Beatrice is well-educated, having earned a degree with honors in English from the University of London, and she holds an important civil service position as an administrator in a state office. She also enjoys writing short fiction, which Ikem reads and admires for its "muscularity" and "masculine" qualities.

Beatrice is characterized by sophistication, intelligence, and independence, but she is also attuned to the common people on an intuitive level. Never having planned on a career in the government, she is very disturbed by accusations that she is ambitious. In reality, she desires what she has desired since childhood—to be left alone in her peaceful solitude and not attract any attention. Achebe places her firmly in the mythic tradition of the people, making her a sort of manifestation of Idemili, a goddess sent to Man to oversee morality. Although Beatrice is unaware of the myths regarding this goddess, she grows into a woman possessed with wisdom, self-knowledge, and compassion as she connects with the culture of her land. At the end of the novel, she participates in the naming ceremony for Ikem and Elewa's baby girl by naming the infant Amaechina, a boy's name meaning "May the Path Never Close." This is bold not only because she has given a boy's name to a girl, but also because the responsibility of naming traditionally belongs to a man.

Professor Reginald Okong

A former Baptist minister and political scientist, Professor Okong was one of the first people Chris recommended for Sam's Cabinet. Chris comes to regret this decision, however, when he sees that Okong "has no sense of political morality."

Christopher Oriko

In his youth, Chris attended Lord Lugard College with his friends Ikem and Sam. Even then, he served as the "buffer" and mediator between the athletic and outgoing Sam and the intelligent and pensive Ikem. As adults, the three occupy prominent roles in Kangan's new military regime, and Chris's role as Commissioner for Information again puts him in the position of go-between as Sam and Ikem engage in a contest of wills. Chris stepped down as editor of the *National Gazette* to accept his position on Sam's Cabinet, after which Ikem became the newspaper's editor. Chris is now Ikem's boss, but he himself reports to Sam, which puts him in the uncomfortable position of trying to get Ikem to comply with Sam's will. Although Chris sees Sam becoming mad with power, he is reluctant to give up his position in the Cabinet. Chris finally asserts himself when Sam orders him to fire Ikem, thus beginning a harrowing series of events. Fleeing for his life, Chris comes into contact with the ''people'' and begins to understand his country better. Chris is killed trying to save a girl from being raped at a chaotic party, and his last words are, ''The last green.'' This is a reference to a running joke he, Ikem, and Sam shared in the early days, when they imagined themselves as three green bottles arrogantly situated on a shelf, each bound to fall.

Ikem Osodi

Ikem is the outspoken and reform-minded editor of the state-owned *National Gazette,* a position that often puts him in conflict with his boyhood friend, Sam, who is the president of Kangan. Part of his duty is to broadcast Sam's messages to the people, which are Sam's way of feeling that he is radiating power from the capitol out to the people. Ikem, on the other hand, believes strongly that the press should be free and independent of government regulation. He and Chris often debate the effectiveness of Ikem's editorials, but Ikem feels that even if they are futile, he should continue publishing them.

Despite the fact that he is a London-educated intellectual, Ikem is very sensitive to the needs of the common people. His editorials are often harsh in their criticism of the new ruling regime, which makes Sam regard him as treacherous. Ikem states that the best weapon against ineffective or unjust governments is not facts, but passion. Unlike Chris, Ikem is an extremist who is not interested in working gradually toward progress and so uses his powerful position as a journalist to call for change. Speaking to a group of students, Ikem discusses the role of the storyteller in depth, insisting that it is the role of the writer to ask questions and make challenges. He concludes his speech to the students by proclaiming, ''Writers don't give prescriptions. They give headaches!'' Ikem also makes a joke about

putting Sam's head on the country's coins, which leads to false reports that Ikem called for the beheading of the president. His fate already orchestrated, Ikem is taken in the night by government secret police and killed. Still, his presence continues to be felt among the people and his friends—a presence strengthened by the fact that he leaves behind a girlfriend close to giving birth to their child.

Major Johnson Ossai

Major Ossai is the head of Sam's security force, the State Research Council (SRC). He is a brutal, menacing, and evil man who calms Sam's insecurities whenever possible. Among his methods of torture is using a simple stapler on the hands of those from whom he needs information.

Sam

Sam is the new president of the military regime in power following a coup, a position he holds due in no small part to the efforts of his schoolmates Chris and Ikem. He is described as being very athletic and very charming, having adopted the ways of an English gentleman. Early in the novel, Ikem comments on Sam's ''sense of theatre,'' adding that Sam ''is basically an actor and half of the things we are inclined to hold against him are no more than scenes from his repertory to which he may have no sense of moral commitment whatsoever.'' Although he attended the prestigious Royal Military Academy at Sandhurst, Sam is fully aware that he is unprepared for his new government leadership role. However, he soon becomes blinded by power, insisting on being called ''Your Excellency'' and seeking to be elected ''President for Life.'' Military school trained Sam and his fellow cadets to remain aloof from political matters, and Sam was, at first, quite terrified in his new role. His solution was to gather together his friends and give some of them government positions from which he could seek their advice. Once he overcame his fear, however, he began to relish his power, becoming extremely upset at even the mildest demonstrations against him.

Chris can see that Sam is now a dictator-in-the-making and considers him a ''baby monster,'' but Sam is only concerned about securing as much power for himself as he can without interacting with the people of the country. In fact, he is starving a dissident province in hopes of forcing them to comply with his authority. He soon becomes consumed with paranoia, anger, and insecurity, and when his political ambitions are disappointed, he recalls being told how dangerous boyhood friends can be. After he arranges for Ikem's murder and Chris has fled, Sam himself is killed during a coup and buried in a shallow grave.

Themes

Overcoming a History of Suffering

The end of the novel offers a little hope but also shows that the political unrest of Kangan cannot be addressed by simple solutions. The people want change and peace but are unsure how to attain a suitable system of government, especially when each successive regime is made up of members of the coup that overthrew the last regime. It is a system driven by sheer might and strength as opposed to justice, philosophy, or respect for the land. The novel also portrays a strong and enduring sense of community among the people, despite the fact that they have no political rights. Achebe suggests that this unity is what keeps the community and its heritage and culture intact even when it is ravaged by unjust political regimes.

Individual Power

In its depiction of Sam, *Anthills of the Savannah* provides a perfect example of the saying, "Power corrupts, and absolute power corrupts absolutely." Unprepared for leadership beyond the military realm, Sam finds himself occupying the position of president of Kangan. Relishing his power, he insists on being called "Your Excellency" and decides that he wants to be elected President-for-Life. At the same time, he makes little effort to connect with the people of Kangan and relies heavily on his Cabinet while simultaneously belittling them. In the end his obsession, paranoia, and insecurity get the better of him, and he goes so far as to have a childhood friend (Ikem) killed because he is perceived as a threat.

At the beginning of the novel, Sam is still a "baby monster," but as the action unfolds, Sam grows into a full-fledged evil dictator. Achebe shows the dangers of blindly pursuing power at the expense of the community. Sam has no regard for the people he is supposed to be leading, and for that they suffer.

Storytelling

Throughout *Anthills of the Savannah* there are references to stories, narratives, and the storyteller.

Achebe writes that "the story is everlasting" and that "storytellers are a threat." Three of the novel's main characters are writers: Ikem is a writer and newspaper editor, Beatrice writes short stories, and Chris is a former journalist who left his post as editor of the *National Gazette* to accept the position of Commissioner of Information. The elder from Abazon speaks at length about the important and lasting role of the storyteller. He argues that in his youth he would have said that the battle was most important, but now that he is older and wiser, he understands that the story is more powerful. Through stories, a community can retain its sense of history and tradition and seek guidance for the future. He explains, "Because it is only the story that can continue beyond the war and the warrior. . .The story is our escort; without it, we are blind." Later, as Ikem addresses a group of students, he expresses his belief that the role of the writer is to ask questions, not to propose solutions. Critics have observed that this is perhaps what Achebe is doing with this novel.

The power of writing is shown after Ikem is taken away in the dark of night and killed. To get the truth about the event into public awareness, Chris uses his contacts within the international press as a means of informing the world about what happened to Ikem.

The Role of Women

Anthills of the Savannah is often noted for portraying strong, believable female characters. In the midst of political strife and injustice, the women maintain a connection with their heritage and culture, and stand for moral strength and sensitivity. Ikem converses with Beatrice about his newfound respect for the position and relevance of women in contemporary society. He explains that women are the most oppressed group of people worldwide and that they must be respected as important to the future of a nation.

At the end of the novel, the naming ceremony takes place for Elewa's infant girl. Although men traditionally name children, Beatrice does so in this case. In this scene, Achebe portrays women as the keepers of tradition, even if tradition must be altered to accommodate modern life. To further blur the lines between masculinity and femininity, the baby is given a boy's name that means "May the Path Never Close." Many critics have commented that Achebe's portrayal of women in *Anthills of the Savannah* suggests that they are critical in the growth of new African societies.

Topics for Further Study

- Consider the rise to power of three dictators in world history and provide a comparison and contrast to Sam's rise to power. In what ways is his background different from those of other dictators? In what ways is it similar? How does each figure handle power and relate to the public? Based on your findings, would you say that Achebe paints a realistic picture of a dictator-in-the-making?

- Read about Idi Amin and his regime in Uganda. Many critics maintain that this was the model on which Achebe based his portrayal of Sam and the fictional land of Kangan. Others believe Kangan is modeled after Nigeria. What are your conclusions? Why do you suppose Achebe chose to create a fictional country rather than making the setting for his novel an actual place?

- Imagine that instead of being killed, Ikem is imprisoned. As an outspoken writer, he will certainly continue his efforts as best he can from behind bars. Write a letter to the people in Ikem's voice. For reference, you might read Martin Luther King Jr.'s ''Letter from a Birmingham Jail.''

- Amaechina is born into a time of tremendous upheaval and instability. Her father is a well-known figure who has been killed and her mother is a simple woman left to raise the child on her own. Given Amaechina's environment, heritage, and family situation, create brief sketches of what you imagine she will be doing at the ages of 20, 40, and 80. Be sure your speculations are supported by the material presented in the novel.

- Research anthills and find out what happens to them during fires. Apply what you have learned to the title and suggest the possible meaning(s).

Style

Point of View

Anthills of the Savannah provides a complete view of the action of the novel by offering multiple points of view. Achebe allows the reader to see the situation from the points of view of Ikem, Chris, and Beatrice, and also, in some passages, from that of a third-person, omniscient narrator. This technique enables the reader to make judgments for him/herself rather than relying on a narrator or a single character to supply descriptions of people and events. This also is a way in which Achebe retains the part of his African literary heritage that focuses on the community rather than on the individual.

Setting

The novel takes place in the fictitious West African land of Kangan. Its borders were arbitrarily drawn by the British colonialists. Some critics maintain that the country is modeled after Achebe's native Nigeria, while others see it as a version of Idi Amin's Uganda. Regardless, Kangan is a contemporary African nation struggling to find stability in postcolonial times. Although the setting is contemporary, there are elements of tradition that reflect consistency in the community and among the people. Tradition is perhaps the strongest source of security and gives the people a feeling of unity.

The setting also takes the reader into the government headquarters—a privilege not afforded to the citizens of Kangan. Whereas the public is forced to rely on hearsay and the press to learn what is happening within the government, the reader can see first-hand how the regime is being run, how it is changing, and how the various forces work together or against each other in the unstable military regime.

Language

Most of the dialogue of the ordinary people of Kangan is written in the dialect of Pidgin English. The unusual grammar and unfamiliar words of this dialect can be difficult for Western readers, but its inclusion gives the novel a strong sense of realism. In addition, it is easy to identify a character's level of education or social standing based on his or her manner of speech. Chris, Beatrice, and Ikem are sympathetic as characters, as they are able to interact with common people by speaking Pidgin English and with powerful political figures by speaking British English. Rather than distance themselves from the ordinary citizen, as Sam does, Chris, Beatrice, and Ikem routinely abandon their British English in favor of being able to communicate in a meaningful way.

Blending of Old and New

Achebe is often praised for his skillful blending of folklore, myth, proverbs, and customs with modern Western political ideologies and Christian belief systems. By presenting these two approaches, Achebe asserts his belief in the power of the past to ease the excesses and confusion of the present.

In a similar vein, Achebe was the first Nigerian writer to apply the conventions of the novel to African storytelling. Well aware of the strong oral tradition of African literature, Achebe found a way to write honestly about Africa in a way that is accessible for an international audience. *Anthills of the Savannah* was originally written in English, and by adopting a structure that is familiar to his English-speaking audience, he makes his African storytelling available without compromising the integrity of his heritage. At the same time, Nigerians can benefit from his writing because English is their official language.

Literary Heritage

Typical of African cultures, Nigeria's storytelling comes from a long oral tradition. This tradition allowed generations to benefit from African literature despite widespread illiteracy. Folktales, legends, verse, myths, and proverbs were preserved in the memories of the people and communicated by performance or simple recitation. As in other societies, myths in African culture explain the wonders of nature, provide creation narratives, and relate the activities of divine beings. Legends, on the other hand, generally describe the actions of people and

often commemorate heroes. The purpose of oral literature is not only to entertain, but also to instruct and honor.

The strong oral tradition in Africa is a major influence for twentieth-century Nigerian writers such as Amos Tutuola, Chinua Achebe, and Nobel Prize-winner Wole Soyinka. Achebe, for example, writes in the traditional novel form in a personalized way that draws from the deep resources of his Nigerian heritage. In her book *Long Drums and Cannons: Nigerian Dramatists and Novelists,* Margaret Laurence observed that beginning in the 1950s Nigeria experienced "the flourishing of a new literature which has drawn sustenance both from the traditional oral literature and from the present and rapidly changing society."

Historical Context

Political Instability

Growing up in Nigeria, Achebe saw for himself how disruptive social upheaval and political instability are and how they affect every facet of a society. He was born during Nigeria's colonial years, a period of tremendous conflict and sociopolitical change. Achebe grew up during the ensuing period of nationalist protest. Once Nigeria gained independence in 1960, vestiges of the colonial years remained, including borders and new political ideas and structures.

When Achebe left his position with the Nigerian Broadcasting Company in 1966, he accepted the position of Biafran Minister of Information. (It is likely that this experience informed his creation of Chris, the Commissioner of Information in *Anthills of the Savannah* .) The Republic of Biafra was a short-lived Ibo state created upon secession. The Ibo decided to found their own state after witnessing the massacre of 10,000 to 30,000 of their people by Islamic Hausa and Fulani people, rival ethnic groups. Anticipating further bloodshed, the Republic of Biafra announced its independence in 1967. Unfortunately, the announcement was not accepted, and a civil war ensued that lasted until 1970, when Biafra surrendered. A food shortage caused by the war brought about the deaths of close to a million people.

At the time *Anthills of the Savannah* was published, political unrest continued to dominate Nige-

Compare & Contrast

- **1787:** The United States wins its independence from Great Britain. Since then, politics has been, among other things, a forum for debate among ethnic and religious groups. At first there was little room for diversity in political office, but over the years this imbalance has improved.

  1960: Nigeria wins its independence from Great Britain. Since then, politics has been characterized by rivalry and distrust between ethnic and religious groups.

- **1787:** The United States Constitution is ratified and remains in place ever since. The American system of government calls for the election of a president to a four-year term and the election of representatives to Congress, made up of the House of Representatives and the Senate. The United States also has a Supreme Court.

  1978: The first Nigerian constitution is ratified. However, it is thrown out in 1983. A new one is

created in 1989, but in 1993 the 1978 version is called back to replace it. Nigeria's system of government calls for the election of a president to a four-year term and for a Supreme Court. The National Assembly, made up of a House of Representatives and a Senate, is dissolved after the 1993 coup.

- **1704:** The United States sees its first continuous newspaper, *Boston News-Letter,* published. The First Amendment is ratified in 1791 and includes protection of freedom of the press. Today, sixty-three million copies of various newspapers are circulated every day.

  1830s: Nigeria establishes its first newspaper. To this day, the federal government has an interest in several of the major newspapers, although censorship is infrequent. By the 1990s over twenty English-speaking daily newspapers are in circulation.

ria. In August of 1985 a military coup, responding to the growing discontent of the people, overthrew the existing authoritarian military regime. The new leader accepted the role of president, banning members of certain past regimes from political involvement for a period of ten years. A few years later, the first tentative steps toward civilian rule were taken.

The Role of Women

Even before Europeans arrived during the colonial period, Achebe's native Nigeria was a male-dominated society. Ikem explains to Beatrice that their culture initially regarded women as lowly and unworthy of respect and then elevated them to a pedestal, where they could remain beautiful and admired but inconsequential. Similarly, the worship of goddesses was an important part of a village's spiritual life but had little to do with decisions regarding power structures. The colonial period widened the gender equality gap by providing African men with educational opportunities while Afri-

can women received schooling in utilitarian skills to prepare them for domestic work. *Anthills of the Savannah*, published in 1987, came at a time when women around the world had made great strides in asserting their relevance in and value to society.

Oral Tradition

As central as the oral tradition is to African cultures, the widespread use of the printed word, radio, and television threatens to render this important tradition obsolete. With *Anthills of the Savannah* Achebe offers a story of the people told by the people (by using multiple viewpoints) and emphasizes the central role of the storyteller in African society. This message comes from various sources, ranging from the village elder of Abazon to the erudite and well-educated Ikem. Achebe reconciles the tension between the oral tradition and the printed word, demonstrating that one does not have to yield to the other as both make worthy contributions to contemporary African society.

Critical Overview

Achebe is revered as one of the founders of modern Nigerian literature for his historically sensitive and insightful novels about his native land and its people. He is praised for his ability to artfully combine traditional folklore and tradition with Western ideologies, and critics are quick to note that Achebe's writing is relevant to a multitude of societies, not just those of Africa. Still, Achebe is first and foremost a contemporary African writer writing novels that carry important messages about and for his people.

Upon the release of *Anthills of the Savannah,* critics responded by praising the author's refined insights and discipline, often attributing them to his twenty-plus-year hiatus. Nadine Gordimer of *New York Times Book Review* commented that the novel "is a work in which twenty-two years of harsh experience, intellectual growth, self-criticism, deepening understanding, and mustered discipline of skill open wide a subject to which Mr. Achebe is now magnificently equal." A. Ravenscroft of *Literary Criterion* commented on the cross-country bus trip taken by Chris and his sympathizers in which Chris comes to appreciate the depth of his heritage. Ravenscroft wrote that if Achebe had ended the novel at this point, "it would have meant that in the twenty-one years since *A Man of the People,* Achebe had learned only to confirm the rather bleak, intellectually cynical vision of political Africa that the earlier novel tends to project. Now, however, the urban masses comprise people with individual lineaments. And the final chapter, even with its acrid question: 'What must a people do to appease an embittered history?' is about the unorthodox, strangely ecumenical naming ceremony for Ikem's child, performed by Chris's woman-friend Beatrice."

Achebe's presentation of the corrupting nature of power is admired by readers and critics alike. Fellow Nigerian Ben Okri noted in *Observer,* "This is a study of how power corrupts itself and by doing so begins to die." Other critics view the senseless deaths of the three former schoolmates as representative of a generation willing to sacrifice its self-knowledge in exchange for power. Related to this idea is Okri's observation that the end of the novel implies that power is better left within the "awakened spirit of the people" than given to the political elite. Similarly, in *Research in African Literatures* Neil Kortenaar described Sam as an illustration of the dangers of a regime or government system that is disconnected from its citizens.

As for most of his novels, Achebe is commended for his use of language in *Anthills of the Savannah.* According to Joseph Swann in *Crisis and Creativity in the New Literature in English,* Achebe's use of multiple narrative voices indicates that history is more than a set of events in the past to be told; it is also the feelings and ideas that different people have about the events. Critics also agree that Achebe writes in Western English without sacrificing the integrity of his characters or their African settings and is capable of writing dignified speech as well as he writes dialect when necessary. The frequent use of Pidgin English in the novel, however, posed a problem for a few critics who felt it might alienate Achebe's international readers. Ravenscroft, on the other hand, found that its inclusion represents unity in diversity: "With political orthodoxies side-stepped, the sounds of hope come through across a range of diverse language levels—the sophisticated English of the educated elite, the demotic [everyday] Pidgin of the people, the proverbial and parable-like cadences of the Abazon elder, the liturgical incantation of Ikem's 'Hymn to the Sun,' the lyricism of Beatrice's temple-priestess lovemaking with Chris, the transformation of traditional kolanut ritual into litany for blessings not only upon the infant being named but upon all life of Kangan."

To many critics, Achebe offers in *Anthills of the Savannah* the message that Nigeria herself must take responsibility for her state of disarray. Certainly, the colonial period ushered in a host of problems, he seems to say, but ultimately the country itself must pick up its own burden and cure its own ills. In *New York Review of Books* Neal Ascherson wrote, "In this new novel . . . Chinua Achebe says, with implacable honesty, that Africa itself is to blame, and that there is no safety in excuses that place the fault in the colonial past or in the commercial and political manipulations of the First World."

Criticism

Jennifer Bussey

Bussey holds a bachelor's degree in English literature and a master's degree in interdisciplinary studies. She is an independent writer specializing in literature. In the following essay, she explores spirituality as a source of hope in Anthills of the Savannah.

Achebe's involvement with Nigeria's political struggle, a struggle marked by coups, a civil war, and elections marred by violence, is echoed in Anthills of the Savannah. *In this picture, villagers watch Nigerian federal troops in a Biafran town.*

Many critics and readers of *Anthills of the Savannah* are left with a sense of hopelessness at the end of the novel. Three of the novel's four main characters have died senseless deaths, and the country is left in the throes of instability. Free of one military regime, it faces another, with no reason to believe that this one will be any better than the last two. Even so, Achebe weaves a story that is not completely devoid of optimism; there are elements of hope and unity, but the reader, like the people of Kangan, must search for them. There is a subtle spirituality running through the novel, and Achebe seems to suggest that the spirit of the people cannot be defeated, even by a series of dictators and corrupt governments. This enduring spirit is what binds the people together and maintains a sense of community that offers the weary Kangans a degree of stability and buoyancy.

Achebe is the son of a missionary and has spent much of his life in Western cultures. Therefore, he is fully aware of the significance of the number three to the Christian belief system, and he uses it twice in *Anthills of the Savannah.* There are three male figures who dominate the novel: the dictator, Sam; the editor, Ikem; and the Commissioner of Informa-

tion, Chris. The three men met in their early teenage years while attending the same school, yet each took a very different path in adulthood. They came from similar backgrounds, which illustrates that predicting the course of a person's life is not a simple task: Tossing three seeds in the same soil may result in three differing plants. Achebe's group of three main characters do not represent religious figures, but they are three aspects of the same entity, and therefore comprise a sort of trinity. They make up a political system that will not work and is destined to fail. Sam represents power driven by self-interest. Ikem represents the desire for reform. He is outspoken and admired by the people, and prefers to do things his way without compromising. Chris represents efforts to work for good within the system. He is a good man in a bad regime, and he is idealistic enough to believe that by staying in the government he can serve his people. By the end, of course, the regime has been toppled, replaced by another that will surely be just like it. When a system dies, so do its components, and as representatives of different aspects of the failed system, each of the three men is killed—Sam by another just like him, Ikem by his own peers, and Chris by an evil man who would rather murder than behave honorably.

What Do I Read Next?

- Achebe's first novel, *Things Fall Apart*, was published in 1958. It is the story of Okonkwo, an extremely proud and brusque man who is ultimately unable to adapt to the collapse of village life as he has always known it.

- *A Man of the People* was Achebe's last novel before his extended leave from novel-writing. When he returned to the literary scene with *Anthills of the Savannah* many critics viewed it as a logical continuation of *A Man of the People*, which predicts the coups that would plague Nigeria.

- *A Good Man in Africa* was published in 1981 by William Boyd. Set in West Africa, it is the award-winning story of a man whose political ambitions are thwarted on every front.

- *Grain of Wheat*, James Ngugi's 1994 novel, is set in war-torn Kenya, where five friends are forced to make choices for themselves, and each takes a very different path. The novel suggests that politicians, not the people, enjoy the greatest benefits of independence.

- Harold Scheub's 2000 collection, *A Dictionary of African Mythology: The Mythmaker As Storyteller*, contains 400 stories and myths gathered on his journeys throughout Africa.

- *African Canvas: The Art of West African Women*, published in 1990, features the pottery, murals, and body art of West African women. The book features a foreword by Maya Angelou.

The story also contains a female trinity in the characters of Beatrice, Elewa, and Amaechina. Beatrice is well-educated, sophisticated, and independent, and she holds an administrative position in the government. Beatrice represents the positive aspects of the present. Elewa is a common woman who is highly emotional and uneducated. She supports herself by working in a small shop. Elewa represents the past. Amaechina is Elewa's infant daughter, and although she does not appear until the end of the novel, she is potential embodied. As Ikem's daughter, she represents the meaning of her name, "May the Path Never Close." She is hope for the future, even though the future currently looks grim.

Beatrice and Elewa do not seem to have much in common, and readers may be surprised by their friendship. Their commitment to each other, however, is undeniable. Upon receiving the news of Chris's death, Beatrice is in complete shock. Achebe wrote, "In spite of her toughness Beatrice actually fared worse than Elewa in the first shock of bereavement. For weeks she sprawled in total devastation. Then one morning she rose up, as it were, and distanced herself from her thoughts. It was the morning of Elewa's threatened miscarriage. From that day she addressed herself to the well-being of the young woman through the remaining weeks to her confinement." Despite their differences, Beatrice and Elewa have a few important qualities in common, most notably that they have lost the men they loved deeply yet remain connected to each other and to the spirit of the community.

Amaechina's naming ceremony is significant because it demonstrates the women's unwillingness to allow tradition to die simply because the father is not present to conduct the ritual. Beatrice resists the trappings of ceremony and takes the place that would normally be filled by a man, that of naming the infant. When Elewa's drunk uncle witnesses this, he responds not by reprimanding the women but by cheering for them. He says, "Do you know why I am laughing like this? I am laughing because in you young people our world has met its match. Yes! You have put the world where it should sit. . .You gather in this. . .house and give the girl a boy's name. . .That is how to handle the world!" The women signify the refusal to let go of the

> There is a subtle spirituality running through the novel, and Achebe seems to suggest that the spirit of the people cannot be defeated, even by a series of dictators and corrupt governments. This enduring spirit is what binds the people together and maintains a sense of community that offers the weary Kangans a degree of stability and buoyancy."

traditions so critical to their culture and in doing so they honor their heritage and maintain a meaningful link to the spirit of the people.

Beatrice is the novel's single most spiritual character. Achebe identifies her strongly with the goddess Idemili, who was sent to Earth by the Almighty to moderate Power. When the Almighty saw how Power was raging across the Earth, he decided to send Idemili "to bear witness to the moral nature of authority by wrapping around Power's rude waist a loincloth of peace and modesty." She was sent to Earth in a Pillar of Water connecting heaven and earth and has been worshipped ever since. On the night Ikem visits Beatrice and they discuss his newfound respect for the important role women should be given in society, Ikem tells her that it was not raining at his house but that when he started out to see her, it "was literally like barging into a pillar of rain"—a clear reference to the goddess. In another scene, Beatrice is summoned to the palace for a dinner. As the evening progresses, she notices that an American reporter is becoming overly familiar and suggestive with Sam. Although Beatrice is not an admirer of Sam's, she is a patriot to her country and cannot stand to see its leader the object of such shameless overtures by a foreigner. In order to avert his attention, she throws herself at him, dancing with him "like the dancer in a Hindu temple." Once Sam is fully aroused and no longer thinking of the reporter, Beatrice leads him outside

and explains her actions to him. Sam calls her a racist and sends her home immediately. This scene shows that Beatrice, like Idemili, is compelled to uphold peace and morality by wrapping a loincloth, so to speak, around Power's rude waist.

There are other, more subtle clues that Beatrice is much more than an everyday government employee or citizen of Kangan. The name Beatrice comes from the Latin root "beatus" meaning "happy," from the past participle "beare," meaning "to bless." Other words with these roots are "beatify," "beatific," and "beatitudes," all related to blessedness and joy. Beatrice is known by this name, not the name her father gave her, Nwanyibuife, meaning "A Woman Is Also Something." Another well-known Beatrice in literature is Dante's guide through heaven in *Paradiso,* the last of the three books in his *Divine Comedy.* As Achebe's Beatrice grows into the fullness of her identity, she acquires wisdom and a presence that commands respect. Her experiences have shown her that the real strength of her people is in their unity and enduring spirit because these are not crushed, even when the land is ravaged by political instability and social upheaval.

Chris comes to grasp the spirit of his community when he embarks on his bus trip to Abazon. Although the purpose of the trip is his flight to safety, he finds himself reconnecting with the people who have committed to helping him. Looking out the bus window, he has the opportunity to revisit the landscape that was so distant to him from the capitol building where he worked. His experiences help him realize that Beatrice was right about his alienation from his own people, and as he reaches into the deep reservoirs of his own culture, he finds that he is on a journey of self-discovery. In his heritage, he begins to find himself. As Chris comes to realize that Bassa is far removed from the rest of Kangan, "the ensuing knowledge seeped through every pore in his skin into the core of his being, continuing the transformation, already in process, of the man he was." Failing to undergo such a reconnection with the land, or even to accept that he was disconnected, was Sam's undoing. By reaching for something so fleeting and fickle as power, he was doomed.

One of the most striking features of the landscape, Chris notices, is the anthills. Achebe offers little guidance as to the significance of the anthills, although the title suggests that they symbolize an idea at the core of the novel's message. Anthills survive the droughts every year, and when fires sweep across the savannah, they are often all that is left on the scorched landscape. To many critics, the anthills represent survival when faced with the harshest of circumstances. Their presence suggests an ongoing life force that endures in the face of the knowledge that another fire is inevitable. For these reasons, the anthills are a fitting symbol for the enduring spirit of the people and their culture.

Source: Jennifer Bussey, in an essay for *Literature of Developing Nations for Students*, Gale, 2000.

Cynthia Bily

Bily teaches writing and literature at Adrian College in Adrian, Michigan. In the following essay, she examines writers and writing in Anthills of the Savannah.

When Chinua Achebe published *Anthills of the Savannah* in 1987, it was his first new novel in more than twenty years. During that time, Nigeria had been governed by a succession of corrupt and greedy rulers, and Achebe had dedicated himself to political activism rather than to his writing. Still, he continued to consider the role of the writer in a nation under severe stress. What might be the best way for a writer to work for change? How should an African writer—or any African—balance the uses of the traditional and the modern, the local and the international, in his work? By populating *Anthills of the Savannah* with a variety of writers, readers, and speakers, Achebe looks at these questions from different angles.

Early in the novel, Achebe sets up a distinction between those who take their direction from literature—either oral or written—and those who pay too much heed to other forms of communication, including print and broadcast journalism. (It is intriguing to speculate on how the availability of the internet would have changed Ikem's crusade, had Achebe written twenty years later.) What emerges is not a strict opposition; the novel is not making a case for old ways over new, or art over objectivity. Nations and individuals must learn to combine old and new, to find a place for adapted tradition in the modern world. But the novel warns against the over-reliance on the so-called truth and objectivity of news, and against making important decisions based upon how the media will describe them.

His Excellency the Head of State is the first to demonstrate his concern for his public image, for how his actions will be reported. In the second

> If Kangan is ever to be a just nation, its rulers and its people must combine old and new, objective and subjective, editorials and poetry. They must use both their heads and their hearts. The precise combination is beyond Achebe's to describe."

chapter he worries that demonstrators might lead Kangan to an episode like the Entebbe Raid, in which Israeli soldiers descended swiftly on the airport at Entebbe, Uganda, to free French hostages. The president tells Professor Okong that he does not rely on his advisors, because if disaster happens he will be the only one blamed: "Yes, it is *me*. General Big Mouth, they will say, and print my picture on the cover of *Time* magazine with a big mouth and a small head." There is, of course, other evidence that the president is not fit to govern a country, but the fact that he is more concerned with how he appears to the outside world than with how his own citizens perceive him is emblematic of his rule. The president is far removed from his people, more concerned with being seen by outsiders as a powerful figure than with actually being one.

Though the president does not perceive how the international news media, and his desire to look good for them, influences him, he has (or thinks he has) a clear sense of how to use the press to manipulate others. He sends Okong to meet with the Abazon delegation, rather than speaking directly with them himself, but he believes he can appease them by giving them a moment of celebrity. He tells Okong, "Before you go, ask the Commissioner for Information to send a reporter across; and the Chief of Protocol to detail one of the State House photographers to take your picture shaking hands with the leader of the delegation." The president has no intention of heeding the Abazon request, and he orders Okong to "make sure that nothing about petitions gets into the papers. . .This is a goodwill visit pure and simple." The reporter and the photographer are only for show, to make the Abazon leader feel important.

The president makes his own decisions based on how he will look in *Time* magazine, and he expects that others share his motivation. He wants the Abazon delegation to have the illusion of being media celebrities for a moment, because he thinks the illusion will distract them from their duty. But he cannot allow their petition to become public knowledge. Particularly, he warns against television coverage: "Before you know it everybody will be staging goodwill rallies all over the place so as to appear on television. You know what our people are." The president deludes himself on two counts in this brief speech. Although he is condescending about how "our people are," he is one of them, as dazzled by the spotlight as he believes them to be. And he appears to have forgotten that he was the one, only minutes before, who labeled the protest a "goodwill visit." In his mind, the connection with television news has already made the label a fact.

Frequently in *Anthills of the Savannah*, Achebe presents a scene featuring one of the three old friends, and then in the next scene shows another of the three saying or doing something that echoes the first. When Chris phones Ikem to request the photographer for the goodwill delegation, he also asks to see Ikem's text before it is printed. Ikem protests, in language that echoes the president's earlier complaint: "You seem to be forgetting something, namely that it is *my* name and address which is printed at the bottom of page sixteen of the *Gazette*."

Though the language is similar, the concerns of the two men are different. The president is willing to make a dishonorable decision rather than appear foolish in print. Ikem is unwilling to act dishonorably—to have his reporting censored or edited—because he is proud of the name that appears on his work. Both men believe in the power of the press. The president believes that his control of the press can help him shore up his power. Ikem believes that his editorials can help bring the presidency down. As it turns out, both men are wrong.

Achebe demonstrates more than once that being in print or being broadcast is not the same thing as being true or solid or valuable. Although Ikem does his best to tell the truth, Chris as Minister of Information "owns all the words in this country." Or does he? After Chris has fled Bassa, Emmanuel the university student manages with "incredible ease" to plant a story in the newspaper with a simple anonymous phone call, and Chris is forced to admit that "the affair put the journalistic profession in Kangan in a very poor light indeed." All of the

characters agree that the Voice of America radio broadcasts are not to be trusted, and the women at the president's dinner choose their inappropriate attire based on what they have heard from "raving American and American-trained preachers on sponsored religious programmes nightly on television."

Separate from journalism and propaganda, Achebe considers literature—poetry, fiction, drama, proverbs, and myths. Chris, Ikem, and Beatrice are all readers and writers, sprinkling their conversation with allusions to the Bible or to great Western writers like Graham Greene and Walt Whitman. Beatrice has drawn praise from Ikem for the "odd short story and poem" she has written. Ikem is an admired poet as well as a journalist, and his prose-poem "Hymn to the Sun" is held in higher regard by his friends than all of his crusading editorials. Only Chris, the former editor of the *Gazette,* does not produce literature (this is only one of the ways that Achebe shows that Chris does not see what is happening around him). Not until he is on the bus heading north and he looks at Ikem's "Hymn to the Sun" again does he begin to learn how to read literature, and to see with the clarity of a writer. The poem reveals "in details he had not before experienced how the searing accuracy of the poet's eye was primed not on fancy but fact."

But even literary writing can be corrupted if the desire for fame overrides the desire to express truth. The most pointed commentary on mass media and its influence is the poetry magazine *Reject,* edited by Dick in Soho, London. *Reject* was intended to publish only poetry that had been rejected by other magazines. The editors soon learned that many people were so hungry to appear in print that they were willing to write fake rejection slips to accompany their submissions. Even a magazine designed to offer rejected work cannot be trusted to be genuine.

As he demonstrates in all of his novels, Achebe reveres oral literature and the honest spoken word. Many critics of *Anthills of the Savannah* have pointed out that the lines spoken in pidgin by various characters of less education often contain the essential wisdom and truth of the culture. Proverbs, snatches of song, and the myth of the priestess Idemili all are presented as demonstrating the goodness and strength of the Kangan people, far removed from the sophisticated upper-class Westernized government officials.

In the often-cited ninth chapter, the Abazon elder honors Ikem for his work on behalf of his people, although he has not read Ikem's writing, "because I do not know ABC." The elder praises those who "tell their fellows that the time to get up has finally come," and also those who, "when the struggle is ended. . .take over and recount its story." With his editorials and his poetry, Ikem is prepared to do both. The elder continues, "The sounding of the battle-drum is important; the fierce waging of the war itself is important; and the telling of the story afterwards—each is important in its own way. . .But if you ask me which of them takes the eagle-feather I will say boldly: the story."

Three chapters later, Ikem delivers his own oration, before a large crowd at the University of Bassa. He has been fired from the newspaper, but follows Beatrice's suggestion that "if you can't write you can surely get up and talk." Like the Abazon elder, whose voice has "such compelling power and magic" that everyone is captivated, Ikem gives a speech that is "so powerfully spoken it took on the nature and scope of an epic prose-poem." It is this oral presentation, far more than anything he has ever written in the *Gazette,* that moves the government to silence him.

Throughout the novel, Ikem is the one among the three old friends who has retained the most of his youthful idealism and vision; the two others are played off him. Like the president, Ikem respects the power of the media, and is aware of his role in the spotlight. Although he has some of the president's sense of self-importance, Ikem tries to use his public forum for the greater good. Like Chris before him, Ikem is editor of the *Gazette,* and like Chris he initially approaches the job with no strong political conviction. But Ikem is politicized when he goes to watch a public execution, something Chris never did. Not until the end does Chris begin to see with "the poet's eye." Ikem has a better perspective on the media than the president does, he is a more effective journalist than Chris was, and he is a better poet than Beatrice. Ikem and the others face similar choices, but Ikem chooses the most nobly. This idea is reinforced by the novel's references to journalism and literature. He combines the best qualities of the other two, but in the end all three die.

Anthills of the Savannah is not a repudiation of journalism or of the notion of objectivity. Instead, Achebe calls for balance. Ikem writes dozens of impassioned editorials, but it is finally through his prose-poem that he connects with Chris, and through his speech that he poses a threat to the president. If Kangan is ever to be a just nation, its rulers and its people must combine old and new, objective and subjective, editorials and poetry. They must use both their heads and their hearts. The precise combination is beyond Achebe's ken to describe. As Ikem shouts to his audience, "Writers don't give prescriptions. . .They give headaches!"

Source: Cynthia Bily, in an essay for *Literature of Developing Nations for Students,* Gale, 2000.

James Marcus

In "Civil Peace," a story he wrote seventeen years ago, Chinua Achebe noted how the violence of civil war inevitably outlives the actual conflict, and barely pausing for breath, extends itself into peacetime. As a band of thieves threatens the protagonist's family with automatic rifles, the leader dwells for a moment on this fine distinction:

> Awrighto. Now make we talk business. We no be bad tief. We no like for make trouble. Trouble done finish. War done finish and all the katakata wey de for inside. No Civil War again. This time na Civil Peace. No be so?

Anthills of the Savannah, Achebe's first major novel since *Things Fall Apart* appeared thirty years ago, unfolds against a similarly euphemistic backdrop of civil peace. The setting is the West African nation of Kangan, a fictional cousin to Achebe's own Nigeria. During the last two years, Kangan has witnessed a scenario of depressing familiarity: a revolution against the civilian government, followed by the rule of an "interim" military government, whose leader soon undergoes a transformation into President-for-Life, First Citizen, His Excellency or whatever job title happens to be in fashion among sitting tyrants. In this case, the aspiring kingpin—a product of Sandhurst Military Academy named Sam—has recently been frustrated in his ambitions. The northern province of Abazon has failed to cast its vote in his favor, spoiling his "unanimous" election. In return, he has refused to provide relief to the drought-stricken province.

In the novel's opening scene, Sam reaffirms his refusal during a meeting of the Cabinet, an assortment of toadies and flacks whose tone Achebe catches perfectly. The meeting is recorded by one of Achebe's multiple narrators, Chris Oriko, Commissioner for Information. A boyhood friend of Sam's, Chris can't help but approach him irreverently; he's also conscious of how rapidly the regime's malevolence has accelerated, "a game that began innocently enough and then went suddenly strange and poisonous." Why, then, does he remain in the Cabinet? Inertia, he speculates, curiosity and "one

> Achebe establishes hope as a given, as the only conceivable response to suffering, the only one that challenges its permanence. It's a courageous act, urging such a thing upon us— neither pessimism nor optimism but a running argument with despair."

last factor . . . namely that I couldn't be writing this if I didn't hang around to observe it all. And no one else would.''

His reportorial instincts notwithstanding, Chris is an insider, with an intelligence faintly poisoned by accommodation. The opposite is true of his old friend Ikem Osodi, poet and current editor of the government-owned National Gazette. Osodi continues to fight the regime via the editorial page. When a perplexed Chris remonstrates with him, Ikem replies, ''But supposing my crusading editorials were indeed futile would I not be obliged to keep on writing them?'' This argument—pragmatism versus idealism—resounds throughout the novel, and not unexpectedly, idealism gets the best lines. Defending his activities on the basis of principle, rather than results, Ikem won't dwell on the ''many successes [his] militant editorials have had.'' Hard facts, he insists, are beside the point:

> Those who mismanage our affairs would silence our criticism by pretending they have facts not available to the rest of us. And I know it is fatal to engage them on their own ground. Our best weapon against them is not to marshal facts, of which they are truly managers, but passion. Passion is our hope and strength, a very present help in trouble.

The two friends' argument over how to respond best to a loathsome regime is complicated by one of that regime's most loathsome features: its constant, theatrical dissembling—government by euphemism. Ikem notes how Sam has turned his rule into a species of performance: ''He is basically an actor and half of the things we are inclined to hold against him are no more than scenes from his repertory to

which he may have no sense of moral commitment whatsoever.'' (It's a performance, too, that American readers can't fail to recognize in the eighth year of the age of Reagan.) With an actor, albeit a dangerous one, at the helm of state, the language of state quickly degenerates. Sam is simply the latest version of Auden's Ogre, for whom ''one prize is beyond his reach, / The Ogre cannot master Speech.''

Achebe passionately opposes this debasement of words by politics, turning upon it all his wit and disgust. ''The story,'' an Abazon tribesman tells Ikem, ''is our escort; without it, we are blind.'' But can any quality of language suffice to oppose the linguistic rot that calls Kangan's head torturer ''Director of the State Research Council''? Achebe can answer this question only obliquely, by placing his book in our hands. In the story itself, Ikem meets his death at the hands of that very same Research Council. (In Idi Amin's Uganda, the state slaughterhouse bore a nearly identical title, the State Research Bureau. And in fact, the account of Wycliffe Kato's incarceration there, published in a recent issue of *Granta*, would fit seamlessly into Achebe's novel.)

Of course, opposing a tyranny, or even enduring it, involves more than precision of language. At the same time as it records Ikem's and Chris's fall from political grace, *Anthills of the Savannah* chronicles their rising consciousness, with respect to both women and that ticklish entity, ''the people.'' Both men begin the novel with conspicuously retrograde attitudes toward women. The agent of their enlightenment, and the novel's third major character/narrator, is one Beatrice Okoh, raised in an Anglican compound, educated at the University of London and now a middle-level bureaucrat in the Ministry of Finance. Beatrice senses Ikim's sexism as ''the only chink in his revolutionary armor.'' And under her prodding, Ikem finally comes around, recanting his ''candid chauvinism'' in a four-page-long apologia. Indeed, after confessing his crimes against the female principle Ikem widens his focus to all oppressed groups. ''Free people may be alike everywhere in their freedom,'' he tells Beatrice, ''but the oppressed inhabit each their own particular hell.''

A fine epigraph. But Achebe's feminism, entirely laudable, doesn't always translate effectively into fiction. In particular, he has resorted throughout to presenting Beatrice as an embodiment of feminine wisdom, ''the village priestess who will prophesy when her divinity rides her abandoning if need be her soup-pot on the fire, but returning again when the god departs to the domesticity of kitchen.'' Perhaps her divinity would sit easier if she were as fleshed-out a character as the two men. Instead, the fuzziness of her portrait conspires with her divinity to keep her symbolic. Yet Achebe is too gifted a novelist to let this mutation take place. He gives Beatrice passion, fear, grief. Still, it's the only element of the novel in which polemic, or even its twin, sentimentality, threatens to displace flesh and blood.

No such problems mar Achebe's treatment of the other target of raised consciousness, the ''people.'' For one thing, he gives them voice throughout *Anthills of the Savannah* by turning again and again to the sprung rhythms of the local patois. (An example, in which a policeman offers his solution to Kangan's problems: ''Make every man, woman and child and even those them never born, make everybody collect twenty manilla each and bring to me and I go take am go England and negotiate with IMF to bring white man back to Kangan.'') Even Chris, Ikem and Beatrice shed their formal speech during moments of intimacy or stress, temporarily lowering the barriers of class and education.

For Ikem, though, these temporary connections aren't enough. How can a writer, in particular, forge a deeper bond with ''the poor and dispossessed of this country, with the bruised heart that throbs painfully at the core of the nation's being''? Ikem's compassion for this ''bruised heart'' is genuine and convincing. It doesn't shield him, however, from the appalling contradictions housed in its chambers. In a brilliant scene, Ikem attends a public execution on a beach near the capital city. A television crew and a bleacher full of V.I.P.s have joined the vast crowd to observe the ''ritual obscenities.'' As he waits for hours in the hot sun, Ikem peers at the crowd around him and wonders at its stamina. ''How,'' he wonders, ''does the poor man retain his calm in the face of such provocation?'' Answering his own question, he decides that ''great good humour'' must explain it. Minutes later, though, he sees the thousands of onlookers jeer as the four condemned men are led out and shot. The terrible laughter—no longer a subversive tool of survival—strikes Ikem as a form of self-mutilation:

> But even the poor man can forget what his humour is about and become altogether too humorous in his suffering. That afternoon he was punished most dreadfully at the beach and he laughed to his pink gums and I listened painfully for the slightest clink of the concealed weapon in the voluminous folds of that laughter. And I didn't hear it.

Ikem's reaction joins disgust, pity, terror, disappointment; characteristically, it doesn't bar hope. The same can be said for Achebe himself. *Anthills of the Savannah* describes a truly dreary historical moment, in which monstrous halfwits wield the instruments of survival and destruction, the ''yam and the knife.'' Yet Achebe establishes hope as a given, as the only conceivable response to suffering, the only one that challenges its permanence. It's a courageous act, urging such a thing upon us— neither pessimism nor optimism but a running argument with despair. And one worth waiting thirty years for.

Source: James Marcus, ''Anthills of the Savannah,'' in *The Nation,* Vol. 246, No. 15, April 16, 1988, p. 540.

Sources

Ascherson, Neal, ''Betrayal,'' in *New York Review of Books,* Vol. 35, No. 3, March 3, 1988, pp. 3-4, 6.

Gordimer, Nadine, ''A Tyranny of Clowns,'' in *New York Times Book Review,* February 21, 1988, p. 1.

Laurence, Margaret, *Long Drums and Cannons: Nigerian Dramatists and Novelists,* Praeger, 1968.

Okri, Ben, review of *Anthills of the Savannah,* in London *Observer,* September 20, 1987.

Ravenscroft, A., ''Recent Fiction from Africa: Chinua Achebe's *Anthills of the Savannah*—A Note,'' in *Literary Criterion,* Vol. 23, Nos. 1-2, 1988, pp. 172-75.

Swann, Joseph, ''From *Things Fall Apart* to *Anthills of the Savannah*: The Changing Face of History in Achebe's Novels,'' in *Crisis and Creativity in the New Literature in English,* edited by Geoffrey V. Davis and Hena Maes-Jelinek, Rodopi, 1990, pp. 191-203.

ten Kortenaar, Neil, '''Only Connect': 'Anthills of the Savannah' and Achebe's 'Trouble with Nigeria,''' in *Research in African Literatures,* Vol. 24, No. 3, Fall, 1993, pp. 59-73.

Further Reading

Arua, Arua E. and Olusegun Oladipo, *Two Perspectives on Chinua Achebe's ''Anthills of the Savannah,''* in *Review of English and Literature Studies,* 1989.
    Two critics from Ibadan discuss their particular interpretations of *Anthills of the Savannah.*

Gikandi, Simon, *Reading Chinua Achebe: Language and Ideology in Fiction,* James Currey, 1991.
    In this book, Gikandi explores fully the role of the language and the storyteller in modern Africa as depicted in Achebe's writing.

Holst Petersen, Kirsten, and Anna Rutherford, eds., *Chinua Achebe: A Celebration*, Heinemann, 1991.
From Achebe's original British publisher comes this volume exploring his life and work. Having been published in 1991, it includes commentary on Achebe's more recent publications.

Moyers, Bill, ''Chinua Achebe,'' in *Bill Moyers: A World of Ideas*, Doubleday, 1989, pp. 333-44.
In this chapter, Moyers recounts his interview with Chinua Achebe.

Aphrodite: A Memoir of the Senses

In the opening sentence of her 1998 book, *Aphrodite: A Memoir of the Senses*, Chilean author Isabel Allende declares: ''I repent of my diets, the delicious dishes rejected out of vanity, as much as I lament the opportunities for making love that I let go by.'' In the height and rigor of physical self-awareness of the late 1990s in America, Allende's literary celebration of sex and food found ample response: her naughty recipe/pillow book ended up on the *New York Times* bestseller list.

Allende's seventh book follows the author's tradition of semi-autobiographical literature; it is a memoir of return to life, written after her 1997 novel *Paula* about the painful loss of her daughter. In the introduction, Allende states that her re-awakening to sensual pleasures marked her exit from the three-year period of sadness. The critics, calling *Aphrodite* an unusually ''light'' work for an author of customarily weightier literature, still praised it as a life-affirming sequel to the grief and anguish of *Paula*.

Aphrodite's anything-but-linear narrative is a mix of the author's romantic and culinary musings and recollections, her friends' stories, world recipes, excerpts from erotic texts, folktales, mythology, anthropology, poetry, travel writing, ancient and historical anecdotes, even gossip. In Allende's words, *Aphrodite* is ''a mapless journey through the regions of sensual memory, in which the boundaries between love and appetite are so diffuse that at times they evaporate completely.''

Isabel Allende

1998

Even the author's California house was inspiring for the writing of her novel: as the author stated in an interview with Fred Kaplan for *The Boston Globe*, "it was the town's first brothel, then it was a church, then it was the first chocolate-chip cookie factory. So we live with all these smells—of the women and the chocolate—wafting in the air."

Author Biography

Isabel Angelica Allende was born on August 2, 1942, in Lima, Peru, to parents Tomas, a Chilean diplomat, and Francisca (Llona Barros) Allende. After her parents' divorce, three-year-old Isabel returned with her mother to Santiago, Chile; she grew up in her grandparents' home and attended a private high school. In 1962, Allende married her first husband, Miguel Frias, an engineer. After several years as a secretary, Allende started working as a journalist, editor, and advice columnist for *Paula* magazine; she also occasionally worked on television and movie newsreels.

In 1973, her uncle, Chilean president Salvador Allende, was assassinated in a right-wing military coup against his socialist government; Allende, her husband, and their two children fled the country and moved to Venezuela, where Allende had trouble finding work. While in exile and under the influence of her memories of Chile, Allende wrote her first semi-autobiographical novel, *The House of the Spirits*, which was inspired by her letters to her grandfather. Published in 1982, the novel became an instant success and placed Allende in the literary category of magic realism, along with Jorge Amado, Jorge Luis Borges, and Gabriel Garcia Marquez. However, Allende's writing also portrays the political reality of Latin America and assumes a decidedly feminine perspective, apparent in her future works.

Allende's other publications include novels *Of Love and Shadows* (1984), *Eva Luna* (1987), and *The Infinite Plan* (1991); a collection of short stories entitled *The Stories of Eva Luna* (1990); and an autobiographical account of her only daughter's death in 1991, entitled *Paula* (1997).

In an interview with Fred Kaplan for the *Boston Globe*, Allende recalled the time after her daughter's death as a gray, painful period void of inspiration and desire—until a night in January 1996, when she had an erotic dream of diving into a swimming pool full of rice pudding, her favorite dessert. "I decided I was never going to diet again but just enjoy what life had to offer. This came slowly—a slow understanding that life is borrowed time, that we are here for a very short time, and we must enjoy what we have," Allende stated.

In the introduction to her 1998 book, *Aphrodite: A Memoir of the Senses*, the author describes this gradual return to life as "reaching the end of a long tunnel of mourning and finally coming out the other end, into the light, with a tremendous desire to eat and cuddle once again." The semi-fictional *Aphrodite* is a book of aphrodisiacs, written in celebration of the inspiring powers of food and sex, a life-affirming and humorous testament of continuing creativity.

Since her second marriage in 1988, Allende has lived in California with her husband, lawyer William Gordon.

Plot Summary

Aphrodite opens with Allende's reflection on her fifty years of life; she emphasizes the way in which memories are based on the sensual experiences that accompanied them. The author further presents her reasons and justifications for writing a book about aphrodisiacs, and offers a brief history of the use of sexual stimulants, consisting of food and many others (from magic rituals to erotic stories). In the "Mea Culpa of the Culpable" section, Allende introduces the people who created the project: the illustrator Robert Shekter, her mother and cook Panchita Llona, her agent Carmen Balcells, and the author herself.

Aphrodisiacs

This chapter defines an aphrodisiac as "any substance or activity that piques amorous desire." The author lists the categories of aphrodisiacs according to their function (the analogy of "the vulva-shaped oyster or phallic asparagus," or the suggestion of certain organs that, when eaten, can convey "strength"), and ruminates on the necessary role of imagination in erotica. Further, she examines the relationship between eating and sexual activity, finding that aphrodisiacs are a "bridge between gluttony and lust."

The Spice Is in Variety

Allende states that "the only truly infallible aphrodisiac is love" followed by the second— variety. However, both infidelity and polygamy are unnecessary if one introduces diversity into sexual practice with some study of erotic manuals or use of sex toys. Nevertheless, Allende warns that excessive and obsessive pursuit of variety can numb one's senses to the full experience of savoring the object of pleasure—be it a sexual partner or "a simple tomato."

The Good Table

Allende describes the culinary attitudes of her family, with a traditionally puritan grandfather, an indifferent grandmother, and a mother "who through one of those incomprehensible genetic accidents had in the midst of that Spartan tribe been born with a refined sensibility."

Cooking in the Nude

This chapter states that "everything cooked for a lover is sensual" and that the processes of cooking, eating, and lovemaking should be approached with pleasure and openness to fun. Allende writes that men proficient in the kitchen are sexually irresistible, and offers anecdotes from her own life and a friend's experience to support this statement.

The Spell of Aromas

The author states the interdependent connection between taste and smell, and proceeds to describe the erotic power of scent (as used by Cleopatra and the French monarchs, among others). After a brief history of perfume and a description of the process, Allende recalls her friend's failed attempt to arouse lovers with a purchased bottle of pheromones. The chapter ends with the significance of scent in the sexual experience, and a claim that the sensuous scent of cooking can have a very erotic result. Allende also includes the story "Death by Perfume" written by Lady Onogoro in tenth-century Japan, describing the revenge of a woman who applies erotic fragrances on the body of her cheating lover, finally killing him with a poisonous dose.

At First Sight

The visual appeal of the human body depends on the teasing and tempting element of the unseen.

Isabel Allende

The erotic appeal of food lies in its resemblance to the body's shapes and colors. The presentation of the table can also be seductive.

Etiquette

Allende calls the rules of table etiquette relative, and describes the pleasures of eating with one's fingers. However, she says that strict rules can also be erotic and imagines such a scenario.

With the Tip of the Tongue

After an analysis of the sense of taste, the author relates it to sexuality and cooking; the key, she states, is in accentuation through opposites.

Herbs and Spice

This chapter contains a history of the use of herbs and spices both in preservation of food and aphrodisiacs, and a list of "Forbidden Herbs."

The Orgy

After a short history of orgiastic celebration and some descriptive examples, Allende gives advice on how to prepare an orgy, along with the recipes: Aunt Burgel's Aphrodisiac Stew, Panchita's Curanto en Olla, and Carmen's Soup for Orgies.

About Taste

The author recalls exotic dining experiences and describes some of the world delicacies that are shunned in the United States. The sections ''Alligators and Piranhas'' and ''Aphrodisiac Cruelties'' describe some unusual dietary practices, as well as certain hair-raising aphrodisiac methods.

About Eroticist

This chapter consists of a letter by the writer of erotica, Anaïs Nin, to her employer, who demanded literature on sex without ''the poetry.'' Nin's reply is Allende's manifesto of pleasure of the sensual vs. the pornographic.

Whisper

The author explains the sexual power of a whispered, spoken, and written word.

A Night in Egypt

This section is an excerpt from a letter from Tabra, Allende's friend, describing an erotic and culinary experience she had on one of her travels.

Sins of the Flesh

The author lists the aphrodisiac properties of different kinds of meat on the menu.

The Gigolo

Allende recalls a conversation with a young male prostitute, and provides the recipe for Aphrodisiac Soup of Acupuncture Master.

Bread, God's Grace

This chapter reviews the kinds of bread, its history, and the sensuousness of making it.

Creatures of the Sea

The author describes uses of seafood for erotic purposes, gives the Bouillabaisse recipe, and quotes Neruda's poem ''Ode to Conger Chowder.''

The Harem

This chapter explores the nineteenth-century European fascination with the harem as an erotic fantasy, the harem's history, and its cuisine.

Eggs

Allende describes the ancient and worldwide belief in the aphrodisiac power of eggs, from chicken to caviar. The section ''Supreme Stimulus for Lechery'' includes Catherine the Great's recipe for Empress' Omelet.

Forbidden Fruits

This section examines the erotic properties of fruit, and lists coffee, tea, chocolate, and honey as ''Other Delicious Aphrodisiacs.''

Cheese

The author describes the sensuality of cheesemaking and lists the most popular kinds of cheeses.

Si Non e Vero. . .

Allende offers some advice on how to ''cheat'' in the kitchen when preparing a complex meal. She also gives the recipe for her seductive Reconciliation Soup.

The Spirit of Wine

This chapter examines the effects of alcohol on the libido and offers some classification of wines according to the cuisine. A similar outline follows the section on ''Liquors.''

Love Philters

The author gives an overview of both legal and illegal—but usually dangerous—potions and substances, from the Spanish fly and powder of rhinoceros' horn to marijuana and cocaine.

The Language of Flowers

Allende reviews the symbolically romantic language of the past, encoded in flowers.

From the Earth with Love

This chapter lists the aphrodisiac properties of vegetables, along with the Shekter's Vegetarian

Aphrodisiac recipe and a ''Subjective List of Aphrodisiac Vegetables.''

Colomba in Nature

This chapter is a rather comic account of an unsuccessful picnic, in which a professor tries to seduce his plump student Colomba. Allende adds an excerpt from the poem ''Eating the World.''

Finally. . .

The author ends the book with thoughts on the best aphrodisiac, love.

Panchita's Aphrodisiac Recipes

The final third of the book contains the recipes for aphrodisiac dishes, including sauces, hors d'oeuvres, soups, appetizers, main courses, and desserts, all introduced with erotic allusions.

Characters

Isabel Allende

In the autobiographical vein that several critics have pointed out in examination of Allende's works, the author herself is a character in this memoir/cookbook/list of aphrodisiacs. She introduces herself at the beginning as a woman at the doorstep of her fifties, ''the last hour of dusk,'' in which she reflects on her life and her past ''relationship with food and eroticism.'' However, Allende's larger focus is the power of sensory experience: she states that her memories are closely ''associated with the senses.'' The reason for writing *Aphrodite*, she explains, is a celebration of her own sensual pleasures reawakening after a three-year period of mourning the death of her only daughter. Allende writes that a dream of diving into a pool filled with her favorite dessert, rice pudding, signaled her return to the joy of living; the book about the connection between food and sex naturally followed.

Allende uses examples from her private life in explaining how she developed her Epicurean philosophy of cooking and lovemaking: she recalls the scents of her childhood, the amorous and culinary

adventures and teachings of her family members, erotic experiences from her youth to the recent days, and past and present sensual perceptions. The first-person narrative of *Aphrodite* allows the author/narrator to sound didactic and sympathetic at the same time. Although both technical and spiritual advice for better cooking and lovemaking abound throughout the text, Allende ''jumps in'' often to remind the reader of her main point—that the goal is to have fun with both of these enterprises. Personal anecdotes are very useful in bringing humor to an instructional text: Allende admits to her many culinary disasters to ease the reader's way through a list of sometimes complex recipes. She justifies her interest in these topics saying that, at her age, most couples need a bit of help in the department of sensual excitement.

Allende is candid about the personal view of her book: she openly and repeatedly declares her own preferences in selecting recipes, literary excerpts, and aphrodisiacs of the world for inclusion in *Aphrodite*. In the chapter entitled ''The Orgy,'' she offers advice by imagining how she would prepare a perfect bacchanal; also, she provides the recipe for her appropriately named ''Reconciliation Soup'' that she prepares for her lover ''after some terrible fight.''

Finally, Allende discusses her romantic and marital experiences, making some generalizations about the erotic and entertaining factors in both. She offers her own recollections and wisdom derived from two marriages and several love affairs, concluding that love is an indispensable aphrodisiac—but, until the end, writing from her own viewpoint is the only reliable basis for her claims.

Carmen Balcells

Allende gives her literary agent a place in the ''Mea Culpa'' section as well, thanking her for the support given for *Aphrodite* and for making her famous Catalan stew whenever the author visits her in Barcelona. Balcells is another hard-core chef, a confident ruler of her kitchen where, ''wrapped in her apron, a kerchief around her head and a string of curses upon her lips,'' she creates miracles of aphrodisiac cuisine. The labor of several hours is always served on a richly embroidered tablecloth, among crystal goblets full of the best wine, in china of superb porcelain and with antique heavy silverware. Allende says the effort is worth it: ''We eat up until our souls rise up sighing and the most hidden virtues of our wretched humanity are renewed as that blessed soup seeps into our bones, sweeping away with one stroke the fatigue of all the disappointments gathered along the road of life and restoring to us the uncontrollable sensuality of our twenties.'' Generous in her cooking as in her profession, Balcells provides her recipe for the Catalan soup in the chapter ''The Orgy.''

John Wayne Bobbitt

Bobbitt is the American husband whose wife, ''fed up with violence and abuse,'' made international news when she cut off his penis. Allende illustrates the civilization's obsession with the male sexual organ, describing how the police on the case diligently searched the highway for the amputated piece which was immediately sewn back on and can now be seen in the pornographic movies starring Bobbitt.

Napoleon Bonaparte

A fan of the female scent au naturelle, the French ruler wrote to his beloved Josephine asking her not to bathe her private parts ''in the weeks prior to his return from the battlefield.'' Josephine also relied on the seductive fragrance of violets to charm her lover.

The Butcher

In a story by the French writer Alina Reyes, a man purchases goat testicles from his butcher every week in order to ''maintain his extraordinary sexual powers.'' Allende mentions the story to emphasize the reverence with which people treat the male organs.

Casanova

Allende describes the aphrodisiac power of oysters with an illustration of the famous lover's technique of seducing young novices by passing oysters from mouth to mouth. Casanova was also a big admirer of a woman's natural, private smell, and knew that the whispered word was a potent aphrodisiac.

Catherine the Great

The Russian Empress reportedly had ''prodigious vitality'' and an insatiable sexual appetite.

Legend accuses her of designing a harness for a horse in her bedroom.

Christian Saints

Allende cites the self-punishment of the saints of the Middle Ages, whose abomination of the flesh as evil illustrates the extreme separation of body and soul in Christianity.

Cleopatra

The Egyptian queen appears in Allende's book as a masterful seductress who used many sensuous approaches to create her feminine fame and power. Cleopatra soaked the sails of her ship in Damascus rose scent, which announced her arrival from miles away and served as her signature fragrance; the scent was a strong political statement during her visit to Rome, where Caesar's opponents were showered with the fragrance which soon became the fashion worn by all aristocratic women except Caesar's wife. The seductive queen also drove her lovers crazy by letting them lick the soft mixture of honey and ground almonds from her intimate parts.

Colomba

Allende's plump friend Colomba was almost seduced by her art professor during a picnic—almost, because a bull chased the unfortunate lovers into the woods and spoiled the professor's plan. The picnic included some highly aphrodisiac dishes, as the seducer wanted to charm his lady by indulging her gluttony.

Comtesse du Barry

Marie Jeanne Isabel Becu du Barry, a French courtesan from the beginning of the eighteenth century, turned orgy into an art; according to the author, her bacchanals were social events that shocked the aristocracy and gave her a reputation as a degenerate. Allende calls Madame du Barry ''a rebellious and fearless spirit.'' The Comtesse died at the age of twenty-four.

The Friend

Allende warns her readers against extreme measures in spicing up one's love life, and tells the story of a friend who, on a wonderful date with a woman, went to see her bedroom to "get an idea of the layout and plot his strategy" but ended up running away in fear, because the lady had a trapeze above the bed.

The Gigolo

The author recalls her conversation with a young male prostitute she met at an airport. The Gigolo does not rely on aphrodisiacs; everything is done naturally.

The Glove Vendor

Allende recalls a sensuous tactile experience she had years ago, when the clerk in a shop helped her buy gloves and aroused her with the touch of his hands on hers. The author lists that incident as an example of Tantric sexuality.

The Grandfather

Allende describes the patriarch of her family in childhood as a man of tradition, who did not like changes in the menu and made the entire family suffer the brewings of their unimaginative cook for years.

The Grandmother

Allende describes an incident in which her grandmother, usually an otherworldly-looking creature completely uninterested in the food on her plate, passed out when an admirer offered her a feast where the main course was a pair of guinea pigs, "intact from the tips of their stiff whiskers to the toenails of their tiny paws, encased in [a] shroud of glassy, shivering gelatin."

Hannah

Hannah is Allende's friend, whose disappointment at the looks of her blind date turned into fascination and powerful attraction when the man cooked an amazing meal for her. Like the author, Hannah serves to prove the argument that men who cook are irresistibly sexy.

Howard Hughes

In her argument that a modern obsession with variety often deprives people of the ultimate sensu-

ality, Allende states that the famous playboy and millionaire died of "poverty of the senses and spirit," wasted from hunger and terrified of germs, alone in a motel room and looking like a concentration camp prisoner.

The Husband

Allende describes falling in love with her second husband despite all odds, mainly because of the skill with which he cooked for her the day after they met.

King Solomon

Allende mentions the old king's epic promiscuity in relation to the aphrodisiac power of variety. She also notes his enjoyment of spices and scents.

Lady Onogoro

A poet in the Court of Heian at the end of the tenth century, Lady Onogoro wrote outstanding and imaginative erotic stories. Allende gives the full text of "Death by Perfume," in which a deceived woman seduces her lover by applying scents and spices to his body, only to poison him with the deadly ones. The author also retells her story "The Cold Fish," in which a carp makes love to a young woman with more success than her human lover does.

Panchita Llona

Llona is the author's mother and the cook who provided (and perfected) most of the recipes included throughout and at the end of the book. Allende writes that her mother has never served the same meal twice, and can decipher any secret recipe by simply tasting the dish. The author further describes Llona's tremendous culinary abilities in an anecdote about their "mortifying" restaurant visits: the thorough chef would look at what other guests were eating ("sometimes so closely that she alarms the diners"), carefully inspect the menu, torture the waiter "with malicious questions that force him to go to the kitchen and return with written answers," make everyone order a different thing on the menu, take a Polaroid picture of the dinner, and then taste each meal so that she can later recreate it in her own kitchen. Llona is mentioned throughout the narrative in the author's memories of childhood as a stern overseeing influence who believes in "impeccable and honest execution,'' versus Allende's ''creative bungling.''

Llona provides the recipe for the elaborate delicacy from Easter Island, the curanto en olla, as well as the recipes in the last third of the book. She once spent weeks travelling from coast to coast in search of the authentic bouillabaisse recipe, which she finally obtained (but ''how she got it is something she will never reveal as long as her husband is alive'').

Lucasta

A renowned poisoner in the Roman Empire, Lucasta used the aphrodisiac irresistibility of mushrooms to commit many a murder during orgies.

Marquis de Sade

The ever-curious Marquis, whose name became a synonym for extreme sexual experimentation, reportedly ended up in jail for using a so-called love philter. Certain ladies, to whom the Marquis had given the stimulant known as the Spanish fly, almost died and experienced rather unpleasant side effects: they ''fell to the floor and gnawed table legs,'' reports Allende.

Lola Montez

A famous nineteenth-century courtesan invented a seductive dance she called the tarantula; the performance, in whose raptures she would remove most of her veils, was so popular that nobody questioned Lola's claim that she was an aristocratic Spanish dancer.

Anais Nin

An early 20th-century writer who, like fellow writer Henry Miller, was paid by the page in the 1940s. They rebelled against their client (''the Collector'') for asking them to ''cut the poetry'' and write pornography instead of erotica in their stories. Allende includes Nin's letter to the Collector as her own manifesto of sensuality.

Tio Ramon

The author's stepfather, her mother's second husband, often went through thorough preparations to create a love nest in the small apartment where the family lived in Beirut. Allende's childhood imagination was awakened by the mysterious activity behind the closed doors, where her stepfather romanced his wife in as much luxury as he could afford.

Scheherazade

The storyteller of the Arabic epic *One Thousand and One Nights*, Scheherazade is a young and wise woman who saves herself with the seductive powers of narrative. A sultan, catching his wife with another upon his sudden return from battle, takes revenge on women by possessing a virgin every night and killing her in the morning, before she has a chance to betray him. Scheherazade puts a stop to the bloody practice by telling the sultan a story and promptly stopping in the morning; the cruel monarch, in eager anticipation to hear how the story develops, lets her live another night—then another, until (after 1,001 nights of stories) the ritual murder is abolished. Allende uses the story as an illustration for the aphrodisiac nature of good storytelling.

Robert Shekter

Allende introduces Shekter, along with the other ''accomplices'' in the creation of her book, in a section entitled ''Mea Culpa of the Culpable''; Shekter is the illustrator of *Aphrodite*. His sketches are the characters that emphasize the protagonists of *Aphrodite*: ''bold nymphs and mischievous satyrs'' that appear throughout the book.

Shekter contributes to the narrative with his memory of an orgy he once attended at a summer house in Sweden, with very little food but plenty of alcohol and marijuana, where participants courteously coupled amongst each other between discussions of Ingmar Bergman's films. A vegetarian ever since he accidentally shot a duck when he was a pilot in World War II, Shekter also provides the aphrodisiac recipe for a vegetable ratatouille.

Miki Shima

Allende's good friend and Japanese doctor, Shima tells her about the famous Japanese pillow-books—ancient erotic manuals closely studied by the male prostitutes in his country.

Tabra

Tabra is Allende's adventurous friend who, in a letter, describes her sensual experience of a feast she attended one night in Egypt.

The Tao Priestess

The most powerful female Tao master claimed that "reality is achieved only through sexual ecstasy." The legend says that she absorbed the male energy of her followers and remained beautiful and young as a seventeen-year-old, until her death at the age of five hundred. Allende tells the tale to depict the connection of carnal and spiritual bliss in some belief systems.

Aunt Teresa

Allende's angelic aunt, who "died with buds of embryonic wings upon her shoulder blades," is preserved in the author's memory along with the scent and taste of violet candy she always gave the children.

Diane de Poitiers

King Henry II of France fell madly in love with this lady, whose success was attributed to her skill in the technique of kabbazah ("squeezing and suctioning contractions of the muscles of their intimate parts").

Themes

Aesthetics

Allende often discusses the concept of physical beauty in her writing, sometimes to emphasize its importance in visual attractiveness, other times to explore the social and cultural differences in what one considers beautiful. In her postscript to several erotic tales of yore, the author laments the modern fascination with the slim and bony female body, recalling the "friendlier" times when a woman's curves were a great feminine asset to her beauty and not a disease called cellulite. However, she adds, the definition of what is erotic is different for each person; her story "Colomba in the Nature" features a man's lust after an obese woman.

In both sex and food, the aesthetic appeal is as crucial for evoking the appetite as any entreaty directed toward the other senses. In the chapter "At First Sight," the author reveals the secret seduction of the flesh according to her grandfather: "Tempta-tion does not lie in nakedness. . .but in the transparent or slinky." Allende claims that partial clothing is provocative and mysterious because it reveals a lot, but excites the spectator's imagination by what it doesn't show. Other bodily adornments used to attract potential lovers include "makeup, hairstyling, jewels, tattoos, and even decorative scars." Also, sexual aesthetics depend on the element of experimentation and surprise: in the chapter "The Spice Is in Variety," the author discusses various decorations used for erotic purposes, especially those used to "sensualize" the setting like Cupid-shaped candles, colorful goblets, satin tablecloths, and evocative plates.

As for the aesthetic appeal of food, Allende presents her mother ("who primps over her table as much as her own attire") as a true culinary artist, always managing to present a dish in an appetizing way and tastefully decorated. According to the author, aphrodisiac meals gather much power from "the association between the shapes and colors of food and those of the body." Allende gives an example of suggestive dishes such as "long, firm asparagus served with two new potatoes at the base of the stem, or two peach halves with raspberry nipples in crème Chantilly."

Flesh vs. Spirit

In her exploration of the relationship between the mind and the body in eroticism and cuisine, Allende discusses the Judeo-Christian division of "the individual into body and soul, and love into profane and divine" as a reason for the shunning of culinary and sensual pleasure in Western culture. After defining aphrodisiacs as "the bridge between gluttony and lust," the author argues that Christian condemnation of both aphrodisiacs and sensuality in general comes from the belief that "the road to gluttony leads straight to lust and, if traveled a little farther, to the loss of one's soul." According to her classification, Lutherans, Calvinists, and "other aspirants to Christian perfection" therefore deny themselves culinary pleasures. Catholics, however, "purified by confession, free to go and sin again," are unhindered in their enjoyment of the delicatessen. Allende cites the expression "a cardinal's tidbit," used to describe something delicious, as support for her claim.

The author further discusses the Christian division between the carnal and the spiritual during the

Topics for Further Study

- Some people believe that aphrodisiacs made out of the body parts of rare animals have amazing powers. Do some research on poaching. How has the belief in these aphrodisiacs led to the endangerment of particular animal and plant species in certain areas of the world?

- Review the recent news (in the past year or two) and find any references to the use of illegal or potentially dangerous stimulants in reported rape cases. According to the news, what are some of the modern-day "love philters"? Are they in any way similar to those of the past? In what way is their reputation today different from their "older relatives," described in Allende's book?

- Research the popular drug Viagra. How does it function? What are its ingredients? Are they in any way related to the aphrodisiacs in *Aphrodite*? What do you think Allende would write about the "erection pill"?

- Conduct an anonymous survey (as broad-based as possible) about what people consider aphro-

disiac in today's society. In your questionnaire, include sections for each of the senses (e.g., "What kind of scent turns you on?") as well as about food, drink, drugs, gestures, situations, media representations, etc. Are your findings different than Allende's? Does the author report aphrodisiacs that your subjects did not mention? Have you received any answers that you did not find in *Aphrodite*?

- The author states that her aphrodisiac recipes worked only when the diners were told what the results should be. Put her statement to the test: prepare a meal following the recipes given at the end of *Aphrodite*, serve it to two middle-aged couples (because, as Allende claims, "even a cup of chamomile tea turns on the young"), and make sure that only one couple knows that the meal is supposedly an aphrodisiac. You don't have to ask them to report to you the next morning, but observe their behavior at the table. Is Allende right?

Middle Ages, when any sensual enjoyment was labeled evil and the Church preached that suffering in this life was the only certain way of achieving a pleasurable eternity. Allende cites the example of those who found virtue and got a title of sainthood in exercises of extreme self-deprivation, equivalent to physical torture.

On the other hand, the author lists some cultures that have embraced the concepts of body and soul as unified in the human pursuit of fulfillment, seen as consisting of both sensual and spiritual elevation. *Aphrodite* contains several references to the Tantric meditation based on sexual ecstasy, the Tibetan practice in which copulation serves as spiritual exercise, and certain Taoist monks who preached that erotic energy is a path to illumination of the soul.

Allende also reflects on the effects of the mind-body binary in the contemporary culture, in which

the art of experiencing sensual pleasure has been lost. One example from the author's neighborhood in California is a "recent rash of workshops for teaching what any orangutan knows without instruction: touching oneself and touching others."

Style

Metaphor

Food and sex are interchanged in metaphoric references throughout the text of *Aphrodite*, as Allende persistently connects food and lovemaking in the language of her recipes and erotic tales. The link between sexual and culinary enjoyment, she claims, is in the senses: people experience both food and sex as physical and sensual pleasures. For example, Allende describes a couple having an elegant dinner while, in their thoughts, they make love "devouring each other" on the table. She also recounts the adventure of her plump friend Colomba, a woman whose "delicious flesh" drove her seducer mad with lust.

Allende lays the ground for her metaphors by explaining that many foods gain their aphrodisiac reputation on the basis of their resemblance to bodily features. Peach and apricot are "perhaps the most sensual of all fruits, for their delectable perfume, soft and juicy texture, and flesh color, an eloquent representation of the female private parts"; strawberry and raspberry are "delicate fruit nipples"; oysters in their shell "suggest delicate vulvae"; and asparagus, carrot, and leek gather their seductive merit from their phallic shape. Also, seafood is considered aphrodisiac because "the human body, especially during sexual excitation, emits a marine odor similar to the smell of crustaceans and fish." These are examples by which visual, tactile, and olfactory properties of one have become evocative of another. In accordance with these comparisons, Allende's language in describing the culinary-carnal connection often has a double meaning: some of the book's chapters are suggestively entitled "Forbidden Herbs" and "Forbidden Fruits," "The Spice Is in Variety," and "With the Tip of the Tongue."

The author also acknowledges the insuperable erotic power of language cited in the legend of Scheherazade, "the prodigious storyteller of Araby who for 1,001 nights captivated a cruel sultan with her golden tongue" by driving him wild with anticipation of the plot development of her stories. The narrative can also arouse amorous anticipation and fuel desire with descriptions of the mundane that allude to the sensual. Allende advises her readers to use the aphrodisiac powers of metaphorically seductive language in the kitchen by giving erotic-sounding names to otherwise ordinary dishes: a boring chicken becomes a sensuous meal when called Valentino, the name that has become an alluring metaphor for sexual temptation.

Humor

Allende carefully weaves her tales of culinary and carnal pleasures with a consistent thread of humor, which comforts the reader just at the moment when recipes begin to look too elaborate and sexual positions too challenging. Some critics have noticed and praised her down-to-earth, easy manner of dealing with touchy issues in food and sex: in a discussion of obesity, Allende includes "Hymn to Cellulite" and shares her personal grief over the fact that feminine curves have fallen out of fashion. In relation to male sexual performance, Allende's suggestions range from eating goat testicles to ingesting the powder of rhinoceros' horn, all in the light of the early proclamation: "As soon as men conceived the curious idea that their superiority over women is based on that organ of their anatomy, they began to have problems."

Every page of *Aphrodite* contains humorous references to the many elements that determine what is acceptable and desirable in food and sex. Allende mentions the Christian division of love into divine and profane, taken to extreme when legs of Victorian dinner tables were covered to prevent impure thoughts, and when virtuous couples would make love through a cross-shaped opening in the wife's nightgown. The author comments that "only the Vatican could imagine something that pornographic!"

Throughout the book, the author stays in touch with her readers by avoiding any pretense that she is either a masterful cook or a grand seductress; she says that sauces are a very useful part of one's cooking because they cover up many mistakes ("I have vast experience in culinary catastrophe," she admits). Allende further describes her research for the book with a self-mocking attitude: in an attempt to test some aphrodisiac herbs, she gave her husband nervous shakes that lasted for days. Also, she argues against exhaustive recipes of full menus that often tire the cook beyond the powers of aphrodisiac revival: after preparing one such elaborate meal and eating it, Allende "fell fast asleep by the dishwasher, clutching a sponge, while the man of the moment. . .awaited in the bedroom, working a crossword puzzle."

The advice Allende repeatedly offers is that both sex and food are enjoyed best when approached with humor: "You're not trying to reach perfection but to laugh along the way." After all, even her elaborate list of culinary aphrodisiacs only worked on her friends who were told the meal was supposed to inspire their sensuality; Allende admits that desire is really in the mind and that, "as in the case of black magic, it is a good idea to notify the participants'' in order to make aphrodisiacs work.

Literary Heritage

Latin American Vanguard

Under Spanish rule, the intellectual centers of Latin America were Lima and Mexico City. These two cities had to share intellectual capital with newly formed independent nations when the Spanish Empire ended. Those countries that encouraged literature as part of nation-building, like Chile, leapt to the fore while nations like Paraguay became backwaters. Due to this encouragement, it is not surprising that when a unique Latin American voice began to emerge around World War I, Chileans would play a major role. This developmental period is called the Vanguard.

Chile's Gabriela Mistral was a member of the Vanguard. She followed the example of Peru's Cesar Vallejo and concerned herself with the oppressed. She became the first Latin American to win the Nobel Prize when it was awarded to her in 1945. Fellow Chilean Pablo Neruda would follow her in 1971. Neruda was also sociopolitically oriented but he is better known now for his love poems beginning in 1924 with *Twenty Love Poems and a Song of Despair.*

El Boom

During the 1960s, the literature of Latin America experienced the height of ''El Boom,'' a revolution that broke away from the nineteenth-century tradition and introduced the modern Latin novel. The result was magic realism, a literary movement that addressed social issues but kept them distorted and veiled in ''magical'' symbolism. Its founder, Cuban novelist Alejo Carpentier, was the first to use the Latin American folk tradition of myth and fantasy to describe the political and historical problems of his day. Other writers of magic realism include the Brazilian Jorge Amado, the Colombian Gabriel Garcia Marquez, and the Argentinians Julio Cortazar and Jorge Luis Borges. The Garcia Marquez generation focuses on the epic and heroic universal ''Truths.''

One of the first successful female novelists from Latin America, Allende is often included among these authors as a magic realist (her 1982 debut, *The House of Spirits*, is often compared to Marquez's *One Hundred Years of Solitude*). However, some critics see her work as a subversion and rejection of the magic realist tradition, since she addresses current issues directly and makes clear references to contemporary political events in her work. Also, Allende's writing approach is often labeled extremely feminine, due to the author's use of the woman's point of view and depiction of the female experience. This literary style, critics argue, places her work in the postmodern opus of personal, down-to-earth, body- and relationship-related works, such as the novels of Diamela Eltit, Albalucia Angel, and Sylvia Molloy, the Latin American female novelists conscious of feminism and post-structuralism.

Historical Context

Food in the 1990s

The 1990s consumer generation in the United States was heavily influenced by the 1970s health-consciousness wave that created huge new markets and considerably raised nutritional awareness. Pesticides and food additives came under scrutiny in the 1970s resulting in the epoch-setting removal of DDT and cyclamates-containing artificial sweetener from the market; nutrition became a hot topic in science as well as popular culture. Numerous books were published about the importance of pure food, which resulted in many new health food stores stacked with organic produce. The movement has proliferated since; many of the products introduced in the 1970s became securely established in the 1990s marketplace and eating habits. However, the trend did not expand beyond a certain slice of the market, and has had arguable influence on the overall concept of food consumerism in the U.S. Healthy eating has not led to reduced or sustainable consumption.

In the 1990s, many authors and critics have noted the reverberating changes in the American attitude toward food. The issue of purity has in some cases developed into an obsession, taking on nation-

Compare & Contrast

- **Chile:** Often heralded as a glowing example of free-market capitalism, 21 percent of this nation's 15 million live below the poverty line; per capita purchasing power is $12,500. In a recent World Bank study, Chile tied with Kenya and Zimbabwe for seventh worst in its list of income distribution: 40 percent of national income goes to workers and 60 percent to capital. According to the *CIA World Fact Book,* that disparity breaks down to the lowest 10 percent of income earners controlling 1.4 percent of the wealth while the highest 10 percent control 46.1 percent.

  United States: The most powerful nation on the planet is no paragon of wealth distribution. Per capita purchasing power for this nation of nearly 273 million (13 percent of whom live below the poverty line) is $31,500. According to the *CIA World Fact Book,* nearly all gains in household income have accrued to the top 20 percent of the income bracket. In other words, the lowest 10 percent of income earners control 1.5 percent of the wealth and the top 10 percent control 28.5 percent.

- **Chile:** Chile, El Salvador, Malta, Andorra, and Vatican City are the sole remaining countries where a woman cannot obtain an abortion even if her life is in peril.

  United States: Although abortion opponents have succeeded in limiting abortion rights, the procedure is still legal throughout the U.S.

- **Chile:** There is no middle class to stabilize the economic disparity, and the working class is poorly paid. Free market policies have caused a dismantling of welfare, which leaves the poor to survive on handouts and solidarity with each other.

  United States: The middle class and working class mesh in the U.S. and, although besieged, are still vibrant. Recent economic growth has brought the unemployment rate down to record lows, but most of the increased employment has occurred in temporary staffing positions and in the service sector. The unskilled are paid a minimum wage, while highly-skilled technology jobs go unfilled.

---

al proportions: in his article "A New Puritanism?", Craig Thompson writes that "American consumer culture is notorious for its Puritanical, self-abnegating, and hyper-controlling orientation toward food, and it is also a culture where junk food, sublimated advertising images of food erotica, obesity, and binge eating abound." Thompson further points out the contrast with other world cultures, especially the French, who "view eating in highly sensual and social terms and, in general, have a far more relaxed and unproblematic relation to food."

The difference between Americans and Europeans over foods has been revealed most markedly in the debate over genetically modified organisms (GMOs), foods that have been modified by agribusiness companies for certain qualities (a usual modification includes the ability to withstand heavy

doses of a particular pesticide sold by the same company). French farmers have dumped such food on the highways in protest, and despite an intensive ad campaign, British consumers refuse to buy GMOs. Such grass-roots concern has prompted the European Union to demand labeling of foods as GMOs, a move that the U.S. dislikes immensely. Protests at the Seattle meeting of the World Trade Organization early in 2000 show that American consumers have begun questions GMOs as well. Meanwhile, farmers who grow foods "organically" continue to make healthy profits and increase market share.

Augusto Pinochet

A few months after the publication of Allende's book in 1998, former Chilean dictator Augusto Pinochet was arrested in London on charges of human rights violation. Pinochet came to power in Chile thanks to the 1973 military coup in which the Marxist president Salvador Allende was killed, while his niece Isabel fled the country with her family. She wrote about the national upheaval in her debut novel, *The House of the Spirits*. In the years since the author's exile, her country was transformed from a developing socialist nation to a corrupt democracy of privatization under right-wing military dictatorship. Chilean political crisis, at a high at the time of Pinochet's arrest, was somewhat resolved in 2000 with the election of a socialist liberal president, Ricardo Lagos.

In 1998, Pinochet was accused of the imprisonment, torture, and murder of thousands of Chilean citizens under his reign, as well as assassinations of his opponents abroad. His arrival to power in 1973 was backed by the United States, financed by the C.I.A., and marked by summary executions. In an unheard-of legal move, the military regime protected itself from prosecution by rewriting the Chilean Constitution and giving itself absolute immunity.

When the political left began to struggle harder against the dictatorship during the 1980s, the regime negotiated a plebiscite with the opposition by which Pinochet would retain power as the military commander if voted out of the presidency; this happened in 1988. Also, the new government was both elected and run under the terms of the dictator's rewritten Constitution, while the secret police and the military were still shielded by amnesty and the judicial system still run as before Pinochet's descent from power. The cosmetic changes did nothing to improve the country's failing economy nor its sink-or-swim market: in the mid-1990s study by the World Bank, Chile was ranked seventh-worst among 65 countries in terms of most unequal distribution of income. However, the international media have much hope for the future of Chile, under the newly elected government, and in planning the trial against Pinochet.

Monica Lewinsky

At the end of the twentieth century, America faced a constitutional crisis due to the sexual relations between President Clinton and White House intern Monica Lewinsky. The Independent Counsel, already investigating the Clintons' Whitewater deal, turned to scrutinize sex in the White House. Although it found no evidence to justify impeach-

ment, the U.S. House of Congress voted along party lines to send the matter to trial before the Senate. The Senate reprimanded the President but did not impeach him for sexual impropriety.

Critical Overview

The critical reception of *Aphrodite* was mostly positive, although several critics pointed out that Allende's writing style has become quite light and overwhelmingly autobiographical. Some have described the book as a literary incarnation of the author herself: in a review for *The San Francisco Chronicle*, Patricia Holt writes that, like Allende, the work "has an eloquence and underlying ribaldry that lends an air of sensuality to every event of the day." Barbara Fisher emphasizes the book's "self-indulgent memoir" quality in a review for the *Boston Globe*, commenting that *Aphrodite* is "too much written by, for, and about the lusty and lovely Isabel Allende." Michele Roberts of the *Times* comments that the book is not "meant to be swallowed too seriously; these are tidbits for grazers; amuse-gueules in the French tradition" and adds that "in one sense this is a manual for women in the old style: how to keep your husband interested."

On the other hand, in a review for the *Boston Globe*, Fred Kaplan sees *Aphrodite* as Allende's "escapist lark [which] restored her contact with the pulse of storytelling, whose links to food and sex are fundamental." Another review for *People Weekly* praises the delight with which the author approaches her topics: "Sex and food, once celebrated as two of life's great joys, suffer a lot of bad press these days. Genuine epidemics, coupled with monthly findings of new things that are bad for us, have pushed otherwise happy souls into programs of agonizing denial and, in severe instances, abstinence. Thankfully, in this sophisticated defense of pleasure, [Allende] puts the joy back into eating and loving with all the panache that marks the best of her fiction."

Several critics have observed Allende's broad inclusion of topics in her discussion of aphrodisiacs, summed up in her statement that "all of creation is one long uninterrupted cycle of digestion and fertility.'' The book's subjects vary greatly in significance and origin, just as the listed aphrodisiacs go from the familiar (peaches, eggplant, and ginseng) to the unusual (canary tongues, virgin's urine, and goat testicles). Elaine Kalman Naves of the Montreal *Gazette* calls the work ''a piquant smorgasbord'' that includes everything from ''arcane information'' about Napoleon's sexual fixation on the scent of Josephine's intimate parts, to ''sensuous and sensory writing'' about the taste of the author's first kiss, to ''homespun philosophy'' (Allende's conclusion that love is the ultimate aphrodisiac) and ''engaging whimsy,'' such as detailed instructions on how to prepare an orgy. In the same vein, Leslie Chess Feller in the *New York Times* describes *Aphrodite* as a plethora of ''forbidden fruits, orgies, whispers, pheromones, erotic poetry and Indian tantric rites''; while Deepti Hajela for *Associated Press* cites the practical uses of the lessons from Allende's book: ''Looking to impress with your knowledge at your next cocktail party? Mention that saffron is considered a stimulant or that fenugreek is thought to provoke sensual dreams. Trying to catch the interest of someone you've got your eye on? Prepare some harem turkey or a few soused pears, and who knows where it could lead.''

Yet, according to Naves, as in all of Allende's books, the power of family ties is at the crux of *Aphrodite* —especially ''the profound professional as well as emotional attachment between mother and daughter.'' Naves claims that the ''delightfully idiosyncratic non-fiction'' is not as much about aphrodisiacs as it is about the ''playful collaboration between Allende and her mother, Panchita Llona, who is responsible for the recipes.''

Most of the reviews of *Aphrodite* note the suggestively erotic illustrations done or selected by the author's friend Robert Shekter; among paintings of femmes fatales and delicious dishes are the tasteful sketches of Shekter's plump nymphs, flirtatious satyrs, and witches looming over aphrodisiac potions.

The style of Allende's prose also received praise from various critics for its tactful approach to the touchy subjects of sensual pleasures. The writer for the *Kirkus Review* states that ''the graceful Allende doesn't kiss and tell. She is never crude or exhibitionistic, and she does not seek to shock her gentle readers''; her prose is ''persuasively warm and inviting, but also down-to-earth.'' The reviewer

commends Allende's skill in maintaining ''the delicate relations between eros and writing,'' adding that her ''tact amplifies the eros that pornography kills.'' Further, in the *New York Times* article, Roberts states that Allende's ''humor and self-deprecation enliven her pages,'' but also that *Aphrodite* shows the author's aphrodisiac of choice in the obvious pleasure with which she writes: ''Telling stories, playing verbal games and flirting with words like shuttlecocks, these are the real turn-on for Allende.''

Criticism

Jeremy W. Hubbell

Hubbell has an M.Litt. from the University of Aberdeen and is currently pursuing a Ph.D. in History at the State University of New York, Stony Brook. In the following essay, he discusses the ways in which Aphrodite, *far from being a lightweight pillow book, fits in with late-twentieth-century postmodernist texts.*

Postmodernism, has been variously defined. Certainly, postmodernism takes the form of montage, the weaving together of information segments to create new narrative identities. For some it is the cultural logic implicit in late capitalism. Others see postmodernism as the condition which results from information floods and information economies. John Barth, in his ''The Literature of Replenishment,'' thinks of postmodernism as a style of literature that replenishes. Each of these definitions can be applied to Allende.

According to some critics of modern Latin American literature, Allende's work belongs to the recently established category of female-written, personal, postmodern, and down-to-earth works, often related to the issues of body and relationships, and written in a tone self-conscious of feminism and poststructuralism. Other writers in this group include Diamela Eltit, Albalucia Angel, and Sylvia Molloy. Although Allende's *Aphrodite* escapes the confines of fiction and has not been included in the theoretical discourse of current literary traditions, in many ways it falls into the category of contemporary Latin American literature by women writers.

What Do I Read Next?

- *The House of the Spirits*, Allende's debut novel published in 1982, became a bestseller and won much critical acclaim. Written partly in the magic realist tradition of the so-called Latin Boom, partly as a social and political representation of the Chilean post-revolution reality, the novel is a semi-autobiographical view of four generations of women.

- *Paula* (1997) is the story Allende intends to tell her daughter if she ever wakes up from a coma. She tells Paula about the kooky relatives she has, about the demise of Salvador Allende, and about growing up in Lebanon and Chile. Amidst the sadness, Allende also tells about her personal love affairs as well as her tale of becoming a writer.

- Laura Esquivel's first novel of 1990, *Like Water for Chocolate: A Novel in Monthly Installments, With Recipes, Romances and Home Remedies*, was a run-away bestseller in Mexico. The novel, set in Mexico around 1900, tells of Tita De La Garza who, as the eldest daughter, must remain single to care for her mother. Therefore, she is reared by the cook, Nacha, and knows all the recipes of the family. But romance cannot be kept from her or her cooking.

- Salman Rushdie's 1980 Booker Prize-winning *Midnight's Children* is an epic novel about the partition of India by the British in 1947. At the stroke of midnight, two children are born into this new divided world. Their life stories in India revolve around the daily happenings of their separate households and the way those households revolve around food.

- *The Cook, the Thief, His Wife and Her Lover* (1990) is a lush, colorful, and often gruesome film by Peter Greenaway about love, lust, cruelty and cannibalism. The film stars Helen Mirren and features magnificent costumes by designer Jean-Paul Gaultier.

- Elizabeth Nash delves into the archive in *Plaisirs D'Amour: An Erotic Guide to the Senses* to reveal the secrets of historical sex icons. Amidst the detailed discussions of the varying qualities of aphrodisiacs and biographical notes on Limt, Courbet, and Rembrandt, the guide includes reprints of selections from Anais Nin and Sappho.

With its mixture of autobiographical revelations, intimate tone, everyday issues, fantastic situations, and time- and world-travel in search of the secrets of aphrodisiacs, Allende's book embraces the postmodern tradition in a potpourri-style combination of recipes, erotica, and the numerous methods of research employed in the writing process.

Aphrodite: A Memoir of the Senses maintains a clearly defined feminine insight throughout the tone of the text: Allende's presence in her writing distinctly marks the point of view, the focus, the attitude, and the flow of the book. On several occasions, the author identifies herself as a representative of the female gender, more or less specified on the basis of ethnicity, age, and personal preferences. For example, in her assessment of culinary skill in men and women, she states that it is "fatal" for a woman to admit she can cook; however, men proficient in the kitchen are not only impressive, but irresistibly sexy as well. Allende describes the way she was smitten by her second husband when he prepared dinner for her, "an experience very few Latin American women have had" because "the machos of [their] continent consider any household activity a danger to their perpetually threatened virility." In the chapter "The Spell of Aromas," the author examines in depth the importance of smell in the female erotic experience, again providing personal anecdotes in support of her argument. Also, the sole chapter-length discussion of prostitution is entitled "The Gigolo." In the book's conclusion, Allende writes about love from the female viewpoint, stating: "I don't know how it is with men, but with women no aphrodisiac takes effect without the indispensable ingredient of the affection, which, when carried to perfection, becomes love."

The personal aspect of *Aphrodite* comes from the intimately autobiographical thread in Allende's writing: from the introduction to the final chapter, the author interweaves her recollections, emotions, and opinions on the book's topics into her "memoir of the senses." In the section "Mea Culpa of the Culpable," the author not only introduces the friends, colleagues, and family members who contributed to the book's creation, but also gives a highly personal account of her own motivation for writing *Aphrodite*: in great detail, she describes the sensual dreams that have brought her back into the world of senses, from the period of grief and depression after her daughter's death. Allende's memoirs further resume in almost every chapter, not following a temporal sequence but rather picked out from her memory according to specific themes in each of the book's sections. In an analysis of the cheese-making process, she remembers the sensuous experience of observing the handsome Don Maurizio, a great Venezuelan cheesemaker, as he stirred milk with the whole length of his arm—"one of [the author's] most pleasant memories of that difficult period as an immigrant in a foreign land." Similarly, in the chapter "The Language of Flowers," Allende recalls how the forget-me-not flower became the symbol of her nostalgia after she had to flee Chile following the military coup in 1973, in which her uncle, socialist president Salvador Allende, was assassinated. Also, the author's family tree plays a consistent part in her sensual memoir: from table manners to attitudes toward food to relationships, Allende introduces her ancestors, grandparents, relatives and immediate family members' adventures to illustrate her own development as a gourmet-lover. The chapter entitled "The Orgy" begins with the author's childhood memory of her stepfather's elaborate preparations for romantic evenings with his wife, involving Turkish cushions, Peruvian waltzes, luxurious cocktails, and toast points with caviar—all of which sparked Allende's youthful imagination.

The everyday element of Allende's writing in *Aphrodite* is summed up in her statement that sex and food are the main pillars of existence; she argues that "all of creation is one long uninterrupted cycle of digestion and fertility," as well as that "everything in life [can be] reduced to a process of

> With its mixture of autobiographical revelations, intimate tone, everyday issues, fantastic situations, and time- and world-travel in search of the secrets of aphrodisiacs, Allende's book embraces the postmodern tradition in a potpourri-style combination of recipes, erotica, and the numerous methods of research employed in the writing process."

organisms devouring one another, reproducing themselves, dying, fertilizing the earth, and being reborn transformed." The author further writes that eating and lovemaking are the two things that men and women have in common; the text predominantly deals with heterosexual desire, as Allende identifies herself as such, save for a few mentions of homosexuality (see "The Gigolo" chapter). The book mainly caters to the heterosexual audience in discussing the male-female relationships; thus, sex and food as parts of the everyday life are explored within this realm. However, any discussion of fertility as a purpose of heterosexual union is dismissed early on in the introduction: the author announces that "everyone else, you will have noticed, already has too many children" and that she will instead "concentrate on pleasure" and write about sensuality in both men and women.

Allende proceeds to discuss everyday issues as she advises readers how to prepare a romantic meal and arrange a seduction, how to shop for the best ingredients, and how to "cheat" with truffle-scented oil. Among other things, the book includes basic descriptions of food groups, "Biology 101" analysis of the functioning of human senses, a brief lesson on which wine to serve with which dish, and the necessity of bringing some "spice" into long relationships. The author also writes in a general way about various issues that are part of daily discussion and awareness if not practice, such as the effects of controlled substances on the libido, allergies to certain foods, religious differences and their influence on one's diet and sexual practices, and the impact of one's background on personal preferences—in cuisine and romance.

Overall, *Aphrodite* is composed of a loosely organized plethora of mythical, historical, and fantastic accounts on the nature, reputation, and effects of aphrodisiacs. In a postmodern style, the author casually and easily crosses the boundaries between the numerous fields of her research to combine erotic literature, folklore, anthropology, history, biology, and various theories in her writing. The items Allende lists in support of a single statement about the aphrodisiac properties of a certain fruit can range from historical anecdotes about the practices of rulers of antiquity, to anthropological examinations of certain patterns of human behavior, to conclusions drawn from personal experience, to scientific analysis of chemical elements of the aforementioned fruit. In a single paragraph in the "Etiquette" chapter, Allende mentions the joy she experiences when making cookies and cleaning vegetables, the sensuality of food eaten with one's hands, the touching of lascivious bodies and delicious dishes at Roman orgies, and the incestuous scene in the 1960s English film *Tom Jones* when the hero and his mother share a Pantagruelian meal.

The author draws on a variety of fields in her narrative to enrich the descriptions of the world's aphrodisiacs. From history, she takes the recordings of the use of love charms and potions; the impact of religious and class systems on the evolution of attitudes toward sex and food; numerous anecdotes from the lives of noted personages (from the notorious to the glorified); and the occurrence of miscellaneous trends in erotica, through the centuries and all over the world. From biology, Allende borrows the analyses of the functions of human bodies; the statistics on sensual and neural experiences, in humans and other species; and the properties and effects of various chemicals present in particular ingredients or substances. The study of anthropology comes in handy with reports on unusual dietary and sexual habits in remote places and times; a discussion of carnivorous, cannibalistic, and otherwise specific practices; the beliefs in certain aphrodisiac powers responsible for poaching, black magic, and fasting; and the notions of beauty, femininity, and masculinity in different civilizations. Further, Allende also turns to many examples in popular culture to prove her points, from the obsessive depravity of Howard Hughes to the fashionable

nouvelle cuisine which the author strongly detests. The book is filled with references to movie scenes in which Epicurean characters devour lush meals, authors of erotica who defended their right to write about passion as they feel it, Latin crooners whose voices are a powerful tool of seduction, and film directors whose recipe for a perfect martini is "allowing a ray of light to pass through the bottle of vermouth and for an instant touch the gin." Allende also makes use of literature, taking excerpts from the Bible, poems by Pablo Neruda, passages from Oriental erotic texts, and various prose and poetry on the topics of romance and cuisine to diversify her assessment of the nature of aphrodisiac.

All in all, Allende's *Aphrodite* abounds with the characteristics that securely place it within the postmodern, Latin-American, female-authored tradition, despite the tendency at first glance to classify this work as a cookbook, a pillow book, or a self-indulgent, self-help memoir—and, in most cases, as all three. The sense of Aphrodite's lightness is created by the author's casual tone and seeming disorganization of her prose; but the numerous threads of themes, arguments, and illustrations that comprise the colorful texture of the book imperceptibly carry the weight of a new theory of meaning. Allende's work reflects her own montage approach to replenishment and can serve as a piece in our own.

Source: Jeremy W. Hubbell, in an essay for *Literature of Developing Nations for Students*, Gale, 2000.

Michele Roberts

In this review, author Michele Roberts calls Isabelle Allende's Aphrodite: A Memoir of the Senses *a "charming" recipe book and treasure trove of advice for sharpening one's culinary and amatory skills. Roberts observes that for Allende, the real joy of the twinned themes of eroticism and food seems to be the words and stories she uses to prepare her novel recipes.*

Just as the pleasures of eating can replace the pleasures of sex, so reading about food can provoke as much satisfaction as flicking through some soft porn. Isabel Allende's charming new book aims to reconcile the two appetites, offering sensual recipes to tempt jaded palates. I don't think her collection of tips and stories is meant to be swallowed too seriously; these are titbits for grazers; amuse-gueules in the French tradition. Not a pot-boiler; rather, a spicy word-salad. The compilation opens with Allende's ruefully honest admission: "I repent of my diets, the delicious dishes rejected out of vanity, as much as I lament the opportunities for making love that I let go because of pressing tasks or puritanical virtue.''

Her solution is that of the novelist: to fantasise, to write it all down, to make it all up. That way she can stay faithful to the husband she assures us she adores, while at the same time hoping to lure him from his computer to experience some new frothy sexual experiences. When you are 50, she explains, and have stayed married to the same man all your life, you have to pep up his flagging interest. So in one sense this is a manual for women in the old style: how to keep your husband interested.

Allende doesn't really seem to imagine that her husband will enter the kitchen and whip up these little feasts for her, though she declares what every woman knows: that a man who cooks for you is a desirable creature. Women are sexier if they don't let on they know how to cook, she warns, but nonetheless her book seems aimed at female chefs. Its male readers, of whom I imagine there could be many, will find it a treasure trove of advice on sharpening up their amatory and culinary techniques. It is, indeed, just the thing to read in bed.

Allende's humour and self-deprecation enliven her pages. She's never known anyone who cooks or makes love from a manual, she tells us, so why should we buy her book, we ''people who work hard to earn a living and who pray in secret, like you and me, improvise in casseroles and bedroom romps as best we can, using what we have at hand, without brooding over it or making too much fuss, grateful for our remaining teeth and our enormous good fortune in having someone to embrace''? Her modesty gives a shrugging answer: ''because the idea of poking about a bit in aphrodisiacs seems amusing to me and I hope it will be to you as well.''

So right away we know that really it's the art and pleasure of reading that's being offered. Allende's testers only found the recipes sexually arousing when told that they were meant to be; the control group reported no surges in libido, though they enjoyed their exquisite dinners and conversation. Telling stories, playing verbal games and flirting with words like shuttlecocks, these are the real turn-on for Allende. In between offering up light, well-flavoured reminiscences sauced with humour she imparts a certain amount of kitchen lore and suggests new ways to make roast chicken romantic; one technique is to call the bird Valentino.

This is mainly a delightful book, juicy with affectionately prepared vignettes that turn out well

> **" This is mainly a delightful book, juicy with affectionately prepared vignettes that turn out well every time like an expert chef's souffles."**

every time like an expert chef's souffles. Occasionally you can feel there are too many loving descriptions of bourgeois dining tables loaded with fine silver and plate and you long for Allende to describe, instead, the stern delights of eating fish and chips in a howling gale on the beach at Skegness.

Her only contact with English eroticism, however, is a practice from ''certain rural areas'' whereby ''the woman kneads flour, water and lard, sprinkles the dough with her saliva, then places it between her legs to endow it with the form and savour of her secret parts. She bakes this bread and offers the loaf to the object of her desire.'' Have Delia and Sophie been keeping this recipe to themselves all this time? I think we should be told.

Source: Michele Roberts, ''Keeping Sex on the Menu,'' in *The London Times,* April 30, 1998, p. 45.

Leslie Chess Feller

In this brief review of Isabelle Allende's Aphrodite: A Memoir of the Senses, *Leslie Chess Feller summarizes Allende's non-fictional exploration of the world of sensual experience using food as an erotic catalyst.*

If this is just a cookbook, then Allende's novels are just potboilers! From the author of such incomparable novels as *House of the Spirits* (1985) and the highly evocative collection *Stories of Eva Luna* (1991) comes a luscious book about aphrodisiacs—the bridge between gluttony and lust. To care less about food preparation with seduction in mind would not prohibit any appreciator of beautiful writing from thoroughly enjoying this extraordinarily seductive book. Yes, Allende does provide recipes, and many of them may spark chemistry between two individuals. But more important than the recipes are her historical and biological ruminations on the inseparability of food and eroticism.

With her "sole focus [being] on the sensual art of food and its effects on amorous performance," the author wanders delectably through the ways food arouses the senses, citing tales and truths, folklore and science, and drawing into her discussions other topics such as the role of language in seduction, the need for physical touch, and the pleasures of drinking wine—an act that "lessens inhibitions, relaxes, and fosters joy, three fundamental requirements for good performance." Readers may view their lunchtime Big Macs and fries in a different light after enjoying Allende's pages, for, as she posits, "all of creation is one long uninterrupted cycle of digestion and fertility."

Source: Leslie Chess Feller, "Books in Brief: Nonfiction," in *The New York Times,* April 5, 1998, sec. 7, p. 25, col. 4.

Brad Hooper

In this brief summary of Isabelle Allende's Aphrodite: A Memoir of the Senses, *Brad Hooper describes Allende's work of non-fiction as a cookbook which, while also providing actual recipes, most importantly provides historical and biological rumination on the "inseparability of food and eroticism."*

"Eggs"—from caviar to the kind produced by chickens—"lend themselves to all sorts of naughtiness," Isabel Allende writes. (She prefers hers "served on my lover's navel with chopped onion, pepper, salt, lemon and a drop of Tabasco.") In *Aphrodite,* Allende turns the joyous preparation and consumption of fine food into an erotic catalyst; it culminates in a collection of serious recipes for your first—or next—bacchanal. Illustrated by Robert Shekter's bold nymphs and mischievous satyrs, *Aphrodite* discusses forbidden fruits, orgies, whispers, pheromones, erotic poetry and Indian tantric rites. Be warned: some aphrodisiacs require more courage and dedication than others. In China, baby cockroaches are tossed into warm rice wine and downed in a single swallow. Although Allende mentions exotica like shark fins, baboon testicles, eye of salamander and the urine of a virgin, her recipes use ingredients that "can be ingested without peril." Serving suggestions, however, can be bold. Regarding a mouthwatering *arroz con leche*: "You can cover your lover from head to foot. . .and slowly lick it of."

Source: Brad Hooper, "Aphrodite: A Memoir of the Senses," (book review) in *The Booklist,* Vol. 94, No. 11, February 1, 1998, p. 875.

Genevieve Stuttaford, Maria Simson, and Jeff Zaleski

In this brief review, authors Stuttaford, Simson and Zaleski call Isabelle Allende's Aphrodite: A Memoir of the Senses *a "sophisticated defense of pleasure," mixing recipes, anecdotes, and advice together for a whimsical view of romance and sex.*

Sex and food, once celebrated as two of life's great joys, suffer a lot of bad press these days. Genuine epidemics, coupled with monthly findings of new things that are bad for us, have pushed otherwise happy souls into programs of agonizing denial and, in severe instances, abstinence. Thankfully, in this sophisticated defense of pleasure, novelist Allende (*The House of the Spirits*) puts the joy back into eating and loving with all the panache that marks the best of her fiction. Though passionate about her subject, she remains consistently whimsical with this mix of anecdotes, recipes and advice designed to enhance any romantic encounter. As always, her secret weapon is honesty: "Some [aphrodisiacs] have a scientific basis, but most are activated by the imagination." Allende's vivacity and wit are in full bloom as she makes her pronouncements: "There are few virtues a man can possess more erotic than culinary skill"; "When you make an omelet, as when you make love, affection counts for more than technique." Her book is filled with succinct wisdom and big laughs. Despite sections titled "The Orgy" and "Supreme Stimulus for Lechery," Allende comes down emphatically for romance over sex and for ritual over flavor in a work that succeeds in being what it intends to be—fun from the first nibble to the last.

Source: Genevieve Stuttaford, Maria Simson, and Jeff Zaleski, "Aphrodite: A Memoir of the Senses," (book review) in *Publisher's Weekly,* Vol. 245, No. 3, January 19, 1998, p. 360.

Sources

"*Aphrodite: A Memoir of the Senses*, by Isabel Allende," in *People Weekly,* Vol. 49, No. 15, April 20, 1998, p. 47.

Chess Feller, Leslie, review, in *The New York Times,* April 5, 1998, Section 7, p. 25.

"An Elegant Grandmother Ponders the Erotic Side of Food and the Most Delicious Aspects of Eros," in *Kirkus Reviews,* February 1, 1998.

Hajela, Deepti, "Allende Blends Two Hot Topics—Food and Sex," in *The Associated Press,* May 4, 1998.

Holt, Patricia, ''Love Is Still the Best Aphrodisiac, Isabel Allende Reports,'' in *The San Francisco Chronicle*, March 24, 1998, p. E1.

Kalman, Elaine, ''The Proof of the Pudding: Isabel Allende Serves Up a Sweet Treat for 'Frightened Men and Melancholy Women,''' in *The Gazette* (Montreal), March 21, 1998, p. J3.

Kaplan, Fred, ''Angel of Gluttony and Lust; Blessings of Food, Eros Heal in Isabel Allende's New Book,'' in *The Boston Globe*, April 1, 1998.

Roberts, Michele, ''Keeping Sex on the Menu,'' in *The Times*, April 30, 1998.

Thompson, Craig, ''A New Puritanism?,'' in *The Boston Review*, Summer 1999.

> Readers may view their lunch-time Big Macs and fries in a different light after enjoying Allende's pages, for, as she posits, 'all of creation is one long uninterrupted cycle of digestion and fertility.'"

Further Reading

Ackerman, Diane, *A Natural History of the Senses*, Vintage Books, 1991.

Ackerman tours history to point out the role the senses have played in historical events. She reports on the curious habits and sensuous delights enjoyed by famous people like Marc Antony and Cleopatra.

Allende, Isabel, *Infinite Plan: A Novel*, translated by Margaret Sayers Peden, Harperperennial Library, 1994.

Allende's first American novel, *Infinite Plan* records the saga of Gregory Reeves. Set in post-WWII America, Gregory has devised a philosophy of life, an infinite plan, and attempts to gain adherents. Then reality begins and Gregory survives law school, Vietnam, two marriages, and the loss of a great sum of money.

Suleri, Sara, *Meatless Days*, University of Chicago Press, 1991.

Another work about the partition of India that also deals with the centrality of the senses and food. Suleri's novel takes place in Pakistan and focuses on a girl coming of age and her role in food preparation in a house that is both Welsh and Hindu.

Toussaint-Samat, Maguelonne, *History of Food*, translated by Anthea Bell, Blackwell, 1994.

Toussaint-Samat's book encompasses, as much as anyone can, the history of eating in Western civilization. The focus of the work looks at the transition of humans to a meat-based diet. Another area of concern is the historical role of culinary habits in the everyday life of humans.

An Astrologer's Day

R. K. Narayan

1947

"An Astrologer's Day" was first published in the newspaper *The Hindu* and then was made the title story of a collection of short stories which appeared in 1947—the year that India gained its independence. R. K. Narayan's first collection of short stories, entitled *Malgudi Days*, appeared in 1941. Two other collections followed quickly: *Dodu and Other Stories* in 1943 and *Cyclone and Other Stories* in 1944. By the time this collection was published, he was already a well-known novelist, both in India and the West. The endorsement given by the eminent British novelist Graham Greene, who wrote an introduction to Narayan's novel *The Financial Expert* (1952), made a great deal of difference to his popularity in the West. By the 1950s he was known as one of the three major writers of India, the other two being Raja Rao and Mulk Raj Anand. "An Astrologer's Day" remains a major work in his corpus and displays all the characteristics associated with his writing. Narayan's sense of irony, his deep religious sensibility, his humor, his consciousness of the significance of everyday occurrences, and his belief in a Hindu vision of life are all revealed in this story.

Author Biography

Rasipuram Krishnaswami Narayan was born in Madras (now known as Chennai), South India, on

October 10, 1907. Although his family moved to Mysore when he was a child, he continued to live in Madras under the care of his grandmother, who ensured that he led a very disciplined life. A Brahmin (one who belongs to the priestly caste) by birth, he learned Sankrit as part of his training in Hinduism. His mother tongue was Tamil, a language spoken by some sixty million people in India. His knowledge of English came from his education. A voracious reader, he learned a great deal of English literature during his school years, and this knowledge was crucial to his own development as a writer. Until he passed his university entrance examination he remained in Madras, and then joined Maharaja's College, Mysore. After considerable effort, he obtained his B.A. in 1930 and decided that he would pursue no further formal education.

After having tried teaching as a profession, Narayan gave it up in exasperation and decided to pursue what he really liked: writing. Financial difficulties forced him to take up journalism for a period of time, but his main objective was to become a full-time writer. In 1933 he married Rajam, a devoted wife who died in 1939. His first novel, *Swami and Friends*, was published in 1935, and since then Narayan's life has been devoted to writing novels, short stories, and essays; during the last sixty years he has produced some fifteen novels, seven collections of short stories, and eight other books, which include his essays and retelling of Hindu myths and epics. His early novels won the admiration of Graham Greene, whose support gave Narayan the opportunity he needed to find an international readership for his writing. Although he has not consciously avoided important issues—such as the struggle for independence, the career of Mahatma Gandhi, the partition of India, or the role of India in South Asia—his primary focus has been the day-to-day lives of ordinary folk in his fictional town of Malgudi. The forces of change have been recorded in his fiction, but the dominant theme of his work is the timelessness of India. What he has projected consistently is a vision of a culture or way of life held together by shared values and a sense of humanity. Narayan continues to live in Mysore and still writes occasional pieces.

Plot Summary

''An Astrologer's Day'' has a deceptively simple plot, although the full significance of the story

R. K. Narayan

becomes evident only after a second or even third reading. Part of the difficulty arises from the fact that the author deliberately avoids markers that would benefit the reader: there is no clear indication where the story occurs or when it does, although it is possible to make an educated guess about both. The story begins almost *in medias res* (in the middle) and concludes on what appears to be an ambiguous note. But, in fact, the story is a tightly knit one in which all parts fit together.

Description

The story begins with a description of the astrologer, who is the central character in the story. In minute detail, his appearance, his clothes, and all the materials he uses to ply his trade are described. The astrologer, who is not given a name, comes across as a type, one of the many street vendors in India, who sit under the shade of a tree or a temporary shed and sell anything from vegetables to newspapers. This astrologer belongs to the same category although, given the nature of his trade, there is a need to dress and behave in a particular manner. He does that effectively by giving the impression of a holy man whose special powers enable him to function as an astrologer.

Almost casually, the surroundings of the astrologer begin to take shape. While there are no clear references to a particular city, it is likely, since Narayan consistently uses the fictional city of Malgudi, that this story too takes place in Malgudi. In any event, one gets the impression of a somewhat backward city which still retains a measure of its rural character. The reference to ''municipal lighting'' is one of the strategies employed by the author to suggest a sense of the place. In addition, the reference to other vendors who sell a variety of goods gives a sense of a bustling community in which the astrologer operates.

Dialogue

The first part of the story provides a sense of the setting and background without providing any real information about the astrologer. In very broad terms, the daily activities of the astrologer are told. The narrator makes it very clear that the astrologer is a charlatan who knows nothing about the future but is a shrewd judge of character. The transition from a type to sharply defined individual occurs when the astrologer is ready to leave for home and one last client stops in front of him. At that stage, omniscient narration gives way to dialogue and the astrologer and client become involved in a discussion. The astrologer treats this client like any other and begins with the same platitudes and comments he always uses, only to find that the client is unusually aggressive and mean-spirited. This client insists on his money's worth and states that if the astrologer does not tell the truth, he should not only return the money given to him but also give an additional sum for having lied. Realizing that he is likely to be exposed, the astrologer gets nervous and does his best to back out of the transaction. The client, on the other hand, is adamant and insists that a challenge is a challenge. The astrologer then has no choice except to agree to the terms.

Just when the reader feels that the client has called the astrologer's bluff, the story takes on a new dimension. The astrologer begins by recounting the story of the client's past and describes how a long time ago he had been stabbed and thrown into a well and left for dead. It was the assistance of a passerby that saved him. The client, who is tremendously impressed by this revelation, is stunned when the astrologer addresses him by name, calls him Guru Nayak, and advises him to go back home and stop looking for the man who stabbed him since he had died in an accident. To further reinforce his point, the astrologer says that if Nayak leaves his

village again, he is likely to face considerable danger. By now, the reader is quite mystified and begins to wonder whether the astrologer has some mystical powers after all. The transition from light-hearted satire to serious narrative is quite striking and the narrator avoids enlightening the confused reader.

Conclusion

Nayak then pays the astrologer and leaves; the astrologer too leaves for home. Since he is late, his wife is at the door waiting for him and insists on an explanation for his delay. This becomes the occasion for the astrologer to give his wife the extra money he earned by winning the wager and to add that now a great load has been lifted off his mind. All these years he had thought that he had killed a man, and that is why he had run away from the village. Today he realized that the victim was in fact alive and well. The wife is mystified and doesn't understand the full story, and the astrologer does not care to elaborate. For the reader, at this moment, the entire sequence of events makes perfect sense. The client was none other than the person who had been stabbed by the astrologer; for obvious reasons, Nayak fails to recognize the astrologer. The author's strategy of ensuring that the encounter takes place late in the evening ensures that the two do not recognize each other initially. In fact, it is only because Nayak lights a cigar that the astrologer gets the opportunity to see his face and recognize him. The story ends with the astrologer going to sleep, completely at peace with himself.

Characters

The Astrologer

The two main characters of the story are the astrologer, who is not given a name, and Guru Nayak, the client who turns out to be a former victim, now on a quest for revenge. The astrologer is not given a name partly because he is intended to be seen, for most of the story, as a typical figure, one of the many who conduct their business in makeshift locations in the city, and partly because the narrative mode does not require that he be given a name. It is only at the end of the story that the astrologer is given an individuality that makes him a distinctive figure. Also, in the story he interacts only with two characters: the first, a passerby who seeks his advice about the future. The relation between the two is purely functional, and there would be no need for the person to address the astrologer by name. The second is the astrologer's wife, who speaks to him at the end of the story. In this instance, convention demands that she should not use his name to address him: In a typical South Indian family it would be rare for a wife to address her husband by name. Hence, despite the latitude of omniscient narration, the author chooses to let the astrologer remain anonymous.

Nonetheless, the astrologer comes across as a sharply defined figure, mainly as a result of the assortment of objects he carries with him in order to create the illusion of spirituality and mystical knowledge. The care he takes over his personal appearance is yet another aspect of his charisma. The profession of an astrologer presupposes a commitment to religious observance, and that is precisely what this character achieves through his eclectic collection of articles. The bundle of palmyra writing (script on the leaves of a palmyra tree) in particular lends a very authentic touch, since such writings reflect both wisdom and a high degree of learning. The combination of holy ash and vermillion on his forehead, the turban on his head, and his whiskers, all taken together, give the impression of a man given to a holy life rather than business. The author ensures that despite the external trappings, the astrologer is not necessarily a negative or rogue figure. Telling the future is a job, not unlike selling peanuts or cloth, and he does this with a sense of purpose and commitment. Within the overall structure of the story, it is important for the astrologer to come across as a somewhat mild and inoffensive person who had left his village to escape a life of poverty. His portrayal as a positive character helps to offset the revelation at the end that he had left the village after having committed a crime. The important aspect of the astrologer's character is that as the story progresses he moves from being a type to a carefully individualized person.

The first three pages of the story are devoted to description of the astrologer and his surroundings. Roadside astrologers are a common sight in India, and the general perception is that they make their living by exploiting the gullibility of people who seek their advice. This astrologer is no different, except that he comes across as a shrewd and intelligent man whose livelihood depends on turning every occurrence to his advantage. Having no light-

ing system of his own, he manages to get by on his adjoining vendor's light. When the groundnut seller closes shop, he has no lighting to conduct his business, and he too leaves for home. Similarly, when his clients seek his advice, he lets them speak long enough in order to gather sufficient information to make an educated guess about their future. His intuitive understanding of human nature and his wit are crucial to the plot of the story, and the relevance of all the details becomes evident at the end of the story. Among the trickster figures that Narayan has created in his work, the astrologer is a memorable and likeable one.

Guru Nayak

Guru Nayak is the antithesis of the astrologer. He appears in the story at midpoint, and almost immediately comes across as both aggressive and mean-spirited. Unlike the astrologer who is described through third-person narrative, Nayak is revealed through his own dialogue. He too remains nameless until the astrologer addresses him by name. The name itself is chosen carefully, for the term "Guru," with all its associations of spiritual leader or teacher, is noticeably different from what we see in the character. Nayak is on a quest for the person who harmed him, and his attempt to solicit the assistance of the astrologer is part of his quest. Unlike other clients, Nayak begins with a skeptical attitude, and rather than accept the astrologer or leave him altogether, insists on a wager. According to the wager, the astrologer must be accurate in his predictions or give up a substantial sum of money. The wager is carefully inserted in the story in order to reveal later that Nayak, with his penchant for gambling, would have been at least partly to blame for the altercation in the past. It is also significant that at the end of story, when the astrologer's wife adds up the coins given by Nayak and announces the total, the astrologer realizes that he has been cheated. A small detail in itself, it establishes that Nayak is the opposite of the astrologer, and in the overall moral scheme of the story, it is the astrologer who is the victim and not the other.

From the perspective of narrative strategy, it is remarkable that while the astrologer is revealed through his actions and the point of view of the narrator, Nayak is shown through his dialogue. Nayak's language is always abrupt and elliptical, and his short sentences suggest a pugnacious nature. Choosing a diction is always a challenge for the writer when the characters would have, in normal circumstances, spoken a different language and not English. In this instance, the chances are that Nayak would have spoken in Tamil. The language he speaks in English is thus a close approximation of the kind of language he would have used in Tamil.

Rather than seek the assistance of the astrologer, Nayak proposes a wager, with the intention of fleecing him. A bully by nature, his objective is to intimidate the astrologer in order to appropriate his money. Curiously enough, at the end of the exchange, it is the astrologer who wins the sympathy of the reader. One of the ironies of the story is that in this encounter, the astrologer's ''supernatural'' knowledge turns out to be the truth, and Nayak leaves after having accepted the astrologer's advice about the future. Nayak's attitude at the end also affirms an interesting aspect of astrological prediction, at least as it is often practiced: the importance of prediction is not so much objective truth as it is the capacity to state what will resolve the conflict in the mind of the client.

Wife

The only other character in the story is the wife of the astrologer, who is also nameless, mainly because husbands rarely refer to their wives by name in the social ethos of the story. The absence of a name also has the effect of casting her as a type, confined to the house, comfortable with attending to household chores, cooking and taking care of their daughter. She is also not from the village—a trivial detail but a necessary one in that it provides the occasion for the astrologer to confess his past indiscretion at the end of the story. Had the wife been from the same village (and this would be more typically the case), the astrologer's confession would have been redundant and would have ruined the economy of the story. The wife is also a means to suggest the overall economic standing of the family, since acquiring twelve and a half annas—a paltry sum by Indian standards—becomes an occasion for celebration. She also serves the fictional purpose of providing the occasion for the astrologer to reveal aspects of his past and the significance of having encountered Guru Nayak on that day. Narayan's women characters are not often as sharply defined as his male characters, and the woman in this story is no exception. She comes across as a type rather than as a sharply individualized person. The very fact that she belongs to the town rather than the city is of considerable sociological interest, although to pursue that would have destroyed the unity of the story.

Themes

Fate

Narayan's world is predominantly a Hindu one in which fate plays an important role. Nothing happens by accident and all human actions have consequences. The entire story is based on the astrologer's sense of guilt at having stabbed another young man in the village and then having absconded in order to avoid punishment. The stabbing is later seen to be an act of youthful folly. Nonetheless, the astrologer lives with the fear of being identified, and the curious irony is that it is he who identifies the victim and not the other way about. He does not pay for his crime, but the story ends on the note that he had spent years regretting his deed and that in itself is punishment enough. The story demands a suspension of disbelief, and if credibility is strained at certain points, it is because the author's notion of fate transcends rational explanation. Narayan's depiction of fate does not lead to an attitude of resignation, and it does not preclude the importance of individual actions. There is, however, a sense of a larger scheme within which human actions function.

Religion

Although religion is never emphasized in this story, or for that matter in most of his fiction, it remains a constant preoccupation in Narayan's writing. In the world that the author depicts religion is a way of life and it becomes an integral part of everyday life. Everything about the astrologer—his palmyra leaves, the holy ash on his forehead, the vermillion—all these are suggestive of an engagement with religion. Ironically, the astrologer is no different from anyone else, and his profession is dependent largely on fooling gullible people. There is no real contradiction between the religious exterior of the astrologer and his profession. The story drives home the fundamental point that religion is not present as a moral force or as an indication of spirituality, but rather as an essential part of life.

Money

For a story that is concerned with moral issues, there is constant reference to money. In fact, for the major part of the story, the astrologer and his client haggle over how much money ought to be paid for the astrologer's services. The story ends with the astrologer's exasperation at having been cheated. Even the wife is described in relation to money, for her concern is with how much her husband earned during the day, and how she would spend the money. The curious juxtaposition of money and spirituality is what gives the story its distinctive texture. While there is an implied contrast between the two, the story also reinforces the coexistence of both.

Modernity

Admittedly, social realism is not Narayan's preoccupation. Issues of caste, gender, class, economic exploitation, and the environment are all incidental aspects of Narayan's work. To say this is not to claim that there is a naive idealism about Narayan that makes him turn away from the realities of modern India. Narayan has lived through a period that witnessed startling changes in India and he reveals in his essays an awareness of their significance. But he is also firmly committed to the idea of a timeless India. Despite all the changes brought about by colonialism, he perceives a fundamental unity in society and a way of life that has remained unchanged. Even in this story the signs of modernization are always present. The casual references to the Town Hall, the different kinds of goods that are being sold, the electric lights and the migration from the village are ways of alerting the reader to the changes that have taken place. At the same time, the texture of life remains unchanged. Institutions such as religion and marriage continue as before and the course of human life is determined by a process that has undergone very little change over time. The juxtaposition of the past and present in a way that privileges the past is one of the distinctive aspects of Narayan's work.

Style

Point of View

The story adopts the traditional mode of third-person omniscience. In other words, the author/narrator relates the entire story to the reader, but since the entire plot is dependent on the revelation taking place at the end, the narrator does not reveal all the aspects of character at the beginning. While the narrator is forthcoming about all the peripheral goings-on in the story, s/he is careful not to reveal to the reader anything more than would be evident to any passerby. The reader sees the plot as it is being enacted, despite the presence of the omniscient narrator. The use of dialogue throughout the story

Topics for Further Study

- Narayan's story often draws attention to light and darkness. To what extent is the imagery of light central to the overall structure of the story? Relate your response to the title of the story.

- The groundnut vendor, whose lighting enables the astrologer to conduct his business, comes across as a very colorful character. Write a brief narrative entitled ''A Groundnut Vendor's Day'' in order to show how different his or her life would have been.

- Narayan's reputation as a significant writer has not waned during the last fifty years. To what extent do you think ''An Astrologer's Day'' demonstrates aspects of his fiction that would account for his popularity?

- The general consensus among critics is that reading Narayan is one way of understanding the real India. How accurately and how comprehensively does ''An Astrologer's Day'' create a sense of the social and cultural conditions in India?

serves the function of providing multiple points of view without altering the overall authority of the narrator.

Style

One aspect of Narayan's writing that has been noted time and again is the remarkably simple style he consistently adopts. For those who are familiar with the South Indian Tamil language, his style would come across as a curious mixture of English and Tamil. While the syntax and grammar conform to English conventions, several of the idioms are clearly influenced by Tamil. Particularly in dialogue, as in the exchange between the astrologer and Guru Nayak, the language moves between standard English and dialect. Sometimes, it is evident that what he is providing is a literal translation of expressions in Tamil. The unself-conscious skill with which he combines the traditions of two languages is yet another reason for his success.

Irony

If there is one aspect of Narayan's writing that has been remarked on by all critics, it is the quality of irony that is always present. Whether it is the narrator informing the reader about the past or the characters interacting with each other, the note of irony is consistent and occurs as a result of the distance between what people profess and, what they do. No one, usually, is free from the ironic perspective of the author. But the irony is never malicious or particularly harsh. The dualities that the author perceives in the characters are subsumed in a larger acceptance of human weakness. Narayan's irony has a quality of acceptance that prevents it from becoming satire or cynicism.

In fact the central irony of the story is that Nayak spends so much time looking for the man who had harmed him and, when he eventually meets him, does not recognize him. By the same token, the astrologer had spent years living in virtual hiding only to discover that he had not committed a crime. These instances of irony operate at the level of structure, while the more obvious use of irony becomes evident when characters speak to each other.

Structure

What gives this story its compelling power is the manner in which the story is constructed. The appearance of artlessness is really a result of a careful structure in which all the details fit together. The initial description of the astrologer gives the impression of a traditional method of introducing a character by describing his appearance. In this particular instance, the astrologer's appearance is a form of disguise, not because he is a fugitive, but because his profession demands that he should give the impression of being in possession of mystical powers. As a result, he hardly looks like the simple villager who left the village years ago. Hence it is no surprise that Nayak fails to identify him. By the same token, it is necessary to provide a context for the astrologer's initial failure to identify Nayak. That is achieved by the simple expedient of having Nayak appear when there is very little light and the astrologer is ready to close shop for the day. Significantly, the astrologer identifies Nayak when the latter lights a cigar and his face is illuminated for a brief moment.

Similarly, casual observations take on a particular significance later in the story. The astrologer's decision to leave the village is mentioned almost as an aside in the story. The strategy here is one of foreshadowing, where the author mentions a detail that appears trivial at that moment but becomes crucial in retrospect. Its relevance is evident at the end when he confesses that he is in some ways a fugitive.

One of the striking aspects of Narayan's writing is that, for the most part, he locates his work in the fictional town of Malgudi. While it is possible to speculate on a precise location for this city, the fact remains that Narayan intended Malgudi to be a microcosm of India. From the landscape to the characters who inhabit this world, there is a strong sense of allegory. The mountains, rivers, houses, city offices, places of religious worship, and shops are all constructed in a manner that would suggest that Malgudi is a typical city whose citizens may be found anywhere in India. It is the insistence with which Narayan does this that gives his work a quality of timelessness.

Literary Heritage

R.K. Narayan was born in Madras, South India, in 1907. A Brahmin by birth (a Hindu priest caste), Narayan was trained in both Sanskrit (as part of his training in Hinduism) and English, although his mother tongue was Tamil, a language spoken by over sixty million people in India. Narayan published his first novel (in English) in 1935, during the turbulent division of India. His writing ranges from retellings of classical Hindu myths and stories to essays, short stories and novels.

Unlike some other Indian authors of the twentieth century, Narayan did not actively avoid writing about the immense political or economic strife of his time and culture, although his primary focus was the day-to-day lives of ordinary Indian people. These depictions of Indian life lend Narayan's work a sense of timelessness, while still recording the forces of change throughout India. Narayan's work has gained an international audience and many critics have praised his work for its ability to impart a sense of Indian life as a native, calling his work a blend of Hindu mysticism and English form. Narayan's work, though in English, is characterized by a Hindu sensibility and a conviction that human lives and problems are part of a larger cosmic harmony.

Compare & Contrast

- **1940s:** India is still under colonial rule, gaining independence in 1947.

  1970s: India has resolved many of its internal and external disputes and taken an active part in the creation of Bangladesh.

  1990s: India emerges as a major industrial nation.

- **1940s:** India is predominantly rural with relatively few urban centers.

  1970s: India is still a controlled economy but major advances are occurring in the shift to urban life.

  1990s: India has become technologically advanced and very urban in its structure.

- **1940s:** In terms of gender relations, Indian society is very patriarchal in its outlook.

  1970s: India sees a number of changes with women joining the work force in large numbers. Indira Gandhi becomes prime minister.

  1990s: Women's movements are very active in the country and major changes have occurred in gender equity. While the country is still patriarchal in many ways, women play a far more active and significant role in the life of the nation.

Historical Context

Politics

Another aspect of Narayan's work that has been consistently pointed out in criticism is the author's refusal to engage with the historical and political events of the time. The author does not completely disregard politics, but that is always less important than the ordinary lives of the people who live in Malgudi.

The collection itself was published in 1947, the year that India gained its independence. It was a time of considerable excitement and turmoil in the country as the British made preparations to leave, and the country was on the brink of a civil war. The conflict between the Hindus and the Muslims was becoming increasingly difficult to control and there was large-scale violence perpetrated by both sides. It was also the time when the nonviolent struggle against the British had achieved international recognition and Gandhi was seen as a major figure. The story does not provide any sense of such events.

Reading the story after five decades is a useful exercise largely because the story has not lost any of its appeal. The timeless quality of the story is also its strength, and as a result the story continues to be relevant. Despite the fact that India has made huge strides in technology and is considered highly advanced in many areas, the pace of Indian life continues to be the same. Street vendors are still a common sight, and the migration from villages to cities continues to be a typical occurrence. In that sense, no aspect of the story appears to be archaic or outdated.

Critical Overview

Among Indian authors, Narayan has probably received the most attention. Apart from a few essays that have expressed some reservation about Narayan's refusal to engage with political social realities, all others have been largely adulatory. Book-length studies of his work have dealt with various aspects of his work, including myth, humor, religion, identity, and so forth. Surprisingly, much more attention has been paid to the novels than to the short stories, although Narayan has published several collections over a career that spans more than six decades. It is to his credit that any major study of Indian writing in English would include at least a chapter on the work of Narayan.

All critical discussions of the story have been positive. ''An Astrologer's Day'' has been perceived as a significant work, comparable to anything else he has written. While many critical accounts have been confined to plot summaries, a few have drawn attention to the quality of irony that accounts for the strength of the story. What has not been stressed adequately is that the quality of harmony that informs all his work also frames this story. There is very little violence in Narayan's writing, and very little by way of tragedy. Not all his fiction ends on a note of optimism, but there is always a sense of reconciliation, a suggestion that contradictions will be resolved. In that sense, Narayan's work is characterized by a very Hindu sensibility, a conviction that human lives and problems are part of a larger cosmic harmony. In this story too, all the potential for violence and revenge is transformed into a vision of harmony.

Criticism

Chelva Kanaganayakam

Kanaganayakam is an associate professor at the University of Toronto and has written for a wide variety of academic journals. In the following essay, he discusses the themes of irony and cosmic harmony in ''An Astrologer's Day.''

Among Indian writers in English, R. K. Narayan is probably one of the most prolific, and he has the distinction of having written fiction for more than sixty years. His first novel, *Swami and Friends*, appeared in 1935, and since then he has written novels, short stories, and essays, totaling more than thirty books in all. Although known predominantly as a novelist in India and the West, his short stories are no less significant than his longer works, and the story ''An Astrologer's Day'' continues to be a heavily anthologized piece. It is of considerable significance that a story which first appeared in 1947 should retain its appeal after more than fifty years.

The deceptive simplicity of ''An Astrologer's Day'' is one aspect of the story that continues to baffle critics. Typically, Narayan's fiction does not depend extensively on the plot to sustain itself. Not much happens in the narrative, and the storyline is relatively straightforward and quite often linear. Sometimes the forward movement of time is arrested, as in this story, but the disruption is such that the reader perceives no real discontinuity in the overall movement of the plot. The shift from the present to the past is necessitated by the plot itself, and as soon as some aspect of the past that needs elaboration is mentioned, the story moves to the present. The spatial element too is kept relatively simple. Despite references to other settings—such as the village—all the action of this story happens in two places which are logically connected to each other. The first is the street where the astrologer runs his ''shop'' and the second is the astrologer's home to which he returns after work. Thus the spatial and temporal aspects of the story are traditional and uncomplicated.

Nonetheless, the story is far from simple. Every facet of the story is crucial to the overall thematic preoccupations of the author. For instance, the astrologer leaves for home when the groundnut vendor closes shop, simply because he is dependent on the groundnut seller for lighting. When this story occurs, the reader is told that after the neighbor closes shop there is still a sliver of light that strays in from somewhere. Although it is a trivial detail in itself, it is this light that enables the astrologer to read Guru Nayak's palm. This incident becomes necessary as a realistic detail and significant as a symbol of mental illumination.

One aspect of the story that requires careful study is the use of the imagery of light and darkness. The setting of the story is such that it needs to begin when there is light and end when it is dark. But it is hard to miss the irony of the title which insists on ''Day'' when the plot really unfolds when it is dark. From another perspective, the issue of light and darkness has an economic angle to it. It reinforces the fact that municipal lighting does not extend to this particular street. And it also points out that, depending on the relative prosperity of the vendors, some of them have their own sources of lighting while others tend to rely on ''borrowed'' light to conduct their business. More importantly, however, the duality of light and dark are obviously symbolic. When there is light, the astrologer conceals his past and the lack of any real expertise in the field of astrology. In that sense, light is associated with the inability to ''see.'' By the same token it is when there is no light that the truth begins to unfold and both the astrologer and his client ''see'' aspects of themselves that had remained hidden. The astrologer realizes that he is no longer a fugitive and that he

An astrologer (right) meets with a client near India's Ganges River.

has paid for his sins. Nayak recognizes that his quest is, in the final analysis, a pointless one, and that he should return home and be at peace with himself.

The curious inversion of light and darkness leads to the notion of irony which is central to an understanding of Narayan's strategy. If there is one aspect of his work that has been praised by critics, it is his unique use of irony. It is unique in that it comes out of a predominantly Hindu sensibility. A Brahmin by birth, Narayan has always been deeply rooted in the Hindu traditions of India and it is this understanding that shapes his vision and sensibility. The fundamental premise of his irony is of course the traditional one of perceiving a dichotomy between the real and the apparent. In other words, when there is a gap between what people profess and what they do, what emerges is a sense of the ironic. In Narayan's fiction, the irony is pervasive, but it is never harsh or misanthropic. Narayan sees human fallibility as part of a larger cosmic system, and views the hypocrisies of individuals with amusement and understanding. Thus, for instance, the groundnut vendor giving his shop a different name each day to attract people is not seen to be fraudulent. The astrologer himself practices a trade about which he knows nothing, and that does not necessarily make the character flawed or negative. The

limitations are not glossed over or sanctioned, but there is no malice in the irony.

The irony also operates at a deeper level. In fact the entire story is built around the central irony of Nayak going on a quest for the man who harmed him and when he finally encounters him, he does not recognize the astrologer as the perpetrator of the crime. A further dimension to the irony is that the potential victim not only escapes but also gives Nayak the advice he needs to resume his life and give up his quest. The philosophical underpinning to this episode is a very religious one in that human beings, regardless of how much they struggle, are governed by a larger scheme. This scheme ensures a form of closure and reconciliation, even if the parties involved are not fully aware of it. In this story both the astrologer and Nayak are guilty to some degree, and both of them suffer in their own ways until the reconciliation occurs at the end. The story is by no means a religious one, but the sensibility that informs and frames the story is, in a broad sense, religious.

Despite the strategy of narrative omniscience (third-person narrative), Narayan himself does not choose to give himself the authority of omniscience. The structure of the story requires that the reader too should be kept in ignorance of many details—

What Do I Read Next?

- *Waiting for the Mahatma*, a novel written by Narayan and published in 1958, is a very popular work that deals with contemporary issues, particularly the campaign against the British led by Gandhi and the impact it had on the people of the time. The novel is a very insightful portrayal of the social upheaval caused by Gandhi's attitudes on caste.

- Narayan's *The Man-Eater of Malgudi* was published in 1962. Arguably one of his finest novels, it deals with the gradual transformation of society as it encounters the forces of change. Written in a manner that is partly allegorical and partly realistic, the novel exemplifies Narayan's attitude toward culture and religion. At the very heart of Narayan's work is a mythical structure, and that comes across very forcibly in this novel.

- *A Passage to India* has earned the reputation of a minor classic. Written by E. M. Forster and published in 1924, it remains a very important attempt, from the perspective of an outsider, to deal with the realities of India. A useful novel to be compared with Narayan's work.

- *Midnight's Children*, published by Salman Rushdie in 1981, is a modern epic about India. Its style, approach, and sweep are very different from anything attempted by Narayan. Rushdie is experimental, discontinuous in his narrative mode, and politically engaged. He presents one version of India and Narayan another.

- *The Idea of India*, published by Sunil Khilnani in 1997, is an excellent introduction to sociocultural conditions and the political situation in India. The focus of the book is postcolonial India—the last fifty years—and the author provides a first-rate introduction to a very complex and confusing topic.

---

hence, the self-imposed limitation of the narrative voice that sees only what the reader sees, for the most part. The first descriptive part of the story simply gives details that any observer would have seen. Later, when Nayak arrives on the scene, more details about the two characters emerge through the dialogue. It is almost as if the narrator too is an observer, who knows a little more than the reader, but not much more. Such a limitation is necessary for the assertion of cosmic harmony, which is an important motif in the story.

Narayan has lived through some of the most important years in India's recent history. Born when India was under British rule, he experienced first-hand the struggle for independence, the remarkable career of Mahatma Gandhi, and the subsequent history of postcolonial India. The creation of Pakistan and Bangladesh, the wars with Pakistan and China, and the period of emergency rule under Prime Minister Indira Gandhi are all events that Narayan is aware of and has discussed briefly in

occasional essays. But none of these changes finds an important place in his writing. Even in ''An Astrologer's Day,'' there is hardly any reference to the economic and political backdrop of the nation. While this refusal to address the realities of India continues to be matter of some debate among critics, the fact is that Narayan makes this a deliberate choice. What appeals to him is a traditional India, held together by a system of values that is ultimately spiritual in origin. And it is this assertion of timelessness, combined with an awareness of the secular world, that gives him a distinctive place in the literary history of India.

Narayan's depiction of society is hardly ever controversial, although his treatment of women sometimes lacks depth of understanding. Seen from a contemporary perspective, Narayan's treatment of gender comes across as somewhat limited and unsatisfactory. He does not consciously celebrate a patriarchal view of the world, but he is more comfortable dealing with male characters rather than female ones. In his novels he has, on occasion, attempted to deal with women more fully, but these attempts are, on the whole, not particularly successful. The treatment of the astrologer's wife in this story is typical of the manner in which Narayan's stories work. Here the wife is introduced at the end, and one of the first impressions she creates is that of a person whose sole interest is money. She is visibly happy when the husband brings home more money than usual, and her immediate plans are to spend the money making sweets for her daughter. She is cast in the form of a stereotype, and is associated with the home and the family, and with domestic life. The astrologer does not even feel the need to give her a full explanation at the end. Of course, it is necessary to recognize that this story was written more than five decades ago, when gender issues were not as important as they are now. Nonetheless, the treatment of women comes across as a flaw in what is otherwise a remarkably well-constructed and insightful story.

Source: Chelva Kanaganayakam, in an essay for *Literature of Developing Nations for Students*, Gale, 2000.

Perry D. Westbrook

In this review of R.K. Narayan's The Astrologer's Day, *author Perry D. Westbrook points out that Narayan, an Indian journalist well before his work as a novelist, published his short stories in Indian newspapers. Westbrook is careful to point out that this is an important aspect of Narayan's short stories. These stories were written by a native Indian and read by a predominantly Native-Indian (English speaking) audience; Narayan was not writing to interpret India for Westerners.*

The first of R. K. Narayan's three volumes of short stories, *An Astrologer's Day and Other Stories* (1947), contains thirty pieces, all of which had previously appeared in the Madras *Hindu*. Thus they had been written for, and presumably read and enjoyed by, the readership of one of India's greatest English-language newspapers. Though this readership would include most of the British, Anglo-Indians, and Americans living in South India, it would be made up overwhelmingly of true Indians. It is an important point. Narayan is an Indian writing for Indians who happen to read English. He is not interpreting India for Westerners. In Europe and America, of course, Narayan's reputation rests upon his novels. The publication in London of *An Astrologer's Day* followed two well-received novels, *Swami and Friends* and *The English Teacher,* but

> " The curious inversion of light and darkness leads to the notion of irony which is central to an understanding of Narayan's strategy. If there is one aspect of his work that has been praised by critics, it is his unique use of irony. It is unique in that it comes out of a predominantly Hindu sensibility."

long before he was a novelist with an enthusiastic Western following, Narayan was an Indian journalist loved by his fellow-countrymen.

Paradoxically, however, though Narayan's short pieces have been welcomed in the *Hindu* for over thirty years, his novels have never been popular in India; indeed, I myself have found that they are obtainable there only with the greatest difficulty. Another book-hunter reports that in the leading bookshop of Bangalore in Narayan's own Mysore State not a single book by Narayan was available. On being queried, a clerk replied that there was no demand for Narayan's works. Narayan himself has stated that in the city of Mysore, where he has lived most of his life, perhaps only 200 of the population of 275,000 have ever read any of his books. And yet Mysore justly has the reputation of being an important centre of education and culture. The fact is that Narayan's books have first been published in England, and more recently in the United States, and have only later appeared in India in unattractively printed paperback editions.

Any reader of Narayan is aware that his stories are cut from very much the same cloth, both in quality and in pattern, as his novels. There is no intrinsic difference to explain why in the same cities where his novels are obtainable, several thousand or more subscribers to the *Hindu* read him with gusto. It becomes even more of a puzzle when we consider that the Indian booksellers do a brisk business in British and American novels and in continental novels in English translation. The most cogent

> Too many educated Indians simply will not accept the possibility of excellence of style in the English writing of a compatriot. In the early years of the independence of the United States much the same prejudice existed. Publishers and readers alike preferred to read books— at least in the category of *belles lettres*—imported from the 'old country'. . . ."

explanation seems to be that of lingering cultural colonialism on the sub-continent. Too many educated Indians simply will not accept the possibility of excellence of style in the English writing of a compatriot. In the early years of the independence of the United States much the same prejudice existed. Publishers and readers alike preferred to read books—at least in the category of *belles lettres*—imported from the 'old country'; American authors were deemed to produce something less than the authentic product.

The newspaper origins of the short stories would tend to place them in the category of reporting on Indian life and thus make them more acceptable to readers who would ignore his longer and more ambitious works. The reportorial quality is especially marked in his second collection, *Lawley Road*, in which the selections are sketches and vignettes rather than plotted stories. In *An Astrologer's Day* the tales also accurately mirror Indian life and character, but most of them appear to have been chosen for the ingenuity of their plots. The title story, ' An Astrologer's Day,' is a good example. The description of the astrologer pursuing his profession on the sidewalk provides an entirely typical glimpse of Indian street life. The astrologer himself, a fake driven into imposture by hard luck, is well drawn. The trickiness of the plot (its O. Henry quality) results from the coincidence of the astrologer's being requested, during a day's business, to

forecast the fortune of a man he recognizes as one whom he had stabbed and left for dead years ago. It was this crime that had forced the astrologer to flee from his village. But the victim recovered, as he informs the astrologer, and has been devoting his life to tracking down his assailant so as to get revenge. The astrologer, who recognizes the man without himself being recognized, informs him that his enemy has died beneath the wheels of a lorry. Thus the astrologer saves himself from attack and learns, to his great relief, that he is not a murderer after all. Though such situations do credit to an author's ingenuity, they do not suit modern taste. Yet they are in a long and honoured tradition, that of Chaucer's 'The Pardoner's Tale,' itself derived from the Sanskrit. As a part of ordinary life, coincidences are legitimate material from any story-teller. At any rate, more than half the tales in *An Astrologer's Day* depend on such twists for their effect. Many of them have other merits as well, such as compelling atmosphere or a memorable character, but perhaps the most justifiable of them are those which present ghosts. 'An Accident ' vividly conjures up on a lonely mountain road the ghost of a man killed in an automobile accident who now devotes himself to helping other motorists in distress. 'Old Man of the Temple ' evokes the mystery and desolation of one of the ruined temples along the South Indian highways. 'Old Bones' exploits the atmosphere of the more isolated of the *dak* bungalows (government-operated overnight hostels). These are skilfully told stories of pure entertainment.

But some of the stories in *The Astrologer's Day* do not depend upon coincidence or some strange circumstance. The most impressive are those that open a window on to the bleak, tedious lives of the white-collar workers of India, that large segment of the population who drag out their lives at forty or fifty rupees a month in government or business employment. Examples are 'Forty-Five a Month ' and 'Fruition at Forty,' accounts of dreary, lifelong wage-slavery. In depicting such prisoned lives Narayan is at his best, even in stories freighted with 'surprise endings.' Thus in 'Out of Business' the destructive mental effects of unemployment on a former gramophone salesman are vividly presented, though the suicide that he narrowly escapes would have been a more convincing conclusion than the gratuitous turn of luck that saves him from it. More believable is the fate of Iswaran in the story of that name. Iswaran, a representative of the vast army of Indian students whose sole goal in life is the passing of government examinations, is driven by repeated failure to a suicide that even his last-minute discovery that he has finally passed with honours cannot deter his crazed will from carrying out. Most prominent in all these stunted lives is the intolerable humiliation that is part of the daily routine. The insults endured by a jewelry-shop clerk in 'All Avoidable Talk' and the clerk's feeble attempt to rebel are unparalleled even in Gogol's and Dostoevsky's fiction on similar themes. Indeed a comparison with the insulted and injured in the works of the great Russian authors is inevitable. The tutor in 'Crime and Punishment', the twenty-ninth story in Narayan's volume, suffers true Chekhovian and Dostoevskian indignities, as does also the porter in 'The Gateman's Gift ', whose employer speaks to him exactly twice in twenty-five years of service. Blighting frustration, of course, figures in all these tales but most severely in 'The Watchman', one of the most powerful short stories Narayan has written. Here a young girl wishes to study medicine but her poverty-stricken family try to force her into a marriage she abhors; she drowns herself at night in a temple tank—at the second attempt, as a watchman stopped her the first time. The pathos lies in the inability of even the best-intentioned person to help a fellow human being in distress. This is the ultimate frustration.

Narayan's second volume of stories appeared in 1956, almost ten years after *An Astrologer's Day*. It is also compiled from writings previously printed in the *Hindu,* but contains fewer elaborately contrived stories. Named *Lawley Road* after a typical thoroughfare in the typical, though fictitious, South Indian city of Malgudi, the volume is made up of sketches, character studies, and anecdotes indigenous to just such a street in such a town. They are the more powerful for the absence of gimmicks, and are marked by naturalness, by the easy pace of Narayan's novels, and the informal style of a leisurely raconteur.

Thoroughly typical of this collection, and indeed of all of Narayan's best short work, is 'A Breach of Promise'. It begins:

> Sankar was candidate 3,131 in the Lower Secondary Examination and he clearly saw his number on a typed sheet, announcing the results, pasted on the weather-beaten doors of the Government Middle School. That meant he would pass on to High School now. He was slightly dizzy with joy.

By way of celebration the boy and two of his companions go first to a restaurant and then to the local cinema. At four the next morning they climb the thousand steps carved a millennium ago in the rocky side of a nearby hill to the temple of the Goddess Chamundi. Thrice the boys make the circuit of the temple and then enter the shrine and remain there while the priest presents their offerings to the Goddess. They give thanks for having passed their examinations and pray for success in all future ones. As they prostrate themselves before the Goddess, Sankar suddenly recalls that before taking his examinations the preceding year he had vowed to the Goddess that he would kill himself if he failed to pass. He had in fact failed that year, but had self-protectively kept the memory of the vow suppressed in his sub-conscious. But now, overwhelmed by his memory, he leaves his friends on the pretense of buying some jaggery in the temple shop. Actually he climbs ten ladders to the top of the lofty gate-tower of the temple, crawls out into the mouth of the huge demon that caps the pinnacle, and is about to jump. At that instant he notices a bleeding scratch on his elbow, and his determination to leap vanishes. Carefully he crawls back into the tower and descends, vowing to give the Goddess two coconuts a year instead of his life. At the bottom he hurries to get the jaggery and resumes a boy's normal existence.

Narayan says that 'A Breach of Promise' is 'almost his first tale', and describes it as being 'very truthful—autobiographical, you know'. Narayan was himself adept at flunking school examinations and after one of his failures he actually did climb to the tower room of Chamundi Temple with the idea—but not, he emphasizes, the intention—of suicide. 'The whole thing was farcical', he says. 'That's the way life is in our temples and our houses'.

This is the way life is in most of Narayan's novels and early stories. What more absurd than the ease with which an irrelevance diverts a boy from a solemn vow and makes him substitute an utterly common-place one? But what is important is that one doesn't feel contempt for the boy; one is delighted that he is saved, and is something of a humbug. He is very human as he celebrates his successful examinations by gorging in a restaurant, attending the cinema, and only as an after-thought running up the hill to give thanks to the goddess Chamundi. In retaining Sankar's humanity, Narayan secures the reader's sympathy, for we see life re-asserting itself against absurdity and solemnity.

If there is an all-pervasive theme in Narayan's work it is that human beings are human beings, not gods. Men and women can make flights toward godhood, but they always fall a bit short. Even Gandhi in the novel *Waiting for the Mahatma* displays an occasional human foible. Other aspirants fall much wider of the mark, of course. In the novel, *Mr Sampath* (entitled *The Printer of Malgudi* in the United States edition), Srinivas tries with his newspaper *The Banner* to arouse the soul of India, but he is sidetracked, at least temporarily, into movie-making. Nataraj, the printer in *The Man-eater of Malgudi,* futilely combats the principle of evil as embodied in the demonic Vasu. Indeed in that novel all of Indian society, as allegorically represented by a poet, a journalist, an inn-keeper, a civil servant, a veterinarian, and a temple dancer, fail to curb Vasu, who is endowed with the strength, cunning and malice of a mythological *asura.* Even the Gods had trouble overcoming the *asuras.* How could a mere human, or nation of humans, even 450,000,000 of them, be expected to blot out evil? Yet Narayan finds the efforts laudable—and at times amusing.

The foibles that Narayan records may be specifically Indian, but they are also generically human. Sometimes they are public and political, as in the title piece of *Lawley Road,* which recounts the agonizings of the municipality of Malgudi over the statue of an Englishman, Sir Frederick Lawley, who had been prominent in the city's history. When Indian independence came, the presence of this statue at a main intersection could not be tolerated, especially as it was discovered that Sir Frederick was 'a combination of Attila, the scourge of Europe, and Nadir Shah, with the craftiness of a Machiavelli. He subjugated Indians with the sword and razed to the ground the villages from which he heard the slightest murmur of protest. He never countenanced Indians except when they approached him on their knees'. The narrator of the story, a private citizen, buys the statue and at great expense removes it to his own premises, where it not only fills his house but protrudes into the road. In the meanwhile the Municipal Chairman receives telegrams from all over India pointing out that there were two Sir Frederick Lawleys—one a despot, the other a humanitarian and an advocate of Indian independence. The statue at Malgudi was of the latter. The result is that the Central Government orders it to be set up again. The owner sells the statue to the Municipal Chairman, who pays for it from his own pocket, thus insuring his victory at the next election.

The story is obviously good-natured spoofing, a rollicking satire on the confusion of the public mind at the time of transition from the British raj to independence. Somewhat more serious as satire is 'The Martyr's Corner'. Rama, a small entrepreneur of the type that abounds in socialist India as in no

capitalist country in the world, has for years made a living selling *chapatis* and other dainties on an advantageously located street corner which he has managed to reserve for himself by a little judicious bribing of the constable and the health department officer. Rama's working day, what with cooking his wares and vending them, begins at three or four in the morning and extends till late at night. His net earnings average five rupees a day. One evening a riot flames up in the town, its cause unknown even to the rioters. A man is killed on Rama's corner, which is then designated as the site for a statue to the martyr in an unknown cause. Rama is of course ousted from this 'holy' ground; in a new location his business falls off to nothing, and he is forced to take a job as a waiter at twenty rupees a month. Who is the martyr? The brawler to whom the statue is erected or Rama who is reduced to penury?

Narayan's fiction is not especially preoccupied with politics; in fact his attitude towards it approaches disdain. (Among his novels *Waiting for the Mahatma* is the only one that is appreciably political.) But disdain becomes dismay in the story 'Another Community', where he writes of religious rioting. Bigotry, fear, ignorance, hate explode into a massacre that sweeps an entire city. Obviously Narayan has in mind the frightful outbreaks between the Hindus and Muslims in 1947. The smouldering, engulfing hate, ready at any moment to erupt into violence, is presented through the consciousness of an educated, rational man, untouched by the popular passions, who considers the whole state of affairs 'absurd'. Detachedly wondering who will spark the conflagration, he unwittingly does so himself in a bicycle collision with a stranger in a dark alley. They quarrel and exchange blows. Unfortunately the stranger turns out to be a member of the other community. With typical restraint Narayan declares that the results 'need not be described . . .'

Narayan has said, 'My focus is all on character. If his personality comes alive, the rest is easy for me.' Certainly in the *Lawley Road* collection, the stories of character are the most absorbing, and where other considerations obtrude, character usually remains the dominant interest. Thus in 'The Martyr's Corner' the focus is always on the *chapati* seller rather than on the rather violent action; always before the reader's eyes is the little vendor—his drab monotonous life, his comments on his customers, his manipulation of the officials who could ruin him, above all his attitude towards existence, his sense of occupying a niche in the social order, the sense of dignity and satisfaction that transforms sheer dreariness into human significance. On every market street in every city, town, and village in India these curb-side merchants spread out their wares—old bottles, tin cans converted into cups and cooking utensils, baubles, and edibles of every kind. What sort of people are they? What can life mean to them? 'The Martyr's Corner' contains at least the beginnings of answers to these questions.

Another ubiquitous frequenter of Indian streets is the beggar. There is one in the story 'The Mute Companions', which records the way of life of a mute mendicant who for a time enjoys the company and added income brought to him by a monkey he accidentally captures and successfully trains. Performing on the streets and in the homes of the wealthy, the mute companions share a good life together till one day the animal escapes and disappears. There is pathos in this story in the dependence of man and beast on one another, despite the unbridgeable differences of species. Narayan skilfully presents the process by which this speechless, gurgling, subhuman wanderer of the streets (one of the homeless, maimed, and starving of the world) regains his humanity through his association with a monkey, and becomes an object of concern and compassion. As for the characterization of the monkey, Narayan has here too achieved a minor miracle. Throughout his work Narayan's skill in depicting animals is noteworthy. In *Lawley Road,* there are several other memorable stories of animals: 'Chippy', which presents two dogs; 'At the Portal', an account of two squirrels; 'Flavour of Coconut', in which the protagonist is a rat! But the most remarkable of all of Narayan's animal portraits is the revered invalid elephant in *The Man-eater of Malgudi.* Narayan certainly bears out the belief that Indians are more understanding than Westerners are of non-human forms of life.

In addition to street-vendors and beggars a score of other types are represented in *Lawley Road,* highly individualized characters like the pick-pockets in 'The Trail of the Green Blazer', the 'coolie' in 'Sweets for Angels,' the black-marketeer in rice, who appears during every famine, in 'Half-a-Rupee Worth', the illiterate *ayah* or nursemaid of 'A Willing Slave', who is a slave first to the family in which she works and later to her husband.

In his first novel, *Swami and Friends*, Narayan proved himself a skilfull portrayer of children. In *Lawley Road* there are at least half a dozen stories of children, in addition to 'A Breach of Promise'. 'Dodu' tells of a boy who has heard that the local

museum has purchased some Palmyra-leaf documents, so he takes ordinary palm leaves to sell to the curator. In 'A Shadow' a boy, Sambu, daily attends a movie in which his dead father played the star role. In the film the father teaches arithmetic to a little girl in exactly the way he had taught it in real life to Sambu. Death is no longer a reality to the watching boy. In 'The Regal' we enter into the activities of a boys' cricket club and share their efforts to find a place where the adults will let them play. In 'The Performing Child' a precocious little girl dancer with a strong instinct for self-preservation refuses to dance before a movie director who her exploiting parents hope will hire her at a large salary. In 'Mother and Son' an adolescent runs away from his mother's home when she is too insistent about his marrying his fourteen-year-old cousin; after spending a night by the temple tank he is found by his mother and returns.

Lawley Road has not been published in the West: it is unobtainable in even the greatest libraries in the United States, nor is it listed in the printed catalogue of the British Museum. Two of the stories have been printed in America: 'The Trail of the Green Blazer' under the shortened title 'Green Blazer', and 'At the Portal', the squirrel story, under the title 'The Mother Bit Him'. Two other stories by Narayan have appeared in American periodicals: the sensitive and humorous 'A Bright Sunday in Madison' (about an American child who gets lost temporarily) and 'A Horse and Two Goats', a piece of humour underlining the lack of communication between East and West.

In 1964 Viking Press published the United States edition of Narayan's third collection, *Gods, Demons, and Others*, a volume that marks a radical departure from his previous tales. Instead of drawing upon contemporary Indian life, Narayan in this book retells myths and legends from the *Ramayana*, the *Mahabharata*, and several other ancient Indian works. In an article in *The Atlantic* Narayan once wrote: 'All imaginative writing in India has had its origin in the *Ramayana* and the *Mahabharata*.' The English influence, to be sure, opened up an entirely new perspective on literature and established a vogue for Western modes and genres. Yet, Narayan believes, the great religious and mythological writings still hold sway over the Indian literary mind, as can be seen in the numerous and usually unsuccessful attempts to reproduce the old legends in cinema form, attempts that Narayan lampoons in several novels, especially *Mr Sampath*. Re-tellings of the great epics or parts of them are commonplace in

Indian literature. In the present generation Aubrey Menon's version of the *Ramayana* is notorious for its irreverence, which caused its sale to be banned in India, and C. Rajagopalachari's versions in Tamil of the *Ramayana* and the *Mahabharata* were later translated into popular English editions. So Narayan's reworking of the age-old stories is completely in the tradition of Indian literature and art.

In his earlier stories Narayan did make some use of legendary material, as in 'The Image' (*Lawley Road*) and 'Such Perfection' (*An Astrologer's Day*), both of which are accounts of sculptors whose skill is regarded as divine rather than human. More important, Narayan's conception of the nature and function of literature seems throughout his writing career to have been influenced by ideas about the nature and function of the epics in Indian life that have been commonly accepted through the ages. In *Gods, Demons, and Others* he describes the composition of the *Ramayana* by Valmiki, 'The greatest story-teller of all times.' According to Narayan, 'Rama, the hero . . . was Valmiki's creation, although the word "create" is not quite apt . . . Rama was not a "character" created by a story-teller and presented in a "work". The "work" in the first place, was not "written"; it arose within the writer. The "character" was not conceived but revealed himself in a vision.' Now this notion, which has much in common with the Greek concept of the Muses and with later theories of the artist as a mere channel for divine revelation, was the theme of 'Under the Banyan Tree', in the final story in *An Astrologer's Day*. Far back in the forested hills, in the sleepy and illiterate village of Somal ten miles from the nearest bus stop, the story-teller Nambi holds sway over the imaginations of the villagers. Illiterate himself, Nambi attributes his stories to 'the Goddess', who causes them to spring up in his own imagination and provides him with the words with which to pass them on to his audience. Nambi's stories are pure flights of fancy, coloured and suggested by the whole body of Indian religious writing. The impression is that Nambi is a lesser Valmiki, in whose mind the Gods have decreed that certain persons and events will spring into being. Later, when Nambi's imagination dries up, he ascribes his failure to the Goddess's pleasure and resigns himself to her will. What Narayan is apparently conveying in this story of Nambi and in his comments on Valmiki is that all creativeness, even that of the humblest village story-teller, depends on something other than the teller's mental energy. Ved Mehta reports Narayan as saying: 'I can't like any writing

that is deliberate. If an author is deliberate, then I can't read him . . .' He says of himself, that he is 'an inattentive, quick writer, who has little sense of style'. With him, as Ved Mehta says, 'a novel well begun writes itself', and elsewhere, as we have seen, he claims: 'I can write best when I do not plan the subject too elaborately . . . If (my protagonist's) personality comes alive, the rest is easy for me.' Narayan's account in *My Dateless Diary* of how he started on his novel *The Guide* bears out these statements.

The art of narration, then, is a talent given to man by God for the benefit of all humanity, for their amusement and edification. In India even at present (as in all other cultures in the past) story-telling is an oral art, an activity in which the listeners and, very likely, the teller are unlettered. The tales in *Gods, Demons, and Others* are presented as told by a village story-teller—in this case, a well-educated one, of whom Narayan gives a detailed and interesting description. But even the stories in the two earlier collections are in many cases told in the words of 'The Talkative Man', a garrulous raconteur of Malgudi who is always ready with some account of personal experience if an audience of one or more is at hand. Narayan believes that modern writers, especially those of the West or under Western influence, have strayed far from their original function of providing pleasure and instruction to the masses. He is uncomfortable about recent academic interest in his own writing. 'Literature', he asserts, 'is not a branch of study to be placed in a separate compartment, for the edification only of scholars, but a comprehensive and artistic medium of expression to benefit the literate and illiterate alike.' Though far from achieving this purpose himself in his own country, where he writes in a tongue known mainly to the educated elite, perhaps he comes nearest to it in his short stories, at least those of the first two volumes, which first appeared in a widely circulated newspaper.

In his preface to *The Bachelor of Arts,* Graham Greene writes of the strange mixture of humour, sadness, and beauty in Narayan's novels, 'a pathos as delicate as the faint discolouration of ivory with age'. In the same preface he comments on Narayan's 'complete objectivity, complete freedom from comment'. Like many critics Greene sees a Russian quality in Narayan: 'Mr Narayan's light, vivid style, with its sense of time passing, of the unrealized beauty of human relationships . . . often recalls Tchekhov.' The vastness of the Indian geography, in which friends are separated never to see each other again, the irrelevance of Indian education which prepares students for nothing: these too remind Greene of the Russia of the tsars and the great novelists. In his introduction to *The Financial Expert*, Greene comments on Narayan's gift of comedy with its undertone of sadness, its gentle irony and absence of condemnation—a type of comedy virtually extinct in the West, where farce, satire and boisterousness are substituted for true comedy. At the basis of Narayan's comedy, Greene points out, is the juxtaposition of the age-old convention and the modern character ... The astrologer is still called to compare horoscopes for a marriage, but now if you pay him enough he will fix them the way you want: the financial expert sits under his banyan tree opposite the new Central Co-Operative Land Mortgage Bank'. Mr Greene's comments are in the main just; and they apply as much to Narayan's short stories as to his novels.

Source: Perry D. Westbrook, ''The Short Stories of R. K. Narayan,'' in *The Journal of Commonwealth Literature,* No. 5, July, 1968, p. 41.

Further Reading

Holstrom, Lakshmi, *The Novels of R. K. Narayan*, Calcutta: Writers Workshop, 1973.

Analysis of individual novels in relation to themes, plots, and style. Attempts to place Narayan in the tradition of Indian writing, and maintains that his novels express a Hindu vision of the universe.

Kain, Geoffrey, ed., *R. K. Narayan: Contemporary Critical Essays*, Michigan State University Press, 1993.

A broad-ranging collection of essays by some of the major critics in the field. Includes essays on individual novels and more general comparative essays. Provides a very good overview of different points of view. The bibliography of both primary and secondary material is likely to be very useful.

vanden Driesen, Cynthia, ''The Achievement of R. K. Narayan,'' in *Literature East and West*, Vol. 21, Nos. 1-4, 1977, pp. 51-64.

A very perceptive and well-written article that deals with the whole corpus of Narayan's writing. Looks closely at the major preoccupations of Narayan's work. It is also one of the first works to suggest that Narayan is a fabulist.

Walsh, William, *R. K. Narayan*, Longmans, 1971.

An early work, but very perceptive in its treatment of Narayan's major themes. Walsh offers a close reading of many texts and his comparative approach provides a valuable overview to Narayan's work.

Bad Influence

Judith Ortiz Cofer

1995

Published in *Stories of the Barrio: An island Like You* in 1995, ''Bad Influence'' details a summer in the life of a young Puerto Rican girl from Paterson, New Jersey. In keeping with the other stories in the collection, ''Bad Influence'' speaks to topics specific to young Puerto Rican Americans, while addressing issues universal to young people. At fifteen, Rita, the narrator, is at odds with the world of her Puerto Rican grandparents, whose eccentric, old-fashioned ways strike her as ridiculous. A typical teenager, she is hypercritical of the adults around her, and finds them invasive and disrespectful of her boundaries. Rita has been sent to the island to stay with her grandparents to keep her out of trouble with boys. Initially she is brutally caustic and critical of everything from her grandmother's telenovelas to her grandfather's spiritual powers (which she satirizes as Ghostbusting). Her take on Papá's approach to curing a family of an evil spirit (or *mala influencia*) is both hilarious and believable. Over time, however, Rita makes a new friend and comes to appreciate her grandparents and life on the island. In the course of the summer, Rita manages to assert her individuality while incorporating her heritage, in her effort to navigate both the American and the Puerto Rican in herself.

Author Biography

Judith Ortiz Cofer describes herself as the product of two worlds, urban America and the island of Puerto Rico, and her work is a reflection of this cross-culturalism. Born in Hormigueros, Puerto Rico, in 1952, Ortiz Cofer spent her early years on the island in the company of her mother, grandmother, and aunt while her father served in the U.S. Navy. Before long, however, her father's military career took the family to Paterson, New Jersey, beginning the family's pattern of moving back and forth between the mainland and Puerto Rico. Ortiz Cofer's parents, J. M. and Fanny, had strikingly different feelings about American life, and this disparity resulted in a feeling of conflict in their daughter. While Ortiz Cofer's father was quiet, serious, and imperative that the family assimilate, her mother was flamboyant and warm, never comfortable in New Jersey. Cofer's mother so longed for her homeland that she refused to learn English and relied largely upon her daughter to communicate outside of Spanish. In her collection of essays, *Silent Dancing*, Ortiz Cofer reports she became a "cultural chameleon, developing early the ability to blend into a crowd, to sit and read quietly in a fifth story apartment for days and days . . . or, set free, to run wild in Mamá's realm." She writes, "I instinctively understood then that language is the only weapon a child has against the absolute power of adults. . . . I quickly built up my arsenal of words by becoming an insatiable reader of books."

Ortiz Cofer spent her last two years of high school in Augusta, Georgia, where her family had moved for a more tranquil lifestyle. She won a scholarship to Augusta College, and earned a bachelor's degree in English in 1971 and a master of arts in English from Florida Atlantic University in 1977. Although she worked as a bilingual teacher for many years, she began to write poetry seriously as a graduate student. In 1989 she published a novel, *The Line of the Sun*, which was nominated for a Pulitzer Prize. In 1990 she published *Silent Dancing*, an essay collection about her Puerto Rican childhood, and another essay collection, *The Latin Deli*, in 1993. In 1995 she published *An Island Like You: Stories of the Barrio*, a collection of short fiction for young adults focused on Puerto Rican expatriate teenagers. Besides her work as lecturer and teacher at numerous schools and universities, Ortiz Cofer has contributed widely to poetry, fiction, and nonfiction anthologies, always tapping into her experiences as a bilingual and bicultural woman. In 1998,

she published *The Year of Our Revolution: New and Selected Short Stories and Poems*.

Plot Summary

Rita arrives in hot, humid Puerto Rico from Paterson, New Jersey with a bad attitude. She has been sent to spend the summer with her grandparents as an alternative to a retreat at a convent, where her friend Meli has been sent. Her parents want her out of contact with her racy boyfriend, Johnny Ruiz, and the result is her exile to the island.

Rita has never spent more than two weeks at a time on the island and she has no desire to get better acquainted with it now. She finds her grandparents and their friends annoyingly gregarious and overwhelming; when she tries to calm herself in the car by practicing deep breathing, her grandmother assumes she's having an asthma attack and harangues her with asthma stories. What Rita really wants is to be left alone.

As soon as the family gets back from the airport, Rita goes to her room to nap and withdraw. When she wakes up, her grandfather is outside her window crooning to his distressed rooster. He tells her (accurately) what she has been dreaming, and reports that the rooster has a skewed sense of time. This is Rita's introduction to her grandfather's talents as a spiritualist. Exasperated, Rita gets up and watches telenovelas with her grandmother, ever critical of Mamá Ana's ongoing dialogue with the television characters. Later that evening, Mamá reports that the next day they plan to travel to the seashore, so Papá can cure a young girl in distress. She explains Papá Juan's powers "that allowed him to see into people's hearts and minds through prayers and in dreams." Rita is skeptical.

The next morning Rita's grandparents awaken her before sunrise. At first Rita fakes an asthma attack so she can stay home alone, but Mamá Ana's dramatic response meets with a miraculous recovery. The three of them head for the beachfront home of the family in need of Papá Juan's help. Having slept in the car on the way, Rita cannot help but enjoy herself on the beach with her grandmother while Papá Juan consults with the señora and Angela in their elaborate, pink house. In the course of the day, Rita learns that the young girl in question refuses to eat or communicate with her mother, and the suspected cause is Rita's mother's boyfriend,

Judith Ortiz Cofer

of being stricken by the news, Rita laughs, and as Mamá Ana reports on the summer to her mother, Rita fantasizes about how she and Meli can get together to move in on the cute boys at the Catholic school.

Characters

Mamá Ana

Mamá Ana is Rita's excitable, gregarious grandmother, with whom she spends the summer. Warm, short, and plump, with a passion for soap operas, Rita finds her attention suffocating. When Rita tries some deep breathing exercises, Mamá Ana interprets them as asthmatic wheezing and clucks over Rita's "condition" throughout the story. Initially Rita finds her grandmother smothering and invasive, but over time she comes to see her as having a way with people and "this talent for turning every day into a sort of party."

Maribel Hernández Jones

Maribel Hernández Jones is Angela's glamorous mother, a famous actress in toothpaste advertisements. She is wealthy from a previous marriage and lives in a pink house that Rita finds ridiculous, but she cares for her daughter enough to take her condition seriously. She calls in Papá Juan to cure Angela, and heeds his advice in cleansing her house of evil spirits and getting rid of her boyfriend.

Angela Hernandez

Angela is the anorexic girl whom Papá Juan is called to cure. She has stopped eating and communicating with her mother because of her mother's abusive boyfriend and his reported "bad influence." At Mamá's and Papá's prompting, the boyfriend is removed from the house, and as a result Angela's health improves. Because she has spent time in New York, Angela speaks English and shares with Rita a certain cross-cultural sophistication. She and Rita develop a friendship that helps make Rita feel connected on the island.

Meli

Meli is Rita's friend from home who gets sent to the convent for the summer. Rita and Meli got caught earlier trying to spend the night at Meli's boyfriend's house, which results in their grounding.

the source of the *mala influencia* in the house. Rita is recruited to invite Angela to eat crab on the beach with them, and during the meal Mamá Ana announces that Rita will be having her fifteenth birthday party in two weeks, and Angela must come.

Rita's party is a huge gathering of neighbors, food, and music, and she gets to wear a blue satin cocktail dress with high heels. Angela and her mother come, and Angela reports that Papá Juan's cure was a success; her mother got rid of her boyfriend and Angela looks much healthier. From then on Rita's summer is greatly improved. She spends a good deal of time with Angela at her home by the beach, and they discuss Rita's story about Johnny, joking that he might be suffering from a *mala influencia* himself. Over time Rita feels disassociated from her experience with Johnny, and it seems like a movie she has seen years ago.

By the time her family arrives in August, Rita feels integrated enough into life on the island to take lessons in perceptiveness from her grandfather, and calls herself a medium. Although at first she plays on her mother's guilty anxiety and holds back from her, she soon warms up and assures her that the summer has gone well. Her mother reports that Meli enjoyed her convent experience so much that she plans to attend parochial school in the fall. Instead

Apparently she likes the retreat at the convent, because she plans to attend Catholic school in the fall.

Joey Molieri

Joey Molieri is Meli's boyfriend and Johnny's cohort in trying to seduce Rita and Meli. When Rita and Meli compare notes on the lines the boys used on them, they are identical.

Papá Juan

Papá Juan is Rita's eccentric, spiritualist grandfather. He is reportedly endowed with special gifts that give him insight into people's hearts. When Rita first arrives on the island she thinks her grandfather is senile because he comforts his emotional rooster and reports the contents of Rita's dreams. Although at first she satirizes Papá Juan's work by calling it Ghostbusting, she comes to recognize that he is an intuitive, perceptive man, and eventually even learns skills from him. His attempt to cure Angela and her mother of their ''bad influence'' sparks Rita's curiosity and draws her into life on the Island.

Rita

Rita is the sarcastic, fifteen-year-old narrator of ''Bad Influence.'' When her story begins, she has been sent from her home in Paterson, New Jersey, to spend the summer with her grandparents in Puerto Rico. The visit is an alternative to a summer in a convent, and intended to keep her away from her boyfriend, Johnny Ruiz. Rita is furious as a result, and much of the story is her sarcastic, adolescent running commentary on her experience in Puerto Rico. Initially she makes every attempt to withdraw from her grandparents and life on the island, and describes their world through critical, and often hilarious, teenage eyes. Over the course of time, however, her interpretations soften as she makes a new friend and becomes engaged in the lives of her family and the ways of her homeland.

Rita's Mother

Rita's mother is responsible for sending her to the island for the summer and impeding her relationship with her boyfriend, so Rita resents her a good deal at the beginning of the story. When her mother joins her on the island later in the summer, she appears nervous, anticipating more of Rita's anger, but Rita has mellowed and they connect warmly.

Johnny Ruiz

Johnny Ruiz is Rita's boyfriend, and the cause for her summer's exile to the island. Rita says he can date any girl he likes, and he usually dates older girls and expects to have sex with them. Rita is caught trying to spend the night with Johnny, and after she is grounded he tells her that although he thinks her family is crazy, he will give her another chance in the fall. Rita's summer in Puerto Rico wears away some of Johnny's attractiveness, and by the end of the story she and Angela characterize him as a troubled young man.

Themes

Fantasy vs. Reality

Rita comes to the island with what she sees as a realist perspective. Her smart-aleck, know-it-all attitude is authoritatively adolescent and grounded in her American upbringing, as evidenced upon her arrival when she reports, ''My friends from Central High would have died laughing if they had seen the women with their fans going back and forth across their shiny faces fighting over . . . who was going to sit next to whom.'' She makes light of her grandparents' spiritual work by calling it Ghostbusting and asserts that her grandfather must be senile because he comforts his troubled rooster. However, as she is drawn into the scenario between Angela, her mother, and her mother's boyfriend, Rita is affected by her grandparents' wisdom and acumen in determining the source of strife in the family. Papá eventually teaches Rita some of his skills of perception, and she comes to call herself a medium. By the end of the story, Rita has assimilated the seemingly mystical in her grandparents' culture into her own version of reality.

Bad and Good Influence

Mala influencia initially refers to the evil spirit that Papá banishes from Angela's house, but the term applies to Rita's summer in several different ways. Rita has clearly been sent to her grandparents in hopes they will be a good influence over her, since her parents think she is on the verge of getting into trouble with boys. Rita and Angela are good influences on each other; in the course of their summer together Angela moves toward wellness and Rita adapts comfortably to island life. Rita and Angela joke about Rita's boyfriend Johnny Ruiz, who was seen by Rita's parents as having a bad

Topics for Further Study

- Critics have noted that Ortiz Cofer's writing emphasizes individual, personal experience. As such, her writing has a more universal, mainstream appeal than the works of some other Puerto Rican authors, which emphasize the exploitation of the Puerto Rican masses. With this in mind, argue your opinion about the role of the personal and the political in fiction.

- Although Rita is critical of her grandparents' world when she arrives on the island, she is a product of both urban New Jersey and rural Puerto Rico. Discuss how Rita's bicultural influences are evidenced in the text.

- Research the relationship between the U.S. and Puerto Rico since 1950. How is Rita typical or atypical of late-twentieth-century Puerto Ricans?

- Ortiz Cofer uses Spanish vocabulary in her narrative in such a way that it is easily comprehensible to non-Spanish speakers. How does she use English/American allusions in a similar way, and what effect does this have upon the narrative?

influence over her. They agree that he sounds like a troubled young man, and joke that perhaps he is himself under a *mala influencia*.

Individual vs. Community

Rita arrives in Puerto Rico from New Jersey sporting an individualist attitude; she sees herself as separate and isolated. She tries to get away from her family and feels suffocated by the way her grandparents push themselves into her bedroom and into her life. They touch her too much and she feels suffocated by so much close contact. She tells an anecdote about trying to make a phone call while the neighbors listen and interpret; her mother explains that Puerto Ricans have different ideas of privacy from Americans, and Rita's desire for more space is a very American quality. Over time Rita becomes accustomed to the island lifestyle, and although she and Angela are allowed to withdraw from others

and assert their identities this way, eventually she becomes more willing to join the community.

Drama and Hyperbole

On the day Rita arrives on the island, Mamá Ana watches telenovelas and Rita rolls her eyes at her grandmother's dramatic relationship to the Puerto Rican equivalent of soap operas. She takes a critical view of the exaggerated, typically Latino reactions to events around her such as Mamá Ana's shrieks and wails at Rita's feigned asthma. As she depicts the conversations around her, the drama inherent in Latin American culture is apparent in the rapid speech patterns and exclamations that pepper the text. Ironically, Rita's brand of adolescent cynicism bears a similarly overblown quality, as when she characterizes her grandmother, at work trapping crabs, as a murderess. Thus she is inextricably part of a culture that strikes her as foreign.

Style

Point of View

"Bad Influence" is a narration of Rita's summer according to her point of view, the account of which shifts over time. At the opening, Rita's narrative is intensely critical, sarcastic, and very funny. She is a classically exasperated, smart aleck teenager with typically hyperbolic, derogatory opinions about her elders. Everything about Puerto Rico is insufferable in her eyes until she spends a beautiful morning at the beach with her grandmother, while Papá Juan attends to Angela and her mother. Once she makes friends with Angela and celebrates her fifteenth birthday with a huge fiesta, her perspective gradually shifts and softens; Rita acclimates to life on the island and begins to enjoy herself, rather than enduring it. Although she by no means drops her sarcastic, know-it-all tone, even her criticisms have a lighter, kinder tone. For example, at the opening of the story she calls her grandfather's car a tiny subcompact, while by the end of the story, when she joins her grandparents in picking up the rest of her family at the airport, she calls it his toy car. Rita's perspective is softened and expanded over the course of the summer to incorporate the Puerto Rican into herself.

Setting

The setting of "Bad Influence" is the core of the story; in essence, Rita's summer is about a sense of place and her identification with location. Although Rita's heritage is Puerto Rican, at age fifteen she identifies strongly with her home, school, and friend in Paterson, New Jersey. As a result, although she has spent two weeks of every year in Puerto Rico on vacation, she predicts her summer there will be, in a word, strange. Her emphasis on this word indicates not only the oddness of the events during the summer, but the fact that she finds the island foreign and apart from herself. Physically Rita finds the place repellent, overly hot, and humid: "it was like I had opened an oven door." Physical climate operates as a metaphor for personal climate in that, like the weather, people in Puerto Rico are intimate, sweaty, hot-tempered, excitable, and very physical.

In Puerto Rico, Rita is forced to deal with a culture that she finds not only foreign in its intimacy but, in her eyes, antiquated and mystical. In keeping with stereotypes of Latin Americans, her grandparents are Catholics who have holy water and an altar in their home, and believe that her grandfather has spiritual powers. Rita is forced to endure a lifestyle that includes rising before dawn and interacting with community members of all ages, rather than a world comprised solely of her peers. By the end of the summer, Rita has taken lessons in mysticism from her grandfather and adapted to life on the island by establishing a friendship with Angela and visiting the beach on a regular basis. In so doing, she incorporates parts of old-world Puerto Rico into her contemporary American self.

Symbolism

Most of the symbolism in "Bad Influence" concerns the disparity between life on the island and life in the United States. When Mamá Ana and Papá Juan pick Rita up at the airport, they have to squeeze into what Rita calls her grandfather's subcompact car. Rita focuses on the tiny, old car as a measure of status, sizing it up by American standards. Similarly, household conveniences like air conditioning are notably absent from Rita's grandparents' home, much to her chagrin. She brings up the absence of A.C. numerous times, so it stands out when she attributes the real and metaphoric chill in Angela's house to the fact that these wealthy people might have air conditioning. Although access to A.C. indicates wealth and status, it is meaningful that Angela's house, in which she and her mother are estranged, is cool inside, while Mamá and Papá's lively, comfortable house is overly warm. Rita complains throughout the story of uncomfortable

heat, an apt metaphor for personal feelings; her grandparents themselves are too warm, too close, and in fact suffocating to her when she first arrives on the island. Over time she does acclimate both physically and personally to the temperature and to the climate, or copes with the discomfort by going to the beach and finding relief in her peer, Angela.

Rita herself operates as a symbol in as far as she is a synthesis of two worlds, the American and the Puerto Rican. It is no accident that on the afternoon of her arrival Papá Juan sees into her dream while comforting his confused rooster, Ramon. Ramon has a skewed sense of time and thinks day is night and night is day. Like Ramon, Rita is out of balance in her new setting, and although she believes she has a clear view of the world around her, she sees through a skewed lens of her own, which is that of an American teenager, and not necessarily reliable. Her view of life on the island is impacted by the fact that she is somewhat of an outsider, and in her own words, Spanish is "not my best language." At the end of the story, having been a catalyst for Angela's healing and to a degree her own, Rita has a more balanced view of life, both in New Jersey and in Puerto Rico. She makes a claim to be a mind-reader herself, and although this is in keeping with her adolescent omniscience, she has a better developed sense of perception by the end of the summer.

Literary Heritage

The literary heritage of Puerto Rico is indebted to its history as an intersection of pre-Hispanic Indian settlement, Spanish colonialism, importation of Africans in the slave trade, and, most recently, American imperialism. The oral history of the Indians and Africans from throughout the Caribbean predate the arrival of the Spanish in 1493. The encounter between the Spanish conquistadors and the Taínos who inhabited the island during the 1500s gave rise to a wave of letters, annals, and poems in Spanish, reporting on the newly discovered place and people. Spanish became the primary language of Puerto Rico, but was enriched and expanded by the Indian vocabulary, which, according to Arturo Morales Carrión in *Puerto Rico, A Political and Cultural History,* "give[s] the Spanish language of the conquistadores a touch of Indian color and a new vision of man and life in a setting unknown to the European before the discovery of

America." He continues, "The vocabulary of Taíno origin gives a special flavor and color to the Spanish language by recalling the prehistory of the Caribbean," which persists today in both geographical names and everyday language. "The oral literature of the island offers glimpses of pre-Colombian Indian poetry in anecdotes, proverbs and legends." The oral tradition has given rise to the contemporary tradition of the jíbaro storyteller, or rural Puerto Rican. Carrión writes that "The jíbaro and the slum dweller continue to tell stories orally, in which daily life and nightmares and dreams become legends that beautify the reality of the island's past and present."

Carrión writes, "From the late sixteenth century until 1897, traditions and customs carried the imprint of the Catholic religion with traces of Taíno and African elements." Catholic religious mysticism combined with the forces of African and Indian spiritualism contribute to the Latin American blend of the real with the fantastic in both written and oral literature, known as magical realism. Of nineteenth- and twentieth-century Puerto Rico Carrión writes, "Country folklore, municipal festivities, and the plantation became the focus of attention for the artist, the poet, the storyteller, and the anonymous bard, while the intellectual began to challenge colonialism in its different aspects." Since colonization of Puerto Rico by Spain, Spanish has been the primary language of the island, but the American presence since 1917 has influenced the language and literature as well; the majority of its people are bilingual. The thematic content of the current oral and written traditions, as well as the recent reemergence of Taíno vocabulary, reflect and chronicle a strong overall impression of cultural resistance. The fact that such a large part of the Puerto Rican population migrates back and forth between the U.S. mainland and the island is also motivation to keep Puerto Rican culture alive in a world divided by a conflicted national identity. This struggle for Puerto Rican identity is embodied not only in Ortiz Cofer's work, but in other Puerto Ricans' as well, in the metaphor of the island for the self—separate from a larger body, yet inextricably a part of it.

Historical Context

Puerto Rico was ceded to the United States in 1898 by the Treaty of Paris as a result of the Spanish-

American War. U.S. citizenship was granted to Puerto Ricans in 1917, and during World War II it became an important U.S. military base. On June 4, 1951, Puerto Ricans voted in approval of a law which allowed them to draft their own constitution, and on July 25 of the following year Puerto Rico was declared a Commonwealth of the United States. As a result, Puerto Ricans share most rights of other U.S. citizens, although they are not allowed to vote and for the most part do not pay taxes. Although several elections have been held since 1952 to reinstate Puerto Rico's commonwealth status, not all citizens are in agreement over it; over the years different factions have advocated independence for the island, sometimes resorting to violence. Since 1968, governmental bodies in Puerto Rico have vacillated over maintaining commonwealth status, achieving statehood, or advocating independence. In 1993, 43 percent of citizens voted to retain commonwealth status, 46 percent advocated pursuing statehood, and 4 percent chose independence.

Since World War II, when Puerto Ricans were drawn into the U.S. armed forces, migration between the Island and the U.S. mainland has been consistent. Ruth Gruber, in *Puerto Rico, Island of Promise*, writes, "New York has the same pull to Puerto Ricans that it had to the America-bound immigrants in the late nineteenth and early twentieth century. Their relatives are in New York; there is security in family." Before 1948, 95 percent of Puerto Rican immigrants to the mainland moved to New York. That statistic has diminished over time, but New York is still the traditional destination for Puerto Rican expatriates. Although Puerto Ricans leave the Island for a variety of reasons, most go in search of work, which is scarce at home, and a higher standard of living. Unlike other immigrants, who often come to the U.S. fleeing persecution or oppressive governments, Puerto Ricans tend to have tremendous national pride. The island of Puerto Rico, however, is too small and has too few natural resources to hold its people. The birth rate continues to soar, and population density is higher per square mile than any state aside from New Jersey and Rhode Island. As a result, unemployment and the resulting poverty is always an issue in Puerto Rico. Many Puerto Ricans, like Ortiz Cofer's family, move back and forth between the Island and the mainland because it can be done with relative ease, and because of the conflicting reception on the mainland. The rapid and voluminous influx of Puerto Ricans into New York in particular has resulted, as with any minority group, in slums, gangs, and a great deal of racial prejudice toward Puerto Ricans. Mainland Americans have tended to forget that Puerto Ricans are American citizens, and Puerto Ricans have historically been treated with the same disregard and exploitation as illegal immigrants. Over the last two decades, however, Puerto Ricans as a community have assimilated at a high rate and much of the community has moved into suburbs such as Paterson, New Jersey, as in Ortiz Cofer's stories.

Critical Overview

Like most of Ortiz Cofer's work, *An Island Like You: Stories of the Barrio* has been met with both critical and popular success. The collection was awarded the Horn Book Farfare Award and the Hungry Mind Book of Distinction award, as well as listings with *Quick Picks for Reluctant Young Readers* and *Best Books for Young Adults*. Hazel Rochman, in her review for *Booklist*, writes, ''The contemporary teenage voices are candid, funny, weary, and irreverent in these stories about immigrant kids caught between their Puerto Rican families and the pull and push of the American dream.'' In her review for *Horn Book* Nancy Vasilakis agrees, writing, ''The Caribbean flavor of the tales gives them their color and freshness, but the narratives have universal resonance in the vitality, the brashness, the self-centered hopefulness and the angst expressed by the teens.''

Sensitivity to voice has been the cornerstone of critique of Ortiz Cofer's work; whether discussing her poetry or her prose, critics have always emphasized its authenticity. Vasilakis writes that ''the teenagers [in *An Island Like you*] speak in characteristic yet very distinct voices and appear in each others' stories the way neighbors step in and out of each others' lives.'' Rochman asserts that ''the teen narrators sometimes sound too articulate, their metaphors overexplained, but no neat resolutions are offered, and the metaphors can get it just right.'' In Bishop's words, ''Cofer's writing is lively, and the characters are memorable. . . . The voices in these stories ring true, as do the stories themselves.''

In his book *Dance between Two Cultures: Latino Caribbean Literature Written in the United States*, William Luís discusses Ortiz Cofer in the context of other Puerto Rican authors. He writes that Ortiz Cofer's work ''touches upon some of the themes of other [Puerto Rican] writers, but she expresses them from a less marginal perspective, in a language that is more polished and mainstream.'' He continues that, unlike some other Puerto Rican writers, ''she is not preoccupied with the exploitation of the Puerto Rican masses who traveled to the United States, as she is with writing about more personal concerns.'' In keeping with this view, Bishop writes that the ''the adolescents in these stories are often reconciling two cultural traditions, and two languages, but Cofer takes this as a given and focuses on the individuals and their everyday problems and concerns.'' The consensus is that Ortiz Cofer manages to give authentic voice to the experience of Puerto Rican young people in such a way that her stories hold universal appeal.

Criticism

Jennifer Lynch

Lynch is a freelance writer in northern New Mexico. In the following essay, she explores the way the main character in ''Bad Influence'' negotiates the boundaries between childhood and adulthood and between New Jersey and Puerto Rico.

The collection *An Island Like You* opens with a poem entitled ''Day in the Barrio''. This poem describes life in the New Jersey neighborhood that Rita, the main character in the story ''Bad Influence'' calls home, a place humming with noise, people, and activity. In its color and music it is reminiscent of Puerto Rico, while in its urbanity it is entirely mainland U.S. The last four lines of the poem sum up the unifying theme of the stories that follow:

> Keeping company with the pigeons, you watch the people below / Flowing in currents on the street where you live / Each one alone in a crowd, / Each one an island like you.

The island metaphor for the mainland Puerto Rican is an apt one, in that it speaks to the interplay between the community and the individual in a displaced island culture. Judith Ortiz Cofer, in her memoir *Silent Dancing*, discusses the way that being a part of two cultures makes one feel an outsider in both worlds. She writes, ''Being the

What Do I Read Next?

- *The Puerto Ricans, 1943-1973* (1973) is a chronology and fact book that explores political, cultural, and legal issues inherent in the relationship between the U.S. and Puerto Rico. It was compiled and edited by Francesco Cordasco with Eugene Bucchioni.

- *Remedios: Stories of Earth and Iron from the History Puertorriquenas* (1998) is a collection of vignettes by Aurora Levins Morales. The stories are comprised of herbal lore from the broad range of women who make up Puerto Rico.

- *The Line of the Sun* (1989) is Judith Ortiz Cofer's first novel and was released to great critical acclaim. It chronicles three generations of a Puerto Rican family through the eyes of Marisol, the youngest of the generations.

- *The Year of Our Revolution: New and Selected Short Stories and Poems* (1998) is Ortiz Cofer's collection of poetry and short stories geared toward adults.

- In *Puerto Rican Tales: Legends of Spanish Colonial Times*, Cayetano Coll y Toste relates twelve Puerto Rican legends of early encounters between the Spanish and native people. The collection is geared toward young people, and is translated and adapted by Jose Ramírez-Rivera.

- *Reclaiming Medusa* (1997) is a collection of stories by and about Puerto Rican women reclaiming their power and challenging racism, sexism, and machismo. It was edited by Diana L. Velez.

---

outsiders had turned my brother and me into cultural chameleons.'' As a fifteen-year-old on the cusp of adulthood, Rita, like the author, struggles to negotiate both the border between two cultures and the line between childhood and adulthood.

At its most basic, ''Bad Influence'' is the story of a teenager at odds with the adult world, who in the course of a summer, comes to terms with that world. At the onset of her summer, exiled from her home and friends to Puerto Rico, Rita resents and criticizes her grandparents. Over time she finds them insightful, spirited, and kind people; she learns from them and adjusts to their world, and, as a result, takes a step toward adulthood. The search for identity Rita undergoes is a universal theme for teenagers, whatever the circumstance, and Rita is like most adolescents. Her critical evaluations of her grandparents and her parents are typical of any teenager sifting through his or her personal legacies, in an effort to accept and incorporate what they choose and reject the rest. Nancy Vasilakis, in her review of *An Island Like You* for *Horn Book*, relates the critical consensus that ''the narratives have a universal resonance in the vitality, the brashness,

the self-centered hopefulness, and the angst expressed by the teens as they tell of friendships formed, romances failed, and worries over work, family, and school.'' Rita's struggle, however, is as much a search for individuality as she approaches adulthood as it is an effort to negotiate two cultures.

''Bad Influence'' opens with Rita's preconception of summer on the island. She begins, ''When I was sent to spend the summer at my grandparents' house in Puerto Rico, I knew it was going to be strange, but I didn't know how strange.'' Emphasis on the word strange calls to mind different interpretations of the word: on one hand bizarre or unusual, on the other foreign or other than oneself. Both function in the story, as Rita sees her grandparents' world as not only odd and nonsensical at times, but finds Puerto Rican culture alien and treats it as something that doesn't belong to her, as an antiquated, foreign world. Notably, she calls Spanish ''not my best language.'' Rita identifies with her current home—Paterson, New Jersey—where her priorities are typical of her peers (boys, sports, and her friends), and in contrast, Puerto Rico holds little appeal. In fact she goes so far as to call it ''my parents' Island," separating it from herself and indicating the gulf between her generation and theirs.

When she gets off the plane, Rita's first reaction is to the heat, which she finds stifling and oppressive. In her typically hyperbolic words, "When I stepped off that airplane in San Juan, it was like I had opened an oven door. I was immediately drenched in sweat, and felt like I was breathing water." The ladies at the airport fan their shiny faces and argue over who carries her luggage, and Rita is mortified. The hot, humid climate operates as a metaphor for Puerto Rico in general: people are too hot, too dramatic, and too loud for Rita's taste. She alludes repeatedly to the fact that everyone in Puerto Rico drinks hot *cafe con leche*, a combination she finds too warm and rich for the heat of the island, and an apt metaphor for her reaction to all things Puerto Rican. The closeness of the weather is akin to the closeness of people on the island, an intimacy that Rita hates when she first arrives. Puerto Ricans are much more comfortable with intimate contact than Rita is; she mentions several times that Mamá Ana sits "real close to me." According to Rita, her parents would never dream of barging into her room the way her grandmother does to wake her in the morning, and she is compelled to discuss her need for privacy with her grandfather when she wakes to find he has opened her window during her nap. She describes her past attempt to call a friend on the mainland, when her conversation was scrutinized and translated by the people around her. Her mother's explanation is that "people on the Island did not see as much need for privacy as people who lived on the mainland."

Rita's grandmother and her neighbors watch telenovelas with unbarred enthusiasm, and participate in the drama as if they were their own communities. After watching one such soap opera with Mamá Ana, Rita speculates about her grandparents' relationship to reality. She reports authoritatively, "Neither one of the old guys could tell the difference between fantasy and reality—Papá with his dream-reading and Mamá with her telenovelas." When she learns of her grandfather's gifts as a spiritualist, she mockingly calls her grandparents a Ghostbuster duo. At one point, when the three of them visit Angela and her mother, her grandfather goes into a trance to meditate on the situation, and Mamá Ana behaves as if nothing is out of the ordinary. Rita takes this as evidence of their craziness, but neglects to consider the way cultural assumptions color her own behavior. For example, she likens her grandparents' spiritist work to televi-

> As a fifteen-year-old on the cusp of adulthood, Rita, like the author, struggles to negotiate both the border between two cultures and the line between childhood and adulthood."

sion shows like *The Twilight Zone* and *Star Trek,* and to rumors she has heard about Haitian voodoo priests in her neighborhood. These cultural references reflect the mass of information she considers normal or native to the U.S. mainland, and comprise her own set of cultural assumptions. Rita is so absorbed in her own, very American view of the world that she cannot help but judge her grandparents' assumption that the spiritual or mystical is a part of everyday life. When she hyperbolically suggests that she would probably go home as one of the walking dead, Rita shows herself to be as dramatic as the grandparents she mocks.

The day Rita spends at the beach outside Angela's house marks the beginning of her transformation in attitude toward her grandparents, as well as the beginning of transformation in Angela's life. Mamá Ana presses Rita to invite Angela to picnic on the beach with them and ends up inviting her to Rita's fifteenth birthday party. In facilitating the connection between the girls, Rita's grandparents succeed in both drawing Angela out of her chilled home and forming a connection for Rita. This connection serves as a bridge for Rita into the world of Puerto Rico. Like Rita and many other Puerto Ricans of their generation, Angela is a person who navigates both island and mainland cultures, since her father lives in New York. In each other's company the girls can speak English and discuss the issues in their lives too private to share with adults. This forum for self-evaluation helps Rita grow out of her infatuation with Johnny Ruiz and see the humor in the situation, as she and Angela speculate that Johnny may be under the spell of a *mala influencia* himself. This kind of peer contact offers Rita the opportunity to honor the part of herself that belongs to the U.S. mainland, while she is immersed in the Puerto Rican.

By the end of the story, Rita characterizes her experience by reporting "I'd had one of the best summers of my life with Angela, and I was even really getting to know my grandparents—the Ghostbusting magnificent duo." Her time on the island has provided her with a new friend and helped her build a bridge between herself and her grandparents, marked by her use of the word magnificent. At her birthday party she notices the way her grandfather makes his way around, "looking at each guest with his kind brown eyes," as if he really does see into their hearts. Over the course of the summer she learns from him how to do the same, to observe how people really feel, and eventually she considers herself a medium in her own right. Rita's assessment of her grandmother is transformed as well; about the woman she previously characterizes as overly gregarious, dramatic, and smothering she says, "She had this talent for turning every day into a sort of party." The time they spend together, shopping for Rita's party dress or cooking crab at the beach, helps bridge the gap in their relationship and their cultures. In a sense they heal the chilliness that Rita brought with her to the island, and this maternal healing extends to Rita's mother as well. When Rita and her grandparents pick up the family from the airport at the end of summer, Rita at first holds back from her mother, deliberately making her suffer for the summer punishment, but then holds her hand in the car, their differences behind them. Thus the healing between Angela and her mother is mirrored in Rita and her mother, thanks to the warm attention of Rita's grandparents.

"Bad Influence" closes with Rita speculating on how she and her friend can get together and meet boys in the fall. Although her summer has helped her bridge the gap between the Puerto Rican and the American in herself, she has by no means lost the part of herself that identifies with Paterson, New Jersey. Rita is every bit the teenager she was when she arrived: caustic, authoritative, and opinionated. Having acclimated to life on the island and come to know her grandparents, Rita is a better integrated version of herself; more at ease in both worlds, she has forged her own identity.

Source: Jennifer Lynch, in an essay for *Literature of Developing Nations for Students*, Gale, 2000.

Liz Brent

Brent has a Ph.D. in American culture, with a specialization in film studies, from the University of Michigan. She is a freelance writer and teaches courses in the history of American cinema. In the following essay, Brent discusses the theme of culture shock in Ortiz Cofer's story "Bad Influence."

In Ortiz Cofer's short story "Bad Influence" the narrator and main character, Rita, is sent from her home in New Jersey to spend the summer with her relatives in Puerto Rico. Rita, who is almost fifteen, and her best friend had been caught attempting to sleep overnight with their boyfriends. Although nothing "happened" between the two girls and their boyfriends that night, their parents still believe the boys to be a "bad influence" on them. In order to keep her away from her boyfriend, Rita's parents give her the choice of spending her summer in a convent or in Puerto Rico. Choosing what she feels to be the lesser of two evils, Rita opts for "*arroz y habichuelas* with the old people in the countryside of my parents' Island." Once in Puerto Rico, Rita experiences various forms of culture shock—meaning that she has trouble adjusting to the habits, customs, and living conditions of a culture which is mostly foreign to her. Although she had spent many summer vacations there in the past with her parents, she had always been surrounded by cousins and preoccupied with playing on the beach. Now, for the first time, she is left to confront this foreign culture by herself. As narrator of the story, Rita uses humor as a means of dealing with her culture shock. In addition, she tries to make sense of things which are foreign to her by relating them back to more familiar elements of popular American culture.

One of the immediate elements of Puerto Rico which Rita must adjust to is the heat. Rita uses exaggeration, figurative language, and humor in order to describe the heat of the Island and its effect on her. As soon as she steps off the airplane in San Juan, the heat strikes her "like I had opened an oven door." Riding in the car from the airport in what she emphasizes is an "un-air-conditioned" car, Rita somewhat humorously attempts to deal with the heat by "practicing Zen." She explains that, "I had been reading about it in a magazine on the airplane, about how to lower your blood pressure by concentrating on your breathing, so I decided to give it a try." This, however, leads to a humorous misunderstanding between Rita and her relatives which she allows them to maintain throughout her visit. Hearing her attempt at Zen-like breathing, her relatives assume that she must have asthma. At her grandparents house, Rita refers to the extreme heat once again; she mentions with a degree of irony that, "Of course, there was no AC"—air conditioning. Again resorting to exaggeration and humor as a means of dealing with her discomfort in the heat, Rita goes to her room, puts a pillow over her head, and "decided to commit suicide by sweating to death."

Rita is additionally disconcerted by the lack of technological devices generally taken for granted in the United States. Because her grandparents do not own a telephone, Rita states ironically that "AT[and]T had not yet sold my grandparents on the concept of high-tech communications."

Another element of life on the island which Rita finds difficult to adjust to is the lack of "privacy." She adopts an ironic tone in describing the crowd of relatives who have come to pick her up at the airport as "my welcoming committee"—a phrase which usually refers to the greeting of an important person on some official occasion. When she decides to call her mother, Rita must use the phone at a neighbor's house, with "a nice fat woman who watched you while you talked." It is in fact impossible for Rita to have a private telephone conversation while on the Island; she explains that, when she had tried to make a phone call the previous summer at the same neighbor's house, "There had been a conversation going on in the same room where I was using the phone, a running commentary on what I was saying in English as understood by her granddaughter. They had both thought that eavesdropping on me was a good way to practice their English." Rita's mother had explained this to her as a cultural difference, as "people on the Island did not see as much need for privacy as people who lived on the mainland." Not only do they not seem to need privacy, but, as Rita's mother had explained, "Keeping secrets among friends is considered offensive." One morning Rita's grandparents come into her room without warning, and Rita observes, "It had been years since my own parents had dared to barge into my bedroom."

Along with the lack of privacy, the level of noise which surrounds Rita among her relatives in Puerto Rico is also difficult for her to adjust to. When her grandmother turns on the TV to watch her telenovela, or soap opera, Rita describes the theme music for the show as "violins wailing like cats mating." Her family members in Puerto Rico seem to have a tendency to play the TV and the radio at higher levels than what Rita is used to in the States. She sarcastically mentions that "I had always suspected that all my Puerto Rican relatives were a little bit deaf." After Rita is told that she and her grandparents must wake up early one morning, she explains, "'Getting up with the chickens' meant

> " Although she had spent many summer vacations there in the past with her parents, she had always been surrounded by cousins and preoccupied with playing on the beach. Now, for the first time, she is left to confront this foreign culture by herself."

that both my grandparents were up and talking at the top of their lungs by about four in the morning." Rita again uses exaggeration in noting that the muffler of her grandparents' car "must have woken up half the island." Rita's use of sarcasm in dealing with the unaccustomed noise of her family life in Puerto Rico is summed up by her rhetorical question, "Why doesn't anyone ever mention noise pollution around here?"

As is the experience of most people in a foreign culture, Rita finds some of the food and methods of food preparation among her relatives on the island to be unpleasant and even disturbing to her. Rita expresses her dislike of the "cafe con leche" which is imposed upon her during her visit in a tone of exasperated irony. Rita describes the drink, which she hates, as "like ultra-sweet milk with a little coffee added for color or something." She goes on to note, "Nobody here asks you if you want cream or sugar in your coffee: the coffee is 99 percent cream and sugar. Take it or leave it."

Strangest of all for Rita are her grandparents' ideas about spirituality, which she interprets as an inability to distinguish between "reality" and "fantasy." Rita tries to make sense of some of the customs of Puerto Rico which seem most bizarre to her by referring to elements of popular American culture, such as movies and TV shows. For example, her grandfather explains to her that his pet rooster, Ramon, likes to sing "when the spirit moves him," and Rita thinks, "I could not believe what I was hearing. It was like I was in a 'Star Trek' rerun where reality is being controlled by an alien, and you don't know why weird things are happening all around you until the end of the show.'' When her grandmother discusses the characters on her telenovelas as if they were real people, Rita thinks, ''It was really going to be 'The Twilight Zone' around here. Neither one of the old guys could tell the difference between fantasy and reality—Papá with his dream-reading and Mamá with her telenovelas.'' Their perceptions and beliefs seem so strange to her that she describes herself as ''spending three months with two batty old people and one demented rooster.''

Rita's grandparents begin to seem even more bizarre to her when they explain that Papá Juan, her grandfather, is ''a medium, a spiritualist,'' who has been called to ''exorcise demons'' from someone's home. This concept is so foreign, unbelievable, and downright disturbing to Rita that she can only make sense of it in terms of the little she has heard in the States about ''voodoo priests.''

> ''Does he sacrifice chickens and goats?'' I had heard about these voodoo priests who went into trances and poured blood and feathers all over everybody in secret ceremonies. There was a black man from Haiti in our neighborhood who people said could even call back the dead and make them his zombie slaves. . . . What had my own mother sent me into? I would probably be sent back to Paterson as one of the walking dead.

Her grandparents' spiritual beliefs seem so foreign and incomprehensible to Rita that she thinks, '' I really should have been given an instruction manual before being sent here on my own.'' Rita's sense of humor about her grandparents' beliefs, however, comes through when she describes their preparations for the spiritual healing in terms which refer to an extremely frivolous element of popular American culture—she refers to her grandfather's holy water and other religious paraphernalia as ''Ghostbuster equipment,'' evoking the Hollywood *Ghostbusters* movie series. As they wait on the beach for her grandfather's visit to the woman and her daughter who have called him in as a spiritual healer, Rita continues to think of these beliefs in terms which are disdainful. She thinks of her grandfather as ''the local medicine man,'' and his spiritual practice as ''mumbo-jumbo.'' Rita again mentions an element of popular American culture—a movie from the 1970s—in describing how she imagines the sick girl in the house where Papá Juan has gone to clean out the evil spirits; Rita thinks of her as ''the girl from *The Exorcist.*''

Once Rita has actually met the sick girl, Angela, they immediately befriend one another, and Rita's visit to the Island takes a turn for the better. Rita is able to bond with Angela when she learns that Angela does not take Papá Juan's spiritual cleansing practices any more seriously than Rita did. By the end of the story, however, Rita becomes more open to her grandfather's spiritual beliefs. She describes herself as ''taking medium lessons'' from her grandparents, whom she now refers to in more positive, although still sarcastic, terms as ''the Ghostbusting magnificent duo.'' Through her grandfather's role as a medium or spiritualist, Rita has learned to be more sensitive to the feelings and needs of other people.

Rita's experience of culture shock in visiting her grandparents becomes an unexpected opportunity for changing her perspective on her own life. Rita ends her narration on an upbeat note, which both acknowledges the ''good influence'' of her grandparents and maintains her characteristic sense of irony, when she claims that she has become ''a mind reader myself.''

Source: Liz Brent, in an essay for *Literature of Developing Nations for Students*, Gale, 2000.

Sheri E. Metzger,

Metzger is a Ph.D. specializing in literature and drama at the University of New Mexico, where she is a lecturer in the English department and an adjunct professor in the University Honors Program. In this essay, she discusses how Judith Ortiz Cofer uses the grandfather's spirituality to envelop the teenage protagonist of ''Bad Influence'' in the heritage and traditions of Puerto Rico.

In her short story ''Bad Influence,'' Judith Ortiz Cofer uses spirituality to help define the family relationship. The young granddaughter is initially unprepared for life in Puerto Rico. She sees herself as a modern, American teenager and her Puerto Rican relatives as antiquated relics of another time and place. Ultimately, it is the grandfather's spirituality that gives direction to Rita's life, first by introducing her to the spirituality of the island, and second by reinforcing a set of morals and expectations by which the people live. Both of these ideas are incorporated into the island heritage that the grandparents pass on to their granddaughter. By the end of her summer, Rita has a new appreciation for her family and her heritage, and she has grown into a more responsible and responsive teenager who accepts and understands the importance of the island's legacy.

In using spirituality, Ortiz Cofer is employing an element of Latin American literature which is often defined by its reliance on magical realism or, in this case, symbolic spirituality. Much of the time, this means that the writer blends together naturalism and supernaturalism seamlessly. Often the literature of Latin America incorporates folktales and legends into the text, making the legends appear a natural part of the author's work. This is the case with Ortiz Cofer's work, which incorporates the grandfather's spirituality and the island's traditional reliance upon such people into Rita's coming-of-age story. Magical realism erases the borders between the characters' reality, the explicable and the inexplicable, and the natural world and the magical world.

Traditional Western literature relies upon literary realism, as it has for more than one hundred years. This traditional realism is what Rita is accustomed to prior to her visit to Puerto Rico. In her American world, healing is given over to conventional medicine and doctors. As is the case with traditional literary realism, which attempts to create a story and characters that are plausible, Rita's New Jersey life is explained as representative of an American teenager's life. In New Jersey, she is a rebellious teenager, easily identifiable to Ortiz Cofer's readers. In contrast, Latin American literature attempts to portray the unusual, the spiritual, and the mystical as ordinary facets of the character's lives, as with the grandfather's journey to heal the evil that permeates Angela's life. For the reader, magical realism requires an acceptance of the coexistence of the real and the imaginary. The author posits these magical events as authentic, with the supernatural events being interwoven seamlessly into the narration. For Ortiz Cofer, this means that the grandfather's spirituality and healing are interwoven into the story as essentially ordinary parts of the island's life. There is nothing exceptional about what he does for his neighbors; the reader accepts this because the author accepts it.

For the people of Puerto Rico, magical realism is an ordinary, accepted, and unquestioned part of their lives. In a 1994 interview with Rafael Ocasio, Ortiz Cofer remarked, "When I write about *espiritismo* [the spiritual healing that Rita's grandfather practices], I am writing about an ordinary, everyday thing that most Puerto Ricans live with." Ortiz Cofer revealed that her own grandfather, who was an *espiritismo,* saw nothing extraordinary or magical about what he did. In this interview, Ortiz Cofer pointed out that when she uses this spiritual tradition in her writing, "there is nothing there that

> It is clear that the stories that Rita's grandparents tell her, the gossip and the myths that permeate their lives, and the folktales that define the role of the *espiritismo* have an important influence on Rita's life—just as they did on Ortiz Cofer's life."

cannot be explained through natural law." For instance, Rita's grandfather seeks to modify his subject's behavior through common sense, rather than cast any spells that change their lives. He employs special teas and prayers, but he also convinces the mother that she must banish her evil boyfriend. As a result, the grandfather's reputation as an *espiritismo,* and the weight afforded his reputation, actually create the healing. In her text, Ortiz Cofer blends the spiritual with morality. Angela is cured, not only because Rita's grandfather appears to work his magic, but also because the cause of her misery is banished. The spiritual teas may also have a role—it is never clear that they do not—and yet, Angela is also healed because her mother banishes her abusive boyfriend. The two influences—the grandfather's spirituality and the mother's actions—work together to resolve the problem. In a sense, spirituality and the appearance of magic give people control. Angela gets her health and life back again because her mother assumes control over her actions. But she is only able to act when the grandfather offers an impetus to do so. The healer's teas and prayers provide that impetus. Consequently, Rita learns to appreciate what her grandfather does when he sets out to heal someone.

Ortiz Cofer does see a difference in how she uses magical realism that makes her use of this rhetorical tradition different from that of other Latin American writers. She told Ocasio that the *espiritismo* are magical "only in that they provide this necessary service and they are connected to the realm of the supernatural." She added that she does not ask her readers to suspend belief in the same way that many Latin American magical realists do. But her distinction is very slight, since the defining element of magical realism is that the reader simply accepts these events as an ordinary part of the character's lives. However, the spirituality found in "Bad Influence" can easily be explained by other means, such as religious or social influences that shape the character's behavior, and so the presence of the *espiritismo* has less importance than it would in a work by Gabriel Garcia Marquez, a leading practitioner of magical realism.

The use of the *espiritismo* is Ortiz Cofer's attempt to live her heritage and to keep it alive for her readers. She told Ocasio that although she lives in Georgia, she has not "stopped relating to the Puerto Rican experience." This is her heritage and it is the heritage that the author also provides for her protagonist, Rita. In the United States, family and friends might intervene to deal with the abusive boyfriend who causes Angela's anorexia. But in Puerto Rico, Angela tells Rita that "it took someone with special powers to drive out the bad influence in my house." The healing of Angela's illness could not have occurred without the *espiritismo*, who orchestrated the evil boyfriend's removal. Was it magic? Probably not, but it was magical in its efficiency. In her summer in Puerto Rico, much of Rita's growth derives from her understanding and acceptance of her grandparents' traditions. In accepting these traditions, and most importantly the tradition of the *espiritismo*, Rita grows into her family's heritage. She leaves behind the New Jersey teenager and recognizes that she is a product of both American and Puerto Rican influences.

Oftentimes, in Latin American literature, magical realism exists in a woman's sphere, as it does in Isabel Allende's novels, but in "Bad Influence," Ortiz Cofer uses magical realism to provide an intergenerational link, rather than a connection between mothers and daughters. Where Allende uses storytelling and magic as interwoven representations of women's lives, Ortiz Cofer uses these two traditions to connect Rita to her Puerto Rican birthright. In "Bad Influence," storytelling and magic are not the exclusive property of women, since Rita's grandfather also possesses this gift. At the story's conclusion, Rita reveals she that has been getting to know her grandparents, and she says, "I had been taking medium lessons from them lately, and had learned a few tricks, like how to look really closely at people and see whether something was bothering them." There is no magic in listening to and paying attention to those with whom Rita comes in contact. But what is new is that she is reaching beyond her own self-absorbed teenage life to appre-

ciate that she needs to show consideration for others, that empathy and compassion are important elements of everyone's life. These are values that her grandparents, and especially her grandfather's *espiritismo*, have taught her. In this way, the traditions of her parents and grandparents are passed down from one generation to the next. This is what Ortiz Cofer suggests is her intention—to keep Puerto Rico alive in her life and to teach its traditions to her readers.

In an earlier interview with Rafael Ocasio, Ortiz Cofer emphasized how important the traditions of Puerto Rico were in her life, and how profoundly those traditions have influenced her writing. In both 1990 and 1992, Ortiz Cofer said that she could not separate her background from her writing and that "the oral traditions of my grandmother's house, the folktales, family stories, gossip or myths often repeated to teach a lesson or make a point educated me and became intrinsic in my writing." It is clear that the stories that Rita's grandparents tell her, the gossip and the myths that permeate their lives, and the folktales that define the role of the *espiritismo* have an important influence on Rita's life—just as they did on Ortiz Cofer's life. Rita learns important lessons about truthfulness, assuming responsibility, and an understanding of the significance of family. By the end of this short story, the young protagonist emerges on the cusp on adulthood. It is her heritage that gives her the means to accomplish this growth.

Source: Sheri E. Metzger, in an essay for *Literature of Developing Nations for Students,* Gale, 2000.

Sources

Bishop, Rudine Sims, review, in *Horn Book*, September-October, 1995, p. 581.

Gruber, Ruth, *Puerto Rico: Island of Promise*, Hill and Wang, 1960, p. 177.

Luís, William, *Dance between Two Cultures: Latino Caribbean Literature Written in the United States*, Vanderbilt University Press, 1997, pp. 27, 95.

Morales Carrión, Arturo, *Puerto Rico: A Political and Cultural History*, W. W. Norton, 1983, pp. 319, 322-25.

Ocasio, Rafael, "The Infinite Variety of the Puerto Rican Reality: An Interview with Judith Ortiz Cofer," in *Callaloo*, Vol. 17, No. 3, Summer, 1994, pp. 730-42.

———, "Puerto Rican Literature in Georgia: An Interview with Judith Ortiz Cofer," in *Kenyon Review*, Vol. 14, No. 4, Fall, 1992, pp. 43-50.

Ortiz Cofer, Judith, *An Island Like You: Stories of the Barrio*, Orchard Books, 1995, pp. 1-5, 13, 22, 25.

————, *Silent Dancing: A Partial Remembrance of a Puerto Rican Childhood*, Arte Publico Press, 1990, pp. 17, 63.

Rochman, Hazel, review, in *Booklist*, Vol. 91, No. 12, February 15, 1995, p. 1082.

Vasilakis, Nancy, review, in *Horn Book*, Vol. 71, No. 4, July-August, 1995, p. 464.

Further Reading

Ortiz Cofer, Judith, contributor, *Puerto Rican Writers at Home in the U.S.A.*, Open Hand, 1991.
    A literary and cultural analysis of contemporary Puerto Rican authors writing from the U.S. mainland.

Sedillo Lopez, Antoinette, *Latino Communities: Emerging Voices, Political, Social, Cultural, and Legal Issues*, University of New Mexico Press, Garland Series, 1998.
    An analysis of contemporary Latin American influences, including artistic movements; it includes an in-depth discussion of magical realism.

Boesman and Lena

Athol Fugard

1969

Fugard began keeping a diary, his "notebooks" as he calls them, in 1959, and the origins of many of his plays can be found in his descriptions of people he has encountered, events he has witnessed, and observations he has made about the condition of his country over the years. In his notebooks, Fugard describes a number of encounters he had with poor black and "coloured" (mixed-race) South Africans that influenced the creation of *Boesman and Lena*, but one in particular stands out above the rest in his mind. On a hot August day in 1965, Fugard and two friends were driving along a rural road when they saw an old woman trudging along with all of her worldly possessions tied up in a bundle on her head. They stopped and offered her a ride. She cried at their unexpected kindness, and during the fifteen-mile trip to a farm up the road, she told them about the death of her husband three days earlier and her nine missing children. If Fugard and his companions hadn't stopped to offer her a ride, she would have followed her plan to sleep in a stormwater drain that night and continue her long journey the next day.

In *Athol Fugard: Notebooks 1960-1977* the author recorded his impression of the old woman. He writes, "In that cruel walk under the blazing sun, walking from all of her life that she didn't have on her head, facing the prospect of a bitter Karoo night in a drain-pipe, in this walk there was no defeat—there was pain, and great suffering, but no defeat."

It was "THE WALK," as Fugard recorded it, that fired his imagination to write *Boesman and Lena*.

Like most of Fugard's dramatic work, *Boesman and Lena* is a small-cast play set in rural South Africa depicting the devastating effects of apartheid on the lives of the author's countrymen. The play, however, is not directly about politics. In his work, Fugard avoids large, scathing political indictments of the white South African government and its treatment of black and mixed-race citizens. Instead, he concentrates on the more immediate struggles of *individuals*—husbands, wives, parents, children, and strangers thrown together by the careless and cruel whims of a racially divided society. Through a handful of people, like Boesman and Lena, the playwright presents a tragic microcosm of South Africa as a whole.

This play about a "coloured" man and woman on a long, hard walk from one shantytown to another was received enthusiastically when it premiered at the Rhodes University Little Theatre in Grahamstown, South Africa on July 10, 1969. Fugard himself was in the cast, portraying Boesman, alongside Yvonne Bryceland as Lena and Glynn Day, a white actor who portrayed Outa in blackface. Jean Bradford, reporting for the *Cape Argus* newspaper, wrote, "When the curtain rang down at the end of the play there was a moment of silence and then followed round after round of applause from the distinguished first-night audience. The cast took eight curtain calls."

Since that first successful performance, *Boesman and Lena* has appeared many times on stages and screens around the world. Well-known actors James Earl Jones, Ruby Dee, and Zakes Mokae performed in the Off-Broadway premiere in New York at the Circle-in-the-Square Theatre in June 1970. In 1971, Fugard was permitted to leave South Africa for a period of one year to direct the play in London at the Royal Court Theatre. Soon afterward, British filmmaker Ross Devenish convinced Fugard to allow him to turn *Boesman and Lena* into a movie. Devenish's film, starring Fugard and Bryceland from the original cast, was released in Great Britain and South Africa in 1973. Subsequently, the play has been translated into French, Dutch, and other languages, performed as a radio play, and filmed again in 1997 in a joint French/South African production starring American actors Danny Glover and Angela Bassett. For works including *The Blood Knot* (1961), *Hello and Goodbye* (1965), and *Master Harold. . .and the Boys* (1982), as well as *Boesman and Lena*, Fugard has earned praise as one of the greatest living playwrights in the English language, and recognition as one of the most outspoken and effective opponents of apartheid.

Author Biography

Athol Harold Lannigan Fugard was born June 11, 1932, in Middelburg, a small village in the semi-desert Karoo region of South Africa. His mother, Elizabeth Magdalena Potgieter Fugard, was an Afrikaner who could trace her ancestry back to the earliest Dutch settlers of 1652. His father, Harold David Fugard, was a South African with English and Irish roots. At his grandmother's request, the boy who would one day become his country's most famous playwright was named Athol after a former British governor of South Africa, the Earl of Athlone.

When he was three years old, Fugard's family moved to Port Elizabeth, where the playwright has since spent most of his life. In his introduction to *Boesman and Lena and Other Plays*, published in 1978, Fugard describes his adopted hometown as "an almost featureless industrial port on the Indian Ocean. . .assaulted throughout the year by strong southwesterly and easterly winds." Port Elizabeth, Fugard explains, is a city of hundreds of thousands of people—blacks, whites, Indians, Chinese and "Coloured" (mixed race) citizens who represent every socioeconomic level. Growing up, Fugard witnessed almost daily the injustice of racial segregation under South Africa's cruel policy of apartheid. Despite its featurelessness, harsh weather, and culture clashes, however, Fugard proudly claims, "I cannot conceive of myself as separate from it," and several of his plays are set in and around Port Elizabeth.

Fugard's father, a musician who led a number of jazz bands, had lost a leg in a childhood accident. Shortly after the family relocated, a lifetime of depression and physical ailments overtook him. In Port Elizabeth, the elder Fugard spent much of his time either drinking heavily or sick in bed. Elizabeth Fugard, meanwhile, operated the St. George's Park Tearoom. Fugard described his father in a 1982 interview for *New Yorker* magazine as a man "full of pointless, unthought-out prejudices." His considered his mother, on the other hand, to be completely color-blind. At the Tearoom, she hired a number of black waiters, and one of them, Sam Semela, became Fugard's closest childhood friend and one of the greatest influences on his life and later career.

One night when his mother was away, Fugard received a call from the nearby Central Hotel. His father was passed out drunk on the floor of the hotel's bar. Young Athol asked Sam for his help, and the two went to the hotel to collect his father. The boy had to ask permission for Sam to enter the whites-only bar, and was humiliated as he walked out past the staring eyes of strangers with his drunken father on Sam's back. The incident, along with Sam's kind treatment of Fugard as an innocent white child in a world that abused its black citizens, became the basis for Fugard's 1982 play *Master Harold. . .and the Boys.*

Though Fugard read constantly and wrote occasionally as a boy, he did not become an artist early in life. After elementary school he studied automobile mechanics on a scholarship at Port Elizabeth Technical College, and later attended the University of Cape Town, majoring in philosophy and social anthropology. He dropped out of school before finishing his degree, hitchhiked the length of the African continent, then, penniless, took a position onboard the *S.S. Graigaur* as an apprentice seaman. Two years later Fugard came ashore back home in Port Elizabeth, determined to become a writer. He worked for a while as a journalist, then met and married Sheila Meiring, an actress working in Cape Town.

Fugard and his new wife founded a theater company, the Circle Players in 1957, then moved to Johannesburg in 1958, where he took a job as a clerk in the Fordsburg Native Commissioner's Court. In the Court, Fugard helped process blacks accused of violating South Africa's "Pass Laws" and witnessed firsthand the terrible atrocities of apartheid. Fugard lamented to the *New Yorker,* "It was just so awful and ugly. We literally disposed of people at the rate of one every two minutes. There was no question of defense—the evidence was rigged. It was like a sausage machine."

Abandoning his clerk's job, Fugard became a stage manager for South Africa's National Theatre Organization and began writing plays in earnest. His first real success was *The Blood Knot* (1961), a play about two South African half-brothers, one black, the other coloured but able to pass for white. Fugard himself starred in the production, something he has done almost continuously ever since.

The Blood Knot set the stage for nearly all of Fugard's later work. Most of his plays are intimate, personal portrayals of tragic events in the lives of two or three characters. Very often his plays contain mixed casts (black, white, and mixed-race characters), and they are all set against the difficult social and political environment of his native South Africa. Plays such as *Hello and Goodbye* (1965), *Boesman and Lena* (1969), *Sizwe Banzi Is Dead* (1972), *A Lesson From Aloes* (1978), *Master Harold. . .and the Boys* (1982), and *My Children! My Africa!* (1989) have won Fugard awards and worldwide recognition and have earned him respect as, in the words of Stephen Gray in *New Theatre Quarterly,* "the greatest active playwright in English."

Plot Summary

Act I

On the surface, the plot of *Boesman and Lena* seems quite simple. In the course of a single evening, two lonely, weathered, beaten down South African "coloureds" (people of mixed race) wander across the bleak mudflats of the Swartkops River near Port Elizabeth, seeking a safe place to settle themselves. They encounter an old black man, briefly take him in, then push onward when he unexpectedly dies in their squalid camp. The real action of the play, however, lies underneath the surface, where Fugard explores a complex mosaic of human emotions, racial politics, and universal questions about existence and the meaning of life in a violent, chaotic world.

The play begins near the end of a long day for Boesman and Lena. Early in the morning, while sleeping in their makeshift "pondok," or hut, in a shantytown outside Korsten, they are awakened by white men with bulldozers who have come to knock down their poor settlement and drive them further away from white civilization nearby. The couple, along with all of the other blacks and coloureds in the segregated settlement, are forced to pick up their few belongings and scatter into the countryside, once more in search of a place to live.

After a long, forced march, when they can walk no more, they arrive at a desolate spot on the banks of the Swartkops River outside Port Elizabeth. There, they drop their burdens and begin to set up camp for the night. Immediately, the strange, abusive relationship they share surfaces. Fugard indicates that the hardship of their lives now obscures

Athol Fugard at Johannesburg's Market Theater.

their ages, but that Boesman and Lena are probably in their fifties. Seemingly, they have spent many of those years together looking out for one another, while at the same time taking out their anger and frustration on each other.

Lena launches the first attack by complaining about the march Boesman has led. ''Why did you walk so hard? In a hurry to get here?'' she rails. ''This piece of world is rotten. Put down your foot and you're in it up to your knee.''

Lena is right. The landscape of the play symbolically mirrors the characters' inner feelings of loneliness, hopelessness, and desolation, as well as the outer political turmoil of the country. The muddy, bleak banks of the Swartkops River, with their sickly vegetation and low-tide stench, are a geographical metaphor for the poverty-stricken, wasted lives of black and coloured South Africans suffering the cruel punishments of apartheid.

For his part, Boesman claims to want merely some peace and quiet while he again tries to build a life and a living for them. Lena's constant talking and complaining, he says, is all nonsense and is driving him mad. In response, Boesman is sometimes simply silent. At other times he ridicules Lena for her ignorance or her emotions, threatens her, and sometimes beats her. Through it all, however, they remain together because there is no one else for them.

While Boesman busies himself with building a shelter out of old corrugated iron and scraps, Lena tries to piece together the many journeys they have taken that have brought them back to this place on the Swartkops. She reels off the names of shantytowns, makeshift villages, and segregated townships they have been forced out of over the years—Redhouse, Veeplaas, Korsten, Bethelsdorp, Missionvale, Kleinskool. It is essential to her that she remembers her past. Putting these towns in order might provide some structure to the chaos of her life. In finding the towns in her mind she may also be able to find herself. But they all run together in her head, and Boesman is no help at all. He mocks her for her ignorance and threatens to beat her again.

The plot of the play, and Boesman and Lena's relationship, turns in another direction when she spots a man sitting in the darkness across the mudflats. Despite Boesman's objections, Lena invites the stranger to join them at their campfire, in hopes that he may be someone she can talk to who will not abuse her the way that Boesman does. As it turns out, the stranger is simply an old, poor black man who doesn't even speak English or Afrikaans, but mutters in Xhosa, a tribal language of South Africa.

Lena is disappointed, but partly out of defiance toward the belligerent Boesman and partly out of loneliness and a need to connect to another human being, she takes the old man in and tries to communicate with him. She calls him "Outa," a respectful name that means "Old Father," and shares her precious bottle of water with him. Disgusted, Boesman stalks off into the darkness to forage for wood and scraps, leaving Lena alone with her new companion.

It is the chance Lena has been waiting for—someone new to talk to who will not mock her or beat her, but will listen attentively, even though he doesn't understand most of what she is saying. In a rush of words and emotions Lena tells the old man all about herself and as much of her past as she can recall. She remembers a dog that followed her around and kept her company for a while. She left the dog behind when the white men chased her away that morning. She tells Outa all about Boesman's abuse, and the way they collect bottles to make enough money to eat. She explains that she has had many children, but only one survived at birth, then died six months later. Throughout her rambling monologue, the old man just sits near their small fire and mumbles.

Boesman's return to the camp a little while later presents a challenge. He demands that Lena run the old man off so the two of them can share their wine and go to bed together on the filthy old mattress in their lean-to hut. Lena, however, wants Outa to stay. Boesman forces her to make a choice—wine, a warm bed, and a bit of a roof over her head, or sobriety and a muttering old stranger outside in the chilly night air. Defiant and fed up with the way he treats her, Lena rejects Boesman and opts for Outa's company. The act ends with Lena and her new friend sharing her bread and bitter tea on the ground near the fire, while Boesman glowers at them from inside his dirty pondok.

Act II

An hour later, Boesman's wine is filling his head, and for entertainment he forces Lena to recall the morning's events in Korsten. In a rude, mocking voice and crude pantomime he imitates her distress when the white men came with their bulldozers to knock down their shantytown. To Lena, it was a travesty, another indignity heaped upon them by their white oppressors. Boesman, however, claims that watching his shabby hut fall actually made him happy and set him free. "Freedom! That's what the whiteman gave us," Boesman cries. "When we picked up our things and started to walk I wanted to sing. It was Freedom!"

With all of his newfound freedom, however, Boesman could still only return to the familiar and the mundane. With all of the world seemingly stretched out before him, he still picked up an old piece of scrap metal and built another pondok on the banks of the Swartkops, just like he had done many times before. In his disgust at this realization, Boesman retreats back into his shelter with his second bottle of wine.

Left alone with Outa again, Lena tries to cheer herself up by talking some more. She describes to the old man the feeling of traveling with all of your belongs on your back, the sweat that comes from hard work in the sun, and the comfort that can be found in a cheap bottle of liquor. Finally, in a desperate attempt to chase away the misery and frustration that is closing in all around her, she begins to clap and sing and dance, working herself into a sweat before crawling under a blanket with Outa again.

Disgusted at the sight, Boesman, who has been unable to find a way to hurt the white men who are his real oppressors, discovers another way to take his frustrations out on Lena. He admits that when he beat her that morning for dropping some of their collected deposit bottles, it was actually he who had broken them when the white men chased them away.

To Lena, this insult is worse than the bruises she received from his beating. ''Why do you hit me?'' she implores. ''To keep your life warm? Learn to dance, Boesman. Leave your bruises on the earth.'' She shakes Outa to prevent him from falling asleep and demands that he be a witness to the next beating Boesman is sure to give her. Their fight escalates, with Lena begging Boesman to beat her and Boesman screaming in his frustration that their lives are not worth the two holes they will someday be buried in.

At the end of Boesman's tirade, Lena stops him short. The old man has finally stopped muttering and has died in her arms. Outa's death at the end of this day is too much for Boesman. His response changes from mockery to accusation to wild defensiveness, and finally he attacks Outa's lifeless body, beating the corpse like he has beaten Lena so many times in the past.

''Look at you!'' Lena screams. ''Look at your hands! Fists again. When Boesman doesn't understand something, he hits it.'' She tells Boesman that now he must leave, and she is staying behind. When the authorities find Outa's body, she threatens, they will find the bruises he left all over it and they will search for Boesman as the old man's killer. As Boesman gathers up all of their belongings for another flight across the countryside, it is Lena's turn to taunt. ''Tonight it's Freedom for Lena,'' she cries. ''Whiteman gave you yours this morning, but you lost it.''

In the end, however, Lena cannot exist without her Boesman. She bids one last goodbye to the old man, who had been a strange sort of friend to her for such a short time, then shoulders some of Boesman's burden and starts to follow him off down the road. ''Where we going?'' she asks. ''Better be far.''

''Coega to Veeplaas,'' he answers. Boesman finally helps Lena remember all of the places they have visited, in their proper order, and she realizes ''It doesn't explain anything.'' Then, with a final

look around their desolate campsite, Boesman and Lena shuffle off into the darkness again.

Characters

Boesman

Much of Boesman's character is defined by his class status in his society. Boesman is of mixed-race descent, and therefore considered ''coloured'' by South African standards. Like the blacks of his world, he has been segregated from white society and denied access to good employment, housing, education, and all of the other things that provide dignity and a quality standard of living to individuals in developed communities. Instead, he has been forced to live on the periphery of the prosperous white world, collecting scraps and constantly moving from one shantytown to the next. His response is to take out his anger and frustrations on the only people in his world who are considered part of a lower class than himself: Lena, his companion and a coloured woman, and Outa, an old black man they meet along the road.

Boesman, a man in his fifties, has obviously mistreated Lena for a long time. At the beginning of the play, she wears bruises from a beating he gave her that morning and complains, ''Ja, that's the way it is. When I want to cry, you want to laugh.'' Boesman has few opportunities in his daily life to feel a sense of power and control, so he seizes them whenever he can. He taunts Lena for her ignorance and drunkenness, which have caused her to forget all of the places they have visited, and continually threatens her with additional beatings. Lashing out physically, however, is his way of covering his own sense of inadequacy and shame. As Lena says, ''When Boesman doesn't understand something, he hits it.''

Outa's arrival presents a challenge for Boesman. The old black man is an easy target for Boesman the bully, but Lena has taken a genuine interest in him, and even Boesman recognizes he can only push so far. He is jealous of the attention Lena showers on the stranger, and he calls the old man a ''kaffer'' (a derogatory term for blacks used in South Africa), but he doesn't seriously harm Outa until after he is dead. Then he takes out all of the frustrations of his miserable day and miserable existence on the life-

Media Adaptations

- *Boesman and Lena* was first adapted as a film in 1973. This South African production was directed by Ross Devenish and starred Yvonne Bryceland as Lena and Athol Fugard himself as Boesman.

- A second film adaptation was produced in 1999. Directed by American John Berry, and starring Americans Danny Glover and Angela Bassett, this *Boesman and Lena* was filmed on location in Cape Town, and produced jointly by South African Primedia Pictures and Pathe Image, a French subsidiary of Pathe, France's oldest film company.

less corpse of the old man. At the end of the play, faced with Lena's very real threat that she will leave him, Boesman gives in to her and recites the names of all the towns and homesteads they have occupied as they shuffle off down the road.

Lena

Lena is a "coloured" woman in her fifties in a society that does not value her race or her gender but, though she occupies one of the lowest rungs on the social ladder, she is probably the strongest character in the play. Lena talks nonstop. Thinking out loud seems to help her bring order to her chaotic world, and the occasional feedback she receives from her companion, Boesman, even though it is usually abusive, is nonetheless affirmation that she still exists and that others hear her cries. At first, Lena seems to be the victim in an oppressive relationship with Boesman. He insults her and beats her regularly, and her body shows the bruises and scars of her hard life on the road as well as his mistreatment. It is soon evident, however, that she is actually a very strong woman. Despite the constant threat of Boesman's abuse, she never hesitates to stand up to him and match his physical blows with her verbal ones.

While Boesman's crutch is violence, Lena leans on alcohol whenever she can to help her get through

cold nights living outdoors and to forget, if only for a while, the hopelessness she often feels. Unlike Boesman, however, Lena also seems interested in finding genuine happiness in her surroundings. It is this interest that causes her to seek out the company of Outa, the old man they meet on the mudflats. While Boesman has only contempt for the ragged old black man, Lena sees in him the opportunity to form a bond with another human being. Even though she can't speak his language, Lena tells Outa all about her travels with Boesman, and even tries to get him to sing and dance with her. After Outa dies, Lena reveals her ability to think more deeply and more philosophically than her companion. Weighing the miserable life she leads against the alternative of death, Lena, much like Shakespeare's Hamlet, concludes, ''Can't throw yourself away before your time. Hey, Outa. Even you had to wait for it.'' In Outa's death, Lena finds a strange sort of release. She agrees to continue her travels with Boesman, knowing all the while that she is free and capable of trekking off on her own should she ever choose to follow that path.

Outa

Outa is the nickname Lena gives to the old black man she and Boesman meet out on the mudflats of the Swartkops River. It is a kindly name that means ''old father,'' and reflects the respect with which she tries to treat the stranger. Lena spots him sitting in the mud not far from their campground and, despite Boesman's protests, invites him to share their campfire, their tea, and their bread. Outa speaks Xhosa, a tribal South African language, and no English, so not much is discovered about his past or his personality. He is obviously weak and sick, and can only manage to prop himself up on a log and mutter continuously while Lena rambles on to him about her life and travels and occasionally spars with Boesman. Outa's most important function in the play is as a foil, a character who does not contribute significantly to the plot of the play, but instead provides other characters a chance to reveal hidden and important aspects of their own personalities. As Lena's foil, Outa provides her the chance to take on the brief role of mother and caregiver, and to extend her contact with people beyond her abusive companion, Boesman. Through Outa's death, Lena achieves a greater sense of understanding of her world and independence from Boesman. She is able to weigh her suffering against the alternative, a death like Outa's, and to choose to look toward the future, whatever it may hold.

Topics for Further Study

- The setting for *Boesman and Lena* is extremely important to the plot and its characters. South Africa in 1969 was a country torn apart by the policies of apartheid, which demanded strict segregation of races. Blacks, whites, and ''coloureds'' were forced to live, work, and attend school and public functions separated from one another, causing a great deal of strife among the different racial groups in South Africa, until they were integrated in the 1980s. The United States has its own history of segregation, strife, and integration. Research America's racially divided past and compare it to South Africa's. What is the timeline for each? What practices did the two countries have in common? What finally led to integration in each country? What race-related problems do the two countries face today as a result of a segregated past?

- Fugard has cited the Irish-born French playwright Samuel Beckett as a major influence on his writing. Read one of Beckett's major plays, perhaps *Waiting for Godot* or *Endgame*, and compare and contrast Beckett's style of ''Absurdist'' theater with Fugard's. Consider such things as setting, plot and character development, and how each author treats important themes in his work.

- Because of its unique history of colonization by many different groups of European settlers, as well as several different native tribes, South Africa recognizes eleven different official national languages, including Afrikaans and Xhosa, two languages used by characters in *Boesman and Lena*. What are the eleven official languages of South Africa? What is the origin of each? Which ones have been especially important in the struggle over apartheid? Why did Fugard choose to use so many ''foreign'' words in an English-language play? What effect does this have on your perception of the characters?

- Watch a film about South Africa and its race relations, such as *Cry, the Beloved Country* (1951/1995), *Cry Freedom* (1987), or *A Dry, White Season* (1989). What are some of the common themes found in both the films and Fugard's drama *Boesman and Lena*? How are the characters in each alike? How are they different? These films were each produced primarily for American audiences, while Fugard's play premiered in South Africa. Can you identify any differences between them based on their intended audiences?

- The relationship Boesman and Lena share is often an abusive one. She assaults him verbally, while he actually beats her physically, leaving bruises and scars. Why do they stay together? Why do they treat each other this way? What could they do differently to improve their relationship?

Themes

Freedom

In a world in which every movement is monitored, controlled and regulated, and every small privilege hard-won and precious, any kind of freedom is a valuable commodity. Because of apartheid and its strict laws governing the separation and rights of races in South Africa at the time of the play, this is the world occupied by the characters in *Boesman and Lena*. The blacks and coloureds of South Africa are told where they can live, work, and travel. Freedom of any kind is not an inalienable right, and complete liberty simply doesn't exist. In its absence, the oppressed minorities of this society have to find their own sense of freedom wherever and whenever they can, even if that means accepting abuse and injustice, and convincing themselves they have found liberation.

Boesman claims to be happy that the white man came with his bulldozers and knocked down his shabby little *pondok* (hut). Where once he had to crawl inside and huddle, cramped, over his food, now he could stand up straight beneath the sky. "Freedom!" Boesman crows, "That's what the whiteman gave us. . .When we picked up our things and started to walk I wanted to sing. It was Freedom!" At least momentarily, Boesman felt liberated. He had no place to live and only the belongings on his back, so the world was open to whatever he might choose to do and wherever he might choose to go. Boesman's freedom, however, was quickly limited by necessity. He had to find another place to shelter himself, and almost immediately he fell into old, familiar habits. He picked up a piece of scrap metal along the roadside to use as a roof for their next *pondok,* and in that simple act he once again fell into the white man's trap and gave away his freedom. "Another *pondok.*" Boesman mourns, "It's no use *baas.* Boesman's done it again. Bring your bulldozer tomorrow and push it over!"

Recognizing this trap, Lena tries to escape with her newfound freedom still intact. "That's not a *pondok,* Boesman," she cries. "It's a coffin. All of them. You bury my life in your *pondoks.* Not tonight." She chooses instead to stay outside, under the sky and next to the campfire, with the old black stranger she has befriended. It is this stranger, whom she calls Outa, who provides her with a different sense of freedom. After she tells him many details of her life and travels, and tries valiantly to feed him and keep him awake and talking, he dies in her arms. Outa's death teaches her about the one freedom she has that cannot be taken away before its time. "I'm alive, Boesman," she observes at the end of the play. "There's daylights left in me." Given the restrictions all around her, it is a meager freedom on which to rely, but it is all she has, and it gives her the strength to resume her journey.

Identity

Both Boesman and Lena are constantly in search of an identity, something that will help them make some sense of the world they inhabit and provide a measure of stability to their frantic, fragile lives. Lena begins the play trying to find some sort of identity in geography. By listing all of the places she and Boesman have traveled together, in order, she hopes to make some sense of her life. But she cannot remember if Missionvale came before Redhouse or after Korsten, and doesn't know in which direction Coega and Veeplaas lie now that she is standing in Swartkops. Boesman is no help at all. He merely insults her or beats her. In his beatings, though, Lena finds another odd sort of identity. If she can be

beaten by Boesman she must exist. "When I feel it," she reasons, "I'll know. I'm Lena." Lena also tries to affirm her being in the eyes of the old stranger they meet. Despite the fact that she cannot speak his language or understand what he is saying, Lena coaxes the old man into saying her name, and is thrilled when he manages to do it.

Despite his best efforts, Boesman usually finds his identity being defined by the white men who rule his world. It is they who have designated him part of the "coloured" class and decreed that he must live in the deserts, mudflats, and other uninhabitable parts of his country. When he finally feels a measure of freedom, after having his ramshackle home destroyed and being driven into the countryside, he immediately lapses into the role his society has handed him and starts scavenging for the white man's junk to build another *pondok.* In the end, both Boesman and Lena discover that, however their identities might change in relation to other people or the world around them, one of the only consistent measurements of their worth and who they are is their relationship with each other. They are Boesman and Lena, and they continue their travels together.

Race Relations

Beneath all of Fugard's plays, including *Boesman and Lena*, is the backdrop of apartheid, or "separateness," the policy of racial segregation followed by the South African government from 1948 until the early 1990s. The apartheid laws classified people according to four major groups—Whites, Blacks ("Bantus"), Coloureds (people of mixed descent), and Asians (mainly Indians and Pakistanis). The laws determined where each group could live and work, and what type of education they could receive, and kept the groups separate from each other, particularly from the ruling white class.

These complicated race relations are an essential component of the plot and character development of *Boesman and Lena*. The title characters, who are both considered coloured, live their lives according to the rules of white society, and find themselves constantly on the move, forced out of one shantytown after another by the bulldozers and soldiers of the white government. Quite obviously, apartheid is a bigoted, unjust system, but its flaws are not the central issue related to race relations in the play. Rather, it is the effect apartheid has had on the minorities it persecutes, and their treatment of one another, that takes center stage.

Both Boesman and Lena feel helplessness and rage at their years of mistreatment by whites, and each deals with his or her emotions in different ways. When confronted and abused by whites, Lena often cries and begs for better treatment. Then, when alone, she seeks solace in a bottle of wine and complains incessantly to her traveling companion, Boesman. For his part, Boesman mocks her for her weakness and cruelly imitates her servility. This is his way of fighting back. Because he cannot mistreat the whites who mistreat him, he passes the abuse along to those who are even more defenseless than he is. In the process, he turns the evil of his white oppressors—interracial hatred—into a greater evil within his own downtrodden class. Because he cannot escape oppression, he chooses to become an oppressor himself. This cruel evolution of abuse is seen most vividly in Boesman's treatment of Outa, the old black man whom Lena invites into their campsite. Boesman angrily calls Outa a "kaffer," a derogatory term for blacks used in South Africa equivalent to the American slang word "nigger." He has no pity for this fellow abandoned soul. He refuses to share his meal and his shelter with the old man, and after he dies, Boesman beats out his frustrations on Outa's lifeless body.

Style

Setting

The setting of a play includes such things as the time period in which it occurs, the location of the action, and important characteristics of the culture in which the characters live. *Boesman and Lena* takes place in the early 1960s in South Africa, when the apartheid movement had a strong grip on the people of that diverse country. Although South Africa at the time was inhabited by many cultures, including Dutch, German, and English white settlers; black Africans representing many different tribes from across the continent; mixed-race people known as "coloureds"; and Asian people from India, Pakistan, and elsewhere, the ruling white class made it very difficult for these other groups to survive and prosper. Strict, oppressive laws governed where these people could attend school, live, and work, and who they could associate with and marry.

Although the landscape of South Africa is marvelously varied and beautiful, containing forests, mountains, enormous grasslands and plateaus,

farmland, and deserts, Fugard chose to set *Boesman and Lena* on a bleak patch of earth that his characters were more familiar with: the mudflats of the Swartkops River outside the city of Port Elizabeth. Here, on the filthy, stinking banks of the river at low tide, Boesman, Lena, and other poor coloureds and blacks were able to scavenge for shrimp and small fish and collect the trash of the whites that floated along the water and collected on the shore.

Circular Structure

One of the hallmarks of plays that are labeled part of the "Theatre of the Absurd" movement of the 1950s and 1960s is that they often contain a circular structure. They end more or less precisely where they began. Samuel Beckett's well-known absurdist tragicomedy *Waiting for Godot* (1953), for example, depicts two tramps waiting near a bare-branched tree for the arrival of a Monsieur Godot at the beginning of the play. By the end, after a series of odd comic and serious scenes filled with metaphysical questions about the absurdity of life, the unlikely pair of clowns remains near the same tree waiting for the same man, with little hope that anything will ever change. The lack of progress becomes a metaphor for the pointlessness of life.

In terms of the characters' development, *Boesman and Lena* does not end exactly where it began. Boesman may have learned to value and respect Lena's companionship just a little more than he did before, and Lena, through Outa's death, discovers a slightly more hopeful way to view her existence. Still, in terms of the play's plot, their lives at the end continue along the same exact journey they were on when the play began. They arrived on the mudflats of the Swartkops running from the oppression of whites and trying desperately to find a place to settle down. When the curtain closes, they are departing in the same mode, running from the death of Outa and the questions of the white authorities and back into the same circle of shabby shantytowns they have visited countless times before.

Literary Heritage

South Africa is inhabited by a broad range of cultures including Dutch, German and English white settlers; black Africans from many different tribes across the continent; "coloreds" (people of mixed descent); and Asian people (mainly people from India and Pakistan). White colonists were first attracted to the South African coast in the eighteenth century for its abundant resources. Since their arrival, the white minority population has sought to control the black majority population of the region.

When Fugard wrote his play *Boesman and Lena* in 1969, all major black African political organizations had been banned, and blacks in the country were segregated and assigned to Bantustans (''homelands''), restricted from travelling outside these areas (except to work for whites in very limited circumstances). The minority white population by this time controlled over eighty percent of the land, all the government, and the vast majority of natural resources, though black African uprisings against white control were frequent throughout the 1960s and 1970s.

The state of the arts, in particular the theater, were hazardous during this time. Although stage dramas were often less censored than were novels, television, and movies (which were often banned before their public release), the laws regarding apartheid made theater production increasingly difficult. Rising international protest against South Africa's apartheid policies caused many countries and playwrights to shun South Africa. At the same time (1965), new apartheid laws were passed prohibiting mixed-race casts and segregating audiences by race. By 1966, British Equity would not allow its performers to act in these conditions. As a consequence, South Africa faced a dearth of plays, performers, and touring companies. While the South African government did provide limited funding for the arts, access to these funds required adherence to the strict apartheid policies governing public performances; because of these restrictions, many artists worked outside subsidized theater.

Some artists, such as Gibson Kent, created all-black touring groups and performed only for black audiences. Other companies (e.g., the Space Theatre and the Market Theatre) devised ways of circumventing the apartheid laws and created works with mixed-race casts and occasionally mixed audiences. The segregation laws regarding casts and audiences were not repealed until 1977, during which time several notable playwrights, performers, and writers (including Fugard) had emerged against the turbulent political background. These performers are often credited with helping to raise national and international awareness of South Africa's apartheid policies.

Athol Fugard, who began (and continued) his writing career while South Africa's apartheid policies were in place, was considered by the South African government to be a ''political risk.'' He was often censored and occasionally prevented from travel from and return to his home country. Today, Fugard is recognized in both his own country and internationally as one of the greatest living playwrights in the English language, and is credited with helping to dismantle the unjust system of apartheid through his drama. Fugard's works are characterized by his personal portrayals of tragic events in the lives of two or three characters, often utilizing casts of mixed-race characters set against difficult political, social and economic backgrounds of South Africa. His dramas depict the devastating effects of apartheid, and represent a microcosm of South Africa as a whole.

Historical Context

Apartheid

South Africa is a land inhabited by many cultures, including Dutch, German, and English white settlers; black Africans from many different tribes across the continent; mixed-race people known as ''coloreds''; and Asian people from India, Pakistan, and elsewhere. Since the eighteenth century, white colonists have been drawn to the southern tip of the African continent for the abundance of resources it has to offer, particularly coal, uranium, diamonds, and gold. From the time they first started to appear in South Africa, the white minority population sought ways to control the black majority.

After decades of creating ''pass laws'' and various segregation legislation, the ruling white class, through the National Party, instituted a policy of *apartheid*, or ''separateness,'' in 1948. The apartheid laws classified people according to four major groups—Whites, Blacks (''Bantus''), Coloreds (people of mixed descent), and Asians (mainly Indians and Pakistanis). The laws determined where each group could live and work and what type of education they could receive, and kept the groups sepa-

Compare & Contrast

- **1969:** After 69 blacks were killed in Sharpeville in 1960 when police opened fire on a crowd of anti-apartheid demonstrators, all black African political organizations, including the African National Congress (ANC) and other opposition groups, are banned.

  Today: In the 1990s, white South African President F. W. de Klerk helped dismantle apartheid policies and restore representative power to black African unions and political organizations.

- **1969:** About a million blacks are arrested each year for violation of the "Pass Laws," a rigid system of rules governing where blacks can live and work, and requiring all black South African citizens to carry with them at all times a "reference book" which lists their personal information and employment history.

  Today: The pass laws were abolished in 1986 when the dismantling of apartheid began, and all citizens of South Africa are now able to move about their country freely, living and working wherever they choose.

- **1969:** Afrikaans and English are the only official languages of South Africa, even though they are spoken as first languages by only a small portion of the population.

  Today: The 1994 constitution added nine languages to the list of officially recognized tongues in South Africa: Zulu, Xhosa, Sesotho sa Leboa, Tswana, Sesotho, Tsonga, Venda, Ndebele, and siSwati. Together with English and Afrikaans, these languages represent 98 percent of the people in South Africa.

- **1969:** Education for blacks and coloureds in South Africa is significantly inferior to that provided for whites. Black students have fewer classrooms, fewer textbooks, and fewer teachers. Few schools have any kind of science laboratories, and per-student spending on blacks is less than 25% that allocated to white students.

  Today: Fourteen separate education departments have been merged into one nondiscriminatory educational system. The government's goal is to provide ten years of mandatory, state-sponsored education for all children, but South Africa still faces a monumental shortage of teachers, textbooks, and classroom facilities and is trying desperately to fund massive educational reforms.

- **1969:** Playwright Athol Fugard is considered a political risk to the government of South Africa. He is subjected to censorship of his plays, limited in his ability to produce for mixed-race audiences, and occasionally prevented from leaving and returning to his country of birth.

  Today: Fugard is recognized in his own country and abroad as one of the greatest living playwrights in the English language, and is credited with helping to dismantle the unjust system of apartheid through his insightful works of drama. He travels freely around the world as a writer, actor, and director.

---

rate from each other, particularly from the ruling white class.

When Fugard wrote *Boesman and Lena* in 1969, all black African unions and political organizations, including the popular African National Congress (ANC), had been banned. Blacks in the country were assigned to *Bantustans,* or homelands, often in the deserts and arid wastelands outside of white cities, and without regard for their true origins. They were restricted from traveling outside of their *Bantustans,* except to work for whites in very limited capacities and for short periods of time. The minority white population controlled more than 80 percent of the land, all of the government, and the vast majority of natural resources, including the workable farmland.

Uprisings against the harsh rules of apartheid were increasingly common in the 1960s and 1970s. During the "Sharpeville Massacre" of March 21, 1960, police killed 69 blacks who were demonstrating against pass laws. In later riots, like the Soweto uprising in Johannesburg in 1976, schoolchildren protested the "Bantu education" they were offered by the white government and boycotted the schools when they were forced to study in the Afrikaans language, the language of the minority white leaders. The Soweto protests sparked similar demonstrations across the country, led mainly by South African youths, which led to the deaths of nearly 600 blacks at the hands of white police and soldiers.

Theater in South Africa

The many divisions of race and class in South Africa at the time of *Boesman and Lena* created a complex and occasionally hazardous environment for theatrical production. Although drama fared better than novels, television, and films, many of which were banned even before their release to the public, government authorities, determined to enforce the laws of apartheid and suppress political opposition, made it difficult for the art of theater to thrive.

The Republic of South Africa was formed in 1961, after the country broke away from the British Commonwealth. Rising international protest over South Africa's apartheid policies and its treatment of black and "coloured" citizens caused many countries to shun the new republic. By 1963, foreign playwrights refused to have their plays staged in South Africa. In 1965, laws were passed prohibiting mixed-race casts on stage and requiring audiences to be segregated into black, white, and "coloured" crowds with separate performances. By 1966 British Equity, the actors' union, would not allow its members to act in these segregated theaters under these conditions. As a consequence of these decisions, South Africa faced a shortage of new plays and hosted practically no touring companies.

While the government provided a small measure of subsidy for theater through a network of Performing Arts Councils, access to this public funding meant accepting harsh restrictions on what could be written and staged, where, and for whom. As a result, many white African playwrights, and practically all black authors, worked outside the subsidized theater where both the risks and the potential rewards were greater.

Some artists, such as Gibson Kente, created all-black touring groups that performed solely for all-black township audiences in a variety of spaces (since none of the townships had actual theaters). Kente mostly avoided obviously political subjects, but was actually jailed for a while in 1976 when *How Long?* (1973), a play of Kente's that criticized the pass laws, was turned into a film and attracted wider public attention. Other "alternative" companies, like the Space Theatre in Cape Town and the Market Theatre in Johannesburg, devised ways to work around the laws segregating theater and staged works by both black and white South Africans with mixed casts and occasionally mixed audiences.

The segregation laws separating casts and audiences were not repealed until 1977, by which time the renegade South African alternative theater had produced many notable playwrights and performers. John Kani, Winston Ntshona, Pieter-Dirk Uys, Fatima Dike (the first black South African woman to have a play published), and Athol Fugard began their careers at the height of apartheid, and are often given credit for helping to raise national and international awareness of South Africa's problems and eventually to end racial segregation and restore the rights of the black majority.

Critical Overview

When *Boesman and Lena* premiered at the Rhodes University Little Theatre on July 10, 1969, Fugard was concerned that he and his cast might run into trouble with South Africa's Censorship Board, the harshest critics he was likely to face. Fugard and other artists had been facing censorship of books, articles, movies, and plays for several years, as the white South African government attempted to control rising opposition to the policies of apartheid. Surprisingly, however, there was no interference, and Fugard was permitted to present *Boesman and Lena* not only to the "whites only" audiences in Cape Town and Johannesburg, but also to the African, Indian, and mixed-race or "coloured" audiences in the outlying townships.

The play, with an all-white cast playing to a predominantly white audience at its world premiere at Rhodes University in Grahamstown, immediately won enthusiastic support for Fugard and his work. The opening night audience cheered the cast onstage (which consisted of Fugard himself as Boesman, Yvonne Bryceland as Lena, and Glynn

Day in blackface makeup as Outa) through eight curtain calls. A review in the *Cape Argus* in Cape Town reported that *Boesman and Lena* "has been acclaimed by critics here as a stunning revelation and as a grim and powerful play with a sustained flow of wit and joy shining off its surface of misery and desolation." Jean Branford, a reviewer for the *Cape Argus,* was particularly impressed by Fugard's blending of the English, Afrikaans and Xhosa dialects in the play. "The language," Branford wrote, "is a vivid and faithful rendering of the mixed dialect of certain coloured people, richly earthy, and humorous and moving by turns."

In "The Poetry of Poverty," a *Guardian Weekly* book review of Fugard's *Three Port Elizabeth Plays* which includes *Boesman and Lena*, Dan Jacobson also emphasized the importance of language in Fugard's plays. Jacobson believed the speech of Fugard's characters "developed out of cultural confusion and disinheritance, out of the historical violence which has thrust together haphazardly a variety of racial groups." He admired the messages Fugard was able to convey through his use of language, and noted, "Without being false to them, or to their mode of speech, he manages to create a poetry of poverty and dislocation that tells the South African reader more about himself and his country than he may wish to admit."

More important than the poetry of Fugard's language, however, is the poignancy of his message. *Boesman and Lena* has been revived many times since it first appeared in 1969. It has been translated into French, Dutch, and other languages, broadcast on the radio, and filmed twice, in 1973 and 1997. Reviewers of all of the play's major productions have consistently praised Fugard for his ability to make powerful political statements and capture some of the best and worst qualities of humanity in intimate portrayals of personal tragedies.

In a review of *Boesman and Lena* for the *New York Times* in 1977, Mel Gussow wrote, "[Fugard's] plays are timeless, a truth that becomes increasingly evident as they are revived and enter the international repertory. He is one of the few living dramatists who can be talked about in terms of greatness." Gussow suggested that there is a "classic purity and clarity" in Fugard's plays. "It is not only black against white, but man against woman, people against people," the reviewer observed.

In a 1980 article for *Canadian Drama*, Derek Cohen praised *Boesman and Lena* as "possibly the finest of Fugard's plays." Remarking on the play-

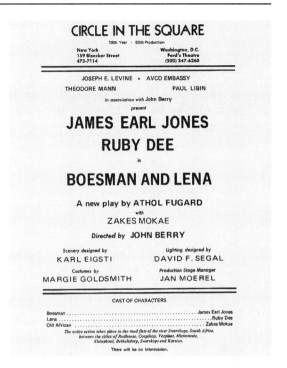

The July 1970 playbill for Boesman and Lena, *starring James Earl Jones as Boesman and Ruby Dee as Lena.*

wright's ability to critique his society and draw national themes from intimate, interpersonal battles, Cohen reported that *Boesman and Lena* was a "drama of unrelieved and immitigable suffering" which becomes "more intense as the characters, impotent against the civilization of which they are outcasts, turn their fury against each other."

By the time the Manhattan Theatre Club in New York City revived *Boesman and Lena* in 1992, African National Congress leader Nelson Mandela had been released from prison and was about to win the Nobel Peace Prize, together with South African President F. W. de Klerk, for their dismantling of apartheid and efforts to unite blacks and whites in the long-troubled country. Still, the play retained its haunting resonance with American audiences. Thomas Disch, a reviewer for the *Nation*, wrote, "I know of no other play that depicts the horror of homelessness and vagrancy so tellingly, and surely the reason for this is that homelessness is not really Fugard's theme. The extremity of the situation in which Boesman and Lena find themselves is like Lear's heath or the desert with its single dead tree in *Waiting for Godot*. Boesman and Lena's straits are presented as emblematic of the human condition and hence not to be protested—only, if possible, endured.''

Criticism

Lane A. Glenn

Lane A. Glenn has a Ph.D. specializing in theater history and literature. In this essay he examines the similarities and differences between Fugard's Boesman and Lena *and Samuel Beckett's Absurdist "tragicomedy"* Waiting for Godot.

There is a moment in Athol Fugard's poetic drama *Boesman and Lena* when the desperate, road-weary Lena begs her traveling companion to please *listen* to her, and to help her remember all the filthy, ramshackle places they have been, and the order in which they visited them. "What difference does it make?" the angry Boesman challenges her, "To anything? You're here now!"

Their debate—as much a matter of metaphysics as geography—is the central conflict in the play. Lena is on a quest to discover her identity, which has been stolen or masked by a dominant white society that systematically marginalizes and abuses its black and mixed-race citizens. Boesman, on the other hand, has built a shaky identity for himself, based on physical aggression and self-deception, and will do almost anything to avoid facing the truth of his existence. Although Fugard writes intimate, realistic dramas in the style of Anton Chekhov or Henrik Ibsen, Boesman and Lena's dilemma—the search for personal meaning in a chaotic, sometimes violent world—is one found more often in the plays of an avant-garde movement of the 1950s and 1960s: the "Theatre of the Absurd."

Theatre scholar Martin Esslin first provided a name for this movement in his 1962 study *The Theatre of the Absurd*. In this book, Esslin describes similarities in the works of several post-World War II playwrights, most notably Eugene Ionesco, Jean Genet, Harold Pinter, Edward Albee, and Samuel Beckett. He examines some of the social and political influences of the twentieth century that he claims have caused playwrights to turn away from more "traditional" forms of drama and accepted meanings, and turn instead toward plays that seem to lack structure and ask many more questions than they are prepared to answer. The Theatre of the Absurd, Esslin writes, is an expression of mankind's search "for a way in which they can, with

dignity, confront a universe deprived of a generally accepted integrating principle, which has become disjointed, purposeless—absurd.''

Because the universe lacks meaning, Absurdist plays often do not contain "plots." Instead, audiences are presented with a handful of characters in a *situation* that begins and ends in more or less the same place. Any attempts to improve this situation, or their lives in general, is doomed to fail, because the human condition itself is viewed as absurd. Characters in Absurdist plays often lack identities, and sometimes do not even have names. Language—the tool most people use to attach meaning to objects and ideas—proves difficult or useless in Absurdist dramas. Time and place—the setting of Absurdist plays—is often unknown, or unreal and unrecognizable.

The best known practitioner of the Theatre of the Absurd is Samuel Beckett, whose 1953 "tragicomedy" *Waiting for Godot* first drew widespread international attention to the new style of drama. The "action" of *Waiting for Godot* is quite simple. Two tramps, Vladamir and Estragon, are waiting near a bare tree for the arrival of a man named Godot. They argue with each other, consider suicide, chew on carrots and chicken bones, meet up with another odd pair—a master and slave named Pozzo and Lucky who perform a strange routine for them—and are told by a young boy that Godot will not be arriving this day, but the next. When the play ends the tramps are sitting beneath the same tree, which now has sprouted a few leaves, still waiting for Godot. The play has not told a "story" or drawn any conclusions from its characters' experiences. Rather, it has presented a meditation on the absurdity of life, and left its audience to pull from that its own lessons.

There is no doubt Beckett and the Theatre of the Absurd had a considerable influence on Fugard in the early part of his career. He began working in earnest as a dramatist, director, and performer just as Beckett was beginning to achieve international recognition for plays like *Waiting for Godot, Endgame*, and *Krapp's Last Tape*. In 1962 Fugard was called upon to direct a black production of *Godot* for the Rehearsal Room in Johannesburg. He recorded the experience in his diary, which was later published in *Athol Fugard: Notebooks 1960-1977*. "In terms of 'satisfactions,' of humility, of feeling that one had made contact with the rare moment of truth in theatre, this production of *Godot* is as important to me as *The Blood Knot*,'' Fugard

What Do I Read Next?

- Fugard has written nearly two dozen plays. All of them are set in his native South Africa, and many share some of the same qualities *Boesman and Lena* possesses: intimate, small-cast, poetic dramas set against the beauty of the South African countryside and the tragedy of its politics. Fugard's first big success, *The Blood Knot* (1961), is about two half-brothers, one black, the other nearly white but technically "coloured," and the effects of apartheid on their lives. In *Master Harold. . .and the Boys* (1982), a young white South African boy learns some lessons about family, love, and dignity from the two black servants in his parents' cafe. *My Children! My Africa!* (1989) explores the devastating effects of anti-apartheid demonstrations and township riots on a black teacher and two of his students, one black, the other white.

- Fugard's *Boesman and Lena* takes some of its inspiration from the works of Absurdist playwright Samuel Beckett, whose plays often explore the themes of loneliness, despair, and the search for order and meaning in a violent, chaotic world. Beckett's masterpiece is *Waiting for Godot* (1953), a tragicomic play about two tramps waiting for a mysterious man named Godot, who never arrives. Some of Beckett's other works include *Endgame* (1957), *Krapp's Last Tape* (1958), and *Happy Days* (1961).

- Nadine Gordimer's novel *July's People* (1981) provides a different perspective on race relations in South Africa in the age of apartheid. July is the black servant of white South African architect Bam Smales and his wife, Maureen. In their minds, Bam and Maureen treat July well and deserve his loyalty. When interracial violence spreads across South Africa, July helps the Smales and their children escape to his distant village, where the tables are suddenly turned and his employers must depend upon July for their survival. In the process, they discover that July is more than a simple servant. He is a human being, a man with a life apart from his servitude to their family, in a complex world of politics and human relations where black and white are kept apart and brought together through the painful system of apartheid.

- Novelist James A. Michener has written several books of historical fiction, including *Hawaii, Alaska,* and *Mexico.* In *The Covenant* (1980), Michener explores the tortuous history of South Africa from the arrival of the first European immigrants in the fifteenth century through the creation of the modern South African nation and the tragedy of apartheid. The saga combines fact with fiction and focuses on Willem van Doorn and ten generations of his descendants as they struggle through the country's colonization, the Great Trek, the Boer War, and other important, defining events in South Africa's history.

- Norman Silver's 1993 collection of stories *An Eye for Color* is narrated by Basil, a Jewish teenager living in Cape Town, South Africa. Basil's tales reflect the world around him, organized by apartheid, where common events take on new meaning because of the rigid class structure system and race laws governing his country. In one story, Basil tells his girlfriend about a beating he saw two blacks endure, and she responds that they must have provoked it. Basil sees a young girl get reclassified from being white, with all its attendant privileges, to being black, which means she must move from their neighborhood and attend another school. This collection is particularly aimed at teenage readers.

> " For all his talk about death and the brevity of life, however, one of the most distinguishing characteristics that separates Fugard from Beckett and the Absurdists is his hope for the future."

admitted. "Yes—above all else—truth—and truth at the level where it is Beauty."

The South African author's admiration of his Irish counterpart's work went well beyond a single play and a lone production. That same year, Fugard read his way through all of Beckett's work, and reported that "Beckett's greatness doesn't intimidate me. I don't know how it works—but he makes me want to work. Everything of his that I have read has done this—I suppose it's because I really understand, emotionally, and this cannot but give me power and energy and faith."

Fugard's empathy and understanding of Beckett found its way into several of his plays, especially *Boesman and Lena*. In many ways the play is similar to Beckett's masterwork, *Waiting for Godot,* and it contains nearly all of the most prominent characteristics of Absurdist theatre—a circular plot structure, characters who lack identities, difficult use of language, and absurd attempts to improve the human condition. Still, though Fugard adopted many of the techniques and attitudes of Beckett and his characters, his brand of "Absurdist" theatre is noticeably different, and distinctly South African.

Like Beckett's tramps in *Waiting for Godot,* Fugard's downtrodden vagabonds in *Boesman and Lena* are insecure about their identities and place in the world, and desperately searching for something to provide them with a sense of purpose and meaning. For Vladamir and Estragon, hope lies in the eventual arrival of Godot, but waiting day after day is meaningless and sometimes fills them with despair. Boesman and Lena, on the other hand, are not waiting; they are walking. Pushed from one shantytown to the next so often that Lena has lost track of where they have been, their search for

meaning is not voluntary. Instead, it has been forced on them by the white men who keep knocking down their homes. As Craig McLuckie suggests in "Power, Self, and Other: the Absurd in *Boesman and Lena*," "It is the walking, not the temporary stops in the towns, that is most important. The absurdity of their condition is found in this incessant, pointless, repetitive cycle of walks. The play could have been called 'Walking for Godot' to emphasize the importance and, paradoxically, the meaninglessness of the action."

Continually running up against chaos and meaninglessness, however, does not deter Lena from seeking greater clarity from the world around her, even though her attempts often fail. Vladamir and Estragon try to find meaning for their lives in arguments about the Bible, contemplation of death, and ridiculous banter. They make no progress, and find themselves as lost at the end of *Waiting for Godot* as they were when the play began. Similarly, Lena seeks to prove her existence by putting together a history of the towns she and Boesman have visited, by singing or dancing, and by talking continuously in the hope that someone will respond and connect with her in a meaningful way. Boesman, however, does not share her need for the human touch. One telling exchange goes like this:

> LENA. Don't be like that tonight, man. This is a lonely place. Just us two. Talk to me.
>
> BOESMAN. I've got nothing left to say to you. Talk to yourself.
>
> LENA. I'll go mad.

Lena needs the reassurance, not only of hearing her own voice, but of hearing the voice of another human being in response, in order to comfort her and bring some sense of belonging and order to her chaotic world. For this reason, the appearance of "Outa," the old man, is vitally important to her. For Lena, Outa represents a new audience—the opportunity to start her stories all over again and get fresh responses and feedback. Of course, it is no small coincidence that Outa speaks only Xhosa and cannot understand what Lena is telling him, or respond to her constant questions and pleadings. Fugard, like the Absurdists, recognizes that even language, ultimately, cannot adequately deliver us from the meaninglessness of life. It is ironic, but appropriate, that Lena has found someone to confide in, to rescue her from the pointless brutality of Boesman and white society, only to discover that he is even more helpless and closer to death than she is.

The subject of death, though not always directly discussed, is one of the motivating themes behind the Theatre of the Absurd. One of the reasons, Absurdists contend, that modern society finds life chaotic and death difficult to contemplate is that people have lost touch with religion, ritual, and any kind of faith that connects them to the universe as a whole. Esslin observes:

> For God is dead, above all, to the masses who live from day to day and have lost all contact with the basic facts—and mysteries—of the human condition with which, in former times, they were kept in touch through the living ritual of their religion, which made them parts of a real community and not just atoms in an atomized society. The Theatre of the Absurd forms part of the unceasing endeavor of the true artists of our time to breach this dead wall of complacency and automatism and to re-establish an awareness of man's situation when confronted with the ultimate reality of his condition.

To Beckett's tramps in *Waiting for Godot* death and suffering are no more or less important than eating lunch or actually finding Godot. They jest at scars, casually joking about hanging themselves, crucifixion, and the existence of God and Christ. Pain and death are more serious and immediate concerns to Boesman and Lena, however, since they must combat them every day. Still, they are resigned to their fates. Lena accepts the beatings and bruises Boesman offers her—even encourages them—as a means of actually *feeling* her existence. Boesman recognizes that, at the end of their struggle for survival, their reward will be simple enough. "One day your turn. One day mine," he observes. "Two more holes somewhere. The earth will get [sick] when they push us in. And then it's finished. The end of Boesman and Lena."

On the surface, Boesman's assessment sounds bleak, and even Fugard himself, who has not suffered like his characters, can seem fatalistic. In "Athol Fugard at Forty," an interview with Peter Wilhelm, the playwright called man's central dilemma "the fact that life dies. The span can literally be measured. . .I know nothing about hereafters. I've not been able to escape being fascinated, depressed, appalled, challenged by the fact that one life is so much, and that is your chance to do it. And the passing of those seconds. . .well man, it's death knocking at the door. Seconds for me is literally the knock at the door."

For all his talk about death and the brevity of life, however, one of the most distinguishing characteristics that separates Fugard from Beckett and the Absurdists is his hope for the future. Both *Waiting for Godot* and *Boesman and Lena* end more or less where they began. Vladamir and Estragon are still beneath the same tree, which has sprouted a few leaves, waiting for Godot. Boesman and Lena, unable to rest for even a single night, have once again shouldered their belongings and are trudging off down the road. While Beckett generates an odd mixture of ridiculousness, wistfulness, and despondency, however, Fugard manages to draw hope and even happiness from the well of desolate despair. Beckett's characters were never real to begin with. They inhabit a world that doesn't exist, and find it easy to mock the world we live in. Boesman and Lena, however, are only too real to Fugard. He has seen people like them suffering in South Africa nearly every day of his life, and to treat them with the casual disregard Beckett shows his comic tramps would be unthinkable. Because they are real, and a part of his world, there must be some hope for their future.

The American playwright Arthur Miller once famously remarked in an essay titled "Tragedy and the Common Man" that tragedy suggests more optimism than pessimism in its author, and that the final result of tragedies should be the "reinforcement of the onlooker's brightest opinions of the human animal." Miller was defending his depiction of Willie Loman as a hopeful tragic hero in *Death of a Salesman* (1949), but the same argument can be been made for the characters and events in *Boesman and Lena*. These two weary travelers are poor, downtrodden, and the victims of South Africa's racially divided society. They live on the edges of affluent white cities in trashy tin "pondoks" created from the refuse of the ruling class. Still, they have a dignity and sense of mission, and small victories may add up to large ones.

At the end of *Waiting for Godot* Vladamir asks "Shall we go?" to which Estragon responds, "Yes, let's go." They remain seated beneath the tree, immobilized, with no place to go. At the end of *Boesman and Lena* Boesman finally gives in and tells Lena the order of the towns they have visited. She realizes then that their history does not help her understand their present or their future, but she is happy she has left a mark. "Somebody saw a little bit," she tells Boesman, "Dog and a dead man." It's a start. And what's more, she reports, "I'm alive, Boesman. There's daylights left in me."

The society Fugard and his characters inhabit may be violent. It may be chaotic and enough to drive a sane person mad, but they refuse to let the absurdity of their situation beat them in the end. As Mel Gussow remarked in a review of *Boesman and Lena* for the *New York Times,* "For all its apparent bleakness, the drama is an uplifting endorsement of the indomitability of mankind."

Source: Lane A. Glenn, in an essay for *Literature of Developing Nations for Students,* Gale, 2000.

Craig W. McLuckie

In this essay, Craig McLuckie compares Fugard's Boesman and Lena, *with the writings of Albert Camus and Samuel Beckett as he discusses* Boesman and Lena's *search for their sense of self in a desperate and absurd world. McLuckie sees Fugard here as being "less rooted in the metaphysical" than either Beckett or Camus, as he places his characters in specific geographical and temporal locations—showing the reader that the absurd presented in his work is a human, not a universal, construction.*

As the substantive body of criticism about Samuel Beckett's theatre attests, it is difficult not to impose a variety of contexts onto his work. Athol Fugard's theatre, alternatively, restricts and focuses one's perceptions so that it is difficult to see more than a single context. More simply put, an audience reads its world into *Waiting for Godot,* while it reads another world out of *Boesman and Lena.* The authors' respective uses of absurdity have led to this state of affairs.

Boesman and Lena is as explicit a title as *Waiting for Godot.* In the latter title, as numerous others have pointed out, unidentified individuals are waiting for God. Control of the individual's fate is placed outside his/her hands into those of a deity; human responsibility is diminished. Others have offered less useful biographical interpretations: Godot is named after a French cyclist, or is the French slang word for boot. While offering an additional dimension to the punning that Beckett indulges in, these latter correlations are not particularly useful for those seeking to explicate the play. Beckett has insisted that the meaning of the title is unimportant. Flippancy, mischievousness, or authorial right may be invoked to explain or support Beckett's position, but the play is an act of communication, a dramatic utterance, which begins with a statement of import. The gerund "waiting" in Beckett's title alerts the reader/audience to the fact that if the communicative act is to mean anything, if grammar means anything, the state of waiting is both subject and action of Beckett's play. What does it mean to wait;

what is it like to wait? The prepositional phrase that completes the title specifies whom (or what) one is waiting for. It clarifies the subject and the act.

Boesman and Lena is simply the names of two characters in a play inhabited by three. Obviously the lack of identification of the third individual gives these two more importance than the unnamed African. More specifically, Lena's song illustrates that "Boesman" is not merely a name, it is also a label and an identification of one's culture: "Boesman is 'n Boesman / Maar hy dra 'n Hotnot hoed" !Boesman is a Bushman / But he wears a Hottentot's hat. "Bushman" is a political label, for the Afrikaners use it as a general term of abuse against the Africans and "coloureds." That Boesman wears a Hottentot's hat should not go unnoticed because a Bushman is considered less civilized, and so lower on the social scale, than a Hottentot. Boesman, therefore, can be said to spurn his identity and falsely attempt to assume another to (re)gain a sense of dignity, albeit in the discourse and practices prevalent in the white scale of values, not his own. Lena, on the other hand, seeks a definition of her being: the questions she poses Boesman in this regard link her to him, and he to her, as inextricably as does the simple coordinating conjunction of the title. Where Boesman seeks validation of his assumed identity through Lena, Lena craves a witness to her existence through Boesman.

An important final point on the titles is the remaining abstraction in Beckett's because neither spatial nor temporal concerns come into play. Fugard's title is more spatially specific, as the assessment of the name Boesman indicates. Lena's exclamation of "Mud! Swartkops!" fixes the location further—they are in the barren Swartkops region of the Eastern Cape, South Africa. Temporally, Boesman and Lena are at one stage in a long cycle of walks:

> Redhouse to Missionvale ... Missionvale to Bethelsdorp. Back again to Redhouse ... Then to Kleinskool. Kleinskool to Veeplaas. Veeplaas to here. First time. After that, Redhouse ... Bethelsdorp, Korsten, Veeplaas, back here the second time. Then Missionvale again, Veeplaas, Korsten, and then here, now.

It is the walking, not the temporary stops in the towns, that is most important. The absurdity of their condition is found in this incessant, pointless, repetitive cycle of walks. The play could have been called *Walking for Godot* to emphasize the importance and, paradoxically, the meaninglessness of the action. Any similarities between the two plays ends here, though, for *Boesman and Lena* know their "Godot" and his purpose: "Blame the whiteman. Bulldozer!" The white, in his "slum clearance," determines their existence with: "Vat jou goed en trek!" Take your things and go! It is an irony that those who commemorate the Great Trek away from the imposition of British rule insist that others undertake a trek away from Afrikaner rule (or, minimally, habitation). Where can they go? Boesman's catalogue of towns implies the same end—a return to the walking, for settlers have claimed all the land.

Fugard, like Beckett and Camus, seeks an answer to Camus' question of why these people do not commit suicide when faced with the absurdity and squalor imposed on their lives. In *Boesman and Lena* the answer to the question is forestalled by the lack of a complete and truthful consciousness of the self. Lena is preoccupied with uncovering her identity, which she believes is held in her past and in an other's recognition of her. Boesman, contrarily, fears an encounter with his self because his false sense of identity might be brought into question.

Lena's arrival on stage immediately sets up their relationship and their identities. She follows Boesman onto the stage and asks "Here?" Both the action and the question are a deferral of power to him. Like Lucky in relation to Pozzo in *Godot*, Lena exists as a slave to Boesman's position as master. And like Estragon in *Godot*, Lena lacks a sense of the chronology of their lives: "Haai! Was it this morning?" In questioning Boesman she gives him the authority to decide her history and identity, while Boesman's remark—that she should have been walking backward—reveals the ties of her sense of self to the past, to history. Boesman is happy to occupy the seat of power in this relationship because he does not have to reflect (look back) on his oppressed life. Instead, he has become the oppressor, white man reincarnated.

Boesman's position is a false one, for he, too, is determined. In the most general sense, the oppressive forces of the white government determine him. His plea that whites set him free from the burden of a squatter's life is a false front, as Lena attests:

> *Holds up a clenched fist in an imitation of Boesman.*
>
> That's how he talks to the world. . . . Ja, so it goes. He walks in front. I walk behind. It used to be side by side, with jokes.

Lena is both bitter and ironic here. She is bitter because their equality (side-by-side) in the face of adversity is gone, as is their earlier happiness. The

> " Fugard . . . provides exact information on his characters' spatial locale and thus defines absurdity as a condition resulting from the human power structures that govern life, not as the condition of life itself."

irony is evidenced by Boesman's bad faith, for his revolt against his condition is not one of solidarity, an acceptance and authentication of the condition; his "revolt" is denial. He talks with anger and beats Lena black and blue, while acquiescing to the real, identified oppressor:

> Whiteman's wasting his time trying to help us. Pushed it [their shanty] over this morning and here it is again. . . . We're whiteman's rubbish. That's why he's so beneukt [fed up] with us. He can't get rid of his rubbish.

Boesman's cowed attitude reveals his inability and unwillingness to make the necessary connection between present conditions and origins. Their food, clothing, shelter, and selves may be considered rubbish by whites, but all rubbish is created: white society is the cause of their status. Boesman fails to take an independent or even a skeptical view of the white perspective that is privileged by raw power. If Boesman made these connections, he would realize that whites could as easily label him valuable (even in the cynical sense of taking the African's labors for white-owned corporations into account). A more humane attitude, trite as it sounds, is a beginning. Failing to connect the cause with the effect, Boesman allows his ignorance and the whites to colonize him.

Similarly, Boesman's utterance of "Dankie, baas" [Thank you, boss], is a reflection of his subservience, of his inability to escape a particular frame of mind. So he becomes an oppressor, bullying Lena into saying "Please, my bassie" [Please, my little boss], in an attempt to dispel his servility. Intellectual engagement with whites, or at least, given the raw power he faces, engagement within himself of the whites' false claim to power, would inhibit this type of intra-race brutality. The stage that Fugard sets is the bleakest: Lena's lack of belief in Boesman's position and his actions reveals her strength (qualified by her need for his "answers") but also causes him to wage psychological and physical warfare on her—just as the white oppressors, because of their false and degenerate humanity, are waging warfare on Africans.

Lena's response to the oppression is to seek human contact, warmth, a sense of community to stave off the madness that their absurd position entails. Boesman denies her these comforts and reaffirms his oppressive role, for the action his role involves helps him to stave off thoughts of the absurdity and the servility of his actions, as well as the related guilt: "Look at you! Listen to you! You're asking for a lot, Lena. Must I go mad as well?" Thus Boesman continues to act in bad faith; he refuses to face his absurdity, to see his reflection in Lena. He is left, his consciousness unawakened, inhabiting despair. So, he will not go to Veeplaas: there are other people there, other reminders of his shame.

Although she is conscious of Boesman's faults, Lena remains inextricably tied to him, for she believes he holds the key to her past, and so her identity:

LENA: Do you really know, Boesman? Where and how?

BOESMAN: Yes!

LENA: Tell me. [He laughs.] Help me, Boesman!

BOESMAN: What? Find yourself?

Unable to extricate a sense of herself from Boesman, Lena pursues the problem alone, and produces a small identity—if she can be hit and bruised, then she exists. Moreover, if she is Lena, identified by her servile, oppressed relationship to him, then he is Boesman, the oppressor. She can affirm, therefore, that they are "Boesman and Lena" a microcosmic world that reflects the positions of groups (rather than individuals) in the larger world they inhabit. This consciousness of their roles, their relationship to one another, is an awareness of a small community, and of the position of the self within that community. We do not find such an explicit awareness in Beckett's characters.

Lena, dissatisfied with this minimal sense of self, seeks witnesses to her existence. The witnesses—"Dog and a dead man"—are as marginal as her Cartesian proof of existence. Similarly, when Boesman gives Lena an exact account of their past she realizes that "It doesn't explain anything"; it is therefore absurd, meaningless. Lena consequently seeks the only path open to her, a sense of commu-

nal interest in her existence. She had instructed Boesman to "Try it the other way. Open your fist, put your hand on me. I'm here. I'm Lena." It is a polemical statement directed both to the individual, who forms the foundation of the community, and to the varying communities of race present within South Africa. The message seems appropriate to South Africa, but the scene depicts two people of the same race; thus Fugard could be criticized on the basis that in the strict sense of South Africa's (thankfully now departed) Population Registration Act the races are separate, apartheid remains in place. This would seem an appropriate interpretation, given the lack of communication between black and "coloured" in the play. Yet, if one gives Fugard the benefit of the doubt, the use of "coloured" people seems an artistically exacting touch—as people of "mixed" blood Boesman and Lena are of indeterminate race, neither black nor white—enabling the characters to represent all races. Whether such generosity in interpretation would "wash" with the people long identified by color/race is a different question. There is a clear political allegory in Lena's acceptance of the black man and the beating of him by Boesman, who takes the white role—"coloureds" must unite with blacks, not aspire to acceptance by whites, if they are to find their true place.

Without a true place for the duration of the play, Boesman and Lena walk. It is an apt metaphor, in all the circularity the act of walking takes on in the play, which justifies Dennis Walder's comment that

"Overwhelmed" by Camus' writings . . . Fugard follows him to the brink of despair, where, nevertheless, may be found "finally the only certainty, the flesh": living "without hope, without appeal," without the traditional certainties of religion or history, we may be able to continue after all, relying on . . . "truths the hand can touch."

Boesman and Lena, in spite of their age, and in spite of the darkness, still have "daylights left in [them]." So Lena's decision to rejoin Boesman is a conscious effort on her part to resolve their problems one way (annihilation) or the other (recognition of self and other and the inherent worth and value of each). The resolution ultimately rests with Boesman (the oppressor) and his ability to change.

Boesman and Lena is a response to the institutionally created absurdity inherent in the lives of Africans, "coloureds," and Indians under the policy of apartheid. Fugard thus seems to view absurdity as something specific to certain social or political contexts; at least this is the view that surfaces because the play is set in South Africa, and race predominates within that society and in Fugard's text. However, Fugard is a more universal thinker than such an interpretation suggests, as a careful reading of his notebooks reveals. Fugard, having set the play in the region he knows best, extrapolates from the situation under apartheid to more universal concerns about the relationship of human beings to each other. Post-apartheid productions of his play will confirm its continued worth and vitality. So, in *Boesman and Lena*, as in Albee's *The Death of Bessie Smith*,

> The racial situation functions . . . as a potent image of man's self-inflicted absurdity. Here . . . is that lack of compassion which Albee [with Fugard] sees as a mark of contemporary society.

Absurdity, for Fugard, is therefore a part of life, an obstacle to be overcome by an equitable awareness of self and other, and the other's reciprocation of this awareness.

Both Beckett and Fugard follow Camus' path into the absurd. In his deliberate omission of spatial and temporal data, Beckett creates a stark world that becomes a universal metaphor for the absurd nature of existence in both the physical and metaphysical realms. Fugard, less rooted in the metaphysical, provides exact information on his characters' spatial locale and thus defines absurdity as a condition resulting from the human power structures that govern life, not as the condition of life itself.

Source: Craig W. McLuckie, ''Power, Self, and Other: the Absurd in 'Boesman and Lena,''' in *Twentieth Century Literature,* Vol. 39, No. 4, Winter, 1993, p. 423.

Derek Cohen

In the following brief review of Fugard's Boesman and Lena, *author Derek Cohen discusses the juxtaposition of the simplicity of the play and the complexity of its structure to demonstrate the play's power to transcend its South African context and present an evil, dark, and hopeless world of society's creating.*

The greatness of Athol Fugard's *Boesman and Lena* lies in its capacity to extend the range of its unnerving protest far beyond its South African context. The play, so utterly and undeniably South African in its language and setting, defines and describes something of the tragedy of civilization itself, and includes in its compass the conviction that the society in which it is set is a microcosm of that civilization in its most evil and vicious details. The world it exhibits is a place where suffering, poverty,

and loneliness are normal. While only the poor and impotent are presented, the existence of the rich and powerful is definitively implied—their indifference is a dire sin.

The characters of the play, Boesman, Lena, and the strange moribund old man, are society's refuse. They embody the poverty and misery of their world and the concomitants of that wretchedness, a brutal internecine hatred which brings with it the grim awareness that their inheritance of pain and confusion have bound them to one another with hoops of steel. However much they crave escape and independence, the essence of their lives is one. Hatred and habit, like love, cement individuals together.

While the story of the play is relatively simple, its structure is curiously complex. All the impetus of the events of the brief yet seemingly incessant movement of the play derives its force from the tortured emotions of Lena. Having been evicted from their shanty town by white men with bulldozers, Boesman and Lena find themselves on the bleak, muddy plain of Swartkops when the play begins. They carry with them their pitiful worldly goods, including the few scraps of corrugated iron and wood which they throw together to provide shelter. Near hysteria, with weariness from the walk and pain from a beating Boesman had given her for breaking three returnable empty bottles, Lena rambles on in passionate confusion, alternating from moods of raucous mirth to outbursts of frantic rage. Her senses of time and place have become dislocated; the past is an amorphous pile of place-names and painful recollections. In despair she begs Boesman to help her make sense and order out of the past by sorting out for her the sequence of places to which they have wandered over the years—to give names to the experiences of the past. Cruelly he taunts her by deliberately confusing the order she has diffidently made. The taunting grows increasingly vicious, verging precariously on violence when the old African appears on the scene, another wanderer into this dark and bitter place. There is morbid comedy in Boesman's immediate repulsion of the old man on grounds of his and Lena's racial superiority; he is black while they, Cape Coloured, are brown. Lena, however, flies to him, entreating him to bear witness to her suffering. She bombards him with laments about her life with Boesman and her past tragedies which include a miscarriage out in the open in the dark, with nothing but a sad old donkey as her witness. With her bottle of cheap wine she purchases from Boesman permission for the lonely old soul to remain the night with them. The old

> The characters of the play, Boesman, Lena, and the strange moribund old man, are society's refuse. They embody the poverty and misery of their world and the concomitants of that wretchedness, a brutal internecine hatred which brings with it the grim awareness that their inheritance of pain and confusion have bound them to one another with hoops of steel."

man's speech is a mixture of Xhosa and guttural, garbled noises resembling language. He learns to say Lena's name after some childlike attempts; and yet throughout his speech Lena adamantly asserts that she can discern words of comfort and sympathy. She huddles under her blanket with him by the fire. Boesman refuses to allow a *kaffer* and his fleas in the shelter with him, and he returns alone into the hovel to get drunk. In loyal defiance Lena elects to remain out in the cold with her new companion.

An hour later, in the second act, Boesman emerges from the shelter and with cruel drunken violence continues his attack on Lena. He explodes in violent tirades against her and his life. A match for his frenzy, Lena responds with a mocking song and dance, at the conclusion of which Boesman announces with quiet hatred: 'I dropped the empties.' It dawns on the incredulous Lena that the beating she suffered was gratuitous. She begs Boesman to explain to her why he beats her. 'What have I done. Boesman? It is my life. Hit your own', she cries in immense uncomprehending rage. He '(*equally desperate, looking around dumbly*)' asks: 'Show it to me! Where is it?' In the desperate haranguing that follows, he angrily tries to explain that the beatings he gives her are beatings he is giving himself. His hatred of life is manifested in his hatred of Lena. She is a loathsome emblem of his endurance, and in smashing and bruising her he is trying to crush his own life. His need of her resides

in this crude perception of his life and his pain as another being. Their attention turns to the old man, their witness. Now they realize that quietly and alone he has died.

In his death the old man has become in relation to Boesman and Lena what they are to the white world. He is now their refuse, an additional burden to them. Boesman, recognizing this, vents his rage on the corpse, kicking and hitting it with impotent hatred. Triumphantly Lena watches the outburst, only to remind Boesman that now the inert body bears his fingerprints and marks. In a fury of panic he begins to pack up to leave. Lena slowly but inevitably helps him and they walk silently off into the darkness.

The development of the play depends upon the explosions of Lena's passions and their dangerous subsidences. The action begins and ends in a white heat of emotion which from time to time flames out. But the outbursts of concentrated rage are no more tortured or significant than those of seething calm when Lena is mumbling her griefs or recollecting the wrongs done to her. The sequence of rises and falls in moral and passional intensity have an ineluctably logical pattern. Lena's emotions determine the tone of each action. And it is evident from the first, as it is evident in the end, that the action is simply and purely continuous; that the events of the evening, terrible as they are, are unremarkable in the lives of the two tormented protagonists. Fugard deliberately locates the action in an unknown, dark place to which the two have come almost automatically; it is a place for which they feel bleak indifference. It has a name to be lumped loosely with the other names of other places where they have stopped in their eternal and eternally damned wanderings. The places where they have remained in the past have meaning for Lena only in so far as they have the power to remind her of her past and of her agonies; they remind her that she has lived a life and that that life has a definable, individual shape.

And yet while what happens in the course of the play seems, by virtue of its relentlessly resigned ending, to be 'normal' for Boesman and Lena, by other standards it is an event (or, rather, a series of events) charged with meaning. The living fact of Boesman and Lena is tragic in and of itself. The tragedy lies not so much in the dreadful antagonism that defines their relationship, and not so much in the fact that, in this evening of unremitting and increasing horrors, they recognize their hapless bondage to one another, but it lies simply in their being and their continuing. When they pack up and leave at the end of the play nothing has changed; Lena it is true pleads with Boesman to kill her the next time:

> I'm alive, Boesman. There's daylights left in me. You still got a chance. Don't lose it. Next time you want to kill me, do it. Really do it. When you hit, hit those lights out. Don't be too late. Do it yourself . . .

But in the act of packing and leaving that desolate place with him she is simultaneously negating the import of the words, and one is left with the disquieting knowledge that the words have been uttered countless times before, and with the same heartfelt sincerity. It is precisely this conviction that informs the conclusion, passive and even static, as it seems, with tragic depth. The passionate debility of the ending crystallizes in as eloquent a fashion the same thoughts and emotional numbness as are conjured up from the depths of helplessness and moral enervation in the celebrated conclusion to *Waiting for Godot*.

Lena's tragedy is twofold. She is a non-white South African and she is a woman. This latter fact determines to a considerable measure the nature of her suffering. However much Boesman is made to suffer and cringe, however victimized he is by his place in this society, there is always someone lower and weaker than himself, and it is she who has to bear the brunt of his rage. Only she feels the effects of his frustration. For Boesman to attack his persecutors is certain defeat; his blows, therefore, have nowhere else to fall than on Lena's body. Her anguish is inevitably the greater. Not only has she her own burden of humiliation to bear, but she must bear the effects of Boesman's as well. This essentially female aspect of her suffering is contained in her description of the miscarriage. While Lena is humanized, made larger, by her experience, Boesman is brutalized by his sense of the wrong done to him and what he sees as Lena's failure.

> *Nee, God, Outa!* What more must I say? What you asking me about? Pain? Yes! Don't *kaffers* know what that means? One night it was longer than a small piece of candle and then as big as darkness. Somewhere else a donkey looked at it. I crawled under the cart and they looked. Boesman was too far away to call. Just the sound of his axe as he chopped wood. I didn't even have rags! You asked me and now I've told you. Pain is a candle *entjie* and a donkey's face. What's that mean to you? You weren't there. Nobody was. Why do you ask me *now*? You're too late for that.

Boesman can recall the event only with disgust and scorn. His voice full of reproach he spews out his hatred of life and Lena in one protracted metaphor of loathing:

> *Sies wereld!*

> All there is to say. That's our word. After that our life is dumb. Like your *moer*. All that came out of it was silence. There should have been noise. You pushed out silence. And Boesman buried it. Took the spade the next morning and pushed our hope back into the dirt. Deep holes! When I filled them up I said it again: *Sies.*

There is a ghastly irony in Boesman's reference to their 'hope', an irony which he is unable to perceive but which the tonal quality of hopelessness throughout dramatically underscores.

In the way that Lena is defined and takes her motive force from pain and suffering, Boesman is motivated by a profound and violent shame. As she, the weaker of the two, is compelled to turn inwards her past experiences in reflective passion, so he turns outwards his shame, venting it in rages of self-pity and savage acts of destruction. Not unlike Dostoesvky's underfloor man, Boesman is a hugely detestable character for whom it is impossible not to have sympathy. Notwithstanding his brutality, his gratuitous cruelty, his carping ugly nature, the fact of his having lived a life overwhelmed by suffering and indignity gives him an undeniable emotional and moral stature and hence authority. The tragedy of Boesman's life is the enforced necessity of acceptance. He is compelled to permit whatever violations of his person and his dignity are inflicted upon them. The life he has been allowed as a poor black man makes him impotent against the ravages of the powerful. The image of the bulldozers of that morning have been burned into his brain; they constitute a symbol of the sheer power that dominates the lives of the downtrodden, who are helpless in the face of such power. They are thus forced to confront the unalterable alternatives of either accepting that power as their master or of fighting it and dying in the struggle. There is no other way, and no compromise. Boesman's rage is most searing in the speech in which he describes his feelings of exhilaration as he watched the bulldozers at work. A note of deep self-loathing permeates the passage. It begins with a description of the inhabitants, who, submissively, 'like baboons', sit watching the destruction of their homes and become by Boesman's frenetic metaphorical leap, freed human beings:

> It was bioscope, man! And I watched it. Beginning to end, the way it happened. *I saw it. Me.*

> The women and children sitting there with their snot and tears. The *pondoks* falling. The men standing, looking, as the yellow *donner* pushed them over and

then staring at the pieces when they were the only things left standing. I saw all that! The whiteman stopped the bulldozer and smoked a cigarette. I saw that too . . .

He wasn't just burning *pondoks.* They alone can't stink like that. Or burn like that.

There was something else in that fire, something rotten. Us!

. . . then I went back to the place where our *pondok* had been. It was gone! You understand that? Gone! I wanted to call you and show you. There where we crawled in and out like baboons, where we used to sit like them and eat, our head between our knees, our fingers in the pot, away so that the others wouldn't see our food . . . I could stand there! There was room for me to stand straight.

You know what that is. Listen now. I'm going to use a word Freedom! *Ja,* I've heard them talk it. Freedom! That's what the whiteman gave us. . . When we picked up our things and started to walk I wanted to sing. It was Freedom!

To which no more eloquent response is conceivable than Lena's barbed observation: 'We had to go somewhere. Couldn't walk around Korsten carrying your Freedom for ever.'

It is perhaps in this tirade of Boesman's that the thought becomes most bitter. Far from being a purifying or liberating fire in which the *pondoks* were burnt, it was a fire that stank, and its stench only served the ironic purpose of reminding Boesman of the humanity he loathes, the humanity of the poor and their obstinate perpetuity. Boesman comes to fathom life through sensuous experience. He says to Lena: 'When you *poep* it makes more sense. You know why? It stinks. Your words are just noises.' And it is by hitting her that he can feel the shape of his own existence, for which there is hardly a more appropriate metaphor than an old, defeated hag to whom he is eternally tied.

The quality of defeat which the characters of the play come to represent suffuses the action with a deep and pure pessimism, a darkness of spirit unlike anything else that Fugard has written. Even *The Blood Knot,* that bleak and terrible work, has its glimmers of hope and its rare moments of beauty through poetic conjuration. Here, in *Boesman and Lena,* the poetry is a poetry of darkness. The author has created a world without even the relief of illusion or emphemerality. All memory is pain and suffering, the past a jumble of poverty and humiliation. The present is only the front of that past. And, even worse, the future is a spectre of easeless death. As Boesman remarks: 'One day your turn. One day mine. Two more holes somewhere. The earth will

get *naar* when they push us in. And then it's finished. The end of Boesman and Lena.' The sense of having lived a shamed, hateful, and useless life is nowhere more evident than in Boesman's assertion that the starved earth will only turn sick when they are buried.

Source: Derek Cohen, ''Athol Fugard's Boesman and Lena,'' in *The Journal of Commonwealth Literature,* Vol. XII, No. 3, April, 1978, pp. 78–83.

Sources

Branford, Jean, review of *Boesman and Lena,* in *Athol Fugard,* edited by Stephen Gray, McGraw-Hill, 1982, p. 80.

Brockett, Oscar G., ''The Theatre of Africa: South Africa,'' in *History of the Theatre,* 8th ed., Allyn and Bacon, 1998, pp. 658-65.

Cohen, Derek, review of *Boesman and Lena,* in *Canadian Drama,* Spring, 1980, pp. 151-61.

Disch, Thomas M., review of *Boesman and Lena,* in *Nation,* March 2, 1992.

Esslin, Martin, *The Theatre of the Absurd,* Anchor Books, 1962, pp. 290-91.

Fugard, Athol, *Boesman and Lena and Other Plays,* Oxford University Press, 1974, pp. vii-xxv.

———, *Notebooks 1960-1977,* A. D. Donker, 1983, pp. 65-7, 124.

Gussow, Mel, review of *Boesman and Lena,* in *Athol Fugard,* edited by Stephen Gray, McGraw-Hill, 1982, p. 94.

Jacobson, Dan, ''The Poetry of Poverty,'' in *Guardian Weekly,* August 10, 1974, reprinted in *Athol Fugard,* edited by Stephen Gray, McGraw-Hill, 1982, p. 82.

McLuckie, Craig W., ''Power, Self, and Other: the Absurd in *Boesman and Lena,*'' in *Twentieth Century Literature,* Winter, 1993, p. 423.

Miller, Arthur, ''Tragedy and the Common Man,'' in *New York Times,* February 27, 1949, reprinted in *Dramatic Theory and Criticism,* edited by Bernard F. Dukore, Holt, Rinehart, 1974, p. 896.

Further Reading

Brockett, Oscar G., *History of the Theatre,* 8th ed., Allyn and Bacon, 1998.

    Brockett's *History of the Theatre* is a comprehensive volume, covering more than 2,000 years of worldwide theatrical tradition. Of special interest, however, is ''The Theatre of Africa,'' a new chapter the author added with the seventh edition of this highly respected theater sourcebook. In this chapter, Brockett covers the history and performance traditions of Nigeria, Ghana, Kenya, Zaire, and countries all across the African continent, including the Republic of South Africa.

Fugard, Athol, *Notebooks 1960-1977*, A. D. Donker, 1983. Athol Fugard began keeping notebooks of his thoughts and experiences in 1959 when he and his wife traveled to Europe. His first entries became the basis for his 1960 play *The Blood Knot*, and since then the brief sketches and ideas he has recorded in his notebooks have provided him with the characters, plots, and themes of his plays. This collection of Fugard's notebooks covers the first half of his career, from the creation of *The Blood Knot* through a production of *Sizwe Banzi Is Dead* at London's Royal Court Theatre in 1977.

Gray, Stephen, ed., *Athol Fugard*, McGraw-Hill, 1982. This collection of scholarship about Athol Fugard is part of the "South African Literature Series" and contains a chronology of events in the playwright's life, reviews of his plays, critical essays, interviews

with the author, and an extensive bibliography suggesting additional resources for study.

Thompson, Leonard, *A History of South Africa*, Yale University Press, 1996. Thompson writes about the entire history of South Africa, from its earliest known inhabitants through the present day, with an emphasis on the black majority population.

Waldmeir, Patti, *Anatomy of a Miracle: The End of Apartheid and the Birth of the New South Africa*, Norton, 1997. Waldmeir is a journalist who became acquainted with Nelson Mandela and F. W. de Klerk, the two men primarily responsible for the dismantling of apartheid, and witnessed the events leading up to the integration of South African society and restoration of political power to that country's black majority. In *Anatomy of a Miracle* she uses interviews and eyewitness accounts to tell the story of the end of apartheid from the unrest of the early 1980s through Mandela's release from prison and inauguration as president in 1994.

Breath, Eyes, Memory

Edwidge Danticat

1994

When *Breath, Eyes, Memory* was published in 1994, Edwidge Danticat was hailed by *Publishers Weekly* as "a distinctive new voice with a sensitive insight into Haitian culture." Although there are some similarities between Sophie's story and Danticat's own life, the work is largely fiction, informed by Danticat's own experience. The book was the culmination of many years of writing, beginning in Danticat's adolescence, when she wrote a story about coming to America to be with her mother; this story was the seed for the later, much longer work.

Danticat continued work on the novel during her pursuit of a Master of Fine Arts degree in writing at Brown University, where she was given a full scholarship. Written as her master's thesis, the unfinished book was eagerly awaited by Soho Press, which offered Danticat a $5,000 advance for it.

Not everyone in the Haitian community approved of the book. In the book, Sophie's mother Martine "tests" her to see if she is still a virgin by putting a finger into Sophie's vagina. Although virginity is highly regarded in Haitian culture, most Haitian-Americans no longer follow this practice, and some felt that Danticat's depiction of it made Haitians seem backward and sexually abusive. Danticat is aware that many people see her as a spokesperson for Haitians, but disagrees with the notion: she is just one person, writing about her own experience, and there are many other voices.

Author Biography

Edwidge Danticat (pronounced "Edweedj Danticah") was born January 19, 1969, in Port-au-Prince, Haiti, and was separated from her father when she was two and he emigrated to the United States to find work. When she was four, her mother also went to the United States. For the next eight years, Danticat and her younger brother Eliab were raised by their father's brother, a minister, who lived with his wife and grandson in a poor section of Port-au-Prince known as Bel Air.

When Danticat was twelve, she moved to Brooklyn and joined her parents and two new younger brothers. Adjustment to this new family was difficult, and she also had difficulty adjusting at school, because she spoke only Creole and did not know any English. Other students taunted her as a Haitian "boat person," or refugee. She told Mallay Charters in *Publishers Weekly,* "My primary feeling the whole first year was one of loss. Loss of my childhood, and of the people I'd left behind—and also of being lost. It was like being a baby—learning everything for the first time."

Danticat learned to tell stories from her aunt's grandmother in Bel Air, an old woman whose long hair, with coins braided into it, fascinated the neighborhood children, who fought each other to comb it. When people gathered, she told folktales and family stories. "It was call-and-response," Danticat told Charters. "If the audience seemed bored, the story would speed up, and if they were participating, a song would go in. The whole interaction was exciting to me. These cross-generational exchanges didn't happen often, because children were supposed to respect their elders. But when you were telling stories, it was more equal, and fun."

Danticat's cousin, Marie Micheline, taught her to read. She told Renee H. Shea in *Belles Lettres,* "I started school when I was three, and she would read to me when I came home. In 1987. . .there was a shooting outside her house—where her children were. She had a seizure and died. Since I was away from her, my parents didn't tell me right away. . .But around that same time, I was having nightmares; somehow I knew."

When Danticat was seven, she wrote stories with a Haitian heroine. For her, writing was not a casual undertaking. "At the time that I started thinking about writing," she told Calvin Wilson in

the *Kansas City Star,* "a lot of people who were in jail were writers. They were journalists, they were novelists, and many of them were killed or 'disappeared.' It was a very scary thing to think about." Nevertheless, she kept writing. After she moved to Brooklyn and learned English, she wrote stories for her high school newspaper. One of these articles, about her reunion with her mother at age twelve, eventually expanded to become the book *Breath, Eyes, Memory.*

Danticat graduated from Barnard College with a degree in French literature in 1990, and worked as a secretary, doing her writing after work in the office. She applied to business schools and creative writing programs. She was accepted by both, but chose Brown University's creative writing program, which offered her a full scholarship. For her master's thesis, she wrote what would later become *Breath, Eyes, Memory* .

After graduating, she sent seventy pages of *Breath, Eyes, Memory* to Soho Press, a small publisher. They bought the book before it was even completed, sending her notes asking if she was done yet and encouraging her to finish.

Breath, Eyes, Memory and her two other books—*The Farming of Bones* and *Krik? Krak!* , a collection of stories—have been hailed for their lyrical intensity, vivid descriptions of Haitian places and people, and honest depictions of fear and pain.

Danticat has won a Granta Regional Award as one of the Twenty Best Young American Novelists, a Pushcart Prize, and fiction awards from *Seventeen* and *Essence* magazines. She is also the recipient of an ongoing grant from the Lila Wallace-Reader's Digest Foundation.

Plot Summary

Edwidge Danticat's *Breath, Eyes, Memory* begins in Haiti in the early 1980s, when Haiti was ruled by the dictator Jean Claude "Baby Doc" Duvalier. Widespread poverty, illiteracy, and government-sponsored violence oppress the population, but Danticat's heroine, twelve-year-old Sophie Caco, has led a relatively sheltered life in the small town of Croix-des-Rosets. Although her family have always been poor agricultural laborers, she and her aunt are better off because Sophie's mother, Martine, moved

Edwidge Danticat

to Brooklyn when Sophie was two, and sends money home every month.

Martine's move to Brooklyn was a form of escape, since she was raped at age sixteen by a *Tonton Macoute,* or guerrilla, one of many allowed by the government to kill, torture, and rape anyone he wanted to. This rape resulted in Sophie's birth, but Martine, unable to bear the painful memories, left Haiti, and Sophie, in search of a new life and release from her emotional pain.

The novel opens a few days before Mother's Day, when Sophie has made a card to give to her aunt, Tante Atie, the only mother Sophie knows. She finds out that Martine has finally sent for her, and wants her to come to Brooklyn. Sophie is fearful and reluctant to go, but has no choice. Atie tells her that her mother wants the best for her, and that if she becomes educated, she can elevate her whole family, that going to the United States will be good for her and everyone else, and that it's the right thing to do.

On the way to the airport they are delayed by a demonstration, and see students fighting soldiers and government officials, an Army truck in flames, and soldiers shooting bullets and tear gas at the demonstrators. They also see a soldier beat a girl's

head in with the butt of a gun, and on the plane, Sophie sits next to a small boy whose father was killed in the demonstration and who has no family left living in Haiti and no luggage.

Adjusting to life in Brooklyn is difficult for Sophie, who is harassed by other students because she is Haitian and does not speak English. For six years, forbidden to date, she spends all her time in the narrow circle of school, home, and church.

When Sophie is eighteen, she falls in love with her neighbor, Joseph, a kind and thoughtful musician who is her mother's age. Aside from Marc, her mother's boyfriend, she does not know any men. ''Men were as mysterious to me as white people, who in Haiti we had only known as missionaries,'' she says.

Although Sophie has not slept with Joseph, her mother suspects that she has, and she makes Sophie lie on the bed and tests her for virginity. ''There are secrets you cannot keep,'' she tells Sophie, meaning that if Sophie has sex, her mother will know about it. Martine herself was tested in this way, as was Atie, and although it has given her emotional scars, she continues to do it to Sophie every week to make sure she is still a virgin.

Sophie does not tell Joseph about the tests, but she feels deeply shameful about her body and avoids him. He goes away on tour, leaving her lonely and confused. She realizes that if she loses her virginity her mother will stop the invasive testing, so she uses a pestle to break her hymen.

The next time she is tested, she fails. Her mother, disgusted, tells her to get out and go to Joseph, and see what he can do for her.

She goes to Joseph and tells him she wants to get married immediately. They move to Providence and have a baby, but Sophie is not happy. For the whole first year of their marriage, she feels suicidal and experiences nightmares. Her sexual secret, her memory and experience of testing and her mother's insistence that sex is filthy and shameful, make her unable to enjoy being sexual with him. ''[My mother's] nightmares had somehow become my own, so much so that I would wake up some mornings wondering if we hadn't both spent the night dreaming about the same thing: a man with no face, pounding a life into a helpless young girl,'' she says. Confused, she leaves without telling Joseph where she is going and takes her baby, Brigitte Ife (named for her grandmother), with her to Haiti.

Sophie's mother does not know that she is in Haiti, or that she is separated from Joseph, but she sends her usual cassette down to Atie and Grandma Ife and mentions that Joseph called her house looking for Sophie. She is frightened because she also does not know where Sophie is. Atie and Ife encourage Sophie to go home, but she isn't ready. Secretly, they ask her mother to come to Haiti and talk to her and convince her to go back.

She talks to her grandmother about the testing, and her grandmother says she did it to her daughters because it was her duty to safeguard the family's chastity and honor. "I hated the tests," Sophie tells her. "It is the most horrible thing that ever happened to me. When my husband is with me now, it gives me such nightmares that I have to bite my tongue to do it again."

Sophie's mother shows up. Sophie asks her why she put her through the tests if she herself hated them so much. She says she did it "because my mother did it to me. I have no greater excuse. I realize standing here that the two greatest pains of my life are very much related. The one good thing about being raped was that it made the testing stop. The testing and the rape. I live both every day."

Eventually, she goes home and calls her husband and tells him she's back. They reconcile, and she begins going to a sexual phobia therapy group, where the therapist says of her mother's rapist, "Your mother never gave him a face. That's why he's a shadow. That's why he can control her. I'm not surprised she's having nightmares. This pregnancy is bringing feelings to the surface that she had never completely dealt with. You will never be able to connect with your husband until you say goodbye to your father." Meanwhile, her mother becomes pregnant with Marc's baby. The pregnancy reactivates all her old fears of rape and violation, and she tells Sophie that when she was pregnant with Sophie, she tried to abort her. She drank "all kinds of herbs, vervain, quinine, and verbena, baby poisons. I tried beating my stomach with wooden spoons. I tried to destroy you, but you wouldn't go away."

The pregnancy reactivates all of Martine's old fears, and eventually she kills herself, stabbing herself in the belly seventeen times with a butcher knife. They take her body back to Haiti, where, at her funeral, Sophie runs into the cane field and beats, attacks, fights back against the cane and the memory of her mother's rapist, as the therapist suggested.

Her grandmother comes to help her, knowing that this is a cathartic moment and that Sophie is releasing the pain of generations. She tells Sophie, "There is always a place where, if you listen closely in the night, you will hear your mother telling a story and at the end of the tale, she will ask you this question: "*Ou libere?* Are you free, my daughter? . . . Now, you will know how to answer."

Characters

Tante Atie

Tante Atie, Sophie's aunt, raises her like a mother. Atie has never married, and carries the secret of a lost love: Monsieur Augustin, the village schoolteacher, once loved her, but married someone else. Illiterate and kind, Atie passes on folklore and family stories to Sophie, telling her that her mother left her in Haiti for a reason, that her mother loves her, but that circumstances out of her control led her to leave Sophie in Haiti for a while. By the end of the book her friend Louise, who may also be her lover, has taught her to read and write, and she is never without her notebook, in which she copies other writers' poems and writes her own. Despite the fact that she began this growth so late in life, she is a much stronger, more self-aware woman.

Martine Caco

Sophie's mother, who is recovering from breast cancer, works as an aide at a nursing home during the day and as a private health care aide at night. She came to the United States when Sophie was two, in an attempt to put Haiti behind her. She is constantly tormented by nightmares of a traumatic event that occurred when she was sixteen: a strange man, wearing a mask, took her into a cane field and brutally raped her. This resulted in Sophie's birth.

Martine was also sexually traumatized by her mother, Grandma Ife, who tested her for virginity until after the rape. Ife meant well when she did this traditional practice, but it resulted in lifelong emotional and sexual scars in Martine. Even though Martine hated being tested and knows that it deeply hurt her, she also does it to her daughter, Sophie, in a desperate attempt to keep her chaste. She is frightened and disturbed by her daughter's growth into a woman, and does all she can to keep her young and away from men. When Sophie becomes interested in a neighbor, Martine is deeply hurt, viewing this as a break in the mother-daughter bond.

Sophie has difficulty integrating her Haitian heritage, which both comforts and frightens her, with her new life in America. Still suffering from nightmares brought on by the rape that resulted in Sophie's birth, and from her mother's "testing" of her virginity when she was a girl, she is burdened by fears and sexual anguish. A new pregnancy reminds her of the rape and increases her nightmares, and she eventually seeks escape from her pain by committing suicide.

Sophie Caco

Sophie Caco, the narrator of the novel, is twelve years old when the novel begins, being raised by her aunt, Tante Atie, in a small Haitian town; her mother has emigrated to the United States. Born after her mother was raped, she doesn't know her father, and because her mother left Haiti when Sophie was two, she doesn't know her mother either. As a child, she imagines her mother as being like the Haitian goddess Erzulie, "the lavish Virgin Mother. . .Even though she was far away, she was always with me. I could always count on her, like one counts on the sun coming out at dawn."

In truth, however, her mother is a wounded woman, with problems of her own, and Sophie must learn to come to terms with them, as they are handed down to her from past generations. "I come from a place where breath, eyes and memory are one," Sophie says, reflecting on the burden of the past, the emphasis on family honor, chastity, and duty that fall on the women in her family, "a place where you carry your past like the hair on your head."

Throughout the novel, she struggles to come to terms with her family's history of pain and loss, to be comfortable with her body and her sexuality, and to avoid passing on her own and her mother's nightmares to her daughter. In addition, when she moves to Brooklyn, she must decide for herself what she wants to keep from her Haitian heritage, and what traditions she wants to drop. In particular, she is frightened and confused by her mother's traditional Haitian practice of testing her to ensure that she is still virgin, and by her mother's mental and spiritual illness.

The rift between Sophie and her mother widens when she falls in love with Joseph, a neighbor who is much older than she is. Ultimately, she chooses to be with him, asserting her own knowledge of what is good and right for her, against inflexible tradition; this move marks her as becoming Americanized.

Joseph describes Sophie as a "deep, thoughtful person," and she is, describing events in a poetic and vivid way, feeling all her emotions deeply, and reflecting on them in solitude.

Marc Chevalier

Marc is Martine's boyfriend, a prosperous Haitian immigrant and lawyer who helped her get her green card. He lives in a well-to-do neighborhood in Brooklyn, unlike Sophie and her mother. He is very traditionally Haitian in outlook, particularly regarding food, and once drove to Canada because he heard of a good Haitian restaurant there. Martine says of him, "Marc is one of those men who will never recover from not eating his [mother's] cooking. If he could get her out of her grave to make him dinner, he would do it." Apart from his wealth and his interest in food, he is not very clearly drawn; although he is the father of a child Martine conceives later in the book, he seems unconnected to the horrifying events connected with her suicide, and only appears again after she is dead.

Grandma Ife

Ife is Sophie's grandmother, a widow who lives in a Haitian village that is so remote that it can only be reached on foot or by mule. A very traditional woman, she has worn black ever since her husband died. When her daughters, Atie and Martine, were young, she followed the traditional Haitian practice of testing their virginity each week, resulting in unintentional sexual and emotional scars in both her daughters. She is a storyteller, passing on old folktales, family stories, and healing wisdom. When Sophie asks her about the testing, she explains that a mother is responsible for her daughter's chastity, and that when a girl is married, if she is not a virgin her new husband can shame the entire family and bring bad luck to them. She doesn't question the practice at all; to her, it's simply an obligation to keep girls "clean," and the right thing to do. However, when she realizes how much the custom has hurt Sophie, she gives her a statue of the goddess Erzulie and tells her, "My heart, it weeps like a river, for the pain we have caused you."

Joseph

Sophie's neighbor, a jazz musician from Louisiana who is the same age as her mother, falls in love with her because she seems like a deep, thoughtful person. She also falls in love with him, although her mother has forbidden her to date. Eventually, he becomes her husband and the father of her child.

Like Sophie, he is deep and thoughtful, and this is what attracts her to him; she realizes that he is the kind of man who would be interested in a woman for more than her looks. She chooses wisely, as he is indeed a kind, wise, and loving man. Later in the book, when she leaves him because physical intimacy with him reminds her of her sexual problems, he is understanding, welcomes her back, and encourages her to stay with him and go to therapy to sort things out.

Themes

Immigration and Assimilation

Throughout the book, Sophie and Martine travel from Haiti to the United States, and back to Haiti. The contrasts between the two settings and cultures are vivid and all-encompassing, and as both women note, it is difficult to find your way in a foreign country. Both women learn to speak English—which Grandma Ife refers to as "that cling-clang talk," and which Sophie says sounds "like rocks falling in a stream," but they also continue to speak their own language, Creole. They eat American food because Haitian food reminds them of the emotional pain they endured in Haiti, but at the same time they long for traditional dishes with ingredients like cassava, ginger, beans and rice, and spices. Sophie hates her school because it is a French school, and she feels she might as well have stayed in Haiti—but she is also uneasy because American students harass her for being Haitian. Sophie's difficulty with assimilation is also shown by her conflicting attitude toward gender roles: she believes women should be traditionally chaste and sheltered, but talks disparagingly of traditional Haitian men, who, she says, will want a woman to stay at home, cooking Haitian food.

Eventually, Sophie becomes Americanized: when she returns to Haiti, a cabdriver is surprised that she speaks Creole so well, and when Martine shows up too, the two of them speak English together without realizing it.

Generational Bonds and Conflicts

"The love between a mother and daughter is deeper than the sea," Martine tells Sophie, and generational bonds and conflicts between mothers and daughters are a major theme in the book. Grandma Ife, the matriarch of the clan, followed the traditional Haitian practice of ensuring her daugh-

Topics for Further Study

- Read about the dictatorship of Jean Claude "Baby Doc" Duvalier in Haiti and discuss how it affected poverty, illiteracy, and crime in Haiti.

- Explore the use of *voudon,* or voodoo, by Jean Claude Duvalier and his father, Francois "Papa Doc" Duvalier, to frighten the population of Haiti into submitting to their rule. How did these dictators use people's spiritual beliefs to enhance their power?

- Research the Haitian deities of *voudon,* particularly the goddess Erzulie, and compare her to Catholic images of the Virgin Mary.

- Find a Haitian cookbook, or if possible visit a Haitian restaurant, and try some Haitian foods. How does Haitian cuisine differ from the food you are used to?

- In the eighteenth century, a slave rebellion ended white rule in Haiti. Read about this rebellion, and compare the plight of the slaves in Haiti to that of slaves in the United States.

ters' chastity and "tested" them each month to make sure their hymens were still intact. This resulted in lifelong emotional scars for both daughters, particularly Martine, whose sexual guilt, pain, and fear only increased when she was brutally raped at age sixteen. Although Martine knows firsthand how emotionally and physically painful the testing is, she still does it to her daughter Sophie, passing on the family curse of sexual phobias and nightmares. When Sophie finally asks why she did this, she says that she has no real explanation or good reason; she only did it to Sophie because it was done to her. Interestingly, although Grandma Ife was also presumably a victim of this practice, she does not seem to be bothered by it, presumably because she has accepted a much more traditional life than either her daughters or Sophie. Sophie realizes that there is a way out of this pain: she manages to exorcise the fear of her mother's rapist, and she vows not to test her daughter or pass on the nightmares and eating disorders that affect both her and her mother. Rather than unthinkingly accepting tradition, she knows that she must shape her own life. She says of her family's emotional pain, "It was up to me to avoid my turn in the fire. It was up to me to make sure that my daughter never slept with ghosts, never lived with nightmares."

Emotional Pain and Liberation

Throughout the book, the female characters suffer from emotional pain that prevents them from living fully, but they seek liberation and in some cases find it. At the beginning of the book, Tante Atie is resigned to being illiterate and unloved, but several years later a friend, who also seems to be her lover, has taught her to read. She carries a notebook everywhere so that she can copy poems and write down her thoughts, and even writes a poem of her own.

Martine also seeks liberation from her pain, but she is unable to do this in a constructive way. For a while things seem to have improved for her: she's involved with Marc, who is a good man, and makes enough money to send some home to Haiti every month. Sophie's arrival disturbs her, however, since Sophie resembles her father, the rapist, and Martine is also disturbed by Sophie's growth into a woman and her relationship with a man. When Martine gets pregnant, it reawakens all her memories of the rape, her pregnancy with Sophie, and her mother's sexual testing. Unable to find a cure for her emotional pain, she eventually commits suicide.

Sophie inherits her mother's fear, sexual guilt, and nightmares, but through a therapy group, she is able by the end of the book to move beyond them and to prevent her daughter from inheriting them. She also realizes that her mother, despite her suicide and the testing she inflicted on Sophie, was a strong, capable woman who was simply overwhelmed by circumstance.

Style

Point of View

Sophie's story is told in the first person and is largely chronological, although some events are not explained or explored until later in the book, when other events give the explanations more depth and context. Sophie is twelve when the novel begins, and nineteen when it ends; the book is told from the grown Sophie's viewpoint. Skillfully, Danticat conveys a child's sense of the world in the early chapters, and a more mature view in the later ones, where Sophie becomes more aware of the suffering of other women in her family and how it relates to her own emotional pain.

Setting

Set in Haiti and in Brooklyn, the book is steeped in Haitian culture, language, folklore, cuisine, and customs. Danticat's description of Haiti is lush and vivid, filled with colors, smells, and sensory experiences, but with an undercurrent of fear brought on by dangerous political unrest and deep poverty. As a child, however, she is largely sheltered from this fear. The bright colors, tropical tastes and scents, and warmth of Haiti are sharply contrasted with the cold, gray, graffiti-covered, and run-down Brooklyn neighborhood she moves to. In addition, in Haiti she is part of a small-town neighborhood where everyone knows everyone else, and where her grandmother and aunt tell family stories and folktales. In Brooklyn, her life in her mother's small apartment still revolves around Haiti, as her mother shops in Haitian stores, sends money home to Haiti, insists that she stay away from American teenagers, and sends her to a French-speaking school. American students tease her, and because she spends all of her time either at school, church, or home, she doesn't have any friends, and also does not know any of her neighbors until, by stealth, she discovers Joseph's name.

Use of Myth and Folklore

Danticat does not directly use myth as a source for her story, but the book is infused with Haitian folklore and the presence of Haitian deities, particularly Erzulie, the goddess whose image is often mingled with that of the Virgin Mary, but who is also considered to be beautiful and sexually enticing. Erzulie, "the healer of all women and the desire of all men," who unites and reconciles these two images—the chaste and the sexual—embodies one of the major themes of the book, the need for sexual healing that all the women characters experience.

In addition, many folktales are told in the book, often as lessons or as ways of deepening the characters' understanding of real life. Sophie's grandmother tells her that some people have more trouble in their lives than others; this is because, though they don't know it, they are special people, spiritually tall, mighty, and strong, who support the sky on their heads. Sophie's father, the unknown rapist, is compared to a cannibalistic bogeyman known as a *Tonton Macoute*—also a name for the real-life guerrilla vigilantes who roam the countryside killing people.

Symbolism

Several symbols recur throughout the book. Daffodils, which are not native to Haiti, are Martine's favorite flower, because they grow in a place they are not supposed to; after Europeans brought the flowers to Haiti, a vigorous kind of daffodil developed that could withstand the tropical heat. To Sophie and her mother Martine, they are a symbol of resilience and survival, qualities the women need to withstand the sexual and emotional torment they have gone through. Danticat writes a Mother's Day poem for her Tante Atie, comparing her to a daffodil, ''limber and strong,'' and as a child is upset when Atie insists that she give the poem to her real mother, whom she has not seen since she was a baby. By the end of the book, however, she realizes that the poem applies to her mother, too.

Stories, which in the book are always told by women, are a symbol of the connections between generations of women, stretching into the past as well as the future. Late in the book, Sophie says, ''I realized that it was neither my mother nor my Tante Atie who had given all the mother-and-daughter motifs to all the stories they told and all the songs they sang. It was something that was essentially Haitian. Somehow, early on, our song makers and tale weavers had decided that we were all daughters of the land.''

Literary Heritage

Haiti is a country long marked by its political unrest and economic depravity as a result of years of dictatorship, government corruption, and a large gap between the wealthy elite and profitable cities and the poverty-stricken non-industrial provinces.

A written or recorded literature was never a priority in Haitian culture, therefore, the number of internationally recognized Haitian authors is understandably few. In addition, Haitian women writers are rare due to the secondary positions they hold within the society, remaining mostly in the home or in non-professional occupations.

Although fiscally poor, Haiti is a culture rich in its language, folktales, customs, and community.

The Haitian people often looked to their families and friends not only for support but also for forms of entertainment. In a sense, it was the effects of poverty and illiteracy that made the practice of storytelling an important and favorite pasttime, allowing this craft to endure throughout the generations, preserving the nation's culture and history.

Haitian literature was not known outside its borders until well into the 1960s, when the Civil Rights and Women's movements pushed for social reforms and gave the Haitian people an impetus to search out and explore their voices. Still, it was not until the 1990s that Haiti and Haitian literature started to receive the attention it deserved. As more and more nations began to learned of Haiti's oppression and the violence its people faced under the Duvalier government, the call for information about the country and its people increased. New emerging writers began to meet this demand, describing the horrors as well as the jewels of this besieged nation. These writers were creating a literature of social consciousness that demanded acknowledgement from the outside world. Their writing also served as a mirror in which to look back and examine their own background and culture.

When Haitian-born writer Edwidge Danticat began to write and record her memories of Haiti, fictionalizing them in her books, her writings became an extension of the oral tradition of her culture, capturing in print what was natural to her at an early age. What is present in Danticat's work is Haiti's painful history but also its uniqueness and beauty. It is this beauty and cultural lushness that are making people more open to Haitian literature and leading to changes in its presence and proliferation.

Historical Context

Political Terror in Haiti

Haiti in the early 1980s was ruled by Jean Claude ''Baby Doc'' Duvalier, son of the infamous dictator Francois ''Papa Doc'' Duvalier. During Papa Doc's regime, the longest in Haitian history, he executed all opponents without trial, and kept troops of unpaid volunteers, known as *Tontons Macoutes*, who were given license to torture, rape, and kill people at will. During his rule, the Haitian economy deteriorated and only 10 percent of the population could read. Papa Doc encouraged the population to believe that he was an accomplished practitioner of *voudon*, or voodoo, and possessed supernatural powers; to rebel against him invited death. After Papa Doc's death in 1971, his son succeeded him, continuing his reign of terror until 1986, when he was overthrown. Even after his overthrow, although the *Tontons Macoutes* were no longer officially condoned, they still terrorized the population.

The *Tontons Macoutes* are ever-present in the book, since Sophie was born as a result of one of them raping her mother when she was sixteen years old. For the rest of her life, long after she has moved to Brooklyn, Martine has terrifying dreams of this event and of the rapist, and passes her fear on to Sophie, who, everyone believes, looks just like the rapist since she does not look like anyone in her family. As a child, Sophie is aware that there is unrest and killing beyond her small town, and sees it for herself on the trip to the airport when she is leaving for the United States. Outside the airport they see a car in flames, students protesting, and soldiers shooting bullets and tear gas at them. They watch helplessly as a soldier beats a girl's head in with his gun. On the airplane, Sophie sits next to a small boy whose father has just been killed in the demonstration but who is traveling alone anyway, because he has no relatives left in Haiti.

The prevalence of poverty and illiteracy in Haiti is also important in the book. Sophie's Tante Atie, who cannot read, tells her, "We are a family with dirt under our fingernails," meaning that they have always been poor agricultural laborers, and says that the only way Sophie will improve her life is to become educated. Atie tells Sophie that when Atie was small, the whole family had to work in the sugar cane fields, and when Sophie's grandfather died in the field one day, they simply had to dig a hole, bury him, and move on. Her mother also tells her, "Your schooling is the only thing that will make people respect you. If you make something of yourself, we will all succeed. You can *raise our heads* ."

Traditional Role of Women

In Haiti, traditional belief holds that a woman's place is in the home. Tante Atie tells Sophie that when she was a girl, Grandma Ife told her that each of her ten fingers has a purpose: Mothering. Boiling. Loving. Baking. Nursing. Frying. Healing. Washing. Ironing. Scrubbing. Wistfully Atie says that she sometimes wished she had been born with six fingers on each hand, so she could have two left over for herself.

Despite the fact that women do so much, they are not valued as much as men. When Sophie returns to Haiti with her baby daughter, one night she and her grandmother sit watching a light moving back and forth on a distant hill. Her grandmother tells her this means someone is having a baby, and the light is the midwife walking back and forth with a lantern in the yard, where a pot of water was boiling. She also says that they can tell from what happens to the light whether the child is a boy or a girl. If it is a boy, she says, the lantern will be put outside the shack and if the father is there, he will stay up all night with the new baby boy. Sophie asks what will happen if the child is a girl, and her grandmother tells her, "If it is a girl, the midwife will cut the child's cord and go home. Only the mother will be left in the darkness to hold her child. There will be no lamps, no candles, no more light."

In Haiti, it is considered very important for a girl to remain a virgin until she is married, because her chastity, or lack of it, affects the reputation of the entire family. Because of this, Martine goes to great lengths to keep Sophie away from men, encourages her to dress in conservative clothes that do not show her figure, and does not allow her to date until she is eighteen. As Sophie says, "Men were as mysterious to me as white people, who in Haiti we had only known as missionaries." In addition, although they have moved to America, Martine follows an old Haitian custom of "testing" Sophie to make sure she is still a virgin by inserting a finger into her vagina and checking to see if her hymen is still intact. This "testing" was done to Martine and Atie by Sophie's grandmother, and presumably her grandmother was tested as a girl, too. Although it has caused great emotional pain to every generation, women have continued to do it to their daughters only because, as Martine explains, it was done to them and because they were told it was the right thing to do.

Culture Clash in Brooklyn

In Brooklyn, both women try to balance the two cultures: Haitian and American. Sophie goes to a French-speaking school but hates it, because it's as if she is still in Haiti, and because American students in the neighborhood taunt her, calling her "Frenchie" and "stinking Haitian," and saying that because she's Haitian and many Haitians have died of AIDS, she must be a carrier of the AIDS virus. Martine, who associates Haitian food and customs with the rape she experienced as a young girl, cooks American foods such as lasagna, but still goes to Haitian shops to buy castor oil to dress her hair, Haitian spices, and images of Erzulie, a Haitian goddess. Martine is aware of the difficulties for immigrants and tells Sophie, ''It is really hard for the new-generation girls. You will have to choose between the really old-fashioned Haitians and the new-generation Haitians. The old-fashioned ones are not exactly prize fruits. They make you cook plantains and rice and beans and never let you feed them lasagna. The problem with the new generation is that a lot of them have lost their sense of obligation to the family's honor. Rather than become doctors and engineers, they want to drive taxicabs to make quick cash.''

When Sophie moves to Brooklyn, although she and her mother live in a poor neighborhood in Brooklyn, she is aware that by Haitian standards, she is rich. Her mother's closet, for example, would have been considered a whole room in Haiti, and any child lucky enough to sleep in it would not have been bothered by the hanging clothes. Both Sophie and her mother suffer from eating disorders after they come to the States, because they are not used to the huge variety and abundance of food. In Haiti, where food is scarce, when people have a lot of it, they eat like they may not see any tomorrow—because they may not. So, in Brooklyn, both Sophie and her mother can't shake their fear of hunger, and when they have food, they can't stop eating. Martine gains sixty pounds during her first year in the United States, and Sophie becomes bulimic, eating huge quantities of food and then vomiting it up.

Critical Overview

Danticat was only twenty-five when *Breath, Eyes, Memory* was published. The book immediately attracted critical notice and acclaim for the clarity and precision of the writing, and its emotional depth. The book was the first novel by a Haitian woman to be published by a major press and to receive wide notice and readership among non-Haitian Americans.

Jim Gladstone wrote in the *New York Times* that the book ''achieves an emotional complexity that lifts it out of the realm of the potboiler and into that of poetry,'' and in *Ms.,* Joan Philpott described it as ''intensely lyrical.'' Danticat was also com-

pared to African-American writer Alice Walker, author of *The Color Purple* and other works. A *Publishers Weekly* reviewer wrote, ''In simple, lyrical prose . . . she makes Sophie's confusion and guilt, her difficult assimilation into American culture and her eventual emotional liberation palpably clear.'' Renee H. Shea noted in *Belles Lettres,* ''To read Danticat is to learn about Haiti—the folklore and myth, the traditions, and the history.''

On May 22, 1998, Danticat's critical praise was augmented by commercial success, when the book was selected by talk show host Oprah Winfrey for her book club. This catapulted it into the number-one spot on the bestseller lists and led Danticat to do a 17-city author tour, as the book sold 600,000 copies. Danticat's agent was flooded with requests for interviews, and Danticat was chosen by *Harper's Bazaar* magazine as one of twenty people in their twenties who will make a difference for the future, and was also named in a *New York Times* magazine article about thirty creative people under thirty who were expected to do great things in the future.

After her television appearance on *Oprah,* Danticat rented an apartment of her own in a Haitian community outside New York, so that she would not have to keep giving interviews in her parents' home. She told Mallay Charters in *Publishers Weekly,* ''I just feel you need a little safe place sometimes, some place that you have just for yourself.''

Since writing the book, Danticat has also published two other books, *The Farming of Bones,* a novel set during the 1937 genocide of Haitians by Dominican dictator Rafael Trujillo Molina, and a collection of short stories titled *Krik? Krak!.*

Criticism

Kelly Winters

Winters is a freelance writer and has written for a wide variety of academic and educational publishers. In the following essay, she discusses the genesis, recurring themes, and critical reception of Breath, Eyes, Memory.

Breath, Eyes, Memory weaves several threads of sexuality, body image, generational bonds and con-

What Do I Read Next?

- Danticat's *Krik? Krak!* is a collection of short stories set in Haiti. The title comes from a traditional Haitian custom of listeners asking "Krik?" before a story is told. The teller answers, "Krak," and begins the tale.

- Danticat's *The Farming of Bones* is a novel set during the 1937 mass genocide of Haitians by Dominican dictator Rafael Trujillo Molina; it vividly shows the brutal existence of workers in the sugar cane fields.

- *Tell My Horse: Voodoo and Life in Haiti and Jamaica,* by African-American writer and folklorist Zora Neale Hurston, examines spiritual beliefs in these two countries.

- *The Rainy Season: Haiti Since Duvalier,* by Amy Wilentz, is a vivid portrait of Haiti in the late 1980s, and provides a clear examination of the parade of dictators and terrorists who have ruled the country since Jean Claude "Baby Doc" Duvalier.

- *All Souls' Rising*, by Madison Smartt Bell, is a historical epic set during the eighteenth-century slave rebellion that ended white rule in Haiti.

- Diane Wolkstein's *The Magic Orange Tree: And Other Haitian Folktales*, is a collection of Haitian folktales and legends, and features an introduction by Danticat.

- *Double Stitch: Black Women Write about Mothers and Daughters*, edited by Patricia Bell-Scott, is an anthology of stories by women writers.

---

flicts, the immigrant experience, and the desperate social and political situation in Haiti, to portray a young girl's coming of age and eventual emotional liberation. It was the first book by a Haitian woman to be published in English by a major publisher and to receive wide readership and attention, and because of this, some have seen Danticat as a voice for all Haitian Americans. Danticat has emphatically stressed in many interviews that this view is inaccurate and that she is one voice among many, telling a Random House interviewer, "My greatest hope is that mine becomes one voice in a giant chorus that is trying to understand and express artistically what it's like to be a Haitian immigrant in the United States." However, she is also aware that not everyone is as articulate as she, and also told the interviewer, "I hope to speak for the individuals who might identify with the stories I tell."

She told *New York State Writers Institute Writers Online*'s Christine Atkins, "[I hope] that the extraordinary female story tellers I grew up with—the ones that have passed on—will choose to tell their story through my voice. . .for those who have a voice must speak to the present and the past. For we may very well have to be Haiti's last surviving breath, eyes, and memory."

She also told Megan Rooney of the *Brown Daily Herald,* "All my conscious life I have wanted to write. I was persistent, I love writing. I wouldn't be stopped."

Although the book is not factually autobiographical, it is emotionally true to her own life. She told a Random House interviewer that one of the most important themes of the book is "migration, the separation of families, and how much that affects the parents and children who live through that experience." Another is the political situation in Haiti—that ordinary people live in fear for their lives and property because of the lawless *Tontons Macoutes,* armed with Uzi rifles, who roam the countryside raping, pillaging, and killing at will. And a third, she noted, was the relationship between mothers and daughters.

The genesis of *Breath, Eyes, Memory* was Danticat's own childhood in Haiti, where she was raised by relatives because her parents had emigrated to the United States when she was very young.

When Danticat was twelve, she joined them in Brooklyn. She told Rooney, "It was a big culture shock. I didn't speak English. I was clueless in school. I was getting readjusted to being with my family. And all of this happened when I was on the verge of adolescence."

Sophie attends the Maranatha Bible Institute, a French-English bilingual school where most of the instruction is in French. Surprisingly, she dislikes the school because, as she says, "it was as if I had never left Haiti." Harassed by American students as a "Frenchie," accused of having "HBO—Haitian Body Odor," and accused of carrying the deadly AIDS virus because of the high rates of the virus among Haitians, Sophie struggles to find a sense of home in Brooklyn, and to learn English. At first, the lone English words in her mother's Creole conversation stand out among others—words such as "TV," "building," or "feeling"—"jump out of New York Creole conversations, like the last kernel in a cooling popcorn machine." Gradually, she learns to read and speak English, although at first the words sound heavy and foreign, "like rocks falling in a stream."

Despite her new language, her mother keeps her sheltered, so that for the next six years, she lives in a narrow world of school, home, and prayer. Martine, trying to keep her daughter traditionally pure and chaste despite the loose American society, forbids her to date until she is eighteen, and takes her to work with her. She has no American friends, no Haitian friends, and no knowledge of men. As she says, in a comment that says as much about relations between the races as it does about those between genders, "Men were as mysterious to me as white people, who in Haiti we had only known as missionaries."

Later, after her marriage to an African-American musician, she learns more about her new country, travels, and even attends a therapy group—something unheard of in Haiti. However, she is still pursued by the ghosts of her own and her mother's past in Haiti—the custom of virginity testing, and her mother's rape by a *Macoute*. Before she can become free and truly live her life fully as a Haitian American, she must come to terms with her Haitian heritage and past.

The experiences and daily lives of women in Haiti are largely unknown to most Americans, who are rarely educated about Haitian culture and history. According to Danticat, Haitian women's lives are defined by what Bob Corbett, in the *Webster*

> The events in the book are shaped by the political, social, and economic chaos in Haiti during the regimes of Jean Claude 'Baby Doc' Duvalier and his successors. During Duvalier's regime, the illiteracy rate in Haiti was 90 percent and the population was oppressed by widespread poverty and disease."

University website, called "the ten fingers of Haitian tradition." According to tradition, each finger on a woman's hand has a purpose: mothering, boiling, loving, baking, nursing, frying, healing, washing, ironing, and scrubbing. Sophie and Atie both struggle to find space for their own needs and wants in this list of services to others, with varying success. As Corbett noted, the novel is about "the struggle of three individuals to rise above the shaping of their history and to take control of their own lives. It's not a story of much success, but of people in motion."

As Danticat makes clear, a girl's virginity and chastity is highly prized in Haiti, where a young woman's conduct can affect the reputation of her entire family. Danticat told a Random House interviewer that the virginity testing described in the book is not unique to Haiti, and cited the apocryphal gospels, in which the Virgin Mary is similarly tested for virginity when it becomes apparent that she is pregnant. Danticat stressed the fact that none of the mothers in the book intended the testing to be abusive, but were doing what they believed was best for their daughters and their families, and because they wanted their daughters to go farther and do better in life than they had.

Because this custom results in emotional harm, Sophie attends a sexual phobia therapy group so that she can heal. She describes her therapist as "a gorgeous black woman who was an initiated Santeria priestess." When Rena, the therapist, hears that Sophie's mother Martine is pursued by nightmares of the rape that led to Sophie's birth, Rena suggests that if Martine is uncomfortable with the idea of therapy, she should have an exorcism. This openness to non-Western and non-American modes of healing marks the therapist/priestess as a bridge between the cultures, an integrator. Rena recommends rituals the members of the group can perform to release their fear and pain: burning slips of paper with the names of their abusers written on them, and releasing a green balloon to the sky. Danticat is realistic in depicting the mixed results of these rituals; Sophie feels better after burning her mother's name, but some time later sees the green balloon stuck in a tree—it has not traveled very far from home. However, Rena does offer some advice that ultimately does result in healing, saying about Martine's rape memories and Sophie's phobia of being with her husband:

> "Your mother never gave him a face. That's why he's a shadow. That's why he can control her. . .You will never be able to connect with your husband until you say good-bye to your father."

She recommends that Martine undergo an exorcism, but Martine commits suicide before she can follow this advice. Sophie, however, ultimately does follow it, revisiting the scene of her mother's rape in the cane fields and experiencing a violent catharsis. Her grandmother and aunt watch, and in the end, acknowledge that she has been liberated from the burden she has carried for so long.

Reviewer Ann Folwell Stanford comments that the therapy section "barely escapes trendy cliche," but in fact the therapist's use of ritual is highly appropriate for Sophie, whose whole life has been enriched by ritual, symbol, and story. This is a language that Sophie understands, since she was raised with stories of Erzulie and other Haitian deities, and since in Haiti even an ordinary bath has ritual elements: at her grandmother's house, they bathe in an outdoor shack using rainwater that has been steeped with healing herbs: "a potpourri of flesh healers: catnip, senna, sarsparilla, *corrosol,* the petals of blood red hibiscus, forget-me-nots, and daffodils." Ritual is part of everyday life in many other ways, from the use of lanterns to mark the sex of a newborn child, the weekly Mass that people attend, and the endless stories of ancestors, deities, and folk heroes and heroines.

The book ends on a hopeful note. Sophie's baby, Brigitte Ife, is a symbol of the integration of her old and new lives and the potential healing in the generational line of women: the child is untouched, untroubled by nightmares, born in America. At the same time, she resembles Sophie's mother so close-

ly that Grandma Ife, on seeing the girl, is astonished. "'Do you see my granddaughter?' she asked, tracing her thumb across Brigitte's chin. 'The tree has not split one mite. Isn't it a miracle that we can visit with all our kin, simply by looking at this face?'"

Danticat emphasizes this possibility later in the book, when Sophie says, "I looked back at my daughter, who was sleeping peacefully. . .The fact that she could sleep meant that she had no nightmares, and maybe, would never become a frightened insomniac like my mother and me." And again, when Sophie, after burning her mother's name in the therapy ritual, wisely realizes, "It was up to me to avoid my turn in the fire. It was up to me to make sure that my daughter never slept with ghosts, never lived with nightmares, and never had her name burnt in the fire."

She will succeed in this, the reader knows, because at the end of the book, when she revisits the scene of the rape, she beats and pounds at the cane, as if she is possessed. The priest walks toward her, but Grandma Ife stops him, knowing that Sophie must do this. Ife and her aunt, Tante Atie, both call, "*Ou libere?*"—"'Are you free?"'—a phrase women traditionally use when one has dropped a heavy and dangerous load. Thus, they acknowledge her freedom from the burden that has oppressed her for so long. Before she can answer their question, Grandma Ife puts her fingers over Sophie's lips and tells her, "Now, you will know how to answer," meaning that she is free, and knows it.

The events in the book are shaped by the political, social, and economic chaos in Haiti during the regimes of Jean Claude "Baby Doc" Duvalier and his successors. During Duvalier's regime, the illiteracy rate in Haiti was 90 percent and the population was oppressed by widespread poverty and disease. In addition, ordinary people lived in fear of the *Tontons Macoutes,* formerly the volunteer secret police and death squad of dictator Francois "Papa Doc" Duvalier. Named for a cannibalistic ogre, the *Macoutes* arbitrarily murdered, raped, and tortured anyone suspected of opposing the regime, or anyone they happened to run into. Sophie's birth is the result of a *Macoute*'s rape of her mother, when Martine was sixteen years old, and throughout the book these figures of terror reappear, shooting students, killing a coal seller, appearing in the market and on a bus Sophie is riding. Sophie herself is a permanent reminder of the power of the *Macoutes,* since she does not resemble anyone in her family, and it is believed that she looks just like the rapist: a physical, daily reminder to Martine of the torture she went through.

In the *Michigan Daily,* Dean Bakopoulos wrote that "in her fledgling career, Danticat has definitely brought a new freshness and vividness to American fiction, a new voice that shows great promise of evolving even further." *Austin Chronicle* writer Belinda Acosta described Danticat as a "gifted, compassionate young writer," and noted that one of the most remarkable aspects of Danticat's career is that she "consistently turns out work that is at turns compelling, beautiful, and breathtakingly painful." Christine Atkins remarked in *New York State Writers Institute Writers Online* that the book "traverses between cultures, negotiating an identity constructed in two sharply distinct worlds." The emotional impact of the book was summed up by a *Publishers Weekly* reviewer, who wrote, "In simple, lyrical prose enriched by an elegiac tone...she makes Sophie's confusion and guilt, her difficult assimilation...[and her] emotional liberation palpably clear."

Source: Kelly Winters, in an essay for *Literature of Developing Nations for Students,* Gale, 2000.

Myriam J. A. Chancy

In the following essay on Edwidge Danticat's Breath, Eyes, Memory, *author Myriam J.A. Chancy discusses the concepts of female and sexual identity within textual and cultural contexts. Chancy shows the reader that the literary structuring used in Danticat's work serves as an illustration of and framework for both Haitian social culture and the alienation of women from themselves, their bodies, and each other. This emphasis on the novel's structure, according to Chancy, further underscores the important theme of the function of literacy for the women in Danticat's novel.*

In Edwidge Danticat's *Breath, Eyes, Memory,* Haitian women are represented through images drawn from folk traditions. The subtext of the story of three generations of the Caco family involves a careful subversion of Haitian tropes of identity. Danticat uses the symbol of the *marassa,* the cult of twins in *vodou,* to highlight the divisions that are created between women who have been brought up to deny their sexuality as well as each other. In invoking *vodou* traditions, she strives, moreover, to disassociate them from their prevalent use as tools of state control during the Duvalier years of terror. Danticat also makes use of the principles of *palé*

andaki, a practice of code-switching particular to Haitian creole, to underscore the complex dimensions of Haitian women's survival in varied social contexts. Danticat thus engages the challenge of Haiti's cultural doubleness in order to emphasize the need to reformulate the traditional Caribbean novel genre to reflect the particularities of Haitian women's lives.

In *Breath, Eyes, Memory,* narrative acts ironically as a metaphor for the absence of writ social existence; in this way, the physical text becomes the manifestation of the social forces at work in Haiti over the span of three generations of Haitian women. It also provides a vital link to indigenous languages while using the vehicle of literary production to supply the context for female liberation. The Cacos of Danticat's novel are a family of women from the working classes who struggle both to maintain continuity from one generation to the next, and to reshape through education the fate of the younger generation, represented by the narrator and protagonist, Sophie. Throughout the novel, education, and, more specifically, literacy, are posited as the only means to salvation; ironically, access to literacy is connected to a life of exile, to a move from valley to city for the older generation within Haiti, from Haiti to the United States for the younger. Resisting this movement, the older generations, represented in part by Sophie's grandmother, cling to their sense of Haiti's "glory days," an invisible African past that is textualized in the novel through the oral folk tales the older generations tell to the younger ones. It is through the thematization of secrecy that the damage resulting from generational disruption is unveiled. The language of the ancestors, which grows increasingly difficult to access, is the key to each woman's freedom.

Sophie is alienated from her natural mother by the latter's memory of the rape of which she is a product, an act that is duplicated by her mother who abuses her sexually in adolescence under the guise of protecting her from future harm. Martine, who wants to make sure that Sophie remains sexually "whole," persists in describing her acts of sexual abuse in terms of a spiritual "twinning" of souls. Presented as a ritual enacted between mother and daughter through the generations, the "testing" that scars Sophie for life is a product of the suppression of female sexuality and the codification of women's bodies as vessels for male gratification in marriage. The Cacos perpetuate this ritual, although none of the women in the family has ever married, in what Danticat terms a "virginity cult."

> Claudine's inability to survive is ultimately a function of her being a woman in Haiti; as a woman, she is denied most privileges, and it is for this reason that she clings so fiercely to those privileges that class alone can provide."

It is because she has internalized the ideology of female inferiority that Sophie's mother is capable of abusing her daughter. Taught to despise the female body for itself and to covet it only as a means by which to acquire a male mate, Sophie's mother commits incest against her daughter, rationalizing her behavior as necessary to her daughter's survival. Social worker and therapist E. Sue Blume notes in *Secret Survivors* that it is rarer for women to incest their children than it is for men. She writes: "Incest often manifests itself in a manner consistent with gender socialization: for a man, the abuse is generally overtly and directly sexual; for a woman, it may be more emotional, more focused on relationship and bonding, or perhaps manifested through care of the child's body, her primary domain." The incest motif overwhelmingly present in the literature by women of the African diaspora—in the works of Toni Morrison, Alice Walker, Joan Riley, Maya Angelou, to name the most notable—clearly demonstrates that Danticat's portrayal of incest between mother and daughter should not be taken as evidence that Haitian women are any more apt than other individuals to commit acts of incest against their daughters and that men are hapless bystanders to such abuse. Rather, Danticat demonstrates (as do the aforementioned women writers) through this aspect of her text the *extent to which the subjugation of women* has led to one mother's sexual oppression of her own daughter. The effect of this subjugation is that the mother believes that she is taking "care of the child's body" when she is in fact subjecting it to very abuse from which she is hoping to save it.

After having been raised for most of her early life by her mother's sister, Tante Atie, in Haiti, Sophie is summoned to New York by her mother.

The community rejoices at what appears to be a "natural" turn of events, the reclamation of a daughter by her mother. As grandmother Ifé says to Sophie: "You must never forget this. . . . Your mother is your first friend." Sophie, however, knows her mother only as an absence; she reacts to her dislocation by withdrawing from the world which until this time had seemed so familiar, so unchangeable. When she is told that she will have to leave Haiti for her mother's New York, she says: "I could not eat the bowl of food that Tante Atie laid in front of me. I only kept wishing that everyone would disappear." Only later do we learn that her inability to eat the bowl of food is symptomatic of what will become a cycle of bodily abuse; once she is in the United States—a place her mother describes to her as a sort of paradise—Sophie becomes bulimic.

For Sophie, the United States is not a garden of Eden; instead, it is a place in which she hungers for the comfort of her true mother, Tante Atie, whom she honors in a poem as a brilliant, delicate, yet nonetheless hardy, yellow daffodil. That image is connected to Erzulie who is the "Goddess of Love, the divinity of the dream. . . . [t]o Haitian women, the goddess . . . signifies escape from a life in which women carry a greater share of work and suffering." Thus Sophie recalls:

> As a child, the mother I had imagined for myself was like Erzulie, the lavish Virgin Mother. She was the healer of all women and the desire of all men. She had gorgeous dresses in satin, silk, and lace, necklaces, pendants, earrings, bracelets, anklets, and lots and lots of French perfume. She never had to work for anything because the rainbow and the stars did her work for her. Even though she was far away, she was always with me. I could always count on her, like one counts on the sun coming out at dawn.

Sophie's mother can never be Erzulie, who is herself most often imaged as a mulatta of the upper classes, and whose power—defined as both erotic and sexual—is derived from these combined class and race distinctions. She nonetheless seeks Erzulie's elusive powers, attempting to transcend Haitian barriers of class, race, and color by exiling herself to the United States, where she appears to find love with Marc Chevalier, a lawyer and a member of the Haitian elite. "In Haiti," she explains, "it would not be possible for someone like Marc to love someone like me. He is from a very upstanding family. His grandfather was a French man." Marc idolizes Erzulie and decorates his home with small busts of her image; it would appear that Sophie's mother has begun to access Erzulie's world. Danticat, however, quickly undermines the association of the mother with Erzulie.

In *The Faces of the Gods,* Leslie Desmangles writes that "[i]n combination with Damballah, Ezili guarantees the flow of human generations," and that "[s]he is believed to have given birth to the first human beings after Bondye [the supreme Being] created the world." Erzulie, or, as Desmangles writes, Ezili, is the mother of us all, that is, of all Haitians, male and female; as such, she is all-powerful and all-controlling. Her power over men is legendary, as is her power over other *vodou loas* [gods]. She is often shown wearing a crown or a halo, "a symbol of her transcendent power and of her radiating beauty." It is crucial to note that Erzulie's power is defined in terms of her relationships, primarily to male deities and human male subjects: she is concubine to all but subjugated to none; she is beyond containment. As much as she seeks to transcend temporality by emulating Erzulie, Sophie's mother is bound to self-negating mores of womanhood embedded in nineteenth-century ideals; for this reason, Sophie is the painful memory of what she perceives to be her failure as a woman.

Sophie's mother never comes to terms with the fact that the man who raped her in her late teens robbed her of her sexual autonomy; she perceives herself as "damaged," incapable, in fact, of being Erzulie, because she is no longer "virginal," or "chaste," a status the Caco women associate with social mobility. It is through marriage that freedom from poverty, and endless toil, can be achieved; marriage, however, is an institution that, historically, has been socially constructed in such a way as to benefit men and deny women their autonomy. Thus, Danticat's protagonist recalls the story of a man who bleeds his young wife to death in order to be able to produce the soiled, bloody sheets of their first marriage night: "At the grave site, her husband drank his blood-spotted goat milk and cried like a child." On the surface, it seems as if Sophie is being led away from such a tragic fate. In the United States, she will be freed from the constraints of class that attend marriage in Haiti; she will gain an education and no man will be able to reject her as one Mr. Augustin rejected her Tante Atie because of her illiteracy. That possibility, however, is as elusive as Erzulie's loyalties, for Sophie knows only what she is in the process of losing. As she leaves Haiti behind, she imagines the friend/twin she has never had: "Maybe if I had a really good friend my eyes would have clung to hers as we were driven away." Sophie has no point of contact, no shared sight, with another human being who can complete for her her sense of self. Identity, Danticat appears to say, is inextricably linked with community, and the image of the twin, the true friend, is the vehicle for communal (re)identification.

Vodou and the Exploitation of Women's Sexuality

In *vodou* culture, the *marassas* are endowed with the power of the gods. Twins are *mystères* (mysteries), who, since they can never be deciphered, must be held in high esteem and revered. As Alfred Métreaux writes: "Some even contend that the twins are more powerful than the *loas.* They are invoked and saluted at the beginning of the [*vodou*] ceremony, directly after Legba." This is no small thing, for Legba is the sun god, the keeper of the gates; he is thus associated with Christ and, as the "guardian of universal and individual destiny," with St. Peter as well. Twins are believed to "share a soul": "Should one die, the living twin must put aside a bit of all food he [sic] eats, or a small part of any gift given him [sic], for the other." Sophie's inability to eat, then, can be understood as having been caused by her separation from the unknown twin, the best friend she wishes she had had in Haiti. On the other hand, because she has been deadened by her loss of family, Sophie can in some sense be regarded as the twin who has died. Her "living twin" on this reading would be the Haitian landscape to which she had last looked to for comfort in her departure from Haiti; it stores away its resources while awaiting her return. Sophie's mother, however, insists on figuring herself as her daughter's *marassa.* The image of her mother as her *marassa* only serves to terrorize Sophie and alienate her from her identity, which becomes both sexualized and demonized in its association (by the mother) with *vodou.*

In the United States, when Sophie has her first love affair, clandestine and innocent, with an older man, Joseph, her mother suspects her of ill-doing; this is the occasion for Sophie's first "test." Characteristically, Sophie prays to the "Virgin Mother" Mary/Erzulie while her mother tells her a story about the *marassas,* "two inseparable lovers . . . the same person duplicated in two." At first, the story seems to be a warning to Sophie to resist her desire for sexual union with a man. Her mother says: "When you love someone, you want him to be closer to you than your *Marassa.* Closer than your shadow. You want him to be your soul. The more you are alike, the easier this becomes." In the story, then, the union between man and woman is presented as a bond that can only be a pale imitation of the union between the *marassa,* who are described as reflections of oneself: ''When one looked in the mirror, the other walked behind the glass to mimic her.'' The story, as does the testing, ends chillingly as Sophie's mother tells her:

> The love between a mother and daughter is deeper than the sea. You would leave me for an old man who you didn't know the year before. You and I we could be like *Marassas.* You are giving up a lifetime with me. Do you understand? There are secrets you cannot keep.

Secrecy is central to the image of Haiti created by Danticat, suggesting that holding on to a sense of renewed options is a narrow, almost non-existent possibility. Secrecy, in the above passage, refers to Sophie's inability to keep her body to herself: it is positioned as her mother's reflection and is consequently not her own. But the truly unkeepable secret is the act of abuse itself, which Sophie attempts to exorcise through the only thing she feels she can still control: food.

Sophie's bulimia is a manifestation of her sexual abuse. As E. Sue Blume explains, eating disorders are manifestations of the ways in which women who have been abused attempt to regain control over their bodies; ironically, these attempts at regaining control perpetuate the cycle of abuse. Blume writes: ''Most men can achieve mastery in the real world, but many women can exercise total control only over their own bodies. Additionally, rigid social expectations define women through their appearance. Body size relates to power, sexuality, attention, self-worth, social status and the aftereffects of incest.'' Unlike anorexics, who try to rid their bodies of the sex characteristics they feel (consciously or unconsciously) have led to their victimization, bulimics attempt to *maintain* the sex characteristics they feel they must possess in order to achieve a ''perfection'' which will put a stop to their abuse. Sophie becomes the prototypical sexual abuse survivor described by Blume as she attempts to control her body—which remains the only socially sanctioned site for her rebellion—precisely because it has fallen beyond her control. She binges and purges in an effort to cleanse herself of her violation.

Sophie's eating disorder will not, however, erase the abuse she has suffered. Through the ''testing,'' Sophie loses her mother a second time and instead of becoming her twin becomes her victim. She clings to an elusive image of perfection, of

Erzulie, which neither she nor her mother can attain. Like Nadine Magloire's protagonist Claudine in *Le mal de vivre,* Sophie cannot reclaim her identity because her *Haitiennité* demands that she deny her desires as well as her need for sexual autonomy. This implicit denial of self, as I will demonstrate below, leads Danticat to reject those cultural markers most associated with Haitian Afrocentricity, such as *vodou* and matriarchal family structure, because they signify oppression rather than liberation; *this is not to say that, in so doing, she abandons what those markers represent.* Rather, Danticat shows that in order to reclaim the landscape of the female body and of Haiti, both must be redefined. Thus, the novel introduces at its start a set of seeming dichotomies that will be reshaped and reimaged as the plot advances: mother versus daughter, food versus starvation, language versus silence, ritual versus violation, *marassa* versus life partner. Each of these seeming dualities reflect the rigid sex roles Haitian women are taught to desire, even though they defy those social sanctions through their very acts of daily survival.

As Ira P. Lowenthal points out in his essay ''Labor, Sexuality and the Conjugal Contract,'' Haitian women of the rural working classes appear to have some power equity due to the fact that many are market women (handling booths at the market, money, trade) while their male counterparts work the fields. Lowenthal writes: ''men make gardens for someone and that someone is invariably a woman. . . . she is a socially recognized spouse of the man. The control of produce, then, as opposed to production itself, falls to women—as men's gardens mature.'' Lowenthal points out that this seeming inversion of sex roles does not guarantee women's economic autonomy. Instead, it suggests a potential that is never realized because male and female sex roles are maintained in such a way as to prevent an equal division of labor. Women continue to have to sustain the home even as they manage the commerce: ''domestic labor is overwelmingly the responsibility of women and . . . [w]hen men cry out, as they sometimes do—especially when actually faced with the unsavory prospect—that they 'can't live without a woman' . . . it is to these basic domestic services provided by women that they primarily refer.'' Put more bluntly, in Haiti, as in other parts of the Caribbean, even though a quasi-matriarchal system seems to be in place, it is one ''that represses women'': ''women are stuck running the household, and if they are tough and strong it is because their children would starve if they weren't.'' The Caco women thus represent the sort of matriarchal family formation that has been celebrated in many Caribbean women's writings (most notably in Audre Lorde's *Zami* and Michelle Cliff's *Abeng,* both semi-autobiographical novels), but which, in most Haitian contexts, is one born both out of necessity and out of the legacy of African social formations where quasi-matriarchal societies did indeed flourish and empower women.

In the Caribbean context, where identity resides at the crossroads of creolization or *métissage,* matriarchal society is a product of a disrupted society (or societies). Sexuality takes on a striking importance in a repressive matriarchal society for it is the ultimate site of women's subjugation and is, by extension, the site of possible empowerment. As Lowenthal explains,

> [f]emale sexuality is here revealed to be a woman's most important *economic* resource comparable in terms of its value to a relatively large tract of land. Indeed, when discussing their relations with men, adult women are likely to refer to their own genitals as *interèm* (my assets), *lajan-m* (my money), or *manmanlajan-m* (my capital), in addition to *tèm* (my land). The underlying notion here is of a resource that can be made to work to produce wealth, like land or capital, or that can be exchanged for desired goods and services, like money.

Lowenthal insists, however, that, just as women wield full control over the goods balanced precariously in weaved baskets upon their heads for sale at market, they have full control of the ways in which their bodies are exchanged or marketed. Yet, if women did, in point of fact, have full control over their bodies and their sexuality, one would expect that they would be endowed with power in whatever social strata in which they were born; this, of course, is not the case. Thus, when women attempt to control their sexual interactions with men, they do so precisely because social and sexual power is taken out of their hands from birth: theirs is an unrelenting struggle.

Danticat's very carefully exposes this truism as one would expose a frame of film to light. The result is not often clear or pleasing to the eye, but it reveals part of what has been obscured by inadequate representations of the difficulties faced by women in Haiti and elsewhere. Haitian women are not immune to what Catharine MacKinnon has called the ''body count [of] women's collective experience in America,'' by which girls are taught to suppress their own ambitions in order to fulfill the sexual needs of men. As Danticat shows, even in a family in which men do not ''exist,'' the threat of sexual violence and subjugation remains a reality too immediate to be ignored.

Learning the Mother Tongue

In many ways, the novel's true heroine is Tante Atie who gains a sense of self and identity only as she grows older. Rejected by a suitor, Augustin, because of her illiteracy, Atie's social role becomes that of caretaker to her aging mother, Ifé. Nonetheless, Atie rebels against her position in the family, and when she has to give up her role as Sophie's surrogate mother-figure, she begins to construct for herself a new life. Her life is reactivated through her being taught to read and write by a market woman, Louise, with whom she develops a strong love relationship. Although both Atie and Ifé have worked diligently to give Sophie and her mother the means to escape the endless cycle of work, poverty, and exploitation, Ifé strongly resents Atie's newfound independence at the same time that she covets it. Through Atie, Danticat presents literacy as a metaphor for the fulfillment of identity and yet she also demonstrates that freedom for the Haitian woman cannot be achieved solely through education; she must also be able to control the passage of her body through a society that rejects her presence and demonizes her sexuality.

Atie defies social convention by severing her relationship to her mother (whom it is supposed she will take care of as she ages since Atie is yet ''single'') in order to have a primary relationship with Louise. Her relationship with Louise is, in fact, subtly coded as a lesbian love relationship. Although there is the merest hint that the two are not sexually involved, suggested through numerous scenes in which Louise leaves at sundown and in which the two only come togther at daylight, theirs is undoubtedly an erotic relationship. They embody the power of the erotic as theorized by Audre Lorde who writes:

> The erotic is a measure between the beginnings of our sense of self and the chaos of our strongest feelings. It is an internal sense of satisfaction to which, once we have experience it, we know we can aspire. For having experienced the fullness of this depth of feeling and recognizing its power, in honor and self-respect we can require no less of ourselves.

This reflects Atie's experience with Louise as she grows in her ''sense of self,'' escaping the strict confines of her role as dutiful daughter and becoming more literate in her own (woman's) language. Access, through education, to both the past and to the future provides an increasingly empowering double-sightedness imaged through the *twinning* of these two women. Louise's descriptions of her relationship with Atie imply as much. She says: ''We are like milk and coffee, lips and tongue. We are two fingers on the same hand. Two eyes on the same head.'' In the end, these two women are the true *marassas* of the novel. Danticat deftly and subtly inverts the linguistic terms with which relationships between women can be described in the Haitian context in a manner akin to that involved in *palé andaki* (as described more fully below), the process of code switching within creole (the equivalent, perhaps, to what Zora Neale Hurston has defined as ''specifyin''' in Black English). Through this code switching, Danticat appears to reject the identifiable markers of *vodou* and to reformulate them in terms which are inclusive of its origins but that also encapsulate the exigencies of working-class and impoverished women. Creole is the mother tongue that links these two women to their Haitian identity, and, thus, to each other, through the process of literacy. Through creole, that literacy retains its oral roots.

Why should literacy be linked so explicitly to Haitian women's process of self-actualization? The languages in which we speak, write, and communicate are signifiers of the societies and/or cultures we live in. Haitians, male and female, have, since Haiti's tragic beginnings, been made to feel as if our ways of speaking are deficient. Creole, to this day, is often referred to as a ''bastard'' tongue, ''denigrated as a lesser language of French,'' even though it has certainly always been the ''dominant'' language of the country despite efforts to enforce French as the language of the polished, accomplished, upper classes. For the last several decades, creole has been taught in the schools and used as the common language of the untutored in various literacy programs. It is a living language that is continuously changing; it accurately reflects a culture that is constantly in flux both socially and politically.

Cultural sociologist Ulrich Fleischmann notes in his article, ''Language, Literacy, and Underdevelopment,'' that in rural Haiti, where the older Caco women live, creole culture distinguishes itself from those ''recognized'' in Western contexts in that it ''cannot be considered as culturally integrated . . . for each member is in some way aware that his [sic] culture seen from a socially more elevated position appears as a 'lower variant' of the dominant culture.'' Haitians are acutely aware of the ways in which linguistic creolization is perceived to be a deviation, but they are also ardently opposed to assimilating.

Fleishmann describes oral creole as follows:

> [T]hough a nationwide intelligible form of Creole speech exists, there is a continuous change and generation of meanings in the narrow local context. Therefore, Creole speech can take on double and even multiple meanings. The information it conveys can vary considerable according to the social context. The diligent use of contradictory explicit and implicit references, for instance, is a highly esteemed art which Haitians call *palé andaki*.

In effect, Danticat's novel is speaking *andaki* to those who are open to the possibilities of cultural doubleness. A little more than halfway through the text, readers are made aware that they have been reading in another language. When Sophie's mother comes to Haiti to reclaim her daughter for a second time, Ifé and Atie complain about their use of English. ''Oh that *cling-clang* talk,'' says Ifé, ''It sounds like glass breaking.'' What should, in effect, be broken in the reader's mind is the illusion that s/he has been reading an English text; the narrative reveals itself to be a masquerade, and the unevenness that is palpable in the passages of dialogue between the Caco women (between those who have stayed in Haiti and those who have emigrated) can be seen as evidence that the text is in fact a creole one.

Danticat's Atie becomes the translator of the camouflaged text, a translator to rival the Dahomean god Eshu, the trickster figure who has become the focus of some phallocentric, Afrocentric criticism, such as in Henry Louis Gates' *The Signifying Monkey*. Like the poeticized women of Dahomey in Audre Lorde's poetry collection, *The Black Unicorn,* Atie embodies a marginalized ancient African *woman-identified* culture in which ''[b]earing two drums on my head I speak/whatever language is needed/to sharpen the knives of my tongue.'' Atie's language is one of covert resistance as she appropriates the French language through creole translations when she learns to read and write and as she appropriates the image of the *marassa* to constitute her own Haitian female identity.

As she becomes literate, Atie creates a new language in order to write down her thoughts in her notebook; Louise ''calls them poems.'' At times, Atie reads to the family from her notebook; one of her most significant creations is an adaptation of a French poem, which remains unidentified in the novel, given to her by Louise. Her poem serves a dual function—one can assume, first, that it is in creole, and secondly, it tells the same story as that of the young husband who kills his young bride because he wants to prove her virginity, or purity, to the community. The important difference, of course, is that the story is now told in Atie's voice:

> She speaks in silent voices, my love. Like the cardinal bird, kissing its own image. *Li palé vwa mwin,* Flapping wings, fallen change Broken bottles, whistling snakes And boom bang drums. She speaks in silent voices, my love. I drink her blood with milk And when the pleasure peaks, my love leaves.

The line Danticat leaves untranslated suggests the interconnectedness of like spirits: she speaks my voice, thus, she is my voice. And since Atie's tongue is creole, it can never be entirely translated, nor does her love attempt that transmutation. The last two lines of the poem echo the traditional tale except that Atie has taken the place of the male hero; she occupies his position but is not male-identified.

This latter distinction leads us to the key element of Atie and Louise's relationship: the partings that figure so prominently in the text are metaphors for the non-acceptance of their union in their community, which denies that women can choose one another as their primary sources of emotional and erotic support. This societal rejection is verbalized by Atie's mother, Ifé, who continuously opposes the relationship, saying "Louise causes trouble" and "the gods will punish me for Atie's ways." But Atie defies her mother and the community: "After her reading, she and Louise strolled into the night, like silhouettes on a picture postcard" (135). And after Louise hears that one of her fellow market workers has been killed, Danticat chooses to reveal the women's closeness in an overtly erotic image: "Their faces were so close that their lips could meet if they both turned at the same time." Their lips "could meet" but do not; what keeps the women from "turning" at the same time is the overt misogyny of Haitian society that Danticat exposes in the shattering of Martine (Sophie's mother) and Sophie's own life; their lives are kept out of view, and silenced. The many departures that occur in the novel symbolize, like the last line of Atie's poem, these women's stifled desires. Their partings culminate in Louise's emigration to the United States; she leaves without saying goodbye to Atie, an event that surprises Sophie. Atie, however, speaks the same language as Louise: there is no need for the articulation of goodbyes, for she knows already the loss she is about to experience: "I will miss her like my own second skin." For Atie and Louise, options are few. They are denied all but each other, but cannot live for and with each other in Haitian society and expect to survive the consequences of that transgressive choice.

In the end, Nadine Magloire's *Le mal de vivre* and Edwidge Danticat's *Breath, Eyes, Memory* resist the romanticization of the Caribbean, and of Haiti specifically, as a culture within which the infinite play of meaning, of subjectivity, can be achieved through the recognition of cultural creolization and/or *métissage.* Magloire reveals the novel genre as inadequate for the textual representation of Haitian women's lives at the same time that she convincingly represents the social and psychological mores that prevent her protagonist from being able to express her own identity. Claudine occupies a position at the crossroads of cultures but is not enabled by that positionality; hybridity, then, can only become a useful force if it is used in the service of disrupting rather than maintaining social and class privilege. Magloire's novel reveals that Claudine's inability to survive is ultimately a function of her being a woman in Haiti; as a woman, she is denied most privileges, and it is for this reason that she clings so fiercely to those privileges that class alone can provide. Similarly, Danticat's Sophie is caught between her memories of happiness in Haiti among women immobilized by their illiteracy and her exile to the alienating U.S. landscape, which will alleviate the oppressions that attend female existence in Haiti. Danticat's use of *andaki* strategies of doubling within the novel form also underscores the need to reformulate the traditional Caribbean novel genre. It is up to us, as readers, to realize that both Magloire's and Danticat's heroines lose "le goût de vivre" because Haitian/North American culture has relegated them to the margins of a text they cannot forcibly rewrite. In that resounding silence, in the absence of textual representations of identity that reflect a vision of hope, we should hear the "cri du coeur [cry of the heart]" of all Haitian women whose bodies are subject to endless commodification in art, in literature, in everyday domestic life. If we fail to do so, then perhaps not even their shapes upon the sea shores will be left behind; their magic will remain as yet unwritten.

Source: Myriam J. A. Chancy, "Lespoua fe viv: Female Identity and the Politics of Textual Sexuality in Nadine Magloire's Le Mal de Vivre and Edwidge Danticat's Breath, Eyes, Memory," in *Framing Silence: Revolutionary Novels by Haitian Women,* Rutgers University Press, 1997, pp. 120–33.

Mary Mackay

In this brief review of Edwidge Danticat's Breath, Eyes, Memory, *Mary Mackay outlines the pain and struggle of the women in the novel, and describes it as a compelling record of the Haiti that Danticat wishes to be remembered, "a rich landscape of memory."*

Edwidge Danticat dedicates her powerful first novel to "The brave women of Haiti . . . on this shore and other shores. We have stumbled but we will not fall." Such optimism is extraordinary, given the everyday adversity faced by the women whose stories are interwoven with that of Sophie, the narrator.

Grandmother Ife, mother Martine, aunt Atie, and daughter Sophie (and later Sophie's daughter, Brigitte) are rooted as firmly in their native Haitian soil as they are bound to one another, despite the ocean, experiences, and years that separate them. The ties to Haiti, the women's certainty of meeting there at the "very end of each of our journeys," affords their only apparent security. "Somehow, early on, our song makers and tale weavers had decided that we were all daughters of this land," Danticat writes. Structurally, the book reflects the centrality of Haiti: the longest of its four sections takes place there, although covering only a few days in a novel that covers years.

The story begins in Haiti. Through Sophie's 12-year-old eyes, the island seems a paradise of bougainvillea, poincianas, and the unconditional love of Tante Atie. Then Martine, the mother Sophie knew only as a photograph, sends for her from New York City. It seems a mean place that has worn out her mother: "It was as though she had never stopped working in the cane fields after all." Sophie is haunted by the hardships of immigrant life, together with the ghosts from the past and the burdens of womanhood in a hostile world. She describes herself as a frightened insomniac, but somehow survives the test. Her older, jazz-musician husband, Joseph, one of the novel's few male characters and certainly the most loyal and gentle, gives her some strength. She copes through a resilient melange of love, ties to home, and therapy. And when she returns to Haiti as an adult, she senses a sinister edge to the place, represented by the Tonton Macoutes (militiamen), the boat people, and her Tante Atie's bitterness.

"There is always a place where nightmares are passed on through generations like heirlooms," writes Danticat. In this book, one of those places is "testing," part of a "virginity cult, our mothers' obsession with keeping us pure and chaste," in which the mother probes her daughter's vagina (sometime violently) to see if she is still whole. She also listens to her daughter peeing to see if the sound suggests a deflowered, widened passage. Even rape has one positive result: the end of "testing" by an otherwise trusted mother. The invasiveness, pain, and humiliation turn daughter against mother generation after generation, Atie against Ife, Sophie against Martine.

But there is reconciliation, too. As mothers and daughters, the women are bound in love as in hate. A mother may inflict on her daughter the same pain that drove her from her own mother. Why? "I did it because my mother had done it to me. I have no greater excuse." The book is a plea to end these divisive rituals. Mothers indeed long to break the cycle of pain, asking pointedly from beyond the grave, "'Ou libere?' Are you free, my daughter?"

Suffering inflicted by a well-intentioned mother is all the more treacherous in a world where the birth of a girl child is marked by "no lamps, no candles, no more light." Danticat leaves the reader with no illusions as to why the welcome is so dark. As well as "testing," the women in this family endure rape, unwanted pregnancy, and violence that lead to mental illness, nightmares, sexual phobias, bulimia, and self-mutilation. Breast cancer seems almost benign in this context; being unmarried and childless does not.

Sophie wants and seems to be the hope for breaking with painful tradition. Returning to Haiti with her mother's body for burial, she reaches an important understanding: the testing was painful for Martine, too. Doing what she had to do as a Haitian woman, "My mother was as brave as stars at dawn." Sophie breaks free as she madly attacks the sugar cane in the midst of which her father had raped and impregnated her mother. We sense that Sophie—and Brigitte—are finally safe.

Despite all the suffering ("'Can one really die of chagrin?' I asked Tante Atie."), Danticat writes with a light and lyrical touch. Her characterization is vivid, her allusive language richly unembellished. Color (literal as well as linguistic) carries the reader from the daffodil yellow associated with Haiti and Sophie's early days in New York, to the more ominous red with which her mother surrounds herself in interior decoration as in death. Occasionally Danticat devotes too many details to a banal incident or action, but this is a minor criticism for a first novel.

In a personal essay, Danticat calls Haiti a "rich landscape of memory." But she is afraid that female storytellers like herself may be Haiti's last surviving breath, eyes, and memory. In this compelling novel, the reader experiences the Haiti that Danticat fears will be lost.

Source: Mary Mackay, *"Breath, Eyes, Memory," (book review) in Belles Lettres,* Vol. 10, No. 1, Fall, 1994, p. 36.

Mary Mackay

The following brief review describes Danticat's Breath, Eyes, Memory *as a graceful first novel outlining the coming-of-age story of Sophie, the novel's protagonist and narrator, in a world where traditions clash and the beauty of Haiti is inexorably mixed with the burden of sexual trauma, mental brutality, and political terror.*

A distinctive new voice with a sensitive insight into Haitian culture distinguishes this graceful debut novel about a young girl's coming-of-age under difficult circumstances. "I come from a place where breath, eyes and memory are one, a place where you carry your past like the hair on your head," says narrator Sophie Caco, ruminating on the chains of duty and love that bind the courageous women in her family. The burden of being a woman in Haiti, where purity and chastity are a matter of family honor, and where "nightmares are passed on through generations like heirlooms," is Danticat's theme. Born after her mother Martine was raped, Sophie is raised by her Tante Atie in a small town in Haiti. At 12 she joins Martine in New York, while Atie returns to her native village to care for indomitable Grandmother Ife. Neither Sophie nor Martine can escape the weight of the past, resulting in a pattern of insomnia, bulimia, sexual trauma and mental anguish that afflicts both of them and leads inexorably to tragedy. Though her tale is permeated with a haunting sadness, Danticat also imbues it with color and magic, beautifully evoking the pace and character of Creole life, the feel of both village and farm communities, where the omnipresent Tontons Macoute mean daily terror, where voudon rituals and superstitions still dominate even as illiterate inhabitants utilize such 20th-century conveniences as cassettes to correspond with emigres in America. In simple, lyrical prose enriched by an elegiac tone and piquant observations, she makes Sophie's confusion and guilt, her difficult assimilation into American culture and her eventual emotional liberation palpably clear.

> As mothers and daughters, the women are bound in love as in hate. A mother may inflict on her daughter the same pain that drove her from her own mother. Why? 'I did it because my mother had done it to me. I have no greater excuse.'"

Source: Mary MacKay, "Breath, Eyes, Memory," (book review) in *Publisher's Weekly,* Vol. 241, No. 4, January 24, 1994, p. 39.

Sources

Charters, Mallay, "Edwidge Danticat: A Bitter Legacy Revisited," in *Publishers Weekly,* August 17, 1998, p. 42.

Gladstone, Jim, review of *Breath, Eyes, Memory* , in *New York Times Book Review*, July 10, 1994, p. 24.

Philpott, Joan, review of *Breath, Eyes, Memory* , in *Ms.,* March/April, 1994, pp. 77-78.

Shea, Renee H., "An Interview between Edwidge Danticat and Renee H. Shea," in *Belles Lettres,* Summer, 1995, pp. 12-15.

Wilson, Calvin, "Edwidge Danticat's Prose Floats in Realm of Sadness and Eloquence," in *Kansas City Star* , September 22, 1999, p. K0779.

Further Reading

Acosta, Belinda, "The Farming of Bones," in *Austin Chronicle*, January 19, 1999.
    This discussion of Danticat's later book also has comments about her writing in general.

Gardiner, Beth, "Writer's Work Evokes Experience of Haitian Regime, Emigration," in *Standard-Times*, April 12, 1998.
    Explores Danticat's experiences in Haiti and how they fuel her fiction.

Maryles, Daisy, "Oprah's Newest Pick," in *Publishers Weekly*, May 25, 1998, p. 20.

A brief article discussing the commercial success of *Breath, Eyes, Memory* following its selection for Oprah Winfrey's book club.

Rooney, Megan, ''Danticat MFA '94 Reads from *The Farming of Bones*, in *Brown Daily Herald*, October 5, 1998. Discussion of Danticat's more recent work, but also includes her reflections on writing and the immigrant experience.

Business

Victor Hernández Cruz
1973

"Business" is the third poem of a suite of five poems in Victor Hernández Cruz's 1973 collection, *Mainland*. Other poems in the suite include "Atmosphere," "Memory," "Love," and "Music." Like the other poems, "Business" relays the sayings of Don Arturo, a wise man who offers parables and cryptic "messages" on universal topics, although unlike the other poems, "Business" is longer, consisting of 34 short, clipped lines of free verse. The poem tells the story of a street vendor and musician who sold puppets and played guitar and was regularly arrested for doing so. Don Arturo relates how detectives and clerks loved the puppet show the man put on during his court appearance and bought puppets and whistles from him. When the judge responds to the detectives' and clerks' enthusiasm for the "criminal's" entertainment with indignance, the musician says that his business is "monkey business." Cruz tells a similar story about Don Arturo, apparently a real person and friend, in his essay "Don Arturo: A Story of Migration."

The subject of the poem is business, and its central theme the conflict between institutionalized ideas of business, as represented by the state, and personal ideas of business, as represented by the musician. Cruz suggests that institutionalized notions of business are impersonal, humorless, and destructive, whereas business rooted in human connection and contact is emotionally satisfying and life-affirming. The fact that the police and clerks fell in love with the musician's puppet show also

suggests that institutionalized business, regulated by licenses, taxes, and the like, is out of step with what most people want and need. Cruz represents the musician as a trickster figure who manages to usurp authority by understanding human beings' desire to be free. The parable-like quality of the anecdote and the fact that it is related in a straightforward and simple manner by someone who speaks from a position of authority not rooted in the state give this poem universal appeal. It is a poem about the triumph of the little guy.

Author Biography

Born in the barrio El Guanabano in the town of Aguas Buenas, Puerto Rico, in 1949 to Severo and Rosa Cruz, Victor Hernández Cruz and his family moved to Spanish Harlem in New York City in 1954. This part of the city teemed with immigrants from Latin America and the Caribbean, and Cruz was surrounded with new sights, smells, and sounds, some familiar and some strange. Learning English along with a new culture was both a challenge and a reward for the young Cruz, who made the intersections between his new home and his old the material for much of his writing. Although he dropped out of high school during his senior year, Cruz became a voracious reader and writer as a teenager, self-publishing his first book when he was only seventeen years old.

The 1960s were exciting times for emerging writers. Small presses sprung up everywhere and increasingly paid more attention to publishing the works of those from underrepresented and neglected populations. Along with writers such as Piri Thomas, a novelist, Cruz developed a reputation as a leading "Nuyorican" writer (the "Nuyo" stands for New York, and "rican" for Puerto Rican). Much of Cruz's poetry addresses life on the streets and the difficulty of negotiating one's ethnic identity and cultural heritage in an often hostile country. Like those he writes about, Cruz is a survivor. Although he writes in English, Cruz often leavens his poetry and prose with Spanish. Critics sometimes refer to this hybrid language as "Spanglish." Like Cruz, many Puerto Ricans are of Indian (Taino) and African descent as well, and Cruz's writing appears frequently in African-American literature anthologies. He often refers to himself as Afro-Latin.

An essayist, novelist, and editor as well as a poet, Cruz remains one of the most prolific and visible spokesmen for minority literature in the United States. His works include *Papa Got His Gun and Other Poems* (1966), *Snaps* (1969), *Mainland* (1973), *Tropicalization* (1976), *By Lingual Wholes* (1982), *Rhythm, Content [and] Flavor* (1989), *Red Beans* (1991), and *Panoramas* (1997), all poetry or poetry and prose collections. Cruz has also published two novels: *Down These Mean Streets* in 1967, and *Savior, Savior Hold My Hand* in 1972. His short-story collection *Low Writings* came out in 1980. Cruz has taught at a number of high schools and universities and frequently gives public readings of his work. He has also successfully participated in poetry "slams," a public event in which poets compete both individually and in teams against one another.

Plot Summary

Lines 1-5

The poem's title, "Business," like the titles of the four other poems included in the suite with "Business," alerts readers that the poem will address a universal subject. The other poems, "Atmosphere," "Love," "Music," and "Memory," are all about figuratively explaining the meaning of their titles. All of the titles are abstract nouns, that is, they are ideas more than images. As with the other poems, "Business" begins by attributing what is said to Don Arturo, a persona Cruz uses to evoke the sense of folk wisdom. The term "persona" derives from the Latin term *dramatis personae* and literally means the mask worn by actors in classical theater. Today persona usually refers to the character that the "I" in a lyrical or narrative poem takes on. Cruz's poem, however, is reported, rather than direct, speech. "Don" means sir, and is a title formerly attached to the last name of a Spaniard of high rank. By beginning his story with the words "There was a man," Arturo signals that the anecdote belongs to the realm of myth. The musician is as much entertainer as he is businessman, and readers are meant to sympathize with him. Although the poem does have a "folklorish" quality to it, it is important to know that Cruz bases the poem on an actual man named Don Arturo, a Cuban immigrant and friend of Cruz who lives in New York City.

Lines 6-15

By first showing the joy people experienced from the street musician's entertainment, and then saying that he was arrested "three times a week" for his work, Cruz underscores how the law can often work against the desires of ordinary people. Not only is the musician penalized for performing on the street, but so are the "huge crowds" who come to see him, as they are now deprived of his music and his toys. The Don Arturo on whom the poem is based used to play his guitar and sell his puppets outside of Gimbel's and Macy's in New York City, two of the largest department stores in two of the busiest parts of Manhattan. As with the character in the poem, Arturo was also arrested regularly.

Lines 16-25

Humor and irony are at work in this poem. Readers don't expect a man arrested for a petty crime to even have the opportunity to perform in court. His performance is funny for two reasons: first, because it involves a puppet show, something usually associated with children and, often, silliness; second, because he performs in a courtroom, a place conventionally associated with somber and dry activity. The detectives' and court clerks' response to the performance is also humorous, as they "rolled on the floor." It is ironic that these people bought puppets and whistles from the man because they are part of the very system that is prosecuting him for selling them. The detectives and court clerks are linked to the crowds that came to see the man perform in shopping areas in that they also belong to the working class. By buying puppets and responding to him the way they do the detectives and clerks show their allegiance to the values of the working class. They demonstrate that although they work for the state, they are not its puppets who blindly behave as they are directed.

Lines 25-34

The judge functions here as a symbol of institutional authority. His anger is the humorless anger of the state responding to something it does not condone nor understand. It is significant that the word "business," the poem's title, is uttered for the first time by the judge. When he asks "What kind of business is this[?]," he is using a rhetorical question, that is, a question which does not expect an answer and is more like a statement. The musician, symbolically representing the "little man," continues his irreverent behavior when he answers, "I am the monkey man / and the / Monkey man sells / Monkey business." These last lines provide the moral, or the message, of Don Arturo's story:

Victor Hernández Cruz

Government may work to keep the little man in his place but in time the little man will win out.

The idea of business in its various guises is suggested in a number of ways in the poem. On a concrete and practical level, the musician is engaged in business, playing his guitar and selling his puppets and whistles to make a living. This kind of business conflicts with the business of the state, which is to regulate trading activity. By breaking the law and actively disrespecting the authority of the state, the musician engages in "monkey business." The musician's attitude at the end of the poem is that what he does is nobody's business but his own.

Themes

Individualism

"Business" takes as its primary message the idea that individuals are more important and, in the long run, stronger than the state under which they live. Individualism, especially in the West, and in America in particular, forms the philosophical basis for modern democracies. The inalienable rights of the individual are codified in the Bill of Rights,

Topics for Further Study

- Interview at least five people, asking them about laws which they believe are unfair, then research the origins of those laws. Are the governmental reasons given for the laws' existence still valid today? Why or why not? How do the reasons of those you interviewed stack up against the government's explanation for the laws?

- Research the regulations for street vending and performing in your city or town and then write an essay speculating on how you think Cruz's vendor would be treated if he were to ply his business in your neighborhood.

- Interview a few recent immigrants to the United States, asking them about the role of street vending or performing in their countries. What differences do you see between their attitudes towards vending/performing and the attitudes of people in this country?

- Spend a day at your local courthouse observing trials and proceedings, then write a description of your observations. Pay attention to the behavior of those being charged with crimes. Write a descriptive essay of your experience.

- Compose an essay about an event in your life when you challenged institutional authority (school, the law, etc.), then craft a poem out of your essay. In what ways is the poem different from the essay?

- Read Cruz's essay "Don Arturo: A Story of Migration" included in his collections *By Lingual Wholes* and *Red Beans*. The last sentence of the essay reads, "The way he got here the story you have been told." What do these words say about the truth of the essay, and what does the essay say about the truth of his poem "Business"?

---

which is the first ten amendments to the Constitution of the United States. Such rights restrict government's interference in the lives of its citizens. "Business" draws on the long history of individualism in America, eliciting sympathy from readers for the plight of a simple street musician who has been denied his right to make a living. Cruz highlights the importance of the individual in the West in two ways: one, he makes the main character in the story a vendor and a musician, someone who both sells things for a living and artistically expresses himself through his music; two, he places the individual in opposition to the law, an institutional branch of government which often squashes the rights of individuals. The judge's angry question, "What kind of business / is this[?]," is rhetorical, and meant to suggest that the kind of business practiced by the musician is against the law. The vendor first violated the law (presumably) by selling his wares and performing on the street, and then showed his contempt for the law by doing the same thing in court and winning over the detectives and

court clerks. The judge symbolically represents not only the law but also the idea of collectivism, which puts the many ahead of the individual. The vendor's "monkey business" is the business of mischief, meant not only to disobey the law but to do it in such a way as to embarrass the law (represented by the judge) as much as possible. The embarrassment is meant to demonstrate that certain kinds of behavior may be illegal but not necessarily wrong, and that individuals are more important than abstract laws.

Law and Order

"Business" implicitly asks the question of how far the law should go in maintaining order in society. Cruz presents us with the dilemma of a person trying to make a living doing what he does best: singing, putting on puppet shows, and selling puppets and whistles. By all accounts the actions of this man are harmless. Indeed, he is giving pleasure to the many who watch him, as evidenced by the "huge crowds" he draws in shopping areas. He, like the crowds who stop to see him, is governed by the more elemental and emotional law of give and take. It is obvious that the public loves the musician. He not only draws "huge crowds" who give him money, but he also wins over the detectives and court clerks, who "rolled on the floor" in laughter after his puppet show. His arrest for accepting money from people is (presumably) because he is performing without a license. Rationales for licensing street performers include the need to maintain public order and the need to protect "legitimate" (i.e., licensed, tax-paying) businesses from competition. Public order, however, is often gained at the expense of joy and more basic human desires and needs. Regulation of street performers also acts in the best interest of those with money who can afford to open nightclubs and other venues where people pay substantially more money to see acts than they would tip performers such as Don Arturo's guitarist. In this way, order is maintained for the many at the expense of the few. The only way for those oppressed by the (unfair) laws of the society to succeed is to be mischievous, like the musician, who flouts the law by flaunting his puppets.

Style

Parable

"Business" is a humorous anecdote in the form of a parable. Anecdotes are short stories, often conversational, told about a particular event. The reported speech in "Business" — the poet's report of Don Arturo and Arturo's of the musician and judge—also underscores that conversational quality, as does the poem's use of nonliterary language.

Parables are short narratives told to make a point or to draw an analogy. The Bible is full of parables that Christ used to illustrate his teachings. In "Business" Cruz employs Don Arturo, a person of unknown origins, but someone Cruz implies holds high status in his community.

Symbolism

"Business" also employs symbolic imagery to point to a moral. Puppets are symbolic of the way the man himself is treated under the state, and highlight the idea that people who do not resist

being manipulated and treated like puppets become puppets. "Monkey man" and "monkey business" are also symbolic terms, meant to suggest the mischief the man embodies in court and the notion that mischief is a form of behavior necessary to avoid becoming a puppet of the state.

Symbols can be public or private. Public symbols, like those Cruz uses, are easy to interpret because they signify an idea or thing familiar to a given culture or society. For example, in the United States the bald eagle symbolizes patriotism and pride in America. Private symbols are much more difficult to interpret because poets imbue them with personal meaning sometimes not accessible to readers, especially readers unfamiliar with a writer's work or life.

Literary Heritage

Victor Hernández Cruz writes out of the Nuyorican (sometimes called Neorican or Nurican) tradition. Either born in the United States, or born in Puerto Rico and raised on the mainland, Nuyorican writers infuse their adopted English language with Spanish and Black English to craft poems and stories about their experience on the United States' mainland. Puerto Ricans have a mixture of Taino, Arawak, Spanish, and African blood. The Taino and Arawak are native peoples that Ponce de Leon largely annihilated before bringing in African slaves to work the Spaniards' sugar plantations.

Because the vast majority of Puerto Ricans who moved to the mainland after World War II in search of economic opportunity settled in New York City or northern New Jersey, their poems and stories often address urban subjects and the difficulties of negotiating a new culture. The implicit subject of much Nuyorican writing is identity, and the ways in which Puerto Ricans often struggle to develop or retain a coherent one in the face of the many linguistic and ethnic barriers of the mainland. Jesus Colon's collection of sketches and essays, *A Puerto Rican in New York* (1961), is one of the first postwar books by a Puerto Rican to examine closely the real-life obstacles and joys of a Puerto Rican living in New York. The 1960s and 1970s witnessed a flourishing of Nuyorican writing, with writers such as Piri Thomas and Cruz helping to bring the Puerto Rican experience to a wider readership.

Compare & Contrast

- **1972:** The first bilingual anthology of Puerto Rican poetry is published, *The Puerto Rican Poets,* beginning the second wave of Nuyorican literature. Cruz is among those included.

  1989: The Nuyorican Cafe in New York City opens, giving Puerto Rican writers, poets, and performers wider exposure.

- **1972:** Almost one-and-a-half million Puerto Ricans live in the United States, up from only 301,000 in 1950.

  1989: The number of Puerto Ricans living in the U.S. has grown to 2,300,000, with most of them living in New York City and northern New Jersey.

Historical Context

In "Don Arturo: A Story of Migration," an essay which originally appeared in Cruz's *By Lingual Wholes,* Cruz tells the story of Don Arturo, the character who relates the anecdote of the street musician in "Business." A musician himself and somewhat of a Don Juan, Arturo migrated to New York City in 1926 from Cuba. Cruz relates how Arturo seduced the wife of the minister who led the Christian band for which Arturo played guitar. Arturo traveled to the United States with the minister and band and played with them until the Great Depression hit, at which point Cruz writes that Arturo quit the band and became a street musician. In this essay it is clear that the street vendor and musician Don Arturo describes in "Business" is, in fact, himself. Cruz has taken language directly from the poem and used it in his story of Arturo. Compare the following paragraph to the poem:

> When the market crashed he [Arturo] became a street musician, taking a position outside Macy's and sometimes Gimbel's. He played many instruments at the same time, even putting a tambourine on his feet. He sang popular Latin-American songs and told jokes. Sometimes he got arrested and he put puppet shows on in the courtroom. The court clerks rolled on the floor.

When Cruz wrote this piece in 1981 he described Arturo as a 78-year-old bon vivant with few regrets in life. Arturo was still in New York City and full of the mischief he showed as the "Monkey man" in "Business." The Don Arturo of Cruz's essay offers witty observations about life and surviving under adverse circumstances just as the Don Arturo of Cruz's poems does.

Although Arturo migrated to the States in the '20s, the wave of Puerto Rican migration came much later, in the '50s and '60s. According to data from the U.S. Department of Commerce, the number of Puerto Ricans in the United States almost quintupled from 1950 to 1970. In 1950, 301,000 Puerto Ricans lived in the states; in 1960, 890,000; by 1970, more than 1,400,000 lived in the states, the overwhelming majority of them in New York City. Today some 1,000,000 live in New York City, and 250,000 live in northern New Jersey. Out of this tremendous influx of Puerto Ricans to the mainland came the Nuyorican literary movement, of which Cruz was a leading figure. In their foreword to *The Puerto Rican Poets,* a seminal bilingual anthology of Nuyorican writing published in 1971, editors Alfredo Matilla and Iván Siláen write that "Puerto Rican poetry of the twentieth century, in Puerto Rico as well as New York, with a few exceptions, is a struggle against the agony of the ghetto (in the colony and the metropolis) and against the imposition of a crushing colonial state of mind." It is this drive for independence and freedom from the petty laws and crushing poverty so prevalent in city life that the musician in "Business" embodies. Cruz writes that "Don Arturo was an expert at survival."

Coming from a culture which values storytelling, many Nuyorican poets such as Cruz also became known for their high-powered readings. Cruz, in fact, is helped by his theater background, having written for and performed with various groups through the years, including the East Harlem Gut Theatre, a Puerto Rican collective of actors, musicians, and writers Cruz helped to found. In 1989 Nuyorican poet Miguel Algarin founded the Nuyorican Cafe in New York City, giving Nuyorican writers and performers a venue for their art. In 1998, poets from the Nuyorican Cafe won the Annual National Slam Poetry Tournament, a competition in which poets from various cities compete against each other by performing their poems and being evaluated by a panel of judges. Cruz himself occasionally performs at these events.

can poet. He is young, together, and his work is heavy pagan feet crushing the necks of the Imperial dead.'' Ginsberg's praise, like his poetry, is almost hallucinatory: ''Poesy news front space anxiety police age inner city, spontaneous urban American language as Williams wished, high school street consciousness transparent, original soul looking out intelligent Bronx windows.'' Ginsberg's reference is to William Carlos Williams, the influential twentieth-century American poet who encouraged poets to discover the American idiom in their own neighborhoods.

Critical Overview

''Business'' is a small poem, both in length and in ambition. Accordingly, critics have not paid much attention to it. However, they have reviewed *Mainland*, the collection in which it appeared. Writing for the *Dictionary of Literary Biography*, Pamela Masingale Lewis notes that ''reviewers of *Mainland* were pleased to see themes which departed from the New York experience. They marveled at the presence of multiple cultures in Cruz's poetry. One critic noted that the *Mainland voice is ''more developed'' and less self-conscious than that of Snaps* [Cruz's previous collection], but felt the abstractions were inappropriate for the sensuous imagery. On the whole, *Mainland* was lauded by critics for its diverse themes and the ease with which Cruz exposes the underside of mainland U.S.A. Reviewing *Mainland* for *Library Journal*, Dorothy Nyren writes that Cruz's ''juxtaposition and intermingling of Latin and Anglo ways of seeing things gives an inner tension to the verse that makes it continually surprising and interesting.'' Laverne González, writing in the *Biographical Dictionary of Hispanic Literature in the United States*, agrees, saying that for Cruz, ''Memory of the island experience invades and informs the mainland experience as images, languages, and allusions mingle with the reality of the Bronx, the United States, particularly California, and finally Puerto Rico again.''

Allen Ginsberg and Ishmael Reed, two poets known for their experiments with poetic form and controversial content, were effusive in their praise of *Mainland*. On the book's dust jacket, Reed writes, ''Victor Hernández Cruz is an original Ameri-

Criticism

Chris Semansky

A widely published poet, fiction writer, and critic, Semansky teaches literature and writing at Portland Community College. In the following essay Semansky examines Cruz's poem ''Business'' in relation to the other poems which accompany it and in relation to the poem's speaker, Don Arturo.

Victor Hernández Cruz's poem ''Business'' is the third poem in a suite of poems in his collection entitled *Mainland*. The other poems in the suite are ''Atmosphere,'' ''Love,'' ''Memory,'' and ''Music.'' All of these poems are both descriptive *and* didactic, that is, they both portray and instruct. This makes sense for a book which takes as its theme life in the United States from the perspective of someone who was born on the small island of Puerto Rico. As a group, then, these poems can be seen as a primer meant to educate readers on what to keep and think about when making the move to the mainland. As a poem, ''Business'' includes within it ideas and themes addressed in the other suite poems. An examination of these poems first will provide the groundwork for an analysis of ''Business.''

Before looking at the poems, however, it is necessary to consider the poems' speakers, for these are poems within poems. Cruz as the poet ''reports'' the words of a man named Don Arturo. Each poem begins ''Don Arturo says''; Don Arturo is both a ''type'' of person and a real person, whom Cruz has written about before. As a type, he personifies the wise man who has lived a full and adventurous life and now dispenses advice about his experience so that others can learn from him. The real Don

What Do I Read Next?

- Turner, Faythe, ed., *Puerto Rican Writers at Home in the USA*, published in 1991, is an anthology of fiction, poetry, and nonfiction from Puerto Rican writers in the United States. Included in the anthology are writers who gained recognition in mid-century such as Piri Thomas and Miguel Piñero, as well as later writers like Cruz.

- Ray Gonzalez's anthology *Currents from the Dancing River: Contemporary Latino Fiction, Nonfiction, and Poetry* collects writing from all Spanish-speaking people of the United States, both immigrants and native-born.

- Cruz's 1997 book *Panoramas* contains many autobiographical essays as well as a hearty dose of his poetry.

- Cruz's essay on Don Arturo, the man who relates the story of the street vendor in "Business," was originally published in his *By Lingual Wholes* in 1982 and reprinted in his 1991 collection of poetry and prose, *Red Beans*. In "Don Arturo: A Story of Migration," Cruz recounts incidents from the life of a now-elderly Cuban man who immigrated to New City in 1926. This essay is indispensable for understanding "Business."

Arturo, the one about whom Cruz has written, is an elderly Cuban émigré with whom Cruz shares wine while listening to his adventures and pronouncements. In "Don Arturo: A Story of Migration," which appears in Cruz's collection *Red Beans*, Cruz describes Arturo in 1981: "Now 78, he still cultivates his famous corner in the Village [i.e., Greenwich Village in New York City, a famous bohemian neighborhood] come spring and summer. He savors memory like espresso coffee. He calls up his beautiful moments with women like an encyclopedia, though his memory sometimes scatters. The details he gives shine like light bulbs and make bridges with each other."

That the poems all begin "Don Arturo says" is significant because these poems carry the power of speech, of being passed down orally. Such a means of cultural transmission tells us that these poems circulate in a close-knit community which has a strong sense of cultural identity. All of them also espouse individualism and the idea that one must live in the present and the present must be seized. They suggest that passion is a greater good than reason, which can often squelch human capacity for joy. There are certain things about living on the mainland that one needs to understand in order to survive. In both "Atmosphere" and "Memory"

Don Arturo tells readers "You have to know." What is it, however, that readers must know? Here is "Atmosphere":

> Don Arturo says: You have to know what the atmosphere is creating You have to know Because if it's good You can go somewhere and make your own.

This small poem underscores the importance of self-awareness, and how the environment contributes to what one feels. It also highlights the capacity that human beings have to make their own way in the world, to create an atmosphere they can live in. Don Arturo's advice on "Memory" also points to the importance of self-awareness, this time in relation to words.

> Don Arturo says: You have to know what you once said / Because it could travel in the air for years / And return in different clothes / And then you have to buy it.

The message here? Choose your words carefully because they could come back to bite you. Much of what Don Arturo offers in the way of advice is standard fare; that is, most of us, whether we are from Puerto Rico, Missouri, or China have heard this kind of advice in some form or another. What makes these poems different is precisely their form. Although the two poems above are straightforward and relatively easy to "decode," his poems on love and music are not. In "Love," for example, Cruz uses surrealist imagery to describe how the emotion can sometimes cripple our ability to think clearly.

> Don Arturo says: If you put your hands in all the time / Some day it will fly away with your mind.

Consistent with his advice to be self-aware, ''Love'' both warns of the danger of falling in love (too often) while also (seemingly) celebrating the euphoria of such an emotion. ''Music'' is similarly contradictory in its message:

> Don Arturo says: There's supposed to be more sauce than fish / It suppose to be like riding on a horse or stepping out of the room / Without a single motion.

Readers are told what music *should* be like, suggesting that they *might* be experiencing it differently. Music, according to the speaker, should be an almost out-of-body experience, where the dancer and the dance become one. Rather than leading to an unawareness of one's environment, something that Arturo cautioned against in ''Atmosphere,'' such mind-body unity allows the dancer to live fully in the present, in harmony with the surroundings. Music plays an integral role in Puerto Rican culture and in Cruz's poetry in general. It is no surprise that the central character in the longest Don Arturo poem, ''Business,'' is a busker. He makes his living selling puppets and whistles and playing his guitar on the city streets. Unfortunately, the law does not condone the entertainer's business, arresting him regularly for what readers can only assume would be not having a license. In court, the same detectives who arrested him were won over by the man's performance and bought toys from him. When this happened

> The judge got angry and yelled: What kind of business is this / And the man said I am the monkey man and the / Monkey man sells Monkey business.

The ''monkey man'' responds as he does because he is appalled by the atmosphere in which he finds himself and so, as Arturo advises, he creates his own. The law in this case hampers the man from enjoying his life and from giving joy to others. ''Monkey'' is used both symbolically and ironically here. Monkeys are mischievous animals, and ''monkey business'' suggests that the man does what comes naturally to him, as a monkey. But mischief is closely aligned to play, to a sense of living in the moment unencumbered by the petty requirements of governmental bureaucracy. Symbolically monkeys signify a prior unconscious part of humanity and are often linked to sorcerers and magic in folklore. The magic of this monkey man is his capacity to seduce others with his music and his

> " Symbolically monkeys signify a prior unconscious part of humanity and are often linked to sorcerers and magic in folklore. The magic of this monkey man is his capacity to seduce others with his music and his puppets, to make them forget about their surroundings and to experience the joy of music and play."

puppets, to make them forget about their surroundings and to experience the joy of music and play. The phrase can also be read as ironic. That is, the musician doesn't really think of himself as a monkey man, but he is merely continuing to flout the law by responding to the judge in this (disrespectful) manner. The ambiguity of this poem's ending points to the lesson that Don Arturo wants readers to understand: be alive to the possibilities of the moment, and don't be beaten down by the system.

The business of ''Business,'' then, is the work of the individual to stay alive in the world, a world often hostile to one's existence. It isn't mere physical survival that Don Arturo wants to teach readers about but emotional survival as well: the capacity to do what one loves best and to make a living at it, regardless of obstacles. The real Don Arturo, Cruz tells us, is also a survivor. After ingratiating himself to a minister and winning a place as a guitarist in the minister's band, Arturo seduced the minister's wife. Then, after tiring of the band, he became a street musician and vendor, selling toys and putting on puppet shows. The ''monkey man'' that Arturo describes in his story is Arturo himself. Cruz has fashioned a set of poems out of his experience with the actual Don Arturo; in this way, his poem can be seen as belonging to the genre of creative nonfiction, a label usually assigned to lyrical prose. This ingenious way of making poetry shows that Cruz, as a poet and storyteller, is also a survivor, refashioning the raw material of his own experience into both entertaining and meaningful forms.

Source: Chris Semansky, in an essay for *Literature of Developing Nations for Students*, Gale, 2000.

Sources

Babáin, Maria Teresa, and Stan Steiner, eds., *Borinquen*, Knopf, 1974.

Cruz, Victor Hernández, *Mainland*, Random House, 1973.

———, *Red Beans*, Coffee House Press, 1991.

———, *Rhythm, Content & Flavor*, Arte Publico Press, 1989.

Gonzalez, Ray, *Currents from the Dancing River: Contemporary Latino Fiction, Nonfiction, and Poetry*, Harcourt Brace & Co., 1994.

Marzán, Julio, *Inventing a Word*, Columbia University Press, 1980.

Masingale Lewis, Pamela, *Dictionary of Literary Biography: Afro-American Poets since 1955*, edited by Trudier Harris and Thadious M. Davis, Vol. 41, Gale, 1985, pp. 74-84.

Nyren, Dorothy, review of *Mainland*, in *Library Journal*, February, 1973, p. 549.

Turner, Faythe, ed., *Puerto Rican Writers at Home in the USA*, Open Hand Publishing, 1991.

Further Reading

Cruz, Victor Hernández, Leroy Quintana, and Virgil Suárez, eds., *Paper Dance: 55 Latino Poets*, Persea Books, 2000.
    Presenting the work of both well-known and lesser-known Latino and Latina poets living in the United States, this anthology explores relationships between tradition and change, Spanish and English, rural and urban, private and public, female and male, and young and old.

Jones, LeRoi, and Larry Neal, eds., *Black Fire: An Anthology of Afro-American Writing*, William Morrow, 1968.
    As a poet with African as well as Spanish and Indian blood, Cruz's writing frequently appears in anthologies of African-American literature. *Black Fire* is one of the first such anthologies to publish Cruz and provides a strong sampling of African-American writers whose reputations would grow in the coming decades.

Matilla, Alfredo, and Iván Siláen, eds., *The Puerto Rican Poets*, Bantam Books, 1972.
    Matilla and Siláen put together the first bilingual anthology of Puerto Rican poetry that spans the twentieth century. This anthology contains many names not included in subsequent anthologies of Puerto Rican literature.

Dream on Monkey Mountain

Derek Walcott

1967

Though St. Lucia native Derek Walcott is primarily recognized as a Nobel Prize-winning poet, he has also written numerous plays for the Trinidad Theater Workshop, including *Dream on Monkey Mountain*. It is Walcott's best known and most performed play. *Dream on Monkey Mountain* was first performed on August 12, 1967, at the Central Library Theatre in Toronto, Canada. After at least one production in the United States, the play made its New York City debut on March 14, 1971, at St. Mark's Playhouse. This production garnered Walcott an Obie Award. Regularly performed since its inception, *Dream on Monkey Mountain* is a complex allegory which, at its heart, concerns racial identity. Makak, the central character of the play, lives alone on Monkey Mountain. He has not seen his own image in thirty years and ends up in jail after drunkenly destroying a café. Much of the play consists of his dream in which he discovers his self-worth as a black man. Critics are divided over many aspects of *Dream on Monkey Mountain*, including the effectiveness of its poetic language. Reviewing a 1970 production of the play in Los Angeles, W. I. Scobie of *National Review* wrote, "In Walcott's dense, poetic text and in the visual images onstage there is a brilliantly successful marriage of classical tradition and African mimetic-dance elements, two strains that are bound as one into the author's British colonial childhood. And in the myth of Makak, an ultimately universal figure, there is achieved some

resolution of the conflict between black roots and white culture. This is a superb play.''

Author Biography

Derek Walcott was born on January 23, 1930, in Castries, St. Lucia, the West Indies. He and his twin brother, Roderick, were the sons of Warwick and Alix Walcott. Warwick Walcott, a painter, poet, and civil servant, died when the twins were one year old. The boys and their elder sister were raised by their mother, a teacher who also supported her family by working as a seamstress. In this middle-class Protestant family, literature and artistry were emphasized.

Like his father, Walcott wanted to become a painter. While he painted his whole life, Walcott's primary focus became words, in English, instead of images while a teenager. Attending St. Mary's College on St. Lucia, Walcott became a poet. Before entering the university, he self-published his first book of poetry at the age of eighteen, entitled *25 Poems*. He borrowed the money to publish it from his mother, and made the money back by selling it himself.

In 1949, Walcott entered the University of the West Indies on Trinidad, from which he graduated in 1953 with a B.A. Even before graduation, Walcott began a teaching career, which he has continued to pursue on the secondary and university levels. While still a student, Walcott also began writing plays. His first was *Henri Christophe* (1951). In both his poetry and plays, Walcott often deals with the racial complexities of the West Indian islands and his own racial heritage. His two grandfathers were white, while both of his grandmothers were black and descendants of slaves.

Walcott's first successful play was *The Sea at Dauphin* (1954). This contributed in part to Walcott obtaining a Rockefeller Fellowship to study playwriting and directing in New York City from 1957 to 1958. Upon his return home to Trinidad, in 1959, Walcott founded the Trinidad Theater Workshop, which provided a forum for his plays. For the workshop, Walcott wrote his best-known play, *Dream on Monkey Mountain* (1967). Other significant titles of his include *The Joker of Seville* (1974) and *O Babylon!* (1976).

While Walcott continued to write plays, over the years he became better known for his poetry. His breakthrough collection was 1962's *In a Green Night: Poems, 1948-1960*, while another important volume was *The Castaway and Other Poems* (1965). In 1990, Walcott published his poetic masterpiece, *Omerus*, a 325-page epic poem which gives a Caribbean twist to Homer's *Iliad* and *Odyssey*. In 1992, Walcott won the Nobel Prize in Literature for his poetry, one of many honors he has received over his career.

Beginning in the early 1980s, Walcott split his time between teaching literature and creative writing at Boston-area universities and in Trinidad. Though the 1990s, Walcott continued to teach and write (including 1997's collection of poetry *The Bounty* and *The Capeman: The Musical* with Paul Simon). He also reestablished his work with the Trinidad Theater Workshop after a decade-long hiatus. Married three times, Walcott has a son and two daughters.

Plot Summary

Prologue

Dream on Monkey Mountain opens in a small jail on an unnamed West Indian island. Corporal Lestrade, a mulatto official, brings in Makak, an older black man. Makak has just been arrested for being drunk and smashing a local café while claiming he was the King of Africa. Two other black prisoners already in cells, Tigre and Souris, try to undermine the corporal as he does his duty. The corporal grows frustrated and compares them to animals.

The corporal asks Makak for basic information, but the prisoner only wants to go home. Makak does reveal that he lives on Monkey Mountain and he is ''Catholique,'' though he does not remember his real name. Next is a trial, where Tigre and Souris don judge's robes and the corporal defends Makak. The corporal presents the facts of the case to the judges. He reveals that Makak claims to have had a dream in which he was told he was a descendant of African kings. Makak was inciting people when he was arrested. Makak asks to be released because he is old. After telling them he has not looked at his reflection for thirty years, Makak relates a dream in which a white woman came to him. He claims to see her at that moment in the prison, but no one else does. Makak believes she gives him strength.

Scene One

The play shifts back to the time before Makak was arrested, though it is part of his dream. In Makak's hut on Monkey Mountain, he lies on the floor. He is found by his business partner and friend, Moustique, a small black man with a deformed foot. Moustique rouses him so they can go to the market and sell their coal. Makak does not want to go. He relates the experience he had the night before. A white woman appeared to him, singing. She knew all about him and wanted to come home with him. When they returned to his hut, she told Makak that he should not live there anymore, believing he was ugly, because he comes from a royal lineage.

Moustique grows frustrated by Makak's insistence that his experience was real. He asks where the woman is now, but Makak does not know. After Makak leaves to get the coal so they can go to the market, Moustique is shaken when he unexpectedly encounters a mother spider with an egg sack. He kills it, but both men believe this is a sign of Moustique's impending death. Moustique finds a white mask under a bench. Makak says that he has not seen it before. He orders Moustique to ready things for their journey to Africa. Moustique is now convinced Makak is crazy, but follows him down the mountain.

Scene Two

Moustique comes upon the family of a sick man. Sisters pray around him hoping to make him well. Moustique joins them in prayers, while asking them for bread. He learns that the sick man has a fever and his body will not break into a sweat. The sick man is basically given up for dead, and Basil, a local coffinmaker, lurks nearby. Moustique convinces them to let Makak help the sick man in exchange for bread.

Makak has everyone kneel around the sick one. He has a woman place a hot coal in his hand. As it sizzles, Makak prays over him. Nothing happens at first, which Moustique and Makak blame on those around the sick man. Still, the sick man's wife gives them food for their effort. Just as they are about to leave, the sick man begins to sweat and heal. After collecting gifts from those present, Moustique teases Basil and obtains his coat and hat. When Moustique and Makak finally depart, Moustique wants to exploit Makak's gift for healing for profit. Makak will only take as much as they need.

Scene Three

At a public market, people talk about Makak's healing miracles. In the meantime, the corporal and the market inspector discuss how they will keep order when Makak makes his rumored appearance. A man claiming he is Makak appears; it is, however, Moustique. Moustique plays to the crowd, asking for cash for his trip to Africa while promising to help them cure themselves. When a spider falls on his hand, he becomes upset. It is removed by Basil, who recognizes that he is not Makak but Moustique. Under duress, Moustique admits the truth and insults the crowd. They beat him for a few moments, before the corporal tells them to disperse. After they leave, Makak appears. Moustique tells him to go back to Monkey Mountain before dying.

Scene Four

At the beginning of Part Two of the play, still in Makak's dream, the action shifts back to the jail. It is the same night that Makak was arrested and the corporal is feeding the prisoners. Souris and Tigre ask him to release the old man, but he will not. Makak offers money to the corporal for his freedom. The corporal will not be bribed, and is disturbed by Makak. After the corporal leaves, Tigre convinces Souris that they might be able to escape from prison and steal Makak's money. To that end, they ask him about his dream and Africa. Tigre convinces Makak that he must kill the corporal— like the lion he claims to be—so they can escape together. Makak reveals that he has a knife. Tigre calls the corporal in, Makak stabs him, and they escape. The corporal is not dead and goes after them.

Scene Five

In the forest, Makak directs Souris and Tigre to rest while he makes a fire. Tigre is impatient, wanting to eat but also anxious to get to Monkey Mountain. Souris is afraid, wondering if there really is any money. As Makak lays out his plans, Souris begins to believe in his words. Tigre grows frightened and impatient. Makak makes him his general. While cooking food Souris has obtained, he and Tigre discuss how they are convinced that Makak is totally crazy.

When they hear someone coming, the three men hide in the bushes. The corporal appears, following their trail and talking in incomprehensible terms. Basil comes out of the bushes and tells the corporal he must repent. Tigre and Souris emerge from the bushes. Tigre encourages the corporal to confess his sins as well. Under pressure, the corporal admits his love of Africa and asks for Makak's forgiveness. Makak appears and declares that the corporal is one of them. Tigre and Souris want to take physical revenge on the corporal, but Makak will not let them. When Tigre wants to shoot the corporal, Souris intervenes for he is now firmly on Makak's side. Makak tries to convince Tigre to join them, but Tigre remains ready to kill. The corporal ends up driving a spear through Tigre with the help of Basil, killing him. Those who remain move on.

Scene Six

Makak is now a royal figure, perhaps in Africa, still followed by the corporal and Souris. Basil reads a list of the accused—figures from history and contemporary society—whom he mentions are all white. Basil lists many letters from those wanting their favor, including the Ku Klux Klan, and an apology from South Africa. None present are appeased. Moustique, now a prisoner, is brought in. Moustique asks Makak for mercy, pointing out that these men might betray him as well. He is taken away. The apparition of the white woman is brought in. The corporal insists Makak must kill her. Makak wants to do this alone, and after much prodding, the others finally leave. Declaring his freedom, he kills her.

Epilogue

The play returns to reality and the jail. It is the next morning. Makak reveals his true identity, Felix Hobain, and does not remember exactly why he is there. Some of his dream returns to his consciousness. The corporal sets the old man free. Just as he is about to leave, Moustique comes, hoping to free his friend. They go home to Monkey Mountain.

Characters

Basil

Basil is a black man (or perhaps apparition) who appears when death is imminent for someone in the scene. Wearing a dark coat and hat, he is described by some as a cabinetmaker. Basil also plays a constant role in Makak's journey after he reaches Monkey Mountain. He compels Corporal Lestrade to confess his sins, resulting in Lestrade's personal epiphany. When the scene shifts to Africa, Basil reads the list of the accused.

Felix Hobain

See Makak

Josephus

Josephus is the sick man who is healed by Makak. He suffers from a fever without sweat until Makak saves his life.

Corporal Lestrade

Corporal Lestrade runs the jail and is responsible for the arrest of Makak. Lestrade is a mulatto, and at the beginning of the play identifies himself with the white authority figures. He follows the rule of the law to the letter and is contemptuous of the three black men. At the beginning of Makak's dream, Lestrade remains like this. In the scene in which Moustique impersonates Makak in the marketplace, Lestrade emphasizes his beliefs on law and law enforcement to Market Inspector Pamphilion. Though Lestrade is stabbed by Makak during the prison escape initiated by Tigre, he later joins Makak's journey after finding the three on Monkey Mountain. Lestrade stabs and kills Tigre when he tries to kill them. Lestrade plays an even bigger role when the three are in Africa. It is he who insists that Makak kill the apparition that started him on this journey. At the end of the play, when the setting is again in reality, Lestrade is somewhat kinder than he was at the beginning of the play and lets Makak go free.

Makak

Makak is the central character in the play, the one who has the dream on Monkey Mountain. Makak is an older man, sixty to sixty-five, of African descent. He works as a coal cutter/burner, in a partnership with Moustique. Makak believes that he is ugly and repulsive, which is why he lives alone in a hut on Monkey Mountain. At the beginning of the play, Makak is thrown in jail for destroying a local café while drunk. He spends the night in jail, which is where he has the dream that forms the bulk of *Dream on Monkey Mountain.*

Makak believes that an apparition, a white woman, appeared to him and told him that he is descended from African kings. He is to go back to Africa to reclaim his heritage. In the dream, Makak begins this journey. He finds that he has healing powers when he cures a sick man's fever. Though Moustique wants to exploit this gift for commercial purposes, Makak is only concerned with the larger goal. After ending up in jail and escaping with the help of fellow prisoners, Makak adds followers to his cause and by scene three is a king, passing judgment on others. Makak's dream ends when he kills the apparition that led him there in the first place. By the end of the play, the setting returns to reality and Makak is released from jail. Through his dream, Makak has gained a better sense of himself as he returns home to Monkey Mountain.

Moustique

Moustique is Makak's partner in business and sidekick in the play. He is a small black man with a pronounced physical deformity in his twisted foot. Makak rescued Moustique from the gutter about four years earlier. Moustique feels Makak is the only one who believes in him. Moustique sells the coal that Makak burns. The pair recently purchased a donkey, Berthilia, together for this business. In Makak's dream, Moustique plays a complicated role and dies twice. Moustique does not believe Makak's apparition was real, and only reluctantly goes on the journey. When Moustique comes upon the sick man and his family, he convinces them to let Makak try to heal the ill one in exchange for bread. It works, and Moustique immediately wants to exploit Makak's gift for commercial purposes. Moustique goes so far as to imitate Makak in the marketplace to make money. But he is caught in the deception and is killed, though Makak tries to save him. Later, when Makak is a king, Moustique is one of the prisoners brought before him. Moustique tries to tell Makak that he should not trust his new followers, but Makak does not believe him. Moustique is killed again. At the end of the play, when reality returns, Moustique shows up at the jail and begs for Makak's freedom, though Makak has already been released. The pair return to Monkey Mountain, their bond seemingly stronger.

Market Inspector Caiphas J. Pamphilion

Pamphilion is a law officer who is under the wing of Corporal Lestrade during Makak's dream. Pamphilion listens to Lestrade's theories and says very little.

Souris

Souris is one of the men in jail when Makak is brought there. He is a man of African descent who has been arrested as a thief. Souris and Tigre seem to be partners of some sort. In reality, Souris agrees with Tigre about Makak's insanity. But in Makak's dream, Souris is more concerned with getting his fair share of food from the Corporal than with

Makak. Souris goes along with Tigre's plan and joins Makak and Tigre's jailbreak. Souris changes sides when the three are on Monkey Mountain together. Though Tigre wants Souris to help him find Makak's money, Souris believes in Makak's vision. Souris does not stand with Tigre when he pulls the gun, much to Tigre's chagrin. Souris follows Makak to Africa. At the end of the play, when reality returns, Souris is still kind to the old man, telling him to "go with God."

Tigre

Tigre is one of the men in jail when Makak is brought there. Like his apparent partner Souris, he is a man of African descent who has been arrested as a thief. Tigre is rather vulgar and, in Makak's dream, convinces Souris that they should take advantage of the old man. Makak tries to pay off the Corporal so that he will be set free, but the Corporal accuses him of bribery. Tigre wants to steal any money Makak has hidden on Monkey Mountain, and to that end convinces Makak that the three should escape together. Makak listens to him, and after leaving the prison the three make their way to Monkey Mountain. Though Makak makes him a general, Tigre is really only concerned with obtaining Makak's money. When the Corporal appears on the mountain and ends up joining them, Tigre pulls a gun on the rest. He is later killed by the Corporal, in part because of his short-sighted greed. Tigre does not understand the journey Makak and the others are on. At the end of the play, when the setting returns to reality, Tigre is in jail, only concerned with himself again.

Themes

Identity/Search for Self

At the heart of *Dream on Monkey Mountain* is a search for and acceptance of one's identity. When Makak is questioned at the beginning of the play, he cannot tell Corporal Lestrade his real name or much about himself. To the question "What is your race?" Makak replies, "I am tired." Makak tells the corporal, Tigre, and Souris that he has not even seen his reflection in thirty years. During his night in jail, Makak has a dream, inspired by an apparition who came to him the night before. The white woman who appeared to him told him that he was a king of Africa and must go there. In his dream, Makak goes on this journey of self-discovery. He heals a sick man thought to be on his deathbed, and his reputation grows. Though Makak is jailed in his

Topics for Further Study

- Compare and contrast Makak from *Dream on Monkey Mountain* with Chantal from an earlier Walcott play, *Malcauchon; Or, the Six in Rain* (1959). Why are both alienated from society? How do they handle their differences? How has Walcott's style evolved?

- Research the history of colonialism in the West Indies. Discuss how this history affects the motivations and attitudes of the characters, especially Corporal Lestrade.

- Research Japan's samurai warriors. Walcott claims to have had them in mind when he wrote the character of Makak. Discuss Makak and his journey in terms of your findings.

- Read psychological research related to race and the formation of personal identity. By what other means could Makak have come to terms with himself?

---

dream, he stabs his jailer, the corporal, and leaves with fellow inmates. The corporal and one of the escapees, Souris, join Makak's journey. When Makak wakes up in reality the next day, he knows his name and has a better sense of himself. He has more hope for his future.

Several of the minor characters have identity issues as well. They include the corporal, a mulatto who, at the beginning of the play, only identifies with the white, ruling side of his heritage. He speaks in disparaging tones to the black inmates. In Makak's dream, the corporal starts out the same way, but has a revelation of his own. He embraces ''tribal law'' over ''Roman law'' and falls in with Makak's journey. At the end of the play, when reality returns, the corporal still is disparaging towards the men of color, but also lets Makak go free.

Death and Rebirth

Throughout *Dream on Monkey Mountain*, there is also a complicated undercurrent of death and, in some cases, rebirth. The first significant event of Makak's journey is his healing of Josephus, a man suffering from a fever and near death. Though Makak initially believes that he has failed to heal the man, Josephus begins to sweat and lives. It is not the first time that Makak has saved someone. He befriended Moustique when he was a drunk in the gutter and made him his business partner. During the play, Moustique dies twice. The first time, he is caught impersonating the now-famous healer Makak in the marketplace and is killed by angry onlookers. He is alive again when Makak is a king in Africa. Moustique appears before Makak as a prisoner, and tries to tell Makak that the men around him will betray him. Makak allows him to be killed a second time. Yet at the end of the play, in reality, Moustique comes to get Makak out of jail. Though Makak is already free, Moustique escorts his newly reborn friend home. Earlier in the play, the corporal is assumed dead after Makak stabs him to get out of prison, but he lives and ends up joining Makak's journey in the woods on Monkey Mountain. In each of these instances, death had a physical symbol with the character of Basil. Each time death is imminent, Basil is present. The ideas of death and rebirth are linked to Makak and the others' search for identity. To understand who they are, they must directly face death in some form and emerge all the stronger. Those who do, survive.

Race and Racism

Another theme in *Dream on Monkey Mountain* directly linked to the search for identity is race and racism. Makak's identity crisis is related to his status as a man of African descent. Makak means monkey, and the old man believes he is not worth looking at. This belief is reinforced by the racist attitudes expressed by Corporal Lestrade, a mulatto himself. Lestrade equates his black male inmates with animals in a zoo. Lestrade identifies only with the white, authoritative side of his heritage. It is only in Makak's dream that Lestrade embraces the African side of his background and joins Makak's journey. At the end of the play, Makak has come to terms with his race because of his dream, but Lestrade has not.

Style

Setting

Dream on Monkey Mountain is an allegory set on an unspecified island in the West Indies at an unspecified time, assumed to be contemporary with the time the play was written. The play's action takes place in several locations, both real and imagined. The most real place is the jail run by Corporal Lestrade, where the play begins and ends. In Makak's dream, the action goes from his hut on Monkey Mountain to a country road where Makak heals the sick man and then to the public marketplace before returning to the jail cell. After Makak, Tigre, and Souris escape, they spend time in the forest before going to a most unreal setting of apotheosis, where Makak is king. All of these settings underscore Makak's journey from a real existence that is harsh, through self-awareness, and back to a reality that he feels better about and in which he functions as a better person.

Symbolism

Dream on Monkey Mountain is replete with complex symbolism, from characters' names to entire subplots. Emphasizing how much of the text is Makak's dream, many words and actions have multiple symbolic meanings. For example, each of the four main characters of African descent—Makak, Moustique, Souris, and Tigre—are the names of animals. They are monkey, mosquito, rat, and tiger, respectively. These names reveal something of each character's personality and perception of themselves, but also play off the corporal's racist remarks about running a zoo. Lestrade's name reflects his dual background, black and white. He literally straddles these cultures. Characters are also symbolic in and of themselves. The prime example is Basil, whose appearance symbolizes a forthcoming death for another character. Nearly everything that happens in Makak's dream has symbolic meaning. When Makak heals Josephus, the man with a fever, it symbolizes the beginning of his awareness of his worth as a human being. When he is a king in Africa, Makak has to kill the white woman who appeared to him as an apparition. She began his journey, and what she symbolizes must be killed to end it.

Language and Dialogue

Walcott uses language and dialogue to underscore diversity in *Dream on Monkey Mountain*. The West Indian island on which the play is set has several kinds of cultures with different languages. The characters of African descent speak English for the most part, but it is often dialect with some local ''patois'' words and phrases, spoken by Makak especially, as well as Souris, Moustique, and Tigre.

Even their names fall under this category. When the corporal is in his authoritative mode, he speaks in a clipped, proper English, throwing in the occasional Latin phrase. During his epiphany in the forest, the corporal's language changes for the moment and becomes more like the other characters. Though the corporal returns to the authoritative tone, the language he then uses is in praise of Makak and that part of the corporal's heritage, instead of against it. Much of the corporal's dialogue is a satiric take on the language of British colonialism. Language defines who characters are and serves as a marker for how they change.

Literary Heritage

Like many countries in the West Indies, Trinidad has a long tradition of folklore with identifiable stock characters. Some of these legends have their roots in animist traditions from West Africa and were brought over by those enslaved. Patois folklore was derived primarily from the slaves of French speakers and has a variety of characters. They include the Soucouyant (evil old hag), Papa Bois (the father of the woods), and Mamadlo, the mother of the water whose form is a snake with human features. Jumbies are anything that could be construed as a bogey-man. Some stories focus on La Diablesse, a female devil in disguise who attracts men and lures them into the forest where they come to harm. Anase tales feature a universal trickster who lives by his wits, though is also greedy and selfish. He is not usually admired because of these characteristics, though stories involving him often try to explain why things are the way they are.

Historical Context

In 1967 as today, Trinidad was a culturally diverse island in the West Indies, with a heritage that includes slavery, colonizers, and island natives. There were many racial and ethnic groups: African, East Indian, and white, with Spanish, British, and French influences. Though English was the official language, many were spoken on the island including Creole, Hindi, Urdu, and Spanish. Each culture had its own religion as well. Catholicism, Protestantism, Hindu, and Muslim faiths were practiced on Trinidad. The groups often thought of them-

Compare
&
Contrast

- **1967:** Trinidad and Tobago has been an independent country since 1962, though it is administered by Great Britain.

  Today: Trinidad and Tobago has been an independent republic within the British Commonwealth for over twenty years.

- **1967:** Trinidad's economy is unstable, with high unemployment, especially among the young. It soon leads to unrest, strikes, and protests on the island.

  Today: Though Trinidad's economy is again unstable, unemployment and inflation are slightly lower and prone to fluctuation. There is more hope, however, because the oil boom of the 1970s proved that a solid economy was possible.

- **1967:** The PNM (People's National Movement) is firmly in power in Trinidad, and though accused of corruption, there are few challengers.

  Today: Corruption scandals and challenges by the NAR (National Alliance for Reconstruction), NDP (National Development Party), and Movement for Unity and Progress have limited the power of the PNM in national politics.

- **1967:** The Black Power movement is prominent in the United States and gaining support in Trinidad.

  Today: Though such a radical, widespread movement does not exist in the same form, many still fight against racism in both countries.

---

selves as distinct, which created problems, social and otherwise, especially during the formation of political parties and unions.

Trinidad (unified with Tobago since colonial days in the nineteenth century) had attained independent commonwealth status in 1962. The country was administered by Great Britain as part of its Commonwealth of Nations, which meant Tobago was ruled by a governor-general appointed by that country's leaders. A locally elected bicameral legislature was controlled by the People's National Movement (PNM), which had been in power since 1956. PNM held a monopoly on power as the first to form a party-based cabinet government.

In 1967, Trinidad's economy was not particularly strong on any front. Two years previously, legislation had been passed that limited the right to strike, making it harder to form nationwide unions. The government tried to stabilize the situation, but high unemployment reigned. This situation created social unrest that would come to a head in 1970 when curfews were imposed. Many black Trinidadians believed there was racial discrimination in employment.

Influenced by and linked to the militant Black Power movement in the United States, demonstrations on the grass-roots level, especially among the young, were presented in an effort to affect change. The demonstrators were critical of the government and accused it of corruption. One particularly radical group was the National Joint Action Congress, related to the University of the West Indies. The Congress believed that white and colored businessmen, both local and foreign, owned most of the nation's businesses. It wanted to form a government that would control the whole economy, all of the land, and the sugar industry. This government would not be a democracy, but would take power by force.

Another part of the economy that was problematic, though on the rise, was farming. Agriculture was supported by the government's five-year development plan, in place from 1962 to 1967. Trinidad supported farming initiatives so the country would not have to import as much food. A significant amount of funding went to the State Lands Programme, which rented government lands at low prices to small farmers. This action did improve the situation in the short term, but did nothing to address the difference between rural and urban areas.

While there were many roads, in rural areas they were often single-laned dirt trails, which limited access to these areas.

Trinidad's future would be bright in the short term for another reason. Oil deposits had been discovered in the early twentieth century, and on-shore oil drilling had been practiced ever since. By the mid-1960s, oil drilling occurred both on and off shore. Because of the worldwide oil crisis in the 1970s, Trinidad oil businesses—which included refining and distributing—would boom. Though life in Trinidad improved greatly as social programs were created with the government's new funds, the boom drained people away from agriculture. The boom was also short-lived. By the 1980s, Trinidad's economy was slumping again.

Critical Overview

Since its earliest performances, critics have been divided over *Dream on Monkey Mountain*. While most found much to praise, especially its poetic nature, some believed it to be bogged down by that very poetry. The complex play also compelled critics to offer their own widely divergent interpretations. Critics of the original New York production in 1971 exemplify this diversity.

Edith Oliver of *The New Yorker* saw the play as pure, successful poetry. She wrote, "*Dream on Monkey Mountain* is a poem in dramatic form or a drama in poetry, and poetry is rare in the modern theatre. Every line of it plays; there are no verbal decorations. A word, too, must be said for the absolute trust that Mr. Walcott engenders in his audience, convincing us there is a sound psychological basis for every action and emotion."

The *New York Times*' Clive Barnes shared Oliver's high opinion. Barnes claimed that this "beautiful bewildering play by a poet" is a "richly flavored phantasmagoria." Even when interpreting Walcott's intentions, Barnes came back to the poetic aspects of *Dream on Monkey Mountain*. He wrote, "I think that what Mr. Walcott is counseling is a twentieth-century black identity rather than an attempt to impose a reversal to a preslave black identity. But much of the play's interest is in its spectacle and poetry."

Another *New York Times* critic, Clayton Riley, generally concurred with Barnes, though he believed the play to be too wordy. Riley argued, "The

Derek Walcott

play is rich and complex; the author's use of fable interwoven with a stark elaboration of historical evidence of oppression illuminates his work, lends it an arresting weight and texture. Walcott's characters are drawn with bold, sometimes extravagant strokes and, prodded by the author, they have an inclination to talk a bit too much." Riley's interpretation also differed from Barnes'. Riley believed that "the thesis, as proposed in *Dream on Monkey Mountain*, is that the West cannot—nor should it—exist forever, given its deplorable record of racist exploitation and butchery throughout the world."

Barnes and Riley's colleague at the *New York Times*, Walter Kerr, thought the poetic tendencies of the play were problematic. He wrote, "It would be easy to misread [the play], in spite of Michael A. Schultz's admirably composed production. . .because the author has a strong bent towards poetic digression. He is long over some scenes that the thread of essential meaning is lost altogether; forward movement is clogged by a waterfall of words."

After the initial productions, *Dream on Monkey Mountain* continued to be presented throughout the world, including regional productions in the United States. Critics' issues with the play remained the same. In 1979, Joseph McLellan of the *Washington Post* reviewed a local production. He found it "a kind of play often written by poets. . .It is too long, loosely organized and specialized in interest for commercial success in this country, but striking in its use of language, fresh and original in its ideas and symbolism.'' McLellan's interpretation focused on the dream aspect of the title. He wrote, ''In a colonial society, one way to compensate for lack of power is to dream. But dreams are also a source of power and a shaping force in its use, if enough people share the dream. This is the central statement of *Dream on Monkey Mountain*.''

Fifteen years later, *Dream on Monkey Mountain* continued to be produced regionally in the United States. Of a Boston production at Playwright's Theatre, Kevin Kelly of *The Boston Globe* wrote, ''Deliberately paradoxical, complex to the point of confusion, *Dream on Monkey Mountain* is so intellectually commanding—and emotionally loaded—that you're constantly being challenged.'' In the same review, Kelly compared the play to the Bible and Walcott to Shakespeare. Like most critics, he saw Walcott's poetic touch. He wrote, ''Derek Walcott's *Dream on Monkey Mountain* is a great piece of work, a mesmerizing, multilayered riff that plays like a black version of the Bible with hardly any specific reference to Christian literature, but, rather, in its myth-making reach, allusive reference to all literature. It's a dense, demanding play, clearly the work of a poet posing inside the proscenium (the same posture applies to Shakespeare).''

Criticism

Annette Petrusso

In this essay, Petrusso compares Makak's journey of self-discovery with that of the one he imagines for Corporal Lestrade in Dream on Monkey Mountain.

Most critics agree that Derek Walcott's *Dream on Monkey Mountain* is an intricate play, full of complicated, sometimes contradictory images and metaphors. Because of the text's richness, *Dream on Monkey Mountain* has attracted numerous interpretations of its many aspects. At the center of numerous critics' reading of the play is Makak and the dream voyage he goes on that leads to his self-acceptance. Some have compared Makak to Christ, while others have focused on his name—which means monkey—and how the play chronicles his emotional evolution to manhood.

From the beginning of *Dream on Monkey Mountain*, it is obvious that Makak is suffering. The old man of African descent has been put in jail for drunken and disorderly conduct after demolishing a local café. When questioned, Makak can only give the name he gave himself to the authorities: Makak or monkey. He has forgotten his real name, symbolic of his nonacceptance of himself. Makak also tells them that he has not seen his own image in over thirty years. In part one, scene one, as his dream begins, the play goes back to the beginning of the day that led to Makak's jailing.

As he relates to his only friend and business partner, Moustique, Makak was visited by a white woman, an apparition, in the light of a full moon. She told him that he was a descendant of African kings and lions, and advised him to live among men. Makak decides to journey to Africa. Moustique accompanies him despite his belief that Makak is crazy. Along the way, Makak learns that he has the power to heal the sick and lead other men. Souris and Corporal Lestrade join his cause.

When Makak makes it to Africa in part two, scene three, he is a tribal king who passes judgment on others and decides their fate. At the end of his dream, Makak must kill the white apparition to free himself from what she represents, that is, the oppression of his soul by white colonials. After he beheads her, he awakens to reality in his cell. Makak now accepts himself and his place in society. He remembers his name and who he is. With Moustique, Makak returns to Monkey Mountain a different man.

Thus Makak's dream is dense and complex. One particularly interesting aspect is how he incorporates Corporal Lestrade into it. Like Makak, Lestrade is a conflicted character. He is a mulatto, who at the beginning of *Dream on Monkey Mountain* identifies only with the white, English, authoritative side of his heritage. This is underscored by his job in both Makak's dream and reality. He is the jailer, the man who explains the ropes to the market inspector in part one, scene three. In the prologue, which is still reality, Lestrade expresses racist opinions about the black men he has jailed. Playing on Makak's appearance and a comment by prisoner Souris (calling Makak ''some mountain gorilla''), Lestrade states, ''Now if you apes will behave like gentlemen, who knows what could happen?'' Yet Lestrade is half ''ape'' himself.

Lestrade plays a prominent role in Makak's dream. Indeed, if we take the dream as solely a product of Makak's imagination, his way of work-

What Do I Read Next?

- *Heart of Darkness,* a novel by Joseph Conrad published in 1902, also concerns a journey of self-discovery.

- *The Gulf,* a collection of poems by Walcott published in 1969, also discusses an internal chasm.

- *Waiting for Godot,* a 1954 play by Jean Paul Sartre, also features a complicated friendship.

- *O, Babylon!* is a play by Walcott from 1976 which also concerns how cultures meet and are integrated internally.

- *Don Quixote,* a two-volume novel by Miguel de Cervantes published in 1605 and 1615, has, at its heart, a relationship similar to that of Makak and Moustique.

---

ing out his problems, he imagines that Lestrade goes on his own journey of self-discovery as well. It begins after Makak has a revelation of his own. He breaks a man's fever and saves his life. Wanting to cash in Makak's gift for profit, his friend Moustique impersonates him in a public marketplace. It is here, in part one, scene three, that the dream Lestrade is introduced.

The dream Lestrade is working with Market Inspector Caiphas J. Pamphilion. Lestrade carries a pistol while accompanying the inspector as he distributes certificates among the vendors. Lestrade tells the Inspector that he has to carry the pistol ''to protect people from themselves.'' Yet he also identifies with the mostly black people present, calling them ''my people.'' He says, ''I would like to see them challenge the law, to show me they alive. But they paralyze with darkness. . .They cannot do nothing, because they born slaves and they born tired.'' Clearly, Makak imagines Lestrade in a kinder light than Lestrade presented himself at the beginning of the play.

Despite such sentiments, Lestrade remains primarily the white-leaning authority figure. He uses racist language similar to that used in the prologue. By part two, scene three, Makak is in Lestrade's jail. Lestrade arrested him when he endangered his friend, the market inspector. Though Lestrade still regards himself as ''an instrument of the law'' with ''white man work to do,'' he also believes, ''In some places the law does not allow you to be black,

not even black, but tinged with black.'' The law is everything to Lestrade; it gives him his identity and his power.

To continue on his own journey, Makak must get out of jail. To that end, he tries to bribe Lestrade. When that does not work, he allows the other prisoners, Tigre and Souris, to talk him into escaping. Makak stabs Lestrade and they escape, leaving the Corporal for dead. Though Makak feels guilty about it, he still takes the opportunity that presents itself. Lestrade, however, does not die. He lives, claiming that he wants them to run ahead so he has an excuse to kill them. Lestrade knows that they are ''attempting to escape from the prison of their lives.'' He will hunt the lion.

In the forest, both Makak and Lestrade undergo further transformations. Makak seems more insane, yet more confident of his journey and his growing self-worth. He makes Tigre his general. As Makak, Souris and Tigre grow closer, Lestrade appears in the forest. The trio hides as Lestrade starts speaking in the same kind of crazy, illogical thoughts as Makak. Lestrade has his own epiphany at this point. Basil, the symbol of death throughout *Dream on Monkey Mountain,* appears and demands that Lestrade confess his sins on the implied threat of death. The other characters present do not see Basil, just like no one else saw Makak's white apparition.

Confessing to Basil, Lestrade comes to terms with his blackness. He tells Basil, ''Too late have I loved thee, Africa of my mind, *sero te amavi,* to

> ❝ The crowning moment of their joint path to enlightenment is when the apparition appears before Makak as a prisoner asking for forgiveness. The Corporal tells him what he must do—behead her—but Makak has a hard time accepting this. Lestrade uses manipulative imagery to get him to finish the deed.❞

cite Saint Augustine who they saw was black. I jeered thee because I hated half of myself, my eclipse. . .Now I see as new light. I sing the glories of Makak!'' After this unbosoming, Makak sees that Lestrade has been transformed, though it takes Lestrade some time. The healer convinces Lestrade to join them, though Tigre immediately resents the Corporal's presence and Souris's loyalty to the old man. Lestrade stabs and kills Tigre with a spear. Though Lestrade and Makak's journeys now follow the same path, some things do not change.

Indeed, Lestrade now seems the leader in giving Makak his African crown. Lestrade pushes the old man forward, following him but acting as his primary advisor and support with the help of Souris. While Makak is unsure where to go, Lestrade remains fundamentally concerned with the rule of law. In part two, scene three, Makak finally reaches Africa and is a tribal king. Lestrade, however, really runs the show. As Makak's right-hand man, he gives the orders for the prisoners to be presented, asks the gathered tribes their opinions on the tribute offers, and keeps Makak making decisions.

The crowning moment of their joint path to enlightenment is when the apparition appears before Makak as a prisoner asking for forgiveness. The Corporal tells him what he must do—behead her—but Makak has a hard time accepting this. Lestrade uses manipulative imagery to get him to finish the deed. His language reflects his acceptance of his dual racial heritage, but also shows how his interpretation of the law is most important of all.

Lestrade tells Makak, ''She is the mirror of the moon that this ape look into and find himself unbearable. She is all that is pure, all that he cannot reach. . .I too have longed for her.'' Makak can only be free of what she represents when he kills her, but he insists on doing it alone. Only then, away from Lestrade's eyes, can Makak symbolically complete his journey. Lestrade has already gone as far as he will go.

At the end of *Dream on Monkey Mountain* , the scene shifts back to reality. Makak knows his real name and is freed by a somewhat kinder, gentler Lestrade. He tells Makak, and later Moustique, that they put the old man in jail because of his behavior but only intended to keep him overnight. When Lestrade frees Makak he tells him, ''Believe me, old man. . .it have no salvation for them, and no hope for us,'' and ''our life is a prison.'' Makak accepts himself for all that has gone on in his head. Lestrade is different, too, though he could not possibly know Makak's dream for him. To Makak, Lestrade will always be the law, but he imagines that the Lestrades of the world will realize their worth as well.

Source: Annette Petrusso, in an essay for *Literature of Developing Nations for Students*, Gale, 2000.

Patrick Colm Hogan

In this essay on Walcott's Dream on Monkey Mountain*, author Patrick Hogan examines the themes of colonization, poverty, and the search for social and personal identity in a world where racial subjugation is absolute and blackness absolutely devalued.*

Establishing both a social and a personal identity which are not determined by the oppressor has been a recurrent theme of subaltern writers, from postcolonials, to women, to racial and ethnic minorities. Whether spoken of in terms of ''decolonizing the mind,'' ''ecriture feminine,'' or the ''black aesthetic,'' it has been a central task of literary artists from dominated groups. A number of writers have chosen to look at this issue from the other side, examining the ways in which oppressive ideologies undermine personal identity and even lead to madness. This approach has been particularly common in feminist critiques of patriarchy. Some of the more obvious instances from the post-colonial canon would include Antoinette in Rhys's *Wide Sargasso Sea,* the narrator in Atwood's *Surfacing,* Elizabeth in Head's *A Question of Power*, Anna in Lessing's *The Golden Notebook,* Nyasha in Dangarembga's *Nervous Conditions,* and the title character in Kincaid's *Annie John.*

Derek Walcott's *Dream on Monkey Mountain* is a particularly complex and interesting example of this genre. Yet it has received relatively little critical attention. This is surprising not only because of Walcott's stature, but because the play presents an important variation on a common theme. Postcolonization literature treating the disintegration of personal identity in the face of oppression has tended to focus on women. Even the male authors who have addressed this issue have often dealt with female insanity (see, for example, Phillips's *The Final Passage*). One result of this is that the disintegrating effects of colonialism and racism have been less fully explored in postcolonization literature than one would expect. While a number of writers besides Walcott have dealt with racial or colonial issues along with patriarchy—Head has done this particularly effectively—the feminist concerns of their works, and the feminist focus of much of the criticism on these works, has tended to limit the literary study of racism and psychopathology. This is particularly unfortunate, because the topic is clearly and necessarily central to the postcolonial situation. Indeed, a number of writers have explored it in theoretical work, most obviously Frantz Fanon in "The Negro and Psychopathology," Chapter Six of *Black Skin, White Masks*. Walcott is one of the few anglophone postcolonial writers to have taken up the problem of racism, identity, and madness, developing and extending Fanon's observations through a literary medium.

In the following pages, then, I should like to consider not only what is going on in *Dream on Monkey Mountain*, but what insight this play can provide into the problems of colonialism and identity In other words, in thinking about the play, I also hope to use the play to think about the world, about the problems which Walcott tries to represent and work through. Before going on to the play, however, it is important to consider some of the more general principles of social and personal identity as they relate both to madness and to the postcolonial condition.

Personal Identity and Social Stratification

Following Lacan and others, we may understand personal identity not as some direct and immediate sense of self, but rather as a "constitution" of the self, a sort of synthetic self-conception. When I think of an object—my car, for example—I think not of some particular isolated detail, but of a complex of elements and relations: its color, its

> As I begin to recognize that the Negro is the symbol of sin, I catch myself hating the Negro. But then I recognize that I am a Negro. There are two ways out of this conflict. Either I ask others to pay no attention to my skin, or else I want them to be aware of it."

shape, how it runs, when it was last serviced, etc. As some cognitive scientists would put it, I "access" a "schema" of my car. When I think about another person, a friend perhaps, I do much the same thing; I access a schema which includes not only his/her appearance, but also typical and particular behaviours, attitudes, beliefs, preferences, etc. When I think about myself, I do the same thing. I access a schema of myself. This too includes a representation of my appearance, my attitudes, my behaviours, etc. What is perhaps most important to note about this self-schema is that it is in large part not the product of introspection, but rather of external attribution. In other words, to a considerable degree, I have been told what I am. My self-schema is formed by the statements and attitudes of others to a far greater extent than we are usually aware. As Lacan put it, our self-image is "more constituting than constituted" (my translation), more a construction of us than a construction by us.

As a simple example, consider body weight. I cannot know by introspection or even observation if I am overweight or underweight or neither. This is, in effect, something I am told, directly or indirectly. And, as research on eating disorders has demonstrated, the advertising and entertainment industries lead many women (and some men) to form a false (and debilitating) conception of themselves as overweight. As Naomi Wolf recently pointed out, a 1984 study indicated that 75% of young women believe that they are overweight, while only 25% are medically overweight; indeed "45 percent of the underweight women thought they were too fat." This is a particularly interesting case, because it illustrates the degree to which even one's perceptual self-constitution, one's conception of one's own appearance, is shaped by attribution, by being told what one is like. People with eating disorders tend, in effect, to see themselves as overweight. Even when looking in a mirror, we do not simply see what we actually look like. Rather, we see what we are told we look like.

The ascriptive character of self-understanding is particularly clear in the case of evaluative terms—such as ''overweight,'' as well as ''beautiful,'' ''ugly,'' and so on. The person who is told he/she is beautiful, treated as beautiful, and so on, will see beauty when he/she looks in a mirror. The same holds for ugliness. Less obvious, but equally true, is the fact that when we look in the mirror we see ourselves in terms of attributed descriptive categories. A white person does, most often, have light skin. But it is due to an attribution of race that he/she sees him/herself as white. A black person does, most often, have dark skin. But it is due to an attribution of race that he/she sees him/herself as black.

More exactly, our self-constitution or self-conception or ''ego'' (as we might call it, following one usage of Lacan) is organized by a hierarchy of physical, mental, and other properties. We believe a range of things about ourselves, but some of these things are more important than others. For example, it is much more central to my self-conception that I am a teacher than that I own many pairs of shorts. The higher we go in this hierarchy, the more important the property is to our sense of our own identity. At the highest levels of this self-schema are the properties which were attributed to us in childhood, the first properties and relations which formed the basis of our later self-conception. These fundamental attributes are themselves determined by a social hierarchy. Specifically, they are the attributes which function to structure the society into which one is born, especially those attributes which structure a society hierarchically. In every society, sex is one of these properties, for it defines a crucial principle of social stratification. Thus being male or female is universally a central property of personal identity. Race, ethnicity, religion, economic class are common and powerful elements of personal identity in societies hierarchically structured by these categories as well.

Clearly, then, the basis of personal identity is nothing other than social identity: being male or female, white or black (or coloured or Indian), European or African (or Asian), Christian or Yoruba (or Ibo or Hindu or Jewish), etc., defines our personal identity as social identity. Whatever one may think of it—whether one finds it a fact to celebrate or to deplore—each of us begins his/her self-constitution on the basis of a series of social categories which are the result of attribution, not experience, and which locate us in one or more social hierarchies. Equally clearly, such a location is problematic, especially for those who have been placed in a socially devalued position. Their basic principles of identity—often undeniable principles concerning the colour of their skin or the nature of their reproductive organs—are not only devalued in themselves, but linked with a series of other devalued attributions which are either putatively absent from the dominant group or are more variable and temporary. For example, in a certain racist aesthetic, which has only recently begun to lose its dominance, black skin is considered to be ugly in and of itself. Individual white people, in this view, may be ugly or may be beautiful; even an ugly white person has some hope of improving his/her looks. But black is ugly by necessity; to be black is necessarily to be ugly. As a result of this sort of constitution, racist, sexist, and other oppressive structures may define a subaltern personal identity which is pervaded by self-denigration and self-hatred.

In considering the social constitution of personal identity, we may distinguish both conceptual and perceptual components of particular relevance to the present study. Specifically, since race (as well as sex) is a socially visible property—in a way that, for example, religion or economic class need not be—we would expect that perceptual self-constitution would be of particular importance in connection with the constitution of a racial subaltern identity. In addition, at the conceptual level, we would expect a close connection between racial identity and social history. Since racist stratification typically justifies claims of racial inferiority by reference to putative cultural inferiority—that is, these two social hierarchies are typically identified—one's relation to one's forebears and to ancestral traditions becomes as definitive and as denigrated as one's face and mind.

Lacan outlines a similar structure of perceptual and cultural/familial factors in identity when he isolates the mirror image and the Name-of/from-the-Father as the two crucial moments in the constitution of the ego. We need not follow Lacanian psychoanalysis in its details to see the particular relevance, to colonial and postcolonial identity, of the mirror image and the ancestral name (whether patronymic, as Lacan assumes, or not), the ways in which these may serve as pivots of subaltern self-constitution. Indeed, in many ways, Lacan's emphasis on naming fits colonial societies, such as those of West Africa or South India, better than it fits European societies. Take, for example, traditional Yoruba culture, to which Walcott frequently alludes as a major force in Afro-Caribbean identity. As Roland Hallgren points out, the name given to a Yoruba child fixed not only sex, but a range of other social relations: "occupation, family traditions, which deity was worshipped," etc. Indeed, Lacan is in a sense recapitulating Yoruba beliefs in his system, for the traditional Yoruba view is that "the name has a psychological effect on the behaviour and character of the bearer." The name thus becomes a particularly important node of social and personal identity. As we shall see, both the name and the image figure importantly in Walcott's exploration of colonial and postcolonial identity.

The Whiteness of Blackness:
Mimeticism and Reactionary Nativism

As we have already indicated, *Dream on Monkey Mountain* is a play which explores the ways in which racism defines an unlivable identity for oppressed people, an identity which pushes toward madness. At various points, Walcott makes this theme explicit. For example, he draws the epigraph for Part One from Sartre's prologue to *The Wretched of the Earth*: as a result of "always being insulted," the self becomes "dissociated, and the patient heads for madness." Or, as the coloured Corporal Lestrade puts it later, in dialogue with the sinister Basil: "My mind, my mind. What's happened to my mind?," he asks; "It was never yours, Lestrade," Basil replies. His mind, we may infer, was never his own because it was always defined by the attributed categories of racism, because his identity was always and necessarily a matter of what he was told he was.

Walcott devotes much of the play to exploring the absolute valorization of whiteness, and the absolute devaluation of blackness, in colonial racist ideology. For example, Moustique explains: "when I was a little boy, living in darkness, I was so afraid. . .God was like a big white man, a big white man I was afraid of." But Walcott is less concerned with the details of racist ideology than with the effects of this ideology on black people. When all value is associated with whiteness, blacks almost necessarily seek to repudiate their blackness—which

is impossible. As Lestrade puts it early in the play: "is this rage for whiteness that does drive niggers mad."

In connection with this, Walcott explicitly defines the issue of subaltern identity in terms of the sort of perceptual and ethnic self-constitutions which we have been discussing. The play centers around a character who foregoes his legal name for the derogatory and implicitly racial epithet "Makak," or "Monkey." When arrested for disorderly conduct, he actually forgets his legal name. The delirium from which he suffers is clearly connected with this inability to link himself to family or culture. He has, in effect, been formed by an ideology which strips him of the individual and human identity implicit in the name and which seeks to structure his personal identity around a racial typology according to which black is to white as monkey is to human. Lestrade summarizes Makak's condition: "this is a being without a mind, a will, a name, a tribe of its own." Lestrade is adopting a colonial and racist perspective, but he nonetheless articulates Makak's complete alienation from any culture which might provide a positive alternative to colonial, racist ideology.

Unsurprisingly, Makak also repudiates any visual self-representation, any image which will remind him of his blackness. Shortly after explaining that he lives "without child, without wife," hence without links to a family and to the culture which such a family might imply, Makak explains that he has also lived without an image of himself: "Is thirty years now I have look in no mirror." The reflection only brings him face to face with his own blackness, thus the impossibility of value in a colonial situation. Indeed, he even takes care not to glimpse himself in water: "Not a pool of cold water, when I must drink, / I stir my hands first, to break up my image" (the fragmentation of the reflection foreshadows Makak's related fragmentation in madness). When Makak looks at himself, he sees what a white racist sees. He is, in effect, a metaphor for those legions of colonized subjects who, in Walcott's words, "looked at life with black skins and blue eyes" ("What the Twilight Says"), suffering the "contradiction of being white in mind and black in body" (or, more accurately, white in self-perception and black in body). His identity, his understanding of the world, his evaluation of himself and of others, all have been determined by white perceptions, white ideas—which is to say, by ascriptions which serve to support racial hierarchies.

Late in the play, Makak comes to consider the situation of blacks in a society structured by white racism. In a moment of despair, he says: "we are black, ourselves shadows in the firelight of the white man's mind." Here, Walcott is alluding to Plato's allegory of the cave, in part to develop the points we have just been considering. One meaning of this line is that, in a world dominated by whites, blacks have no more free volition, no more power, than shadows. It also suggests that the selves or egos of blacks are reduced to shadows by the white racist's perception of them. Whites are like the men in Plato's cave who confuse shadows with reality. The white understanding of blacks is as distant from black reality as the understanding of a shadow is from the understanding of a man or woman. But Makak does not say, "We are black, appearing to whites like shadows in the firelight of their minds." Rather, he says that "we are. . . ourselves shadows," implying that blacks have accepted and internalized the racism which reduces them to shadows. In this sense, Walcott presents blacks as prisoners in the cave. And the shadows they see on the wall are not images of others, but of themselves, the only images they have of themselves

Of course there is more to Makak than a disvalued and disrupted constitution, a disintegrating ego formed from shadows deep in the mines of racist ideology. Makak experiences himself and other blacks as human, and whites as a force of natural or supernatural evil. Indeed, this is what brings about his delirium, for he can neither resolve this contradiction nor live with it. In his hallucinations, Makak becomes a saviour of his people, the man who will revive their culture, return them to the time before colonial degradation, lead them out of the cave where they see only shadows, and bring them into the light where they will see the truth. He links himself to his ancestry, proclaiming himself "the direct descendant of African kings." And he will save his race in part because he is "a healer of leprosy"; he can cure the disease that turns its victim white with decay and causes him/her to disintegrate bit by bit. The people he seeks to lead have, like Makak, lost their identity—their names, their link with a tradition. He addresses them: "I see you all as trees,/like a twisted forest,/like trees without names,/a forest with no roots!"

Elsewhere, Walcott speaks about "racial despair," by which he seems to mean the sense of complete human denigration which drives Makak mad. He links this to the sense of being "rootless," of having no connection with a tradition which gives one personal value—even of having no home, of being a stranger in a home owned by someone else, by whites. After Makak is arrested, Lestrade mockingly asks him, "Where is your home? Africa?" The implication is that he has no home, no homeland. Makak replies, "Sur Morne Macaque," which he translates as "on Monkey Mountain," but which means something more like "on despondent Makak"—he lives, in a sense, on racial despair. In his delusions, Makak's first project is to return to Africa, to find his home, his "roots." Later, he tells his followers, "We will see Africa"; he explains that they will be transported, suddenly, when they open their eyes after making a wish, just as if they "have eaten a magic root." Africa is, in effect, that magic root which he wishes will fix him deep in the soil of a homeland.

But this project is always uncertain. Unlike Souris, when Makak looked at God, he saw not "a big white man," but "blackness." A good thing? It is hard to say. As Lestrade asks: "What did the prisoner [i.e., Makak] imply? That God was neither white nor black but nothing? That God was not white but black, that he had lost his faith? Or..or. . .what." The alternatives are significant, but none is satisfactory. As to the last option, even those who do not believe in God are likely to admit that a despairing loss of faith is not a good thing. And if Makak has lost his faith, it is almost certainly not a positive development—an achievement of human community, for example, a turning away from the promises of an afterlife to a social affirmation of this life. It is, rather, a sign of racial despair. On the other hand, suppose Makak has decided that God is black. Certainly, this is better for Makak, and for other people of African descent. But one thing that Souris makes clear is that the first problem with thinking of God as white is that it racializes divinity, and thus value. To make God black is to repeat this racialization, if in an inverted form.

Asserting God's racial blackness is part of what I refer to in the title as "reactionary nativism." By "reactionary nativism," I mean the general inversion of colonial and racist hierarchies such that members of the oppressed group affirm their racial and cultural authority in precisely the manner of the colonizers. This is a reactionary tendency in that it is a reaction to the physical and mental brutality of the oppressors, which it denies but does not overcome. As I am using the term, the relation between reactionary nativism and colonial racism is analogous to the relation between conscious and unconscious impulses in "reaction formation." Suppose, for example, that I have strongly aggressive impulses toward someone, which disturb me so much that I repress them. As part of my defense against these impulses, I may develop a "reaction formation" and come to behave toward this person with excessive affection and care. Though my outward behavior and conscious attitude are solicitous and loving, they are both in fact determined by my defense against aggression and hatred. Reactionary nativism is similar in that it is an affirmation of one's racial and cultural superiority which is based upon and guided by an underlying denigration of one's race and culture. In other words, it is a sort of reaction formation against colonial racism.

Thus reactionary nativism is a rejection of colonial racist ideology which presupposes the acceptance of that ideology. Put differently, reactionary nativism is the obverse of mimeticism—mimeticism being the formation of one's identity in terms of the concepts and values ascribed to one by one's oppressors. Mimeticism is what leads to racial despair, to the sense that one has no value, as well as to the imitation of white culture, devotion to white law and rule, white ideas and language (i.e., ideas and language which are categorized by whites as superior and as their own—even when those ideas had their origin outside of Europe). Mimeticism creates both Makak's madness and Lestrade's pathetic and cruel conformity. It is also what creates reactionary nativism. Anti-colonial and postcolonial theorists from Frantz Fanon to Ashis Nandy have noted the close connection between a desire to become European and a subsequent repudiation of all things European. As Walcott puts it, "Once we have lost our wish to be white we develop a longing to become black, and those two may be different, but are still careers."

Three Moments of Subaltern Identity

To a great extent, the plot of *Dream on Monkey Mountain* is organized by reference to mimeticism and reactionary nativism. It in effect maps the development of the latter out of the former. More exactly, Walcott implicitly isolates three stages of development in the social and personal identity of his characters. Moreover, in each stage he implicitly distinguishes what we might call "popular" and "anti-popular" versions, which is to say, versions which arise out of or in solidarity with the people (or some sub-group of the people) and versions which arise out of an individualist or careerist alignment with the foreign oppressors. (As shall become clear, the "popular" versions do not necessarily contrib-

ute to the well-being of the people; the fact that they are "of the people" does not imply that they operate in the objective interests of the people.) In exemplifying these alternatives, Walcott presents us with a valuable, if tacit, anatomy of subaltern identity.

Specifically, Walcott begins with mimeticism divided into the figures of racial despair and mimetic collaborationism. The former—exemplified in Makak—is what I am calling the "popular" tendency, for those who suffer racial despair identify themselves with the people. Though they see themselves and the people through "blue eyes," they do not set out to distance themselves from the people. In contrast, the collaborationist tendency—exemplified in Lestrade—is marked by an insistence on difference. Lestrade is proud of being part white and he repeatedly refers to blacks in brutally racist terms: "Animals, beasts, savages, cannibals, niggers."

Makak's mimeticism manifests itself in many ways. Most obviously, his "name" alludes not only to the racist identification of blacks with apes, but also to the adage "Monkey see, monkey do." Indeed, at one point, Lestrade—representing white power and authority—has Makak imitate him in a series of meaningless actions. He concludes: "Everything I say this monkey does do, / I don't know what to say this monkey won't do. / I sit down, monkey sit down too, / I don't know what to say this monkey won't do." But the most significant image of Makak's mimeticism is probably the mask. When arrested, Makak is carrying a white mask. This is the mask of mimicry, the mask which imitates white people. Makak is, of course, not unique in wearing such a mask. It is a mask that all blacks learn to wear as children. When Moustique finds the mask in Makak's hovel, he calls it "cheap stupidness black children putting on." Later, Moustique confronts a crowd seeking release from oppression, and makes the connection explicit: "you all want me, as if this hand hold magic, to stretch it and like a flash of lightning to make you all white." Of course, he cannot. All he can do is train them in mimicry. "All I have is this," he says, pulling out the mask, and explaining: "black faces, white masks!"

Mimeticism manifests itself not only in relation to authority and divinity, but also in relation to desire. Within a racist society, the dominant racial group assumes official authority for all evaluation, and enforces that authority. In the cases we have been discussing, the mimic seeks the respect of his/ her oppressor. But there are other cases in which imitation aims at love. And just as respect is definitive only if it comes from a white person, so too is love absolute only if it comes from a white person—a white woman, in this case. Thus, for Makak and for others whose identity has been formed by racism, the white woman becomes, a sort of alternative to racial despair. To be loved by a white woman—that would mean one has value. In *Dream on Monkey Mountain,* the white woman is represented by the moon. Thus, Tigre imagines Makak "masturbating in the moonlight," which is to say, fantasizing the carnal love of a white woman. And later, in a moment of despair, Makak explains that "I can [never] reach that moon; and that is why I am lost." Connecting the desired white woman with the mother—a connection which will become important later on—Souris explains what "they teach me since I small": "To be black like coal, and to dream of milk," milk being the whiteness he can never achieve, but also the white woman and the white mother he can never have.

When Makak begins to go mad, he hallucinates the visit of a white woman who loves him. This love inspires him, seemingly returns his identity. First, he explains, "she call out my name, my real name," thereby restoring to him his culture, the sense of ethnic and racial connection he had lost. In addition, her love gives him pride in this heritage: "She say that I come from the family of lions and kings." And, yet, this new ethnic valorization is not unproblematic. Makak is still linked with nature, not humanity; as a lion, he is "king of the jungle." More importantly, in making him a lion, this imaginary white woman makes him white. Later in the play, Walcott sets up three parallels: milk and coal, day and night, lion and monkey. The primary significance of "lion" in this sequence is as a signal of whiteness. Through the imagined love of the white woman, Makak has to some extent gained access to values which need not constrain his identity to that which is worthless. But even so, those values are defined precisely by their whiteness. Indeed, the substitution of "lion" for "Makak" is colonial in another way. Etymologically, "lion" derives from Greek and Hebrew roots, making it firmly Judeo-European, "Makak," in contrast, derives from Fiot, a Bantu language; indeed, "Makak" avoids the French/English, Portuguese, and Latin spellings ("macaque," "macaco," and "macaca"), employing instead the standard transcription of the Fiot (see, for example, the entry for "macaque" in *The American Heritage Dictionary*). Thus, while the value placed on Makak by the white woman does

give him a sense of worth, it is worth which in virtually every way derives from colonial valorization of whiteness and European culture. This is why Moustique identifies her with the white mask. The values she allows Makak to celebrate are ultimately mimetic, however anti-mimetic they may appear.

Nonetheless, Makak does move out of mimeticism per se into a form of reactionary nativism—a transition adumbrated at the beginning of the play through the identification of "the round moon" (representative of whiteness and, particularly, the white woman) with "the white disc of an African drum" (representative of a rediscovered African tradition). Specifically, Walcott represents two stages of reactionary nativism. The first, which tends to precede national independence, is what I will call "Romantic Nativism," in its popular form, and "Opportunistic Nativism" in its anti-popular or individualist form.

Romantic nativism is a celebratory idealization of (what one perceives to be) the culture and history of the subordinated group. Walcott is harshly critical of this view. Elsewhere, he calls it "a schizophrenic daydream of an Eden that existed before. . .exile" ("What the Twilight Says"). Unsurprisingly, Makak accepts the colonial view of black Africans as living in a natural state, at one with the jungle. His romantic nativism tends to be a romantic naturalism related to his new self-image as the (white) lion, king of the jungle. Specifically, Makak urges Souris to find himself "at home" as "One of the forest creatures" and makes himself, in the words of Souris, "Half-man, half-forest." Along similar lines, when Lestrade is converted to nativism and affirms his race rather than rejecting it, he is suddenly naked in the jungle. Makak then identifies him and all his African forebears with nature, asking: "Don't you hear your own voice in the gibberish of the leaves? Look now how the trees have opened their arms. And in the hoarseness of the rivers, don't you hear the advice of all our ancestors?"

In connection with this turn from law to nature, from the court to the jungle, from civil authority to natural authority, the object of love shifts from the nubile white woman and inaccessible moon to Mother Earth or Mother Africa, black with fertile soil, the true home, always there, always waiting. In this context, love becomes a return to the patient, everloving mother or motherland, one's origin and destiny. Though only humoring Makak, Tigre presents this theme when he exclaims, "Ah, Africa! Ah, blessed Africa! Whose earth is a starved mother waiting for the kiss of her prodigal.'' And as he approaches his conversion, Lestrade cries out to ''Mother Africa, Mother Earth''; as he removes his clothes in preparation for his rebirth as African, he announces, ''I return to this earth, my mother.''

In contrast with this naive view, opportunistic nativism is the cynical manipulation of the people's hopes and desires through an insincere celebration of non-European values and customs—a celebration aimed merely at one's own advancement. The obvious example of this is Moustique's fraudulent preaching and impersonation of Makak, after Makak has achieved success as a political and religious leader. Walcott criticizes such demagoguery. But at the same time he allows Moustique alone to recognize the close connection between romantic nativism and mimeticism (in the passage already quoted concerning the Fanonian ''black faces, white masks''). Moustique's cynicism is not entirely misplaced.

Indeed, the kernel of truth in Moustique's cynicism is made evident when there is a sudden change in the situation. Independence has been achieved. But instead of the expected peace and harmony, Africans are fighting against Africans. There is violence and brutality everywhere. Makak is at the head of an unstable state with many enemies. This is the third moment of post-colonization identity, and it too has a communal and an individual version. I will refer to these as Sectarian Nativism and Neo-Colonial Nativism. Neo-colonial nativism here is in effect a version of the mimetic collaborationism of the first moment. The primary difference is that it is not overtly mimetic. Neo-colonial nativists celebrate indigenous traditions in order to advance their own interests as junior partners of the former colonies. They frequently do so by supporting sectarian nativism, the affirmation of small-group identities within the former colony. Sectarian nativism involves the affirmation of narrow linguistic, religious, ethnic, or other identities—for example, Hindu vs. Muslim in India or Yoruba vs. Ibo in Nigeria. This is clearly the same sort of affirmation as initially created the broader sense of identity in romantic nativism, where an identification with Africa relied on a specific repudiation of Europe. In other words, sectarian nativism continues the identification of all value with one particular culture, but narrows that identification (e.g., from ''Africa'' to ''Yoruba''). Indeed, it narrows the identification in a way which can be extremely brutal. Finally, it maintains the mimetic basis of romantic nativism. Value is still understood as white value—even

though both sectarian and neo-colonial nativists may violently reject all whiteness (the former sincerely, the latter cynically).

Makak describes the situation after independence, as sectarian nativism spreads: ''The tribes! The tribes will wrangle among themselves, spitting, writhing, hissing, like snakes in a pit. . .devouring their own entrails like a hyena.'' He also explains that this is the direct outcome of the racist ideology of colonialism and the mimeticism of the colonized. They devour ''their own entrails'' because they are ''eaten with self-hatred.'' ''The tribes! The tribes!,'' he laments, ''One by one they will be broken.'' But Makak too succumbs to sectarianism. The people who ''rejected'' his ''dream'' ''must be taught, even tortured, killed.'' The reign of terror begins: ''Their skulls will hang from my palaces. I will break up their tribes.''

Unsurprisingly, Lestrade, formerly the mimetic collaborationist, is now the neo-colonial nativist. He names himself: ''Hatchet-man, opportunist, executioner.'' He initiates the sectarian violence by killing Tigre, and encourages the reign of terror, telling Makak: ''those who do not bend to our will, to your will, must die.'' His work is to manipulate the nationalist leader (Makak) and the people in his own interests, and implicitly in the interests of the former colonizers Now when he says, ''I have the black man work to do,'' we can hear, echoing just below the surface, his earlier statement: ''I got the white man work to do''; the repetition is not accidental. He establishes his cynical strategies: ''Wow, let splendour, barbarism, majesty, noise, slogans, parades, drown out that truth. Plaster the walls with pictures of the leader.'' But even in this, they all remain mere shadows in the fire of the white man's mind. Speaking of Makak, he says: ''He's a shadow now.'' The pomp and circumstance only thicken the shadows, but do not make them real. Referring to Makak's coronation, he calls out, ''magnify our shadows, moon, if only for a moment.

Perhaps most interestingly, Lestrade deploys the rhetoric of nativism in order to support westernization. He urges, ''Onward, onward. Progress'' and, in keeping with his idea of progress, faces Makak toward the moon in order to ''go forward,'' clearly connecting ''forward'' movement and progress with the ideal of whiteness. Makak has a brief vision of what this means: the breaking of the tribes, the replacing of tradition by commerce, ''the gold and silver scales of the sun and the moon. . .that is named progress.'' But his response to this is mistaken, a deepening of reactionary nativism which continues to accept colonial racist ideology even as it denounces whiteness more vehemently and completely. When praises are sung in the new kingdom, they are pervaded with the images of whiteness. Makak is lauded as he "Whose plate is the moon at its full,/ Whose sword is the moon in its crescent." His peace is "gentler than cotton; his "voice is the dove," his "eye is the cloud," and his "hands are washed continually in milk." And yet, as emperor, Makak proclaims whiteness to be guilt. He presents a list of names, explaining: "Their crime. . .is, that they are. . .white." He continues, explaining the new official history which parallels and inverts the official histories written by whites: "a drop of milk is enough to condemn them, to banish them from the archives of the bo-leaf and the papyrus, from the waxen tablet and the tribal stone." Again, the nature of this rejection is clear. It is a reaction formation; its vehemence is directly proportionate to the force of the mimeticism which it simultaneously represses and manifests.

In this context, the object of desire again becomes the white woman. But here, in a reaction formation, she is reconstrued as the object of hate and violence. Before his execution, Moustique accuses Makak: "Once you loved the moon, now a night will come when, because it white, from your deep hatred you will want it destroyed." In reply, Makak asserts his blackness, his rejection of whiteness: "My hatred is deep, black, quiet as velvet." But Moustique, as always, recognizes the mimeticism just below the surface: "you are more of an ape now, a puppet" and he sings "I don't know what to say this monkey won't do," recalling the earlier scene with Lesnade and implicitly indicating Lestrade's manipulative and collaborationist role in the new society. Subsequently, Lestrade does drive Makak to kill the white woman—indeed, not merely to kill her, but to brutalize her: "Nun, virgin, Venus, you must violate, humiliate, destroy her." Like all successful propagandists, Lestrade mixes truth with lies. He is right that this idealization of whiteness "is the mirror of the moon that this ape look into and find himself unbearable"; it is "white light that paralysed [Makak's] mind" and Makak must free himself from whiteness, "as fatal as leprosy," if he is ever to achieve "peace." But this repudiation of an idea is too easily mixed up with the repudiation of people—in this case, a woman, then all women. It turns too easily to misogyny—a frequent component of reactionary nativism, and

yet another hierarchization which mirrors or repeats the stratification of colonial racism. Lestrade tells Makak that he must strive "to discover the beautiful depth of [his] blackness," but such a project remains squarely within the racist problematic of colonialism: all self-understanding and value are based on race. Moreover, the supposed purity and "blackness" of this project is denied by the sectarian brutality of the regime and by its imagery of whiteness. Indeed, when Makak beheads the white woman, he does so with "the curved sword," which was described at the beginning of the scene as "the moon in its crescent" (though it is at the same time reminiscent of Islam; perhaps Walcott is also criticizing the reactionary violence which Islam has been used to justify).

And yet, for Walcott, this reactionary, sectarian, misogynist brutality seems not to be entirely negative. When beheading the white woman, Makak announces, "Now, O God, now I am free." Immediately thereafter, he recalls his name. It is now dawn—with all the symbolism this implies. Suddenly, he is part of no organized religion, but "I believe in my God"—he has found an alternative to both religious despair and religious mimeticism. Most importantly, when Lestrade offers him the white mask, Makak refuses it. He leaves, perhaps for the first time since childhood, without the mask. In his final monologue, he claims that he has now found "roots" and a "home" and the chorus sings that he returns to his "father's kingdom," which, one is left to assume, he finds by accepting himself, his image, his name, rejecting the white mask.

I am not the only critic to be uncomfortable with this ending. Jan R. Uhrbach tries to solve the problem of the execution by maintaining that the decapitated woman "is not the same figure who spoke to [Makak] in his dream," but is instead "Lestrade's vision." In this view, the execution is more like an attack on Lestrade than on any woman. Uhrbach's argument rests on her claim that the white woman is identified with the moon only late in the play. However, she is identified with the moon in the same sentence in which she is introduced: "I behold this woman. . . / Like the moon." On the other hand, even if she were not immediately identified with the moon, Uhrbach's conjecture seems unsupported and implausible. In the only lengthy recent treatment of the play, Samad also addresses the execution, maintaining that the white woman represents "the polarized and static romanticized vision of his ancestral past," a polarized vision ended by the execution. But, as we have seen, the brutality of the execution, its association with Lestrade and sectarian nativism, and the imagery surrounding the act, all indicate that it is necessarily part of such a polarization.

Perhaps Walcott is following Fanon here in linking violence with catharsis. Fanon wrote: "violence is a cleansing force. It frees the native from his inferiority complex and from his despair" and "is closely involved in the liquidation of regionalism and tribalism." It is what prevents demagoguery, for "When the people have taken violent part in the national liberation they will allow no one to set themselves up as 'liberators.'" People are "Illuminated by violence." Indeed, "Violence alone, violence committed by the people, violence organized and educated by its leaders, makes it possible for the masses to understand social truths and gives the key to them." Unfortunately, this does not really solve the problem. Admittedly, revolutionary violence is often unavoidable. And we should not fall into the trap of condemning the small violence of the revolutionaries while ignoring the massive violence of the oppressors. Yet, Fanon seems to be just wrong here. The history of revolutions hardly indicates that violence ends mimeticism or demagoguery, that it leads to social harmony or justice. Violent revolution brings the most violent leaders to the fore, habituates everyone to conceiving of problems and solutions in terms of force, power, weapons, terror. At best, violence is an unfortunate necessity. But it will almost invariably function to perpetuate itself. Moreover, it will tend to operate through and thus support the sort of stratified thinking, and thus identity, promulgated by colonial racism.

Elsewhere, Fanon presents a different solution to the problem of colonial identity: "the individual should tend to take on the universality inherent in the human condition." More exactly,

> As I begin to recognize that the Negro is the symbol of sin, I catch myself hating the Negro. But then I recognize that I am a Negro. There are two ways out of this conflict. Either I ask others to pay no attention to my skin, or else I want them to be aware of it. I try then to find value for what is bad—since I have unthinkingly conceded that the black man is the color of evil. In order to terminate this neurotic situation, in which I am compelled to choose an unhealthy, conflictual solution, fed on fantasies, hostile, inhuman in short, I have only one solution: to rise above this absurd drama that others have staged round me, to reject the two terms that are equally unacceptable, and, through one human being, to reach out for the universal.

Here, Fanon advocates the universalism also found in such writers as Bessie Head and Rabindranath Tagore, Ngugi wa Thiong'o and Samir Amin. Though unfashionable amongst academics (except, of course, those in linguistics), it is perhaps the one option which need not presuppose and repeat the structure of colonial racism.

But that is the topic of another essay, for universalism is not a solution which Walcott considers in *Dream on Monkey Mountain*. In 1967, when the play was first produced, perhaps the consequences of revolutionary violence were not so obvious. Perhaps the resolution, the discovery of name and roots, the rejection of mimeticism through the humiliation and murder of the white woman, would not have seemed so mistaken, so brutal, so close to misogyny. In any event, whatever one's view of its problematic ending, Walcott's play presents us with a powerful literary analysis of the constitution of colonial identity, its varieties and development (or dialectic). And the anatomy we have sought to abstract from his work should be of value not only in understanding other literature, but, one might hope, in conceptualizing and responding to the far more important issues of social and personal identity in the real world—the issues toward which, after all, Walcott sought to draw our attention and inspire our action.

Source: Patrick Colm Hogan, "Mimeticism, Reactionary Nativism, and the Possibility of Postcolonial Identity in Derek Walcott's *Dream on Monkey Mountain*," in *Research in African Literatures,* Vol. 25, No. 2, Summer, 1994, p. 103.

Robert J. Willis

In this review of Walcott's Dream on Monkey Mountain, *Robert J. Willis describes the two major themes of this satirical play as racial inferiority and the "thwarted potential of a human spirit." He describes the protagonist, Makak, as a mythic and microcosmic representation of the lives of West Indians and of the legacy of racial subjugation and poverty they have endured.*

Derek Walcott, a Third World poet and dramatist, born in the Castries, St. Lucia, began writing poetic dramas in 1948 with his first play, *Henri Christophe,* a play about the Haitian Revolution. Walcott has written 15 plays, which have been produced and published, and 10 volumes of poetry, seven of which must be called major collections. His own life as a "divided child"—he is the son of parents of mixed European and African descent—embodies one of the prime tensions of the West Indian experience.

Walcott's arch hero, Makak, in *Dream on Monkey Mountain* is taken from the author's early years in St. Lucia where Walcott recalls a childhood memory of an old, undisciplined woodcutter, who reflects regional history. Two of the major themes of the play are racial inferiority (Makak's French Patois name implies an apelike figure) and the thwarted potential of an independent spirit, "living on his own ground, off its elemental resources." Walcott's drama illuminates the tragic struggle of Makak, his hopes, his fears, and his temporary freedom, which is itself a dream. Makak is a microcosm of all poor West Indians who suffer; he is offered a seeming identity only to return to his mountain hermitlike life, with dreams defeated again. The play, however, leaves the audience with a hopeful vision: Makak must and will descend again from his mountain isolation to face reality, regardless of the cost.

Walcott, in his introduction to *Dream on Monkey Mountain*, credits the theater as an outlet to show the legacy of racial oppression and subjugation of the West Indian natives. "[B]eing poor, we already had the theatre of our lives which we share with the agony of actors of all time."

Dream on Monkey Mountain is a mythic drama, a ritualized play of the West Indies, combining fantasy, obeah, music, dance, and poetry to expose the deeper, unconscious sources of identity and the nature of freedom. The cast includes seven black men, one white woman dancer-singer, a male chorus, drummers, and music. The play was first presented by the Trinidad Theatre Workshop in Toronto in 1967. Other productions were presented in the Eugene O'Neill Memorial Theatre in Connecticut; the Mark Taper Forum in Los Angeles; and in New York, where the play won the Obie Award for the best foreign play in 1970–71. In the 1971 production at St. Mark's Theatre, the White Goddess appeared singing in a huge cutout of the moon. When Makak's hallucination is over, the moon sinks into the sea. Edith Oliver, in her review of the play, tells how the setting, choreography, costumes, and lighting enhance the mood of the play. In this play, characters exchange roles, assume aspects of the protagonist's dominant personality traits, and serve as symbols; one who is twice killed returns alive again in the epilogue.

The play, ripe with satire, is structured around a series of interrelated themes within dream sequences

echoing Cervantes' *Don Quixote*. In these dream episodes, the protagonist, Makak, discovers his true self, neither God nor beast, only a man, an old black man who eventually learns his name and identity.

Walcott generously credits Brecht, Oriental artists, and Robert Graves's *The White Goddess*, who appears in Makak's dream as the white apparition representing inauthentic and limited African identity, for his inspiration. The play is also rich in puns, metaphors, and verbal play of fast-paced Calypsonian rhetoric. Unlike Brecht's productions, Walcott's plays demand a different kind of disciplined actor, dancer, and singer more like those who perform in Kabuki theater. All of these elements, including dream sequences and the introduction of the White Goddess, merge in *Dream on Monkey Mountain*.

Walcott's protagonist, Makak (monkey), who is an extension of Walcott's hero in his drama *Henri Christophe*, is a coal-burner who represents not only the blacks' righteous rebellion against the white master but also the heretical step of rejecting the equally oppressive role imposed by black racists. In a note on the production, Walcott, somewhat reminiscent of Strindberg, allows the producer freedom to amplify: "The play is a dream, one that exists as much in the given minds of its principal characters as in that of its writer." Walcott also suggests Sartre's prologue to *The Wretched of the Earth* as another source of his theme: "Thus in certain psychoses the hallucinated person, tired of always being insulted by a demon, one fine day starts hearing the voice of an angel who pays him compliments."

In the Prologue, Makak has been jailed for being drunk and disorderly. He shares his cell with two fellow prisoners, Tigre and Souris, who merge with his hallucination and share his quixotic experiences, as does Makak's jailer, Lestrade. The names of the characters suggest fable: Lestrade, neither black nor white, is a straddler. *Makak* means *monkey*, taken from the name of the mountain where he lives. His two companions are the tiger and the mouse. Corporal Lestrade, like Charles Fuller's Sergeant Waters in *A Soldier's Play*, ridicules backward blacks. He attempts to prove that Makak is an old ape who must be told how to act and what to do: "Animals, beasts, savages, cannibals, niggers, stop turning this place into a stinking zoo."

When Lestrade interrogates Makak about his race, Makak replies, "Tired," a one-word declaration of long-standing prejudice. Then Makak relates his dreams, claiming "All I have is my dreams and they don't trouble your soul." The prisoner goes on to tell about his vision of the White Goddess on Monkey Mountain who calls out his "real" name and not the one he uses.

In Scene One, Makak is on Monkey Mountain with his friend, Moustique, whom he tells about his dream and the lady, the root of his problem, in his vision. Makak declares that the lady, after talking all night, commands him to regain his African birthright. He has been living all of his life, without a wife or children, on Monkey Mountain, working at his charcoal pit. Moustique does not believe his story but, like Sancho Panza, decides to accompany his "king" on his misadventures. The two men mirror the play's black consciousness in that both lack any positive identity, underscored by Moustique: "You black, ugly, poor, so worse than nothing. You like me, small, ugly with a foot like an 'S.'" Obviously, Makak had one identity throughout his life—subhuman. His hallucinations slowly give him dignity and eventually his God-given identity of a man. The two travelers set out to prove Makak's birthright in a series of misadventures. The episodes are laced with satire and humor: "Saddle my horse, if you love me, Moustique, and cut a sharp bamboo for me. . . . Makak will walk like he used to in Africa, when his name was Lion!" Reluctantly, Moustique agrees to follow his master, but adds, "Is the stupidest thing I ever see." To the music of flute and drum, they sally forth down the mountain to glory.

On their first encounter, Makak is instrumental in restoring a dying man to life. Corporal Lestrade, informed about the local "savior" appears in wig and gown, deriding the crowd's delusions: "It's the cripples who believe in miracles. It's the slaves who believe in freedom." Moustique is quick to seize the opportunity for gain, like many other trickster heroes of West Indian folklore who convert faith and trust into a profitable enterprise. Caught impersonating his master, Moustique is beaten to death by a crowd of villagers who discover his attempt to be the miracle-working Makak.

In what appears to be reality, Makak is back in his cell with Souris and Tigre, enduring Lestrade's pointedly contradictory defense of white justice. In an attempt to sublimate his own problem of racial identity, Lestrade—once again echoing Fuller's Sergeant Waters—screams: "This ain't Africa. This is not another easy-going nigger you talking to, but an officer!" Angered, Tigre plans an escape for him-

" Walcott's drama illuminates the tragic struggle of Makak, his hopes, his fears, and his temporary freedom, which is itself a dream. Makak is a microcosm of all poor West Indians who suffer; he is offered a seeming identity only to return to his mountain.**"**

self, Souris, and Makak, who pretends madness to bring Lestrade to his cell where he stabs him. After they leave the jail, the corporal rises and explains to the audience that the act is only what they dream of—their dream of revenge. As Lestrade begins his hunt for the fugitives, he warns: "Attempting to escape from the prison of their lives. That's the most dangerous crime. It brings about revolution." Going through the forest on their way to Monkey Mountain (Africa), the fugitives become hungry. Makak dries ganja to smoke and tells Souris and Tigre that they will not need food when they smoke the plant. As the chorus chants, "I am going home to Africa," Makak announces "The mind can bring the dead to life. It can make a man a king. It can make him a beast."

Lestrade, searching for the escaped prisoners, meets Basil, another apparition, a coffin maker and spirit of death, who admonishes the corporal and demands he repent his sins. Lestrade does not know if he is in the real world or in a dream himself. Coming upon Makak and the others, who see Lestrade apparently talking to himself, the officer, thinking of his sins, "goes native" and becomes the most fanatic convert to Makak's back-to-Africa movement. At this point, Makak himself is caught up in the frenzy for power and revenge. Makak promises to make Tigre a general when they arrive in Africa. Meanwhile, Makak is crowned king by his three followers. Souris is also converted totally to Makak's dream. Throughout the play all of the major characters, at one time or another, question their racial identity, their place in life. Makak wavers between reality and illusion. Another dream-death takes place when Lestrade drives a spear through Tigre, who, like Moustique, seeks only monetary gain from his newfound position of power.

In a quick change of scene, they are transported to Africa, and Makak sets up court and judgment is passed on the history of racial oppression. Lestrade insists on death for all the accused, including Makak's White Goddess. In one of the wittiest and most entertaining scenes in the play, Basil, who reappears in Africa, reads a list of the offenders, including Aristotle, Shakespeare, The Phantom, Mandrake the Magician, and Al Jolson.

The revolutionists then consider the enemies' fate. Basil asks if the Pope is to be spared. A unanimous negation is the tribe's response. The same reaction is rendered at the names of the President of the United States, the Republic of South Africa, and the Ku Klux Klan. Also in this dream sequence, congratulatory letters arrive from several golf and country clubs. A gilt-edged doctorate from Mississippi University arrives, along with the Nobel Peace Prize, an autograph of Pushkin, the Stalin Peace Prize, an offer from the United Nations, a sliver of bone from the thigh of Lumumba, and an offer from Hollywood. The scene then shifts from satire to "tragedy." With the beheading of the White Goddess, Makak gains his total freedom—by killing his "problem": "She is the white light that paralysed your mind, that led you into this confusion. It is you who created her, so kill her! Kill her!" Moustique is also executed (his second death) for having betrayed the original dream. In this court, there is no room for personal relationships; there is only racial retribution.

The Epilogue makes it clear that the play's action has been real only in Makak's mind. He has cut through illusion to discover his essential self. Makak, the "Being" without an identity, without manhood, now has rejoined the world, taking on his ancestral name. His name is his identity; Makak, as the world has considered him, is a new man, equal to all other men and women. When he wakes in his jail cell, he recollects that his legal name is Felix Hoban. Moustique comes to take him from the jail and discovers Makak to be a new man. Together they set out for Monkey Mountain. Makak's last words are a prayer for the future: "Makak lives where he has always lived, in the dreams of his people! Other men will come, other prophets will come, and they will be stoned, and mocked, and betrayed. But now this old hermit is going home, back to the beginning of this world."

Walcott dismisses revenge as uncreative. Makak, after experiencing his dream, realizes he is a man, a man living off his own land and its native resources. He has found his own roots, which are just as sacred to him as the white man's roots are to the white man. It is his self-imposed image that Makak has learned to dismiss, not by seeking revenge on the oppressors such as Lestrade but by seeking in himself a positive image. His racial identity has been made up of a complex historical legacy, but this should not deter him from creating a new vision of renewal with dignity and purpose. This theme is reiterated throughout Walcott's work.

Makak has thus gone through the whole cycle from woodcutter to king to woodcutter again, but his experiences will keep alive the dreams of the people of the Caribbean, a dream of freedom that must be maintained in the colonized world. The play reawakens the anger at the legacy of bondage in the minds of the oppressed, but it also, in glorifying and idealizing Africa, displays the power of the theater in everyday life. The awakening of the colonized consciousness is seen in the acting out of the hallucinations of this old charcoal maker who refuses to accept the forced identity of a subhuman.

As the play ends and the house lights go on, the audience may doubt the fantasy of the play, for outside of the world of the theater, humans are still irrational. They still consult the astrologer; they still cross their fingers and knock on wood; and they are still, in a sense, religious. Then, as the house lights again dim, the actors renew their cult of nakedness. Life begins again every night when the house lights go out. Rehearsals are also life. They have accepted the twilight. Walcott teaches us that in the theater all the races are one race. He believes that there is no such thing as black or white literature. He notes that the reception of this play in New York (the critics viewed the play as part of the "Get Whitey Syndrome") would not be acceptable to a West Indian audience. What Makak recognizes after he awakes from his nightmare-dream is the lesson he learned from the horror of the blacks' actions in Africa—tribes slaughtering each other—that human cruelty is raceless. Makak has come to realize that the first step in getting rid of his fear of everything white is his need for freedom and identity. The world can and must dispossess prejudice at all levels. Makak has given us a new meaning of life.

Source: Robert J. Willis, "*Dream on Monkey Mountain*: Fantasy as Self-Perception," in *Staging the Impossible: The Fantastic Mode in Modern Drama*, Ed. Patrick D. Murphy, Greenwood Press, 1992, pp. 150–55.

Robert Elliot Fox

In the following essay on Walcott's Dream on Monkey Mountain, *author Robert Elliot Fox examines the use of metaphor and meaning in a play he—and Walcott—have described as "a dream," and discusses the social implications that the dreams, spirit-talks, and fantasies of the novel's protagonist carry.*

In Derek Walcott's own words, "The play is a dream, one that exists as much in the given minds of its principal characters as in that of its writer, and as such, it is illogical, derivative, and contradictory. Its source is metaphor . . ." This statement is crucial to any profound understanding of the work, and my purpose in this essay shall be to examine the nature and function of dreams in the play in an effort to elucidate one essential level of meaning in Walcott's *magnum opus.*

I

In the world of the work—that is, within the context of the play itself—we are presented with a dream and a dream-within-a-dream. But in the context of the work within the world—that is, beyond the text or enactment of the drama—we are also confronted with a dream: Walcott's creative vision which informs the play, and which is itself a part of a larger dream in the mind of mankind, an edenic dream of elemental freedom. Beginning on a "realistic" level in the play we move rapidly into the realm of *poetic* reality, spiraling evermore inward toward an essential core of meaning before ascending once more to the "logic" of the waking world. But this essential core of meaning, discoverable by the individual through an internal voyage, exists beyond the individual—or any individual work of art—in a collective consciousness which Art as a spiritual endeavour has always striven to articulate. So, at the play's conclusion, when we are told that "Makak lives where he has always lived, in the dream of his people," the world within the work and the work within the world merge at the crossroads of the imagination. Makak comes from, and he returns to, the world of myth.

One of the perennial motifs of myth is that of the seeker, the defier of odds and gods, and his redemptive quest; and one of myth's lessons to mankind lies in the articulation of the rhythms of recurrence, the repetitive nature of experience. Walcott grasped these concepts early. He "recalls

> Makak, after all, is no king; he is merely himself—but that self is now endowed with dignity and a certain prophetic wisdom. As long as the dream remains a dream, we can awaken from it or dream it again."

the familiar scene in his childhood when the story teller would sit by the fire to narrate stories involving a 'hero whose quest is never done', and explains how it became necessary for him to appropriate the image of that hero in his plays." And his brother, Roderick Walcott, has noted that "The legends of Papa Diablo, Mama Glos, lajables, and the sukuya can remain if only we tell them over and over again."

Imagination solidified itself in the ambiguous person of an actual individual whom Walcott vividly remembers. "My Makak comes from my own childhood. I can see him for what he is now, a brawling, ruddy drunk who would come down the street on a Saturday when he got paid and let out an immense roar that would terrify all the children . . . When we heard him coming we all bolted, because he was like a baboon . . . This was a degraded man, but he had some elemental force in him that is still terrifying; in another society he would have been a warrior."

These images from Walcott's past, folkloric and literal, are fused in the character of Felix Hobain, whose metaphoric identity is Makak, the monkey-man, the lion and king. Makak, one of the lowliest of the low, is the one in whom the dream is invested. The dream that transforms Makak is, in a very real sense, Walcott's own dream, his artist's vision which espies the potential for greatness in "a degraded man," which recognizes the raw power behind seeming impotence.

> These dead, these derelicts, that alphabet of the emaciated, they were the stars of my mythology.

Makak then becomes representative of the downtrodden and impoverished blacks who long to be redeemed, and of the transformation that brings about, or at least prefaces, such redemption.

II

Speaking specifically of the anguish of the West Indian, Walcott says, "we have not wholly sunk into our own landscapes," thus defining an inherent rootlessness. It is a concern that numerous writers share, but Walcott, like Wilson Harris, attempts the absorption into the indigenous landscape along with a corresponding exploration of a mind—or dreamscape: "a country for the journey of the soul" as Walcott calls it. Both of these geographies—the literal and the imaginative—are recreated and fused through *language*.

It is through language, in fact, that Walcott envisions the salvation of "the New World Negro." "What would deliver him from servitude was the forging of a language that went beyond mimicry, a dialect which had the force of revelation as it invented names for things, one which finally settled on its own mode of inflection, and which began to create an oral culture of chants, jokes, folk-songs and fables...." The poet in his primal role as maker is the one who can forge this recreative language that will provide a vehicle for the liberation of consciousness from its colonized state. But it is obvious here that the way forward is the way back: to roots. "For imagination and body to move with original instinct, we must begin again from the bush. That return journey, with all its horror of rediscovery, means the annihilation of what is known ... On such journeys the mind will discover what it chooses...." But a choice made via the annihilation of the known can only be instinctual, unconscious, intuitive; it will not be *rational*.

The true arena of the drama, then, is that of the mind, of imagination. Its vehicle is dream, which enables Walcott to dispense with normal logic, linearity, literalness, and emphasize instead myth, recurrence, ambiguity. When the cages rise out of sight during Makak's deposition—his first recital of his dream—we have a graphic representation of the liberating power of the imagination. This is Walcott's strategy throughout: to demonstrate the disparities between a consciousness that is creative and metaphoric, and one that is straightforward and imprisoning. Makak, for instance, is said to be in a state of "incomprehensible intoxication." He may literally be drunk, or this could be merely a pejorative characterization of his dream and madness by someone who remains untouched by them. Especially the dream is described as "vile," "obscene" and "ambitious." The charges of being "uppity" and sexually depraved are those traditionally levelled at blacks by racists, and Corporal Lestrade has absorbed this mentality, or rather, he has been possessed by it.

"Incomprehensible intoxication" might be one label a modern, scientific mind would apply to the trance states of mystics, seers and shamans. When Makak declares, "Spirits does talk to me," a "rational" person would perhaps dismiss this as hallucination, but a "primitive" individual would know that Makak is in touch with the traditional world, which encompasses a nonmaterial reality. Makak is a visionary, and the visionary stance is fraught with peril. He is able to exorcise a dying man's sickness when "priest," "white doctor," and "bush medicine" fail, and he tries to do the same with his people, only to be rejected by them because they are incapable of belief. Makak is struggling with a pejorative limitation on his psyche and being which his dream helps him transcend. Failure to "dissolve in his dream" means that one remains imprisoned. Moustique, for example, masters the rhetoric of salvation but he lacks vision; he has not experienced the power of the dream but merely wishes to exploit it. Hence Basil says of him, when unmasking him in the marketplace, "The tongue is on fire, but the eyes are dead."

In his recital of his dream, Makak describes himself as walking through white mist to the charcoal pit on the mountain. He is ascending the slope of consciousness, journeying through whiteness to blackness, through vagueness toward a solid identity. "Make the web of the spider heavy with diamonds/And when my hand brush it, let the chain break"—that is, the chain of slavery, both psychological and actual. The spider's web represents the entanglements of history, racism, colonialism; the diamonds are the oppressed. In his role as saviour, Makak is able to shatter this evil beauty with an almost casual gesture. The dream transcends time, telescopes spiritual and physical evolution, so that Makak moves, in the infinite space of a poetic moment, from ape to God:

> I have live all my life / Like a wild beast in hiding.... / And this old man walking, ugly as sin, / In a confusion of vapour, / Till I feel I was God self, walking through cloud.

Again, in the healing scene, Makak stands with a burning coal in his palm, chanting a formula for salvation, striving to save the sick man from an actual death and his people from the living death of degradation and despair. "Faith! Faith! / Believe in yourselves." The energy released by the burning charcoal symbolizes the spiritual energy released by Makak's positive confirmation of his blackness.

"You are living coals," he tells them, "/ you are trees under pressure, / you are brilliant diamonds ..." The decomposed matter from primeval vegetation was transformed into coal, and diamonds are the result of coal under enormous pressure, over great periods of geological time. Burning coal brings light; diamonds reflect and refract light. Hence Moustique's echo, in the marketplace, of Makak's metaphor: "One billion trillion years of pressure bringing light, and is for that I say, Africa shall make light." Here, of course, Moustique is speaking better than he knows. The "revelation of my experience" that he talks of is that of his people, the broader dimensions of which Makak's dream calls back from a darkness of oppression, forgetfulness and ignorance.

The dream which redeems, the imaginative reversal that transforms a poor charcoal burner into royalty, has its roots in historical fact. In his book *The Loss of El Dorado*, V.S. Naipaul relates how the black slaves in Trinidad at the beginning of the nineteenth century created kingdoms of the night, with their own kings, queens and courtiers, elaborate uniforms, and other regal paraphenalia. During the day the blacks laboured and endured the cruelty and contempt of their masters; but beneath the moon these same slaves were for a time themselves metamorphosed into masters, issuing commands and miming splendours, while their white owners became the objects of mockery and fantasies of revenge. One of these nocturnal regiments, led by a King Sampson, was known as the Macacque regiment. In light of the condemnations meted out during the apotheosis scene in *Dream*, it is significant to note as well from Naipaul's account that "the role of the Grand Judge, who punished at night as the overseer punished by day, was important."

This nighttime pageantry was redemptive drama, an elaborate masquerade which enabled the oppressed to vivify their ancestral memories while at the same time reversing, if only momentarily, the bitter realities of the present. Naipaul remarks, "Negro insurrection, which seemed so sudden in its beginnings and so casual in its betrayals, was usually only an aspect of Negro fantasy; but an adequate leader could make it real." It never came to this. In 1805, the imaginary kingdoms were revealed—practically voluntarily, as if the secret were too good to keep—and the slave aristocracy was executed or whipped. Still, until such time as the powers of rebellion proved to be sufficiently substantive, the dream remained as a possible vehicle of escape from despair; and, while they lasted, the

kingdoms of the night must have been a positive force, a means of sustaining the slave in what were otherwise intolerable circumstances. There are those who would argue —and indeed the same criticism has been directed against *Dream*—that the blacks would have been better off had they refrained from fantasy and resorted instead to violence. But this is itself a form of romanticism. When you have been reduced to a dehumanized state, you must first regain your dignity; when you have been relegated to physical toil, the mind must sometimes soar above the body. If you are an animal, why not be a lion? If you are a slave, why not dream of being a king (especially when you may be the descendent of kings?) Dreams may be attacked as nothing more than dreams, but in the beautiful words of Delmore Schwartz, "In dreams begin responsibilities."

III

Monkey Mountain is depicted in the Prologue as "volcanic," which suggests unpredictability, slumbering violence, submerged and smouldering energies that will one day demand release. Makak's dream touches and taps these hidden energies and gives them form and substance in a way that the criminality of Tigre or Souris or the oppressive mentality of the corporal (themselves crude manifestations of the need for self-assertion, of a refusal to accept identitylessness) cannot. Makak repeatedly insists that his dream is not a dream, whereas others characterize it, not only as a dream, but a *bad* one. They are literalists, fatalistic and unimaginative, like the politicians whom Walcott describes as "generation after generation / heaped in a famine of imagination." Even though the charges that the corporal addresses against Makak clearly include incitement to rebellion, even though Makak himself declares that it is "better to die, fighting like men, than to hide in this forest," *Dream on Monkey Mountain* cannot be said to advocate revolution in the circumscribed political sense. What Walcott thinks about colonialism, racism, oppression—the "dream of milk" as he calls it —ought to be evident from the play; but Walcott is equally clear about an opposite but attendant danger, characterized by him as "Witchdoctors of the new left with imported totems." The solution is not politics. "The future of West Indian militancy lies in art."

One reason why this should be so can be adduced from the tension in the play between a fulfilling, integrative sensibility—represented by Makak and his dream—on the one hand, and divisive, reductionist tendencies—manifested in the likes of the corporal and Moustique—on the other. Plurality of experience is suggested by the number of doublings and pairings we find in the play. Makak and Moustique provide one dual, complementary partnership; Tigre and Souris present another pair who offer a similar contrast. Basil seems sometimes to be paired with the dancer, sometimes with the white apparition. The corporal is really a double in himself: he is both black and white, and shifts from one pole of being to the other partway through the play. The sun and the moon form another pair, the former representing ''reality'' and the latter ''dream.'' The prevailing tendency—which the play implicitly condemns—is to emphasize *one* aspect of identity or experience at the expense of all others. The corporal tries to be white, then reverses the process and strives to be as black as possible. The pragmatic aspect of Makak, symbolized by Moustique, dies twice. The moon is slain in order to free the sun. White supremacy is established on the myth of black inferiority, then black supremacy asserts itself.

According to Walcott's stage directions, the moon reversed becomes the sun; the two are opposed but joined, Janus-like. Makak ''kills'' the moon so that the sun can rise and free them all from the dream in which they are locked ''and treading their own darkness.'' Sun and moon each have their particular clarity; it is only that all things appear equal under the sun (Makak, Moustique, the corporal, the thieves are all ''imprisoned''). It is the moon and its attendant world of dreams beneath which we experience vital contrasts, revealing differentiations.

In the contradictory dreamworld, these differentiations become ambiguous; distinctions between things keep shifting, altering. But characters with restrictive, ''logical'' mentalities keep struggling to reduce things to simple black and white, and Corporal Lestrade is perhaps the pre-eminent example of this behaviour. In his role as the upholder of the rules of Her Majesty's government, the corporal functions as Makak's prosecutor. Later, in the important apotheosis scene, where the power of shaping history now lies with Makak and his retinue, the corporal is still functioning as a prosecutor, but this time upholding the law of the tribes against the threat of whiteness. He has changed his allegiance but retains his legalistic devotion, with its logic and rationalism. (When the corporal says of Makak, ''I can both accuse and defend this man,'' he is articulating his ability to switch sides easily, a testimony to his innate opportunism and uncertain sense of identity.) For him, the white goddess, who represents the negative aspect of his own previous possession (by ''English'' and all that it implies), is much more of a threat than she is to Makak, for whom she functions as muse. The corporal has reduced her to one (especially for him) damaging context: the mother of (Western) civilisation—in other words, Europe. (Eur-opë = ''she of the broad face''—that is, the full moon.)

IV

Walcott himself characterizes the apparition as having four roles (or phases): the moon, the muse, the white goddess, a dancer. All of these manifestations coalesce into a simultaneous complex of meaning, splendidly articulated by Robert Graves in *The White Goddess*. He writes, ''Her name and titles are innumerable. In ghost stories she often figures as 'The White Lady', and in ancient religions, from the British Isles to the Caucasus, as the 'White Goddess'.'' She is the Muse, ''the Mother of All Living, the ancient power of fright and lust—the female spider or the queen-bee whose embrace is death.'' The Night Mare is one of her cruellest aspects. But it is she who inspires the magical language of poetic myth which ''remains the language of true poetry.'' Hence the goddess has complementary moods of creation and destruction.

One of the further aspects of the muse is Mnemosyne, ''Memory,'' and this is important for the play in that it is through the dream inspired by the white goddess that Makak journeys back to the roots of his heritage, to the time when he was both ''lion and king.'' Before his inspiration, Makak could declare, like the speaker in Walcott's poem ''Names'': ''I began with no memory. I began with no future.'' And when he does make a beginning, it is ''where Africa began: / in the body's memory.''

Since Makak is clearly posited in the play as a kind of Christ-figure, one is likely to question the simultaneous emphasis on the rather pagan white goddess, since, as Graves reminds us, the concept of such a creative anima was banned by Christian theologians nearly two thousand years ago and by Jewish theologians even earlier. But if we move outide the mainstream of orthodoxy, as artists are wont to do, there is no real contradiction or incompatibility, for the ancient Irish and British poets ''saw Jesus as the latest theophany of the same suffering sacred king whom they had worshipped under various name from time immemorial.'' Furthermore, the Gnostics held that Jesus ''was conceived in the mind of God's Holy Spirit, who was female in Hebrew''—which is enlightening in view of the fact that Makak refers to himself as "responsible only to God who once speak to me *in the form of a woman* on Monkey Mountain." Graves goes on to remark that the "male Holy Ghost is a product of Latin grammar—*spiritus* is masculine—and of early Christian distrust of female deities or quasi-deities." The corporal's indictment of the apparition—"She is the wife of the devil, the white witch"—contains strong echoes of this intolerance.

Makak in his role as the King of Africa and the saviour of his people is an image of the Sacred King who is the moon goddess's divine victim, who dies and is reborn in the cycle of perpetual renewal; and, as the madman, the dreamer, the visionary poet, he is also the muse's victim, for the two roles interpenetrate. But Makak refuses to die this death, slaying the white goddess instead, under the pressure of the corporal's vehement prosecution and the collective animosity of the tribes. In doing so he frees himself from the dream, but only on one level—a level on which, as Moustique correctly diagnoses, a betrayal of the true cause is taking place, blindness replacing vision, maleficent madness driving out beneficent madness. It is Moustique who dies, and, in so doing, attains wisdom; he who had himself betrayed the dream by attempting to market it is later able to see that the dream is now being prostituted by others for political ends. And the corporal has to go to the verge of death before he experiences a necessary (but not thoroughgoing) transformation.

Makak has to kill the white goddess for several reasons: one, because he cannot forever go on depending upon his source of inspiration but has to begin to rely upon himself (just as he had earlier insisted that the people have faith in themselves as well as in an outside force); two, he has to come back from the world of visionary truth to the everyday world, in order to translate and transmit the fruits of his experience; and, three, he has to escape from the somewhat perverted role of tyrant which the corporal and others have thrust upon him, as well as from the complementary role of saviour that is so fraught with agony and peril.

When Makak divests himself of his royal robe before he beheads the apparition, he is symbolically freeing himself from the bondage of kingship as well as that of the dream and all externally-imposed definitions of selfhood. Indeed, Makak's real name, Felix ("happy") is only revealed in the epilogue, after he has finally discovered who he is. It is not quite as simple as waking up, because, paradoxical-

ly, on one level the dream continues right to the play's end. What happens is that Makak moves from his personal dream back to the realm of collective dream, where his experience becomes universalized and undifferentiated.

In an early poem by W.B. Yeats, Fergus of the Red Branch tells a druid of his desire to "Be no more a king / But learn the dreaming wisdom that is yours." Taken as an admonition, these words could apply appropriately enough to Makak, who in the apotheosis scene witnesses the clarity of his vision being distorted by the blindness of revenge, the salvational role of leadership reduced to a rallying-point for fanaticism. Just as he must escape from the thrall of the muse, Makak must free himself from the perversions of power. The recognition of kingliness, the possibility of triumph, are sufficient for the satisfaction of the psychic hunger for reinforcement. It is similar to the realization that it is enough to travel to Africa in one's mind; indeed, that such an imaginative journey may be ultimately preferable to an actual one. Ironically, the dream seems to reassert reality once more, though on a higher plane of recognition. Makak, after all, is no king; he is merely himself—but that self is now endowed with dignity and a certain prophetic wisdom. As long as the dream remains a dream, we can awaken from it or dream it again. The danger is when people like Corporal Lestrade try to make the dream literal. Then there is no more imagining and no more awakening; no true freedom, only another confining structure.

Source: Robert Elliot Fox, "Big Night Music: Derek Walcott's *Dream on Monkey Mountain* and the 'Splendours of Imagination,'" in *The Journal of Commonwealth Literature*, Vol.XVII, No. 1, 1982, pp. 16–27.

Sources

Barnes, Clive, "Racial Allegory," in *New York Times*, March 15, 1971, p. 52.

Kelly, Kevin, "The Poetic Power of Walcott's *Dream*," in *Boston Globe*, July 26, 1994, p. 57.

Kerr, Walter, "How to Discover Corruption in Honest Men?," in *New York Times*, March 15-21, 1971, sec. 2, p. 3.

McLellan, Joseph, "Powers of the *Dream*," in *Washington Post*, November 30, 1979, p. C10.

Oliver, Edith, "Once Upon a Full Moon," in *New Yorker*, March 27, 1971, pp. 83-5.

Riley, Clayton, "A Black Man's Dream of Personal Freedom," in *New York Times*, April 4, 1971, sec. 2, p. 3.

Scobie, W. I., "The West Coast Scene," in *National Review*, November 3, 1970, p. 1174.

Walcott, Derek, *Dream on Monkey Mountain*, in *Dream on Monkey Mountain and Other Plays*, Farrar, Straus, 1970, pp. 207-326.

Further Reading

Colson, Theodore, "Derek Walcott's Plays: Outrage and Compassion," in *World Literature Written in English*, April, 1973, pp. 80-96.

This article discusses the importance of the plays included in the volume *Dream on Monkey Mountain and Other Plays* (1970).

Hamner, Robert D., "Mythological Aspects of Derek Walcott's Drama," in *Ariel*, July, 1977, pp. 35-58.

This essay looks at several of Walcott's plays, including *Dream on Monkey Mountain*, through elements of mythology.

Montengro, David, "An Interview with Derek Walcott," in *Partisan Review*, Spring, 1990, pp. 204-14.

In this interview, Walcott discusses his inspirations and life as a writer.

Olaniyan, Tejumola, "Derek Walcott: Islands of History at a Rendezvous with a Muse," in *Scars of Conquest/Masks of Resistance: The Invention of Cultural Identities in African, African-American, and Caribbean Drama*, Oxford University Press, 1995, pp. 93-115.

This chapter considers *Dream on Monkey Mountain* and other writings by Walcott from several historical perspectives.

Fable

Octavio Paz
1954

Octavio Paz's beautiful and mysterious poem reflects many of the ideas that characterize his work in the early 1950s after his return to Mexico from Paris. Like the other verses in the volume *Semillas para un himno* (*Seeds for Hymn*) in which it appears, the style of the twenty-two-line, visually rich, unrhymed, unpunctuated poem shows the influence of surrealism, an aesthetic movement that aimed to expand human self-expression by rejecting rational control and deliberate intent in favor of uncensored images springing from the subconscious. The poem describes a mythical landscape at the beginning of creation whose unity is suddenly shattered. With the fragmentation of this previously undifferentiated world comes human language. The images presented in the poem are unexpected and startling while having familiar echoes from myths of the Christian tradition and ancient Mexico.

The imagery, tone, and subtle allusions in the poem combine with powerful effect to present a picture of a paradise lost. The poem may be read as a depiction of a world corrupted by humans' attempt to express it in intellectual terms. It may also be viewed as a commentary on the modern predicament where humans are removed from each other because their lives lack the cohesion and meaning found in the sacred ancient myths. Another understanding of the poem is of the limitations of language to express the raw human experience that resides in the subconscious. The related themes of myth and language that figure in much of Paz's

poetry are explored in "Fable" with characteristic insight, elegance, and erudition, but ultimately the poem offers no simple explanations about the nature of these subjects. Like the ancient myths themselves, the poem presents a story whose universal truths are not explicitly told but which lie buried, to be discovered using imagination and an opening up of the subconscious mind.

Author Biography

Paz enjoyed a distinguished career as a diplomat, playwright, essayist, and poet, and is regarded as one of the greatest writers and intellectuals of the twentieth century. He was awarded the Nobel Prize for Literature in 1990, the first Mexican to be so honored, in recognition of a body of work that includes more than thirty volumes of poetry and over forty prose works on subjects ranging from Mexican culture to literary theory and Eastern philosophy.

Paz was born Octavio Paz Lozano in Mexico City in the middle of the Mexican Revolution in 1914. He was raised in the small town of Mixcoac by his mother, his aunt, and his paternal grandfather, a prominent liberal intellectual and novelist. Paz came into early contact with literature in his grandfather's extensive library. His father was a journalist and lawyer who had joined the uprisings led by Emiliano Zapata, the peasant leader of Mexico's 1910-to-1920 revolution. At age sixteen Paz published his first poem and founded a literary review. Three years later he published his first book of poems, *Luna silvestre* (1933), and founded another literary magazine. He attended Mexico City's National Autonomous University, where he joined a Marxist student group, marking the beginning of a long involvement with leftist causes. While in college he married writer Elena Garro, a union that would last twenty years and which produced a daughter, Helena.

In 1937 Paz left his formal university studies, committed to combining the ideals expressed in his poetry with tangible social action. He traveled to the Yucatan, where he helped to set up a school in a poor rural area. Later that year he went to Spain to join the Republican forces fighting General Francisco Franco in the civil war. He never saw active fighting, perhaps because his commitment to leftist ideals was doubted. Throughout his life Paz had disagreements with leftist leaders and intellectuals, despite his sympathies with the cause. Upon his return to Mexico via Paris, Paz continued to demonstrate his opposition to fascism by writing articles for left-wing journals and giving speeches. In 1938 Paz helped to found *Taller*, a literary journal that signaled the emergence of a new generation of writers in Mexico. As a Mexican living in the shadow of the European war, Paz found himself becoming increasingly dissatisfied with political revolution as a means of changing society. In 1943 he went to the United States on a two-year Guggenheim Fellowship, where he became immersed in Anglo-American Modernist poetry and founded a literary review that translated major contemporary poets into Spanish.

After completing his fellowship, Paz moved to Paris, where he lived from 1946 to 1951 and served as the Mexican cultural attache. In Paris he became friends with the Surrealist poet and artist André Breton, who had perhaps the greatest influence on Paz's poetry. Paz was to say later that his turning to Surrealism was a way of coming to terms with the problems of writing poetry in a godless world of existential alienation. Paz was engaged with various activities and publications organized by the Surrealists during his Paris years, and he developed the voice that would appear in some of his most important early poetry. Also during this time he published his seminal study of Mexican identity, *El laberinto de la soledad* (1950), translated as *The Labyrinth of Solitude* in 1961.

After living abroad for eleven years, Paz returned to Mexico in 1953. A year later he published *Semillas para un himno* (1954; *Seeds for Hymn*), the volume in which the poem "Fable" appears. The collection was not well-received by Mexican critics, who charged that Paz had been overly influenced by European Surrealism and that he was not ideologically committed or engaged in ideas that were important for Mexico. His next two works, the collection of essays *El arco y la lyra* (1956; *The Bow and the Lyre*) and the volume of poetry *Piedra del sol* (1957; *Sun Stone*) were well-received by critics and confirmed Paz's status as a thinker and poet in his country. These works, like *Semillas para un himno*, are concerned with how language has separated humans from the world but yet must become a bridge between them using the powers of poetry.

By the early 1960s, Paz had established his reputation as a poet in Mexico and throughout the world. In 1962 he was appointed Mexican ambassador to India, where he was influenced by Indian philosophy and myths and produced two important works, *The Grammarian Monkey* and *East Slope*. During this time he married his second wife, Marie-Jose Tramini. In 1968 Paz resigned from the diplomatic service in protest against the government's suppression of student demonstrations during the Olympic Games in Mexico. Paz continued to write poetry and prose, translate poetry, and edit literary journals during the 1960s. Much of his writing during this period is infused with his experiences of living in the East. In the 1970s Paz taught at various universities, including Cambridge and Harvard, and wrote several collections of essays. His poetry and prose after the 1960s began to argue more openly for democracy. In several of his writings he severely criticized the leftist regimes of Cuba and Nicaragua, which led to charges by his critics that he was a neoconservative.

Throughout the 1980s Paz lectured, traveled, edited journals, translated poetry, and published prose works. In 1987 he published *Arbol adentro*, his first collection of poetry in eleven years. His contribution to world literature was recognized with numerous awards in addition to the Nobel Prize of 1990, including the International Poetry Prize (1964), the Jerusalem Prize (1977), the Golden Eagle Prize (1979), the Olin Yoliztli Prize (1980), an honorary degree from Harvard (1980), the Cervantes Prize (1981), the Neustadt Prize (1982), and the Frankfurt Peace Prize (1984). He died in Mexico City in 1998 at the age of eighty-four.

Octavio Paz

Everything belonged to everyone

Everyone was everything

Only one word existed immense without opposite

A word like a sun

One day exploded into smallest fragments

They were the words of the language that we speak

They are the splintered mirrors where the world can see itself slaughtered.

Poem Text

The age of fire and the age of air

The youth of water springing

From green to yellow

From yellow to red

From dream to vigil

From desire to act

You needed only one step and that taken without effort

The insects then were jewels who were alive

The heat lay down to rest at the edge of the pool

Rain was the light hair of a willow tree

There was a tree growing within your hand

And as it grew it sang laughed prophesied

It cast the spells that cover space with wings

There were the simple miracles called birds

Plot Summary

Title

The poem's title is important, as it alerts readers to its subject. A fable is a legendary story of supernatural or marvelous happenings, a tale with connotations of the mythic, the allegorical, and the fabulous. It can also be a story that is not true but that is nevertheless instructive of the truth through its underlying meaning. The title, then, leads readers to expect that the content of the poem will be not of this world yet perhaps contain within it a truth that is applicable to human life and experience.

Lines 1-7

The opening lines of the poem take us to a primordial age, to the very beginnings of time when there is nothing but the most basic elements of fire, air, and water. It is the period when the world, and even water itself, is still in its youth. The grounding element of earth is notably missing from the list, and the sense conveyed is that of freedom, lightness, and freshness. In the third line we learn that out of these elements comes life. It is at first green, signifying its newness, then matures to yellow and ripens to red. The act of creation that brings forth this world is performed completely effortlessly. There is "only a step" between a thing being a dream (an internal state of seeing) and a vigil (an external act of watching), between the desire for something and its being done. The unidentified creator who brings forth this life, referred to in line 7 as "you," may be God or Nature or some other principle of generation.

Lines 8-14

The next seven lines describe the paradaisical world that has been born. There is a sense of brightness and, again, lightness and freedom in the images of the created things, which are transformations of the elements of air, fire, and water: airborne insects are living jewels; heat in the air lies down to rest at the edge of a pond; rain cascades down gently as loose hair of a willow tree. The hand of creation (again referred to as "you" but not specifically identified) has a tree growing from its palm. This tree reminds us of the Tree of Knowledge in the Christian garden of Eden. However, this tree is not associated with reason but with laughter, song, and prophecy. The tree has an element of the magical as it casts spells to fill the air with wings and bring about the "simple miracles" that are birds.

Lines 15-18

In this primitive paradise, there is no division, and everything is held in common. Things are in fact completely unified so that there is no separation at all between people and objects: everything is one. Only a single word exists. This word has no opposite, because all ideas and things are contained within it. It is like the sun, the source of all life, round and perfect and indivisible. There are echoes here of the Christian creation myth in which in the beginning there is nothing but the "word" as well as of ancient Mexican myths in which the sun is worshipped and held as sacred because of its power to make things grow.

Lines 19-22

The last four lines offer a dramatic contrast to the fluidity and airy, dreamlike nature of the earlier part of the poem. Paradise is shattered when the word, the sun, explodes and breaks into tiny pieces. Human language is born and, like fragments of a mirror, reflects in myriad ways the multitude of things in the world. This language does not see the world unified as in the innocent state of paradise, but presents a fractured, splintered reality. Words in human language reflect back to the world, which was single and unified in its sacred and original state, how its beauty and innocence have been destroyed.

Themes

Reason vs. Imagination

In a very important sense, any attempt to explicate the "themes" of "Fable" does a disservice to the poem, because it speaks to readers on a subconscious rather than a conscious level. It seems to try to tell readers about a truth that cannot be explained in intellectual, reasoned terms but which are meaningful and representative of the human experience nonetheless.

One way to see the poem is as a visual representation of the subconscious mind unbounded by the fetters of rational thought. In the harmonious age that is described, there are free associations of images and ideas. Connections are made effortlessly and the fantastic is commonplace. Paz uses and overturns the biblical symbol of the Tree of Knowledge in the Garden of Eden, for in his dreamlike Eden the tree is not a symbol of reason but of imagination. He describes it as having grown out of the hand of Nature (or some other creator) and says that it "sang laughed prophesied," casting spells and creating miracles. The entire description of the paradise is one that requires readers to use imaginative power, to make connections between what would otherwise be thought of as disparate images. But these ideas and connections are possible in the imagination and in the subconscious. At the end of the poem, paradise is destroyed and its unity is fragmented. A possible interpretation of this is that reasoned discourse or description, in trying to capture the unified, uninhibited experiences of the subconscious, cannot do justice to it. The explanation of it is doomed to be fragmented and partial.

Language

Related to the idea of the tension between reason and imagination is the concept of the limitations of language. Again it seems dangerous and counter to the spirit of "Fable" to try to tease out a single "meaning" about the nature of language in its lines to explain what is being expressed. Paz seems to be pointing to the idea that there is a gap between an experience and the expression of it in language. Or perhaps he is saying that human experience cannot be expressed in certain types of language. He talks about the unity of the "word." It should be mentioned that the concept of the "word" was important for surrealists, who aimed to restore language to its original purity by releasing it from constricting rules so it could do justice to humans' inner vision. In "Fable," the "word" encompasses all things in the universe. It may be thought of as the true expression of truth that is corrupted by an attempt to recount it in "the language that we speak." When we understand the "word" we understand the primordial nature of human existence, but any attempt to explain what this is in ordinary language is bound to fail. Or it may be that for Paz the "word" is all the facts and feelings of the world that are conveyed in poetry but which cannot be expressed in non-imaginative language, for example in the languages of philosophy or politics or science. So then the "word" may be seen as poetic language that reflects the world in its unity, while its fragmentation symbolizes the attempt of discursive language to explain those things that only poetry can convey.

Myth

Myth is centrally important in Paz's poetry and is connected with his ideas about language and the subconscious. In many of his writings, Paz emphasizes the alienation and isolation of twentieth-century humans from each other and the world. Ancient people, he believed, found meaning and cohesion in their lives through the understanding of sacred stories and rituals. Myths communicate the common values and experiences of people across cultures and histories by tapping into and trying to make sense of humans' basic and common experiences. Myths then are a reflection of humans' subconscious longings and visions of themselves and the world. Paz hoped that a return to an understanding of humans' stories, recreated for the modern world by the poet, could reconnect humanity with its lost soul. Early in his life Paz sought

Topics for Further Study

- Research the creation myths of various cultures and note their similarities and differences. Does the idea of a "golden age" of paradise figure prominently in many of these myths?

- Examine the surrealist movement in literature and art. What particular techniques do surrealist artists use to express their ideas in visual form and in using the written word?

- Write an essay about what you view to be the possibilities and limits of language when it comes to expressing ideas. Do you think poetry can communicate complex ideas better than prose? Why or why not?

- Investigate the ancient Mexican practice of sun worship and discuss why the sun was considered sacred in ancient agrarian Mexican societies.

through politics to effect change in society and return people to a more harmonious existence, but became disillusioned and gave up hope for the transformation of society through political revolution. Paz felt also that in the modern age people were removed from religious beliefs that traditionally served to connect them to the sacred, to each other, and to the world. In this secularized and fragmented society, people needed a new world image, new mythology, to give meaning to their existence.

In "Fable" myth functions on various levels. Most obviously, the setting of the poem is a mythical time. It presents a creation myth and a myth of a "golden age" where there is unity and harmony among all things. The poem also calls up biblical and ancient Aztec myths. There is, as mentioned earlier, an allusion to the Tree of Knowledge from the Garden of Eden. There is a symbol of the sun, which was the principle of creation and the source of life in Aztec mythology. The image of the word that appears later in the poem calls up ideas from Christian mythology; in the Christian New Testa-

Media Adaptations

- The Nobel Committee maintains a page on Paz that includes a bibliography of his works and useful links to other sites at http://www.nobel.se/laureates/literature-1990.html.

ment, the word or "logos" is all that exists at the beginning of time. With the explosion of the word and the introduction of language, the ancient mythical world is shattered. A feeling of dislocation and disharmony enters where before there was unity. So then the poem may be seen as portraying a wondrous world in which myth and the sacred pervade the landscape but which when destroyed give rise to fragmented, isolated modern existence.

Style

Surrealism

"Fable," like many poems set in a surrealist mode, is difficult to make sense of at first, since nothing is said literally. The poem moves through a series of images that displace the reader into an altered state of understanding and consciousness. The recipient of these surreal images is forced to make connections between pictures and ideas that he or she would not ordinarily make. Yet at the same time the subject matter of the poem, a fable or myth, leads the reader to expect the supernatural and marvelous in the poem. The effect, then, is of being transported to a fantastic but not unsettling world. But at the end of the poem disharmony enters this blissful state, and the reader is made to experience a sense of dislocation.

Style

"Fable" was originally written in Spanish, and there are no doubt stylistic elements in the poem that are not captured in the English language. However, it is very much a poem that relies on visual images and ideas, which are effectively rendered in transla-

tion. The first fourteen lines of the poem, in which paradise is described, move slowly and languidly. There is a clear absence of grammatical structure from the beginning—in the first six lines of the poem there is no complete sentence at all—yet there is a clear sense of movement and easy rhythmic flow. Creation bursts forth but it is expressed in terms that effect a feeling of simplicity and calm. Life begins green, becomes yellow, then turns to red. Each transition and phase of growth is simple and effortless. As lines 6 and 7 express, there is only one step taken by the creator between the desire for something and its action, and the diction echoes the grace and ease of that step. Punctuation is also notably absent from the poem. This works also to convey a sense of freedom and uninhibited flow. As the things of paradise are described, similes are not used, but a sense of magic and, again, freedom is imparted by the use of direct metaphors. The insects are not *like* jewels; they *are* jewels. Rain *is* the hair of a willow tree. Birds *are* simple miracles. The startling images are presented too in a matter-of-fact way to emphasize that this blissful world is simply the way things are, a harmonious and perfect paradise. The poem says that a tree grew out of the creator's hand, and as it grew, "sang laughed prophesied." The lack of punctuation between the verbs again presents a feeling of effortlessness and a sense that these three actions are one and the same thing. The general feeling of lightness in the early part of the poem is highlighted with the creation of birds and other winged creatures.

The tone shifts slightly with the fifteenth line. The visual description ends and the images presented become abstract. The descriptors used are general (everyone, everything, immense), and the explanation of the unified world given tersely. In contrast to the direct analogies used earlier, the word here is likened to the sun, not said to be the same thing. Suddenly with line 19 the tone changes again, this time more dramatically, with the shattering of the single, unified word. The use of the word "explode" comes as a violent outburst on the peaceful landscape of the poem. Immediately the "immense word" is contrasted with the "smallest" pieces of the mirror. The diction used (fragment, splintered, slaughtered) comes in stark contrast to the words used before, presenting a feeling of dislocation after the wondrous experience of harmony.

Imagery

The early part of the poem is full of interesting and unexpected images. The birth and burgeoning of the created world is presented by using colors—green, yellow, red—that are not really images but raw visual experiences that capture all the possibilities of generation, maturation, and ripening. More unexpected images come with insects who are jewels, heat resting by a pool, rain that is hair on a tree, and a tree growing from within a hand. Many of the images are elemental and primordial. There are the elements of fire, air, and water, and the very basic images of a tree, pool, birds, and sun.

The most powerful image, at the end of the poem, is that of the mirror. This image figures in many of Paz's surrealist poems. It is a symbol of outer reality, or the world, reflected in a partial way. The understanding of reality that comes with this sort of reflection is necessarily inadequate because it cannot capture inner longings. The mirror indicates a sense of imprisonment in time and space, as all of reality is rendered as static rather than dynamic. The broken pieces of the mirror here are the words of human language, perhaps an indication that language reflects only a partial reality even as it seeks to express inner human experience.

Literary Heritage

Modern Mexican society has its roots in two diverse cultures, those of the indigenous Indians and the Spanish. Mexico's language, religion, and the racial composition of its people—Spaniards, Indians, and mestizos (those of mixed ancestry)—clearly reflect these elements. The official language is Spanish, but many Mexicans still speak only indigenous tongues. Some 90 percent of the people are Roman Catholic, but the practice of Catholicism in Mexico is heavily influenced by pre-European religious ideas.

In ''Fable,'' Paz takes readers back to the dawn of time and offers mythical retelling of the creation of the world. Much of Paz's poetry is influenced by mythology from Mexico and other cultures, and this poem seems to have elements of both Christian and ancient Mexican mythology. Before the arrival of the Spanish in Mexico in the early sixteenth century, the great indigenous civilizations of the Olmec, Aztec, Maya, Toltec, Mixtec, and Zapotec flourished in Mexico. There are many similarities to the religions and myths of all these peoples, and resemblances between the myths of these cultures to those of Christianity.

The indigenous group that dominated central Mexico at the time of the Spanish conquest were the Aztecs (also known as Mexicas), and they are regarded by many as the ancestors of the Mexican people. They practiced a polytheistic religion, and their chief god was Huitzilopochtli, a god of the sun and war. The Aztecs viewed the development of the universe as a steady evolution during successive periods of ''suns.'' This evolution, it was believed, could only be interrupted by catastrophic revolutions or by natural catastrophes during the transition of one sun to the next. They also believed that within each sun only those forms of earthly life could flourish that were organized according to the principles governing the order of the prevalent constellation. Many Aztec myths also have similarities with those found in the Christian tradition. The world, it is said, began with the creation of a man and a woman in a delightful garden. There is a legend also of a pyramid built that threatens to touch the sky, displeasing the gods, which is much like the Christian story of the Tower Of Babel. Another tale with likenesses to the Tower of Babel story is that of Teocipactli and Yochiquetzal, the man and woman who were saved from the Great Flood. It is said that they had many children, but they were all dumb until a dove from the branches of a tree taught them to speak. Their tongues, however, were so diverse that they could not understand one another.

When the Spanish conquered the indigenous people, Christian priests were quick to see parallels between the Aztec and Christian religions and used the similarities in order to convert them more effectively. Mexican culture today reflects the heritage of its Indian and Spanish ancestry with rituals that are not found in European Catholicism but which can be traced back to pre-Hispanic origins. Mexico's most popular celebration, the Day of the Dead, can be traced to the festivities held during the Aztec month of Miccailhuitontli, ritually presided by the goddess Mictecacihuatl and dedicated to children and the dead. In the Aztec calendar, this ritual fell roughly at the end of July, but it was moved by the priests to coincide with the Christian holiday of All Hallows Eve to transform it from a ''profane'' to a Christian celebration. The result is that Mexicans now celebrate the Day of the Dead during the first two days of November, and the modern festivity is characterized by a blend of ancient aboriginal and introduced Christian features. In myriad other ways

Mexican culture reflects the fusion of European and Indian ideas.

Historical Context

Mexico from the 1910 Revolution to the 1930s

Paz's political beliefs and artistic concerns were shaped by events and ideas that he was exposed to at home and abroad. His early experiences growing up in Mexico in the shadow of the 1910-20 Revolution no doubt influenced his leftist leanings. The Revolution, which was begun by Francisco Madero, came in response to the gross inequality of land holdings between the wealthy and peasant classes under Porforio Diaz. Even after Diaz's overthrow, the fighting continued, and numerous revolutionary leaders (including peasant leaders Emilio Zapata and Pancho Villa) and a million others were killed in a bloody struggle for power. From 1921 to 1933 a series of presidents held office in Mexico. Despite making some gains in economic growth, government became increasingly corrupt and conservative, and large pockets of discontent remained among the Mexican populace. Some improvement came with the 1934 election of Lazaro Cardenas, who carried out land reform and established state-managed collective farms. As a student in the 1930s, Paz sympathized with the leftist cause, which he saw as offering hope for reforming Mexican society and closing the widening gap between rich and poor.

The Rise of Fascism in Europe

In 1936 Paz left his university studies to set up a school in a poor rural area in the Yucatan. He wanted to put into action those political ideals that had already started to manifest in his poetry, about improving the lives of those living with the alienating effects of an abstract capitalist economy. His poetry of this period is highly political and reflects a bright hope for revolution. This idealistic fervor continued when he moved to Spain to aid in the civil war and fight against right-wing forces. In this conflict, conservative forces in Spain overthrew the second Spanish republic. The war pitted Nationalists, led by the wealthy landowners and aristocracy, Catholic Church, military leaders, and fascist Falange party against the Loyalists, which consisted of liberals, anarchists, socialists, and Communists. Paz was one of many young idealistic volunteers from around the world who went to Spain to fight for the Loyalists. The Nationalist cause was aided by the fascist

governments of Italy and Nazi Germany, and the Loyalists received supplies from the Soviet Union. Franco eventually wore down the Loyalists, conquering Barcelona and Madrid in early 1939. But for Paz, saving the Spanish republic was an idealistic cause, and during his year there he was firm in his socialist dream of equality among all people brought through revolution. However, Paz was to remark later in his life that the year he spent in Spain sowed the seeds for his rejection of a purely political revolution as a hope to reform humans and the world.

Mexico in the Early 1940s

Back in Mexico, Paz continued his fight against fascism by founding and editing several revolutionary literary journals. He began also to consider the place of the poet in the world, as a historical agent and an agent of change. The events of the early 1940s, with the entire world engaged in war, made Paz despair about the world situation and the possibility for change. In Mexico, President Cardenas stepped down and was replaced by Avila Camacho. Camacho and his successor, Miguel Aleman Valdes, placed heavy emphasis on industrial growth while downplaying redistributive social reforms and economic nationalism. This policy led to the uneven distribution of wealth once again. Income inequalities, inflation, intellectual ferment, and government repression were a feature of Mexican political life in the 1940s. The squabbles among various socialist groups, with their rival opinions about the duties of writers and intellectuals, forced Paz into retreat from political engagement. In 1943 he left for the United States, where he reflected on his position as a Mexican in the shadow of the European war, before moving to France for six years and then traveling in Asia.

Surrealism

Paz's years in Paris mark a significant period of development in this thinking as an artist, as he moved further away from the ideals of political change and embraced the principles of surrealism. It would be misleading to say that his contact with surrealist modes of thought in France influenced or changed Paz's approach to poetry, but rather he found in surrealism many of the ideas that he had been drawn to throughout his artistic and intellectual life. Founded in the 1920s by the Frenchman André Breton, with whom Paz became friends during his Paris stay, the movement began as a revolt against the control exercised by rationality over accepted modes of expression. Breton attacked pre-

Compare & Contrast

- **1910:** Only one percent of the Mexican population holds ninety percent of the land. More than ninety-seven percent of the rural poor own no land at all.

  1934: The Mexican government begins a major program of land distribution to farmers.

  1999: A group of farmers and other protesters ride on horseback to Mexico City to publicize the plight of Mexican farmers, who have become indebted to large banks. Authorities block their way and repress the march all along its route.

  Today: In the United States, particularly in California, American farmers hire illegal Mexican immigrants to work as laborers at low wages.

- **1936-39:** Volunteers from around the world, from Mexico to the United States to Britain, join the Loyalists to defend the left-wing cause against General Franco's forces in Spain.

  1975: Franco dies after almost four decades as ruler of Spain.

  1978: The Spanish people approve by an eighty-eight-percent majority the new constitution, which defines Spain as a parliamentary monarchy.

  1982: The Spanish people elect a socialist government by an overwhelming majority.

  2000: The right-wing Popular Party wins an outright majority in the Spanish general election. Meanwhile, in the U.S., the socialist presence in political life is minimal. The dominant forces in the political landscape are, as they have been since the establishment of the nation, the Democratic and Republican Parties.

- **1924:** The surrealist movement is born with André Breton's publication of the *Manifesto of Surrealism.*

  1950s: The pop-art movement begins in Britain and the United States. It uses the images and techniques of mass media, advertising, and popular culture, often in an ironic way.

  1960s: The primarily Latin American literary movement called magical realism arises. Magical realist writers mingle realistic portrayals of events and characters with elements of fantasy and myth, creating a world that is at once familiar and dreamlike.

  Today: The late-twentieth-century postmodernist movement is popular among left-leaning academic intellectuals in the United States. The movement, which grew out of a movement in architecture, eschews definition and touches on a range of subjects, including literary criticism and cultural theory. One of its aims is to destabilize the myth of fixed meaning in language.

---

conceptions about the nature and function of words and advocated free expression of uncensored images that well up from the subconscious using a technique of "automatic writing." Paz was impressed by the revolutionary principles of the movement, with its faith in the power of the imagination to revitalize poetry and art to compensate for the sociopolitical forces that he had begun to find so oppressive and stultifying. Some of the other interests of the surrealists, who were greatly influenced by Sigmund Freud's new theories of psychoanalysis, were the exploration of the whole self through the individual's dream and fantasy worlds as well as conscious life; the restoration of the "word" or expression to its original purity; a desire to step beyond the bounds of human experience; and the tension between imagination and reason. "Fable," written after Paz's return from France, shows a clear affinity with surrealism, with its dreamlike quality, lack of inhibition, and unusual imagery that shocks readers into an awareness of areas of the subconscious that had not previously been called upon. Although Paz's work continued to be shaped by his exposure to different cultures and ideas that he came into contact with on his extensive travels, even his later poetry has affinities with surrealism, with its concerns about the constraints of language, the use of unexpected images, and the desire to expand the range of human expression. Paz's engagement with surrealism was crucial to his artistic development, as it offered him the possibility for radical social change not in the political arena but beginning in the arena of human subconscious.

Critical Overview

Although Paz's work has been extensively reviewed and analyzed in Spanish and English, there are no sustained critical treatments of "Fable" in English. The work is generally discussed with the other poems in the 1954 volume *Semillas para un himno* (*Seeds for a Hymn*), which is often viewed as representing a particular phase in Paz's career as a thinker and a poet. Its initial reception in Mexico was mixed. Paz published the volume shortly after returning to his native land after eleven years abroad, six of which were spent in Paris among André Breton and other French surrealists. The surrealist elements and tone of *Semillas para un himno* are obvious. Many Mexican critics were appalled at the work, which they said had no social or political relevance to what was happening in Mexico at the time. Jason Wilson, in his study of Paz's life and career, explains the reaction of critics and poets to the volume: "The period of the mid-1950s in Mexico saw the term 'surrealist' become the 'forbidden word'. . . . For Raúl Leiva the poems [in *Semillas para un himno*] were hermetic with a total loss of feeling for humanity. Silva Villalobos found them inhuman and not Mexican. . . . That surrealism could still provoke reactions in 1954 may surprise. Augusto Lunel, reviewing the same book, claimed that the term surrealist became an adjective for whatever could not be understood." There were also favorable reviews of the collection, but in general critics viewed *Semillas para un himno* as evidence that Paz had been "corrupted" by his stay in Europe.

The interest in and popularity of "Fable" in English is indicated by its inclusion in two important English-language collections of Paz's early poetry. The poet Muriel Rukeyser translated the poem and included it in *Early Poems: 1935-1955*, and it appeared in Eliot Weinberger's *Octavio Paz: Selected Poems*, which appeared in 1969 and was reissued several times. Unfortunately, only a few

critics have offered any remarks at all on the poem, and those who mention it do so only in passing, summarizing it in a sentence or two. Rachel Phillips, writing in 1972, in discussing mirror imagery in Paz's work, notes that the mirror motif in "Fable" "acts as one of the threads unifying Paz's great themes of epistemology, solitude, and language." Gordon Brotherston's 1975 discussion of Latin American poetry offers the provocative suggestion that the "golden age" Paz describes is an ironic reminder of the triteness of the perfect society as a political entity. Jason Wilson, is his 1986 study of Paz's life and work, sees the poem as depicting an original world where there is no alienation. He sees it as a world "bound by interlocking metaphors . . . the original metaphorical quality of language itself released from its twentieth-century straitjacket."

Although the poem "Fable" itself has not received much notice by English-language critics, this is by no means an indication of Paz's general reputation among readers outside Mexico. He is admired throughout the world not only as one of the masters of the Spanish language but, as indicated by the Nobel committee, as a giant figure in world literature whose work is marked by "impassioned writing with wide horizons, characterized by sensuous intelligence and humanistic integrity."

Criticism

Uma Kukathas

Kukathas is a freelance writer and a student in the Ph.D. program in philosophy at the University of Washington, where she is specializing in social, political, and moral philosophy. In the following essay, she argues that in "Fable" Paz expresses what he takes to be the limitations of language by using poetry to move beyond its confines.

Upon initial reading, most people no doubt find Octavio Paz's "Fable" to be a curious poem. Many readers have difficulty discerning its meaning at first sight. The poem begins by presenting a series of strange visual images that appear not to hang together, and then moves on to offer equally odd abstract images. However, the beauty and challenge of his poem, like so many of Paz's works, is that it requires the imagination of the reader to be exercised in order for the poem to be fully appreciated and understood. The poem expresses its message or

What Do I Read Next?

- *The Labyrinth of Solitude: Life and Thought in Mexico* (*El labertino de la soledad*, 1950) is Paz's powerful nonfiction work that contains elements of autobiography, literary criticism, and social commentary. The book probes Mexican identity by examining the nature of political power in Mexico after the Spanish conquest as well as the relation of Native Americans to Europeans.

- In his lecture given upon receiving the Nobel Prize in 1990, entitled "In Search of the Present," Paz discusses language, history, myth, and poetry. He speaks about the bridge between tradition and modernity as new life is constantly breathed into antiquity, and also of his "pilgrimage in search of modernity" that led to a recognition of the "real time" of the present.

- *A Tale of Two Gardens: Poems from India 1952-1995* collects the poetry from over forty years of Paz's relationship with India—as ambassador,

student of Indian philosophy and mythology, and poet.

- Joseph Campbell discusses the primitive roots of mythology, examining them in light of discoveries in archaeology, anthropology, and psychology in *The Masks of God: Creative Mythology* (1968). His *Hero of a Thousand Faces* (1949) explores the world's interwoven mythology and sees their common themes as indicating distinctly human reactions to the riddles of life.

- Paz's early poems, with their elements of eroticism, political questioning, and surrealism, are well represented in *Early Poems: 1935-1955*, which are translated and collected by the American poets William Carlos Williams, Muriel Rukeyser, Denise Levertov and others. Paz's later poetic visions are beautifully rendered by the poet Elizabeth Bishop in *The Collected Poems of Octavio Paz, 1957-1987*.

---

story not by using overt explanations or descriptions, but taps into the reader's innermost mind and subconscious to draw out its multiple possibilities. This is especially effective in the case of "Fable" since it seems in fact to be a work *about* the limits of literal or static descriptions that are given in language. "Fable" offers readers an understanding of the limits of language using—paradoxically—the medium of language. But it does this by showing that the "word" of poetry allows readers to move beyond language to understand the truth that lies behind it.

Paz wrote "Fable" after his years in Paris, where he associated with the French surrealists. For the surrealists, the notion of the "word" was central. The many techniques of composition they employed, such as "automatic writing," sought to "release" the energy of the word from the prison of rational thought. Their goal was to allow a person's introspection and subjective ideas, those thoughts

and sensations and experiences deep in the unconscious, to emerge and be expressed despite the limitations of the conscious mind. The word, once it was removed from the strictures of what seemed to "make sense" in logical terms, could, it was hoped, express what might otherwise be thought of as inexpressible.

In "Fable," Paz offers a view of language that is compatible with the surrealists' conception of it in a form that is true to the inner vision that surrealism seeks to clarify. In the poem Paz offers a picture of the unconscious mind using terms that don't "make sense," or cannot be captured in rational terms, but which express an inner experience. In the early part of the poem, the reader is presented with a lush visual description of a paradise. The images that are supplied are remarkably simple but contain within them a wealth of associations. When the reader tries to understand them literally, or to see them in the strictures of the rational mind, they mean nothing.

"'Fable' offers readers an understanding of the limits of language using—paradoxically—the medium of language. But it does this by showing that the 'word' of poetry allows readers to move beyond language to understand the truth that lies behind it."

But when pedantic understanding is cast aside, the words start to make sense in a much different way.

The poem opens by establishing the setting. It is an age of fire and of air, an age when water is in its youth. Right away the images used show that this is a primordial, primitive world. And the associations the reader is likely to have with them—of the basic elements that produce all of life—make it a very real and concrete and sensual world. But the absence of the element of earth also is significant because it calls into question the concreteness of this world. In the fourth line the description slips without warning to that of created things growing and maturing and ripening: ''From green to yellow / Yellow to red.'' The account makes little sense if it is read literally. But the associations that the reader makes—of green with growing things in their youth, yellow with organic objects as they mature, and red with things as they ripen—make clear what idea is being conveyed. What is required for it to be understood is, again, for the reader to look beyond language to ideas that reside in the subconscious. Paz is relying on the reader's ability to move beyond the confines of the literal word and the conscious mind to be able to make free associations with images and ideas to understand the truth behind his words.

The series of surprising images that are offered in lines 8 to 10 also require readers to move beyond discursive thought to be fully appreciated. The visual descriptions given are of insects that are jewels, heat that lays down to rest, rain that is the hair of a tree, and a tree that grows out of somebody's hand. All these representations cannot be explained in rational language or justified in terms of what the conscious mind knows to be true. But the existence of these things is possible in the subconscious. Just as in dreams when strange and disparate images come together to tell a story that is understood by the dreamer, these images come together to tell a story if the mind allows itself to be open to it. The use of direct metaphors (the rain is not simply *like* the hair of a willow tree but *is* the hair of a willow tree) creates a sense of fusion, oneness, and synthesis among all things in the universe. And once more the free association between images allows readers to understand this unity without it being explicitly stated.

The tree growing from within a hand is a fantastic picture. As Rachel Phillips points out in her study of Paz's work, the image of the tree in Paz's poetry often symbolizes humans' rootedness and is used to stand for humans' physical bodies. Here there are no roots in the earth (as was pointed out earlier, earth is noticeably absent from the landscape), which reinforces the idea of freedom and possibility. But the symbol of the tree seems to indicate a sense of belonging, suggesting that there is some real connection between humans and this marvelous and dreamlike world.

The various associated images in the first part of the poem combine to create a sense of a landscape or time or place that is at once fabulous but strangely familiar. Making sense of these images has required the reader to exercise certain non-rational powers, and the place being understood using those powers feels oddly close to home. This is because what is being described in the poem is in fact that place from which these powers spring—the subconscious. The poem uses the reader's imagination and the immediate experiences he or she has had in calling upon associations to build, without using overt explanation, a most vivid picture of the subconscious mind. This depiction of the subconscious is shown through language on the one hand, since the medium is the poem. But in another way poetry cuts through the confines and clumsiness and inexactness of discursive language to speak to the subconscious in a voice that it can better understand—and allows it to recognize itself.

In the latter part of the poem the imagery shifts from being visual to being abstract. Although the images are still unusual, the tone of the poem changes so that the reader is no longer left with a strange but familiar *feeling* but must try to *understand* what is going on in the poem in a quite different way. It is explained that this world that has been depicted is a single, unified world: "Everything belonged to everyone / Everyone was everything." These two lines have overtones of a socialist utopia, where there is no ownership and there is perfect harmony. The lines call up associations, but they are not the same sorts of sensuous, basic images that were given earlier in the poem. The reader does not even have to make any associations to understand these lines; they are simple and expository. The very tone indicates a movement out of the realm of the subconscious to a more conscious understanding.

The poem goes on to say that in this world only a single word existed. It was immense and without opposite. Everything that may be described or talked about existed within that single word. Returning to the earlier discussion of the "word," this can be seen as showing that in this subconscious, primitive world, there is a true expression of how things "are," of what deep human experiences feel like, of what truth without the rules of consciousness is in actuality. But this word that expresses all things and the harmony of the world explodes into fragments. All that there is now are pieces of a mirror that reflects partially and statically the truth that before was whole. The truths of the subconscious mind cannot be told literally. Once this is even attempted, the images that are projected are not reflective of that deep reality, but of the world seen by the conscious mind.

That Paz uses the medium of a poem to express this idea of the limits of language might be seen as undercutting what he says in the last lines of the poem about a splintered reality viewed through language. But the presence and form of the poem itself works as a very important factor in "Fable." Most forms of language cannot describe those feelings and ideas that well up from the unconscious or even explain the subconscious in any meaningful way at all. When a person tries to describe a dream he or she had at night to someone else the next day there is simply no way the experience can be conveyed fully. Even the person who had the dream might remember his or her own experience in a dim way in the light of conscious thought. But poetry, like the original "word," does not do such disservice to the ideas of the subconscious. Poetry does not offer a fragmented reality because it not only uses language but the silences between words. It allows the mind to reach down into itself and understand the world not only at a conscious level but at an unconscious one as well. It reveals the truth to us that is behind our rational thoughts, by opening up

our minds. Paz does not explain this in any of the words of "Fable" but shows it by having the poem itself work on the reader's subconscious to better understand itself.

Source: Uma Kukathas, in an essay for *Literature of Developing Nations for Students*, Gale, 2000.

John M. Fein

In this essay on Selected Poems *of Octavio Paz, author John M. Fein discusses the use of the mirror as both image and theme in the works of Paz. Fein sees the mirror as symbolic of the endless possibilities for the poet to both find and lose himself in the act of creation.*

One of the principal reasons for the success of the poetry of Octavio Paz is that it can be meaningful without being inaccessible and highly refined in form without being meaningless. It is axiomatic that the poet of the 20th century, no matter what language he uses to declare himself, must express his personal feelings and reactions. Even when discoursing on absolutes and infinites, he must maintain a close relationship between his views and his own experiences. The demands on his readers, accordingly, have been proportionately greater, and in Mexico as in the United States, have made the reading of vanguard poetry a trying task in the last quarter of a century. The reader never knows what kind of intellectual wardrobe he may be called upon to pack for his esthetic voyages. But recent years have seen a return to sanity in poetry, not only by individual poets who write understandably, but also as a perceptible literary movement. For many midcentury poets, this signifies the ability to blend the personal and the universal, the particular and the general, and to strike a balance in technique as well as in choice of subject.

The fact that the new poetry is accessible, however, does not mean that it is easy; there are still many aspects of it that remain obscure. Although there is seldom one explanation which clarifies everything in a poet's work, there are frequently key ideas that can be of help, and it is with one of these, the device of the mirror, that we wish to concern ourselves here. What we propose is to observe the ways in which the poet has used the mirror as image and as theme, and to deduce from these uses conclusions which may be applied to all of Paz's work, especially with respect to his concept of reality and his reaction to it.

> The fact that the new poetry is accessible, however, does not mean that it is easy; there are still many aspects of it that remain obscure."

There are two primary reasons for selecting the mirror as the point of departure instead of other abstractions which the poet also dwells upon. First is the fact that the mirror is referred to with much greater frequency and intensity than any of the others, particularly in *Libertad bajo palabra*, in which the mirror occurs in the introduction, the last section of the concluding poem, and repeatedly in the pages in between, to such an extent that the reader's first impression is that the mirror is an obsession or at least a fixation of Paz. Its importance for the poet is also indicated by its repeated appearance in articles and in poetry published subsequent to *Libertad bajo palabra.* Secondly, Paz has given the problem of reality a dominant place in his work, and the mirror, as tradition would lead one to expect, is ideally suited for the exploration of this subject.

There is no significant appearance of the mirror in Paz's collections of poetry before *A la orilla del mundo* or in his latest volume of poems (1954). The poems which concern us most here, therefore, are those of *A la orilla del mundo* and *Libertad bajo palabra.* In fact, the former contains only a limited number of references to the mirror, and of these the majority apply to descriptions or to objects not having a direct and close relationship to the poet's interior life; in these cases, the mirror, if it is mentioned at all—it is suggested more frequently than stated—tends to be a brief image which is engulfed in the procession of other images and other subjects which follow it in close order. Such is the case in ''Palabra'':

> Palabra, voz exacta
> y sin embargo equívoca;
> oscura y luminosa;
> herida y fuente: espejo;
> espejo y resplandor;
> resplandor y puñal,
> vivo puñal amado,
> ya no puñal, sí mano suave: fruto.

In any case, glimpsed briefly or not, the mirror in *A la orilla del mundo* is always subordinate to the description of something else, as a secondary element of the poem, an incidental instrument of poetic reconstruction applied to something beyond the limits of the poet's emotional life. We might say that the mirror, in the small space it occupies in this book, only foreshadows a larger concept which Paz was to form at a later date.

Surveying the cases in which the mirror is used as an image in *Libertad bajo palabra,* we observe that there is one common denominator which stands out above all others: the vision of the mirror as an object which suggests absence of limits, an object which by definition is not subject to the usual laws of spatial measurement. ''Atrás mis uñas y mis dientes caídos en el pozo del espejo,'' for example, suggests the irretrievable loss.

''Un olvido reciente y ya olvidado, espejo en un espejo'' postulates the endless repetition of two mirrors reflecting each other. ''Su propia soledad doblada: un desolado espejo negro'' conveys the idea of solitude extended to infinite proportions. Repeatedly the image of the mirror involves the opening of a new dimension, a dimension of endlessness, spacelessness, so that its use here might be termed a kind of window into infinity:

> Insomnio, espejo sin respuesta
> Anegado en mi sombra-espejo
> La conciencia, laberinto de espejos,
> hipnótica mirada en sí misma abstraída
> La noche nace en espejos de luto
> El silencio es un espejo negro
> donde se ahogan todas las preguntas
> Adiós al espejo verídico,
> donde dejé mi máscara
> por descender al fondo del sinfín
> Mas a solas de pronto
> un espejo, unos ojos, un silencio,
> precipicios abrían, inflexibles
> El mal sabor del mundo, el impasible,
> abstracto abismo del espejo a solas

These passages also suggest that a look through the window into a dimension that is formless and timeless can only be disquieting to the subject. In some cases this uneasiness becomes a more extreme emotion, and the image of the mirror is used to suggest resentment, hostility, and fierceness. The poet's fear of the void is thus expressed in his antagonism towards the object which represents it. The poet wishes to ''probar la soledad sin que el vinagre / haga torcer mi boca ni repita / mis muecas el espejo, ni el silencio / se erice con los dientes que rechinan,'' the night is filled with ''espejos que combaten,'' or the sea is wrecked by its own ''voraz espejo.'' It is not the concrete reflection in the mirror which is feared as destructive, but what the reflection does towards nullifying the poet's vision of his own identity and independent existence. ''El espejo que soy me deshabita.'' Since what he sees furnishes no answer, but merely repeats a question or statement, the poet's attitude is one of hostility. In two cases where the mirror is not named but is implied, Paz declares: ''Lo que devoras te devora, / tu víctima también es tu verdugo''; ''Frente de mí yo mismo, devorado.''

If it is true that the principal quality of the mirror as Paz sees it is infinite repetition, it is equally true that this repetition is never utilized to glorify the subject's vanity. There is never the slightest implication that the face in the mirror is an object of admiration. The person who looks in the mirror, on the contrary, rarely sees what we would expect him to see, and what is reflected to him, far from being a source of satisfaction and pleasure, is the cause of a variety of adverse reactions ranging from boredom through rejection to the deepest despair. The lack of any trace of narcissism in poetry which is constantly haunted by the appearance of the mirror is in itself distinctive and sets Paz apart from other writers such as Paul Valéry, a narcissist of the intellectual variety, or a newly popular Mexican contemporary of Paz, Guadalupe Amor, who frankly admits her narcissism in her fondness for mirrors.

What the image of the mirror constantly suggests here, then, is its use as an entry into a dimension of infinite repetition, which the poet frequently associates with a bottomless void and which is related to an emotional reaction of strife and violence. The mirror as repetition, as a world of its own, is not particularly illogical nor far removed from the realm of experience. Considerably less clear so far is the poet's reaction to this concept; the reader may find himself confused when he tries to determine why the mirror is disturbing to the poet. The possible cause of the restlessness, the feelings of violence, is not revealed in the imagery itself. The fuller symbolic significance of the mirror is reserved for several entire poems—or sizable sections of poems—where it appears as the theme. These do not contradict or amend the ideas which we have pointed out as characteristic of the mirror up to this point; they add the philosophical implications, particularly relating to the poet's vision of reality, which are too extensive to be summed up completely by the image alone.

* * * *

Before turning to an analysis of the mirror as theme, we should note the significance of another theme which has a relationship to it, that dealing with Paz's concept of poetry. It is not due to caprice that ''La poesía,'' the concluding poem of *A la orilla,* appears in a revised form as the first poem of *Libertad bajo palabra,* the only item in these two collections of his verse which the author has chosen to honor by repetition. Throughout both books, indeed, there is a predominant concern for the form that the poems are taking in the author's mind; he gives us a picture of a man constantly aware of the demands of his craft while he is in the throes of creation. Part of this concern centers around the forging of a language which will express his personality, which he seems to view as a means of personal revelation more than as a literary medium. Even more important than this, perhaps, is his view of poetry as a source of order and meaning in a disordered world. To the extent that he succeeds in finding words to express himself, to that extent does he shape a part of life and control a segment of existence:

> El arte opera con la vida real como Dios con
>   el tiempo.
> No sólo da unidad a la vida dispersa, abandonada
>   a su propio
> fluir o a los estrechos cauces en que el hombre
>   la encierra;
> también le ''pone un hasta aquí'' a esa
>   inagotable marea.

The great reverence for the mission of poetry helps to explain the absence of the narcissistic variety of self-contemplation which has already been noted in the imagery. Just as the poet is not content with the appearances of the world as he finds it, so does he reject the first appearances of his own personality as superficial. If poetry must give order to life, it will seek what the face in the mirror *implies* rather than dwell on a description of it as it is. In fact, a self-centered interpretation of the face in the mirror would be incompatible with the poet's reverence for the aims of art.

It is particularly in reference to time—or rather to the suspension of time—that a transformation of reality is felt. This experience is what the poet treats in ''Arcos,'' in which he looks at the process of artistic creation with a schizophrenic eye by identifying himself with the river of his own poetry. The river flows along, divides, and goes separate ways to find itself once again. Although the mirror is not mentioned, it is strongly implied in the poet's reflection of himself in the river of imagery. The idea of a somewhat mystic union with poetry, a union which suspends time, helps to clarify passages of the poem:

> ¿Quién canta en las orillas del papel?
> Inclinado, de pechos sobre el río
> de imágenes, me veo, lento y solo,
> de mí mismo alejarme; oh letras puras,
> constelación de signos, incisiones
> en la carne del tiempo, ¡oh escritura,
> raya en el agua!

Writing itself may be as fleeting as a line in the water, but the effect it achieves, ''incisiones en la carne del tiempo'' puts experience out of time's reach. This immobilization of time, moreover, is involved in the paradox (a device which Paz is obviously fond of) which he suggests in ''me veo, lento y solo, de mí mismo alejarme,'' a situation which would be impossible except in a timeless world. The same kind of magic is applied to the river, which also has paradoxical characteristics (''que se desliza y no transcurre'') and which, like the poet, is in two places at once, leaving itself to find itself, just as the poet, not only here, but in other poems, leaves his identity to find it, most often with the aid of the mirror:

> Voy entre verdores
> enlazados, voy entre transparencias,
> entre islas avanzo por el río,
> por el río feliz que se desliza
> y-no transcurre, liso pensamiento.
> Me alejo de mí mismo, me detengo
> sin detenerme en una orilla y sigo,
> río abajo, entre arcos de enlazadas
> imágenes, el río pensativo.
> Sigo, me espero allá, voy a mi encuentro,
> río feliz que enlaza y desenlaza
> un momento de sol entre dos álamos,
> en la pulida piedra se demora,
> y se desprende de sí mismo y sigue,
> río abajo, al encuentro de sí mismo.

The river of art, then, is not a reflection of life, but a distillation:

> El arte no es un reflejo de la vida. Tampoco es solamente una profundización de la vida, una visión más pura y limpia. Es algo más; limita el acontecer, extrae del fluir de la vida unos cuantos minutos palpitantes y los inmoviliza, sin matarlos.

This same impression of the blissful suspension of time which the poet feels when he is successful in achieving self-expression is also observable in ''Delicia'':

> . . . naces, poesía, delicia,
> y danzas, invisible, frente al hombre.
> El presidio del tiempo se deshace.

The release from the domination of time, which the author continues to develop in the stanza following this, emerges in the concluding lines as the principal theme of the poem, and fully defines the nature of ''delicia.''

The poet's search is not always so well rewarded, and the references to his work are not always the reflection of satisfaction in his mission, as can be seen in ''La poesía'' and ''Las palabras.'' Occasionally the poet finds poetry not a reward but a punishment, and his feelings indicate frustration, uncertainty, and disillusionment. Such is the case of ''El sediento,'' in which the hopeful search for poetry ends in failure when the poet faces reality. The reality here is of special interest to us because it takes the form of the mirror, and connotes the barriers of the poet's own personality which he feels he must break to attain his aims:

> Por buscarme, Poesía,
> en ti me busqué:
> deshecha estrella de agua,
> se anegó mi ser.
> Por buscarte, Poesía,
> en mí naufragué.
> Después sólo te buscaba
> por huir de mí:
> ¡espesura de reflejos
> en que me perdí!
> Mas luego de tanta vuelta
> otra vez me vi:
> el mismo rostro anegado
> en la misma desnudez;
> las mismas aguas de espejo
> en las que no he de beber;
> yen el borde del espejo
> el mismo muerto de sed.

The thirst is the poet's desire to lose himself in poetry (see ''Destino del poeta'' for another variation on the theme of ''Delicia''), the mirror is his hope of attainment (and his attainment of his hope) in his goal, and the conclusion is his forlorn objective glimpse of himself in the action of the search.

It is this consciousness of himself in the act of creation which unites the theme of poetry with the theme of the mirror, although not always as concretely as Paz has mingled them in ''El sediento.'' There is a significant relationship between the two suggesting that perhaps they represent, not separate problems, but different aspects of the same problem—perhaps the unique and gigantic problem in the case of Paz—which the poet is called upon to solve. Paz is probably aware in his discussion of Quevedo's poetry of the significance of this question for an understanding of his own work:

En los salmos y sonetos que forman las ''Lágrimas de un Penitente,'' Quevedo expresa la certidumbre de que el poeta ya no es uno con sus creaciones: está mortalmente dividido. Entre la poesía y el poeta, entre Dios y el hombre, se opone algo muy sutil y muy poderoso: la conciencia, y lo que es más significativo: la conciencia de la conciencia, el narcisismo intelectual. Quevedo expresa este estado demoníaco en dos versos:

> las aguas del abismo
> donde me enamoraba de mí mismo.

It is no coincidence that Paz uses the same term ''abismo'' to refer to his own search for himself, and that his comments here are in essence an exact paraphrase of ''El sediento.''

Continuing his discussion of Quevedo's poetry, Paz remarks that Quevedo is the first of modern poets to attribute a sinful content to ''conciencia,'' not because it sins in imagination, but because it tries to sustain itself by itself, and, all alone, to satiate its thirst for the absolute. While Paz may not take the bitter and proud pleasure in ''conciencia'' which he finds in Quevedo, his attitude partakes of the same solitude, the same sin of isolation. When he declares ''contemplo el combate que combato,'' or when he addresses poetry to say ''Insiste, vencedora, /porque tan sólo existo porque existes,'' he is simply bearing witness to the lucidity, almost unbearable in its brightness, of his sense of awareness. As was true in the case of his tribute to poetry, here too the mirror serves as a link between his ideas:

> Romperé los espejos, haré trizas mi imagen—que cada mañana rehace piadosamente mi cómplice, mi delator—. La soledad de la conciencia y la conciencia de la soledad, el día a pan y agua, la noche sin agua. Sequía, campo arrasado por un sol sin párpados, ojo atroz, oh conciencia, presente puro donde pasado y porvenir arden sin fulgor ni esperanza. Todo desemboca en esta eternidad que no desemboca.

When the poet is confronted with his awareness of the world, which he tries to view objectively, he ends by asking himself where reality lies. The nature of the question is such that only a paradox can be the answer. ''Epitafio para un poeta'' at first glance is mere word play, but in fact contains a rather profound riddle:

> Quiso cantar, cantar
> para olvidar
> su vida verdadera de mentiras
> y recordar
> su mentirosa vida de verdades.

The clue to the riddle is found in his article, ''Poesía de la soledad y poesía de comunión.'' Quevedo, Paz finds, refuses salvation and denies the grace of poetry because he is absorbed in the world.

''Nada me desengaña, / el mundo me ha hechizado'' are lines written by Quevedo which introduce *A la orilla del mundo.* Paz notes that Quevedo rejects redemption because he is absorbed in appearances:

> Y es que no sólo la hermosura vacía del mundo lo sujeta (ni es ella a la que se abraza, en todos los sentidos y con todos los sentidos), sino su conciencia de sí.

This statement recalls the concluding lines of ''Insomnio'' :

> Insomnio, espejo sin respuesta,
> páramo del desprecio,
> pozo de sangre ardiente,
> orgullosa conciencia ante sí misma.

It is no wonder, then, given the power of self-awareness and of all that it implies, that Paz's poetry is frequently characterized by anguish, by striving, by unfulfillment, and occasional glimpses of his own kind of paradise. Significantly, Paz uses the mirror to explain what the poet represents in relation to the grace of poetry and the pain of perception:

> La poesía es inocencia, pero el poeta no es inocente. De allí su angustia. La poesía es una gracia, un don, pero también es una sed y un padecimiento. La poesía brota del dolor como el agua de la tierra. Con la poesía el poeta recobra la inocencia, recuerda el Paraíso Perdido y come de la manzana antigua. Pero,¡qué duros páramos, qué desiertos, hay que atravesar para llegar a la fuente! Una fuente que a veces es sólo un espejo resplandeciente y cruel, en el que el poeta se contempla, sin saciarse, sin hundirse, reflejado por una luz impía. El poeta es una conciencia: la baudeleriana ''conciencia del pecado,'' la conciencia de la embriaguez, la reflexión del vértigo. La conciencia de la existencia. Y de su conciencia brota, no la ceguera ni el abandono, sino una más profunda lucidez, que le permite contemplar y ser contemplado, ser el delirio y la conciencia del delirio.

This too helps to explain what might seem the chaos of lines such as the following:

> Vuelvo el rostro: no soy sino la estela
> de mí mismo, la ausencia que deserto,
> el eco del silencio de mi grito.

The concluding portion of ''Envío'' states the same idea with a cool intensity (''ardor helado''), which serves to heighten the effect of a metaphysical mystery. Paz treats this theme more fully and dramatically in ''La calle'':

> Todo está oscuro y sin salida,
> y doy vueltas y vueltas en esquinas
> que dan siempre a la calle
> donde nadie me espera ni me sigue,
> donde yo sigo a un hombre que tropieza
> y se levanta y dice al verme: nadie

''Encuentro'' in *Águila o sol* is a prose variation of the same subject.

Seen in connection with the poet's pain of awareness, the device of the mirror acquires philosophical connotations: it is the symbol of the conflict between his general quest (the search for the absolutes) and his subjective point of view (the knowledge of his own limitations). It is also the point of conflict between the poet's reverence for the mission of poetry in general and his dissatisfaction with the way in which he has chosen to express himself. It is as if Paz held up his written words to see himself reflected in them. The mirror, basically, is Paz's poetry and at the same time, his reaction to his poetry.

This reaction, which can be noted particularly in the poems which have the mirror as a theme, is the source of the dimension of endless repetition and the violence associated with it, which are inexplicable when the mirror images are seen alone. The mirror constitutes an infinity in that it is only through the presentation of an endless series of perspectives in his poetry that the poet can orient his search for an ultimate objective view of reality. Yet he must start his search with himself since he is the only reality he knows. The violence is a result of his frustration at not getting beyond himself in his search, for what he invariably sees is a picture of the poet observing the poet observing the reflection.

*   *   *   *

There are several entire poems in *Libertad bajo palabra* which are especially significant for a study of the poet's vision of himself. These are, in addition to some already referred to in the preceding pages, ''El prisionero,'' ''Insomnio,'' ''El espejo,'' ''Pregunta,'' ''La caída,'' the sixth part of ''Crepúsculo de la ciudad,'' ''Medianoche,'' ''La calle,'' and the fourth part of ''Cuarto de hotel.'' In four of these the mirror is specifically mentioned as the source of the reflected image; in the others it is strongly implied. What they all have in common, as a point of departure for the development of the theme, is that the poet uses a reflection of himself as a means of probing the meaning of reality.

It is interesting to note that in all cases the poet does not use the mirror at the outset of the poem. There is an introduction—varying from several words to several paragraphs—before the actual appearance and recognition of the reflection. This gradual approach to the dominant idea has the effect of increasing the impact and heightens the drama of the confrontation when it actually occurs. The meeting takes place without any strong break in the association of ideas, so that the reader suddenly

becomes aware, with the same surprise that the poet himself must feel, that another identity, perhaps unbidden, has made an appearance. The passage from ''Cuarto de hotel'' is representative of all the poems under discussion in the way it slips into the question of dual identity easily, casually, and passively:

Roza mi frente con sus manos frías
el río del pasado y sus memorias
huyen bajo mis párpados de piedra.
No se detiene nunca su carrera
y yo, desde mí mismo, lo despido.
¿Huye de mí el pasado?
¿Huyo con él y aquel que lo despide
es una sombra que me finge, hueca?
Quizá no es él quien huye; . . . .

At first we are told only that the poet is evoking memories; a chain of them which he reviews in his mind's eye. In the second sentence, the poet makes a separation of himself from the procession of memories (a separation which is indispensable for what is to follow, but which suggests nothing more so far than his awareness that there is a part of him which is not actively engaged in the process of evocation). In the question which follows, the separation between memory and himself is sharpened and made more concrete, but as yet does not involve a second personality. But in the next question—and the transition is made even smoother by the parallelism of the form—a subtle but vital change has been effected: the poet has shifted his point of view. Instead of seeing his memories from the vantage point of his consciousness, he has now identified himself with the memories themselves—but without submerging his voluntary consciousness completely, so that he now looks back at the person who was viewing the spectacle. What follows is a perfectly logical and rational doubt, and an implied debate as to the real identity of the poet: ''Aquel que fuí se queda en la ribera. / No me recuerda nunca, ni me busca.'' We have, therefore, been led into the problem somewhat unawares. The poet has begun with a perfectly rational and normal set of circumstances and without our realizing it, has entered the realm of the abstract, a confused world where the standard concepts of reality do not always apply.

In this poem we have observed that the poet's vision of himself is obtained when he identifies himself with his recollections, and that he sees a shadow imitating him. In ''La calle,'' the same sort of subtle change of vantage point is made with the same effect: the poet sees himself as he had described himself a moment before. In ''El sediento,'' after becoming lost in a forest of reflections, the poet finds himself again: ''y en el borde del espejo / el mismo muerto de sed.'' This, the final line of the poem, is particularly interesting, for it signifies that the poet has repeated in objective terms the same desires which he described at the beginning of the poem in very subjective terms. In ''Envío'' the process we have noted is reversed; instead of proceeding from the subjective view of himself to the objective, he begins with the objective (''Alguien escribe en mí'') and concludes with the return to himself (''y vuelve a ser yo mismo''). The general impression, however, is the same: the poet sees himself as another person in his own situation (''Con un ardor helado /contempla lo que escribo''). In ''Arcos'' (''Sigo, me espero allá, / voy a mi encuentro''), the same situation is repeated, as it is somewhat less clearly in ''La caída'' (''El espejo que soy me deshabita'') and as it is very clearly in ''Pregunta,'' ''El espejo,'' and ''El prisionero .''

What Paz sees first, then, is a new dimension of his personality —we might call it his unconscious self—which he reveals to us in the contrast between subjective and objective description, and with the exception of ''Insomnio'' and of ''Crepúsculo de la ciudad,'' all the poems we are discussing here return the image of the poet in the act of observing his image, thus giving an unusual depth of perspective.

There is, of course, a basic paradox here, which Paz has not failed to develop for its poetic effect. For how is it possible for the poet to be at the same time the observer and the observed, the victim and the executioner, the departing one and the person to whom he says farewell?

> Estoy con uno como yo,
> que no me reconoce y me muestra mis armas;
> con uno que me abraza y me hiere
> —y se dice mi hijo—;
> con uno que huye con mi cuerpo;
> con uno que me odia porque yo soy él mismo.

''La caída'' summarizes the paradox of the reflection when the poet writes ''Frente de mí yo mismo, devorado'' and ''El espejo que soy me deshabita.'' Unusual definitions of paradoxical situations are found in the concluding stanza of ''Envío'':

> Pero este juez también es víctima
> y al condenarme, se condena:
> no escribe a nadie, a nadie llama,
> a sí mismo se escribe, en sí se olvida,
> y se rescata, y vuelve a ser yo mismo . . .

and in ''Crepúsculo de la ciudad'' :

> Vuelvo el rostro: no soy sino la estela

> de mí mismo, la ausencia que deserto,
> el eco del silencio de mi grito.

Many more examples, not only in the poems built around the mirror, but throughout Paz's work, indicate that he takes pleasure in the exploitation of the paradox. In the case of the mirror, we should add that this device is a fundamental aspect of the poet's vision of himself. It is an organic part of the reflection in the mirror because Paz sees, not a repetition of the same thing in isolation, but a different aspect of reality, and not only a different perspective, but an opposite one:

> todo lo que contemplo me contempla
> y soy al mismo tiempo fruto y labio
> y lo que permanece y lo que huye.

The paradox at first seems an insoluble riddle, for how can one person be two opposing things at the same time? In the real world of events, in life ruled by an inescapable chronology, there would be no answer, but in the dreamlike world of the mirror, time does not exist, at least not in the form in which we know it. In one passage, as applicable to the question of reality as it is to the question of time, we read: ''¿ Y somos esa imagen que soñamos, / sueños al tiempo hurtados, / sueños del tiempo por burlar al tiempo?'' Lines which Paz wrote for the sixth part of ''Cuarto de hotel'' could be applied to the mirror:

> No hay antes ni después. ¿ Lo que viví
> lo estoy viviendo todavía?
> ¡Lo que viví! ¿Fuí acaso? Todo fluye:
> lo que viví lo estoy muriendo todavía.
> No tiene fin el tiempo: . . . .

Like Paz's concept of poetry, the mirror is a world without time (here we are reminded of the Surrealists, who have capitalized on the abolition of limits of time and space), where it is completely appropriate for two opposites to be viewed in conjunction.

As an illustration of the poet's reaction to what he sees in the mirror, the major portion of ''Pregunta'' is particularly revealing. The first lines of the poem, with the deliberate confusion regarding the identity of the being the poet is addressing, lead up to the presentation of the vision:

> Déjame, sí, déjame, dios o ángel, demonio.
> Déjame a solas, turba angélica,
> solo conmigo, con mi multitud.

The fact that the same thing can be taken as a god or angel, devil and angelic throng, the paradoxical statement of the poet's being alone with himself and alone with his multitude, prepare us for the dualities which are to follow.

The second stanza is the confrontation ''Estoy con uno como yo,'' which we have already discussed above. The stanza which follows describes Paz's usual reaction to the image in the mirror:

Mira, tú que huyes,
aborrecible hermano mío,
tú que enciendes las hogueras terrestres,
tú, el de las islas y el de las llamaradas,
mírate y dime:
ese que corre,
ese que alza lenguas y antorchas
para llamar al cielo—y lo quema—;
ese que vive entre las aguas,
en un pedazo oscuro de tierra deliciosa;
ese que es una estrella lenta que desciende;
aquel que es como un arma resonante,
¿ es el tuyo, tu ser, hecho de horas
y voraces minutos?

The question which introduces the fourth stanza is a logical outgrowth of the preceding one. What the poet has seen, we have pointed out, is another facet of his own personality. ''¿Quién sabe lo que es un cuerpo / un alma, /y el sitio en que se juntan?'' This question, unanswered, leads to still another: ''¿Y somos esa imagen que soñamos, / sueños al tiempo hurtados, sueños del tiempo por burlar al tiempo?'' The three questions, all centering around the identity of the reflection, might be reworded, resorting to oversimplification, as follows: Is he my soul? Who knows what body and soul are? Are they both unreal?

This question of identity, the reaction to the vision in the mirror, is primarily an intellectual matter, a rational inquiry, but its secondary effect on an emotional level is one of acute anguish:

Muros, objetos, cuerpos te repiten.
¡Todo es espejo!
Tu imagen te persigue.
El hombre está habitado por silencio y vacío.
¿Cómo saciar esta hambre,
cómo acallar este silencio y poblar su vacío?
¿Cómo escapar a mi imagen?
Sólo en mi semejante me trasciendo . . .

Frequently the question asserts emptiness, as it almost does in ''Pregunta'' above. Or again:

¿ qué soy, sino la sima en que me abismo,
y qué, si no el no ser, lo que me puebla?
El espejo que soy me deshabita;
un caer en mí mismo inacable
al horror de no ser me precipita.

And again:

Hacia mí mismo voy; hacia las mudas,
solitarias fronteras sin salida:
duras aguas, opacas y desnudas,
horadan lentamente mi conciencia
y van abriendo en mí secreta herida,

que mana sólo, estéril, impaciencia.

In another poem the poet wonders if he is alone in time, if he is only time: ''¿Soy un llegar a ser que nunca llega?'' One of the concluding sections of ''Pregunta,'' immediately following the three questions, sums up the extreme discomfort the interrogations have brought about, a discomfort expressed, logically enough, in terms of self-inflicted hurt:

En soledad pregunto,
a soledad pregunto.
Y rasgo mi boca amante de palabras
y me arranco los ojos
henchidos de mentiras y apariencias,
y arrojo lo que el tiempo
deposita en mi alma,
miserias deslumbrantes,
ola que se retira . . . .

What does the questioning lead to? What answer does the poet find? The conclusions he draws in ''El espejo'' are the conclusions of all the poems with the mirror as a theme:

y entre los juegos fatuos del espejo
ardo y me quemo y resplandezco y miento
un yo que empuña, muerto,
una daga de humo que le finge
la evidencia de sangre de la herida,
y un yo, mi yo penúltimo,
que sólo pide olvido, sombra, nada,
final mentira que lo enciende y quema.
De una máscara a otra
hay siempre un yo penúltimo que pide.
Y me hundo en mí mismo y no me toco.

This is equivalent to an admission of failure, to a certain extent, failure at least in an inability to determine the nature of reality. The reflection is false, and after observing it carefully, the poet feels that what it reflects is false too. Both then are masks, as he has declared above. ''Y entre espejos impávidos un rostro / me repite a mi rostro, un rostro / que enmascara a mi rostro.'' He ends up being a reflection of a reflection. Yet with all this, in spite of the rejection of both faces, of all the faces that he may see, the poet is aware of his own observation and of his own unsatisfied need for something else. Between one mask and another, ''hay siempre un yo penúltimo que pide,'' which asserts the existence of the ''último yo,'' the object of his search.

The mirror illustrates, in its connection with reality, an idea fundamental for all of Paz's poetry: the pursuit of the absolute, which frequently leads to feelings of anguish at its unattainment. What underlies the majority of his poems, analogous to his search for his true reflection in the mirror, is a desire to define the subject with which he is dealing. Definition seems to involve, first, a rejection of the appearances, and then a simplification, a stripping away of superfluous attributes, in an impassioned effort to arrive at the heart of things. Finally, the poet in most cases is left with the feeling of frustration that comes when he sees that somehow there is a reality beyond his reach.

Whether he is dealing with a chair, the Mexican landscape, or love, Paz cannot help but be an abstractionist in his treatment of the topic. This does not mean generalizing, so that he attempts to write about all chairs, all the landscape, all love, but rather to find the essence of his own vision of the subject. If it can be found, he seems to say, in it will be found the common ground which is universality. For all of his vision of reality, as for his search in the mirror, his aim is to find an absolute value—not so much in himself as *through* himself.

Quite clearly the goal has not been attained in his poems dealing with the mirror. The reality he seeks usually concludes in the nothingness the poet feels at the conclusion of ''El espejo'' and which in another poem, he has described in similar terms:

Adiós al espejo verídico,
donde dejé mi máscara
por descender al fondo del sinfín
(y nunca descendía:
¿ no tienes fondo, sólo superficie?)

It is the same negative result that gives rise to another thought which occurs several times to the poet: perhaps we do not exist even in the form that we imagine we exist in:

olvidos que alimentan la memoria,
que ni nos pertenecen ni llamamos,
sueños del sueño, súbitas presencias
con las que el tiempo dice que no somos,
que es él quien se recuerda y él quien sueña.

An interesting parallel to this concept of man as related to idea is found in the work of Paul Valéry, who was also fascinated by the mirror. Valéry, too, suggested that it is not the self that finds the idea, but the idea that adopts the self. The similarity between the two writers, moreover, does not end there; the mirror, as a method of encouraging complication in order to think better, is a token of a great area of thought which the two have in common. Like Paz, Valéry had moments of annoyance with the defectiveness of words and the meaning they convey; like Paz, too, and as the title of Elizabeth Sewell's interesting study indicates, Valéry was bewitched by the sight of his own mind in action: ''Je suis étant et me voyant, me voyant me voir.''

There is at least one notable difference between the two, however. Paz probably would agree with Valéry that we have the faculty of producing an inner antagonism against ourselves. In Paz, however, it is produced, not while looking at his image in the mirror, but before, and it is the frustration of not being able to overcome it which takes the form of resentment against the image in the mirror. Hence when Valéry speaks of the mind vibrating in an infinity of mirrors, he is speaking of creation and movement, of a pleasurable sensation. The same image for Paz is one of frustration, limitation, and anguish.

Although Paz's only firm conclusion after looking in the mirror is a negative one, the certainty of nothingness, we may well suspect that he seeks certainty of a different kind. The thirst for eternity which torments him seldom appears in his poetry in positive form. One of these few cases of blissful longing occurs in ''Himno entre ruinas,'' the concluding poem of *Libertad bajo palabra:*

La inteligencia al fin encarna en formas,
se reconcilian las dos mitades enemigas
y la conciencia-espejo se licúa,
vuelve a ser fuente, manantial de fábulas:
Hombre, árbol de imágenes,
palabras que son flores que son frutos que
        son actos.

Some lines of William Butler Yeats, from a poem which is not particularly metaphysical (''Before the World Was Made''), perhaps provide a definition of Paz's goal:

From mirror after mirror,
No vanity's displayed.
I'm looking for the face I had
Before the world was made.

Paz's search in the mirror, then, is a search typical of 20th-century man. It is paradoxical, as many of Paz's ideas are, that the more personal his search becomes, the more it acquires characteristics of the universal. This is not the unfathomable, intricate labyrinth of the ego that we often find in the Surrealists, but a search that concerns many men of today's world.

Source: John M. Fein, ''The Mirror as Image and Theme in the Poetry of Octavio Paz,'' in *Symposium,* Vol. X, No. 2, Fall, 1956, pp. 251–70.

Sources

Brotherston, Gordon, ''The Traditions of Octavio Paz,'' in *Latin American Poetry: Origins and Presence*, Cambridge University Press, 1975, 228 p.

Paz, Octavio, *Early Poems: 1935-1955*, translated by Muriel Rukeyser et al., Indiana University Press, 1993, 145 p.

Phillips, Rachel, *The Poetic Modes of Octavio Paz*, Oxford University Press, 1972, 168 p.

Weinberger, Eliot, editor, *Octavio Paz: Selected Poems*, New Directions, 1984, 147 p.

Wilson, Jason, *Octavio Paz*, Twayne Publishers, 1986, 165 p.

Further Reading

Chiles, Frances, *Octavio Paz: The Mythic Dimension*, Peter Lang, 1986, 224 p.
    Study of myth and mythmaking in Paz's poetry based on an analysis of the central theme of solitude versus communion.

Duran, Manuel, "Octavio Paz: The Poet as Philosopher," in *World Literature Today: A Literary Quarterly of the University of Oklahoma*, Vol. 56, No. 4, Autumn, 1982, pp. 591-94.
    Duran writes that Paz belongs to a select group of poets "who can expand the limits of poetry until they invade the realm of philosophy."

Ivask, Ivar, ed., *The Perpetual Present: The Poetry and Prose of Octavio Paz*, University of Oklahoma Press, 1973, 160 p.
    A collection of essays on a variety of subjects in Paz's poetry, including water imagery, the concept of universalism, irony and sympathy, the status of the reader, and the use of images.

Quiroga, Jose, *Understanding Octavio Paz*, University of South Carolina, 1999, 194 p.
    A study of Paz with regard to his literary and historical position, emphasizing his earlier work.

Wilson, Jason, *Octavio Paz: A Study of his Poetics*, Cambridge University Press, 1979, 192 p.
    Wilson explores Paz's affinities with André Breton's surrealism as the basis for Paz's vision of the poet and poem.

Family Ties

Clarice Lispector
1960

"Family Ties" is the title story of Clarice Lispector's *Lacos de Familia* (*Family Ties*). A play on the word "ties" suggests the tension of the story, between the ties that connect and the ties that bind one to family members. Like many of the other stories in the collection, "Family Ties" concerns men and women who, when faced with a moment of epiphany in their relations with others, tragically choose not to communicate openly, but to perpetuate a sense of alienation within family bonds. The story concerns a woman, Catherine, who is relieved when her mother departs after a visit, because their relationship is strained and artificial. They cannot reach each other emotionally and fear doing so. They ignore the deepest part of their feelings for each other, since both hate and love reside there. Almost in retaliation for her own imprisonment, Catherine begins the process of re-creating the same bonds with her young son at the end of the story. She has learned the nature of her anguish from a moment of epiphany, yet rather than right this wrong, she commits it to her son's legacy. The phenomenological narrative style of the story was a landmark in Brazilian literature, opening the door to experimentation with form and language. Clarice Lispector's fiction spans the modern and postmodern eras, representing the human mind in an eloquent and fluid style and probing metaphysical questions of being, identity, and language. This is a story that does not preach, but that exposes essential and tragic human qualities in a quiet, haunting way.

Author Biography

Clarice Lispector, the youngest of three daughters, was born in Tchetchelnik, Ukraine, to Ukrainian parents on December 10, 1920. At the time the family was en route to Brazil, where they lived first in Alagoas, then Recife, and finally in Rio de Janeiro. The year of her birth has been established only recently, since Lispector routinely lied about her age, either from feminine modesty or to give the illusion of having been an early blooming writer. Thus her birth year is variously cited as 1920, 1921, 1924, and 1925, depending upon the date of the publication. Her mother, Marieta, was paralyzed during Clarice's childhood and died when Clarice was nine. Her father, Pedro, could not afford to buy the books that he and his daughters loved, so Clarice made use of the local library. She was a good student, and one of the very few women to earn a secondary degree in law in Brazil in the 1950s. During and after law school she also worked as a reporter and news agency editor. She married a fellow law student, Mauro Gurgel Valente, and accompanied him on his diplomatic journeys to Italy in 1944, during the end of World War II. Being a Jew in Mussolini's Italy, Lispector refrained from commenting in her letters or her journal about the political climate she found in Europe. In fact, Lispector, like Jorge Borges, whose work she read and admired, went against the grain of contemporary writing in her native land and usually avoided political commentary. The couple lived in Europe until 1949 and then in the United States from 1952 until 1960. During these years away from Brazil, Lispector experimented with short stories and produced two more novels. After divorcing her husband in 1959, she and their two sons returned to Rio de Janeiro.

As a student, Lispector had begun to write stories and to send them to newspapers to be published, and she served as editor of the school newspaper. Her first published work, *Perto do Coraca Selvagem* (1943) [*Near to the Savage Heart*], was an autobiographical novel, for which she was awarded Brazil's Graca Aranha Prize. Her fourth and most acclaimed novel, *A Paixao Segundo G. H.* [*The Passion According to G. H.*] was published in 1964, after she returned to Rio de Janeiro. Her prevalent themes of gender, imprisonment, psychology, existential metaphysics, and their relationship to language appear from her earliest writings. In the midst of writing a confessional treatise on the creative relationship between writing and life in 1977, *Um sopro de vida* [*A Breath of Life*], Lispector died of cancer. This last work was published posthumously in 1978.

When she once visited Clarice Lispector's home in Rio de Janeiro to conduct an interview, Elizabeth Lowe reported being "struck by the great number of portraits that stared out from every wall of the room with the eerie effect of fragmenting my perception of the author as she stood in front of me." The interviewer's observation seems a fitting tribute to Lispector's obsession with perception, introspection, and identity, which drove her to write haunting and evocative prose throughout her life. She is credited with changing the course of Brazilian literature by opening up new possibilities in narrative style with her existentialist stories and novels.

Plot Summary

The story opens with a mother and daughter in a taxi on the way to the train station for the mother's departure, after a visit to her married daughter's family. The daughter, Catherine, is relieved that the tensions of the visit will soon end. She had nearly laughed aloud at her husband's discomfort when her mother made a general and insincere-sounding apology for her comments, which apparently mostly centered on the couple's "thin and highly strung" son. Tony, suffering from a cold, had hidden behind a cough rather than respond meaningfully to his mother-in-law. In the taxi ride, both women have the sense of something left unsaid, and they ask each other what they may have forgotten, but keep the conversation on the relatively safe topic of the child. Their composure is momentarily shaken when the taxi driver slams on the brakes and the two women briefly collide. They rearrange the suitcases and handbags quickly, to avoid the sense of "physical intimacy long since forgotten." Catherine had had a closer relationship with her father, and she is anxious to be away from her mother. Only when the train lurches away do they call out to each other, "Mother" and "Catherine," and when the daughter sees her mother's tremulous hand adjusting the hat she had bought at Catherine's milliner's shop, she has a sudden urge to ask her if she had had a happy marriage with her father.

Having never made the connections both women longed for and feared, they are parted, and

Catherine walks with her usual brisk step, now that she no longer has to keep pace with her aging mother. She feels beautiful and fixes her pleasure on "the things of the world." Catherine heads straight for her own son, after answering yes to her husband's terse query, "Has *she* gone?" The child is a distant and preoccupied young thing, four years old. She finds him playing with a wet towel, and feels a sudden desire to "fasten the child forever to this moment." As she hangs up the towel, the child calls her "Mummy," in a way he hadn't before, without following it with some kind of request. Not understanding why, Catherine enjoys the moment, and bursts into a wheezing laugh, which the child promptly pronounces "ugly." Now Catherine is more than ever determined to attach him to her. She brusquely gathers him up and spirits him to the elevator, telling her surprised husband they are going for a walk. Coughing and blowing his nose from his cold, Tony does not have time to respond or to stop them, even though he feels left out.

Tony watches the pair from the height of the apartment window, seeing them now as "flattened," without their familiar perspective. The child's hair blows in the breeze of the nearby sea. A fear grips Tony that his wife might transmit something—at first he does not know what—to his son. "Catherine, this child is still innocent," he thinks. He realizes that it is imprisonment that she will transmit, and that she will impose it with a "morose pleasure." He foresees how the child will stand by the same window and be imprisoned, "obliged to respond to a dead man." Tony feels alone in the efficient apartment his engineering job has provided for his family. They have escaped him to form a bond he will not join. He realizes that beneath her serenity, Catherine hates him and what they have achieved, as a family as well as economically, but he also knows that he is bound to perpetuate both. He sees their petulant child as excised from the safe life Catherine and he have fashioned; the child is the expression of irritation and frustration that they refuse to express to each other.

Tony's thoughts turn to dinner, the return of routine, and he decides to go to the cinema after dinner, to bide the time until dark, when "this day would break up like the waves on the rocks of Arpoador." Tony just barely acknowledges the irritating sound of the elevator coming up, bearing his family. Either the noise or the idea of its not stopping "even for a second" seems to remind him how little control he has over his family's progression toward eternal imprisonment.

Characters

Catherine

Catherine is a serene thirty-two-year-old woman who has a distant relationship with her mother, husband, and four-year-old son. She is "modern" and pretty, slightly plump, with short hair tinted reddish brown, and a slight squint. With her husband, Catherine lives tranquilly if not happily, refusing to break the peace with the kind of talk that could lead to intimacy. With her mother, she maintains a safe distance, even though she longs, in a way, to ask her intimate questions such as whether she was happy with her father. To Catherine, "'mother and daughter' means 'life and repugnance.'" She is filled with relief after her mother leaves, but the lingering sense of a connection drives her to build the same neurotic and imprisoning relationship with her tiny son.

The Child

"Thin and highly strung," the child, whose name is not given, speaks "as if verbs were unknown to him" and "observe[s] things coldly, unable to connect them among themselves." His mind is always "somewhere else." When his mother laughs in a wheezing way at his calling her "Mummy," it prompts him to pronounce his mother "ugly." He has no attachment to his family, but Catherine is about to forge one.

Severina

Severina, Catherine's mother, adopts a tone of "challenge and accusation" with Tony that is really directed at her daughter. She pronounces their son "too thin" and waits until the day of her departure to apologize, in an offhand and general way, for her harsh treatment of her son-in-law. Severina is an old woman, wrinkled, with dentures, but with the silly vanity of a hat that falls over her eyes when the train lurches forward. The hat, "bought from the same milliner patronized by her daughter," was a futile and misguided attempt at intimacy as well as a form of advertisement of her stylishness to the other train passengers. The unsaid words, "I am your mother," haunt her parting with Catherine. Severina, looking like a madonna, is most vulnerable when the train moves off and it is too late for her to repair the damage of her mothering of Catherine.

Tony

"A slightly built man with a dark complexion," Catherine's husband has a slight cold, which he uses to mask his discomfort around his mother-in-law. His having a cold is a metaphor for all of the family relations: sickness, self-absorption, and fragility. He is an engineer who has provided well for his family and who on typical Saturdays "pursued his private occupation" of reading. Tony realizes that when Catherine takes their son for a walk, she is beginning to build that tight bond between mother and child that will imprison the young boy just as he was imprisoned by his own mother and Catherine by her mother, yet Tony can do no more than think to himself, "Catherine, this child is still innocent." He cannot move himself to follow them or to stop her, but stands looking wistfully out the window at them walking away from him. He takes refuge in the thought of going to the cinema with his family after dinner, a way of passing the evening safely and quickly, with no threat of intimacy.

Themes

Existentialism

Existentialism is a philosophy that places tremendous responsibility on humans, because it posits no meaning to life except that which each person makes of it. The existentialists (Sartre, Heidegger, Kierkegaard, Dostoyevsky, Nietzsche, Jaspers, Camus) in their various formulations of this philosophy of being (ontology), either deny the existence of God or point out that because God does not reveal the purpose of life, the consequence for humankind is the same as if God did not exist. With no purpose in life, each human is totally free—but also totally responsible for his or her own actions. The meaninglessness of existence coupled with ultimate responsibility causes angst, a physical and emotional rejection of an unwelcome truth. Life is absurd, and humans shrink in horror from its absurdity and fear to take responsibility to create themselves. How does one decide how to live, how to create oneself in a meaningless world? Jean-Paul Sartre, the "father of existentialism," coined the term to describe the creation of the self as a necessary reaction to awareness of the existence of others: "I see *myself* because *somebody* sees me." Without others to remind one of one's existence, a person's state of mind is simply "unreflective consciousness," an inert state. Being aware of the presence of others is a reminder that the world, meaningless as it is, cannot be escaped. Being seen by another does not result in morality, however, since each person is alone in creating a self and a purpose in life. The presence of others only serves to remind one of one's own existence, and of the other's freedom, not of any particular moral code. Sartre explains in *Being and Nothingness* (1943), "*nothing*, absolutely nothing, justifies me in adopting this or that particular value, this or that particular scale of values." The loneliness of mutual but unconnected co-existence is described in Sartre's novel *Nausea*, where a couple cannot sustain their relationship in the face of the absurdity of life. As depressing as existentialism may seem, there is a way out of its prison of absurdity. Sartre describes the "man of good faith" as one who fully governs his life responsibly, even though no moral consequences exist. The "man of bad faith" harms himself and others through hypocrisy or selfishness, or by withdrawing from the world. Thus existentialists find it crucial to make responsible choices. Another way to fight against absurdity and nausea is to create. In a world without values, the freedom to create one's own meaning can be liberating, at least to those with the strength of character to face the responsibility implied in the creative act or gesture. The narrator of *Nausea* overcomes his despair by imagining he will write a perfect novel, a redeeming act of creativity.

One of the hallmarks of the existentialist writer is to probe the consciousness, searching for understanding of oneself, and exposing self-contradictions, in an attempt to achieve total honesty. The self, because it is always creating itself, is always in flux and thus always in need of re-evaluation. Clarice Lispector (who had read Sartre and loved Dostoyevsky) shares the existentialist concern for soul-searching and responsibility. Her writing surveys her character's fluid consciousness, moving from one thought to another, without fixing or defining her character definitively through assertion, using a combination of deliberate vagueness and specificity. Giovanni Pontiero in his translator's introduction to *Family Ties* says that "Clarice Lispector shares the Sartrean conviction that we are not content to live. We need to know who we are, to understand our nature, and to express it. Her vision of reality gives identity to being and nothingness and satisfies the need 'to speak of that which obliges us to be silent.'"

Phenomenology

Phenomenology is a philosophy centered on psychological processes. It concerns the way that objects are perceived or registered in the consciousness. Edmund Husserl, the founder of phenomenology, sought to make of it a science that would give philosophy the same status as the sciences of psychology and math. Therefore, he posited not only the philosophy, but a way of approaching it. Since phenomenology involves only the registering of objects in the mind, it is necessary to "bracket out" any preconceived notions, inferences, or valuations of the object. In phenomenology, the only acceptable emotive or intellectual process is the notion of "intention" which comprises the conceptualization of the object and empathic response to it. The world and the self are thus constructed through the subjective human consciousness. There are several implications for writing implicit in a phenomenological approach. One is the necessity to describe consciousness as a temporal flow that moves from one encounter with objects to the next, incorporating the past, present, and future. Such accounts would tend to be first-person accounts, bordering on solipsism, or self-centeredness. Given this personal point of view, the individual's history of experiences affects or molds the possible "horizon of meanings" that a given object will summon up in the mind. While objects and the world exist independently, they can only be perceived through the consciousness, and thus any description of the world and its objects is necessarily subjective and idiosyncratic.

Clarice Lispector has been called a phenomenological writer and thinker due to her obsession with portraying the ever-changing consciousness. As she has explained, her approach is to let her own thoughts flow freely: "When writing I have insights that are 'passive' and so intimate that they *write themselves* the very instant I perceive them without the intervention of any so-called thought process." In other words, Lispector tries to "bracket out" her editorial mind as she writes, in an attempt to reproduce the actual flow of her own consciousness.

Feminism

Existentialism has a particular importance to women, as shown by Simone de Beauvior, Sartre's life partner. If, according to existential philosophy, each person constantly recreates herself in reaction to awareness of the other, then women are doubly subjected, because of oppression by male others who use women, and their power over women, as a

Topics for Further Study

- Why does Catherine have the urge to laugh at her husband's discomfiture when her mother apologizes to him for "anything [she] might have said in haste"? Why does she suppress her laughter?

- What is "normal" about the relationship between Catherine and her mother? What is "abnormal" about it?

- What is "normal" about the couple's marriage? What is "abnormal" about it?

- What is the significance of the phrase "no one would know on what black roots man's freedom was nourished"?

- Why does Tony not run after Catherine to prevent her from giving their son a "prison of love"?

- In what ways is "Family Ties" representative of existential literature?

means to define themselves. De Beauvoir explains, "Woman. . .finds herself living in a world where men compel her to assume the status of the Other." Existential feminism does not place the burden of female identity solely on males, however, but recognizes female complicity in the formation of woman's gender identity. Women are compliant to their own oppression to the extent that they accept their subordinate role and to the extent that they create their own identity as a subordinate identity. Feminism is the study of the construction of gender identities and the impact these identities have on women's lives and writing. If, as Sartre had shown, writing is a creative outlet for working out problems of identity, then women's writing can be an act of subversion against oppression. According to feminist critic Elaine Showalter, feminist criticism is concerned with "woman as the producer of textual meaning, with the history, themes, genres, and structures of literature by women. Its subjects include the psychodynamics of female creativity; linguistics and the problem of a female language; the trajectory of the individual or collective female literary career; literary history; and, of course, studies of particular writers and works.''

Clarice Lispector was not a feminist in the political sense, but her work has been appropriated by numerous feminist critics, most notably Helene Cixous, who reads into Lispector's fiction her own feminist viewpoint. In Cixous' hands, Lispector becomes a feminist who portrays ''libidinal economies'' by recounting which sexual energies are invested in and which are not. Cixous sees Lispector as a writer who recognizes and exposes her own complicity in the creation of a subordinate female identity, and who, at the same time, mildly subverts male authority through writing. Cixous dissects Lispector's stories and novels and reconstitutes them as evidence supporting her own feminist philosophy, a process for which she has been criticized. Maria Jose Barbosa, another feminist critic, sees Lispector's work as empowering language ''to combat discourses that seek to dominate and corrode women's power as authors and as subjects within Brazilian culture.'' However, Lispector quite consciously avoided writing with political intent, feminist or otherwise, a move of departure from the mainstream of Brazilian literature in the 1960s when the full-length work *Family Ties* was published. It is doubtful that Lispector would identify herself as a feminist, either in the 1960s political sense of the word or in the current linguistic/semiotic/ontological sense of it as expressed by Cixous. Although she said that the status of the Brazilian woman ''still leaves much to be desired; she is enslaved,'' her writing is more focused on human consciousness and the perils of intimacy than on the politics or semiotics of gender.

Style

Point of View

Point of view, as defined by C. Hugh Holman and William Harmon in *A Handbook to Literature, 6th edition* (1992), is ''the vantage point from which an author presents a story.'' The vantage point takes into account several aspects, including the narrator's physical perspective (what she or he sees, as a camera would take it in), the narrator's emotional perspective (mood) and the narrator's related social or relational perspective (attitude toward what is seen). Thus a narrator will record physical observations of items seen, such as a hat, and the vantage point from which it is seen, on another character's head. The narrator would also speak of this item in a certain mood, which could be happy, as expressed in ornate or playful description, or miserable, as expressed in a flat tone and sparsely worded description. Finally, the narrator's reaction to the item as, for example, threatening or congenial, will also be evident. One may also speak of the focalization of a work. Focalization is formed by the triad of the narrating agent (who tells), the narrator's perspective (the vantage point), and the focalized (what is seen). The narrating agent may be omniscient, and be able to read the thoughts of the characters; a restricted omniscient narrator can only read one character's thoughts. Lispector employs a restricted omniscient point of view in ''Family Ties,'' but the perspective shifts after the first two-thirds of the story is told. It begins from the restricted perspective of Catherine, telling what she observes as well as what she thinks. Then after Catherine takes their son for a walk, the story is told from Tony's viewpoint, with his thoughts and observations narrated. The narration is ''restricted'' in the sense that only one viewpoint is treated at a time. If the narration described thoughts from both Catherine and Tony (as well as Severina) at the same time, the point of view would be unrestrictedly omniscient.

Motif

A motif is a recurring image, phrase, or device that enhances the meaning of a story. Often, the motif takes on symbolic importance as part of the story's theme. For example, the Bible contains motifs of light and dark imagery as well as the devices of the prodigal son and the messiah, and these important elements contribute to the meaning of Biblical stories. A motif can be a seemingly minor detail that is repeated in a meaningful way, or it can be a commonly occurring story event around which the story coheres. In ''Family Ties,'' the motif of the window repeatedly occurs as an image that both separates and also joins family members. Another motif is that of departure, as symbolized by the taxi, train, and elevator. There is also a subtle motif in the form of the ''gaze,'' which can border on tender, as when Catherine notices her mother's tremulous hand as she adjusts her hat, or hostile, as when Catherine watches the fumbled apology of her mother to her husband, or it can be fearful, as when Tony watches his wife take their son away for a walk. In all cases, the gaze is impotent, yet judging. The central, organizing motif is that of the relationship between mother and child, first exemplified in the tension between Catherine and her mother, and then the regeneration of that tense bond between

Catherine and her young son. The motif of insects or a swarm of them appears just once in "Family Ties" in a brief allusion to moths around the dinner table, but is a common one in the other stories of the collection *Family Ties* and in other Lispector stories and novels.

Literary Heritage

Lispector is considered one of the leading Latin American writers of the twentieth century. The literary heritage of her fiction can be understood in the historical context of Latin-American literature, and more specifically Brazilian literature. Before conquest and colonization by European forces, particularly Spain, the native Indian cultures of Latin America had a well-developed tradition of written and oral literature. After colonization Latin-American literature emerged from the narratives of the conquered native Indian peoples as well as the European conquerors themselves, and later from the struggles of native peoples against colonial domination, a "literature of oppression." Brazil produced the first Latin-American novel in 1844, with *A moreninha* ("The Little Brunette") by Joaquim Manuel de Macedo. Latin-American fiction in the latter half of the twentieth century developed a concern with experimental narrative and linguistic style as a means of expressing social concerns. Lispector herself served as a forerunner to the flowering of Latin-American fiction by women authors that developed in the 1960s.

Historical Context

The 1960s in Brazil

Brazil is a country whose economy has been largely dependent upon the world price of coffee. It did not obtain independence from Portugal until 1822, and coffee has carried the economy for the fledgling nation ever since, even though Brazil has recently diversified both its agricultural and its service products. Brazil was the only South American country to send troops to Europe to fight the Axis powers in World War II, having had the resources as well as a percentage of expatriate Europeans to encourage participation. The economy accelerated under relatively stable leadership during the late 1950s and very early 1960s. In 1960, President Juscelino Kubitschek established Brasilia

as the new national capital in an effort to shift economic strength to the geographic center of Brazil. Clarice Lispector wrote several *cronicas* (chronicles) in the news applauding Brasilia and its architecture. In 1964, a military coup attempted to control the nation's political unrest (between communist, democratic, and republican supporters) and to ease economic uncertainty, but the move initiated twenty years of military rule and a reign of police terror against those seeking political reform.

Although women in Brazil had received political equity with the right to vote in 1937, they still struggled in the 1960s to shrug off the myth of the tanned, exotic, and willing female from the tropics. In Brazil as in other countries, women did not find equality in the job market and their status was reinforced through sexual stereotyping. Lispector was unusual in having completed a law degree in the 1950s and in having been the first female journalist at a major news agency. Lispector's stories do not actively engage in a critique of gender politics, but portray the urban Brazilian woman as imprisoned by her own inertia as well as by society. In a 1979 interview, Lispector said that the status of the Brazilian woman "still leaves much to be desired; she is still enslaved."

Modernist and Postmodern Literature Movements

The Week of Modern Art of 1922 in Sao Paulo, Brazil, set off a modernist movement among the literati of Brazil that would last for fully fifty years, with a galvanizing effect on artists and writers comparable to the effect of the Impressionist Exhibit of 1874 on Paris. On one hand it introduced the art of Cubism, while on the hand other it inspired an interest in Brazil's folkloric history and native arts. A new artistic movement was spawned whose artists wanted to infuse their art with "light, air, ventilators, airplanes, workers' demands, idealism, motors, factory smokestacks, blood, speed, dream," according to Brazilian poet Menotti del Pichia. Marxist and naturalist writers such as Jorge Amado and Graciliano Ramos wrote of the poverty and hardships of the barren northeast region of Brazil, setting a tone of political and social purpose in Brazilian literature. The 1960s was a period of literary "Boom" in all of Latin America, including Brazil. Modernism represented a break with traditional forms of writing, which had included romantic socialism, realism, and regionalism. The "new" literature of Brazil was cosmopolitan, stylish, poetic, and "arty." Brazilian writers such as Mario Raul

Compare & Contrast

- **1960:** In Brazil, President Juscelino Kubitschek encouraged nationalism through public works projects sponsored by the government, but his spending on these improvements resulted in a higher national debt and inflation, such that the cost of living tripled in Brazil during his presidency. He was also accused of graft and corruption, a not-uncommon problem in Brazil and other Latin American nations. The weakness of his successor, Jânio Quadros, nearly led the country into civil war.

  Today: After a period (from 1964 until 1985) of military rule rife with corruption and police terrorism, increased demands for democratization resulted in local elections (1982 for states and 1989 for president), but the two succeeding presidents were impeached for alleged corruption. President Fernando Henrique Cardoso, an academic rather than a military leader, came to power in 1994 on a campaign platform of democratic reform. His measures have resulted in progress in human rights (against Brazil's police force), economic reform, and education.

- **1960:** The cost of living tripled in Brazil during a period of high inflation under President Kubitschek. Over two-thirds of the population subsisted on agriculture in rural areas. A small percentage of wealthy people controlled the government and the arts.

  Today: Radical economic reforms instituted by President Fernando Henrique Cardoso, including a radical devaluing of the *real* (the currency of Brazil) in 1999, have succeeded in holding back inflation where other South American countries have gone into deeper and deeper recession. Currently Brazil's economic strength outweighs all of its South American neighbor nations together. At the same time, currently 75 percent of Brazil's population now resides in cities. A handful of wealthy influential people still govern the masses, however, who continue to suffer from high rates of illiteracy and poverty.

- **1960:** Modernist literature either sought social change or expressed a sense of pessimism and exhaustion through flat characters who move relentlessly through a complex and absurd world.

  Today: Postmodern literature attempts to express the uniqueness of the individual through the theme of relative values. At the same time themes' transcendence are on the increase, as writers reassert the presence of shared values and experiences.

de Morais Andrade wrote of the urbanity of Sao Paulo, and Jorge Amado elevated the folkloric form to art. Clarice Lispector is often included among modernist writers because of her interest in consciousness and the poetic quality of her prose.

The postmodern movement was slower to come in Brazil. Postmodernist writing self-consciously exposes the act of writing itself, which involves a rejection of standard forms of plot and character and the idea of the "death of the author" in a world of literary "exhaustion," where every story has been told. Postmodernists attempt to capture the illusory or relative quality of meaning through "playing with" narrative schemes, language, and genre. The focus therefore is on formal properties of writing and the act of writing itself more than content. Postmodern fiction also often involves the elevation of marginalized voices.

Brazilian writer Joao Guimaraes Rosa was a formalist, postmodern writer in the sense that he introduced "magic realism" to Brazilian writing, and he expanded on the unique language of eastern Brazil to fuse his own new language in a move similar to *la negritude* of the Caribbean. Rosa profoundly affected the future of Brazilian writing by demonstrating that literature did not have to have a socially reforming agenda. According to Antonio Candido, Clarice Lispector likewise influenced Brazilian literature, due to her ''impressive attempt to elevate Brazilian Portuguese to a plane hitherto unexplored, by adapting it to mental processes imbued with mystery—whereby fiction was no longer a mere exercise or sentimental adventure but rather a genuine instrument of the spirit, capable of helping us penetrate the most recondite labyrinths of the mind.'' Lispector straddled the modernist and postmodern movements. She was a modernist writer who also participated in the postmodernist concern for expressing states of consciousness and she experimented with narrative extensively.

Critical Overview

The short story ''Family Ties'' was first published in 1952 in a collection of Lispector's stories called *Alguns contos* (*Stories*), but it did not receive much notice. Eight years later, in 1960, Lispector republished the story in *Lacos de familia* (*Family Ties*), along with other pieces, some already published and some new, all about family relationships. This time, her collection was reviewed favorably. In *Luso-Brazilian Review,* Rita Herman called *Lacos de familia* ''a personal interpretation of some of the most pressing psychological problems of man in the contemporary western world. Liberty, despair, solitude, the incapacity to communicate, are the main themes that unite the separate stories into a definite configuration of the author's pessimistic perception of life.'' However, since the book, like all of Lispector's original writings, was written in Portuguese, her audience was quite limited. A new translation into English by Giovanni Pontiero, *Family Ties* (1972), launched the collection into a wider literary market, where it was appraised highly. Bruce Cook of *Review* noted the work's ''intense concentration,'' and Lispector's book was cited, along with Guimarares Rosa, as a landmark of Brazilian literature in *Contemporary Latin American Literature* (1973). In general, the seventies found many of Lispector's works being translated into English as well as French, German, Spanish, and Czechoslovakian. With her work in the hands of a worldwide audience eager for texts with a feminist slant, Lispector's writing gained positive attention.

Lispector's writing career as a whole had taken off with the publication of her first novel, *Close to the Savage Heart*, in 1944, when she was just

President Juscelino Kubitschek receives the key to the new Brazilian capital, Brasilia, on April 21, 1960.

twenty-four. That semi-autobiographical novel won the Graca Aranha Prize and showed how Brazilian literature, according to Earl Fitz, ''could benefit from such staples of modern fiction as the interior monologue; temporal dislocation; rejection of external orientation; structural fragmentation; and an emphasis on the ebb and flow of psychological, rather than chronological, time.'' However, it would be another twenty-two years before the appearance of a book-length study of her, by Benedito Nunes (1966). He and other early critics noticed the metaphysical focus of Lispector's writing, especially the influence of Sartre and Camus. In 1979, with the publication of *Vivre l'orange*, feminist French critic Helene Cixous began a decade of promoting Lispector as a paradigm for ''l'ecriture feminine.'' Cixous found in her writing a feminine kind of ''effacement of the subject,'' which has to do with the power of tolerance and acceptance that she finds in Lispector's female characters. Cixous presented her poetic musings about Lispector in a series of lectures that introduced Lispector to a wide, international audience; the lectures have been transcribed in her book *Readings with Clarice Lispector* (1990). The first English biography of Lispector, by Earl Fitz, was published in 1985. At that time, issues of narrative structure joined issues of gender in criticism of Lispector's fiction. Raymond Williams classified her as a feminist writer whose female characters search for ''self-realization and freedom,'' and whose ''constant focus is *nordestinas*, women from the Northeast of Brazil who are characterized as faceless beings who are disenfranchised.'' Others have discussed her narrative strategies, such as Maria Nunes, who notes Lispector's creative use of the interior monologue: ''Lispector's originality lies precisely in the fact that her stylistic control and coherence are used to create influential chaos in the consciousness of her characters.'' On the other hand, irritation with her stream-of-consciousness style of writing has also been registered. Philip Swanson, in his 1995 book *The New Novel in Latin America,* asks, ''Is Clarice's revolutionary new language little more than just vagueness after all?''

Upon the occasion of Lispector's death in 1977, Earl E. Fitz wrote in the *Luso-Brazilian Review,* ''Given the vigor and innovativeness of what we see here, one must wonder about the wonderful stories we could have expected from Clarice Lispector had she not died so prematurely. With her untimely passing, one of Latin America's most original and powerful voices has been stilled.'' Lispector continues to gain credence for her stylistic innovations in narrative. Her writing is now being appreciated for its craft, as well as its dramatic and disturbing portrayal of the human condition.

Criticism

Carole Hamilton

Hamilton is an English teacher at Cary Academy, an innovative private school in Cary, North Carolina. In this essay she analyzes the dramatic unity in the vague elements of Lispector's ''Family Ties'' that cohere into a formal tragedy.

The tight form of the tragedy, in which a character moves relentlessly towards catastrophe, seems to lie in direct opposition to the amorphous flow of a phenomenological or existential work such as ''Family Ties.'' However, because Lispector's fluid narrative concerns the epiphanies of life, what the character does in response to his or her epiphanies constitutes a decision that is not unlike those made by the more traditional tragic hero, who, because of some inherent tragic flaw, can make no other deci-

sion than to fulfill his or her tragic destiny. In a conventional tragedy, the catastrophe results in death or madness, but in Lispector's hands, the tragedy is the perpetuation of existential nausea, from which the character fails to break free.

''Family Ties'' portrays fluidly changing states of consciousness. The story has been called existential for its portrayal of anguish in an absurd and uncaring world, metaphysical for its philosophical feel, and phenomenological for its style of rendering states of consciousness. Giovanni Pontiero, who translated ''Lacos de familia'' (''Family Ties'') into English, notes in an essay titled ''The Drama of Existence in 'Lacos de Familia,''' that Lispector has forged ''a highly unusual style among contemporary writers in Brazil. It is a style that is particularly effective when she creates the image and atmosphere of the world bordering on the realm of phenomenology. Like her characters, the reader is invited to examine experience from inside. Thus her prose style comes close to achieving that 'fertility and fluency' of expression discussed by Virginia Woolf in *Writer's Diary* (1953). Like the English novelist, Clarice Lispector also appears to be learning her craft under the most fierce conditions, now overcome by the brutality and wildness of the world, now overcome by the poetry of life.''

Lispector achieves a phenomenological mood through a fragmented style with sudden shifts in narrative point of view, from outside of the character's mind to inside it, and back. The character's actual thoughts are interposed with the author's narration from that character's perspective. For example,

> Preoccupied, he watched his wife leading the child away and he feared that at this moment, they were both beyond his reach, she might transmit to their son. . .but what? ''Catherine,'' he thought, ''Catherine, this child is still innocent!'' At what moment was it that a mother, clasping her child, gave him this prison of love that would descend forever upon the future man.

In the passage above, the first sentence is presented from the point of view of an omniscient narrator. Then in the next, Tony's thoughts are given in direct discourse. The third sentence is in indirect interior monologue, where the author narrates Tony's ideas. Moving freely among these presentations results in the sensation of perceiving the story through Tony's consciousness, as he sees, and reacts to what he sees.

Phenomenology is about perception and seeing objects, and the phenomenological approach of

What Do I Read Next?

- Jean-Paul Sartre's *Nausea* (originally published in 1935 and issued in English translation in 1965), an existentialist novel about a man who reacts physically to the absurdity of life, inspired Lispector's work.

- Lispector also admired Virginia Woolf. An excellent example of Woolf's work is *To the Lighthouse* (1927), a psychologically oriented portrayal of a young painter who struggles to express her fluid perceptions of life, which contrast markedly with the compass-ordered observations made by men.

- Lispector related to Katherine Mansfield's novel *Bliss* (1920), about which she remarked, ''This book is me.''

- Chilean writer Maria Luisa Bombal's *House of Mist* (1935) did for Chile what Lispector's works did for Brazil—shifted focus away from politics and into the feminine mind.

''Family Ties'' is further emphasized by a motif of seeing that pervades the story. One instance is Catherine watching her mother's hat fall over her eyes, then seeing her mother's watchful but unseeing face from the train window. Seeing occurs literally and in metaphor. The story is narrated almost entirely through the seeing eyes of its characters, first from Catherine's view of her mother, and then from her husband's watchful view of Catherine taking their son for a walk. Throughout the story, the characters' gaze takes in the action, which is then reported from their interior perception of it. There is little effort to portray the characters as characters, with personalities, but rather as interior minds perceiving the world. Pontiero notices that Lispector's ''characters. . .cannot be described as 'types''' but rather ''as images of different states of mind.'' Metaphorically, Tony ''sees'' that Catherine intends to create a bond with their son. In phenomenology, seeing and perceiving are the main mental processes, the physical seeing leading to metaphoric seeing as understanding.

The flow of consciousness is not totally amorphous, despite Lispector's assertion that her writing is mysterious because she lets it flow directly from her mind and does no editing. She claims to be ''incapable of transposing feeling in any clear way without falsifying it—to falsify thought would be to rob writing of its only satisfaction. So I often find myself assuming an air of mystery—a phenomenon that I find extremely irksome in others.'' Whether or not she edited her writing, it succeeds in evoking shifts in consciousness quite realistically, yet her craft is most apparent in the way in which the amorphous flow of thought proceeds in a forward, plotted movement. Tragedy requires plot to unfold the causal sequence that ultimately leads to death or madness. Without a plot, catastrophic events may be sad, but not tragic. Tragedy requires a chain of events, with a fatal decision made by the protagonist. The plot line of ''Family Ties'' is tight, but it occurs internally, in the form of epiphany.

As Lispector's characters perceive and react to the world, they continually generate and modify a self that consists of consciousness. Through acts of perception, the characters confront the world and make decisions that mold their internal character, thus affecting what they observe, in a yin-and-yang relationship between person and perception. The characters experience an epiphany because of the interaction between observation and self-making, and these epiphanies form a very conventional tragic plot line. Catherine's epiphany takes place in two stages. First she reacts to her mother's adjusting the brim of a hat she had bought at her daughter's milliner's with a ''somewhat tremulous'' hand. Catherine realizes at this moment that her mother loves her, and that her mother is aging and frail. Her internal response is loving: ''Catherine felt a sudden urge to ask her if she had been happy living with her

> Epiphany leads to tragic results in this story because the characters fail to respond adequately to the moment, due to a tragic flaw. All of the characters in 'Family Ties' have a tragic flaw that prevents them from growing and benefiting from their moments of epiphany. In fact, the characters seem almost to revel in their misery."

father.'' However, Catherine fails to act on this impulse, and the train takes her mother away. The epiphany inherent in the event fails to change Catherine, however, because instead of acting consistently with her feelings, she hides behind formality and merely shouts, ''Give my love to Auntie!'' She walks away with relief, tinged with regret. Regret is a powerful emotion, as Lispector described in a *cronica* entitled, ''Learning to Live'': ''There are moments in all our lives which we regret having ignored, allowed to pass, or refused, and that regret is as painful as the deepest sorrow.'' Catherine's regretful epiphany leaves a residue that colors her reaction in the next stage of the story's climax, when Catherine' son calls her ''ugly'' because of the wheezing way in which she laughs, with pleasure, at his calling her ''Mummy.'' Her second epiphany is apparent from her physical reaction, coloring, and in her instant decision to take the boy off for a walk. There is a causal relationship between her first and second epiphany, corresponding to rise and the climax of a tragedy. Massaud Moises finds evidence of ''a dramatic unity'' in the ''internal action'' in Lispector's stories. That climax is ''the existential moment on which the characters stake their destinies.'' It is revealed ''by a sudden profoundly psychological revelation which lasts a fleeting second, like the flashing light of a beacon in the dark, and thus escapes being captured in words.'' Catherine's tragic step of taking her son for a walk results from the residue of regret she felt after failing to respond intimately to her own mother. She

creates a new bond with her son in the faint hope that she will succeed where her mother failed. That her mission is doomed from the start is spelled out by Tony, when he thinks that she will transmit a ''prison of love that will descend forever upon the future man.''

Epiphany leads to tragic results in this story because the characters fail to respond adequately to the moment, due to a tragic flaw. All of the characters in ''Family Ties'' have a tragic flaw that prevents them from growing and benefiting from their moments of epiphany. In fact, the characters seem almost to revel in their misery. Catherine associates ''mother and daughter'' with ''life and repugnance,'' yet she walks away from the train station in a exuberant state. She has, she thinks, escaped the moment of truth through avoidance. But she does not realize that she has only taken another step into the human morass. Through her point of view, the narrator asserts that ''nothing would prevent this little woman who walked swaying her hips from mounting one more mysterious step in her days.'' However, she takes her son down to the beach, away from the intimacy of home, to form her imprisoning bond with him. The phenomenological symbolism of her abrupt leave-taking suggests strength, but misplaced strength—a strength in failure. Likewise, the overbearing and criticizing but needy mother Severina shrinks back from being thrown physically against her daughter and tries to uphold an image of success and happiness to her fellow train passengers. She is not unusual in wanting to maintain appearances at the cost of risking a real bond with her daughter. Catherine decides to form the same unhealthy bond with her tiny son, giving him the same legacy that she resents in her relationship with own mother, yet she is happy in doing so. She enjoys the power and avoids thinking about the painful consequences. In a similar way, Tony decides to go to the movies after dinner to avoid being alone with the wife who is reattaching herself to their son instead of to him; he is avoiding confronting her with the comment he repeats impotently out of her hearing, that the child is ''still innocent.'' Moises links these decisions to the existential philosophy that underlines Lispector's stories. Hers is an existential world, and ''this world is inhabited by people who, not knowing the reason for life, commit endless gratuitous acts, fail to communicate among themselves, are impermeable to the 'other' and are condemned to an irremediable solitude.'' While existentialism certainly underlies the tragic circumstances in this story, it follows the very traditional form of tragedy, within its phenomenological framework.

The tragic recognition that Lispector exposes in ''Family Ties'' is that love has hate in it. An analysis of the title of the story underscores this reading. Giovanni Pontiero points out ''the double significance of the word *Lacos* (ties)—referring on the one hand to the chain of conformity with social conventions that link each human to his fellow men [sic]; on the other hand to the bonds of solitude and alienation inherent in our humanity.'' Despite its seeming amorphous flow, ''Family Ties'' is not just a tragic tale told in the phenomenological form. The phenomenological approach supplies the axis of the conflict, the climax, since the heart of the tragedy occurs not outside of the characters in a contest with a formidable enemy, the forces of nature, or fate, but internally, within their hearts. Their tragic flaws prevent them from learning and growing from their epiphanies. The real enemy lies within the character as a fatal inability to embrace intimacy. Each family member is bound by tragic family ties and is doomed to re-recreate these bonds of love and hate in an endless cycle like those of the Greek tragedies.

Source: Carole Hamilton, in an essay for *Literature of Developing Nations for Students*, Gale, 2000.

Liz Brent

Brent has a Ph.D. in American culture with a specialization in film studies from the University of Michigan. She is a freelance writer and teaches courses in the history of American cinema. In the following essay, Brent discusses family relationships in Lispector's story ''Family Ties.''

As its title implies, Lispector's short story ''Family Ties'' is concerned with relationships among family members. The story dwells upon the relationships between the characters in seven different juxtapositions, including: mother/daughter, daughter/father, mother-in-law/son-in-law, grandmother/grandson, mother/son, father/son, and husband/wife. Each relationship is characterized by coldness, distance, and alienation.

As the story opens, Catherine is riding in a taxi with her mother, Severina, to the train station after a two-week visit. Catherine's attitude toward her mother is described by the look in her eyes, which bears ''a constant gleam of derision and indifference.'' Her mother expresses constant anxiety through her continual counting and recounting of her two suitcases. The mother also repeatedly asks Catherine if

All of the family relationships described in this story are characterized by coldness, distance, and alienation. A recurring image which captures the atmosphere of these 'family ties' is one of imprisonment. While observing her child, Catherine imagines that she is 'escaping from Severina,' her mother. Tony imagines that mothers bestow upon their children a 'prison of love,' and that their son will grow up to feel 'imprisoned' in their home.''

she has ''forgotten anything.'' Her anxiety over having forgotten something symbolizes an absence in the relationship between mother and daughter; they have both ''forgotten something'' important about their relationship. They seem to have forgotten the ''family tie'' of mother/child intimacy, however remote in the past, which continues to bind them. They are only reminded of this long-forgotten intimacy when the taxi driver suddenly slams on the brakes, and the two women fall against each other: ''Catherine had been thrown against Severina with a physical intimacy long since forgotten, and going back to the days when she belonged to her mother and father.'' However, this accidental moment of physical intimacy between mother and daughter is not characteristic of their relationship, even when Catherine was a child, as ''they had never really embraced or kissed each other.'' While this could have been an opportunity for an acknowledgment of what they had ''forgotten,'' both women respond with anxiety and further distance: ''after the collision in the taxi and their composure had been restored, they had nothing further to say to each other—both of them feeling anxious to arrive at the station.'' While waiting for the train, mother and daughter still do not know what to say to each other.

From Catherine's perspective, their mother/daughter relationship is one of distance and disdain: "As if 'mother and daughter' meant 'life and repugnance.'" In fact, "she could not say that she loved her mother." However, as the train is pulling out of the station, and mother and daughter exchange a final glance, Catherine does feel a sense that something has been "forgotten." And what they have "forgotten" is to acknowledge the "family ties" which bind them to one another as mother and daughter, despite their differences and the emotional distance they feel: "What had they forgotten to say to each other? It seemed to her that the older woman should have said one day, 'I am your mother, Catherine,' and that she should have replied, 'And I am your daughter.'" But it seems that it is literally too late for this acknowledgment, as the train pulls out of the station, and her mother's face disappears from view. The implication is that the inherent intimacy of this mother/daughter relationship will once again be "forgotten," and the relationship between the two women, despite their "family ties," will always be one of distance, disdain, and alienation. However, the strong maternal image left with Catherine is indicated when, as the train pulls away, she sees that "her mother's face disappeared for a second and now reappeared, hatless, the topknot on her head undone and falling in white strands over her shoulders like the tresses of a madonna." This image refers to the Christian iconography of the mother of Jesus, often depicted in artistic representation as "madonna and child."

Although her relationship with her mother has always been one of distance, Catherine had a closer connection to her father. This intimacy between father and daughter, however, seems to have been built upon their mutual and clandestine sense of alienation from Catherine's mother: "When her mother used to fill their plates, forcing them to eat far too much, the two of them used to wink at each other in complicity without her mother ever noticing." Thus, Catherine's only experience of intimacy in her family of origin is one in which two family members secretly take sides in bonding over their distance from a third family member. Along with her sense of distance from her mother, Catherine's ideas about intimacy with her father are also indirectly based on alienation.

While Catherine's relationship with her mother is characterized by a mutual "forgetting" of the mother/daughter bond, as expressed through their coolness toward one another, her husband's relationship with her mother is even chillier: "During

the older woman's two-week visit, the two of them had barely endured each other's company; the good-mornings and good-evenings had resounded constantly with a cautious tact which had made [Catherine] smile." Catherine seems to take a certain delight in observing the alienation between her husband and mother, as if it confirmed her own alienation from her mother. At the moment of departure, however, her mother attempts to reconcile with her son-in-law, as "before getting into the taxi, the mother had changed into the exemplary mother-in-law and the husband had become the good son-in-law." Catherine seems to enjoy observing her husband's discomfort at being "forced into being the son of that gray-haired little woman." Catherine's inability to think of her mother as a mother is indicated by the fact that she describes her as "that gray-haired little woman." Furthermore, Catherine's coolness toward her own husband is suggested by the fact that she seems to enjoy seeing him squirm; she even has to repress the urge to laugh at him.

Even the relationship between Severina and her grandson, Catherine and Tony's son, seems to be unpleasant. While the relationship between a grandmother and her grandchild is traditionally one of warmth and affection, this one is characterized by distance and antagonism. Severina complains to Catherine that her son is "thin and highly strung." The little expressions of endearment traditionally bestowed by a grandparent upon a beloved grandchild in this family have become perverted into a negative experience on the part of the grandchild. "During his grandmother's visit he had become even more distant and he had started to sleep badly, disturbed by the excessive endearments and affectionate pinching of the older woman."

Like her relationship with her mother, Catherine's relationship with her own son is characterized by distance and alienation. The son seems to have inherited Catherine's sensibilities in his coolness, distance, and inability to express childish affection for his own mother. Like Catherine, her son lacks the ability to form any emotional attachment or connection, or express any human warmth, to other people. Catherine notes that "he observed things coldly, unable to connect them among themselves." In playing with an inanimate object, he is "exact and distant." Even when she tries to scold him, "the child looked indifferently into the air, communicating with himself." She finds that "his mind was always somewhere else. No one had yet succeeded in really catching his attention." Even when he addresses her as "Mummy," it is because he wants something. However, after returning from seeing her mother off at the train station, Catherine hears him address her as "Mummy" for the first time in a warmer tone. She momentarily feels that this is a "verification" of her maternal connection to him. However, this is immediately undermined when he looks at her and says "ugly." Catherine's inability to feel a maternal connection or sense of warmth toward her own mother is thus reproduced in her son's distant, cold, and even cruel regard for her.

The relationship of Tony, Catherine's husband, to their son seems to be even more distant and indifferent than any of the other relationships in the story. It is mentioned that Tony "had never really given much attention to his son's sensibility."

The relationship between Catherine and her husband Tony is almost as cool and distant as that between Catherine and her mother. Tony has always designated Saturdays as "his own," meaning that he is exempt from paying attention to his wife and son. When Catherine returns from the train station, he "scarcely raised his eyes from his book." It is implied that his indifference toward her seems to extend beyond his Saturdays. However, when Catherine spontaneously leaves the apartment with their son to take a walk, Tony becomes keenly aware that he is now literally alone. From this point, the perspective of the story changes from that of Catherine's to that of Tony's, as he watches his wife and son from the window. Tony reflects that, although the couple live "tranquilly" and "peacefully" and "everything worked smoothly" in their home, there is something lacking in their relationship. Catherine's coldness and distance from him is indicated by his description of her as "that serene woman of thirty-two who never really spoke, as if she had lived since the beginning of time." He knows that, although he is a successful engineer with a promising future, Catherine "despises" their home life, and will grow to "hate" their life together.

All of the family relationships described in this story are characterized by coldness, distance, and alienation. A recurring image which captures the atmosphere of these "family ties" is one of imprisonment. While observing her child, Catherine imagines that she is "escaping from Severina," her mother. Tony imagines that mothers bestow upon their children a "prison of love," and that their son will grow up to feel "imprisoned" in their home. He imagines that, in leaving the house to take a walk with their son, Catherine is "escaping" from him

and their marriage and home life. This story thus presents an extremely cynical and bitter depiction of the "ties" which constitute three generations of a family.

Source: Liz Brent, in an essay for *Literature of Developing Nations for Students*, Gale, 2000.

Rena Korb

Korb has a master's degree in English literature and creative writing and has written for a wide variety of educational publishers. In the following essay, she discusses the isolation among the family members in "Family Ties."

With the short story collection *Family Ties*, Brazilian author Clarice Lispector firmly established her reputation. Though she has also written novels, in examining her life's work most critics agree that her true medium lies in the shorter fiction form. The stories in *Family Ties* explore those issues most crucial to the author. Writes Giovanni Pontiero in his introduction to the English translation of *Family Ties*, "[T]he stories of *Laços de Familia* give a comprehensive picture of the author's private world of deep psychological complexities. The narrative in these stories often appears to evolve from smoke—from some momentary experience or minor episode that seems quite insignificant in itself. Action, as such, is virtually nonexistent, and the threads of tension are maintained by use of stream-of-consciousness techniques and interior monologues." Indeed, the plot of the story that lends its name to the collection could hardly be given such a weighty label, and the narration essentially takes place within the minds of two main characters, a husband and wife, who are estranged from each other as well as from the people who inhabit their world.

"Family Ties" can be divided into two sections. The first section features a thirty-two-year-old woman, Catherine, who is accompanying her mother to the train station at the end of a two-week visit. The women have very little proper communication, but an opportunity arises for them to make a connection, which both refuse. The second section takes place at Catherine's home. She decides to forge a bond with her son, and she takes him away, leaving her husband to wonder where they are going, what they are doing, and when they will return.

At the heart of the story is humankind's essential loneliness and alienation. As such, Lispector demonstrates the influence of existentialist writers, who were concerned with issues of freedom, human

> At the heart of the story is humankind's essential loneliness and alienation. As such, Lispector demonstrates the influence of existentialist writers, who were concerned with issues of freedom, human suffering and failure, and alienation."

suffering and failure, and alienation. On a more personal level, however, Catherine, and to a lesser extent, her husband, show the effects of living a life apart. Their actions have ramifications for their son as well, but the reader is left not knowing whether Catherine's experience and her reaction will have any significant change on the relationship between mother and son, and possibly father and son.

The first section of the story makes clear the isolation in which the members of the family—Catherine, her husband Tony, their four-year-old son, and her mother Severina—exist. Nobody in this family makes any pretenses to true closeness or even derives pleasure in each other's company, not even husband and wife, or child and parent. Severina and Tony "had barely endured each other's company" throughout the visit. Severina, who thinks her grandson is too "thin and highly strung," scares him. "During his grandmother's visit he had become even more distant and he had started to sleep badly, disturbed by the excessive endearments and affectionate pinching of the old woman." Significantly, it is the very act of receiving attention that frightens the child and disrupts his sense of self. Clearly, the child is not accustomed to being the focus of love, or more likely, accustomed to being the focus of any sort of emotion.

The section also shows that Catherine and Severina have never had any kind of close relationship themselves. Both women shy away from drawing together, as physically demonstrated in the taxi "when a sudden slamming of brakes threw them against each other." This unexpected occurrence shocks Catherine "because something had, in fact, happened. . .Catherine had been thrown against

Severina with a physical intimacy long since forgotten." The contact reminds Catherine that she once "belonged to a father and a mother," though she immediately reveals that it was with her father that she had always had the "much closer relationship." For her part, after being thrown against her daughter, Severina reacts by paying attention to her luggage. "I haven't forgotten anything?" she asks her daughter, who gives her the gloves picked up from the floor of the cab. What both women have forgotten, however, is how to be a family, indeed, how to express emotion for each other or even how to *feel* emotion for each other. As Catherine admits, the words "mother and daughter" to her mean "life and repugnance." In fact, "she could not say that she loved her mother. Her mother distressed her, that was it."

At the moment of leave-taking, however, Catherine feels some strange stirring. She notices that her mother had "aged and that her eyes were shining," as if with unshed tears. When the bell announcing the departure of the train rings, the women "exchanged frightened glances." Suddenly, both of them feel their disconnection from each other, and ironically, this alienation is explicitly demonstrated to the reader by their similar thoughts. At the same moment that Catherine is about to ask her mother if she had forgotten anything, Severina again poses that question, "I haven't forgotten anything?" as she had in the cab. The women "looked apprehensively at each other—because, if something had really been forgotten, it was too late now." Catherine anxiously wants to open some line of communication. She wants to establish that a relationship actually exists between them. Her mother "should have said one day, 'I am your mother, Catherine,' and. . .she should have replied, 'And I am your daughter.'" With these words, Catherine and Severina would prove not merely their familial bond but a bond between two humans that exists because they want it to be so. All Catherine is able to say, however, is a warning not to sit in a draft.

As soon as the train pulls out of the station, however, Catherine returns to her usual persona. Moving from the platform, "she had recovered her brisk manner of walking," for "alone it was much easier." Ironically, as she walks, she moves in "perfect harmony" and demonstrates to any interested passerby "the relationship this woman had for the things of the world." Although she never openly manifested having a similar interest for her mother, her body retains the memory of what just transpired.

The second section of the story takes place at Catherine's home, and the action rises directly from Catherine's leave-taking with her mother. Catherine feels both the lack of connection with her mother and relief at "escaping" from her. These contradictory feelings affect how she treats her son, whom she is intent on reaching, both physically, in his room, and emotionally. The first glimpse of the child shows his isolation from his parents—that he has been forced to live in a fairly solitary world—for he amuses himself by "playing with a wet towel, exact and distant." When Catherine speaks to him, he "looked indifferently into the air, communicating with himself." (And later, Tony's narration shows the son's inherent difference from his parents: "he stamped his feet and shouted in his sleep.") In the interaction between mother and son, the boy shows his disinterest—even his distaste—for his mother. He calls her "ugly" when she wheezes while laughing (an action that symbolically shows her transformation and her desire to be more open, for earlier the narration revealed that "she never in fact laughed when she felt the urge"). She grabs the child *"by the hand"* [italics mine] and leads him from the apartment where so little affection has been sown.

At this point, the story shifts to the mind of the husband, Tony. He, the man who had seemed disinterested in his wife's return (he "scarcely raised his eyes from his book" when she came in) and in his son's activities, suddenly feels the emptiness of the apartment. He reveals that while he liked Saturdays to be "his own," he also desired that Catherine and the boy be at home "while he pursued his private occupations." His narrative shows Tony's dual desires. He wants to be perceived as an adequate provider for a family but he is essentially a solitary man who wants both to be alone and to control his surroundings. While he values the relationship between himself and his wife, which he calls "tranquil," others might very well call it distant or even perverse, for his most in-depth revelation about his treatment of his wife is his confession that "he tried to humiliate her by entering the room while she was changing her clothes, because he knew that she had detested being seen in the nude. (Why did he find it necessary to humiliate her?)" The answer is clear—he seeks to maintain some, any, connection with his wife—though he does not even recognize it as such.

What provokes Tony's unhappiness at his wife's departure is his innate understanding that his wife is about to attain some sort of connection with their son: "Now mother and son were understanding each other within the mystery they shared." Though Tony has no true desire to share in any "mystery," either with his wife or his son, he does not want them to join without him. He would prefer that all members of the family continue to exist in their isolated boxes. In the end, Tony cannot handle his own explorations of his feelings. Instead of investigating why he is reacting so strongly, he, a man who treasures a life in which "everything worked smoothly," jettisons his thoughts into the future, when his wife will return with their son and all will return to normal. "When Catherine returned they would dine. . .'After dinner we'll go to the cinema,' the man decided. Because after the cinema it would be night at last, and this day would break up like the waves on the rocks of Arpoador."

Source: Rena Korb, in an essay for *Literature of Developing Nations for Students*, Gale, 2000.

Sources

Ayer, A. J., and Jane Grady, eds., *A Dictionary of Philosophical Quotations*, Basil Blackwell Reference, 1992, pp. 401, 404.

Borelli, Olga, *Clarice Lispector: um esboco para um possivel retrato*, Nova Frontiera, 1981, p. 66.

Cook, Bruce, "Women in the Web," in *Review*, Vol. 73, Spring, 1973, p. 65.

Fitz, Earl E., *New York Times Book Review*, Winter, 1982, pp. 195-208.

Herman, Rita, review of *Lacos de Familia*, in *Luso-Brazilian Review*, Vol. 4, No. 1, June, 1967, pp. 69-70.

Holman, C. Hugh, and William Harmon, *A Handbook to Literature, 6th edition*, Macmillan Publishing Co., 1992, p. 366.

Lispector, Clarice, *Selected Cronicas*, New Directions, 1992, p. 55.

MacAdam, Alfred J., review of *Lacos de Familia*, in *New York Times Book Review*, September 3, 1967, pp. 22-23.

Moises, Massaud, "Clarice Lispector: Fiction and Cosmic Vision," translated by Sara M. McCabe, in *Studies in Short Fiction*, Vol. 8, No. 1, 1971, pp. 268-81.

Pontiero, Giovanni, "The Drama of Existence in *Lacos de Familia*," in *Studies in Short Fiction*, Vol. 8, No. 1, 1971, pp. 256-67.

Popkin, Richard H., ed., *The Columbia History of Western Philosophy*, Columbia University Press, 1999, p. 730.

Swanson, Philip, *The New Novel in Latin America: Politics and Popular Culture after the Boom*, Manchester University Press, 1995, p. 135.

Williams, Raymond L., *The Postmodern Novel in Latin America: Politics, Culture, and the Crisis of Truth*, St. Martin's Press, 1995, p. 118.

Further Reading

Cixous, Helene, *Reading with Clarice Lispector*, University of Minnesota Press, 1990.
    A transcription and translation of French feminist Cixous' lectures about Lispector's fiction.

Fitz, Earl E., *Clarice Lispector*, 1985.
    The first full-length biography of Lispector in English.

———, "Clarice Lispector," in *Dictionary of Literary Biography*, Volume 113: *Modern Latin-American Fiction Writers*, edited by William Luis, Gale, 1992, pp. 197-204.
    A brief biography of Lispector.

Lindstrom, Naomi, *Women's Voices in Latin American Literature*, Three Continents Press, 1981.
    Lindstrom examines the narrative techniques used in *Family Ties* to demonstrate the confines of the expected female social roles and women's reactions to those roles.

Lowe, Elizabeth, "The Passion According to C. L.," in *Review*, Vol. 24, June, 1979, pp. 34-37.
    An interview that focuses on Lispector's writing habits and her interest in social issues.

Lucas, Fabio, "Contemporary Brazilian Fiction: Guimaraes Rosa and Clarice Lispector," in *Contemporary Latin American Literature*, edited by Harvey L. Johnson and Philip B. Taylor, University of Texas Press, 1973.
    An assessment of Lispector's place in modern Brazilian literature.

Nunes, Maria Luisa, "Narrative Modes in Clarice Lispector's *Lacos de Familia*: The Rendering of Consciousness," in *Luso-Brazilian Review*, Vol. 14, No. 2, 1977, pp. 174-84.
    Nunes applies the various and somewhat contradictory terms for interior narration to Lispector's *Family Ties*.

Pontiero, Giovanni, "The Drama of Existence in *Lacos de Familia*," in *Studies in Short Fiction*, Vol. 8, No. 1, 1971, pp. 256-67.
    Pontiero, translator of many of Lispector's works into English, discusses the philosophical underpinnings of the stories in *Family Ties*.

Severino, Alexandrino E., "Major Trends in the Development of the Brazilian Short Story," in *Studies in Short Fiction*, Vol. 8, No. 1, 1971, pp. 199-208.
    Puts Lispector into the context of other modernist writers in Brazil.

A Far Cry from Africa

Derek Walcott
1962

Derek Walcott's "A Far Cry from Africa," published in 1962, is a painful and jarring depiction of ethnic conflict and divided loyalties. The opening images of the poem are drawn from accounts of the Mau Mau Uprising, an extended and bloody battle during the 1950s between European settlers and the native Kikuyu tribe in what is now the republic of Kenya. In the early twentieth century, the first white settlers arrived in the region, forcing the Kikuyu people off of their tribal lands. Europeans took control of farmland and the government, relegating the Kikuyu to a subservient position. One faction of the Kikuyu people formed Mau Mau, a terrorist organization intent on purging all European influence from the country, but less strident Kikuyus attempted either to remain neutral or to help the British defeat Mau Mau.

The ongoings in Kenya magnified an internal strife within the poet concerning his own mixed heritage. Walcott has both African and European roots; his grandmothers were both black, and both grandfathers were white. In addition, at the time the poem was written, the poet's country of birth, the island of St. Lucia, was still a colony of Great Britain. While Walcott opposes colonialism and would therefore seem to be sympathetic to a revolution with an anticolonial cause, he has passionate reservations about Mau Mau: they are, or are reported to be, extremely violent—to animals, whites, and Kikuyu perceived as traitors to the Mau Mau cause.

As Walcott is divided in two, so too is the poem. The first two stanzas refer to the Kenyan conflict, while the second two address the war within the poet-as-outsider/insider, between his roles as blood insider but geographical outsider to the Mau Mau Uprising. The Mau Mau Uprising, which began in 1952, was put down—some say in 1953, 1956, or 1960—without a treaty, yet the British did leave Kenya in 1963. Just as the uprising was never cleanly resolved, Walcott, at least within the poem, never resolves his conflict about whose side to take.

Author Biography

Derek Walcott was born January 23, 1930, in the capital city of Castries on the eastern Caribbean island of St. Lucia, a territory at that time under the dominance of Britain. While the official language of St. Lucia was English, Walcott grew up also speaking a French-English patois. Both of his grandfathers were white and both grandmothers were black. From the beginning, Walcott was, in terms of St. Lucia, a bit of an outsider. In a poor, Catholic country, his parents were middle class and Protestant: his mother was a teacher at a Methodist grammar school who worked in local theater, and his father was a civil servant by vocation and a fine artist and poet by avocation. Walcott's father died shortly after Derek and his twin brother were born. The Walcott home was filled with books, paintings, and recorded music. Walcott studied painting and published, at age fourteen, his first poem. At eighteen, Walcott borrowed $200 from his mother to publish his first book, *25 Poems*. To pay back his mother, he sold copies of the book to his friends.

In his early years, Walcott was schooled on St. Lucia, but in 1950, he attended the University of the West Indies in Jamaica, getting his degree in 1953 but staying on one more year to study education. From 1954 to 1957, Walcott taught in Grenada, St. Lucia, and Jamaica, and wrote and produced plays along with his brother, Roderick. In 1954, Walcott married. Since then he has been married three times and has had three children. In 1958, his play *Drums and Colours* earned him a Rockefeller grant to study theater in New York City. Alienated in the United States, Walcott returned to Trinidad in 1959 to found, with his brother, The Trinidad Theater Workshop, a project that lasted until 1976. From 1960 to 1968, Walcott also wrote for the local newspaper, the *Trinidad Guardian*.

Walcott has taught in both America and the West Indies and has earned numerous awards. He has taught at New York University, Yale, Columbia, Harvard, and, since 1981, at Boston University. Walcott has won numerous awards: in 1965 he received the Royal Society of Literature Heinemann Award for *The Castaway and Other Poems*; his play *Dream on Monkey Mountain* earned the 1971 Obie for the most distinguished off-Broadway play; in 1977 he was awarded a Guggenheim and in 1981 a MacArthur Foundation Award. In 1992, however, Walcott received literature's highest honor, the Nobel Prize. The author of more than twenty books, Walcott continues to write, paint, and direct.

Poem Text

A wind is ruffling the tawny pelt

Of Africa. Kikuyu, quick as flies

Batten upon the bloodstreams of the veldt.

Corpses are scattered through a paradise.

Only the worm, colonel of carrion, cries:

'Waste no compassion on these separate dead!'

Statistics justify and scholars seize

The salients of colonial policy,

What is that to the white child hacked in bed?

To savages, expendable as Jews?

Threshed out by beaters, the long rushes break

In a white dust of ibises whose cries

Have wheeled since civilization's dawn

From the parched river or beast-teeming plain.

The violence of beast on beast is read

As natural law, but upright man

Seeks his divinity by inflicting pain.

Delirious as these worried beasts, his wars

Dance to the tightened carcass of a drum,

While he calls courage still that native dread

Of the white peace contracted by the dead.

Again brutish necessity wipes its hands

Upon the napkins of a dirty cause, again

A waste of our compassion, as with Spain,

The gorilla wrestles with the superman.

I who am poisoned with the blood of both,

Where shall I turn, divided to the vein?

I who have cursed

The drunken officer of British rule, how choose

Between this Africa and the English tongue I love?

Derek Walcott

Betray them both, or give back what they give?

How can I face such slaughter and be cool?

How can I turn from Africa and live?

Plot Summary

Background

"A Far Cry from Africa" discusses the events of the Mau Mau Uprising in Kenya in the early 1950s. In the mid-twentieth century, British colonialism was a fading but still potent force in the world. In the African nation of Kenya, British colonists had settled and introduced European concepts to the local people: money, taxation, and ownership of land. When the British asked, "Who owns this land?" tribal people responded, "We do," and the British assumed that "we" referred to the tribal government, although the land was actually owned by individual families. Because the British were replacing the tribal government with their own, they then claimed all the land in the name of the new British government. Naturally, the Kenyan people were outraged. Now, instead of owning and farming their own land, they were reduced to being laborers for the British owners. As employees, they were further insulted by being paid only a fraction of the amount a British worker received for doing the same work.

The Kikuyu tribe was the largest in Kenya, and the most educated. In 1951, some Kikuyu outbursts of violence against the British occurred, and in 1952 a secret Kikuyu society known as the Mau Mau began a war of violence against the British and any Africans who were loyal to them. By October of 1952, the situation was so serious that the British called out troops to fight the rebels, and a three-year war ensued, during which 11,000 rebel warriors were killed and 80,000 Kikuyu men, women, and children were locked up in detention camps. One hundred Europeans and 2,000 Africans loyal to them were killed. Later, the leader of the rebellion, Jomo Kenyatta, was elected prime minister of Kenya when Kenya became independent from Britain in 1963.

In the poem, Walcott presents some graphic images of the conflict and asks how he can be expected to choose one side over the other, since he is of both African and European descent. He cannot condone the colonialism of the British, or the violence of the Mau Mau, because choosing either side would mean he is turning against that part of himself.

Lines 1-3:

The first three lines depict the poem's setting on the African plain, or veldt. The nation itself is compared to an animal (perhaps a lion) with a "tawny pelt." Tawny is a color described as light brown to brownish orange that is common color in the African landscape. The word "Kikuyu" serves as the name of a native tribe in Kenya. What seems an idyllic portrayal of the African plain quickly shifts; the Kikuyu are compared to flies (buzzing around the "animal" of Africa) who are feeding on blood, which is present in large enough amounts to create streams.

Lines 4-6:

Walcott shatters the image of a paradise that many associate with Africa by describing a landscape littered with corpses. He adds a sickening detail by referring to a worm, or maggot, that reigns in this setting of decaying human flesh. The worm's admonishment to "Waste no compassion on these separate dead!" is puzzling in that it implies that the victims somehow got what they deserved.

Lines 7-10:

The mention of the words "justify" and "colonial policy," when taken in context with the preceding six lines, finally clarifies the exact event that Walcott is describing—the Mau Mau Uprising against British colonists in Kenya during the 1950s. Where earlier the speaker seemed to blame the victims, he now blames those who forced the colonial system onto Kenya and polarized the population. They cannot justify their actions, because their reasons will never matter to the "white child" who has been murdered—merely because of his color—in retaliation by Mau Mau fighters or to the "savages," who—in as racist an attitude as was taken by Nazis against Jews—are deemed worthless, or expendable. "Savages" is a controversial term that derives from the French word *sauvage* meaning wild, and is now wholly derogatory in English. Walcott's use of "savage" functions to present a British colonialist's racist point of view.

Lines 11-14:

Walcott shifts gears in these lines and returns to images of Africa's wildlife, in a reminder that the ibises (long-billed wading birds) and other beasts ruled this land long before African or European civilization existed. The poet also describes a centu-

ries-old hunting custom of natives walking in a line through the long grass and beating it to flush out prey. Such killing for sustenance is set against the senseless and random death that native Africans and European settlers perpetrate upon each other.

Lines 15-21:

These lines are simultaneously pro-nature and anticulture. Animals kill merely for food and survival, but humans, having perfected the skill of hunting for food, extend that violent act to other areas, using force to exert control—and prove superiority over—other people; they seek divinity by deciding who lives and who dies. Ironically, wars between people are described as following the beat of a drum—an instrument made of an animal hide stretched over a cylinder. Walcott also points out that for whites, historically, peace has not been the result a compromise with an opponent, but a situation arrived at because the opposition has been crushed and cannot resist anymore.

Lines 22-25:

These lines are difficult to interpret, but they appear to be aimed at those judging the Mau Mau uprising from a distance—observers who could somehow accept brutality as necessary and who are aware of a dire situation but refuse to become involved in it. The poet appears to condemn such an attitude by comparing the Mau Mau Uprising to the Spanish Civil War (1936-39). Leaders of France and Great Britain wanted to avoid another war that would engulf all of Europe, so they introduced a nonintervention pact that was signed by twenty-seven nations. Nonetheless, the Insurgents, or Nationalists (under the leadership of General Francisco Franco), were aided by and received military aid from Germany and Italy. The Loyalists, or Republicans, had no such backing; they fought valiantly but were outmanned, lost territory, and were eventually defeated in March of 1939. Line 25 presents a cynical view of the Mau Mau Uprising as just another colonial conflict where gorillas—negatively animalized Africans—fight with superman—a negative characterization of Europe.

Lines 26-33:

This stanza is a change of scene from primarily that of Africa to that of the poet. Walcott, being a product of both African and English heritage, is torn, because he does not know how to feel about the Mau Mau struggle. He certainly is not satisfied with the stock response of those from the outside. Walcott is sickened by the behavior of Mau Mau just as he has been disgusted by the British. By the end, the poet's dilemma is not reconciled, but one gets the sense that Walcott will abandon neither Africa nor Britain.

Themes

Violence and Cruelty

The wind "ruffling the tawny pelt of Africa" refers to the Mau Mau Uprising that occurred in what is now independent Kenya, roughly from October 20, 1952, to January of 1960. During this span, the white government called an emergency meeting against a secret Kikuyu society that came to be known as Mau Mau and was dedicated to overthrowing the white regime. Against the backdrop of a cruel, long-lasting British colonialism erupted the more short-term cruelty of Mau Mau insurrection. While some versions have it that Mau Mau was put down by 1953 and others by 1956, the government kept the state of emergency in place until the beginning of 1960. It is the violence of Mau Mau that most disturbs Walcott, apparently because it makes Africans look even worse than their British oppressors. There were many stories of Mau Mau violence directed at whites, the animals owned by whites, and at other Kikuyus who refused to join Mau Mau. The violence was especially grisly since many of the Kikuyus used a machete-like agricultural implement, the *panga,* to kill or mutilate victims after killing them. One such murder—one that Walcott could be describing in "A Far Cry from Africa"—was reported of a four-and-a-half-year-old white child. And on March 26, 1953, in the Lari Massacre, Mau Maus killed ninety-seven Kikuyu men, women, and children, apparently for collaborating with the British. But it was not only the violence of insurrection that terrorized animals, whites, and Kikuyus, but also the reportedly gruesome Mau Mau oathing ceremonies in which initiates pledged allegiance to the Mau Mau cause. A Kikuyu schoolmaster gave this account of a ceremony initiating seven members: "We were . . . bound together by goats' small intestines on our shoulders and feet. . . . Then Githinji pricked our right hand middle finger with a needle until it bled. He then brought the chest of a billy goat and its heart

Media Adaptations

- Bill Moyers interviewed Walcott, primarily on the subject of empire, for his *A World of Ideas,* released by PBS videos in 1987.

- A cassette titled *Derek Walcott Reads* (1994) is available from Harper Collins.

still attached to the lungs and smeared them with our blood. He then took a Kikuyu gourd containing blood and with it made a cross on our foreheads and on all important joints saying, 'May this blood mark the faithful and brave members of the Gikuyu and Mumbi [analogues of Adam and Eve] Unity; may this same blood warn you that if you betray secrets or violate the oath, our members will come and cut you into pieces at the joints marked by this blood.'" Before Mau Mau, one gets the impression that Walcott was not so torn between Africa and Britain; he may have viewed British colonialism as arrogant, ignorant, and cruel, and Africa as victimized. But then, when Africans themselves turned violent, Walcott was torn and could not so easily side with Africans against the British.

Culture Clash

There are many clashes in this poem. The first image signalling conflict is the hint of a storm brewing in the opening lines where Kikuyu flies feed upon the land and maggots upon dead Mau Mau. Here is the first of several culture clashes: pro-Mau Mau pitted against anti-Mau Mau Kikuyu. And within this, a subconflict also exists between those Kikuyu believing that the rights of the individual ("these separate dead") do not necessarily violate those of the group and those convinced that individual rights do violate group rights (the Mau Mau philosophy). In lines six through ten, there is also the clash between the culture of those outside the uprising and those killed by it, outsiders ("scholars") with the luxury of judging the conflict, and insiders (victims) for whom no explanation is sufficient. There are also the outsiders of stanza three, surmising that the conflict is not worth their compassion or involvement, a position against which victims would vehemently argue.

Within the poet, all of these exterior clashes also rage. Walcott is pro-African and pro-Kikuyu but anti-Mau Mau, is pro-English (as in culture and language) but anti-British (as in colonialism), an outsider to the conflict, but an insider in the sense that within his body exists both English and African blood. These conflicts yield up the main confrontation of the poem, that between Mau Mau and the British, and the conflict within the poet about which side to take. Walcott is, then, completely conflicted: while both an outsider and insider he is ultimately unable to be either. While both British and African, he is unable to sympathize with either. While both pro-revolution and anti-violence, he cannot defend the uprising or completely condemn it. Still, he feels he must face these clashes, rather than wish or rationalize them away. From the cultural clash on the continent of Africa, the poem moves to the battlefield within the poet—a place less violent but more complex, since Walcott is, at the same time, on both sides and neither side.

Style

"A Far Cry from Africa" contains four stanzas of mostly iambic tetrameter. Actually, the poem starts off in iambic pentameter, the prevalent form of poetry written in English, but it soon veers off course metrically—a change that reflects the changing scene and perspective in the poem—with lines of varying length and number of stresses. A point of consistency is Walcott's use of masculine endings (lines ending with accented syllables) and masculine rhymes (one syllable rhymes). Rhyme is as irregular as meter. The rhyme scheme of the first stanza might be rendered *ababbcdecd* or *ababbaccad*. On the other hand, both of these schemes leave out the related sounds in "Jews," "flies," "seize," and "policy" that give this stanza two basic end sounds upon which lesser or greater variation occurs. The second stanza has its fourth and seventh lines rhyming and also lines five, ten, and eleven. In stanza three, the scheme is *abba*, but in stanza four there is only the rhyme of its sixth and eighth lines. In sum, then, a loose rhyme scheme for two stanzas is present, but none for the other two. Fluctuation

between rhyme and non-rhyme, rhyme and near-rhyme, between iambic tetrameter and iambic pentameter echoes the poet's own unresolved schism between Africa and Britain.

Literary Heritage

Derek Walcott considers himself a Caribbean writer, but he is also viewed as a cosmopolitan, cultivated poet who draws heavily on European, and particularly British, sources. Despite the fact that English was his second language, he is acknowledged to be one of the finest poets writing in English today. However, he was also nurtured by African-Caribbean folktales and slave narratives, and these inspire many of his plays. Ethnically, Walcott comes from a diverse heritage, with African, English, and Dutch ancestors; this diversity is also apparent in his writing.

Historical Context

Most of the area of contemporary Kenya was made a suzerain by the Imperial British East African Company in 1888. The British government then took over administration in 1895, calling the area a "protectorate." White settlers started moving in, cutting down trees, and amassing estates (some of the largest were over 100,000 acres). The migration of both whites and Indians continued, unabated. The settler built roads and a railroad, and, over time, dispossessed a great many Kenyans—mostly Kikuyus—of their land. Once dispossessed, Kikuyus were forced, through tax, work, and identity-paper schemes—and by outright force—into employment, primarily as servants on white estates. To gain back self-government and their land, the Kikuyu Central Association sent representative Jomo Kenyatta to England in 1929. During the next sixteen years, Kenyatta tried unsuccessfully to convince England to alter its method of government in Kenya; he returned to his home country in September of 1946.

In 1947, Kenyatta became president of the Kenya African Union (KAU), a nationalist party demanding an end to the numerous injustices of white rule. These demands were met with British resistance or excuses. While Kikuyus at large were becoming increasingly angry at white rule, a militaristic wing emerged, The Kenya Land Freedom

Compare & Contrast

- **1958-64:** This period of civil war in Africa's largest country, Sudan, comes to an end in the October, 1964 revolution when a student is shot and killed. A general strike and protests bring down the military junta.

  1999: CBS News reports that slavery is "alive and well in Sudan." Islamic groups, taking only women and children of the Dinka tribe in raids, use them as sexual servants, housekeepers, and farmhands. Dinka slaves are sold for about $50, the price of a goat.

- **1962:** The long, immensely expensive Ethiopian-Eritrean War (1962-1991) begins after Ethiopia cancels Eritrean autonomy within the Ethiopian-Eritrean federation, in effect since 1952.

  1999: In January, Eritrean news reports that 243 Eritreans are rounded up, jailed, and deported from Ethiopia. To date 49,500 Eritreans have been deported from Ethiopia.

- **1962:** Civil war begins in Rwanda (1962-63), as Tutsi military forces try to gain control of the new country after the majority Hutus had won control in free elections.

  1998: In Rwanda, during the course of the year, 864 people are tried for the 1994 genocide in which between five hundred thousand and one million are slaughtered in the Hutu government's attempt to wipe out the Tutsi minority. Civil war follows the 1994 genocide, and the Tutsi Rwandan Patriotic Front defeat the Rwandan military, which, with an estimated two million Hutus, flee Rwanda into neighboring countries.

Army, from which the organization Mau Mau grew (origins of this term are unknown but most agree it began as a derogatory label of settlers). On August 4, 1950, Mau Mau was declared illegal, even though the government knew little about it except that militant Kikuyus were winning over, coercing, or forcing other Kikuyus to take an oath against foreign rule. Then, on October 20, 1952, after Mau Mau killings of European cattle and the execution of a Kikuyu chief loyal to the British, a state of emergency was declared and an order sent out for the arrest of 183 people. Kenyatta was one of those arrested and, after a trial, was incarcerated for masterminding Mau Mau. Though this charge was never confirmed, he was imprisoned for seven years.

While fearful whites collected guns to protect their lives and property, the first Kikuyu murder of a white settler occurred a week after the emergency: the settler was hacked to death with a machete-like tool, a *panga*. Some thirteen thousand people and untold animals were to be killed in the Mau Mau anticolonial struggle, most of them Kikuyus. By 1953, the guerilla fighting force of Mau Mau had largely been defeated, and by 1956, the fighting had mostly stopped; the unequal political, economic, and social conditions leading to Mau Mau's rise, however, were still in place. While the state of emergency continued, governmental reforms between 1953 and 1960 did attempt to appease further threats from Mau Mau. The state of emergency finally ended end in 1960, likely well after Walcott finished writing "A Far Cry from Africa." Kenyatta was released from prison in 1961, Kenya gained its independence in 1963, and Kenyatta assumed the presidency in 1964, the same year Martin Luther King received the Nobel Peace Prize.

Walcott was most likely in the English-speaking Caribbean when he wrote "A Far Cry from Africa," an area, like Kenya, under the domination of the British. It was not until the 1930s, at a time of Caribbean social unrest, that even political parties were allowed and universal suffrage introduced. The growth of nationalism and the effects of World War II led to increasing pressure from West Indians for Britain to loosen its grip. So, in 1958, a federation including most of the English-speaking Caribbean islands was formed to prepare for eventual independence. Increasing friction between the archipelago and Britain led to Trinidad and Tobago, as well as Jamaica, withdrawing from the federation and becoming independent in 1962. Walcott's home island, St. Lucia, would not gain its independence until 1979, sixteen years after Kenya attained hers. During the period of greatest Mau Mau activity, Walcott was attending university in Jamaica. Until 1960, he spent most of his time teaching in West Indian schools and working in theater with his brother. It is likely that Walcott's West Indian origins, linked back to part of his family's original homeland in Africa, and the domination of both his country and Kenya by Britain spurred him to take special note of events in Kenya—events that at the time could have been a specter of a similar future for England's Caribbean colonies.

Critical Overview

When analyzing "A Far Cry from Africa," most critics comment on the poem's message and what it reveals about the poet, rather than the technical aspects of its creation. In an article titled "West Indies II: Walcott, Brathwaite, and Authenticity," Bruce King remarks, "The poem is remarkable for its complexity of emotions" and that it "treats of the Mau Mau uprising in terms that mock the usual justifications for and criticisms of colonialism." King notes that the narrator is stricken with "confused, irreconcilably opposed feelings: identification with black Africa, disgust with the killing of both white and black innocents, distrust of motives, love of the English language, and dislike of those who remain emotionally uninvolved." In his article "Ambiguity Without a Crisis? Twin Traditions, The Individual and Community in Derek Walcott's Essays," Fred D'Aguiar also deals with the division at the heart of the poem: "Already there is the ambivalence which hints at synthesis at the heart of the proclaimed division, a wish to artificially expose long buried oppositions between ancestries in need of reconciliation if the artist—and his community—are to grow." Though the poet seeks reconciliation, he does not appear to achieve it, which only accentuates his dilemma, a point Rei Terada makes in his *Derek Walcott's Poetry*: "His often anthologized early poem 'A Far Cry from Africa' (1962), for example, places the poet 'Between this Africa and the English tongue I love.' Even in this poem, however, betweenness is not a solution, but an arduous problem. Even here, betweenness cannot adequately conceptualize the poet's position,

since betweenness doesn't necessarily question the authenticity of the oppositions supposedly surrounding the poet.''

Criticism

David Donnell

David Donnell, who teaches at the University of Toronto, has published seven books of poetry. His work is included in the Norton Anthology of Modern Poetry, *and his volume* Settlement *received Canada's prestigious Governor General's Award. In the following essay, Donnell analyzes "A Far Cry from Africa" as the poet's personal credo.*

A Credo in Isolation

Even the title itself of Derek Walcott's lovely poem "A Far Cry from Africa" suggests that the author is writing about an African subject and doing so from a distance. It's an apt title, to be sure; Walcott is of African descent but was born and raised in what we might call the southeast corner of the American sphere without in any way encroaching on West Indies' independence. Writing from the beautiful island of St. Lucia, Walcott feels, as a well-educated and totally independent black West Indian, that he is indeed at some distance from Africa and the brutal atrocities of whites against blacks and blacks against whites that he has been reading about in Kenya, a large African state famous for its Veldt and for its extraordinary wildlife—giraffes, antelope, even rhinoceros.

The title "A Far Cry from Africa" may have a second meaning in addition to the obvious geographic and personal sense the author feels. The title also seems to say, "well, look, this is a far cry from the Africa that I have been reading about in descriptions of gorgeous fauna and flora and interesting village customs." And a third level of meaning to the title (without pressing this point too much) is the idea of Walcott hearing the poem as a far cry coming all the way across thousands of miles of ocean—the same routes, perhaps, as the Dutch ships of the late seventeenth century—to land in his accepting ear on the island of St. Lucia. He hears the cry coming to him on the wind. He writes, in the first line of his poem, "A wind is ruffling the tawny pelt / Of Africa." He has seen photographs of Kenya. He knows that light brown and yellow, of various shades, are two of the most prominent colors of this

Military officials round up suspects in Kenya's Mau Mau Uprising, an extended and bloody battle during the 1950s between European settlers and the country's native Kikuyu tribe. This rebellion figures prominently in Walcott's poem.

large African state; they are veldt colors, and there are lions out on the veldt.

"Kikuyu," in the second line, is the only African word in the poem. The Kikuyu were a Kenya tribe who became Mau Mau fighters in a grass-roots effort to oust the British colonial administration of Kenya. Walcott, as if mesmerized, describes the Mau Mau fighters as moving with extraordinary speed—they know the geography of their country and they "Batten upon the bloodstreams of the veldt." The use of the word batten is interesting; it generally means to fasten or secure a hatch on a ship. The upsurge of violence is justified in some ways perhaps, but what rivets Walcott's attention, because he is a well-educated man and a humanist, is given very simply in the following image, still from the powerful opening stanza: "Corpses are scattered through a paradise." Walcott, born on St. Lucia, a lovely island with a fairly low economy, would like to believe that Africa is just as paradisal and peaceful as the West Indies.

Most of Walcott's poems since the early 1960s have been written in very open but quite controlled language. "A Far Cry from Africa" is such a compressed and tightly structured poem that the

author tends to cover the ground he wants to talk about point by point and sometimes with what we might call caricatures, or images verging on caricature. "Only the worm, colonel of carrion cries: / Waste no compassion on these separate dead!" He follows this surprising image with two very sharp lines about the foolishness of statistics and alleged political scholars who want to discuss fine points. And then he ends his powerful opening stanza by saying, "What is that to the white child hacked in bed?" Or to Kenyans, he says, who are being treated as if they were "expendable." What appears to horrify Walcott partly in the case of Kenya is that the conflict and savagery taking place are happening on the basis of color; his reaction is almost Biblical in its unusually compressed and angry personal credo. At no time in this poem does he waste his time referring to any particular historical agreement. He sees the tragedy as essentially human tragedy, and the violence on both sides as essentially inhuman.

Walcott's dilemma seems to be very much in synch with some of the participants in this poem. "Threshed out by beaters," he says at the beginning of the second stanza. The poet has dealt with his

What Do I Read Next?

- The anthology *Modern African Poetry* (1984), edited by Gerald Moore and Ulli Beier, includes poems by sixty-four poets from twenty-four African nations, including three poets from Kenya of the same generation as Walcott.

- *Orientalism* (1979) by Edward Said is a pioneering work in postcolonial studies. Although it mostly centers on the Muslim world (including North Africa), the book is a must for the student wanting to understand the roots of Western imperialism as its ideas were disseminated through intellectual practice.

- Ella Shohat and Robert Stam's *Unthinking Eurocentrism* (1994), a text of multicultural media studies, links the often separated studies of race and identity politics on the one hand, and on the other, third-world nationalism and (post)colonial discourses.

- Gayatry Chakravorty Spivak's *The Post-Colonial Critic: Interviews, Strategies, and Dialogues* (1990) speaks to questions of representation and self-representation, the situations of postcolonial critics, pedagogical responsibility, and political strategies.

---

initial horror at these events in Kenya and has outlined his initial focus on the general area of comment. He seems to see in this second stanza what he regards as the acceptable violence of nature or "natural law" as having been turned into a nightmare of unacceptable human violence based on color. "Beaters" on big game safaris in Africa are the men who beat the brush, sometimes singing or chanting as they do so, and flush out birds and animals for the hunt. Of course, in a lot of cases, beaters will flush out a variety of animals they hadn't expected.

"A Far Cry from Africa" continues this meditation on the landscape of the Kenyan veldt by saying, "the long rushes break / In a white dust of ibises whose cries / Have wheeled since civilization's dawn / From the parched river or beast-teeming plain." Walcott's image of Africa may strike some readers as a bit innocent, but it doesn't seem to be in any way affected or insincere as he expresses himself in this personal credo. Quite the contrary; it seems idealistic and uplifting, although it does leave the reader—and perhaps Walcott as well—in the position of saying, "How can we prevent these outbreaks of violence?" Or, perhaps more specifically, "How can we be fair?" Should the United Nations have intervened on behalf of the

Kenyans? This is a very intense and bitter poem—a lashing out at injustice and an attempt to formulate both some distance for the writer as well as a sense of his own eventual or fundamental juxtaposition to the uncomfortable and agonizing subject.

Anthropologists, both American and European, have published an enormous amount of material in the twentieth century on different questions of social personality, physicality, and to what degree many of our fundamental social responses—for example, defensiveness, lust, comfort, and pride—seem to have an animal basis. Walcott lashes out at both sides of the Kenyan situation from a position in which he strongly and intensely believes that human and animal are not only different but should be regarded at least as absolute opposites, yet he seems to know that this is not the case. But a large portion of the middle of this poem is Walcott's expression of his coming to terms with human nature and the mixed good and bad, up and down, nature of history.

"A Far Cry from Africa" is such an agonizing and didactic personal poem, and such a tightly structured poem in which Walcott never relaxes and explains to the reader in casual asides that he himself is of African descent, that some readers may at first feel that the poem is more a comment on news of the day than it is a personal response, and a credo, and to some extent a partial deconstruction of his own credo. The narrator weighs different examples from the Kenyan upsurge in this poem, and the writer obviously wants to come out on top of his own material. He wants to see the argument in a perspective that makes some kind of sense, and he doesn't want to get swallowed by his own feelings of anger and outrage at these events.

And so we have the "Kikuyu" and violence in Kenya, violence in a "paradise," and we have "Statistics" that don't mean anything and "scholars" who tend to throw their weight behind colonial policy. Walcott's outrage is very just and by the standards of the late 1960s, even restrained. His sense of amazement and awe, and his desire to love the Africa he describes, surges at one point when he notes what is probably a fairly salient and typical detail of Kenya, how "the long rushes break / In a white dust of ibises whose cries / Have wheeled since civilization's dawn. . . ."

Of course the African continent is nothing if not enormous. The range of geography and of fauna and flora is extraordinary. Different cultures are in different kinds of motion in various parts of the continent. The north of Africa contains some of the old Arabic civilizations of the eastern half of our world, including Libya, which is across the Mediterranean from Italy, and Egypt, where historical records show at least one or more black African Pharaohs before the period of time described in the Bible's New Testament. Walcott may or may not be interested in these ideas; he may or may not have visited Africa at some time. We have to concentrate on the poem and on what happens in the poem. How does he develop his sense of weighing these different negative facts of violence in a paradise of ibises and different cultures?

Walcott could be a little more informative in this poem. For example, he could allude to some of the newspaper reports that he's been reading; he could mention a particular town in Kenya, or a local hero. Even though he identifies Kenya and the great veldt and begins with a powerful opening line that sets the tone and motion for the whole poem ("A wind is ruffling the tawny pelt / Of Africa"), he still wants this poem to be timeless and to apply to other situations in different parts of the world. Near the end of the poem, however, having accomplished his first objective, the charting of the Kenya upsurge and his own humanistic denunciation of brutality,

> What appears to horrify Walcott partly in the case of Kenya is that the conflict and savagery taking place are happening on the basis of color; his reaction is almost Biblical in its unusually compressed and angry personal credo."

Walcott does come into "A Far Cry from Africa"—and he does so very dramatically.

Perhaps the most brutal and categorical movement in the whole poem occurs after that lovely image of the "ibises" wheeling in historical patterns since "civilization's dawn." Frustrated with every aspect of this brutal color war in Kenya, Walcott comes up with an image that more or less generalizes the history of English, European, and African wars: "his wars / Dance to the tightened carcass of a drum, / While he calls courage still that native dread / Of the white peace contracted by the dead." In this powerful image, coming to the penultimate point of the poem, Walcott says basically that everybody dances, everybody gets emotionally intoxicated with the egoism of taking sides, everybody in that kind of situation is listening to a drumbeat of some kind or another. "Brutish necessity," he calls it, comparing the Kenyan fighters to the revolutionaries in Spain: "A waste of our compassion, as with Spain / The gorilla wrestles with the superman." At this point, Walcott seems to have spoken out on the issue, identified the problem, and to some degree disposed of the whole subject.

But there is more to "A Far Cry from Africa" than what we have read so far. There is, as a matter of fact, the very fulcrum of his being so involved and so intense about the subject in the first place: not just humanistic anger, but also a very personal outrage. "I who am poisoned with the blood of both, / Where shall I turn, divided to the vein?" he says as a beginning to the last stanza. Born and raised in St. Lucia, educated in the British system, and an omnivorous reader by the time he was in high school, Walcott is very much a citizen of the world.

Quite a well-known poet by the time he was in his twenties, Walcott had, by the time he wrote ''A Far Cry from Africa,'' spent considerable time in Trinidad, working on different theater projects, and he had also been exhibited as a talented painter.

One of the most moving aspects of this poem, once the reader accepts the very terse, basic, logical arguments regarding the struggle in Kenya, is the general image of the poet/author at the end of the poem. He has no choice but to watch both sides rather sadly continue their violence against each other. But he ends this powerful polemic with six devastating lines: ''I who have cursed / The drunken officer of British rule, how choose / Between this Africa and the English tongue I love? / Betray them both, or give back what they give? / How can I face such slaughter and be cool? / How can I turn from Africa and live?'' And of course, Walcott has never turned from Africa or gone to live there. He has continued writing and publishing and has, since the 1980s, become famous all over again for an enormous book-long Homeric poem about the islands, the Caribbean, the Mediterranean, and the coming together of a multiple of cultural convergences.

Source: David Donnell, in an essay for *Literature of Developing Nations for Students*, Gale, 2000.

Jhan Hochman

Jhan Hochman, who holds a Ph.D in English and an M.A. in cinema studies, is the author of Green Cultural Studies: Nature in Film, Novel, and Theory *(1998). In the following essay Hochman examines the role of animality in ''A Far Cry from Africa.''*

When most Westerners think of Africa, one of the first things that comes to mind are the animals—lions, elephants, zebras, giraffes, rhinos, hyenas. And although the issues of Walcott's ''A Far Cry from Africa'' are cultural—are concerned with people—animals materialize throughout the poem in generally two ways. As kinds, such as flies and ibises, animals are compared similarly to particular groups of people. But as a kingdom, as in ''animal kingdom,'' animals are largely contrasted to humankind, even though Walcott does acknowledge a shared animality.

The opening image of ''A Far Cry from Africa'' is ''A wind . . . ruffling the tawny pelt / Of Africa.'' A pelt, in this case, most likely refers to the furry or hairy skin of an animal, such as a wild cat, dog, or antelope. Not only is the continent of Africa

associated with animals in Walcott's poem, but it is represented as an animal. The specific topography referred to is the ''veldt,'' a Dutch Afrikaans word meaning a field or a flat grassland or prairie with few or no trees. Within this landscape are (as one might expect to find around large animals) insects, specifically flies. The flies Walcott mentions, however, are not really flies, but metaphors for the Kikuyu, a tribal people of Kenya living in the region long before Europeans arrived. This is a controversial metaphor, indeed: likening African tribal people to pesky insects sucking the blood out of Africa.

The metaphor of the Kikuyu as flies is developed further. As flies lay eggs that turn into maggots (Walcott's ''worms''), the Kikuyu also brought forth something considered unappealing by Walcott: Mau Mau, a secret terrorist organization. The Kikuyu were an influential people whose economy revolved around agriculture. Their land was increasingly taken by white ''settlers'' when Britain, in 1895, turned what is now The Republic of Kenya into the East African Protectorate. The Kikuyu were forced off their land and into servitude. Kikuyu anger over this predicament increased and reached its peak with the Mau Mau Uprising against the British regime. Mau Mau began as a militant faction of the Kikuyu, the Kenya Land Freedom Army, and became a secret society bent on expelling the British from Kenya. From 1952 to 1956, it engaged in a bloody terrorist campaign; Mau Mau was infamous for its hackings and mutilations of whites, animals owned by whites, and Kikuyus who refused to join Mau Mau or who collaborated with the British. (Though the British defeated Mau Mau, the country of Kenya earned its independence in 1963 from colonial rule.)

It was reports of this violence that reached other parts of the world and must have appalled Walcott to the extent that he compared Mau Mau to maggots eating away at a field of corpses. One might infer here that Walcott is not just appalled, but ashamed at Mau Mau because he is, himself, part African. His problem is that Mau Mau might synecdochically (in a substitution of part for whole) become all Africans, even all black peoples. Mau Mau became so infamous that it was used as a verb in American slang; ''to Mau Mau,'' meant to threaten or terrorize. In comparing Mau Mau to maggots, Walcott is distancing himself from Mau Mau and against the synecdoche that Mau Mau equals all black peoples.

The second stanza begins with ibises, large birds related to herons and storks. The ibis was a favorite animal of the ancient Egyptians, becoming not only the incarnation of the god Thoth—patron of astronomers, scribes, magicians, healers, and enchanters—but a bird whose appearance heralded the flooding Nile, the season of fertility. In this stanza, (white) ibises are apparently being hunted by black Africans, which could be read as a metaphor of black Mau Maus "hunting" white estate owners and farmers. Some reading this poem are apt to synecdochically understand the white ibis, intuitively or intellectually, as a good symbol. Once the association is made, whites hunted by Mau Mau can seem blameless, guiltless, and good. Further, calling white ibises inhabitants of Africa since "civilization's dawn," makes it seem as if whites resided in Africa even before the Kikuyu. While the metaphor of "ibis equals white person" may work with the thrust of the poem, it is far too positive an image to represent the whites who took Kenya away from Kenyans.

The third stanza may be read as two comments made by an outsider to the Kenyan conflict that justify complacency. The word "brutish" comes from the Latin *brutus*, meaning heavy, inert, and stupid; it most commonly refers to beasts. Walcott's outsiders to the uprising complacently remark that nothing is to be done since Africans are possessed by "brutish necessity" to wipe their bloody hands upon "napkins of a dirty cause." "Napkins" indicate a "civilized" nicety, and the "dirty cause" of the British is known as the "white man's burden"—the purported altruistic duty of white people to "civilize" black people. The other comment in this same stanza made by outsiders about the Mau Mau Uprising is: "The gorilla wrestles with the superman." The "gorilla" represents black Africans and the "superman," white Brits. Walcott's outsider considers both sides of the conflict reprehensible: that Africans, like gorillas, are not civilized, and that Brits, like Nietzsche's overweening superman, are too civilized—so arrogant as to think it their destiny to rule the nonwhite world. The speaker of this section apparently wants nothing to do with Africans, Mau Mau, or imperialism. Walcott is disgusted by both views put forth in this stanza, not only because they are distasteful, but because he cannot so easily remove himself from the conflict since he is "poisoned with the blood of both."

Walcott, or the persona of the outsider, has compared people to animals, but, in the second stanza, animals are contrasted with people:

> The violence of beast on beast is read
> As natural law, but upright man

Seeks his divinity by inflicting pain

The "is read" makes the speaker seem just barely willing to go along with the thrust of the first statement. He does seem, however, in agreement with the second idea—that man does indeed seek "his divinity by inflicting pain." With these two thoughts, beasts come out better than "upright man" since animals do what they must do, and do not seek divinity through inflicting pain.

Although Walcott never solves—within the poem—his problem of loyalty, one thing does look clear-cut: Walcott believes that humans, unlike animals, have no excuse, no attractive rationale, for murdering noncombatants in the Kenyan conflict. While we cannot be sure if Walcott, at this point in his life, was a pacifist, he does make plain in "A Far Cry from Africa" that whatever the rightness of the Mau Mau cause, its mode of operation was shameful. Geographical outsiders might be apt to agree. Still, Mau Mau's swift, rude terror would better represented if juxtaposed against the gnawing, polite oppression of British imperialism. Unfortunately, Walcott only briefly mentions the vivid extremity of British practice ("The drunken officer of British rule" and "dirty cause" do not do justice to the extent of British injustice), making it far easier to condemn Mau Mau. Walcott's dilemma (and the reader's) might have been more righteously difficult had the poem added a few stanzas condemning the British. Instead, Walcott displaces a political situation in which large numbers of people suffered and died to the "action" inside himself—personal shame and confusion. In the process of shaming Mau Mau by claiming its members do not even measure up to animals, both Mau Mau and animals are demeaned. At the end of "A Far Cry from Africa," Walcott appears as torn about his identity as both animal and human as his identity as both African and European.

Source: Jhan Hochman, in an essay for *Literature of Developing Nations for Students*, Gale, 2000.

Aviya Kushner

Aviya Kushner, who is the poetry editor for Neworld Renaissance Magazine, *earned an M.A. in creative writing from Boston University, where she studied under Walcott, among others. In the following essay, Kushner analyzes "A Far Cry from Africa" as the speaker's quest self-description.*

Island boy. That's how Nobel Prize-winning poet Derek Walcott often describes himself, in both his poems and his conversation. However, that simple self-portrait can be misleading. At best, it's only part of the story of a man whose wanderings have produced rich, skillful, multilayered poems that draw on the poetic tradition of many nations, ranging from modern England, Russia, and Spain to ancient Greece.

Of course, the island bit has some truth to it. Walcott is a major English-language writer who was born—and still lives, for part of the year—in the multilingual Caribbean. His accent and warm manners are from the tiny, tourist-attracting island of St. Lucia, but his heroes in both his reading and writing have taken him far past the sunny, postcard blue-and-green Caribbean landscape. Walcott's historical conscience also extends far past the island's borders, and his readers live all over the world.

Walcott is so admired in England that he was mentioned in leading newspapers as a possible candidate for the position of Poet Laureate when Ted Hughes died. For a son of the colonies, being named England's chief poet would certainly be an impressive turn of events. But that irony of personal success amid his native country's history as a conquered land has not been lost on Walcott. His precarious perch between two cultures has become a key subject for him.

In fact, this lifelong conflict between his tiny native island and the wider world, between his love of English and his knowledge that it is the colonizer's tongue and the oppressor's language—and thus part of its power—is a factor in the depth and strength of Walcott's poems.

Many poems are built on ambivalence, and "A Far Cry from Africa" is an example of how a masterful poet can mold ambivalence into art. In this poem, Walcott extends his ambivalence about the English language and the heritage it bears to everything—meter, subject matter, and even the choice of English as a language to write in. While the poem starts off in the iambic pentameter Walcott has mastered—the bread and butter of poetry in English—the poem soon veers course metrically, just as it changes place, perspective, and point of view. Like ownership of countries and empires, everything here is subject to change.

Much of the poem can be read in more than one way, starting with the title. At first glance, if "a far cry" is read as "a subject far removed from daily reality," "A Far Cry from Africa" is a title that might apply to most of Walcott's work. With a few exceptions, he is not influenced by the sound or

tradition of Africa, but rather the titans of Western poetry. Personally close to Russian-born Joseph Brodsky and Canadian-born Mark Strand, a deep admirer of Britons Edward Thomas and W. H. Auden and Russian poet Marina Tsvetaeva, Walcott frequently writes homages to his favorite writers. African writers, however, rarely figure among Walcott's models.

But the "far cry" of the title can also be taken literally, as simply a cry from a far place. This is supported by the poem's opening lines, which detail human misery and the cries that must come with it. The phrase then leads into a questioning of colonization and the pain it has brought. The poem subsequently details a deep, personal division that is paralleled by the double meanings of the title and much of the poem. As the poem progresses, it questions itself, and it ends in a series of questions.

This division mirrors the speaker's feelings about Britain's colonization of so many countries. Despite the violence, Walcott the poet cannot fully condemn the colonizers because he has taken so much from them. His vocation—English—comes from the colonizer, and yet, as a moral human being, he feels he must condemn colonization.

Naturally, this produces an inner division. By the final passages, the rumbling references to a divided self have reached a shriek. This division is the heart of the poem, but it is only clear at the end. Therefore, all of the stanzas fall more easily into place if they are read as steps to the crucial line in the last stanza: "I who am poisoned with the blood of both / Where should I turn, divided to the vein?"

Now it makes sense to return to the beginning. Every word in the poem is part of the step-by-step march to that deafening moment of self-division at the end. The poem starts with a personification of the entire continent, and this speaker-Africa parallel continues to some extent throughout. For a poem that moves to the grandiose, its first step looks modest: "A wind is ruffling the tawny pelt / Of Africa." But like Walcott's characterization of himself as merely "a man who loved islands," this first line is misleadingly simple. A trip to the dictionary is one way to uncover the layers of the poem.

The word "pelt" is normally defined as the skin of an animal (with fur or hair still on it), and so the opening line compares the continent to an animal, with "tawny pelt" possibly evoking the color of the African desert. But there's more. "Pelt" can also be human skin, and here, the wind is ruffling the pelt of a person. What seems modest is actually horribly frightening. Finally, ''pelt'' as a verb means ''to strike,'' an image that begins a few lines later.

In the second line, the pace quickens. ''Kikuyu, quick as flies, / Batten upon the bloodstreams of the veldt.'' After the confident iambics of the first line and a half (trademark Walcott), the poem draws on alliteration, forsaking meter as primary device for other poetic tools. The alliteration of ''Kikuyu/ quick'' and ''batten/bloodstreams'' physically speeds up the poem; the action parallels the sound. Kikuyu are indigenous African people, and here they are rushing to feed upon the streams of blood in the level grassland of the continent. In this landscape, people feed off people. This is a ghastly paradise, populated with scattered corpses.

Amid all of the hubbub, the smallest of creatures—the worm—wily and slinky, loudly warns those who would be compassionate. Walcott injects some humor into the gruesome scene, with the characterization ''colonel of carrion'' depicting the worm as king of those who prey on flesh. Suddenly, Walcott takes us out of this frightening, jumbled-up world and anchors it in ''statistics'' and ''scholars'' who try to justify colonial policy. Once again using alliteration to point to a turn in the poem, the speaker puts the spotlight on those who write and think but don't really look at a hacked child or a dead savage rotting in the desert.

The reference to ''statistics'' and ''scholars'' borrows from W. H. Auden's famous poem ''The Fall of Rome,'' in which an ''unimportant clerk'' writes ''I DO NOT LIKE MY WORK'' on a pink official form. Here, too, Walcott mixes the fall of an empire with a humorous jab at bureaucrats and their statistics.

Apart from that slight tangent for some humor, stanza one sticks to its mission—to set a scene. It also shows off some poetic gymnastics, pushing alliteration and rhyme as far as they can go. Slant rhymes such as ''pelt/veldt'' and ''flies/paradise'' share space with conventional rhymes such as ''bed/ dead.'' Most important in its role of scene-setting, the first stanza ends with questions, which are integral to this poem. Just as the title proclaims ''A Far Cry from Africa'' and then the first line proceeds to set a scene in Africa, the questions announce that the poem will offer a far cry from answers. This is a poem about far cries, about divisions of the self, a gulf as wide as a continent— all contained within one man.

> ... 'A Far Cry from Africa' is an example of how a masterful poet can mold ambivalence into art."

While the first two lines of stanza one were all iambs, for a lulling, ta-tum sound, the second stanza begins quite differently. Instead of a light ruffling, there is the loud ''Threshed by beaters, the long rushes break.'' The plants that are used for mats or furniture bottoms are literally broken by beaters, which are revolving cylinders that chop up stalks or brush. ''Beaters'' also recalls ''to beat'' or ''to conquer,'' a major theme of the poem. This technique of a noun that also resonates as a verb was seen earlier with the word ''pelt.''

Once again, as in the first stanza, sound is king. ''Threshed'' is a single, forceful syllable, placing a clear stress on the stanza's first word. ''Rush'' and ''break'' reinforce the sensation of power and violence. The speaker is getting ready to roll out some grand ideas, with that kind of drumbeat sound. And so ''have wheeled since civilization's dawn'' does not come as a huge surprise. The phrase ''civilization's dawn'' lets the poem shift from a scene in Africa to a rumination on the world itself—to the history of man.

''Civilization's dawn'' also recalls the Bible's book of Genesis, which is why the poem's quiet opening followed by loud, active rumbling seems so familiar. In the next few lines, Walcott takes that opening image of paradise marred by violence coupled with a personal conflict and expands it into a tale of humanity—a sorry story repeated throughout human history:

> The violence of beast upon beast is read
> As natural law, but upright man
> Seeks his divinity by inflicting pain

While English naturalist Charles Darwin may have proclaimed survival of the fittest as natural law, and while in the creation story God may have granted animals to men to eat, the speaker here sees man as a conqueror attempting to mimic God. According to the Biblical story, God has power over all things, including, of course, the power to give life. Man can be God-like by literally lording power over his fellow man. The speaker here questions the wisdom of having mere people possess so much power over their fellow men.

The next stanza begins with another shake to the reader and another powerhouse image—"brutish necessity" wiping its hands "upon the napkin of a dirty cause." The word "Again" signals the stanza will continue what the other stanzas have done. As we have seen, each stanza's first few words are crucial to the poem's overall structure, and this stanza is no exception.

"Again" means that this story has happened many times over, and the repetitive questions at the end reinforce the feeling of a cycle. These are questions the speaker has asked himself many times before. This is a story of conquest and divided loyalties that snakes back to the Bible, and later, to the great empires that rose and fell and figure so prominently in Walcott's work. Here, for example, Walcott deliberately alludes to the Bible and mentions Spain. ("A waste of our compassion, as with Spain . . .") Finally, like the earliest Greek epic poets, Walcott is fascinated by senseless brutality of man over man and how even great humans are tripped up by their simple human nature.

These grand ideas should not distract from the tools of poetry that are used here, since they point to meaning. The careful rhyme throughout the poem is especially important as the ending nears. The "flies/ paradise" lines that came early on have already focused a spotlight on line endings, and the last few create an interesting juxtaposition of "live" and "love." The speaker seems to be realizing that how he lives and what he loves are not compatible. Though his elegant, Westernized lines that draw on the classical epic and lyric traditions are indeed "a far cry from Africa," Walcott nevertheless realizes that his life—what makes him live—is wider than the Western canon. He must address those close to him who are struggling to live. He cannot turn from Africa, despite all the years, the accolades, and the devotion to its oppressors' tongue.

And so, in this poem that evokes a continent, a world, and an entire history of the world in four stanzas, the speaker faces Africa and uses its desert and its violence as a means of looking at himself. The only conclusions he reaches, however, are a series of questions. All of the violence and self-division reach an intense pitch with those final questions:

> I who am poisoned with the blood of both,
> Where shall I turn, divided to the vein?
> I who have cursed
> The drunken officer of British rule, how choose
> Between this Africa and the English tongue I love?
> Betray them both, or give back what they give?
> How can I face such slaughter and be cool?
> How can I turn from Africa and live?

Fittingly, the poem ends in the word "live." For this speaker, questioning and living are one and the same. Forming questions into art—in perfectly controlled lines, displaying all of poetry's power— is how this poet approaches a crisis of identity. Somehow, a speaker nearly ripped apart by inner conflict produces a poem that races up and down but, in the end, seems overwhelmingly whole. Despite the questions, the mission of self-description within the context of history is accomplished.

Source: Aviya Kushner, in an essay for *Literature of Developing Nations for Students*, Gale, 2000.

Kelly Winters

Winters is a freelance writer who has written for a wide variety of academic and educational publishers. In the following essay, she discusses issues of race and heritage in "A Far Cry from Africa."

In "A Far Cry from Africa," Walcott writes about the bloody war of African against European during the Mau Mau Rebellion, when members of local tribes, particularly the Kikuyu, rebelled against the British seizure of their land. The poem opens with graphic lines describing the blood and brutality of conflict; as if these descriptions were not enough, Walcott makes it clear that this is an unnecessary war, describing it as "a dirty cause."

Walcott saw his own life mirrored in this larger conflict, because he was of mixed African and European ancestry and thus felt an ancestral connection of loyalty to both sides involved in the conflict. As he writes in the poem,

> I who am poisoned with the blood of both, / Where shall I turn, divided to the vein? / I who have cursed / The drunken officer of British rule, how choose / Between this Africa and the English tongue I love?

The outer war brings up an inner paradox: how could Walcott, who is part of both sides, choose sides? How can one man fight himself? It's impossible, and he seems to be using this fact as a way of saying that all of humanity is one—these race wars and ethnic conflicts are as futile as one man fighting against himself would be. He sees the falseness of this "dirty cause"—the British propaganda that violence against the Mau Mau is a noble cause, while African violence is viewed as "animal" and the Africans themselves as "savages" and "expendable."

Despite the fact that the Kikuyu were right to be angered over British colonialism, however, Walcott could not condone the violence they used to achieve their goals, nor could he condone the colonialism and subsequent bloody acts of the British even though he loved their language and art. He does not, and will not, take sides; he cannot reduce the conflict to a simple "right versus wrong," or even to a metaphorical or actual "black-and-white" problem, with clear answers. There is no solution: both sides are wrong, both sides are right, and Walcott as observer has compassion for them both, as he has compassion for himself as a child of both sides.

The poem is one of the first in which Walcott began exploring the implications of his mixed heritage; it was published in his first collection of poems, *In a Green Night*, in 1962. Since then, many critics have remarked on Walcott's use of traditions from both sides of his ancestry, and the cultures he has inherited from both sides of his family, in his work. Peter Balakian wrote of "A Far Cry from Africa" in *Poetry* that Walcott's "ability to embrace his Black West Indian identity and to accept, with the ingenuity of an artist, the language of his inherited culture accounts for much of the genius and richness of his idiom. Using the English tongue he loves does not preclude his moral outrage at the crimes that the Empire has committed against his people."

Walcott epitomizes the mixed heritage of the Caribbean—born on the island of St. Lucia, with African, Dutch, and English ancestors, he spoke a local Creole dialect at home, but in school learned to speak formal English and read the classics of British literature. On both his mother's and father's sides, he had a white grandfather and a black grandmother. According to Mark A. McWatt in *Third World Quarterly,* Walcott was aware from a very young age of this split; Walcott said, "In that simple, schizophrenic boyhood one could lead two lives: the interior life of poetry, the outward life of action and dialect." Walcott's ancestry epitomized the larger racial and ethnic composition of the Caribbean islands, and he has often called himself a "divid-ed child" because even as a youth, he was aware of the contradictions he embodied.

Walcott loved the English literature he read at school, and its power and beauty filled him with the ambition to write about his Caribbean home and fill it with the same kind of power and life. Even as he was thrilled by the English language, however, he was aware that the British had brought slavery and slaves to the Caribbean, including some of his ancestors. This ambivalence about his heritage would stay with him for decades and would constitute a major theme in his writings, including "A Far Cry from Africa."

As Robert D. Hamner noted in *Derek Walcott,* Walcott "is a living example of the divided loyalties and hatreds that keep his society suspended between two worlds." But as Walcott makes clear in "A Far Cry from Africa," Caribbean society is not the only one touched by these conflicts: they occur in Africa, in America, anywhere there is oppression and racism. As Hamner wrote, because of Walcott's awareness of the paradoxes in his heritage, "inevitable questions of origins, identity, and the creation of meaningful order in a chaotic world lead Walcott to themes that transcend race, place, and time."

Racial conflict, and the conflicts associated with it throughout history—conflicts between master and slave, colonizer and colonized—have been a constant theme in Walcott's work since the publication of "A Far Cry from Africa." More than any other poet, he epitomizes and embodies the forces that shaped the new world—every country in the western hemisphere has been shaped by the flowing-together of races, but this fact is often ignored by other writers. Many of Walcott's other poems, for example "The Schooner Flight." feature people of mixed race. In that poem, a mariner from Trinidad, who is very similar to Walcott, describes his mixed English, African, and Dutch ancestry, and says, "either I'm nobody or I'm a nation."

In a 1977 interview with Edward Hirsch, reprinted in William Baer's *Conversations with Derek Walcott,* the poet made it clear that he was still thinking about the issues brought up in "A Far Cry from Africa." Walcott told Hirsch, "There is no West Indian who is black, or even one who is not black, who is not aware of the existence of Africa in all of us. . . . The fact is that every West Indian has been severed from a continent, whether he is Indian,

Chinese, Portuguese, or black. . . . It would be equally abhorrent to me to say 'I wish we were English again.' The reality is that one has to build in the West Indies." In other words, to live with all facets of one's heritage, not denying them, not elevating one over the other.

Not everyone is as comfortable as Walcott with the racial paradoxes of his heritage and of the real world; as a result, throughout his writing career, critics have sought to label him in narrower ways than he himself is comfortable with. Because he is a very cosmopolitan, cultured poet who is black, he has been both praised and blamed not so much for his writing as for his race. Some white critics have patronizingly thought him amazing because he is so articulate, and some black critics have accused him of sounding too white and betraying black sensibility. For example, McWatt wrote that the Nobel-prize-winning poet Joseph Brodsky believes that describing Walcott as a "West Indian poet" or "a black poet from the Caribbean" does not do him justice. Rather, Brodsky prefers to think of Walcott as "the great poet of the English language."

Regarding his place in literature, Walcott feels differently. He told Edward Hirsch in the *Paris Review,* "I am primarily, absolutely a Caribbean writer. The English language is nobody's special property. It is the property of the imagination: it is the property of the language itself. I have never felt inhibited in trying to write as well as the greatest English poets. Now that has led to a lot of provincial criticism: the Caribbean critic may say, 'You are trying to be English,' and the English critic may say, 'Welcome to the club.' These are two provincial statements at either end of the spectrum."

As in the poem, where he refuses to settle for an easy answer and embraces both sides, painful though that may be, Walcott has chosen to embrace the whole of his heritage. As Robert D. Hamner noted in *Derek Walcott,* "As inheritor of two vitally rich cultures, he utilizes one, then the other, and finally creates out of the two his own personalized style." In the interview with Hirsch, Walcott said, "Once I knew that the richness of Creole was a whole uncharted territory for a writer, I became excited." And, he said, "I have always locked in on the fact that there is a living tradition around me, a tradition of chanting, of oral theater in terms of storytelling and the enjoyment of rhetoric. I was lucky to be born as a poet in a tradition that uses poetry as demonstration, as theater. . . . The chant, the re-sponse, and the dance are immediate things to me: they are not anachronistic or literary."

Source: Kelly Winters, in a essay for *Literature of Developing Nations for Students,* Gale, 2000.

Paul Witcover

Paul Witcover is a novelist and editor in New York City with an M.A. in creative writing and literature from the City University of New York. In the following essay, he discusses the personal and the political in Derek Walcott's poem, "A Far Cry from Africa."

In his 1993 critical biography, *Derek Walcott,* Robert D. Hamner observes, "It is not a simple choice between cultures for Walcott, but a matter of laying claim to his mixed heritage." This "mixed heritage," which the Swedish Academy, in awarding Walcott the Nobel Prize for Literature in 1992, referred to as "the complexity of his own situation," takes a variety of often-paradoxical forms. For example, Walcott is of both English and African genetic ancestry. The blood of colonizers and colonized, oppressors and oppressed, flows in his veins. Culturally, too, he is a hybrid. As a native of St. Lucia, a small island in the Lesser Antilles, Walcott grew up immersed in West Indian culture, yet received a thorough English-style education, including exposure to the European literary tradition which soon fired his own ambitions as poet and playwright—ambitions further complicated by a linguistic inheritance including English, French, and Creole patois.

Although Walcott has long since incorporated the tug-of-war of these competing traditions, expectations, and loyalties into his mature verse and drama, successfully "laying claim to his mixed heritage" and forging it into something wholly his own, his early work reflects the personal, political, and poetic struggles of an extraordinarily gifted young writer faced with a variety of difficult, urgent choices, none of which seems fully satisfying. "A Far Cry from Africa," written in 1957, is exemplary in these respects.

The title is a pun alluding to the poet's dilemma of divided loyalties. It refers to a cry coming from faraway Africa which the poet nevertheless hears all too clearly, but it also states, through the ironic, self-mocking use of the colloquial expression "a far cry from," that the poet, despite his sympathy to that distant cry, is far from Africa in more than just a geographical sense. Walcott is almost obsessively drawn to such tangled conundrums of identity and language. In his best work, like the book-length epic poem *Omeros*, these questions are examined with the highest literary artistry and a profoundly moral, though never simplistically judgmental, intelligence.

"A Far Cry from Africa" was occasioned by events taking place in the country of Kenya, which at the time was a British colony. Following World War II, a veritable epidemic of independence movements swept Africa and Asia as places like Kenya, long under the political, military, and economic yoke of European countries, sought the basic freedoms of self-governance. It is a tragic fact of history that many of these movements were marked on both sides by extremes of violence, and such was the case in Kenya. There, the majority tribe, the Kikuyu, under the leadership of the charismatic Jomo Kenyatta, stood at the forefront of anti-British rebellion. Even so, many Kikuyu sided with the British, who exploited tribal differences in a classic strategy of "divide and conquer." As civil war spread, the British sought to demonize the rebels by attributing the worst excesses of the fighting to the soldiers of a secret society called the Mau Mau. Historians generally agree that there was no such secret society. The Mau Mau were a fabrication invented for international public relations purposes, to justify the harshly repressive tactics employed by the British and their tribal allies in putting down the rebellion. Ironically, however, certain rebel factions seized the opportunity to use the widespread panic engendered by this propaganda to their own advantage. A secret society calling itself the Mau Mau emerged as if out of the worst nightmares of the British Empire and proceeded to cast a bloody pall of terrorism over the war-torn country. In the process, they gave the conflict the name by which it became known to history: the Mau Mau Rebellion. By the time the rebellion was crushed in the late 1950s, more than 11,000 rebels had been killed and 80,000 Kikuyu herded into camps. Despite the propaganda of the British, only 32 white civilians were killed in the rebellion, and the total number of European deaths in combat did not greatly exceed 100. Jomo Kenyatta ultimately served as an independent Kenya's first president.

For Walcott, the Mau Mau Rebellion, pitting Africans against British, is a metaphor for his own psychological and cultural conflict, a conflict neatly summed up in the last eight lines of the poem: "I who am poisoned with the blood of both, / Where shall I turn, divided to the vein? / I who have cursed / The drunken officer of British rule, how choose / Between this Africa and the English tongue I love? / Betray them both, or give back what they give? / How can I face such slaughter and be cool? / How can I turn from Africa and live?"

The answers Walcott ultimately found to these questions lie beyond the scope of this essay. What is important to note here is the artistry and anguished emotion with which the young poet raises his questions, as well as the mingling of the personal and the political in almost every line. The poem is divided into three stanzas of 10, 11, and 12 lines, respectively. The majority of these lines are of ten syllables, in the meter known as iambic pentameter, which has been called the natural rhythm of the English language. Iambic pentameter simply means a line of Five (penta) metric "feet" (units of two or three syllables) whose stresses (or accents) most often follow the pattern of light-heavy, light-heavy, etc. Of the eight lines quoted above, six are in iambic pentameter. The sonnets of William Shakespeare feature some of the most beautiful uses of iambic pentameter in the English language, but even colloquial speech, if written down and parsed, will often work out to be iambic pentameter.

Indeed, Walcott is consciously alluding to the sonnet form in this poem, although he has adapted it, cut it down—even, one might say, done violence to it, suiting the form to its violent subject matter. There are many different kinds of sonnets: the Petrarchan, the Shakespearean, the Miltonic, to name but a few. All are characterized by distinctive rhyme schemes and lengths, though in most cases the convention of fourteen iambic pentameter lines is maintained. Walcott has introduced variation in meter, rhyme scheme, and length. Moreover, a sonnet is a poem meant to stand alone, to be complete in itself (although sonnet sequences are not uncommon), but Walcott makes each stanza of his poem into a kind of quasi-sonnet. Thus, while the poem as a whole is not a sonnet, it is put together with the stuff of sonnets, as if the stones from an ancient but tumbled cathedral had been used to build an edifice whose origins remained noticeable but whose purpose was entirely different. It is a display of breathtaking virtuosity and confidence, but the poet's purpose is more than simply to show off his mastery of English verse forms and traditions. As mentioned above, Walcott does violence to the traditional sonnet form in order to mirror the violence of his two subjects: the war between African and European going on in Kenya, and the similar struggle going on within the soul of the poet between "this Africa and the English tongue I love."

Walcott compares Africa to an animal, perhaps a lion. It possesses a "tawny pelt," and the veldt, a word meaning grassland, is likened to the bloodstream. Contrast this with the image of the Kikuyu introduced in line 2: "Kikuyu, quick as flies, / Batten upon the bloodstreams of the veldt." In the poet's extended metaphor, Africa is a beautiful animal, while the Africans living there are little more than blood-sucking insects. Africa may be "a paradise," but if so, it is a paradise strewn with corpses. What or who is responsible? While statisticians and scholars argue over "the salients of colonial policy," the poet rejects such inquiry as useless. "What is that to the white child hacked in bed? / To savages, expendable as Jews?" The unblinking ferocity of these two lines is shocking. The butchery of an innocent white child by natives is equated to the attitude of hypocritical whites who, despite professing horror and revulsion at the Holocaust, treat Africans analogously to the Nazi extermination of Jews.

There are no good guys here. Only vast and ancient Africa, symbolizing the natural world where violence is not evil but simply an inevitable result of evolution, and the Europeans and Africans who see themselves as superior to nature, representatives of competing civilizations both of which mock the beauty and purity of nature with their murderous ways. "The violence of beast on beast is read / As natural law, but upright man / Seeks his divinity by inflicting pain." Walcott, sickened by the spectacle as "the gorilla wrestles with the superman," would turn away, but cannot, for he carries that same grotesque wrestling match in his own bloodstream, in his own brain. Africa, the mother country, and English, the mother tongue, call to him with equal force, demanding he choose between them. He knows he cannot choose one or the other. Nor can he reject both. The litany of questions, posed as paradoxes, that constitutes the final eight lines of the poem poignantly and powerfully express the poet's existential dilemma, a dilemma that remains unresolved. Yet in the structure of the poem, Walcott has already begun to answer these questions by taking what is worthwhile from mother country and mother tongue and blending them into something that is both and neither. "Where shall I turn, divided to the vein?" The answer, perhaps still unconscious, is nevertheless plain: to poetry.

Source: Paul Witcover, in a essay for *Literature of Developing Nations for Students*, Gale, 2000.

Sources

Brown, Stewart, ed., *The Art of Derek Walcott*, Seren Books, 1991.

D'Aguiar, Fred, "Ambiguity Without a Crisis? Twin Traditions, The Individual and Community in Derek Walcott's Essays," in *The Art of Derek Walcott*, edited by Stewart Brown, Seren Books, 1991, pp.157-70.

Delf, George, *Jomo Kenyatta: Towards the Light of Truth*, Doubleday, 1961.

Hamner, Robert D., *Derek Walcott*, Twayne, 1993.

Hamner, Robert, D., ed., *Critical Perspectives on Derek Walcott*, Three Continents, 1993.

King, Bruce, "West Indies II: Walcott, Brathwaite, and Authenticity," in *The New English Literatures: Cultural Nationalism in a Changing World*, St. Martins, 1980, pp. 118-39.

Terada, Rei, *Derek Walcott's Poetry*, Northeastern University Press, 1992.

Further Reading

Baer, William, ed., *Conversations with Derek Walcott*, University Press of Mississippi, 1996.
    This text contains eighteen interviews spanning the period from 1966 to 1993. Also included is a good bio-chronology of Walcott's life.

Balakian, Peter, "The Poetry of Derek Walcott," in *Poetry*, June, 1986, pp. 169-77.
    Balakian comments on Walcott's *Collected Poems, 1948-1984.*

Breslin, Paul, "I Met History Once, But He Ain't Recognize Me: The Poetry of Derek Walcott," in *Tri Quarterly*, Winter, 1987, pp. 168-83.
    Breslin reflects on Walcott's career and work.

Dickey, James, "The Worlds of Cosmic Castaway," in *New York Times Book Review*, February 2, 1986, p. 8.
    Dickey reviews Walcott's *Collected Poems, 1948-1984.*

Grant, Nellie, *Nellie's Story*, William Morrow, 1981.
    For those wanting a firsthand account of what it was like to be a white farmer in Kenya during the period of 1933 to 1977, this is a valuable text.

Hamner, Robert D., ed., *Critical Perspectives on Derek Walcott*, Three Continents Press, 1993.
    These 52 essays, eight of which are by Walcott, present an exhaustive compendium of commentary on Walcott's life and works.

Hirsch, Edward, ''An Interview,'' in *Paris Review*, Winter, 1986, pp. 197-230.

  Hirsch's conversation with Walcott provides fascinating insight into Walcott's background and childhood, as well as his writing.

Hirsch, Edward, ''An Interview with Derek Walcott,'' in *Conversations with Derek Walcott*, edited by William Baer, University Press of Mississippi, 1996, pp. 50-63.

  Hirsch and Walcott converse about the author's poetry, prose, and plays, and his heritage as a West Indian.

Huxley, Elspeth, compiler, *Nine Faces of Kenya*, Viking, 1991.

  For firsthand accounts by both blacks and whites who lived in Kenya during Mau Mau, this is an excellent source. The book is divided into themes: Exploration, Travel, Settlers, Wars, Environment, Wildlife, Hunting, Lifestyles, Legend, and Poetry.

McWatt, Mark A., ''Derek Walcott: An Island Poet and His Sea,'' in *Third World Quarterly*, October, 1988, pp. 1607-15.

  McWatt examines Walcott's place in Caribbean literature and Walcott's theme of artistic isolation.

Walcott, Derek, *Collected Poems: 1948-1984*, Farrar, Straus and Giroux, 1986.

  This collection contains ''A Far Cry from Africa'' and 135 other poems, from Walcott's first major books, *In a Green Night* to *Midsummer*.

The Farming of Bones

Edwidge Danticat

1998

The Farming of Bones, Danticat told Megan Rooney in *The Brown Daily Herald,* is a survivor's story, based on the true story of a woman who was killed in the massacre. "But I wanted her to live," Danticat says, and in the book, she does. The book, which has received almost universally favorable reviews, is based on historical facts, filtered through Haitian tales and oral history, "a collage of various characters and experiences from my upbringing in Haiti," she told Rooney.

Although Danticat was still in her twenties when her first book, *Breath, Eyes, Memory,* was published, it received critical acclaim and was selected for Oprah Winfrey's book club, rocketing it to the top of the bestseller lists and commercial success. This success eventually led Penguin to pay $200,000 for the paperback rights to *The Farming of Bones*.

Danticat spent several years researching the events in *The Farming of Bones,* traveling to Haiti as many as four times a year. After visiting the Massacre River there in 1995, she realized that she wanted to write a book about the 1937 massacre of Haitians by Dominican dictator Rafael Trujillo. When she visited, there was no sign of the mass killings that occurred so many decades ago: a woman was washing clothes in the water, a man was letting a mule drink, and two boys were bathing. The river itself was small and slow, nowhere near the high-water mark that once swallowed hundreds

of bodies. "I had come looking for deaths," she wrote in *Kreyol,* "but I found habitualness, routine, life."

Despite this peace, or perhaps because of it—because the event and the people who suffered in it seemed to have been lost and forgotten—she decided to memorialize them by writing the book. "I felt like I was standing on top of a huge mass grave, and just couldn't see the bodies," she told Mallay Charters in *Publishers Weekly,* and reflected, "It's part of our history as Haitians, but it's also a part of the history of the world. Writing about it is an act of remembrance."

Danticat does not merely write about Haiti, but is still active in the Haitian community. With writer Junot Diaz, she runs Haitian-Dominican youth groups in New York, and also works with the National Coalition for Human Rights as part of a grant from the Lila Wallace-Readers Digest Foundation.

Author Biography

Edwidge Danticat (pronounced "Edweedj Danticah") was born January 19, 1969, in Port-au-Prince, Haiti, and was separated from her father when she was two and he emigrated to the United States to find work. When she was four, her mother also went to the United States. For the next eight years, Danticat and her younger brother Eliab were raised by their father's brother, a minister, who lived with his wife and grandson in a poor section of Port-au-Prince known as Bel Air.

When Danticat was twelve, she moved to Brooklyn and joined her parents and two new younger brothers. Adjustment to this new family was difficult, and she also had difficulty adjusting at school, because she spoke only Creole and did not know any English. Other students taunted her as a Haitian "boat person," or refugee. She told Mallay Charters in *Publishers Weekly,* "My primary feeling the whole first year was one of loss. Loss of my childhood, and of the people I'd left behind—and also of being lost. It was like being a baby—learning everything for the first time."

Danticat learned to tell stories from her aunt's grandmother in Bel Air, an old woman whose long hair, with coins braided into it, fascinated the neighborhood children, who fought each other to comb it. When people gathered, she told folktales and family stories. "It was call-and-response," Danticat told Charters. "If the audience seemed bored, the story would speed up, and if they were participating, a song would go in. The whole interaction was exciting to me. These cross-generational exchanges didn't happen often, because children were supposed to respect their elders. But when you were telling stories, it was more equal, and fun."

Danticat's cousin, Marie Micheline, taught her to read. She told Renee H. Shea in *Belles Lettres,* "I started school when I was three, and she would read to me when I came home. In 1987. . .there was a shooting outside her house—where her children were. She had a seizure and died. Since I was away from her, my parents didn't tell me right away. . .But around that same time, I was having nightmares; somehow I knew."

When Danticat was seven, she wrote stories with a Haitian heroine. For her, writing was not a casual undertaking. "At the time that I started thinking about writing," she told Calvin Wilson in the *Kansas City Star,* "a lot of people who were in jail were writers. They were journalists, they were novelists, and many of them were killed or 'disappeared.' It was a very scary thing to think about." Nevertheless, she kept writing. After she moved to Brooklyn and learned English, she wrote stories for her high school newspaper. One of these articles, about her reunion with her mother at age twelve, eventually expanded to become the book *Breath, Eyes, Memory.*

Danticat graduated from Barnard College with a degree in French literature in 1990, and worked as a secretary, doing her writing after work in the office. She applied to business schools and creative writing programs. She was accepted by both, but chose Brown University's creative writing program, which offered her a full scholarship. For her master's thesis, she wrote what would later become *Breath, Eyes, Memory .*

Breath, Eyes, Memory and her two other books—*The Farming of Bones* and *Krik? Krak!* , a collection of stories—have been hailed for their lyrical intensity, vivid descriptions of Haitian places and people, and honest depictions of fear and pain.

Danticat has won a Granta Regional Award as one of the Twenty Best Young American Novelists, a Pushcart Prize, and fiction awards from *Seventeen* and *Essence* magazines. She is also the recipient of an ongoing grant from the Lila Wallace-Reader's Digest Foundation.

Edwidge Danticat, signing her book for Ixel Cervera.

Plot Summary

After her parents drown in the flooded Massacre River that marks the border between Haiti and the Dominican Republic, young Haitian Amabelle Desir becomes a housemaid to Dominican landowner Don Ignacio, and a companion to his daughter, Valencia. As the book opens, Valencia and Amabelle are grown women, and Amabelle attends the birth of Valencia's twins. Valencia is now married to a Dominican army officer seeking to rise in the ranks, and he is soon assigned to assist in the brutal slaughter of Haitians in the Dominican Republic.

Amabelle's lover, Sebastien, works in Ignacio's sugar cane field, a brutal job known to workers as "farming the bones" because of its killing, exhausting harshness.

Amabelle has a pleasant but distant relationship with the family she serves, and the novel juxtaposes her moments in their home with her conversations with other Haitian workers in the cane fields, as they slowly realize that Dominican dictator Trujillo is against them, and that their lives are worthless to those who hire them. This tension increases when a cane worker is accidentally killed by Duarte's poor

driving, and he is not brought to account for the murder; no one, other than the Haitians, seems to care.

When the roundup and killing of Haitians begins, Sebastien disappears, presumably killed. Amabelle manages to escape, fleeing toward Haiti over mountain trails. Many others, also escaped, are pursued, forced to jump off cliffs, beheaded, or beaten to death before they ever cross the border into Haiti. The Dominicans identify Haitians by language, since despite the fact that Dominican propaganda states that Dominican origins are in Spain and the Haitians' are "in darkest Africa," there are no color differences between the two groups—the only difference is that the Haitians cannot pronounce the r in *perejil,* the Spanish word for "parsley." Some of the refugees in the book, in fact, are Dominicans who were attacked or killed because at first sight they appeared to be Haitian, and even Valencia's twins show this racial mix— one is dark, the other light, though they both grew in the same womb.

The most perilous part of Amabelle's journey back to Haiti occurs in Dajabon, the Dominican town closest to the Massacre River, which marks the border between the two countries. She and other refugees are herded together, attacked, and choked with parsley, while the Dominican attackers demand that they say "perejil." Because their language is Creole, not Spanish, they are unable to pronounce it correctly, and some are choked to death on handfuls of the herb; people throw stones at them, attack them with machetes, and brutally punch and kick them. She and some others escape only because the crowd is distracted by the arrival of the Dominican dictator, Trujillo, and they flee toward the river.

The river is filled with the corpses of slaughtered Haitians, and soldiers are throwing more bodies off a nearby bridge. As they swim across, one of the other refugees is shot, and his wife panics. Amabelle, in an attempt to keep her quiet and thus prevent the soldiers from noticing them and killing them too, covers the woman's nose and mouth with her hands. Although Amabelle does not intend to kill her, the woman dies.

Amabelle goes home with Yves, another refugee, and lives with him as if they are married, but is never intimate with him: she is still grieving for Sebastien. She finds Sebastien's mother's house and talks to her, but his mother soon moves to a distant city, because she can no longer bear talking to people who tell her that her son is dead.

In the wake of the massacre, the government sends officials to pay off surviving family members and to hear the stories of survivors. Amabelle and Yves go to the city to tell their stories, and after they wait for several days, they are turned away. They later find out that they will not receive any compensation after all. Danticat describes the scene: "The group charged the station looking for someone to write their names in a book, and take their story—they wanted a civilian face to concede that what they had witnessed and lived through did truly happen."

Much later, Amabelle, still seeking answers to her questions about why this all happened and what happened to Sebastien, crossed the river again and returns to Alegria, the Dominican region where she used to live. But the familiar landmarks are gone, she is disoriented and confused, and even Valencia has moved to a new house and does not recognize her at first. Eventually, she finds the cave she used to meet Sebastien in, but there are no answers there. At the end of the book she returns to the river, still seeking answers; as the book ends, she is lying in the current, giving herself up to fate and the forward flow, with faith for a new life.

Characters

Amabelle Desir

Amabelle is orphaned at a young age when her parents drown in the river between Haiti and the Dominican Republic, as they try to cross over to attend a market on the far side. Distraught, she tries to follow them, but two river-crossing guides hold her back, saying, "Unless you want to die, you will never see those people again." She is found on the riverbank by kindhearted and wealthy landowner Don Ignacio, who asks her, "Who do you belong to?" "To myself," she answers. He takes her in as a house servant, where she grows up with his daughter Valencia; as Valencia grows up, Amabelle becomes her personal maid, altering the relationship from personal companion to respectful servant. When Valencia has twins and there is no one else to attend her unexpected and early delivery, Amabelle serves as midwife, having picked up a smattering of

knowledge about this from her parents, who were both traditional healers back in Haiti.

Alone and alienated, a stranger in a strange land, Amabelle clings to her lover Sebastien, who works at brutally hard labor in the sugar cane fields. They meet often in a secret cave behind a waterfall, and she says of him, "When he's not there, I'm afraid I know no one and no one knows me." Having taken the place of her family, he is her rock in life. Like her, he has suffered loss—his father was killed in a hurricane—and their shared sadness bonds them together.

When Dominican dictator Rafael Trujillo begins a genocidal campaign against all Haitians in his country, Amabelle must flee for her life. She is a survivor at all costs: determined, driven, she will do whatever it takes to live. When, in the ensuing chaos, Sebastien disappears and is presumed killed, she must once again rely on her own instincts.

Amabelle makes it across the border to Haiti, but not without paying a heavy price in physical and emotional suffering. For many years afterward, she grieves for Sebastien, even going back to the Dominican Republic in an attempt to find their old secret cave. Driven to find answers to the questions that haunt her—why people suffer, why they die, why she lived when others perished—she returns to the river, hoping "that if I came to the river on the right day, at the right hour, the surface of the water might provide the answer. . .But nature has no memory."

Don Ignacio

A wealthy Dominican landowner, Valencia's father, and employer of Amabelle and Sebastien. He was born in Spain, and constantly looks back to his lost homeland. Each night he listens to the radio for broadcasts of the progress of the Spanish Civil War. As Amabelle notes, "He felt himself the orphaned child of a now orphaned people." Sympathetic to the suffering of others, he takes Amabelle into his household when he finds her orphaned on the riverbank; this sympathy comes from the fact that although he is wealthy now, his background was humble. Back in Spain, he says, "My father was a baker. . .There are times when he gave bread to everyone in our quarter for nothing. I was his only son but he would never let me eat until everyone else had eaten." When his son kills a Haitian worker with his car, Don Ignacio is sympathetic and wants to visit the grieving father, but he is human and has limits—when his own grandson dies, he forgets all about this, wrapped up in his own pain.

Doctor Javier

An intense, educated man, he admires Amabelle's intelligence and determination and invites her to work in a clinic in Haiti with him when he finds out that her parents were healers and that she has successfully midwifed Valencia's twins. "You can be trained," he says. "We have only two Haitian doctors for a large area. I cannot go there all the time, and I know of only one or two midwives in that region of the border. You are greatly needed." When he hears about the genocide, he warns Amabelle and others to run and tells her he and others have room in their trucks for her, but before this happens, he is arrested and is never seen again.

Kongo

An old mask maker and carpenter, whose true name is unknown. His son is struck and killed by Pico Duarte's car. When the genocide begins, he tells Amabelle that she must escape. He does not try to escape, saying that he is too old to run, but he performs a ritual for safe passage and tells her how to follow mountain trails and then cross the river.

Sebastien Onius

Amabelle's lover, who works in Don Ignacio's sugar cane fields. His father was killed seven years before the story begins, in a devastating hurricane; this led him and his sister to seek work in Dominica, though his mother remains in Haiti. He is a strong, calm man, her friend and protector; when the genocide begins he disappears, presumably killed, and is never seen again. He is an enigmatic figure: intensely strong and physical, often sweaty and dirty from his hard work, but he speaks like a poet when he and Amabelle lie together in their secret cave, telling stories of his dreams and the past, of the hurricane that killed his father. He likes to talk; he dislikes silence, because "to him [it] is like sleep, a close second to death." He disappears early in the book, apparently killed by the Dominicans, but he is an almost tangible presence throughout, as Amabelle grieves and asks everyone she meets if they know what happened to him.

Papi

See Don Ignacio

Man Rapadou

Mother of Yves, who has her own secrets: when she found that her husband, a Haitian, was planning to become a spy for American interests, she cooked him a meal filled with ground glass and rat poison, and killed him. She tells Amabelle, "Greater than my love for this man was my love for my country."

Father Romain

A Haitian priest who works with the poor Haitian workers and who runs a school for their children. He often speaks of their home in Haiti, and how common language, customs, and memories bind them all together as a community. Amabelle says of him, "His creed was one of memory, how remembering—though sometimes painful—can make you strong." During the genocide, he is tortured by the Dominicans and goes insane, but eventually is healed when he leaves the priesthood, marries, and has three children. "It took more than prayers to heal me after the slaughter," he tells Amabelle. "It took a love closer to the earth, closer to my own body, to stop my tears. Perhaps I have lost, but I have also gained an ever greater understanding of things both godly and earthly."

Valencia

Daughter of Don Ignacio, wife of Pico Duarte, and mother of twin babies, a boy and a girl. She and Amabelle grew up together, and later, during the genocide, she helps hide Haitians from the killers because she remembers how close she was to Amabelle: "I hid them because I couldn't hide you. . .I thought you'd been killed, so everything I did, I did in your name." She is one of the few characters in the book who does not murder, injure, or neglect someone else; despite being married to a man who carries out the orders to kill as many Haitians as possible, she works to save them.

Yves

A sugar cane worker, a refugee. Amabelle escapes with him, and not knowing where else to go, follows him to his mother's house in Haiti. They live together as if they're married, and his mother assumes they are lovers, though they are not—Amabelle is still grieving for Sebastien, who has disappeared. Yves spends long days working in his fields, only coming home at night and going to sleep immediately. He is a good man, and Amabelle regrets that they have not found more comfort in each other.

Themes

Exile

As Scott Adlerberg observed in the *Richmond Review*, "Exile increases the poignancy of memory," and many of the characters in the book are exiled, cut off from their families or homes by death or distance. Amabelle remembers her parents constantly, replaying their death by drowning in the swollen river, and talks about them with her lover Sebastien, who likewise tells her about his lost childhood in Haiti. The poor, displaced Haitians in the book all share this sense of a lost home, and it serves as a bond to unite their community—as Amabelle notes, "In his sermons to the Haitian congregants of the valley he often reminded everyone of common ties: language, foods, history, carnival, songs, tales, and prayers. His creed was one of memory, how remembering—though sometimes painful—can make you strong." The Haitian sugar cane workers consider themselves to be "an orphaned people, a group of *vwayaje*, wayfarers."

The Haitians in the book are not the only exiles; Amabelle's employer, Don Ignacio, though born in Spain, came to the Caribbean to fight in the Spanish-American War in 1898. Now, each night he scrolls up and down the radio dial to hear reports from Spain about the progress of the Spanish Civil War. Amabelle notices his homesickness and is aware that "he felt himself the displaced child of a now orphaned people."

Despite these warnings, Amabelle, Sebastien, and the other Haitians are unprepared for the bloodbath about to occur, which will further exile those who are not slaughtered in it. The survivors, cut off from their past, those they love, and their own sense of safety and purpose, are spiritual exiles, looking for meaning and a sense of purpose; some find it, and some never do.

Genocide

The mass killing of Haitians is the central event in the book, and is described with nightmarish clarity; the book may remind readers of more recent atrocities in Bosnia and Rwanda, and the refugees flowing over the borders of these and other countries. Danticat is aware that despite the fact that events like these are visible on the news almost every night, these events seem very far away. She told Calvin Wilson in *The Kansas City Star*, "People don't want to believe that there is that kind of danger, if there is no precedent for it that they know

Topics for Further Study

- Research the 1937 massacre of Haitians by Dominican dictator Rafael Trujillo and compare it to more recent ethnic genocides in Rwanda and Bosnia.

- Choose another dictator, such as Adolf Hitler or Haitian leader Francois "Papa Doc" Duvalier, and compare him to Rafael Trujillo. What methods did these men use to gain and keep control over their countries?

- Investigate the hurricane of 1931 and the damage it caused in Haiti and the Dominican Republic. Other than destruction of property, what long-term effects did the storm have on the economy, society, and culture of these countries?

- Consider the society you live in. Is there any evidence that a dictator like Trujillo could come to power in your own culture?

of. They don't want to believe that, all of a sudden, thousands of people can be killed." The book is a vivid reminder that these events do happen, that they can happen to everyone, and that no one is left out of the whirlpool of death and destruction when they do occur.

Remembrance

The themes of exile and of remembrance are related: the exiles' pain is alternately increased or soothed by their remembrance of the past. In addition, however, the book is permeated with a sense of remembrance of the actual people who suffered through these events, and the unnamed, unrecorded tens of thousands who were killed. As a man says near the end of the book, "Famous men never die. . .It is only those nameless and faceless who vanish like smoke in the early moning air." Danticat sees changing this fate as part of her mission as a writer, wanting to create a kind of memorial in words for all the "nameless and faceless." As Amabelle says, "All I want to do is find a place to lay it [the slaughter] down now and again, a safe nest where it will neither be scattered by the winds, nor remain forever buried beneath the sod.''

The River of Death

The Massacre River, named for a mass slaughter in the seventeenth century, lives up to its name in the events of the book. Throughout the book, the river is a place of actual and symbolic death: many people die in it, corpses float down it, and once people cross it, their lives are never the same. Crossing it a second time is even harder, leading to alienation: you can never truly go back to the other side.

Amabelle's life is marked early by the river: when she is a child, her parents try to cross it to get to a market in the Dominican Republic. Though the water is visibly rising and the young boys who work carrying people and goods across refuse to go, her father insists that they enter the current. ''My father reaches into the current and sprinkles his face with the water, as if to salute the spirit of the river and request her permission to cross,'' Amabelle says. ''My mother crosses herself three times and looks up at the sky before she climbs on my father's back.'' Despite these ritual precautions, Amabelle's parents are swept away. Amabelle is prevented from going after them by the river boys, who drag her away, saying, ''Unless you want to die, you will never see those people again.''

Later, during the mass slaughter of Haitians, she and some other refugees reach the river. ''From a distance,'' she says, ''the water looked deep and black, the bank much steeper than I remembered.'' They hear splashing: the Dominicans are throwing corpses into the water. When they cross, they must swim to avoid the bodies and the belongings of slain Haitians: the water is literally a river of death. And when Odette, another refugee, panics because her husband has been shot while he swims across, Amabelle covers her nose and mouth to keep her quiet, ''for her own good, for our own good.'' Odette does not struggle, but gives up to the lack of air and the motion of the river, as if she has already decided to die.

Near the end of the book, Amabelle crosses the river again, returning to the Dominican Republic, and tries to find Alegria, the region she lived in for so long. All is unrecognizable, the landmarks changed or gone, the people gone or moved, and when she finally finds her former employer Valencia, Valencia does not recognize her until she tells the story of her parents' death in the river. Valencia apologizes for this, and Amabelle tells her she understands and says she feels ''like an old ghost had slipped under my skin.''

Style

Pace

Danticat's story begins slowly, told with a languid, measured pace, set in a traditional agrarian society, and the first scene, after a dreamlike encounter between Amabelle and her lover Sebastien, involves the birth of twins, a boy and a girl, to her wealthy employer. At first, the book seems very much like many weighty classics of nineteenth-century literature, which begin with the birth of the protagonist.

Danticat turns this expectation upside down, however: the real hero of the story is not either of the children, but Amabelle, the servant, who midwifes them using half-remembered skills taught by her healer parents. Tinges of violence creep into the story: the twins' father kills a sugar cane worker when he runs into him with his car, but is never officially brought to justice, because the cane workers' lives are considered expendable and because he is a ranking military officer. In addition, Amabelle and Sebastien have both lost one or both parents at a young age, hinting at the precarious nature of their lives—or, as Danticat makes clear, everyone's life: no one is exempt from the possibility of violence that lurks in every person and every society.

As the story moves on, the violence escalates, along with the pace. Rumors of an impending slaughter of Haitians begin circulating. One of the twins, the boy, dies of crib death. Haitian workers begin telling stories they've heard of other workers who were killed in recent weeks. Amabelle is almost killed by a stray bullet from her employers' target practice. And when the genocide begins, people are stabbed, shot, drowned, crushed by trucks, forced to jump off cliff, and choked with bunches of parsley—because their inability to say the word properly in Spanish marks them as Haitians.

Point of View

Throughout, Danticat's narrator Amabelle tells the story in the first person. She is there, she suffers through all these events, and Danticat's choice of this point of view, and her vivid imagery and sensory detail, gives everything an almost choking immediacy. Amabelle's narrative style is flat, almost documentary in style, as in the following paragraph:

> Her face flapped open when she hit the ground, her right cheekbone glistening as the flesh parted from it. She rolled onto her back and for a moment faced the sky. Her body spiraled past the croton hedge down the slope. The mountain dirt clung to her dress, her arms, her face, her whole body gathering a thick cloud of dust.

Danticat deliberately avoids depicting too much emotion in the body of the book, capturing the numbness inherent to the survivors of catastrophes. Instead, she presents the scenes and allows the reader to view them and fill in the emotional impact of the slaughter, torture, and dislocation of the refugees. This participation on the reader's part makes the scenes hard to dismiss, and hard to forget. As Danticat said in an interview with Calvin Wilson in the *Kansas City Star,* "The things that I have written so far are things that almost give me nightmares."

Separation of Emotions

In the beginning and end of the book, Danticat allows Amabelle to speak more openly of her feelings in short sequences, in which she describes her dreams, her memories of her departed parents, her wishes, and her fears. These sequences are deliberately separated from the main story of the book, since Amabelle only feels safe to express them when she is alone, enclosed, in a secret cave where she hides with Sebastien, or at the end of the book, when she has reached some measure of peace with his loss and is able to come to terms with her life as a survivor apart from him. As she says, "I sense that we no longer know the same words, no longer speak the same language. There is water, land, and mountains between us, a shroud of silence, a curtain of fate."

Literary Heritage

Haiti is a country long marked by its political unrest and economic depravity as a result of years of dictatorship, government corruption, and a large gap between the wealthy elite and profitable cities and the poverty-stricken non-industrial provinces.

A written or recorded literature was never a priority in Haitian culture, therefore, the number of internationally recognized Haitian authors is understandably few. In addition, Haitian women writers are rare due to the secondary positions they hold within the society, remaining mostly in the home or in non-professional occupations.

Although fiscally poor, Haiti is a culture rich in its language, folktales, customs, and community. The Haitian people often looked to their families and friends not only for support but also for forms of entertainment. In a sense, it was the effects of poverty and illiteracy that made the practice of storytelling an important and favorite pastime, allowing this craft to endure throughout the generations, preserving the nation's culture and history.

Haitian literature was not known outside its borders until well into the 1960s, when the Civil Rights and Women's movements pushed for social reforms and gave the Haitian people an impetus to search out and explore their voices. Still, it was not until the 1990s that Haiti and Haitian literature started to receive the attention it deserved. As more and more nations began to learned of Haiti's oppression and the violence its people faced under the Duvalier government, the call for information about the country and its people increased. New emerging writers began to meet this demand, describing the horrors as well as the jewels of this besieged nation. These writers were creating a literature of social consciousness that demanded acknowledgement from the outside world. Their writing also served as a mirror in which to look back and examine their own background and culture.

When Haitian-born writer Edwidge Danticat began to write and record her memories of Haiti, fictionalizing them in her books, her writings became an extension of the oral tradition of her culture, capturing in print what was natural to her at an early age. What is present in Danticat's work is Haiti's painful history but also its uniqueness and beauty. It is this beauty and cultural lushness that are making people more open to Haitian literature and leading to changes in its presence and proliferation.

Historical Context

The Massacre River

In an essay in *Kreyol,* describing a 1995 visit to the river, Danticat writes, "Between Haiti and the

Dominican Republic flows a river filled with ghosts.'' The Massacre River was named for a seventeeth-century bloodbath, but as Danticat makes clear, it has continued to live up to its name. The river divides the small Caribbean island of Hispaniola into the countries of Haiti and the Dominican Republic. Because the countries are so close, their fates have historically been intertwined. *The Farming of Bones* begins in the Republic, during the regime of General Rafael Trujillo.

Trujillo's Regime

From 1930 to 1961, the Dominican Republic was ruled by General Rafael Leonidas Trujillo, whose ascension to power was inadvertently aided by American efforts to bolster stability in the Caribbean. American leaders were interested in the Caribbean because it was a gateway to the Panama Canal, central to U.S. shipping and trade interests, and the U.S. wanted to keep the area stable and free from European intervention. Because the nations in that area were poor, politically unstable, and, in the case of the Dominican Republic, still recovering from past Spanish rule, the U.S. took over Dominican finances, occupying the country from 1911 through 1916.

The harshness of this occupation offended Dominicans, and when the American marines left the island in 1924, they left behind an armed National Guard. Trujillo, one of the officers of the guard, used his military connections to foster a coup six years later, remove then-President Vasquez from office, and establish his own dictatorship, which lasted over three decades.

Once in office, Trujillo killed anyone opposing him and sent his thugs through the countryside, armed with machine guns, to terrorize the population. Money and ownership of land was funneled to him, resulting in widespread poverty and uprooting of entire communities. Mail was censored, telephones were monitored, and citizens needed government permission to move or practice any profession.

In 1931, a devastating hurricane struck Haiti and the Dominican Republic, killing 2,000 people and injuring many more. Trujillo used the destruction to his advantage, taking absolute power in the crisis and controlling all medicine and building supplies. He imposed ''emergency'' taxes, never repealed. Naturally, resentment against him grew, and he murdered, tortured, or imprisoned anyone he suspected of disloyalty.

During this period, many Haitians crossed the border into the Dominican Republic, seeking work in the wake of the devastating hurricane. Their sheer numbers began to make some Dominicans uneasy, and there was a racist tone to this unease. As the book notes, Dominicans were told, ''Our motherland is Spain, theirs is darkest Africa, you understand? They once came here only to cut sugarcane, but now there are more of them than there will ever be cane to cut, you understand? Our problem is one of dominion. . .Those of us who love our country are taking measures to keep it our own.''

Trujillo Orders Genocide

In 1937, to stop this tide of humanity and implement these ''measures,'' Dominican troops killed between 10,000 and 15,000 Haitians. As Scott Adlerberg remarked in the *Richmond Review,* ''None of those killed is anyone famous, nearly all the slaughtered are poor Haitians working as cheap labor in the neighboring country.'' Danticat also notes that there is often no difference in color between the two sides, despite the insistence that ''our motherland is Spain, theirs is darkest Africa.'' Language is the only differentiating feature, and Dominican troops use the Haitians' inability to pronounce the trilled Spanish ''r'' in *perejil,* the word for parsley. ''Que diga perejil,'' the soldiers demanded, and anyone who answered ''pewejil'' would be shot as a Haitian.

Critical Overview

Danticat is the first Haitian woman to write in English, be published by a major American press, and earn wide publicity, so she is the first one to open the door of her culture to mainstream America. Her work has received almost universally favorable reviews, and she has won numerous awards and honors for her two novels, *Breath, Eyes, Memory* and *The Farming of Bones,* and her short story collection, *Krik? Krak!*

An interesting aspect of criticism of Danticat's work is that, unlike discussions of many other writers, commentary on her work always also includes a lengthy discussion of her life, even though she is relatively young. Perhaps this is because Haiti and its culture and history are not well known to most American and European readers, so there is a certain fascination inherent in Danticat's life and in her unfamiliar culture. Perhaps it's because her first novel, *Breath, Eyes, Memory* was the semi-autobiographical story of a young girl raised by an aunt, who comes to the United States at age twelve and must deal with her family's generational issues and the dislocation of immigration to a strange place. A book like this makes readers ask about the author's life in an attempt to determine how much of the novel is "true."

Dan Cryer, who wrote one of the few unfavorable reviews of *The Farming of Bones*, in *Salon*, seemed to be reacting to this seemingly excessive interest in Danticat's life, mainstream Americans' fascination with her "exotic" settings, and her lionization as a spokeswoman for Haitian Americans (a position that Danticat says she does not want). "Pity the young novelist surfing the wave of novelty and hype," he wrote. "Sooner or later, she's going to wipe out." Regarding the awards she's won, he asked, "A prized seat among the literati-in-waiting of *Granta* magazine's 20 Best American Novelists and a National Book Award nomination for *Krik? Krak!*? Oh, please! Has anyone actually read these books?" Cryer criticized Danticat's characterization, saying that Amabelle and Sebastien are depicted only with the broadest brush, making it "hard to care, except in the most abstract way," about their fates. "This is by far Danticat's longest book, and the stretch shows," he commented. "Only 29, Danticat has plenty of time to achieve her considerable potential. But overpraising her work won't help her get there."

Cryer seemed to be alone in his opinion, however, as other critics praised the work. "No antiseptic, nothing for the pain, just the serrated slice of her words," wrote Christopher John Farley in *Time*, "...every chapter cuts deep, and you feel it." Farley also remarked that Danticat's prose "never turns purple, never spins wildly into the fantastic, always remains focused...[and] uncovers moments of raw humanness." Scott Adlerberg, in the *Richmond Review*, praised *The Farming of Bones* as an "indelible work of art," remarking on Danticat's "effortless style" and "simple but sensual language [that] brings her tropical world to life; one can feel the heat, see the luxuriant colors, taste the spicy foods...Amabelle is a flesh and blood woman...we share in her joys and sorrows, her dreams, memories, and day-to-day struggles." In *Newsweek*, Sarah Van Boven cited Danticat's beginning the book with the birth of a wealthy child, while the true hero is the servant girl Amabelle, as one of many "masterful inversions" in the book; among others, she noted, "joyful reunions turn hollow,

damnation masquerades as salvation, big questions are met with a silence more profound than any answer."

As Van Boven suggests, Danticat does not provide any neat conclusion, moral lesson, or encompassing answer to the horrific events that take place in the novel. Sebastien, who is named in the first line of the book ("His name is Sebastien Onius"), soon disappears and is never seen again, and his fate is uncertain—he's presumed killed, but Amabelle, and readers, never have the satisfaction of knowing exactly what became of him. Amabelle herself, by the end of the book, is still grieving, still alone, deeply scarred by the genocide—and she always will be. Nothing in the book is predictable except that inevitably, pain and sorrow will enter everyone's life. A *Publishers Weekly* reviewer noted that when violence does erupt in the book, the story develops the "unflinching clarity" of a documentary. The review also praised Danticat's realistic characterizations, the dignity of the people described, and her "lushly poetic and erotic, specifically detailed" prose. Calvin Wilson, in *The Kansas City Star*, wrote, "There's little doubt that, at a time when some writers gain attention simply by emphasizing the glib, the trendy and the superficial, Danticat will continue to create works of enduring weight."

Criticism

Kelly Winters

Kelly Winters is a freelance writer. She has written for a wide variety of academic and educational publishers. In the following essay, she discusses themes of remembrance, racism, and hope in The Farming of Bones.

In her afterword to *The Farming of Bones*, Danticat writes:

> In *The Farming of Bones*, Amabelle is similarly obsessed with the loss of the past, and the unrecorded or forgotten stories of thousands of lives cut short or stunted. Even before the slaughter, she ritualistically tells herself the story of her parents' drowning, keeping alive every word and gesture; but she realizes that the older she gets, the more her memories of them are fading. At the end of the book she knows, painful though it is, that her memories of her lost lover Sebastien will fade in the same way.

She is not the only one who believes in the importance of stories and memory. The Haitians in the book share their stories, and Amabelle com-

What Do I Read Next?

- Danticat's *Krik? Krak!* is a collection of short stories set in Haiti. The title comes from a traditional Haitian custom of listeners asking ''Krik?'' before a story is told. The teller answers ''Krak'' and begins the tale.

- *Breath, Eyes, Memory*, also by Danticat, tells the story of a twelve-year-old Haitian girl, raised by an aunt, who comes to the United States and is reunited with her mother for the first time since infancy.

- *Trujillo: The Death of the Dictator,* by Bernard Diederich, documents Trujillo's ascension to power, rule over the Dominican Republic, and assassination.

- Philip Gourevitch's *We Regret to Inform You That Tomorrow We Will Be Killed with Our Families* is a collection of harrowing first-person accounts of the genocide in Rwanda.

---

ments: ''This was how people left imprints of themselves in each other's memory, so that if you left first and went back to the common village, you could carry, if not a letter, a piece of treasured clothing, some message to their loved ones that their place was still among the living.''

Later, after the slaughter, in a refugee camp run by nuns, the survivors call out their stories, testifying to what they have seen, telling tales of wanton killing and destruction. Desperate to tell what happened to them, they interrupt each other, ''the haste in their voices sometimes blurring the words. . .One could hear it in the fervor of the declarations, the obscenities shouted when something could not be remembered fast enough, when a stutter allowed another speaker to race into his own account without the stutterer having completed his.''

Later, she hears that the government supposedly will give reparation money to the survivors of the massacre and record their stories. Amabelle and Yves go to see the Justice of the Peace and tell about their experiences, and find over a thousand other people waiting. They wait for several days, and in the end, find that their story will not be recorded and no money will be paid; the government simply does not have the resources to deal with everyone who was affected. Amabelle and Yves are more upset by the fact that no one will listen to them than by the loss of money: money disappears, but stories, if recorded, endure forever.

But, as they see, listening and recording all this suffering is an arduous and painful task; even when Amabelle goes to visit the priests of the cathedral, they tell her that they too have stopped listening to the survivors' tales, since they can do nothing to bring back those who have died or to change the suffering that people have already experienced. ''It was taking all our time, and there is so much other work to be done,'' one priest tells her. He is focusing on the future, not the past, an act that Amabelle later realizes is the only thing that can be done.

The only way to reconcile these two conflicting urges—to constantly keep the past alive, and to move beyond it into the future—is to record the past in a safe place, somewhere outside an individual's memory, some place where facts will remain and not fade, but where the person won't have to carry the memory daily. Amabelle says, ''The slaughter is the only thing that is mine enough to pass on. All I want to do is to find a place to lay it down now and again, a safe nest where it will neither be scattered by the winds, nor remain forever buried beneath the sod.''

That safe place, Danticat invites readers to say, is this book.

In addition, *The Farming of Bones*, in telling the stories of so many ordinary people whose lives were disrupted or destroyed, tells us that this could happen to anyone. No one is safe from disaster, grief, or pain. Even before the genocide, many people have been uprooted by a hurricane that devastated the island. Amabelle's parents die on a routine marketing trip across the river. Throughout the book, Danticat makes clear that everyone is born to suffer and that no one can afford to be complacent.

This applies especially to the beaten-down workers in the cane fields, but also to the wealthier, more established Haitians, the ones who don't have to work in the cane fields, but have houses made of wood or cement, with metal roofs, beautiful gardens, and fruit trees. "We all regarded them as people who have their destinies in hand," Danticat says, but when the genocide begins, it's clear that they don't, that in fact there is no difference between their fates and those of the poor laborers. Even before the slaughter, some of these people begin to realize that the Dominicans regard them as alien and unwanted, that they don't have Dominican identification or birth certificates, and that they could be pushed out of their settled existence at any time. People begin telling stories of poor Haitians who have been killed. As Amabelle notes, "Poor Dominican peasants had been asked to catch Haitians and bring them to the soldiers. Why not the rich ones too?"

And Danticat doesn't stop there. She makes it clear that no one—not even the Dominicans—is exempt from suffering. Some Dominicans are slaughtered or injured, as the killers mistake them for Haitians. Even for those who are not attacked, the changes wrought by the massacre are so far-reaching and all-encompassing that when Amabelle revisits her Dominican neighborhood, nothing there is recognizable. Haciendas have been transformed into guarded fortresses surrounded by walls topped with broken glass and metal spikes; the landscape is so changed that she can't find her old home, and the people are so changed that she sees no one she recognizes, and no one recognizes her until she tells the story of her parents' drowning.

As a man who was shot and left to die in a pit full of dead bodies says, "It is no different, the flesh, than fruit or anything that rots. It's not magic, not holy. It can shrink, burn, and like amber it can melt in fire. It is nothing. We are nothing."

This existential despair touches everyone, Dominican and Haitian—after all, the division between the two nations is false, an arbitrary marker—the river—and both sides suffer. They share the

> " The only way to reconcile these two conflicting urges—to constantly keep the past alive, and to move beyond it into the future—is to record the past in a safe place, somewhere outside an individual's memory, some place where facts will remain and not fade, but where the person won't have to carry the memory daily."

same island, Hispaniola. This false division and misplaced hatred is made apparent in Pico Duarte, the racist military officer, whose wife has twin children. One is "coconut-cream colored, his cheeks and forehead the blush pink of water lilies." The other is "a deep bronze, between the colors of tan Brazil nut shells and black salsify," and this child's grandfather remarks that she got her color from Duarte's side of the family. There is no such thing as racial purity, and the island cannot be neatly divided into two sides, one white, one black. Both sides are a mix of many skin colors and many heritages; in hating people of African descent, Duarte must also hate himself and his child. Each time he sees the baby, he displays a "stinging expression of disfavor growing more and more pronounced. . .each time he laid eyes on her," despite the fact that she looks like him.

In the same way, Danticat points out, there is also no such thing as moral purity. Most of the characters are guilty of many sins: Amabelle murders another refugee and shows little remorse, brushing it off as something she had to do in order to survive; Man Rapadou, a respectable matriarch, reveals that she killed her own husband to prevent him from becoming a spy; Kongo, the honorable old carpenter, reveals a senseless prejudice against a perfectly good woman simply because her grandfather once stole a hen, and he fears that thievery is in her blood; the refugee Tibon tells Amabelle that when he was ten, he almost killed a Dominican boy simply to make him say that even if he lived in a big house, he was no better than Tibon was. Sebastien seems to understand this complexity of the human heritage, both physically and spiritually; as he strokes Amabelle's skin, he tells her he sees "all the shades of black in you, what we see and what we don't see, the good and the bad."

In the same way that some Haitians are capable of evil acts, some of the Dominicans are capable of good. Some pity the Haitians instead of hating them, and others hide them from the killing mobs. Valencia in particular hides many refugees, even though her husband is involved in the slaughter. She does this out of remembrance and friendship for Amabelle, whom she grew up with, and whom she believes is dead.

So how, Amabelle and others in the book ask, can one escape this feeling of existential despair and fear? The only way out of suffering, Danticat shows, is not to forget the past, but at the same time, to renew one's relationship with the flow of life. Father Romain, who is tortured and brainwashed by the Dominicans so severely that he becomes insane, is eventually healed—not by the church, but because he marries and has three children. Holding their lives against his heart, loving his wife, he finds something to live for, despite his grief for all those who were lost. He has acknowledged the loss, but is now more invested in the future. We have to let go and go on, his healing shows.

Amabelle also learns this lesson at the end of the book, when she goes to the river, thinking that if she visits it enough—the site of her parents' deaths, and the massacre—that she will find some answers to the questions that torment her: why people die, why people suffer, why she has survived. In the end, she realizes, nature has no answers, but she literally lies down in the river, surrendering herself to its flow, "looking for the dawn," in faith that some-day, she will be at peace.

It's a lesson Danticat knows well, as she wrote in *Kreyol.* When she visited the river in 1995, and saw no sign of the slaughter, her hope for the future was renewed by the sight of people from both sides—Dominicans and Haitians—washing and fishing in the water. To her, they seemed to be "part of a meaningful celebration. Not only of the continual flow of a boundless body of water, but essentially of the resilience of life itself."

Source: Kelly Winters, in an essay for *Literature of Developing Nations for Students,* Gale, 2000.

Dean Peerman

In the following review of Danticat's The Farming of Bones, *Dean Peerman characterizes the author's work as a distinctive and poetic blend of fully realized characters, seamlessly interweaving history, politics, and fiction in a compelling manner.*

"El Corte," the cutting, it was called—a euphemism akin to "ethnic cleansing." It was one of the worst massacres of modern times, though much of the world seems to have forgotten about it. It took place in the Dominican Republic in 1937. Raphael Trujillo, a military leader and former sugar plantation guard (and former hoodlum) who had been trained by U.S. Marines during the 1916–1924 U.S. occupation of his country, managed to get himself elected president in 1930 (there were more votes than eligible voters). Seven years into his rule, Trujillo secretly ordered the killing of thousands of immigrants—most of them sugarcane cutters—from Haiti, the country with which the DR shares the island of Hispaniola. In his view, the Haitians, whom he considered inferior beings, had simply become too numerous. The military police were instructed to use machetes in their murdering, in the hope of putting the blame on civilians. Some Haitians were given a choice, however, of jumping off a high cliff rather than being hacked to death.

The novel *The Farming of Bones*, by Haitian-American writer Edwidge Danticat, is set in that terrible time, but while politics, race and class are among its subjects, it is far from being an ideological tract. Danticat writes a poetic, evocative prose that is replete with vivid human details, and her characters are distinctive, fully realized individuals. In this work, history and fiction are interwoven in a seamless and compelling fashion.

Amabelle Desir, the novel's Haitian-born narrator, is a servant in the home of a prominent Dominican family—a family that has raised her since the age of eight, following her parents' death by drowning (an event she observed helplessly from the riverbank). When Senora Valencia, the mistress of the house, is about to give birth, Amabelle unexpectedly has to serve as midwife. The senora has twins—a boy, who shortly dies, and a dark-skinned daughter. At one point she says to Amabelle—in words she no doubt thinks are inoffensive: "Do you think my daughter will always be the color she is now? My poor love, what if she's mistaken for one of your people?" Senor Pico, the twins' father, a colonel in service to "the Generalissimo" (as Trujillo is referred to throughout), cannot bear even to look at his swarthy daughter after her twin brother dies.

Mature for her 25 years and remarkably confident despite her servant status, Amabelle allows herself to show a more tender and vulnerable side only in the presence of her lover, a canecutter named Sebastien Onius. When the crackdown comes and Amabelle and Sebastien realize they must flee for their lives, circumstances separate the two, and Sebastien is arrested (by Senor Pico, we learn much later) along with Father Romain, a liberal priest who had arranged to smuggle a group to Haiti. Eventually Amabelle finds out that Sebastien has been executed. She and Sebastien's friend Yves do manage to escape, and after a harrowing odyssey (including a near-fatal ordeal that leaves Amabelle disfigured) they finally reach Haiti. Amabelle survives, working as a seamstress, but she never marries, and she remains troubled by her painful memories. At age 50—after the Generalissimo has been assassinated—she returns to visit the senora, but communication is awkward and difficult between them after so many years. The senora tries to apologize—and make excuses—for her husband's role in "El Corte."

Danticat's semiautobiographical first novel, *Breath, Eyes, Memory*, was an impressive debut, but *The Farming of Bones* is a richer work, haunting and heartwrenching.

Tensions continue between the Dominican Republic and its much poorer and culturally different neighbor. Just last year, for example, at least 14,000 Haitians were repatriated in many cases minus possessions and paycheck. One faint sign of hope: also last year, direct mail service was established between the two countries; previously mail between them had to be routed by way of Miami.

Source: Dean Peerman, "Bookmarks," (book review), in *The Christian Century,* Vol. 116, Issue 25, September 22, 1999, p. 885.

Jacqueline Brice-Finch

In this brief review of Danticat's The Farming of Bones, *Jacqueline Brice-Finch gives the reader an overview of Danticat's memorialization of the genocide of Haitian immigrants as framed by a love story between two Haitians involved in the political machinations of their times.*

Readers of Caribbean literature are no strangers to the harsh conditions of the cane field, particularly in the French Antilles during the early twentieth century. Joseph Zobel in *La Rue Cases-Negres* (1950;

> Danticat writes a poetic, evocative prose that is replete with vivid human details, and her characters are distinctive, fully realized individuals."

Black Shack Alley) and Simone Schwarz-Bart in *Pluie et vent sur Telumee Miracle* (1972; *The Bridge of the Beyond*) graphically related the degradation that workers endured to eke out a subsistence living. However, it is the second novel by Edwidge Danticat, *The Farming of Bones,* which is the focus of another aspect of the history of cane workers, the massacre of Haitians in the Dominican Republic in 1937.

Due to a growing xenophobia under the rule of Generalissimo Rafael Leonidas Trujillo Molina, the Dominicans were told:

> Our motherland is Spain; theirs is darkest Africa, you understand? They once came here only to cut sugarcane, but now there are more of them than there will ever be cane to cut, you understand? Our problem is one of dominion. . . . Those of us who love our country are taking measures to keep it our own.

Thus, a wave of genocide which decimates the Haitian emigre population is justified. What is striking about this historical fact is how relevant the situation is to current immigrant backlash in many countries around the world. While the workers were initially welcomed to build or to create a thriving infrastructure, they become an encumbrance when they choose to stay in the host country. This story of emigres is particularly revolting because the slavelike conditions endured by the Haitians are imposed on them by their neighbors sharing the island of Hispaniola. Danticat is careful to illumine just how perverse is the prejudice. Color is not the determinant, for the melanin is apparent in both groups. Only language separates these people. For example, while Dominicans could trill the r in parsley, in response to the question "¿Que diga perejil?," many Haitians could only voice "pewegil." Thus, when Trujillo ordered their roundup, Haitians would be spared if they "knew as well how to say the Spanish 'pesi' as to say the French 'perejil.'"

The Farming of Bones is a stark reminder of the massacre as well as a tribute to the valor of those

> **"**Danticat is careful to illumine just how perverse is the prejudice. Color is not the determinant, for the melanin is apparent in both groups. Only language separates these people."

Haitians who escaped the terror. The love story of Amabelle Desir and Sebastien Onius frames the novel. After her parents drown, Amabelle becomes a maid to the Dominican officer Pico Duarte and his wife. Sebastien, her Haitian lover, works in the Duarte cane field. During the roundup, Amabelle manages to escape, but Sebastien dies, presumably shot by Duarte's regiment. Many of the pursued are forced by soldiers to jump from cliffs; others face being beheaded or beaten to death by civilian thugs before reaching their homeland.

While Danticat's novel is a searing indictment of Dominican barbarism, the Haitian government also merits some censure. In the aftermath, Haitian President Stenio Vincent dispatched government officials to various sites only to record the testimonies of victims and to give them stipends. The citizens wondered why the Haitian government did not avenge the slaughter of its people. By writing her vivid account, Danticat memorializes this farming of human bones and all those "nameless and faceless who vanish like smoke into the early morning air."

Source: Jacqueline Brice-Finch, "Haiti," (book review) in *World Literature Today,* Vol. 73, Issue 2, Spring, 1999, p. 373.

Sources

Adlerberg, Scott, "The Farming of Bones," in *Richmond Review* (online), 2000.

Charters, Mallay, "Edwidge Danticat: A Bitter Legacy Revisited," in *Publishers Weekly*, August 17, 1998, p. 42.

Cryer, Dan, "The Farming of Bones," in *Salon* (online).

Danticat, Edwidge, "A Brief Reflection on the Massacre River," in *Kreyol* (online), May 19, 1999.

"The Farming of Bones," in *Publishers Weekly*, June 8, 1998, p. 44.

Rooney, Megan, "Danticat MFA '94 Reads from *The Farming of Bones*," in *Brown Daily Herald*, October 5, 1998.

Van Boven, Sarah, "Massacre River: Danticat Revisits Haiti," in *Newsweek*, September 7, 1998, p. 69.

Wilson, Calvin, "Edwidge Danticat's Prose Floats in Realm of Sadness and Eloquence," in *Kansas City Star*, September 22, 1999, p. K0779.

Further Reading

Acosta, Belinda "The Farming of Bones," in *Austin Chronicle*, January 19, 1999.
  This discussion of Danticat's book also has comments about her writing in general.

Brice-Finch, Jacqueline, "Haiti," in *World Literature Today*, Spring, 1999, p. 373.
  Brief review of *The Farming of Bones* in the context of Haitian history.

Farley, Christopher John, "The Farming of Bones," in *Time*, September 7, 1998, p. 78.
  Farley discusses Danticat's writing career and her books.

Gardiner, Beth, "Writer's Work Evokes Experience of Haitian Regime, Emigration," in *Standard-Times*, April 12, 1998.
  Explores Danticat's experiences in Haiti and how they fuel her fiction.

Gladstone, Jim, "Breath, Eyes, Memory," in *New York Times Book Review*, July 10, 1994, p. 24.
  Brief review of the book.

Jaffe, Zia, "The Farming of Bones," in *The Nation*, November 16, 1998, p. 62.
  Brief review.

Shea, Renee H., "An Interview between Edwidge Danticat and Renee H. Shea," in *Belles Lettres*, Summer, 1995, pp. 12-15.
  Shea and Danticat discuss her life and works.

Fear

Gabriela Mistral
1924

"From her maternal hand this poet offers us her potion, which has the savor of earth and which quenches the thirst of the heart." These words are from the citation that offered Gabriela Mistral the Nobel Prize for Literature for the year 1945. The same speech also noted that "Gabriela Mistral shared her maternal love with the children whom she taught." "Fear" was published in Mistral's second collection of poetry, *Tenura* (*Tenderness*). The poems in this book are referred to as children's poems, even though they have decidedly mature themes, and they have, in the years since it was first published in 1924, become standards of elementary-school education in Chile and throughout Latin America.

In a section at the end of the book called "Colophon by Way of Explaining," Mistral discussed why she chose to write a book about mothers and children. She wrote, "The woman who has never nursed, who does not feel the weight of her child against her body, who never puts anyone to sleep day or night, how can she possibly hum a *berceuse* (lullaby)?" Ironically, though she dedicated her life to children through her profession as an educator, Mistral herself never married and never had a child. Her ideas about the bond between mothers and children, which have come to mean so much to generations of mothers who are thrilled to at last find their feelings expressed in print, came to the author second-hand, through observation of the hundreds of children that she worked with as a

teacher and her experience in growing up in a household of teachers. As is apparent by the popular and critical acclaim lavished upon her work about motherhood, Mistral was able to touch upon the very real emotions of the experience even though she did not live the experience herself.

Author Biography

Gabriela Mistral was one of the most famous poets to come out of Chile, and the first poet from a Latin American nation to win the Nobel Prize for Literature. She lived a colorful and active life, visiting foreign cities as a representative of Chile, and was recognized as an expert in education throughout the Americas. Her father was a schoolteacher who married a widow who already had a fifteen-year-old daughter. On April 7, 1889, Mistral was born as Lucia Goday Alcayaga in Vicuna, in the Elqui valley in northern Chile. When she was three, her father abandoned the family, and she was raised and educated by her mother and her half-sister Emilina, who were both teachers. She spent her childhood in the natural, rural setting of the Elqui valley.

By the time she was fifteen, she was already a teaching assistant. At eighteen she met Romello Ureta, a railroad engineer, and fell in love, but their relationship did not work out; not long after they broke up, for reasons unrelated to his relationship with Mistral, he committed suicide. His death was to affect her throughout her entire life. In 1910 she received her official teaching certificate, and by 1912 she was recognized across the country for her work in teaching poor people. In 1914 she won a national poetry competition with three sonnets that she titled *Los Sonetos de la Muerte* (*Sonnets of Death*). This was the first time she used the pen name ''Gabriela Mistral,'' which she would be known by for the rest of her life—Gabriela after the angel Gabriel, and Mistral after the fierce cold wind that blows over the south of France.

In 1922, Mexico's Secretary of Education invited Mistral to collaborate with him on reforming that country's education system, and so she lived in Mexico City for two years. At the same time, in 1921, a professor at Columbia University in New York gave a lecture about her poetry, and when interested members of the audience tried to look up her work they found that no books of her work had ever been published; this led to the publication of *Desolacion* (*Desolation*) in 1922. The book that ''Fear'' is from, *Ternura*, or ''Tenderness,'' followed in 1924. It is a book about children and motherhood, with poems familiar to generations of children who grew up in Latin America.

Mistral continued to publish influential prose pieces and to travel the world as a consultant in affairs of education. Her only other two books of poetry, published at wide intervals of time, were *Tala* (1938; the title means ''Felling,'' as in ''felling trees'') and *Lager* in 1954. She received the Nobel Prize for Literature in 1945, the year that World War II ended. Starting in 1933, and for the next twenty years, Mistral was Chile's consul to several cities throughout the world, including Lisbon, Los Angeles, and Madrid. Near the end of her life she served as the Chilean delegate to the United Nations, retiring in 1954 to Rosalyn Bay, Long Island, where she died in January of 1957. On her tomb is the inscription, ''What the soul does for the body so does the poet for her people.''

Plot Summary

Lines 1-2

Swallows are small, fast birds known for being gregarious—that is, for socializing with other birds and forming large colonies. They also are known for the long distances of their migrations. When the speaker of this poem infers that someone who is unidentified, referred to as ''they,'' could turn her little girl into a bird, she is speaking metaphorically, by referring to aspects of the swallow that the girl would have if she went through such a transformation. In this case, the fear expressed is that the girl will, as she grows up, start socializing with others of her kind and fly away, traveling with them rather than staying near her home. Moreover, the speaker is not just worried that her girl will turn into a swallow, but that ''they'' will turn her into one. Readers naturally wonder to whom this refers. At first, it appears to point to a particular mysterious group that wants control of the daughter, but, with no other evidence offered, the best answer seems to be that ''they'' simply refers to the people that a young girl will come into contact with while growing up: the world of school, teachers, and classmates that directs a child's attention outside of the home.

Lines 3-4

A parent's fear of losing his or her child is so powerful that it is natural to associate it with watching the child disappear off into the vast unknown, as mentioned in the third line. Mistral was certainly well familiar with air travel, but she spent her childhood in a rural, provincial area of Chile during the end of the nineteenth century, with neither automobiles nor air travel that would later conquer great distances. She was well aware of the intimidating vastness of the open sky, of the ways that a simple rural person could feel that someone was hopelessly gone once they had disappeared beyond the field of vision. It would be the same way that a parent would feel upon losing sight of her or his child. This connection between a poor person rooted to one place and a parent is made even more directly in line 4, in which the speaker of the poem refers to "my straw bed." A straw bed is the sign of a country person who has no means to buy a feather bed but has plenty of straw on hand to make her own. This image also refers to a bird's nest, extending the "swallow" imagery. The daughter actually is presented as some kind of bird, meant to fly from home, just not as a swallow, which would fly far away.

Lines 5-6

While the opening lines of the poem indicate that the speaker's fear is caused by the thought that her daughter will fly far away, this section indicates that she does not even want her going a short distance. It would seem, in the natural progression of life, that a parent would be glad to have her child "nest under the eaves"—that is, to have her child attached to the same house where she grew up, with a stable home (nest) that is easily in her mother's sight. Rejecting this distance from her daughter means that this speaker is not willing to put up with even the normal distances that will come between a mother and her growing child. The act of combing the child's hair mentioned in line six symbolizes any type of taking care of the child, as long as it involves the very personal act of touching that is implied in combing.

Lines 7-8

Repeating the first two lines gives the poem a song-like quality, with a refrain that reminds readers of the most important fact, which in this case is the cause of the speaker's fear. Aside from the obvious key element, which would be turning the

Gabriela Mistral

child into a bird, the key elements in this simple statement are "them" and "my little girl," emphasizing the daughter's helplessness and the threat to the girl that comes from mysterious outside forces.

Lines 9-10

The diction here is just slightly different than it was in the first two lines. Where the first statement like this expressed the fear that "they" would "turn" the child into a swallow, this second stanza starts with the fear that they will "make" her into a princess. The verb "make" shows less aggression than "turn," indicating that it would take less force on the part of the outside forces to perform this transformation. This is, in fact, quite likely, since it would seem that the daughter (and, in fact, her mother) would welcome her transformation into a princess. This slight change in verb subtly indicates the fact that the daughter might be open to change, even though the mother does not want it. Just as the first stanza surprises the reader with the idea that someone might be able to change a child into a bird, this stanza draws attention by stating the mother's opposition to the world glorifying her daughter. Often, parents refer to girl children as "princess," indicating that they are privileged by birth, that they should have no duties other than being themselves, and the wealth of the world will be handed to them. When this speaker wishes that her daughter not be given such easy privilege, readers sit up and take notice.

Lines 11-12

There is an implicit love of nature here that the poem just presents, without supporting. The speaker of the poem wishes against her daughter's social success because she does not want the girl to lose touch with nature, to become unable to play in the meadow. The way that this is presented emphasizes the idea that pampering the girl would separate her from nature. The poem assumes that she would, as a princess, wear golden slippers, and the word ''tiny'' in reference to her feet brings to mind ancient Oriental practices of binding girls' feet, to keep them small and dainty and impractical for romping across uncultivated ground.

Lines 13-14

Like lines 5-6, this section in the middle of the stanza contains a direct statement of the speaker's personal desire to keep her daughter to herself, away from the outside world. This time, however, there is less reason to believe that the fear of losing her daughter is about the girl's welfare, and more reason to see it as a fear of being alone. While the earlier statement emphasized the selflessness of the act by stating the speaker's wish to serve her daughter, by combing her hair, this stanza states her wish as directly for the speaker's, not the daughter's, benefit. Rather than expressing the fear that the mother could no longer sleep at her daughter's side, the fear expressed here is that ''no longer / would she sleep at my side,'' which indicates that the speaker is concerned with her own loneliness.

Lines 15-16

Once again, repeating the first lines of the stanza has the effect of a refrain from a song, emphasizing the main idea to make it easier for a listener or reader to remember. This time, however with the added measure of desperation of the speaker, with her own self-interest more plainly on display, the repetition seems like a way of reminding and assuring herself that what she fears cannot hurt her.

Lines 17-18

One would expect that nothing but benefit would come to the daughter from becoming a queen, from attaining the ultimate in power in the human social world. Being a queen would certainly be better than being a princess, because a queen holds true power while a princess only has potential. Once again, however, this poem challenges expectations by presenting a mother's wish that she would like her daughter to be a queen ''even less'' than she would like her to be a princess. An element of reality is implied in the fact that the mysterious ''they,'' who are assumed to have the power to make all of the transformations in this poem take place, would not be able to make the daughter into a queen immediately, only ''one day.'' Their powers to change the girl's species and her social class do not extend to altering time.

Lines 19-20

In these lines, the speaker's fear reaches its emotional height. She fears that her daughter's social ascendancy would create an insurmountable division between them. In the scenario that she suggests here, the daughter may have the ability (through the power of ''them'') to rise up to the level of royalty, but she, the speaker, is so humble that she could never even be in the presence of royalty, not even if the queen is her daughter. Psychologically, it makes sense that a mother would worry that her daughter would be able to transcend her own humble roots to the extent that she could find herself in company that would keep her own mother out. The odd psychological element in this poem, as it is throughout, is the projection of the unnamed ''they,'' used to represent social forces that would take the daughter away from her mother. Her fear of losing her daughter, which is a natural by-product of a parent's love, is personified, but incompletely, by characters that are not given names or identities.

Lines 21-22

These lines indicate the selfless concern for the child that is missing from the parallel lines in the previous stanza. Lines 13-14 indicate the speaker's wish for comfort by not wanting to lose the feeling of having the daughter ''by my side'': here, the mother wants to be able to rock her daughter in the night, to give comfort to her. The use of the night as the time of fear, when either of them would need comfort, is fairly standard in poetry, based on a normal fear of the dark and discomfort about the mystery of being unable to see. Bringing this fear back for a second time in this last stanza helps to emphasize the idea that this poem is not just about a mother's natural concern that her daughter will grow up and leave her, but that it has its roots in deeper, more powerful, psychological mysteries.

Lines 23-24

The same pattern that ended the other two stanzas—the repetition of the first two lines—is played out again here, with one slight difference, which is the addition of the final exclamation mark. Since this thought has already been expressed in lines 17-18, the effect of the exclamation point is not to add any new information, just emotion. This speaker *really* does not want her little girl made into a queen. Repetition and the exclamation mark push the speaker's fear even higher, almost to a degree of terror, making it difficult to read her case as a normal discomfort about her little girl growing up. Mistral presents this speaker as a complex character who has a right to be concerned but who has let her maternal fear, especially her fear of what might be done to her by unidentified forces called ''they,'' take control of her mind.

Themes

Return to Nature

From the details provided, it is clear that this speaker lives in a rural setting: she sleeps on a straw bed and she knows enough about birds to imagine which type of bird her daughter would become if she were to become one. She knows that swallows travel with large flocks of other swallows and that they cover vast distances in their migrations, which means that they leave for long periods of time. Ironically, the transformation to a swallow in the first stanza is not presented as a return to nature but as a corruption of nature, forcing a little girl to separate from her mother. One of the primary fears worrying the speaker of this poem is that her little girl might no longer be able to play in the meadow if she becomes too deeply a part of society, which is symbolized here by tiny golden slippers. She would prefer her daughter to not be pampered by the excessive delicacy of culture, to instead keep in touch with her surroundings (as long as her surroundings are the rural area that the speaker knows as home). The image of playing in the meadow is an idealized way of imagining that the child can remain one with nature, presenting childhood play as part

Topics for Further Study

- Find a fairy tale that has a person turned into a bird or an animal, and use its situation to illuminate the situation described here.

- A modern-day equivalent to turning a little girl into a princess might be turning her into a music star. Think of several similar possibilities that might concern a modern American mother and use them to write additional verses for this poem.

- Pick a contemporary politician and report on the relationship she or he has with her or his mother.

- Do you think that this poem could have been written in Chile today? Why or why not?

- Write a letter from this little girl to her mother, explaining what she wants to be when she grows up.

of nature and little golden slippers as the opposite of it.

Change and Transformation

This poem presents a parent fearing the changes that will happen to a little girl. Change is inevitable, and it is natural that a parent would fear that change might cause her daughter to drift away, a fear that reflects the intensity of the parent's involvement in the child's life currently. The likelihood of change is treated creatively here, described in terms of transformations that have less to do with reality than they do with the parent's emotional state. Of course a child cannot transform from a human into a bird, but the parent might feel as if the child is a bird when she leaves, like a bird flying from its nest. Children from humble backgrounds are not spontaneously turned into princesses, either, but to a parent, looking on as society gives the girl the adoration she used to get from her mother, it might feel like she is a princess. She also does not need to fear the girl being turned into a queen, but if the girl some day became a woman of power and influence it would feel the same to her mother as if she were a queen.

Media Adaptations

- Babbitt Instructional Resources produced a video-cassette with accompanying teacher's guidebook and script called *Gabriela Mistral: Poems of Chile*, in 1999.

- Mistral is one of the poets featured on the bilingual filmstrip and cassette package *Twentieth Century Poetry / Poesia del Siglo Veinto* from Films for the Humanities, Princeton, N. J., 1979.

- *Gabriela Mistral Reading Her Own Poetry* is available on a vinyl record. Read in Spanish. Released in 1971 by the Library of Congress, catalog number LCM 2055-2056.

The poem speculates that all of these changes and transformations would be brought about by some power known only as "them," who would want to make the girl into a sparrow, a princess, or a queen for unexplained reasons. The most reasonable understanding of "them" is that they are the people whom a growing child would meet throughout her life, and that her transformation would then be just the normal result of the influence of other people.

Public vs. Private Life

The speaker of this poem has, like all parents, a special bond with her daughter: it is a small, private society with just two members, shared by them when the speaker rocks her child and combs her hair. Beyond their small world is a larger one inhabited by people who want to change the daughter in ways that would take her away. If they were to succeed in turning the daughter into a swallow, a princess, or a queen, she would be a successful part of their world, but she would not be part of the mother's any more. The poem's title refers to a mother's fear of losing her daughter—not to death, not to disagreement, but to the general social world of other people. This fear is expressed most directly and most poignantly in the poem's third stanza, in which the mother hopes against her daughter's social success by visualizing a scenario in which her daughter would be made queen, with all of the command over society that a queen has, but when she is placed on the throne her mother would not be able to see her any more. This reflects the social responsibilities of a queen, who would not be allowed to associate with a commoner even if it was her parent. Social allegiances would, in such a case, become more important than private bonds.

As much as readers can sympathize with the poem's speaker for her fear of losing the intimate relationship she shares with her daughter, it is based on her fear of society in general, and that must be accepted for readers to truly accept her feelings. She fears that a public life will give her daughter freedom like a bird's, and will offer the honors due a princess or, even worse, the power due a queen. By imagining that society could or would bestow such honors, the narrator proves herself to be unfamiliar with the ways of public life, uncertain what it might do. She is a woman who sleeps on a straw bed, who rocks her child to sleep and combs her child's hair—she understands the small world, not society at large. Not understanding the public world, she fears it, and her fear makes her imagine the public world coming to take away the thing she values most.

Style

Even in its original Spanish, "Fear" follows no strict rhyming or rhythmic pattern. This is appropriate because the speaker of the poem, sleeping on a straw mattress and worrying that her daughter will one day be too good to associate with her, is a simple woman and would naturally not have a voice that is too polished or refined. Still, there are sections that follow rhythmic structures, which has more to do with displaying the poet's skill than the character's personality. This poem is predominantly, but loosely, iambic, which means that the rhythm that occurs most frequently is the iamb. An iamb is a combination of one unstressed syllable with one stressed syllable. A line like "and *nev*-er *fly* a-*gain* to my *straw bed*" starts out iambic before losing the pattern at the end; the line "and *when* night *came* no *lon*-ger" is iambic with one extra syllable at the end. The quantity of iambs in this poem gives it something like an iambic structure, but it would not entirely be correct to say that the poem has a definite rhythm. There is also a strong presence of the "Cretic foot," which follows a pattern of stressed-unstressed-stressed. The line that appears with variations at the beginning and end of each stanza has two Cretic feet: "*I* don't *want / them* to *make*." There are definite rhythmic patterns in "Fear," but they do not add up to an overall rhythmic design.

Other elements help to give readers a sense that the author has a firm control on the ideas expressed here. Each stanza has eight lines, and each begins and ends with a variation on the same two lines. There is no set length for the individual line. They do not all have the same number of syllables, but there is not any great degree of variance, either. For instance, there are no very short or very long lines. This speaker is a person of moderation—the whole poem is about fear of change—but she is too simple to have her ideas presented in an ornate, complex pattern.

Literary Heritage

When Mistral was writing "Fear" in the 1920s the Modernism movement that influenced artistic theory across the world was settling into maturity. Literary theorists use the term "modernism" to describe a wide variety of changes that came about at the beginning of the twentieth century. It is generally used to explain the backlash against literary tradition, a reaction caused by the way psychoanalysis changed the understanding of personal behavior and that Marxism changed the way that social behavior was understood. In poetry, Modernism entailed casting away traditional forms and concepts of beauty and using words that were concerned with evoking an emotional impression over those that had a beautiful sound together. Many strains of modernism, such as surrealism, imagism, and dadaism, were more concerned with striking readers with a powerful feeling than with overall logic.

In Latin American countries, literary trends generally followed European trends at the time. A unique literary theory had not been developed, and much of the literature that was read and discussed then was from Europe or the United States. For instance, when Mistral's collection *Tenderness* was published, there was no body of children's literature in Latin America. She had to make what she could out of the modernist sense of using direct language and out of the folktales of her native country.

In many ways, her poems in *Tenderness* anticipate what may be Latin America's greatest contribution to world literature, which is the magical realism movement that started in the 1960s and continues today. Magical realism, usually associated with fiction, is a joining of the serious tone of fatalism associated with Realism with supernatural occurrences that readers know do not really happen in this world. Some of the earliest and most widely read examples of this genre are Colombian author Gabriel García Márquez' 1967 novel *One Hundred Years of Solitude* and Argentine writer Julio Cortazar's *Hopscotch*, from 1966. Both of these works presented elements that would be called "fantasy" in other books, treating them with dead seriousness. As Marquez, who won the Nobel Prize for Literature in 1982, explained it, the tone he was trying to achieve "was based on the way grandmother used to tell stories. She told things that sounded supernatural and fantastic, but she told them with complete naturalness."

Historical Context

Chile is a long narrow country that runs along the western coast of South America. The Andes mountain range runs the length of the inland border. It was originally inhabited by Araucanian natives, but was colonized by the Spanish in 1550. Unlike many South American countries, Chile does not have abundant deposits of gold or silver ore, and for this reason its growth as a colony was slow. It does, however, have great stores of iron, copper, and nitrates. During the Industrial Revolution that swept the world in the nineteenth century, these elements became crucial for manufacturing. Especially influential was Chile's nitrates, which were essential in fertilizers that became increasingly valuable as countries all over the world moved from farm economies to urban industrial societies, and for the manufacture of explosives. Chile became a rich country by the dawn of the twentieth century from nitrate production.

The country's greatest problem was that its nitrate wealth was not evenly distributed. The country's wealth was in the hands of a small proportion of people. As the economy grew, the cities grew at a tremendous rate, too fast to control, and they ended up breeding slums. The government looked after the interests of the wealthy: starting in 1891, Chile was a Parliamentary Republic, with the parliament appointing the president and his cabinet. The parlia-

Compare
&
Contrast

- **1924:** United States interest in Chile and other South American countries is limited to their production of rich ores. In Chile, the Chuquicamata copper mine and Tofo Iron Mines produce metals of greater purity than those found in North America.

  Today: Chile still produces about forty percent of the world's copper, but advances in transportation have made Chile a major exporter of fish and fruit to the world market.

- **1924:** Farmers in rural California, feeling that their water was being stolen by the government (reflected by the poem's suspicion of a monolithic "them"), dynamited the Los Angeles aqueduct seventeen times in open rebellion.

  Today: Ranchers in the western states still fight openly and sometimes violently with the government over water rights.

- **1924:** A right-wing military coup ousts Arturo Alessandri, who had been president of Chile since 1920. Supporters of Alessandri helped him gain back the presidency the following year.

1973: General Augusto Pinochet becomes president of Chile after a coup, backed by the United States' Central Intelligence Agency, helps him depose the elected president, Salvador Allende. Pinochet rules the country as a dictatorship for nearly twenty years.

Today: Pinochet, faced with trial in Spain for crimes that he committed as president, has been declared too ill to stand trial, and returned to Chile, where he has received full immunity for crimes committed in office.

- **1924:** British author A. A. Milne publishes *When We Were Very Young*, his first book of poems written for his child, Christopher Robin.

  Today: Milne's name will live on forever because of his *Winnie-the-Pooh* books, which were written for Christopher Robin. The Disney corporation holds the copyright and sells millions of dollars each year in Pooh licensed videos, toys, games, and apparel.

---

ment was elected, but the elections were controlled by wealthy business people.

Labor organizations started to gain in popularity at the beginning of the twentieth century, advocating socialist and anarchist policies that would take wealth from the rich and put it in the hands of the common people. In cities and in the nitrate and copper mines in the north, where Mistral grew up, unions encouraged workers to fight against their employers to increase their financial positions and working conditions. Because the government was, essentially, an arm of the owners of industry, government forces were used to fight the workers. One particularly stirring episode in the struggle for labor reform was a massacre at the miners' camp at Iquique in 1907, where government troops killed striking workers. Economic tensions became even

more strained during the following decade when, during World War I from 1914 to 1918, the world's usage of nitrates dwindled. Even worse was the fact that during the war Germany developed synthetic nitrates for its explosives, which devastated the Chilean economy.

In the 1920s, when "Fear" was written, the government of Chile was changing. In 1920, Arturo Alessandri was made president, in an attempt to keep the people from rebelling and taking over the government. While the Parliament had appointed Alessandri to be a moderate and to look after their own interests, he turned out to be a true reformist once in office. He was popular with the people, but he had trouble getting any measures passed by Parliament, and therefore the country sank into deeper financial trouble during his presidency. In 1924,

Alessandri went past the legislators and straight to the people who elected them, and with the people's support he was able to have his reform legislation passed. This caused a coup by military right-wingers, who took control of the government in September of 1924. The reformists had enough power by then to perform a second coup in January of 1925, and a new constitution was drawn up that gave more power to the common people but that also compromised with the wealthy landowners to assure their cooperation. This constitution served the country until the early 1970s, when Salvador Allende became the first president elected with a Marxist agenda in a non-Communist country. Three years into Allende's administration, he was ousted by a coup led by General Augusto Pinochet, with American support. Pinochet ruled the country for almost twenty years and had himself declared a Senator for Life.

Critical Overview

Through the decades, Mistral has remained continuously popular in South America, especially her native Chile, but in North America her reputation has been kept alive mainly by the good word of critics. It was, in fact, good critical response that led to the publication of her first book, *Desolacion*: it was not until a professor at Columbia University in New York, Federico de Onis, talked about Mistral's poetry in a lecture that interested readers created a demand that a publisher filled. Margaret Bates, in her introduction to *Selected Poems of Gabriela Mistral*, pointed out why it has been so difficult to capture the flavor of Mistral's poetry for North American readers. They are especially difficult to translate, she said, because "the effect of utter simplicity is backed up by a subtle, complex, hidden machine that extracts from each word, from each sound and accent, its maximum challenge." Bates quoted Marcel Bataillon, author of *Erasme et L'Esoagne*, saying that he had "found even more reason to love the Spanish language after reading Gabriela."

Critics examining Mistral's poetry, especially the poems from *Tenura*, try to separate the attitude of rural simplicity in her work from the actual simplicity of her humble origins. In an essay called "Gabriela Mistral, the Restless Soul," Majorie Agosin noted, "The Elqui Valley, Chilean women and children, created Gabriela Mistral's voice; it sprang from her depths, and was destined for the exterior world." It was the combination of this rural, home-bound persona and her worldliness as an international traveler that gave Mistral her distinct voice, according to Agosin.

Critics credit the book *Ternura* for being especially skillful in doing precisely what it set out to do, which is to examine the bond between mothers and children. Among volumes of praise for the book that have been published, the general consensus is perhaps best captured by Cuban writer Jorge Manach in his 1936 book *Gabriela Mistral: Vida y obra*: "The art of speaking to childhood is one which only those who have a very deep sense of the spiritual and the concrete can master. The fusion of tremulousness with plasticity, of malice of beautiful expression with the innocence of the emotions—what a faultless achievement in the pages of *Ternura*!"

Since winning the Nobel Prize for Literature in 1945, Mistral's reputation with critics in Europe and North America has been unimpeachable. In South America and among Chileans, she is a sentimental favorite, a source of pride and a symbol of the culture. "She carried within her a fusion of Basque and Indian heritage," said Margot Arce de Vasquez, then the chair of the Department of Spanish Studies at the University of Puerto Rico: "Spanish in her rebellious individualistic spirit; very Indian in her long, deep silences and that priestly aura of stone idol. To this representative cultural value must be added the great value of her literary work, an incomparable document for what it reveals of her person and for its unique American accent."

Criticism

David Kelly

Kelly is an instructor of creative writing and composition at two colleges in Illinois. In the following essay, he looks at several of the poems from Mistral's book Ternura *and how they successfully capture the idea of motherhood.*

The poems in Gabriela Mistral's second collection, Ternura, are supposed to be about mothers and their relationships with their children. The author called them "colloquies the mother holds with her own soul, with her child, and with the Earth Spirit around her, visible by day and audible by night." Addressing the wide, emotion-laden subject of motherhood is an ambitious thing to try, ten times so because

What Do I Read Next?

- Isabel Allende is the niece of slain Chilean President Salvador Allende. Her 1986 novel *The House of the Spirits* tells the story of one powerful family that captures the spirit of the country. It became an international bestseller.

- Short stories by contemporary Chilean women are compiled in the anthology *What is Secret*, edited by Marjorie Agosin (White Pine Press, 1995).

- Alfonsa Storni was an Argentine woman who wrote poetry at about the same time as Mistral. Her poems are available in English and Spanish in *Seleccion Poetica De Alfonsa Storni/Selected Poetry*, a 1999 paperback published by Editories Mexicanos Unidos.

- Pablo Neruda is another poet from Chile who, in 1971, won the Nobel Prize for Literature. His first book of poetry was published a year before "Fear" was. Neruda's best works are available in English and Spanish in *Pablo Neruda: Selected Poems/Bilingual Edition*, published in 1990 by Houghton-Mifflin.

- An American poet who, like Mistral, wrote more from understanding than experience was Emily Dickinson, the famous Belle of Amherst. After years of various Dickinson poems showing up in various places, they were collected in 1960 in a definitive edition, edited by Thomas H. Johnson, called *The Complete Poems of Emily Dickinson.*

Mistral was not a mother herself. Like Emily Dickinson, she knew that she knew what she knew about her subject and did not feel the need to justify herself with the weak excuse of experience, which proves nothing (you can't, for instance, expect everyone who has a spleen to be qualified by that intimate experience to explain what it does or where in the body it is located). Unlike Dickinson, who published hardly anything in her lifetime, Mistral put her theoretical works out in the open for all who had really experienced motherhood to see and criticize, and she traveled the world, living in different countries as an emissary of her government, while Dickinson only left her hometown a few times in her lifetime. What are readers to learn from this? That Gabriela Mistral, living among mothers and children as an educator since age fourteen (and a child before that), did more research on the subject she was theorizing about than Emily Dickinson did, and that she was more confident about her conclusions. We know that she was successful in capturing the bonds of motherhood and that Dickinson was successful in capturing the complexities of romantic love. Neither case gives any conclusive evidence about experience, observation, or popular sentiment.

It is, in fact, its bold departure from popular sentiment that marks Gabriela Mistral's greatness. The aspects of the maternal state of mind that she captures in *Ternura* are not aspects that we are accustomed to seeing on paper, and yet, as she did, we know they are right once we see them. Much of the public face of motherhood is about selflessness, about extending beyond oneself, about giving up all one has that is good, if necessary, and taking on another's troubles. Motherhood, in short, is the drama of life's most noble moments.

The problem, as even those of us who are not mothers can realize, is that this view of nobleness is incomplete. That which has life's greatest moments must logically be balanced with some rough spots as well. We seldom see art that probes the deeply troublesome things about being a mother. We hear that it's a lot of work with little thanks, but these apparent negatives actually add to the positive side of the equation, pointing out the superior character of one who can put up with such trouble. Sometimes, we hear macabre stories about negligent mothers, abandoning or abusing their children, but these stories are news precisely because they are so unusual. In patriarchal societies like the United

States and Mistral's Chile, where men dominate the economies, mothers are paid for their labors with honor—this is referred to as "the cult of the mother," in which society assigns special privileges to motherhood as well as special responsibilities. Unfortunately, honor is too often taken too far, blotting out the dishonorable instead of recognizing it.

What Mistral brought to the discussion with *Ternura* was a piercing examination of the subject, putting it into a quiet place, beyond all of the surrounding cultural noise and clutter in the atmosphere. She did not have to emphasize negative examples of motherhood because the truth is deeper and more profound than could ever be conveyed through specific examples about bad events. At the heart of the beauty of motherhood she found the psychological truths of sadness, loneliness, and fear.

The titles of the poems in *Ternura* are not the kinds of titles we see in the upbeat version that literature—not just the popular kind, but the most intellectual, too—often presents. They include "The Sad Mother," "Bitter Song," and "Fear." The poems with titles that are less disturbing are no less forlorn in the stories that they tell about women who look at their children and see their own continuance (for whatever that's worth) and at the same time their own vulnerability. These women measure their own lives by how close or far their infants are to them.

"Bitter Song," for instance, starts with the mother/speaker suggesting that her son play a game with her, imagining that they are a king and a queen, and it goes on to say the bounties of nature are his, working into each stanza the refrain "Whose else could it be?" The son's birthright, granted to him because—well, because he is her beloved—includes "this green field," "this whole valley," "sheep and pasture," and "the gleanings of the harvest." A common paean to motherhood would be content listing the glories this mother wishes for her child, but Mistral includes a stanza in parentheses about the child shivering and the breasts of the mother "dry with suffering," and later in the poem she repeats the entire stanza. The sense of motherhood is conveyed by the abundance she can see around her while watching her child do without, while the bitterness of the title comes from the repeated question that makes us think about who really does own this land, and how they could possibly deserve such wealth more than a son who is loved so much. The reason Mistral is able to introduce the darkness that is left out of so much other literature about

> " The only way to reconcile these two conflicting urges—to constantly keep the past alive, and to move beyond it into the future—is to record the past in a safe place, somewhere outside an individual's memory, some place where facts will remain and not fade, but where the person won't have to carry the memory daily."

motherhood is that there is a scapegoat, someone to blame for the suffering in this poem: the landowners.

And what of "The Sad Mother"? If there is one thing that the traditional uplifting ideal of motherhood does not have room for, it is sadness, except for the momentary sadness that occurs with a glimpse of life's difficulties. In the ideal of the selfless mother that popular culture promotes, it is the woman's place to keep quiet about her own suffering while tending to her child's; here, the mother openly discusses her existential terror and openly admits that her child is a way of blocking out what is frightening in her life. There are three four-line stanzas, culminating in this: "In you, my fear, my trembling / let my body sleep, / Let my eyes close on you / In you my heart finds rest." The unsettling thing about this is not that it admits that a mother can be sad—as mentioned before, the mother's suffering often serves to make her seem more noble—but that she so blatantly uses her child as a tool. Mistral broke new ground on the concept of motherhood in *Ternura* by allowing selfishness into the same poem as maternal love, not claiming that either leads to or causes the other, only admitting that a respectable person may have both at once.

"Fear" is all about selfishness. The title refers to the fear that the child will one day go off and leave the mother alone. This in itself is a natural fear—no one wants to be alone, and the whole point of being a loving mother is that she wants to be with her child. But the courageous thing that Mistral does

> " As in the case of all true creative artists, attachment to her own familiar world did not exclude a strong feeling for other languages and cultures."

in "Fear" is having the poem's speaker admit that she would not want to be separated from her child even if it meant that the child would have a better life. She does not want her child turned into a queen, the speaker says, because "They would put her on a throne / where I could not go see her. / And when nighttime came / I could never rock her. . ." The poem does not look at the situation of the queen on the throne, which, presumably, would be pretty good: the mother, for once in literature, is lamenting her own loss at the child's gain. Like "Bitter Song," there is an external society that is the cause of the problem between the mother and child in "Fear" —the three stanzas are about resistance to "them" turning the child into a sparrow, a princess and a queen, respectively—but this time the offensive intruders pose no threat to the child, only to the mother's self-interest.

Motherhood is not a fragile thing. There is no reason for our literature to view only a narrow range of what it involves, ignoring the fear and the sorrow, as if to talk about them would somehow be disrespectful to mothers (accusing them of not being able to transcend? suppress? of not being perfect?). It is understandable that one would want to focus on motherhood's brighter aspects as a sign of respect, but there is a greater respect in truth. Even those of us who are not mothers can tell that Gabriel Mistral had the truth in hand in her collection *Ternura.*

Source: David Kelly, in an essay for *Literature of Developing Nations for Students*, Gale, 2000.

Carl Mowery

Mowery has a Ph.D. in literature and composition from Southern Illinois University. In the following essay he examines the themes of loss and separation and the bond between a mother and her daughter.

In her *Lecturas para mujeres* (*Readings for Women*) (1923), Gabriela Mistral reflects on the role of women and mothers in society. She believes that mothers and motherhood represent the means to national formation in both the physical sense and the figurative sense. But she is in constant fear that mothers and women will be victimized and abandoned by the nation and their men. The conflicts between the expectations, creating life and then being abandoned by their offspring, are at the root of much of her writing, including her poetry. In the poem "Fear," she examines the conflict between traditional family values and family structures and the loss of those traditions.

Mistral has illuminated her deeply held belief in maintaining strong family bonds in *Lecturas*. In them she expressed a concern and uncertainty about what she saw as the dissolution of the family unit. She raised questions about the loss of husband/wife bonds as a result of the increase of outside activity by the wife, even though these were not the most important bonds. As Elizabeth Marchant notes, "the bonds between mother and child lie at the core of Mistral's" concerns. Her poem "Fear," published in 1924, echoes a specific fear: the loss of the maternal bond between mother and daughter.

The importance of the role of the Latin-American mother to hold her children close is emphatically presented here. The plea for the child to sleep with the mother is strong and falls within the normal structure of Latin-American families. Mistral uses this image of the closely bonded pair to lend artistic power to the point she is making.

In Latin cultures there is a strong family bond built on affection between the same-sex members of the family, fathers for their sons, mothers for their daughters. Fathers develop a relationship with their sons that involves instructing the son in the ways of *machismo*, a typical Latin attitude that does not allow boys and men to show emotion, pain, or weakness of any kind. Mothers develop a relationship with their daughters and try to keep their daughters close, to instruct them in the ways of the household and how to be a nurturing mother themselves in the future. For mothers, it is important to keep their daughters free from outside influences as long as possible and to help them cultivate the sense of what is or is not important.

One important cultural aspect of the mothers' attempts to control their daughters' interactions with boys was through the role of a chaperone. When young people became attracted to one another or when the families of young people decided on mates for their sons and daughters, the mother of the girl often took the role of chaperone for the couple during social engagements. Some of these practices have since been forgotten, but Latin-American mothers still have great care and concern for the welfare of their daughters. For the mother, anyone or anything that comes between her and her daughter is an intruder and must be kept at bay.

There are three characters in the poem: a mother, who is the narrator; the daughter, who is the object of the mother's fears; and "them," an unnamed entity who has an effect on the other two. In "Fear" the intruders are different in each stanza, but they accomplish the same disturbing result: separation of the mother and daughter. In the first stanza the intruder is symbolized by the image of the swallow, a bird that seemingly flits to and fro without purpose or direction. The loss of the sense of direction is contrary to the mother's wishes. Mistral's statements about this sense of direction are found in her *Lecturas* when she urges her contemporaries to follow the ancient and eternal roles and models of the past. They are defined by her beliefs that "gender roles were stable and bonds between women and children were privileged," according to Marchant. Therefore, any violation of these privileged roles was unacceptable. Such a violation was an interruption of traditional family roles and contributed to a loss of the opportunity for affection between the mother and her daughter, which constitutes her fear in this stanza.

The intruder in the second stanza is more sinister because it adds materialism to the distractions which interfere with the maternal bonds. The "golden slippers" are symbolic of the increasing materialism of society (even in the 1920s). The mother fears that the daughter will become so interested in material things that the mother will be neglected or forgotten. Mistral also addresses this issue in a prose poem, "To the Children." (A prose poem is one in which the poetic wording is presented in paragraph form, not in the typical stanza form.) In this poem, the mother encourages her children to take the dust of her body after she has died and to use the dust for play and as a vehicle for remembering her after she is gone. She warns the children against letting her dust become part of a brick (a symbol of materialism) but rather to let her dust be a part of the road where the children play. In this way the mother will still be a part of the children's lives. In "Fear" the mother wonders how the daughter can play when encumbered by materialistic objects

(the golden slippers). The loss of play then becomes the loss of the maternal bond when the daughter "no longer would sleep at my side."

For the mother the worst kind of departure is found in the last stanza. She warns her daughter against allowing someone else to make the decisions for her. Leaving under such circumstances will create a barrier between the two that is insurmountable. Here the mother fears that her daughter will take on airs and postures and that the daughter will assume that she is better than the mother and she will not allow her mother to comfort her. The mother says "I could never rock her . . ." continuing the theme that the mother wants to provide comfort and nurture for her daughter. In this final stanza the ellipsis implies more in this line than is directly stated.

The inclusion of the ellipsis hearkens back to the previous ideas. But there is more than just the rocking, playing, and combing, the total ideal of comfort, nurture, and support that the mother desires to give to her daughter. The emotional impact of these three dots is theatrical, as when at the most intensely dramatic moment the actor's voice drops off and the sentence is left unspoken. The stanza finishes with a sense of desperation, ending with an exclamation mark.

In the third stanza the mother fears the most significant loss of all: the alienation of affection from her daughter. The simple pleasures of giving comfort, for example by combing her hair (symbolically maintaining the maternal bond with the daughter), will be lost forever. In her poem "Nio Mexicano" ("Mexican Boy") the act of combing a child's hair is mentioned four times and is the major symbol of keeping the maternal bond with her child.

The theme of the poem is loss and separation and is a concern that lies at the heart of Mistral's beliefs. But despite never having married nor borne children, Gabriela Mistral had what Herman Hespelt called "a deep but never satisfied maternal longing" which left "sadness on (her) life and work." Examination of many of her poems will reveal a great affection for children and for the role of the mother in tending to her children. In the *Lecturas*, Mistral urges her contemporaries to follow the patterns of the mothers of the past. In this publication, she presses for a cohesive family unit with an educated mother as the central figure, says Marchant. This little poem makes the same point, as the mother cajoles, urges, and finally warns about the difficulties ahead if the daughter were to leave the mother under dubious circumstances.

In her poem "Close to Me", she is even more graphic and passionate in her beliefs that the mother/child bond ought not be broken. "Little fleece of my flesh / that I wove in my womb, / little shivering fleece, / sleep close to me." Additionally, the last line in the poem "Close to Me" is even more dramatic. "Don't slip from my arms. / Sleep close to me." These are the sentiments she expresses in "Fear," although not as directly. The importance of the role of the Latin-American mother to hold her children close is emphatically presented here. The plea for the child to sleep with the mother is strong and falls within the normal structure of Latin-American families. Mistral uses this image of the closely bonded pair to lend artistic power to the point she is making.

Source: Carl Mowery, in an essay for *Literature of Developing Nations for Students*, Gale, 2000.

UNESCO Courier

In the following brief overview of the writings of Mistral (1889-1957), the reviewer characterizes her work as "harsh," philosophical, and ultimately universal as she united poetry and humanism in one powerful voice.

The life of Gabriela Mistral, who was born on 7 April 1889 in a village in northern Chile and died in New York in 1957, was devoted to an intellectual and spiritual quest. From her early days in Chile's Elqui valley to her European travels on cultural and diplomatic assignments, the story of her career reads almost like a myth. The needy peasant girl becomes the doyenne of Latin-American literature. The humble rural schoolteacher is awarded some of the world's highest honours, including the Nobel Prize for Literature in 1945.

Gabriela Mistral's poetry, from her 1922 collection *Desolacion* ("Desolation") to *Lagar* ("The Wine Press") of 1954, was written in harsh, powerful and colloquial language. Like her massive output of prose, it is informed by a visionary, prophetic sense of the destiny of Latin America. But readers in Europe and countries as culturally diverse as Israel, China and Japan, also found a meaning in the humanism and poetry of her work.

In many books, theses, poetic and philosophical reflections, it is possible to trace the influence of this Latin-American writer from a country which, within a mere half century, produced three writers of world stature: Gabriela Mistral, Vicente Huidobro and Pablo Neruda.

Why has Gabriela Mistral's work had a universal impact? As in the case of all true creative artists, attachment to her own familiar world did not exclude a strong feeling for other languages and cultures. She acknowledged her debt not only to Saint Theresa and to the Spanish poet Luis de Gongora y Argote but to Dante, Rabindranath Tagore, and the great Russian writers, and, Christian though she was, to the great sages of Buddhism.

Closely identified with her country and with her people ("I am and will remain, she said, "a daughter of my land"), Gabriela Mistral described her personal experience with a voice which all humanity could recognize, drawing from a tragic love affair a song of love and tenderness which speaks to people everywhere. In her sympathy for the downtrodden and her readiness to defend their cause, poetry and humanism become one: "We must give expression to the soul in all its intensity, and boldly utter the message which springs from the heart before it ceases to beat."

Source: *UNESCO Courier,* November, 1989, p. 49.

Sources

Acre de Vazquez, Margot, *Gabriela Mistral: The Poet and her Work*, New York University Press, 1964.

Agosin, Marjorie, "Gabriela Mistral, the Restless Soul," in *Gabriela Mistral: A Reader*, White Pine Press, 1993, pp. 17-24.

Bates, Margaret, "Introduction," in *Selected Poems of Gabriela Mistral*, translated and edited by Doris Dana, Johns Hopkins Press, 1973, pp. xv-xxvi.

Hespelt, E. Herman, "Gabriela Mistral," in *An Anthology of Spanish American Literature*, F. S. Crofts and Company, 1946, p. 730.

Marchant, Elizabeth A., "The Professional Outsider: Gabriela Mistral on Motherhood and Nation," in *Latin American Literary Review*, Vol. 27, No. 53, January/June, 1999, pp. 49-66.

Further Reading

Castro-Klaren, Sara, Sylvia Molloy, and Beatriz Sarlo, eds., *Women's Writing in Latin America: An Anthology*, Westview Press, 1991.

The introduction to this book is interesting but complex for students; the examples included, however, offer a good variety.

Hughes, Brenda, *Folk Tales from Chile*, Hippocrene Books, 1997.

Intended primarily for a young audience, this book retells some fascinating traditional tales which capture the flavor of the transformations in ''Fear.''

Rodriguez, Ileana, *House/Garden/Nation*, Duke University Press, 1994.

This book is an academic exploration of issues of gender and ethnicity in Latin America after the colonial period. It does not specifically examine Mistral, but it does give a good background to the period in which she worked.

The Friends

Rosa Guy

1973

The Friends, published in 1973, is the first in a trilogy of young adult novels portraying the interconnected relationship between two families, the Cathays and the Jacksons. *Ruby* (1978) and *Edith Jackson* (1979) complete the series. All three of the novels have received an American Library Association citation. Each is told from the perspective of the title character and focuses on different problems young black adolescents faced growing up in the 1960s. Author Rosa Guy provides both a rich portrait of Harlem and insight into the lives of the Caribbean immigrants who settled there. Her view of the 1960s is unflinching; the tension in the neighborhood provides a catalyst for the story's action. Guy's novel is important because it graphically presents issues of race and class prejudice which had rarely been explored in young adult novels. She was one of a group of novelists who emerged during the late 1960s and 1970s to enrich the world of children's literature by providing stories centered around black characters and their world. Alice Walker, in her review of *The Friends* in the *New York Times*, describes the void which Guy's novel filled. Walker speaks for an entire generation when she notes that she was a "young black girl who spent the first twenty years of her life without seeing a single book in which the heroine was like herself." In an article in *Hornbook*, Guy characterizes herself foremost as a storyteller who wishes to create characters that her readers will learn to know. She adds, "If I have proven to be

popular with young people, it is because when they have finished with one of my books, they not only have a satisfying experience—they have also had an education.''

Author Biography

In *The Friends*, Rosa Guy provides a vivid portrait of two cultures, demonstrating the immigrant's struggle to integrate old and new ways of life. Many of these details come from her own experiences.

Guy was born in Diego Martin, Trinidad, on September 1 of either 1925 or 1928; she has declined to confirm either date. Her early years bear many similarities to the lives of the Cathay sisters in the novel. When Guy's parents, Henry and Audrey Cuthbert, moved to New York City, she and her sister, Ameze, remained in Trinidad. In 1932, they rejoined their parents. Unfortunately, shortly after their arrival, Audrey Cuthbert became seriously ill. The sisters then moved in with a cousin, a political activist who supported Marcus Garvey's philosophy of political and economic independence for blacks. Guy traces the social awareness of her novels for young adults to these years.

In 1934, Guy's mother died. The sisters returned to live with their father, but he also died a few years later. At fourteen, Guy was forced to leave school in order to support her older sister who was ill and unable to work. She married Warren Guy in 1941 and one year later gave birth to a son, Warren Jr. While her husband was away in the service during World War II, she became involved with the American Negro Theater. After his return, however, the family moved to Connecticut. When the couple divorced in 1950, she resumed her life in New York City, continuing her literary and political activities.

With John Killens, Guy helped form the Harlem Writers Guild, a workshop which inspired writers such as Maya Angelou, Paule Marshall, and Lonnie Elder. The workshop gave Guy the determination to continue writing, a difficult task for a single working mother. Since she had dropped out of school so early, it also provided a means for her to develop her education, which she later continued formally at New York University.

During this period, the civil rights movement had acquired increased momentum both in the United States and in Africa. Guy took an active role in the efforts of the artistic community to support political action. She and novelist Maya Angelou led a demonstration at the United Nations to mourn the assassination of the Congolese leader Patrice Lumumba. Her role in this protest led to her meeting and subsequent friendship with Malcolm X.

The turmoil and racial unrest of the 1960s made it a difficult period for Guy. Her husband's murder in 1962 caused her to move to Haiti for a while. After Malcolm X's death, she produced her first novel, *Bird at My Window*. Her next book, *Children of Longing*, a collection of essays, revealed the thoughts of black youth on the recent past. This was followed by the trilogy *The Friends*, *Ruby*, and *Edith Jackson*.

Throughout her career, Guy has been an experimenter, working in a wide range of genres: novels for children, young adults, and adults; plays; folktales; essays; and cultural criticism. Recently, she was honored by the Harlem Writers Guild for a lifetime of achievement.

Plot Summary

Part One

The Friends describes a transitional period in the life of Phyllisia Cathay as she learns about herself, as well as the responsibilities involved in both family life and friendship. As the novel opens, Phyllisia, the first-person narrator, is sitting in her classroom contemplating her dislike for Edith Jackson, a poorly dressed classmate who is determined to become her friend. When Edith enters the room, typically late, she is mocked by Miss Lass, the teacher. Edith simply disregards the snub, trying instead to speak to Phyllisia, who ignores her.

Phyllisia, who has recently moved from the West Indies to Harlem, feels lost and unhappy. The other children constantly mock her and call her names. They dislike her accent, her intelligence, and her willingness to respond in class. Their hostility culminates in a fight between Phyllisia and Beulah, a much larger and tougher classmate. Phyllisia astonishes everyone (including herself) by butting Beulah with her head, which enables her to escape. Running home, she feels even more alone since no one, child or adult, had tried to help her. She contrasts this with her previous life on the island where ''everybody cared about everything.'' When her mother, Ramona, questions Phyllisia about her disheveled appearance, she learns that

Rosa Guy

both Phyllisia and her sister, Ruby, have had problems at school because they are seen as outsiders.

That evening, Calvin Cathay, Phyllisia's father, brings two strangers home, Cousin Frank and Mr. Charles. Introducing the men to his family, he hugs Phyllisia, then heartlessly dismisses her as ugly. This makes Phyllisia feel even more isolated, the ugly duckling in a handsome family.

The next day, when Phyllisia walks into the classroom the students boo her, while Beulah enters to cheers. Miss Lass refuses any assistance; Edith, however, warns that no one should pick on her best friend, Phyllisia. Astonishingly, Phyllisia feels the hostility of the students dissipate. Initially, she is grateful, but this soon turns to anger because she doesn't want to be linked in any way to this dirty and disheveled girl.

Although Phyllisia had been looking forward to warmer weather, the summer bring several disturbances. Gradually, Phyllisia becomes aware that her mother is very ill. As the heat mounts, tension in the neighborhood escalates and the newspapers predict a "long, hot summer" where the cities will explode in riots. Even in the classroom, the heat affects everyone. Miss Lass eventually explodes into a virulent racist attack on her students, driving Phyllisia

from the room. Edith follows her and the two girls explore New York City. For the first time, Phyllisia enjoys Edith's company. However, when she witnesses Edith stealing, it brings back her dislike. When they return to Harlem, Phyllisia is determined to abandon Edith and find her own way home, in spite of the fact that Edith has warned her that there will be trouble soon. Just as Phyllisia turns to escape, the police charge the crowd. Edith again saves Phyllisia, pulling her out of the melee. As the two girls flee, Phyllisia glances back and sees Calvin struggling with a mounted policeman.

The girls run to Edith's apartment where Phyllisia meets the Jackson family. Phyllisia notices that Edith suddenly seems older under the weight of the responsibly of caring for her four younger sisters. When she returns home, Calvin is angry with her, not for being in the riot but for associating with Edith. He warns her never to socialize with any "ragamuffins" again.

Part Two

The section opens in Central Park where Phyllisia is picnicking with Edith and her sisters. Although she knows it is cruel, Phyllisia is bragging about the elegant new clothes that she'll be wearing to high school. Edith shifts the subject, asking about Phyllisia's mother and criticizing Calvin for not treating Phyllisia fairly. When they are about to leave, Edith picks some flowers for Phyllisia's mother. Ramona, who is delighted to learn that her daughter has a friend, wishes to meet her. However, Phyllisia refuses because she is too ashamed of Edith's clothes: this automatic betrayal of her only friend stuns her.

Five days later, Phyllisia visits the Jacksons' apartment, learning that Mr. Jackson has disappeared. Edith swears her to secrecy because she is afraid that the family will be separated. Soon Edith drops out of school. Gradually, Phyllisia discovers that she is becoming paired with Miriam Robbins. Just a few months ago, Phyllisia desperately wanted this friendship, but now she finds Miriam to be shallow and uninteresting compared to Edith. As Ramona becomes increasingly ill, her moods become erratic. When Phyllisia attempts to comfort her mother by mentioning that Miriam thinks she's beautiful, Ramona bares her chest, showing the scars where one breast has been removed. Desperately, she warns the girls against relying on something as superficial and transitory as beauty.

Phyllisia doesn't see Edith for over two months. During that time, Norman, one of the boys in the neighborhood, has been flirting with her. Ramona, who is now certain that she is dying, seems to have moved into another world. Finally, Phyllisia goes to see Edith, only to discover that she is at an employment agency. Edith eagerly accepts when Phyllisia invites her home. Both Ramona and Ruby are charmed by Edith, which angers Phyllisia. When Ruby compares herself and Phyllisia to Edith, Phyllisia strikes out in fury, shouting insults directed at Edith. Calvin enters in the middle of the scene and throws Edith out, which secretly pleases Phyllisia. That evening, Ramona tells Phyllisia that she is dying. She then reminds Phyllisia that she will have to deal with her guilt over the incident with Edith in some way: ''You must not forget this day—what you have done today—easily.''

Ramona's death, coupled with her own betrayal of friendship, forces Phyllisia into a trancelike state where she is scarcely aware of the world around her. At the funeral, convinced that Edith is waiting to comfort her, Phyllisia runs outside screaming Edith's name.

Part Three

Ruby wakes Phyllisia from a recurring nightmare where both her mother and Edith appear. Phyllisia has been unable to eat; she is weak and too ill to attend school. Ruby tries to entice her with her favorite food, but all Phyllisia wants is to be left alone. She believes the spirit in the dream won't allow her to eat. Eventually, Calvin decides to force-feed Phyllisia. Every day, he threatens her with a beating unless she eats, and gradually her health returns.

Throughout her illness, Phyllisia longs to see Edith, but once she recovers she is afraid to defy Calvin. She spends most of her time studying, socializing only when Ruby forces her. One evening when Ruby drags her to a party at Miriam's, she learns that Randy, Edith's brother, has been killed by the police. She rushes to Edith's building, only to find herself afraid to go in. When she returns home, Calvin is enraged because he caught Ruby kissing her boyfriend, Orlando. He keeps both girls virtual prisoners in the house. Cousin Frank and Mr. Charles try to reason with him to no avail.

Ruby obeys his rules, hoping to regain his trust, but Phyllisia rebels. She starts skipping school, picking up a boy in the park. When Calvin learns of this, he decides to send the girls back to the island.

After visiting Calvin's restaurant, Phyllisia learns that she has been deceiving herself about her family's wealth and status in order to feel superior to those around her. She decides that she has to see Edith in order to renew their friendship. When she gets to Edith's apartment, however, she learns that Ellen, the baby of the family, has died and the other children have been taken away. Edith, too, will be going to the orphanage soon. Phyllisia tells Edith that she will always be her friend, and will visit her no matter where she goes.

When Phyllisia returns home, she makes her first real attempt to communicate with her father in order to convince him not to send them to the island. She finally breaks through to him, and he indicates that they can stay in Harlem. Phyllisia will be able to keep her promise to Edith.

Characters

Beulah

Beulah, who is the toughest girl in Phyllisia's class, intimidates Miss Lass, the teacher. She dislikes Phyllisia, starting a fight with her after school. When Phyllisia manages to escape, Beulah plans to resume the fight the next day, this time really hurting Phyllisia. However, Edith intervenes, placing Phyllisia under her protection.

Calvin Cathay

Calvin Cathay is a proud, domineering man who has brought his family from the West Indies to Harlem. He likes to brag about his possessions, which include his beautiful wife, Ramona, and daughter Ruby. He is hardworking and determined to succeed, putting in long hours with strenuous labor at his restaurant. He announces to Mr. Charles, ''I'm going to be one of the richest men in Harlem.'' He is also intolerant, usually judging people by their appearance. From the novel's beginning, he makes it clear that he doesn't want his family to associate with anyone who is poorly dressed.

Although he loves his family, he is accustomed to showing his caring through domination rather than communication. As the head of the family, his orders must be obeyed. When defied, he flies into a rage. He is unable to express gentler feelings and is completely unable to cope with the fact that his daughters are growing up. Although he is harsh because he is afraid for them, he cannot express this sentiment. His struggles with Phyllisia are particu-

Media Adaptations

- Scenes from the novel are mixed with teens interviewing Guy about her life, writing, and move from the West Indies to Harlem in *The Friends*, released in 1985 and available from The Media Guild.

larly contentious because they are both very strong-willed and both convinced of the righteousness of their own behavior.

Cousin Frank Cathay

Cousin Frank, along with Mr. Charles, seems to function as the voice of reason in the novel. The two men, who are introduced to the children at the novel's beginning, always appear together. Because Calvin often acts rashly, the two function as a restraining force, often giving him helpful advice on how to deal with family problems.

Phyllisia Cathay

Phyllisia, the novel's first-person narrator, is intelligent, sensitive, and introspective, qualities which increase the difficulties she finds in her new environment. She is extremely unhappy at having been torn from her happy childhood in the West Indies and moved to Harlem where she is scorned for her accent and her scholastic ability. Like her father, Calvin, she is also rigid, inflexible, and snobbish, often looking down on others because of their appearance. She rejects Edith Jackson, as well as many other children in her class, because she sees them as ''ragamuffins.'' When she finally spends some time with Edith, enjoying her company, the pleasure is marred by her conviction that everyone is looking at the holes in Edith's socks, and judging not only Edith but herself also.

Phyllisia is strong-willed. She refuses to placate her classmates in order to make life easier. She often battles with her father. The conflicts between the two continue throughout the novel since neither is willing to give in to the other. Although she loves her mother, the bond between the two has been weakened by her mother's cancer. Phyllisia is forced to cope with two shattering events in a row: her betrayal of Edith and her mother's death. When these incidents force her to reexamine her values and attitudes, she realizes that she has been unfair to almost everyone: Calvin, Ruby, and most of all Edith. This new self-awareness allows her to establish a connection with her father which also enables her to fulfill her promise to Edith.

Ramona Cathay

Ramona Cathay, Phyllisia's mother, is an exceptionally beautiful woman whom Phyllisia compares to a fairy-tale queen. Her gentle voice, with its rich island accent, creates poignant memories of their beloved island home. She has much in common with both of her daughters. She shares Ruby's striking beauty. Like Phyllisia, she is both a reader and thinker; each has a strong need for privacy, which makes them, at times, lonely.

Unfortunately, she is seriously ill throughout the first part of the novel. Although she has already had one breast removed to combat cancer, the disease has returned. Since Ramona has always been physically beautiful, this disfigurement is difficult for her. At the same time, it allows her to recognize that dependence on external appearances is foolish, placing too much value on characteristics that are superficial. She tries to convey this to her family, particularly to her daughters, who are vulnerable in a society which judges women, in particular, by appearance. She is unable to deal with the difficulties her daughters are experiencing since her illness tires her, making her moody. She knows that she is dying. When Phyllisia brings Edith to visit her, Ramona treats Edith with respect. This angers Phyllisia, who insults Edith. Instead of scolding Phyllisia, Ramona reminds her that she will have to find a way to deal with her own guilt. Her death shortly after this incident devastates Phyllisia.

Ruby Cathay

Ruby, Phyllisia's sister, is pretty, easygoing, and wants to get along with everyone. Even though her beauty enables her to make friends easily, she tries to please the people around her, even if it means disguising her true feelings or abilities. She is not as introspective as Phyllisia, but she likes caring for people. She spends hours with her mother and with Phyllisia during their illnesses, performing simple tasks for them. She also is fun-loving and enjoys gossip and socializing.

Mr. Charles

Mr. Charles is a large man, so big that at first sight he appears frightening. However, he has a gentle, reassuring voice. With Cousin Frank, he helps to guide Calvin Cathay.

Bess Jackson

Edith's ten-year-old sister. After the death of their youngest sister, Ellen, Edith sends her to the welfare department in order to make arrangements for a funeral. Although Edith warns her not to say they are orphaned, Bess is too young to keep the secret. When she reveals that they have been living on their own, Edith's sisters are taken away.

Edith Jackson

In spite of the fact that she bears most of the responsibility for taking care of her family, Edith Jackson is a cheerful and generous person. Throughout the novel, she is an object of scorn: Miss Lass, the teacher, attacks her appearance; Calvin throws her out of the Cathays' apartment, commenting that people like her ''don't go with my furniture''; Miriam Robbins calls her ''a beat up looking chick.'' Most distressing of all, Phyllisia is ashamed of her. However, Edith never retaliates. The only time she seems affected by negative opinions is when Phyllisia is cruel to her.

Edith is intense and interested in everything around her. She is continually thoughtful, stopping to pick flowers for Ramona when she is ill, always remembering to compliment Phyllisia. Eventually, the burden of caring for her family takes its toll. When Phyllisia finds her in the employment agency, she looks as if she has aged. However, she is always forceful and determined.

Ellen Jackson

At four, Ellen is the baby of the Jackson family. She is a delightful child, warm and affectionate. Because of her wholehearted admiration, Phyllisia begins to develop a sense of confidence that she did not get at home where she felt that she was the ugly duckling of the family. Ellen's sudden death destroys Edith's attempts to hold her family together.

Minnie Jackson

Edith's seven-year-old sister.

Mr. Jackson

Mr. Jackson appears very old and tired-looking to Phyllisia. He is obviously unable to take care of his family, leaving most of the responsibility for raising the children to Edith. He watches the young children when they are well, but if they show the slightest sign of sickness, Edith has to stay home from school to care for them. He is an almost invisible presence in his own home, sitting quietly in his chair without speaking.

Randy Jackson

Randy, Edith's sixteen-year-old brother, is tall and intense. Although he gets a job to help support the family after their father disappears, he is fired because he is unwilling to take orders. His murder by the police fuels further tension in the neighborhood. Ironically, he had wanted to go to the police for help when his father disappeared, but Edith dissuaded him.

Suzy Jackson

Edith's eight-year-old sister.

José

José is a handsome Puerto Rican boy whom Phyllisia meets in the park while she is cutting school in order to defy her father's strict restrictions. Although she likes him at first mainly for companionship, after an intense kiss she decides she is in love with him.

Miss Lass

Miss Lass, Phyllisia's teacher, is an insecure and cruel white woman who both scorns and is afraid of her class. She is especially hostile to Edith Jackson, continually disparaging her appearance and behavior. When she insists on holding Phyllisia up to the rest of the class as a symbol of proper behavior, Phyllisia realizes that she is only doing this to divert hostility away from herself. Eventually she reveals the extent of her prejudice by calling all of her students ''filthy pigs'' and attacking their families.

Norman

The first boy ever to flirt with Phyllisia, Norman bolsters the newfound self-esteem she has gained through the affection of Edith's family. However, while Phyllisia is sick, he gives his pin to

Miriam Robbins. His father is a doctor who is planning to move his family upstate.

Orlando

Norman's brother, Orlando, admires Ruby, and the two begin to date. Interest in the two brothers brings Miriam and Ruby together in a casual friendship centered around gossip about boys and clothes, one which Phyllisia scorns. After Calvin sees Orlando kissing Ruby goodnight, he explodes, hitting Orlando, then keeping both of his daughters virtual prisoners in the house.

Miriam Robbins

Miriam Robbins, one of Phyllisia's classmates, lives across the street from the Cathays and belongs to a clique of well-dressed, middle-class teens. Because her father is a professional, she believes she is better than most of the other students. Although she rejects Phyllisia's first attempts to be friendly, finding her too unattractive and different to be a part of this select group, Miriam later seeks out an acquaintanceship because she admires the rest of the Cathay family. By then, however, Phyllisia finds her shallow and uninteresting.

Mrs. Robbins

Like her daughter Miriam, Mrs. Robbins is interested in social roles and status. She dislikes Harlem and would like to move to a better neighborhood. Phyllisia is rather scornful of the fact that she attempts to take part in her daughter's social affairs.

Carole Smith

A shy and quiet classmate whom Miss Lass shames in front of the entire class.

Themes

Prejudice

Against the backdrop of Harlem during a season of violence, rioting, and police-neighborhood confrontations, *The Friends* portrays many different kinds of prejudice. The opening scene of the novel alone introduces three separate and different examples of bigotry. Phyllisia's classmates taunt her because of her West Indian background and accent. She, in turn, scorns Edith Jackson, who would like to befriend her, simply because Edith has holes in her clothes and frequently appears dirty. The teacher, whose disdain for the entire class in this scene later erupts in virulent racist comments, manages to maintain her limited control over the class primarily by focusing their hostility against Phyllisia. This sets the discordant mood of the novel where groundless antagonisms and failures in communication frequently separate the characters, ultimately contributing to the tragedy at the story's conclusion.

Phyllisia faces mockery daily from her classmates. She insists on demonstrating her knowledge and intelligence to the rest of the class, and this simply fuels their dislike of her. Her sister, Ruby, advises her not to draw attention to herself in order to adapt to this new situation in Harlem. Even at home, Phyllisia becomes the victim of another type of bigotry. Her own father mocks her appearance, cruelly describing her as ugly when he introduces her to Cousin Frank and Mr. Charles, subsequently praising Ruby for her beauty. Mournfully, Phyllisia notes that it far easier to laugh at ugly people that pretty ones.

However, Phyllisia is also guilty of intolerance. Beulah, the class bully, could have seriously hurt Phyllisia if Edith had not intervened. In spite of that, Phyllisia continues to be ashamed of Edith. Even when the two girls have formed a friendship, Phyllisia intellectually distances herself from Edith and the life she lives. Phyllisia believes that her way of life, and therefore she too, is superior. When Ruby describes going barefoot on the island, Phyllisia is enraged. She cannot bear to think that her life is, in any manner, similar to Edith's. Shortly after this, when Calvin throws Edith out of their house, Phyllisia is almost happy. It reinforces her belief about her own worth—a belief which is based, like Calvin's, on clothes, money, and material possessions.

Coming of Age

In the novel, Phyllisia is forced to deal with a variety of adult responsibilities. On the island, her life had been carefree, her role that of a child. After she arrives in New York, she confronts a series of incidents which test her character. The prejudices of her classmates and teacher force her to examine what behavior she should adopt as a young adult. Throughout the novel, she is tested by her father's frequently unreasoning domination. She must discover how to communicate with him, a man who is unable to express his feelings. Eventually, she assumes the adult role in the relationship, explaining to her father how they might survive as a family. The most difficult of her trials is her mother's death. This forces her to reexamine what is most valuable in her life.

Friendship

In spite of the title, throughout most of the novel, Phyllisia fails at friendship. While Edith is open and willing to share, Phyllisia withholds her family and her approval. She sneaks away to be with Edith. In an odd way, her behavior mirrors that of a lover who is conducting a hidden and disreputable affair. The relationship is exciting, but no one else may be aware of it. This continues until Phyllisia's betrayal of Edith in front of the entire Cathay family. Phyllisia must then slowly rebuild the relationship.

Failure of Adult Authority

On every level, the adults in the novel are unable or unwilling to protect the children in their care. Although Calvin is a strong, domineering figure who is determined to supply his family with all of their physical needs, he nonetheless avoids developing a relationship with his children. He likes Ruby because she is pretty and compliant. However when he catches her kissing Orlando, he beats her. Until the final scene of the novel, he uses force and domination to get his way. Ramona Cathay, a loving and communicative parent, unfortunately is dying. She cannot provide Phyllisia with the support she needs. Cousin Frank and Mr. Charles, who are also voices of reason in the novel, are only occasionally around.

Edith's life has even less support. Her father seemed invisible even when he was there. Although Phyllisia had been in the room with him for quite some time, it was only when he got up to leave that she noticed him. Traditional figures of authority provide absolutely no assistance to Edith and her family. In fact, most of them do far more harm than good. The police kill Randy. Miss Lass seems to hate Edith, regularly abusing her verbally. After Ellen's death, Phyllisia tries to figure out how the tragedy could have been prevented. ''Why hadn't I been able to talk to Mother—to Calvin? Why hadn't we at least thought of Miss Lass? But thinking of Miss Lass made me shudder again. We could have gone to a policeman. Which one? The one who had killed her brother because he was running? Why hadn't there been some way out of our ignorance? I didn't know. The only thing I did know was that Edith was the only blameless one.''

Topics for Further Study

- Research the experiences of recent teenage immigrants; if it is possible, conduct some interviews with foreign-born students. Compare and contrast their experiences with those of Phyllisia Cathay.

- Police/neighborhood hostilities create the tension in the novel's setting. Develop a timeline showing major events in police-community relations in New York City. Write an essay discussing what has transpired over the years.

- Rosa Guy describes herself as a storyteller, an important role in many Caribbean and African societies. Describe the traditional aspects of this role.

- *The Friends* is set in Harlem during the riots of the 1960s. Investigate the causes and the result of these riots.

Style

Point of View

The Friends uses a first-person ''I'' narrator, Phyllisia Cathay. Telling the novel from Phyllisia's perspective allows the reader to develop along with her. Since she is learning to adjust to a new society, she possesses an outsider's awareness of the world around her. The reader discovers Harlem and New York City through her eyes. Her growing insights operate on a psychological level as well, since Phyllisia is introduced to a world of prejudice that had been previously unknown to her. Part of the novel's depth comes from the fact that Phyllisia's own intolerance is obvious to the reader long before it becomes apparent to her.

Guy occasionally breaks into the first-person perspective to include sections of dialogue between other characters. The use of these breaks signals that Phyllisia has withdrawn inside herself. The dialogue swirls around her while she struggles to cope with her inner turmoil. These scenes occur first after

Calvin rejects her, next at her mother's funeral, and finally when she attempts to confront her own prejudice.

Setting

The setting of the novel is central to the story. Most readers already possess an awareness of Harlem as the long-standing center of New York City's black community. Its reputation mingles elements of civil protest and artistic creativity. However, Phyllisia resents that her father brought her away from her island home "to this miserable place called Harlem." Through the eyes of the main character, the reader observes two different cultures and discovers some of the immigrant's struggles to integrate old and new ways of life.

Shortly after the novel's opening, Harlem is poised at the beginning of a "long, hot summer." Guy uses the tension in the neighborhood to mirror the plot. Miss Lass nervously paces the room before she explodes at her class. When Edith and Phyllisia abandon school and head out to the streets, Guy vividly describes the gathering crowds sweltering in the heat. These scenes shift to a brief escape by subway to the zoo and Central Park, providing a few moments of calm where Edith and Phyllisia are able to form the beginning of a relationship. When the girls return to Harlem, however, Phyllisia is furious with Edith for stealing. Again the internal turmoil has a parallel in the streets, which are even more explosive as police patrol through the restless crowd on horseback.

The tension of Harlem is countered by the remembered calm of the islands. Phyllisia contrasts the city's noises to the island's quarreling birds. The tranquility and ease of play there cause her to regret her life in the city.

Contrast

Guy develops several elements of the story through the use of contrast. The location is perhaps the most obvious, as Phyllisia compares the world of Harlem with her memories of the island. However, other elements in the setting use contrast as well. The heat of summer, which Phyllisia had been longing for because she thought it would make Harlem seem more like the island, brings violence: the fight with Beulah and later the riot. However, it also provides the opportunity for her to begin her friendship with Edith. The summer days are filled with picnics in the park. When fall and winter come,

Edith is forced to drop out of school and the two girls lose touch with each other.

Guy also contrasts Phyllisia's family with Edith's. Calvin is almost too strong, attempting to dominate every aspect of his family's behavior, while Mr. Jackson has abdicated all responsibility. Both girls lose a parent during the course of the novel, but they react quite differently. Edith is forced to assume an adult life, while Phyllisia withdraws from the world around her. Even simple details, such as Ramona's moods, contribute to the novel's rich use of juxtaposition.

Language and Dialect

The island accent of the Cathay family is an important element in the story. The other children tease Phyllisia because of it, mimicking the way she speaks. "Someone else shouted in a mock West Indian accent: 'Run her into the sea, mahn.'" For Phyllisia, however, her mother's rich French Creole voice is soothing and filled with overtones of the island she loves.

While the use of dialect in the novel is not overpowering, Guy allows the reader to hear the island sound, particularly in Calvin's language. He frequently uses phrases and word order in his sentences that illustrate West Indian speech: "when you old-talk about pretty people," "minding me own business." Ramona interjects French words into speech as well.

Literary Heritage

Rosa Guy's novels for young adults draw on her rich and varied cultural heritage. *The Friends*, whose vivid setting is infused with the atmosphere of both Harlem and the West Indies, reflects several aspects of this heritage.

The cultural heritage of the Caribbean has been created by successive waves of immigrants. Today, it is a rich blend formed from the many groups who live there. Some of the earliest inhabitants were the Arawaks and Caribs who came to the islands from South America. After the arrival of the Europeans, however, disease wiped out most of the native population. Several European nations—France, England, Spain, and the Netherlands—colonized the region during the 16th and 17th centuries. With the introduction of sugar cane to the islands in the 17th century, many Africans were brought over as slaves.

After the emancipation of the slaves in the 19th century, plantation owners imported Chinese and East Indian workers as indentured servants. The culture of the islands reflects this blend of ethnic groups with its representatives from Africa, Europe, and the Orient. Even a cursory examination of the literary output of the region demonstrates the wide range of ethnic and social backgrounds.

Although the Caribbean region is influenced by several cultures, some of the most prominent influences come from Africa. The musicality and pronounced rhythms which produced such Trinidadian innovations as the steel band and calypso have their origins in African tribal tales. When Rosa Guy subtitled her article in *The Horn Book Magazine* ''I Am a Story-teller,'' it reflected these roots since the storyteller has held a prominent role in many African countries. African tribal tales were communal, relying on dialog and rhythm, requiring audience participation. It is possible to hear their overtones in the distinct rhythms of the language in the West Indies, language which Guy introduces to her readers in *The Friends*.

Presenting Rosa Guy opens with a quotation in which the author sums up her cultural heritage:

> My life in the West Indies, of course, had a profound influence on me. It made me into the type of person I imagine that I am today. The calypso, the carnival, the religion that permeated our life—the Catholic religion—superstitions, voodoo, the zombies, the djuins, all of these frightening aspects of life that combine the myth coming over from Africa, had a genuine effect on me. . . . So when I say I am West Indian, I have all of these little things—all of that broad background—that makes up the thinking, the searching of a person when art becomes relevant.

Historical Context

Several reviewers have commented on Guy's effective portrayal of Harlem in novels such as *The Friends*. Since she arrived in the United States from Trinidad in 1932, Harlem has played a key role in her life and work. It has also played a central role in the cultural, political, and intellectual life of black America.

At the turn of the twentieth century, however, Harlem was primarily occupied by the English and Germans, although a wave of Jewish immigrants had begun to move into the area. In 1904, Phillip A. Payton Jr., a black real estate agent, initiated a project which would eventually turn Harlem into a black community. He began leasing empty buildings in order to rent them to African-American families. This opportunity, blended with an increased migration of blacks from the southern states, precipitated a rapid growth in the area. Caribbean immigrants, as well, swelled the population during the years between 1910 and 1920, since several hurricanes caused severe damage in the West Indies during that decade. In 1914, Harlem was home to approximately 50,000 blacks; by 1930, the number had reached 200,000.

As early as 1920, Harlem was home to a burgeoning artistic community. It was known for its social gatherings, clubs, and music. During the 1920s and 1930s, the Harlem Renaissance drew black artists and intellectuals from throughout the United States. Writers such as Langston Hughes and Zora Neale Hurston made the area famous.

Harlem was also the home to several political and social movements. The struggle for civil rights existed in Harlem almost as long as the black community itself. Caribbean activists played a prominent role in many of these movements. Marcus Garvey, the Jamaican who founded the United Negro Improvement Association (UNIA), visited Harlem in 1916. His message of self-pride, economic independence, and freedom from social exploitation resonated in the community. As poverty and violence against blacks exploded across the United States, Garvey proclaimed a clear and positive counter-message. In 1917, the first branch of the UNIA in the United States opened in Harlem. Although Garvey was later jailed and then deported, his followers continued to preach his message.

During the 1930s, Harlem was home to many early civil-rights campaigns. In 1933, black activists, along with members of the black churches, held boycotts to protest stores which would not hire black workers. Although the boycotts met with some success, critics such as Ralph Bunche noticed that the benefits of these struggles mostly affected the middle-class and educated while little was being done to alter the living conditions for the entire community.

Harlem was the scene of riots in 1935 and again in 1943. Both protests began in response to police conflicts with citizens. During the 1950s, those problems which caused the earlier boycotts and riots intensified. Rents were raised, while the living conditions in the buildings deteriorated. Landlords refused to listen to tenant complaints. Discrimination in the workplace made it very difficult for laborers to find adequate jobs. Crime increased, yet frequently the police presence was viewed as even more of a threat that the crime. While Harlem still remained the artistic capital of the African-American community in the United States, it had a growing, angry core.

This is the community in which *The Friends* begins. The situation in the novel parallels the 1964 riot. On June 16, 1964, James Powell, a fifteen-year-old male, was shot by the police. Accounts of the incident varied widely. While some witnesses said Powell had a knife, others swore he was unarmed. Two days later, an angry crowd protested in the streets. Four nights of violence resulted. *The Friends*, like most of Guy's novels, enables her readers to see the individual stories which underlie history.

Critical Overview

Although literature for young adults is seldom reviewed widely or in depth (unless the author is relatively well known), *The Friends* received several favorable reviews. Elizabeth Haynes in *Library Journal* described the novel as powerful and praised the realism of its characters, setting, and language. A *Kirkus Reviews* critic also found *The Friends* memorable, particularly because of the complex development of Phyllisia's character as she learns to cope with the difficulties of life in Harlem. The reviewer admired the skillful presentation of the comparisons between Phyllisia and her father, concluding that she is a character "worth knowing even when she's least lovable." Both journals included the novel among their selections for the best books of the year.

In particular, Guy received praise for her sensitive and perceptive handling of potentially controversial subject matter such as prejudice and racism. In addition, *The Friends* was mentioned for its pioneering role in the development of several strong, black female characters since up until the 1960s books for children and young adults seldom employed minority characters in prominent roles. In the opening paragraph of her review in the *New York Times*, Alice Walker noted that novels such as *The Friends* filled a gaping void, providing sustenance for black adolescents who had been "hungry for heroines." The struggles that Phyllisia goes through in having to deal with hostile classmates, a

racist teacher, a cold and domineering father, and, most tragic of all, a dying mother create a vivid portrait of the growth of a young girl struggling to survive in a new country. Walker commented on the novel's valuable insights into this process of growing up: "And so begins the struggle that is the heart of this very important book: the fight to gain perception of one's own character; the grim struggle for self-knowledge and the almost killing internal upheaval that brings the necessary growth of compassion and humility *and courage*, so that friendship (of any kind, but especially between those of notable economic and social differences) can exist."

All reviews, however, were not favorable. The novel was criticized for plot weaknesses and stilted dialogue. M. R. Hewitt in *The Junior Bookshelf* found it hard to sustain interest in the book because the characters were so unappealing: "... one a rather priggish girl from a proud West Indian family, the other a sluttish, thieving but ever loyal and loving drudge struggling to keep her parentless family together." While the review in *Booklist* found the novel's characterizations complex and admired the realistic portrayal of life in Harlem, the overall conclusion was negative: "The plot is nonexistent, the dialog is sometimes awkward, and several scenes are jolting."

Over the years, critical acclaim for *The Friends* has increased. As the other two books in the trilogy emerged, the full range of Guy's portrait of family and neighborhood became clearer and the depth of her characterizations received more notice. In 1980, the American Library Association declared it one of the best novels of the previous fifteen years. When the *English Journal* asked several teachers at the Virginia Polytechnical Institute to select a handful of young adult novels that they believed would become "classics," they chose Guy's trilogy for its expert plotting, perceptive presentation of characters, and skillful use of language and idiom. In their opinion, the three books raised the standards of novels for adolescents.

Interestingly, the novel has been part of the standard curriculum in the United Kingdom since the 1970s. There is even a magazine devoted to explaining the neighborhood where Phyllisia and Edith live. Guy points out the irony of this in an article in *Horn Book Magazine*: "Young people in England can speak with authority about a place called Harlem in America, of which Americans—some living a mile away—know nothing. A young Londoner can describe conditions in American 'in-

Slums in East Harlem, New York. Guy moved from Trinidad to Harlem as youngster, and her novel The Friends *uses this setting to explore relationships strained by the harsh realities of ghetto life.*

ner cities'—places which Americans drive miles to avoid, even as they discuss how to bring 'democracy' to El Salvador and Nicaragua.''

Criticism

Mary Mahony

Mahony is an English instructor at Wayne County Community College in Detroit. In the fol-

lowing essay, she discusses The Friends *as one of a group of novels which raised the literary level of young adult literature in the 1970s.*

Up until the late 1960s and 1970s, the majority of the novels written for young adults were not particularly impressive. Characters tended to be conventional and underdeveloped; plots plodded along to a predictable happy ending. Most were eminently forgettable, and were duly forgotten. In 1980, four teachers from Virginia Polytechnic Institute—Lin-

What Do I Read Next?

- The other novels in Guy's trilogy, *Ruby* (1976) and *Edith Jackson* (1978), continue the story of the three main characters, focusing on Ruby's relationship with another girl and Edith's struggles to regain her family.

- *Journey of the Sparrows*, a 1991 novel, describes the journey of a fifteen-year-old girl and her family from El Salvador to Chicago.

- Gripping first-person narratives recount the realities of immigrant life in *Teenage Refugees from Cambodia Speak Out*, a 1995 book from Rosen Press. Other works in this series include *Teenage Refugees from Iran Speak Out* and *Teenage Refugees from Bosnia-Herzogovina Speak Out*.

- *The African American Experience* (1997) provides an informative, easily readable overview of African-American history for young adults.

- *The Graywolf Annual Seven: Stories from the American Mosaic* (1990) is a collection of tales featuring immigrants from many countries as they deal with a frequently prejudiced mainstream America.

- The immigrant experiences of an Indian teenager in England receive a rich portrayal in 1993's *The Roller Birds of Rampur*.

---

da Bachelder, Patricia Kelley, Donald Kenney, and Robert Small—collaborated on an article in the *English Journal* entitled ''Looking Backward: Trying to Find the Classic Young Adult Novel.'' When they sought a classic from before the late sixties, they found ''nothing praised by literary critics or read by anyone other than kids, a few English teachers, and school librarians, and by no one three or four years after publication.''

However, by 1970, the world of young adult literature had been shaken by some of the same forces which dominated the history of the period. A formerly staid and conventional field opened up as writers began to introduce complex characters who faced situations and choices that precluded an automatic happy ending. Rosa Guy's *The Friends* holds a prominent place in this vanguard. Because of this fact, the critical stature of her work has increased over the years as it became increasingly apparent that this was one of a handful of novels which enlarged the scope of young adult fiction.

One of *The Friends'* most important characteristics is its focus on strong, central minority characters and settings. In addition, the fact that the Cathays have a West Indian background provides the novel with an international scope as well, introducing to a young adult audience the consequences of the African diaspora. During the period in which the book was written, this was not at all common. Nancy Larrick published a groundbreaking article in the *Saturday Review* in 1965. Titled ''The All White World of Children's Books,'' it presented the results of a survey given to major book publishers; ninety percent responded. Fewer than six percent of the books published even included a single black character. Even worse, fewer than one percent told a story that centered around black characters.

In the introductory paragraph of her review of *The Friends* in *The New York Times*, Alice Walker commented on the emotional toll of such neglect. ''I am thinking of a young black girl who spent the first 20 years of her life without seeing a single book in which the heroine was a person like herself. . .But now, with books like Rosa Guy's heart-slammer, *The Friends*, I relive those wretched, hungry-for-heroines years and am helped to verify the existence and previous condition of myself.'' In Phyllisia Cathay and her family, Guy worked to fill that void with her richly developed portrait of an immigrant family in Harlem.

The Friends is also important for its literary quality. Guy has utilized both a sophisticated and a complex development of characterization and plot. Although the novel is geared to the young adult market, the evolution of the characters is presented with subtlety and attention to psychological authenticity. Typically, earlier young adult novels had relied on stock characters who tended to be basically good or evil. The leading character might falter or face a crisis of conscience, but the conclusion was never in doubt. It is interesting to contrast this stance with *The Friends* where most of the major characters display an intriguing duality.

This is clearly apparent in Guy's portrayal of Phyllisia. While the reader's sympathy may lie with her in the beginning of the novel because she is under attack by her classmates, it becomes quickly apparent that she is just as judgmental as the children who are harassing her. When she finally overcomes her snobbishness and enjoys a pleasant day with Edith, her narrow-mindedness still intrudes. She cannot overlook the holes in Edith's socks. Guy allows the reader to watch the same pattern appear over and over. Phyllisia enjoys Edith, but at the same time she is ashamed of her, and feels that their friendship somehow endangers her standing in the world. Few young adult novels have demonstrated so clearly the fact that it is possible for adolescents (like everyone else) to feel two contradictory emotions at the same time. In fact, Guy elicits this response from the reader who can regard Phyllisia with two opposing feelings. She can be a sympathetic character, even as she behaves very badly.

Nowhere is this duality more evident than in Part Two of the novel. Almost every time Edith and Phyllisia interact, Phyllisia experiences some kind of tension. While she appears to accept Edith, she ultimately withholds her total approval since she is never able to reconcile Edith's appearance and poverty with her own self-view. Thus, she frequently and deliberately wounds Edith. When the girls are picnicking in the beginning of Part Two, Phyllisia cruelly brings up the new clothes she'll wear to school, explaining her behavior with this comment: ''I never really intended to hurt Edith, but there was this little streak of wickedness that kept popping out of me. I didn't understand why.''

Later that same day, Phyllisia actually gives voice to her conflicting emotions. When her mother asks to meet Edith, she makes up all kind of excuses:

> "Although the novel is geared to the young adult market, the evolution of the characters is presented with subtlety and attention to psychological authenticity. Typically, earlier young adult novels had relied on stock characters who tended to be basically good or evil. The leading character might falter or face a crisis of conscience, but the conclusion was never in doubt."

I was making it up because I did not want her to see my friend. And I did not want to see her because I was ashamed of Edith. I loved her but I was ashamed of her. As the enormity of my betrayal of Edith hit me, it stunned me.

In many novels this self-knowledge would be the conclusion of the story. In *The Friends*, it is only a prelude, for although Phyllisia is finally aware of her true feelings, she finds herself unable to change. The very next time the two meet, Phyllisia explodes in anger when she thinks Ruby is comparing their lives to Edith's. In *Presenting Rosa Guy*, Jerrie Norris discusses the impact of this scene. ''Phyllisia, who has camouflaged her ambivalent attitudes toward her friend throughout their summer together, launches a vicious, although indirect verbal attack upon her friend, brutally humiliating her in front of the Cathays. The friendship shattered, Phyllisia is left alone.''

The last part of the novel describes Phyllisia's attempts to deal with the loss of her friend, followed shortly after by the loss of her mother. Self-knowledge does not come easily to her. Only after she realizes that her father's restaurant is a simple diner for working men does the ''voice'' of her interior dialogue finally convince her that she had been deceiving herself all along so that she could feel superior. At last, then, she is able to change: ''If I understood anything now, it was that I *was* almost sixteen and I had never accepted any responsibility. I had even blamed Calvin for my treatment of Edith. But I was the one who had made her suffer. She was my friend.''

However, when Phyllisia rushes to Edith she discovers that Edith's little sister is dead and the rest of the family has been taken away to an orphanage. Although Guy creates a reconciliation between the girls, there is no happy ending. The novel's end opens doors of communication for Phyllisia to remain in the United States so that she can continue her friendship with Edith. But Edith is on her way to an orphanage, her family is separated, and Phyllisia's relationship with her father is tenuous.

Guy uses the same ambiguity in her development of Calvin Cathay. It is easy to respond to him as an extremely negative figure, since the first-person narrator, Phyllisia, often presents him that way. Indeed, even at the novel's beginning, his many flaws are extremely apparent. His abrupt rejection of Phyllisia because she is ugly is described in a truly brutal manner. In her review in *The New York Times*, Alice Walker vividly describes him: ''Calvin is a menacing braggart who can show concern for his daughters in only the most tried, trusted, and useless ways: he beats them, locks them in, and makes constant comments on the salaciousness of their characters.''

Guy, however, does not allow Calvin to remain a stock villain. Through Ramona, the novel projects his vulnerability. It is clear that he loves his wife. Her illness reduces him to helplessness so that Phyllisia notices that he is no longer ''big and awesome,'' even wishing to touch and comfort him. When Ramona reminds him that he had been poor as a boy, his pride and determination to succeed become understandable.

Both Calvin and Phyllisia have similar flaws. A *Kirkus Review* writer describes it as a ''mixture of pride and snobbism.'' Each of them makes an adjustment in their behavior that is difficult for them because of that pride. Phyllisia's change is more dramatic. She accepts responsibility for her behavior. However, Calvin also demonstrates an ability to admit a portion of wrongdoing. He eventually admits that he is strict with his daughters because he is afraid for them. He cares, but does not know how to show it. When Phyllisia tells him what happened to Edith's sister, he shows a ''flash of guilt.'' Nothing is neatly tied up at the novel's end. Guy is too sophisticated a storyteller to impose an unnatural conclusion. However, the story hints at hope for the future, which is perhaps all that anyone can expect from life.

The Friends is an important young adult novel because of its complex view of reality and its clear portrait of life in Harlem. In her article in *Horn Book Magazine*, Guy explains her success: ''A novel is an emotional history of a people in time and place. If I have proven to be popular with young people, it is because when they have finished one of my books, they not only have a satisfying experience—they also have had an education.''

Source: Mary Mahony, in an essay for *Literature of Developing Nations for Students*, Gale, 2000.

Rena Korb

Korb has a master's degree in English literature and creative writing and has written for a wide variety of educational publishers. In the following essay, she discusses how Phyllisia reacts to those people who populate her new life in America.

Rosa Guy's award-winning novel *The Friends* is the first in what would become a trilogy concerning two vastly different families: the Cathays, native West Indians relocated to New York City, and the Jacksons, poor African Americans struggling through life in Harlem. *The Friends* is primarily Phyllisia Cathay's story. Young and willful, Phyllisia cannot adjust to life in the United States, partially because she cannot see beyond herself. As she learns to care for the needs of others, Phyllisia takes her first steps to developing into an adult. *The Friends* is also an important novel for younger readers in its exploration of the misunderstandings and conflicts that exist within families, friends, and communities. The American Library Association named it as one of the Best of the Best Books published in the last few decades.

At the heart of the novel rests the unlikely friendship between two teenage girls, Phyllisia and Edith. Phyllisia has recently moved from the West Indies to Harlem, where she is befriended by tough, street-smart Edith. The two girls are a study in contrasts. Phyllisia is an excellent student whereas Edith appears disinterested in school. Phyllisia's family lives comfortably. Her father owns a restaurant, and her mother is cultured and refined. Edith's family is very poor. Her father works for the subway system and her mother is dead, so Edith takes on much of the responsibility of taking care of the family. Edith, however, turns out to be the only person Phyllisia can turn to. Through the relationship, Phyllisia learns how to grow up and look beyond herself.

When the novel begins, Phyllisia, who has only been in the United States for five months, feels isolated both from her family and her community. She resents being taken from her aunt's home in the West Indies, where she felt loved and treasured, to be "set. . .down in this trap of asphalt and stone called Harlem." When she asks Calvin, her tyrannical father, why he brought her and her sister to New York, he answers, "To control your rudeness better," a succinct statement that early on defines the antagonistic relationship between father and daughter. To make matters worse, her sister Ruby is already popular at school while the other students only notice Phyllisia to mock her accent and her interest in education.

While Phyllisia feels like a stranger to America, she also desperately wants to fit in, but she is utterly unable to do so. For instance, she is drawn to her neighbor Marian because she is "so brown and round and pretty" and wears "the prettiest dresses to school and those thick, ribbed socks that were all the rage." Phyllisia, however, has nothing to offer Marian, who rebuffs her rudely. The superficiality—on both girls' parts—is underscored by the narration. Phyllisia notes that Marian "looked me up and down" before turning from Phyllisia to join her friends. Still, Phyllisia "longed so much for her friendship." Phyllisia wants to be friends with Marian *only* because she is popular and pretty, not for more valued reasons.

At the same time that Phyllisia wants acceptance, she knowingly sets herself apart from the other students. While she describes herself as physically gawky, "too tall for fourteen years, and without any shape," when in class she admires the picture she presents: "I pulled myself tall in my seat, made haughty little movements with my shoulders and head, adjusted the frills on the collar of my well-ironed blouse, touched my soft, neatly plaited hair and pointedly gave my attention to the blackboard." Phyllisia also acknowledges that in school she relishes her role of "star pupil," the person who is "always jumping up to let others know how smart I was." Even when she knows she will draw the ire of her fellow students by showing off, she continues to do so. For instance, when the teacher specifically calls on her in class to answer the question of where Egypt is located, Phyllisia answers the question, and "despite a sixth sense warning me to remain silent," she gives an extremely detailed answer.

> **Instead of praising Edith for her hard work, Phyllisia silently looks down upon Edith's shabby life. While Phyllisia embraces Edith and her family when it suits her—away from the eyes of her family or when Edith's younger sister is bestowing affection upon her—she still keeps Edith at a distance."**

Tellingly, Phyllisia equates "sitting there and not answering" with "begging," and she is too proud to beg—in this case, beg for friendship from the other students. Ruby, in notable contrast, does not experience Phyllisia's inherent difficulty of adjusting to a new culture, for she follows a deliberate pattern of not "calling attention to oneself," even if it means pretending not to know the right answer.

Phyllisia's isolation is also underscored by the attitude of her teacher, Miss Lass, a woman who openly resents and dislikes her students. The day after one of the other girls physically attacks Phyllisia, in response to the catcalls in class, Miss Lass only reminds the students, "What you do out in the street is your business." Like the other adults in her world, Miss Lass makes no effort to ease Phyllisia's adjustment. Miss Lass even draws attention to the way Phyllisia is different from the other students in her educational diligence. Phyllisia is hit by the sudden realization that Miss Lass is setting her up "as a target" in order "to keep the hatred of the children away." She is the "natural choice because I was a stranger and because I was proud."

Phyllisia knows that one of the reasons the other students dislike her so much is that her isolation makes her appear an easy target. She "had reasoned that the children singled me out for abuse because I walked alone. They might leave me in peace if I walked with a friend." However, the only person who wants to be with the real Phyllisia is Edith, who "had made up her mind, from the first day I entered this class, that she would be my friend whether I wanted it or not.'' Edith is drawn to Phyllisia for the same reason that other students hate her: ''Girl, you sure are smart,'' she says. Phyllisia, however, does not like Edith, as she firmly asserts on the first page of the novel. Edith speaks ungrammatically, chews gum loudly, and ''always came to school with her clothes unpressed, her stockings bagging about her legs with big holes.'' Phyllisia grudgingly becomes friends with Edith, despite herself. One thing she likes about Edith, however, is that her new friend always compliments her—the only person who does so.

From the start, however, the friendship is unequal and tenuous. For example, Edith constantly compliments Phyllisia—her clothes and her appearance—while Phyllisia takes little note of the hardship that Edith goes through simply to keep her family fed and clothed. Instead of praising Edith for her hard work, Phyllisia silently looks down upon Edith's shabby life. While Phyllisia embraces Edith and her family when it suits her—away from the eyes of her family or when Edith's younger sister is bestowing affection upon her—she still keeps Edith at a distance. Her relationship with Edith takes place amid strangers, in the park for instance. Phyllisia also deliberately makes clear to Edith that she is superior—financially and intellectually—for in truth, she is ''ashamed of Edith.'' Phyllisia's father owns a restaurant, while Edith's father is a laborer. Phyllisia's family lives in a comfortable apartment, while Edith's family lives in a ramshackle tenement. These are details that Phyllisia cannot forget, nor does she want to forget them, for they contribute to her sense of self-worth.

As time progresses, Phyllisia's life changes dramatically. Edith's father disappears, and Edith drops out of school so she can work to support her family. Phyllisia becomes friends with Marian, whose former best friend has moved to the suburbs. At the inception of the relationship, Phyllisia compares Marian to Edith: ''[H]er eyes lacked expression. They did not have the levels of interest that had always forced me to probe into Edith's eyes, no intense fires to feed on. . .Hers were toneless.'' Yet, Phyllisia is forced to acknowledge that ''everything about her, the pores of her brown skin, her carefully arranged hair, shouted good care.'' Here, Phyllisia's words hearken back to her earlier self-appraisal, when she notes her own good grooming. Clearly, Phyllisia values someone who mirrors her own image. Phyllisia also raises a perhaps more important issue: ''No one would ever dare question Marian as a choice for a friend.''

Of the Cathays, only Calvin questions Phyllisia's friendship with Edith, which comes to a head after Phyllisia brings Edith home for the first time, to meet her mother, who is ill with cancer. Both Ruby and Mrs. Cathay enjoy Edith's company and conversation. Unlike Phyllisia, they look beyond the surface. As Phyllisia acknowledges, upon meeting Edith, ''Ruby's pleasure seemed genuine. Perhaps she had not noticed Edith's clothes. . .It was as though I was the only one who noticed how untidy Edith was.'' Phyllisia is actually discontented to have Edith in her home, for she doesn't truly feel that Edith belongs in so ''elegant'' a place. She also resents Edith's ability to speak to adults in a ''calm, relaxed manner,'' an ability that she lacks. Phyllisia gets increasingly upset as she sees Edith being elevated and is forced to confront her own family's poverty in the West Indies. When Calvin comes home, he yells at seeing a ''picky-headed ragamuffin'' in his house, and Phyllisia does not defend her friend because she secretly believes his insults to be true.

After her mother's death, Phyllisia is forced to grow up quickly. Through a series of events, Phyllisia comes to the realization that she is like the father she claims to despise. ''I had wanted to be the unhappy princess living with the cruel king of a father,'' she realizes. ''I had wanted to be the daughter of the owner of a big restaurant. . .I had wanted to be rich, to live in luxury, so that I could feel superior to them—to people like Edith.'' With this mature comprehension, Phyllisia is able to renew her relationship with Edith and become a true friend, for the first time: ''Don't you ever say again you don't have anybody,'' she tells Edith. ''You have me. And you'll have me as long as I live.'' Her newfound maturity and compassion also gives her the strength to convince Calvin not to send Ruby and her back to the West Indies. In so doing, she makes the commitment to forming a true family, a commitment to openly communicating with her family as well as with herself. ''And Daddy,'' she says, ''I-I-I'm much older today than I was yesterday.'' With these words, Phyllisia signifies her transformation from a selfish girl to a caring and considerate young woman.

Source: Rena Korb, in an essay for *Literature of Developing Nations for Students*, Gale, 2000.

Karen D. Thompson

In the following essay, Thompson asserts that Guy's treatment of an adolescent friendship besieged by prejudice and violence rings true in almost every way, but not in its characterization of the protagonist, Phyllisia.

Rosa Guy's young adult novel *The Friends* begins with the same dark urgency as Richard Wright's *Native Son*. Within very few pages the reader learns that Phyllisia Cathay, a fourteen-year-old girl born in West India and recently moved to Harlem, is not only unaccepted but also persecuted by the other students in her classroom. She is ostracized because of her different physical features, accent, and intellect. Ironically, she is also rejected by the larger society in which she lives. The largely white, largely prejudiced society of the 1960s groups her with all other Harlem blacks and leaves her without a social circle. Further compounding Phyllisia's hardships is a seemingly tyrannical father, a mother too ill to provide much comfort, and a self-absorbed sister who, because she is willing to disguise her own intelligence and willing to modify her appearance to fit in with her peer group, offers no support.

Enter Edith Jackson, a young woman whose spirit and confidence seem unquenchable. Wiry and disheveled with holes in her stockings and her shoes worn down at the back, Edith Jackson commands the respect of the other students in Phyllisia's homeroom and effectively stops their mistreatment of Phyllisia, whom she has decided to befriend for no apparent reason. By the second chapter Phyllisia and Edith have cemented their friendship by running away from school together and spending the day sharing the simple pleasures of New York City including subway rides, refreshingly cool department stores, and Peter Paul Mounds chocolate bars.

From this point, a reader might expect the story to move along predictable lines and tell a tale of girlhood friendship. To her credit, Guy did not continue along a predictable path. Instead, she introduced a series of crises in Phyllisia's life and a corresponding series of crises in Edith's life that kept the two girls apart for much of the book and kept their friendship unsure at best.

Guy is a gifted writer. Her knowledge of her setting, her gift for description, and her characterization of some of the characters provide a readable, and at times compelling, book. However, because Guy is ultimately unconvincing in her characterization of Phyllisia, leaving readers with the impression that Phyllisia is not trustworthy (an absolutely necessary quality in friends), the story rings hollow at the end and leaves the reader with unfulfilled

> " To her credit, Guy did not continue along a predictable path. Instead, she introduced a series of crises in Phyllisia's life and a corresponding series of crises in Edith's life that kept the two girls apart for much of the book and kept their friendship unsure at best."

expectations, unanswered questions, and an uncertain feeling toward the protagonist.

Guy knows her setting well and presents the streets of Harlem with sensory details that bring the story immediately into focus. Phyllisia moves to Harlem in winter, and the cold reception she receives from her classmates mirrors the cold weather. Several classmates follow and bully her for blocks when she leaves school before ultimately surrendering to the cold. With relief Phyllisia watches them "hunch their shoulders up to their ears and go home." However, as winter passes and the weather heats up, so do the tempers of Phyllisia's classmates, and their anger breaks loose on the first hot day. Just before a throng of students attacks her, Phyllisia looks for help to the adults standing on stoops around the school and looking out the windows of adjacent buildings. The sense of crowding from the surrounding buildings is as palpable as the crowding of the mob. By the time Phyllisia escapes her attackers, dashes through street crossings, and hears "horns blowing, brakes screeching, blending with the jeers which seemed a very part of the air," the reader is running along with Phyllisia, dodging cars and jeers.

Guy is as effective at describing characters as she is at describing the setting. She introduces Edith in this way:

> Edith always came to school with her clothes unpressed, her stockings bagging about her legs with big holes, which she tried to hide by pulling them into her shoes but which kept slipping up, on each heel, to expose a round, brown circle of dry skin the size of a quarter.

Edith has a wiry body with a square little face and an impish grin that readers can see as clearly as if they had spied a picture of her peering out of a magazine or television screen.

Yet, it takes more than description to bring a character to life. Guy animates several of her characters effectively. Calvin, with his booming voice, is every bit as imposing in his personality as in his appearance. Broad gestures accompany his speeches, which may be accurately described as performances, and he speaks in short, effective phrases of the type used when issuing commands or running for elected office. The first time readers encounter him he has been drinking, and he is lively and uninhibited, basking in the approval of his friends, encouraged by the material goods he has provided for his family. When he cries pathetically to his wife that he only "tells the lies that I can make come true," he becomes totally human, therefore imperfect, but deserving of forgiveness.

Guy's gifts for description and animation should easily turn this into a memorable story, but sadly, her characterization completely fails with the protagonist, Phyllisia. Guy handles the physical description of Phyllisia well, which can be difficult to do with a first-person narrator. As her father praises Ruby and Ramona's beauty, Phyllisia reflects on her own physical self:

> I was plain and tall, too tall for fourteen years, and without any shape. At home it had not mattered. On The Island my Aunt loved me. She had promised that soon my breasts would begin to develop. She had promised too that one day my nose would stand up straight on my face and look like my mother's. But up to this time none of her predictions had come true. My nose still remained undefined. My chest was still flat. The only things constantly changing about me were my arms and legs, getting longer and skinnier with the years.

Later, in Chapter Nineteen, Phyllisia shares that her "breasts were fuller than Ruby's now, so were my legs and thighs. I had even grown an inch or two taller than she." These descriptions are important because so much of Phyllisia's self-image is tied to her appearance. A generous critic could assert that Phyllisia's absorption with personal cleanliness and neatness exists because she realizes that her inner self falls far short of such beauty. Such an interpretation might stir up sympathy for Phyllisia. But an average reader will have grown tired of Phyllisia's preoccupation with appearance and her unfair derision of Ruby's and Marian's appearance-consciousness. In the case of Ruby and Marian, readers can almost forgive them their pre-

occupation because they use style and appearance as means of entering and belonging to a group rather than as a way to exclude. Ruby does not shun Edith when Phyllisia brings her to the apartment, but Phyllisia bristles when Ruby reveals that on The Island, Phyllisia ran around without shoes. Phyllisia's anger is the result of her unacknowledged need to feel that she is better than Edith. In this scene as in many others, Phyllisia uses appearance to separate and disenfranchise people, most tragically Edith.

Phyllisia fails as a character for another reason. Though we are asked to believe that she has grown as a person by the end of the book, we have no reason to believe it. Time and time again Phyllisia makes promises that she does not keep and proclamations that lack conviction. She shuns Edith from the moment Edith offers her friendship, then desperately wants Edith to return to school and be her friend later the same day. After Edith subdues the entire class with her speech on Phyllisia's behalf, Phyllisia turns to Edith to thank her, but upon seeing Edith's shabby dress, her "feeling of gratefulness changed to one of annoyance. Did this mean then that I actually had to accept this girl's friendship? Why, she might even want to make it a habit of walking with me!" When Phyllisia and Edith run away from school together, Phyllisia thinks, as she rides the subway with Edith, that "I found that I was really having fun. I liked Edith. I really liked her." However, within a short time span, after Edith has shoplifted from a store counter, Phyllisia confesses silently, "my confidence came surging back and with it all of my former revulsion, my dislike for Edith." This pattern occurs over and over in the book until the reader cannot believe Phyllisia's statements, cannot forgive her treatment of Edith, and cannot like her character.

In the end we are asked to accept that Phyllisia has changed. We are given to believe that she has learned many lessons throughout the book and that she is now a better person and, most importantly, a true friend to Edith. A discerning reader cannot believe this because while Phyllisia asserts often that she has learned some important lesson, we do not see her understanding translate into action. Time and again in the story Phyllisia has revelations. These revelations often follow powerful events, yet readers do not see Phyllisia's revelations as a natural result of these events. Instead of working her way through conflicts or confusion, Phyllisia pushes ahead blindly until confronted by an epiphany or visited by a spirit; she suddenly "sees." Because she has not invested energy, emotion, or intellect in changing her behavior, change seldom occurs, and when it does, it is temporary. On page eight, Phyllisia has one of her revelations:

> I knew it suddenly. Standing in front of the room, her blond hair pulled back to emphasize the determination of her face, her body girdled to emphasize the determination of her spine, her eyes holding determinedly to anger, Miss Lass was afraid!! She was afraid and she was using me to keep the hatred of the children away from her. I was the natural choice because I was a stranger and because I was proud.

This insight comes to Phyllisia after Phyllisia has answered one of Miss Lass's questions, elaborated on her answer to dispel any thought that she might be guessing, then been praised by Miss Lass who says, "If some of you would follow Phyllisia's example and study your books, then perhaps the intelligence rate in this room might zoom up to zero." Readers are shocked by Phyllisia's epiphany because while we have witnessed the entire exchange, we could not possibly have reached Phyllisia's conclusion on our own because no evidence warrants it.

One of the most important scenes in the book happens in this same, miraculous way. Phyllisia is examining her feelings about Calvin, his restaurant, his sternness, and his pride:

> Then, just like that, it was clear. I had seen things the way I wanted them to be. I had wanted to be the unhappy princess living with the cruel king of a father. I had wanted to be the daughter of the owner of a big restaurant. Perhaps it was because the kids in school had been so hard on me. I didn't know. But I had wanted to be rich, to live in luxury, so that I could feel superior to them—to people like Edith. Calvin had never lied to me. I was the fraud.

Real people do not come to self-knowledge this suddenly or this completely. Self-knowledge comes one bit at a time like adding pieces to a jigsaw puzzle. If it does come suddenly and completely, it is usually years after the fact when the subconscious has been fashioning the puzzle all along. Phyllisia seems to receive bulletins from a supernatural source, but because she has not worked hard for them, readers do not want to credit her with perception or maturity.

In Guy's next novel, she made Edith Jackson the hero. Edith deserves to be one. She is honest, sincere, loving, and lovable. Beside her Phyllisia appears self-centered, affected, and dishonest. On only one occasion do readers find themselves in complete agreement with Phyllisia. When she is thinking about Calvin and how many people love him, Phyllisia thinks, "I would never understand what made some people love other people." Sadly, we share Phyllisia's bewilderment because we cannot understand why Edith, unselfish and unflinchingly honest, loves Phyllisia.

Source: Karen D. Thompson, in an essay for *Literature of Developing Nations for Students*, Gale, 2000.

Sources

Bachelder, Linda, and others, "Looking Backward: Trying to Find the Classic Young Adult Novel," in *English Journal*, Vol. 69, September, 1980, pp. 86-89.

Guy, Rosa, "Young Adult Books: I Am a Storyteller," in *Horn Book Magazine*, Vol. LXI, No. 2, March-April, 1985, pp. 220-21.

Hewitt, M. R., review, in *The Junior Bookshelf*, Vol. 38, No. 6, December, 1974, p. 378.

Norris, Jerrie, *Presenting Rosa Guy*, Twayne, 1988.

Review, in *Booklist*, Vol. 70, No. 10, January 15, 1974, p. 542.

Review, in *Kirkus Reviews*, Vol. XLI, No. 19, October 1, 1973, p. 1107.

Walker, Alice, "The Friends," in *New York Times Book Review*, November 4, 1973.

Further Reading

Guy, Rosa, "The Human Spirit," in *Caribbean Women Writers: Essays from the First International Conference*, edited by Selwyn R. Cudjoe, Calaloux, 1990.
Guy discusses her experiences as both an immigrant and a minority in America, focusing on the importance of the human spirit in survival.

Haynes, Elizabeth, "The Friends," in *Library Journal*, Vol. 98, November 15, 1973, p. 3464.
A positive review of the novel.

James, Winston, *Holding Aloft the Banner of Ethiopia: Caribbean Radicalism in Early Twentieth Century America*, Verso Books, 1998.
James's book provides an excellent background for understanding the experiences of Caribbean immigrants in America.

Johnson, Dianne, *Telling Tales: The Pedagogy and Promise of African American Literature for Youth*, Greenwood Press, 1990.
Johnson discusses themes in *The Friends*.

Livingston, James T., ed., *Caribbean Rhythms*, Washington Square Press, 1974.
The introduction traces the development of Caribbean

literature over the centuries, while the book itself provides several examples of a variety of types of writing.

Osa, Osayimwense, ed., *The All White World of Children's Books and African American Literature*, Africa World Press, 1995.

This work contains several excellent articles on books for black children.

Richardson, Judy, "Black Children's Books: An Overview," in *Journal of Negro Education*, Vol. 43, Summer, 1974, pp. 380-98.

Richardson traces the development of books written about black children through the decades, providing descriptions of excellent works including Guy's trilogy.

The Garden of Forking Paths

Jorge Luis Borges

1941

First published in 1941, ''The Garden of Forking Paths'' (''El jardin de senderos que se bifurcan'') marked a turning point in the literary career of Jorge Luis Borges. In fact, the story helped to establish his reputation as a fiction writer.

His fiction received immediate critical acclaim in Argentina, even though he failed to win an important prize the year of the book's release. Outraged, other Argentinean writers and critics devoted an entire issue of the prominent literary journal, *Sur*, to Borges and his work.

As in his other stories, Borges uses fiction as a vehicle to explore philosophical and literary issues. Consequently, the characters in his stories seem less developed. In ''The Garden of Forking Paths,'' he uses the genre of the detective story—a genre that requires clue-gathering and puzzle-solving—in order to explore the way time branches into an infinite number of futures.

Widely anthologized, ''The Garden of Forking Paths'' continues to generate interest among scholars and students. Its clever plot and sophisticated philosophical exploration of the nature of time inspires much critical commentary.

Author Biography

Jorge Luis Borges was one of the most important and influential writers of the twentieth century.

Born on August 24, 1899, in Buenos Aires, Argentina, Borges was a poet, an essayist, and a short story writer, and his career spanned six decades.

Borges was born into an old, wealthy Argentinean family. He learned both English and Spanish as a child and later studied French, German, Latin, and Old English. His early fascination with language and words became a defining characteristic of his later work. His family traveled extensively when he was a boy.

The Borges family lived in Geneva, Switzerland, during World War I. During this time, Jorge attended college in Geneva and earned his degree in 1918. When the war ended, the Borges family resumed their tour of Europe, spending the next three years in Spain. It was during this period that Borges began to write poetry and became acquainted with a group of young avant-garde Spanish poets known as the "Ultraistas."

In 1921 the Borges family returned to Buenos Aires. Jorge published his first book, *Fervor de Buenos Aires,* in 1923. This first publication was followed by two more books of poetry. In addition, he also published three books of essays between 1925 and 1927. These works served to establish him as a leading literary voice of Argentina.

In 1938 the death of his father and subsequent financial difficulties forced Borges into accepting a position as a municipal librarian. In the same year, he suffered a serious head injury. Some biographers suggest a link between the fall and his turn toward prose fiction in the following years. Between 1938 and 1954 he wrote several stories that elevated him to the pinnacle of Argentinean literary life. Moreover, as his stories were translated into other languages he became a writer of international reputation.

Borges' first major collection of short stories, *El jardin de senderos que se bifurcan* (*The Garden of Forking Paths*) was published in 1941 and included the title story, "The Garden of Forking Paths." These stories were later collected in *Ficciones (1935-1944),* published in 1944. This volume was translated into English in 1962.

Although Borges' stories garnered critical acclaim, the jury charged with selecting the 1941 National Literary Prize did not choose *The Garden of Forking Paths* as the recipient of the award. Many Argentinean writers and critics were outraged, and they subsequently dedicated an entire issue of *Sur,* an important literary magazine, to a consideration of his work.

Borges continued to write poetry, short stories, and essays despite the blindness that plagued him during his final twenty-five years. Although Borges published little new work after 1977, he remained actively involved in literary life until his death in Geneva, Switzerland, in 1986.

Plot Summary

The story opens with a brief passage from a history of World War I, presented by an unnamed narrator. The narrator refers to a statement by a character, Dr. Yu Tsun, made during World War I. The narrator suggests the first passage is connected to Yu Tsun's statement.

Dr. Yu Tsun, a Chinese national and a former professor of English, reveals in his statement that he is a German spy. He recounts the events leading to his arrest, beginning with when he discovers that his contact has been killed. He knows he must devise a way to get an important message to the Germans. He looks in a telephone book and finds the name of a man, Stephen Albert. Yu Tsun thinks Albert will be able to help, although he does not reveal how he knows this.

Yu Tsun then recounts how he travels to Dr. Albert's house, pursued by Captain Richard Madden, an Irishman in service to the English. When Yu Tsun arrives, Dr. Albert mistakes him for a Chinese consul that he knows; Dr. Albert assumes that the Chinese man is there to view his garden. Yu Tsun discovers that Dr. Albert is a sinologist, which is a scholar who studies Chinese culture.

By a strange coincidence, Dr. Albert has created a garden identical to one created by Yu Tsun's ancestor, Ts'ui Pen, a writer who worked for thirteen years on a novel called *The Garden of Forking Paths*; he also was working on a labyrinth before being murdered by a stranger. In addition to recreating Ts'ui Pen's garden, Dr. Albert further reveals that he has been studying the novel. Dr. Albert tells Yu Tsun that he has solved the riddle of the lost labyrinth, arguing that the novel itself is the labyrinth.

Furthermore, Dr. Albert tells Yu Tsun that the *The Garden of Forking Paths* is "an enormous riddle, or parable, whose theme is time." Albert explains that the novel reveals that time is not singular, but rather a "dizzying net of divergent, convergent, and parallel times." Like the labyrinth, each turn leads to different possible futures. Dr. Albert shows Yu Tsun a letter written by his ancestor that says, "I leave to the various futures (not to all) my garden of forking paths." This letter has provided the key Dr. Albert needs to make sense of both the novel and the missing labyrinth, that the "forking" referred to by Ts'ui Pen is not a forking of space, but a forking of time.

Yu Tsun experiences for a moment a sense of himself and Albert in many other times. Suddenly, he sees Madden approaching. Yu Tsun asks Albert to let him see once again the letter written by his ancestor. When Albert's back is turned, Yu Tsun shoots and kills him.

In the last paragraph of his statement (and the story), Yu Tsun is awaiting his death on the gallows as punishment for his crime. He reveals that he has shot Albert in order to send a message to the Germans. The name of the town the Germans needed to bomb was Albert. By shooting a man of the same name without apparent motive, Yu Tsun was sure that the information would appear in newspapers the Germans would read. Because the city was bombed the day before Yu Tsun makes his statement, he knows that his message had been received.

Jorge Luis Borges

Characters

Stephen Albert

Dr. Stephen Albert is a noted sinologist, or student of Chinese language and culture. A former missionary in China, he is a student of the works of Yu Tsun's ancestor. Indeed, he has solved the mystery of the missing labyrinth, revealing that the novel of Ts'ui Pen is the labyrinth itself.

Through Albert, Borges offers a philosophical discussion of the nature of time. Albert's role in the story is to explain Ts'ui Pen to his great-grandson— and to be murdered, simply by the coincidence that his name is identical to the name of a town in Belgium.

Richard Madden

Captain Richard Madden is an Irishman who works for English intelligence. After he kills Yu Tsun's contact, Viktor Runeberg, he stalks Yu Tsun to prevent him from passing along the information. Yu Tsun characterizes Madden as "a man accused

of laxity and perhaps of treason." Madden tracks Yu Tsun to Albert's house, and arrests him for the murder.

Narrator

The narrator's words open the story, directing the reader to a particular page in a history of World War I. The narrator then introduces the statement made by a Dr. Yu Tsun.

Yu Tsun

Dr. Yu Tsun is a Chinese professor living in England during World War I. He is also a German spy. Yu Tsun takes on the role of narrator of the story as the original narrator provides Yu Tsun's statement to the reader.

The document is a statement made by Yu Tsun after his murder of Dr. Stephen Albert. Yu Tsun, in order to get vital information to the Germans after his contact is killed, describes how he devises a plan to relay the site of the British artillery park in Belgium.

Yu Tsun is a contradictory character; although he is Chinese, he teaches English. Although he does not like the Germans, he works for them as a spy. Yu Tsun is also the great-grandson of a Chinese writer,

Media Adaptations

- "The Garden of Forking Paths" was recorded on an audiocassette collection of Borges' stories titled *Selected Fictions*. The recording was made in 1998 by Penguin Audio Books, and is six hours long on four cassettes. Andrew Hurley and George Guidall read the stories.

Ts'ui Pen, whose goal it was to write a huge novel and a build a great labyrinth. Yu Tsun visits Dr. Stephen Albert for the sole purpose of murdering him so that his name will appear in the newspaper and reveal to the Germans the name of the city Albert.

He discovers that Dr. Albert has studied the work of Ts'ui Pen and understands it. Nevertheless, he carries through with his plan to murder Dr. Albert, thus revealing to the Germans the information they need to bomb the English artillery.

Themes

Time

Dr. Stephen Albert tells Yu Tsun, "*The Garden of Forking Paths* is an enormous riddle, or parable, whose theme is time. . . ." Likewise, Borges seems to be implying that the major theme of the short story "The Garden of Forking Paths" is also time. Yu Tsun reflects early in the story, "everything happens to a man precisely *now*. Centuries of centuries and only in the present do things happen. . . ."

With this, Yu Tsun describes time in a linear manner. That is, humans experience time as a series of present moments, one following the other. As soon as the moment is experienced, however, it no longer exists. On account of this, the past is no more real than the future. Both exist nowhere but in the human mind: the past belongs to the realm of memory, while the future belongs to the realm of imagination.

When Yu Tsun arrives at the home of Albert, however, the notion of time as linear is challenged. Albert argues Yu Tsun's ancestor "did not believe in a uniform, absolute time. He believed in an infinite series of times, in a growing, dizzying net of divergent, convergent, and parallel times." In this construction of time, all presents, pasts, and futures exist simultaneously. Further, each decision a person makes leads to different future. The branching, or forking, of all these decisions suggests that time is not a line, but rather is a web or a network of possibilities. The image of the labyrinth, thought of as a forking of time, rather than space, is the clue that Albert needs to rethink the concept of time.

For a moment, Yu Tsun experiences time as Albert describes it: "It seemed to me that the humid garden that surrounded the house was infinitely saturated with invisible persons. Those persons were Albert and I, secret, busy, and multiform in other dimensions of time." The appearance of Madden, however, pulls Yu Tsun into the future he chose when he got on the train. In this moment, in *this* present, Yu Tsun murders Dr. Albert.

Order and Disorder

In addition to the consideration of time in "The Garden of Forking Paths," Borges also seems to be exploring the concepts of order and disorder. Indeed, Thomas P. Weissert argues that the subject of the story is "chaos and order." Within the short story there exists a novel by Yu Tsun's ancestor. The novel is described variously as "incoherent," "chaotic," "an indeterminate heap of contradictory drafts," and "confused." In short, the novel appears to represent the very essence of disorder.

However, Albert believes that he has solved the mystery of the lost labyrinth and the chaotic novel. He argues that if one assumes that the novel itself is the labyrinth, and is the author's attempt to represent the webbing nature of time, the novel is not an example of chaos, but of order. Furthermore, Albert works to create order out of the disorder of the novel. He says, "I have compared hundreds of manuscripts, I have corrected the errors that the negligence of the copyists has introduced, I have guessed the plan of this chaos, I have re-established . . . the primordial organization."

In other words, Albert acts as an ideal reader of this text, imposing form and structure to what might otherwise be seen as nonsense. Like a labyrinth, which only *seems* chaotic to someone who does not hold the key to its solution, the novel itself becomes, in Weissert's words, "an ordered maze" once Albert discovers the key.

Borges seems to be implying that while the universe may appear to be chaotic and disordered, the chaos itself may represent an order-as-yet-not-understood. Certainly, the tension between Yu Tsun's reading of his ancestor's text as incoherent and Albert's reading of the same text as ordered parallels the human experience of trying to render meaningful the apparently random events of life.

Style

Narrator and Narration

One of the most interesting tricks Borges plays in "The Garden of Forking Paths" is his narrative technique. As the story opens, an unknown narrator speaks directly to the reader: "On page 22 of Liddell Hart's *History of World War I* you will read. . . ." The narrator summarizes Hart's position that rain delayed a British attack.

In the second paragraph, the narrator suggests that rain may not have been the reason for the delay. He offers as evidence a statement from a Dr. Yu Tsun, but the first two pages of the document are missing. Consequently, the narrator throws the reader into the statement mid-sentence. The effect of this is to disconcert readers momentarily as they try to piece together the missing portion of the text and to absorb the sudden introduction of a new narrator. Interestingly, although it appears that the original narrator drops completely out of the story after introducing the statement, there is one further intrusion by the original narrator in the form of a footnote.

The footnote serves several purposes in the narration. In the first place, footnotes are generally found only in scholarly works, not short fictions. Consequently, the appearance of the footnote seems to suggest that Borges wants to place the story within a certain genre of work—a nonfiction report. In the second place, the inclusion of the footnote suggests that Yu Tsun's account of his murder of Dr. Albert may not be entirely trustworthy.

Although Yu Tsun says that Viktor Runeberg has been murdered by Richard Madden, the narrator in the footnote calls this "an hypothesis both hateful and odd." The narrator offers another point of view: Richard Madden acted in self-defense. This defense of Madden causes readers to wonder if the narrator and Madden might not be one and the same. At the

very least, it casts serious doubt in the minds of readers over the missing two pages of the document. What else has the narrator chosen to hide from readers?

Although superficially the footnote helps to preserve the fiction that this is a factual report, its presence offers yet another troubling detail for the reader to absorb: throughout Yu Tsun's long statement, there is a narrator standing behind him, ready to edit or excise or add bits of text. Furthermore, by calling attention to the narrator that stands outside the margin of the story, Borges also calls attention to himself as the writer. The writer stands behind the narrator, manipulating and formulating plot, character, and setting. Thus, through the use of the narration inside the narration and the footnote inside the inner narration, Borges confuses the fiction of his story. He makes it simultaneously more and less "real" by his inclusion of the footnote.

Detective Story

Critics often refer to "The Garden of Forking Paths" as a detective story. The genre was invented by Edgar Allan Poe in the 1840s. In detective stories, details are very important. A writer of a detective story is obligated to follow certain rules and conventions, including the inclusion of clues and details that will allow the reader to solve the mystery at just the same moment the detective does. Sometimes, the resolution of a detective story requires some small bit of information that the writer withholds from the reader until the very last moment.

Certainly Borges follows the conventions. His protagonist, Yu Tsun, is a spy. He has a secret he must transmit. He has limited time. He offers clues to the reader without revealing the final secret. Borges even places another mystery within the framework of Yu Tsun's mystery. That is, he offers readers the mystery of Yu Tsun's ancestor and his labyrinth, a mystery that Dr. Albert solves.

However, although "The Garden of Forking Paths" fills the conventions of the detective story, it only resembles a detective story in structure. In reality, the story is more of a philosophical treatise, masquerading as a detective story. Yet even here, Borges plays games with his reader. Because the story is not only about time and mystery, but also about the making of fiction, it seems as if Borges is questioning the rules of fiction.

Consequently, the reader is left wondering: is this a detective story that appears to be about philosophy, or is this a philosophical treatise that resembles a detective story?

Literary Heritage

The literary heritage of Borges' fiction can be understood in the broader context of Latin-American literature, and more specifically, Argentine literature. Before conquest and colonization by European forces the native Indian cultures of Latin-America had a well-developed tradition of written and oral literature. Latin-American literature since colonization emerged from the narratives of the conquered native Indian peoples as well as the European conquerors themselves. Later, the literature sprang from the Native Indian's struggles against colonial domination, which became known as a "literature of oppression." Latin-American literature in the latter half of the twentieth century developed a concern with literary and linguistic form, as exemplified by the experimental short stories of Borges, first published in the late 1940s. Borges also imported the avant-garde poetic movement of "Ultraism" (*Ultraismo*, named for the literary journal *Ultra*, to which he was a regular contributor) from Spain to Buenos Aires, Argentina, in 1921. Although Borges later moved away from Ultraist principles, revising much of this early poetry, his influence upon other Argentine and Latin-American writers remained significant.

Historical Context

Buenos Aires and Europe

In 1816 Buenos Aires gained independence from Spanish colonial rule. Argentina was becoming a wealthy country, most notably for its beef, wheat, and wool. In spite of their growing wealth, many of the old families of Argentina, including the Borges family, looked to Europe for culture and education.

Consequently, the Borges family left for an extended vacation in Europe in 1916. After World War I broke out, the Borges family chose to stay in Geneva, Switzerland, for the next four years. Consequently, the historical and cultural milieu that shaped Borges during this period was not Argentinean at all, but continental.

While in Switzerland, Borges discovered a number of influential writers: Chesterton, Schopenhauer, Nietzsche, and Kafka. Although the war raged across Europe during this time, it seems to have had little effect on Borges or his work.

With World War I new forms of literature and art emerged throughout Europe. T. S. Eliot, Ezra Pound, Miguel de Unamuno, James Joyce, and Luigi Pirandello, among many others, published a new kind of literature that was classified as Modernist literature. Experimental art also flourished in the form of Dada and Surrealism. As Borges continued his travels across Europe in the years after the war, he found himself surrounded by new thinking and new ideas.

The Borges family returned to Argentina in 1921. During the 1920s, Argentina flourished; both mining and oil exploration were well under way, and Buenos Aires even had a subway system for the city. At the same time that Argentineans embraced all things modern, they also rediscovered the traditional Argentine dance form of the tango.

While the economy was healthy, the Radical party government of Hipólito Irigoyen maintained power through the 1920s. However, the economy crashed in 1930 and Argentina slumped into depression. A military-Conservative coalition came to power and continued to rule throughout the period.

Borges continued to publish short stories throughout the 1940s. Politically, a new power began to take shape in Argentina. Juan Perón was elected president, and effectively became dictator of Argentina. Just before Perón was elected, Borges had signed a petition protesting fascism and military rule. Consequently, Perón fired him as a city librarian. He also offered Borges a post as a poultry inspector in order to embarrass him. Borges, in an uncharacteristically political gesture, denounced dictatorships at a banquet given in his honor. The Perón years were difficult ones for Borges as well as for Argentina.

Some critics have suggested that the fantastic and imaginative prose that Borges produced during the years of World War II and the Perón years was in response to the grim realities and horrors of daily life. Still others believe that he was a man ahead of his time, prefiguring many of the concerns of Postmodernism some thirty years early. Whether he

Compare & Contrast

- **1940s:** World War II rages all over Europe as England, France, and the Allied Powers fight Hitler's Nazi regime. When Japan bombs Pearl Harbor on December 7, 1941, the United States enters the war on the side of the Allies.

  Today: Although the decade is free of large-scale war, several regional conflicts threaten pose threats to world peace. Problems in the Middle East, in Africa, and in the Balkans force the United Nations to send troops around the world.

- **1940s:** In Argentina, Juan Perón is elected to the presidency, but quickly becomes a dictator with the support of the military.

  Today: After decades of repression—particularly of the press and intellectuals—Argentina moves toward a more open government with the return of a civilian government in the 1980s. The government puts forth a concerted effort to find the bodies of people who "disappeared" during the 1970s.

- **1940s:** Building on the work of Albert Einstein and others, scientists build a cyclotron, which leads to the creation of the atomic bomb. Einstein's theory of relativity continues to be hotly debated, and Newtonian physics is displaced by quantum mechanics.

  Today: Unified field theories, chaos theories, and nonlinear dynamics occupy mathematicians and physicists attempting to explain the nature of the universe.

- **1940s:** Science fiction and fantasy literature become popular genres, particularly in North America. Pulp magazines such as John W. Campbell's *Astounding Science Fiction* flourish.

  Today: Science fiction and fantasy continue to generate wide readership. In addition, films such as the *Star Wars* and *Star Trek* series attract large audiences.

- **1940s:** Philosophical existentialism, developed in the works of writers like Jean-Paul Sartre, Albert Camus, and Franz Kafka, becomes an important movement. Existentialists believe that existence is of the greatest importance; however, an individual's understanding of him or herself as alone in the universe results in a sense of meaninglessness, alienation, and anxiety.

  1990s: Postmodern philosophers such as Jacques Derrida and Michel Foucault move away from the consideration of the individual human being. Derrida "deconstructs" language, demonstrating that the meaning of words and texts is not stable. Foucault examines texts as cultural artifacts—that is, as products of a given culture at a given time.

---

was a man of his times, or a man ahead of his time, Borges is considered an innovative and evocative author.

Critical Overview

When Borges' collection of short stories *The Garden of Forking Paths* initially appeared in Argentina in 1941, reviewers were quick to recognize something new. Most critical commentary had concentrated on his poetry, although in 1933, a special issue of the magazine *Megafono* devoted to a discussion of him reveals that critics had begun to treat him as a writer of prose as well.

The rejection of *The Garden of Forking Paths* for the 1941 National Literary Prize did much to solidify support for his work among the literary intelligentsia of Argentina, who were outraged at the oversight. Nevertheless, even among those crit-

Buenos Aires, Argentina, the capital of Spanish American Cosmopolitanism, a literary and artistic movement championed by Borges.

ics who felt he should have received the award, there was some reservation. Most commonly, these reservations focused on his cerebral style and his esoteric subject matter.

Other critics, however, found Borges' work to be important and original. In his book *Jorge Luis Borges*, Martin Stabb cites, for instance, Pedro Henriquez Urena's famous comment: "There may be those who think that Borges is original because he proposes to be. I think quite the contrary: Borges would be original even when he might propose not to be."

In the early 1940s the translation of his work into English began in literary magazines, although it was not until the early 1960s that whole collections were translated and published. However, the work made an immediate impact. John Updike presented an important survey of his work in the *New Yorker* in 1965, a review in which he noted his fascination with calling attention to a work of literature *as* a work of literature.

Another seminal article on Borges by the novelist John Barth appeared in the *Atlantic Monthly* in 1967. In the article, Barth discussed the literature of the 1960s, placing Borges at the center of such literature. In addition, Barth paid careful attention to his use of the labyrinth as image in his work.

In the years since its initial publication and subsequent translation into English, Borges' work in general and ''The Garden of Forking Paths'' in particular have continued to inspire critical attention. Many commentators point to the influence he has had on a whole generation of South and North American writers, including Gabriel Garcia-Marquez and John Barth, among others. Moreover, as Roberto Gonzalez-Echevarria points out in the essay ''Borges and Derrida,'' Borges has exerted considerable influence on the postmodern philosophers Jacques Derrida, Michel Foucault, and Roland Barthes.

Other critics attempt to trace the influences on Borges' work. Andre Maurois, in a preface to Donald A. Yates and James E. Irby's edition of *Labyrinths*, directly addresses his sources. He cites H. G. Wells, Edgar Allan Poe, G. K. Chesterton, and Franz Kafka as important influences on Borges' writing. Borges himself noted in several places the debt he owed to Chesterton, Robert Louis Stevenson, and Rudyard Kipling.

As James Woodall indicates in *The Man in the Mirror of the Book*, ''Chesterton's compact, witty-short-story style was to have a lasting influence on the way Borges structured his stories over twenty years later.'' Kafka's influence seems also clear to many critics; Borges was largely responsible for introducing Kafka into Argentina through his translations of the Czech writer. Indeed, the image of the labyrinth is important both in Kafka as well as Borges.

Borges' choice of detective fiction as his favorite genre recalls both the stories of Poe and Chesterton's Father Brown mysteries. A number of critics have concentrated on this connection. John Irwin, for example, examines his construction of an analytic detective story in his article, ''A Clew to a Clue: Locked Rooms and Labyrinths in Poe and Borges.'' In so doing, he also suggests that Borges associates the word ''clue'' with the word ''thread,'' and in so doing, makes an allusion to the story of Theseus and the Minotaur in the labyrinth.

In other critical essays, scholars contend that Borges' early prose is essentially nihilistic. In other words, he denies any ground of objective truth in his stories. John Fraser examines the stories of *Ficciones*, including ''The Garden of Forking Paths,'' maintaining that Borges both creates the threat of nihil-

ism in the character of Pierre Menard in an early story, ''Pierre Menard, Author of *Don Quixote*,'' and overcomes it through ''his concern to connect rather than disjoin values, fictions, and action. . . .''

A number of commentators have explored the metafictional nature of the story. That is, they interpret ''The Garden of Forking Paths'' to be a story about stories, a fiction about the writing of fiction. In her *Jorge Luis Borges: A Study of the Short Fiction*, Naomi Lindstrom, for example, argues that the ''spy plot is tangled with a second narrative concerning the reading and appreciation of literature.''

Didier T. Jaen offers a book-length study of metafiction in Borges, *Borges' Esoteric Library: Metaphysics to Metafiction*. In this book, Jaen asserts that using a ''first-person impersonal narrator is one of the most characteristic metafictional devices used by Borges.''

Finally, several recent critics view Borges as a writer who, years before the Postmodern era, prefigures both Postmodernism and chaos theory. Thomas P. Weissert, for example, in *Chaos and Disorder: Complex Dynamics in Literature and Science*, argues that ''Jorge Luis Borges discovered the essence of bifurcation theory thirty years before chaos scientists mathematically formalized it.''

Because Borges created a large body of highly esoteric, allusive prose, as well as poetry, it is likely that critical attention will continue to focus on his work. Although it is sometimes difficult for readers to grasp, his fiction, essays, and poetry offer great rewards for interested scholars and readers.

Criticism

Liz Brent

Brent has a Ph.D. in American culture, with a specialization in film studies, from the University of Michigan. She is a freelance writer and teaches courses in the history of American cinema. In the following essay, Brent discusses narration in Borges' story ''The Garden of Forking Paths.''

Critics have noted that Borges often incorporates elements of nonfictional narrative genres into his fictional short stories. Borges also often composes his stories from fragmentary pieces of documentary-style narrative. In so doing, Borges created his own distinctive style of short story in which the

What Do I Read Next?

- *Detective Fiction,* (1996) edited by James Robert Smith, offers a collection of classic detective stories, including Edgar Allan Poe's "The Murders at the Rue Morgue" and "The Purloined Letter." The collection offers students a good opportunity to examine the genre closely.

- Edited by Raymond Tostevin Bond, *The Man Who Was Chesteron: The Best Essays, Stories, Poems, and Other Writings of G.K. Chesterton* (1945) provides a glimpse into the man who influenced Borges.

- *Borges: A Life* (1998), written by James Woodall, has been called by the *The New York Times Book Review* the best general biography of Borges available today. The writing is accessible and well-researched.

- David Van Leer's edition of Edgar Allan Poe's *Selected Tales* (1998) also provides a good selection of mysteries from the master, including his famous detective stories.

- Borges' *Labyrinths* (1962), edited by Donald A. Yates and James E. Irby, is an excellent translation of a collection of Borges' work. For the student interested in reading more of Borges' fantastic fictions, this is a good choice.

---

conventions of fictional storytelling are integrated with elements of factual (or, more often, pseudo-factual) reportage. Borges thereby addresses the self-referential theme of the nature of authorship and questionable nature of "facts" and truth in the telling of stories.

Borges' short story "The Garden of Forking Paths" is presented as a compilation from fragments of fictionalized written documents presented as factual. The first two paragraphs introduce the body of the story, which is composed of an archived "statement," which has been "dictated, reread and signed" by one Dr. Yu Tsun. The introductory paragraphs are thus presented as an excerpt from what the reader can conjecture is a published book of historical scholarship, probably regarding the history of World War I. The presentation of this short story as historical "document" is further developed through reference to previous history books written on the same topic. Thus, Borges' story begins, "On page 22 of Liddell Hart's *History of World War I,* you will read that . . ." This opening introduces themes central to the story's concern with the nature of narrative. The reader is immediately and directed addressed as "you," and specifically as a reader. This highlights the preoccupation of the story with the nature of reading, and

the reader's relationship to the author, as well as the text itself. Further, the theme of fragmentary evidence is central to Borges' presentation of various "documents" which comprise the story. The abruptness of such an opening to a short story creates the effect on the reader of having entered this chapter of a history book somewhere in the middle of a broader discussion. This creates the impression of having been presented with a fragmentary piece of a larger historical narrative.

In addition, although it is not immediately clear to the reader, one can assume that Borges has invented this fictional historian (Liddell Hart) as well as the history book he is purported to have written. Borges thus creates an artificial universe of inter-textual references—meaning that he refers the reader to texts, or books, outside the scope of the story, which in fact do not exist. Yet, in the context of this fictionalized scholarly discourse, Borges focuses on various pieces of information specifically associated with factual evidence—namely, dates, times, precise numbers, and exact geographical locations. As is stated in the opening sentence, "you will read" in Hart's *History of World War I* that "an attack against the Serre-Montauban line by thirteen British divisions (supported by 1,400 artillery pieces), planned for the 24th of July, 1916, had to be postponed until the morning of the 29th.'' However, while focusing on reported ''facts,'' Borges also composes his story of, not just fragmentary documents, but such questionable conclusions as scholarly commentary, conjecture, theory, and hearsay. For instance, the reader is told that the historian Hart ''comments'' that ''the torrential rains. . .caused this delay. . .'' The word ''comments'' alerts the reader to the possibility that the conjecture of one historian may not necessarily be a historical fact. The reader is then presented with a further piece of documentary evidence which ''throws an unsuspected light over the whole affair.'' The narrator's preoccupation with legitimate, valid, and accurate documentation is indicated by the assurance that ''the following statement'' has been ''dictated, reread and signed by Dr. Yu Tsun.'' The fragmentary nature of such documentary evidence, however, is indicated by the statement that, ''The first two pages of the document are missing.'' Later, within this document, an ellipsis (''. . .'') silently indicates that, not only are the first two pages of the document missing, but that the reader is presented with only a fragment of what is left of the document. It is not indicated whether or not the ''editor'' has presented only the parts of the document he deems relevant, or if perhaps the government which holds the document has seen fit to keep certain parts of it classified, containing sensitive information not to be made available to the public. Either way, it is further indicated to the reader through use of the ellipsis that he or she is given access to only a fragment of the document. Thus, the reader is in effect positioned vis à vis the text (Borges' story) as having begun reading in the middle of a chapter of a history book which begins by referring to a fictionalized previous history book, and which presents an excerpt from a statement beginning on page three. Already, then, the fragmentary nature of the documentation presented to the reader has been indicated at two levels: it is a fragment of a history book which presents a fragment of a historical document.

To further the narrative format of a published piece of historical scholarship, Borges has added a footnote to the fragmentary document. Footnotes are traditionally associated with scholarship and not with literary fiction. The inclusion of a footnote emphasizes the author's attempt to present his fictional story in a format similar to that of a factual narrative. The footnote is credited as an ''(Editor's note).'' This creates yet another level of extratextual discourse to the story. The ''Editor'' is a fictionalized character who enters the text in the service of correcting the ''document'' which makes up the central text of the story with a factual statement. A footnote also conventionally connotes authoritative commentary on the main body of a text. The reader is thus positioned between what may be termed two ''competing discourses''—that is, within Borges' story itself, the reader is invited to make distinctions between ''true'' and ''false'' statements about the fictional events of the story. Furthermore, the footnote explains that the ''Prussian spy Hans Rabener'' went by the ''alias'' of Viktor Runeberg. Again, the fictional ''editor'' of the document invites the reader to question the validity of the ''statement,'' as already a character has been referred to by a false name. The reader is thus positioned on shaky ground in terms of her or his ability to sort out ''fact'' from ''fiction'' within the universe of this fictional story.

Borges' narrative structure, involving fictionalized inter-textual references (references to documents and books existing outside of the story itself), continues throughout the story. Within the main body of the story, the narrator of the fragmentary document, Tsun, makes reference to, and draws his own information from, the sources of various authoritative texts external to the story, as well as fragments of texts. He imagines the Chief in Germany, ''examining newspapers'' for a communication from his spies in England. In examining his own pockets, Tsun finds ''a notebook,'' and a letter. In order to find someone by the name of ''Albert,'' Tsun consults a telephone book. On the train, Tsun notices ''a young boy who was reading with fervor the *Annals of Tacitus*'' In the library of Stephen Albert he sees ''several volumes of the Lost Encyclopedia, edited by the Third Emperor of the Luminous Dynasty but never printed.'' In addition to fictionalized extra-textual references, Borges makes reference to several actual authors, philosophers and works of literature which exist in reality outside of the story itself. Tsun refers to Stephen Albert as a man ''no less great than Goethe,'' and concludes that, from his perspective, the man ''was Goethe.'' Goethe is Germany's preeminent classic poet and playwright, akin in literary status and national pride in Germany to Shakespeare in England.

The layering of fragmentary documents which make up the story culminates in the discussion between Tsun and Albert of the ''chaotic manuscripts'' of Ts'ui Pen. Albert, who is a Sinologist (scholar of Chinese history) explains to Tsun, who is a descendent of Ts'ui Pen, his research on these manuscripts. Tsun explains that, from his perspective, the publication of the manuscripts was "senseless" because of their fragmentary and nonsensical nature: "The book is an indeterminate heap of contradictory drafts." As evidence of his theory about the manuscripts, Albert presents Tsun with a "fragment of a letter" from Ts'ui Pen. The multiplication of fragmentary manuscripts, which puts into question the validity of any one, is indicated by Albert's assertion that "I have compared hundreds of manuscripts, I have corrected the errors that the negligence of the copyists has introduced."

Albert, in explaining to Tsun his speculations about the meaning of the fictional novel by the fictionalized character Ts'ui Pen, refers to the character and narrator Scheherazade of the ancient stories of the *Thousand and One Nights*, which is in reality a classic piece of literature. In this ancient story, also called *The Arabian Nights*, the character Scheherazade tells a king a series of tales every night in order to delay his decision to kill her. The reference to Scheherazade in Borges' story points again to his interest in the nature of storytelling and authorship. Just as "The Garden of Forking Paths" includes a narrative embedded within a narrative-the story told by Tsun as embedded in the "frame narrative" of the fictionalized scholarly text—so the *Thousand and One Nights* is characterized by the series of stories told by Scheherazade within the frame narrative of the story of Scheherazade herself. Borges' reference to the *Thousand and One Nights* is also significant to the concerns of his own story in that it is in effect a compilation of ancient folk tales from Eastern and Middle Eastern cultures, which were collected, translated, and retranslated by a series of authors over a thousand years, dating back to the ninth century. This reference is suited to Borges' theme of the fragmentary and debatable nature of the "documents" which make up any narrative. In fact, discussion of the scholarly evidence on the *Thousand and One Nights* in the *Encyclopaedia Britannica* sounds very similar to the encyclopedic tone of Borges' fictional story:

> Though the names of its chief characters are Iranian, the frame story is probably Indian, and the largest proportion of names is Arabic. The tales' variety and geographical range of origin—India, Iran, Iraq, Egypt, Turkey, and possibly Greece—make single authorship unlikely; this view is supported by internal evidence—the style, mainly unstudied and unaffected, contains colloquialisms and even grammatical errors such as no professional Arabic writers would allow.

In discussing the *Thousand and One Nights*, Albert refers to the fragmentary and debatable ori-

gin of this real piece of literature. Again, the *Encyclopedia Britannica* sums up scholarship on the origins of this ancient text in a tone which matches that of Borges in describing the scholarship of his fictional ancient "manuscript."

> By the twentieth century, Western scholars agreed that the Nights is a composite work consisting of popular stories originally transmitted orally and developed during several centuries, with material added somewhat haphazardly at different periods and places. Several layers in the work . . . were distinguished by 1887. . . . By the mid-20th century six successive forms had been identified: two 18th-century Arabic translations of the Persian . . . ; a 9th-century version . . . ; the 10th-century work . . . ; a 12th-century collection, including Egyptian tales; and the final version, extending to the 16th century and consisting of the earlier material with the addition of stories of the Islamic counter-crusades and Oriental tales brought to the Middle East by the Mongols.

Furthermore, the *Thousand and One Nights* was first translated into a European language (French) in 1717; but many different versions and translations were produced over the following centuries, each drawing from different sources and versions of the text. The standard English translation to date is that by Richard Burton in 1885. In Borges' fictional story, Albert explains a point of repetition in the *Thousand and One Nights*, which he attributes to "a magical oversight of the copyist." Like the *Thousand and One Nights*, Borges' story is composed of the multiple authorship of a layering of fragmentary "documents," any one of which is of questionable validity.

Source: Liz Brent, in an essay for *Literature of Developing Nations for Students*, Gale, 2000.

Diane Andrews Henningfeld

Henningfeld is an associate professor at Adrian College who writes widely on literature for educational publishers. In the following essay, she discusses Borges's use of metafiction in "The Garden of Forking Paths."

Before the publication of his first collection of short stories, *El jardin de senderos que se bifurcan* [*The Garden of Forking Paths*] in 1941, Argentine readers knew Jorge Luis Borges as a writer of poetry and essays.

The publication of his first short stories, however, marked a shift in his reputation. Soon, Borges would achieve an international reputation because of his short stories. By the late twentieth century, critics and scholars listed Borges as one of the most important writers of the century.

Although Borges is widely considered an important writer, not all critics appreciate his work—particularly his short stories. There are those who find his work overly cerebral and erudite, too filled with esoteric allusions and philosophical argument to qualify as literature at all. On the other hand, there are those such as Martin Staab who admire his "literary gamesmanship . . . playful philosophizing. . . linguistic dabbling and . . . urbane humour." It seems that with Borges, readers feel strongly one way or another.

"The Garden of Forking Paths," first published in 1941 in the collection of the same name, is a typically Borgesian story, if there is such a thing. James Woodall, in his book *The Man in the Mirror of the Book: A Life of Jorge Luis Borges*, maintains that the story "is the densest, and perhaps philosophically most nihilistic, story Borges ever wrote."

Moreover, he contends that Borges constructs an elaborate discussion of time, using "[s]inology, the philosophy of labyrinths and gardens, espionage and premonition" to demonstrate the "essentially fictitious and yet . . . inescapable" nature of time.

Readers of Borges, therefore, are left with many questions when reading this story. Is it a detective story? A philosophical treatise? Is it about time? About future(s) in potential? To these questions, it is possible to add one more: can "The Garden of Forking Paths" be read as an example of metafiction, fiction that takes as its subject the creation of fiction itself?

Metafiction is an important term in postmodern literature, yet Borges' story appeared some thirty years before the self-consciously metafictional texts of the postmodern era. Thomas Weissert identifies Borges as "a transitional figure between modern and postmodern literature," and it is through his use of metafiction that this seems most clear.

Indeed, writers such as Didier Jaén, Weissert, and others explore Borges' use of metafiction. The concept of metafiction may seem at first strange to readers used to reading realistic or mimetic texts, that is, texts that are constructed to reflect or mimic reality. However, by examining first the characteristics of metafiction, and second how "The Garden of Forking Paths" illustrates those characteristics, readers can grow in their understanding of both the concept of metafiction and the story itself.

> " The characters that exist in the pages of the text—no matter how real they seem—are no more than ink on paper. They have no existence before the beginning of the text, and they have no future at the end of the text. They are, pure and simple, creations of language and narration."

A metafictional text, according to Patricia Waugh in her book *Metafiction: The Theory and the Practice of Self-Conscious Fiction*, is one that "self-consciously and systematically draws attention to itself as an artifact in order to pose questions about the relationship between fiction and reality." "The Garden of Forking Paths" does this in a number of ways.

In the first place, the story opens with a reference to a historical event and a historical text, followed by the statement by Yu Tsun. This clearly calls into question the "relationship between fiction and reality." By suggesting that the statement to follow offers yet another historical explanation for the event referred to in the historical text, Borges undermines the truth of the historical text itself.

In addition, the impersonal narrator mentions that the first two pages of the document are missing. The information serves to remind the reader that what is to follow is a description of a series of events constructed after the fact. That the two pages are missing also serves to remind the reader that the editor of the statement can change and manipulate the material in the statement.

The fact is further emphasized by the inclusion of a footnote early in the story. The unnamed narrator corrects a statement made by Yu Tsun that Richard Madden murdered Viktor Runeberg. The narrator tells the reader that even the name used by Yu Tsun for Viktor Runeberg is incorrect. As a result, the reader does not know which narrator to trust: the unnamed opening narrator or Yu Tsun.

Indeed, the inclusion of the footnote forces the reader to question the reality of the narrator, a violation of the unspoken agreement that readers enter into with writers of realistic texts. Narrators have to at least *seem* real or they cannot function as narrators.

As this further illustrates, metafictional texts often function at several narrative levels. In other words, there are stories within stories within stories in this text. At the first level, there is the unnamed narrator who instructs the reader to connect Yu Tsun's statement with a passage from a history text.

At the second level is Yu Tsun's statement describing his journey and conversation with Dr. Stephen Albert. Within this level is the story of Yu Tsun's ancestor who withdraws from the world to write a book and build a labyrinth. At the inner most level is the novel itself, "an indeterminate heap of contradictory drafts," according to Yu Tsun, or according to Dr. Albert, a brilliant novel that reveals the labyrinthine nature of time.

By naming the novel at the innermost narrative level *The Garden of Forking Paths*, Borges call attention to the fact that there is yet another narrative level above the unnamed primary narrator. That is, the story itself, "The Garden of Forking Paths" contains the first narrator and all of the narrative levels below it.

Therefore, if the novel at the center of the story is a fictional creation of the fictional Ts'ui Pen, then the story "The Garden of Forking Paths" is also a fictional creation. What, then, does this imply about Borges himself? Is he suggesting that the author is a fictional creation, someone constructed by the language and the reader?

Borges violates another unspoken agreement between writer and reader that the text will follow in a linear fashion from start to finish. Storytelling works because of the linear arrangement of the text. Borges, however, introduces the possibility that texts may not be linear.

He does this by revealing the nature of the fictitious novel at the center of the story. The novel, according to Albert, puts forward an infinite number of futures—many of them contradictory. According to Albert, "In the work of Ts'ui Pen, all possible outcomes occur; each one is the point of departure for other forkings."

Likewise, metafictional texts, because they are texts about texts, introduce the possibility of multiple meanings. As Peter Stoicheff argues, "This is one way of saying that within the finite space of any text are an infinite number of possible meanings, whose hierarchy metafiction refuses to arbitrate."

In other words, in the world of fiction no one meaning has any more connection to reality than any other meaning. Therefore, all meanings and no meanings are simultaneously possible, just as all of the futures in "The Garden of Forking Paths" are possible within the fictional world. However, since it is a fictional world, none of the futures exist in reality.

Furthermore, metafictional texts differ from realistic texts in that they often contain both contradictions and coincidences that force readers to question the "reality" of the universe created by the writer. In a realistic text, there is an agreement between the writer and the reader that the reader will believe the world the writer has created as long as the writer stays within the conventions of that fictional world. In a realistic text, natural law must be obeyed and characters must act as if they were real people.

However, in a metafictional text like "The Garden of Forking Paths," the coincidental nature of many of the events forces the reader to accept that the story has no connection to reality. For example, Yu Tsun picks a name out of a phone book. The person he chooses is a noted sinologist who has spent years studying a novel written by Yu Tsun's ancestor. Such coincidence calls attention to the fact that in the world of fiction, anything can happen. The writer controls the story because it is a story, not reality.

What a story like "The Garden of Forking Paths" reveals, then, is that all fiction, whether realistic or fantastic, is a product of language. The characters that exist in the pages of the text—no matter how real they seem—are no more than ink on paper. They have no existence before the beginning of the text, and they have no future at the end of the text. They are, pure and simple, creations of language and narration.

Consequently, the implications that a metafictional text like "The Garden of Forking Paths" finally introduce are profoundly disturbing. As the character Yu Tsun tells the reader early in the story, "everything happens to a man precisely, precisely *now*." Once an event is past, it exists nowhere but in memory and narration.

Likewise, the future exists nowhere but in the imagination and in narration. By calling attention to itself as fiction, the metafictional text also calls attention to the nature of reality itself, at least suggesting that the lines between fiction and the narration of lived experience are perhaps fuzzier than anyone wants to admit.

Source: Diane Andrews Henningfeld, in an essay for *Literature of Developing Nations for Students*, Gale, 2000.

John T. Irwin

In Borge's first collection of pure fictions, *The Garden of Forking Paths* (1941), the game of chess is mentioned in four of the volume's eight stories and alluded to in the epigraph to a fifth. Let me recall briefly three of these references. In the volume's final tale (the detective story that gives the collection its title), Stephen Albert, the murder victim, asks the killer Dr. Yu Tsun, ''In a guessing game to which the answer is chess, which word is the only one prohibited?'' To which Yu Tsun replies, ''The word is chess.'' In the volume's sixth story, ''An Examination of the Work of Herbert Quain,'' the narrator, summarizing Quain's literary career, outlines the plot of his detective novel *The God of the Labyrinth*: ''An indecipherable assassination takes place in the initial pages; a leisurely discussion takes place toward the middle; a solution appears in the end. Once the enigma is cleared up, there is a long and retrospective paragraph which contains the following phrase: Everyone thought that the encounter of the two chess players was accidental. This phrase allows one to understand that the solution is erroneous. The unquiet reader rereads the pertinent chapters and discovers another solution, the true one. The reader of this book is thus forcibly more discerning than the detective.'' The third example is from the volume's opening story, ''Tlon, Uqbar, Orbis Tertius.'' In the tale Borges recalls a figure from his childhood named Herbert Ashe, an English engineer and friend of his father, who, Borges later realizes, was part of a group involved in the creation of the idealist world of Tlon and in the secret project of insinuating that fictive world into the real one. Borges remembers that when he was a boy the childless widower Ashe and Borges's father ''would beat one another at chess, without saying a word,'' sharing one of those English friendships ''which begin by avoiding intimacies and eventually eliminate speech altogether.''

One would assume that if an image occurs in half the stories in a collection, it reflects some central concern of the volume as a whole, and part

The labyrinthian style of Borges's detective and philosophical story, in which he intentionally tries to lose the reader's attention, parallels this surrealistic artwork created by Borges's contemporary, Salvador Dali.

of the rationale for listing these three examples in the reverse order of their appearance in the book is to move backward toward the origin of that concern. In the first instance cited, chess is evoked as the answer to a riddle, the solution to a mystery; in the second, it is linked to the structure of a detective story; and in the third, it is associated with Borges's father and with the invention of a world of ''extreme idealism'' (''Tlon''), a world created, as Borges says, by ''the discipline of chess players'' (T).

Chess has, of course, a long-standing connection with the detective genre. In the first Dupin story, ''The Murders in the Rue Morgue'' (1841), the narrator cites it as an example, along with draughts and whist, to illustrate the workings of the analytic power; and in the third Dupin story, ''The Purloined Letter,'' Poe presents us with a scenario strongly reminiscent of a chess game - there is a king and queen, and a battle between two knights (Dupin is a Chevalier, and we must assume that his double the Minister D—— is at least of equal rank), a battle for possession of a letter that concerns the

" 'When I was still quite young, he showed me, with the aid of a chessboard, the paradoxes of Zeno—Achilles and the tortoise, the unmoving flight of the arrow, the impossibility of motion. Later, without mentioning Berkeley's name, he did his best to teach me the rudiments of idealism.'"

queen's honor and that in the minister's hands could reduce the queen to being a pawn. Moreover, a chess game is one of the most frequently used images for the battle of wits between detective and criminal in the tradition of the genre, an image of the detective's attempt to double the thought processes of his opponent in order to end up one move ahead of him. This doubling of an opponent's thoughts, in which one plays out possible variations against an antithetical mirror image of one's own mind, is reflected in the physical structure of the game itself, for the opposing chess pieces at the start of the game face each other in a mirror-image relationship. Borges's association of the detective story with chess is, then, fairly easy to explain. But this still leaves the question of the game's link with Borges's father and with idealist philosophy. In making these associations in his first book of pure fictions, Borges seems simply to have transposed into art connections already present in real life. Borges's father was a chess player; he taught his son the game; and, as Borges tells us in ''An Autobiographical Essay,'' he used the chessboard to begin his son's philosophical education: ''When I was still quite young, he showed me, with the aid of a chessboard, the paradoxes of Zeno—Achilles and the tortoise, the unmoving flight of the arrow, the impossibility of motion. Later, without mentioning Berkeley's name, he did his best to teach me the rudiments of idealism.''

During Borges's visit to Hopkins in 1983, I asked him about the way his father had demonstrated Zeno's paradoxes at the chessboard. He said that he had used the pieces aligned on the first rank,

showing him that before he could travel the distance between the king's rook and the queen's rook he had first to go half that distance (that is, from the king's rook to the king), but that before he could go from the king's rook to the king he had first to go half that distance (that is, from the king's rook to the king's knight), and so on. To the extent that the paradoxes of Zeno reveal ''the impossibility of motion,'' they are in effect tropes of helplessness, of impotence. Their moral is that nothing can really be accomplished in this world. A person cannot even move from point A to point B, since between the two points yawns an abyss of infinite regression. And if motion is impossible, then our physical world in which motion seems constantly to occur must be an illusion. This world does not have a real, independent (that is, material) existence; its existence is wholly apparential, a function of mental states. From the paradoxes of Zeno, then, it is a short step, as the passage from ''An Autobiographical Essay'' implies, to the ''rudiments of idealism'' and the philosophy of George Berkeley. But if the paradoxes of Zeno are, as we have suggested, tropes of impotence, then a father's decision to teach them to his young son might seem at best ill considered and at worst faintly hostile. Indeed, if there is an element of veiled hostility in this act—a sense on the father's part that he has accomplished little of what he set out to do, not because he failed, but because nothing could really be achieved in a world where motion is an illusion; and a warning to the son not to show his father up, not to defeat him, by trying to accomplish something on his own—then certainly the chessboard is the right place for the father to convey that message, since virtually every psychoanalytic reading of the game's structure and symbolism sees it as a ritual sublimation of father murder.

The game's goal is, of course, the checkmate of the opponent's king. One seeks to place the king under a direct attack from which he is powerless to escape, so that on the next move he can be captured and removed from the board. (Indeed, the word checkmate derives from the Persian Shah mat, ''the king is dead.'') But this capture and removal (the killing of the king) never actually takes place, for the game always ends one move before this with the king's immobilization in check. Which is simply to say that in the game's sublimation of aggression, the murder of the father even in a symbolic form is repressed. According to the psychoanalyst and chess master Reuben Fine, since ''genetically, chess is more often than not taught to the boy by his father, or by a father substitute,'' it naturally ''becomes a means of working out the father-son rivalry.'' In this ritual mime of the conflicts surrounding the family romance, the mother plays a major role. In his essay on the American chess champion Paul Morphy, Ernest Jones points out that ''in attacking the father the most potent assistance is afforded by the mother (Queen),'' the strongest piece on the board. As one chess critic has noted, ''chess is a matter of both father murder and attempts to prevent it. This mirror function of chess is of extreme importance; obviously the player appears both in a monstrous and a virtuous capacity—planning parricide, at the same time warding it off; recreating Oedipal fantasy, yet trying to disrupt it. Yet the stronger urge is the monstrous one; the player wants to win, to kill the father rather than defend him, although one could clearly speculate on the problems of players who habitually lose at last.'' Fine argues that the king not only represents the father but, as a hand-manipulated, carved figure, ''stands for the boy's penis in the phallic stage, and hence rearouses the castration anxiety characteristic of that period. . . . It is the father pulled down to the boy's size. Unconsciously it gives the boy a chance to say to the father: 'To the outside world you are big and strong, but when we get right down to it, you're just as weak as I am.''''

That Borges understood this Oedipal component of chess is clear from a passage in the last book he published before his death, *Atlas* (1984), a collection of short essays devoted for the most part to geographic locales associated with the psychic terrain of his past. The essay on Athens begins:

> On the first morning, my first day in Athens, I was proferred the following dream. In front of me stood a row of books filling a long shelf. They formed a set of the *Encyclopaedia Britannica*, one of my lost paradises. I took down a volume at random. I looked up Coleridge: the article had an end but no beginning. I looked up Crete: it concluded but did not begin. I looked up the entry on Chess. At that point the dream shifted. On an elevated stage in an amphitheater filled to capacity with an attentive audience, I was playing chess with my father, who was also the False Artaxerxes. (His ears having been cut off, Artaxerxes was found sleeping by one of his many wives; she ran her hand over his skull very gently so as not to awaken him; presently he was killed.) I moved a piece; my antagonist did not move anything but, by an act of magic, he erased one of my pieces. This procedure was repeated various times.

> I awoke and told myself: I am in Greece, where everything began, assuming that things, as opposed to articles in the dream's encyclopedia, have a beginning.

It seems only fitting that this dream, with its images of castration and father murder, should have

been ''proferred'' to Borges in Athens, the city where the blind parricide Oedipus ultimately sought shelter and where he was welcomed by Theseus, who, according to Plutarch, cannot himself ''escape the charge of parricide'' because of his ''neglect of the command about the sail'' that caused his father's death. (Recall that when Theseus left for Crete to slay the Minotaur, his father Aegeus, the ruler of Athens, told him to have his crew hoist a white sail upon returning if Theseus was alive and a black sail if he was dead. Theseus forgot his father's command, and when his ship returned flying a black sail, Aegeus, in despair at his son's supposed death, leapt from a cliff.)

Borges's dream in Athens begins as a search for origins, an attempt to recover or return to a ''lost paradise'' represented in the dream by a set of the *Encyclopaedia Britannica*. In terms of an individual's biological origin, that lost paradise is the maternal womb, and the fact that Borges's attempt to penetrate the ''lost paradise'' of the encyclopedia (by delving into one of its volumes) leads almost immediately to an image of conflict with the father and the threat of castration suggests that the *Britannica* functions here as a figure of the mother's body. In the dream Borges takes a volume of the Britannica from the shelf (the volume for the womblike letter C, to judge from its entries) and finds that in the first two articles he reads (on Coleridge and Crete) the attempt to return to origin is frustrated: each article has an end ''but no beginning.'' The reference to Crete seems to be a fairly straightforward allusion to the island's legendary labyrinth, that underground enclosure of winding passageways that Freud interprets as an image of the matrix, an enclosure which the hero Theseus enters and from which he is reborn, with the help of the umbilical thread, after having slain the monster, who symbolizes the fear of castration or death that the son must face when he tries to rival the father by entering the mother's body.

In contrast, the dream reference to Coleridge seems less clear at first glance, but a passage from Borges's essay on nightmares in the 1980 volume *Seven Nights* gives us a clue. According to Borges, Coleridge maintains that

> it doesn't matter what we dream, that the dream searches for explanations. He gives an example: a lion suddenly appears in this room and we are all afraid; the fear has been caused by the image of the lion. But in dreams the reverse can occur. We feel oppressed, and then search for an explanation. I, absurdly but vividly, dream that a sphinx has lain down next to me. The sphinx is not the cause of my fear, it is an

explanation of my feeling of oppression. Coleridge adds that people who have been frightened by imaginary ghosts have gone mad. On the other hand, a person who dreams a ghost can wake up and, within a few seconds, regain his composure.

I have had—and I still have—many nightmares. The most terrible, the one that struck me as the most terrible, I used in a sonnet. It went like this: I was in my room; it was dawn (possibly that was the time of the dream). At the foot of my bed was a king, a very ancient king, and I knew in the dream that he was the King of the North, of Norway. He did not look at me; his blind stare was fixed on the ceiling. I felt the terror of his presence. I saw the king, I saw his sword, I saw his dog. Then I woke. But I continued to see the king for a while, because he had made such a strong impression on me. Retold, my dream is nothing; dreamt, it was terrible.

The progression of images in this passage forms an instructive gloss on the associative logic of Borges's dream at Athens. Starting with the name of Coleridge and the dictum that "the dream searches for explanations" by creating images which correspond with, and thus account for, emotions we feel, the passage introduces the example of a lion as a symbolic expression of fear; to which Borges adds the example of his own dream that a sphinx has lain down beside him, the image of the sphinx serving as "an explanation of my feeling of oppression." The associative link between the images of lion and sphinx seems plain: the multiform sphinx is traditionally depicted with a lion's body. But the sphinx is, of course, the monster associated with Oedipus. She threatens the hero with death if he doesn't solve her riddle; her name (strangler, from the Greek sphingein, origin of the English sphincter) evokes the dangerous, constricting passageway out of and into the mother's womb; and her form, with one shape issuing from another, suggests the child's body emerging from the mother's at birth, according to Otto Rank.

The passage's imagery now shifts from the figure of a sphinx to that of a ghost, with the dictum that people frightened by an imaginary ghost in waking life have gone mad but that those who dream a ghost can wake up and regain their composure. The connection between sphinx and ghost is unclear at first, until we recall that in Borges's third detective story, "Ibn Hakkan al-Bokhari, Dead in His Labyrinth," the three faceless corpses found in the labyrinth are those of a king, a slave, and a lion and that the explanation for the crime contrived by the killer is that the three have been murdered by the ghost of the king's vizier. The murderer is in fact this same king's vizier Zaid, who, along with his

black slave and lion, had come to the small Cornish village of Pentreath masquerading as the king Ibn Hakkan, built the labyrinth, lured the real king into it, killed him and then obliterated his face (along with that of the slave and lion) to cover the previous imposture and effect his escape. Given the associative link between sphinx and lion in Borges's discussion of nightmares and that between king, ghost, and lion in "Ibn Hakkan al-Bokhari," the progression of images in the nightmare passage becomes easier to follow: The image of the lion (the king of the beasts) serves as a middle term connecting the image of the sphinx (with its lion's body) to that of the king. But this linking of sphinx and king also implicitly connects the images of sphinx and ghost, for the king in Borges's nightmare is clearly coded as a spectral apparition. Thus the associative chain underlying the passage from the nightmare essay runs: lion (king of the beasts) / sphinx (creature with a lion's body who tests King Oedipus) / king / ghost (of a king). But in the passage Borges reverses the order of the last two links in the chain by moving directly from the dream image of the sphinx to a discussion of ghosts in waking life versus ghosts in dreams, and only then going on to describe his "most terrible" nightmare about "a very ancient king." Since it is dawn and the king is at the foot of Borges's bed, one assumes that in the dreamed scene Borges is just awakening from a night's sleep and that the uncertainty as to whether he is, within the dream, awake or dreaming, whether the figure of the king is an imaginary ghost or a ghost in a dream, forms part of the dream image's terror, a frightening sense of ambiguity that is confirmed when Borges actually awakens and yet continues "to see the king for a while" because the image has "made such a strong impression."

That the figure of the "ancient king" is coded as a ghost seems obvious from the way in which the account of Borges's nightmare grows out of his comment about the difference between thinking we see and dreaming we see a ghost. Moreover, I would suggest that this "King of the North" is a very specific ghost indeed. Borges identifies him as the king of Norway, but that is undoubtedly a displacement within the dream. He is the king of Denmark, the ghost of Hamlet's father returned to confront his son with the Oedipal task of avenging the father's murder and with the epistemological dilemma of whether this demanding appearance is a real ghost, a dream, or a hallucination. (Recall that at the start of Shakespeare's play we are told that Hamlet had killed Fortinbras, the King of Norway, in combat, thus causing young Fortinbras to seek revenge for his father's death.) In the dream the king's "blind stare" is "fixed on the ceiling," at once a reminder of the punishment which Oedipus inflicted on himself for incest and parricide, for usurping the true king's place, and an evocation of Borges's own father who went blind from a hereditary eye ailment, an ailment which he in turn passed on to his son who also went blind.

Indeed, the imagery of the dream suggests the extent to which Borges may have experienced his blindness on some unconscious level as an Oedipal transmission. In the dream, Borges sees the king, his sword, and his dog. The sword would seem to be both a phallic symbol of the father's authority and a metonym for the punishment (castration) meted out to those who would usurp that authority; while the king's dog probably bears something of the same relationship to the dreamer that the Sphinx does to Oedipus and the Minotaur does to Theseus—a symbol of the animal (that is, sexual) realm, who confronts the aspirant (son) with a life-threatening test by which the real king (or his lawful successor) is distinguished from usurpers or impostors. At the end of "Ibn Hakkan al-Bokhari," one of the characters describes the cowardly murderer of the king as "a good-for-nothing who, before becoming a nobody in death, wanted one day to look back on having been a king or having been taken for a king." The message seems plain enough: though the usurper might be able to murder a king, he could not take the king's place; not every son who can kill his father can become a father.

Now if we are correct in thinking that the image of the encyclopedia entry on Coleridge in Borges's dream at Athens represents the dreamwork's condensation of the chain of associations grouped around Coleridge's name in the essay on nightmares, then it seems clear that the progression of images in the Athens dream is essentially the same as that in the nightmare essay, with two revealing substitutions in the signifying chain. Starting with the name of Coleridge, the passage in the essay from *Seven Nights* moves first to the image of a lion, and then to that of a sphinx, a lion-bodied animal whose name evokes the figure of Oedipus. From the sphinx, the passage shifts to the image of ghosts (either hallucinated or dreamed) and then ends with the nightmare figure of an ancient, blind king holding a sword, the reference to ghosts serving to associate the dream's image of the king of Norway (that is, Denmark) with the opening of Hamlet and thus code the blind king as the ghost of a murdered father appearing to his son. In a similar manner the chain of associations in Borges's dream at Athens begins by invoking the name of Coleridge but then instead of moving on to the image of the sphinx (that is, to a direct allusion to Oedipus), the dream obliquely calls up a screen-figure of Oedipus (Theseus) through the reference to the encyclopedia entry on Crete (that is, the Cretan labyrinth, the Minotaur, and the Minotaur's slayer). In place of Oedipus, who kills his father and marries his mother, stands Theseus, the man who penetrates the symbolic womb of the labyrinth and accidentally causes the death of his father through an act of forgetfulness. From the reference to Crete, the dream then shifts to the encyclopedia entry on Chess, the veiled allusion to the womblike, Cretan labyrinth giving way to the image of the labyrinthine network of a chessboard on which one symbolically kills the father. And this image in turn suddenly shifts to that of a real chess game and brings us to the second major substitution in the signifying chain. For instead of culminating, as the passage from Borges's essay on nightmares did, with the terrifying image of a blind king holding a sword, the Athens dream ends with an image of Borges's own father (who went blind) as a false king mutilated by a sword. And with this final figuration the reason for the substitutions in the associative chain becomes obvious.

In the passage from the essay on nightmares, Borges can directly allude to Oedipus through the mention of the sphinx precisely because the blind king is not explicitly identified as Borges's father. But in the Athens dream the figure whom Borges confronts in a chess game (a ritual sublimation of father murder) is so identified; and consequently, the direct Oedipal allusion which followed the mention of Coleridge's name in the nightmare essay is repressed by Borges in favor of a veiled reference to the Oedipal screenfigure Theseus, the man who welcomed the aged, blind Oedipus to Athens (remember that the aged, blind Borges is dreaming this dream in Athens) and who became Oedipus's spiritual son.

Perhaps the most striking detail in the Athens dream is the description of Borges's father as "the False Artaxerxes," whose ears had been cropped. It seems only fitting that since the dream begins with the image of the *Encyclopaedia Britannica*, we should turn to that work for an explanation of this figure. The eleventh edition of the *Britannica* identifies the false Artaxerxes as one "Bessus, satrap of Bactria and Sogdiana under Darius III": "When Alexander pursued the Persian king [Darius III] on his flight to the East (summer 330), Bessus with some of the other conspirators deposed Darius and shortly after killed him. He then tried to organize a national resistance against the Macedonian conqueror in the eastern provinces, proclaimed himself king and adopted the name Artaxerxes.'' Taken prisoner by treachery, Bessus was sent by Alexander to Ecbatana where he was condemned to death: ''Before his execution his nose and ears were cut off, according to the Persian custom; we learn from the Behistun inscription that Darius I punished the usurpers in the same way.'' Bessus, the false Artaxerxes, was then a usurper, someone able to kill a king but unable to take the king's place, an impostor like Zaid, the murderer in ''Ibn Hakkan.'' In Borges's dream the cutting off of the usurper's ears is an obvious image of castration, reminiscent of the destruction of Oedipus's eyeballs with the pin of Jocasta's brooch; and the suggestion of maternal complicity in the attack on the father is present as well: ''His ears having been cut off, Artaxerxes was found sleeping by one of his many wives; she ran her hand over his skull very gently so as not to awaken him; presently he was killed.''

While the image of paternal mutilation and death in Borges's dream would seem to be simply an expression of the son's desire to inflict on the father the same violence with which he feels threatened, the nature of the paternal threat to the son's power, as figured in the moves of the chess game, is more complex than that reading suggests. For the image of the father in Borges's dream is not that of a true king, an absolute ruler with complete power to inflict whatever injury he chooses on the son, but that of a false king, a usurper, who is castrated and put to death. Which is to say that the father in Borges's dream threatens the son's potency by presenting himself as a castrated son trapped within a generational line and doomed to death, threatens him by showing that the father is not an absolute source but merely the son's immediate predecessor who has been rendered helpless, made unoriginal, by his own predecessor. Describing the moves of the chess game, Borges says, ''I moved a piece; my antagonist did not move anything but, by an act of magic, he erased one of my pieces. This procedure was repeated various times.'' One cannot help but recall that Borges's father had used the chessboard not only to teach his son the game but to acquaint him with the paradoxes of Zeno, tropes of impotence figuring, as Borges says, ''the impossibility of motion.'' The logic of the scene is plain: To play a game of chess, one must move pieces from one square to another until finally one places the king in a check from which he cannot escape. But if checkmating the king is a symbolic murder of the father, then the father who teaches this game to his son might well try to protect himself from the Oedipal combat for paternal power by convincing his son that no such power exists for them to fight over. Thus in the dreamed chess game, Borges moves a piece, but his father does not move anything (motion is impossible). Instead, ''by an act of magic'' (the paradoxes of Zeno which reveal the magical, that is, illusory, nature of action), he erases one of his son's pieces; he makes it vanish like the dream it is. In erasing his son's chess piece with these magical paradoxes, the father castrates him not physically by exercising superior strength, but psychologically by showing him that in this illusory world nothing can be done, that everyone is helpless, father and son alike. (Recall in this regard that Borges's poem ''Chess'' [1960] concludes by questioning the traditional scholastic explanation of the origin of motion which traces movement, through a series of intermediate causes, back to an unmoved first mover, the All-Father: ''God moves the player, he, in turn, the piece. / But what god beyond God begins the round / of dust and time and dream and agonies?'' No wonder, then, that when Borges awakens from this dream in Athens of unreachable origins and illusory grounds, this dream in which he discovers, during the course of a chess game, the person who conceived him depicted as a sleeping king (that is, when Borges discovers himself [the dreamer of the Athens dream] as a figure in the dream of the Other), no wonder that the force of the dream persists into waking consciousness as a doubt about whether origins and original power exist in real life, a persistence of the dream state that seems to blur the distinction between reality and illusion (as when Borges awakened from his nightmare of the blind King of the North yet ''continued to see the king for a while''): ''I awoke and told myself: I am in Greece, where everything began, assuming that things, as opposed to articles in the dream's encyclopedia, have a beginning.''

When one sees the psychological point of Borges's association of his father with the game of chess, then ''the encounter of the two chess players'' (the elder Borges and Herbert Ashe) in the story ''Tlon, Uqbar, Orbis Tertius'' seems far from ''accidental'' indeed, to use Herbert Quain's words from his detective novel *The God of the Labyrinth.* And the encounter takes on still greater significance when we consider that ''the faded English engineer

Herbert Ashe'' is, according to Borges's friend Jose Bianco, simply ''a portrait'' of Borges's father.'' That Borges should imagine a chess game in which his father competes against ''a portrait'' of himself is not surprising, given his use of the game's mirror-image structure to evoke the mental duel between antithetical doubles in the detective story. But this encrypted image of a specular chess game played by the father against himself becomes even more interesting when we recall that, at the beginning of ''Tlon, Uqbar, Orbis Tertius,'' fatherhood and mirroring are invoked as analogous forms of duplicating human beings. Borges says that he owed the discovery of the idealist worlds of the story's title to ''the conjunction of a mirror and an encyclopedia.'' He and his friend Bioy Casares had dined one evening and talked late into the night. During their conversation, Borges noticed that ''from the far end of the corridor, the mirror was watching us; and we discovered, with the inevitability of discoveries made late at night, that mirrors have something grotesque about them. Then Bioy Casares recalled that one of the heresiarchs of Uqbar had stated that mirrors and copulation are abominable, since they both multiply the numbers of man'' (T). Asking for the source of this ''memorable sentence,'' Borges is told that it comes from the article on Uqbar in the Anglo-American Cyclopaedia. As it happens, the villa where they are staying has a copy of the reference work, but try as they might, they cannot find the article on Uqbar. The next day Bioy telephones to say that he has found in another copy of the work the article in question and that the passage he had paraphrased the night before reads: ''For one of those gnostics, the visible universe was an illusion or, more precisely, a sophism. Mirrors and fatherhood are abominable because they multiply it and extend it'' (T). Borges and Bioy compare the two versions of the encyclopedia and find that the sole difference between them is the additional four pages of the article on Uqbar, a discovery that ultimately reveals the existence of a secret project pursued by a band of intellectuals over the years to introduce the idealist world of Tlon into this world and thereby alter the shape of reality.

The opening image of ''Tlon, Uqbar, Orbis Tertius'' (''the conjunction of a mirror and an encyclopedia'') is almost certainly an allusion to the fact that in the Middle Ages a work of encyclopedic knowledge was commonly referred to in Latin as a speculum, a mirror (for example, the thirteenth-century *Speculum majus* of Vincent of Beauvais), a name that figures the encyclopedia as a written

mirror of the universe. Given the sexual overtones of ''conjunction,'' the opening image also sets the stage for the subsequent association of a mirror, first with copulation, and then with fatherhood. And if, in this conjunction of a mirror and an encyclopedia, the mirror is equated with the male principle, then the encyclopedia would obviously be equated with the female (the matrix)—the same association found in Borges's dream at Athens where the *Encyclopaedia Britannica* is described as a ''lost paradise'' and then immediately linked to the image of the womblike labyrinth through the reference to Crete. (Significantly enough, the Anglo-American Cyclopaedia in ''Tlon, Uqbar, Orbis Tertius'' is ''a literal if inadequate reprint of the 1902 *Encyclopaedia Britannica*'' [T].)

If for Borges mirror and encyclopedia are gender coded as male and female respectively, then the description Borges gives in *Seven Nights* of two of his recurring nightmares, two dreams that frequently blend into one, seems like a gloss on that conjunction of a mirror and an encyclopedia that begins ''Tlon, Uqbar, Orbis Tertius'':

> I have two nightmares which often become confused with one another. I have the nightmare of the labyrinth, which comes, in part, from a steel engraving I saw in a French book when I was a child. In this engraving were the Seven Wonders of the World, among them the labyrinth of Crete. The labyrinth was a great amphitheater, a very high amphitheater. . . . In this closed structure—ominously closed—there were cracks. I believed when I was a child (or I now believe I believed) that if one had a magnifying glass powerful enough, one could look through the cracks and see the Minotaur in the terrible center of the labyrinth.
>
> My other nightmare is that of the mirror. The two are not distinct, as it only takes two facing mirrors to construct a labyrinth. . . .
>
> I always dream of labyrinths or of mirrors. In the dream of the mirror another vision appears, another terror of my nights, and that is the idea of the mask. Masks have always scared me. No doubt I felt in my childhood that someone who was wearing a mask was hiding something horrible. These are my most terrible nightmares: I see myself reflected in a mirror, but the reflection is wearing a mask. I am afraid to pull the mask off, afraid to see my real face, which I imagine to be hideous. There may be leprosy or evil or something more terrible than anything I am capable of imagining.

As the dream at Athens begins with the image of a book (the Britannica) and immediately moves (via the reference to Crete) to the image of the labyrinth, so this passage from the nightmare essay begins with the image of the labyrinth and moves immediately to the image of a book—a French book in which Borges saw a steel engraving of the laby-rinth when he was a child. Though Borges does not say what kind of book it was, the mention of a ''steel engraving'' recalls a remark from his ''Autobio-graphical Essay'' about the books he enjoyed most as a child in his father's library: ''I have forgotten most of the faces of that time . . . and yet I vividly remember so many of the steel engravings in *Chambers's Encyclopaedia* and in the *Britannica*'' (''An Autobiographical Essay'').

In the engraving in the French book the laby-rinth is shown as ''a closed structure,'' a ''very high amphitheater,'' a description that gives added mean-ing to the setting for the chess game in the Athens dream: ''On an elevated stage in an amphitheater filled to capacity with an attentive audience, I was playing chess with my father, who was also the False Artaxerxes.'' That Borges imagines the laby-rinth as an enclosed amphitheater suggests yet again that the amphitheater which serves as the site of the chess game with his father, a game of kings and queens played out on a labyrinthine network of squares, represents the maternal space of origin for whose possession they are competing. And the fact that the labyrinth as symbol of the matrix, as the scene of the contest with the father, is closely associated in these passages with another womb symbol (the image of a book as a ''lost paradise'') suggests that the real-life arena into which the Oedipal struggle between Borges and his father had been displaced was not the game of chess but the realm of literature in which the virgin space of the page, inseminated by ink from the phallic pen, can produce an offspring longer-lived than any child, an offspring almost immortal if the author only be original enough. Borges's father in addition to be-ing a lawyer had, of course, been a minor poet and fiction writer before he went blind, and, as Borges recalls in his ''Autobiographical Essay,'' ''From the time I was a boy, when blindness came to him, it was tacitly understood that I had to fulfill the literary destiny that circumstances had denied my father. . . . I was expected to be a writer'' (A). An oddly contradictory legacy: that the son fulfill the literary destiny denied to the father by becoming the successful writer his parent had never been, in effect surpassing, defeating, the father in an implicit liter-ary competition.

If the images that dominate Borges's two recur-ring nightmares (the mirror and the labyrinth) are associated respectively with fatherhood and moth-erhood, then Borges's assertion that ''the two are not distinct'' suggests a union of male and female

principles reminiscent of ''the conjunction of a mirror and an encyclopedia'' at the beginning of ''Tlon, Uqbar, Orbis Tertius.'' This blending of mirror and labyrinth in Borges's dreams, like the conjunction of mirror and encyclopedia in the tale, seems to be the symbolic figuration of a primal scene, an evocation of the dreamer's parents in the act of engendering the dreamer. And to judge from the imagery that follows from this blending of mirror and labyrinth in Borges's account, the prod-uct of that union is experienced as something mon-strous—a masked figure whose mask conceals ''something more terrible than anything'' the dreamer is ''capable of imagining.''

According to the associative logic of the pas-sage, two of Borges's nightmare images, in becom-ing ''confused with one another,'' are in effect equated with one another—the labyrinth and the mirror. As the labyrinth contains a monstrous figure (the Minotaur with a man's body and a bull's head), so the mirror contains an equally monstrous figure (a masked man with a human body and a concealed face). In one case the bull's head, in the other the masked face, makes the figure terrifying. But what is that frightening content at once concealed and evoked by the masked face and animal head? Recall that in his entry on the Minotaur in *The Book of Imaginary Beings* (1967), Borges says that the Cretan labyrinth was built ''to confine and keep hidden'' Queen Pasiphae's ''monstrous son,'' the product of an unnatural union of animal and human. And if the bull's head is the visible trace of a monstrous copulation, then are we to assume, given the equation of the bull-headed monster of the labyrinth and the masked figure in the mirror, that the masked face also evokes the image of a mon-strous copulation, or more precisely, evokes the image of copulation as something monstrous? Not-ing the ''revulsion for the act of fatherhood . . . or copulation'' found in ''Tlon, Uqbar, Orbis Tertius,'' Borges's biographer Rodriguez Monegal wonders how much this feeling ''has to do with the discovery of the primal scene through the complicity of a mirror'' when Borges was a child. He points out as evidence for this possibility a passage from Borges's poem ''The Mirror'':

> Infinite I see them, elementary executors of an old pact, to multiply the world as the generative act, sleepless and fatal.

Monegal notes that in the tale ''The Sect of the Phoenix'' (1952) Borges imagines a pagan cult bound together by a shared secret that assures its members immortality, a secret hinted at in the tale but never named—the act of copulation. In the story Borges says that though the secret "is transmitted from generation to generation . . . usage does not favor mothers teaching it to their sons." He continues, "Initiation into the mystery is the task of individuals of the lowest order. . . . The Secret is sacred, but it is also somewhat ridiculous. The practice of the mystery is furtive and even clandestine and its adepts do not speak about it. There are no respectable words to describe it, but it is understood that all words refer to it, or better, that they inevitably allude to it. . . . A kind of sacred horror prevents some of the faithful from practicing the extremely simple ritual; the others despise them for it, but they despise themselves even more." To many members of the sect, the secret seemed "paltry, distressing, vulgar and (what is even stranger) incredible. They could not reconcile themselves to the fact that their ancestors had lowered themselves to such conduct." When asked by the critic Ronald Christ about the secret shared by the sect of the Phoenix, Borges replied, "The act is what Whitman says 'the divine husband knows, from the work of fatherhood.'—When I first heard about this act, when I was a boy, I was shocked, shocked to think that my mother, my father had performed it. It is an amazing discovery, no? But then too it is an act of immortality, a rite of immortality, isn't it?"

If, as we have suggested, the masked figure in the mirror evokes for Borges the bull-headed monster of the labyrinth ("it only takes two facing mirrors to construct a labyrinth"), that is, evokes the monstrous offspring of an unnatural copulation, and if that bullheaded figure symbolically represents in turn the act of copulation as something monstrous, as the assault of a male animal on the mother (Freud notes that in the fantasy of the primal scene the child frequently misinterprets parental intercourse as an act of sadomasochistic violence by the father against the mother), then the terror that Borges feels at the nightmare image of seeing his masked reflection, a terror both of the mask and of pulling off the mask to see the real face beneath, seems to be compounded of two related emotions. First, there is probably, in Monegal's words, a "revulsion for the act of fatherhood . . . or copulation" (*Jorge Luis Borges*), a sense (left over from childhood or adolescence) of the reproductive act as terrifying or humiliating, as an act unworthy of those godlike beings one's parents, and as an origin unworthy of oneself, unworthy of that spiritual entity which finds itself imprisoned in the earthy cave of the body (with its physical constraints and

sexual drives) as surely as the Minotaur (a symbol of the sun during its daily descent into the underworld) is imprisoned in the subterranean labyrinth. And what is particularly terrifying in this regard about the dream image is that while the mirror, a traditional figure of reflective self-consciousness, appears to contain, to restrain within its verge, the frightening visage that evokes the animal body, we know that the reflective self which the mirror symbolizes is equally contained within, and subject to the instinctual imperatives of, that body.

The second emotion the dream image seems to express is the son's feeling of helplessness, his feeling of being trapped in the cycle of generation, doomed to repeat and transmit this cycle by doing the thing his father did. Indeed, for Borges, part of the peculiar terror of the masked figure in the mirror seems to be that it not only evokes the primal scene as the bestial copulation of a male animal with the mother, it also suggests that the face hidden beneath the mask worn by the son's mirror-image is not his own but his father's, suggests that, in this reversal of the master/slave relationship between self and mirror-image, the son is simply a reflection of the father helplessly repeating his physical gestures, trapped within a corporeal body and a material world only because he has been physically engendered.

All of which brings us back to the image of Borges's father teaching him the paradoxes of Zeno and idealist philosophy at the chessboard and to the question of what it was that Borges learned from that teaching. For to judge from the number of stories in which the theme recurs, the lesson would seem to be that the most powerful defense the self can muster against external threats to its own integrity, against sexual conflict and the threat of checkmate, is a massive reinterpretation of the surrounding world that substitutes mind for body, the intellectual for the sexual—a substitution whose autobiographical dimension is almost always present in the Borgesian text. In "Tlon, Uqbar, Orbis Tertius," for example, this sublimation of the bodily is carried to an extreme in the image of a world (Tlon) where mental states are the only reality: "The men of that planet conceive of the universe as a series of mental processes, whose unfolding is to be understood only as a time sequence" (T). Since "the nations of that planet are congenitally idealist" (T), there is "only one discipline, that of psychology" (T). Consequently, "among the doctrines of Tlon, none has occasioned greater scandal than the doctrine of materialism. . . . To clarify the general understanding of this unlikely thesis, one eleventh century heresiarch offered the parable of nine copper coins, which enjoyed in Tlon the same noisy reputation as did the Eleatic paradoxes of Zeno in their day'' (T).

The irony, of course, is that in an idealist world like Tlon a parable of materialism seems as paradoxical as the antimaterialist parables of Zeno seem in ours. But this mention of the paradoxes of Zeno also suggests the autobiographical link between the imaginary world of Tlon and the detail of Herbert Ashe's chess games with Borges's father. For if the fictive chess games between the elder Borges and Ashe (a veiled portrait of Borges's father) are based on those real games during which the elder Borges taught his son the paradoxes of Zeno, and if, as Borges suggests in ''An Autobiographical Essay,'' it was a natural transition from these paradoxes to his father's instructing him in ''the rudiments of idealism'' without ever ''mentioning Berkeley's name'' (T), then that trajectory in Borges's personal life—from paradoxes at the chessboard demonstrating ''the impossibility of motion'' to a philosophical system that treats the material world as an illusion—is evoked in the story by having the same person who plays chess with Borges's father be one of the secret inventors of an imaginary idealist world, a world created through the writing of its fictive encyclopedia, through fiction writing.

In effect, Tlon is a world of perfect sublimation, and its significance for Borges is a function of the way in which his knowledge of Berkeley's idealism originated from a scene of sublimated conflict with his father at the chessboard, a scene which suggested idealist philosophy as an effective means of extending to life as a whole chess's sublimation of (sexual) violence, its transformation of physical conflict into a mental duel where opponents match wits but remain ultimately untouchable because physical motion is an impossibility. No wonder, then, that the world of Tlon is described as exhibiting ''the discipline of chess players'' (T) or that one of the members of that ''benevolent secret society'' which ''came together'' in the seventeenth century ''to invent a country'' (the society which counted Herbert Ashe among its latterday members) was ''George Berkeley'' (T).

The imaginary world of Tlon represents for Borges, then, the substitution of a mental life for a physical one, of inventing stories for living them. Recalling his boyhood in ''An Autobiographical Essay,'' Borges says, ''I was always very nearsighted and wore glasses, and I was rather frail. As most

of my people had been soldiers . . . and I knew I would never be, I felt ashamed, quite early, to be a bookish kind of person and not a man of action'' (A). In one of the essays in *Other Inquisitions*, Borges speaks of his as ''a lifetime dedicated less to living than to reading,'' and he recalls that ''Plotinus was said to be ashamed to dwell in a body'' so devoted was he to the life of the mind, a remark that Borges applied to himself and to his own lifetime devotion to the imagination in a conversation we had during his visit to Hopkins in 1983.

Given that Borges's predilection for idealist philosophy is to some degree a function of this philosophy's valorization of mind at the expense of body (a valorization that precisely suited the temperament of a bookish child who knew that he was not destined to be a man of action), and given further that Borges's acquaintance with the principles of idealist philosophy began as a child within the context of a combative game that favored mental acuity rather than physical strength, a game of sublimated father-murder taught him by his own father, it is certainly not surprising that in those stories of Borges's concerned with idealist philosophy there is usually present some form of veiled father/son competition, a competition in which the son not infrequently tries to effect a wholly mental procreation, tries to occupy the place of the father by imagining or dreaming into existence a son of his own. Thus in ''The Circular Ruins'' the magician sets out ''to dream a man'' into existence, ''to dream him in minute entirety and impose him on reality.'' But the relationship of dreamer and dreamed soon becomes in the story that of father and son: ''When he closed his eyes, he thought: Now I will be with my son. Or, more rarely: The son I have engendered is waiting for me and will not exist if I do not go to him.'' In order to keep his son from ever knowing that he is merely a mental apparition, the magician wipes out ''all memory of his years of apprenticeship'':

> Of all the creatures that people the earth, Fire was the only one who knew his son to be a phantom. This memory, which at first calmed him, ended by tormenting him. He feared lest his son should meditate on this abnormal privilege and by some means find out he was a mere simulacrum. Not to be a man, to be a projection of another man's dreams—what an incomparable humiliation, what madness! Any father is interested in the sons he has procreated (or permitted) out of the mere confusion of happiness; it was natural that the wizard should fear for the future of that son whom he had thought out entrail by entrail, feature by feature, in a thousand and one secret nights.

But what the magician finally discovers is that father and son share the same substance, that he (the magician) can dream a phantom man into existence only because he is himself a phantom dreamed by another—a realization that comes to the magician when the ruined temple in which he dwells is engulfed by a forest fire, a fire that, as its flames caress him "without heat or combustion," claims him as its own.

As I said at the start, the game of chess is mentioned in four out of the eight stories in *The Garden of Forking Paths* and alluded to in the epigraph to a fifth. That fifth is "The Circular Ruins," and its epigraph, taken from chapter four of Lewis Carroll's *Through the Looking Glass,* runs "And if he left off dreaming about you. . . ." The line occurs in the scene where Alice, in the company of the mirror-image twins Tweedledum and Tweedledee, comes upon the sleeping Red King. As you recall, at the start of the book Alice falls asleep in the drawing room and dreams that she climbs through the mirror above the mantelpiece into the drawing room of Looking-glass House. When she steps outside the house, Alice finds that the garden is laid out like a chessboard, and her subsequent movements become part of a bizarre chess game. Gazing at the sleeping Red King, Tweedledee asks Alice what she thinks he's dreaming about. When she says that nobody can guess that, Tweedledee replies,

> "Why, about you! . . . And if he left off dreaming about you, where do you suppose you'd be?"

> "Where I am now, of course," said Alice.

> "Not you!" Tweedledee retorted contemptuously. "You'd be nowhere. Why, you're only a sort of thing in his dream!"

> "If that there King was to wake," added Tweedledum, "you'd go out—bang!—just like a candle!"

In the kind of Aleph-like oscillation of container and contained that obsessed Borges, Alice dreams the Red King, who dreams Alice, who dreams the Red King, and so on in an endless progression/regression. And just as Alice's mental existence as "a sort of thing" in the Red King's dream is evoked in an image of fire (if he awakens, she will go out like the flame of a candle—the traditional figuration of mind as light), so in "The Circular Ruins" fire is also invoked as a figure of a purely mental existence ("Of all the creatures that people the earth, Fire was the only one who knew his son to be a phantom").

What the epigraph to "The Circular Ruins" does in effect is to assimilate the relationship be-

tween the magician and his son, each of whom is an image in the dream of another, to that between Alice and the Red King, who dream one another, thus associating the context of the latter scene (a chess game) with the phantasmatic father-son relationship of the former. (Recall that when Alice comes upon the Red King, she is playing the role of a white pawn in the chess game, so that there is a mutually threatening quality to their encounter: if the King awakens, Alice goes out of existence, say the mirror-image twins; but on the other hand, when Alice, as a white pawn, finally reaches the eight rank and is promoted to a queen, she checkmates the Red King, which is to say that at the end of the game it is she who awakens from her dream and the Red King who goes out of existence.) "The Circular Ruins" and its epigraph bring together, then, in one spot those themes of fatherhood, mirroring, chess, dreams, and idealist philosophy that haunt Borges's work, images whose conjunction was established for Borges in a childhood scene of instruction in which a father faced, across the mirror-image alignment of pieces on a chessboard, his son (a diminutive image of himself) and, in demonstrating the paradoxes of Zeno and Berkeleyan idealism, showed him the dreamlike status of reality. In thinking back on that scene, perhaps Borges was reminded of Alice's words near the end of *Through the Looking Glass*: "So I wasn't dreaming, after all . . . unless—unless we're all part of the same dream. Only I do hope it's my dream, and not the Red King's! I don't like belonging to another person's dream."

Source: John T. Irwin "The False Artaxerxes: Borges and the dream of chess," in *New Literary History,* Vol. 24, No. 2, Spring, 1993, pp. 425–446.

Ralph Yarrow

The "aesthetic aim" Jurado refers to suggests that Jorge Luis Borges is concerned with the effect of his work, and that this effect may have something to do with the mental processes that give shape to what is then called reality. To suggest that Borges is concerned with stimulating the creative faculties of his audience appears legitimate; he says his work is a means of "fusing the world of the reader and the world of the book."

This possibility implies an intention similar to Robbe-Grillet's demand for the active participation of the reader in the creation of the work. More than that, it is—as with Robbe-Grillet, or Proust or Coleridge before him—a recognition that "imagination" is precisely that process of constructing significance for oneself. Borges's "games" are

> " We must never forget that Borges's intelligence . . . is at the service of games rather than convictions. . . . The purpose of the game is not to discover incognizable reality; it has an aesthetic aim."

designed to extend the "field of play" as far as possible and to make the reader aware that he or she is playing. Borges is aware, too, that the way in which this happens is through the physical changes induced in the brain by the demands made by his text: he states that "what is essential is the aesthetic factor, the thrill, the physical effect brought about by reading."

Looking at what happens when reading a story by Borges, one sees that the work necessarily and openly accepts the commitment made by the reader in entering the fictional sphere. Although the story may ultimately wish to correct the reader's notions about the relationship of fiction and reality, it first of all welcomes the assumption that these spheres are different and similar in the ways in which the reader has conventionally come to believe. The writer welcomes even more the reader's desire to gain something from the reading. This drive may be blocked, deflected, or turned upon itself, but it remains a necessity for reader and writer. The desire rests on assumptions much profounder, perhaps, than even a belief in the ability of language to signify—to say something meaningful about the world. It may reflect the sense that actions move towards some kind of completion, that there is some kind of shape to a succession of lived and willed events. That is, fundamentally, an intuition of order which is aesthetic in nature rather than merely intellectual. Thus the satisfaction gained from reading a book in its entirety has as much, if not more, to do with a grasping of pattern and plan, as with the simple knowledge of "what happens in the end."

A book draws, then, on two kinds of rather crucial awareness—about the nature of reality, and about the way in which relating to it is a matter of perceiving a growth of plan and order. These con-

cerns have perhaps become oversimplified and reduced to superficiality by conventional ideas about reading (both the mental and the physical operations involved) and by the large amount of easily "consumable" reading material available. So, in fact, Borges and others may not be making totally new demands, but rather attempting to reestablish the fundamental issues of reading; a "revolution" in the sense of returning to something. That which has been forgotten must be reestablished, and in order for this to happen, the forgotten must be highlighted. The text will, therefore, at first appear extraordinary; indeed it *has* to appear extraordinary, so that people can see the process of reading as something "new" and worth investigation. Shock tactics may be in order at this stage in the process. Just as Rilke said that poetry needed to respond to the earth's wish to become "invisible," so reading must become a new and strange experience in order for it to register. Readers must be made aware of the fact that they are reading, otherwise they will never perceive the extraordinary richness and importance of this old and familiar process. So Borges's work, like that of Robbe-Grillet and Gombrowicz, hovers incessantly around the borders of the "normal" and the "abnormal," constantly interrelating and juxtaposing the two.

The text needs, therefore, to be doing at least two things at once: inviting and stimulating the sense that something is to be discovered, some "point" to the reading; and subverting or distorting the over-hasty assumptions that tend to be made about how that point is reached. A title may do the job quite well. Take, for instance, the well-known Borges story, "The Garden of Forking Paths."

The title both seduces and subverts. Like other Borges stories, it offers a prospect of mystery but also suggests the opposite of a closed or simple solution. The garden and the labyrinthine implications have vaguely esoteric, Eastern, or exotic connotations. The detective format of the story (like "Death and the Compass") is similar not only to G. K. Chesterton, whom Borges certainly liked, but also to Robbe-Grillet (detectives in *Les Gommes, La Maison de Rendez-Vous*, labyrinths in *Dans le Labyrinthe, Topologie d'une Cite Fontome*). Butor (*Passage de Milan*) and Beckett (*Molloy*) also have something of the detective formula. Detective stories traditionally play a kind of game with the reader; they also traditionally offer a number of blind alleys, red herrings, spurious "clues," and so on. Whatever the "truth" may be, it will not be reached easily. In addition, the *nouveau roman* and other post-modernist writing (e.g., new American fiction in works like Pynchon's *The Crying of Lot 49*) often reverse the implicit assumption encoded into the structure of detective fiction and deliberately refuse any single or definitive solution that will ultimately be "revealed" to the reader. All of these possibilities float about in Borges's title, promising in addition a kind of intimate and bizarre pleasure. Getting caught up in the forking paths is a kind of Baudelairean *invitation au voyage*, leading readers to engage both narrative and mental processes, and the ways in which they may interact.

The story advertises its dubious wares clearly enough; it lays them out more fully in the combination of seductive and suggestive settings, themes, and appellations which follow. A summarization of the narrative in linear fashion is unnecessary, but the ingredients are clearly chosen for their effect: a Chinese spy for the Germans; a sinologist holding the key to the labyrinthine work of the spy's ancestor; a plot involving murder, attempted killing, and a message that will result in many deaths; the conjunction of modern (1916) war and Chinese culture; the sending of a secret message. The structure of the narrative is a typical (for Borges, as for Robbe-Grillet) "Chinese-box" affair, moving from the apparent neutrality of the opening paragraph ["On page 22 of Liddell Hart's *History of World War I* you will read . . ." (*Labyrinths*)] to a statement by the Chinese spy-cum-professor, to the English sinologist Albert's outline of Ts'ui Pen's work, to direct quotation from and involvement in that work. Version is enclosed within version, each narrative with its own range of reference and association, its own standards and horizons of "truth." Borges's fictional composition includes and comments upon the confessions of a spy, the philosophical exegesis of an academic, the traditionally inscrutable joke of a complex mind. The interference of the narratives incites reference back and forth, setting up analogies between contemporary historical events and cultural reflections, betwen the various levels of personal existence of Dr. Yu Tsun, between nationalities, beliefs, and codes.

This interaction is deliberately sought after in the structure and detail of the narratives. It is apparent even at the simple level of names and nationalities, with a Chinese-German spy, an English-Chinese expert, and an Irish-English secret service agent (who speaks German at the outset). The Chinese spy was formerly "professor of English at the *Hochschule* in Tsingtao" (*Labyrinths*). The result of his actions in Staffordshire will be under-

> " Each central symbol, theme, or idea is assimilated into a successively more extensive context, which displaces it from central to relative importance. In this way the reader is gradually pushed into a state in which he or she doesn't totally accept or reject anything."

stood in Berlin and translated into action in France. This confusion of nationality and identity can suggest various aspects: the complexity of political interaction and its implications for national identity; the increasing difficulty of simplistic notions about culture and genealogy; twentieth-century doubts about the singleness and stability of personality; the issue of how much our behavior is affected by the language we speak.

What happens, in general terms, is that each notation (here and in other Borges stories) works less as an attempt to "clarify" someone's identity and role than as a kind of magnetic field for associations. The stories are so short, and the details so few, that "realistic" character-portrayal is clearly not intended. (The same is true for Robbe-Grillet's longer fictions: "characters" frequently change names, and in *La Maison de Rendez-Vous* many of the names they adopt are aliases or have theatrical connotations, e.g. "L'Americain," "Lady Ava.") Names (and other details), become a kind of vibratory charge—not so much a definite symbol as a means of calling up associative possibilities (Chineseness, distinguished professorship) which themselves are usually deliberately vague. In this respect, the brevity of Borges' stories produces a highly-charged symbolism of doubt and possibility, which is intensified by many other techniques including the switch between narrative levels—realism and fantasy, for instance, or the confessional and the exegetic. Or the shifting or playing between psychological exploration and fantastic inventiveness; or the typical Borges mixture of genuine quotation and "spurious" scholarship. Uncertainty is produced whichever way you "read" the story, and principally if one manages to read it all ways at once—which is what the labyrinth at the center of the story suggests. It is "a labyrinth of symbols" (*Labyrinths*). These symbols point, however, not to some definitive grand interpretive scheme, but to the conjunction of apparently antagonistic possibilities: all four alternative endings, Albert explains, are possible for Ts'ui Pen's work.

Yu Tsun, however, chooses one of the endings and shoots Albert, in order to convey his secret message (the name Albert, as reported in the press, will also indicate the town in France that the Germans must attack). He, by a combination of historical necessity and psychological condition, opts for a single solution, which will inevitably result in his death as a murderer. In Robbe-Grillet and Gombrowicz, as here, and elsewhere in Borges, killing as closure is always suspicious—it is usually heavily ironized, and virtually never achieves the kind of solution it promises.

Murder, then, or sudden death, is a means of presenting one of the two poles between which the story oscillates. Mentioned also is that Yu Tsun's ancestor was murdered, and Albert refers to excerpts from his book concerned with a battle and with the various possible outcomes of a meeting between a man with a secret and a stranger. Albert claims that Ts'ui Pen meant the reader to choose not one alternative outcome, but all of them: the book is intended as a demonstration of what Valery called *noeuds* and contemporary critical theory describes as *generateurs*. That is to say, there are points in a text (any point, by implication) where the reader, like the writer, may seize not only upon the self-perpetuating inventiveness of narrative and decide to draw on any prticular association or link to give the text a new twist, but the reader or writer is also aware at that moment of holding within his grasp (in his imaginative or magical power) the secret or possibility of all future developments of that text. He is at the point where the paths fork. Any path is a potential murder/death because it can lead to closure; but the dominating single-mindedness (obsession or terrorism, for Robbe-Grillet) of each textual departure can always be arrested, and hauled back to any point from which the plurality of possibility becomes available again.

Yu Tsun has a secret (Albert's name) that he must encode and transmit. Albert has a secret (the nature of Ts'ui Pen's book and of his labyrinth). The garden is a "secret" kind of location (with medie-val, Chinese, mystical, erotic, biblical-genetic connotations). Borges's story teases us with its secretive atmosphere and offers a few clues (some helpful but hidden, others unhelpful and overt) as the reader is put in the position of trying to figure out what Yu Tsun is trying to do. In all cases, the real nature of the secret is generative rather than unitary. (A brief aside to The Sect of the Phoenix, whose aura of arcane profundity and talk of the Secret is a joke on the phoenix's propensities for sex.) Even Yu Tsun's message, when transmitted, has more than one possible outcome, and is important to him in more than one way. As an Oriental, he despises the Western conflict in which he finds himself caught up, but he needs to complete his mission to justify himself (and by implication his family and his race) in the eyes of his narrow-minded German boss (described as a "sick and hateful man—in his arid office"— *Labyrinths*). The import of the secrets is that in messages, in wisdom, and in all encoded texts (as shown by the successive frames of the story) reside not closed "answers" but structures of possibility.

That kind of structure is represented by Albert's proposition (fascinating to Yu Tsun and frequent in Borges) stating Ts'ui Pen's work reveals a conjunction of all time and identity. That is to say, when you actually stand at the point where paths fork, you hold sequence and causality in your power. This bifurcation is the "now" point of reading in contemporary critical theory, the point where reader and text converge. (Do battle, as in Simon's *La Bataille de Pharsale* (= *la phrase*) or Ricardou's *La Prise* (= *la prose*) *de Constantinople*: hence the battle quoted from Ts'ui Pen, of which two versions are given, and the battle Yu Tsun's act will influence.) It is the location of moral choice, in existentialist theory: the place from which the self is constructed, or—consistent with phenomenology—consciousness wills or intends a new perception and construction of reality.

Borges's games are not trivial, because as L. A. Murillo contends, "The conjecture is about radical questions of human existence, time, personal will, consciousness, and destiny." Such questions are pertinent to the protagonist (Yu Tsun) of "The Garden of Forking Paths," and are mediated through him, and through the structure of interlocking narratives Borges builds around him, to the reader. Thus "The Garden" is a "representation of the very process by which . . . events acquire their symbolical significance in the consciousness of the protagonist and . . . reader." The games, then, are centrally "about" the exploration by the reader (where else can the story "take place"?) of certain states and procedures in consciousness: those states and procedures that concern the way in which we invest our experience with understanding or significance, by which we arrive at our ability to interact creatively and purposively with our environment. The elements of game play that Borges uses here are for the purpose of propelling the reader towards this exploration.

Murillo, in *The Cyclical Night*, suggests that Yu Tsun is presented as being in an ethical vacuum: existentially aware of his responsibility in a world whose political, social, and psychological upheaval has negated a priori values, and conscious of his need to locate himself and make a choice that endows being and acting with meaning. Again one sees the confusing intersection of personal, cultural, and historical identities in the story. The "vacuum," also presented to the reader through the mystery, paradox, and symbolic condensation of the narrative, demands to be grasped and developed as text, as another way of pinpointing the source of moral choice.

Yu Tsun takes, perhaps, the easy way out. He opts for the single, deadly solution, though knowing, as his wry admission at the end makes clear, that it is not really so simple. ("He does not know . . . my innumerable contrition and weariness."—*Labyrinths*). The odd adjective indicates Yu Tsun's acknowledgment of the chance of plurality, a chance he passes over. Yu Tsun tries, by recalling his murder of Albert, to construct around the event a narrative that gives it the status of irrevocability (all incidents seem restrospectively compelling and essential). His "confession" is thus fundamentally spurious. Its format proposes an acquiescence that, in fact, is quite the reverse of the confession's purpose. His narrated version, like his act of murder, seeks to impose a unique and dominant reading.

That uniqueness and dominance is, however, undermined by the multiplicity of narratives within which Borges frames the story. It is, moreover, further placed in perspective by the contrast between Yu Tsun (actually Chinese but betraying his culture and his identity) and Albert (a Westerner who is far more an incarnation of traditional Chinese wisdom). Yu Tsun disregards or distorts Albert's possibilities; he uses him only as a cipher in a code of language and action. Yu Tsun tries uneasily to justify his action as inevitable in terms of historical necessity. Albert is, however, also the sign of

many other possibilities, more inclusive than the use to which his name is put as indicating a place to be destroyed. In addition to his grasp of the fluid dynamism of the labyrinth, he seems to Yu Tsun a person of Goethean stature, endowed with wisdom and easy grace. Living within the procreative garden, or labyrinth, Albert is at the junction of East and West, uniting the contemplative and the active, the English and the German, in a harmonious and lively balance, like that of nature and the "sparkling music" through which he is approached. He is the kind of multiple possibility that Yu Tsun ignores.

Murillo describes the labyrinthine structure by which consciousness is represented as a "metaphysical ground" (*The Cyclical Night*). The "hesitation" (Todorov's term)—characteristic of postmodernist texts and here instilled by the confusions and paradoxes, the ironic juxtaposition of versions, and so on—produced in protagonist and reader is the moment of absence (of choice, significance) that impels selection of world and action. The existentialist reading suggests that the motive force is an *angst*, a desperate need to fill the vacuum by projecting anything. That is certainly one factor, and it may be the principal one in Yu Tsun's case. But the contradictions, blocks, and ironic perspectives of the story's structure, together with its repeated indications about the plural significance of secrets, and the balance of forces harmonized in Albert, offer an alternative mode of response.

Such a response is also offered to Yu Tsun. As he moves towards Albert's house, he experiences a kind of detachment combined with a liveliness of perception. The "slope of the road . . . eliminated any possibility of weariness," and he feels himself to be "an abstract perceiver of the world" (*Labyrinths*). At this point he becomes aware of the "living countryside" and of an "almost syllabic music," which he later realizes is Chinese. Here, as always in Borges, the topology is not realistic scene-setting but directions to a mental state. Robbe-Grillet clearly works in a similar fashion in *Topologie d'une Cite Fantome*, but the parallel is not quite exact. Robbe-Grillet maps out with ironic geometrical precision the moves of an imagination confined by its own obsessions and by a passion for linguistic symmetry. Borges's landscapes have perhaps more in common with the *terrains vagues* of Beckett: they present not so much a process as a condition in which a process may take place. Beckett's world, for example, in *Molloy*, is one in which objects are cherished precisely because they are "*en voie de disparition*": the protagonists are in the process of ridding themselves of inherited assumptions about reality and its relationship with language. What we have is a curious kind of precise vagueness, a very persistent and subtle attempt to render a state in which "meaning" is loosening its hold, dissolving the links between word and experience. (Everything dissolves or disintegrates in Beckett: bicycles, limbs, relationships—the onions in Moran's Irish stew in *Molloy*: "*On n'est pas lie?*" is what the tramps in *Godot* ask each other.) Borges's descriptions, though they are in a way more detailed, frequently operate with a similar combination of the vague and the precise. That is to say, they are attempting to pinpoint a condition of increasing "vagueness," or distance from the restrictions of conventional levels of thinking and perceiving.

What increasing vagueness leads towards is exactly that moment when no single interpretation is dominant and possibility has re-established itself. Yu Tsun is in a kind of suspended animation in which the possibilities of harmony present themselves most fully to him. His state of physical ease matches the time of day (late afternoon) and the surroundings: "the afternoon was intimate, infinite" (*Labyrinths*); his consciousness is freed from its preoccupation with limited ends—he feels that it is not possible to be the enemy of a country, in the sense that he is now experiencing it. He is integrated with his surroundings, acting spontaneously, and feeling at home (he instinctively accepts the music and does not remember whether he knocks at Albert's gate or rings a bell). He is, in short, in a condition of very lively and expanded awareness in which his doubts about identity are replaced by a kind of oneness with nature as the source of order and mobility—"fireflies, words, gardens, streams of water, sunsets." Yu Tsun's state is what brings him to the center of the labyrinth, and Albert comes to open the gate, holding a symbolic lantern.

Yu Tsun is in fact blinded by the light, and cannot make out Albert's face. That is to say, in this situation where he becomes aware of himself as a center of possibility, an organizing potential, a consciousness which can shape and form, he is not able to pin Albert down as a limited and thus expendable identity. This "awareness of awareness" is both positive and negative, a sense of hesitation in which simplistic single interpretations are found inadequate, and the pluralistic is on the verge of presenting itself.

Thus the two versions of the battle in Ts'ui Pen's book offer as reasons for victory apparently

contrary states of mind: the warriors experience situations that make them feel either existential angst or joy. On the one hand, individual identity is felt to be insignificant; on the other it is merged in a communal celebration. In both cases an apparent negation of individual significance leads to a "victory" or fruitful outcome. In a similar way, the postmodernist "negative aesthetic" is a way of continually emphasizing the apparently negative in order to reveal hidden possibilities. Whatever is said also provides a way of *not* saying everything else: it puts off, conceals, and defers (differer, pace Derrida) all the other possibilities of language. So what is said is frequently contradicted or revealed to be inadequate, in order that it may be seen to have those other possibilities lurking behind or within it, as linguistic history for example, or as association, or as alternative readings.

In the one "direct quote" Borges gives us from Ts'ui Pen's text, the warriors are referred to as "heroes, tranquil their admirable hearts, violent their swords, resigned to kill and to die" (*Labyrinths*). The line might have come out of the *Bhagavad Gita*, an epic much concerned with the problems of fighting in the proper way. (Although Borges may not have actually taken it from there, he did use the *Gita* as one source among many for esoteric references.) Taking a leaf out of Maharishi Mahesh Yogi's commentary on the *Gita*, Borges would probably interpret the quotation something like this: "swords" refer to the "outer" organs of action, "hearts" to the inner state of mind. An apparently contradictory condition here renders the mind still and the body violently active. This condition actually allows the warriors to perform action without attachment to the result (however drastic that may seem), and because of that the action is in fact most successful and the warriors can be classified as heroes. Taking the gloss further, one can see that this kind of neutrality is the mark of being in the state where the possibilities are held in play. "Negative" or "positive" outcomes (apparent surrender or destruction of one "side") are balanced, or perhaps perceived to be equally false. At this point one is the master of the opposites (as Thomas Mann puts it in *The Magic Mountain*), as is the figure of Stephen Albert and his interpretation of Ts'ui Pen's narrative, and as is Borges with his construction of interlocking versions, and as the reader may be.

This interpretation is not inconsistent with Borgesian practice, but it does suggest a further point: "suspended animation" may be a more exact term than we suspected. It may be necessary to look further at this condition, since it does seem to be represented both by Yu Tsun and by the warriors. Useful parallels may be drawn between what occurs in reading and in certain states of consciousness closely analyzed in psycho-physiological terms by Maharishi Mahesh Yogi. His theory, together with experimental evidence derived from scientific investigation, can provide some interesting angles on the nature of aesthetic experience. One of the most crucial conditions for the experience is precisely the one in which stillness and activity appear to be present simultaneously.

What appears to happen is that a kind of neutral expectancy may be produced, as a background against which a variety of possibilities may be generated. I think this happens in ''The Garden of Forking Paths'' and in other Borges texts as a result of what Murillo calls ''displacement.'' In a phenomenological reading of the story, the narrator is realized via the narrative as a process; that is, as a succession of different vantage points, perceptions, or versions: the various styles and readings are a record of successive states of consciousness. (They move from the ''outer'' historical account of the war, through the deceptively confessional spy story, to Yu Tsun's more intimate sensations on approaching Albert's house, to Albert's gloss of Ts'ui Pen's work, and finally to the ''direct quotation'' given above: a graded progression towards the condition described and which Yu Tsun then reluctantly rejects.) The narrator presents this succession as a record of successive locations of his being-in-the-world, much as, for instance, Sartre's Roquentin in *La Nausee* tries out a variety of styles in an attempt to express the shifts and variations of identity. But just as from the mock-detective perspective, none of the versions offers the whole truth, so too each style is relativized by the next frame that the narrative adopts. Each central symbol, theme, or idea is assimilated into a successively more extensive context, which displaces it from central to relative importance. In this way the reader is gradually pushed into a state in which he or she doesn't totally accept or reject anything. The movement of the narrative into new frameworks takes the reader along, and at the same time serves as a block to any once-and-for-all opting for the previous perspective. One has to take part in the process by which meanings are created, but one is prevented from attributing finality to any one interpretation. The movement is something like closing and opening a pair of nutcrackers, as each possibility is grasped, then released as its kernel is found to be generative

rather than final. Murillo neatly explains Borges' semi-invented locality for the 1916 battle in this vein: *Serre-Montauhan* suggests a tension between ''compulsion'' and ''freedom''—which is both that of Yu Tsun's moral dilemma and of the reader's progress through the text. Interestingly, Ludovic Janvier describes Robbe-Grillet's narrative as built around the ''*couple fascination-liberte*.'' This ''disengaging compulsion toward ironical displacement'' allows the reader both to experience and to judge the progress of the protagonist/narrator. It further allows the reader to locate the source of creative and moral action, but forces him or her to return again and again to its nature as potential, and not to get carried away into one-sided choice.

The key to the production of this state is repetition. One reads on and on, and keeps getting blocked. Readers are somewhere between remembering and not remembering, between believing and not believing. They are in one sense getting lost in a labyrinth, and in another discovering that the secret of a labyrinth can be found only in that way. The reader becomes both active—in that she or he continues to read and to weigh up further possible additions and outcomes—and nonactive, in that everything is somehow held in abeyance, given a kind of nonfinite status, its seeming definitiveness undermined in advance by the ''let's wait and see'' mood established at the center of our consciousness. As a parallel to Yu Tsun's exposition of his state, with its moral and psychological implications, the text operates its own aesthetic procedure upon us. The state which Yu Tsun enters, in the labyrinthine center of Albert's enclave, but never fully explores, is offered as the means by which the thematic and structural development of Borges's tale can be most completely judged.

Irony gives more of a perspective so that more of the game can be judged. And yet one can only judge by being involved as well as detached. ''Critical distance,'' so often held up as the aim of literary study, does not mean a kind of owlish glare that reduces a text to the status of a dead mouse. It does not mean the cultivation of a spurious and self-delusive ''objectivity'' swathed in biographical detail or critical jargon. It means, and it requires, precisely the kind of participation in the reading of a text on all levels which Borges is here working to produce. The reader must ''get lost'' in the text. Ts'ui Pen ''renounced worldly power in order . . . to construct a labyrinth in which all men would become lost'' (*Labyrinths*). The labyrinth is *the* text, in the sense of the network of meanings through which people make the world known to themselves. If we go on using this text unthinkingly, we never really own the world at all, and perhaps never really experience it either. We have to make it *our* text, which means first of all forgetting the one convention dictates, and secondly becoming aware of our own propensity for memory and organization. Yu Tsun discovers his own past where he least expects it. Borges's narratives weave their spell of mystery, symbolic density, suggestiveness, and disruption in order to propel the reader into the area, the kind of mental activity, where dream and memory and imagination operate. But more than this, the narratives offer the chance to be and to perceive that operation in process. The reader must learn to manipulate symbol, metaphor, strange registers, and rhythms; to familiarize himself or herself with the most powerful properties, the generative structures of language.

Reading this story can show us our own linguistic and moral capacity. So "dreaming" is not evasion, but rather (as Borges suggests with inevitable irony in "The Circular Ruins") a very precise kind of work. Playing this sort of game—especially if engaged in repeatedly—could very well serve as useful training for everyday activity, even if authors—and critics—tend to overplay the game for its own sake and forget the application.

Source: Ralph Yarrow, "Irony Grows in My Garden: Generative Processes in Borges's 'The Garden of Forking Paths,'" in *The Fantastic in World Literature and the Arts*, edited by Donald E. Morse, Greenwood Press, 1987, pp. 73-86.

Stephen Rudy

"Ah, bear in mind this garden was enchanted." — E. A. Poe

". . . Magic is not the contradiction of the law of cause and effect but its crown, or nightmare." — Borges

Michel Foucault in his magnificent preface to *The Order of Things* quotes a text by Borges, a taxonomy of animals, which is attributed by Borges to a certain Dr. Franz Kuhn, who in turn attributes it to "a certain Chinese encyclopedia entitled *Celestial Emporium of Benevolent Knowledge.*" The text reads:

Animals are divided into: (a) belonging to the Emperor, (b) embalmed, (c) tame, (d) suckling pigs, (e) sirens, (f) fabulous, (g) stray dogs, (h) included in the above classification, (i) frenzied, (j) innumerable, (k) drawn with a very fine camelhair brush, (l) et cetera,

(m) having just broken the water pitcher, (n) that from a long way off look like flies.

Foucault's exegesis of this passage leads him to conclude that Borges is here creating a "heterotopia," a place that is an impossible and frightening non-place, a place of language and of mind which manages to contain words "in sites so very different from one another that it is impossible to find a place of residence for them, to define a common locus." This procedure, according to Foucault, "destroys . . . that less apparent syntax which causes words and things (next to and also opposite one another) to 'hold together.'" I think it could be argued that what Foucault finds Borges doing with words in general, we find the same writer doing with *plots* in "The Garden of Forking Paths," a story from the celebrated collection *Ficciones*. Plot emerges in this story in typically Borgesian fashion as a central symbolic element which embodies the author's subversive metaphysics as much as do the elements of theme or imagery more often discussed in the critical literature on this most sophisticated of contemporary writers.

I. The Frame

The first paragraph of "The Garden of Forking Paths" acts as a frame to the body of the text, a first-person confessional "document" written by Yu Tsun, a Chinese spy for the German Empire operating in England during the First World War. Ostensibly this framing paragraph serves to ground the confessional narrative in historical fact and provides the question to which Yu Tsun's "deposition" is supposedly an answer. The historical fact is the delay of a few days suffered in the British offensive on the Somme River in July, 1916. Borges (or more exactly, the "editor") cites Captain Liddell Hart's *A History of the World War* to the effect that "torrential rain caused this delay—which lacked any special significance." The reader assumes that Yu Tsun's "deposition" will prove (a) that "torrential rains" were not the decisive factor in the delay and—perhaps—(b) that the delay did have significance. This seems innocent enough if the reader is unaware, as no doubt he is, that the action on the Somme took place a month earlier than Borges quotes Liddell Hart, falsely, as having stated. He will be all the more surprised to discover that an obscure Chinese spy caused this delay by murdering a man who is, it seems, a reincarnation of his ancient ancestor Ts'ui Pen and that the delay thus had a significance of a most unsettling sort, indirectly and on another plane of "reality."

Yet Borges' intention in introducing us to the story via history is not simply to give his fiction an innocent motivation, that of answering the "official" account of a historical event, of attempting, on the basis of later "documentation," to assert historical "truth," whatever that may be. Rather, this frame is there for the purpose of exploding on itself: it is subversive. History, chronological time, has no place in Borges' universe, and since his universe so often appears as the "Book" or model of our universe, ours is left on shaky ground when he has completed his supposedly innocent operation of ascertaining the "truth." The historical work to which Borges refers is itself a "Borgesian" work: it is a startling narrative of "real" events which seem more fantastic than any fiction an author could invent. Borges understandably likes Conrad's thought "that when one wrote, even in a realistic way about the world, one was writing a fantastic story because the world itself is fantastic and unfathomable and mysterious.") The historian Liddell Hart, who is of a positivistic bent to say the least, admits of his enterprise that "it is difficult to pick out salient features where there are either none, or else so many that they tend to merge into a formless mass." Nevertheless, he plods along, sorting out causes and effects, making judgments, interpolating the various "factors" of chance involved in a given battle (with the thoroughness of an Avalon-Hill war game)—and ends up with a fantastic narrative. Borges takes the model of this fantastic but literal narration of "real events" as his starting point: he will correct Liddell Hart (ostensibly in the interests of historical truth), outdoing the very concept of cause and effect to the point that it turns on itself, and all notions of history, causal time, and truth are overthrown by the "unfathomable."

Such a strategy is quite typical of Borges. As Ronald Christ, in his excellent book *The Narrow Act*, states: "On the one hand Borges taints the reality which his sources describe; on the other he corrupts the authenticity of those sources themselves; in both cases the motive is to penetrate the metaphysical world which lies beyond fact and substance. . . ." In view of this critic's fine understanding of the meaningful distortion which even the simplest quoted text undergoes in Borges' hands, it is surprising that he completely misses the point of the reference to Liddell Hart in "The Garden. . . ," the opening of which, in his view, "shows Borges operating out of an historical background, grafting his fiction, once again, *on the stock of fact*" (italics mine). The mechanism of quotation, particularly

> In returning to 'The Garden . . . ,' one can see clearly how essential a role details play in cementing the two plots together in line with Borges' aesthetics of 'anticipation' and 'prefiguration.'"

quotation from an authoritative, non-fictional source, may be used as a device to mark the "factual," as opposed to "fictional," nature of a narrative. This is certainly the *overt* purpose of the opening paragraph of "The Garden. . . ." (This purpose is further served by the presentation of Yu Tsun's narrative as a "deposition," i.e., a genuine, if personal, account of an actual event, by its naturalistic fragmentation ["the first two pages are missing"], and by the "editor's note," which cantankerously corrects a supposedly slanderous accusation voiced in the deposition.) But the *covert* purpose of the opening, which, as we shall see, is more important for the story's total effect, is clearly to lull the reader into a type of false security as regards the status of "real" events, a security he will be forced to give up—if nothing else, in befuddlement. For the expectation of a "factual" type of narrative which the frame sets up is destroyed by Borges' play with two parallel yet incompatible plots, one of a detective, the other of a metaphysical, nature.

II. The Detective Plot

Into the frame of a historical plot, an effort to sort out the cause and effect of a historical event, Borges inserts a detective plot, a more modest (or usually so) effort to find the hidden order underlying a crime. Borges himself has characterized "The Garden of Forking Paths" as a "detective story": "its readers will assist at the execution, and all the preliminaries of a crime, a crime whose purpose will not be unknown to them, but which they will not understand—it seems to me—until the last paragraph" (*Ficciones*). The reader learns early in the story that Yu Tsun has a secret—the site of a new British artillery park on the Ancre—to communicate to his Chief, a "sick and hateful man . . . sitting in his arid Berlin office," and that his message will result in the bombing of the site by the Germans and a consequent delay in the British offensive. The reader also learns that Yu Tsun is being pursued by his arch-enemy, the British secret-service agent Madden, and is desperate, and that he is contemplating, and then has planned, a crime— viz., the emphasis on the "revolver with a single bullet" and his various meditations of the sort, *"Whosoever would undertake some atrocious enterprise. . . ."* Furthermore, this planned crime is somehow connected with his communicating the necessary information to his Chief, but all we learn relative to the *means* of the communication is that "the telephone directory gave [Yu Tsun] the name of the one person capable of passing on the information." Only in the last paragraph of the story do we learn that the crime is the murder of a man named Albert, whose elimination will signal to the Chief the necessity of eliminating the depot at Albert on the Ancre River. (This is, incidentally, a typical "fantastic" replacement of the inanimate [the name, a sign] by the animate [the unfortunate person who happens to bear the name].) Thus the name, not the man, is to communicate the spy's secret; the murder is a coded message, the solution of which hinges on a semantic notion, that of elimination, and a key word, the name, to express location.

III. The Metaphysical Mystery Plot

The second plot develops out of a coincidence, namely that the man named Albert, chosen by Yu Tsun as his victim-message, is a Sinologist who has solved the metaphysical mystery of the novel-labyrinth left by Yu Tsun's illustrious ancestor, Ts'ui Pen. The second plot is also a detective plot, though of a literary-critical nature, whose solution is also based on the decoding of a message. This message is Ts'ui Pen's will (just as the newspaper article on Albert's murder is in some sense Yu Tsun's will), which is decoded on the basis of the key word *time*, which Ts'ui Pen eliminated from his novel (just as the key word *Albert* was "eliminated" by proxy to insure the success of Yu Tsun's plan). The unique novel left by Ts'ui Pen, considered by posterity to be "a shapeless mass of contradictory drafts" and decoded by the ingenious Albert, is actually a symbolic labyrinth of time in which the various possible futures of the characters are depicted simultaneously. As Albert puts it:

"In all fiction, when a man is faced with alternatives he chooses one at the expense of the others. In the almost unfathomable Ts'ui Pen, he chooses—simul-

taneously—all of them. He thus *creates* various futures, various times which start others that will in their turn branch out and bifurcate in other times. This is the cause of the contradictions in the novel.

"Fang, let us say, has a secret. A stranger knocks at his door. Fang makes up his mind to kill him. Naturally, there are various possible outcomes. Fang can kill the intruder, the intruder can kill Fang, both can be saved, both can die and so on and so on. In Ts'ui Pen's work all the possible solutions occur, each one being the point of departure for other bifurcations. Sometimes the pathways of the labyrinth coverge. . . ."

This novel conception of narrative echoes Borges' own view of time, presented throughout his stories and essays, a view which stresses the cyclical nature of history and the concept of the Eternal Return, resulting in a negation of the concept of "individuality" and, on the literary side, the radical assumption that all authors are ultimately one, all texts forming the collective text of a universal and eternal Author. Borges' theories of time have been admirably discussed by various critics and need not detain us here, though one could note in passing that certain pronouncements of Yu Tsun are rephrasings of Borges' own statement on the subject. In terms of plot, however, it should be stressed that the metaphysical plot parallels the murder plot in abstract form: both involve messages to be decoded on the basis of the elimination of a key term. The fact that one message relates to a man's life and the other to a literary work immediately suggests a disturbing parallelism between the universe (the "real" plane) and the book (the "fictional" plane).

IV. The Crossing of the Plots

Coincidence brings the two plots together, and the second is contained in the first just as the first is framed historically. The reader expects the second plot to illuminate the first (or at least have some direct bearing upon it) just as the first supposedly illuminates the historical event referred to in the framing paragraph of the opening. Actually, it does so only indirectly, on a different level, and thus again subversively. Before exploring the devices by which the first and second plot are linked, let us turn briefly to one of Borges' most famous theoretical statements on narrative, which is of relevance for an understanding of the overall structure of "The Garden. . . ."

In an essay on "Narrative Art and Magic," first published in Spanish in 1932 (i.e., before Borges began writing the stories in *Ficciones*) and only recently translated into English, Borges outlines a primitive typology of narrative alternatives. His statements refer primarily to the genre of the novel, but are actually of little critical use in approaching that domain; they read more like a manifesto for the future poetics of the short stories in *Ficciones*. The main problem of the novel for Borges is that of cause and effect, or the motivation of fictional events. He sees two possible approaches. The first, which typifies fiction of "the slow-moving psychological variety," is grounded in character and depends for its success on a chain of cause and effect which may be termed "naturalistic": it is "the incessant result of endless, uncontrollable [psychological] processes." This approach Borges finds wholly unacceptable: as he puts it, citing Mallarme in his support, "the pleasure of reading is in anticipation, and the ideal lies in suggestion." The psychological novel succeeds through a consistency of motivation which, for Borges, is as tiresome as it is predictable. The second approach he discusses is based on "magic," and in it, "—clear and defined—every detail is an omen and a cause." In defining magic, "that craft, or ambition, of early man," Borges quotes the general principle formulated by Sir James Frazer, "the Law of Sympathy, which assumes that 'things act on each other at a distance through a secret sympathy,' either because their form is similar (imitative, or homeopathic, magic) or because of a previous physical contact (contagious, or contact, magic)," or in more contemporary terms, through association based on similarity or contiguity (respectively metaphoric or metonymic relations). According to Borges, "the only possible integrity" for the novel is to be found in "narrative magic." The novel should be "a rigorous scheme of attentions, echoes, and affinities." "Every episode in a painstaking piece of fiction," Borges writes, "prefigures something still to come."

It is not surprising that Borges supports his argument with references to the adventure novel, the detective story, and the "endless spectacular fictions made up in Hollywood." The first two, despite the primitiveness of many of their practitioners, offer manifold possibilities for intricate plotting, in which characters act as "functions" (much as they do in the folk tale) rather than as determiners of the action. The suppression of the psychological element in Borges may be regarded not merely as a philosophical and aesthetic reaction against "the psychologism bequeathed to us by the last century," as he puts it, but also as a reflection of a more general poetics of narrative. The emphasis on plot entails a reduction in the importance of character and necessitates a concomitant increase in embedded, structurally significant details of description which prefigure the action and thus form a sort of "secret plot," to use Borges' term.

In returning to "The Garden . . . ," one can see clearly how essential a role details play in cementing the two plots together in line with Borges' aesthetics of "anticipation" and "prefiguration." It is precisely the undercurrent of signification, the "secret plot" formed by connecting links between the two plots, which renders neither plot adequate in explaining the action and results in the disorienting "heterotopia" typical of Borges. The role of detail is most obvious on the level of imagery, where the emphasis on the circle reinforces the theory of cyclical time advanced in the metaphysical plot; as Ronald Christ has pointed out, "cyclical time is evinced in the portentous detail." On the level of plot Yu Tsun's meditation on his ancestor's labyrinth before meeting by "accident" the man who has solved its riddle—a meditation which would seem initially to be a mere "digression"—motivates the meeting with Albert, which does not in the least surprise Yu Tsun. Furthermore, as E. Rodriguez Monegal has shown, Yu Tsun's meditation actually anticipates on an intuitive level the intellectual solution later offered by Albert: "I thought of a maze of mazes, of a sinuous, ever growing maze *which would take in both past and future and would somehow involve the stars*" (italics mine). The details embodied in Albert's discussion of Ts'ui Pen's novel also serve to link the detective and metaphysical plots. In describing the novel's structure, besides the rather portentous example of the character Fang, a stranger, and a murder, Albert has recourse to an illustration based on the present situation, Yu Tsun's appearance at his house: "Sometimes the pathways of the labyrinth converge. For example, you come to this house; but in other possible pasts you are my enemy; in others my friend." And further:

"... your ancestor ... believed in an infinite series of times in a dizzily growing, ever spreading network of diverging, converging and parallel times. This web of time—the strands of which approach one another, bifurcate, intersect or ignore each other through the centuries—embraces *every* possibility. We do not exist in most of them. In some you exist and not I, while in others I do, and you do not, and in yet others both of us exist. In this one, in which chance has favored me, you have come to my gate. In another, you, crossing the garden, have found me dead. In yet another, I say these very same words, but am an error, a phantom."

Yu Tsun replies: "In all of them . . . I deeply appreciate and am grateful to you for the restoration of Ts'ui Pen's garden." Albert's response, his last words before being assassinated by Yu Tsun, seem to reveal an intuition of his death at the spy's hands: "'Not in *all*,' he murmured with a smile. 'Time is forever dividing itself toward innumerable futures and in one of them I am your enemy.'" In terms of the metaphysics of repetition, Albert's death may be interpreted as a reenactment of Ts'ui Pen's "assassination by a stranger" centuries before. Yu Tsun experiences the "pullulation" of past and future identities, a state in which he becomes an "abstract spectator" of his own life, which seems directed by a will other than his own. His last words to Albert, "The Future exists now . . . ," seem almost ironic. We are abruptly returned to the detective plot by the sudden appearance of Madden, whom Yu Tsun sees coming through the garden (as if emerging out of his vague hallucinations) to arrest him. The spy's enactment of his plan, the murder of Albert, occurs simultaneously on the level of the mundane causality of the detective plot and on that of the inscrutable causality of the metaphysical; the moment of the murder is on the borderline between the "real" and the "fantastic."

The use of two plots, of a murder mystery and a metaphysical mystery which runs imperceptibly parallel and counter to it, is motivated by Borges' desire to upset any notion of plot understood as simple chronological causality, as well as the conception of reality which underlies such a notion. The disjunction of the two plots, the impossible distance which separates the realms to which each pertains, is so startling precisely because of their apparent and less obvious parallelisms. The two plots are connected with history through the framing device and make it (a potential model for plot in general) seem as fantastic as the time of Ts'ui Pen's labyrinth. The "delay" Yu Tsun has caused becomes more significant as having been the cause of his primal reenactment of Ts'ui Pen's assassination than it was in "real" history, and the total significance of the story is caught up in the unfathomable metaphysics of repetition. As one critic temptingly formulates it: "The labyrinth and the book are one and the same. But they are also something else as Borges insinuates—the universe."

Source: Stephen Rudy, "The Garden *of* and *in* Borges' 'Garden of Forking Paths,'" in *The Structural Analysis of Narrative Texts*, edited by Andrej Kodjak, Michael J. Connolly, and Krystyna Pomorska, Slavica Publishers, Inc., 1980, pp. 132-144.

Sources

Barth, John, "The Literature of Exhaustion," in *Atlantic Monthly*, Vol. 220, No. 2, August, 1967, pp. 29-34.

Borges, Jorge Luis, *Labyrinths*, preface by Andre Maurois, edited by Donald A. Yates, and James E. Irby, New Directions Books, 1964.

Fraser, John, "Jorge Luis Borges, Alive in His Labyrinth," in *Criticism*, Vol. 31, Spring, 1989, pp. 179-91.

Gonzalez-Echevarria, Roberto, "Borges and Derrida," in *Jorge Luis Borges*, edited and with an introduction by Harold Bloom, Chelsea House, 1986.

Irwin, John, "A Clew to a Clue: Locked Rooms and Labyrinths in Poe and Borges," in *Raritan*, Vol. 10, Spring, 1991, pp. 40-57.

Jaen, Didier T., *Borges Esoteric Library: Metaphysics to Metafiction*, Lanham, 1992.

Lindstrom, Naomi, *Jorge Luis Borges: A Study of the Short Fiction*, Twayne, 1990.

Stabb, Martin, *Jorge Luis Borges*, Twayne, 1970, p. 138.

Stoicheff, Peter, "The Chaos of Metafiction," in *Chaos and Order: Complex Dynamics in Literature and Science*, edited by N. Katherine Hayles, University of Chicago Press, 1991, pp. 85-99.

Updike, John, "Books: The Author as Librarian," in *New Yorker*, October 31, 1965, pp. 223-46.

Waugh, Patricia, *Metafiction: The Theory and the Practice of Self-Conscious Fiction*, Routledge, 1988.

Weissert, Thomas P., "Representation and Bifurcation: Borges' Garden of Chaos Dynamics," in *Chaos and Order: Complex Dynamics in Literature and Science*, edited by N. Katherine Hayles, University of Chicago Press, 1991, pp. 223-42.

Wheelock, Carter, "Borges and the 'Death' of the Text," in *Hispanic Review*, Vol. 53, 1985, pp. 151-61.

Woodall, James, *The Man in the Mirror of the Book: A Life of Jorge Luis Borges*, Hodder and Stoughton, 1996.

Further Reading

Bloom, Harold, ed., *Jorge Luis Borges*, Chelsea House, 1986.
A collection of important critical essays, including the chapter-length essay, "Doubles and Counterparts: 'The Garden of Forking Paths'" by Shlomith Rimmon-Kenan.

Lindstrom, Naomi, *Jorge Luis Borges: A Study of the Short Fiction*, Twayne, 1990.
Offers an introduction to Borges, as well as an interview, selected criticism, a chronology, and a bibliography.

Sorrentino, Fernando, *Seven Conversations with Jorge Luis Borges*, translated by Clark M. Zlotchew, The Whitson Publishing Company, 1982.

A collection of seven interviews with Borges, considered to be among the best books of its kind. Includes a helpful appendix identifying personalities mentioned by Borges.

Weissert, Thomas P., ''Representation and Bifurcation: Borges' Garden of Chaos Dynamics,'' in *Chaos and Order: Complex Dynamics in Literature and Science*, edited by N. Katherine Hayles, University of Chicago Press, 1991, pp. 223-43.

Provides an interesting account of chaos and bifurcation theory in lay terms. Weissert uses the theories to demonstrate Borges' fundamental determinism and modernism, as opposed to chaotic postmodernism. A good choice for the advanced student interested in both literature and science.

Woodall, James, *The Man in the Mirror of the Book: A Life of Jorge Luis Borges*, Hodder and Stoughton, 1996.

An accessible biography of Borges. Includes photographs and bibliography as well as a listing of films based on Borges' work.

Girl

Jamaica Kincaid

1978

First published in the June 26, 1978, issue of *The New Yorker*, "Girl" was the first of what would become more than a dozen short stories Jamaica Kincaid published in that magazine. Five years later, "Girl" appeared as the opening story in Kincaid's collection of stories, *At the Bottom of the River* (1983), her first book.

"Girl" is a one-sentence, 650-word dialogue between a mother and daughter. The mother does most of the talking; she delivers a long series of instructions and warnings to the daughter, who twice responds but whose responses go unnoticed by the mother. There is no introduction of the characters, no action, and no description of setting. The mother's voice simply begins speaking, "Wash the white clothes on Monday," and continues through to the end. Like all of Kincaid's fiction, "Girl" is based on Kincaid's own life and her relationship with her mother. Although the setting is not specified in the story, Kincaid has revealed in interviews that it takes place in Antigua, her island birthplace.

When *At the Bottom of the River* was reviewed in major publications, reviewers praised the rhythm and beauty of the language and found the mother-daughter relationship fascinating, especially as it changes and develops throughout the volume. But a few, including the novelist Anne Tyler, found them too opaque. Tyler called the stories "almost insultingly obscure," but still encouraged readers to read the volume and to follow the career of

"a writer who will soon, I firmly believe, put those magical tools of hers to work on something more solid."

Author Biography

Raised in Antigua, a small and beautiful island nation in the Caribbean, Kincaid experienced first-hand the colonialism that affects so many of her characters. Antigua was a colony of Great Britain when Kincaid was born on May 25, 1949, and given the name Elaine Potter Richardson. Elaine's mother, Annie Richardson Drew, was a believer in obeah, a West Indian religion incorporating magic and ritual. For nine years Elaine was an only child, and felt happy and loved. She began school when she was four, the same year her mother taught her to read. She was a bright student. When her three brothers were born, she felt that her mother turned away from her; a longing for a reconciliation with a distant mother is a recurring theme in Kincaid's work.

Elaine's adolescent years were turbulent. She became aware of various ways that black Antiguans were made to serve the British, and she rebelled, especially at school, where the children were taught English history, geography, and literature instead of Caribbean. In June, 1966, at seventeen, Elaine left Antigua to become an au pair in New York. Over the next seven years she worked as an au pair, a receptionist, and a secretary; studied photography; and eventually began a career in publishing. Her first publication was an interview with feminist Gloria Steinem for *Ingenue* magazine. Soon afterward, she changed her name to Jamaica Kincaid, "Jamaica" for the Caribbean country, and "Kincaid" because it "just seemed to go together with Jamaica."

As Jamaica Kincaid, she wrote articles for various magazines and became a staff writer for the *New Yorker* magazine in 1976. She would write more than eighty essays for the magazine in the next decade. One afternoon, after reading an Elizabeth Bishop poem, "In the Waiting Room," Kincaid sat down and wrote the short story "Girl" in one sitting. As she tells it, she found her voice as a writer that afternoon: "I somehow got more confident in what I knew about language. Finding your voice brings great confidence." The story, which is one long sentence spoken by a Caribbean mother to her daughter, appeared in the *New Yorker* in the June 26, 1978, issue, the first of many short stories she would publish there. It also became the first story in her first book, *At the Bottom of the River*, a collection of ten stories about childhood in the Caribbean. This writing experience taught Kincaid that the Caribbean and her mother would always be her true subjects.

Kincaid married, had two children, moved to Vermont, and continued to write. She has published six books of autobiographical fiction and received numerous awards. Her work has attracted critical as well as popular success, as the writer's voice she found has changed and evolved.

Plot Summary

The story begins abruptly with words spoken by an unidentified voice. "Wash the white clothes on Monday and put them on the stone heap; wash the color clothes on Tuesday and put them on the clothesline to dry; don't walk barehead in the hot sun. . . ." The voice continues offering instructions about how a woman should do her chores, and then about how she should behave: "on Sundays try to walk like a lady and not like the slut you are bent on becoming." At the end of the first third of the story, another voice, signaled by italics, responds, *"but I don't sing benna on Sundays at all and never in Sunday school."* This speaker is presumably the daughter of the main speaker. Without any reply to the daughter, and without missing a beat, the mother continues with her litany. She suggests how to hem a dress "and so to prevent yourself from looking like the slut I know you are so bent on becoming."

As the story progresses, the mother's tone becomes more insistent and more critical. The chores and behaviors are more directly related to a woman's duties to men, such as ironing a man's clothes. The mother again comes back to her earlier admonition: "this is how to behave in the presence of men who don't know you very well, and this way they won't recognize immediately the slut I have warned you against becoming." The lines of advice are loosely grouped into sections of related lines. In a section that recognizes the powers of obeah, a mystical religion based on African beliefs, she cautions the daughter against taking appearances for granted, and explains how to make several medicines to cure disease, bring on an abortion, and catch a man. Finally she shows the daughter how to squeeze bread to tell whether it is fresh. For the second time, the daughter speaks: *"but what if the*

Jamaica Kincaid

Characters

Daughter

The daughter is an adolescent or pre-adolescent girl in Antigua, learning from her mother how to be a proper woman. She speaks only twice in the story, voicing impulsive objections to her mother's accusations and warnings.

Mother

The mother is a woman in Antigua who understands a woman's "place." She lives in a culture that looks to both Christianity and obeah, an African-based religion, and that holds women in a position of subservience to men. She recites a catalog of advice and warnings to help her daughter learn all a woman should know. Many of her lines

baker won't let me feel the bread?" This time the mother replies to her daughter, "you mean to say that after all you are really going to be the kind of woman who the baker won't let near the bread?" With that, the story ends. There is no action, no exposition of any kind, and no hint of what happens to the characters after this conversation.

are practical pieces of advice about laundry, sewing, ironing, sweeping, and setting a table for different occasions. Other harsher admonitions warn the daughter against being careless with her sexuality, "so to prevent yourself from looking like the slut I know you are so bent on becoming."

Themes

Mothers and Daughters

Like much of Kincaid's fiction, "Girl" is an examination of the relationship between the "girl" of the title and her mother. The mother's instruction to "soak your little cloths right after you take them off" refers to the cloths woman in many parts of the world use to absorb their menstrual flow and indicate that the girl is a young adolescent. Kincaid has said that all of her fiction is based on autobiography, and that her own relationship with her mother has been difficult since Kincaid was nine years old. In an interview with Selwyn R. Cudjoe she explains, "the fertile soil of my creative life is my mother. When I write, in some things I use my mother's voice, because I like my mother's voice. . . . I feel I would have no creative life or no real interest in art without my mother. It's really my 'fertile soil.'"

Nearly all of the text of "Girl" is the mother's words to the daughter. Although the mother does nearly all of the talking and there is no action or exposition, there is much that can be guessed about the relationship between the two. The mother is preparing the girl to take her rightful place as a daughter and then a wife, and teaches her how to do the chores expected of a woman. If the mother feels that the tasks allotted to a woman are demeaning or subservient, she does not say so, but neither does she describe the satisfactions of her life. She simply shares information about washing, sewing, ironing, gardening, cooking, and making medicine, trying to be objective and thorough. But there is a steady current of suspicion and fear lying under the surface, and the mother is unable to talk very long without something reminding her of the dangers of sex, and of "the slut you are so bent on becoming." When she thinks of sex, and of her daughter's supposed or real flirtation with it, her tone becomes colder, even angry.

The daughter's reaction to her mother's litany can only be imagined, because Kincaid does not reveal it. How would any young teen react to hearing such a long list of suggestions from one's mother? Twice the daughter interrupts with a defensive comment, both times beginning with the word "but." The first time, the mother does not respond, but simply goes on with her speech. The second time, near the end of the story, her growing anger causes her to irrationally hear the daughter's innocent question, *"but what if the baker won't let me feel the bread?"* as confirmation of her suspicions, that the girl is thinking about "sluttish" behavior, that she is going to become "the kind of woman who the baker won't let near the bread."

This conflict between mother and daughter is not unusual. Many mothers, because they know what their daughters may not know—that sexual promiscuity tends to hurt women more than it does men—grow angry and fearful at the thought of their daughters behaving recklessly. However, in this mother's entire long speech there is not a single gentle line, not one word of love or reassurance. The words the mother leaves out reveal as much about the relationship as what she includes.

Culture Clash

Although Kincaid herself has denied that she thought much about politics when she was writing *At the Bottom of the River*, Diane Simmons demonstrates that the British colonial powers governing Antigua during Kincaid's youth stand behind many of the lessons of Kincaid's fictional mothers. "As the child in both *At the Bottom of the River* and *Annie John* approaches puberty, the mother increasingly imitates the colonial educational system, which seems bent on erasing all that is native to the child, rewarding only that which imitates the European rulers." Thus, the mother suddenly institutes a number of programs to make a "young lady" out of her daughter.

Clearly the family lives simultaneously in two cultures. They sing *benna* (calypso music), but know enough not to sing it in the European church. They practice obeah, a system of belief derived from Africa, but they also attend Sunday school. They eat bread pudding and doukona, a spicy plantain pudding, but also know how to "set a table for tea." The mother's attempt to train her daughter in the ways of the colonizers—ways that will help her be successful but that will turn her against her true self—may account for the mother's growing coldness throughout "Girl." She becomes angry because, however dutifully she passes along her knowledge, her heart is not in it. Kincaid remembers her own training with some anger. "I was brought up to be sexless and well-behaved. . . . I was supposed to

Media Adaptations

- "Girl" is available on audiotape, read by the author. The tape, produced in 1991 by the American Audio Prose Library, is titled *Jamaica Kincaid Reading Annie John (The Red Girl), At the Bottom of the River ("Girl" and "My Mother"), Lucy (Excerpts)*.

be full of good manners and good speech. Where the hell I was going to go with it I don't know."

Style

Point of View

"Girl" does not have a narrator in the conventional sense, because it does not have action in the conventional sense. There is no event, or series of events, acted out or told about by the characters or by a third-person narrator outside the action. Instead, the story is for the most part one speech delivered by the mother. The mother speaks in the first person referring to herself as "I" when she mentions "the slut I know you are so bent on becoming" and "the slut I have warned you against becoming." Far more important than the pronoun "I," however, is the pronoun "you." The mother directs her speech to her daughter, the "girl" of the title, and every instruction contains either the word "you" ("this is how you set a table for tea") or the implied "you" ("cook pumpkin fritters in very hot sweet oil").

In its handling of point of view, "Girl" is more like a type of lyric poetry called the dramatic monologue than it is like most short prose fiction. The dramatic monologue places one character in a dramatic situation and has her speak to a listener who can be identified but who does not speak herself. Through the words of the speaker, a personality and a conflict are revealed. Of course, "Girl" does have two lines spoken by the listener, the daughter. These lines, also spoken in the first person, move the story beyond pure dramatic monologue into the realm of fiction, where the exchange between the characters, limited though it is, becomes the central action.

As Moira Ferguson points out, however, the complete lack of exposition in the story opens up another possibility: ''the entire section could be the daughter's own internal monologue. What if the daughter is simply imagining this oracular, maternal discourse, extrapolating certain worries expressed by the mother in day-to-day asides?'' In that case, the words assumed to be the mother's would be memories of things she has said over time, not necessarily one long speech, and the italicized responses from the girl could be rehearsals for things she might say the next time the mother criticizes. Whether the mother is speaking or the girl is remembering, Kincaid uses the first-person point of view to create immediacy and tension; even with no description of people or places, the reader cannot help but visualize these two women and feel the charged atmosphere between them.

Setting

Although there are no descriptive passages in ''Girl,'' there are several clues to the story's Caribbean setting in the mother's instructions. In the first lines, for example, the mother mentions putting laundry ''on the stone heap'' and ''on the clothesline to dry,'' indicating a way of life without electrical appliances. Later, she tells ''how you make ends meet,'' again indicating relative poverty. The foods she mentions help place the story in the Caribbean: pumpkin fritters, salt fish, okra, dasheen (also called taro, a tropical starchy root), bread pudding, and pepper pot. Kincaid grew up on the island of Antigua, in a home without electricity or running water, and although she does not name the place, in her mind it is set there.

Literary Heritage

Because Kincaid was born and raised in Antingua, an island in the West Indies, and emigrated to New York as a young adult, her fiction may be categorized as emerging from both Caribbean and American literary traditions. The virtual genocide of indigenous peoples of the West Indies by European colonizers in the sixteenth century explains why there is no surviving indigenous oral or literary

tradition of the islands of the West Indies. Until the 1900s, literature emerging from the region was derived from the literary traditions of the conquering nations, including Spain, France, Great Britain, and the Netherlands. In the 1920s, however, a movement of writers influenced by Spanish-American Modernism began to develop a distinctive West Indian literature identified with the segment of the region's population largely of African descent. Distinguishing themselves from European literary aesthetics, these poets drew from oral folkloric traditions to strive for ''the construction into poetic forms of the rhythmic and tonal elements of the islands' rituals and speech patterns, using Symbolist and Surrealist techniques'' (*Encyclopaedia Britannica*). Kincaid's writing style, which utilizes a non-standard form of written English, follows this tradition in its success at capturing both the speech patterns and folkloric elements of West Indian culture.

Historical Context

Antigua: British Colony

''Girl'' was first published in *The New Yorker* magazine twelve years after Kincaid left Antigua for New York City. Even at that distance of time and space, Kincaid drew on her experiences growing up in Antigua for the setting and themes of ''Girl,'' as she has done for the rest of her fiction. From the time Kincaid was born in 1949 until she left in 1966, Antigua was a colony of Great Britain. England had gained control of the island in 1667, after thirty years of fighting with the Carib Indians, who inhabited the island, and the Dutch and French, who wished to own it. In 1674 the first great sugarcane plantations were established, and slaves were brought in from Africa to do the work on them; the slaves were freed in 1834, and their descendants make up most of the population of the island. Antigua also became an important naval base for the British, and remained so until the beginning of the twentieth century, when battles between the British and the French for control of the New World waned.

Antigua under the British had a small, wealthy population of whites from Europe, and a large, poor black population descended from imported African slaves. The Carib Indian population had been eliminated. Like her peers, Kincaid attended schools based on the British educational system. The child-

Compare & Contrast

- **1978:** Antigua is a semi-independent "Associated State" under British domain, no longer a full colony, but not an independent nation.

  1990s: Antigua, Barbuda, and the uninhabited island of Redonda make up the independent nation of Antigua and Barbuda.

- **1970s:** The economy of Antigua is largely based on farming, particularly fruits, vegetables, cotton and livestock. Its former reliance on sugar production has ended abruptly and catastrophically in the 1960s.

  1990s: The economy of Antigua is based on services, particularly tourism and off-shore banking.

- **1970:** Approximately 41 percent of Antigua's population is fourteen years old or younger.

Many adults leave the country, or die in middle age.

1995: Only 25 percent of the population is fourteen years old or younger. Adults are living longer, and staying in Antigua.

- **1974:** Although Antigua is a small and poor island, it is densely populated. There are 70,000 people, with an average of 412 people per square mile.

  1995: The population of Antigua has decreased to about 65,000 people, as many Antiguans have moved to the United States and elsewhere to escape poverty and to make a better life. The United States has 263 million people, with an average of 71 people per square mile.

---

ren were taught to speak "proper" English, studied British history, and read and memorized the works of British writers including William Wordsworth and John Milton. They did not learn about the Carib peoples, or about African or even Antiguan history. There were no books by Caribbean writers available.

As a young child Kincaid did not feel the effects of colonialism. In an interview with Donna Perry she comments, "the political situation became so normal that we no longer noticed it. The better people were English and that was life." But as she grew older she began to rebel, as she told Selwyn R. Cudjoe, "When I was nine, I refused to stand up at the refrain of 'God Save Our King.' I hated 'Rule, Britannia'; and I used to say we weren't Britons, we were slaves."

Because Antigua was so poor, it was easily dominated by Great Britain, and the economy grew worse in the 1960s when the international sugar market declined and Antigua was forced out of the business. However, in 1967, after Kincaid had left for New York, Antigua and another island, Barbuda, became one semi-independent "Associated State."

They attained full independence from Great Britain on November 1, 1981.

Antigua: Daily Life

Although it is the wealthiest island in the Eastern Caribbean, Antigua is poor by North American standards, and was even poorer during the time of Kincaid's youth. Most families, like the mother and daughter in "Girl," grew most of their own fruits and vegetables and ate little meat beyond the fish they caught themselves. Foods mentioned in the story were typical: pumpkin fritters, doukona (a pudding made from cornmeal, green bananas, coconut, sugar, and spices), and pepper pot (a stew made from spinach-like greens and other vegetables, reheated each day with new ingredients added). Their homes did not have running water or electricity, and they treated illnesses with home-made medicines rather than with doctors and pharmacies.

Many Antiguans, especially the older generations, practice a woman-centered, African-based religion called obeah, similar to voodoo. Even those who are members of Christian churches will often practice obeah as well, using spells and secret medicines when the situation calls for them. Because objects may conceal spirits, believers in obeah do not trust appearances. This lies behind the mother's warning, "don't throw stones at blackbirds, because it might not be a blackbird at all." Kincaid's mother and grandmother practiced obeah, and the writer explained in an interview with Selwyn R. Cudjoe, "I was very interested in it; it was such an everyday part of my life, you see. I wore things, a little black sachet filled with things, in my undershirt. I was always having special baths. It was a complete part of my life for a very long time."

Critical Overview

Because "Girl" and several other Kincaid stories had first been published in the influential magazine *The New Yorker,* when Kincaid's collection *At the Bottom of the River* came out in 1983 it attracted more critical attention than volumes of short stories usually do, particularly for a writer's first book. Early reviewers were drawn to the language of the stories, though some were put off by the overall obscurity. Anne Tyler, writing for *The New Republic,* praised the stories for Kincaid's "care for language, joy in the sheer sound of words, and evocative power." Edith Milton, in *The New York Times Book Review,* also cited the language, "which is often beautifully simple, [and] also adopts a gospel-like seriousness, reverberating with biblical echoes and echoes of biblical echoes." Both writers commented briefly on "Girl" and its theme of the mother-daughter relationship, and David Leavitt, writing for *The Village Voice,* proclaimed, "The tangled love between child and mother, so clearly articulated in 'Girl,' is the major preoccupation of Kincaid's work."

Though impressed by the language and interested in the themes, early reviewers found the stories in *At the Bottom of the River* needlessly opaque. Tyler called them "often almost insultingly obscure." Milton wondered "if her imagery may perhaps be too personal and too peculiar to translate into any sort of sensible communication." Barney Bardsley warned in *New Statesman* that the book could be "irritatingly difficult to read unless you let yourself go." Ultimately, however, all of the national reviewers saw promise in the volume and recommended it.

Since that time, "Girl" has been selected for several important anthologies, including *Wayward Girls, Wicked Women: An Anthology of Stories* (1987), *Green Cane and Juicy Flotsam: Short Stories by Caribbean Women* (1991), *Images of Women in Literature* (1991), and *Beyond Gender and Geography: American Women Writers* (1994). Most critical work on Kincaid has focused on her first novel, *Annie John,* considered a richer and more accessible examination of Kincaid's themes.

Kincaid's work has been the subject of two book-length studies, each published in 1994, and each of which analyzes "Girl" as an early articulation of her central concerns. Moira Ferguson's *Jamaica Kincaid: Where the Land Meets the Body* examines the personal and political conflicts in Kincaid's writing. She finds that in "Girl," "the mother-daughter relationship appears to be framed principally in terms of maternal-colonial power, mixed with probable rage and frustration in the daughter. A polyphony of messages fuses with conflicting reactions." Diane Simmons, author of *Jamaica Kincaid,* revisits the sound of Kincaid's language noticed by early reviewers and explains how "Girl" "may be read as a kind of primer in the manipulative art of rhythm and repetition." The mother's speech, she believes, "not only manipulates the girl into receptivity to the mother's condemning view but also teaches the art of manipulation."

One question that has interested readers of *At the Bottom of the River* from the beginning is the nature of the pieces. Though many critics have been content to call the pieces "stories," others have looked for a better term. Barney Bardsley claims, "This is not a story. There is no linear progression, no neat plot. *At the Bottom of the River* is instead a beautiful chaos of images, murky and tactile, which hint at the dreams and nightmares involved as a girl shakes off her childhood." Tyler writes that "this book is more poetry than prose." David Leavitt calls them "prose pieces," and Moira Ferguson consistently calls them "sections." For Simmons they are "dreamlike stories" or "surrealistic short stories."

Kincaid herself has spoken about the voice in her first book. In an interview with Donna Perry she comments, "I can see that *At the Bottom of the River* was, for instance, a very non-angry, decent, civilized book, and it represents sort of this successful attempt by English people to make their version of a human being or their version of a person out of me.

It amazes me now that I did that then. I would never write like that again, I don't think. I might go back to it, but I'm not very interested in that sort of expression any more.''

Criticism

Sarah Madsen Hardy

Madsen Hardy has a doctorate in English literature and is a freelance writer and editor. In the following essay, she explores ''Girl'''s form, discussing how Kincaid uses a list-like monologue to evoke a complex set of emotions and social factors.

In ''Girl'' Jamaica Kincaid tells a story in a mere page and a half—and, no less, in a single breathless sentence. The story has no proper plot, and readers are denied basic biographical facts about its two characters. It doesn't tell us their names, where they live, or any details of their background. What ''Girl'' *does* do is relate the rules of proper behavior as told to a teenager by her mother, or, at any rate, a mother figure. Behind these very explicit rules is an implicit message—one relating a complex vision of the intricate line a girl must walk as she enters into womanhood. In this one-sentence tour-de-force, Kincaid sketches a mother-daughter relationship and a view of the world as it appears to women—the woman that the mother is and one that the daughter will soon become. Through a simple list of instructions—including when to wash the clothes, how to sit when playing marbles, how to cook various dishes, and how to spit in the air—Kincaid performs a precise sociological analysis and evokes a complicated interpersonal relationship.

The only event or action in the story is that the mother speaks and the girl listens (with the two notable exceptions, set off in italics, when the girl asserts her own voice against the mother's barrage of advice). What, then, makes ''Girl'' a story? Out of the list of instructions, the attentive reader gleans a narrative. The list tells the story of the rhythm of life for women in West Indian culture, and, specifically, that of the mother character that Kincaid has created. Though the list has no particular chronology—the mother's harangue starts with Monday, but travels quite randomly through its miscellaneous topics—its progression and repetitions suggest certain issues that dominate the life of the mother, as well as the concerns that she has for her daughter as she enters the passage into womanhood. Behind the

mother's injunctions on how to sew on buttons and how to smile at people one likes to varying degrees is a self-portrait. These are the codes by which the mother lives, the rules she has gleaned from experience about the best way to get by within the strictures of the feminine social role. Implicit in this same list of commands is the mother's vision of her daughter's unfolding future—her story of what her daughter's life will entail as she comes of age. Of central concern is the daughter's sexual reputation and the danger that sexuality poses to a young girl who wishes to grow up to be a ''proper'' woman—the kind of woman the baker will trust to squeeze his bread. The mother, from a position of experience, understands the delicate enterprise that it is to make this passage. If a plot can be said to entail, at its simplest, a character that wants something, then the plot of ''Girl'' involves the mother's multitude of desires and fears for her daughter's life as a woman.

The question that logically follows is: Why did Kincaid choose to tell this story as a list-like monologue, rather than through more traditional descriptive narration? The answer, I believe, lies in the power of the mother's voice. Throughout Kincaid's fiction, she has given special credence to the unique power and intensity of the mother-daughter bond. She has frankly and sensitively portrayed the tension and ambivalence that often develop between mother and daughter with the separation in identity that comes during adolescence. In Kincaid's novels *Annie John* and *Lucy*, which are more conventional narratives, these issues are explored from the daughter's point of view. In ''Girl,'' Kincaid clears away all extraneous narrative details and allows the mother an (almost) uninterrupted forum. But, after all, the story is not called ''Mother.'' A portrayal of the girl emerges as if in relief, through the near silence that meets the mother's dominating vision of her and her future. The unique form of the story suggests how the power of the mother's voice shapes the girl's sense of herself.

Though it creates a rich sense of character through its oral speech rhythms, the list of instructions that makes up the story is not intended as a realistic sample of mother-daughter conversation. That is, the text of ''Girl'' is not what the mother actually says in a single interaction, but rather a condensation that creates the *effect* of the mother's influence on the daughter's sense of self. It illustrates the way mothers communicate with daughters about issues that are important to both of them, using a method that may not be quite as direct as it seems. The forceful barrage of instructions that

What Do I Read Next?

- *Annie John* (1983) is an episodic novel in eight parts by Jamaica Kincaid. Annie John, a young girl living on the island of Antigua in the Caribbean, endures a painful adolescence in which she both adores and hates her mother. As she matures she struggles to come to terms with her parents, her faith, her culture, and her sexuality.

- *At the Bottom of the River* (1983) is Kincaid's first collection of short stories, and the collection in which "Girl" appears. Like "Girl," many of the ten stories about growing up in the Caribbean are told in dreamy, stream-of-consciousness prose.

- *Krik? Krak!* (1996), by Edwidge Danticat, is a collection of nine short stories about women in Haiti. The stories are sad and beautiful, and the volume was a National Book Award finalist.

- *The Penguin Book of Caribbean Short Stories* (1997) collects forty short stories ranging from pre-Columbian myths and legends to stories by Jean Rhys, V. S. Naipaul, Claude McKay, and other major twentieth-century writers.

- *Reading Black, Reading Feminist: A Critical Anthology* (1990) is edited by Henry Louis Gates, Jr. In twenty-six essays, this collection traces the history of African-American women's writing in the United States. Works studied include prose and poetry, fiction and nonfiction.

---

makes up the story represents how the mother *sounds* to the daughter. Her seemingly endless stream of rules has the effect of overwhelming the reader, much as the daughter is overwhelmed. When the girl does dare to interrupt her mother the first time, defending herself that she doesn't sing beena on Sundays as her mother has accused her, it is after her mother has already gone on to reel off several other unrelated commands. The girl can't keep up with the pace of her mother's tirade. The mother's voice is both critical and affectionate, creating a sense of the ambivalent feelings that the adolescent and this most powerful figure in her life have for each other.

This condensation of the mother's speech functions as a form of hyperbole, and its effect is simultaneously ominous and ironic. When viewed from a sociological perspective, this compressed list of rules speaks to women's limitations within a male-dominated society. This, the mother seems to say, is how you *must* live because you are growing to be a woman, and she goes on to describe a host of housework tasks and other forms of service to men. All the while, the girl's budding sexuality (described by her mother as the daughter's will to become a "slut") is seen as a negative force that

threatens the girl's downfall with every small gesture. Conduct such as eating fruit on the street, giving "wharf-rat" boys directions, and letting one's hem come unstitched are codes for "loose" or immoral sexuality, actions that would threaten the girl's position in the social order and the whole quality of her future prospects. In this sense, the mother's list of rules describes the state of women's lack of freedom. The mother delivers her list of instructions briskly and sometimes harshly, but with an ultimately loving intent. Though she comes close to calling her own daughter a slut, her real bitterness is directed at the codes that she feels duty-bound to pass on.

However, this same condensation expresses not only the force of the social strictures of womanhood, but also the force of the mother's personality as well. Like that of a person who always exaggerates, her rhetoric is intended for effect and is cumulatively funny. This cuts against the grim picture of women's social disempowerment described above. Indeed, the mother's frank, bullying nature belies the fact that women must conduct themselves in a manner that is always demure and respectable. The mother is full of information and secrets, in full control of her world, even if it is a limited world.

Furthermore, among the instructions on how to be a good housekeeper and proper young lady, the mother sneaks in information on how to break the rules as well: "This is how to make a bread pudding; this is how to make doukona; this is how to make pepper pot; this is how to make a good medicine for a cold; this is how to make good medicine to throw away a child before it even becomes a child." Though the mother seems strongly censorious when it comes to the issue of the girl's sexual conduct, the fact that she informs her of how to induce abortion suggests both that the mother herself is less than utterly proper and that she is less strict in her personal views of sexuality than many of her rules would indicate. What matters, she implies, are appearances. And by showing the girl that it is possible to maintain the appearance of propriety while actually experiencing or experimenting with sexuality, she allows the girl a measure of covert power.

Toward the end of the story, there are other indications that the limitations of a woman's life are not so rigid as the list initially implies as well. The mother tells her daughter both "how to bully and man" and "how a man bullies you." In another acknowledgment of the girl's developing sexuality, the mother imparts knowledge about "how to love a man," adding "if this doesn't work there are other ways, and if they don't work don't feel too bad about giving up." Both of these pieces of advice imply a potential agency on the girl's part that is denied in the earlier part of the story. Furthermore, the mother's instructions on how to "spit up in the air if you feel like it" also suggest the value of preserving some sense of self that is outside of the codes and roles of womanhood. A space for doing something just because "you feel like it" is also within the realm of women's experience that the mother envisions for her daughter. The girl must unravel this complex and sometimes contradictory set of advice as a step toward to developing her own idea of womanhood and her own individual voice.

Source: Sarah Madsen Hardy, in an essay for *Literature of Developing Nations for Students*, Gale, 2000.

Adrian Blevins

Adrian Blevins, a poet and essayist who has taught at Hollins University, Sweet Briar College, and in the Virginia Community College System, is the author of The Man Who Went Out for Cigarettes, *a chapbook of poems, and has published poems, stories, and essays in many magazines, journals, and anthologies. In this essay, Blevins discusses the poetic devices Kincaid draws upon in*

> "Girl," *revealing how the story* "work[s] by way *of rhythm and image, opening up gateways to the reader's senses and enlightening her to a more ample awareness of the complex and primordial nature of the emerging feminine psyche."*

Most fictions evolve by way of the labors of four main narrative devices. These are a predominate, or commanding, focus on (1) voice, which includes the writer's tone; on (2) character, or the narrative's main protagonists and players; on (3) plot, which is the cycle of events that lead the story to its conclusion; and finally, on (4) agenda, which is the writer's social message. Few serious fictions are driven by just one of these devices, engines, or powers: most voice-driven fictions, for instance, are also character-driven in the sense that a voice must always represent a personality, and many literary works move forward by way of the plots within which their characters are entwined. Still, this method of classification can help us discriminate between literary works and their more commercial counterparts, which are fictions whose major device is either a plot in which the main concern is what is going to happen next, or fictions whose major device is a social notion that the author wishes to put forth to the reader, such as one might find in after-school specials.

One of the many glories of Jamaica Kincaid's fiction is that it is urged forward by voice, tone, and—often—image. While one can read Kincaid's novels and stories in terms of agenda, or isolate certain themes rising from her experience as a black woman from the Caribbean island of Antigua, such readings are reductive, since Kincaid's work is far more universal than a mere concentration on these social themes would suggest. *At the Bottom of the River*, the collection of stories from which we take "Girl," is by far Kincaid's most difficult work, mainly because it violates traditional notions of narrative in favor of more poetic methods of discourse. Thus, many of the stories in this collection stand on the boundary between story and poem; they do not rely on plot or even character development for their movement, but, like poems, work by way of rhythm and image, opening up gateways to the reader's senses and enlightening her to a more ample awareness of the complex and primordial nature of the human—and in this case, emerging feminine—psyche.

Many of Kincaid's books explore the complex relationship between mothers and daughters. Critics have suggested that *Annie John*, one of Kincaid's later novels, can be read, as Wendy Dutton says in *World Literature Today*, as a "companion [piece] or sister [text]" to *At the Bottom of the River*. While a look at Kincaid's novels will illuminate the reader of her short stories, Kincaid's stories do stand on their own, operating independently of the later work.

"Girl" is, first and foremost, a voice piece, written in one long, present-tense sentence. It relies on repetition and refrain and on the physical images of the Antiguan landscape and customs—the stone heap in the yard, pumpkin fritters, pepper pot, dasheen—for its progression. Stripped of plot and other traditional storytelling methods, the story offers us, quite simply, two speaking voices. The text's main voice is the mother's, translated and recorded by the writer/girl, and the second or countering voice is the writer or girl's own voice, which is offered in response to the mother-voice's litany of orders and commands. By comparison to the mother's voice, the girl's voice is barely audible; it is separated from the main text by being set off in italics, and thus seems almost a whisper. It is significant that the mother gets the first and the last word of this story. It is also significant that "Girl" is written in one long sentence. This choice reveals the sheer psychological weight of the mother's advice; when the girl does respond to her mother's orders and questions, it is as though she is speaking from the bottom of a well. Yet nothing the girl says seems to have any impact on the mother's opinions; the mother is quite strong-minded about how she expects her daughter to behave, thus revealing who she expects her daughter to become. The mother is also quite forthcoming about what she fears to be the girl's fate, which is to become "the slut I have warned you against becoming."

Fiction writer Susan Neville, in "STUFF: Some Random Thoughts on Lists," argues beautifully in favor of the power of the list in prose texts: "with their repetitions, their song rhythmic qualities—lists are often the most musical section of a piece of prose, as though the writer suddenly broke into song—they contain time like a jeweled box; they let you know what to expect with the next breath, the next heartbeat." "Girl," of course, is one long list of a mother's orders to her daughter, containing instructions having to do with the domestic, or daily, arena of human experience and the way a girl should conduct herself in public. The fact that most of the mother's orders center around the domestic arts—cooking, sewing, washing, ironing, and so on—tells us that the mother has traditional attitudes about the nature of a woman's place in the world. She tells the girl:

> Wash the white clothes on Monday and put them on the stone heap; wash the color clothes on Tuesday and put them on the clothesline to dry . . . cook pumpkin fritters in very hot sweet oil; soak your little cloths right after you take them off; when buying cotton to make yourself a nice blouse, be sure that it doesn't have gum on it.

The mother's orders regarding her daughter's behavior serve equally well to communicate the mother's values. Critic Helene Pyne Timothy, in *Caribbean Women Writers: Essays from the First International Conference*, says of the novel *Annie John*, which centers around the same autobiographical characters as those in "Girl," that:

> the Caribbean mother who is bent on seeing her daughter rise from the lower classes to the middle ranks must not only teach her useful housekeeping tasks, cleanliness, good manners, and practical knowledge of her environment, but also European norms and the need to desist in the practice of African ones. . . . Thus in the mother's perception, Christianity, Sunday school, good manners (the ability to curtsy), and piano lessons are all essential to her daughter's acceptability and respectability.

In "Girl," the mother tells the daughter: "always eat your food in such a way that it won't turn someone else's stomach, on Sundays try to walk like a lady and not like the slut you are so bent on becoming; don't sing benna in Sunday school; you mustn't speak to wharf-rat boys, not even to give directions . . ." The mother doesn't want her daughter to sing benna songs, or folk/African tales, in Sunday school because she wants her daughter to rise from the customs and habits of the Caribbean island she and her daughter, like their mothers before them, were born on. The girl's whispering response to the mother—"but I don't sing benna on Sundays at all and never in Sunday school"—is a meek statement the girl poses in her own self-defense, revealing that she does wish to please her mother. Her question about the bread—"but what if the baker won't let me feel the bread?"—exposes the girl's limited self-worth, since she is afraid she can command no authority, even with the baker. While the mother could use this question to subdue her daughter's fears, she chooses instead reinforce her own negative ones. These center around the girl's emerging sexuality.

The refrain in "Girl" concerning this sexuality ("the slut you are so bent on becoming") serves to hold the piece together. This refrain is, again, a poetic device. Although the mother's comment about the girl becoming ''a slut'' probably comes from her fear for the girl, it serves only to isolate the two, representing a gap in the mother between her fears for her daughter, which are that her daughter will become sexually promiscuous and make a bad wife, and her goals for her daughter, which are that her daughter must behave in ways becoming to a Christian ''lady'' and marry well.

In *Annie John*, this gap—represented also by the mother's contradictory advice both to follow Caribbean traditions and customs (''this is how to make a good medicine to throw away a child before it even becomes a child'') and to reject them in favor of more European notions of conduct—causes the girl to have a mental breakdown. All we get in ''Girl,'' however, is the mother-voice's litany of instructions. The fact that ''Girl'' is written in the present tense also underscores the mother's power over her daughter, since it makes past-tense commands predominate in the psychological present.

Any culture standing on the wavering bridge between values that teach young women to live the lives their mothers lived and values more dedicated to teaching each individual woman to find her own way will produce an estrangement, especially between mothers who expect their daughters to follow precisely in their footsteps and daughters who have more worldly ambitions. This estrangement, as it played out in her own life with her own mother, is one of Jamaica Kincaid's most dominating themes. As critic Roni Natov says of the novel *Annie John* in *Mothers and Daughters: Jamaica Kincaid's Pre-Oedipal Narrative*, ''focusing on the painful struggle to separate from the mother that characterizes early adolescence for many girls, Kincaid evokes with intensity the wrenching many of us shudder to remember.'' This struggle is prefaced in the stories of *At the Bottom of the River*, ''Girl'' among them evoking the most representative portrait of the traditional mother's convictions and her efforts to see them borne out in the life of her daughter. ''Girl'' is also a good example of Kincaid's skill with English, a skill which incorporates a remarkable talent for employing devices most often reserved for poetry. The effect, for readers, is a very haunting narrative experience. In the end, it is her skill with English that makes Jamaica Kincaid a writer worth watching—a writer, as Suzanne Freeman has said, branded by ''images that are as sweet and mysterious as the secrets children whisper in your ear.''

Source: Adrian Blevins, in an essay for *Literature of Developing Nations for Students*, Gale, 2000.

Cynthia Bily

Bily teaches English at Adrian College in Adrian, Michigan. In the following essay, she discusses expectations and opportunities in ''Girl.''

In her 1984 *New York Times Book Review* piece about Kincaid's *At the Bottom of the River* , Edith Milton singles out ''Girl'' as ''the most elegant and lucid piece of the collection,'' and observed that the mother's exhortations ''define in a few paragraphs the expectations, the limitations, and the contents of an entire life.'' If this is an accurate assessment, and I believe it is, what kind of life does it describe? What will the future hold for the girl if she follows her mother's suggestions?

Many of the instructions give purely practical advice for doing daily chores in a developing nation where running water and electricity are not common. Even in a society where people do not have many clothes, obtaining and maintaining them is hard work, and that work typically falls to women. ''Girl'' begins with laundry: ''Wash the white clothes on Monday and put them on the stone heap; wash the color clothes on Tuesday and put them on the clothesline.'' Before the one-sentence story is done, the mother will come back to clothing many times, explaining how to buy fabric for a blouse, sew on a button and make a buttonhole, and hem a dress. And of course, women are also responsible for men's clothing, and the mother demonstrates ''how you iron your father's khaki shirt so that it doesn't have a crease'' and ''how you iron your father's khaki pants so that they don't have a crease.''

Women are also providers of nourishment, and the mother explains how to grow and prepare different foods. In this family, the girl is expected to catch fish and to ''soak salt fish overnight before you cook it.'' She learns to shop for bread, to grow okra and dasheen, a root vegetable, and to prepare pumpkin fritters, bread pudding, doukona (a cornmeal, banana and coconut pudding), and pepper pot, the staple of poor Caribbean families that involves reheating a large pot of greens with whatever fresh ingredients might be added on a given day. By preparing these humble dishes, a woman can ''make ends meet.''

The mother rounds out her list of womanly duties with guidance on cleaning (''this is how you sweep a corner; this is how you sweep a whole house; this is how you sweep a yard''), setting a table for any occasion, and making different kinds of ''good medicine.'' In a culture where there is a

> The relationship that concerns the mother is the relationship between a man and a woman. If she derives any pleasure or pride from her own experiences with parenthood, she does not reveal it here."

lot of work to be done, it is important that everyone do a fair share, and this is a woman's share.

Just as important, that the girl must learn how to behave in front of other people, especially men. Several of the instructions have to do with how one appears to others, such as the command to "always eat your food in such a way that it won't turn someone else's stomach." A woman must learn to hide her true self, her true feelings, and wear the mask that is right for the occasion: "this is how you smile to someone you don't like too much; this is how you smile to someone you don't like at all; this is how you smile to someone you like completely." Most of all, she must "try to walk like a lady and not like the slut I know you are so bent on becoming." A woman may have thoughts of "sluttish behavior" (by which is meant, I suppose, acting as though she wants or enjoys sex), but "this is how to behave in the presence of men who don't know you very well, and this way they won't recognize immediately the slut I have warned you against becoming."

Apparently the mother has learned to do all these things, and they are probably not beyond the girl's capacity either. But if she learns her lessons well, what will she have to look forward to, to be excited about? Where is the pleasure in this life? The litany of instructions in "Girl" is a far cry from the advice given to women in today's popular women's magazines, which suggest that taking long aromatherapy baths to regenerate will make one a better mother, or advocate "making time for yourself."

Just as important as the advice the mother gives in "Girl" is what she leaves out. The advice is practical, "how to make ends meet." There are no instructions for how to make beautiful things, or how to make oneself happy. The Caribbean is celebrated all around the world for its exuberant music, but the only reference to music in the story is to music that must not be made: "don't sing benna in Sunday school." Tourists travel great distances to Antigua to admire its beautiful flowers and birds. In "Girl," the mother refers to flowers only once: "don't pick people's flowers you might catch something." Her one mention of a bird is strangely cautionary: "don't throw stones at blackbirds, because it might not be a blackbird at all."

In an early essay in *The New Yorker*, Kincaid described the beauty of Antigua, and explained that Antiguans get up to begin their work very early in the morning, when the island is at its loveliest. In an interview, Kincaid remarked, "But it wasn't to admire any of these things that people got up so early. I had never, in all the time I lived there, heard anyone say, 'What a beautiful morning.' Once, just the way I read it in a book, I stretched and said to my mother, 'Oh, isn't it a really lovely morning?' She didn't reply to that at all." People who live in the midst of rare beauty, it would appear, lose their ability to notice it, to find pleasure in it. A child could be taught to observe and enjoy the natural world for its beauty and elegance, but this daughter will not learn it from this mother.

There are no tender words in the mother's litany. She does not use "dear" or any other terms of endearment, or even address the daughter by her name. She gives no advice about how to be a friend, or how to sense which women to confide in. There are no tips about changing a diaper or wiping a tear or nurturing a child in any way; she mentions children only when she shows "how to make a good medicine to throw away a child before it even becomes a child." The relationship that concerns the mother is the relationship between a man and a woman. If she derives any pleasure or pride from her own experiences with parenthood, she does not reveal it here.

Finally, there are no words in the mother's speech about possibilities beyond home and family. She does not speak of school or books, nor of travel, nor of a career. She speaks about only what she has to offer: a set of instructions for a successful life as the mother understands it and lives it. That Kincaid wanted more is evident. She left Antigua and found a different sort of life for herself, as she explained in an interview with Kay Bonetti in *The Missouri Review*: "I did not know what would happen to me. I was just leaving, with great bitterness in my heart towards everyone I've ever known, but I could not have articulated why. I knew that I wanted something, but I did not know what. I knew I did not want convention. I wanted to risk something.''

The story ends before we find out what happens to the girl. Does she heed all her mother's advice and become a competent homemaker? Does she follow Kincaid's lead and find something else? If she stays, is her life as joyless as her mother's? If she leaves, can she find a way to create a new family and a new home? What of the mother? If her life is as joyless as it seems, what sense of responsibility compels her to train her daughter for the same life? Kincaid might say that these questions and their answers are irrelevant, that she is revealing a truth about a moment and that should be enough. In an interview with Marilyn Snell in *Mother Jones*, she complains that Americans want pleasant solutions. ''Americans find difficulty very hard to take. They are inevitably looking for a happy ending. Perversely, I will not give the happy ending. I think life is difficult and that's that.''

Source: Cynthia Bily, in an essay for *Literature of Developing Nations for Students*, Gale, 2000.

Liz Brent

Brent has a Ph.D. in American Culture, with a specialization in cinema studies, from the University of Michigan. She is a freelance writer and teaches courses in American cinema. In the following essay, she discusses the use of language, the mother-daughter relationship, and the significance of African cultural heritage in ''Girl.''

The Mother/Daughter Relationship

Jamaica Kincaid's short story ''Girl'' is the opening piece in a collection entitled *At the Bottom of the River*. Critics have noted that the use of language in ''Girl,'' as well as in the other stories of this collection, is one of its most notable features. ''Girl'' is unusual in that it is a short story written in the ''second person'' voice, meaning that the narrator addresses the reader as ''you.'' The narrator here is a mother giving advice to her daughter, who is the ''you'' in the story. Kincaid's use of language in this story is key to understanding the nature of the mother/daughter relationship which it conveys. Grammatically, the entire story is a single sentence, which reads like a list or string of statements made by the mother to her daughter. The use of repetition and rhythm renders the mother's words almost

hypnotic. In her article ''The Rhythm of Reality in the Works of Jamaica Kincaid,'' Diane Simmons explains that, ''in the long, seemingly artless, list-like sentences, the reader is mesmerized into Kincaid's world.'' She goes on to say that ''like the girl to whom the mother speaks, the reader is lulled and drawn in by the chant of motherly admonitions.''

The central theme of ''Girl,'' as in many of Kincaid's stories, is the mother/daughter relationship. An important element of the use of language in this story is the sense that the mother's ''chant of information and advice'' (as Simmons calls it) threatens to completely engulf the girl, leaving her no language with which to formulate her own sense of identity as separate from her mother. Simmons has pointed out that the use of rhythm and repetition in the mother's words ''enfolds and ensnares the daughter, rendering the girl nearly helpless before the mother's transforming will.'' It is as if the mother's incantatory speech pattern is so all-enveloping that it prevents the daughter from asserting any individuality, opinion, or will outside of the narrowly defined world of advice and warning her mother has created through her speech. In the two instances in which the girl does attempt either to question her mother's advice or to defend herself against her mother's judgement, the rhythm and repetition of the mother's voice only works to overwhelm and engulf this meek voice of dissent.

The power of the mother's words to envelop the daughter within the strict confines of her own set of values and expectations is most apparent in terms of her references to sexuality. What is striking in this piece is the power of the mother's words to impose upon the girl a ''sluttish'' sexuality which must always be contained and hidden. The mother's ''advice'' comes in the form of a condemnation for behavior or tendencies the girl herself might not even have considered: ''On Sundays try to walk like a lady and not like the slut you are so bent on becoming.'' The power of this condemnation of the girl's sexuality, perhaps before it has even formed, comes in part from the way in which the mother integrates references to sexuality into advice on even the most mundane tasks: ''this is how to hem a dress when you see the hem coming down and so to prevent yourself from looking like the slut I know you are so bent on becoming.'' The insistence of the mother's repetition of this condemnation gives it all the more power: ''this is how to behave in the presence of men who don't know you very well, and this way they won't recognize immediately the slut I have warned you against becoming.''

> **"**The power of this condemnation of the girl's sexuality, perhaps before it has even formed, comes in part from the way in which the mother integrates references to sexuality into advice on even the most mundane tasks . . . .**"**

The sense that this restricted definition of sexuality which the mother imposes upon the daughter is all-encompassing is most strongly emphasized in the closing lines. What begins as another mundane and harmless piece of advice "always squeeze bread to make sure it's fresh" becomes, upon the daughter's questioning, yet again an opportunity to condemn the girl to the inevitability of becoming a "slut," despite all these warnings. When the daughter, with good reason, asks "but what if the baker won't let me feel the bread?" the mother replies, "you mean to say that after all you are really going to be the kind of woman who the baker won't let near the bread?" As this closing line suggests, the mother's words create a world so all-encompassing that the daughter is unable to escape its judgments.

Growing Up Female

A good portion of the "chant of information" the mother passes onto the daughter is made up of specific directions on how to carry out the domestic work for which the girl is clearly being trained. The mother's advice concerns such "woman's work" as washing clothes ("Wash the white clothes on Monday and put them on the stone heap; wash the color clothes on Tuesday and put them on the clothesline to dry"); sewing ("this is how to sew on a button; this is how to make a button-hole for the button you have sewed on"); and cleaning house ("this is how to sweep the house; this is how to sweep the yard"), as well as setting the table, ironing, and buying fabric. The use of repetition here is suggestive of the repetitive nature of the endless domestic chores which the girl seems condemned to spend her life performing: "this is how you set the table for tea; this is how you set the table

for dinner; this is how you set the table for dinner with an important guest; this is how you set the table for breakfast." The tedium implied by this simple repetition mimics the tedium and dullness of the domestic duties the girl is expected to take on.

In addition to the repetitive daily domestic work for which she is training her daughter, the mother also includes messages which assume a role of subservience to a man: "this is how you iron your father's khaki shirt so that it doesn't have a crease; this is how you iron your father's khaki pants so that they don't have a crease." The messages which the mother gives her daughter about relationships with men also include warnings which suggest the potential for violence: "this is how you bully a man; this is how a man bullies you." The potential hazards of sexual relationships with men are also indicated in terms of reference to unwanted pregnancy: "this is how to make a good medicine to throw away a child before it becomes a child." And, despite all the warnings about not being a "slut," the mother also instructs the girl in "how to love a man."

A simple instruction by the mother, toward the end of the story, is suggestive of her underlying motivation in passing on such specific instructions to her daughter. One of the items on her list of instruction is "this is how to make ends meet." This statement by the mother in some ways clinches all of her previous statements. The underlying message which the mother imparts to her daughter, through all of these detailed instructions, is a message about how to survive as an African-Carribean woman in a harsh world with limited resources.

Christianity and African Heritage

The mother's litany of advice, warning, and condemnation in "Girl" also contains a string of confusing and contradictory messages about the daughter's relationship to her African heritage and culture. On the one hand, the mother insists on warning the daughter against integrating African folk culture into her Christian education. "Is it true you sing benna songs in Church?" the mother asks. As benna songs are African folk songs, the mother's question is designed to warn the daughter against maintaining cultural practices derived from her African heritage.

Yet, on the other hand, the mother's list of advice contains rich elements of this African heritage, which she clearly intends to pass on to her daughter. Thus, while warning against mixing African traditional songs with the Western practice of

Christianity, the mother is sure to pass on information based on folk beliefs derived from African culture. As Helen Pyne Timothy explains, in her article "Adolescent Rebellion and Gender Relations in 'At the Bottom of the River' and *Annie John*," "when dealing with the real problems of life," the mother's advice "falls back on the belief in folk wisdom, myth, African systems of healing and bush medicine, the mysteries of good and evil spirits inhabiting the perceived world of nature." Thus, the mother's advice includes such folk beliefs as "don't throw stones at blackbirds, because it might not be a blackbird at all," or "this is how to throw back a fish you don't like, and that way something bad won't fall on you." She also includes references to folk medicines or remedies, such as "this is how to make a good medicine for a cold."

A rich African-Carribean cultural heritage is also passed on from mother to daughter through the importance of advice and directions concerning food preparation. These elements of the mother's litany add an important element of warmth and nurturing to her warnings and condemnations. Food preparation is described in cookbook-style, matter-of-fact detail, such as "cook pumpkin fritters in very hot sweet oil," and "soak salt fish over night before you cook it." Other references to food evoke strong sensory associations, such as "this is how to make bread pudding" and "this is how to make pepper pot." In these instances, the mother's insistence on conveying such an overwhelming "chant of information" to her daughter takes on a deeper significance in terms of the role of the mother-daughter relationship in the context of African-Carribean cultural heritage. In "Mothers and Daughters: Jamaica Kincaids' Pre-Oedipal Narrative," critic Roni Natov explains that, "Jamaica Kincaid's fiction focuses on the importance of continuity and community as they are preserved and kept alive by mothers, through their stories and through their connection with their daughters." In this way, the mother is maintaining an oral tradition whereby cultural traditions and survival skills are passed down from mother to daughter, and from generation to generation, by way of a rhythmic flow of words such as that conveyed in this story.

Source: Liz Brent, in an essay for *Literature of Developing Nations for Students*, Gale, 2000.

Diane Simmons

Kincaid's "Girl" may be read as a kind of primer in the manipulative art of rhythm and repeti-tion. The story begins with the mother's voice giving such simple, benevolent, and appropriately maternal advice as "Wash the white clothes on Monday and put them on the stone heap; wash the color clothes on Tuesday and put them on the clothesline to dry." Like the girl to whom the mother speaks, the reader is lulled and drawn in by the chant of motherly admonitions, which go on to advise about how to dress for the hot sun, how to cook pumpkin fritters, how to buy cloth for a blouse, and how to prepare fish. Seduced in only a few lines, readers, like the listening girl, are caught unaware by an admonition which sounds like the previous, benevolent advice but has in fact suddenly veered in a new direction, uniting the contradictions of nurture and condemnation: ". . . always eat your food in such a way that it won't turn someone else's stomach; on Sundays try to walk like a lady and not like the slut you are so bent on becoming." As the brief, one-sentence story progresses, we come to see that the mother's speech, inviting with nurturing advice on the one hand and repelling with condemnatory characterization on the other, not only manipulates the girl into receptivity to the mother's condemning view, but also teaches the art of manipulation. The mother incorporates into her indictment of the girl's impending sluttishness the task of teaching her how to hide that condition: ". . . this is how to hem a dress when you see the hem coming down and so to prevent yourself from looking like the slut I know you are so bent on becoming." As the contradictions draw closer together—as nurture and manipulation become increasingly intertwined—the language seems to become even more rhythmic.

> . . . this is how you smile to someone you don't like too much; this is how you smile to someone you don't like at all; this is how you smile to someone you like completely; this is how you set a table for tea; this is how you set a table for dinner; this is how you set a table for dinner with an important guest; this is how you set a table for lunch; this is how you set a table for breakfast; this is how you behave in the presence of men who don't know you very well, and this way they won't recognize immediately the slut I have warned you against becoming. . . .

In the last third of "Girl" the mother's voice continues the litany of domestic instruction, but added now is comment on a frighteningly contradictory world, one in which nothing is ever what it seems to be. The continued tone of motherly advice at first works to lighten the sinister nature of the information imparted and then, paradoxically, seems to make these disclosures even more frightening; eventually we see that, in a world in which a recipe for stew slides into a recipe for the death of a child, nothing is safe.

> ... don't pick people's flowers—you might catch something; don't throw stones at blackbirds, because it might not be a blackbird at all; this is how to make bread pudding; this is how to make doukona; this is how to make pepper pot; this is how to make a good medicine for a cold; this is how to make a good medicine to throw away a child before it even becomes a child; this is how to catch a fish; this is how to throw back a fish you don't like, and that way something bad won't fall on you.

Source: Diane Simmons, "The Rhythm of Reality in the Works of Jamaica Kincaid," in *World Literature Today*, Vol. 68, No. 3, Summer, 1994, pp. 466–72.

Laura Niesen Abruna

Some of the finest fiction from the West Indies has been written by Jamaica Kincaid. Her fiction, specifically her collection of short stories *At the Bottom of the River*, makes interesting use of dream visions and metaphor as the imaginative projections of family life and social structure in her West Indian society. In the short stories Kincaid explores the strong identification and rupture in the daughter-mother relationship between the narrator and her mother. The process is mediated through metaphor and, when it is threatening, through surrealistic dream visions.

Each of these stories demonstrates tensions in the daughter-narrator resulting from a prolonged period of symbiosis between mother and child, especially because the mother views her daughter as a narcissistic extension of herself. In "Wingless," the narrator dreams the story as a mirror of her own situation and then imagines herself as a wingless pupa waiting for growth. The narrator uses a dream vision to mediate her sense of helplessness as a child dependent on her mother's care and attention.

In this dream, the mother is perceived to be powerful, even more potent than the male who attempts to intimidate and humiliate her. Because the narrator still views her mother as powerful, an incident of potential sexual violence becomes instead an easy victory for the mother:

> I could see that he wore clothes made of tree bark and sticks in his ears. He said things to her and I couldn't make them out, but he said them so forcefully that drops of water sprang from his mouth. The woman I love put her hands over her ears, shielding herself from the things he said. ... Then, instead of removing her cutlass from the folds of her big and beautiful skirt

and cutting the man in two at the waist, she only smiled—a red, red smile—and like a fly he dropped dead.

The strong mother is a potential threat of death to those who confront her. But there is also a wonderful parable here of the integrity of the woman who shields herself from assault by refusing to listen to the tree-satyr who is trying to assert his power over her.

The story that best demonstrates the daughter's ambivalent relationship with her mother is "Girl." The voice is the girl's repeating a series of the mother's admonitions:

> Wash the white clothes on Monday and put them on the stone heap; wash the color clothes on Tuesday and put them on the clothesline to dry ... on Sundays try to walk like a lady and not like the slut you are so bent on becoming ... this is how to hem a dress when you see the hem coming down and so to prevent yourself from looking like the slut I know you are so bent on becoming ... this is how to behave in the presence of men who don't know you very well, and this way they won't recognize immediately the slut I have warned you against becoming.

The first of the mother's many rules concerns housekeeping. Unlike the girl's father, who can lounge at the circus eating blood sausage and drinking ginger beer, the woman is restricted to household duties. The many rules, which make the father's circus-going a female impossibility, are experienced by the narrator as unnecessarily restrictive and hostile. The mother's aggression is clear in the warnings of the price a girl will pay for ignoring her mother's advice. The penalty is ostracism—one must become a slut, a fate for which the mother is ironically preparing the daughter. The mother's obsessive refrain indicates hostility toward her adolescent daughter, activated when the growing daughter is no longer an extension of the self but a young woman who engenders in the older woman feelings of competition and anger at losing control of her child. Her anger may also result from the pressures felt by every woman in the community to fulfill the restrictive roles created for women. Of the ten stories in the collection, "Girl" is the only one told as interior monologue rather than as dream and thus seems to be the least distorted vision. The ambivalence of the mother-daughter relationship is presented here in its most direct form. The reasons for their mutual distrust are very clearly stated: resentment, envy, anger, love.

Source: Laura Niesen Abruna, "Twentieth-Century Women Writers from the English-Speaking Caribbean," in *Modern Fiction Studies*, Vol. 34, No. 1, Spring, 1988, pp. 85–96.

Sources

Bardsley, Barney, review of *At the Bottom of the River*, in *New Statesman*, Vol. 108, No. 2790, September 7, 1984, p. 33.

Bonetti, Kay, interview with Kincaid, in *The Missouri Review*, Vol. 21, No. 2, August 17, 1998; available online at http://www.missourireview.org/interviews/kincaid.html.

Cudjoe, Selwyn R., "Jamaica Kincaid and the Modernist Project: An Interview," in *Callaloo*, Vol. 12, Spring, 1989, pp. 397, 402, 408.

DeVries, Helen, interview, in *Christian Science Monitor*, May 2, 1985, p. 41.

Dutton, Wendy, "Merge and Separate: Jamaica Kincaid's Fiction," in *Biographia Literaria—Word Literature Today*, Vol. 63, No. 3, Summer, 1989, p. 406.

Edwards, Audrey, "Jamaica Kincaid: Writes of Passage," in *Essence*, Vol. 22, No. 1, May, 1991, pp. 86-89.

Ferguson, Moira, *Jamaica Kincaid: Where the Land Meets the Body*, University Press of Virginia, 1994, p. 18.

Freeman, Suzanne, *Ms.*, 1984, quoted in *Contemporary Authors Online*, Gale, 1999.

Leavitt, David, review of *At the Bottom of the River*, in *The Village Voice*, Vol. 29, No. 3, January 17, 1984, p. 41.

Milton, Edith, "Making a Virtue of Diversity," in *The New York Times Book Review*, January 15, 1984, p. 22.

Natov, Roni, "Mothers and Daughters: Jamaica Kincaid's Pre-Oedipal Narrative," in *Children's Literature*, Vol. 18, 1990, pp. 1-16.

Neville, Susan, "Stuff: Some Random Thoughts on Lists," *AWP Chronicle*, Vol. 30, No. 4, February, 1998, p. 6.

Perry, Donna, *Backtalk: Women Writers Speak Out*, Rutgers University Press, 1993, p. 132, 133.

Simmons, Diane, *Jamaica Kincaid*, Twayne, 1994, p. 30, 48, 49.

Snell, Marilyn, "Jamaica Kincaid Hates Happy Endings," in *Mother Jones*, Vol. 22, No. 5, September-October, 1997, pp. 28-31.

Timothy, Helen Pyne, "Adolescent Rebellion and Gender Relations in 'At the Bottom of the River' and *Annie John*," in *Caribbean Women Writers*, edited by Selwyn R. Cudjoe, Calaloux Publications, 1990, pp. 233-242.

Tyler, Anne, "Mothers and Mysteries," in *The New Republic*, Vol. 189, No. 27, December 31, 1983, pp. 32-33.

> The many rules, which make the father's circus-going a female impossibility, are experienced by the narrator as unnecessarily restrictive and hostile."

Vorda, Allan, "An Interview with Jamaica Kincaid," in *Mississippi Review*, Vol. 20, No. 8, 1991, p. 15.

Further Reading

Bloom, Harold, ed., *Jamaica Kincaid: Modern Critical Views*, Chelsea House, 1998.

Eleven essays of criticism and interpretation, particularly of Kincaid's work after *At the Bottom of the River*. Most of these essays were written for scholarly audiences.

Cudjoe, Selwyn R. *Caribbean Women Writers: Essays from the First International Conference*, Calaloux Publications, 1990.

Three dozen essays and interviews about the works and lives of English-speaking women Caribbean writers, as well as overviews of the writing by Spanish-, French-, and Dutch-speaking women. Two pieces explore Kincaid directly, and the others provide context for her work.

Dachner, Don, and Dene Dachner, *A Traveler's Guide to Caribbean History*, Travelers Press, 1997.

An accessible and sensitive overview of the region's historical development, written for the general reader.

Nasta, Shusheila, ed., *Motherlands: Black Women's Writing from Africa, the Caribbean and South Asia*, Rutgers University Press, 1991.

The Glass of Milk

Manuel Rojas

1927

In 1927, Manuel Rojas published his first significant collection of short stories, *Hombres del sur* (*Men of the South*), which included his short story "El vaso de leche". It is one of Rojas' best known and most widely anthologized tales.

"El vaso de leche" ("The Glass of Milk") is an intensely written short story that examines a brief moment in the life of a youth who is out of work and very hungry. The unnamed youth is refused work and refuses free food. He finally is overcome with a hunger stronger than his pride. He accepts some milk and cookies from the woman in the milk bar and experiences a powerful emotional release. She understands, and he leaves the cafe without paying.

Grafton Conliffe identifies Rojas as one of the premiere Chilean writers. He was innovative in character development, portraying hard-working, down-and-out people in a sensitive, sympathetic fashion. Cedomil Goic reports that Rojas was the first Chilean writer to use the subjective narrator, a narrator who makes comments on and takes part in the telling of the story. However, the narrator in "The Glass of Milk" is an objective narrator. Rojas acknowledged being influenced by the American writers Ernest Hemingway and William Faulkner.

In his fiction, Rojas often included autobiographical material derived from his youth, when he and his family wandered about in the mountains of southern Chile and Argentina. However, this story is not about himself. It is a tale about the plight of

the lower classes in his adopted homeland, as witnessed through the life of one young lad. Rojas does not preach; he lets his readers come to their own conclusions about the problems these people face.

Author Biography

Manuel Rojas was born on January 8, 1896, in Buenos Aires, Argentina; he died on March 11, 1973, in his adopted homeland, Chile. His family moved to Chile in 1899 and from then until 1922 they wandered back and forth between Chile and Argentina, working a variety of jobs to earn a meager living. He probably settled permanently in Chile in 1924. In 1927, he published his first collection of short stories, *Hombres del Sur*, which included the story ''El vaso de leche'' (''The Glass of Milk'').

It was about this time that Rojas became associated with the political group called the Anarchists, who opposed the oppressive Chilean government. He wrote articles for the Anarchist newspapers, *La Batalla* (in Chile) and *La Protesta* (in Buenos Aires, Argentina). The Popular Front political party took control of the government in 1936. In 1938 Rojas published a collection of essays, *De la poesía a la revolución* (*From Poetry to Revolution*), many of which were written during the struggles with the government in the 1920s and early 1930s.

From then until 1951 Rojas did not publish anything in book form, concentrating on making contributions to the journal *Babel*. His most influential novel, *Hijo de ladrón* (literally ''Son of a Thief,'' but published in English as *Born Guilty* in 1955) was published in Santiago de Chile. This novel draws heavily on his childhood experiences when his family wandered from town to town looking for work and food. In it he looks at the plight of the poor and indigent peasants who lived at the bottom of South American society at that time. His protagonist Aniceto is the son of a common thief and it is he who bears the weight of his father's crimes. The police and others in the story expect him to have adopted his father's illegal lifestyle. This novel, along with *Lanchas en la bahía* (1932) and *Mejor que el vino* (1958), form an autobiographical trilogy and are thought to be his best and most important works.

Rojas is thought by many critics to be the best Chilean writer of the first half of the twentieth century, if not the best of all time. His output includes poetry, short stories, essays, and novels. These works look sympathetically at the lives of the people in Chile during Rojas' lifetime. He takes a compassionate look at thieves, bums, and other members of the lowest stratum of society. He does not glorify their lives nor does he condemn them.

His short story ''El vaso de leche'' (''The Glass of Milk'') is a tightly written tale that draws the reader into the complexities of the issues raised in it. It is one of his most widely anthologized stories. The main character is a youth who is out of work and very hungry, much like the protagonist in *Hijo de ladrón*. As in his novel, there are no simple answers to the questions posed by the situations encountered in the story. Rojas lets the reader arrive at the answers.

Rojas received several awards during his lifetime, including the Chilean National Prize for Literature in 1957.

Plot Summary

In ''The Glass of Milk,'' a youth who has been expelled from a ship as a stowaway finds himself walking around the port looking for work to earn money to buy some food. He has not eaten in three days, yet he refuses a handout from a sailor and then watches hungrily as a ''gaudy tramp'' accepts the food and eats it. He finds some work unloading a vessel. After the first day he asks for his pay, but the foreman tells him that he will be paid at the close of the whole job. The foreman then offers him some money as a loan but the lad again refuses.

Soon his hunger gets the better of him and he decides to go to a cafe and eat, with the intention of not paying for the food. He does not care what they might do to him. He finds a milk bar and, after waiting for another customer to leave, he enters and sits alone. He orders some milk and wafers. But as he finishes the cookies, he begins to weep. The woman offers him a second helping of milk and cookies. After he eats, he leaves without paying. He resolves to pay her but as he walks back to the wharf he forgets his pledge. He sits on some burlap and watches the night activities at the docks. He falls asleep facing the sea.

In 'The Glass of Milk,' a destitute young man wanders the dock of a Chilean port like this one in Puntas Arenas seeking both food and work.

Characters

The Milk Bar Woman

The cafe attendant is soft-spoken and gentle. She takes the youth's order and offers him a second helping after he finishes the first. She understands his need for food and his reluctance to accept charity. When the lad weeps, she comforts him. After he stops weeping he looks to her, but she is looking away. She does not ask for payment for the food.

The Old Sailor

He is a pipe-smoking seaman who offers a bundle of food to the lad. The thin youth refuses his offer. The sailor smiles when a second fellow accepts his offer without saying thanks.

The Thin Youth

This young fellow is an itinerant laborer on the waterfront who is in constant search of work. He is very hungry because he has not eaten in several days, but his pride keeps him from accepting hand-outs from others. When he asks the foreman for his daily wages, he is refused payment until the job is completed. He refuses to take a loan from the foreman. He wants to meet his own needs without accepting charity from others.

But his hunger pushes him to the brink of despair, and he decides to "eat anywhere, without paying, even if they shamed him, beat him, sent him to jail." He is willing to accept shame and disgrace for a meal.

He accepts food and comfort from the milk bar woman. He does not offer to pay for the food. He plans to repay her, but by the time he reaches the wharf, he has forgotten this.

Themes

Reality vs. Imagination

The youth leaves his home to live and work on the sea. But his life there is not as fascinating and orderly as he imagined. The reality he faces is a life of difficult, hard-to-find work and gnawing hunger.

Loneliness

This theme finds its place in much of the fiction of Rojas. In his best known novel, *Hijo de ladrón (Born Guilty)*, the main character, Aniceto, struggles to overcome his loneliness. His father is a common criminal, and society believes that he too is a criminal. Aniceto is pushed to the lonely edges of society.

The youth in "The Glass of Milk" fights loneliness as he tries to fit in with other stevedores on the waterfront. Ironically, he remains outside the circles of other workers. When they eat lunch he goes off by himself. When he goes to the milk bar, he waits until it is empty before he enters, alone. Despite his search for companionship he remains alone throughout the story.

Style

Literary Style

Manuel Rojas began writing at the mid-point of the Naturalist Period in the history of Chilean literature. Naturalism is an extreme type of Realism in which the writer portrays the most grisly aspects of human nature. The characters in such stories

Topics for Further Study

- In the story ''The Glass of Milk,'' the walls of the city are symbolic of the youth's internal psychological walls. What other symbols can you find in the story and how would understanding them help you to better understand the story?

- Have you ever experienced the kind of hunger the youth experiences in the story? How did this change your behavior or attitudes then, and does that change still affect your life today? Explain in detail.

- If *machismo* is the governing aspect of the youth's daily life, why and how does he allow himself to accept the comfort and ministrations of the woman in the milk bar?

- Explain the change in attitude of the boy between the time he leaves the wharf to find the milk bar and his arrival back at the wharf. What physical and psychological differences do you see that account for any differences in his attitude?

- Do you know any other stories in which an individual experiences a similar set of circumstances? How would you compare that tale with this one and what are the major differences between the two? If you do not know a fictional story, do you know any real-life tales of similar circumstances?

---

usually come from the lowest stratum of society and their behavior is often unsavory.

Point of View

The storyteller in ''The Glass of Milk'' is a limited third-person narrator, sometimes called a non-participant narrator. A third-person narrator is one who is able to see all the actions of all the characters, all the time. But in this tale, it is limited because the narrator does not reveal what is happening inside the mind of every character, only that of the youth.

Setting

The setting for the story is the waterfront of a seaport on the Chilean coast. This area includes the wharf, some of the streets nearby, and a small milk bar on a side street. Rojas does not provide detailed descriptions of these areas but he includes enough for the reader to know that this is a rough part of town.

Irony

Rojas' writings are filled with irony, which is a way of writing in which the intended meaning is contrary to the meaning seemingly expressed. For example, in ''The Glass of Milk'' the youth says he

is not hungry when in fact he is painfully hungry. He says this in an attempt to maintain his dignity.

Symbolism

A symbol is an object in a story that suggests something else. The pile of burlap is a symbol of the working world to which the youth returns at the close of the tale. The eyes of the youth, the woman, and the old man are symbols of entrances or portals through which their souls may be seen or shown.

Literary Heritage

The Roman Catholic Church exerted a great influence on the people of Chile. The Church came to South America with the first conquerors and, in addition to providing religious teaching for the Spanish conquistadors, it undertook an effort to convert the native population. Therefore the majority of the Chileans are governed by their religious affiliation with the Roman Catholic Church. The Church has been successful in imprinting its social and ethical value system on the country.

Additional social influences come from the indigenous people who still live in the area. These include the descendants of the ancient peoples, the Araucanians, who were living there when the Spanish first occupied the country. Mystical and animistic beliefs still exist in these peoples' local communities. In some instances these combine with the Roman Catholicism and create a hybrid religion that blends native rituals with Church festivals.

An important aspect of "The Glass of Milk" involves the role of *machismo* in the lives of Latin American men and boys. It is very important for male members of this society to maintain an attitude and bearing of strength, self-sufficiency, and pride in the face of any and all situations. For the lad, he is unable to acknowledge his hunger even as it causes him to double up from pain.

Historical Context

Political History

Chile was the object of Spanish conquest in 1536 and 1537, when Diego de Almagro made the first contact with the indigenous populations, the Araucanians. He was an associate of Pizarro and later was given jurisdiction over the area. After his death his successors divided the country into portions that were given to wealthy Spanish patrons and associates. However, the native populations were not included in the division of the lands. They did not enjoy the benefits of the resources that were taken from the country, a fact that would eventually lead to uprisings in the late nineteenth and early twentieth centuries.

Spain controlled the area until Napoleon invaded Spain early in the nineteenth century, diverting Spanish attention to a defense of their homeland. Chile was granted independence on September 18, 1810, but it was not fully established until 1818, after a series of skirmishes between the Chileans (indigenous people and colonial Europeans) and the Spanish. The issue was finally settled in 1818 when Chile formed a navy that could protect the coast from the Spanish fleet. Still the country was plunged into anarchy until 1831, when a republic was established. From then until 1891 a series of republican governments came and went.

The government in Chile from 1891 to 1918 was a parliamentary system. But this time was also a period of unrest as the ruling parties, both political and economic, resorted to fraud and bribery to maintain their status and to gain more political and financial control of the country. These nefarious maneuvers created an ever-widening separation between the upper classes and the lower working classes. Then in the 1910s foreign demand for the country's minerals decreased, as did the wages for the laborers. In 1912 the Socialist Party was established in a bid to garner support from the workers. Labor unrest was exacerbated by worldwide economic pressures created by World War I, which reduced the demand for Chilean exports. By September 5, 1925, the situation had deteriorated to the point where a military junta was established. This junta was replaced by another in October of 1925.

In that month a *coup d'état* was engineered by the minister of war, who ruled from 1925 until 1931. The worldwide Great Depression was in full swing by then, and in 1935 the Radical Party took control, which lasted until 1952. Carlos Ibañez was elected to the presidency as an independent and remained in office until 1958. In this year Jorge Alessandri narrowly defeated a five-candidate slate which included Salvador Allende, who was elected in 1972. After Allende's assassination in 1973, Augusto Pinochet took control of the country and ruled as a military dictator until he was voted out of office in 1990. The election of presidents has been orderly since then.

Literary History

It was in these unsettled times that Rojas began writing. His first works were written in the second part of the Naturalist Period of literature of Chile. The Naturalist Period (1890-1935) was first dominated by Lastarria and his novel, *Salvad las aparencias!* But Vicente Grez (1847-1909) was the most prominent novelist of the generation. The second part of this period was strongly influenced by the writings of Eduardo Barrios, who created the psychological novel out of naturalist techniques.

Rojas was one of the more important short story writers of the period. His writings were not as grotesque as other writers' works. He focused on the people from the low classes and their struggles in life, but his characters were more sympathetically presented. Rojas was the first Chilean writer to use the subjective narrator, a narrator who was involved in the action in part or in whole. (An objective narrator, like the one in *"The Glass of Milk,"* tells the story without making judgmental comments about it.)

Compare & Contrast

- **Early Twentieth Century:** In the 1920s and 1930s, economic and political life in Chile was in turmoil. By the middle of the 1930s the worldwide Great Depression was at its worst and had left its mark on the country, especially the working classes. This often led to violent political upheaval and the beginning of a series of ineffective presidencies.

  Late Twentieth Century: In the 1990s, the political situation in Chile had begun to settle, beginning with the removal of the brutal dictator Augusto Pinochet in 1990. Democratic elections were held in 1999 and the freely elected government was installed in early 2000.

- **Early Twentieth Century:** In the 1920s and 1930s, the literary culture in Chile was just beginning to expand. Manuel Rojas was the most important writer of the times.

  Late Twentieth Century: In the 1990s, more writers emerged who have made significant contributions to the body of Chilean and world literature. A new generation of writers is focusing on the political events in Chile between 1973 and 1985. Their works deal with issues of internal repression and exile. In the 1990s folk literature has found an audience in Chile and elsewhere.

- **Early Twentieth Century:** In the 1930s, the working classes were oppressed by both the political powers and the upper-class owners of the businesses in the country.

  Late Twentieth Century: In the 1990s, political stability has been established. The economic situation in the country, while not as strong as many would like, has begun to produce a larger middle class. The workers receive higher wages and have more opportunity to enjoy the fruits of their incomes.

The latter part of the Naturalist Period included writers like Juan Marín and Salvador Reyes. These men voiced strong criticism and denunciation of the working conditions in the Chilean mining industry. Their works were condemned by the government when they were first published.

Early in his life, Rojas was an active participant in the opposition political party often called the Anarchists. Much of his early writings were contributions to the opposition's newspapers and other publications. These efforts were his attempts to draw attention to the plight of the working classes and to achieve a better life for them. Many of his novels and short stories tell of the struggles of the working classes.

World Recognition

Rojas' early writings exposed the lives and experiences of the lower classes, the *rotos* (the broken ones). His ability to create sympathetic characters from this part of society "earned him a vaunted place among Chilean novelists" according to Grafton J. Conliffe. Jaime Concha calls him "the outstanding Chilean writer of the first half of the 20th century." He won the Chilean National Prize for Literature in 1957.

Despite the Chilean setting for many of his stories, his writings received international admiration. He created characters that attain a universal appeal, teaching what Fernando Alegría calls "lessons about humanity." Because of his universality, his stories have been translated into many languages, including English, and his short fiction has been anthologized frequently.

Critical Overview

The short story "The Glass of Milk" has long been a favorite of readers in South America and in the

United States. It is a tightly written story that captures the frustrations and desperation of a youth who is down on his luck. But just as with Rojas' other writing, it does this without preaching or demeaning the characters. Rojas' characters are largely drawn from his personal experiences when, as a lad, he wandered around the mountains of Chile and Argentina with his family in search of work and food.

His literary style is easily understood, without a lot of confusing detail. The action in his stories is concise, intense, and direct. Little extraneous information is included. His style is often called plain, according to Naomi Lindstrom. His narrators seldom make commentary on the actions of the characters. Much of his writing falls within the general category of Naturalism, a literary style that attempts to depict the life and times of characters in a brutally real manner. Its characters are drawn from the lower classes of society. Giovanni Pontiero says of Rojas' approach to character development, "his characters and situations are drawn with vigor and conviction." But even though they are from the lowest class of society they are creatures who maintain their "dignity and pride. . .even under the most abject conditions" according to Fernando Alegría.

In "The Glass of Milk" Rojas explores a day in the life of a down-and-out youth who is trying to make his way as a stevedore. Herman Hespelt says that the youth is portrayed with a "deep sensitivity and a warm understanding" that lets readers arrive at an affection for the lad. But Rojas does not preach and beg for this result. His writing is fraught with intensity and a strong dramatic impact but the story is the most important aspect of his writing.

In his fiction he is interested in telling a story, not so much in making a philosophic statement. As Mary Cannizzo states, "his novels reflect a social consciousness, but instead of being a propagandist he is primarily an artist." It is precisely his artistry that keeps readers coming back to his works. Another of his well-known tales, "El hombre de la rosa," "draws the reader back irresistibly, inviting a closer look," says Susan M. Linker. Rojas' works can be viewed "as a long biographical narration," but without the injection of his own person, says Fernando Alegría. Rojas calls upon his own youthful experiences to fill out the characters in his stories.

Rojas' short story "The Glass of Milk" is a widely anthologized and published tale. It was included in his first collection of short stories, *Hombres del sur*, published in 1927 and "acclaimed by Chilean critics as one of the best collections of short stories ever published in the country," according to Cannizzo. These tales are the first fictional works that look at the lower stratum of Chilean and Argentinean society with the same compassionate approach that would mark Rojas' major novels and later short stories. Cannizzo adds that his success as a writer on the world scene derives from the fact that he depicts Chilean characters and cultural customs in a universal manner by "attributing human significance to them." Their localized behaviors therefore become universal behaviors. According to Grafton Conliffe, Rojas' "innovative techniques and ability to delineate memorable characters" are those aspects of his style that elevate his work to the position of high acclaim among Chilean writers.

Criticism

Carl Mowery

Mowery has a Ph.D. in writing and literature from Southern Illinois University, Carbondale. In the following essay he examines the psychological struggles of a lad trying to make his way among stevedores on the waterfront in Chile.

Henry David Thoreau wrote: "The mass of men lead lives of quiet desperation." In the story "The Glass of Milk," the main character, a thin youth, engages his sense of desperation as an internal quest for personal identity. He "was gripped by that fascination of the sea which molds the most peaceful and orderly lives as a strong arm a thin rod." He left the comfort of his family for the rough exotic life among the tramps and criminals, hoping to become a man among the stevedores who worked on the docks. He has spent several months working with some success at various tasks on ships plying the coasts of Chile. However at the start of the story he is down on his luck, out of work and out of food.

The boy's home life has seemed confining to him, so he seeks the freedom that he imagines he will find at sea. But along his way to becoming a free man, he becomes more and more constricted by the walls he builds to protect himself from everyone he meets. As he constructs them higher, he becomes more isolated from those among whom he desires acceptance. He is "without an acquaintance, without a penny, and without a trade." Even those skills he has are "almost useless on land." His pride

What Do I Read Next?

- The short story "The Man and the Rose" by Manuel Rojas, published in 1963, is a tale of a clash of mysticism and religion in the natural world. It presents an interesting conflict between illusion and reality.

- *Hijo de ladrón* (*Born Guilty*) by Manuel Rojas was published in 1951 in Santiago de Chile. This novel examines the life of a lad who tries to overcome his father's reputation as a criminal. The people the lad meets expect him to be as unsavory as his father. A theme from this story is the youth's fight against loneliness. It is part of a trilogy that is somewhat autobiographical and includes *Lanchas en la bahía* (1932) and *Mejor que el vino* (1958).

- Rojas' collection of political essays, *De la poesía a la revolución* (*From Poetry to Revolution*), comes from the 1920s and 1930s. It was first published as a collection in 1938. These essays offer insight into his thinking and activism on behalf of the workers in Chile and Argentina.

- *Invisible Man* (1952) by Ralph Ellison depicts the isolation and struggles of a southern black man in New York City. The protagonist faces many of the same kinds of situations that Aniceto faces in *Hijo de ladrón*.

---

becomes his most important possession and he sacrifices everything in order to keep it.

His pride keeps him from accepting anything that he perceives as a handout or charity. The sailor offers him a package of food, which he "heroically" refuses, believing that he must not show any sign of weakness. As a Latin-American youth he knows that to accept a handout would cost him his dignity. The "gaudy tramp" confirms his loss of dignity by accepting the package from the sailor. The youth's heroic arrogance makes him feel superior to the tramp who accepts the package. The lad knows that he could never rely on charity or he would lose the sense of manliness that he has cultivated. Indeed, this refusal of the package is not the first time he has done this. "And when, just as now, someone did offer him a handout" indicates a pattern of refusing offers of food.

Since he has been out of work for six days and has not eaten for three days, his hunger grows more and more intense. The pain of his hunger convinces him that "he could not hold out much longer." Then he decides "to resort to any means to get some food." His internal desperation has come to the surface. It is no longer Thoreau's "quiet despera-

tion." He is determined to act. However, before he can act rashly, he gets work loading grain onto a ship.

In his search for acceptance among the men of the docks, he develops a strong sense of pride, which he uses to gird himself psychologically and to insulate himself from them. Despite his desire to be one of the guys, he remains apart from them. He does not eat with them at lunch time and when he looks for a place to eat in the evening he avoids the cafes where these men might congregate. At other times his timidity keeps him from waiting "by the gangways at mealtimes" hoping to be offered some leftovers by the sailors.

As time moves on, the boy finds himself trapped by his walls as he searches for places to hide from the other stevedores. The high walls of the city, symbolic of the walls he is building within himself, are dark and threatening. The people are loud and intimidating. He wanders around looking for work or a place to eat, overwhelmed by the oppressive city surroundings. He is held back by his fears that the people would be able to see his pain and shame and that this would be seen as a weakness. His psychological walls will not allow him to accept a

> The boy's home life has seemed confining to him, so he seeks the freedom that he imagines he will find at sea. But along his way to becoming a free man, he becomes more and more constricted by the walls he builds to protect himself from everyone he meets."

loan from the foreman. The irony of refusing the loan is that it reinforces his feelings of self-sufficiency by avoiding any obligation to anyone other than himself. But this false sense of self-sufficiency drags him deeper into despair.

When he has the vision of his home, it appears only "as if a window opens before him." This invisible barrier was once an obstacle that kept him confined at home but now, since he is on his own, it is the barrier preventing him from going back home. He does not want to admit that he could not make it on his own. But despite his strong desire to live on the open sea, he keeps looking for some job that would keep him "until he could get back to his home grounds." He is homesick. He yearns for his mother and his siblings.

Later as he is seated in the milk bar, "a blonde lady in a very white apron" comes to his table and wipes it off. She speaks "in a soft voice" asking what he wants to eat. When she leaves to get the milk and wafers, he rejoices in the knowledge that he will soon eat. As he prepares to eat he feels her eyes "watching him with curiosity and attention," but he refuses to look back at her. The quiet power of her maternal nature overcomes his timidity and shame and he accepts her tenderness.

However, he rejects any offerings of assistance from the men in the story. They are father figures to the boy, and because it is inappropriate for a Latino boy to show weakness of any kind, he rejects their assistance. It is unmanly for a man to show need of any sort, even though he could feel "his hunger increase with the refusal." The sailor offers him the food and he refuses because he was "ashamed that he had seemed to need charity." Later he rejects the foreman's offer of a loan "with an anguished smile." He does not want to let any adult male see his weaknesses. For him to accept a "handout" is demeaning, since the word handout implies condescension on the part of the giver and loss of dignity for the recipient, confirms Michael Waag.

Coupled with his reluctance to show weakness to stronger male figures, he is also concerned with a sense of morality. Included with this is a feeling that an individual must accept responsibility for one's actions, and that every responsibility brings with it a consequence that must be accepted. The youth accepts the responsibility to work in the boiler room on the ship after he is found as a stowaway. The irony is that he hides on the ship like a common criminal but gets to work like any other hired hand. Moreover, he is satisfied that, despite the illegality of being a stowaway, he has fulfilled his manly duty by working his way to the next port, where he is immediately put off the ship.

This sense of fulfilling an obligation no matter how it is obtained also arises as he determines to steal food to assuage his hunger. He accepts the obligation to pay for the food no matter what that entailed, whether they "shamed him, beat him, sent him to jail, anything." He is operating by the slogan "If you can't do the time, don't do the crime." For him it is an accepted obligation to be fulfilled after eating stolen food. And it is part of maintaining his idea of manhood. But by making this decision to accept the punishment, he breaches his own carefully established set of rules that keep him from being shamed. Now he turns this aversion into an obligation he must fulfill for getting something to eat.

Just as his search for the right cafe takes him to the outskirts of the city, his internal search takes him to the edges of his emotional self. After he selects a quiet milk bar, he refuses to enter when he sees an old man sitting there reading a newspaper and drinking a glass of milk. As he waits, his anxiety grows more intense and he begins to think of the man as "his enemy" who knew his plight and intent to steal a meal. His sense of pride is whipped into a new sense of fear and paranoia. He feels that he must demonstrate his strength of manhood by insulting the old man. His mental confrontation with the old man is yet another rejection of a father figure for the youth. His reaction to the man is ironic because he condemns him for taking so long to sit and read "for so small a purchase," when the boy intends to steal a meal. He is angry because the man is an inconvenience to the boy's entrance to the milk bar.

He does not act on his impulses to accost the old man because his sense of morality does not allow him to do so, knowing that it is not proper to insult anyone. His reluctance to act on his impulses occurs as he is face to face with his victim. His sense of outrage and anger at the man are diminished. The youth would have to look him in the eye to accost him and he could not reveal his own eyes to the man. The man puts on his glasses and walks away reading.

This fear of looking someone directly in the eyes happens again after he has accepted his meal from the woman. His sense of propriety now causes him to lose composure when he is face to face with the woman from whom he intends to steal the meal. It is only after she gives him a second helping that his feelings of guilt are eased and he feels comfortable enough to leave without paying. His only payment is his departing words: "Thank you very much ma'am; good-bye."

His walls are breached when he allows the woman to see his inner self. After she gives him the plate of cookies and the glass of milk, he refuses to look at her directly. He fears that "she would guess his situation and his shameful intentions" (eyes and glasses are symbolic portals to the soul). As his hunger is diminished, his inner burning begins to release itself. He weeps. After the woman strokes his head, he weeps more intensely and deeply.

In these poignant moments the boy has lowered his walls and let the woman comfort him and soothe his internal turmoil. In the vision that sent him on this quest for the milk bar, he saw his family, mother, sisters, and brothers, and he remembers the comfort of his home. Thus began the slow disassembly of his walls. The acceptance of his family bonds, not the bonds of "slavery" to the work on the docks, causes him to relax the walls he had so carefully built over the past few months. He releases himself from the bonds of pride. Just as he lets go of those bonds, he finds himself outside the city. He has freed himself from the intimidation of the city's walls and the walls of his pride.

After he allows the woman to stroke his head and feed him, he regains his composure and leaves the bar. He has been fed physically and psychologically. He strides confidently as he hums on his way back to the wharf and the life of a stevedore. He returns to the dock thinking that he will repay the woman. But just as the tears on his face have disappeared, so too has that thought vanished. He enters the rough, working world when he sits on a pile of burlap and stares out at "the grand sweep of the sea," his idealized fantasy world. As he falls asleep, he is content with himself; he has eaten and he is reinvigorated, "like a new man. . .reassembled and united."

Source: Carl Mowery, in an essay for *Literature of Developing Nations for Students*, Gale, 2000.

Sheri E. Metzger,

Metzger is a Ph.D. specializing in literature and drama at the University of New Mexico, where she is a lecturer in the English department and an adjunct professor in the University Honors Program. In this essay, she discusses the divisions and implications of the feminine and masculine spheres present in Manuel Rojas' "The Glass of Milk."

Manuel Rojas' short story "The Glass of Milk" offers two distinct images, each one in direct opposition to the other. One image is that of the male sphere, the public sphere of male employment and masculine strength, a world of independence and self-sufficiency. This is the sphere that the boy seeks to join. This male sphere is balanced by the feminine sphere, the domestic world of comfort and nurturing, of tenderness and security. This is the world from which the boy has traveled on his journey to manhood. In spite of the unnamed youth's desire to locate himself solely in the masculine sphere, he is unable to completely break free of the feminine sphere, not yet understanding that for a man to find true balance, he must be able to exist in both worlds. The youthful protagonist of Rojas' story thinks that if he is to be a man and live successfully in the male world, he must first extradite himself from his mother's world.

The reader's first glimpse of the boy presents his conflict between hunger and pride, between those images that he thinks must exist in separate worlds. In his desire to be a man, the boy assumes that the only way he can prove his independence and self-sufficiency is by denying any offer of assistance. To accept food from the sailor is to admit that he cannot survive on his own. But, he is still an adolescent, and as such, he is in need of tenderness and nurturing, two things that the sailors on the docks do not have to give. Moreover, the boy thinks that men do not need tenderness and nurturing. For the boy, the docks are a man's world. The sailor with his pipe, the gaudy tramp begging for food, the

> While the boy cannot admit to his needs while in the male world, he can reveal his hunger and his loneliness to the woman in the dairy bar. For the boy, this is the essential difference between the male sphere and female sphere, the ability to admit to fallibility and vulnerability."

men loading heavy sacks of wheat—these are all men, performing men's work and functioning as with strength and self-sufficiency. The boy is still too insecure in his adult maleness to approach these men for help; he cannot even acknowledge that he needs their help.

Rojas provides the boy with many of the elements of manhood. He has served as a mess boy on an earlier ship and been a stowaway on another. He has spent sufficient time on his own, earning a wage and supporting himself, and yet, insecurity still consumes him. In his study of the psychological conflict in ''The Glass of Milk,'' Robert Scott suggests that the boy's inability to accept help is the insecurity of early adolescence. As evidence of this insecurity, Scott points to the boy's hesitancy:

> When he first appears on the scene, he seems doubtful as to which direction to take; he vacillates out of timidity and shame before refusing the food from the sailor; he waivers again, watching the stevedores, before asking for the job unloading cargo; he is reluctant to join the other men at lunch and remains alone; he waits until all the men have left the scene before asking the foreman for an advance in pay and will not enter the milk bar until the old man leaves; when he finally goes in, he stumbles over one of the chairs; he chooses a table in a corner; and finally, he is both unable to look the woman in the eye and incapable of any extended conversation with her.

In his hesitancy, the boy is timid, doubtful, and ashamed of his hunger. The homeless man is also hungry, but he is not ashamed of his hunger. He is older and more secure in his manhood, and for him, being hungry and accepting a handout does not exclude him from the male world. For the boy, however, hunger is a sign that he has not net earned full admission to this male realm.

When the day's work is finished, the boy is desperate enough for food that he asks for an advance on his earnings. This request denied, as he walks away the youth is very near collapsing. When he is at his most desperate time of need, the boy sees his home:

> Suddenly he felt his entrails on fire, and he stood still. He began to bend down, down, doubling over forcibly like a rod of steel, until he thought he would drop. At that instant, as if a window opened before him, he saw his home, the view from it, the faces of his mother, brothers and sisters, all that he wanted and loved appeared and disappeared before his eyes shut by fatigue. . .Then, little by little, the giddiness passed and he began to straighten up, while the burning subsided gradually.

In his moment of most extreme urgency, the boy sees the faces of his mother and siblings. He sees the feminine world of his mother and the safety that it offers. This vision gives him the strength to continue on. He does not see his father's face, and it is not the masculine world that gives him the strength to survive. It is, quite simply, the image of his mother's world that carries him toward the dairy bar.

The boy's need for the feminine sphere becomes evident in his selection of the dairy bar as his destination. Before he stops there, he passes up several nearby cheap grills. The grills are really representative of the male world, public places filled with people who gamble and drink. The dairy bar, on the other hand, is a child's world. This is the world of his mother, represented by milk and cookies and a sympathetic woman. Of course the boy does not know she is sympathetic, except intuitively. But like his mother, the woman in the dairy bar represents comfort and safety, and the familiarity of home—something he badly needs at this moment. The boy may desire manhood, but he is still a boy who has not eaten in three days, and who cannot manage even one more day without sustenance. While the boy cannot admit to his needs while in the male world, he can reveal his hunger and his loneliness to the woman in the dairy bar. For the boy, this is the essential difference between the male sphere and female sphere, the ability to admit to fallibility and vulnerability.

Certainly men can admit to these emotions, but the Latin *machismo* does not encourage this, and in the boy's effort to be a man, he does not yet understand that the essential strength of men can include an acknowledgment of need. Scott maintains that "it is indicative of the degree of insecurity in the youth that he cannot allow himself even a simple act of kindness from another man." Even the elderly man in the dairy bar is a threat, according to Scott, because the youth cannot allow any male "to witness such lack of manly dignity" as will occur when the boy eats without paying for his food—as he plans to do. To permit even the old man to see him would deny the boy the adult male status that he desires, whereas the woman's help does not compromise his maleness. The woman in the dairy bar assumes the mantle of the maternal, the feminine world of nurturing. In this private, domestic sphere of women, the boy can be a child again, drinking milk and eating cookies, much as he would in his mother's house. He needs the warmth and comfort of his mother, and so he instinctively seeks out this world, just as a small child refreshes himself in the warmth and safety of his mother's kitchen.

After the boy has eaten his cookies and milk, he is finally able to ask for the comfort that he needs. In the male world, he cannot cry, but in the women's world, tears and weeping are not badges of disgrace. With the woman, the youth can give in to his despair and loneliness. He can weep openly because she offers him the opportunity to do so. When he leaves the dairy bar, it is with stomach soothed and soul healed. Scott argues that through this show of community support, "the youth has 'learned' to accept support from others in a period of difficulty. This time he has opened himself to a mother figure; next time perhaps he will be able to be more open with men." But Scott's reading of Rojas' story is a psychological reading. A feminist reading of "The Glass of Milk" could posit that the youth has not learned to accept support from others. He has always known how to ask support of his mother, and at his moment of greatest need, he reverts back to what has always been acceptable—asking support of the feminine world. The boy is not any more ready to accept help from men than he was previously, and there is no reason provided in Rojas' text that suggests he will be comfortable accepting help from the masculine world until he is more comfortable with his newly acquired manhood. There is a reason that weeping before this woman creates "a great refreshing sensation . . .extinguishing the hot something that had nearly strangled him." After his tears, the boy eats "as if he were at home and his mother were that woman who was standing behind the counter." For the boy, that woman represents all

the love and security of his mother's world. She represents the feminine sphere, and the boy's experience illustrates how essential both worlds are to his existence.

Source: Sheri E. Metzger, in an essay for *Literature of Developing Nations for Students,* Gale, 2000.

Liz Brent

Brent has a Ph.D. in American culture, with a specialization in film studies, from the University of Michigan. She is a freelance writer and teaches courses in the history of American cinema. In the following essay, Brent discusses descriptions of hunger in Rojas's story "The Glass of Milk."

Rojas's short story "The Glass of Milk" concerns a sailor boy, in a port town far from home, without money or a job, his body wracked with hunger, who is nonetheless too proud to admit to his hunger or accept the charity of others. Much of the story focuses on descriptions of the boy's experience of hunger, in terms of his perceptions of the world around him, his physical sensations, his thoughts and feelings, and his interactions with others.

As the story opens, a sailor, leaning on the rail of a ship, holds a package of food which he first offers to the boy as he passes by on the dock, and then gives to a tramp. This scene establishes a contrast between the reaction of the boy to this offer of charity and the reaction of the tramp, while also indicating that the boy's hunger is no less extreme, and his situation no less desperate, than that of the tramp. The first indication that the package held by the sailor contains food is that it is "grease-spotted." Upon first appearance on the scene, the boy's demeanor does not betray his hunger. He walks along the wharf "with his hands in his pockets, idling or thinking." At this point in the story, the narrator describes the scene as if from the perspective of the sailor, or any onlooker. Upon rereading, however, the reader, knowing that the boy is terribly hungry, can re-interpret this description of the boy as "idling or thinking" as an expression of his state of hunger and desperation. He may seem to the onlooker to be "idling" either because his hunger has put him in a state of listlessness, or because he is not sure what to do or where to go to obtain food. He may be "thinking" of ways out of his predicament. At the same time, he may have his hands in his pockets in an attempt not to betray to anyone how desperate he is. When the sailor calls out to the boy, asking if he is hungry, the boy's outward response at first seems ambivalent: "There was a brief silence during which the youth seemed to be thinking, and took one shorter step as if to stop. . . .'' Although he denies to the sailor that he is hungry, the reader may interpret his behavior as an expression of the struggle within himself between his desperate need for food and his sense of pride, which prevents him from accepting the handout. He replies to the sailor ''smiling feebly'' that he is not hungry. His feeble smile in part indicates that he is so terribly hungry he can barely smile, yet his sense of pride causes him to try his best to appear unconcerned with food.

The ''gaudy tramp'' who does accept the sailor's offer of food represents an outward expression of the boy's feelings of hunger which he is too proud to demonstrate. While the boy is hesitant, and then refuses the charity, the tramp is overly eager to accept it, which he does so without pride or gratitude. The sailor asks the tramp if he is hungry, and ''He had not yet finished the phrase when the tramp looked with shining eyes at the package the sailor held in his hand. . . .'' While the boy lies, responding that he is not hungry, the tramp expresses outwardly what the boy experiences inside: ''Yes, sir; I'm very much hungry!'' The tramp's eagerness to accept this charity is further indicated by the description of the package landing ''in the eager hands'' of the tramp. The tramp's happiness and eagerness in accepting this charity is further described by the way in which he ''happily rubbed his hands'' at the sight of the food.

The story goes on to describe in a variety of ways how hunger affects the boy, both physically and mentally. ''He had not eaten for exactly three days and three long nights.'' Although he cannot bring himself to accept handouts, from both ''timidity and shame,'' his refusal of the sailor's offer seems to exacerbate the hunger, as ''he felt his hunger increase with the refusal.'' The boy's internal state of hunger affects his perceptions of the world around him, so that his impression of the port town in which he has been wandering hungrily takes on a dark, oppressive, and horrible demeanor: ''It seemed a place of slavery; stale, dark, without the grand sweep of the sea; among its high walls and narrow streets people lived and died bewildered by agonizing drudgery.''

Although he refuses to accept charity, the boy finally decides ''to resort to any means to get some food.'' When he is hired to work loading cargo onto a steamship, he takes his place ''enthusiastically'' among the workers. However, his extreme hunger affects his ability to work, and he ''began to feel

tired and dizzy; he swayed as he crossed the gangplank, the heavy load on his shoulder. . . .'' His hunger and exhaustion again cause him to look at the world around him as a dark, dirty, and unsightly place; he looks down at the water below the wharf, ''stained with oil and littered with garbage.'' Because of his extreme hunger, he ends the workday ''completely exhausted, covered with sweat, at the end of his rope.'' Although he decides to ask the foreman for an advance on his pay, his hunger leaves him ''confused and stuttering.'' Refusing the foreman's paltry offer of the forty cents in his pocket, the boy thanks him ''with an anguished smile.'' Again, as with the sailor, the boy attempts to hide his hunger and despair with a smile, but his true state of mind is expressed by his ''anguish.''

At this point, the story's description of the boy's hunger becomes more extreme and anguished, the physical sensations brought on by hunger more painful:

> Then the boy was seized by acute despair. He was hungry, hungry, hungry! Hunger doubled him over, like a heavy, broad whiplash. He saw everything through a blue haze, and he staggered like a drunk when he walked. Nevertheless, he would not have been able to complain or shout, for his suffering was deep and exhausting; it was not pain, but anguish, the end! It seemed to him that he was flattened out by a great weight.

The narrator uses several literary devices in depicting the extremes of hunger experienced by the boy. Repetition, such as in the phrase ''hungry, hungry, hungry!'' is used throughout the story to emphasize the boy's condition. The narrator also makes use of figurative language to depict the boy's state of hunger. The hunger ''doubled him over, like a heavy, broad whiplash''; because of the hunger ''it seemed to him that he was flattened out by a great weight.'' The narrator further describes the ways in which hunger affects the boy's physical abilities; his vision is affected, as he ''saw everything through a blue haze,'' as is his ability to walk, in that ''he staggered like a drunk.'' Eventually, the hunger causes a burning sensation in his gut, as ''he felt his entrails on fire, and he stood still. He began to bend down, down, doubling over forcibly like a rod of steel, until he thought he would drop.''

Recovering slightly from this spell of dizziness caused by the hunger, ''he made up his mind to eat anywhere, without paying, even.'' Again, the narrator uses the literary device of repetition to emphasize the boy's hunger and his determination to eat: ''the main thing was to eat, eat, eat. A hundred times he mentally repeated the word: eat, eat, eat, until it lost its meaning, leaving his head feeling hot and empty.'' He imagines that he will eat somewhere, and then explain to the owner, ''I was hungry, hungry, hungry, and I can't pay.''

After the boy enters the milk bar and begins to drink the glass of milk and eat the wafers, the narrator describes the process by which his hunger subsides, leaving him with a new physical sensation in his body, and new vision of the world around him. As he begins to eat, ''he felt the burning in his stomach diminishing, dying away.'' After he cries from relief, the food begins to restore the physical sensation of his body: ''. . . he felt a great refreshing sensation spread inside him, extinguishing the hot something that had nearly strangled him.'' Unlike the tramp at the beginning of the story who did not bother to thank the sailor for his charity, the boy thanks the waitress at the milk bar for allowing him to eat and drink without paying for it. After he leaves the milk bar, the sensations in his body, previously wracked with hunger, are refreshing and energetic. ''The wind blowing from the sea refreshed his face. . . .'' His entire attitude and outlook on life are refreshed, as well. As he walks along, ''he straightened up happily, strode on with assurance and determination.'' He walks along the sea, ''with a spring in his step; he felt like a new man, as if his inner forces, previously scattered, had reassembled and united solidly.'' Whereas, in his hunger, the sea, the wharf, and the port town had seemed to him dirty and oppressive, the story ends, once he has eaten, with an image of the sea as life-giving and full of hope: ''He just felt alive, that was all. Then he fell asleep with his face toward the sea.''

Source: Liz Brent, in an essay for *Literature of Developing Nations for Students*, Gale, 2000.

Sources

Cannizzo, Mary, in *Hispania*, Vol. 41, May, 1958, pp. 200-01; collected in *Modern Latin American Literature*, edited by David William Foster and Virginia Ramos Foster, Frederick Ungar, 1975, pp. 273-77.

Castro, Raoul Silva, *Historia crítica de la novela chilena (1843-1956)*, Ediciones Cultura Hispánica, 1960, pp. 319, 326-27; collected in *Modern Latin American Literature*, edited by David William Foster and Virginia Ramos Foster, Frederick Ungar, 1975, pp. 273-77.

Concha, Jaime, ''Manuel Rojas,'' in *Encyclopedia of Latin American Literature*, edited by Verity Smith, Fitzroy Dearborn, 1997, pp. 724-25.

Conliffe, Grafton J., trans., Introduction to ''The Man and the Rose,'' in *Latin American Literary Review*, Vol. 18, No. 36, July/December, 1990, pp. 78-86.

Goic, Cedomil, ''Chile,'' in *Encyclopedia of Latin American Literature*, edited by Verity Smith, Fitzroy Dearborn, 1997, pp. 195-201.

Lichtblau, Myron I., in *Modern Latin American Literature*, edited by David William Foster and Virginia Ramos Foster, Frederick Ungar, 1975, pp. 273-77.

———, ''Ironic Devices in Manuel Rojas' *Hijo de ladrón*,'' in *Symposium*, Fall, 1965, pp. 214-25.

Lindstrom, Naomi, ''Realism and Naturalism,'' in *Twentieth Century Spanish American Fiction*, University of Texas Press, Austin, 1994, pp. 52-3.

''Manuel Rojas,'' in *An Anthology of Spanish American Literature*, edited by E. Herman Hespelt, F. S. Crofts and Co., 1946, p. 707.

Richardson, Maurice, in *Modern Latin American Literature*, edited by David William Foster and Virginia Ramos Foster, Frederick Ungar, 1975, pp. 273-77.

Scott, Robert, ''The Psychological Conflict in Manuel Rojas' 'El vaso de leche,''' in *Studies in Short Fiction*, Vol. 24, No. 1, Winter, 1987, pp. 49-56.

Waag, Michael, Chairman, Department of Foreign Languages, and Professor of Spanish Language and Literature, Murray State University, interview conducted March 28, 2000.

Further Reading

Fleak, Kenneth, *The Chilean Short Story: Writers from the Generation of 1950*, Peter Lang, 1989.
    Chapter Two contains a section of general information on Manuel Rojas and his impact on Chilean short fiction.

Goic, Cedomil, ''Chile,'' in *Encyclopedia of Latin American Literature*, pp. 195-201.
    This section from the *Encyclopedia of Latin American Literature* contains information that gives a broad overview of Chilean literature from the beginning of the nineteenth century up to the end of the twentieth century.

The Handsomest Drowned Man

Gabriel García Márquez

1968

"The Handsomest Drowned Man" is one of Gabriel García Márquez's later short stories, reflecting the growth of an accomplished writer. In this story, the author tells a simple story of the recovery of a drowned man and the effect the man has on the group of villagers who must now bury him. Through the act of cleaning and dressing the body, the drowned man's humanity moves the villagers to change their lives. They grow to love a man they never knew in life, and before they can bury him, they must bestow upon him family, kinship, and the village's love. The villagers represent the ideal world, one in which strangers take responsibility for another human being. It is also a world where people unite for the common good, and where people take the time to listen to one another, even when they do not share a language. The dead man cannot speak, but he speaks to the villagers through a universal language of humanity. This, of course, is the utopian world of García Márquez's imagination. But it is also a world where the villagers are able to imagine the pain and grief the man must have felt in being different. Their compassion for this man allows them to transcend their small village so that, within hours, they can visualize another village— one more glorious and beautiful, one that will be admired by any visitor.

Author Biography

Gabriel García Márquez was born in Aracataca, Colombia, in 1928. He lived with his grandmother until he was eight years old, and it was her storytelling and the myths of the townspeople that helped form García Márquez's imagination. When war forced the closure of the University of Bogota's Law School in 1948, García Márquez transferred to the University of Cartagena, where he also worked as a journalist. Within two years, García Márquez left the study of law to focus on journalism. He began writing short stories during this period, even as he continued to work on a daily paper, *El heraldo*. García Márquez's short stories were published in regional periodicals; at the same time, he joined a circle of local writers, where he became acquainted with the works of such authors as Franz Kafka, William Faulkner, Virginia Woolf, and James Joyce. After returning to Bogota in 1954, García Márquez published a novella, *La hojarasca* (1955; *Leaf Storm*, translation published in 1972). During this period, García Márquez also gained some political notoriety for his published newspaper accounts of a sailor who survived a shipwreck in the Caribbean. This series exposed the Colombian navy as incompetent, and as a result the author left his country to avoid government retribution, eventually settling in Paris.

Generally, critics have labeled García Márquez's earliest short stories, those written in the late 1940s and early 1950s, as unsuccessful and too self-conscious in their use of unconventional narrative techniques. Additional collections of short stories, such as *Los funerales de la Mama Grande* (1962; translated in *No One Writes to the Colonel and Other Stories*, 1968) are considered more successful. García Márquez's first novel, *La mala hora* (1962; *In Evil Hour*, 1979) was followed by the commercially successful *Cien anos de soledad* (1967; *One Hundred Years of Solitude*, 1970), which critics called a masterpiece. García Márquez continued to publish additional novels and collections of short stories, including *El otona del patriarca* (1973; *The Autumn of the Patriarch*, 1975), *Cronica de una muerte anunciada* (1981; *Chronicle of a Death Foretold*, 1982), *El amor en los tiempos del colera* (1985; *Love in the Time of Cholera*, 1988), and *El general en su laberinto* (1989; *The General in His Labyrinth*, 1990). Garcia was awarded the 1982 Nobel Prize for Literature, and is regarded as one of the world's most influential living authors.

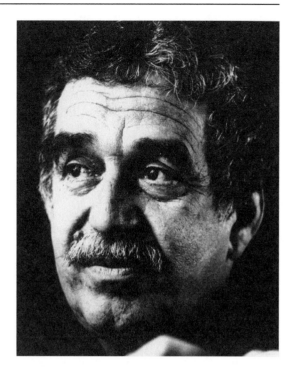

Gabriel García Márquez

Plot Summary

The Discovery

The story opens with the discovery of the body of a man. Children find a body washed up onshore, covered in seaweed, and at first they play with the body, burying it and digging it up again and again. Eventually, another villager sees the corpse, and the body is brought into the nearest house. The villagers observe that the corpse is unusually heavy, weighing almost as much as a horse, and he is also taller than other men, barely fitting into the house. Another notable difference is that the man's body is covered with a crust of mud and scales, giving him the appearance of something scarcely human. It is clear to the villagers that the man is not one of them, since their village is so small and everyone knows everyone else.

The Village

The village of twenty homes sits on a cliff, with so little land that the mothers worry a strong wind will blow their children out into the sea. With so little land available, when a villager dies the body is thrown off the cliff instead of being buried, because there is no room for a cemetery. While the men in the village go to neighboring villages to inquire about the missing man, the women clean the body, first washing away the mud, then scraping off the scales. The women note that the debris from the sea is from faraway oceans and the man's clothing is tattered, as if he had passed through a sea of coral. After he is cleaned, the women notice that the man is the "tallest, strongest, most virile, and best built man they had ever seen." He also appears proud and lacks the lonely look of other drowned men.

The Man

The drowned man is too tall for anyone's bed and too heavy for any table, and dressing him for the wake proves especially difficult since there are no clothes in the village that will fit him. The women decide to sew clothing in which to bury him, using a sail and some bridal linen. As the women sew, they imagine what the man was like and decide that he would have had a much sturdier house than anyone else in the village, and that he would have made his wife very happy. He would have also had great luck as a fisherman, having to expend no energy to draw the fish from the sea. The women also compare the drowned man to their own husbands, finding their husbands lacking in comparison. Eventually, one of the women decides that the man looks like his name was Esteban, and the others agree. But in giving him a name, they also give him a life. In personalizing the man, the villagers are struck by how difficult his life must have been, as he was always too large for doors, beds, and clothing. The women are able to visualize the man frightening people who did not know him and being uncomfortable in the presence of others. When they finally cover the man's face with a handkerchief, he at last looks dead and defenseless, and the women cry because he reminds them of their own helpless husbands.

When the men return they bring news that the body is not from any of the neighboring villages, and the women rejoice, since now Esteban belongs to the village. The men prepare a litter to draw the body to the cliffs, where they will then throw him into the sea. But the women keep interfering and wasting time, decorating the body with many small trinkets, until finally the men grow angry. Finally, when the women remove the handkerchief and the men see the man's face, they too recognize Esteban's humanity. Instantly, the men can see how ashamed Esteban would have been at the inconvenience he was causing the villagers.

The Funeral

The men now agree with the women that Esteban should be honored, and so a splendid funeral is held for the drowned man. When the women go in search of more flowers, the women of neighboring villages come to see the man, and they too bring flowers. As the villagers prepare to return the body to the sea, they name members of the village as his family, so that he will not be buried as an orphan, and so through his family, everyone in the village will be the man's kin. As they carry Esteban to the cliffs, the people become aware of the desolation of their village. As they watch his body fall into the sea, the villagers decide to rebuild their village, with houses having wider doors, higher ceilings, and stronger floors, so that if ever Esteban decided to return again, he would never need to worry about his size. They decide to plant flowers and glorious gardens, to tempt the cruise ships that pass by the cliffs and to make Esteban's memory eternal, so that the ships' captains might point to their village and exclaim that it was Esteban's village.

Characters

Esteban

Esteban is the central character in this short story, and the only one to have a name. He is a corpse, and nothing is known of his life, except for what the villagers attribute to him. Since he cannot speak, the villagers must interpret his story from what they discover about his body. His appearance informs the villagers of his kindness and his pride, and they imagine that he must have also been so commanding a presence that even the fish would obey his every command. His excessive size is at first a measure of his greatness, but eventually the villagers realize that Esteban's size might also have made his life difficult. The villagers imagine the awkwardness that must have greeted his every move, and the concerns that he might have had about peoples' insincerity. The women initially compare Esteban to their husbands, and eventually, as they grieve for him, they also grieve for their husbands. The villagers open their homes and their hearts for this man, sharing their families as they formally adopt him into their village. As they return his body to the sea, Esteban enables the villagers to see their lives as the drowned man would have seen them. They see their small village, with their smaller homes, and they see the desolation in their life upon the cliffs. Because of his presence, the villagers are inspired to beautify their village and enlarge their homes, so that if Esteban returns again, he will feel comfortable and welcome in their homes. Although he never lived in their village, nor even spoke a word, the drowned man inspired these people to open their hearts and their homes, and he inspired them to improve their lives. Esteban, who began the story as a nameless corpse, received the funeral of an honored citizen, and like any great man, he changed the lives of everyone he came into contact with, even after death.

The Villagers

None of the villagers have names, since community functions as one person in this story. The villagers' lives are hard; their tiny fishing village sits on such a narrow space of land that they cannot bury their dead in the dirt near their community, but must drop them from the cliffs into the sea. The village is so small that the community knows immediately that the drowned man is a stranger, since all the men from the village fit into seven boats. The women are captivated by the drowned man, and it is they who name him. They admire him, and they sympathize with him, understanding the anguish he must have felt as someone who was so very different from those around him. The men are initially jealous, even irritated that the women are so entranced by the stranger, but when they see his face, they are equally enchanted. It is Esteban's humanity that speaks to the villagers, and although he never speaks a word, his language is one of love, as the villagers embrace this stranger. The village acts as one as they prepare for Esteban's funeral. Everyone takes responsibility for burying the drowned man, and as they watch him fall into the sea, the village unites in a common goal: the improvement of their village. The villagers represent the ideal world, where the people function as a community for the betterment of the common good.

Themes

Beauty

When the women assume the task of cleaning and preparing the drowned man for burial, they are struck by his beauty. Even in death the man's pride shines through, and the women feel the strength of that beauty. They immediately imagine that the drowned man would have had command of the sea, simply calling the fish to their capture. The women are so struck by the man's beauty that they cannot

Topics for Further Study

- Research the political atmosphere in Colombia in the 1960s and compare the way this society functioned with the idealist socialist village that García Márquez constructs in "The Handsomest Drowned Man."

- Explain how Esteban talks to the villagers.

- Discuss how Esteban's humanity is reflected in the love the villagers express toward him.

- Research the lives of the small village fishermen along Colombia's coast and compare their lives with those of fishermen in the United States.

- Explain the role of the sea in the lives of the villagers in this story, and discuss what the sea contributes to their lives.

- Research funeral practices in Colombia, and compare them with the funeral Esteban receives.

resist comparing their husbands to him, and their husbands are reduced in stature next to such an attractive figure. The man's beauty is so significant that the women are inspired to name him, and they call him Esteban, which means Crown, since they see him as royal. Esteban is, indeed, the handsomest drowned man.

Generosity

Esteban creates in the villagers a need to open their community and their hearts to this stranger. They share of their time when they prepare him for burial, and they share in what small wealth they possess when they make his burial clothes. Their village is a humble one, sustained by the men's fishing. They have little, living in simple wooden houses, and yet they attempt to clothe the man, who is too large to wear any of their husbands' clothes. The villagers share their wealth in other ways, as they invite this stranger into their community, adopting him and giving him kinship within their village. Esteban may have been alone when he washed up on the beach, but he is not alone when he is returned to the sea. He takes the villagers' love and giving spirit with him, and in return he teaches them about sharing their lives.

Humanity and the Role of the Community

When the village unites to give Esteban a splendid funeral, they become a utopian community, one willing to open their hearts and their homes to a stranger. This is the ideal community, filled with love and caring for a stranger. Esteban's humanity moves the villagers to change their lives. They see themselves through his eyes, and they see their desolation and the bareness of their existence. The drowned man inspires them to unite, first in sewing clothing for the man, then in burying him as a community, and finally in remaking their community into a welcoming village, one which Esteban might again visit. In accepting Esteban into their lives, in adopting him into their families, the villagers respond to the drowned man's humanity with their own humanity, and through this they become a community filled with love.

Imagination

Imagination is an important theme in this story, since it is the catalyst for most of what occurs. When the women prepare Esteban's body for burial, they are at first awed by his size and beauty, and in their imaginations they visualize what his life must have been like. They see him as a fisherman with the power to command the fish, and they see him as a husband with a wife who is the envy of every other woman in their village. But within a short time, they also imagine how he must have felt as someone who was different, someone who never quite fit in. The women see the awkwardness with which Esteban moved around his home and the homes of his friends. The women also imagine that others must have been intimidated by someone so large, and that perhaps he was lonely. Through this use of their imaginations, the women find compassion for an outsider and they respond by making him a welcomed member of their village, so that he does not have to be buried as a stranger.

Tolerance

García Márquez uses "The Handsomest Drowned Man" to teach his readers about tolerance. The drowned man is different from the villagers who discover his body. He is larger than any other man they have seen, and the villagers imagine that he must have had much pride in his size and beauty. But when they realize that being different must have also created pain, they respond with love and warmth. Esteban tells the villagers of a lifetime of being different, of having to squeeze through doors and of breaking a host's chair when he was invited to sit down. Of course, Esteban is dead, and so his story is told through a different kind of language, the language of compassion. When the villagers are able to understand that even beauty and size can create obstacles, they respond with love. This love is born out of the tolerance they learn from Esteban. Seeing the drowned man's life as filled with difficulties teaches the villagers tolerance for those who are different, and their ability to learn leads them to a greater existence as a united community.

Style

Character

The actions of each character are what constitute the story. Character can also include the idea of a particular individual's morality. Characters can range from simple stereotypical figures to more complex multifaceted ones. "Characterization" is the process of creating a lifelike person from an author's imagination. To accomplish this the author provides the character with personality traits that help define who he will be and how he will behave in a given situation. García Márquez does not provide his characters with a great deal of depth in "The Handsomest Drowned Man." Most of what the audience knows about the villagers is provided in very brief vignettes. But the reader does realize that the villagers are kind and caring, and that they unite as a community out of love.

Fiction

Fiction is any story that is created out of the author's imagination, rather than factual events. Sometimes the characters in a fictional piece are based on real life, but their ultimate form and the way they respond to events is the creation of the author. In "The Handsomest Drowned Man" the villagers are fictional, but there are certainly many villagers living in Colombian fishing villages. Thus the villagers exist, but perhaps not precisely as they are depicted in García Márquez's story.

Folktale

A folktale is a story deriving from the oral tradition. The story may be based upon a myth or legend prevalent in a particular culture, but folktales are also sometimes based on historical figures and events. Typically, these stories are passed on by word of mouth and are often a part of rituals, such as summer camp and other coming-of-age experiences. Most communities have folktales as a part of their history, and typically, the stories contain elements that are exaggerated or improbable. ''The Handsomest Drowned Man'' contains elements of improbability, such as Esteban's height.

Genre

Genres are a way of categorizing literature. Genre is a French term that means ''kind'' or ''type.'' Genre refers to the format in which a work is written, such as novel, short story (of which ''The Handsomest Drowned Man'' is one), or poem, and also to the type of story it tells, such as tragedy, comedy, epic, pastoral, mystery, science fiction, or romance.

Plot

This term refers to the pattern of events in a work of literature. Generally plots should have a beginning, a middle, and a conclusion, but they may also sometimes be a series of episodes connected together. The plot provides the author with the means to explore primary themes. Students are often confused on the difference between plot and themes. Themes explore ideas, and plots simply relate what happens. The plot of ''The Handsomest Drowned Man'' surrounds the finding of a man's body and the villagers' coming together as a community to give him a splendid funeral. The theme is how a drowned man teaches a community about humanity and generosity.

Setting

The time, place, and culture in which the action of the play takes place is called the setting. The elements of setting may include geographic location, physical or mental environments, prevailing cultural attitudes, or the historical time in which the action takes place. The location for ''The Handsomest Drowned Man'' is a small village overlooking the sea. All of the action occurs within a day.

Literary Heritage

Much literature of Latin America is defined by the use of magical realism, sometimes referred to as symbolic mysticism. Much of the time, this means that the writer blends together naturalism and supernaturalism seamlessly. Often the literature of this area incorporates folktales and legends into the text, making the legends appear a natural part of the author's work. Magical realism erases the borders between the character's reality, the explicable and the inexplicable, and the natural world and the magical world.

Traditional Western literature has relied upon literary realism for more than one hundred years. This ''realism'' attempts to create a story and characters that are plausible, a representation of our everyday lives. The literature of magical realism attempts to portray the unusual, the spiritual, and the mystical as ordinary facets of the character's lives. For the reader, magical realism requires an acceptance of the co-existence of the real and the imaginary. The author posits these magical events as authentic, with the supernatural events being interwoven seamlessly into the narration. For García Márquez, this element of mysticism is presented in an objective and unemotional voice. García Márquez also relies on a monosyllabic style of writing that puts the emphasis on the content, which is complex, while making the text itself accessible to the reader.

Historical Context

Much of what the world knows about Colombia has been derived from the media. Films, newsreels, and newspapers emphasize the illegal trade from this Latin American country, but there is much more to modern Colombia than the drug trade. Much of Colombia's population, which has tripled in the past fifty years, lives in the large urban areas, such as Bogota and Medellin. However, about thirty percent of the population still lives in rural areas, where many people are illiterate and often impoverished. Many of these rural workers have been moving to larger towns and cities, hoping to improve their lives, but often their lack of skills or education

Compare & Contrast

- **1968:** The Second Latin American Bishops' Conference is held in Colombia. The bishops denounce the oppression of the poor and call for social and political reform.

  Today: The Catholic Church has continued to be a strong presence in Latin American countries, where it is alternatively praised for its helping of the poor and condemned for its stance on birth control and overpopulation.

- **1968:** The Peruvian government is overthrown by a military junta, and the Panamanian government falls in a coup. Both changes in government reflect the desire for change growing among Latin American countries, which are moving toward expelling big business interests (Standard Oil in Peru) and foreign governments (the United States' puppet government in Panama).

  Today: In recent years, many Latin American countries have continued to experience political turmoil, but much of this conflict has been in the form of guerrilla attacks and politically and economically inspired kidnappings. Recently, the United States pledged emergency aid to prevent the collapse of Colombia's democratic government.

- **1968:** It is estimated that 15 million fish in the United States are killed each year due to pollution. Because of this, 58 percent of all fish consumed in the United States are imported from other countries. However, global warming will devastate the South American fishing industry by 1972.

  Today: Pollution and global warming continue to be important issues for scientists who seek ways to prevent the extinction of species. The world's oceans have become a dumping ground for chemicals and garbage, and this threatens the survival of many fish and, in turn, of fishing economies.

- **1966:** A world food crisis threatens as production in Latin American countries falls 2 percent below the previous year's output.

  Today: Another food crisis threatens because of the effects of weather patterns that have caused significant flooding in Latin America over the past two years, destroying crops and farmland.

- **Mid- to Late 1960s:** Literature by Latin-American writers, especially by Gabriel García Márquez, creates a literary market ''boom'' that extends to writers of many nationalities.

  Today: Despite concerns that the Internet will make books obsolete, authors continue to publish new novels and the public continues to purchase them.

---

makes them unlikely to find work. Women can usually find jobs as housekeepers, but men have a difficult time finding even the most menial of jobs. Because of this migration to the cities, the population in rural areas of Colombia has continued to decline since the 1920s. As a result of high unemployment throughout Latin America, the 1970s and 1980s brought chronic economic problems to much of Latin America, and Colombia was no exception.

Unemployment and economic problems often lead to military solutions, but Colombia has been one the few Latin-American countries to avoid falling victim to military dictatorship. In the 1950s and early 1960s, the government instituted reforms that led to some economic stabilization. However, the next government made no moves to build upon this economic base, and by the middle 1960s declining economic conditions led to social unrest. Eventually the economic situation improved, and subsequent governments attempted to institute socialist reforms. But none of these reforms did much to improve the lives of rural Colombians, who found that most of the available land was held by a few large landowners. As has been the case for the past thirty years, leftist guerrilla movements and drug traffickers have contributed to a significant number of kidnappings and assassinations of government officials. In the past several years, there has been an escalation of violence, which has left many Colombians facing a bleak future. This somber reality stands in stark contrast to the Colombia of "The Handsomest Drowned Man." Instead, the reader is presented with an idyllic story of love and community awareness, where the villagers unite for the common good. There is no time period established in García Márquez's short story, nor is the location exact. The author leaves these details to the readers' imaginations. But if this place is 1960s Colombia, then the village represents the possibilities that García Márquez wishes for his country.

Critical Overview

In general, reviews of García Márquez's books, short stories, and novellas have been positive, even enthusiastic. Marquez has been embraced by critics and readers since the English publication of *One Hundred Years of Solitude* in 1970, which many reviewers labeled a masterpiece of Latin-American fiction. García Márquez also received a Nobel Prize in Literature in 1982, further acknowledging his acceptance into a modern literary canon of Latin-American writers. Most reviews of García Márquez's work focus on his novels and novellas, since these genres tend to be considered more important by critics. At the 1995 release of the novel *Of Love and Other Demons,* Hilary Mackenzie, in a review for *The Ottawa Citizen,* labeled the book "classic García Márquez—a rich pageant of phantasmagorical events and reality." This novel captures the essence of García Márquez and delivers what his previous works had also supplied—a blending of myth and reality. Mackenzie called García Márquez "one of the most fertile literary imaginations of our time." When *Love in the Time of Cholera* was released in 1988, *Christian Science Monitor* reviewer Merle Rubin pointed out that García Márquez's novel was "about people who choose hope over despair, self-knowledge over self-dramatization, in the belief that love can transform age and time." Similar qualities are found in "The Handsomest Drowned Man," where the small group of villagers find a reason to look to a happier future and do so with love. As Rubin observes of García Márquez's 1988 novel, the author's work is "profoundly imagina-

tive"; it is a "fully imagined work of fiction that expands our sense of life's infinite possibilities."

García Márquez's novellas have also captured the attention of reviewers. When *Collected Novellas* was published in 1991, the *Ottawa Citizen*'s Christopher Levenson declared that these three novellas provide "a clear demonstration of the way Marquez's techniques have expanded and grown in complexity over the years." Levenson also wrote that the second novella, *No One Writes to the Colonel,* "concerns itself less with power than with hope." This is also an important element of "The Handsomest Drowned Man," which concedes that the small village has little conventional power, but the end of the story makes clear to the reader that the villagers have hope for their future, which they see as vastly improved since Esteban was washed up from the sea. Levenson found García Márquez's "imaginative power" as worth a trip into the "mysterious, ambiguous, and, yes, magical world he has created." Another endorsement of García Márquez's work was offered by George R. McMurray in a general review of the author's cumulative work. After first citing García Márquez as having almost singlehandedly saved the novel from extinction, McMurray stated that García Márquez "has emerged as a mature, consummate craftsman." McMurray also noted the author's use of "mythical time. . .[which] blurs sordid reality and thrusts the reader into a kind of temporal void where the laws of cause and effect tend to become meaningless." This creates a "greater emphasis on the absurdities of human existence." These elements of the myth and the absurd are also present in "The Handsomest Drowned Man," as they are in many of García Márquez's works. As McMurray noted, García Márquez is able blend fantasy and reality to create a place where "the commonplace takes on an aura of magic and the impossible is made believable."

Criticism

Sheri E. Metzger

Metzger is a Ph.D. specializing in literature and drama at The University of New Mexico, where she is a lecturer in the English department and an adjunct professor in the university honors program. In this essay, she discusses García Márquez's use of imagination in "The Handsomest Drowned Man" and suggests that this use of imagination functions to blend fantasy and reality into a magical world

*A young boy fishes near a small,
Colombian coastal village.*

where people are able to exceed society's expectations and seek out a happier future.

When a drowned man is swept ashore in "The Handsomest Drowned Man," the recovery of his body and the villagers' attempts to identify him seem very ordinary. But as Gabriel García Márquez moves into a description of the body, which "weighed more than any dead man they had ever known, almost as much as a horse," the reader has the first signal that the body is not that of an ordinary man. To reinforce that image, García Márquez relates that the townspeople "could not find a bed in the village large enough to lay him nor was there a table solid enough to use for his wake." Within a short time, the women succumb to awe as they clean and prepare the body for burial. Still, while out of the ordinary, there is nothing magical in this description. Nor does the fact that "the tallest man's holiday pants would not fit him, not the fattest ones' Sunday shirts, nor the shoes of the one with the biggest feet" signal anything other than the appearance of a larger than ordinary man. In fact, it is not the man's size that is magical at all; it is the magic his presence creates that reveals so much about the villagers, and the readers' ability to believe in magic.

In a 1985 interview with Marlise Simons, García Márquez told the interviewer that often the source of his writings is an image. In "The Handsomest Drowned Man" the image is of a man, one who is larger than life, but a man who is a corpse. Still, perhaps this initial image is not the image García Márquez visualized for this short story. Instead, consider the image of a community united in generosity and love, and working together to create a better community in which to live. This image is one of renewed life, and this is the final image of García Márquez's short story. Later in the same interview, García Márquez explained to Simons that the subject of his work is life, and "that the subject gets larger the longer I live." Once again, the correlation with "The Handsomest Drowned Man" is clear. This story is about a dead man who brings a village to life. To accomplish this goal, the villagers had to be able to listen to the dead man speaking to them, and García Márquez's readers had to be equally ready to accept the story related to them. Giving the dead a voice is a difficult task for any writer, who must give a voice to someone who has never existed for the reader and who has never spoken. Neither the villagers nor the readers know Esteban's story. The challenge, then, is to give the character a way to speak, without the artifice of flashbacks. In a second interview with Simons in 1988, García Márquez described how he gives voice to the dead, recounting a story about the writing of *Love in the Time of Cholera*. He described being unable to visualize a character because he could not see her as present in the story. But when he realized that the woman was dead, "she became alive and real." The woman had a story to tell, but it was the story of a life already ended. This is also Esteban's story, which never exists in the story, except as the villagers construct it. The reason his story can come alive, even without the character's ever actually speaking, is that the villagers know his story. It is their story, and this is the element of García Márquez's work that appeals to the reader. These readers are the ones who write to García Márquez, asking where he has learned their stories, where he met their families. This easy identification happens because García Márquez is able to capture the stories within all of his readers. This is the same identification that the villagers feel with they hear Esteban's story and so easily identify with his loneliness.

This ability to relate the story of a dead man, to hear his voice, reveals García Márquez's ability to grasp the villagers' hearts and, through them, the

What Do I Read Next?

- *A Very Old Man with Enormous Wings* (1968), also by García Márquez, is the story of another man who is washed up from the sea. In this case the man is still alive, but his appearance has a profound effect on the small village that finds him.

- *Love in the Time of Cholera* (1988), also by García Márquez, is a love story that transcends time.

- *Captain's Verses* (1988), by Nobel Prize-winner Pablo Neruda, is a collection of his love poetry published in a bilingual edition.

- *Cruel Fictions, Cruel Realities: Short Stories by Latin American Women Writers* (1997), edited by Kathy S. Leonard, contains the work of twelve Latin American authors. Each story is preceded by a short biographical sketch.

- *A Cultural History of Latin America: Literature, Music and the Visual Arts in the 19th and 20th Centuries* (1998), edited by Leslie Bethell, provides a cultural history of Latin America. This book contains essays that place the artistic expressions of Latin America into a historical context.

- *Based on a True Story: Latin American History at the Movies* (1999), edited by Donald Stevens, offers a glimpse into how movies have depicted the history of Latin America. This book covers history from the 1500s to the present, as depicted in film.

- *Children of Cain: Violence and the Violent in Latin America* (1992), by Tina Rosenberg, is a journalistic account of the effect of the violence in Latin America. The book includes individual stories that help capture the reality of this world.

---

reader's imagination. The story is recounted so matter-of-factly that the reader never questions the authenticity of the experience. Certainly, the reader knows that Esteban is dead, and yet how do we account for our complete belief that the villagers know both his name and his story? Ricardo Gullon suggests, in an article that focuses on García Márquez's technique as a storyteller, that his talent lies in his ability to report the events as a journalist would. García Márquez, Gullon points out, "does not doubt or question events or facts," and thus neither does his audience. The readers do not question the dead man's story because García Márquez does not question it. Gullon says that this is because for this author, "there is no difference between what is likely and what is not; he fulfills his mission—his duty—of telling all, speaking as naturally of the dead as he does of the living, associating with the greatest of ease the intangible with the tangible." This continuity of tone, this acceptance of all things, is what makes the reader so easily accept the imaginary as real. There are many examples in

"The Handsomest Drowned Man" of real life. The reader learns of the villagers' homes, of their livelihood as fishermen, and of their marriages. Alongside this information, there are descriptions of scales covering the dead man, his larger than ordinary size, and the villagers' assurance that even having once been placed in the sea, Esteban will return to them again. The real world and the fantasy world work well together because, as Gullen suggests, García Márquez integrates these two sides of village life so smoothly. Gullon indicates that in the author's works, "prodigious events and miracles mingle with references to village and household events. The narrator never allows it to become evident, by interjection or amazement, that there may be a substantial difference between the extraordinary and the commonplace." The reader believes because García Márquez believes; he never questions, and neither does the reader. This allows the reader to escape from a world where news and current events quickly become repetitive and even frightening, into a world where magic occurs.

It is not the man's size that is magical at all; it is the magic his presence creates that reveals so much about the villagers, and the readers' ability to believe in magic."

This magic is obvious in "The Handsomest Drowned Man" when the readers witness the metamorphosis of a village into a community, all because a dead man told the villagers a story of loneliness. In response, the villagers adopted this man and gave him a family. They reached this point because García Márquez blurred the real with fantasy. Through their ability to imagine Esteban's life, the villagers first named him, and then gave him a story from which they could learn the lessons they needed in their own lives. The villagers are able to imagine this man's reality, and it is their imagination that becomes the catalyst for most of what occurs. When the women prepare Esteban's body for burial, they are at first awed by his size and beauty, and in their imaginations, they visualize what his life must have been like. They see him as a fisherman with the power to command the fish, and they see him as a husband, with his wife the envy of every other woman in his village. But within a short time, they also imagine how he must have felt as someone who was different, someone who never quite fit in. The women see the awkwardness with which Esteban moved around his home and the homes of his friends. They see the fear his neighbors felt when he came to visit, and the villagers see that Esteban would have been afraid to sit in his neighbor's homes. The women also imagine that others must have been intimidated by someone so large, and that perhaps he was lonely. Through this use of their imaginations, the villagers find compassion for an outsider and they respond by making him a welcomed member of their village, so that he does not have to be buried as an outsider. Equally important is the villagers' ability to imagine Esteban's return, since this moves them to recreate their village, improving their homes and planting gardens. The villagers never question that Esteban may choose to return; he is dead, but his burial is only a

temporary state. This assurance that the dead can return is another facet of García Márquez's writing, according to Gullon: "[García Márquez's] authentic presentation of events (that is to say, his tone) allows him to dispense with explanations and justifications. There is no need to justify the fact that a character dies, or appears to die, and later comes back to life, or appears to, twenty, a hundred, or five hundred years later; there's no reason to follow the clock's chronology or the calendar's." Nor is there any reason to follow our accepted knowledge about the dead. Esteban can return because the villagers need him to live, and because he needs them to go on living.

Writers make us, the readers, see what we cannot see on our own. As Joseph Epstein suggests, "Literary artists make us see things, and differently from the way we have seen them before; they make us see things their way." Gabriel García Márquez makes us see the poetry in his writing, and he forces us—no, trusts us enough—to slip into another world, a world where reality and fantasy blend together perfectly. In this world, we do not question that the dead can speak, or even that they can return to our lives. García Márquez's writing does, as Epstein observes, look to the future. It is a future where many of his readers happily sojourn.

Source: Sheri E. Metzger, in an essay for *Literature of Developing Nations for Students,* Gale, 2000.

Liz Brent

Brent has a Ph.D. in American culture, with a specialization in film studies, from the University of Michigan. She is a freelance writer and teaches courses in the history of American cinema. In the following essay, Brent discusses the element of fantasy in García Márquez's story "The Handsomest Drowned Man."

García Márquez's short story "The Handsomest Drowned Man" is about a drowned man who washes up on the shore of a tiny village. Although no one in the village knows who he is, they determine that he must have been named Esteban, and the reaction of various segments of the village inhabitants to his arrival results in a complete and permanent transformation of the village. Before this longer term transformation occurs, however, the arrival of Esteban's body becomes a catalyst for evoking the fantasies of the men, women, and children of the village. García Márquez's story is concerned with the realm of fantasy and the imagination which is activated in the minds of the people of the village by the arrival of Esteban's body.

The children are the first to spot "the dark and slinky bulge" of the drowned man drifting ashore. The children immediately allow their fantasies to determine what it must be; the narrator states that they "let themselves think it was an enemy ship." The statement that they "let themselves think" this indicates that they were indulging in a fantasy, in which the arrival of an enemy ship would bring excitement and adventure to their village.

It is the women of the village, however, whose fantasies are most actively sparked by the arrival of the enormous, handsome drowned man. The body of the drowned man is brought to the women, who clean away the ocean debris which has covered his body.

> But only when they finished cleaning him off did they become aware of the kind of man he was and it left them breathless. Not only was he the tallest, strongest, most virile, and best built man they had ever seen, but even though they were looking at him there was no room for him in their imagination.

The response of the women to the presence of the drowned man they call Esteban is specifically eroticized in the narrative. Their first real glimpse of the man's body "left them breathless." They determine that he is the "best built" man they have ever seen, a description which implies that their response to his body is of a sexual nature. Furthermore, they see him as the "most virile" man "they had ever seen," meaning that they determine him to be especially sexually potent. The sight of him is so overwhelming to the women that "there was no room for him in their imagination"; this implies that his body represents an ideal of masculinity beyond their wildest dreams, more handsome and virile than they could ever have imagined before his arrival. His presence thus ultimately inspires the entire village to expand the horizons of their dreams and fantasies, and therefore to strive for higher ideals in their own lives.

The attentions of the women to the body of the drowned man, and to preparing him for a funeral, are further imbued with eroticism and expressive of sexual desire. The women are "fascinated by his huge size and his beauty." They sit around "gazing" at the body; the word "gaze" implies desire on the part of those who are gazing. The women imagine Esteban to have embodied their ideal of masculinity, and, by comparison, their own men seem lacking: "They secretly compared him to their own men, thinking that for all their lives theirs were

> *"...Only when they finished cleaning him off did they become aware of the kind of man he was and it left them breathless. Not only was he the tallest, strongest, most virile, and best built man they had ever seen, but even though they were looking at him there was no room for him in their imagination."*

incapable of doing what he could do in one night, and they ended up dismissing them deep in their hearts as the weakest, meanest, and most useless creatures on earth." The women find themselves "wandering through that maze of fantasy"; in other words, the body of the drowned man inspires them to become lost in fantasies of what they would like their own men to be. And these fantasies are specifically sexual; the narrator describes them as looking upon the drowned man "with passion." The women attach their own personal fantasies to the body of the drowned man, to the extent that each maintains the "illusion" that his name is in keeping with their own erotic fantasies. An older woman determines that his name is "Esteban," but the more passionate of the women hang on to their own imaginary image of him: "The more stubborn among them, who were the youngest, still lived for a few hours with the illusion that when they put his clothes on and he lay among the flowers in patent leather shoes his name might be Lautaro." Yet, the narrator states that "it was a vain illusion"; this statement attests to the erotic power of the women's "illusions" about the drowned man, which are based on erotic fantasy. The women romanticize the drowned man to the extent that they imagine that the outfit they have sewn for him is too small due to "the hidden strength of his heart" which "popped the buttons off his shirt." The sexualized nature of the women's conception of the drowned man is indicated by the description of him "stretched out like a sperm whale"; the image of a "sperm whale" expresses the fantasies of the women that he represents an ideal of masculine virility. During the funeral preparations, the women ''released in sighs what they did not in tears''; the ''sighs'' of the women are expressive of their feelings of passion and their fantasies of romance in regard to the dead man. The women even feel possessive of the drowned man, as if he were one of their own husbands, and they do not want to learn that he belonged to another village. So when their own men determine that he does not come from one of the neighboring villages, the women ''felt an opening of jubilation''; '''Praise the Lord,' they sighed, 'he's ours!'''

The men of the village at first react very differently to the arrival of the drowned man. Their initial response is purely practical. They travel to the other villages in order to identify the origins of the drowned man. They are then concerned only with disposing of the body in an efficient and practical manner, for ''all they wanted was to get rid of the bother of the newcomer once and for all.'' The men at first dismiss the undue attention their women pay to the corpse of the drowned man, thinking that ''the fuss was only womanish frivolity.'' But, as the women ''thought of more ways to waste time'' before letting the body of Esteban leave their sight, the men become aware that the drowned man represents some form of competition for the attention of their women, and they ''began to feel mistrust in their livers and started grumbling.'' Yet, the men continue to adopt a practical attitude toward disposing of the dead man's body, thinking that the ministrations of the women are pointless because ''the sharks would chew him all the same.'' The men think of him merely as a dead body, ''a drifting corpse, a drowned nobody, a piece of cold Wednesday meat.'' The narrator later describes what must have been Esteban's own conception of his oversized body as a nuisance and a ''filthy piece of cold meat.''

The attitudes of the men change, however, once the women uncover the face of the dead man, and they, too, are taken with how handsome he is. Before this sight, the men had perceived the drowned man as a threat, an element of competition for the love and ''dreams'' of their wives. But, once they have seen his face, they are softened in their attitude by the look of ''sincerity'' on the face of the dead man: ''There was so much truth in his manner that even the most mistrustful men, the ones who felt the bitterness of endless nights at sea fearing that their women would tire of dreaming about them and begin to dream of drowned men, even they and

others who were harder still shuddered in the marrow of their bones at Esteban's sincerity.''

Once the men have seen what the women see in Esteban, his presence changes from one which divides the women from the men of the village to one which unites them in their attentions to the drowned man. Because they decide to appoint a set of relatives for the unknown drowned man, ''through him all the inhabitants of the village became kinsmen.'' Both the women and the men together decide to ''hold the most splendid funeral they could conceive of.'' The idealization of the drowned man thus motivates the people of the village to strive for ideals above and beyond what they had previously attempted. As Esteban represents for them an ideal of perfection, they become aware of the lacking in their own lives, and are motivated to improve their village. The ''men and women became aware for the first time of the desolation of their streets, the dryness of their courtyards, the narrowness of their dreams as they faced the splendor and beauty of their drowned man.'' Whereas before their ''dreams'' had been ''narrow,'' this image of perfection inspires them to expand the scope of their dreams, and therefore to improve their own lives. They ''knew that everything would be different from then on.'' In Esteban's memory, they improve their homes, paint them in ''gay colors,'' and determine to break their backs ''digging for springs among the stones and planting flowers on the cliffs.'' In essence, the arrival of the drowned man expands the minds of the inhabitants of the tiny village by presenting to them a fantasy of a perfect man which goes beyond anything they could have imagined. Eventually, the fantasies which are inspired by his presence motivate the people of the village to improve their own lives, and particularly to improve their community.

Source: Liz Brent, in an essay for *Literature of Developing Nations for Students*, Gale, 2000.

Dean Rader

Rader has published widely in the field of American and Latin American art and literature. Taking as his point of departure the notion of identity, he discusses how Esteban and the villagers acquire new senses of identity in ''The Handsomest Drowned Man.''

Generally, folktales and myths are deeply concerned with issues of identity, and ''The Handsomest Drowned Man'' is no exception. Through tales and myths, a culture, a person, and sometimes even a place establishes a sense of identity through codes, practices, descriptions, and values. The Grimm Brothers' fairy tales are famous for evoking a sense of German identity; Native American tales almost always include indigenous animals and local natural landmarks; even early American folktales define what life and landscape were like for the colonists in burgeoning New England. In all of these cases, the stories carve out an identity that distinguishes them from other kinds of stories.

García Márquez claims that he acquired his sense of the fantastic (what others have called "Magical Realism") from his grandmother's stories, which contained a series of unlikely events, but which she told with a deadpan realism. He has also remarked that he grew up in a small town (probably not unlike the village in the story) in which the only thing of importance was the past—that is, myths, history, memories. In "The Handsomest Drowned Man" García Márquez uses the death and subsequent "adoption" of Esteban not only to establish an identity for the village that finds him but also as how the village creates an identity for Esteban himself. Through this dual construction, García Márquez makes the construction of identity for the village and Esteban contingent on each other. Without the other, neither entity is able to claim any sense of identity.

The most obvious change in identity occurs within the village and the villagers. They become obsessed with making the village a place worthy of a man like Esteban, whom they have elevated to the level of mythic hero. The men become jealous of his immense size, both physically and imaginatively, and the women dream about what it must be like to have him as a guest. They compare him to their own husbands and find that the men cannot compare, just as their village before Esteban cannot compare to their village after Esteban's serendipitous arrival. In fact, one can divide the history of the village into two eras: B.E. (Before Esteban) and A.E. (After Esteban). Before Esteban, the villagers led lives of quiet desperation. They had no magic, no sense of purpose. They were a nameless, faceless, undistinguished village in need of something magical to transform their mere existence into life. After Esteban, everything is different. Rena Korb agrees, suggesting that the change in honor of Esteban is not simply for the moment but forevermore: "The lives of the villagers will continue to change over the next twenty-four hours and on into the future." Indeed, the villagers will paint their houses bright colors and plant flowers, and they will expand the doorways in their houses so Esteban's ghost can pass through

A Bogota, Colombia, neighborhood. García Márquez began writing fiction while working as a journalist in this capital city.

with ease. They will keep his memory alive and perpetually remember that both God and Esteban chose their village for the delivery of Esteban into their lives (Esteban's watery arrival stands as a sort of mythical "birth" from the amniotic fluid of the sea, much like Aphrodite's). Passengers on ocean liners, who normally would cruise by the seaside village and think nothing of it or its residents, will now smell the flowers, see the newly painted houses, and say to each other, that is the village of Esteban. In other words, the private love for Esteban is simultaneously transformed into a public determinant of identity. The village will always be known as Esteban's Village by those both inside and outside of it. According to Korb, this transformation gives their lives a sense of purpose as well as a sense of reputation: "by making their home a place good enough for Esteban, they are enriching themselves as well."

There are a number of cities around the world who achieve an identity because of individuals. Washington, D.C., is inscribed as the city of George Washington; Florence, Italy is the city of Dante and Michelangelo; Chicago has become linked with

> Perhaps, after reading this story, your life will mirror the lives of the residents of the Village of Esteban who believe that, at any moment, the essence of everything they believe in might rise out of the foamy seas or walk, like the happiest ghost in the world, through a doorway wide enough for a god."

Michael Jordan and Oprah Winfrey. So, to suggest that a small town might develop a new personality because of an individual is not necessarily an unusual concept; however, what gives García Márquez's story its own sense of identity is how the villagers construct the identity of this dead man washed to their shores. When he is first discovered, he possesses nothing that might offer any clue to his identity. He has no papers, no identifying marks—nothing. But, after spending time with him, a woman comments that he has the face of one who is called "Esteban." From that moment forth, he could not be referred to by any other name. Additionally, the villagers begin to invent a life for him. They imagine his difficulty in visiting someone's house. They endow him with a graciousness commensurate with his stature. They wonder about how his back burned as he bent over in people's houses and how he would decline a chair out of fear of breaking it. Even though his destiny placed him at this village, the residents agree that even in death he feels shame for causing them so much trouble. No matter what horrendous or scandalous deeds the man may have committed in his life, in death he is transformed into a kind of patron saint (the reference to St. Stephen, the first Christian martyr, is no coincidence here) embodying the best human traits imaginable. Speculating about his adventures at sea, the villagers assemble a history for him from the scraps of their previously dormant imaginations. The great irony of the story is that in death, Esteban becomes a model on how to live life. Thus, as they invent an identity for Esteban, Esteban is busy

inventing an identity for them. The same structure is at work in "A Very Old Man with Enormous Wings." In both texts, a kind of cultural symbiosis occurs in which a duality engenders two separate but connected identities.

Korb rightly notes that Esteban resembles various mythical characters, most notably Odysseus who, like Esteban, washed up on more than one shore on his ten-year trek back to Ithaka. For Odysseus, his homecoming is absolutely critical to the establishment of his identity as a hero, a man, a father, a husband, and a king. Furthermore, how Odysseus behaves in the poem serves as a model for behavior for Greek males. Without question, the poem situates Greek identity through the character of Odysseus. Similarly, Esteban's homecoming (to his own village) is necessary for the establishment of his identity and that of the town. And, as the *Odyssey* does with Greek identity, this story offers a possible glimpse at Latin-American identity. García Márquez wants to inscribe into the identity of Latin America an awareness for magic, imagination, and the unexplained. In both this story and "A Very Old Man With Enormous Wings," García Márquez uses the micro to help create cultural identity on a macro level. To what degree is this village a metonym for Latin America itself? García Márquez has always associated the magical, the unexplained, the mystical, the miraculous with Latin American culture. Similarly, one of his main themes has always been the lengths to which Latin-American individuals and communities go to define their identities.

Finally, the story forces readers to wonder about their own identities. In Rainer Maria Rilke's "Archaic Torso of Apollo," Rilke ends the poem, a musing on the magic of transforming how one sees the world, with this famous line: "You must change your life." Can reading a poem or a short story change your life? Perhaps. Tales for children always have a moral. The moral of this story might be to expect the magical or to take advantage of the miraculous when it arrives on your doorstep. According to Raymond Williams, García Márquez's "A Very Old Man with Enormous Wings" and "The Handsomest Drowned Man" are stories about how one interprets unexpected events in one's life: "Both stories demand that the reader approach interpretation—and the process of reading these stories—with an awareness of the problems of interpretation and the limits of one's strictly rational faculties." For Williams, these two texts turn the focus of the story away from the author and place it on the reader. Is the life of the reader like that of the villagers Before Esteban? Perhaps, after reading this story, your life will mirror the lives of the residents of the Village of Esteban who believe that, at any moment, the essence of everything they believe in might rise out of the foamy seas or walk, like the happiest ghost in the world, through a doorway wide enough for a god.

Source: Dean Rader, in an essay for *Literature of Developing Nations for Students*, Gale, 2000.

Sources

Epstein, Joseph, "How Good is Gabriel García Márquez?" in *Commentary*, Vol. 75, No. 5, May, 1983, pp. 59-65.

Gullon, Ricardo, "Gabriel García Márquez and the Lost Art of Storytelling," translated by Jose G. Sanchez, in *Diacritics*, Vol. I, No. 1, Fall, 1971, pp. 27-32.

Korb, Rena, overview of "The Handsomest Drowned Man," in *Short Stories for Students*, Gale, 1997.

Levenson, Christopher, "Novellas Provide Background to Nobel Winner's Success," in *Ottawa Citizen*, September 7, 1991, p. H4.

MacKenzie, Hilary, "Once Again, a Tale Only García Márquez Could Tell," in *Ottawa Citizen*, August 13, 1995, p. C3.

McMurray, George R., *Gabriel García Márquez*, Ungar, 1977.

Rubin, Merle, "García Márquez's Tale of Love, Illusions, and Life's Possibilities: *Love in the Time of Cholera*," in *Christian Science Monitor*, May 12, 1988, p. 20.

Simons, Marlise, "The Best Years of His Life: An Interview with Gabriel García Márquez," in *New York Times*, April 10, 1988, p. 48.

———, "Love and Age: A Talk with García Márquez," in *New York Times*, April 7, 1985, p. 1.

Williams, Raymond, *Gabriel García Márquez*, G. K. Hall & Co., 1984.

Further Reading

Bell, Michael, *Gabriel García Márquez: Solitude and Solidarity*, St. Martin's Press, 1993.
This book offers an examination of García Márquez's life and his work, offering the hypothesis that the reason for the author's popularity lies in the inability of critics to interpret his works, and that writings themselves are too elusive for interpretation.

Bell-Villada, Gene H., *García Márquez: The Man and His Work*, University of North Carolina Press, 1990.
Bell-Villada creates a portrait of García Márquez as an artist and as a human being. This book discusses the impact of *One Hundred Years of Solitude* on the author's subsequent works, and examines the many influences on García Márquez's writing.

Bloom, Harold, *Gabriel García Márquez*, Chelsea House, 1992.
This book is a collection of essays about García Márquez's work.

Dolan, Sean, and Rodolfo Cardona, *Gabriel García Márquez*, Chelsea House, 1989.
This book discusses García Márquez's life and work. Its primary focus is on the author's early celebrity.

Fau, Margaret Eustella, *Gabriel García Márquez: An Annotated Bibliography*, Greenwood, 1980.
Although only covering the early years of García Márquez's work, this book still offers valuable assistance in locating information about the author's work.

Hahn, Hannelore, *The Influence of Franz Kafka on Three Novels by Gabriel García Márquez*, Peter Lang, 1993.
This text demonstrates García Márquez's use of Kafka's thematic and stylistic influences, looking at how both authors use solitude, spirituality, and personal freedom in their works.

McMurray, George R., *Critical Essays on Gabriel García Márquez*, G. K. Hall, 1987.
McMurray reprints reviews and critical articles on García Márquez's work. This text offers much valuable information, including reviews of the author's less commercially popular works.

The House of the Spirits

Isabel Allende

1982

Isabelle Allende's *The House of the Spirits* is often compared to Gabriel García Márquez's *One Hundred Years of Solitude.* The obvious similarities are that both novels relate the saga of a family, both make liberal use of magic and fantasy, and both established their authors' literary reputations. But where García Márquez's words create a poetic picture of Latin-American life, Allende's words offers an explicit commentary on the political situation in Chile. On the surface, Allende's novel is the story of Esteban Trueba, his wife, his children, and his granddaughter. But *The House of the Spirits* is also the story of political corruption, patriarchal authority, feminine oppression, and the movement from the old world into the new. The action in the novel spans four generations and covers more than fifty years of history. During those fifty years, the country changes, first through technology and modern communications, and later through the desire to find a better life. Nivea and Clara become suffragettes, and Jaime works to improve people's lives, while Alba becomes involved in a protest movement that will ultimately ask great sacrifices of her. Throughout all these events, Esteban will be little more than an angry observer. But by the end of the novel, he will have undergone a significant change, having grown from a selfish, self-centered man into a fair, loving grandfather. *The House of the Spirits* is filled with violence and corruption, but it is also filled with love and magic.

Author Biography

Isabel Allende was born in Lima, Peru in 1942. Her father, Tomas Allende, was a diplomatic representative from Chile; when her parents divorced, Allende moved to Chile, where she lived with her maternal grandparents. Although Allende had little contact with her father, she remained close to his family, including her uncle and godfather, Salvador Allende, president of Chile from 1970 to 1973. Allende spent much of her adolescence in Bolivia, Europe, and the Middle East with her mother and stepfather. As an adult Allende returned to Chile and became a journalist, where she worked in television and wrote for a radical feminist magazine. When her uncle, Salvador Allende, was assassinated during the overthrow of the Chilean government, Allende was shaken, and after realizing that she, too, was in danger, she left the country, moving to Venezuela in 1974.

Allende's literary career began with a letter to her grandfather, who was dying. She began the letter as a response to his idea that people only died when they were forgotten. The letter, which was never mailed, became Allende's first novel, *La casa de los espiritus* (1982; *The House of the Spirits*). The matriarch and patriarch in this first novel were based on Allende's grandparents. Her second novel, *De amor y de sombra* (1984; *Of Love and Shadows*) also takes place in a country recognizable as Chile, where a military regime oppresses the people. A third novel followed in 1987, *Eva Luna*, and was followed in 1989 with *Cuentos de Eva Luna* (*The Stories of Eva Luna*), a collection of short stories based on the biographical sketches of the character Eva Luna for the previous book. A fourth novel, *El plan infinito* (1991; *An Infinite Plan*), followed. Allende's 1995 memoir, *Paula*, evolved out of an effort to understand her daughter Paula's death at age 26. Allende is also the author of *Afrodita: Recetas, cuentos y otros afrodisiacos* (1998; *Aphrodite: A Memoir of the Senses*). Allende has won several awards for her work, including the Feminist of the Year Award from the Feminist Majority Foundation. Allende also received honorary doctorate of letters degrees from Bates College and Dominican College in 1994. Allende was divorced from her first husband in 1987, after 25 years of marriage and the birth of two children. She has remarried and currently lives in California.

Plot Summary

The House of the Spirits is an epic story focusing on four generations of women of the Trueba family and their dreams, hopes, love affairs, spiritual yearnings, and connections with each other. At the same time, the book portrays the tumultuous social and political changes occurring in Chile. Although the country in the book is never named as Chile, its history and events correspond to events that occurred there, from the ownership of huge tracts of land by the wealthy, through land reform in the 1960s, to the popularly elected government of Salvador Allende (who was Isabel Allende's uncle and godfather) and his overthrow by a political dictatorship.

Ch. 1: Rosa the Beautiful

The first chapter introduces the two main characters in the novel. Esteban and Alba alternate telling the story, with Alba relating what her grandmother Clara has recorded in her diary. This chapter begins with the story of Clara's mother, Nivea, who was the mother of fifteen children, eleven of whom are still living. Clara is the youngest child, and her sister, Rosa, is the oldest surviving daughter. In the opening pages, Marco, Clara's brother, is returned home for burial. He has died of some sort of tropical plague on his journey home. Accompanying him home is a large dog, Barrabas, who adopts Clara. Marco is an explorer and inventor, and Clara inherits his magic books, since Clara also has something magical about her. Esteban's story is also interwoven into Clara's story. Esteban is engaged to Rosa, from whom he has been separated for two years. He has been working in the mines to earn money so that they can marry. Meanwhile, Rosa becomes ill and dies, poisoned by some brandy that was intended for her father, Severo. Clara feels guilty at having predicted Rosa's death, as if in predicting the death she has somehow caused it to happen.

Ch. 2: The Three Marias

This chapter opens with Esteban deciding that he will leave his mother and sister and move to the abandoned family estate in the country. There he will take the money he has saved and try to make his fortune. Esteban makes Pedro Segundo Garcia his foreman and sets about repairing the house, clearing the fields, planting the crops, and raising some livestock. Esteban is a hard *patron*, violent and cruel. He rapes many young women, and the countryside is littered with his illegitimate children.

Isabel Allende

Esteban hates communism, a political philosophy that will have important ramifications later in the novel. He also begins frequenting a brothel, the Red Lantern, where he becomes friends with Transito Soto, to whom he lends money. This chapter ends with the news that Esteban's mother is dying; he makes plans to return to the city to visit her.

Ch. 3: Clara the Clairvoyant

Clara has not spoken since Rosa's death nine years earlier. Nana, the family nanny, has made many attempts to frighten Clara into speaking, but Clara has resisted all efforts. Instead of speaking,

Clara has been studying her uncle's magic books and learning to interpret dreams, move objects, and predict the future. Her uncle's dog, Barrabas, is devoted to her, and Clara is spoiled by her siblings, parents, and Nana. Nivea has told Clara of the family's history and traditions, and she also interests Clara in social protest, since Nivea has became a suffragette after Rosa's death. When she is nineteen, Clara announces that she will marry Rosa's former fiancé, Esteban. Meanwhile, Esteban has returned to see his dying mother. He needs a wife and remembers that Rosa's family had once accepted him as a prospective son-in-law. Clara agrees to marry Esteban. At the engagement party, Barrabas enters with a large knife sticking out of his back and dies at Clara's feet. This is considered a bad omen. After a year's wait, the couple marry and move into the grand new house that Esteban has built. Esteban's sister Ferula cares for the now pregnant Clara, who gives birth to Blanca by caesarian section.

Ch. 4: The Time of the Spirits

Clara treats Blanca like a miniature adult instead of a child. After several years in the city, the family decides to go to Tres Maria, the country estate, for a summer visit. Blanca spends the summer playing with Pedro Tercero Garcia, the foreman's six-year-old son. Both Esteban and Clara are happy in the country, and Clara becomes interested in helping the peasants have better lives. Ferula hates the country life, and with Clara again pregnant, the family returns to the city. Clara announces that she will have twin sons, and she has chosen their names, Jaime and Nicolas. Just before she is due to give birth, Clara's parents are killed in an automobile accident, and Clara is determined to find her mother's decapitated head, which she locates just as she is going into labor. The house becomes more crowded when Nana comes to live, and Clara becomes the center of a mystical community of young women. A jealous Esteban, who hates sharing Clara, finally sends his sister from the house. As the years pass, the children grow, with the boys educated at British boarding schools and Blanca sent to a convent school. In the visits to the country estate, Blanca and Pedro Tercero Garcia continue to play together.

Ch. 5: The Lovers

Blanca is fourteen and becoming a young woman. When she and Pedro are reunited that summer, they still play together as children, but by summer's end, they are in love. When the family returns to the city, they are visited by Ferula's ghost. Clara and Esteban find Ferula's body and arrange her funeral. Ever since Esteban threw his sister out of their house, Clara has been distant from her husband, and Ferula's death will not bring them back together. Blanca and Pedro have continued to write to one another, although in secret. Pedro becomes a talented singer as he grows up, but he is also an activist whose ideas scare Esteban. For the next several years, Blanca and Pedro continue to spend their summers together, falling more deeply in love. Then a serious earthquake destroys the house in the

country, severely injuring Esteban. In the city, Nana is killed when the city house is damaged. As Esteban recovers, Blanca manages to be sent home from the convent school, and she and Pedro continue their affair, which grows more passionate as they get older.

Ch. 6: Revenge

Esteban and Clara have continued to grow apart, and she has installed a lock on her bedroom door, although he still continues to force himself on her whenever he gets the chance. But the more Clara withdraws, the more Esteban wants and desires her. A French count, Jean de Satigny, arrives and suggests that he and Esteban set up a chinchilla farm as a way to make money. When the count asks to marry Blanca, Esteban gives his approval, but an angry Blanca refuses. Blanca is twenty-four years old now, and her brothers, who are also visiting, have developed into young men. Jaime is generous and compassionate and very interested in the peasants who work the farm. He is also sentimental and interested in politics. In contrast, Nicolas has turned into a male version of his mother, with her interest in mystical things. Nicolas is the more intelligent of the twins, and he uses his cleverness to seduce all of the young women in the neighborhood. When the count, who has been spying on Blanca and following her, discovers her affair with Pedro, he tells Esteban of the affair. Esteban beats Blanca and strikes Clara when she intervenes, knocking out several teeth. Clara removes her wedding ring, resumes using her maiden name, refuses to speak to Esteban again, and leaves their country home with Blanca, and both women return to the city. Esteban attempts to kill Pedro but only succeeds in cutting off three of his fingers.

Ch. 7: The Brothers

When he discovers that Blanca is pregnant, Esteban forces her to marry de Satigny, after telling her that he has killed Pedro. But Clara tells Blanca that Pedro is still alive. Esteban gives his new son-in-law a large check and the couple are sent away, where no one will notice the new bride's advanced pregnancy. Blanca is gone, and the two brothers are also changing. Nicolas has become a playboy and is involved with a young woman, Amanda, who is soon pregnant. Jaime is studying to become a doctor and gives his clothing and money to help the poor, and he also performs an abortion on a pregnant Amanda, whom he secretly loves. Meanwhile, Esteban runs for political office and is elected senator.

Ch. 8: The Count

Blanca discovers that her husband has a secret life of sexual decadence and pornography. She escapes, with whatever she can carry, and returns to her mother.

Ch. 9: Little Alba

Alba is born as soon as Blanca arrives at her mother's house in the city. The young child is raised in a carefree atmosphere by her mother, grandmother, and uncles. All the love that Esteban had to give is now directed toward Alba, since everyone else in his life has disappointed him in some way. However, Esteban's estrangement from the rest of the family only increases. Pedro, who has become a successful singer, reenters Blanca's life and meets his daughter. Blanca and Pedro continue to see one another when they are able to. Esteban Garcia, the son of Esteban Trueba's illegitimate son, reappears, as a threat to Alba. Garcia both hates and desires all that belongs to the Truebas. When Alba is seven years old, her grandmother, Clara, dies, and Esteban is devastated.

Ch. 10: The Epoch of Decline

Without Clara, Esteban becomes an old man, and the house begins to disintegrate. Nicolas has become aligned with Indian Mysticism and whatever other exotic ideas he encounters. Alba is enrolled in a British school, where Esteban had hoped she would get a good education. Pedro and Blanca continue to see one another, but Alba is not told that he is her father. Esteban has a large mausoleum built for Clara, Rosa, and himself.

Ch. 11: The Awakening

Alba, who is now eighteen, is the lover of Miguel, Amanda's younger brother. He organizes protests at the university, and Alba becomes involved. Jaime has also become involved with politics, as a supporter of the new Socialist candidate. When Amanda is ill, Jaime, who has always loved her, takes her to a detoxification hospital for help.

Ch. 12: The Conspiracy

The Socialist candidate is elected, and Esteban begins plotting ways to overthrow the government. The political situation leads to economic instability and life becomes very complicated for everyone. When Esteban visits the country estate, he is captured by the peasants, and Blanca asks Pedro to rescue her father. This is how Alba learns that Pedro is her father. After they have returned to the city, one of Clara's old friends arrives with a message from Clara, who wants to warn Alba that she is facing great danger.

Ch. 13: The Terror

There has been a coup, and the president is murdered. When Jaime refuses to help cover up the murder, he is tortured and murdered as well. Esteban celebrates the overthrow, not knowing his own son has been killed by the insurgents whom he is supporting. Miguel has been forced to flee and is in hiding. The initial euphoria that greeted the coup dissipates in the face of economic problems and social and political repression. Pedro, who has been hiding since the coup, and Blanca escape the country together with her father's help. But Alba is arrested late in the night and turned over to Esteban Garcia.

Ch. 14: The Hour of Truth

Alba is tortured repeatedly, but she will not tell her captors where Miguel is hiding. It soon becomes clear that Esteban Garcia is torturing and raping Alba not to learn Miguel's location, but out of revenge for all the hurts of his childhood. When the torture becomes too much to bear, Alba wishes for death. But her grandmother, Clara, appears to tell her that she must survive, and Alba becomes determined that she will survive and write down what has happened. Outside the prison, Esteban visits Transito Soto, whom he had helped many years before. He asks her to help find Alba and return her to him.

Epilogue

After Alba is released, she and Esteban decide to write down their family story. Esteban tells his part, and they use Clara's diaries and Blanca's letters to tell much of the rest. When they are finished, Esteban dies in the bed he once shared with Clara. Alba is pregnant with a daughter, but she does not know if it is Miguel's child or the child of the rapist, Esteban Garcia. But Alba is determined not to live her life with hatred, and so the novel ends with hope for the future.

Characters

Alba

Alba is Blanca's daughter, the result of a love affair with Pedro Tercero Garcia, the son of Esteban's foreman, Pedro Segundo Garcia. Alba is the story's narrator in the last half of the book. Her grandfather, Esteban, is so angry at the circumstances of her parentage that he will not acknowledge Alba's real father as her parent. Alba reminds everyone of Rosa, and her birth brings much happiness to Esteban. Like Rosa, Alba is blessed with the family's unusual green hair. When Pedro Tercero rescues Esteban from the peasants, Alba learns that he is her father. As a young adult, Alba becomes involved with student protests, and she is soon arrested and tortured by her grandfather's illegitimate son, Esteban Garcia. Clara tells Alba to use her imagination to create stories that would allow her to escape Garcia's torture. She is eventually freed from jail after her grandfather asks his friend Transito Soto to help. Alba, who is now pregnant, decides to write her family's story, with the help of her grandfather, Esteban. Alba represents the future of Latin-American women. She is strong, a survivor, whose desire to preserve her family's story leads to the creation of the book.

Amanda

Amanda is Nicolas's girlfriend. She becomes pregnant and goes to Jaime for an abortion. She is also the older sister of Miguel. When Amanda nearly dies of drug addiction, it is Jaime who saves her life. She later dies after being arrested and tortured.

Esteban Garcia

This Esteban is the grandson of the illegitimate son of Esteban Trueba and his servant, Pancha Garcia, also named Esteban Garcia. He will become a sadistic policeman and colonel. When he arrests Alba, he also tortures her and rapes her. He may be the father of her unborn child. Esteban Garcia is filled with hate for the Trueba family and thinks that they have stolen all that he should have possessed, had he been born to the legitimate son of Esteban Trueba.

Pedro Segundo Garcia

This Pedro is the father of Blanca's lover. He is Esteban's foreman and helps Esteban rebuild the estate after Rosa dies. He is devoted to Clara, and there is an implication in the novel that they are in love in a pure, nonsexual way. Pedro helps Clara rebuild the estate after an earthquake destroys it and injures Esteban.

Media Adaptations

- *The House of the Spirits* was released as a film in 1994 starring Meryl Streep, Jeremy Irons, Winona Ryder, Antonio Banderas, Vanessa Redgrave, Glenn Close, Armin Mueller-Stahl, and Maria Conchita Alonso.

Pedro Tercero Garcia

Pedro is the son of Trueba's foreman and the father of Alba. Pedro and Blanca fall in love as children and continue to love one another throughout their lives. After he and Blanca are caught, he loses three fingers when he is attacked by Esteban. Pedro goes into hiding for a short time, and Blanca is forced to marry someone else. Pedro becomes a popular Latin singer and supports the socialist government. Eventually, he is reunited with Blanca and with his daughter, Alba. Pedro finally receives Esteban's respect after Esteban is captured by peasants and freed by Pedro, who has become a Socialist revolutionary. With the help of Esteban, Pedro and Blanca are able to flee the country and live together in Canada.

Marcos

Marcos is Clara's uncle, a carefree but mad inventor, who leaves Clara a set of books that will help her develop her magical powers. He also leaves her a wonderful dog, whom she loves.

Miguel

Miguel is Amanda's brother and a member of the lower social class. He gets Alba involved in student protests and becomes her lover. He is finally forced to flee and hide to save his life. He may be the father of Alba's unborn child.

Nana

Nana is the family nanny. She has spoiled Clara throughout her childhood and later spoils Blanca. Nana is a possessive and jealous woman who does not want to share Clara and who is happy to see Ferula sent away.

Transito Soto

Transito is a long-time friend of Esteban. Esteban meets Transito at a brothel called the Red Lantern and gives her money to set up her own business. Over the years, Esteban visits Transito several times, often just for comfort and advice. Later, she will help free Alba from jail at Esteban's request.

Blanca Trueba

Blanca is the daughter of Esteban and Clara. She is also the mother of Alba. Blanca is rebellious, and resembles neither her mother nor her father in personality. Blanca is forced to attend a convent school, while her brothers are sent to a British school. When Blanca falls in love with Pedro Tercero, her father reacts with anger and attacks Pedro. Esteban tells Blanca that Pedro is dead and forces the pregnant Blanca to marry de Satigny. Eventually, Clara tells Blanca that Pedro is still alive, and after leaving her philandering husband, Blanca is reunited with Pedro. After Clara's death, Blanca assumes control of her family's estate. Eventually, a contrite Esteban helps Blanca and Pedro escape to a life of freedom in Canada. Blanca's letters form an important element of the narrative that Alba puts together after she is released from jail.

Clara Trueba

Clara is Esteban's wife, and the mother of Blanca, Jaime, and Nicolas. Her diary tells the story that is recounted in the first half of the book. Clara is clairvoyant, and as a child she was able to predict the future, read fortunes, and make objects move. After the death of her sister, Rosa, Clara is mute for nine years, and when she does finally speak, it is to announce that she will marry Esteban Trueba when she is nineteen. Clara has foreseen that Esteban, who was once engaged to her sister, Rosa, will become her husband. She does not love him and refuses to allow him to control her. She is compassionate and concerned about the poor and is very much the opposite of her new husband. After Clara and Esteban marry, they move to his country estate. When her parents die in an accident, Clara saves her mother's decapitated head in a hatbox. Over the years, Clara comes to resent the controlling anger that Esteban uses to manipulate everyone. Clara never again speaks to Esteban after he hits her and

beats Blanca, at the discovery of Blanca's affair. Clara dies when Alba is seven years old, leaving Esteban devastated. When Alba is in danger, Clara's spirit returns to protect her granddaughter. Clara represents strength, morality, and a willingness to fight oppression.

Esteban Trueba

Esteban is married to Clara, and is the father of Blanca, Jaime, and Nicolas. When he is thirty-five, Esteban returns to the city from his country estate to visit his dying mother and to find a wife. Esteban was Rosa's fiancé, and he spent several years grieving for Rosa after her death. Esteban is a stern man, often given to rage, but he is also very lonely. Somehow, Clara has telepathically summoned Esteban, and he will fall passionately in love with her and remain so for the rest of his life. Esteban is a self-made man. After Rosa's death, he took the money he had been saving for the wedding and used it to rebuild his family's ruined country estate. During this period, he raped many of the young women who lived on his estate or in the nearby town, and fathered many illegitimate children, including Esteban Garcia, the son who resulted from Esteban's rape of Pancha. Esteban is moody and often violent. He demands his own way and is used to getting it. Esteban cares little for the servants on his own estate, even raping them when it pleases him. One of the children born of these rapes will, in turn, rape Esteban's own granddaughter. Eventually, Esteban enters politics, becoming a senator. Esteban, who is opposed to communism, foolishly helps to arrange a military coup, which leads to the overthrow of the socialist government and the murder of the president. Later, when Esteban is captured by the peasants, he is rescued by Pedro Tercero. The changing political climate causes Esteban to question his previous actions, and he decides to help Blanca and Pedro Tercero flee the country. By the end of the novel, Esteban has emerged as a sympathetic character because of his willingness to accept responsibility for his own mistakes. His deep love for Clara, who never loves him, adds to the picture of sadness. Esteban represents the tragedy of the *machismo* Latin male.

Ester Trueba

Ester is Esteban's mother; he returns to her bedside when she is close to death. Ester's inheritance was squandered by her husband, and she now lives in poverty.

Ferula Trueba

Ferula is Esteban's unmarried sister. She moved in with Clara and Esteban at Clara's request, and in return she pampers Clara and angers a jealous Esteban. Ferula loves Clara more than anyone else ever has, and Nana is jealous of this love. Ferula leaves when Esteban orders her from the house. After she dies, her ghost appears to the family.

Jaime Trueba

Jaime is Nicolas's twin brother and is one of Clara and Esteban's sons. Jaime is a quiet boy who grows into a reflective adult and becomes a doctor to the poor. In personality, he is very different from his twin brother. Jaime loves his brother's girlfriend, Amanda, and when she turns to Jaime for an abortion, he unhappily agrees. Jaime's socialist views lead him to support the new government, but when he refuses to accept the demands of the revolutionary military leaders, he is tortured and murdered.

Nicolas Trueba

Nicolas is Jaime's twin brother and is one of Clara and Esteban's sons. Nicolas toys with mysticism, magic, and Eastern religions, but focuses mostly on being a playboy. He carelessly gets his girlfriend, Amanda, pregnant, and then moves on to other interests. He is very intelligent, but lacks any direction and wastes the potential that he has been given.

Jean de Satigny

De Satigny is a French count who tells Esteban about Blanca's affair with Pedro Tercero. Esteban forces Blanca to marry de Satigny, but she eventually leaves him when she learns that he is devoted to pornography and to an underground lifestyle of sex and torture.

Clara del Valle

See Clara Trueba

Nivea del Valle

Nivea is Clara's mother. She has borne fifteen children, of whom Clara is her youngest. After Nivea's death in an automobile accident, Clara saves her mother's decapitated head in a hatbox.

Rosa del Valle

Rosa is often referred to as Rosa the Beautiful. Her green hair is a distinguishing element of her beauty. She was engaged to Esteban but died after accidentally sipping poisoned brandy. Rosa represents the blending of magic and reality, which results in a sort of ethereal beauty that enchanted Esteban.

Severo del Valle

Severo is Clara's father. He dies in an automobile accident while Clara is pregnant with her sons.

Themes

Alienation and Loneliness

Although Esteban does very little to make the reader like him, by the end of the book he has become a sympathetic character. In large part, this is because of his loneliness. His anger has so isolated him from everyone he loves that he exists without friends. After a lifetime of bullying and ordering people around, no one wants to be near him. He has alienated his family through his own selfishness. He abandoned the illegitimate children that he fathered, and when they displease him, he abandons his legitimate children as well.

Anger and Hatred

Anger is the central trait of Esteban's personality. He seethes with rage at nearly everyone he meets. He rapes the young girls on his estate and in the neighboring towns, not out of desire but out of hate. His anger is also an element of his jealousy, and this leads him to banish his own sister from his life. He wants to own Clara's mind and body, but he cannot, and so in anger to banishes Ferula. When Esteban discovers his daughter's love for Pedro, he responds with anger, beating her. And when Clara objects, he hits her so hard that he knocks out several of her teeth. Esteban attacks Pedro and forces his only daughter to marry a man she hates, all out of anger. Esteban's anger roars through all their lives, costing him Clara's companionship, his daughter's love, and his sons' affection.

Class Conflict

One of the many tragedies in *The House of the Spirits* revolves around Blanca's love for Pedro. Pedro is the son of the foreman, and Blanca is the daughter of the *patron*. The former is little more than a servant, and the latter is comparable to a plantation owner from the nineteenth-century American South. Esteban decides this man and his daughter are not an acceptable match. Much of the politi-

Topics for Further Study

- Research the political events of 1970–1975, and determine how closely Allende's novel depicts historical reality.

- What role does magic play in this novel? Decide what the use of mysticism contributes to the story and how it is used to foreshadow events. Do the many ghosts function as an omen or just as a device to foreshadow events?

- Examine the role of patriarchy in this novel and discuss how the Latin *machismo* of the men oppresses the women characters in Allende's novel.

- Note the references to nature and animals and discuss how nature functions in this novel. Is there is a connection between nature and the supernatural?

- Throughout the novel, there are many events in each woman's life that are repeated. At the conclusion, Alba remarks that the cycle of rape will probably continue. Discuss the cyclic nature of these women's lives, paying close attention to their relationships with men.

- Discuss the undercurrent of political corruption, intrigue, graft, and influence peddling in Allende's novel.

- Examine closely the character of Esteban Trueba. What qualities does he represent? Many critics feel that he deserves the reader's sympathy. Put together a well-constructed argument supporting this point.

---

cal drama of the book is also focused on class issues. It is the peasants who kidnap Esteban, and it is the lower class who protests for change. When Miguel falls in love with Alba, he is dismayed to discover that she is from the upper class, since he has no respect for that element of society. When Nivea and Clara speak of human rights to factory women, they do not even notice that they are speaking from the wealthy classes to people who have few rights. They mean well, but they have spent their lifetimes insulated from reality and the problems that afflict the poor.

Duty and Responsibility

When Clara arrives at the country estate, she understands at once the responsibility that they have to the peasants who live on the estate and who work for them. She is concerned with their well-being and health. But Esteban has never seen the peasants as anything other than labor. He has exploited them since the day he arrived to rebuild the estate. When he has wanted a woman, he has simply seized the first young girl he found. Then, when an illegitimate child was born, Esteban refused to acknowledge his paternity or his responsibility. Instead, he looked for another young woman to seize. This failure to accept responsibility leads to the torture and rape of his only granddaughter. The son of one of Esteban's illegitimate sons, Esteban Garcia grows into an adult filled with rage at being excluded from all that he thinks he should have received. But Esteban never extends responsibility to the lower classes. He does assume financial responsibility for his mother and sister, but he denies emotional responsibility for excluding his sister from his family. She dies alone in poverty because of Esteban's jealousy. Only at the end of the novel does Esteban take responsibility for the events that have occurred.

Magic

Magic is an important theme in *The House of the Spirits* and one that runs throughout the novel. Many of the characters have special powers that enable them to survive in their world. Clara has magical powers, which permit her to escape Esteban's oppressive control. But she is not the only member of her family to have something magical about her.

Rosa, with her ethereal beauty and green hair, has magic in her as well. Clara's uncle Marco is also magical, and later Nicolas will try to awaken the family's magical inclination from his own psyche. Most often, the magic is used to foreshadow events in the family's lives. Clara predicts Rosa's death, and she uses magic to summon Esteban when she foresees that she is to marry him. Clara knows the sex of her unborn children, just as Alba does in the book's final chapter. This final use of magic allows the novel to end with a sense of hope. Often magic is used to impart good news, such as when Clara announces that she is carrying twin sons, but many other times it is used to predict death or danger. Alba grows up in an atmosphere of magic, and when she is in danger, she uses her magical powers to call Clara to her, and it is Clara who is able to help Alba find a way to survive. In many other novels magic would be a contrivance, but in *The House of the Spirits* magic is merely another element of Latin-American culture, and its use becomes a natural and accepted part of the novel.

Style

Character

A character is a person in a dramatic work. The actions of each character are what constitute the story. Character can also include the idea of a particular individual's morality. Characters can range from simple stereotypical figures to more complex multifaceted ones. "Characterization" is the process of creating a lifelike person from an author's imagination. To accomplish this the author provides the character with personality traits that help define who he will be and how he will behave in a given situation. Allende provides her characters with a great deal of depth. This is made easier because they are loosely based on people that she has known in the past.

Fiction

Fiction is any story that is created out of the author's imagination, rather than factual events. Sometimes the characters in a fictional piece are based on real life, but their ultimate form and the way they respond to events is the creation of the author. In *The House of the Spirits* the characters are fictional, but they are based on people from Allende's

life. Thus the people did exist, but not exactly as they are depicted in Allende's novel.

Foreshadowing

Foreshadowing is a device in literature that is used to create expectation and tension in the story. This device is one way to build anticipation and to keep the reader interested in the story, or even worried about a character's future or well-being. Allende uses ghosts, such as Ferula or Clara, to predict future events.

Genre

Genres are a way of categorizing literature. Genre is a French term that means "kind" or "type." Genre refers to the format in which a work is written, such as novel (of which *The House of the Spirits* is one), short story, or poem, and also to the type of story it tells, such as tragedy, comedy, epic, pastoral, mystery, science fiction, or romance.

Memoir

A memoir is an autobiographical form of writing in which the author gives his or her personal impression of significant events or people. This is different from autobiography, since the work does not center around the writer's own life or experiences. Although *The House of the Spirits* is not strictly a memoir, Allende does use the novel as a means to explore the important events of her own family's history.

Plot

This term refers to the pattern of events in a work of literature. Generally plots should have a beginning, a middle, and a conclusion, but they may also sometimes be a series of episodes connected together. The plot provides the author with the means to explore primary themes. Students are often confused on the difference between plot and themes. Themes explore ideas, and plots simply relate what happens. In *The House of the Spirits* the plot covers the events of more than fifty years, but the theme is of growth and change amid the political upheaval that threatens the country.

Setting

The time, place, and culture in which the action of the story takes place is called the setting. The elements of setting may include geographic location, physical or mental environments, prevailing cultural attitudes, or the historical time in which the action takes place. The location for *The House of the Spirits* is vague, but it is understood that the events take place in Chile. The action spans more than fifty years.

Literary Heritage

Much literature of Latin America is characterized by magical realism, sometimes referred to as symbolic mysticism. Much of the time, this means that the writer blends together naturalism and supernaturalism seamlessly. Often the literature of this area incorporates folktales and legends into the text, making the legends appear a natural part of the author's work. Magical realism erases the borders between the character's reality, the explicable and the inexplicable, and the natural world and the magical world.

Traditional Western literature has relied upon literary realism for more than one hundred years. This "realism" attempts to create a story and characters that are plausible, a representation of our everyday lives. The literature of magical realism attempts to portray the unusual, the spiritual, and the mystical, as ordinary facets of the character's lives. For the reader, magical realism requires an acceptance of the coexistence of the real and the imaginary. The author posits these magical events as authentic, with the supernatural events being interwoven seamlessly into the narration. For Allende, this means that Clara's ability to move objects or predict the future are interwoven into the story as essentially ordinary parts of her life. There is nothing exceptional about the ghosts who appear, and the reader accepts this, because Allende writes with authority. She claims this novel is based on her family's story, and so the magic and the ghosts must also be a part of that history. Because the author is so accepting of these details, the reader must also accept them.

Historical Context

The events in *The House of the Spirits* take place during a period of more than fifty years, from about 1920 to 1975. Allende sets her family saga against a backdrop of political change, in an occasionally violent era, but her novel also functions as an examination of women's lives during this period in Chile. In the early sections of the novel, both Nivea and Clara are involved in the suffragette movement. During this period, women were confined by traditional gender roles, with most women performing the work traditionally designated for women: marriage and family, or, if employed outside the home, teaching. The right for women to vote in all elections, an interest of both Nivea and Clara, was not granted to women until 1949, much later than in other Latin American countries. With regard to education, Chilean women have moved slowly toward greater access. Women have been admitted to universities since the middle of the nineteenth century, and Chile was one of the first countries to graduate a woman physician. But the number of women attending universities and working in traditionally male careers, such as law and medicine, has been, and remains, significantly lower than in most western countries. One reason that women have been so slow to gain equal rights in Chile is the tradition of *machismo,* which posits male superiority and control over women. This is evident in *The House of the Spirits* when Esteban, with impunity and without fear of reprisal, seizes and rapes any woman he wishes. He is also able to demand that his daughter Blanca marry a man she hates, so that her father need not be embarrassed by an unwed and pregnant daughter—a shame he has inflicted on countless other fathers. Esteban also has the right to control who his wife spends time with, even throwing his own sister out of the house when he chooses. And yet, *machismo* is not the only ideology that oppresses women. Women also have a cultural designation that leads to their repression, *marianismo,* which is a belief in the spiritual superiority of women, based on women's sisterhood with the Virgin Mary. This affiliation means that women are expected to emulate the Virgin Mary, both in piety and in purity. All of the women in Allende's novel display this piety, and some, such as Ferula, embrace purity as well. When Ferula observes Clara as an eager sexual partner to her husband, she is shocked and immediately devotes herself to praying for Clara. The idealism of *marianismo* is difficult for any woman to meet, as the novel makes very clear. But in spite of the difficulty, men expected women to maintain this ideal.

Religion, and its influence in Chilean society, also had an important impact on women's lives. In

The House of the Spirits, the story begins with the family in church. Their priest is an important part of the family's lives, and the influence of the church is an important factor in the family's social and cultural existence. Chile is one of the last countries in the world where divorce is still not legal; thus, Clara leaves Esteban and spiritually divorces him, changing her name and removing her wedding ring, but legally she remains his wife. If it appears in Allende's novel that there is little that women can do to prevent pregnancy, that is because birth control information, which has been readily available elsewhere in the world since the 1960s, in Chile is only available to married women who have had a child. Such information is disseminated only during prenatal and postpartum checkups. Both Nivea, whose pregnancy predates the availability of birth control, and Alba, whose pregnancy coincides with the 1973 revolution, were single and had no access to birth control information. Abortion, which was available as a therapeutic procedure during the period 1931-1989, is now absolutely against the law under any circumstances.

Ironically, women began to gain more control under the repressive dictatorship of General Augusto Pinochet, who controlled the country from 1973 to 1989. The coup which set Pinochet in control is the political event that controls the action at the end of the novel. This is because with so many men dead or in prisons, women began to protest on behalf of their families and their missing men. As a result, women today have more freedom in Chile than ever before. But during the period outlined in *The House of the Spirits* women were little more than chattel, owned and controlled by the men of Chile.

Critical Overview

Reviews of *The House of the Spirits* have often focused on comparisons between Allende's first novel and Gabriel García Márquez's *One Hundred Years of Solitude*. Despite the similarities, Allende's novel offers some important distinctions and contains strengths that set the work apart from novels written by other Latin-American writers. In a review of *The House of the Spirits* for *The Christian Science Monitor*, Marjorie Agosin declares that Allende's novel "captivates and holds the reader throughout its 400 pages." Agosin agrees that the

critical acclaim of readers and critics that greeted the publication of Allende's novel is richly deserved. Calling *The House of the Spirits* "a moving and powerful book," Agosin argues that the book is far more than a novel. Instead, according to Agosin, it is "a double text." This is because Allende's novel incorporates two different goals: "On one level it is the story of the Trueba family and its progeny, both legitimate and bastard. On the other level, it is the political and social history of Chile." Agosin notes that real events form the background of the novel, and also refers to the elements of magic and spirituality which contribute to the story's strengths, asserting that "the unbridled fantasy of the protagonists and their enchanted spirits is played out against the story of the demented and tragic country once free, now possessed by the evil spirits of a military dictatorship." According to Agosin, all of these elements—the family saga, the historical background, the spirituality of the women, and an excellent translation—make this novel "an unforgettable experience."

Jonathan Yardley, a reviewer for *The Washington Post,* is equally enthusiastic about *The House of the Spirits*. Although Yardley observes that this novel contains a "certain amount of rather predictable politics," he suggests that the humanity of the book transcends this predictability. Finding that "the only cause it wholly embraces is that of humanity," Yardley is fervent about the way the book embodies "passion, humanity and wisdom that in the end. . .transcends politics." One element of the book that appeals to Yardley is the depiction of Esteban Trueba, who is not allowed an easy "political conversion." Even when Esteban understands and accepts responsibility for his actions, he does not simply admit defeat; instead, he realizes, as Yardley notes, that "nothing is immutable." It is a simple distinction that reveals Allende's strength as a writer: "Allende has both the tolerance and the wisdom to understand that there is lamentable human loss when any world crumbles, even if it was not a good one, and thus the cantankerous Esteban emerges at last as a deeply sympathetic figure." That the reader is able to sympathize with Esteban, after all the destruction he has caused, is one the strengths of *The House of the Spirits*. The novel's success, suggests Yardley, is due to its status as "a novel not about ideas or causes but about people."

Not every reviewer offers an unqualified endorsement of Allende's novel. The *Los Angeles Times*'s Richard Eder finds *The House of the Spirits*

Salvador Allende, Isabel's uncle.

to have strengths but also weaknesses. Among the book's strengths, says Eder, is its ability to make the victims of these events, as depicted in the book, "humanly, if not altogether ideologically, quite a bit like a Californian's son at Berkeley, a Bostonian's lawyer cousin, a New York professional serving on her school community board, or anyone's occasionally imprudent younger brother or sister. We meet the atrocity statistics and, in Pogo's words, they are us." The people in Allende's novel are real, and the reader is able to recognize them as such. Eder also acknowledges that Allende has created a novel that is "a mix of romantic nationalism and revolutionary zeal." But, Eder also points to some weaknesses in the novel. Among these is the author's use of magical realism, which Eder says Gabriel García Márquez does "better than anyone else" and in her attempt to appropriate this device, Allende "rarely manages to integrate her magic and her message." This difficulty of cohesion is actually due to Allende's characterization, Eder states, with the result being that some characters lack enough depth to make effective use of the magic. Instead of the cohesion that García Márquez's novels contain, Eder asserts, Allende's novel is "populated too tidily with representative figures, possessing a richness of incident and detail, if not of character, and decorated rather than transformed by

the magic." The result is that "there are times when the women's [Clara and Alba's] small miracles resemble the stories of saints recounted with pedagogical intent and unalloyed ravishment in the children's devotional literature used in Latin America a generation or two ago."

Criticism

Sheri E. Metzger,

Metzger is a Ph.D. specializing in literature and drama at The University of New Mexico, where she is a lecturer in the English department and an adjunct professor in the university honors program. In this essay, she discusses how the women in Isabel Allende's The House of the Spirits *use the supernatural as a mechanism for escape from the patriarchy of Latin-American family structure.*

During the more than seventy years that *The House of the Spirits* spans, each of the women in Esteban Trueba's life finds a way to escape his obsessive control. Although externally, Clara, Blanca, and Alba continue to exist within Esteban's world and in

What Do I Read Next?

- *Daughter of Fortune* (1999), also by Isabel Allende, is the story of a young woman's journey to California during the gold rush of the ninetheenth century.

- *Paula* (1995), by Isabel Allende, is a memoir that was begun when Allende's daughter became ill.

- *A Cultural History of Latin America: Literature, Music and the Visual Arts in the 19th and 20th Centuries* (1998), edited by Leslie Bethell, provides a cultural history of Latin America. This book contains essays that place the artistic expressions of Latin America into a historical context.

- *Based on a True Story: Latin American History at the Movies* (1999), edited by Donald Stevens, presents an overview of how movies have depicted the history of Latin America. This book covers history from the 1500s to the present as depicted in film.

- *Speaking of the Short Story: Interviews with Contemporary Writers* (1997), edited by Farhat Iftekharuddin, includes interviews with many Latin-American writers, including Isabel Allende, Rudolfo Anaya, and Arturo Arias.

- *Children of Cain: Violence and the Violent in Latin America* (1992), by Tina Rosenberg, is a journalistic account of the effect of the violence in Latin America. The book includes individual stories that help capture the reality of this world.

---

his house, each one is able to escape, to create an internal place where she can go. With the use of the supernatural, the Trueba women can escape to a spiritual world, a magical world from which Esteban is excluded. This is one place where Esteban cannot follow, since it is a world without defining structure, without rules. In the spiritual world, there is no patriarchy, and there are no social constructs that define women as subordinate to men. The supernatural is an ethereal world of shifting boundaries; and as such, it is a world that offers Clara, Blanca, and Alba an identity separate from that of wife, daughter, granddaughter.

In the patriarchal world of Chile, women are little more than chattel, property which men possess, exploit, and even reject, as a facet of male privilege. Women have few rights, and so they must find their own means to control their lives. Isabel Allende provides the Trueba women with a tool—magic—that will simplify their escape from a patriarchal world. In a way the women's ability to escape into magic is a defeat for Esteban. In a critical study of Allende's work, Ronie-Richelle Garcia-Johnson suggests that Esteban exists within traditional codes of honor, which direct him to "possess and confine these women." But rather than succumb to Esteban's control of the home, his women move onto a spiritual plane within the same home. Esteban's home space, which he possesses and controls, becomes a woman's space, which she can then possess and control. As Garcia-Johnson notes, "The Trueba women confronted Esteban in his own space, usurped his control of that area, expanded their lives into alternative spaces, or left Trueba's property altogether." Instead of the male-dominated hierarchy that Esteban craved, the women dominated the familial spaces, and Esteban was defeated. His defeat lies within Clara's magic. Magic is the only mechanism that Clara has to escape Esteban's unrelenting desire to possess her. Clara's husband is not content to love his wife and share his life with her. His love is an obsessive need to own Clara, to own not only her body but her mind and soul. His unwillingness to share any element of Clara's life leads to his rejection of his own sister, whom he banishes from their home. To own herself, Clara can only escape into the supernatural world. In the real world, Esteban can break down locked doors to possess his wife, but in the spiritual world, her mind

> " Clara's ability to find a voice, to create an interior life that offers escape from a patriarchal husband, provides her with something that she can leave to her daughter, and by extension, her granddaughter. In a patrilineal world, Clara has little that she owns and which is hers to bequeath to her daughter, but she does have her magic, which she can offer to Blanca and Alba. "

is free of him. Esteban's obsessive need to possess his wife does not end when her life ends. Clara cannot even escape into death, since even there Esteban can find her. Garcia-Johnson suggests that Esteban's decision to build an elaborate tomb, one that will house Rosa, Clara, and himself, is a way to make sure that he will have in death what he could not own in life—Clara's entire being. Esteban's idea that he can confine Clara is forced to wait until their deaths, because, during her life, she finds freedom by claiming something that Esteban cannot control. The spiritual world offers Clara her own place, a woman's place, something she can claim, while defeating her husband's idea that she must be confined in his place.

In a patriarchal society, such as exists in Chile, one element of male control is silence. Traditionally men have used silence as a mechanism of control. Patriarchy is founded upon the biblical injunction that women must obey their husbands, and they must obey without complaint. In defending their domination of women, men cite Paul's instructions in the New Testament. In his epistle to the Ephesians, Paul tells wives that they must "submit yourselves unto your own husbands" and that "the husband is the head of the wife, even as Christ is the head of the church" (Eph. 5.22-23). This hierarchy is again reinforced in verse 24: "Therefore as the church is

subject unto Christ, so let the wives be to their own husbands in every thing." Paul also notes that women were subordinate to men in matters of religion. Specifically women were not permitted to instruct or preach the word of God. To do so is "to usurp authority over the man" (1 Tim. 2.12). Consequently, women must be silent in church where the word of God is spoken. In the years since Paul wrote these words, patriarchal societies have used these biblical verses as a means to silence and control women. As is the case with much of the Bible, Paul's words are taken out of context to support an agenda. In this case, the agenda is patriarchy. Whereas in a patriarchal society, a woman is expected to be silent, in the Trueba household, Clara uses silence to her own best advantage. Instead of being silent as a signal of female oppression, Clara evokes silence as a way to control her own place within her husband's house. Clara cannot escape Esteban through divorce, but she can escape him through silence, and it is silence that permits her escape into the spiritual world. Clara defeats male domination by creating a separate interior life, while using silence in the exterior world, the world of men. In a discussion of the spirituality of *The House of the Spirits*, Ruth Y. Jenkins points out that Allende's novel "explore[s] the double bind of articulating female voice in cultures that ordain silence as the appropriate expression of female experience." Clara is silent because she chooses to be, not because Esteban orders her to be silent. Silence is her way of discovering her voice in a society that says she should not have a voice. She is not subordinate to Esteban; he cannot control her because her magic gives her a voice, and he cannot control her magic. Jenkins suggests that supernatural fiction, when used within a culture that "embraces the other-worldly," can be used to "explore the authority provided by ghosts and spirits to articulate an alternative story from those endorsed by patriarchal cultures." The Trueba women use the supernatural to tell their own story in a culture that would not otherwise be willing to hear their story. The spiritual world disguises Clara's strength and makes her struggle visible, by subtly and indirectly rejecting the patriarchal world. Clara can replace patriarchal silence with spiritual silence, and she can use her own silence as a way to voice her story. Through their connection to the spirit world, the Trueba women share an authentic feminine experience, to the detriment of the male-structured world. Jenkins proposes that these women are empowered by the spirit world and that they pose a threat to Chilean society, which, "while in transition, remains nonetheless patriarchal.'' If, in a patriarchally organized society, women can create an identity separate from that extended by the men in their household, then such women will pose a threat to the culture's social construct.

Clara's ability to find a voice, to create an interior life that offers escape from a patriarchal husband, provides her with something that she can leave to her daughter, and by extension, her grand-daughter. In a patrilineal world, Clara has little that she owns and which is hers to bequeath to her daughter, but she does have her magic, which she can offer to Blanca and Alba. This inheritance, which Clara offers, results in Alba writing down the family story. When Alba has been captured, tortured, and raped, she wishes for her grandmother to bring her death. But instead, Clara tells her grand-daughter that she must survive. To do so, Alba must escape into her mind, where she begins to write her grandmother's story. The resulting book is Alba's inheritance from her grandmother. Jenkins suggests that when Alba reconstructs her family's story, she is ''assert[ing] the value of individual female experience while weaving it into generations of female history.'' Thus in writing down and preserving Clara's story, the female experience acquires a value it would not otherwise have in this patriarchal society. Ambrose Gordon maintains that when Clara leaves her parents' home and enters Esteban's home, she brings her spirit world ''as a kind of dowry,'' and that these ''spirits are an extension of her own clear spirit. . .her rich and loving femininity.'' But the spirit world is more than a dowry for Clara. In Esteban's house, she needs much more, and the spirit world offers Clara her own personal existence. Instead of a dowry, the spirit world provides Clara with an escape from patriarchy and an inheritance to leave her daughter and granddaughter. In a way, Clara leaves Blanca and Alba with their own escape from an oppressive world, which confines and restricts a woman's means of expression.

Source: Sheri E. Metzger, in an essay for *Literature of Developing Nations for Students*, Gale, 2000.

Kelly Winters

Kelly Winters is a freelance writer and has written for a wide variety of academic and educational publishers. In the following essay, she discusses feminist themes in The House of the Spirits *.*

''Critics are terrible people,'' Allende told Farhat Iftekharuddin in *Conversations with Isabel Allende.*

After the September 1973 coup Santiago's National Stadium was turned into a detention center for members of the political opposition.

''They will label you no matter what, and you have to be classified. I don't want to be called a feminist writer, a political writer, a social writer, a magic realism writer, or a Latin-American writer. I am just a writer; I am a storyteller.''

Despite her objections to being categorized, Allende is a feminist, as she made clear in the same interview. She told Iftekharuddin, ''Because I am a woman and because I am an intelligent women, excuse my arrogance, I have to be a feminist. I am aware of my gender; I am aware of the fact that being a woman is a handicap in most parts of the world. . .in any circumstance, a woman has to exert double the effort of any man to get half the recognition.''

And, she told Marjorie Agosin in *Conversations with Isabel Allende*, ''All the women in my book [*The House of the Spirits*] are feminists in their fashion; that is, they ask to be free and complete human beings, to be able to fulfill themselves, not to be dependent on men. Each one battles according to her own character and within the possibilities of the epoch in which she happens to be living.''

All the women in my book *The House of the Spirits* are feminists in their fashion; that is, they ask to be free and complete human beings, to be able to fulfill themselves, not to be dependent on men. Each one battles according to her own character and within the possibilities of the epoch in which she happens to be living."

In *The House of the Spirits* although Esteban Trueba is a central figure, women are the true main characters, and the main focus of the book is the bonds and interrelationships among the generations of mothers and daughters. Trueba is a traditional Latin-American man, with traditional ideas about honor, *machismo,* sexuality, and the roles of women—who should be quiet and under a man's control. The women in the book all defy these notions in very distinct ways. As characters, they are richly portrayed; all are uniquely talented, and all are influenced by the lives of their mothers and grandmothers.

As Allende notes, each woman in *The House of the Spirits* asserts herself against patriarch Esteban Trueba in her own way. Nivea is an enthusiastic early feminist; Clara lives in a time when divorce is impossible and is married to a controlling man, so she frees herself by maintaining her own mental and spiritual dominion, which Trueba cannot enter or control. Blanca defies him to be with the man she loves, and Alba is a member of a more modern generation: she is interested in work and politics, and allies herself with radical leftists, using Trueba's home and wealth to help them.

In addition, all the women in the book are creative in some way: they are all artists who create their own worlds. Clara is a spiritualist who keeps notebooks that "bear witness to life"; Rosa embroiders a huge tablecloth with phantasmagorical birds and beasts; Blanca works with clay to create creches of similar mythological and imaginary animals; and Alba retrieves Clara's notebooks and continues the tradition of keeping them. Allende told Agosin, "I chose extraordinary women who could symbolize my vision of what is meant by *feminine*, characters who could illustrate the destinies of women in Latin America." It is not surprising, since all of these women are intelligent and creative, that they are all feminist in their own way.

All of the women manage to escape Trueba's dominion by ignoring him, evading him, using his house for their own purposes, and changing the house that he built to suit their own needs. As Ronie-Richelle Garcia-Johnson noted in *Revista Hispanica Moderna,* "With spatial symbols, Allende communicates the message that, although the patriarchy may seem to be in control, women and traditionally feminine spirits prevail behind the facade."

Allende has been angered by some feminist interpretations of the book as not being feminist enough. She told Inez Dolz-Blackburn in *Conversations with Isabel Allende* that some feminists object to the fact that at the end of the book, Alba goes back to her grandfather's house and calmly waits optimistically for the birth of her baby, disregarding the fact that the child is the result of rape. Also, she notes, some critics feel that even her politically active characters, such as Alba, become that way only because they fall in love with a man who is active. "And that's not a feminist attitude," Allende said. "[They think] she should go out on the streets and fight."

However, Allende says, the women in her book do defy the rules of patriarchal society, mainly the rule that women should not voice their opinions. Collectively, all the women in the book defy this rule by keeping a journal of their experiences. And, according to Allende, the baby Alba is expecting at the end of the book is a symbol of the new society she hopes for—one in which men and women are equal and free.

The women in *The House of the Spirits* draw their strength from their common bond of blood, which, Allende told Agosin, "goes beyond mere biology; it's a chain of love that goes from mother to daughter and which conveys some special qualities that are not transmitted to men. . .It links all women who've had similar experiences and makes them capable of understanding, of making sacrifices."

Allende's emphasis on the spiritual and emotional bonds between women is drawn from her own family, in which the women were, and are, very close. She has always been close to her mother, and told Magdalena Garcia Pinto in *Conversations with Isabel Allende,* "My mother was the most important person in my childhood, and she has been the most important person in my life. She's my friend, my sister, my companion. . .Her love has always nourished me." In addition, many of the characters in the novel are drawn from Allende's own life. The character of Clara, for example, is Allende's own grandmother, only slightly exaggerated; like Clara, her grandmother had psychic gifts.

Allende told Marie-Lise Gazarian Gautier in *Conversations with Isabel Allende,* "My great-grandmother, my grandmother, my mother, my daughter, and I all communicate with each other telepathically, even after death. My grandmother died thirty-seven years ago but she still speaks to me. My mother who lives in Chile also speaks to me telepathically because calling by phone is very expensive. So there is very much of a female focus in my work because of my understanding of women."

Despite this emphasis on feminism and on women's lives, Allende is not interested in writing what others call "women's fiction." "I don't think literature has any gender," she told Garcia-Pinto, "and I don't think it's necessary to come up with a plan to write like a woman, because that seems like a kind of awkward self-segregation to me. . .You have to write like an authentic person as much as possible. . .and those qualities are independent of gender."

Allende is aware that not many women writers from Latin America are known outside Latin America, and that in the literature written by men, there are seldom well-developed women characters; the women in most Latin American fiction are stereotypes, "the mythical woman." She believes this is a result of traditional Latin culture, in which men and women had very different roles and lived largely separate lives. "That generation was brought up in a segregated world where men and women went to different schools, we only danced together, we didn't even sleep together very often," she told Dolz-Blackburn and colleagues. "And so, we knew about each other very little." As a result, she added, except for works by Jorge Amado, who "had great female characters. . .I think that literature written by women in Latin America has better knowledge of our feminine reality."

In response to a critic who remarked that Allende would never be "a writer of worth" until she created a male character who was as strong as her female characters, Allende told Garcia Pinto, "I wonder how many male writers have good female characters. Very few. And that doesn't mean that they write badly or that they aren't recognized as writers. . .I'm not asking for any concessions because I'm a woman, nor do I permit superfluous demands to be made of me because I'm a woman."

She told Linda Levine and Jo Anne Engelbert in *Conversations with Isabel Allende,* "I think that men and women are really not so different. If we were left alone, if we were not mutilated, so to speak, by an education that alters our course of development, we would all be persons who did not have such rigid roles and would lead happier, fuller, more integrated lives." And, she told Iftekharuddin, "I think that is what being a feminist means, the awareness and the strength to fight for what you believe."

Although her books often deal with political events and political realities that affect people's lives, Allende does not intend them to have a particular political message or easily stated moral. She told Michael Toms in *Common Boundary,* "I don't intend to deliver any sort of message, because I don't have any answers. I just have the questions, and these are the same questions that everyone asks. Maybe what a writer has to do is just tune into the question and repeat it in such a way that it will have a ripple effect and touch more people."

Source: Kelly Winters, in an essay for *Literature of Developing Nations for Students*, Gale, 2000.

Katy Butler

In the following interview with Allende, interviewer Katy Butler discusses Allende's novels, including her work The Infinite Plan *and the history of both Allende's life and of California as backdrops for her writing.*

Isabel Allende, the daughter and stepdaughter of Chilean diplomats, is one of California's most famous literary immigrants. The author of *The House of the Spirits* and other books, she is probably best known for her memoir, *Paula*, chronicling the year she spent at the bedside of her comatose daughter, watching her die after being stricken with porphyria and a series of ultimately fatal medical misadventures. We met with Allende recently to talk about her new novel, as well as about the true history of

General Augusto Pinochet depicted here in 1978. Pinochet named himself president of Chile and drafted a new constitution in 1980 that assured his leadership for the rest of the decade.

the American Gold Rush, the creative process and her experience of making a new family in a foreign land.

KATY BUTLER: A historical novel like this is a departure for you. How did you come to write it?

ISABEL ALLENDE: In 1991, after I finished *The Infinite Plan*, I had fallen in love with California, and I realized that San Francisco was only 150 years old. Before that, there was a little town called Yerba Buena with 300 people, and nothing was happening there. The pioneers coming West were stopping in Oregon and other places that they felt were better for agriculture, less wild than California. So California was inhabited by nomadic Indian tribes, Mexican haciendas, farmers who had lived there in large communities forever—this belonged to Mexico. And Mexico lost California in a war with the United States nine days after the gold was found.

The Gold Rush, in a year's time, brought a large number of people here motivated by greed. And they formed this place very fast. It would have taken probably 50 more years to bring all those people

here without the gold. I was fascinated by the Gold Rush because it is like war. It is a time when all human faults and human virtues become enlarged, highlighted. You see people with very strong characters; there's adventure, with bandits and prostitutes; and there's courage, idealism, irrational hope, all the things that in a novel are great ingredients.

I planned to start writing on Jan. 8, 1992. I knew only that it would be about a Chilean woman, not a prostitute, who comes north to the Gold Rush. Then my daughter fell sick and, during 1992, I was at her bedside. [She would die in 1993, after spending a year in a coma.] In 1993, I was very depressed and I wrote *Paula*. In 1994 and 1995, I was totally blocked and depressed and taking Prozac. I couldn't write anything.

BUTLER: What would happen?

ALLENDE: Nothing. When I write, there are voices that I listen to. There was no voice. It was just emptiness and void and silence and a sense of terrible frustration. I would have ideas. And I would sit down and I could never get the tone right. It never sounded natural and never seemed to flow. It was just stuck there, like playing with Legos, where you put one piece on the other piece but it never looks real. I thought I would never write fiction again.

So I gave myself a subject as far removed from death as possible, and I ended up writing *Aphrodite* [a collection of erotic stories and recipes] about lust and gluttony. It unblocked me, I think, because it brought me back to my body, to the sensuous, to the joy of life.

Finally, I began to write. It just happened. The characters just walked into my house! In seven months the book was written. What I have learned in all these years is that you have to let go of things in life and in the writing. And if you just follow your characters around, you will get the story in a more natural way. They are not flat comic book characters that you can order around. You just let them live.

BUTLER: How did you research the book?

ALLENDE: First at Bancroft Library at UC Berkeley. I bought books. I watched documentaries. I went to exhibits at the Oakland Museum. I found that almost everything written in the history books— and this is what they teach in school—had been written by the victors. The white males. That was how the story was told: the epic thing of white males coming to the Gold Rush. But the truth is, they were a minority. The majority of the people here were not white until October of 1849, when 40,000 people, most of them white men, crossed the continent.

In 1848, when the panning began, the majority were people of color: Mexicans, who were miners by trade, who taught the whites what to eat, how to find food, how to get the gold; Chinese people; people from South America; people from all over. Then the white men [the Forty-Niners] came overland, and they took over. They took the mines away and made laws against people of color and took away everything from them until many of them became bandits.

There was the story that we have seen so often, the story of greed and violence and abuse and racism. However, the people of color stayed. They helped form this society, but in the history books they are invisible, so my interest was to tell the story from the perspective of a woman and an immigrant of color.

BUTLER: You say that people of color were actually the majority. How did you find that out?

ALLENDE: I read a lot of letters written by wives of miners or pioneers who came, and by miners themselves. And those letters tell about life in the Gold Rush better than any history book. And then there is a fantastic collection of photographs.

BUTLER: And they show that people are not all white?

ALLENDE: Of course. You see the Chinese settlements; you see the Mexican settlements, the Indians panning for gold. You discover, for example, that the Indians did not scalp the whites; the whites scalped the Indians and collected the scalps.

BUTLER: Do you see parallels between the time of the Gold Rush and today?

ALLENDE: The racism. There is always racism. In that era, there were signs all over saying no dogs or Mexicans or Chinese allowed. Now, it is more hidden. I live in San Rafael, where there is a large Hispanic community. One day, United Markets published the life story of a little immigrant boy who came from El Salvador on one of the paper bags they give you for groceries. There was picketing in front of United Markets by white women who said they were going to boycott the market because they were promoting immigration.

People want immigrants of color to do the work, to take care of their children, walk their dogs,

> They took the mines away and made laws against people of color and took away everything from them until many of them became bandits."

wash their cars, do their gardens—but then they want them to disappear at 6 o'clock. They don't want to know that they live crowded four or five families in a small apartment.

People who come here have never heard of welfare. You come because you are desperate—so desperate that you are willing to leave behind your extended family, your village, your community. You decide to come to a country like the United States, come north, to a place where you don't know the rules, the clues, the codes of the society. You have never driven a car. You have never lived away from your village. You don't speak the language. And then you come here, and you are usually very exploited for a long time.

There is overt fear of the immigrant. We always fear everything that is different. So when the women who go to United Markets see men who look dark waiting at the corner for the truck, any truck, to pick them up and give them a menial job for the day, they are scared. Because they see them as different. They don't see the misery.

The first generation comes here out of hardship only. But they have the hope that their children will be Americans. And their children will do well. My housekeeper, to give you an example, is from Nicaragua. She will probably die exhausted. But her kids will be professionals. One is studying to be a chef, another is a public accountant and another is studying administration. In Nicaragua, they wouldn't have a chance. Her grandchildren will be totally American; they will look American and they will not speak Spanish, just like my grandchildren. And they will probably look for their roots. They will say, ''Oh, let me talk to my grandmother. I will go back to Nicaragua and find out about her!'' While her children don't want to know anything about it. They want to be Americans.

BUTLER: Are there any parallels between your experience and that of your heroine in ''Daughter of Fortune,'' or the experience of other immigrants?

ALLENDE: I am very privileged. I speak English. I am married to an American and therefore I am legal. I do not need a job. I have paid my way. Very few come like this. My photograph is in the newspapers so people know who I am. They know I am Latin but they bear with me! But I see how my [former] daughter-in-law, who looks very Latin and speaks with a strong accent, can be discriminated against, and how angry that makes her. My grandkids are probably the only brown kids in their school. But if they do [face some discrimination], it's OK. I think it's good for them. It makes them aware of their race and makes them strong, and maybe they will have more dignity and more courage.

BUTLER: Will you ever feel like an American yourself? Do you define yourself as an exile or as an immigrant?

ALLENDE: I define myself as an immigrant. A first-generation immigrant. I think in Spanish, dream in Spanish, write in Spanish, cook and make love in Spanish. So there is always this thing that you have to express yourself in another language. But I feel very comfortable here and very happy in the United States. When I fell in love with my husband, Willie, I decided that I would adapt myself. I never had when I lived in Venezuela; I was always looking south, always wanting to go back to Chile, always nostalgic for my extended family. When I came here, I said, ''No, I will cut off all this. I will be Willie's wife, and I will form another extended family here.''

BUTLER: How is this extended family different from what you had in Chile?

ALLENDE: In Chile it was larger, it was natural. This is artificial. I have to make a tremendous effort to put it together and keep it together. Because everything here tends to separate people, not bring them together.

BUTLER: Was it hard for you to adapt to American ways? Or was it like learning a different dance step?

ALLENDE: I think of myself as a person who is always moving. That was my fate, my karma. And I accept. I would love to have had roots and have my grandchildren around me with a sense of belonging and all that. That's not going to happen. My grandchildren spend a week in their father's house and a week in their mother's house. And that's OK. You can't have everything. I have a lot.

BUTLER: And how about your own background? Is it American Indian as well as European?

ALLENDE: My family would say that we are fully European. But I do not believe that. I don't believe that anybody in Chile is fully anything; that we are the result of mixture. And even if we do not have it in the blood, we have it in the culture. And I think we should be very proud of that and rescue that from our background.

BUTLER: My favorite line in your new book is this: When Eliza is leaving for the north, you write that she ''had the clear sensation of beginning a new story in which she was both protagonist and narrator.'' Did this ever happen to you?

ALLENDE: Yes. When I started writing *The House of the Spirits*, I was writing about myself and my family, but I realized I was the narrator. I had the incredible possibility of turning things around, for better or worse, to highlight some things and keep other things hidden, to create the legend of my own life.

BUTLER: Did that affect your sense of control of the narrative of your real life?

ALLENDE: No.

BUTLER: You already had a sense that you controlled your life?

ALLENDE: No. I had the idea that I was in control for a while. But when Paula fell sick I realized I didn't control anything. I looked back at my life and I realized that most of the things that had happened to me had happened by chance. I had not chosen. My karma seems to be to get what I never aimed for and to lose what I most love. So that is what my fate has been about. I don't have any feeling of control.

BUTLER: What did you get that you never aimed for?

ALLENDE: Success, celebrity. Never aimed for. I never expected that I would make enough money to support an extended family all by myself. Never hoped to do that.

BUTLER: What did you lose?

ALLENDE: I lost Paula. I lost my extended family. I lost my country. I lost a sense of belonging. I lost control over the things I would have wanted to control. But it's OK. I never expected I would find a man like Willie and fall in love late in my life and 12 years later still be madly in love. So that is unexpected. It is a gift that I never aimed for.

I learned the hard way losing Paula—her year of agony, in which I witnessed her slow death, unable to help her in any way. I learned that if I could not keep her alive, I could not make the lives of the people I love easier. I can't.

BUTLER: How did you let go?

ALLENDE: When she died. It took her a day and a night to die. This thing inside me broke. I let go of the anger against the things that had gone wrong in my destiny. About Paula's death. I had been very angry at the hospital. But the sadness took over, and I realized that it was nobody's bad intention. It had been a misfortune. And somehow I accepted that. It was like unfolding, unfolding of things. During the whole year that I wrote "Paula," this unfolding continued. Every single day.

I am a happier person now because I don't cling. I know that I can't have most of the things I wish I could have. To give you an example: We were going to buy a house up in the hills. And then it all turned out wrong and it's not going to happen. I promise that it didn't take me 30 seconds to let go. Willie's still angry, and he's hitting his head against the wall, and I say, "Willie, just let go." We have a nice house. We are going to be dead, naked, underground, some day very soon. So what is the problem?

BUTLER: Has anything changed for you recently?

ALLENDE: Paula's agony was too long, and too painful. I could not remember her dancing and laughing. I could only remember her in the wheelchair or hooked to all those machines with a respirator. Slowly, I think that has started to change. I went to Alaska on a cruise with my mother last spring, and one day we were in the front part of the ship, slowly going into a bay, where all the glaciers were. There was absolute silence and whiteness. Everything was white but the sky and the water. There was a sense of solitude and beauty. And I thought that Paula was OK. I started seeing her happy again. I started having a few dreams in which I didn't see her sick. The other day I dreamed that I saw her with lipstick. She never in her life wore any lipstick. But I saw her with lipstick, and she was talking to me. I woke up and told Willie. It was such a wonderful thing to meet her in a dream and she was OK.

Source: Katy Butler, "Isabel Allende on California's Mythic Past," (interview) in *Los Angeles Times,* October 10, 1999.

Sources

Agosin, Marjorie, "Powerful Chilean Saga Blends Fact and Fiction," in *The Christian Science Monitor*, June 7, 1985, p. B5.

Eder, Richard, "*The House of the Spirits* by Isabel Allende," in *Los Angeles Times*, June 16, 1985, p. 3.

Garcia-Johnson, Ronie-Richelle, "The Struggle for Space: Feminism and Freedom," in *Revista Hispanica Moderna*, Vol. XLVII, No. 1, June, 1994, pp. 184-93.

Gordon, Ambrose, "Isabel Allende on Love and Shadow," in *Contemporary Literature*, Vol. 28, No. 4, Winter, 1987, pp. 530-42.

Jenkins, Ruth Y., "Authorizing Female Voice and Experience: Ghosts and Spirits in Kingston's *The Woman Warrior* and Allende's *The House of the Spirits*," in *MELUS*, Vol. 19, No. 3, Fall, 1994, pp. 61-74.

Yardley, Jonathan, "Desire and Destiny in Latin America," in *Washington Post*, May 12, 1985, p. 3.

Further Reading

Agosin, Marjorie, *Tapestries of Hope, Threads of Love: The Arpillera Movement in Chile, 1974-1994*, University of New Mexico Press, 1996.

This book examines the lives of ordinary women as they tried to survive general Pinochet's oppressive military rule. The Arpilleras are tapestries made with scenes of everyday life which served as memorials to lost loved ones. The book contains a forward by Isabel Allende.

Bethell, Leslie, *Chile Since Independence*, Cambridge University Press, 1993.

This book focuses on the economic, social, and political history of Chile since it achieved independence from Spain in 1818. It contains much of the detail that establishes the background for Allende's novel.

Galeano, Eduardo, *Open Veins of Latin America; Five Centuries of the Pillage of a Continent*, Monthly Review Press, 1997.

This book provides a history of Latin America from a Marxist perspective. Since many of the characters in Allende's novel espouse socialist ideology, this book contributes some helpful background in understanding the political framework of the novel.

Kovach, Claudia Marie, "Mask and Mirror: Isabel Allende's Mechanism for Justice in *The House of the Spirits*," in *Postcolonial Literature and the Biblical Call for Justice*, University Press of Mississippi, 1994, pp. 74-90.

Kovach discusses symbols of the mask and the mirror in *The House of the Spirits*.

Rodden, John, ed., *Conversations With Isabel Allende*, University of Texas Press, 1999.

This book is a collection of 24 interviews with Allende from the 1980s and 1990s. In these interviews, Allende discusses her work and her life, offering readers insight into her perspective and motivations.

Tayko, Gail, ''Teaching Isabel Allende's *La casa de los espiritus*,'' in *College Literature*, Vols. 19-20, Nos. 3-1, October 1992-February 1993, pp. 228-32.
This essay discusses how *The House of the Spirits* could be used in the classroom. This author argues that Allende's novel works well to raise important issues about sexual, political, and economic oppression.

Toms, Michael, interview in *Common Boundary*, May/June, 1994, pp. 16-23.
Interview in which Allende discusses her writing methods and how her personal experience influences her work.

I, Rigoberta Menchú: An Indian Woman in Guatemala

When Menchú's autobiography was first published in 1984, it catapulted her and her story, describing the exploitation and mistreatment of her people, to the forefront of international attention. The book imbued her work in organizing the Guatemalan peasantry with added authority and credibility. The voice of the Guatemalan peasants, which had been heretofore silenced by government oppression, illiteracy, and linguistic barriers, was now available to the global public, and Menchú's narrative encompassed the story of oppressed people everywhere. Critics alleged that parts of Menchú's story were exaggerated or untrue, some even pursuing years of fieldwork to prove their allegations. Supporters have insisted that the verisimilitude of her story extends from the commonality of her experience with that of other Guatemalan peasants, in fact, most Guatemalan peasants. Menchú eloquently delineates the conflicts between ladinos and Indians, landowners and peasants, the government and the resistance, men and women, and change and tradition.

Rigoberta Menchú

1984

Author Biography

In this autobiography, Rigoberta Menchú details the two stages of her life: before political organizing, and after. Because she was born into a life of varied suffering and extreme poverty, and because hunger and crippling labor were constants, she was always

conscious of the repercussions of Guatemalan politics in her personal life.

Every year of her childhood was divided between her home in the *Altiplano*, where Indians cultivated their own land and made every attempt to live as their ancestors had, and the coast, where the *fincas* were located. For most of each year, her family would leave the *Altiplano* and go down to the *fincas*, or plantations, on the coast, and endure inhumane work and living conditions picking cotton or coffee. Many children accompanied their families to the *fincas*, and many of the younger ones died of malnutrition or disease.

It is when Menchú becomes a worker in the *finca* at the age of eight that she experiences the true magnitude of the exploitation by the landowners. Indian workers always incurred debt at the plantation's cantina, pharmacy, and general store, so Menchú's family would sometimes leave the *finca* at the end of eight months with little or no money to show for their work. Simultaneously, what little land the Indians had managed to cultivate successfully in the mountains was constantly being seized by the government, or by landowners with government ties.

Menchú's community had always impressed upon her the importance of maintaining the ways of their ancestors, and they saw the encroachment of *ladino* as a direct threat to their way of life. Menchú saw, quite readily, the discrimination suffered by her people, and the divisive measures employed by the *ladino* society to keep the different Indian groups separate, so that the Indians, who were the majority population in Guatemala, could not unite and resist the discrimination and exploitation. Her growing awareness about this dire situation sparked her entry into activism, and she risked her life to organize the peasants against this abuse.

Menchú's father, Vincente Menchú, a leader in their Indian community, was also well aware of this exploitation, and worked most of his life to improve working and living conditions; he, his wife, and his son were brutally killed by the government for their activism. Menchú left Guatemala for a short period, when her own life was most in danger, but she ultimately returned to continue her resistance work. She was awarded the Nobel Peace Prize in 1992. She used some of the money accompanying the prize to establish a foundation in honor of her father, and continues to travel and write extensively, speaking out against social injustice. In 1998 she pub-

lished a sequel to her autobiography, titled *Crossing Borders*.

Plot Summary

From the time she begins working on the *finca* at age eight, Menchú sees that the position of Indian workers is beyond grim. Workers make the long journey to the plantation by truck; because they are covered with a tarp, and not permitted to get out during any stops, the smell of human and animal excrement is unbearable. A large lean-to made of branches with one crude outdoor toilet is meant to serve four hundred or more workers. The landowners find various ways to cheat the workers, by changing quotas or charging exorbitant prices at the plantation cantina, where many workers would go to drink away their suffering. Landowners spray pesticides on the fields while workers are present; one of Menchú's friends dies as a result, one of many who is killed by pesticide poisoning.

One year, on the *finca*, her youngest brother dies, and her mother is faced with going into debt to bury him on plantation grounds, or waiting until they return to the *Altiplano*; she elects to go into debt and bury him right away, as Indian custom demands, and the other workers provide what they can to help Menchú's family. Menchú recalls, "Those fifteen days working on the *finca* was one of my earliest experiences and I remember it with enormous hatred. That hatred has stayed with me until today." When the family, who had been scattered among various *fincas*, reunites at their home in the *Altiplano*, the news of her brother's death is the greeting Menchú and her mother bring.

When she is almost thirteen, Menchú becomes a maid in Guatemala City, the capital. She works with another maid, Candelaria, an Indian who has become "ladinized," that is, she has learned Spanish and abandoned some of her Indian ways. Nonetheless, Cande, as she is called, is kind to Menchú and helps her learn her duties, and also shows Menchú how to stand up to the mistress, who is a petty, demanding woman. During her time as a maid, Menchú witnesses the full force and cruelty of *ladino* discrimination against Indians; Menchú sees that the dog is fed better than she, that Cande is given a bed while she must sleep on the floor. Fearful of losing her ties with her family, and unable to contain her anger at the way she is treated, Menchú leaves. When she returns home, she learns that her father has been imprisoned for resisting the government's takeover of Indian land. Given that illiterate Indians have virtually no recourse in the justice system, it takes a combination of superhuman effort and luck to get him out.

In 1967, Menchú's village in the *Altiplano* is "repressed" by the army for the first time. When land cultivated for years by Indians finally began to produce, landowners appeared, ransacked the village, and forced the Indians out. Government authorities, in collusion with the landowners, took advantage of the Indian's illiteracy by coaxing them to sign documents which the authorities claimed gave Indians the deed to the land. In reality, the documents stated that the Indians would be allowed to remain on the land for two years, after which they must move to another area. It is during these early conflicts with the landowners and the government that Menchú discovers the power of language, and the multiple ways that Indians are cheated, divided, and abused because of their illiteracy. She vows to learn Spanish, which she knows is, in many ways, a break with her community, since in learning Spanish, she will learn many other ways of *ladinos*. It is also at this time that the CUC is created—the Comité Unidad de Campesina, or the United Peasants Committee. Both Menchú and her family are active leaders of the CUC at different points in its history.

The government's next step is to disrupt the communal structure of Indian village life by giving each Indian family a parcel of land, too small to cultivate efficiently. The Indians resist, and combine their parcels into a common area, divided into cultivated land and living areas for all. Since Menchú's parents had long been the leaders of their community, they are elected to live in the center, with others surrounding them. The government's response to this resistance is to send in soldiers to break up the villages by force; the soldiers, some of them recruited Indians, engage in mass looting, murders, rape, and torture. Menchú's community decides to defend itself by placing booby-traps all around the village, and they are successful, even managing to capture one of the soldiers. In accordance with their respect for human life, they do not kill the solider, but impress upon him how wrong his actions are, and beseech him to tell his comrades the same. After this success, Menchú travels to nearby villages and organizes them in a similar way.

One of Menchú's earliest experiences with organizing was facilitating Bible study meetings in

Rigoberta Menchú

her community, which was largely Christian, thanks to the influence of Catholic Action, a religious organization started in 1945 to spread Catholic doctrine among the Indians. Menchú explains that Indians took to Catholicism readily because the Bible and Indian culture had many elements in common, such as veneration of ancestors, expression of thanks to a God, and the promise of a better afterlife for suffering endured on earth. Once she decides to learn Spanish in order to better organize the peasant population, Menchú receives most of her tutelage from sympathetic priests. She does recognize, however, that there are two Catholic churches in Guatemala: the church of hierarchy, which turns a blind eye to the Indians' plight, teaching Indians to be passive and accept "God's will," and the church of the poor, which actively joins the struggle, with priests and nuns risking their lives in the same way, for the same cause.

As Menchú and her family become more active in the CUC's resistance activities, they become wanted by the government. Menchú's younger brother is kidnapped and brutally tortured by the military, and her family is called to watch him and other prisoners be burned alive. If they refuse, they would be arrested as accomplices. After the death of her brother, Menchú's father, as part of a mass protest, occupies the Spanish embassy, where they are killed when troops set fire to the building. Menchú's mother is captured, raped, tortured, and left to die of exposure on a hilltop, her open wounds infected and suppurating. Her body is guarded by soldiers, to ensure that no one comes to save her or claim the body; they guard the corpse until it completely disintegrates.

Ultimately, Menchú renounces marriage and motherhood, for several reasons. Although she acknowledges that having children is natural, and that family planning is another abomination placed on Indians by the *ladino* society, she cannot bear the thought of bringing children into the world who will suffer as she has. Also, she knows that her work will be limited by having children, and while many men in the organizing movement are very enlightened about their common plight, that many are also trapped in the chauvinist ways of thinking which place men above women.

Forced to go into hiding after the death of her mother, Menchú barely avoids capture while hiding in a church. She works briefly for a group of nuns at a convent, until she learns that they are often visited by a member of the secret police. She escapes to Mexico with the help of non-peasant members of the resistance movement, and is reunited with her four sisters. She rejects the offer of European supporters to go to Europe, and returns to Guatemala, where she begins to work as an organizer for the Vincente Menchú Revolutionary Christians, a group formed in memory of her father, an unceasing activist and devout Christian.

Characters

Candelaria

Candelaria is the "ladinized" Indian maid with whom Menchú works in the city. Cande is unimpressed by the mistress' fits and threats, and stands up to her without hesitation. She even plans a small rebellion in the house, to annoy the mistress, but is thrown out when her plot is discovered. Cande refuses to sleep with the sons of the house, inciting more mistreatment from the mistress, but still, she is able to demand that the mistress give Menchú's father some money when he appears one day, penniless.

Petrona Chona

Doña Petrona Chona is the "first dead body" Menchú had ever seen. She had been hacked to pieces by the landowner's bodyguard because she refused the landowner's son. She was married and had a small son, whose finger was chopped off during the attack.

Petrocinio Menchú Tum

Petrocinio Menchú Tum was Menchú's younger brother, who was kidnapped, tortured, and killed by the army for his organizing work. His family was called to witness his murder by the army; the army lined up all the prisoners, doused them with petrol, and lit them on fire as their families watched. He was Menchú's second brother to die.

Juana Menchú

A community leader alongside her husband, Juana Menchú was a woman of varied talents; in addition to running an ever-growing household in strict accordance with Indian customs, she was immensely knowledgeable about natural medicines, and her services as a healer and midwife called her away from home much of the time. Menchú admits that because of her patience and resourcefulness, her mother was the one "who coped with the big problems in our family." Also an activist in the peasant's struggle, she is ultimately captured by the military and tortured in unspeakable ways, and dies an agonizing death.

Rigoberta Menchú

Menchú describes herself as "shy, timid," during her younger years. She was her father's favorite, and her father's staunchest supporter, sympathizing with his need to drink to drown his overwhelming sorrows. As for her mother, she regrets not having taken the time to learn as much from her mother as she did from her father, particularly when, after the death of her mother, she notes that women bear most of the suffering of families, and know the most secrets. Perhaps due to the influence of her parents, who were leaders of the community and wholly Indian to the core, Menchú also becomes a leader in both the Christian and peasant organizations without sacrificing her Indian beliefs. She does, however, consciously decide not to be married or become a mother, identities which are integral to womanhood in the Indian culture; she decides, with difficulty, that her mission to work for social justice is one which cannot accommodate the challenges of motherhood. She is a tenacious and intelligent figure, able to learn Spanish without formal schooling, without being able to read or write. Her narration of her story is replete with an understanding of political struggle: why barriers exist between people, what fuels injustice and exploitation, what will precipitate change. She is astute enough to look at Catholicism critically, although she is a devout Christian, and select those elements of Christianity that will help her struggle and which will not. Her courage and unceasing stamina allow her to organize other villages on her own, to venture into the city at the age of twelve to work as maid, and to risk her life organizing all peasants, *ladino* and Indian, as a leader in the CUC.

Vincente Menchú

Orphaned as a teenager, Vincente Menchú is the driving force behind the village's resistance. In the army, he learned ''a lot of bad things, but he also learned to be a man.'' He was often away from the house, petitioning government authorities, organizing workers, or imprisoned, but he was Menchú's favorite, and she his. He is killed while occupying the Spanish Embassy, when troops set fire to the building. He was very intent on teaching his children to fight, as he had been taught, and passes down the ideology of cultural pride and resistance.

The Mistress

The *ladino* who employs Menchú as a maid, the mistress is a symbolic representation of all *ladinos* who discriminate and oppress Indians. Her appallingly unfair treatment of Menchú is Menchú's wake-up call to the true nature of racist *ladinos*.

Themes

Community

The book contains detailed descriptions of Quiché Indian ceremonies, traditions, and customs, which Menchú gives in order to explain the profound sense of community which fuels Indian village and family life. The village is an extension of the family, and all previous generations are represented in the village through remembrances of ancestors and their ways.

Topics for Further Study

- Research ancient Mayan culture, with particular emphasis on respect for nature and family and rites of passage. Compare and contrast the salient elements of ancient Mayan culture and modern Quiché Indian culture. What has remained intact? What has evolved?

- Investigate the United States' involvement in Guatemalan politics and economy from 1960 to 1990, with emphasis on the U.S. anti-Communist policies of the Cold War. What were the effects of U.S. intervention on Indian land holdings and family structure?

- Trace the development of Menchú's feminist sensibility, and the way she acknowledges, confronts, preserves, and adapts traditional notions of family, motherhood, womanhood, and *machismo*.

- Analyze the structure and recurring themes of Menchú's story as testimony. Compare and contrast her testimony to African-American narratives, such as those of Frederick Douglass and Malcolm X. What themes of struggle and oppression, as well as triumph and resilience, are present in both narratives?

The ceremonies for childbirth, marriage, and death all emphasize the importance of community involvement. A pregnant woman is given all the comforts and attention that the village can afford, and the birth itself is one of the rare occasions when the village will kill an animal to celebrate. Indians engage in intricate ceremonies to ask the earth's permission before sowing and harvesting; it is considered blasphemous to abuse the land, when the earth is the mother and father of all that exists upon it. Marriage is undertaken only after an elaborate series of visits by the prospective groom and his parents to the bride's family; the bride makes the ultimate decision. Even after marriage, if the situation becomes untenable, the bride can leave her husband and his family and return to her village, where the community will care for her, feeding her out of a communal surplus which she, in turn, contributes to with her labor. For death rituals, the community, not the family of the dead, bears all the expenses of the burial. It is one of few occasions when flowers are cut, to be placed around the coffin. Before his death, an Indian will offer his secrets to one chosen person, and all of his advice and his recommendations to his family. Menchú says, "We can only love a person who eats what we eat," explaining that when encountering non-Indians, the willingness to accept Indian ways is a crucial sign of empathy.

One other significant aspect of all these rituals, which has developed since the appearance of the *ladino*, is the pact that all Indians make at certain milestones (birth, ten years of age, marriage) to uphold and maintain the ways of their ancestors and to "destroy the wicked lessons we were taught by [the White Man]," since "if they hadn't come, we would all be united, equal, and our children would not suffer." Even these century-old ceremonies have adapted to include not only an acknowledgment of the Indian's history, but a call to consciousness of the Indian's present situation at the hands of ladinos, and a promise to battle the forces which endeavor to corrupt Indian ways.

Language and Literacy

Menchú's community has an oral tradition through which they pass information about traditions and history from one generation to the next. Because of the variety of language spoken among the larger Indian population, however, Menchú finds that Indians cannot communicate with one another, despite their similar circumstances. Menchú's family is afraid that she will acquire other undesirable *ladino* traits if she learns Spanish, but *ladinos* have kept Indians from learning Spanish anyway, by keeping them out of their homes and schools. Menchú learns how disempowering it is not to be literate, particularly in Spanish, when her family is cheated into signing documents they did not understand, which ultimately left them landless. The chapter where Menchú describes her decision to learn Spanish to organize peasants more effectively is titled "Farewell to the Community: Rigoberta decides to learn Spanish." Her decision is based on the logic that "Since Spanish was a language which united us, why learn all the twenty-

two languages in Guatemala?. . .I learned Spanish out of necessity."

Natural World

Menchú refers to the earth as "the mother of man," because she "gives him food." Animals, water, and maize are considered pure and sacred, and are often invoked in prayer. Menchú also notes that "they" call the Indians polytheistic because they acknowledge the God of water, the earth, and the son, but she explains that all are expressions of the one God, "the heart of the sky." All life originates with this one God, and for that reason, Indians promise to respect all life, killing neither trees, plants nor animals without good cause or first asking permission to do so from the earth. Even when the Indians begin to organize the villages to protect themselves from the army, they ask the "Lord of the natural world, the one God," for permission "to use his creations of nature to defend" themselves. For this reason, the indiscriminate killing of people and animals by the army is still more shocking to the Indians.

When Catholic Action began to spread the Christian doctrine among the Indians in 1945, the Indians willingly accepted it as not a discrete religion, but another means through which to express their existing indigenous beliefs and practices, such as prayer. Menchú delineates the similarities between Catholicism and Indian beliefs: "it confirms our belief that, yes, there is a God, and yes, there is a father for all of us. . .we believe we have ancestors, and that these ancestors are important. . .the Bible talks about forefathers too. . .We drew a parallel [between Christ] and our king, Tecŭn; Umãn, who was defeated and persecuted by the Spaniards." Later, Menchú finds that the Indians can use the Bible as a weapon in the struggle for social justice, observing that the Kingdom of God where all humans are equal should be created here on earth, despite some teachings of the Church that compel Indians to be passive and accept "God's will."

Migration and Dislocation

Movement and relocation are the two primary modes for Indian living conditions, since Indian families can only spend a third of the year cultivating their own land at home in the *Altiplano*, spending most of the year away at the *finca*. When traveling to the *finca*, Indians attempt to replicate a sense of home by bringing their animals, utensils, and other small possessions, although doing so makes the long journey by truck uncomfortable and sometimes unbearable. The dislocation is underscored by the fact that Indians are covered by a tarp while traveling, making it impossible to see the countryside they cross. Furthermore, when the government begins to force Indians off their own communally developed land and onto individual parcels or uncultivated land, it exacerbates the sense of dislocation by forbidding the use of basic natural resources that are critical to the Indians survival, such as trees. The Guatemalan Forestry Commission begins to require advance permission for cutting down trees, and when permission is granted, charges the Indians exorbitantly for them, although corporations are seen freely cutting down hundreds of trees for business use.

elaborate ceremonies before the first yearly harvest of maize. Childbirth ceremonies reaffirm that humans are made of maize, and how the essence of humans can be found in maize. Maize is the lifeblood of the Quiché Indian culture.

Talk is another important representation of Quiché culture; it is through talk, spoken language, that those near death pass on their recommendations and secrets, and it is through talk that young people and newlyweds reiterate their commitment to the community and its ways. It is the inability to talk to one another that keeps the different Indian ethnicities from uniting effectively against their common oppressors, the *ladino* landowners and government. When tortured by the army, Indians have their tongues cut or split, so they will not be able to talk of the atrocities they have suffered, or pass along warnings and true stories of brutality.

Style

Setting

Menchú's story begins with the story of her parents, her orphaned father and her abandoned mother, who both matured under the same impoverished conditions as Menchú herself. In her narration, Menchú takes the reader from the dreadful conditions of the *finca* to the difficult but fulfilling communal life.

Point of View

The book is written in first person, from the point of view of Menchú, who has learned to speak Spanish through immersion. She is in her early twenties when she dictates her story to ethnographer Burgos-Debray, and she describes not only her life story, but the stories of her father and mother, other villages, and the evolution of the CUC (The United Peasants Committee).

Symbolism

There are two salient symbols which Menchú weaves through her narrative: maize and talk. Maize (corn) is the center of the Indian economy; they eat, sell, and feed their animals with maize. They hold

Literary Heritage

I, Rigoberta Menchú: An Indian Woman in Guatemala has a dual literary heritage, descending from ancient Mayan/Quiché Indian culture and shaped by modern Guatemalan social forces. As a spoken narrative which was transcribed and put into print by ethnographer Elizabeth Burgos-Debray, and translated into English by Ann Wright, Menchú's story was left virtually intact the way it was narrated. The act of telling her life story, replete with recommendations, explanations, as well as concealed information, is one of *testimonio*, a form common to Indian culture. Testimonio, or testimony, is, according to Zimmerman, ''a culminating life act,'' and Menchú's testimonio is ''like that of one who is going to die.'' In describing the funeral ceremonies in the Indian community, Menchú notes that before death, the dying will call his family to him and ''tells them his secrets, and advises them how to act in life, towards the Indian community, and towards the *ladino*. That is, everything that is handed down through the generations to preserve Indian culture.'' Essentially, that is what the peasants struggle is as well: a persistent attempt to preserve Indian culture, their way of life, in the face of *ladino* encroachment. The purpose of Menchú's narration is not only to describe this struggle, but to be a part of it.

During times of crisis, Zimmerman notes that writers evolve new forms of expression, and in Guatemala, this new form embraced the use of metonymy, using one entity to represent other things associated with it. Menchú acknowledges right away, on the first page, that her story "is the story of all poor Guatemalans." Although it seems impossible, her story is the story of all Guatemalans, not only through the use of metonymy, but accumulation. Just as the recommendations of the dying integrate the story of his life and the advice of all those who came before him, Menchú's story encompasses not only her family's life but the lives of all families like hers.

In *Teaching and Testimony*, Arata describes a "flexibility of expression" which was a "crucial part of Mayan resiliency," facilitating their survival through centuries of invasion, oppression, and hardship. Arata contends that this "ability to adapt without giving up what is most important provides a continuity through change," a statement which further clarifies how Menchú's people have managed to remain so consistent and true to the ways of their ancestors despite the relentless modernization going on around them. It is also true of the structure of her story, which is fluid, moving seamlessly between a chronological narration of events to detailed descriptions of Indian customs. Burgos-Debray explains that she left all the parts of Menchú's story in the order that it was told, despite worries that it might be confusing or boring to the reader; her editorial decision preserved the fluid, flexible structure of Menchú's narrative which places it so firmly not only in her native oral tradition, but her cultural imperatives.

Historical Context

A Thirty-five Year Civil War

When Guatemala's economy changed from an agrarian economy to an trade economy based on coffee in the late 1800s, the government needed more and more land on which to grow this lucrative cash crop. To satisfy its need for land, the government employed a strategy known as "land grabs," whereby arable land was forcibly taken from Indian villages and used to grow coffee and other cash crops. Because coffee was labor intensive to process, the government began to pressure Indian communities to work on plantations, as Pratt explains, by "passing a 'vagrancy law' requiring all landless peasants to work for at least 150 days per year for either the *fincas* or the state." This law, in conjunction with the military's takeover of Indian land (thereby rendering Indians "landless" in the eyes of the law), is the reason why Menchú's family and so many others had to migrate to the coast for most of every year to work on the *fincas*.

A new government came into power in 1944, beginning a period known as the "Ten Years of Spring," with Arbenz as president. Labor and land laws were modified to favor peasants' rights, land was taken from corporations and redistributed back to peasants. Unfortunately for the peasants, the largest corporate landowner was United Fruit Company, a U.S.-owned conglomerate, who cried foul and "Communism" back in the States, which was experiencing the McCarthy anti-Communist juggernaut; United Fruit had a monopoly on fruit exports from Guatemala, and it "stood to lose 400,000 acres," in the land redistribution, according to Pratt. The Arbenz government was overthrown in a U.S.-backed military coup in 1954, part of the United States' worldwide anti-Communism campaign, and was replaced by a military dictatorship.

Organizers such as Menchú and her family members, and Indians in general, because of their communal ways and organizing work, were labeled as Communists and became government targets nearly overnight. It was during the period of authoritarian rule following Arbenz' administration that the "land grabs" were in full force; peasant lands were once again forcibly reappropriated and peasant resistance crushed. The guerrilla movement developed in response to the government's brutal tactics, in tandem with a groundswell of grassroots organizing, such as literacy campaigns, farming cooperatives, and health initiatives for the poor. The government responded to guerrilla reprisals by organizing death squads, such as the notorious "La Mano Blanco," or the White Hand. During a peaceful occupation of the Spanish Embassy, against the protests of the Spanish ambassador, the army set fire to the building, killing all but one protester, including Menchú's father.

An irony is that the *finca* system actually brought groups of Indians into contact, a gathering which would have been difficult otherwise, given the remoteness of most Indian villages. Indians from different groups were able to meet and compare experiences and, eventually, communicate and organize. Perhaps one of the largest triumphs of the resistance was the coalition established between *ladino* peasants and Indians, manifested during the strike of over 75,000 workers in 1980. It was a coalition which could only develop when racist, classist, and linguistic barriers were finally minimized.

Critical Overview

Menchú's autobiography has been attacked by critics for being an "inauthentic" text. Critics charge that there has been "interference" from editor and ethnographer Burgos-Debray, who interviewed Menchú, or that Menchú herself exaggerated or fabricated parts of her story to make it more dramatic. One of Menchú's earliest and most vocal critics, Dinesh D'Souza, former editor of the conservative college paper the *Dartmouth Review* and author of *Illiberal Education*, questioned the veracity of Menchú's status as an impoverished victim of centuries-old discrimination, exploited by corrupt landowners. He offers her vocabulary, her later travels, and her conversion to Catholicism as dubious proof of her victimization. David Stoll, a professor at Middlebury College in Vermont, conducted years of fieldwork in Guatemala and claims to have found people whose recollections of events described by Menchú differ greatly from hers. He asserts that the truth about Guatemalan politics at that time was far less extreme and polarized than Menchú suggests, and that "the people" were more ambivalent about which side—the guerrillas or the government—to believe.

Advocates of Menchú's counter that the structure and content of Menchú's story are both accurate and typical of the period during which Menchú matures and tells her story. Zimmerman argues that in a "crisis period" such as that of the 1960s-1980s in Guatemala, that writers create "new forms representing new perspectives. . .each. . .straining to express. . .the social whole," such as the form created in Menchú's autobiography. Menchú explains her-

self, on the first page, that her story is the story of all poor Guatemalans: "My personal experience is the reality of a whole people." Menchú's supporters contend that it is not the sheer veracity of her facts that determines the value of her story in a political-social context, but that the verisimilitude of the Guatemalan peasant experience is revealed, made accessible, and honored.

Zimmerman, and others, note that Menchú does not use metaphor to develop her descriptions, but metonymy. Metonymy is a literary device which uses the name of one entity to represent the idea of all other entities associated with it. In reference to Menchú's story, that means Menchú's story, and her name, invoke the story and names of all other poor peasants. Her use of the pronoun "I," Zimmerman reasons, "is imbedded and absolutely tied to a 'we.'" In this sense, Menchú's supporters are not acknowledging and excusing falsehoods in her story, but asserting that an inconsistency or contradiction in her story does not render it an inauthentic or unimportant text, because in the balance, it tells the true story of poor Guatemalan peasants who were, in fact, exploited, tortured, and killed.

Another critical aspect of Menchú's story is the method through which it came to print. This book requires an unusual definition of authorship; is the author the person who tells the story, or the one who writes it down? Burgos-Debray, the editor of Menchú's story, assures the reader in her introduction that the narrative that Menchú relayed orally was not altered in the slightest. This book has a special status as literature, spoken narrative, autobiography, and historical text, since it is the true-life story of Rigoberta Menchú, a Quiché Indian woman. Menchú did not actually put pen to paper to write the book; it is the unabridged transcription of her story, which she told in Spanish, to ethnographer Elisabeth Burgos-Debray over the period of a week. (An ethnographer, simply put, is someone who studies other cultures.) Burgos-Debray recorded Menchú's story, transcribed it, organized it, and put the words in print, in Spanish. That book was then translated into English by Ann Wright. The exact words and the flow of the story are Rigoberta Menchú's, but others put her story into book form.

As the book is essentially the printed version of an oral narration, theorists have placed Menchú's autobiography in the genre of "testimonio," or

A Quiché woman working at her loom. Menchú, a member of this same tribe, became a leading Guatemalan activist for Indians' rights.

testimony, an oral form prevalent in Quiché culture, and a literary form common in Latin American literature, whether printed or oral.

Criticism

Lydia Kim

Lydia Kim is a teacher of world history and English literature at Cary Academy in Cary, North Carolina. In the following essay, she explains how the testimonial nature of I, Rigoberta Menchú: An Indian Woman in Guatemala *makes it difficult to judge, or even categorize, the book by Western standards of literature, including those of autobiography and biography.*

Although *I, Rigoberta Menchú* is classified as autobiography, it is, in many ways, inaccurate to call the book an autobiography or a memoir, because those texts are written largely for purposes of recalling and celebrating a life, whereas Menchú told her

What Do I Read Next?

- *Crossing Borders* is Menchú's 1998 sequel to her autobiography *I, Rigoberta Menchú: An Indian Woman in Guatemala*. In it she details her continuing work and struggles after receiving the Nobel Peace Prize in 1992.

- *Rigoberta Menchú Tum: Champion of Human Rights* is a biography of Menchú appropriate for secondary-school readers.

- *Guatemalan Women Speak*, is a collection of translated statements from *ladino* and Indian women on a broad range of topics including ''Earning a Living,'' ''Being Indian,'' and ''Fighting Back.''

- *Rigoberta Menchú and the Story of All Poor Guatemalans*, by David Stoll, is decried by supporters of Menchú as a conservative attack on Menchú's purpose in telling her story, and praised by others as an enlightening analysis of inconsistencies in Menchú's story.

- *Teaching and Testimony: Rigoberta Menchú and the North American Classroom,* a collection of essays written by college professors and teachers about the use of *I, Rigoberta Menchú: An Indian Woman in Guatemala* in their classroom, offering a comprehensive analysis of historical context, literary form, and critical theory.

- *Kaffir Boy: The True Story of a Black Youth's Coming of Age in Apartheid South Africa* is a powerful autobiography of a young man confronting the horrors of discrimination, abject poverty, and police terrorizing, and, against all odds, becoming a tennis player who eventually wins a scholarship to an American university.

---

story for the purposes of informing a larger public about human rights abuses in Guatemala. It is precisely that designation as autobiography, however, which has caused so much controversy about the veracity of her story. Critics of Menchú have alleged that Menchú includes many falsehoods and exaggerations throughout her story, events which did not occur at all or transpired differently. Her supporters contend that even if every detail of her story was not witnessed by Menchú, as a verbal account in both the oral tradition of Quiché Indians and its more recent permutation into *testimonio*, that her story cannot be judged by conventional standards of autobiography, since it was not written with the same intention or by familiar methods. Menchú's story retains its value not as autobiographical literature, but as a singular voice for thousands of silenced Guatemalans.

Her critics further allege that her claims to being a poor, uneducated Quiché Indian woman, the child of impoverished Indian peasants, are also false. They assert that she was actually the daughter of an Indian landowner, and the recipient of extended schooling well into her adolescent years. David Stoll, a professor at Middlebury College, published a book in 1998 titled *Rigoberta Menchú and the Story of All Poor Guatemalans* in which he disputes Menchú's claims that she had no formal schooling, that a brother of hers died of starvation as a child, and that another brother was murdered, burned to death before her eyes after being tortured. He claims to have found eyewitnesses who recall the situations differently. CNN.com reported on December 15, 1998, that the *New York Times* had also found such eyewitnesses who recall events differently. They assert that the land dispute Menchú details in her book as a twenty-two-year struggle between her father and *ladino* landowners was in fact a dispute between her father and his in-laws. Stoll claims that most peasants were far more ambivalent about making allegiances, given their options: the brutal and unjust Guatemalan government, or the violent and unforgiving guerilla movement. Stoll claims he is not out to debunk or delegitimize Menchú, but that he is concerned about the political momentum

> Menchú's *testimonio* is replete with recommendations, explanations, as well as secrets; it is, according to Zimmerman, 'a culminating life act,' which aggregates the experiences of many Guatemalans into one narrative."

created by what may be a falsified story, momentum which led to Menchú being awarded the Nobel Peace Prize in 1992.

Menchú has explained these inconsistencies with a combination of cultural background and political imperative. In a response reported on CNN.com on January 21, 1999, Menchú stated, "I still haven't written my autobiography. . .what you have is a testimonial." She counters reports that there was no brother who died of starvation on the *finca* by explaining that Indian families often give the same name to more than one child; in her family there was a Nicolas I and Nicolas II. She also chides Stoll, saying that as the expert, he should have known that. She confirms that she did participate in literacy classes run by nuns at a Catholic boarding school, but that she was there as a maid, not a student. Stoll, for his part, insists he never called Menchú a liar, but that as "[t]he book expresses 500 years of Native American experience in the eyes of a woman born in 1959. . .It can't be a literal truth." Given that he believes this, it is baffling that he would spend ten years trying to find and substantiate falsehoods in Menchú's account.

Menchú narrated her story in a tradition that is both centuries old and shaped by modern forces. Her Quiché Indian heritage relies heavily on oral tradition to pass precepts, information, morals, and history from one generation to the next. As a twentieth-century Guatemalan peasant, her story is also told in the ritual manner of *testimonio*, or testimony, a form which is common in modern Latin American narratives. In both, there is a sense of shared history to be recounted, a collective memory and experience which any narrator adds to when telling his or her story. Menchú's *testimonio* is replete with recommendations, explanations, as well as secrets; it is, according to Zimmerman, "a culminating life act," which aggregates the experiences of many Guatemalans into one narrative. Her use of the pronoun "I," Zimmerman explains, "is imbedded and absolutely tied to a 'we.'" In a CNN report from February 12, 1999, Menchú declared, "The book that is being questioned is a testimonial that mixes my personal testimony and the testimony of what happened in Guatemala. . .The book that is being questioned is not my biography." Menchú agrees and acknowledges that the book is not her biography; indeed it was never intended to be read as a biography or autobiography. In Indian (and to some extent, Latin American) culture no one's story exists in an individualized vacuum, distinct from this collective memory and experience.

The purpose of Menchú's *testimonio* is twofold: to inform the global community about the plight of her people, and to be of service to her people by being their voice. In her book *Reconstructing Womanhood: The Emergence of the Afro-American Woman Novelist*, Hazel Carby describes a similar process undertaken by Frances Ellen Watkins Harper, a black female writer in the crisis period of post-Reconstruction, in writing her novel *Iola Leroy*. Addressing the horrors of slavery and its effects, Harper writes passages which "shift from the individual experiences of her character to the experience of a race." Harper undertakes an endeavor similar to Menchú's in attempting to give voice to her community, previously silenced by exclusion from the government and the press, as well as from language and literacy acquisition.

This is not to say that lies are acceptable if the text is written for purposes of political persuasion or enlightenment, but Menchú does counter and explain each of Stoll's charges. Menchú affirms, on the first page, "This is my testimony. I didn't learn it from a book, and I didn't learn it alone." This statement underscores the fact that her testimony was *learned*, both from other people, and from her own experience, not something which merely happened that she is now just retelling. As reported on CNN.com on February 12, 1999, she asked a New York audience to read her book and "focus attention on the need to investigate and prosecute massacres, kidnappings, and widespread torture during Guatemala's 36-year civil war." Her supporters contend that detailed authenticity does not determine the worthiness of Menchú's activism.

Since Western academic categories do not recognize *testimonio* as a familiar narrative form, Menchú's book is erroneously categorized as autobiography. But why apply standards of accuracy, plot development, or narrative form of autobiography to a form which is inherently different in purpose and heritage? Western-style autobiography attempts to dramatize one's life story so that the reader may vicariously experience or genuinely empathize with the events in others' lives. *Testimonio* seeks to accumulate and recount one's own experiences and those of one's community, in order to enlighten and provoke others to action. Stoll's and other's challenges to Menchú's *testimonio*, even if proven true, will not mitigate her status as a Nobel Prize laureate, or her international prominence as a human rights activist. The implication that the mere taint of fiction should diminish the credibility of Menchú's story and her purpose is clearly a political argument, one which denies the altogether different structure, intent, and history of *testimonio* and oral tradition, its standing as a widespread cultural practice, and its legitimacy in Menchú's cultural sphere.

Is the point, then, to discredit Menchú's book as literature, thereby rendering it unfit for use in the classroom? If so, one must return to the point that Menchú's book does not fit neatly into the category of autobiography and its dramatic requirements of a captivating plot, well-developed characters, and handily resolved conflicts. Her story is a testimony of events which occurred in Guatemala, events which she wanted to bring to the world's attention for purposes of ending the suffering and exploitation of her people. Menchú's story does not make use of literary conventions that Western readers are accustomed to, expressly because hers is a "resistant literature." She does not want the reader to identify with her, like a sympathetic character in a novel, but to listen to her; she keeps the reader at a distance, rather than develop her character in the book and invite the reader to have complete empathy. As Ann Wright, the translator of Menchú's book, puts it, "Her words want us to understand and react." The book is not recognizably canonical, but it can, however, play an important part in classes where the purpose is to investigate and analyze oral history and political narratives.

In addition, readers of the translated English version are reading a text which is, in Moneyhun's words, "several times removed from whatever we might recognize as Menchú's 'real world,'" because translation is not "simply a negotiation between language but between mind sets and world

views." So critics who challenge and denounce Menchú for inconsistencies in her story are doing so based on a text which is not in its original, authentic form. Menchú told her story to ethnographer Elizabeth Burgos-Debray over the course of a week, who then transcribed it and put it into print in Spanish; that Spanish print version was then translated by Ann Wright. Subsequent to Menchú's oral testimony, the printed version was shaped by Burgos-Debray, although she denies doing so in the introduction, only to contradict herself a paragraph later. Burgos-Debray has her own worldview and literary and linguistic influences, as does translator Ann Wright. It is possible that this process of translating, first into Spanish print and then into English, transforms Menchú's story from *testimonio* to oral history. The difference between oral history and *testimonio*, according to John Beverly, is that "in oral history, it is the intentionality of the recorder— usually a social scientist—that is dominant. . .In *testimonio*, it is the intentionality of the narrator that is paramount. . .*testimonio* has to involve an urgency to communicate, a problem of repression, poverty. . .[a] struggle for survival, implicated in the act of narration itself." In other words, Menchú's story does not have to be entirely hers, nor entirely personally true, for it to be effective, edifying, motivating, or provocative.

Since she is taking advantage of a rare opportunity to be the voice of a previously silenced people, she is responding to the pressure to tell the story of the whole accurately and poignantly. It is not the sheer veracity of her facts that determines the value of her story in a political-social context, but that the truth of the Guatemalan peasant experience is revealed, comprehended, and honored.

Source: Lydia Kim, in an essay for *Literature of Developing Nations for Students*, Gale, 2000.

Norma Stoltz Chinchilla

In the following essay, Norma Stoltz Chinchilla examines Rigoberta Menchú's autobiography, I, Rigoberta Menchú)*, the charges made by author David Stoll that the autobiography is not authentic, and Stoller's assertion that Menchú's actions functioned to prolong the war.*

Long before David Stoll's book appeared and the *New York Times* journalist Larry Rohter (1998) gleefully proclaimed it a definitive expose of Guatemala's only Nobel Prize winner since Miguel Angel

Asturias (and the only indigenous female, let alone Guatemalan, to become an international icon), there were articles and interviews purporting to summarize Stoll's argument and his motives for advancing it. From exposure to a few of these I formed my first impressions of his project and was willing to give his motives for devoting ten years of his life to it the benefit of the doubt.

I seriously questioned the timing of a book that would most certainly tarnish the reputation of one of the few objects of international pride Guatemalans have had in the past few decades and worried that its appearance would make an already difficult process of reconciliation more so. But I was willing to concede that Stoll's inquiry, however uncomfortable and disagreeable, might lead to a useful reexamination of the idealizations that inevitably emerge during a war. I was interested in honest discussions of a revolutionary strategy that, in retrospect, had underestimated the power of the enemy and carried such a high cost in human lives, particularly those of indigenous Guatemalans. I knew from experience that complexities, nuances, and contradictions are typically overlooked or go unmentioned in the course of mobilizing support for one or another side in a war or in efforts to stop widespread human rights violations.

If, I reasoned, all Stoll intended to do was to show that Rigoberta's autobiography might have been partly a composite or an oversimplified account, crafted in a historical context that required a certain amount of clandestinity and dissimulation to survive, that could be useful information for those who studied and used oral histories. Again, if it was an account partially shaped by the international audience with whom she was trying to communicate—the First World anthropologist to whom she first told her story and later the audiences in the United States whose sympathy with the plight of indigenous peoples, human rights victims, and activists for change she sought—that might be important to know. Furthermore, different regions of Guatemala had undoubtedly experienced the army, the revolutionary movement, and the violence differently, and reconstruction of events in specific communities could be useful in spite of methodological difficulties such as the fact that many witnesses are dead and survivors tend to shape interpretations to fit those of the victors. Reconstruction of village experiences might be useful even if, as in this case, the villages were not representative of those most sympathetic to the revolutionary movement or those most subject to army retaliation.

Reading the book, however, disabused me of my original generosity about Stoll's agenda and intentions. His aim is to question not only whether Rigoberta Menchu was an eyewitness to the events she describes and whether the story she tells about her family and community coincides with that of others but whether her testimony is a valid account of how the violence began and whether Indians who sided with the revolutionary movement did so out of conviction or out of pragmatism, fear, and manipulation. He suggests that, in fact, Rigoberta and the solidarity movement promoted a mythical interpretation of the origins of the war and that Rigoberta's telling of "her" story around the world actually prolonged the war.

Revisionist History

In Stoll's revisionist version of recent Guatemalan history (one supported by few sources other than army apologists), the real cause of poverty is not conflicts between impoverished peasants, mostly Indian, and landed oligarchy, mostly ladino, but rapid population growth. As he sees it, the primary source of conflict in the countryside is tensions among indigenous peasants over land, and the real cause of genocide is not the systematic implementation of counterinsurgency plans (such as Plan Ixil and President Efrain Rios Montt's Plan Victoria '82, devised in consultation with U.S. military advisers and implemented by military officers trained in the United States in the 1960s and 1970s) (Black, 1984) but the actions of "panicked" soldiers and "a homicidal sector" of the officer corps baited by the guerrillas. The "indiscriminate" massacres of many innocent civilians, in Stoll's view, were an understandable if regrettable response to the strategy of "irregular war," in which combatants and civilians cannot be clearly distinguished. Army and guerrilla violence are roughly equivalent. He never discusses the historical links between Guatemalan army violence and U.S. training and advice and never asks why torture, extrajudicial disappearances, and attacks on unarmed civilians have been hallmarks of counterinsurgency campaigns in Latin American countries without rural insurgencies or why the repression extended to villages with little direct involvement in the revolutionary movement.

In Stoll's version, Guatemalan Indians were recruited to a strategy that had "failed" even before the movement's heyday in the 1970s and the army massacres of the 1980s. He implies that guerrilla leaders knew of the risks involved but failed to give peasants and Indians adequate "consumer protection warnings'' before joining. Anyone who knows the history of armed revolutionary movements in Latin America knows, however, that the defeat of Che in Bolivia had little to do with the Guatemalan guerrilla movement in the 1980s. Che and his band never managed to get to first base with Bolivian peasants. But Guatemalan revolutionaries incorporated Indian as well as Christian (liberation) philosophy into their theoretical frameworks, learned some of the local languages, spent years studying local conditions, and, unlike Che in Bolivia, recruited successfully from local populations in their areas of greatest strength. One movement was based on the foco guerrilla war strategy and the other on ''popular war'' more akin to the Vietnam experience (which eventually resulted in independence).

Given the long history of racial/ethnic division, state-sponsored repression, and generalized mistrust in Guatemalan culture, what is extraordinary is the degree of support the revolutionary movement had among rural Indians and ladinos in the 1970s and early 1980s. Not all rural Indians and ladinos, perhaps not even the majority, supported the revolutionary movement. Rarely does any social change movement that has a high degree of risk mobilize a majority of those who are supposed to benefit from it. Nor was there a perfect fit between the goals and dreams of those who supported the movement and those who led it or a homogeneity of motives among the active and passive supporters affiliated with it at different times in different places. There never is. Gaps between the rhetoric and coherent narrative of leaders and the agendas and experiences of followers are a given in social movements, as are exaggerated claims of representation. But what is undeniable is that, after the victory of the Sandinista revolution in 1979 and prior to the Rios Montt coup that implemented a coherent counterinsurgency strategy and centralized military command in 1982, both the Central Intelligence Agency (CIA) and revolutionary sympathizers believed that the Guatemalan revolutionary movement was a real contender for power. Through the 1970s, popular (unarmed) movements demanding land, better wages and working conditions, and an end to repression were strong, heterogeneous, and broadly based. It was partly their strength, particularly in indigenous areas, and, later, the threat of an indigenous insurrection, rather than the threat of the guerrillas alone, that caused the army's response.

Thus, the armed revolutionary strategy adopted in the 1970s did not seem doomed then as it may appear to have been today. If, in retrospect, it is important to question whether it was justified, given its human costs, the counterinsurgency capacity of the army, and the international context (particularly the resolve of the United States not to let another Nicaraguan revolution take place in the region), as some former guerrilla strategists and activists themselves have done, it is with the benefit of hindsight. And if the adoption of an armed revolutionary popular-war strategy indeed closed off opportunities for other forms of resistance, this was not evident in the 1970s when organizing within this framework began.

The Human Agency of Indigenous Revolutionaries

Despite denials, Stoll seems to believe that Indians who joined the revolutionary movement in the 1970s or participated in the beginnings of rural insurrections between 1970 and 1982 (not led or directed by the National Guatemalan Revolutionary Unity [Unidad Revolucionaria Nacional Guatemalteca-URNG]) were not really capable of pursuing their own political agenda but were misled or used. Indians, like other poor people, are thus better understood as victims or dupes rather than historical agents. He also seems to believe that the presence of economically better-off rural or urban leaders or intermediaries (priests, nuns, missionaries, university and high school students, middle peasants, etc.) undermines a movement's claims to be fighting poverty, illiteracy, and inequality. More literate and educated people are always catalysts for social movements on behalf of the poor, disenfranchised, and dispossessed. Few social movements would qualify if we removed those led by individuals who came from more literate and economically comfortable backgrounds.

> "...I was willing to concede that Stoll's inquiry, however uncomfortable and disagreeable, might lead to a useful reexamination of the idealizations that inevitably emerge during a war."

Stoll recognizes that a number of Indians were guerrilla combatants and cadres, including middle-level leaders, in several revolutionary organizations, but he uses the fact that leaders at the highest levels were ladino to diminish the significance of their participation. While we can and should be critical of the relative absence of women and Indians in high-level leadership positions in the Guatemalan guerrilla movement, this criticism should not be allowed to obscure the significance of the hundreds who joined the movement with agendas that both paralleled and diverged from those of top leaders. Women, for example, frequently saw participation in the revolution as a vehicle through which sexism and discrimination could be addressed, despite the reluctance of leaders to raise these issues directly (see Chinchilla, 1998), and Indian women and men joined the revolution to address issues related to racism as well as economic exploitation.

Rigoberta and the Human Rights and Solidarity Movements

There is no doubt that many people in the United States who met Rigoberta for the first time in the early 1980s were impressed, moved, and even transfixed by her. She was young, articulate, and intelligent. For those of us who knew Guatemala, the fact that an indigenous woman from a country where Indians had been marginalized and subordinated could connect so well with audiences of people so different from her was extraordinary. Rigoberta left lasting impressions on cynical journalists and television interviewers as well.

Powerful as Rigoberta's book and, even more, her persona were in reaching uninitiated audiences, heads of state, and international diplomats, however, *I, Rigoberta Menchu* was hardly the human rights and solidarity movement's "little red book," and Rigoberta was never its leader. If it turns out to be true that scholars were not skeptical enough about Rigoberta's representations of her particular family and village, it is because the outlines of her account coincided with those of many other reputable sources, including a landmark study of land concentration and landlessness by the U.S. Agency for International Development published in 1982 and eyewitness and secondhand accounts by missionaries, priests, nuns, ministers, anthropologists, Peace Corps volunteers, journalists, refugees and immigrants, and United Nations workers.

While the popularity of Rigoberta's book on college campuses may have made it a key source for some students and teachers who knew little else about Guatemala, for the Guatemalan solidarity, human rights, and scholars groups it was hardly the only or even the most important one. At the national and international level, people concerned about Guatemala were never dependent solely on URNG representatives for their information about political conditions and human rights. Amnesty International, Americas Watch, scholars, journalists, and a myriad of church groups took great pains to document the situation and design campaigns for stopping the repression.

Even the National Network in Solidarity with Guatemala (NISGUA), formed in the early 1980s, had a wide range of groups and members as its affiliates-pacifists, armed-struggle supporters, liberals, socialists, human rights activists, atheists, clerics, missionaries, ordinary churchgoers, students and professionals, Spanish teachers, artists, anthropologists, archaeologists, world travelers, hippies, (U.S.) Native Americans, weavers and importers of indigenous crafts, and others. The URNG analysis of events and strategies was always available in NISGUA, but it was certainly not embraced without question. The most enduring point of unity in NISGUA was working to end serious human rights violations and changing U.S. policy. As Marilyn Moors, who worked closely with Washington, DC, groups and the national office, told me in a recent conversation, "Never have I known a network made up of more contentious groups and individuals than NISGUA in the 1980s." Her observation coincides with my own firsthand experience.

Groups affiliated with the solidarity and human rights networks included many Guatemalan activists, some of them recent immigrants, representing a variety of ages and classes, ethnic, religious, and political backgrounds. The Guatemalan solidarity committee with which I worked in Los Angeles always had access to a wide variety of opinions from families of committee members and the large Guatemalan immigrant community, numbering somewhere between 100,000 and 200,000, including some 2,000 to 3,000 Q'anjob'al Indians. These voices included those of URNG supporters and combatants, former government soldiers and deserters, Q'anjob'al Indians who had worked with the Ejercito Guerrillo de los Pobres (Guerrilla Army of the Poor-EGP) and others who claimed to have been victimized by it, priests who supported the movement and priests who did not, Guatemalans who were Marxists and Guatemalans who were staunch anticommunists, and a variety of political party activists from left to right. People in the solidarity movement who had grown up in Guatemala or who had deep roots there were very familiar with the complexities and contradictions and the many levels of meaning, overt and hidden, of a social reality characterized more by repression than by democracy and trust.

Likewise, the Guatemala Scholars' Network, which began with some 20 members in the early 1980s and grew to some 350, has always been a politically and philosophically diverse group, as Stoll, who himself has been a member for some years, undoubtedly knows. The Scholars' Network included well-informed individuals with long experience in Guatemala. If we add together the Guatemalan activists, the scholar activists, and other students, journalists, and ex-missionaries and clerics, we undoubtedly had more people with firsthand knowledge of Guatemala in all its complexity than any other similar support movement in recent history. Behind the activism was a deep appreciation for historical context that Stoll, despite his anthropology training, surprisingly lacks.

If Stoll wishes to be taken seriously, he must do more than substitute one superficial, unidimensional stereotype for another. His portrayal of the Guatemala solidarity movement and the network of activist scholars who undertook human rights and solidarity work in the 1980s is little more than a caricature.

Reaction to the Book in Guatemala

Stoll asserts that anyone who subscribes to a historical view of the origins of army violence by dating it to the 1960s or to elite fears generated by land reform and the mobilization of workers and peasants during the 1944–1954 reform movements (violently brought to an end through a CIA-supported coup) and anyone who believes that poverty, discrimination, repression, and inequality created fertile ground for revolution has "bought into" the URNG line. Human rights agencies, solidarity organizations, the United Nations, European governments, scholars, religious people, and ordinary citizens have fallen for this URNG-propagated myth, Stoll believes, because Rigoberta's testimony has given it credibility.

But this version of history, in one form or another, is also shared by many Guatemalans, including those not necessarily sympathetic to the revolutionary movement. Guatemala's foreign minister, who recently spoke at my university, for example, cited poverty, discrimination, political repression, inequality, and a lack of democracy as the principal reasons for the war. The local deputy consul general talks in similar terms. Furthermore, most Guatemalans believe that Rigoberta's narrative is essentially true, if not for her and her family then for the many other Indians who suffered during the war. They remark on the naivete of a white North American anthropologist's traipsing through areas controlled or previously controlled by the army that have suffered repression asking questions about politics and clandestine organizations. They are stunned to learn, for example, that a trained anthropologist could ask the mayor of Uspantín if people in his town had been organized by the Committee for Campesino Unity and take his answer ("I don't recall calling a CUC meeting") at face value. With the indigenous poet Humberto Akabal, they believe that "in Guatemala, it is not that the rocks can't talk; it is that they don't want to." The debate over Stoll's critique of Rigoberta's book in the Guatemalan press was intense for little more than two weeks and then became insignificant. More important, most Guatemalan writers or politicians, including notoriously conservative and anticommunist ones such as Jorge Skinner-Klee and Carlos Manuel Pellecer, have found little in Stoll's argument with which they could identify. Skinner-Klee has gone so far as to call Rigoberta's book "a Guatemalan epic" on the order of the *Odyssey* or the *Iliad*.

Stoll's version of the U.S. human rights and solidarity movements is naive at best and opportunist at worst. He must impeach not only Rigoberta but the whole of the human rights and solidarity movement to create space for his idiosyncratic version of recent Guatemalan history. He attempts to do this by caricaturing the movements and arguing that Rigoberta's testimony was their centerpiece. He gives little consideration to how his own positionality may have shaped his choice of an entry point into developed-country culture wars. He is unapologetic about his use of an inherently problematic methodology and insufficiently concerned about how the time and circumstances of his first entries into the region (in the middle of the worst of the war in the 1980s, when reportedly only the army and people sympathetic to it trusted him) might have shaped his understanding of rural indigenous Guatemala or how his conducting interviews in areas where he does not speak the local language may have influenced what people chose to tell him. In the end, it is Stoll the journalist rather than Stoll the scholar who pursues what some have called the ''symbolic impeachment'' of Rigoberta Menchu's testimony.

Source: Norma Stoltz Chinchilla, ''Of Straw Men and Stereotypes: Why Guatemalan Rocks Don't Talk,'' in *Latin American Perspectives,* Vol. 26, No. 6, November, 1999, pp. 29–37.

Roger N. Lancaster

In the following review of Rigoberta Menchú's I, Rigoberta Menchú, *Roger N. Lancaster examines controversies over the authenticity of the author's autobiography (developed originally as testimony emerging from relationships between U.S., European and Latin-American solidarity movements) by examining the literary form by which her testimony was developed and the goals she sought to meet with it.*

Two recent news items on Guatemala have made headlines in North American papers. One is the publication of the report of the UN Commission for Historical Clarification, which found the Guatemalan army overwhelmingly responsible for the political massacres that left some 200,000 Mayans dead or missing in the course of that country's 36-year civil war. The other comes from reports questioning the veracity of the biography of the best-known spokesperson for Guatemala's indigenous peoples, Rigoberta Menchu.

Clearly, the present airings of doubt about Rigoberta Menchu's life story are emblematic of the political skepticism of the 1990s—a decade that witnessed the collapse of really-existing socialism, the failure of Sandinismo in Nicaragua and the retreat of progressives everywhere from any semblance of a radical engagement or a global vision. We have to understand the present zeitgeist to understand why such stories now show up on the front pages of *The New York Times.*

The present controversies surrounding *I, Rigoberta Menchu* also require an understanding of how its literary-polemical form, the testimonio, or testimony, emerged in the 1970s and 1980s. The testimony grew out of the unique relationship between popular movements in Latin America—especially Central America—and solidarity movements in the United States and Western Europe. The goal of the testimony was to didactically convey salient sociological facts to a Northern audience through an exemplary life history, and to thereby solicit moral, political and economic support for local struggles.

Revolutionary upheavals in Central America were in no small part struggles over basic material resources. These conflicts acquired horrific scale and brutality owing to the racist legacies of colonialism and the entrenchment of landed elites in authoritarian governments and abusive militaries. Communicating complex historical lessons like these has always been difficult, but it proved well-nigh impossible to convey the salient facts against a Reagan propaganda offensive demonizing Communist aggression in ''our backyard.''

The testimony offered an end-run around these obstacles. It attempted to convey an analysis of indisputable facts of scale—inequality, racism, repression and struggle—through the details of an individual life. Like its antecedent—the ethnobiographies collected by Oscar Lewis—the testimony condensed a life history into a single argument about a big picture. Therein lay the polemical strength but also the analytical weakness of the form. The testimony is convincing, not because it offers a studied, exhaustive analysis of social structures or historical developments, but because it weaves a narrative of discovery as an autobiographical tale: The author comes to the Truth simply by knowing his or her own experiences, by claiming his or her own voice, by possessing his or her self. The appeal of the story is thus based on the authoritative voice of the speaker, who stands as a representative of larger social groups.

Rigoberta Menchu's life story was more successful than myriad other testimonies of the period because, in the circulation of meanings on a global scale, it better reflected the tastes and interests of its intended audience in the United States and Western Europe. Page by page, Menchu's life appears as a straightforward morality play about the coming-to-consciousness of a poor Indian peasant woman. As with didactic Hollywood movies, nothing complicates the picture, where poor Indians struggle against rich Ladinos. Menchu's struggles are those of Everywoman, her story is the story of all poor Guatemalans.

But individual life history seldom dovetails so clearly with the larger course of social history, much less with the demands of an audience craving clear-cut tales of unmediated authenticity. Individuals cannot really exemplify the singular experiences or uniform interests of larger groups. Poor Indian peasant women invariably turn out to have varied experiences, opinions and interests.

What was long whispered in solidarity circles and suspected by academics who used *I, Rigoberta Menchu* now appears to have been empirically documented: Some of the narrator's details do not quite square with the facts, at least the facts as recalled by other eye witnesses. With a middle-school education, Menchu was undoubtedly better educated than her story lets on. Three of Menchu's siblings died, apparently under circumstances bearing some resemblance to but not quite identical with events she describes. The central land struggle in Menchu's autobiography undeniably happened in the context of a highly stratified social system in which Spanish-speaking Ladinos wield power and wealth, but this particular conflict occurred not between poor Indians and rich Ladinos but, as is so often the case, between related indigenous families, neither of whom could be described as wealthy or powerful. And so on.

In short, Menchu appears to have told her story in a manner that force-fits her and her family's experiences into the social analysis she wished to dramatize. The narrator thus becomes Exemplary Rigoberta, the very personification of Maya struggles, edited and airbrushed into an icon who stands outside the course of real-life events (which are always complex) to embody a simplified lesson, a clear purpose, a Pure Idea.

Narrative devices like these—the use of composite personas, shadings of events—would have scarcely raised an eyebrow in a properly qualified ethnographic work or in an historical novel. But they undercut the authority of a text that purports to tell us the unvarnished truth—indeed, that reports to embody the truth, in a singular persona—without proviso or caveats. It cannot be said that anyone has come out very well in the ensuing brouhaha.

After casting himself as the Matt Drudge of anthropology, David Stoll has insisted that he never intended to attack or discredit Menchu. This is not very convincing. Stoll suggests in an interview in the March/April 1999 issue of *NACLA* that his real aim is to contribute to a critical reassessment of the guerrilla struggles of the 1970s and 1980s. But poking holes in Menchu's autobiography does not demonstrate his by-now familiar refrain that violence only begets more violence. If one's goal were a balanced assessment, it would be far more logical to suggest that whatever semblance of formal democracy that now exists in Guatemala, El Salvador and Nicaragua owes its existence to the very revolutionary movements Stoll now disparages.

> Individuals cannot really exemplify the singular experiences or uniform interests of larger groups. Poor Indian peasant women invariably turn out to have varied experiences, opinions and interests."

Menchu, for her part, has responded by questioning the timing of Stoll's book and *The New York Times* reporting it stimulated. She has suggested that such unflattering reportage is part of a conspiracy designed to cast doubt on the findings of the Guatemalan truth commission. In *NACLA*, the *Times*, and other vehicles, Menchu falls back on two standard defenses: Are you saying my brother isn't dead? Are you saying Indians are all liars? Once again, Menchu conflates her own persona with the people and with the movement.

Perhaps most disappointing have been the responses coming from the North American academic left. "I don't care whether it's true or not," huffs one scholar in *The Chronicle of Higher Education* . Others insist that Menchu's account is, in effect, still true, even if it is not. The Guatemala Scholars Network insists that Menchu was awarded the Nobel Peace Prize not because she watched her brother being burned alive or because she was eye-witness to horrific violence, but because of her role as a public spokesperson for the indigenous rights movement. Such a statement evades the obvious. Menchu was awarded the Prize precisely because she wove a convincing narrative about the deaths of her family members into a story about ethnic, class and political conflicts. Her family indeed met gruesome deaths at the hands of the state. But would her tale have had the same force, would it have received the same accolades, had it begun in the real-life complexity of land conflicts between related indigenous families?

Although Menchu's testimony has never much affected the course of indigenous rights or political mobilization inside Guatemala, her impact on solidarity politics, higher education and multiculturalism in the United States and other Northern countries has been more profound. For a time, she stood as an object lesson on the truth of identity and the power of authentic voices. Her testimony was touted as a new model of writing, one that superseded the traditional canon, standards of argumentation, and demands for ethnographic verification. She was appropriated as the most accessible of the postcolonials, and an image of Menchu was shaped that compounded the bases of identity politics—poor, Indian, peasant, woman. On this count, the left, in effect, fell prey to its own worst impulses—a tendency to romanticize noble natives and to oversimplify the nature of social struggles in stratified societies.

It is not just for academic reasons that editorial airbrushing and oversimplification are bad practices. Iconization is a bad practice for the left because it offers a fake resolution for the real complexities and dilemmas of history. The emotional work performed by icons is good for rallying the faithful, but proves incompatible with effective struggle. Halos illuminate nothing. The facts matter. Details matter. Complexity matters. Any left incapable of working through the facts in all their complexity will be by definition inadequate to the task it poses.

This is no small point. Accuracy about the shape of local struggles is of critical importance, as Alejandro Bendafia's study of demobilized Contras, *Una Tragedia Campesina: Testimonios de la Resistencia,* illustrates. When the triumphant Sandinistas brought the revolution into remote areas of Nicaragua after their 1979 victory, they were drawn into pre-existing land feuds between contending campesino kin groups and political factions—disputes much like those to which Menchu's relatives were party. Preaching the gospel of redistributive justice and class empowerment, inexperienced cadre took an oversimplified approach to the crazy-quilt patchwork of alliances they encountered in the countryside. In consequence, they sometimes took land from poor peasants to give to other poor peasants. Such mistakes, repeated wherever the FSLN had shallow roots or failed to understand local conflicts, embittered a section of the rural poor and created the Contra base that was so effectively mobilized by Washington.

But mistakes in practice and interpretation notwithstanding, some basic facts remain: Large numbers of people in Central America joined revolutionary struggles in the 1970s and 1980s not because they were deceived by clever storytellers who wielded details in a slippery manner, but because gross inequalities and political repression led them to the conclusion that only revolutionary movements could implement the desired changes.

Who is telling that story in a plausible, methodical manner today?

Source: Roger N. Lancaster, ''Rigoberta's Testimonio,'' in *NACLA Report on the Americas,* Vol. 32, Issue 6, May–June, 1999, p. 4.

Jo-Marie Burt and Fred Rosen

*In the following interview with Rigoberta Menchú (author of the autobiography,*I, Rigoberta Menchú*), Burt and Rosen discuss the controversies over the authenticity of the author's biography and the Recovery of Historical Memory (REMHI) project, which collected evidence of civil-war abuses in Guatemala.*

Rigoberta Menchu, who was awarded the Nobel Peace Prize in 1992 and has been a tireless activist for indigenous and human rights, has become the subject of controversy. Last fall, anthropologist David Stoll, a professor at Middlebury College, published a book entitled *Rigoberta Menchu and the Story of All Poor Guatemalans* (Westview Press, 1998), in which he questions many aspects of Rigoberta's life story presented in *I, Rigoberta Menchu: An Indian Woman in Guatemala* (Verso, 1984). On December 15, *The New York Times* ran a front-page story reporting on the controversy, and sent one of its sleuthing reporters to Guatemala to corroborate some of Stoll's findings. In the midst of the controversy, Guatemala is still struggling to consolidate its fragile peace and to find ways of addressing the legacies of 36 years of war. In this interview, which took place on February 10 in the NACLA offices, Rigoberta discusses the controversy and its impact on the current political situation in Guatemala. NACLA correspondent Steve Dudley interviewed David Stoll by telephone on January 26.

Last year, the Recovery of Historical Memory (REMHI) project, which documented the testimonies of the victims of Guatemala's civil war, made public its final report. The UN Commission on Historical Clarification is scheduled to release its final report in late February. How would you describe these two processes and their relevance to building peace in Guatemala today?

The REMHI and the UN Commission are tremendously important because they have exhaustively documented the nature of the crimes committed by the Guatemalan armed forces during the 36-year conflict. We now know the names and stories of many of the victims—as well as of the victimizers.

The REMHI was particularly important because it established a new methodology for recovering the testimonies of the thousands of people who suffered these crimes. Most investigations are run by a few experts who show up and ask questions and tell people how to present their testimonies. But the REMHI was designed to be a participatory investigation, in which community leaders—many of whom were Mayan—interviewed over 6,000 victims and eyewitnesses. This made it possible to collect information about more than 50,000 cases of human rights violations, and out of these individual memories to begin to construct a collective memory.

Monsignor Gerardi, who led the REMHI, paid with his life so that this project could materialize. The Monsignor's death was a tremendous blow to us, but we continue to work in defense of human rights in honor of his memory.

REMHI has been described as a process of recovering memory ''from below.'' How would you characterize this process and its relationship to the work of the UN Commission?

The REMHI set the standard for truth-seeking; this was important because that meant that the UN Commission had to rise to the level of the REMHI report. In many ways, the two reports are complimentary, and together they have succeeded in breaking the fear and terror that have dominated Guatemalan society for so long.

More than 80% of all the testimonies collected by REMHI were of indigenous people. The REMHI made it possible that their great and painful story be heard. It marks the first time in our history that indigenous people were active participants in the writing of their own history. And they were also participants in drawing up the recommendations for the future to ensure that these atrocities never happen again. It was also a small compensation to the victims for all they had suffered—for the first time they could tell their stories without fear and be certain that it was not in vain.

The other main achievement of the REMHI project is that no one can now deny what happened in Guatemala. There was a systematic campaign of genocide and ethnocide against the indigenous peoples of Guatemala. REHMI represents a struggle against forgetting. A struggle against indifference. Many people have been victims of the violence, and

❞ We believe there is a malicious element in all of this, and, moreover, that it is politically motivated. We are unsure where this political campaign is coming from. But we have no doubt that there are sectors who do not want the people to tell their stories."

not everyone has told their story. But it is no longer a question of individual guilt; it is a national tragedy.

Our hope is that this will contribute to a process of reconciliation, of coming together, of rebuilding confidence in the future. For finding and uncovering the truth gives us an opportunity to start all over again.

Isn't it true that there are social forces in Guatemala who do not want this process of truth-telling to continue?

Clearly. For example, REMHI and the UN Commission were denied access to the secret files of the G-2, one of the most feared secret police forces in the past. Nor did they have access to the important files of the army or the national police.

The Association of Military Veterans reportedly has its own files, which it has not made available. There are also those who say, ''Well yes, the indigenous people were killed, but it was necessary. The army was just carrying out its mission. Rios Montt didn't want to kill. He just wanted to bring things under control. The Communists and theologians manipulated the situation and exposed the people by creating a myth.''

So there is a tendency to want to clean up the image of the dirty war. But the truth uncovered by the REMHI can no longer be hidden. It cannot be undone. It is now part of the historical record.

How do you respond to the charges by numerous critics, stemming from the book published by David Stoll questioning aspects of your first book, *I, Rigoberta Menchu,* that your story is at least partly fabricated? Has this controversy had any effect on the process you have been describing?

We have had many meetings with human rights groups and various indigenous organizations in Guatemala, and we are all concerned because the discussion has been brought to a personal level, to attempt to dispute the story of Rigoberta Menchu.

In many ways, during the 1980s, I was a solitary indigenous voice, the only survivor, upon whom fell the task of traveling the world, going to the UN and to human rights groups around the world to tell them of what was happening in Guatemala. Now there is an effort to say that this solitary voice is not valid. But this is not the 1980s, when people were silent and there were many reasons to worry; now we are over 30,000 strong, and every story being told, every testimony gathered by REMHI and the UN Commission, is part of the broader tapestry of thousands of stories that are being woven together to write our history. Mine is just one page among thousands that have confirmed what really happened in Guatemala.

The implication of the charges is that if Rigoberta Menchu—the best-known Indian from Guatemala, a Nobel laureate—is lying, then these Indians who are unknown must also be lying. We believe there is a malicious element in all of this, and, moreover, that it is politically motivated. We are unsure where this political campaign is coming from. But we have no doubt that there are sectors who do not want the people to tell their stories. In some way, there is a complicity here. If during the 1980s someone said that I was telling lies, and those charges had been investigated, they would have discovered the extreme violence going on in my country. The onslaught against the indigenous population was just beginning when I fled Guatemala, so they might have helped prevent the 422 massacres that took place.

Of course there are omissions in my book. Among the most evident omission is in relation to my brother Patrocinio. The names of the witnesses who saw the torture and who told the story are left out. These were conscious omissions because in the context of the 1980s this was necessary to protect the lives of those who remained in Guatemala. If I had said my sister Anita was with my mother when they burned my brother Patrocinio, I would have been exposing her to death. And so many more people who were witnesses also would have been put at risk. Perhaps these omissions do not make any sense today because we are in a different

period. So a more constructive way of responding is to say that the collective testimony of REMHI and the UN Commission is adding to the pages of the history of the Guatemalan people.

It is true, as Mr. Stoll says, that I spent a lot of time with the Belgian nuns of the Order of the Holy Family and the school they run, which provides education mainly to middle and upper-middle class Guatemalans. I was there for a long time, but as a servant. I mopped floors and cleaned toilets, work that I am very proud to have done. It was not an "elite" school as Mr. Stoll says. In Guatemala there are very few elite schools—the elite sends its children to Harvard. I will never complain about the time I spent there, because the Sisters protected me and taught me many things.

Another of Mr. Stoll's charges is that the land conflict I describe was a simple dispute between my grandparents. Now my grandparents have been dead for some time. The fact is that there was a dispute among my grandparents because they had bought a farm together and they never could decide who owned which part, but that was not the problem. The problem was a large old-growth forest which the big landowners coveted and which my father, with a group of people, was also soliciting from the government because these were public lands. So, Mr. Stoll tells only a part of the truth. He doesn't say that there were more actors involved— in fact there were seven actors—and the dispute still hasn't been resolved. We hope that the land census can resolve these ongoing land disputes. But to say that it was a dispute among Indians—among brothers—is malicious and only a partial version of the truth. Mr. Stoll says he consulted an official file of 600 pages. But the file is a thousand pages long; what do the 400 pages that he does not mention say?

I think that the intention is to divert the question of collective memory by bringing the discussion to a personal level. Of course, there are other intentions here as well. I think that underlying this is the fact that the "official history" is always written by others. The conquistadors, the victors, the victimizers have always written history. It is unfathomable for certain sectors in Guatemala that we have written our own history, that we have insisted on our rights to our own memory and our own history. They would liked to see us remain victims forever.

I am concerned, however, that at this particular moment, this controversy might negatively affect the process of establishing the collective truth of the victims of this war. If it had erupted prior to the

REMHI report, the official version of Guatemalan history might have triumphed.

Your book has also been questioned as a political tool. How do you respond to these charges?

It is obvious that Mr. Stoll is obsessed with his own conclusion. For some time he has tried to talk with me and I haven't wanted to do so. He also tried to interview various friends. He would say, "Look, I know your history, and I know who your parents were and I have information about them." His only intention was to corroborate his own version of events, and he never had the respect to listen to the people, and that's why I never wanted to talk to him. For my own dignity, I didn't want to engage in this discussion.

But the question is this: For many years it has been said that we Indians are useless and ignorant, that we can't make our own decisions, that we are manipulated by the Communists and the theologians, that the theologians turned me into a myth. In reality, the intention is to destroy the myth of Rigoberta Menchu. But he doesn't realize that this myth called Rigoberta Menchu has blood in her veins, believes in the world, believes in humanity, believes in her people. This myth is not carved out of stone, but is a living, breathing person.

My book was a cry in the silence. It had no objective other than to expose the carnage being deployed against the Guatemalan people. It was the cry of a survivor, one of the first survivors who managed to cross the border alive. I also traveled all over the world to tell about what happened to my parents. In those years, I was very conscious that my only mission in the world was to not permit that those atrocities continue. And I think I have fulfilled that mission.

I am happy that it fell on me to take part in the Peace Accords, the dialogues, the negotiations, and that I even had the human ability and the sensitivity as a woman to shake hands with the military officers on the day following the signing of the Peace Accords. We planted a tree in the Ixcan together— the Minister of Defense, a guerilla commander and myself. It was not just theater. It was something very deeply felt.

I don't want to say that I forgive what happened in the past. I think that forgiveness will evolve as part of a much larger process. I want to see justice. I want to see respect. I want to see that we can live together peacefully so that forgiveness can take place. But yes, a demonstration of a willingness to

begin again was important. It is the same with my book. If some people didn't hear my cry back in 1982 or heard it and remained complicit in what happened in Guatemala, that too is part of our collective history.

But many people did hear, and therefore we were able to obtain the support of human rights organizations and the UN. In 1984 we succeeded for the first time in having a special UN rapporteur named to Guatemala. But this testimony no longer belongs only to me. It belongs to Guatemala and to the world; it belongs to the memory of indigenous people everywhere, and especially to all those who are survivors.

Tell us about the work you see ahead of you.

Most importantly, I am not alone. There is a team of people who work with me at the Rigoberta Menchu Tum Foundation. We have worked tirelessly to assist local efforts to address the problems of reconciliation and reconstruction. We have especially worked hard to promote political participation on both a municipal and regional level. Remember that most of those assassinated during the war were community activists. We have to rebuild local leadership, and it is our hope that young people will become more and more involved in this task.

We have also been involved in the debate over constitutional and educational reforms. Rather than remaining on the sidelines saying, "we like this" or "we don't like that," we have made concrete proposals. And in the case of education, we believe that unless it is intercultural, interethnic and multilingual, then intolerance will continue, racism will continue, and so will impunity.

It is not true—and I want to say this very clearly—that I am working to be the next president of Guatemala. Many sectors fear this because they don't see me as an ally, but as an adversary. The same thing happened to Martin Luther King and many other world leaders who were seen by those in power as adversaries.

What I do want to do is be a part of the international campaign to promote a culture of peace in the year 2000. But I hope we can establish a new peace ethic in which justice is considered an essential part of peace. Without justice there is no peace. And there can be no justice without democracy, without development, without respect, without equity.

Source: Jo-Marie Burt and Fred Rosen, ''Truth-telling and Memory in Postwar Guatemala: An Interview with Rigoberta Menchu,'' in *NACLA Report on the Americas,* Vol. 32, Issue 5, March-April, 1999, p. 6.

Janet Varner Gunn

In the following essay, Janet Varner Gunn examines the ethics of reading Third World autobiographies in the context of Rigoberta Menchú's autobiography I, Rigoberta Menchú. *Varner Gunn discusses the narrative form of both the autobiography and the more collective form of ''testimony'' as presented in Menchú's work.*

I'll never forget the first time I stood in front of a university classroom in the fall of 1966. It was packed with the composition students I would be teaching as a part-timer at a large urban campus in Chicago. Names like Mary Ellen Arpino, Lois Leposky, Joan Krishko, and Ron Sigada reminded me of my own classmates back in the Western Pennsylvania mining town where I was born. Part of the Anglo-Saxon minority in Portage, I had grown up feeling both superior to and excluded from the Italian and Eastern European Catholics whose lives I observed with both fear and envy through the window of my Republican childhood.

Those people were the ''foreigners,'' according to my great-Aunt Mary who had come to the United States from Scotland when she and my grandmother were still toddlers. Annie Dillard's Western Pennsylvania childhood was spent in fear and envy of the Irish Catholic Jo Anne Sheehys who, in Dillard's *An American Childhood,* ice-skated in the winter street outside her Point Breeze house in Pittsburgh. In my own adolescence, I was in awe of the Mary Ellens and the Joanies whose bodies glided with their own ''radiance'' across the teen canteen dance floor.

As soon as I began calling the roll on that first day of composition class, I knew that I would be canceling most of the supplementary texts I had added to the anthology of essays departmentally required for all composition sections. I would make room on the syllabus for my students' lives. The course, I hoped, would be a larger window on American ethnicity.

After leaving Chicago for Chapel Hill some ten years after I began my teaching career, Annie Dillard's autobiography, had it been published by then, might have been the model of the book I wanted to write about growing up in Western Pennsylvania. Having left the flat plain of the Middle West, I found myself again in the Back Country whose low mountains chained down the Alleghenies to the Carolina Piedmont. But instead of writing my own autobiography, I returned to graduate school at the end of my first year in North Carolina so that I could develop a theory of autobiography that employed the writing of others.

Four years after publishing my dissertation, I left for a city among other hills halfway around the world. Divorced by then and taking my first sabbatical since starting out in that Chicago classroom, I decided that I wanted to turn fifty in Jerusalem, not Greensboro, North Carolina where I was a tenured professor of religion and literature. It was on my subsequent return to Jerusalem that I first read Dillard's *An American Childhood.* Having taken the sabbatical to begin a book on the autobiography of the Holocaust, I later went back to Jerusalem to work and study on the Palestinian West Bank.

It was in the third world, then, that I first read Annie Dillard's autobiography and, as it turned out, began writing my own. I say, ''as it turned out,'' because I didn't realize how much of my own life was implicated in a book I began to write about a Palestinian refugee family. Gaining access to the life of that family was not a matter of getting outside my own window but of acknowledging that it was there: I was looking at them from somewhere. How the window of my own life both blocks and facilitates the telling of Palestinian lives was part of the story I wanted to tell.

The information I have been supplying thus far is not personal background but critical foreground to the more explicit argument I want to develop about an ethics of reading third world autobiography, which begins with the reader, not with the text. Defining the location of that reader is the first interpretive task for such an ethics. The next interpretive task requires the interrogating of that location. Defining and interrogating the reader's location finally affords the reader what Edward Said calls a ''wider optics''—a new and expanded location which can move interpretation toward transformation or what George Yudice has recently called an ''ethics of survival,'' which engages the autobiographical activity of the first world reader as well as the third world text. Along the way, I will be addressing the differing functions of the ''other'' in first and third world representations of selfhood and identity.

I, Rigoberta Menchu: An Indian Woman in Guatemala is the third world autobiography I want to use. A life history set in a country that accounts for more than half of the disappeared in Latin America, *I, Rigoberta Menchu* is a counter-story that works against such disappearance to the extent that it testifies to the appearance of her people on the stage of history and names the harsh reality in which they live. It is furthermore a resistance story about directing that history and transforming that reality.

Life stories like Menchu's emerged in Latin America after the Cuban Revolution and were elicited by other more privileged women like the Venezuelan anthropologist Elisabeth Burgos-Debray, who edited and inscribed Menchu's story. She interviewed Menchu in Paris, where the Guatemalan had been invited in 1982 to participate in a conference sponsored by the 31 January Popular Front. The organization's name commemorates the day in 1980 when Menchu's father and other early leaders of the Committee of Campesino Unity had been burned to death during their peaceful occupation of the Spanish embassy in Guatemala City to protest military repression in their villages.

Latin American women like Burgos-Debray were trying to overcome their own marginality in a patriarchal culture. Through such testimonials as Menchu's, they wanted to show that oppressed people were subjects and not merely objects of national histories. The inscribers of these testimonials were also raising questions about the negative aspects of the concept "third world" with its connotations of dependency and racial backwardness. They were helping to redefine "third world" as a positive term of radical critique against colonialist policies both inside and outside Latin America.

When I returned to my teaching career in the United States, I decided to use *An American Childhood* as a point of embarkation for the course on third world autobiography which I team-taught with an anthropologist. An autobiography like hers, we agreed, could be useful in defining our own location since most of us, like Dillard, had had a middle-class American childhood. More than that, Dillard would help us to measure the distance between our lives and Menchu's, in their differing modes of self-representation as well as their material conditions.

In beginning the course with Dillard, we began to appreciate some of the differences between what I called autobiography of nostalgia and the testimonial. The former represents a mainstream tradition of self-writing in the industrialized West and North. A strategy of recovering what would otherwise be lost, autobiography of nostalgia is directed toward

" 'How much noticing could I permit myself without driving myself round the bend? Too much noticing and I was too self-conscious to live. . .Too little noticing, though . . . and I would miss the whole show. I would awake on my deathbed and say, What was that?' "

the past. The autobiographer's identity depends not only on recovering this past but on individuating his or her experience of the past. Childhood memories are especially important since it is in that period that the process of individuation has its start. That process is experienced as separation, painful but necessary to establish a self/world boundary that must be kept essentially intact to assure the unique individuality on which identity is based. Growing up requires the self's outward movement into the world, but in such a way that a sense of boundary is maintained and even sharpened by experiences of otherness. The other, alluring but dangerous, continues to reset those limits that keep alive one's sense of having a self.

Unlike nostalgic autobiography of the first world, the testimonial's understanding of selfhood is based on collective identity, not individuality. Early in her account, Menchu is quick to insist that her "personal experience is the reality of a whole people." What follows in the first half of her book is the description of rituals which establish the bond between the community and each of its members. Those rituals begin with the practice of the mother who, "on the first day of her pregnancy goes with her husband to tell . . . elected leaders that she's going to have a child, because the child will not only belong to them but to the whole community."

Like other third world autobiographies, the testimonial is oriented toward creating a future rather than recovering a past. It is a form of utopian literature that contributes to the realization of a liberated society based on distributive justice. A form of resistance literature as well as utopian literature, the testimonial resists not only economic and political oppression, but also any nostalgic pull towards an idealized past—pre-Hispanic origins, for instance, which promise false comfort. To resort to such indigenism would implicate Menchu in the very culture from which her testimonial wants to free itself.

While autobiography of nostalgia welcomes and, in fact, needs the other, the testimonial has to find ways of deconstructing it, since otherness in the third world is the most basic structure of colonial control. It is a construction by means of which the oppressed are kept ''barbarian'' and the colonizer securely defined as the bearer of civilization's burden. The operative existence of the other justifies a colonialist structure of domination.

Through autobiography of nostalgia like *An American Childhood,* I tried to define and establish the location from which the first world reader listens to the voice of Rigoberta Menchu. The reader I constructed is a reader very much like myself some ten years ago when I developed a theory of autobiography based on the self-writing of Thoreau, Wordsworth, and Proust—all of them writing in the romantic tradition of an Annie Dillard and all of them members of a culture that already has a voice (Gunn, *Autobiography*). Although I raised questions about an autobiographical tradition that privileged the private and ahistorical self, it was not until I spent time in the third world that I began to see that another set of questions had to be raised about the ''narrative space of familiarity'' that my very choice of texts constructed (Kaplan). That space was first of all defined by the first world citizenship of my informants. To be sure, I ended my project with Black Elk, but even there I was reading his testimonial out of the location I had established by means of the others. It is that location I began to interrogate with the help of Menchu.

Were the reader to respond to Menchu from an unexamined mainstream location in the first world, she would, I think, be disturbed or simply incredulous at the suffering that fills Menchu's world and frustrated at how little she could do to alleviate that suffering. She might conclude much like Jane Tompkins did in her essay on American Indians: ''The moral problem that confronts me now is not that I can never have any facts to go on, but that the work I do is not directed towards solving the kinds of problems that studying the Indians has awakened me to.'' Such limits must be acknowledged in establishing an ethics of reading third world autobi-ography that gets us beyond a conventional ethics of altruism to an ''ethics of survival.''

An American Childhood epitomizes a nostalgic mode of self-representation. The following passage illustrates several of its main characteristics:

> How much noticing could I permit myself without driving myself round the bend? Too much noticing and I was too self-conscious to live; I trapped and paralyzed myself, and I dragged my friends down with me, so that we couldn't meet each other's eyes, my own loud awareness damning us both. Too little noticing, though ... and I would miss the whole show. I would awake on my deathbed and say, What was that?

Replete with echoes from Thoreau's famous words about going to the woods to live deliberately, Dillard's passage underscores three features associated with a mainstream autobiographical tradition of the industrialized world. First of all, its ''loud awareness'' calls attention to a Cartesian singularity of consciousness. Second, the passage calls attention to an aesthetics within which individuation and style are coterminous. Third, Dillard's exact noticing combines with exact expression to situate the passage in a tradition which privileges inner selfness as both the spring of artistic activity and the starting-point of ontological reckoning. The world is significant to the extent that it enters and is ratified by one's consciousness: Dillard writes, ''. . . things themselves possessed no fixed and intrinsic amount of interest; instead things were interesting as long as you had attention to give them.''

Nostalgic autobiography seems to hold out the promise that memory can achieve perfect rapport with the past. Dillard writes her autobiography to rescue the sensuous details of her childhood from what she calls a ''cave of oblivion.'' She understands memory to be an empty space individually filled rather than a cultural activity practiced in and informed by an historical and ideological situation. In order to maintain a centered ''I'' by defining itself against the other, Dillard's autobiographical agenda has to remain fixed. In the sense that Menchu's testimonial ''I'' represents the communal and resistant ''we,'' its agenda must remain open.

The comfortable Pittsburgh neighborhoods of Point Breeze and Squirrel Hill where Annie Dillard had her American childhood are worlds away from the inhospitable mountains and fincas of Guatemala where Menchu grew up. Even so, Dillard has her dangerous places: the ''dark ways'' of the Roman Catholic Sheehy family, the ''greasy black soil'' of Doc Hall's alley, the Frick Park bridges under which the bums had been living since the Great Depression, and, in the earliest memory of all, her own bedroom into whose corners a slithering, elongated ''thing'' would burst nightly to search her out. In the process of figuring the ''thing'' out as the lights of passing cars, young Annie was ''forced'' to what she calls ''the very rim of her being, to the membrane of skin that both separates and connects the inner life and the outer world.''

In the daily mapping of her world, it is important for Dillard to name those experiences of what might be called the other but at the same time to keep them on the outside of that membrane. Like the ice-skating figure of Jo Anne Sheehy whom she watches from the ''peace and safety'' of the Dillard house, they are experiences which take place on the outside of her skin's rim—dark, dangerous, criminal, but also beautiful, mysterious, and ''radiant.'' Dillard's child is careful to keep the membrane virginally unbroken, but she needs nonetheless to be taken to her ''edge'' with that combination of ''desire and derision'' which communicates the anxiety involved in the construction of otherness (Bhabha).

Not surprisingly, Menchu's autobiographical agenda is quite different. But in a world more literally dangerous, it is surprisingly more open. The telling of her story is a matter of cultural survival. In telling that story to Burgos-Debray, she makes it clear that she used the story of her own past as a strategy for organizing her people against landowners and the larger system of oppression whose interests they represented. ''I had some political work to do, organizing the people there, and at the same time getting them to understand me by telling them about my past, what had happened to me in my life, the reasons for the pain we suffer, and the causes of poverty.''

In no way unique, Menchu's story is intended to elicit recognition and, in naming the suffering she shares with her people, to deliver them and herself from muteness. Such muteness is a product of oppression. As recently observed by a fellow-member of the Committee of Campesino Unity, ''a person can be poor, dirt poor, but not even realize the depth of their poverty since it's all they know'' (MacGregor). To take notice of the oppression and to give it a name is the first step beyond it. Noticing, it turns out, is an even more important activity in Menchu's culture of ''silence'' than it is in Dillard's culture, whose voice is secure. But it is a noticing of material conditions, not a noticing of noticing.

Menchu's testimonial is a story of resistance as well as a story of oppression. More precisely, her testimonial is itself an act of resistance. Solidarity growing out of resistance as much as membership in a community of the oppressed produces the circumstances of her identity. Menchu has to be reminded of these circumstances by a twelve-year-old when she is on the verge of hopelessness following the torture deaths of her brother and then her mother. '''A revolutionary isn't born out of something good,''' the young girl told her; '''she is born out of wretchedness and bitterness.''' The twelve-year-old goes on to add something very foreign to an autobiographer of consciousness like Dillard: ''We have to fight without measuring our suffering, or what we experience, or thinking about the monstrous things we must bear in life.'' Menchu's testimonial is instead an autobiography of conscientization.

Menchu leaves behind the communal rituals that have long anchored her and her people in order to enter resistance activity that keeps her on the run outside her own community. Far from mourning her loss, she opens herself to new and potentially conflicting strategies of survival, especially in learning Spanish and turning to the Bible. Spanish is the language of her enemy; those who learn it, as her father cautioned her, often leave the Indian community. The Bible had been used by many priests and nuns to keep her people ''dormant while others took advantage of their passivity.'' Menchu, however, uses both, especially the Bible, as ''weapons.'' Far from being ''an unlikely, movie-set world'' as it was for Dillard, the Bible became a document by means of which Menchu could understand her people's reality. Moses ''gets pluralized and Christ turns into a political militant'' (Sommer). Biblical stories allowed Menchu and her people to give yet another name to their oppression.

Instead of constructing a single map within whose boundaries a Dillard can hold safely onto a sense of individual identity, Menchu superimposes many ''conflicting maps'' in a collective and incorporative struggle for communal survival (Sommer). Yudice notes (in words that echo liberation theologian Enrique Dussel), ''her oppression and that of her people have opened them to an unfixity delimited by the unboundedness of struggle.''

Dillard's autobiography set side-by-side with Menchu's testimonial raises a new set of issues that can move us in the direction of Yudice's ''ethics of survival.'' A third world testimonial like Menchu's serves to destabilize the nostalgic structure of autobiography based on a loss and recovery ostensibly beyond the marketplace that gives force to those very terms. More important, it lays the ground for exposing otherness as that construction which keeps women, blacks, Jews, Palestinians, and Guatemalan Indians in their subordinate place.

In order that interpretation become transformative and reading of third world autobiography be ethical, we need to re-insert texts into political cultures and what Raymond Williams calls the ''life of communities'' (Said). The Pittsburgh of the Fricks and Carnegies is also the Pittsburgh of the unemployed steelworkers and the black slums. That the latter are outside Dillard's ken has everything to do with the fact that the former are not. Gerald Graff has recently reminded us that ''what we don't see enables and limits what we do see.'' He was offering a personal account of how his teaching of *Heart of Darkness* has changed as a result of confronting a very different reading of the text from the third world perspective of the Nigerian novelist Chinua Achebe. Simply out of sight from this or that location, huge chunks of the world are blocked out.

Dillard's memories of Pittsburgh block out the Polish and Slovak steelworkers and the Hill District ghetto except, in the case of the latter, as a place where boarding-school boys carouse. To acknowledge such unavoidable blocking is to open the way for examining the emancipatory potential of autobiographical practice in testimonials like *I, Rigoberta Menchu*. With that ''wider optics,'' we might find a way of breaking through the membrane of critical isolation and solitude to an ethical criticism practiced ''in solidarity with others struggling for survival'' (Yudice).

Cornel West identifies as an Enlightenment legacy ''the inability to believe in the capacities of oppressed people to create cultural products of value and oppositional groups of value.'' In any ethical reading of third world autobiography, the racism inherent in this legacy must be exposed and rejected. George Yudice turns this legacy on its head when he concludes his essay ''Marginality and the Ethics of Survival'' by defining ''ethical practice'' as the ''political art of seeking articulations among all the 'marginalized' and oppressed, in the interests of our own survival.'' ''We need not speak for others,'' he says, ''but we are responsible for a 'self-forming activity' that can in no way be ethical

if we do not act against the 'disappearance' of oppressed subjects.''

Autobiography like *I, Rigoberta Menchu* calls on first world readers to take responsibility, not for the third world but for the locatedness and therefore the limitations of our own perspective. Acknowledging those limitations might contribute to the survival of us all. The ultimate window of opportunity is to stand with Menchu and, acknowledging the cost borne by the third world for our own selfhood, to affiliate at the borders between us.

Source: Janet Varner Gunn, '''A Window of Opportunity': An Ethics of reading Third World Autobiography,'' in *College Literature,* Vol., 19, No. 3, October–February, 1992, p. 162.

Sources

Arata, Luis O., ''The Testimonial of Rigoberta Menchú in a Native Tradition,'' in *Teaching and Testimony: Rigoberta Menchú and the North American Classroom*, edited by Allen Carrey Webb and Stephen Benz, SUNY Press, pp. 82-83.

Bell-Villada, Gene H., ''Why Dinesh D'Souza Has It In for Rigoberta Menchú,'' in *Teaching and Testimony: Rigoberta Menchú and the North American Classroom*, edited by Allen Carrey Webb and Stephen Benz, SUNY Press, pp. 50-51.

Beverly, John, ''The Margin at the Center: On *testimonio* (Testimonial Narrative),'' in *De/Colonizing the Subject: The Politics of Gender in Women's Autobiography*, edited by Sidonie Smith and Julia Watson, University of Minnesota Press, 1992, p. 94.

Carby, Hazel, *Reconstructing Womanhood: The Emergence of the Afro-American Woman Novelist*, Oxford University Press, New York, 1987, p. 74.

Moneyhun, Clyde, ''Not Just Plain English: Teaching Critical Reading with *I, Rigoberta Menchú*,'' in *Teaching and Testimony: Rigoberta Menchú and the North American Classroom*, edited by Allen Carrey Webb and Stephen Benz, SUNY Press, pp. 238-39.

Pratt, Mary Louise, ''*Me llamo Rigoberta Menchú*: Autoethnography and the Recoding of Citizenship,'' in *Teaching and Testimony: Rigoberta Menchú and the North American Classroom*, edited by Allen Carrey Webb and Stephen Benz, SUNY Press, pp. 60-65.

Rochelson, Meri-Jane, '''This Is My Testimony': Rigoberta Menchú in a Class on Oral History,'' in *Teaching and Testimony: Rigoberta Menchú and the North American Classroom*, edited by Allen Carrey Webb and Stephen Benz, SUNY Press, p. 249.

Zimmerman, Marc, ''Resistance Literature, Testimonio, and Postmodernism in Guatemala,'' in *Literature and Resistance in Guatemala: Textual Modes and Cultural Politics from El Senor Presidente to Rigoberta Menchú*, Center for International Studies of Ohio University, 1995, pp. 25-26 (Vol. I), 54-55 (Vol. 2).

Further Reading

hooks, bell, *Feminist Theory: From Margin to Center*, South End Press, 1984.

    A series of easily accessible essays addressing the topic of feminist political and personal action, in practical terms, from solidarity with other women to the nature of work, relationships with men, education, and struggle, among others.

Gómez-Quiñones, Juan, *Chicano Politics: Reality and Promise 1940-1990*, University of New Mexico Press, 1990.

    A political history of Mexico and in the United States, delineated along chronological and ideological lines, clarifies similarities and differences in the conditions of laborers and their fight for social equality and justice.

Roediger, David R., *The Wages of Whiteness: Race and the Making of the American Working Class*, Verso, 1991.

    A dense but thought-provoking investigation into the process of racial identity formation, and the effects of this racial identification on the size, strength, unity, structure, and progress of the American working class and labor movement. Sheds additional light on why the barriers between *ladinos* and Indians remained intact for so long, so tenaciously.

Jasmine

Bharati Mukherjee

1989

Bharati Mukherjee's *Jasmine*, the story of a widowed Punjabi peasant reinventing herself in America, entered the literary landscape in 1989, the same year as Salmon Rushdie's *Satanic Verses*. Rushdie, also an Indian writer, received international attention for his novel when a fatwa (or death threat) was issued against him. The fatwa essentially proclaimed it a righteous act for any Muslim to murder Rushdie. Michelle Cliff's *No Telephone to Heaven*, Jill Ker Conway's *The Road to Coorain*, Tsitsi Dangarembga's *Nervous Condition*, Jamaica Kincaid's *A Small Place*, and Amitav Ghosh's *The Shadow Lines* were all published around this time. Each of these writers is considered to be a contributor to the genre of postcolonial literature. Although there is considerable debate over the term ''postcolonial,'' in a very general sense, it is the time following the establishment of independence in a (former) colony, such as India. The sheer extent and duration of the European empire and its disintegration after the Second World War have led to widespread interest in postcolonial literature.

Partly because of the abundance of such postcolonial works, some critics suggested *Jasmine* was part of a fad. *The New York Times Book Review*, however, named it one of the year's best works.

Mukherjee's time as a student at the University of Iowa's acclaimed Masters of Fine Arts program, the Writer's Workshop, almost certainly informed the setting of *Jasmine*. She began studies there in

1961 and took her MFA in 1963. She stayed on to earn a Ph.D. in English and comparative literature in 1969. Though Iowa City is a small college town, the state is 95 percent farm land. In the 1980s, when *Jasmine* is set, many family farmers on the outskirts of Iowa City faced the same dilemma as Darrel Lutz, a character in *Jasmine*. The hard life of farming coupled with tough times economically persuaded many farmers to sell out to large corporate farms or to non-agricultural corporations. Other farmers struggled on determined to save the farm their fathers and grandfathers had built up, as well as to preserve this unique way of life.

Author Biography

Mukherjee was born in 1940 into an elite caste level of Calcutta society. A Bengali Brahmin, Mukherjee grew up in a house cluttered with extended family, 40 or 45 people by her own count. In a 1993 interview with Runar Vignisson in *Journal of the South Pacific Association for Commonwealth Literature and Language Studies*, Mukherjee said she "had to drop inside books as a way of escaping crowds."

Mukherjee was educated as a proper Indian girl of a good family: she spoke Bengali her first three years, then entered English schools in Britain and Switzerland. Back in India, she attended the Loretto School run by Irish nuns, and subsequently universities in Calcutta and Baroda, where she earned a master's degree in English and Indian Culture. She immigrated to the United States in 1961 to attend, on scholarship, the Writer's Workshop at the University of Iowa. There, she earned her M.F.A. in fiction writing, and subsequently a Ph.D. in English and comparative literature. She also met and married writer Clark Blaise, thus avoiding a traditional Hindu marriage to an Indian nuclear physicist, arranged back home by her father. As of the year 2000, she has collaborated with her husband on three major writing projects.

Mukherjee's body of work, which includes three novels, two short story collections, and five works of varied nonfiction, returns to the theme of crossing cultural boundaries. Though Mukherjee has been a citizen of India, Canada, and the U.S., she clearly identifies herself as American. In *American Dreamer*, an essay published in 1997 in *Mother Jones*, she wrote, "I choose to describe myself on my own terms, as an American, rather than as an Asian-American. Why is it that hyphenation is imposed only on nonwhite Americans? Rejecting hyphenation is my refusal to categorize the cultural landscape into a center and its peripheries; it is to demand that the American nation deliver the promises of its dream and its Constitution to all its citizens equally."

Jasmine represented Mukherjee's return to the novel form. It had been fourteen years since *Wife*, her last published novel. *The New York Times Book Review* listed *Jasmine* as one of the best of 1989. Among others, Mukherjee has received awards from the Guggenheim Foundation (1978-79) and the National Endowment for the Arts (1986). She earned the National Book Critic's best fiction award for *The Middleman and Other Stories* in 1988, the same year she became an American citizen.

In the same *American Dreamer* essay, Mukherjee wrote, "As a writer, my literary agenda begins by acknowledging that America has transformed me. It does not end until I show that I (along with the hundreds of thousands of immigrants like me) am minute by minute transforming America. The transformation is a two-way process: It affects both the individual and the national-cultural identity. Others who write stories of migration often talk of arrival at a new place as a loss, the loss of communal memory and the erosion of an original culture. I want to talk of arrival as a gain."

Mukherjee has taught creative writing at Columbia University, New York University, and Queens College. She currently resides as professor of English at the University of California at Berkeley. She and Blaise have two children.

Plot Summary

Synopsis

Jasmine, the title character and narrator of Bharati Mukherjee's novel, was born approximately 1965 in a rural Indian village called Hasnpur. She tells her story as a twenty-four-year-old pregnant widow, living in Iowa with her crippled lover, Bud Ripplemeyer. It takes two months in Iowa to relate the most recently developing events. But during that time, Jasmine also relates biographical events that span the distance between her Punjabi birth and her American adult life. These past biographical events inform the action set in Iowa. Her odyssey encompasses five distinct settings, two murders, at least

Bharati Mukherjee

one rape, a maiming, a suicide, and three love affairs. Throughout the course of the novel, the title character's identity, along with her name, changes and changes again: from Jyoti to Jasmine to Jazzy to Jassy to Jase to Jane. In chronological order, Jasmine moves from Hasnpur, Punjab, to Fowlers Key, Florida (near Tampa), to Flushing, New York, to Manhattan, to Baden, Iowa, and finally is off to California as the novel ends.

Opening Chapter

The novel's opening phrase, "Lifetimes ago..." sets in motion the major motif, or theme, the recreation of one's self. Jasmine is seven years old. Under a banyan tree in Hasnpur, an astrologer forecasts her eventual widowhood and exile. Given the traditional Hindu belief in the accuracy of such astrological forecasts, this is a grave moment in the young girl's life. It foreshadows her first husband's death and even her move to the isolated Iowa farm town of Baden.

Life in Iowa

The action shifts, at the end of the first chapter, into the most recent past tense. This clues the reader into the narrative strategy of the novel. The twenty-four-year-old Jasmine currently lives in Baden,

Iowa. The next four chapters provide details about her current situation. It is late May during a dry season, which is significant because the farm community relies on good harvests. She is pregnant. Bud, her partner, became wheelchair-bound some time after the onset of their relationship. Bud wants Jasmine to marry him. The neighbor boy, Darrel Lutz, struggles to run his family's farm, which he inherited after his father's sudden death a year before. Darrel entertains the idea of selling off the farm to golf-course developers, but Bud, the town's banker and thus a powerful figure to the independent farmers, forbids it. Bud has close, though sometimes strained, ties with all the farmers. Though change—technological, social, and sexual—seems inevitable, Bud resists it. Du, Jasmine and Bud's adopted Vietnamese son, represents this change. He comes from an entirely different culture than his sons-of-farmers classmates.

Jasmine describes her introduction to Bud and their courtship, introduces her would-be mother-in-law, Mother Ripplemeyer, and Bud's ex-wife Karin. She hints at sexual tension between her and Du, and her and Darrel. When Jasmine makes love to the wheelchair-bound Bud, it illustrates the reversal of sexual power in her new life. Desire and control remain closely related throughout the novel. Du's glimpse of the lovemaking adds another dimension to the sexual politics: there are those in control, those who are helpless, and those bystanders waiting to become part of the action. This resonates with ideas later chronicled about Indian notions of love and marriage.

In these early chapters, the narrator, Jasmine, alludes to more distant events. These hint at important people and events: her childhood friend Vilma, her Manhattan employers Taylor and Wylie, their child and her charge Duff. These allusions begin to create the more complicated and full circumstances of the story, but remain sketchy until later, when the narrator gives each their own full treatment.

Childhood in Hasnpur

In Chapter 6, Jasmine dips back in time to her birth. She was born during a bountiful harvest year, which for a male would have signified enormous luck. But Jasmine was the fifth daughter (the seventh of nine children) in a poor family. What little money there was would go to the older daughters. She seems destined, since she would have no dowry, to become an old maid, a grim prospect in a male-dominated society. A dowry is money or property brought by a bride to a husband at their wedding.

Jasmine's childhood in Hasnpur is humble, maybe even impoverished. Her family had been forced to move there from Lahore after their village was sacked by Muslims during the Partition riots. This historical event, like others in the novel, is rendered true to actual events. The Partition riots of 1947 were a consequence of the attempt to create separate Hindu and Muslim states. More than 200,000 people died as Hindus fled their homes in Pakistan and Muslims theirs in India. Her father, who wore fancy clothes despite having no money, clung to nostalgic notions of his past life. He, like so many Indians, exchanged relative wealth for squalor. In Lahore, the family lived in a big stucco house with porticoes and gardens. In Hasnpur, they live in mud huts. Jasmine, of course, never knew Lahore. She distinguishes herself during her Hasnpur childhood as beautiful and exceptionally smart, none of which seems to matter, given that she was a poor girl. Her first teacher, Masterji, and her mother lobby for her right to stay in school. With her mother and teacher's backing, Jasmine is allowed to stay in school six years, or twice as long as the average girl.

Jasmine fends off a mad dog with a staff. It's a scene filled with underlying meaning about the young woman's power to effect the trajectory of her life. This relates to one of the novel's philosophical questions, namely, ''Does free will exist?'' Pitaji, Jasmine's father, gets killed by a bull a short time later.

Marriage

Jasmine eavesdrops on the impassioned arguments of her brother and their friends: they speak of political and social turmoil in their homeland. She hears the voice of Prakash, whom she soon after marries.

Jasmine lives with Prakash Vijh in a two-bedroom apartment, a break from the tradition of living with relatives. Prakash studies to be an engineer and works several demeaning jobs to save money. Jasmine and Prakash plot their move to the United States and a ''real life.'' Their dreams of opening an electronics store are fueled by a letter from Prakash's old teacher Professorji, who pronounces America a land of vast opportunity and riches. Prakash's efforts result in acceptance to a technical college in Florida. They decide that Prakash will move to Florida to begin his studies, and Jasmine will follow in a few years. She is just 17 years old. On the brink of Prakash's departure,

Sukhwinder, a political terrorist from her brother's circle of acquaintances, plants a bomb. Prakash dies, thus fulfilling the astrologer's prophecy of widowhood for Jasmine.

On To America

Jasmine goes to America alone. She secures illegal immigration papers and journeys across the sea. She plans to kill herself on a makeshift pyre of Prakash's clothes. Eventually, she lands, alone, in a desolate Florida coast town. After docking, Half-Face, the deformed captain of The Gulf Shuttle, drives Jasmine to a seedy hotel called Flamingo Court, where he rapes her. Jasmine uses a knife given to her by Kingsland, another crew member, to kill her rapist. She burns the suitcase filled with her late husband's American suit and her bloody sari.

Reincarnation

As the narrative moves back to the most present past, Mary Webb, an Iowa acquaintance, talks to Jasmine of her past lives. She's part of a network of women who believe, literally, in rebirth. Mary believes she once was a black Australian aborigine. Mary's guru, Ma Leela, inhabits the body of a battered Canadian wife. The placement of this chapter is important: it raises the issue of literal rebirth just as Jasmine begins to tell her story of figurative rebirth in America.

Fowlers Key, Florida

Lillian Gordan, an elderly Quaker woman, rescues Jasmine and nurtures her back to health in an informal halfway house. Three Kanjobal women also stay there. Lillian teaches Jasmine American mannerisms to protect her against possible arrest and deportation. Lillian puts Jasmine on a Greyhound bus, destined for the New York home of Prakash's former teacher.

Flushing, New York

Jasmine stays five months in the Flushing apartment of Professorji, his wife Nirmala and his two octogenarian parents. A pseudo-Indian culture has been recreated in their neighborhood, particularly in their apartment building, where 32 of 50 families are Indian. Here, Jasmine is expected to live the life of an Indian widow. Professorji's family watches Indian movies and television, eats Indian food, socialize with other Indians of similar class. This life disappoints, even depresses, Jasmine, who is without money or a green card. Professorji finances and arranges for Jasmine's forged green card.

Manhattan

Through Lillian's daughter, Kate Gordan-Feldstein, Jasmine obtains work as an au pair for a young professional couple, Taylor and Wylie. She cares for Duff, and for the first time in her life earns a paycheck. Taylor and Wylie treat Jasmine with respect and love. Though there are minor tensions, Jasmine settles into a safe, happy existence. She eventually takes on extra work, making what seems to her to be fantastical amounts of money. Jasmine, the caregiver, learns from her charge. "I was learning about the stores, the neighborhood, shopping, from [Duff]." Jasmine feels part of the family, and may be a little in love with Taylor, who also might be a little in love with her. In the summer of her second year with the Hayes, Wylie leaves to be with another man. Jasmine and Taylor become even closer, acting very much like a family. Finally, at a park, Taylor declares his love, but seconds later, seconds from the realization of Jasmine's American bliss, Prakash's killer appears. Jasmine, in fear, makes the immediate decision to move to Iowa, the place she knows to be the home of Duff's natural mother.

Back to Baden

The Iowa narrative goes back to Jasmine's first fall, about a year after her move to Iowa. Two days before Christmas, Harlan Kroener comes to their home looking for Bud. Jasmine has a chance to alert police, but she fails to understand what is happening. Harlan shoots Bud twice in the back with a rifle, and then kills himself.

During this first year in Iowa, Jasmine encounters tension with Bud's ex-wife Karin. Jasmine still thinks about Manhattan. She remembers her final days. She and Taylor consummate their love and then she leaves for Iowa. She explains that "Iowa was a state where miracles still happened." Duff was born there, and her birth allowed her mother to attend college (the Hayes paid for it as part of the deal to adopt Duff), and thus gave Jasmine opportunity to break out of Flushing.

In Baden, Jasmine receives a postcard from Taylor saying that he and Duff are on the way to Iowa. Though this turns out to be a false alarm (several similar postcards follow), the novel's tension revolves around this impending visit. Will Jasmine stay with Bud or leave with Taylor?

Darrel invites Jasmine over to his house. He is in a strange mood. He has prepared, poorly, an Indian dish. He begs Jasmine to run away with him,

to New Mexico, to run a Radio Shack. Jasmine flees, and once home calls Karin to convey her fears for Darrel's sanity. Du, meanwhile, plots to leave Iowa, to find his sister in California.

Karin goes with Jasmine to Darrel's, to see if they can help. But when they arrive, Darrel is hard at work on the hog house. Jasmine lies to Bud about Du's trip, says it's temporary, and he'll be back for school. Bud works out a loan for Darrel, but it's too late: he has hanged himself above the hogs.

Finally, Taylor and Duff show up. Though Jasmine is torn between her former family and her life in Iowa, and her obligation to Bud, she goes off with Taylor and Duff.

Characters

Arvind-prar

Jasmine's brother co-inherits the responsibility of caring for his large family upon his father's death. He quits technical college in Jullundhar, sells the family farm, and opens a scooter repair shop. His political activism brings Jasmine in contact with her future first husband, as well as her husband's killer. He is given no character traits which distinguish him from his brother.

Astrologer

Under a banyan tree, he tells the young Jasmine's fate of widowhood and exile.

Sant Bhindranwale

Leader of all fanatics.

Dida

Jasmine's maternal grandmother aggressively supports traditional Indian values. Dida opposes Jasmine's efforts to extend her formal education. When Jasmine is 13, Dida unsuccessfully tries to arrange a marriage with a Ludhiana widower. In reference to Jasmine's bleak prospects, she says, "You're going to wear out your sandals getting rid of this one."

Stuart Eschelman

Stuart, an economist, has an affair with Wylie Hayes. Eventually, it breaks up their comfortable family, and allows Taylor to pursue Jasmine. He is tall, extremely thin, and pleasant.

Kate Gordon-Feldstein

The photographer daughter of Lillian Gordon, Kate puts Jasmine in touch with her friends Taylor and Wylie Hayes.

Lillian Gordon

The kind Quaker lady rescues Jasmine from a road just east of Fowlers Key, Florida. She lives in a wooden house on stilts and runs a sort of halfway house for refugee women. Three Kanjobal women who lost their husbands and children to an army massacre stay in her daughter's old bedroom. She earns the description ''facilitator'' of ordinariness by coaching Jasmine on being American: the clothes, the walk, the attitude. Lillian continues to be Jasmine's benefactor, sending money and gifts long after her departure. She is arrested for harboring undocumented immigrants.

Hari-prar

Jasmine's brother co-inherits the responsibility of caring for his large family upon his father's death. He quits technical college in Jullundhar, sells the family farm and opens a scooter repair shop. His political activism brings Jasmine in contact with her future first husband, as well as his killer. He is given no character traits which distinguish him from his brother.

Duff Hayes

Duff is the adopted daughter of Taylor and Wylie. Jasmine is hired to be Duff's au pair. Through Duff, Jasmine learns about their Manhattan neighborhood. She sleeps with Duff at night. During this time, Jasmine, due in large part to her attachment to Duff, develops a sense of family. Duff's natural mother accepted the price of tuition at Iowa State University as a kind of adoption fee. Jasmine eventually moves to Iowa because she knows it as Duff's birthplace.

Taylor Hayes

Taylor, a Columbia University physics professor, falls in love with his au pair, Jasmine. When his wife Wylie leaves Taylor for another man, he expresses his love to Jasmine. Eventually he drives to Iowa and convinces her to go with him to California. He is in his early thirties, with crooked teeth and a blonde beard. He convincingly speaks to Jasmine of a person's ability to create change. His advice to Jasmine to pull down the imaginary shades and block out the evil world beyond is a recurring image.

Wylie Hayes

A tall, thin, serious woman, Wylie leaves her husband Taylor in favor of her lover, Stuart Eschelman. This creates an opportunity for Taylor to pursue Jasmine. In her early thirties, Wylie is a book editor for a Park Avenue publisher.

Mr. Jagtiani

Prakash's boss at Jagtiani and Son Electrical Goods. He forces Prakash to doctor the accounting books on his illegal income.

Karin

Bud's ex-wife remains in Iowa after her husband leaves her for Jasmine. She answers phones for a Suicide Hot Line, the existence of which shows the desperation and tension in dry farm communities like Baden. She lives in the house Bud built.

Harlan Kroener

Harlan expresses his sense of betrayal toward Bud with two rifle shots to the banker's back. His dramatic action represents the frustration, anger, and helplessness of the Baden farmers. He kills himself just after shooting Bud.

Don-jin Kwang

The artificial inseminator of Jasmine.

Orrin Lacey

An advisor to Bud, Orrin suggests ways to solve Darrel's problem.

Ma Leela

Mary Webb's thirty-six-year-old guru.

Carol Lutz

The Ripplemeyers' neighbor moved to California after her husband's death. When she returns to sell the farm after her son Darrel's death, she blames Bud for the tragedy.

Darrel Lutz

Darrel struggles to manage the 1,000-acre, 150-hog farm he inherited from his father Gene. Just twenty-three years old and alone, Darrel variably thinks about modernizing the farm and selling it off to a golf course developer. Bud, Darrel's neighbor, family friend, and the town's banker, appeals to his sense of tradition. Some community members, such as Bud, consider it almost sacrilegious to give up farm land for non-agricultural uses. Darrel, a shy young man, secretly longs for Jasmine. With an awkward presentation of poorly prepared Indian food, Darrel declares his love and lays out all his desperate plans. Jasmine rejects him, and shortly afterwards Darrel hangs himself to death above his hog pit. The hogs chew his feet to stumps.

Gene Lutz

The 300-pound father of Darrel is dead prior to the start of the action. Gene choked to death on a piece of Mexican food one year before the novel begins, during a vacation with his wife. His farm goes to his son Darrel.

Masterji

An elderly teacher in Hasnpur, Masterji advocates Jasmine's continued education. He loves America, and has a nephew in California. A gang of boys humiliate and kill Masterji in front of his school children.

Mataji

Jasmine's mother, she begs Pitaji to let their daughter study English books. Her pleas help Jasmine stay in school six years, as compared to the customary three for girls.

Nirmala

Professorji's nineteen-year-old wife, who works in a sari store.

Pitaji

Jasmine's father, Pitaji remains nostalgic for Lahore, the village in which his family lived before the Partition Riots, right up until his death. He lived in relative prosperity in Lahore before being forced to move Hasnapur. He gets gored from behind by a bull in a country lane.

Potatoes-babu

Vimla's father.

Bud Ripplemeyer

Bud hires Jasmine to work in his bank, a family business started by his father, and soon after leaves his wife to be with her. Bud is the pillar of Baden, Iowa, a small farm town experiencing drought. He wields the power to loan farmers money. As a result, he creates some resentment, particularly from Harlan Kroener, who cripples him with two rifle shots in the back. Bud wants Jasmine to marry him, espe-

cially now that she carries their unborn child. He is twice Jasmine's age, and an avid Cardinal's baseball fan.

Mother Ripplemeyer

The seventy-six-year-old gets Jasmine a job at her son Bud's bank. Bud is one of her nine kids. Jasmine compares Mother Ripplemeyer favorably with Lillian Gordon as a representation of kindness.

Vern Ripplemeyer

Vern, Bud's father, is dead before the start of the novel.

Scott

Du's friend.

Vancouver Sing

A land prospector, Vancouver Sing buys Jasmine's family farm in Hasnpur and some of the neighbors' land as well. He attended agriculture school in Canada. It is rumored, by the village's political activists, that his newly acquired land is being used as a haven for drug pushers and gunmen.

Mr. Skola

Du's teacher.

Sukhwinder

A political extremist, Sukhwinder, or Sukkhi, kills Prakash in an Indian sari shop. He turns up later in a Manhattan park as a hot dog vender. His threatening presence drives Jasmine away from an idyllic, American life, to Iowa.

Du Thien

The adopted Vietnamese son of Jasmine and Bud, Du came from a large family in Saigon. He survived refugee camp, and therefore shares with Jasmine memories of torture, violence and a fight for life. Jasmine and Bud got Du when he was fourteen, three years prior to the start of the novel. He is called Yogi in school. Du hoards things and experiments with electronics. He feels unloved by Bud. As the novel ends, Du leaves Iowa to find his only living sister, the one who fed him live worms and lizards and crabs to keep him alive in the detention camp.

Professorji Devinder Vadhera

Prakash's benefactor and teacher during first year of technical school, Professorji lodges Jasmine during her five months in Flushing, New York. Professorji fueled Prakash's dreams of American riches. He lent Prakash money to bolster his efforts at procuring an education. He preceded Prakash to America, and in his letters back to India exaggerated the vast potential for riches and employment in the country. Professorji poses as a professor at Queen's College, but really works as an importer and sorter of human hair.

Jasmine Vijh

Jyoti is a beautiful, smart, dowryless girl born eighteen years after the Partition Riots in a makeshift birthing hut in Hasnapur, Jullundhar District, Punjab, India. She is the fifth daughter, the seventh of nine children. An astrologer tells the young Jasmine's fate of widowhood and alienation, and both predictions come true. She attends school twice as long as most Indian girls, and impresses her teachers with her intelligence. Jyoti's name and identity change and change. Her grandma names her Jyoti, meaning ''light.'' Prakash, her Indian husband killed by a terrorist bomb, calls her Jasmine. Lillian Gordan calls her Jazzy, Taylor names her Jase, and Bud Ripplemeyer gives her the moniker Jane. Jasmine originally shares Prakash's dream of an American life of prosperity. After his murder, she travels abroad to burn herself on his pyre. Upon landing in America, Half-Face, the captain of the boat that carried her over, rapes her. She then kills him. Lillian Gordan saves Jasmine, coaches her, and sends her to Flushing, New York. There, she spends five oppressive months with Professorji, an Indian immigrant, and his family. From there, she goes to Manhattan to be Duff's au pair. She falls in love with her employer, Taylor, who eventually entices her to run away to California with him. In Iowa, she is Bud's lover Jane, a caregiver to a crippled man. She becomes pregnant through artificial insemination. Du, their adopted teenaged child, also flees to California.

Jyoti Vijh

See Jasmine Vijh

Prakash Vijh

Prakash marries Jasmine two weeks after they first meet. He is twenty-four and she fifteen at the time. She had already fallen in love with his voice, overheard during a conversation with her brothers. She is called Jyoti until Prakash gives her a new name and identity: Jasmine. Prakash lost his parents when he was ten. A modern man, Prakash rents a two-bedroom apartment rather than live with his family. He studies engineering and works several demeaning jobs in pursuit of his dream to move to America. Just prior to leaving India to attend Florida's International Institute of Technology, Prakash is killed by a bomb. Sukhwinder, a Sikh extremist, probably intended the bomb for Jasmine. With Prakash, so too die Jasmine's American dreams.

Vimla

Jasmine's rich childhood friend Vimla has the fanciest wedding in their village. Her husband dies of typhoid when she is twenty-one, and a year later she burns herself to death. Her suicide, or sati, illustrates the culture's gender politics: a widow's future seems endlessly gloomy.

Dr. Mary Webb

Part of a group of women who believe in past lives. In one past life, she was a black Australian aborigine.

Themes

Rebirth

The major theme of rebirth plays out literally and figuratively in *Jasmine*. In literal language, every word is truthful, whereas figurative language is used for a certain effect. Figurative language might be exaggerated, or embellished, or used to help access otherwise difficult-to-grasp concepts. The opening line, ''Lifetimes ago,'' hints at all the transformations the title character has undergone. Mukherjee consistently highlights this theme, making authorial connections between the fictional action and its significance as a subject under investigation. The narrator says, ''There are no harmless, compassionate ways to remake oneself.'' And, ''I picked [Sam] up and held him. Truly I had been reborn.''

Jasmine undergoes life transformations, or metaphorical rebirths. Dr. Mary Webb shares with Jasmine her belief in literal rebirth, or reincarnation. Mary claims to have been a black Australian aborigine in a past life. When channeling this past life, she speaks tribal languages. Ma Leela, Mary's guru, inhabits a battered, suicidal Canadian wife's body. Mary has presumably confided in Jasmine because she is Hindu. Mary understands that Hindus keep

Topics for Further Study

- When Dr. Mary Webb and Jasmine meet for lunch at The University Club, they discuss reincarnation. What is reincarnation? Name at least three distinct religions in which reincarnation is accepted as truth.

- In studying Bharati Mukherjee's work, you'll often encounter the term ''postcolonialism.'' What does the term mean, and how does it relate to Jasmine's India?

- Jasmine's childhood friend Vimla burns herself after her husband's death. This act is called ''sati'' or ''suttee.'' Define ''sati'' and discuss its cultural, historical, and religious origins.

- Prakash and Jasmine, in plotting their move to the United States, confront problems getting their ''green cards.'' Later, in Flushing, Jasmine again worries about procuring her green card, even equates it with freedom. Pretend you are a modern-day citizen of India. Explain the requirements you would have to meet in order to legally make a permanent move to the United States. What obstacles might you encounter?

- In literature and film, farmers are often stereotyped as being rather simple, sometimes crude, people. In Darrel Lutz we see a more complicated portrait of the farmer: a young, hard-working person who must understand sophisticated technology and high financing. Do some research into the state of the American farm. How big is the average farm, and how much does it cost to run?

revisiting the world. Jasmine admits that, ''yes, I am sure that I have been reborn several times, and that yes, some lives I can recall vividly.''

This further blurs the distinction between the figurative and the literal. Jasmine never gets into details of these rebirths. When Jasmine, the narrator, considers the concept of an eternal soul, she thinks of distinct stages of her present twenty-four-year-old-life: her youth in Hasnpur, her blissful time in Manhattan, her life in Baden, Iowa. Are these the past lives she means to confide to Mary Webb?

This melding of literal and figurative underlines the importance of the metaphors. It's as if Mukherjee means to say that the experience of a person's self-reinvention is so powerful as to be real.

Identity

Tied to the theme of rebirth is the theme of identity. This is the most persistent motif in *Jasmine*, infiltrating every aspect of the story. The most obvious manifestation of identity comes in the title character's name.

When Jyoti marries Prakash, a modern Indian man, she becomes Jasmine. Lillian Gordon calls her Jazzy, Taylor names her Jase, and Bud Ripplemeyer gives her the name Jane. With each name comes a new identity, a rebirth of sorts, replete with new personality traits.

The narrator says, ''I shuttled between two identities.'' Other characters, and Jasmine herself, even speak of these splinter personalities in the third person, as if they really did exist independently. She says, ''Jyoti of Hasnapur was not Jasmine.''

Prakash says, ''You are Jasmine now. You can't jump into wells.'' Prakash characterizes Jyoti as feudal. Prakash wants Jasmine to call him by his first name, rather than the pronoun used in traditional address between women and men. This identity helps create a semblance of equality between husband and wife in the male-dominated society.

Jasmine seems to like most the name Taylor gave her. ''Jase was a woman who bought herself spangled heels and silk chartreuse pants.'' Indeed, each of Jasmine's identities has distinct characteristics. ''Jyoti would have saved. . .Jasmine lived for the future, for Vijh & Wife. Jase went to the movies and lived for today. . .''

The theme of identity also pertains to place. Jasmine's name, her identity, changes with each locale. The notable exception to this is Flushing, New York, where the narrator's name is never mentioned. Whereas Jasmine forged a distinctive identity in every other place, the Flushing apartment building filled with Punjabis did not represent significant change.

Free Will vs. Predestination

Hinduism and Western notions of self-reliance oppose each other in this debate. Believers in predestination accept the idea that a higher power designs all events. Believers in free will think that each person has the power to change the course of events. In the opening chapter, the astrologer accurately predicts Jasmine's fate of widowhood and exile. This seems to support predestination, which is sometimes loosely referred to as fate. As the novel ends, however, Jasmine boldly decides to change her life, to exert free will.

> Adventure, risk, transformation: the frontier is pushing indoors through uncaulked windows. Watch me re-position the stars, I whisper to the astrologer who floats cross-legged above my kitchen stove.

Jasmine's childhood is a time when she seeks to break free from her inherited circumstances. In one dramatic scene, Jasmine kills a mad dog with a staff. A Westerner would surely credit Jasmine for having saved her own life. Dida, however, knows God willed it to happen that way.

The scenes in which Jasmine's partners are assaulted heighten the debate. Prakash, an Indian, gets killed by a bomb. During the death scene, a voice shouts ''The girl's alive. This is fate.'' Later, Dida claims that God, displeased with Prakash and Jasmine's modern ways, sent Sukkhi to murder him. Jasmine, even at this early stage of her development, shows an unsteady relationship to fate. She says, ''if God sent Sukkhi to kill my husband, then I renounce God. I spit on God.'' Before Bud gets shot, he tries to communicate covertly his grave situation to Jasmine. But she doesn't understand that Harlan Kroener is about to shoot her partner, and cannot process any of the signals. In retrospect, she realizes that her son Du or Bud's ex-wife Karin would surely have summoned the sheriff and halted the assault. In other words, an act of free will would have changed Bud's fate.

Jasmine clearly exerts free will in her decision to join Taylor and Duff on their trip to California. Earlier in the novel, Jasmine and Taylor disagree about that very topic. The narrator takes a humble position, though the question marks indicate that she leaves room for error. ''The scale of Brahma is vast, as vast as space in the universe. Why shouldn't our lives be infinitesimal? Aren't all lives, viewed that way, equally small?'' Taylor believes that Jasmine's take on the subject is a formula for ''Total fatalism.''

Gender and Sexual Politics

Sex and power are closely linked in Jasmine's life. As a Punjabi peasant woman, Jasmine would naturally have a servile relationship to men. She would be expected, in her homeland, to make herself useful to the male society. We see this even in her relationship to Prakash, a modern Indian man. There is never a thought that Jasmine will pursue an education, get work, and in that way help the couple realize their dreams. Rather, she plays a supporting role to Prakash's education and work. Jasmine carries this attitude with her to America, where she spends five months in Flushing living the life that Professorji plots for her. She even kisses his feet when he agrees to help her get a green card.

Jasmine says, ''I have had a husband for each of the women I have been. Prakash for Jasmine. Taylor for Jase. Bud for Jane. Half-Face for Kali.''

But Mukherjee depicts sex as being an act that somehow shifts the power balance. Prakash encourages a free exchange of ideas with Jasmine. He is nine years older, however, and always demonstrates a superiority in reasoning. Mukherjee juxtaposes a scene in which Jasmine is defeated intellectually with a scene of the couple in the throes of sex. Prakash says, ''Jasmine. . .help me be a better person.''

Taylor, another sensitive and liberal man, pays Jasmine's salary. He provides her food and shelter. Though he promotes equality, Jasmine cannot treat him as anything but a superior—until the night when they consummate their relationship: ''I am leading Taylor to a bed as wide as a subcontinent, I am laying my cheek on his warm cheek, I am closing his eyes with my caregiving fingertips, I am tucking the mosquito netting tight under his and Wylie's king-sized mattress.'' Here, again, Jasmine wrestles the power away from her male counterpart.

Bud, despite his disability, manages to be the head of the household. He manages, still, to be a leader in the community. When it comes to sex, however, Jasmine is entirely in charge. ''It shames Bud that now, for sex, I must do all the work, all the moving, that I will always be on top.''

With sex comes power and with power violence. Half-Face rapes Jasmine on her first day in America. He surely will rape her again. She might not survive his brutality. She kills him not out of revenge, it seems, but rather fear.

Alienation

The astrologer predicts Jasmine's exile. Throughout the novel, Mukherjee reminds the reader of Jasmine, the immigrant's, alienation in a foreign land. The most dramatic example of this is when Taylor sends her a postcard of a revolutionary's wife who ended up living among strangers.

Fear

Mukherjee returns again and again to the imaginary window shade Jasmine pulls down to close out the world: ''Taylor the Rescuer is on his way here. He taught me to yank down that window shade.''

Style

Setting

In Jasmine, the time, place, and culture of the action constantly shifts. The narrator tells of events that happened in the past (thus the use of the past tense), but not in chronological order. Some events happened in a distant past, some in a more recent past. The reader understands the order of events partly in relation to place. Events in Hasnpur, Punjab, happened during Jasmine's childhood, and references to Lahore indicate events that happened before her birth. When the setting shifts to Florida, the reader knows the action is set during Jasmine's first weeks in America. Scenes in Flushing, New York, precede scenes in Manhattan, just as scenes in Manhattan come before scenes in Iowa.

To what purpose does the narrative timeline shift back and forth? There is a sense of urgency in the Iowa scenes because Jasmine's life is moving forward, possibly in the direction of monumental change. The past events are critical to the reader's understanding of Jasmine's dilemma, but they are not as urgent. The narrative strategy, then, is to maintain this sense of urgency through the Iowa

story line, while working in all the important people, places and things from prior times.

Foreshadowing

This device, used in literature to create expectations or set up an explanation of later developments, is used frequently throughout Jasmine. The astrologer's forecast of Jasmine's widowhood and exile operates in this way. It alerts the reader to future events. Viewed in hindsight, Prakash's death seems linked to this forecast. Were it not for foreshadowing, however, the reader would not make the connection between the theme of fate and the death.

In other instances, foreshadowing is used to build tension. Jasmine says, ''That day I found the biggest staff ever, stuck in a wreath of thorny bush. I had to crawl on stony ground, and of course thorns bloodied my arms, but the moment my fist closed over the head of the staff, I felt a buzz of power.'' The strong imagery and language—the blood, the thorns, the fist—clue the reader into the importance of this scene. It insists that the reader wonder, ''What's she going to do with that staff?'' In due time, Jasmine kills the mad dog with the staff.

The knife Jasmine receives from Kingsland operates in the same way. There's an old adage that if a writer puts a gun into the story, then he or she better make the gun go off later. That's because a weapon, like the knife, signifies great danger and makes the reader expect future violence. In other words, it foreshadows danger. Jasmine's knife goes off, so to speak, when she kills Half-Face.

Symbolism

A symbol is something that suggests or stands for something else without losing its original identity. In literature, symbols combine their literal meaning with the suggestion of an abstract concept. Mukherjee uses symbols to help reader's understand a complex fabric of ideas.

Jasmine grasps a drowned dog in a stench-filled river and as she does it breaks in two. The reader accepts the literal action, the breaking apart of the dog. Given Mukherjee's treatment of the theme of identity, the reader must also associate the broken body with the splitting apart of life. The dog becomes two parts from one, just as Jyoti splits into Jasmine and Jyoti.

One symbol repeats itself throughout the novel. The narrator explains that when a pitcher breaks, the air inside is the same as outside. The author returns to this symbol when Vimla sets herself on fire, and in a discussion of Jasmine's father. "Lahore visionaries, Lahore women, Lahore ghazals: my father lived in a bunker. Fact is, there was a difference. My father was right to notice it, and to let it set a standard. But that pitcher is broken. It is the same air this side as that. He'll never see Lahore again and I never have. Only a fool would let it rule his life."

Another, more subtle, symbol is the small crack in the television set at the Flamingo Court hotel room. A reader detects symbols due to their placement and importance in the context of a scene. The highly charged rape scene, on Jasmine's first day in America, shows an ugly, imperfect aspect of the country. The television represents a medium of Hollywood fantasies and fables. The crack in the television, then, can be read as a crack in the American dream. That Jasmine's head causes the crack lends even more power to the symbol.

Irony

Irony is the use of words to express something different than and often opposite to their literal meaning. Mukherjee uses irony to show Jasmine's confusion with American culture.

Jasmine finds irony in the revolving door. "How could something be always open and at the same time always closed?" Also in the escalator. "How could something be always moving and always still?"

Metaphors

A metaphor is a figure of speech that expresses an idea through the image of another object. Metaphors suggest the essence of the first object by identifying it with certain qualities of the second object.

Sukkhi's appearance in the Manhattan park terrifies Jasmine. The image of him behind the hot dog cart stays with her even after she moves to Iowa. She says, "Sukkhi, the New York vendor, pushes his hot dog cart through my head." The reader does not think that there's an actual hot dog cart in Jasmine's head. Rather, the reader understands that Sukkhi, and all the violence and fear he represents, constantly invades Jasmine's thoughts.

A persistent metaphor derives from Taylor, "Just pull down the imaginary shade, he whispers, that's all you need to do." Again, Jasmine does not literally pull down a shade. Rather, she men-

tally blocks out all the outside influences that cause her fear.

Literary Heritage

Though not particularly interested in being known as an Indian writer, Mukherjee has placed herself in the long tradition of immigrant writers such as V. S. Naipaul and Bernard Malamud. She claims to have learned much from their fiction. She dedicated *Darkness* to her friend Malamud and even named one of her sons after him.

The predominant mode of American fiction in the 1980s was a minimalism exemplified by such writers as Raymond Carver. Minimalism used short sentences, understatement, and very little elaboration. Mukherjee positioned herself against this style, preferring instead a more elaborate one that allowed her to explore the layers of meaning and significance in the layered lives of her immigrant characters. She believes that a writer's status as immigrant gives her a great subject about which to write, and the subject deserves a great style.

Historical Context

The Partition Riots

Jasmine, the title character and narrator of Bharati Mukherjee's novel, was born 18 years after India's Partition Riots, or approximately 1965, in a rural village called Hasnpur. The time of her Indian birth would have been one of political and social upheaval. Two wars between Pakistan and India were fought that year.

The Partition Riots, which play such a key role in Jasmine's family's plight, were an attempt to create separate Muslim and Hindu States. More than 200,000 people died as Hindus fled their homes in Pakistan and Muslims theirs in India. The province of Punjab was divided between India and the newly-created Pakistan. It became the home to many Hindus.

Jasmine's family, like many Hindus at the time, left behind relative riches in exchange for squalor during the Partition Riots. It was a time of violence and upheaval. Families abandoned not only material wealth, but established roots. The Muslim-Hindu religious divide continues to be a source of tension in India. Nearly 80 percent of Indians are Hindu, and Muslims constitute 11.4 percent of the population.

The Sikhs are a religious group that made up about two percent of India's population in 1991. After India gained independence in 1947, virtually all Sikhs wound up on the India side of Punjab. They have a social identity separate from other Punjabis. The new Punjabi-speaking Punjab, established in 1966, had a Sikh majority. In *Jasmine*, there would have been natural tensions between Sukhwinder, the Sikh extremist, and Prakash Vijh.

The Green Revolution

Punjab, like many Indian states, cherishes its own subnational identity, including its own language. A Punjabi would possess a much different cultural identity and characteristics than, say, a Bengali. India has some 46 officially listed mother tongues, seventeen of which have achieved the status of recognized languages. Of these, Hindi is spoken by the largest number of people, though not by a majority. Jasmine spoke Punjabi, Hindi, and, of course, English. The first two were natural to her culture and the other made possible, in part, by pre-Independence British influence and rule.

Punjab is a largely agricultural province, much like Iowa is to the United States. The majority of India's wheat is grown in Punjab. During Jasmine's childhood, rapid technological advancement was being made in the agricultural sector. She says, ''When I was a child, born in a mud hut without water or electricity, the Green Revolution had just struck Punjab. Bicycles were giving way to scooters and cars, radios to television. I was the last to be born to that kind of submission, that kind of ignorance.''

The green revolution of the late 1960s brought in some gains in productivity and made the country self-sufficient in food grains. Poverty, however, remains a chronic problem in India. As of 1991, approximately forty percent of the nation's 800 million people were classified as poor. Life expectancy was 54 years and the annual per capita income approximately $300 U.S., ranking India among the very poor countries of the world. Paradoxically, India also possesses a sophisticated scientific, technical, and financial infrastructure.

This paradox is embodied in Jasmine's family. Though they lived in a mud hut with no electricity or plumbing, her brothers attended technical college and later repaired scooters. Television, which first came to India in 1959, was becoming a common household item in Jasmine's Hasnpur.

Women's Position in Indian Society

India, during Jasmine's childhood and today, is a male-dominated society. Men hold economic and political power. Dowries have been officially banned, but in reality the practice of giving them remains a prevalent practice. The debate over the wisdom of dowries is discussed openly in newspapers and in government. A dowry is money or property brought by a bride to a husband at their wedding. Essentially, a dowry acts as an incentive package to entice prospective husbands. The better the dowry, the better the husband, at least in theory. Jasmine entered young womanhood in the late 1970s, when her family would have been expected to offer a dowry to her perspective husband. For somebody like Jasmine, whose little family money would go to the older four daughters, the future seemed grim.

A Hindu wife, indeed, saw her role as subservient to her husband. When her friend Vimla burns herself after her husband's death, she is following a now-illegal Hindu practice called sati, or suttee. The widow cremates herself on her husband's funeral pyre in order to fulfill her true role as wife. Jasmine intended to follow the same ritual after Prakash's death. She brought his suit to America in order to make a pyre.

She says, ''I had not given even a day's survival in America a single thought. This was the place I had chosen to die, on the first day, if possible. I would land, find Tampa, walking there if necessary, find the college grounds and check it against the brochure photo. Under the very tree where two Indian boys and two Chinese girls were pictured, smiling, I had dreamed of arranging the suit and twigs. The vision of lying serenely on a bed of fire under palm trees in my white sari had motivated all the weeks of sleepless, half-starved passage, the numbed surrender to various men for reward of an orange, a blanket, a slice of cheese.''

Divorce in India is becoming more common, but it is highly stigmatized.

Critical Overview

When Bharati Mukherjee's *Jasmine* was published in 1989, it received wide critical praise in the mass media, but less kind treatment among academic scholars. Mukherjee had just had her greatest success in becoming the first naturalized American citizen to win the National Book Critics Circle Award for Fiction. She won that award in 1988 for *The Middleman and Other Stories.*

The New York Times Book Review called *Jasmine* "One of the most suggestive novels we have about what it is to become American." At the year's end, it named the book one of the best of 1989. *The San Francisco Chronicle* and *The New York Times* praised the author's poetic writing style. *The Library Journal* said, "The novel has delicious humor and sexiness that make it a treat to read." The *USA Today* and others chose to focus more on its importance in raising awareness of both Indian and American cultures.

"A beautiful novel, poetic, exotic, perfectly controlled," *The San Francisco Chronicle* wrote.

In *Bharati Mukherjee: Critical Perspectives, Jasmine* is seen in less generous terms. Debjani Banerjee, in an essay published in *Perspectives,* indicates that Mukherjee fails "to contextualize the historical and political events of India" and is unable to "perceive the complex workings of postcolonial and neocolonial forces." In this article, Banerjee articulates a backlash among South Asians to Mukherjee's work. She writes that Mukherjee represents Indians in such a way that implies "one must escape from the disillusionment and treachery of postcolonial history." In sum, Banerjee accuses Mukherjee of "catering to a First World audience while stilling mining the Third World for fictional material."

Gurleen Grewal, another critic writing in *Perspectives,* accuses Mukherjee of perpetuating certain lies about the American Dream. She claims that Mukherjee overlooks the barriers of education, race, and history that would have prevented Jasmine, a Punjabi peasant girl, from becoming a liberated and articulate New World woman in a relatively short time. Grewal further indicts Mukherjee for perpetuating stereotypes of Indian-American speech patterns and other social and psychological aspects of immigration.

Still another *Perspectives* writer, Alpana Sharma Knippling, takes offense with Mukherjee's perspective on immigration. Knippling feels Mukherjee's views are skewed by her own upper-class background.

Other critics insist that Mukherjee is exploiting a fad of postcolonial literature. Despite these criticisms, Mukherjee is generally well regarded in literary America. Wendy Lesser, writing on the United States in 1997's *The Oxford Guide to Contemporary Writing,* credits Mukherjee with a "talent for cultural mimicry that verges on ventriloquism." She does, however, point out that, "Mukherjee is known for her novels but her best writing is in her short stories."

Criticism

Donald G. Evans

Evans is a novelist, journalist, and instructor of writing. In the following essay, he explores the conflict between duty and desire inherent in Jasmine.

Desire is the root of American fairy tales: desire for riches, desire for fame, desire for better this different that. Duty suppresses desire. Jasmine, the Punjabi heroine and title character of Bharati Mukherjee's novel, debates whether to act according to desire or duty. The Indian consciousness in which she was raised, embodied by Dida, her grandmother, supports duty. In her culture, there is a greater connectedness, a sense that individual acts affect so much more than the individual. The Western consciousness, embodied by her Manhattan employers Taylor and Wylie Hayes, encourages desire. The notion of America as a free country seems, in this mindset, to be an invitation to pursue one's wildest inclinations, with little respect for those left behind.

The novel opens with the phrase, "Lifetimes ago. . ." This phrase seems deliberately ironical, recalling the classical fairy tale phrase, "Once upon a time." The ensuing scene, in which an astrologer predicts Jasmine's widowhood and exile, frames the discussion of whether fate or free will dictate one's life trajectory. This is the core of existential philosophy: a focus on the conditions humans create for their existence, rather than those created by nature. This relates closely to the idea of desire and duty: does one necessarily follow the prescribed path, or can one make their own path?

The young Jasmine, due to her religious and cultural orientation, has been programmed to believe in predestination. She knows, "Bad times were on their way. I was helpless, doomed." Outwardly, however, she whispers to the astrologer, "I don't believe you." That she whispers—rather than says, or states, or shouts—indicates the tentativeness of Jasmine's position as an agent of change.

A scene of a Punjabi village in India. Jasmine*'s title character, a widowed Punjabi peasant, creates a new life for herself in the United States.*

The astrologer plays an all-important role in the novel: he is there, under the banyan tree, as the story opens, and he is there, in Jasmine's thoughts, as the novels ends.

Dida, the grandmother, firmly believes in duty. Dida knows that a girl must marry, that she must bear a son. It is the family's burden, their duty, to ensure that the girl find a husband. To tinker with this tried-and-true formula requires a certain amount of arrogance and, in Dida's mind, disrespect. Her pronouncement that, "Some women think they own the world because their husbands are too lazy to beat them" demonstrates her unflinching belief in the social order.

When Jasmine fends off a mad dog with a staff, Dida refuses to credit her granddaughter, claiming, instead, that God didn't think her ready for salvation. "Individual effort counts for nothing," she says. Later, Dida explains Prakash's death according to religious beliefs. "God was displeased" that Jasmine did not marry the man Dida chose for her, that she called her husband by his proper name, that they spent money extravagantly, that her husband planned to go abroad. Reward and retribution: God controls it all.

But Jasmine all along shows an inclination to veer from the prescribed path. She tells her father she wants to be a doctor. This is the first hint that she harbors fantastical Western-like dreams. For Dida, education for a woman seems frivolous, and even dangerous: it defies her future duty.

Jasmine eventually marries a modern Indian man. On the surface, it seems like her life merely represents a breaking of tradition, an exchange of new values for old. Certainly, that's part of it. But in the deeply ingrained mindset of the Hindu Indian, change puts the whole culture at risk. Who will care for Prakash's uncle, now that his nephew has chosen to live in an apartment?

Danger accompanies desire. Mukherjee creates at least three characters who wind up bloody, in part, because they eschew duty for desire. Prakash gets blown to pieces holding the money that would purchase the clothes in which he would follow his American dreams. Darrel, who made a desperate, futile attempt to follow his desires, hangs limp from an electrical cord, chewed on by the hogs who represent his duty. Bud winds up in a wheelchair, partly because the wife he left—his duty—could not apply her relative wisdom to the task of saving him.

What Do I Read Next?

- In *The Mistress of Spices* (1997), a novel of magic and everyday life by Chitra Banerjee Divakaruni, the heroine, Tilo, forgoes a life of special powers to live and love as an ordinary woman.

- *What's Happening to India? Punjab, Ethnic Conflict, Mrs. Gandhi's Death, and the Test for Federalism,* by Robin Jeffrey (1986), is a survey of events leading to the Golden Temple incident and Indira Gandhi's assassination, with a focus on the roles of media and modernization.

- *Days and Nights in Calcutta* (1977), by Mukherjee and Clark Blaise, is a journal of the couple's 1973 visit to India.

- In *The Holder of the World* (1997), a novel by Mukherjee, a diamond called Tear Drop connects a contemporary woman, Beigh Masters, to a 19th-century Puritan woman, Hannah Easton.

- In *Leave It To Me* (1997), a novel by Mukherjee, the heroine, Debbie DiMartino, searches to find her origins and identity.

- The short stories in *The Middleman and Other Stories* (1988), by Mukherjee, trace the lives of Third World immigrants and their adjustments to becoming Americans.

- *The Tiger's Daughter* (1972), a novel by Mukherjee, provides a satiric look at Indian society from the point of view of expatriate Tara Banerjee Cartwright.

- In *Wife* (1975), a novel of morals by Mukherjee, Dimple moves to the United States with her husband and becomes torn between Indian and American cultures.

- In *A House for Mr. Biswas* (1961), a deeply comic novel by V.S. Naipaul, the title character yearns to be something greater than a henpecked sign writer.

- In *How I Became A Holy Mother and Other Stories* (1981), a collection of short stories by Jhabvala Ruth Prawer, the characters are divided into two essential categories, Seekers and Sufferers.

- *The Great Indian Novel* (1989), an irreverent novel by Salman Rushdie, chronicles modern Indian political history.

(Jasmine thinks that Karin, under the same circumstances, would have understood to call the sheriff and thus stop Harlan Kroener's assault).

Darrel, like Jasmine, internally debates the value of acting out his desires at the price of neglecting his duty. "Crazy, Darrel wants an Indian princess and a Radio Shack franchise in Santa Fe. Crazy, he's a recruit in some army of white Christian survivalists. Sane, he wants to baby-sit three hundred pound hogs and reinvent the fertilizer/pesticide wheel."

Mukherjee's careful use of imagery and sensory details in Darrel's suicide scene demonstrates the danger of both desire and duty. The fantastical images of far-off galaxies and the pleasantly strong smell of cumin stand in contrast to the word "rawness."

> The frail man who is still slowly twisting and twisting from the rafter with an extension cord wrapped around his stiffly angled neck isn't the Darrel, would-be lover, would-be adventurer, who only nights ago in a cumin-scented kitchen, terrorized me with the rawness of wants. This man is an astronaut shamed by the failure of his lift-off. He keeps his bitter face turned away from the galaxies that he'd longed to explore.

Desire, however, does not necessarily end in blood. The danger is always there, but Mukherjee allows for success. Du, Jasmine's adopted Vietnamese son, represents this opportunity. In following his own desire, he betrays Jasmine's sense of duty. In Du's departure scene, he bends over a rifle to kiss

> **❝** This is the core of existential philosophy: a focus on the conditions humans create for their existence, rather than those created by nature. This relates closely to the idea of desire and duty: does one necessarily follow the prescribed path, or can one make their own path?"

Jasmine. The two are fairly close in age, seven years apart, and given their history it's fair to assume an undercurrent of sexual tension. At least, the tenderness goes beyond that normally exchanged between mother and son. The kiss seems to symbolize so much desire, just as the rifle symbolizes so much violence. Mukherjee might be suggesting that it's necessary to pass through violence to fulfill desire.

> Suddenly, I'm bawling. How dare he leave me alone out here? How dare he retreat with my admiration, my pride, my total involvement in everything he did? His education was my education. His wirings and circuits were as close to Vijh & Vijh as I would ever get. . .This time his face is smiling, confident. He's mastered his demons. For the first time in our life together, he bends down, over the rifle, to kiss me. You gave me new life, I'll never forget you. I hear the crunch of gravel. He undoes the lock, announces it's John, not Darrel, not Bud, and on a hot Iowa night, he steps into the future.

Make no mistake: Mukherjee's novel supports the Western notion of self-determination and individual initiative. Of all the settings in the novel, only Manhattan allows for the possibility of freedom, which seems closely tied to happiness. Hasnpur is mud huts and arranged marriages and a lifetime of servitude. Prakash and Jasmine experience a certain kind of bliss in plotting their escape from Hasnpur. Florida is economic and sexual shame. Jasmine gets raped and wanders penniless, sure to die if not for the saint-like kindness of Lillian Gordon. Flushing is India all over again, in costly replication. Jasmine lacks the power, financial and otherwise, to purchase her escape. Baden, Iowa, is India with white people: an agricultural community bound, in so many ways, to tradition. Jasmine plays the role

of dutiful wife. The postcards Prakash received from his old teacher—"CELEBRATE AMERICA. . .TRAVEL. . .THE PERFECT FREEDOM"—don't ring true.

Manhattan is different. It is where Jasmine claims to become an American. "On Claremont Avenue I came closest to the headiness, dizziness, porousness of my days with Prakash. What I feel for Bud is affection. Duty and prudence count. Bud has kept me out of trouble. I don't want trouble. Taylor's car is gobbling up the highways."

The Hayes, an urban professional couple, represent the antithesis of Dida's stubborn relationship with duty. The Hayes possess confidence, wit: they seem happy. Their inclination, surely, is to act according to desire. Wylie Hayes on the surface lives an idyllic life. She's involved in an equal-partnership relationship with her husband Taylor, who is smart, caring, and sensitive. She loves her darling daughter Duff. The family has sufficient financial means and meaningful work. Yet, when she falls in love with Stuart Eschelman, she sees an opportunity to improve upon all that. Forget the ripples of pain Wylie's divorce from Taylor will cause. It isn't about those other people, it's about Wylie. "It's all so messy," Wylie says. "Taylor's such a sweetheart, and there's Duff and Stuart's three kids, but this is my chance at real happiness. What can I do? I've got to go for it, right?"

It's as natural for Wylie to act out her desires as it is for Jasmine to suppress them. Taylor, though hurt, never seems to begrudge Wylie's decision. Taylor, like Wylie, does not seem to consider it a wife's duty to remain with her loving husband and daughter.

Earlier, Taylor and Jasmine exchange ideas on the subject of free will. Jasmine explains, in Hindu terms, how "a whole life's mission might be to move a flowerpot from one table to another; all the years of education and suffering and laughter, marriage, parenthood, education, serving merely to put a particular person in a particular room with a certain flower. If the universe is one room known only to God, then God alone knows how to populate it." Taylor responds angrily to this, saying that a world in which rearranging a particle of dust ranks with discovering relativity is "a formula for total anarchy. Total futility. Total fatalism."

This argument frames Jasmine's ultimate dilemma: to remain as caregiver to the crippled Bud Ripplemeyer, or run away with the man of her dreams, Taylor Hayes. Jasmine finds safety in her duty to Bud, in being a caregiver. She understands responsibility, such as raising her child there in Iowa, as not only practical but expected. She cannot, however, deny the oppression that comes with the duty. "I am not choosing between men. I am caught between the promise of America and old-world dutifulness. A caregiver's life is a good life, a worthwhile life. What am I to do?"

Notice the similarities between Wylie's rhetorical question, "What can I do?" and Jasmine's more sincere question, "What am I to do?" Jasmine, of course, chooses to run away with Taylor, to once and for all show that a person can determine their own fate. Jasmine will not end up like Darrel. Earlier, she disagreed with Bud's insistence that Darrel keep up the farm. "What I say is, release Darrel from the land." Jasmine, in the end, releases herself. As Taylor says, "Why not, it's a free country?" In doing so, Jasmine executes all the traditional values held by Dida. She leaves a crippled lover to fend for himself. She takes a baby away from his father. She trades security for the unknown.

Mukherjee in the end circles back to the astrologer. "It isn't guilt I feel, it's relief. I realize I have already stopped thinking of myself as Jane. Adventure, risk, transformation: the frontier is pushing indoors through uncaulked windows. Watch me re-position the stars, I whisper to the astrologer who floats cross-legged above my kitchen stove." Here, the astrologer, the teller of fate, seems to symbolize old-world duty. The astrologer's position above the stove recalls Vimla's suicide scene. In the Hindu practice called sati, or suttee, the widow cremates herself on her husband's funeral pyre in order to fulfill her true role as wife. Jasmine intended to follow the same ritual after Prakash's death. She brought his suit to America in order to make a pyre. This practice is predicated on the idea that a wife's duty to her husband is absolute and eternal. Now, Jasmine mentally has the astrologer hover above the stove, as if to commit a kind of sati. The image seems to symbolize a ritual death of duty.

The ending of the novel recalls so many Hollywood endings in which the happy couple ride off into the sunset. "I am out the door and in the potholed and rutted driveway, scrambling ahead of Taylor, greedy with wants and reckless from hope." The tone and language, along with the final word "hope," suggest that Jasmine does not regret her decision to act out her desires. The author draws very little attention to the sorrowful image of an abandoned Bud, and rather focuses on the thrill of Jasmine's liberation.

Source: Donald G. Evans, in an essay for *Literature of Developing Nations for Students*, Gale, 2000.

Amy Levin

In the following essay, author Amy Levin discusses Bharati Mukherjee's novel Jasmine *in conjunction with two other novels in an exploration of female perspective on domestic and farm ideologies, as well as the quest for self, in the American Midwest.*

During the 1980s, Republican administrations glorified nostalgic visions of family life. These visions coexisted with social and fiscal policies that had negative ramifications for small farms, families, and women. This paper analyzes three contemporary novels— *Jasmine* by Bharati Mukherjee (1989), *A Thousand Acres* by Jane Smiley (1991), and *A Map of the World* by Jane Hamilton (1994)— in which the heroines' lives on their farms are influenced by contemporary myths. Like some of their predecessors, today's novelists express nostalgia for a harmonious homestead; however, they reveal the flawed nature of such visions and question their public acceptance. Ultimately, the heroines leave their farms for anonymous lives in town, indicating some resignation to the power of dominant ideologies. At the same time, the three novels offer distinct perspectives on region and narrative, as well as more specifically on what it means to be a Midwesterner. These perspectives complicate the connections among farming, families, and ideology, throwing into relief global events such as the surge in undocumented immigrants, as well as questions of identity.

During the 1980s, the American press documented hardships experienced by rural families as a result of shifts in public policy and attitudes. More recently, women novelists have provided another record of these events, focusing on the interrelated effects of government regulations and domestic ideology on the lives of farm women. Specifically, three novels—Jane Smiley's *A Thousand Acres* (1991), Jane Hamilton's *A Map of the World* (1994), and Bharati Mukherjee's *Jasmine* (1989)—use first person narratives to comment ironically on the farm woman as popular icon. Yet, even as the authors offer a critique of social and political values, their heroines remain enmeshed in powerful ideologies regulating gender, sexuality, and the family. The

> They emphasize that protest arises out of women's need to construct their own identities. Thus, by definition, such regionalist works address issues of difference and in particular of 'how foreignness is constituted,' literally and figuratively. By implication, they are 'essential to understanding how the United States constitutes itself.'"

novels reflect on the nature of literary regionalism as well, illustrating how it may give voice to some of those neglected by the dominant discourse, while it may silence still others.

In *The Land Before Her: Fantasy and Experience of the American Frontiers, 1630–1860,* Annette Kolodny has traced the existence of connections between social ideology and domestic fiction back to novels written prior to the Civil War. She indicates the ways in which some nineteenth-century women's novels about the West perpetuated nostalgic visions of the American home, and she outlines how several authors reinforced contemporary ideals of frontier farms and ranches. Such portraits of farm life, accompanied by pastoral imagery, were opposed to views of corrupt, dirty towns and cities. Kolodny links this theme in fiction to nineteenth-century conceptions of women's roles, indicating how novels at once supported and subverted popular values. Carol Fairbanks (1986) expands on Kolodny's theory, writing about later authors. Fairbanks suggests that these women, like some of those described by Kolodny, "wanted to undermine or, at a minimum, modify the public's image of the lives of women on the frontier" (1986). Works about farming in the Midwest during the turbulent 1980s suggest that these points apply to contemporary literature as well.

In their edited collection of articles, Sherrie Inness and Diana Royer go beyond Kolodny and Fairbanks, arguing that regionalism "offers a forum for social protest"(1987). Yet even protest is complicated because of women's liminal status as community insiders and outsiders: "As regional writers present their communities, real and imagined, they engage in multiple discourses born out of those communities, discourses that embody cultural conflict and reflect social tension even as they seek to resolve those very issues." They emphasize that protest arises out of women's need to construct their own identities. Thus, by definition, such regionalist works address issues of difference and in particular of "how foreignness is constituted," literally and figuratively. By implication, they are "essential to understanding how the United States constitutes itself." The importance of this concept is evident when one considers the historical context of the novels to be discussed. During the 1980s, the Reagan and Bush administrations, spurred on by the Moral Majority and other conservative coalitions, glorified visions of family life, even though—or perhaps because—many Americans were convinced that the family as they knew it was rapidly disintegrating. Magazines such as *Newsweek* devoted special issues to the plight of the family, including articles such as one wondering, "What Happened to the Family," which lamented, "marriage is a fragile institution," and the "irony here is that the traditional family is something of an anomaly" (Footlick 1990).

At the same time, farms were portrayed as a refuge from the forces pulling families apart, as well as from isolating and corrupting aspects of urban survival. For many, the Midwest remained a metonym for rural living, and farms took on metaphorical associations with a prelapsarian America, where families enjoyed prosperity, togetherness, and a certain moral certitude. In this almost mythical realm, women kept impeccable houses and baked bread, and people of color were virtually invisible.

In the first half of the decade, country was, quite literally, the fashion. In 1979, Mademoiselle featured an article entitled "Barn Makeover," offering readers advice on purchasing items necessary to replicate the effect. In 1985, Vogue chronicled socialite Robin Duke's conversion of a barn on Long Island into a "haven for simple pleasures after decades of globe-trotting" and a "dream house, a pleasingly rustic, French-accented country retreat" (Talley 1985). Never mind that the old horse stall separating the dining and living areas was probably as close as the socialite and her guests would get to farming, or that the homes on most Midwestern farms lacked imported French antiques. What such texts recorded was an enduring fantasy of mythic proportions.

Idealized visions coexisted with increasingly conservative social and fiscal policies that had negative ramifications for small farms, families, and women. The same week that *Time* magazine reviewed the film *Witness*, noting the "tone of civilized irreconcilability" between the heroine's rural, Amish life and the hero's spiritually starved urban existence as a policeman (Schickel 1985), its cover stories recorded the crisis facing America's farms. Popular magazines throughout the year ran articles about the farm bill, the administration's attitudes toward price supports and credit, and their negative effects on family operations.

Specialized magazines, such as *Successful Farming*, recorded similar circumstances as the decade progressed. The April and May 1979 issues of *Successful Farming* hinted at trouble with articles entitled "Loan Request Denied" (Kellum 1979) and "He Sold His Cow Herd in the Face of Rising Prices" (Kruse and Baxter 1979). Yet, such troubles seemed scattered and remediable; the farmer who had to relinquish his cow, for instance, turned to raising corn. An article by Carol Tevis, who reported on women and families, was optimistically entitled "Mom is the Key," and noted the importance of women to successful farm transfers and keeping the family together (Tevis 1979).

Thus, in the first part of the decade, farming and general interest magazines revealed that for many the vitality of the Midwestern farm belt was associated with and perceived as a reflection of the condition of the American family. Any threat to the farm represented a potential assault on the family, as well as on the moral values in which the family was grounded. The government crackdown on farm and price supports met bitter anger, having provoked in farmers a sense that their way of life was under attack, with "partisans . . . waging the battle with nearly religious intensity" (Church 1985).

Ironically, these perceptions of a direct relationship between the fate of the family and of the farm, between moral and economic stability, may have facilitated the administration's pursuit of its agricultural policy. In the middle of the decade, public personages such as David Stockman and Agriculture Secretary John Block presented farmers as irresponsible financial managers who failed to provide for their families and thus undercut the stability of the nation. Concomitantly, what had been portrayed as valuable, fertile "real estate" (to

use a category proposed by Carol Fairbanks) was increasingly referred to as a kind of "waste land," over cultivated or left fallow in crop plans designed to yield maximum federal subsidies (1986). The 1985 issue of *Time* on farming prominently featured Stockman's reproach: "For the life of me, I cannot figure out why taxpayers of this country have the responsibility to go in and refinance bad debt that was willingly incurred by consenting adults who went out and bought farmland when the price was going up" (Church 1985). Through such rhetoric, politicians were able to weaken popular nostalgia surrounding agricultural life. This strategy made policies hostile to farming interests more palatable to taxpayers in towns and cities, who felt they had something to gain—morally and financially—with the elimination of easy credit and price supports for their neighbors. Farmers themselves blamed the "greed" of their colleagues (Tevis 1992), as well as the government and bankers, but not their own practices.

By the end of the decade, *Successful Farming* testified to the devastating effects of the 1980s on farms and their families. In "Diminished Expectations," Carol Tevis (1992) compared 1974 and 1991 surveys of thousands of families. The results were discouraging. Federal policies were frequently blamed for the desperate plight of farms; the author reported that "A strong sense of disillusionment prevails regarding government." More specifically, said a woman from Kentucky, "I believe the government wants the family farm out." Respondents also linked government policies to the collapse of the family: "Many farm men and women point to the increase in off-farm employment [necessitated by the economy] as a factor behind the erosion of social relationships, and the decline in neighboring in their communities." Not only did the survey indicate that "[t]he feeling that family life is threatened is more pronounced," (1992) but it cited a farmer who took a stab at earlier rosy pictures of rural life: "I hate the way farm magazines glorify the farm with all the sentimental slop." In light of such disgruntlement, it is not surprising that in the 1991 survey, only 63 percent of the respondents thought the family farm would survive.

Similarly, sociological and anthropological studies of women in rural America have noted increasing anxiety and tension, which they locate historically and contemporaneously. Their methodologies include large samples, as well as interviews and case studies, and some of them take an explicitly feminist perspective. For instance, Deborah Fink traces the history of the myth that "farm people were happier, healthier, and more virtuous than city people" back to Jeffersonian idealism (1992), entrenching perceptions of rural America in the political ideology of the new Republic. Fink further argues that visions of the "frontier West as a place where women could shake free" are feminist reconstructions of the past, whereas many farm women have lived and continue to live in virtual isolation. She indicates that "the organization of labor within the nuclear family undermined its liberating potential" and permitted the elision of women from study, as well as the neglect of farm women's troubles. Her work chronicles "subtle acts of sabotage," or women's modes of resistance, in contrast to the portraits of united families in popular farm publications.

In *Open Country, Iowa: Rural Women, Tradition, and Change*, Fink (1986) takes a feminist anthropological perspective in focusing on women since World War II. In this work, Fink emphasizes the importance of economics in farm country, in particular in such changes as increased mechanization and women's difficulties in finding adequately paying off-farm jobs that might reduce their dependence on men. She also identifies land transfers and a lack of social services to help with domestic violence, child care, and other needs as difficulties for farm women. And, unlike the reporters in popular farm publications, she contends that the patriarchy itself is a major source of tension and unhappiness in farm life. To the extent that other social and political structures support the patriarchy, she finds them complicit as well. Thus, while farmers in the public press blamed many of their problems on external forces, and the government accused farmers of fiscal irresponsibility, scholarly researchers noted internal family tensions as well.

These connections between the health of the family and of the farm, between political policy and domestic ideology, which researchers such as Kolodny documented in nineteenth-century novels, are central in *Jasmine, A Thousand Acres*, and *A Map of the World*. Smiley's novel is set in 1979, and Hamilton's at the end of the 1980s or beginning of the 1990s. Mukherjee's focuses primarily the middle of the 1980s. The novels thus span the decade and offer a retrospective on its events. At the same time, the three texts provide distinct perspectives on the region and what it means to be a Midwesterner: the heroine of Smiley's work is born and bred in Iowa, the family in Hamilton's book has chosen to farm in Wisconsin, and Mukherjee's protagonist

arrives in Iowa after a long odyssey that began in Punjab. These different temporal and spatial removes complicate the connections among farming, families, and ideology, throwing into relief global events, such as the return of Vietnam war veterans or the surge in undocumented aliens, as well as questions of national and regional identity.

The effects of these various removes are particularly significant, because they exemplify theories developed by contemporary scholars on regionalism in literature. First, these novelists contest the idea of a single, monologic definition of a region, instead "[v]iewing geography as a two- or three-tiered field, as a combination or dialectic of what there is and what people believe or imagine there is" (Loriggio 1994). Every one of these texts supports Marjorie Pryse's assertion that the region that is experienced by marginalized individuals, including women, minorities, and ideological "outsiders," is very different from the Midwest experienced by members of the dominant population (1994). This difference generates conflict and plot (Loriggio 1994).

Second, these novels illustrate a distinction made by Marjorie Pryse between regionalist literature, written or narrated by insiders, and regional literature, which is written or narrated by outsiders and captures "local color" (1994). The literature of insiders tends to elicit "empathy" (Fetterley and Pryse, 1992) and to express an "implicit pedagogy" (Pryse 1994), while outsiders maintain an ironic remove. While all three novels include characters whose perspectives exemplify this duality, Mukherjee's text ultimately challenges and collapses the distinction.

Third, the novels enact various, contested views of region by presenting conflict not only among differing factions in the local population, but also between inhabitants and government outsiders, or between long-term residents and newcomers. Thus, just as the article from *Vogue* (Talley 1985) cited above offers a view of farming that differs from the representations in *Successful Farming*, these novels contain myriad perspectives on farms and their owners. At their best, these novels are about the (re)possession of space, and of memories or myths of that space, which inhabit it and affect individual constructions of it.

Specifically, in all three novels, the heroines' lives on their farms are influenced by myths of "an idyllic rural life" (Hardigg 1994). Moreover, the ultimate collapse (or near collapse) of their families and modes of living is directly related to economic policy, government farming regulations, and social ideologies that offer oppositional views of their efforts. Because citizens of neighboring towns represent or carry out government threats, the distinctions between farm and town life become critical.

Within the novels, these issues are embedded in contemporary discourse pertaining to sexuality and sex crimes. Just as the fate of the family farm is directly related to who holds political and financial control, so is the fate of the protagonist's body. The heroine of Smiley's book finds herself deeply affected by her experiences as an incest victim; Hamilton's protagonist is accused of molesting children; Mukherjee's Jasmine is raped (and her husband is crippled by an angry farmer). Ultimately, the novels might be considered maps of a world, charts not only of the limited acreage the heroines possess and are possessed by, but also topographical surveys of an important segment of American society and reflections on the forces that shape and dominate regions. As Mukherjee's heroine notes repeatedly, the Midwest has much in common with Punjab, a reference to the presence of violence and factionalism, as well as to agrarian life.

The question of whether and how much difference is tolerated by the community is even more pronounced in Mukherjee's *Jasmine*, another novel concerning a woman's attempts at self-definition. Even though the novel was not written by a Midwesterner, *Jasmine* offers significant variations on the themes developed in Hamilton's and Smiley's texts. Beginning in India and ending with a journey to California, Mukherjee's text presents a "map of the world" that is embedded in a regional setting even more explicitly than *A Thousand Acres* or *A Map of the World* itself.

Moreover, *Jasmine* invokes the distinction between regional and regionalist texts or characters only to throw it into question. On one level, *Jasmine* renders the very distinction moot, because the heroine takes different perspectives during various points in her life. On another level, the novel offers both regional and regionalist perspectives simultaneously. *Jasmine* is a regional work in the sense that it is written and narrated by an outsider with critical distance from the milieu. At the same time, it offers a regionalist perspective, giving voice to the increasing numbers of Asian immigrants in the Midwest, individuals who may be marginalized on the basis of linguistic, racial, and cultural differences. Most importantly, the novel draws attention to the fact that distinctions between insiders/outsiders are questionable, because they are based on discriminations made by those empowered and rendered visible by their status as members of the majority.

These distinctions between insiders and outsiders come into play as Jasmine travels around the world, adopting different personas. She is given various names—Jyoti, Jasmine, Jase, and Jane—to indicate the shifting phases of her existence. Having emigrated to the United States and served as a nanny in New York for several years, Jasmine chooses exile in Elsa County, Iowa, because it is the birthplace of Duff, the adopted little girl she looked after. The money from the adoption covered Duff's mother's college tuition, and the opportunity to be her nanny offers Jasmine an escape from the stifling Indian community in Flushing. Consequently, Jasmine decides, "Iowa was a state where miracles still happened" (Mukherjee 1989). For Jasmine, Duff—and, by extension, the county of her birth—initially represents openness, acceptance, freedom, and caring.

Once again, the Midwest—with the community of Baden—is presented as an idyllic environment. Jasmine is offered a job as a teller and rapidly enters a relationship with Bud Ripplemayer, the bank's manager and "secular god of Baden." The breakup of Bud's first marriage causes a stir, but as Jasmine and Bud adopt Du, a Vietnamese child, and Jasmine becomes pregnant, they appear to blend back into the community of families.

Like Smiley's Ginny, Jasmine offers advice about understanding the Midwest and farmers' lives. She explains that unfed hogs sound like abused children and that farmers need to get away from their reponsibilities in winter. Additional information is reported, often originating with Bud or his ex-wife Karin: "Bud always says, of young farmers or the middle-aged ones with shaky operations, Look out for drinking." In this community, too, character and the success of a farm are inextricably linked: "The First Bank of Baden has survived in harsh times because Bud can read people's characters. Out here, it's character that pays the bills or doesn't, because everything else is just about equal." This determination of character exists as part of a network of gossip, which is communicated over the telephone and at events such as quilt sales.

Community gossip reveals danger under the town's bucolic veneer. In contrast to the towns in the other two novels, in Elsa, violence is so frequent as to seem almost banal. "Over by Osage a man beat his wife with a spade, then hanged himself in his machine shed,'' comments Jasmine flatly. Bud is shot and paralyzed by Harlan Kroener, ''a disturbed and violent farmer,'' and Darrel Lutz, the owner of a neighboring farm, adopts the rhetoric of hate groups and eventually commits suicide.

The violence is driven both by a literal drought and the drying up of credit, which in turn is caused by government policy. Whereas Bud ''used to welcome'' the state inspectors' visits,

> it's become impersonal. Cranky bureaucrats, men with itchy collars and high-pitched voices, suggesting that this looks like a bad loan, and this and this, saying in pained voices that a banker who cosigns his neighbor's loan . . . is getting that farmer in a tougher spot.

In the communities in Smiley's and Hamilton's books, bankers are associated with the external forces destroying farms; here ''[e]ven a banker is still a farmer at heart.'' The enemies are functionaries enforcing policies that trap farmers in debt and despair, tearing apart their families.

A few farmers are able to leave for winter or to negotiate loans to develop and sell their land. Others are rooted like crops in the soil. As Karin comments bitterly (and somewhat comically), ''I won a Purple ribbon in a 4H state fair with my How-to-Pack-a-Suitcase demo . . . but I never got to travel.'' Yet economics alone do not determine who will go. Karin notes that ''She could have [left], but she chose to stay.'' What really traps local residents is an inability to conceptualize other parts of the world as distinct: ''In Baden, the farmers are afraid to suggest I'm different. . . . They want to make me familiar.'' Bud never questions Jasmine about India because ''it scares him''; to the extent that he recognizes her past, he does so in cliched terms that cast Asia as Other, unknown: ''Bud courts me because I am alien. I am darkness, mystery, inscrutability.'' ''The family's only other encounter with Asia'' was when Bud's brother Vern was killed in Korea, adding to the aura of danger and silence surrounding the continent. Torn between ignoring difference and fearing its perils, the inhabitants of Elsa County have no compelling reason to leave home.

Even Jasmine denies difference. Of Florida, she says, ''The landscape was not unfamiliar: monsoon season in Punjab.'' Iowa is flat like Punjab, and the farmers there remind Jasmine of the ones she ''grew up with.'' The Indians in Flushing ''had kept a certain kind of Punjab alive, even if that Punjab no longer existed,'' so that after a while, Jasmine notices that ''I had come to America and lost my English.'' Unlike the inhabitants of Elsa County, however, Jasmine is repulsed by such similarities, especially since the greatest resemblance is in the area of regional or factional prejudice.

To the extent that Midwestern characters acknowledge the existence of otherness, they do so only to tame or domesticate it. Asia and Africa provide the women of Baden and Elsa County multiple opportunities for charitable events, such as quilt sales. These allow the women to socialize and trade news. At a fair to raise funds for starving Ethiopians, the women seem oblivious to the fact that ''[e]very quilt auctioned, every jar of apple butter licked clean had helped somebody like me [Jasmine].'' The merchandise consists of little more than cast-offs from local families. Instead of representing genuine compassion for the sufferings of others, the objects seem designed to elide any sign of difference or exoticism:

> There was a model tractor commemorating John Deere's fortieth anniversary. All the dolls had yellow hair. It had been a simpler America. The toys weren't unusual or valuable; they were shabby, an ordinary family's cared-for memorabilia. Bud's generic past crowded in display tables. I felt too exotic, too alien.

The surface of Baden, with its deliberate and continual references to a ''simpler America,'' obscures violence and difference in the same way that the apparent fertility of the farm in *A Thousand Acres* hides subterranean pollution. As in *Map of the World*, the locals blame outsiders for the violence, but like Alice, Jasmine shows repeatedly that it is inherent in the community. Moreover, even though Jasmine remarks, ''Every night the frontier creeps a little closer,'' immigrants remain invisible. At the hospital, Asian doctors treat women, but one has to ''poke around'' to find them. The stories of people like Jasmine and Du remain undocumented, outside the law and the ''official'' versions of the television newscasts. The silencing of foreignness exemplifies the ''conservative, nostalgic'' qualities of regionalism described by Warren Johnson, who notes that ''[r]egionalism would seem to be the converse of exoticism. The depiction of the foreign and exotic frequently seeks to evoke what is repressed in the dominant culture for being extreme or excessive'' (1994) and is thus perceived as threatening.

Despite its international flavor, then, Mukherjee's novel insists on fragmentation and regional conflict in a way that the other two works do not. From the beginning, for instance, *Jasmine* specifies that Baden is neither Danish or Swedish, but German. The early sections of the novel show the effects of Sikh separatism and of a terrorist attack that kills Jasmine's first husband. Not only does the murderer reappear in Central Park, but when Darrel Lutz begins to lose his sanity, he accuses Bud of being a tool of the Eastern establishment. There is even a pecking order among immigrants; Du, who is from urban Saigon, looks down on the Hmong emigres. Ironically, even though such prejudices constantly invoke difference, they ultimately render it impossible to distinguish between insiders and outsiders; the policies that create have and have-nots also spawn endless numbers of factions, and factions within factions.

Rather than embracing such fragmentation, Jasmine leaves Bud for the "perfectly American" Taylor, choosing a myth of nationality over the actuality of factionalism, a fiction of self-development over a narrative of entrapment. Jasmine's departure echoes Ginny's abandonment of the farm in Smiley's novel. Jasmine has changed with her names from the timid Indian widow who wanted to immolate herself to the self-sufficient Iowa farm woman tending a handicapped husband. Her ability to transform herself, gained through years of traveling and suffering, distinguishes her from the rooted Iowa women: "The world is divided between those who stay and those who leave."

In much canonical literature, the quest is presented as a male prerogative, while females remain at home. One could therefore argue that much regional literature is gendered as female because "characters in regional fiction are rooted" (Fetterley and Pryse 1992), too. In her discussions of some of the nineteenth-century texts she analyzes, Kolodny (1984) supports these assertions, tracing the historical efforts of pioneer women to cultivate their environment, rendering it homelike and familiar. Yet, even as these three novels about farming in the 1980s question ideological and social traditions, they break with literary convention by presenting female characters who choose, or are forced, to journey. Their itinerancy is instigated by the devastation of the land and the accompanying cruelty of its owners. Women such as Ginny in *A Thousand Acres* and Alice in *A Map of the World* ultimately must forge urban existences, contradicting stereotypes that gender the earth as female and portray it as freer and somehow purer than the city. Similarly, Jasmine is a traveler leaving behind natives and other migrants who have walled themselves in: "the frontier is pushing indoors through uncaulked windows" (Mukherjee 1989).

With its reference to the frontier and "uncaulked windows" of makeshift abodes, the conclusion of Mukherjee's novel reinscribes itself within the lore of America's past, reinforcing a notion that anything is possible for someone with the correct spirit. Indeed, *Jasmine* constitutes a female version of the myth of the self-made American: "We murder who we were so we can rebirth ourselves in the images of dreams" (1989). If, as she claims, the people of Elsa County are "puritans," then Jasmine is one of the Elect (1989), protected by the trinity of Brahma, Vishnu, and Shiva.

Jasmine's "Rescuer" (1989), the man who encourages her to escape from Iowa, is Taylor. Yet Jasmine's decision to follow Taylor is ambiguous. Jasmine presents the choice as liberatory: "I am not choosing between men. I am caught between the promise of America and old world dutifulness." The America she claims for herself is one where "Adventure, risk, [and] transformation" are possible. Taylor is not taking her back to New York but to the Western edge of the country—California— which is also Du's new home. The novel concludes with the heroine "reckless from hope" (1989) like a male adventurer in a nineteenth-century novel.

But what has Jasmine chosen? She is initially attracted to Taylor because he seems "entirely American": "I fell in love with what he represented to me, a professor who served biscuits to a servant, smiled at her, and admitted her to the broad democracy of his joking, even when she didn't understand it" (1989). This statement makes an essentialist equation between being an upper middle class intellectual and being American, as if to be a banker/ farmer in the Midwest were somehow less American (a comment that reverses many stereotypes, even as it colludes with 1980s political rhetoric against farmers). Although Jasmine denies being a "gold digger" (1989), one cannot help wondering about Taylor's increased attraction after Bud is paralyzed and his bank is increasingly controlled by outsiders, given the importance of financial success in the myth of the self-made American. Similarly, Jasmine's astoundingly rapid acquisition of knowledge of literary classics such as Jane Eyre, together with her ready acceptance outside the immigrant world, obscures the realities and prejudice in American society.

The world Jasmine chooses, then, is not free of the ideological illusions surrounding the Midwest of the 1980s. Like the heroines in Smiley's and Hamilton's works, one could argue that Jasmine has chosen a diminished realm and a fractured or weakened family. Taylor offers not wholeness but an ''unorthodox family'' (1989), appropriately, as he is a physicist specializing in subatomic particles. Moreover, Jasmine's departure leaves traditional family structures and roles intact; although Jasmine claims that she is relinquishing her role as a ''caregiver'' (1989), she initially met Taylor when she was his child's nurse, and she will continue to tend Duff. It is questionable, therefore, whether the move is truly liberatory, or whether her narrative merely reinscribes conventional gender and power relations: ''As exotic caregiver, homemaker, and temptress, Jane is the model immigrant woman who says and does nothing to challenge the authority or ethnocentrism of the white American male'' (Grewal 1993). If this is the case, the manual embedded in the text is not so much a guide to the Midwest as a revision of Benjamin Franklin's autobiography, another work that equates character and worldly success.

To the extent that Jasmine has learned about America, she has familiarized herself with a 1980s ideology that lays claim to classlessness but looks down on farmers, that values technology and money over the vagaries of crops, livestock, and the weather. Even though Jasmine bears the psychic and physical effects of rape, she seems reborn after killing her attacker and slicing her tongue, effectively silencing herself. The effects of this violence do not seem indelibly written on her body, although Bud is permanently crippled and can only father a child with the assistance of technology. The novel seemingly liberates Jasmine, but fails to challenge a system that traps and oppresses many Midwesterners. Similarly, the novel elides the fates of most immigrants, who continue their undocumented existences on the margins of the American economy. By leaving such social and political structures in place—and suppressing alternative stories—Jasmine bows to their power. The book gestures toward a regionalist perspective that ''speaks for us, the new Americans from nontraditional immigrant countries'' (Mukherjee 1988), but ultimately settles for a critical distance from the newly reconstituted Midwest.

Taken together with *A Thousand Acres* and *A Map of the World*, *Jasmine* demonstrates that fiction continues to document the complicated effects of social beliefs and economic trends on individuals, as well as the silencing of women, immigrants, and the otherwise marginalized. Like their predecessors, today's novelists express nostalgia for a more harmonious form of life; however, they reveal the flawed nature of earlier social visions and question the public's acceptance of them. In the end, the heroines leave their farms for lives in town, indicating a certain resignation among the authors to the overwhelming power of dominant ideologies concerning women, farming, and family in 1980s America.

Ultimately, the ambiguous endings of all three novels, including the heroines' mixed success at finding a more liberated existence, have significant implications for our readings of contemporary women's regionalist fiction. While this fiction succeeds in giving voice to the unheard and offering a critique of agrarian idealism, the authors are unable to conceive of a world where women can extricate themselves from powerful discourses pertaining to gender, social policy, and politics. The protagonists offer readers advice, but the advice is not what it seems, outdated, or useless. The strength of regionalist fiction—that it comments from inside the region rather than from outside—is also its weakness, for it cannot rise above community structures and social ideology. For women heroines, this means that their narratives must express nostalgia for a past that never was and dream of future unity that may never be.

Source: Amy Levin ''Familiar Terrain: Domestic Ideology and Farm Policy in Three Women's Novels About the, 1980s,'' in *NWSA Journal,* Vol. 11, March 22, 1999, p. 21, Jasmine.

Abha Prakash Leard

In the following brief review of Mukherjee's novel Jasmine, *author Abha Prakash Leard writes that Mukherjee is offering the reader a unique, female Hindu bildungroman. As the novel's protagonist, alternately known as Jyoti, Jasmine, or Jane, travels from one circumstance and geographical location to another, so is her inner self travelling the journey of rebirth toward a higher plane.*

Despite postcolonial readings of Bharati Mukherjee's novel *Jasmine*, Western critics have not placed in context the pivotal play of migrations, forced and voluntary, literal and figurative, found in the plural female subjectivity of the novel. With the connotations of both dislocation and progress within the tangled framework of the narrator's personal history, journey as metaphor in the novel stands for the ever-moving, regenerating process of life itself. In presenting a woman capable of birthing more than one self during the course of her lifetime, Mukherjee invests her novel with the unique form of a Hindu *bildungsroman*, where the body is merely the shell for the inner being's journey toward a more enlightened and empowered subjectivity.

But the material self exists and is the site of oppression and transformation. Cognizant of the formidable interventions of gender, class, religion, and historical circumstance, Mukherjee shapes her heroine as a "fighter and adapter," who is perpetually in the process of remaking her self and her destiny. Set in the seventies and eighties when the violent separatist demands of the militant Sikhs forced many Hindus to migrate from Punjab, *Jasmine* centers around the experiences of Jyoti, a teenage Hindu widow, who travels all the way from Hasnapur, India, her feudalistic village, to America. These experiences are told in first person by a woman who identifies herself as Jane Ripplemeyer, the pregnant, twenty-four-year-old, live-in girlfriend of Bud Ripplemeyer, a Jewish banker in Baden, Iowa. But the "I" in the past and present fragments of this first-person narrative belongs to a woman who sees herself as more than one person. Officially known as Jyoti Vijh in India, the narrator, in America, is a many-named immigrant with a fake passport and forged residency papers. By giving her protagonist more than one name, usually through the character of a husband/lover, Mukherjee subverts the notion of a fixed, uniform subject. Simultaneously, the narrator's plurality of names—Jasmine, Jazzy, Jase, Jane (which successively became more Westernized)—helps to mask her ethnic difference and enable her to survive in a hostile, alien land.

Jasmine's decision to leave her homeland coincides with her desire to escape the confines of her cultural identity. This desire, articulated in the dramatic recollection of the opening chapter, is a subtext that continually spurs the narrative's critique of the patriarchal underpinnings of Hindu culture and its social fabric. The little girl's refusal to accept the astrologer's prophecy translates into the adult narrator's unwillingness to imprison herself within traditional, predetermined codes of femininity. As Jyoti matures into a young woman, her resistance against a determinate existence continues in her unconventional marriage to Prakash, a "modern man," who wants them to leave the backwardness of India for a more satisfying life in America. Within a cultural context that privileges arranged marriages, Jyoti's romance, that she has engineered, can indeed be seen not only as nontraditional but also as a subversive tactic against the established cultural norm. Her marriage is not only liberating but transforming as well. Comparing her husband to

> **" By giving her protagonist more than one name, usually through the character of a husband/lover, Mukherjee subverts the notion of a fixed, uniform subject."**

Professor Higgins, the benevolent patriarch of Pygmalion, the narrator recollects the early days of her marriage when Prakash, in an attempt to make her a "new kind of city woman," changes her name to Jasmine. Although "shutt[ling] between identities," the narrator is eager to transcend the name/identity of her child self in the hope of escaping the doomed prophecy lurking in her future. To leave the country of her birth would mean new beginnings, "new fates, new stars." But before the seventeen-year-old bride can embark on a new life with her husband, he is killed in a terrorist bombing.

The motif of the broken pitcher in Jasmine epitomizes not only the temporality of one life journey within the ongoing Hindu cycle of rebirth, but also the fragility of constructed boundaries, whether of the self, the family, or the nation. The author parallels the violence of the Khalistan movement that is responsible for Jasmine's widowhood and her subsequent displacement and exile to the bloody communal riots between the Hindus and Muslims at the time of India's independence in 1947. Despite her distance from this historical event, which rendered millions of people homeless and destitute overnight, the narrator can still empathize with her parents' anguished memories of the Partition that forced them to leave their ancestral home in Lahore and flee to Punjab. The fragmentation of the nation and the family as well as the haunting journey from terror to refuge have seeped into Jasmine's subconscious—"the loss survives in the instant replay of family story: forever Lahore smokes, forever my parents flee."

Directly or indirectly, historical conflicts (sparked by religous intolerance) within India determine the problematic constitution of Jasmine's shifting individuality. Her "illegal" migrant life in America is an extension of an existence that began in the shadow of political refuge and later, with her husband's death, almost ended in her widowed status. Within the enclosures of the Hindu culture, a widow must atone the death of her husband for the rest of her life. Jasmine's widowhood cancels her right to material fulfillment. It entails a life of isolation in the "widow's dark hut," on the margins of Hasnapur society. For Jasmine, to live the life of a widow is to live a fate worse than death.

Jasmine's difficult "odyssey" to America and her initial experiences in an alien society parallel the emergence of a new selfhood despite the vulnerability of her youth and material circumstances. Her brutal rape at the hands of Half-face, a man who represents the worst of America in his racist and inhuman treatment of the Asian and black refugees aboard his trawler, is a climactic moment in the text which signals the sudden awakening of Jasmine's "sense of mission." Refusing to "balance [her] defilement with [her] death," a traditional ending for most rape victims in orthodox Indian society, Jasmine, infused with the destructive energy of the goddess Kali, murders the man who symbolizes the "underworld of evil" and begins a new "journey, traveling light."

Given a world where violence and bloodshed, exploitation and persecution are constants, Jasmine's plurality of selves is her only strategy for survival. Knowing only too well that there are "no harmless, compassionate ways to remake oneself," Jasmine views her multiple selves with a detachment that has been forged in pain. But beneath this carefully maintained distance is the terrible agony of a woman who cannot free herself from the collective memory of her haunting past:

> Jyoti of Hasnapur was not Jasmine, Duff's day mummy and Taylor and Wylie's au pair in Manhattan; that Jasmine isn't this Jane Ripplemeyer. . . . And which of us is the undetected murderer of a half-faced monster, which of us has held a dying husband, and which of us was raped and raped and raped in boats and cars and motel rooms?

Having lived through "hideous times," Jasmine, in her arduous journey of survival, has accomplished the rare mission of transcending the boundaries of a unitary self and identifying with all the nameless victims of gender, culture, class, and imperialism. The narrative ends on a note of optimism where Jasmine, "cocooning a cosmos" in her pregnant belly, and about to "re-position her stars" again, is ready to plunge into another life and another journey of transformation.

Source: Abha Prakash Leard, "Mukherjee's 'Jasmine,'" in *The Explicator,* Vol. 55, No. 2, Winter, 1997, pp. 114–118, Jasmine.

F. Timothy Ruppel

In the following essay on Mukherjee's novel Jasmine, *F. Timothy Ruppel suggests that* Jasmine *disrupts the traditional narrative process, thematizing narration and identity by illustrating, through the circumstances of Jasmine's character, how identity can be ascribed by outside influences that desire to define her character as known, or as conforming to, their own social, economic or hierarchicalized mythos.*

> We are the outcasts and deportees, strange pilgrims visiting outlandish shrines, landing at the end of tarmacs, ferried in old army trucks where we are roughly handled and taken to roped-off corners of waiting rooms where surly, barely wakened customs guards await their bribes. We are dressed in shreds of national costumes, out of season, the wilted plumage of intercontinental vagabondage. We only ask one thing: to be allowed to land; to pass through; to continue. (Mukherjee)

Who are these "strange pilgrims"? Certainly, we see them infrequently on the evening news en their "vagabondage" becomes intolerable, when their passage can no longer be ignored, when they put spectacular pressure on our borders. Then, these "outcasts and deportees" emerge into a brief visibility beneath Western eyes. Watching TV the other night, I saw Haitian "boat people" crammed on their small, overcrowded crafts off the Florida shore. Through its spokesman, the United States administration reasonably explained its policy of denying these refugees entry, citing a benevolent and humanitarian concern with the possible loss of life. In other words, their "vagabondage" was being treated as an issue of water safety, of laudable nautical rigor, rather than as an issue of political and material conditions. In addition, and due to the interests of electronic brevity, the Haitians had been resolutely fixed into the already known, and therefore available, category of "boat people," a distinction that defined them as a collective identity. As Chandra Mohanty writes, "the idea of abstracting particular places, peoples, and events into generalized categories, laws, and politics is fundamental to any form of ruling."

We are thus insulated from the historical trajectories that set this population in motion, the contradictions and ruptures that have propelled them out of their native culture. This insulation involves a substitution, a metalepsis, where a sociopolitical effect is identified as a cause. As a result, these "strange pilgrims" become the originary cause of scrutiny, interest, or benevolence of a discourse that seeks to situate them in teleological narratives of Western civilization and progress, rather than as the effects of these same narrative gestures. In this paper, I want to suggest that texts such as Bharati Mukherjee's *Jasmine* attempt to disrupt this even flow of narrative historiography with a counter-discourse that thematizes prior narratives of enforced identity—narratives that through accumulation and repetition seek to define and circumscribe identity as a fixed and available resource, constituted wholly by another's desire. At the same time, *Jasmine* illustrates the inherent difficulty of such an attempt, since Mukherjee's overt critique of debasing stereotypes based on gender and exoticism tends to impede a sustained critique of problematical representations of India.

Although *Jasmine* is a narrative of emergence, I do not wish to assert, in any sense, that this novel relates an immigrant's success story, charting a steady and inevitable progress that culminates in the achievement of an autonomous, unified self. Nor is it a completely realized postcolonial text, since Mukherjee's portrayal of India relies on the trope of the manichean allegory and the demonization of the Sikh community. Rather, *Jasmine* is a novel that resists closure and suggests a strategy of continual transformation as a necessary and historically contingent ethic of survival. This continual remaking of the self invokes "two temporalities: that of oppression, memory, and enforced identity, and that of emergence after the 'break,' the counter memory, and heterogeneous difference" (Radhakrishnan, "Ethnic Identity"). On the one hand, *Jasmine* thematizes narration and identity by bringing into focus how differences are social products of interested desire. At the same time, it offers the symbolic possibility of the emergence of a reinvented, paralogical, heterogeneous "family," based on affinity and multiplicity rather than fixed identity. Thus, I will be reading *Jasmine* as a counter-narrative where "re-inventing ourselves a million times" becomes a reflexive, historically situated strategy for negotiating power.

Discussing narrative history, Frantz Fanon writes that when the colonizer comes to write the history of the colonial encounter "the history which he writes is not the history of the country which he plunders

> "*Jasmine* is a novel that resists closure and suggests a strategy of continual transformation as a necessary and historically contingent ethic of survival."

but the history of his own nation . . . ." Such interested productions become, for Lila Abu-Lughod, "the great self-congratulatory literature of the rise of the West, which for so long has shaped our view of the past . . . ." Suggesting that this literature should be "revaluated" and "remade," Abu-Lughod recommends an analysis based on triangulation, or multiple, contradictory points of view. It is just this voice of the excluded and marginalized respondent that feminist, Afro-American, and multicultural studies try to recover. But, at the same time, this voice is seen as a threat to the accomplishments and values of Western culture simply because it has been historically marginalized and may have a different story to tell. In other words, the silent, demarcated subject who is the product of Western and patriarchal historiography built upon theories of synchronous development is again resituated just at the very moment of emergence, at the very moment s/he speaks.

Moreover, as Edward Said suggests, when the postcolonial subjects speak, they are considered by many Western intellectuals to be merely "wailers and whiners," denouncing the evils of colonialism. They are thus implicated in the politics of blame. As Said explains, such a politics proceeds from a willingness to assert that colonialism has ended. Therefore, "any claims about or reparations for its damages and consequences into the present are dismissed as both irrelevant and preposterously arrogant" ("Intellectuals"). The phrase "into the present" is crucial. As I mentioned earlier, the former colonial subject becomes an originary cause, a source of discourse. Instead of being grateful for what "we" have historically done for them, "they" are constituted in the present as a pack of unappreciative whiners. They have declined the invitation, refused the call to step up into a world that is not of their own making. They are then implicated in a failure of recognition that only confirms their essential and underdeveloped nature.

This rhetorical and strategic resituating of the resisting respondent tends to maintain boundaries of exclusion. What is at risk here is the erasure of those traces of resistance that might disrupt the inevitability of the Western narrative of progress and benevolence. These exclusions occlude the complete record of colonialism, even as they resolutely try to define the excesses of colonialism as the product of aberrant individuals, a succession of Kurtzes, rather than as effects of the system that produced them. Such an experience of colonialism does continue into the present, producing an endless ripple of effects. For specific reasons, different in each case, the historical discourse produced by the colonizer created a system of representations (mostly centered around, and justified by, supposed traits of the native) that effaced the possibility of resistance. Resistance to domination was portrayed as an essential misrecognition on the part of the native.

This is the complex of concerns articulated by *Jasmine:* resistance, hierarchical distinctions, and boundaries that exclude and include. In what follows I will be examining these in light of what Chandra Mohanty calls (following Dorothy Smith) ''relations of ruling''—a model for cultural analysis that ''posits multiple intersections of structures of power and emphasizes the process or form of ruling, not the frozen embodiment of it.'' In *Jasmine* these concerns, embedded in relations of ruling, reveal themselves through the actions of the religious fundamentalist, Sukhwinder, the rapist, Half-Face, and the seemingly benevolent banker, Bud Ripplemeyer, individuals who continually attempt to place *Jasmine* into prior narratives of desire that would define her as a known, visible, and essential self conforming to one or another of the myths that their narrativized knowledge of her authorizes and legitimizes.

Confronted by the repeated pleas from Bud Ripplemeyer, the father of her unborn child, the narrator of *Jasmine* reflects upon how much he doesn't know about her. In fact, he has studiously avoided such knowledge, since her ''genuine foreignness frightens him.'' Instead, his desire and interest are spurred by his image of ''Eastern'' women. For her prospective husband, she is ''darkness, mystery, inscrutabllity. The East plunges me into visibility and wisdom.'' This visibility then involves an identity as an already-known subject. But she knows differently: she has been ''many

selves'' and has ''survived hideous times.'' In contrast to her, Bud lives innocently within ''the straight lines and smooth planes of his history.''

Two versions of history and narration emerge in the narrator's comments. For Jasmine, history is the discontinuity and rupture produced by material and political events and, as a result, the self becomes plural and contradictory. Her survival depends upon a flexible strategy of appropriation and transformation. For Bud, history is a straight line, a teleological and progressive ordering of existence where the phenomenological world is transparent and the self is unified and autonomous. It is ''a history whose perspective on all that precedes it implies an end of time, a completed development'' (Foucault). The narrator's displacement of fixed identity and these two views of history provide a point of entry into Mukherjee's *Jasmine*. In the course of the novel, the narrator is Jyoti, Jasmine, Jane, and Jase. Each of her names represents a transitional self as she travels from Hasnapur, India to Baden, Iowa. Rather than a recapitulation of the stereotype of the deceitful, mendacious Asian, these name changes can be seen as a response to the still ongoing effects of colonialism. She must change to survive and to continue her journey. In fact, the narrative structure is that of a journey and passage, a liminal state, which places the third world inside the first world. In the process, the narrator must continually remake herself to avoid the threat posed by enforced identity. She must avoid the limiting boundaries that seek to confine her in traditional and specific gendered roles, both in India and America.

As a village girl from Hasnapur, she is ''born to that kind of submission, that expectation of ignorance.'' Her transformation from Jyoti to Jasmine represents her ability to escape from ''a social order that had gone on untouched for thousands of years.'' This social order can be seen as symptomatic of the relations of ruling I discussed earlier. For Jyoti and the other women of Hasnapur, these relations of ruling involve a submission to the patriarchal order, which demands limited education, arranged marriages, and constant reproduction. These gendered restrictions are also configured along the lines of class and religion in *Jasmine*. Jyoti's expectations as a bride are limited by the fact that she is undowered. Her husband dies in sectarian religious violence. As the fifth daughter of nine children, Jyoti is born into a culture where daughters are a curse, since they must have dowries—which her family is unable to provide. Jyoti's mother, in an effort to spare Jyoti from a history similar to hers, a history of incessant childbearing and beatings, tries to kill her at birth. This is a culture that brings up daughters "to be caring and have no minds of our own." Nevertheless, her mother fights to keep Jyoti in school for six years and to prevent her from being married at the age of eleven to a widowed landlord.

When Jyoti does marry, it is to Prakash Vijh, a city man whose values are those of Gandhi and Nehru. In contrast to the other men of the traditional culture, Prakash does not see marriage as the cultural sanctioning of patriarchal control and enforced obedience. He renames Jyoti as Jasmine, a symbolic break with her feudal past. Yet this break causes Jyoti/Jasmine deep conflict. As a traditional woman she wants to get pregnant immediately to prove her worth and to validate her identity. Indeed, in this society, pregnancy is the only available identity. Jyoti still feels "eclipsed by the Mazbi maid's daughter, who had been married off at eleven, just after me, and already had had a miscarriage."

The point to note here, as Jasmine later realizes, is that Prakash does exert a Pygmalion effect on her, since he wanted "to make me a new kind of city woman"—a new woman for his new India. Thus, Prakash is entirely determining Jyoti's new identity. He tells her that it "was up to women to resist." Despite his modern views, Prakash is first defining Jyoti's role in the new political landscape of India, and then he is telling Jyoti how to be this new woman. As such, Prakash exerts a more subtle form of patriarchal control, disguised as benevolence and demanding her active complicity. Jyoti fully recognizes her husband's limitations. She instinctively hides her detergent sales' commissions from Prakash. "For all his talk of us being equal, was he possessive about my working?" she wonders. Indeed, his talk of equality contradicts his belief that a "husband must protect the wife whenever he can." At the same time, Jyoti begins to read, even reading Prakash's repair manuals. Her ability to read and understand technical manuals leads to the turning point in their marriage: the night when they work together, repairing a VCR with an equal division of labor. They dream of opening their own business, Vijh & Vijh. This vision is important in the narrative economy of Jasmine, since it provides the first model of the reconstituted family in the novel.

This possibility is decisively put to an end by the religious fundamentalist, Sukhwinder, who has "unforgiving eyes" and a "flat, authoritative voice." Conveniently forgetting the history of violence that followed Partition, Sukhwinder wants to create the new, separatist state of "Khalistan, the Land of the Pure" for believers who renounce "filth and idolatry." Within this codified economy of sameness, "whorish women" would be kept off the streets. Indeed, "all women are whores," and "'the sari is the sign of the prostitute.'" Sukhwinder thus wishes to uphold the traditional rigid segregation of the sexes and the exclusion of women as a corollary of his religious beliefs. For Sukhwinder, the nation-state is an exclusionary border, an enclave that celebrates the will to sameness in its univocal narrative of historical and human destiny. In her desire for stark narrative contrast, Mukherjee, however, demonizes the entire Sikh community, portraying them solely as violence-crazed fundamentalists. Here, as in her portrayal of the asymmetrical relationship between India and the West, Mukherjee succumbs to those relations of ruling that, at other points, she struggles to dismantle.

Jasmine and Prakash cannot escape the sectarian violence that has spread from the provinces to the city. Prakash is killed by a bomb wired into a radio as his assassin yells "'Prostitutes! Whores!'" The bomb is meant for Jasmine, who becomes a political target because her aspirations pose a threat to the social order built on women's subjection. Like Jasmine's father, and later Professor Devinder Vadhera, Sukhwinder and his cohorts desire to return to an imagined, timeless, and seamless moment that, to them, reflects the natural order. For Jasmine, this political killing means an abrupt end to the dreams of Vijh & Vijh. Instead, she must join her mother in enforced widowhood. As she laments, "I am a widow in the war of feudalisms." In spite of this temporary recognition, however, she is still balanced precariously between Jyoti and Jasmine. Her place, her "mission," is to travel to the United States and commit ritual suicide, suttee, where Prakash intended to go to school. As such, she is still ensnared in the same imaginary relations as her contemporary from the village of Hasnapur, Vimla. When Vimla's husband dies of typhoid, Vimla, although just twenty-two, douses herself with kerosene and flings herself on the stove. "In Hasnapur, Vimla's isn't a sad story."

At this point in the novel, India merely serves as a regressive and repressive background to further Mukherjee's thematic aims. It is a timeless India that is forever feudal, undeveloped, and barbaric, and, hence, still in need of Western guidance. On strictly literary grounds, Mukherjee argues that "I had to give her [Jasmine] a society that was so regressive, traditional, so caste-bound, genderist, that she could discard it'' much easier than ''a fluid American society'' could be discarded (''Interview''). Here, India's stalled backwardness is unfavorably contrasted to the more attractive fluidity of Western society. Following Abdul JanMohamed, we can see that Mukherjee deploys the trope of the manichean allegory in her representation of India, since ''the putative superiority of the European'' depends upon ''the supposed inferiority of the native.'' As JanMohamed explains, the manichean allegory exerts such a powerful influence, consciously or subconsciously, that ''even a writer who is reluctant to acknowledge it and who may indeed be highly critical of imperialist exploitation is drawn into its vortex.'' Mukherjee's interests in *Jasmine* do not include such a critical attitude towards ''imperialist exploitation'' or the practice of suttee. Instead, her focus remains on the gendered subject in transit from the third world to the first world. For Mukherjee, then, a critique of stereotypes based of gender and exoticism supersedes a critique of imperialist influence in India. In many ways, this omission points to the inherent difficulties involved in avoiding the powerful attraction of the manichean allegory and, again, indicates the pervasive effects of colonialism continuing into the present.

These effects become more apparent in Mukherjee's novel when Jasmine leaves Hasnapur. She joins the dangerous, unstable category of ''refugees and mercenaries and guest workers,'' slipping into ''a shadow world'' of interchangeable bodies. This floating population only asks to be allowed ''to continue,'' while it journeys, simultaneously and side-by-side, with the tourists and businessmen who travel through legal channels of access and availability. These pilgrims are thus seen and unseen. They are ignored because of their obscene message that colonialism is not over yet. Colonialism has merely shifted into a different register. As Donna Haraway writes, the international economy of electronics and capital has redefined the notion of work. This new worker is ''female and feminized,'' conforming to the twin imperatives of constant vulnerability and availability, as she is thoroughly ''exploited as a reserve labor force.''

For the refugees, the goal is simply to survive. However, this survival is threatened at the moment of their emergence into visibility. They then become the locus of suspicion and discourse. As a ''''visible minority,''' these refugees are enveloped in an ''atmosphere of hostility'' based upon a whole series of ''''crippling assumptions''' (''Interview'') that are the product of prior colonialisms, textualities,

and cultural myths. These myths then represent and influence behavior towards the native. For Jasmine, these myths of the available and passive Eastern woman create the climate that legitimizes her rape.

Jasmine's journey has taken her from Hasnapur to the United States aboard unregistered aircraft and ships. As an illegal immigrant traveling on a forged passport, she must complete her pilgrimage to Tampa aboard *The Gulf Shuttle*, a shrimper engaged in ''the nigger-shipping bizness.'' She ends up in a motel room at the run-down Florida Court with the captain of the trawler, Half-Face, whose name derives from the loss of an eye, an ear, and half his face in Vietnam, where he served as a demolitions expert. Half-Face, a character ''from the underworld of evil,'' is thus marked by his neocolonialist experience in Southeast Asia, and in this sense is like the young man at the bar later in the novel who reacts to Jasmine's entrance with the remark that '''I know whore power when I see it.''' Recognition and association are immediate: ''His next words were in something foreign, but probably Japanese or Thai or Filipino, something bar girls responded to in places where he'd spent his rifle-toting youth.'' The young man and Half Face, both veterans of the East, respond similarly because Jasmine represents an already known and gendered subject.

With banal conviction, Half-Face tells Jasmine, ''You know what's coming, and there ain't nobody here to help you, so my advice is to lie back and enjoy it. Hell, you'll probably like it. I don't get many complaints.'' For Half-Face, Jyoti's vulnerability is a '''sort of turn-on,''' and his boast implies a prior knowledge/narrative of known Eastern women and an entire history of others who have not complained. In other words, for Half-Face and his cohorts, women have not complained because ultimately they accepted the inevitability of the hierarchical situation and their presumed sexual nature, thus discovering that they ''really'' liked it after all. In this interested configuration of desire, cause and effect are conflated, and the threat of violence occluded. The myth of the available and passive Eastern woman eliminates any possibility of resistance, any possibility that these women did not ''really'' like it. For Half-Face, Jyoti is merely '''one prime piece,''' a gendered marking of the body that ''cancels out'' any other considerations. With mechanical and perfunctory obliviousness, Half-Face drinks, rapes, and then falls asleep. As a consequence of her ''personal dishonor,'' Jasmine considers killing herself as Half-Face snores in the next room.

Occurring at the exact center of the novel, Jasmine's rape signals a crucial moment in her successive transformations and in the formation of her ethics of survival. Instead of killing herself and passively conforming to an identity politics that would define her solely as a victim, she decides instead to kill her attacker. With ritualistic attentiveness, she first thoroughly cleanses her body, and then she purifies her soul through prayer. She has a small knife, given to her by Kingsland, a savvy fellow nomad traveling aboard The Gulf Shuttle. She first uses it on herself, cutting a strip across her tongue. As Mukherjee explains, Jasmine becomes Kali, the goddess of destruction, since "Kali has her red tongue hanging out" ("Interview"). In addition, this gesture of marking and naming reclaims her body. It is an active intervention in the relations of ruling that provided the justification of her rape and her subsequent conception of herself as a victim.

One further observation here has implications for Jasmine's later desertion of her crippled husband. Mukherjee has remarked that Kali is "the goddess of destruction, but not in a haphazard, random way. She is the destroyer of evil so that that world can be renewed" ("Interview"). As such, this restructuring and renewing function of Jasmine as Kali provides a key to the possibility of a postcolonial politics where resistance to the myths, histories, and narratives of the metropolitan center involves an active thematizing of the structures of enforced identity, and an affirmative transformation that involves appropriating the weapons and technologies that have served to maintain the center. Jasmine's killing of Half-Face involves a reappropriation—a violent sundering and subsequent adapting of the controlling strategies of violence and desire—and the reinscription of active resistance into the patriarchal narrative of vulnerability and availability. She appropriates the knife/phallus, and she penetrates his body. Then, instead of committing suttee—burning the suit of her dead husband and then lying on the fire, the "mission" that controlled her journey to the United States—Jasmine burns Prakash's suit and her Indian clothes in a trash can next to the motel. She breaks the chain of causality, the metalepsis that continually tries to substitute cause for effect in the relations of ruling, the terrible causality that led to her being "raped and raped and raped in boats and cars and motel rooms" on her journey to America. With the killing of Half-Face, Jasmine passes from innocence and enacts a radical break, suggesting a form of resistance that is contingent, disruptive, and strategic.

Rather than reifying a past that is continuous and identical with itself, Jasmine suggests a history dislodged from origins and a self fractured from organic wholeness.

As R. Radhakrishnan writes, "[t]he task for radical ethnicity is to thematize and subsequently problematize its entrapment within these binary elaborations with the intent of stepping beyond to find its own adequate language" ("Ethnic Identity"). For Jasmine, this "adequate language" involves the ability "to adjust, to participate," without succumbing to the desire to hold on to the past and certainty. To do so would be to become like Professor Vadhera and his family, who recreate an artificially maintained Indianness. In contrast, Jasmine must seek to negotiate and resituate, continually, the horizon of her fears and desires. This process of constant adjustment propels her to New York, where she acquires an illegal green card and comes to work as a domestic in the Hayes household. In the process, she is again renamed. Like Prakash, Taylor Hayes acknowledges her liminal state: "Taylor didn't want to change me. He didn't want to scour and sanitize the foreignness. My being different. . . didn't scare him." In contrast to her earlier transformations, she asserts that "I changed because I wanted to." She thus becomes "Jase, the prowling adventurer."

But Sukhwinder reappears in New York. To protect her new family, Jase escapes to Baden, Iowa. Here again, she changes, exchanging Jase for Jane. The point to note here is that she is actively changing her name, rather than passively accepting a name as she had with Prakash. But this new role requires a "regression, like going back to village life, a life of duty and devotion" ("Interview"). Settling in Baden as the wife of Bud Ripplemeyer, the head of the local bank, would be the same as remaining in Hasnapur, since becoming Bud's wife would be merely another form of enforced identity. As Jane, she only feels affection for Bud. Crippled by a distraught farmer whom his bank has foreclosed on, Bud appeals to her feelings of responsibility to be a caregiver as she had been in the Hayes family. To become Mrs. Jane Ripplemeyer, therefore, would require renouncing her desire to gain control of her body and destiny.

I began my reading of Jasmine with Jane and Bud by noting their two different conceptions of narrative and history, and I want to return to the connection between these conceptions and the production of enforced identity through another's desire. These two contrasting views become apparent when Bud and Jane are driving through Baden and pass ''half-built, half-deserted cinder-block structures at the edge of town.'' The ''empty swimming pools and plywood panels in the window frames'' remind her of the Florida Coast motel where she was raped because as constructed by prior narratives of female identity she could be imagined as provocatively vulnerable and available.

Bud reacts differently to the cinder-block structures. Contemplating these undeveloped resources, Bud ''frowns because unproductive projects give him a pain.'' In fact, Bud sees these unproductive resources and can only wonder ''who handled themr financing.'' For Bud then, individuals, resources, and land are only understandable within an economy of productivity and efficiency. Thus, ''Asia he'd thought of only as a soy-bean market,'' presumably tended by productive and silent natives. And, indeed, Bud imagines the natives of his own region in terms of similar evaluative categories. A ''good man'' is one who displays ''discipline, strength, patience, character. Husbandry.'' To Bud, individuals like Darryl who do not want to be tied down by the family farm, who want to make ''something more of his life than fate intended,'' are irreducibly ''flawed.''

Bud Ripplemeyer is like a series of characters in this novel—Sukhwinder, Professor Vadhera, and Jyoti's father—who want to preserve a vision of the past as a pure, uncontested, and originary terrain. This nostalgia precludes change while it authorizes relations of ruling that seek to deny the interested subordination of oppositional voices and knowledges. Thus, the narrator can easily ''wonder if Bud ever sees the America I do.'' The answer is no. Bud's desire manifests itself in the will to possess and to define. Jasmine has learned a different lesson from history.

Rather than preservation, stasis, and attachments, Mukherjee's novel proposes a counter-narrative that suggests that ''transformation'' must be embraced. Such a strategy questions the drive to essentialize that characterizes Sukhwinder, Half-Face, and Bud Ripplemeyer. It also suggests a different relationship between former colonial partners, a resituating of history that involves a thematizing of prior myths of enforced identity and a breaking into a new space, provisional and based on affinity, not identity. This postcolonial space is portrayed symbolically as the reconstituted family that emerges at the end of the novel: Jase is carrying

Bud's child, Duff is an adopted child, and Taylor is emerging from a failed marriage. In addition they are going to California to be reunited with Du and his sister, victims of Vietnam's colonial past.

In the reconstituted family, they do not have the certainty of Bud's straight line of history, but neither do they have those benevolent assumptions that authorize exclusions based on fear of immigrants. Here, individuals survive through a flexible strategy of ''scavenging, adaption, and appropriat[ing] technology,'' not exactly because they want to, but because they must in order to survive. It is not coincidental that the skills of Prakash and Du involve the rewiring of the circuitry of electronic machinery. Yet, this skill can also be turned to destructive ends, since Sukhwinder and his cohorts, the Khalsa Lions, wire bombs into radios. In this sense, an affinity that recognizes difference and contradiction, rather than an affiliation solely based on identity politics, becomes a necessity.

But survival also depends on a recognition of the historical and material forces that set this floating population in motion. As I indicated earlier, such a recognition might have informed Mukherjee's portrayal of India and her understanding of the ideological complexity of suttee. With its title character scarred by history, Mukherjee's *Jasmine* concludes with an image of affiliation through affinity—a hopeful imaging of a postcolonial world where difference is acknowledged and history is reconfigured. Yet, at the same time, this achieved state or topos of the reconstituted family cannot be seen as fixed and realized. Instead, Jasmine wonders how many ''more selves'' are in her. There are no answers to these questions in *Jasmine*, since any answer would involve a refutation of the novel's ethic of survival, adaptation, and transformation.

''Re-inventing ourselves'' may be seen as an active strategy that implies the possibility of resistance and reappropriation through a reconfiguring of the received knowledges that constitute colonial hmstory. As JanMohamed and Lloyd note, such a critical reinterpretation ''assert[s] that even the very differences which have always been read as symptoms of inadequacy are capable of being re-read transformatively as indications and figurations of values opposed to the dominant discourse.'' Thus, this archival work involves a strategy of re-reading the received history of the past, with particular attention to its silences, ruptures, and contradictions. It strives to avoid mistaking effects for causes, and to maintain a critical activity that sees differences as a product of competing discursive fields. Identity is never reducible to one stable and essential position, but is an effect of these discourses and contestations. To think only in terms of the implacable opposition of center to margin is to revalidate the essentializing binary grid of identity. To think in terms of shifting the center, de-centering, is to imagine an ascendancy of the margins, a simple reversal, where "interested" versions of heterogeneity vie for prominence. A third option is to illuminate the borders where centers and margins rub against each other in often contradictory ways. It is to bring the border into visibility, while resisting the urge to speak for it.

Jasmine examines this play of borders. As such, the novel avoids becoming a simple attack upon identity-based discursive formulas. Instead, it addresses the multiplicity of material forces and discursive regimes that seek to position the gendered subject. Put another way, *Jasmine* examines the doubleness involved in being "always moving and always still," a shifting and multiple identity that is in a state of perpetual transition. This novel presents the possibility of the acceptance of a plural self, one that resists the impulse towards certainty and totalization. In addition, resistance and transgression become viable alternatives, since, as the narrator remarks, "[t]here are no harmless, compassionate ways to remake oneself." Remaking oneself becomes the only possible response to enforced identity and subjugated knowledge.

It is a mistake, I think, to seek agency at the conscious level of enactment. Even when there is a face on the machine—for instance, Half-Face or Bud Ripplemeyer—it is only one of many replaceable faces. The task for the intellectual is to delineate the workings of the machine, the relations of ruling, at its tentacle extension, at the extended point where it is most vulnerable, disputed, and diffused. Such a strategy involves a reappropriation, but also a negotiation, since negotiation recognizes difference as a site of both affinity and contestation. Negotiation is a desire to open up larger spaces in a common field of dialogical interaction. Yet, at the same time, there is the persistent danger noted by R. Radhakrishnan, related to the "profound contradictions that underlie the attempt to theorize change," that "our attempts to change the subject" may be "potentially wrong and repressive, even barbaric" ("Changing Subject"). In other words, there is the real danger of reproducing the very same relations

of ruling that we have identified. To some extent, these processes occur in Jasmine.

Rather than locating agency in a unified subject position capable of correctly reading the real, a subject who has somehow "successfully" resisted its interpellation, Mukherjee's Jasmine struggles to articulate another form of knowledge. This negotiated knowledge is a modality of action predicated on a series of shifting subject positions. These temporary roles then become vectors of intersection and intervention, and, because they are temporary and mobile, possibly prevent succumbing to the desire for certainty and completeness. A "role" is not originary, unique, or substantial. In fact, it points to the fictiveness of the gesture towards complete, realized development and continuity. It reveals discontinuity beneath the "role," the mask. Rather than a frozen category, Identity, then, becomes an historically specific strategy: not a "free" subject acting, but an available site for negotiation. Mukherjee has argued that an ability to adapt and appropriate is transformative, establishing the "sense of two-way traffic" ("Interview"). This "two-way traffic" captures the sense of Said's call for "a tremendously energetic attempt to engage with the metropolitan world in a common effort at re-inscribing, re-interpreting and expanding the sites of intensity and the terrain contested with Europe" ("Intellectuals").

No doubt, this "common effort" does not in any way help the Haitian "boat people" that I began this paper with. Nor will it probably help the next floating population of refugees and deportees. The failure lies in the too-easy conflation of cause and effect and the ready availability of abstract categories, so that these people are not seen as the effects of colonialisms "into the present." We can, however, continue to create the conditions where these silent people might speak of a different history. I think Mukherjee's strategy of "re-inventing ourselves" does open up the transformative possibility of not only interrogating these structures of power and knowledge, but also suggesting a historically-situated strategy where borders serve as multiple sites of contestation, transformative rereadings, and affinity. As such, the visible border becomes the site for critical interruption and discontinuity, for rewiring the circuitry.

Source: F. Timothy Ruppel, "'Re-inventing ourselves a million times': narrative, desire, identity, and Bharati Mukherjee's 'Jasmine,'" in *College Literature,* Vol. 22, No. 1, February, 1995, pp. 181–92, Jasmine.

Eleanor Wachtel

In the following review of Mukherjee's novel Jasmine, *Eleanor Wachtel describes the life journey of a Punjabi woman, Jyoti, as circumstance moves her through varying geographical locations and personalities, and calls Mukherjee's depiction of clashing cultures and philosophies as narrated by Jyoti, or Jasmine, as "powerful", "ambitious" and "impressively compact."*

In Bharati Mukherjee's new novel, the inhabitants of Hasnapur, a fictional village in India's Punjab state, dream of better lives in richer lands. As a girl, the title character of *Jasmine* listens with fascination as the men around her debate over which countries would be best for making a new start. Her brothers talk of well-paid jobs in the United Arab Emirates. But Prakash, their friend—and Jasmine's future husband—says that guest workers there are mere slaves, even if they are rich ones. He insists that the place to go is the United States. "When I go to work in another country," he declares, "it'll be because I want to be part of it." In the end, the brothers stay at home when their father is gored by a bull in a freak accident, and Prakash is killed in Hasnapur by a bomb planted by Sikh extremists. It is only Jasmine who becomes part of America.

The novel grew out of a story that appeared in Mukherjee's *The Middleman and Other Stories*, a collection that won last year's prestigious U.S. National Book Critics Circle Award. And it elaborates on a theme that Mukherjee, 49—who was born in Calcutta but moved to the United States in 1961 (she later lived in Canada for 14 years)—has carved out as her own: the assimilation of Third World immigrants into the American melting pot, which is itself enriched by those she describes as "new pioneers." Jasmine is one of those pioneers, a survivor with courage, wryness and a hopeful streak at odds with her fatalism. At the end of the short story, even though Jasmine was a domestic worker without a visa, papers or a birth certificate—and had been seduced on the Turkish carpet by her boss, an academic—she was still happy, "a girl rushing wildly into the future." By the time the novel's complex, textured and violent story comes to a close, Jasmine is still "greedy with wants and reckless from hope."

Using flashbacks and crosscuts, the novel weaves the story of the heroine's life from her early days in Hasnapur to her extraordinary adventures in the United States. The narrative begins when Jasmine is 7 and an astrologer in her home town foretells a future of exile and widowhood. As Jasmine evolves, she is given different names. Born Jyoti, she is renamed Jasmine at 14 when she weds the modern-thinking Prakash. When his murder leaves her widowed three years later, Jasmine emigrates to the United States. There, she undergoes a series of metamorphoses as she struggles to leave her old self behind and find a new, American identity.

She lands in Florida, where a kind Quaker woman nicknames her "Jazzy" in response to her quick take on American-style walking and dressing. She goes to work for a New York City academic—a variation of the one depicted in the short story—and he names her Jase. Then, she leaves him and travels to rural Iowa, where she meets her second, common-law husband, Ben, an invalid banker with whom she adopts a refugee teenage boy from Vietnam. Ben calls her Jane. The naming underlines her mutability—it is part of the melting process.

While Jasmine remains curiously passive and adaptable to her new country, ready to reinvent herself, she is also tough and resilient. She has to be to endure all of the violence that she encounters. Violence has always characterized Mukherjee's work, but in Jasmine the body count is so staggeringly high that it reinforces one of the novel's many aphorisms: "Dullness is a kind of luxury."

Jasmine's devoted schoolteacher, Masterji, who recognizes her intelligence and saves her from an arranged marriage at 14 to an old widower, is murdered by Sikh punks on scooters—"emptying over 30 bullets in him." Her girlfriend douses herself with kerosene and flings herself on a stove after her husband's death. During her migration to Florida, Jasmine is raped by a Vietnam veteran who lost half his face in a paddy field. She murders him with a small, sharp knife.

Even one of her Midwest American neighbors chokes to death on a piece of Mexican food while vacationing in California. Another hangs himself from the rafters of his unfinished hog barn. Still another maims Ben and then kills himself. Mukherjee suggests that people everywhere—whether they are Indian victims of Sikh extremism or Iowa farmers distraught by bankruptcy—are ripped apart by terrorism, passion and despair.

In her powerful depiction of clashing cultures and philosophies, Mukherjee has created an ambitious and impressively compact work. The writing is vivid and economical as the author moves easily between the Punjab and Iowa, Florida and New

York City. In one of the novel's more poignant sequences, Jasmine discovers that her husband's old teacher, Professorji, now living in an immigrant enclave in Flushing, N.Y., is not a professor in his adopted country but an importer and sorter of human hair.

Working in the basement of the Khyber Bar BQ, he measures and labels the length and thickness of each separate hair, which is then sold for wigs and scientific instruments—which use human hair as a gauge for humidity. "A hair from some peasant's head in Hasnapur could travel across oceans and save an American meteorologist's reputation," Mukherjee writes. "Nothing was rooted anymore. Everything was in motion."

But the author seems unafraid of change. Her heroine surveys the havoc of American farm country and observes: "I see a way of life coming to an end. Baseball loyalties, farming, small-town innocence." It is clear that Jasmine feels no regret. Her fatalistic Eastern perspective—the long view—assumes that everything has a purpose and change is as it should be. At the same time, Jasmine is willing to push fate to elude its hold. That is how American she becomes.

Source: Eleanor Wachtel, "Jasmine," (book review) in *Maclean's,* Vol. 102, No. 43, October 23, 1989, p. 72.

Sources

Banerjee, Debjani, article, in *Bharati Mukherjee: Critical Perspectives*, edited by Emmanuel S. Nelson, Garland Press.

Lesser, Wendy, "United States," in *The Oxford Guide To Contemporary Writing*, edited by John Sturrock, Oxford University Press, 1996, 406-31.

Mukherjee, Bharati, "American Dreamer," in *Mother Jones*, Jan/Feb 1997.

Vignisson, Runar, "Bharati Mukherjee: an interview," in *Journal of the South Pacific Association for Commonwealth Literature and Language Studies*, edited by Vijay Mishra, Number 34-35, 1993.

Further Reading

Chua, C. L., "Passages from India: Migrating to America in the Fiction of V.S. Naipaul and Bharati Mukherjee," in

> In her powerful depiction of clashing cultures and philosophies, Mukherjee has created an ambitious and impressively compact work. The writing is vivid and economical as the author moves easily between the Punjab and Iowa, Florida and New York City."

Reworlding: The Literature of the Indian Diaspora, edited by Emmanuel S. Nelson, Greenwood Press, 1992, pp. 51-61.
    Discusses Mukherjee and V. S. Naipaul's portrayal of Indian immigrants in North American, and their struggle to realize the American Dream.

Hofstede, Geert, *Cultures and Organizations*, McGraw-Hill, 1997.
    Provides a method for understanding cultural differences.

Kriefer, Joel, ed., *The Oxford Companion To Politics of the World*, Oxford University Press, 1993.
    Provides comprehensive coverage of international affairs and domestic politics throughout the world.

Lesser, Wendy, "United States," in *The Oxford Guide To Contemporary Writing*, edited by John Sturrock, Oxford University Press, 1996, 406-431.
    Explores the recent writing of various cultures, including the literary and cultural contexts for authorship in each area.

Mukherjee, Bharati, "American Dreamer," in *Mother Jones*, Jan/Feb 1997.
    In this essay, Mukherjee clearly identifies herself as an American and rejects other, more limiting labels.

Nelson, Emmanuel S., ed., *Bharati Mukherjee: Critical Perspectives*, Garland Press.
    Provides an assortment of critical essays on Mukherjee's work.

Vignisson, Runar, "Bharati Mukherjee: an interview," in *Journal of the South Pacific Association for Commonwealth Literature and Language Studies*, edited by Vijay Mishra, Number 34-35, 1993.
    Vignisson's 1993 interview with Mukherjee where she explains her initial attraction to literature.

The Kiss of the Spider Woman

Manuel Puig

1976

Kiss of the Spider Woman is Manuel Puig's fourth and best known novel. It was first published in Spanish in 1976 as *El beso de la mujer arana*, then translated and published in English in 1979. Puig became most popularly known to the English-speaking public for the critically acclaimed 1985 screen adaptation of *Kiss of the Spider Woman*, starring William Hurt, Raul Julia, and Sonia Braga.

Kiss of the Spider Woman focuses on two characters: Valentin, a Marxist revolutionary, and Molina, a homosexual window-dresser, who share a prison cell for six months. Molina passes the time by telling Valentin the stories of his favorite movies in great detail. Valentin at first reluctantly listens to Molina's narration of these tales of melodramatic romance, criticizing Molina for indulging in escapist fantasies rather than in political activism. But Valentin eventually becomes enthralled with the stories, as he becomes emotionally drawn to Molina. Molina, meanwhile, has secretly agreed to elicit information from Valentin in order to pass it on to the prison authorities. Over the course of their confinement, however, the two men fall in love and ultimately become lovers. Upon his release from prison, Molina agrees to help Valentin in his political cause by passing on important information to his fellow revolutionaries.

Kiss of the Spider Woman focuses on the theme of the conflict between personal emotions, relationships, and desires vs. political idealism and activ-

ism. Valentin begins as a revolutionary who disregards pleasure and romance, while Molina begins as a man obsessed with the escapist fantasies provided by movies. As a result of their interactions, however, the two men transform one another, Valentin eventually succumbing to his emotional and physical desire for Molina, and Molina agreeing to sacrifice himself for Valentin's political cause. Puig's novel also employs experimental narrative techniques in its use of dialogue and fragmentary information such as letters and prison reports, as well as in the extensive use of footnotes which present a discussion of the psychological literature on homosexuality throughout the novel. *Kiss of the Spider Woman* is also characteristic of Puig's fiction in its extensive reference to classic cinema and its profound effect on the lives of his characters as a means of escapist fantasy.

Author Biography

Manuel Puig was born on December 28, 1932, in General Villegas, in the pampas of Argentina. His father, Baldomero, was a businessman, and his mother, Maria Elena, was a chemist. As a young boy in a provincial town, Puig was enchanted by the Hollywood movies which his mother regularly took him to see. In 1950, Puig entered the University of Buenos Aires. In 1953, he joined the Argentine Air Force, serving as a translator. Beginning in 1955, Puig studied cinema at the Centro Sperimentale di Cinematografia. From 1955 to 1956, he worked as a translator and a language instructor in London, England, and Rome, Italy. From 1957 to 1958, he was an assistant film director in Rome and in Paris, France. From 1958 to 1959, he lived in London, and in Stockholm, Sweden, working as a dishwasher. In 1960, he returned to Argentina and worked as an assistant film director in Buenos Aires. From 1961 to 1962, Puig worked again in Rome, translating film subtitles. In 1963, he moved to New York, working as a clerk for Air France until 1967.

Puig's serious writing career began while he lived in New York. He had originally planned to write a film script, but found that his extensive notes for the script were turning into a novel. In 1968, the result of this effort became Puig's first novel, *La traicion de Rita Hayworth* (translated as *Betrayed by Rita Hayworth*), which soon became a best seller and was chosen by *Le Monde,* a French periodical,

as one of the best foreign novels of the 1968-69 season. His second novel, *Boquitas pintadas: Folletin* (translated as *Heartbreak Tango: A Serial*) was published in 1969. Both of these novels utilize experimental narrative techniques to follow the concerns of inhabitants of a small, provincial Argentine village. Puig's third novel, *The Buenos Aires Affair: Novela political* (1973) was translated as *The Buenos Aires Affair: A Detective Novel* and published in English in 1976.

It was Puig's fourth novel, *El beso de la mujer arana*, first published in 1976 (translated as *Kiss of the Spider Woman*), for which Puig has become best known. The novel is written primarily in dialogue form and centers on two men, one a Marxist revolutionary and the other a homosexual window-dresser, who share a prison cell. In 1979, Puig was awarded the American Library Association Notable Book Award for *Kiss of the Spider Woman*. In 1985, he won the Plays and Players Award for most promising playwright for his dramatic play version of *Kiss of the Spider Woman*. In 1985, *Kiss of the Spider Woman* was adapted to the screen in a critically acclaimed English-language film starring William Hurt, Raul Julia, and Sonia Braga. Subsequent novels by Puig include *Maldicion eterna a quien lea estas paginas* (1980; published in English in 1982 as *Eternal Curse on the Reader of These Pages*) and *Cae la noche tropical* (1988; published in English in 1991 as *Tropical Night Falling*). Puig died in 1990 from complications after a gallbladder operation.

Plot Summary

The story begins with two men, Molina, a homosexual window-dresser, and Valentin, a Marxist political activist, sharing a prison cell. Molina has been convicted of a sexual "perversion," while Valentin has been arrested for his revolutionary activities. In order to pass the time, Molina describes in great detail to Valentin a movie he once saw. Although the movie is not named directly in the story, it is recognizable as the classic Hollywood movie *Cat People,* which was released in 1943. In this movie, a woman is transformed into a panther who attacks people at night. Although he reluctantly listens in order to relieve the boredom of prison, Valentin makes fun of Molina for his obsession with what he perceives to be a shallow, inane movie. But

Manuel Puig

ably because, realizing that he is being followed, they don't want him to hand the information over to the authorities. Valentin, meanwhile, still in prison, has been severely beaten and tortured by the prison officials, who have inflicted third-degree burns on him. In the hospital ward, he is administered a strong dose of morphine by a sympathetic clinician who wishes to relieve him of the physical pain. Valentin slips into a morphine-induced dream. The novel ends with Valentin's dream, in which Marta, his former lover, leads him out of the prison and to an island in the ocean, where he makes love with a native girl while maintaining an internal dialogue with Marta, telling her that he is pretending the native girl is in fact her. Through this dream, Valentin considers the fact that he has learned of Molina's death. The novel ends, still in Valentin's morphine fantasy, with Valentin admitting to Marta that he loves her, and Marta assuring him that he will never lose her, because, in the enigmatic words which end the story, Marta says, ''This dream is short but this dream is happy.''

Valentin grows to like hearing about Molina's movies, and becomes increasingly engaged in the stories. Although Valentin continues to be disdainful of Molina, when he becomes sick from food poisoning the prison officials have put in his dinner Molina takes care of him, thus winning his increased affection and gratitude.

Molina is secretly asked by the prison officials to try to get Valentin to reveal to him information significant to his revolutionary cause. Molina tries to gain Valentin's trust for this purpose, but becomes emotionally attached to Valentin in the process. Valentin likewise becomes increasingly emotionally attached to Molina. Molina meanwhile attempts to stall the prison officials in order to be given more time with Valentin, without actually having to betray him. Eventually, the two men make love. When Molina is released from prison, Valentin asks him to convey some important information to his revolutionary comrades. Molina is at first reluctant, but agrees to do it.

After Molina is released from prison, he contacts Valentin's revolutionary comrades and agrees to meet them in order to convey the information Valentin has passed on to him. Molina is followed and surveyed by government officials, who witness Molina being shot by the revolutionaries, presum-

Characters

Valentin Arregui Paz

Valentin is a Marxist revolutionary, imprisoned for his political activism. His cellmate, Molina, is a homosexual window-dresser with no political convictions whatsoever. Valentin is at first disdainful of Molina because of his homosexuality. Nevertheless, Valentin is willing to listen to Molina's descriptions of some of his favorite classic Hollywood movies in order to pass the time. Valentin becomes increasingly tolerant of Molina, and, after Molina selflessly cares for him during his illness, Valentin becomes increasingly emotionally attached to Molina. Eventually, Valentin, despite his initial anti-homosexual prejudices, becomes Molina's lover. When Molina is released from prison, Valentin asks him to pass important information on to his revolutionary comrades. Soon after Molina leaves, however, Valentin is severely beaten and tortured by the prison officials, who inflict third-degree burns on his body and his groin. While he is in the prison hospital ward, a clinician offers secretly to inject him with a strong dose of morphine in order to ease the pain. As the story ends, Valentin slips into a morphine-induced fantasy in which his former lover, Marta, takes him out of the prison and to a fantasy island in the sea.

Marta

Marta is Valentin's former lover, whom he renounced because she was from the upper classes and therefore considered the oppressive enemy against whom his political ideals caused him to struggle. Valentin finds, however, that, despite his political convictions, he still loves Marta. When, at the end of the story, he slips into a morphine-induced fantasy, he imagines that Marta has come to release him from prison and lead him to a fantasy island in the sea. The novel ends with Valentin's fantasy of Marta assuring him that he will never lose her because "This dream is short but this dream is happy."

Molina

Referred to as "Molina" throughout most of the novel, this character's full name is Luis Alberto Molino. The "masculine" ending of "o" in Molina's last name has been changed in his nickname to the "feminine" ending of "a," as an expression of his desire to be thought of as a woman. Pamela Barcarisse has referred to the "'hyperfeminine'" Molina as "one of the truly great creations in modern fiction." Molina is a homosexual window-dresser in prison for sexual "perversion." While in prison, he tells the stories of some of his favorite movies in great detail to Valentin, his cellmate, a Marxist revolutionary, in order to pass the time and relieve the boredom. While Molina is obsessed with the romantic fantasy elements of these movies, Valentin is disdainful of them, and makes fun of Molina. Yet Valentin reluctantly asks Molina to continue describing the movies. Valentin, however, continues to express disdain for Molina, based on his sexual orientation and his desire to think of himself as a woman. Molina is eventually requested by the prison authorities to try to win Valentin's trust in order to elicit information from him about his revolutionary comrades, in exchange for Molina's early release from prison. Molina, however, becomes increasingly emotionally attached to Valentin, and does his best to stall the process of providing the prison officials with any information. When Valentin becomes ill from the food poisoning which has been planted in his meals, Molina selflessly takes care of him. Out of gratitude, Valentin softens to Molina and the two men eventually become lovers. When Molina is eventually released from prison, without having given away any important information from Valentin, he agrees to pass important information from Valentin to his revolutionary comrades outside of prison. This becomes a self-sacrifice, however, as Molina is followed by government agents on this mission, and is then shot by the revolutionaries themselves, in order to keep him from confessing anything to the authorities. Molina dies as a result, his sacrifice ultimately ineffective.

Themes

Fantasy and Escapism

As in many of Puig's novels, *Kiss of the Spider Woman* focuses on the theme of escapism through fantasy. In particular, Molina uses his memories of classic movies as a means of escape. He is particularly drawn to melodramatic movies with a strong romantic theme, which is the central focus of his retelling of the movies. On one level, Molina wishes to escape the oppression and boredom of his prison cell. He retells the movies to Valentin as a means to entertain them both during their long hours of imprisonment. For Molina, however, the movies also function as a form of escapism from the social oppression he suffers as a homosexual. Furthermore, Molina identifies with the female characters in all of his movies; the movies then represent for him an escape from his designated sex as a man, for he prefers to think of himself as a woman. Valentin is at first disdainful of Molina's romantic obsessions; to Valentin, such fantasies are trivial and self-indulgent compared to his political idealism and activism. But Valentin slowly becomes drawn into the movies, and, in the process, to a romantic relationship with Molina. In the end, Valentin completely succumbs to a world of escapist fantasy. After Molina is released from prison, Valentin is severely beaten. In the hospital ward, an attendant mercifully gives him a strong dose of morphine to relieve him of the physical pain. In accepting the morphine, Valentin gives in to the escapism he has been resisting all along. The film ends with Valentin's morphine-induced fantasy of romance in a dream of paradise. This represents the defeat of Valentin's

Topics for Further Study

- Puig is a prominent twentieth-century Latin American writer. Learn more about another Latin American writer, such as Jorge Louis Borges, Pablo Neruda, or Gabriel Garcia Marquez. What Latin American country is this writer from? What are some of his or her principal works? What are some of the central themes and stylistic characteristics of this writer's works?

- Learn more about the history of Argentina, Puig's nation of origin, including the pre-colonial era, the period of colonization by Spain, or the era of national independence. What were the major political conflicts, changes, and events of Argentina during this period? Or, learn more about contemporary political and social struggles and conditions in Argentina today.

- Based on his own childhood fascination with Hollywood cinema, Puig's fiction is characterized by his many references to the influence of popular culture, particularly American movies, on his characters. Can you write a short story, essay, or autobiographical memoir about the influence of a particular movie on yourself, someone you know, or a fictional character? In what ways can you incorporate references to a movie into a written medium? What kind of impact can movies, or one movie in particular, have in a person's life?

- Puig's novel *Kiss of the Spider Woman* is written almost entirely in dialogue, much like a stage play or screenplay. Can you write a short sketch entirely in dialogue? How can important action and characterization be conveyed strictly through dialogue?

- The screen adaptation of *Kiss of the Spider Woman*, released as a movie in 1985, is at least as well known, and as critically acclaimed, as the novel. How do the movie and the novel compare? In what ways did the filmmaker employ cinematic techniques in order to convey action and characterization which was originally conveyed in written form? In what ways does the film version enhance your appreciation of the novel? What elements of the novel are "lost" or left out in the film version? What changes have been made in the characters of Valentin and Molina in the adaptation from novel to screen?

---

political principals, which the prison officials have effectively beaten out of him.

Political Idealism

Puig is concerned with the struggle between the ideals of Marxist political philosophy and the human urge to fulfill personal desires. The character of Valentin, imprisoned for his revolutionary activities, begins the novel with a strong dedication to his political ideals, which he prioritizes over personal relationships and the satisfaction of physical desires. However, the inconsistency of Valentin's idealism is indicated by the fact that he still loves an upper-class woman who politically represents the oppressive enemy of the working people. Valentin thus struggles with the disjunction between his emotions and his politics. Molina, on the other hand, is pointedly apolitical in the beginning of the novel. Molina is homosexual, but shows no interest in a political analysis of his oppressed position in society, or in any efforts at social and political empowerment of homosexuals. Through the influence of Valentin, however, Molina ultimately makes the decision to sacrifice himself for the sake of Valentin's political cause. He agrees that, once released from prison, he will relay important information to Valentin's comrades. Molina, however, seems to be aware of the fact that he is risking his life by committing to this action. Thus, while Valentin succumbs to the escapist fantasy of a morphine-induced hallucination, Molina rises to the level of political idealism Valentin has espoused. In the end, however, Molina's sacrifice is completely ineffective, accomplishing nothing.

Homosexuality

Puig in this novel addresses the issue of homosexuality as a social and political subject. In the footnotes which accompany the body of the story, Puig presents a rather dry, scholarly explanation of various psychological theories regarding homosexuality. The character Molina, a homosexual, represents the oppression of the homosexual in Latin American society. Valentin, although a Marxist revolutionary, at first embodies all of the standard prejudices against Molina as a homosexual. He is disdainful of Molina, mocks and insults him for his sexual orientation, and even physically abuses him for his resistance to traditional masculine behavior. Valentin, however, eventually grows to love Molina, as a friend and then as a lover. Valentin's softening from an aggressively masculine man to the point of loving another man forces him to question and then reevaluate his attitude toward homosexuality.

Style

Setting

This novel is set in an unnamed Latin American country, but clearly refers to the political climate of Puig's native Argentina during the period of its history known as the "dirty war." During the 1970s, Argentina was ruled by a military junta which exercised extreme measures of political repression against its citizens. Thousands of people were killed, imprisoned, or "disappeared" during this time at the hands of the government for their alleged political activities. The fictional character of Valentin is clearly representative of such government action against Argentine citizens. Valentin is a political activist who has been tortured and imprisoned for his revolutionary activities. Jonathan Tittler has pointed out the significance of the fictional character of Valentin to the realities of Argentine politics during the 1970s, when the novel was written. Tittler asserts, "With legitimate movements of opposition banished and forced to move underground, it was not uncommon for educated, sensible young people to associate with guerrilla bands and, indeed, to carry out acts of sabotage or subversion against the government. When caught,

these political enemies of the State were of course frequently treated with little regard for civil rights or due process." The character of Valentin is, therefore, "a plausible example of the measures many people of conscience were driven to take under the extremely repressive conditions reigning in Puig's homeland at the time."

Narration

Puig is known for his experimental narrative style, which combines dialogue, letters, official reports, and even footnotes into a composite story without a traditional narrative voice. Critics have noted that this narrative style causes the reader to more actively participate in the narrative process, for he or she must do the work of filling in the blanks left by what is left out of the story.

Characterization

Puig's novel consists of a very limited number of principal characters, namely Molina and Valentin, as well as Marta. However, each character represents not just an individual, but a social and political cross-section of the population. Thus, the character of Valentin represents the young political radicals active in revolutionary activities in Argentina during the 1970s; Molina represents not just one homosexual, but the condition of homosexuals in general in Latin American culture. Puig uses characters, therefore, as a means of exploring specific social issues of concern to him, particularly homosexual rights and political activism. Furthermore, certain characters represent a particular social strata in Argentine society; Marta, for instance, represents, especially for Valentin, the privileged sector of society against which Marxist revolutionaries struggle. The fact that Valentin is unable to reconcile his personal desires with his political ideals functions as a commentary on the part of Puig about the internal struggles faced by revolutionary activists in general. Likewise, the fact that Molina, although clearly a member of an oppressed segment of society, is unable to conceptualize his sexual orientation as a political issue functions as a commentary on the part of Puig regarding the need of homosexuals to engage in political struggle for their rights.

Literary Heritage

Latin American literature is most often distinguished by its use of magical realism. Magical realism is a literary style that addresses social concerns but masks them in a veil of magical or fantastical symbolism. Magical realism can be seen in the works of Gabriel Garcia Marquez, who is considered a pioneer of this style, and in the works of other writers such as Julio Cortazar, Jorge Luis Borrges, and Carlos Fuentes. These writers were all a part of the Boom period in the 1960s when Latin American literature was reaching worldwide attention and praise.

Manuel Puig is considered one of the most prominent of the Latin American Post-Boom authors. Puig's writings are noted by their experimental narrative style and non-conventional forms, which stem from his interest in popular culture and early work in films and screenwriting. Although Puig has helped usher in a new era in Latin American literature that blends literary and nonliterary forms, his works still hold those elements that have distinguished this culture for decades. Puig's works are not only concerned with creating a new fiction that challenges conventional notions of literature and art, but are also expressing social and cultural criticisms. In his critically acclaimed *Kiss of the Spider Woman*, Puig addresses the issues of Marxist political philosophy and its influence on the public and political arenas within this society, and in particular, on the citizens who question their place within it. One can also find threads of magical realism within his novel as both of the main characters engage in acts of fantasy and escapism.

Historical Context

Argentina: History

The process of colonization of Argentina by Spain began in the sixteenth century and developed through the nineteenth century. Before the coming of the Europeans, the area now known as Argentina was populated by approximately 300,000 Indians. The colonization of the area was accomplished in part through the efforts of Catholic missionaries. The drive for national independence began in the early nineteenth century. Argentine independence from Spanish rule was first declared in 1816, although the country did not achieve a stable internal unity until 1880.

The first time an Argentine president was chosen by a popular vote (rather than by appointment of the previous president) was in 1916. The period from 1916 to 1930 in Argentina is referred to as the era of the "radical regime," followed from 1930 to 1943 by a "conservative" rule. A military coup in 1943 eventually led to the election of Juan Peron as president of Argentina in 1946. Peron had become a popular politician among working class Argentines for his support of unions and of various social welfare efforts. Peron was re-elected in 1951, after which he developed a more conservative political agenda. His wife, Evita Peron, a powerful political figure in her own right, died in 1952, as a result of which his popularity was diminished. In 1955, Peron was overthrown in a military coup, and from 1955 to 1958, Argentina was run by a military dictatorship. A series of elected presidents were followed by a coup in 1966 by Peron supporters. However, there were coups in 1970 and in 1971, and Peron himself was not re-elected president until 1973. Peron had turned against leftists at this point in favor of an oppressive right-wing leadership. When Peron died in 1974, he was succeeded as president by his widow, Martinez de Peron, who continued Peron's staunchly right-wing policies until 1976, when she was overthrown in a coup.

The period in Argentine history which followed, called the "dirty war," was characterized by the rule of a military junta, and the violent subjugation of thousands of people through execution, imprisonment, or the notorious "disappearances" carried out by the government. A change in leadership in the early 1980s resulted in a more democratic rule in Argentina, during which there was some attempt at convicting those responsible for the excessive political repression carried out in the 1970s.

Hollywood Cinema

Puig is known for his fascination with classic Hollywood cinema, which began at an early age, and his fiction frequently makes reference to old movies and their role in the lives of provincial Argentine people. The period in film history known as the Classic Hollywood era can be dated roughly from the birth of sound cinema in 1927 through the 1950s and early 1960s. *Kiss of the Spider Woman*, for instance, begins with Molina's description of the classic film *Cat People,* directed by Jacques Tourneur in 1942. A remake of *Cat People* was released in 1982, directed by Paul Schrader. Puig has also made reference to such B-quality horror films as *I Walked with a Zombie* (1943), also directed by Tourneur. Puig's first novel focuses on the classic movie star

Rita Hayworth (1918-1987), a glamorous Hollywood icon known for such films as *Gilda* (1946) and *The Lady from Shanghai* (1948).

Critical Overview

Manuel Puig has been most prominently noted for his novels, which make use of experimental narrative techniques and include extensive references to popular cultural genres such as classic Hollywood movies and various forms of popular fiction (including the serial, romance, and detective novel). Puig's success as a novelist is indicated, according to Jonathan Tittler, by "the broad dissemination of his works" which resulted in "considerable financial success and artistic independence."

"The name of Manuel Puig has for almost 25 years brought with it associations with popular and mass culture," Tittler claims, noting that, while "widely recognized as an innovator of narrative technique," Puig was early on criticized for his blatant use of mass-cultural genres and references: "He was for many years mistakenly viewed as either a parodist of vulgar, mass-produced cultural products or a victim and purveyor of bad taste." Pamela Barcarisse also makes note of a general dismissal of Puig on the part of critics, stating that "the fact is that none of Puig's novels has been immune to adverse criticism; this has ranged from a total lack of understanding in the late sixties to expressions of disappointment, condemnation, even antagonism, in more recent years." Tittler points out that later critics began to interpret Puig's pop-cultural references in greater depth: "Only recently has literary criticism come to. . .appreciate the depth of his ambivalence about melodrama and the extent of his commitment to subverting structures of authority, in whatever guise they might appear." Barcarisse also makes note of the generally celebratory tone of more recent criticism of Puig's work, stating that "it is gratifying to note that at the present time some journalists and many academic commentators are beginning to take the entire corpus of his writings very seriously indeed, the latter classifying him as one of Latin America's first postmodern authors and by far the most impressive representative of the Latin American Post-Boom. Indeed, there is little to complain about in current Puig criticism." Tittler contends that "Puig's writ-

ing as a whole fleshes out surprising depth from a world of pure surface" and goes on to note the importance of Puig's influence on the Latin American novel, particularly in terms of his references to mass-cultural forms of media: "In breaking through to a postmodern, culturally unpretentious space. . .Puig made an impact that was so immense that soon such leaders as Cortazar, Vargas Llosa, and Donoso were producing fictions based on movie stars. . . melodramatic soap operas. . .detective novels. . .and erotic mysteries." Lucille Kerr notes the impact of Latin American fiction, as influenced by Puig, on international literature, stating, "Puig's work exemplifies modern Latin-American writing's most adventurous contribution to contemporary literary trends, which include a return to popular culture." Kerr describes the combined influence of Puig's experimental narrative style and his references to popular culture, asserting that "Puig's writing challenges conventional notions of literature and art as it draws on literary, subliterary, and nonliterary forms and languages to fashion new narrative models and radical ways of thinking about fiction." Kerr also makes note of Puig's concern with political issues, as expressed through his fiction: "Puig's novels are works of literary experimentation as well as social and cultural criticism."

Puig's first novel began as a set of notes for what he intended as a film script; however, Puig eventually realized that it was turning into what became his first published novel, *La traicion de Rita Hayworth* (translated as *Betrayed by Rita Hayworth*), published in 1968. Loosely autobiographical, Puig's novel makes use of experimental narrative techniques in focusing on a boy who grows up in an Argentine town in the pampas. The title refers to the role of escapist fantasy which classic Hollywood movies play in the lives of the novel's provincial characters. His second novel, *Boquitas Pintadas* (1969; translated as *Heartbreak Tango*), was based on the genre of the serialized novels, popular in Argentina, which are considered to be non-literary. His third novel, *The Buenos Aires Affair* (1973), is based on the genre of the detective novel and focuses on the sexual obsessions of the characters.

First published in 1976, Puig's fourth novel, *Kiss of the Spider Woman*, was banned in Argentina until 1983, when a change in government resulted in greater tolerance. Tittler has stated that *Kiss of the Spider Woman*, "widely considered his greatest work," is also "Puig's most generally successful novel because it is, far and away, his most power-

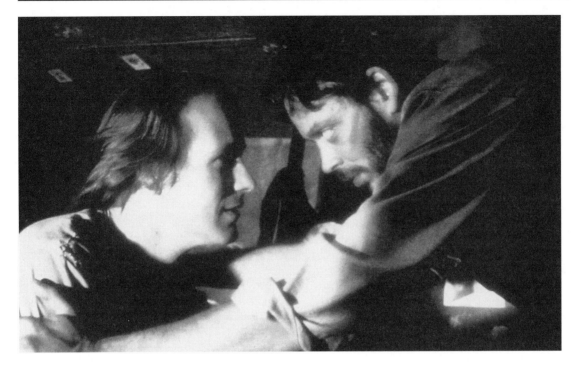

William Hurt and Raul Julia star as cell mates Luis Molina and Valentin Arregui in the 1985 film adaption of Kiss of the Spider Woman.

ful.'' Tittler also notes that it is ''an uncommonly good read.'' Kerr points out the political implications of this novel: ''The success of [*Kiss of the Spider Woman*] clearly speaks not only of the power of Puig's fiction and style but also of the public's interest in the issues about which he chose to write.''

Puig's final novel, *Tropical Night Falling*, was first published in Spanish in 1988, and then published in English translation in 1991, after his death.

Criticism

Liz Brent

Brent has a Ph.D. in American culture, specializing in film studies, from the University of Michigan. She is a freelance writer and teaches courses in the history of American cinema. In the following essay, Brent discusses narrative technique in Puig's novel Kiss of the Spider Woman.

Puig is known for his experimental narrative techniques, and *Kiss of the Spider Woman* is no exception. The narrative fabric of this novel is woven from the threads of embedded narrative, dialogue, footnotes, official reports, and internal subjective voice, from which the reader is invited to piece together the story. Puig is also known for his concern with social and political issues, as expressed through the struggles of his individual characters in socially and politically oppressive environments. Each specific narrative technique in this novel has the effect of further developing central social and political themes of the story: homosexuality as a social and political issue, the nature of storytelling as a means of escapist fantasy, the struggles of the politically committed individual, and the questionable nature of objective, versus subjective, renditions of reality.

A central narrative technique of *Kiss of the Spider Woman* is that of *embedded narrative*. This means that a character within the *frame story* tells a story, usually to another character within the story. Thus, Molina's narration to Valentin of his favorite movies constitutes an embedded narrative. Furthermore, the fact that Molina is narrating the *story* presented in a fictional movie presents the narrative at a further remove. The reader is presented through the narrative technique of dialogue with the story of a man (Molina) telling another man (Valentin) the

What Do I Read Next?

- *Betrayed by Rita Hayworth* (1968), Puig's first novel, is a loosely autobiographical account which focuses on a boy growing up in a provincial town in Argentina who fantasizes about movie stars as a means of escapism.

- *Heartbreak Tango: A Serial* (1969), Puig's second novel, is a parody of the melodramatic serial novels popular in Argentina.

- *The Buenos Aires Affair* (1973), Puig's third novel, is based on the popular detective novel genre and focuses on the sexual obsessions of the characters.

- *A Curse upon the Reader of These Pages* (1980), Puig's sixth novel, focuses on the dialogue between two characters: Larry, a twenty-six-year-old former history teacher, and Ramirez, a seventy-four-year-old Argentine exile.

- *Tropical Night Falling* (1988) was Puig's last novel. The English translation was not published until a year after his death.

- *Eva Peron* (1996), by Alicia Dujovne Ortiz and translated by Shawn Fields, is a biography of Eva Peron (1919-1952), a popular political figure in modern Argentina.

- *The Dirty War* (1994) by Charles H. Slaughter is a young adult novel set in Argentina in 1976.

- *Argentina* (1999) by Michael Burgan provides an overview of Argentine history, geography, and culture.

- *A Hammock beneath the Mangoes: Stories from Latin America* (1991), edited by Thomas Colchie, is a collection of short stories, including "Relative Humidity 95%" by Puig.

---

story he was told through the fictional medium of the movie. This narrative technique is significant to broader themes of the novel on several levels. The focus on the storytelling *process* indicates to the reader that Puig is concerned with the *medium* of fiction, as well as the content of the story he is telling. Puig's fiction has been noted for its concern with the ways in which his characters utilize popular narratives, such as movies or romance novels, as a means of escapism from societal restrictions. In this novel, stories, either in oral, written, or cinematic form, are central to the fantasy lives of the characters.

This novel consists primarily of dialogue between the two principle characters. The emphasis on dialogue is in part rooted in Puig's early career plans as an aspiring screenwriter. In *Kiss of the Spider Woman*, Puig skillfully develops his characters and his story without standard narrative explanation or description. This puts the reader in the position of having to actively work to "fill in the blanks," so to speak, by constructing the details of the story solely from the dialogue. This is particu-

larly significant in the lovemaking scene between Molina and Valentin the night before Molina is released from prison. The reader is provided with only minimal dialogue between the two men, devoid of any graphic or physical description of their interaction with one another:

> You're not cold taking your clothes off?. . .How good you look. . .Ah. . .Molina. . .What? Nothing. . .I'm not hurting you? No. . . Ow, yes, that way, yes. It hurts you? Better like last time, let me lift my legs. This way, over your shoulders. . .Like this. . .

Clearly, Puig would have been aware that, given broad social prejudice against homosexuality, particularly in terms of the details of homosexual acts, this scene would be inherently controversial. In some ways, the use of dialogue without description avoids a narrative approach which could have dwelt upon the graphic details. On the other hand, the silences implied by this minimalist dialogue force the reader to piece together the physical details of what it is these two men are doing. It could be argued that this was a quite radical choice on the part of Puig because of the way in which it invites

---

> In addition to embedded narrative, dialogue, and footnotes, the story is presented to the reader through official police reports based on surveillance of the principal characters."

the reader to mentally internalize a scene of homosexual lovemaking.

One of the most strikingly unusual elements of this novel is Puig's use of *footnotes* to accompany the fictional text. Jonathan Tittle has described the tone and scope of the footnotes as follows:

Here we have not a case study in quasidramatic form (as we find with Molina) but a disembodied, erudite voice that offers an overview of some extant scholarship on the subject of homosexuality as it has been studied by the social sciences in this century. Theories by such prominent figures as Sigmund Freud, Anna Freud, Norman O. Brown, Wilhelm Reich, Herbert Marcuse, and Kate Millet on the sociopsychological origins and ramifications of homosexuality are proposed, debated, and, in most cases, rejected, relativized, or countered.

Footnotes are traditionally used to accompany scholarly essays in order to provide factual evidence or information supporting the body of the text, to further elaborate on a side-point made within the text, or to refer the reader to previous scholarship on the topic at hand. Puig makes use of footnotes in this novel to provide explanations of the psychological scholarship on homosexuality as an accompaniment to the portrayal of a fictionalized homosexual character (Molina) and homosexual relationship (between Molina and Valentin). To some extent, the often dry, sometimes misguided discussion within the footnotes as juxtaposed with the dramatic portrayal of homosexuality within the body of the novel work to highlight the insufficiency and often wrongheadedness of the field of psychology on the topic of homosexuality.

Puig ultimately puts into question the nature of factual, or scientific, discussion of this topic when, toward the end of the novel, his footnotes describe the theories of a fictionalized psychologist and her theories of homosexuality. The impact of this addition of fictional to factual footnotes is described by Tittler, who asserts, "the author outdoes himself by introducing in the last entry the figure of the Danish scholar Dr. Anneli Taub." The boundary which has been drawn between the fictional body of the novel and the factual footnotes is here transgressed. Tittler states, "Like Molina and Valentin, she is an invented figure whose 'presence' in the footnotes effaces the neat distinction between reality and fiction maintained until that point." Thus, the made-up, or fantasy, element of the story itself eventually bleeds into, and takes over, the factual element of the footnotes. This innovative narrative technique is central to the theme of homosexuality in the novel. The final "false" footnote provides the reader with a set of clearly defined values and ideals in regard to this issue; Tittler explains that Taub's footnoted comments toward the end of the novel are "tantamount to an exhortation for homosexuals to organize themselves and participate in the political process." The footnotes, both factual and fictional, function in counterpoint to the escapist fantasy narratives related by Molina and based on movies. Through the footnotes, the reader is provided with a non-escapist, realistic (though stated by a fictional character) political agenda in regard to the issue of homosexuality. The fact that it is stated in footnote form effectively legitimizes this assertion.

In addition to embedded narrative, dialogue, and footnotes, the story is presented to the reader through official police reports based on surveillance of the principal characters. The reader learns of Molina's attempt at political action, once released from prison, and his demise, through the reports filed by the agents who have been following him. The chapter which describes Molina's activities begins with the explanation: "Report on Luis Alberto Molina, prisoner 3.018, paroled on the 9th, placed under surveillance by CISL in conjunction with wiretap unit of TISL." The report is then presented without additional narrative explanation, as a series of entries, each headed by a date and time. This presentation emphasizes the official, bureaucratic, objective perspective of the government or police officials on a character whom the reader has come to know from a much more personal, emotional, subjective perspective. The reader thus learns of the death of Molina only through this cold, impersonal, "objective" reporting:

...two agents of the CISL, already in close contact with our patrol unit, proceeded to make the arrest. Subject demanded to see credentials. At that moment, however, several shots were fired from a passing automobile, wounding CISL agent Joaquin Perrone, along with subject, both of whom immediately fell to the ground. The arrival of our patrol unit, minutes later, was too late for pursuit of extremist vehicle. Of the wounded, Molina expired before arriving patrol unit could administer first aid.

The distance and lack of emotion with which Molina's death is recorded allows the reader to supply the appropriate emotional response. This narrative technique thus increases the impact of Molina's death on the reader, rendering it all the more powerful. The nature of the report also parallels the dry, objective style which characterizes the footnote passages. Thus, the dry, objective, factual tone of both the footnotes on homosexuality and the official report on Molina's death are contrasted with the reader's personal, emotional attachment to the homosexual Molina based on his character as developed through dialogue.

The ending sequence of the novel is written from the perspective of Valentin's *internal subjective voice* as he drifts into a morphine-induced fantasy. An internal subjective voice is a narrative voice from the subjective point of view of one character, and represents his internal thoughts. These final pages of the novel are written in *italix* print, in order to set them off as the depiction of a fantasy, and not to be taken as an objective reality. This ending narrative technique is significant to several important themes in the story. It demonstrates that Valentin has succumbed to escapist fantasy (aided by the morphine) as a response to the torture and beating inflicted upon him by the prison authorities. The narrative makes clear that Valentin has *chosen* to accept the morphine, and that it has not been injected into him against his will. The "dialogue" between Valentin and the clinician, during which Valentin does not actually speak because he is in too much pain, indicates in no uncertain terms that Valentin has nodded his head in acceptance of the offer of morphine:

> Listen. . .you won't tell anyone, promise me. . .Nod your head whether you want it or not. God, what they did to you it's barbaric, you'll be in a lot of pain for quite a few days. . .Listen to me. Nobody's around here in first aid right now, so I can take a chance and give you some morphine, that way you'll be able to rest. If you want it, nod your head. . .Okay, you'll get some relief in just a minute.

This exchange is important to the development of Valentin's character, because it makes clear that he has succumbed to the very type of escapist fantasy for which he criticized Molina. This represents the final breakdown of Valentin's political

idealism, which called for resisting escapism in favor of political action.

Furthermore, the morphine dream itself resembles Molina's movies, with its fantasy tropical island and strong element of romance. The internal subjective fantasy sequence is also set up in stark contrast to the "objective" factual narrative segments based on the scholarly footnotes and the official reports filed by the government agents. The novel closes with Valentin's fantasy of Marta's assurance that he will never lose her because "This dream is short but this dream is happy." Just how one may interpret this final, fantasized statement is left open to the reader. However, there is an edge of cynicism to this ending, implied by the fact that "happiness" can only be achieved by the characters in the novel through fantasy—and, more to the point, that fantasy is equivalent to death. One may speculate that Valentin will mercifully be given enough morphine that he may in fact die. Or that, even if he lives, he will exist in a state of living death, because he will become addicted to the morphine, and therefore lose all ties to reality. For Molina, too, fantasy ultimately leads to death. It is clear that his decision to pass on important political information to Valentin's comrades outside of the prison is motivated not by an awakening to political conviction, but by his love for Valentin. Molina only agrees to do this after he and Valentin have made love. Furthermore, even Molina's political act is, for him, the embodiment of one of the romantic movies about which he fantasizes. Valentin's speculation, through his morphine dream, is that Valentin, rather than "sacrificing himself for a just cause," has in fact "'let himself be killed because that way he could die like some heroine in a movie, and none of that business about a just cause. . .'"

Puig thus utilizes a variety of experimental narrative techniques as a means of further developing central social and political themes of particular concern to him.

Source: Liz Brent, in an essay for *Literature of Developing Nations for Students*, Gale, 2000.

Jonathan Tittler

In the following essay on Argentinian author Puig's Kiss of the Spider Woman, *author Jonathan Tittler speculates on the success of the novel to transcend its boundaries of genre (from novel to film, play, drama, and musical comedy). Tittler proposes that this is Puig's most powerful—and most explicit—novel, not only because of the taboo themes it addresses (most notably homosexuality and revolution), but also how the writing itself interacts with these themes.*

On 14 May 1990, *Newsweek* ran an article on a renewed concept in American theater, a series of productions called "new musicals," the most recent avatar of "off-off-off-Broadway." This collaborative venture between a local college and recognized theater mavens was touted as a bold initiative that would allow "a radical change, away from the high-stakes crapshoot of producing new musicals on Broadway." The first of the maverick theater's productions was slated to be, uncannily enough, *Kiss of the Spider Woman*, "based on the Argentine novel by Manuel Puig that inspired the 1985 film" [Kroll]. My letters of inquiry to both the show's producer-director Harold Prince and SUNY Purchase's impresario, Martin Bell, as to the feasibility of acquiring copies of the libretto of their adaptation, went unanswered. Involved for the moment in other projects, I let the matter rest.

Puig's name next appeared in *Newsweek* some three months later. A jarringly brief entry in the "Milestones" section read "died: Argentine novelist Manuel Puig, 57; of a heart attack, in Cuernavaca, Mexico, July 22. Puig's work *The Kiss of the Spider Woman* was made into an Academy Award-winning movie in 1985." Having maintained a periodic correspondence with Puig since 1981, when he participated in a festival of Ibero-American culture at Cornell University, I was shaken to learn via the mass media that an important aspect of my textual relationship with the author was over. It was not till later, however, that another realization dawned on me: if these two journalistic entries were any indication, Puig would be known to future generations not so much for the diverse textures of his unorthodox novels as for a film in whose production he figured secondarily, a by-product of one of his narratives, *El beso de la mujer arana*.

All the ink spilled in representing stock characters, everyday situations, vernacular dialogue, commodified cultural references, parodies of stereotypes, and the like, and what earned the artist a piece of immortality was the chance conversion of some of his words into images on celluloid. As Puig was, practically from birth, fascinated with the world of film (and this novel is clearly his most "filmsy"), there is some justice or at least a twisted symmetry to this eventuality. But to appreciate the consonance of the author's fate is not to understand why this novel—rather than the seven others he published—

has transcended its generic borders, spilling over into the realms of film, drama, and, now, musical comedy. What is there about *Spider Woman* that sets it apart, marking it as especially meaningful?

The most accurate and honest answer to this sort of question—one critics nowadays are reticent to ask—is that I don't know for certain. Neither does anyone else, although, as usual, there may be no shortage of opinions on the subject. Success, both commercial and critical, is no less difficult to explain than it is to achieve. It inevitably depends on such intangibles as balance (between tension and release, emotion and reason, action and dialogue) and timing (both within the text and within history), elements that, even if mastered once, do not transfer easily from one work to the next. Of course, the mechanical repetition of one's past accomplishments is probably the surest way to *avoid* producing a valid artistic representation, let alone a masterpiece. On the contrary, the freshness that comes with venturing into uncharted terrain, occasioning the felicitous juxtaposition of disparate elements—what I call here "odd coupling"—seems like a more reliable guideline for authentic artistic creativity. Even then, however, there are incomparably more ways to get lost than to hit the mark, whatever "hitting the mark" may be taken by publishers, consumers, and critics to mean. These considerations notwithstanding, *Kiss of the Spider Woman*, since long before the author's premature death, has stood out (for me, for many of my colleagues, for the public at large) as Puig's most complete work, the one that addresses the issues that haunted him in the most satisfying, integrated fashion. Let us, in an appropriately eulogistic vein, probe the wherefores of its perceived greatness.

I start with the conviction that *Kiss of the Spider Woman* is Puig's most generally successful novel because it is, far and away, his most powerful. My contention is that, whereas his other novels allude to, but eventually skirt, several suppressed and even taboo themes (homosexuality as social practice, revolution as political activity, film as culture), this work confronts these issues in a candid and sustained manner that is likely to have an impact on contemporary Western readers. The topics, "hot" in themselves, interact, moreover, by means of a minimalist technique such that time, space, the number of characters, and other plot elements are judiciously reduced to their bare essentials, thereby enhancing the novel's dramatic compression and intensity. These unique ingredients—the particular signs and the numerous pregnant silences that constitute the text—combine to empower the reader to respond creatively on a number of fictional and psychological levels. The response is particularly acute and significant because, again, Puig manipulates images that touch our collective contemporary nerve. In short, the highly pertinent problematics dovetail precisely with the audacious technique (although the technique is part of the problematics and vice-versa) such that they give rise to a sense of aesthetic and intellectual fullness. All of which, despite or perhaps because of the effort entailed, amounts to an uncommonly good read.

The novel's thematic power base can be thought of initially as a three-legged stool. But in addition to the three strongest explicit motifs—homosexuality, revolutionary politics, the world of film—there is a fourth thematic strand—writing itself—that not only conveys the other themes but interacts with them as well. Through the adjacency of disparate kinds of discourse (Molina's nostalgic cinematic evocations, Valentin's dialectical syllogisms, the impersonal voice of psychoanalytic theory, that of the cellmates' unconscious, a police report), writing acquires opacity and calls attention to itself—a major instance of the "odd coupling" noted above. Each of the main themes is by itself potentially subversive vis-a-vis the dominant ideology—heterosexual, bourgeois, logocentric—of contemporary Western culture. Together they have the potential to function explosively, unsettling mainstream values and practices and, if reading is not yet totally irrelevant to other realms of our cultural life, threatening to destabilize the balance of power in society.

To be sure, this novel is not the first in which Puig has broached these controversial topics. With regard to homosexuality, the quasiprotagonist Toto in *Betrayed by Rita Hayworth* is portrayed as effeminate or sexually ambivalent and barely escapes being the victim of a homosexual attack. And Leo Druscovich's sodomitic violation and bludgeoning of a male homosexual in *The Buenos Aires Affair* brings him so much guilt that it nearly drives him crazy and does eventually lead to his own violent self-destruction. But neither of these episodes is central to the fictions in which they figure, nor is the question of homosexuality developed systematically. *Kiss of the Spider Woman*, however, through two main vehicles—the character of Molina and a series of apparently scientific footnotes that intermittently break the illusion of the primary fictional discourse—removes the issue of sexual preference from its

> *Kiss of the Spider Woman,* since long before the author's premature death, has stood out (for me, for many of my colleagues, for the public at large) as Puig's most complete work, the one that addresses the issues that haunted him in the most satisfying, integrated fashion."

discreet Victorian closet and subjects it to thorough scrutiny.

That scrutiny, to be sure, is far from disinterested. Rather, it takes the form of an apologia and acquires the quality of a defense of homosexuality. Crucial to Puig's strategy for counteracting Western culture's intolerance toward deviance from the "straight" norm is to portray the gay character Molina as sympathetically complex. The windowdresser's eye for the fine details of design, his sensitive identification with the heroines of the films he narrates, his genuine fondness for his mother and his cellmate, and his attempts (largely hapless) at defending himself intellectually against Valentin's cutting ratiocinations all help dispose the reader positively toward this middle-aged queen (*loca* in the original Spanish) convicted of impairing the morals of a minor.

It should be noted that Molina is not just a typical sexual dissident but rather an individualized subject who identifies not so much with women as with the pervasive stereotype of the subjugated woman. Referring to himself as a female (''I can't believe what a stupid girl I am), he refuses to play a penetrative role in his sexual relations and cannot imagine enjoying sex with a man unless the pleasure is mixed with pain and fear. Men are, according to Molina, serious, responsible, consequential, whereas the other queens Molina associates with tend toward the fickle and feckless, as indicated by their trivial game of exchanging names with those of starlets of the silver screen. Politically inert, socially outcast, lacking in self-respect, untrained in the rigorous methods of Marxian analysis, Molina must somehow marshal his scanty resources to confront the challenges thrust upon him by the State and by his assertive interlocutor Valentin.

To meet those challenges and gain his release from prison, Molina does the only thing he can do. He converts himself into the Spider Woman, the seductive spinner of webs who devours her mate after coupling with him. Each film segment Molina narrates constitutes a strand designed to weaken Valentin's resistance and eventually to trap him into revealing the identity of his comrades in arms, data the informant hopes to pass on to the warden. If successful, this treacherous plan—another manifestation of the betrayal motif that courses through Puig's fiction—is likely to alienate Molina from our affection. But it does not succeed, at least not in the form in which it was conceived, for as Molina seduces Valentin he also seduces himself. When, like a Hollywood ingenue, he falls in love with his cellmate and sacrifices his life in order to pass information on to Valentin's revolutionary cohorts, he demonstrates to what extent he has been caught in the very web of allure he fashioned.

A hero(ine) despite himself, Molina ultimately embodies the ragtag vestiges of virtues—valor, fidelity, magnanimity—commonly associated with an earlier age and possible today only in an impure, parodic, mass-mediated form. It is not an abuse of figural language to aver that his characterization amounts to the author's planting a mischievous kiss on the lips of the (male, Western) reader. By addressing the question of homosexuality directly (the love scenes, although carefully constructed so as not to offend, cannot be taken for anything other than love scenes between men), Puig shows his willingness to play with fire. And by according Molina such sympathetic treatment, Puig enacts a revindication of sexual practices whose marginality has only increased with recent historical events (witness the persistent homophobic hysteria pursuant to the AIDS epidemic).

But the novel's vehicle for dealing with homosexuality is not limited to this one character or, for that matter, to the level of fiction where characters normally dwell. In a series of eight footnotes, spanning chapters 3 through 11, the text also explores the same question, but from a radically different perspective. Here we have not a case study in quasidramatic form (as we find with Molina) but a disembodied, erudite voice that offers an overview of some extant scholarship on the subject of homosexuality as it has been studied by the social sciences in this century. Theories by such prominent figures as Sigmund Freud, Anna Freud, Norman O. Brown, Wilhelm Reich, Herbert Marcuse, and Kate Millet on the sociopsychological origins and ramifications of homosexuality are proposed, debated, and, in most cases, rejected, relativized, or countered.

Rather than revisiting cliches about the role of repression, narcissism, paternal domination, maternal castration, and the like in contributing to the incidence of homosexuality, I propose to take a global stance before this aspect of the novel. Most noteworthy from such a perspective is that no single theory or group of theories glossed can explain satisfactorily either the phenomenon of homosexuality in general or the situation of Molina in particular. I do not conclude out of hand from this limitation, however, as some critics have done, that the footnotes function to burlesque psychoanalytical or sociological theory. Instead, I take at face value Puig's comments as to his felt need to disseminate information on the matter, even if the scholarship represented, especially in the area of non-Freudian and particularly feminist psychoanalysis, is far from the last word on the subject. The sort of play going on here, rather than mere spoof, is the endless freeplay of signifiers, as Derrida would put it, or the polyphonic interplay of indeterminately authoritative voices, in Bakhtinian terms. Puig's mistrust of power, and the lengths he will go to in order to diffuse it in his texts, is by now amply documented. But instead of simply playing out that obsession through the risky technique of the footnotes (numerous students have complained to me about how this feature momentarily interrupts their reading enjoyment), the author outdoes himself by introducing in the last entry the figure of the Danish scholar Dr. Anneli Taub.

What makes Taub so important in the context of the quasiscientific discourse of the annotations is that, whereas the Freuds, Brown, Reich, Marcuse, Millet, et al. are thinkers and writers whose titles can be found in the card catalog of any research library, Taub is something of a nonentity. Like Molina and Valentin, she is an invented figure whose ''presence'' in the footnotes effaces the neat distinction between reality and fiction maintained until that point. Perhaps this roguish tweak of our nose derives from Puig's familiarity with the works of his senior compatriot Jorge Luis Borges, whose spurious footnotes are legion and who even went so far as to invent an author, H. Bustos Domecq, for three books he coproduced with Adolfo Bioy Casares.

Possible influences aside, however, Anneli Taub's fabricated contributions to the scholarship on the issue of homosexuality do attain a privileged status for the license Puig takes in her name. The conclusions attributed to her read at first like a behavioral explanation for Toto's development in *Betrayed by Rita Hayworth.* And her closing remarks, tantamount to an exhortation or homosexuals to organize themselves and participate in the political process, tend to support the course of action Molina finally chooses for himself. This female authority figure, whose name consists of the same number of vowels and consonants as those of Manuel Puig, whose theories encompass the alpha and omega of Puig's novels to that date, and whose very appearance in the text implies the sort of self-erasure at the heart of Puig's ideal vision of power (see chapter 5 of this volume), demonstrates the enormous personal investment the author has in giving priority to a balanced understanding of homosexuality—a priority long overdue on the agenda of Western culture.

Despite Molina's initially apolitical stance, the novel shows that to speak candidly of homosexuality, let alone of gay liberation, is to engage in meaningful political praxis. The text's second high-risk thematic venture is to try to envisage a way for homosexuality to insert itself creatively into revolutionary politics. Now, lest the novel look unduly fanciful and extremist, we must distinguish between North American and Latin American politics. Whereas the 1980s saw a flowering of democracy in such Latin American countries as Chile, Uruguay, Paraguay, and Argentina, the decade before (that of the novel's writing) was marked by a preponderance of brutal military governments whose repressive regimes tended to curtail or abolish entirely freedom of speech and of the press, not to mention their engagement in acts of torture, rape, pillage, and the like. With legitimate movements of opposition banished and forced to move underground, it was not uncommon for educated, sensible young people to associate with guerrilla bands and, indeed, to carry out acts of sabotage or subversion against the government. When caught, these political enemies of the State were of course frequently treated with little regard for civil rights or due process.

The Argentine military dictatorship of the 1970s was particularly savage in this respect, mounting a "dirty war" (*guerra sucia*) that involved torturing, killing, or "disappearing" thousands of citizens suspected of political dissidence. North Americans have come to take for granted the right to criticize

their government, and they even (somewhat naively) expect the government to defend that right for them. What they are not often aware of, however, is the exceedingly narrow options offered to them by the two-party political system, a system in which Republicans and Democrats are frequently indistinguishable as to the conservatism or liberality of their views. There are even instances of complete inversions from the norm: North Carolina's Democratic senator Jesse Helms, for example, stands clearly to the right of New York's Republican senator Alphonse D'Amato on the question of artistic freedom. Neither of these politicians, of course, espouses guaranteed free postsecondary education or medical treatment, as Cuba's Fidel Castro or Peru's Alan Garcia have done with enormous popular support. Which is to say that the urban revolutionary Valentin Arregui Paz is neither a lunatic nor a legendary figure, as he might be if the novel were set in the United States. He is, rather, a plausible example of the measures many people of conscience were driven to take under the extremely repressive conditions reigning in Puig's homeland at the time.

These distinctions, often necessary when dealing with cross-cultural phenomena, are especially pertinent in the light of Puig's residence in New York while writing this novel. In addition to wanting to discredit the Argentine military in the eyes of the rest of Latin America (the novel was censored in Argentina until the democratically elected Alfonsin government came to power in 1983), it is quite likely that the author also had a North American reader in mind. The film version, in fact, unequivocally speaks to the North American viewer: despite the Brazilian location (Sao Paulo), an Argentine director (Hector Babenco), a Brazilian leading lady (Sonia Braga), and a Puerto Rican supporting actor (Raul Julia), the language of the original soundtrack is English. Notwithstanding the text's lush aesthetic dimension, this is not a work for complacent speculative consumption. It is an instructive exercise in Latin American realpolitik.

As with the motif of homosexuality, that of radical sociopolitical change is one Puig has flirted with in at least two of his previous novels, *Betrayed by Rita Hayworth* and *The Buenos Aires Affair.* Again, on those occasions the author deals with the question only tangentially or allusively. While most of the characters in *Rita Hayworth* are too young, too old, or too preoccupied with the details of everyday domestic life to actively pursue politics in the conventional sense, the promising premedical student Esther does channel her idealism into the Peronist (military populist) slogans she inscribes in her diary. But these sporadic outbursts of youthful zeal lead nowhere and are in a sense neutralized by the protofascist remarks found in Hector's monologue ("long live the united jerks of my beloved country"). Leo Druscovich's brush with unionism in *The Buenos Aires Affair* is likewise short lived and furthermore at odds with his lust for personal power. Until the advent of *Spider Woman,* in fact, Puig's fiction focuses almost exclusively on the micropolitical, that level where power is wielded over one subject by another, where events are so meaningful to the individual and so trivial to society at large. The sustained treatment accorded to the possibility of a macropolitical solution to human problems marks not so much a turning point (as he never returns to address the question with equal seriousness) as an apex in the trajectory of large-scale political investment in his narrative.

The representative of a certain kind of class struggle in the novel is Molina's cellmate, Valentin Arregui Paz. It would be comforting to brand Valentin as simply a Marxist, but, like Molina, he is too individualized and complex for us to dismiss him so summarily. And like Molina, he undergoes a fundamental metamorphosis. From an initial position of narrowly doctrinaire militancy, he evolves into an ostensibly sensitive, caring person capable of sharing his feelings and thoughts on a nonjudgmental, egalitarian basis. Despite his near reversal of roles with Molina, and contrary to the dominant interpretations of the novel to date, though, I do not see Valentin as a figure of equal sublimity or significance, however formidable a challenge he mounts to Molina's discourse of seduction.

Valentin's secondary status within the fiction derives, characteristically for Puig, from the position of superior power he initially enjoys relative to Molina. Trained at the university level in political science, practiced in the art of Marxian dialectic, and tempered in the forge of physical torture, Valentin thinks and acts with a rigor and discipline that critically undermine ("deconstruct") Molina's sentimentally escapist film narrations. These are qualities certainly worthy of respect, but they do not overcome an inevitable antipathy that stems from, among other sources, the revolutionary's haughty disdain toward his apolitical interlocutor ("What an ignoramus! When you know nothing, then say nothing"). Before long, Valentin's insistence on consistent reasoning cannot help but underscore certain inconsistencies in his own modus operandi, incon-

sistencies that lead him to reduplicate, within the isolated space of their cell, the very relations of power he has dedicated his life to overthrowing. His inability to apply the high-sounding values of his abstract theories to the simple and concrete situation in which he finds himself erodes his credibility almost from the outset.

To his credit, Valentin becomes increasingly aware of these contradictions and makes a Herculean effort to resolve them. He manages to unblock a good part of his emotions and to admit not only that he cares more deeply for a woman in his revolutionary movement than for the movement itself but also that the woman he really loves belongs not to the movement at all but to the hated ruling class. His acquiescence to coupling sexually with Molina, surely the most sensational manifestation of significant change in Valentin, reflects not desire for his partner but a desire to please Molina and to exchange affection with him on Molina's own terms. Even his readings of the films Molina narrates to him, at first severe allegorical reductions, eventually become more highly nuanced appreciations of the diverse textures of human experience. Valentin's evolution, grossly summarized, runs from an inconsistent dogmatism to a tolerant pluralism, the latter terms bearing a markedly positive charge in Puig's narrative system. But Valentin's sentimental education, financed through a debt not collected in full by his mentor Molina, never becomes the text's primary object of focus.

The contention of Valentine's secondary role vis-a-vis Molina, itself hierarchical in nature, rests on two key aspects of the novel: the dominant subject matter of the footnotes and certain revelations included in Valentin's concluding dream sequence. As we have already seen, the footnotes deal chiefly with homosexuality, the motif embodied in Molina, not with the topic of guerrilla movements of liberation. There is, to be sure, an exception to that rule: one long annotation, located in chapter 4, that represents officially sanctioned (by the Third Reich) publicity material concerning the second, pro-Nazi film Molina narrates, "the superproduction entitled *Her Real Glory.*" This note does bear an explicit political message, but not of the sort that would resound sympathetically in Valentin. In fact, it quite severely contextualizes the version of the film the reader receives from Molina.

Instead of speaking directly to any particular ideology, however, the note's primary function is to emphasize the relativity of all ideologies and discourses. Since the character with the ideological hang-up is Valentin (Molina, who can barely muster a consistent attitude, has no pretensions of maintaining anything so authoritative as an ideology), the note serves as a necessary corrective to his obsessive and imperious Marxist cant. In sum, then, by airing the questions most important to Molina personally (albeit in an erudite manner quite foreign to him) or by justifying his nonauthoritarian position in the ongoing debate in which he is embroiled, the marginal notes work to bolster Molina's protagonistic, and even heroic, status.

That still leaves open the matter of the novel's conclusion, taken by some to embody a sort of apotheosis for Valentin, who in a literal sense has the novel's last words. That is, once Molina is eliminated by the urban guerrillas, only Valentin remains as a focus of readerly interest and, especially, empathy. Having been subjected to further torture, which according to the attending physician has produced third-degree burns in the groin area, Valentin is mercifully given a drug to alleviate the pain. His morphine-induced delirium shows the extent to which he has assimilated some of the key concepts implicit in the interlude with his deceased cellmate. In touch with his emotions and forthright in his relations with others (he carries on an imaginary dialogue with his beloved Marta), Valentin closes the novel by demonstrating how he has become humanized, spiritually enriched by the process. Let us see where such an ostensibly sound interpretation fails to do justice to the text.

Beginning with the drug-induced state of the monologue, which marks Valentin as Other with respect to himself, we should consider some of the ways in which the novel critiques the idea of a stable, discrete identity underlying such an account. Those burns in the groin area, for instance; are they not the mark of a *castrato*, of a man who is not (in the conventional sense) a man, of a man who is perhaps Molina, or more precisely both Molina and not Molina? This contradictory statement, rather than embodying a logical absurdity, carries the full force of Puig's vision of both the ideal subject and the sort of intersubjective relations that would constitute the ideal society. When, after making love with Valentin, Molina says "It seemed as if I wasn't here at all . . . like it was you all alone. Or like I wasn't me anymore. As if now, somehow . . . I . . . were you," he posits the principle of a porous, fluid personal identity, one where the subject is not viewed as an elemental, unassailable fortress. It takes the form, rather, of an open-ended construct consisting of myriad influences, prominent among which, in addition to one's genetic constitution, are the events, persons, images, and words that comprise one's environment.

In Valentin's monologue, the instability of such a contextualized subject is reflected in the protean figure of his interlocutor. At first taken to be the physician ("if it weren't for your knowing the way out of here, doctor, and leading me, I couldn't go on"), that figure quickly transforms into Marta, Valentin's long-standing object of desire ("Marta . . . where are you? when did you get here?"). Marta, however, soon blends with an island girl ("'Can I ask you to pretend that she's me?' yes, 'But don't tell her anything, don't be critical of her, let her think she is me'"), who later changes into an island ("she's lying in the sea and she lifts her hand and from up here I can see that the island is a woman") and finally into the spider woman ("the spiderweb is growing out of her own body, the threads are coming out of her waist and her hips, they're part of her body"). This fantastic figure, who appears in a scene thoroughly stylized in the manner of a Hollywood production and who provides him with sustenance, is of course a hallucinatory version of the deceased Molina, both quasisubject and quasiobject of the dream. Through all these metamorphoses, to be sure, Valentin is talking to no one but himself, but that self is not the same self who began the dynamic interaction. It is a self that has incorporated Molina's notion of a commutable, constructed subject. It is a selfless self, not just in the sense of altruism (though there is plenty of that) but also that of alterity, of otherness, such that the only trace that remains of the initial entity "Valentin" are the linguistic signs of his ventriloquy. Within such a framework, the character is reduced to little more than a simulacrum, a name over a void, and the possibilities of his playing a conventionally protagonistic role are accordingly negligible.

Dissident sexual preference and radical political practice are, in the context of Western culture, topics almost certain to outrage or at least titillate. But to what extent can the same be said for film, a medium that is by now not only commonplace but also in some sense superseded by that of video, which in turn is rendered obsolete by the graphic capacities of the personal computer? Are we not in the Age of the Image, where reading is largely replaced by viewing and where life is reduced to electronic impulses that register within the confines of a small, two-dimensional monitor? Surely the representation of the world of film, even in the mid-

1970s, could not be expected to imprint sensationally on the reading public.

To appreciate the force of the film motif in *Spider Woman*, we must first specify precisely what kind of films are involved and how they function within the text. The films Molina narrates do not belong to the world of ''serious'' cinema, to that of a Bergman, an Antonioni, or a Godard. They are, with one exception, grade B American commercial flicks, unashamedly riven with the facile gimmicks of melodrama, suspense, nostalgia, chintzy glitter, and the like. Such films normally have but one appeal: entertainment. They hold the power of spectacle and are designed to distract us from the tedium or problems of everyday existence, but nothing more transcendent than that. Escape from his mediocre-cum-sordid existence is presumably Molina's primary motive for viewing the films in the first place, and it is certainly one of his principal reasons for retelling the films as stories to Valentin during their incarceration (more about his other possible motives shortly). Valentin, for his part, with unlimited time on his hands, listens attentively not because he expects to be edified, but because he seeks relief from the boredom of his sentence.

Failing to qualify as Art, these commercial artifacts lack legitimacy in the world of high culture—that of museums, symphonic concert halls, or traditional universities. And here is precisely where Puig works a neat inversion of the established cultural axes. Whereas the term *cell* in the novel connotes imprisonment and repetition ad nauseam of the same, a configuration with a markedly downward vector, *celluloid* brings with it associations of liberation, of passage into a realm of inexhaustible novelty and difference. Escapism is not disparaged out of hand. On the contrary, it is studied detainedly, in depth, with an eye to its less-than-obvious complexity, its motivations, its unforeseeable effects. In short, then, what is remarkable about the treatment of film in *Kiss of the Spider Woman* is not so much its presence in the text (a mere reflection of the superabundance of passe technology in postindustrial society) as the unpretentious nature of the examples provided and the unflagging respect that attends their narrative representation.

If escapism serves to motivate the cellmates to start narrating the films, it is certainly not their only reason, nor does it continue for long as their chief purpose. Although the reader is not aware of this level of meaning until chapter 8, Molina has another

sort of escape in mind, for he has made a deal with the warden to wear down Valentin's resistance and extract information about his comrades' whereabouts and planned activities. Poisoning the revolutionary's food is one means toward this end, but Molina's preferred tactic is to gain Valentin's confidence. The film narratives are thus designed to promote a sinister, one-sided intimacy (the spider woman scenario): the gay yarn spinner would appear to reveal his feelings, values, and memories, and the pliant guerrilla would be conned into revealing political secrets of utility to the authoritarian State.

Molina's downfall occurs because the above plan works too well. Not only is Valentin's physical resistance eroded, he responds to Molina's invitations to intimacy by uncovering elements of his own psyche that Molina finds irresistible. Here at last is a ''real man,'' the kind Molina has been searching for all his adult life! Once Molina realizes he is in love with Valentin he must revise his objective: rather than relay information to the warden in order to gain his own release, he must play a stalling game in order to stay in Valentin's company as long as possible. He must not elicit information from Valentin, lest he betray both his love and himself. The film narrations continue through the second half of the novel almost as intensely as in the first (approximately 84 pages in part 1 as opposed to 57 pages in part 2), but their function and meaning undergo a drastic transformation.

For Valentin, the change—lacking an analogous ethical reversal—is less radical but still significant. From an inconsequential pastime, the films evolve into the matrix for an almost primal experience. Through their narration and discussion Valentin reawakens to aspects of life—the joy of eating, of erotic imagining, of intimate sharing, of crying—he had allowed to wither and almost die. After Molina dies in attempting to make contact with Valentin's band of subversives, Valentin wonders whether his cellmate acted out of political conviction or just in emulation of Leni, the heroine of one of his narrations. He never learns of Molina's duplicitous collusion with the State and so never fully understands the irony of his miraculous rebirth. The new meaning he finds in life comes about through his exposure to an illusion, or a series of illusions on a variety of planes. These include the patently idealized films, which are filtered through Molina's memory, then translated into language, and finally are received under a set of assumptions not shared by both parties. Rather than undermine the value of the narrated movies, however, such dynamic equivocality attests to the importance of such mass-cultural objects as a force in contemporary life. By incorporating the rudimentary structures of the films into the nuanced and shifting structure of the text, Puig both legitimates the marginalized artifacts and implicitly questions the boundaries of serious literature.

Some of the ways in which the dominant motifs of homosexuality, revolution, and film interact should by now be obvious. Homosexuality is treated with a candor that, within mainstream society, is outrageous. The seductive power of Molina's discourse is such, moreover, that it invades the space of Valentin's discourse (even as the other discourse impinges on it as well). Revolutionary politics becomes sexualized, sexual dissidence becomes politicized. And the narration of film proves to be a crucial vehicle for sexual-political change in both directions. The cultivation of an aesthetic sensibility within a doctrinaire Marxist, of course, may not satisfy many militants on the left, but the idea that an effeminate gay male could achieve such humanizing results through the use of passe commercial films qualifies as nothing short of startling. And Molina's ultimate determination to act in a politically subversive (though still romantic) manner is no less noteworthy. Puig has always held out more hope for gains in the micropolitical, intersubjective arena than in the national or global theater of macropolitics. But for Puig, unlike Jean Baudrillard, the social is not dead; social progress is still conceivable. Freedom and justice come about, however, not through mass mobilization (which leads to dangerously high concentrations of power) but with and in one interlocutor at a time, one viewer at a time, one reader at a time. Perhaps it was Puig's appreciation of the pivotal role of even the humblest individuals in society that moved the author to adopt the minimalist technique he so successfully wields in *Spider Woman*.

At a time when it looked like the Latin American novel was in peril of painting itself into the exuberant but ultimately confining corners of the neobaroque or of encyclopedic metafiction, Puig championed the refreshing current move away from "literary language." His styles, or lack of them, at times reminiscent of Barthes's degree zero of writing, work at reconnecting fiction with the worldly context in which it is produced. In *Kiss of the Spider Woman*, however, while maintaining his allegiance

to plain parlance and popular myths, he achieves a maximum of economy and efficiency in the structure of the fictional universe itself. As we shall see shortly, temporal and spatial coordinates, as well as other plot elements, are reduced to the barest of essentials. But these economies are insignificant in comparison to the constraints introduced with regard to narrative technique: there is none. That is, the figure of the narrator itself, long considered an indispensable component of narrative fiction, is eliminated altogether. Puig's regard for the unempowered manifests itself in an aesthetic of spareness wherein less is more and thinking small is its own reward.

Spider Woman is, after all, an exceedingly simple tale. With counted exceptions (the warden, a guard, a shopping list, a police report, the footnotes), the novel depends on only two characters talking to move from start to finish. And even though the themes of their conversations range widely in time and space, the coordinates of the action are limited almost absolutely to the restricted space of their prison cell and the weeks or months when they occupy it. Props consist of little more than the characters' clothing, some sheets and towels, the food Molina manages to bring in, their beds, the bars that enclose them. With no narrator to provide background information or even stage directions, reading difficulties can arise. When, for instance, Valentin in a fit of pique throws their prized marble cake on the floor, it is only through the reader's inference that the action can be said to take place.

The scene in which such significant silences play their most capital role is, of course, the first of the cellmates' love scenes, but the use of the almost-blank space (graphically rendered as "-...") is certainly not limited to moments when words might be offensive or too graphic for the lyrical nature of the scene. They appear throughout the text (see 9, 96, 180, 276, and passim) and, as in much contemporary fiction, invite the reader to participate actively in the completion of the fiction, to "write" it into coherent signification. In addition, the particular junctures where the fissures appear seem to indicate an awareness that language, so important in life and definitely no less crucial in literature, is really not adequate at the peak moments of either. Language is troping, figuration, approximation, not the "thing itself" it tries to represent. At any rate, the presence of so much silence in this colloquial text further supports the hypothesis that Puig's writing, despite the lush embroidery of some of Molina's descriptions, inscribes a logic of austerity.

To say that the reader must function as a coauthor is to evoke Cortazar's figure of the "lector complice" (accomplice reader), by now a critical commonplace in contemporary fiction. In view of the critique of power Puig articulates in *Spider Woman*, however, the reader must be seen as more than routinely engaged in a collaborative interpretive act. The reader here constitutes an utterly crucial link in a social transaction begun with the author and transmitted through the text. Nonfeasance on the reader's part aborts the process entirely, not only producing nonsense but also reinstalling the despotic power structure in its place of comfortable dominance. Let us look at this transaction in some detail.

Within the text, two sets of transactions are set in motion, one between the two main characters and another, on a discursive level, between the discourse of oral fictiveness (the "main plot") and the discourse of written scientificity (the scholarly footnotes). Despite their considerable differences, what these textual debates have in common is their tendency to blur the distinctions between what are normatively taken to be binary opposites. We have already established the ways in which Molina and Valentin come to partake of each other's personal identities, such that they merge, acquire some of each other's traits, share dreams, and the like. In similar fashion we might demonstrate the "truth" conveyed through fiction (not a terribly controversial notion) and the fictionality of writing within the domain of the humanities (perhaps less immediately apparent but, as the work of Hayden White and Dominick LaCapra indicates, still easily demonstrable). In both cases we observe an interpenetration of formerly distinct conceptual fields, with a more nuanced and dynamic understanding of the overall configuration. Higher on Puig's agenda than this appreciation, however, is the removal of power from one pole (the "scientific" one, in both Valentin's Marxian sense and the scholar's psychoanalytic sense) and an equitable redistribution of forces over the entire field (now properly called "fictive/scientific" or simply "narrative"). The newly transformed structure of power now grants as much validity to fiction (Molina's film narratives, the novel's entire imaginary dimension) as to what is conventionally thought of as nonfiction.

Something analogous occurs between the reader and the text. Conventionally conceived of as separate from the text and relegated to a subaltern, passive role, the reader of *Spider Woman* is invited to reflect upon several heady matters. First are the ways in which the reader is in the text (as Valentin, the listener, and as Molina, the unauthorized speaker, for instance) and the text is within the reader (the stock gambits of Hollywood films, along with Molina's familiar emotional responses; the identifiable fragments of Marxian orthodoxy as well as Valentin's predictable turns of logic). In addition, there is the question of how this mutual interpenetration of text and reader empowers the reader to respond creatively to the text (to imagine love scenes, to fathom Molina's motives for sacrificing himself, to write an ending to Valentin's concluding dream sequence, or to choose not to do any or all of these things). By responding creatively, rather than merely determining the meaning of the text for him- or herself (thereby "consuming" the text as the commodifiers of art would prefer), the reader/text realizes the networking potential of the liberated (autonomous but interconnected) subject represented and sanctioned within the text/reader. In short, to read *Kiss of the Spider Woman,* internalizing its structure, is to subscribe to a utopian program, a self-effacing, quasimystical process where one is prodded to imagine a secular, nonalienated state in which world and word recouple oddly and flow through each other like (troping unabashedly) warm salted butter and sugar syrup.

That recipe may be too high in cholesterol and calories for some, but there is no question that the images and ideas represented in *Kiss of the Spider Woman* have made a deep impression on our collective psyche. Again the question arises: why? Have we gotten to the crux of the matter? Convinced we have not (nor will we ever), I suggest (vainly) one more possible explanation for this work's singular importance: death. Not the mere incorporation of this universal motif in the text but, again, the procedure by which the theme is transmitted. Death in the novel, to be sure, is always "out there," lurking beyond the prison bars as a threat against those who challenge the given social order. It is the ultimate coercive force, one that Molina and Valentin are dedicated to resisting by forming an oasis of solidarity within their cell.

As you read this novel, in which unarmed individuals are pitted against the mammoth powers of the State, you have to suspect that one or both characters is eventually going to meet with death and that their storytelling, much like that of

Scheherazade in the *1001 Arabian Nights*, is designed mainly to defer that inevitable encounter. But when the expected happens, and Molina finally perishes, you are not accorded the finality you have come to associate with death. Rather, you are given a set of equally plausible choices as to Molina's motives, choices that span the heroic and the bathetic, and you are then assured that his reasons are "something only he can know, and it's possible that even he never knew." Likewise, you are kept in the dark about Valentin's death. Are the (remarkably upbeat) words with which the novel ends the words with which he terminates his earthly existence? Does he live on in order to be tortured again, in a repeated enactment of death-within-life? Or does his newfound sensitivity move him to confess to his torturers? In any case, death is a latent presence that never quite crystalizes, a specter, an enigma or question rather than an entity or answer.

These reflections on death as an ongoing process and an insoluble human mystery arise within the context of another "death," that of the narrator. Far from tragic, the death of the narrator is a ritual sacrifice necessary to the destabilization and reallotment of power within the text, so that other, less authoritative voices (narrators in their own right) may be heard. It is therefore a silence and an absence that engender a deferred meaning, however decentered and disunified the textual surface may appear. That death, of course, dwells in the shadow (now, for us) of the death of the author, the biological, historical subject who will write no more. Perhaps the oddest coupling of all is the marshalling of so many images of death to constitute a work that amounts to a celebration of vitality ("this dream is short but this dream is happy"), a work whose signifying life has only just begun.

Source: Jonathan Tittler, "Odd Coupling: *Kiss of the Spider Woman*," in *Manuel Puig* in *Twayne's World Authors Series Online*, G. K. Hall & Co., 1999, Chapter 4.

Barbara P. Fulks

In the following review, Barbara P. Fulks outlines the theme of Puig's Kiss of the Spider Woman, *the polemical nature of sexuality and revolutionary politics. Fulk calls attention to Puig's "innovative" narrative techniques, as well as his uses of themes and techniques which call into question such wide-ranging issues as assumptions of gender identity, language, and psychoanalytic and Marxist theory.*

Puig's fourth novel, published in Spain in 1976 and in English translation in 1979, deals with the po-

lemical nature of the relationship between sexuality and revolutionary politics. The conflict between power and sex, and their functions in society, is embodied in the two protagonists, Valentín Arregui Paz and Luis Alberto Molina. The isolated setting of the novel, a prison cell, emphasizes the problem of language and communication between two individuals who experience different realities. Molina, a male homosexual who feels that he is a woman, colours his world with images of the silver screen of the 1930s and 1940s. Valentín, a heterosexual leftist, expresses himself in the rhetoric of Marxist ideology.

In order to fill the empty space between and around them, Molina narrates films to Valentín. The films become a form of metaphorical displacement for the two men—as they identify with or reject characters and actions in the films, they expose themselves to each other and to the reader. In addition to this major concern of interpersonal communication, there is a sub-plot of intrigue and possible betrayal which gives the flavour of a mystery story to the novel and also ties the two men to the larger social world outside the womb-like existence of the prison cell. The prison officials have offered Molina a lighter sentence in exchange for information about Valentín's political activities. Valentín, then, may be victimized by Molina. When Valentín asks Molina to risk his life to deliver a message to the revolutionaries, Molina is put in the position of potential victim. Thus, personal allegiances are pitted against larger social forces.

Puig's innovative narrative techniques are inextricably connected to the novel's theme of language and its social uses. Various types of discourse—dialogue, interior monologue, film and song texts, bureaucratic documents, footnotes, and letters—are presented without the traditional guiding voice and manipulative power of a third-person narrator. The reader must fill in the gaps, a process which reveals the reader's own preconceptions and ideological framework. How one feels about homosexuality and left-wing politics will determine in part how one judges the actions of the characters.

The novel begins with unattributed dialogue. No names are given, and there is no 'he/she said'. One speaker is describing a woman, and the details of the description (clothing, colours, emotions) may lead the reader to believe a woman is speaking. The other speaker is oddly antagonistic, interrupting to question the details and objecting frequently. Only

> Puig's innovative narrative techniques are inextricably connected to the novel's theme of language and its social uses. Various types of discourse—dialogue, interior monologue, film and song texts, bureaucratic documents, footnotes, and letters—are presented without the traditional guiding voice and manipulative power of a third-person narrator."

much later in the novel are the gender and the enforced cohabitation of the characters explained. This technique exposes the connections between interpreting language and interpreting gender.

Because the characters have trouble communicating with each other—the text is filled with the ellipses of unfinished sentences—Molina narrates films he has seen. These are standard Hollywood potboilers, with the addition of a Nazi propaganda film. Film narration, however, is different from film viewing. The plots may be familiar, but what the reader sees is Molina's and Valentín's identification with character. Molina becomes the heroine and Valentín the male love interest. With the Nazi film, however, Valentín's knowledge of history makes him refuse to participate, while Molina sees it as just another romantic love story. In all of the films there are outside social forces that defeat the lovers' relationship. The identification process is also taking place at the level of the reader. Which character in this dialectic confrontation elicits the reader's sympathy? Readers also identify by gender and by ideology.

The footnotes present an unfamiliar interpretive problem in fiction. In them, Puig presents various historical and contemporary explanations of homosexuality in chronological order. Both famous and obscure experts are named, but the references are paraphrased and not in any standard format. Moreo-

ver, their authority is undermined by the inclusion of part of the Nazi film in footnote form. When the film switches from Molina's voice to footnote form, its hyperbolic fascist content becomes clearly evident. The discourses of the state and academe are both manipulative, and thus suspect.

The prison documents presented in the text are another manifestation of the language of power. The State's obsession with proper names, hierarchical titles, dates, times, and gender contrasts with the absence of all these features in the dialogue between the two men and with Molina's emotionally charged recounting of the films. Language in these forms is divorced from an individual voice and assumes a mask of objectivity and authority. The documents also fulfil the plot function of portraying the effects of a malevolent exterior reality on the lives of the protagonists. The real confrontation is not between two men of different worldviews, but between the individual and the state.

The themes and techniques in this novel make it almost a display text for current trends in literary theory. Puig's questioning of the assumptions of gender identity is also a concern of feminist theory. He shows that language is not a unified monolithic system, but rather a set of conventions particular to use or function. The novel is self-deconstructive in its various discourses. Reader-response theorists can experience a step-by-step manifestation of the process of reading in the beginning of the novel. And finally, Puig exposes the weak links in both psychoanalytic and Marxist theory: Marxism's lack of a theory of the individual and Freud's inadequate explanation of both the female and the homosexual.

Source: Barbara P. Fulks, ''Kiss of the Spider Woman: Overview,'' in *Reference Guide to World Literature, 2nd ed.,* Ed. Lesley Henderson, St. James Press, 1995.

Sources

Barcarisse, Pamela, *Impossible Choices: The Implications of the Cultural References in the Novels of Manuel Puig,* University of Calgary Press, 1993, pp. 2, 4.

Kerr, Lucille, *Dictionary of Literary Biography*, Volume 113: *Modern Latin-American Fiction Writers,* First Series, Gale, 1992, pp. 235-47.

Tittler, Jonathan, *Manuel Puig,* Twayne, 1993, pp. vii, viii, 1, 5, 47, 51-52, 123.

Further Reading

Borges, Jorge Luis, *Collected Fictions*, Viking, 1998.
   A collection of short stories by the internationally renowned Argentine writer.

Martinez, Tomas Eloy, *Santa Evita*, Vintage, 1996.
   A fictional novel based on the life of the popular Argentine political figure Eva Peron.

Mitchell, Mark, ed., *The Penguin Book of International Gay Fiction*, Viking, 1995.
   A collection of short stories and selections, including a selection from Puig's *Betrayed by Rita Hayworth.*

Glossary of Literary Terms

A

Aestheticism: A literary and artistic movement of the nineteenth century. Followers of the movement believed that art should not be mixed with social, political, or moral teaching. The statement "art for art's sake" is a good summary of aestheticism. The movement had its roots in France, but it gained widespread importance in England in the last half of the nineteenth century, where it helped change the Victorian practice of including moral lessons in literature. Edgar Allan Poe is one of the best-known American "aesthetes."

Allegory: A narrative technique in which characters representing things or abstract ideas are used to convey a message or teach a lesson. Allegory is typically used to teach moral, ethical, or religious lessons but is sometimes used for satiric or political purposes. Many fairy tales are allegories.

Allusion: A reference to a familiar literary or historical person or event, used to make an idea more easily understood. Joyce Carol Oates's story "Where Are You Going, Where Have You Been?" exhibits several allusions to popular music.

Analogy: A comparison of two things made to explain something unfamiliar through its similarities to something familiar, or to prove one point based on the acceptance of another. Similes and metaphors are types of analogies.

Antagonist: The major character in a narrative or drama who works against the hero or protagonist. The Misfit in Flannery O'Connor's story "A Good Man Is Hard to Find" serves as the antagonist for the Grandmother.

Anthology: A collection of similar works of literature, art, or music. Zora Neale Hurston's "The Eatonville Anthology" is a collection of stories that take place in the same town.

Anthropomorphism: The presentation of animals or objects in human shape or with human characteristics. The term is derived from the Greek word for "human form." The fur necklet in Katherine Mansfield's story "Miss Brill" has anthropomorphic characteristics.

Anti-hero: A central character in a work of literature who lacks traditional heroic qualities such as courage, physical prowess, and fortitude. Anti-heroes typically distrust conventional values and are unable to commit themselves to any ideals. They generally feel helpless in a world over which they have no control. Anti-heroes usually accept, and often celebrate, their positions as social outcasts. A well-known anti-hero is Walter Mitty in James Thurber's story "The Secret Life of Walter Mitty."

Archetype: The word archetype is commonly used to describe an original pattern or model from which all other things of the same kind are made. Archetypes are the literary images that grow out of the "collective unconscious,'' a theory proposed by psychologist Carl Jung. They appear in literature as incidents and plots that repeat basic patterns of life. They may also appear as stereotyped characters. The ''schlemiel'' of Yiddish literature is an archetype.

Autobiography: A narrative in which an individual tells his or her life story. Examples include Benjamin Franklin's *Autobiography* and Amy Hempel's story ''In the Cemetery Where Al Jolson Is Buried,'' which has autobiographical characteristics even though it is a work of fiction.

Avant-garde: A literary term that describes new writing that rejects traditional approaches to literature in favor of innovations in style or content. Twentieth-century examples of the literary *avant-garde* include the modernists and the minimalists.

B

Belles-lettres: A French term meaning ''fine letters'' or ''beautiful writing.'' It is often used as a synonym for literature, typically referring to imaginative and artistic rather than scientific or expository writing. Current usage sometimes restricts the meaning to light or humorous writing and appreciative essays about literature. Lewis Carroll's *Alice in Wonderland* epitomizes the realm of belles-lettres.

Bildungsroman: A German word meaning ''novel of development.'' The *bildungsroman* is a study of the maturation of a youthful character, typically brought about through a series of social or sexual encounters that lead to self-awareness. J. D. Salinger's *Catcher in the Rye* is a *bildungsroman*, and Doris Lessing's story ''Through the Tunnel'' exhibits characteristics of a *bildungsroman* as well.

Black Aesthetic Movement: A period of artistic and literary development among African Americans in the 1960s and early 1970s. This was the first major African-American artistic movement since the Harlem Renaissance and was closely paralleled by the civil rights and black power movements. The black aesthetic writers attempted to produce works of art that would be meaningful to the black masses. Key figures in black aesthetics included one of its founders, poet and playwright Amiri Baraka, formerly known as LeRoi Jones; poet and essayist Haki R. Madhubuti, formerly Don L. Lee; poet and playwright Sonia Sanchez; and dramatist Ed Bullins. Works representative of the Black Aesthetic Movement include Amiri Baraka's play *Dutchman,* a 1964 Obie award-winner.

Black Humor: Writing that places grotesque elements side by side with humorous ones in an attempt to shock the reader, forcing him or her to laugh at the horrifying reality of a disordered world. ''Lamb to the Slaughter,'' by Roald Dahl, in which a placid housewife murders her husband and serves the murder weapon to the investigating policemen, is an example of black humor.

C

Catharsis: The release or purging of unwanted emotions—specifically fear and pity—brought about by exposure to art. The term was first used by the Greek philosopher Aristotle in his *Poetics* to refer to the desired effect of tragedy on spectators.

Character: Broadly speaking, a person in a literary work. The actions of characters are what constitute the plot of a story, novel, or poem. There are numerous types of characters, ranging from simple, stereotypical figures to intricate, multifaceted ones. ''Characterization'' is the process by which an author creates vivid, believable characters in a work of art. This may be done in a variety of ways, including (1) direct description of the character by the narrator; (2) the direct presentation of the speech, thoughts, or actions of the character; and (3) the responses of other characters to the character. The term ''character'' also refers to a form originated by the ancient Greek writer Theophrastus that later became popular in the seventeenth and eighteenth centuries. It is a short essay or sketch of a person who prominently displays a specific attribute or quality, such as miserliness or ambition. ''Miss Brill,'' a story by Katherine Mansfield, is an example of a character sketch.

Classical: In its strictest definition in literary criticism, classicism refers to works of ancient Greek or Roman literature. The term may also be used to describe a literary work of recognized importance (a ''classic'') from any time period or literature that exhibits the traits of classicism. Examples of later works and authors now described as classical include French literature of the seventeenth century, Western novels of the nineteenth century, and American fiction of the mid-nineteenth century such as that written by James Fenimore Cooper and Mark Twain.

Climax: The turning point in a narrative, the moment when the conflict is at its most intense. Typically, the structure of stories, novels, and plays is one of rising action, in which tension builds to the climax, followed by falling action, in which tension lessens as the story moves to its conclusion.

Comedy: One of two major types of drama, the other being tragedy. Its aim is to amuse, and it typically ends happily. Comedy assumes many forms, such as farce and burlesque, and uses a variety of techniques, from parody to satire. In a restricted sense the term comedy refers only to dramatic presentations, but in general usage it is commonly applied to nondramatic works as well.

Comic Relief: The use of humor to lighten the mood of a serious or tragic story, especially in plays. The technique is very common in Elizabethan works, and can be an integral part of the plot or simply a brief event designed to break the tension of the scene.

Conflict: The conflict in a work of fiction is the issue to be resolved in the story. It usually occurs between two characters, the protagonist and the antagonist, or between the protagonist and society or the protagonist and himself or herself. The conflict in Washington Irving's story ''The Devil and Tom Walker'' is that the Devil wants Tom Walker's soul but Tom does not want to go to hell.

Criticism: The systematic study and evaluation of literary works, usually based on a specific method or set of principles. An important part of literary studies since ancient times, the practice of criticism has given rise to numerous theories, methods, and ''schools,'' sometimes producing conflicting, even contradictory, interpretations of literature in general as well as of individual works. Even such basic issues as what constitutes a poem or a novel have been the subject of much criticism over the centuries. Seminal texts of literary criticism include Plato's *Republic,* Aristotle's *Poetics,* Sir Philip Sidney's *The Defence of Poesie,* and John Dryden's *Of Dramatic Poesie.* Contemporary schools of criticism include deconstruction, feminist, psychoanalytic, poststructuralist, new historicist, postcolonialist, and reader-response.

D

Deconstruction: A method of literary criticism characterized by multiple conflicting interpretations of a given work. Deconstructionists consider the impact of the language of a work and suggest that the true meaning of the work is not necessarily the meaning that the author intended.

Deduction: The process of reaching a conclusion through reasoning from general premises to a specific premise. Arthur Conan Doyle's character Sherlock Holmes often used deductive reasoning to solve mysteries.

Denotation: The definition of a word, apart from the impressions or feelings it creates in the reader. The word ''apartheid'' denotes a political and economic policy of segregation by race, but its connotations—oppression, slavery, inequality—are numerous.

Denouement: A French word meaning ''the unknotting.'' In literature, it denotes the resolution of conflict in fiction or drama. The *denouement* follows the climax and provides an outcome to the primary plot situation as well as an explanation of secondary plot complications. A well-known example of *denouement* is the last scene of the play *As You Like It* by William Shakespeare, in which couples are married, an evildoer repents, the identities of two disguised characters are revealed, and a ruler is restored to power. Also known as ''falling action.''

Detective Story: A narrative about the solution of a mystery or the identification of a criminal. The conventions of the detective story include the detective's scrupulous use of logic in solving the mystery; incompetent or ineffectual police; a suspect who appears guilty at first but is later proved innocent; and the detective's friend or confidant—often the narrator—whose slowness in interpreting clues emphasizes by contrast the detective's brilliance. Edgar Allan Poe's ''Murders in the Rue Morgue'' is commonly regarded as the earliest example of this type of story. Other practitioners are Arthur Conan Doyle, Dashiell Hammett, and Agatha Christie.

Dialogue: Dialogue is conversation between people in a literary work. In its most restricted sense, it refers specifically to the speech of characters in a drama. As a specific literary genre, a ''dialogue'' is a composition in which characters debate an issue or idea.

Didactic: A term used to describe works of literature that aim to teach a moral, religious, political, or practical lesson. Although didactic elements are often found in artistically pleasing works, the term ''didactic'' usually refers to literature in which the message is more important than the form. The term may also be used to criticize a work that the critic finds ''overly didactic,'' that is, heavy-handed in its delivery of a lesson. An example of didactic literature is John Bunyan's *Pilgrim's Progress.*

Dramatic Irony: Occurs when the reader of a work of literature knows something that a character in the work itself does not know. The irony is in the contrast between the intended meaning of the statements or actions of a character and the additional information understood by the audience.

Dystopia: An imaginary place in a work of fiction where the characters lead dehumanized, fearful lives. **George Orwell's** *Nineteen Eighty-four,* and Margaret Atwood's *Handmaid's Tale* portray versions of dystopia.

E

Edwardian: Describes cultural conventions identified with the period of the reign of Edward VII of England (1901-1910). Writers of the Edwardian Age typically displayed a strong reaction against the propriety and conservatism of the Victorian Age. Their work often exhibits distrust of authority in religion, politics, and art and expresses strong doubts about the soundness of conventional values. Writers of this era include E. M. Forster, H. G. Wells, and Joseph Conrad.

Empathy: A sense of shared experience, including emotional and physical feelings, with someone or something other than oneself. Empathy is often used to describe the response of a reader to a literary character.

Epilogue: A concluding statement or section of a literary work. In dramas, particularly those of the seventeenth and eighteenth centuries, the epilogue is a closing speech, often in verse, delivered by an actor at the end of a play and spoken directly to the audience.

Epiphany: A sudden revelation of truth inspired by a seemingly trivial incident. The term was widely used by James Joyce in his critical writings, and the stories in Joyce's *Dubliners* are commonly called ''epiphanies.''

Epistolary Novel: A novel in the form of letters. The form was particularly popular in the eighteenth century. The form can also be applied to short stories, as in Edwidge Danticat's ''Children of the Sea.''

Epithet: A word or phrase, often disparaging or abusive, that expresses a character trait of someone or something. ''The Napoleon of crime'' is an epithet applied to Professor Moriarty, arch-rival of Sherlock Holmes in Arthur Conan Doyle's series of detective stories.

Existentialism: A predominantly twentieth-century philosophy concerned with the nature and perception of human existence. There are two major strains of existentialist thought: atheistic and Christian. Followers of atheistic existentialism believe that the individual is alone in a godless universe and that the basic human condition is one of suffering and loneliness. Nevertheless, because there are no fixed values, individuals can create their own characters—indeed, they can shape themselves—through the exercise of free will. The atheistic strain culminates in and is popularly associated with the works of Jean-Paul Sartre. The Christian existentialists, on the other hand, believe that only in God may people find freedom from life's anguish. The two strains hold certain beliefs in common: that existence cannot be fully understood or described through empirical effort; that anguish is a universal element of life; that individuals must bear responsibility for their actions; and that there is no common standard of behavior or perception for religious and ethical matters. Existentialist thought figures prominently in the works of such authors as Franz Kafka, Fyodor Dostoyevsky, and Albert Camus.

Expatriatism: The practice of leaving one's country to live for an extended period in another country. Literary expatriates include Irish author James Joyce who moved to Italy and France, American writers James Baldwin, Ernest Hemingway, Gertrude Stein, and F. Scott Fitzgerald who lived and wrote in Paris, and Polish novelist Joseph Conrad in England.

Exposition: Writing intended to explain the nature of an idea, thing, or theme. Expository writing is often combined with description, narration, or argument.

Expressionism: An indistinct literary term, originally used to describe an early twentieth-century school of German painting. The term applies to almost any mode of unconventional, highly subjective writing that distorts reality in some way. Advocates of Expressionism include Federico Garcia Lorca, Eugene O'Neill, Franz Kafka, and James Joyce.

F

Fable: A prose or verse narrative intended to convey a moral. Animals or inanimate objects with human characteristics often serve as characters in fables. A famous fable is Aesop's "The Tortoise and the Hare."

Fantasy: A literary form related to mythology and folklore. Fantasy literature is typically set in non-existent realms and features supernatural beings. Notable examples of literature with elements of fantasy are Gabriel Garcia Marquez's story "The Handsomest Drowned Man in the World" and Ursula K. LeGuin's "The Ones Who Walk Away from Omelas."

Farce: A type of comedy characterized by broad humor, outlandish incidents, and often vulgar subject matter. Much of the comedy in film and television could more accurately be described as farce.

Fiction: Any story that is the product of imagination rather than a documentation of fact. Characters and events in such narratives may be based in real life but their ultimate form and configuration is a creation of the author.

Figurative Language: A technique in which an author uses figures of speech such as hyperbole, irony, metaphor, or simile for a particular effect. Figurative language is the opposite of literal language, in which every word is truthful, accurate, and free of exaggeration or embellishment.

Flashback: A device used in literature to present action that occurred before the beginning of the story. Flashbacks are often introduced as the dreams or recollections of one or more characters.

Foil: A character in a work of literature whose physical or psychological qualities contrast strongly with, and therefore highlight, the corresponding qualities of another character. In his Sherlock Holmes stories, Arthur Conan Doyle portrayed Dr. Watson as a man of normal habits and intelligence, making him a foil for the eccentric and unusually perceptive Sherlock Holmes.

Folklore: Traditions and myths preserved in a culture or group of people. Typically, these are passed on by word of mouth in various forms—such as legends, songs, and proverbs—or preserved in customs and ceremonies. Washington Irving, in "The Devil and Tom Walker" and many of his other stories, incorporates many elements of the folklore of New England and Germany.

Folktale: A story originating in oral tradition. Folktales fall into a variety of categories, including legends, ghost stories, fairy tales, fables, and anecdotes based on historical figures and events.

Foreshadowing: A device used in literature to create expectation or to set up an explanation of later developments. Edgar Allan Poe uses foreshadowing to create suspense in "The Fall of the House of Usher" when the narrator comments on the crumbling state of disrepair in which he finds the house.

G

Genre: A category of literary work. Genre may refer to both the content of a given work—tragedy, comedy, horror, science fiction—and to its form, such as poetry, novel, or drama.

Gilded Age: A period in American history during the 1870s and after characterized by political corruption and materialism. A number of important novels of social and political criticism were written during this time. Henry James and Kate Chopin are two writers who were prominent during the Gilded Age.

Gothicism: In literature, works characterized by a taste for medieval or morbid characters and situations. A gothic novel prominently features elements of horror, the supernatural, gloom, and violence: clanking chains, terror, ghosts, medieval castles, and unexplained phenomena. The term "gothic novel" is also applied to novels that lack elements of the traditional Gothic setting but that create a similar atmosphere of terror or dread. The term can also be applied to stories, plays, and poems. Mary Shelley's *Frankenstein* and Joyce Carol Oates's *Bellefleur* are both gothic novels.

Grotesque: In literature, a work that is characterized by exaggeration, deformity, freakishness, and disorder. The grotesque often includes an element of comic absurdity. Examples of the grotesque can be found in the works of Edgar Allan Poe, Flannery O'Connor, Joseph Heller, and Shirley Jackson.

H

Harlem Renaissance: The Harlem Renaissance of the 1920s is generally considered the first significant movement of black writers and artists in the United States. During this period, new and established black writers, many of whom lived in the region of New York City known as Harlem, published more fiction and poetry than ever before, the first influential black literary journals were established, and black authors and artists received their first widespread recognition and serious critical appraisal. Among the major writers associated with this period are Countee Cullen, Langston Hughes, Arna Bontemps, and Zora Neale Hurston.

Hero/Heroine: The principal sympathetic character in a literary work. Heroes and heroines typically exhibit admirable traits: idealism, courage, and integrity, for example. Famous heroes and heroines of literature include Charles Dickens's Oliver Twist, Margaret Mitchell's Scarlett O'Hara, and the anonymous narrator in Ralph Ellison's *Invisible Man.*

Hyperbole: Deliberate exaggeration used to achieve an effect. In William Shakespeare's *Macbeth,* Lady Macbeth hyperbolizes when she says, "All the perfumes of Arabia could not sweeten this little hand."

I

Image: A concrete representation of an object or sensory experience. Typically, such a representation helps evoke the feelings associated with the object or experience itself. Images are either "literal" or "figurative." Literal images are especially concrete and involve little or no extension of the obvious meaning of the words used to express them. Figurative images do not follow the literal meaning of the words exactly. Images in literature are usually visual, but the term "image" can also refer to the representation of any sensory experience.

Imagery: The array of images in a literary work. Also used to convey the author's overall use of figurative language in a work.

In medias res: A Latin term meaning "in the middle of things." It refers to the technique of beginning a story at its midpoint and then using various flashback devices to reveal previous action. This technique originated in such epics as Virgil's *Aeneid.*

Interior Monologue: A narrative technique in which characters' thoughts are revealed in a way that appears to be uncontrolled by the author. The interior monologue typically aims to reveal the inner self of a character. It portrays emotional experiences as they occur at both a conscious and unconscious level. One of the best-known interior monologues in English is the Molly Bloom section at the close of James Joyce's *Ulysses.* Katherine Anne Porter's "The Jilting of Granny Weatherall" is also told in the form of an interior monologue.

Irony: In literary criticism, the effect of language in which the intended meaning is the opposite of what is stated. The title of Jonathan Swift's "A Modest Proposal" is ironic because what Swift proposes in this essay is cannibalism—hardly "modest."

J

Jargon: Language that is used or understood only by a select group of people. Jargon may refer to terminology used in a certain profession, such as computer jargon, or it may refer to any nonsensical language that is not understood by most people. Anthony Burgess's *A Clockwork Orange* and James Thurber's "The Secret Life of Walter Mitty" both use jargon.

K

Knickerbocker Group: An indistinct group of New York writers of the first half of the nineteenth century. Members of the group were linked only by location and a common theme: New York life. Two famous members of the Knickerbocker Group were Washington Irving and William Cullen Bryant. The group's name derives from Irving's *Knickerbocker's History of New York.*

L

Literal Language: An author uses literal language when he or she writes without exaggerating or embellishing the subject matter and without any tools of figurative language. To say "He ran very quickly down the street" is to use literal language, whereas to say "He ran like a hare down the street" would be using figurative language.

Literature: Literature is broadly defined as any written or spoken material, but the term most often refers to creative works. Literature includes poetry, drama, fiction, and many kinds of nonfiction writing, as well as oral, dramatic, and broadcast compositions not necessarily preserved in a written format, such as films and television programs.

Lost Generation: A term first used by Gertrude Stein to describe the post-World War I generation of American writers: men and women haunted by a sense of betrayal and emptiness brought about by the destructiveness of the war. The term is commonly applied to Hart Crane, Ernest Hemingway, F. Scott Fitzgerald, and others.

M

Magic Realism: A form of literature that incorporates fantasy elements or supernatural occurrences into the narrative and accepts them as truth. Gabriel Garcia Marquez and Laura Esquivel are two writers known for their works of magic realism.

Metaphor: A figure of speech that expresses an idea through the image of another object. Metaphors suggest the essence of the first object by identifying it with certain qualities of the second object. An example is ''But soft, what light through yonder window breaks?/ It is the east, and Juliet is the sun'' in William Shakespeare's *Romeo and Juliet.* Here, Juliet, the first object, is identified with qualities of the second object, the sun.

Minimalism: A literary style characterized by spare, simple prose with few elaborations. In minimalism, the main theme of the work is often never discussed directly. Amy Hempel and Ernest Hemingway are two writers known for their works of minimalism.

Modernism: Modern literary practices. Also, the principles of a literary school that lasted from roughly the beginning of the twentieth century until the end of World War II. Modernism is defined by its rejection of the literary conventions of the nineteenth century and by its opposition to conventional morality, taste, traditions, and economic values. Many writers are associated with the concepts of modernism, including Albert Camus, D. H. Lawrence, Ernest Hemingway, William Faulkner, Eugene O'Neill, and James Joyce.

Monologue: A composition, written or oral, by a single individual. More specifically, a speech given by a single individual in a drama or other public entertainment. It has no set length, although it is usually several or more lines long. ''I Stand Here Ironing'' by Tillie Olsen is an example of a story written in the form of a monologue.

Mood: The prevailing emotions of a work or of the author in his or her creation of the work. The mood of a work is not always what might be expected based on its subject matter.

Motif: A theme, character type, image, metaphor, or other verbal element that recurs throughout a single work of literature or occurs in a number of different works over a period of time. For example, the color white in Herman Melville's *Moby Dick* is a ''specific'' *motif,* while the trials of star-crossed lovers is a ''conventional'' *motif* from the literature of all periods.

N

Narration: The telling of a series of events, real or invented. A narration may be either a simple narrative, in which the events are recounted chronologically, or a narrative with a plot, in which the account is given in a style reflecting the author's artistic concept of the story. Narration is sometimes used as a synonym for ''storyline.''

Narrative: A verse or prose accounting of an event or sequence of events, real or invented. The term is also used as an adjective in the sense ''method of narration.'' For example, in literary criticism, the expression ''narrative technique'' usually refers to the way the author structures and presents his or her story. Different narrative forms include diaries, travelogues, novels, ballads, epics, short stories, and other fictional forms.

Narrator: The teller of a story. The narrator may be the author or a character in the story through whom the author speaks. Huckleberry Finn is the narrator of Mark Twain's *The Adventures of Huckleberry Finn.*

Novella: An Italian term meaning ''story.'' This term has been especially used to describe fourteenth-century Italian tales, but it also refers to modern short novels. Modern novellas include Leo Tolstoy's *The Death of Ivan Ilich,* Fyodor Dostoyevsky's *Notes from the Underground,* and Joseph Conrad's *Heart of Darkness.*

O

Oedipus Complex: A son's romantic obsession with his mother. The phrase is derived from the story of the ancient Theban hero Oedipus, who unknowingly killed his father and married his mother, and was popularized by Sigmund Freud's theory of psychoanalysis. Literary occurrences of the Oedipus complex include Sophocles' *Oedipus Rex* and D. H. Lawrence's ''The Rocking-Horse Winner.''

Onomatopoeia: The use of words whose sounds express or suggest their meaning. In its simplest sense, onomatopoeia may be represented by words that mimic the sounds they denote such as ''hiss'' or ''meow.'' At a more subtle level, the pattern and rhythm of sounds and rhymes of a line or poem may be onomatopoeic.

Oral Tradition: A process by which songs, ballads, folklore, and other material are transmitted by word of mouth. The tradition of oral transmission predates the written record systems of literate society.

Oral transmission preserves material sometimes over generations, although often with variations. Memory plays a large part in the recitation and preservation of orally transmitted material. Native American myths and legends, and African folktales told by plantation slaves are examples of orally transmitted literature.

P

Parable: A story intended to teach a moral lesson or answer an ethical question. Examples of parables are the stories told by Jesus Christ in the New Testament, notably "The Prodigal Son," but parables also are used in Sufism, rabbinic literature, Hasidism, and Zen Buddhism. Isaac Bashevis Singer's story "Gimpel the Fool" exhibits characteristics of a parable.

Paradox: A statement that appears illogical or contradictory at first, but may actually point to an underlying truth. A literary example of a paradox is George Orwell's statement "All animals are equal, but some animals are more equal than others" in *Animal Farm.*

Parody: In literature, this term refers to an imitation of a serious literary work or the signature style of a particular author in a ridiculous manner. A typical parody adopts the style of the original and applies it to an inappropriate subject for humorous effect. Parody is a form of satire and could be considered the literary equivalent of a caricature or cartoon. Henry Fielding's *Shamela* is a parody of Samuel Richardson's *Pamela.*

Persona: A Latin term meaning "mask." Personae are the characters in a fictional work of literature. The persona generally functions as a mask through which the author tells a story in a voice other than his or her own. A persona is usually either a character in a story who acts as a narrator or an "implied author," a voice created by the author to act as the narrator for himself or herself. The persona in Charlotte Perkins Gilman's story "The Yellow Wallpaper" is the unnamed young mother experiencing a mental breakdown.

Personification: A figure of speech that gives human qualities to abstract ideas, animals, and inanimate objects. To say that "the sun is smiling" is to personify the sun.

Plot: The pattern of events in a narrative or drama. In its simplest sense, the plot guides the author in composing the work and helps the reader follow the work. Typically, plots exhibit causality and unity and have a beginning, a middle, and an end. Sometimes, however, a plot may consist of a series of disconnected events, in which case it is known as an "episodic plot."

Poetic Justice: An outcome in a literary work, not necessarily a poem, in which the good are rewarded and the evil are punished, especially in ways that particularly fit their virtues or crimes. For example, a murderer may himself be murdered, or a thief will find himself penniless.

Poetic License: Distortions of fact and literary convention made by a writer—not always a poet—for the sake of the effect gained. Poetic license is closely related to the concept of "artistic freedom." An author exercises poetic license by saying that a pile of money "reaches as high as a mountain" when the pile is actually only a foot or two high.

Point of View: The narrative perspective from which a literary work is presented to the reader. There are four traditional points of view. The "third person omniscient" gives the reader a "godlike" perspective, unrestricted by time or place, from which to see actions and look into the minds of characters. This allows the author to comment openly on characters and events in the work. The "third person" point of view presents the events of the story from outside of any single character's perception, much like the omniscient point of view, but the reader must understand the action as it takes place and without any special insight into characters' minds or motivations. The "first person" or "personal" point of view relates events as they are perceived by a single character. The main character "tells" the story and may offer opinions about the action and characters which differ from those of the author. Much less common than omniscient, third person, and first person is the "second person" point of view, wherein the author tells the story as if it is happening to the reader. James Thurber employs the omniscient point of view in his short story "The Secret Life of Walter Mitty." Ernest Hemingway's "A Clean, Well-Lighted Place" is a short story told from the third person point of view. Mark Twain's novel *Huckleberry Finn* is presented from the first person viewpoint. Jay McInerney's *Bright Lights, Big City* is an example of a novel which uses the second person point of view.

Pornography: Writing intended to provoke feelings of lust in the reader. Such works are often condemned by critics and teachers, but those which can be shown to have literary value are viewed less harshly. Literary works that have been described as pornographic include D. H. Lawrence's *Lady Chatterley's Lover* and James Joyce's *Ulysses.*

Post-Aesthetic Movement: An artistic response made by African Americans to the black aesthetic movement of the 1960s and early 1970s. Writers since that time have adopted a somewhat different tone in their work, with less emphasis placed on the disparity between black and white in the United States. In the words of post-aesthetic authors such as Toni Morrison, John Edgar Wideman, and Kristin Hunter, African Americans are portrayed as looking inward for answers to their own questions, rather than always looking to the outside world. Two well-known examples of works produced as part of the post-aesthetic movement are the Pulitzer Prize-winning novels *The Color Purple* by Alice Walker and *Beloved* by Toni Morrison.

Postmodernism: Writing from the 1960s forward characterized by experimentation and application of modernist elements, which include existentialism and alienation. Postmodernists have gone a step further in the rejection of tradition begun with the modernists by also rejecting traditional forms, preferring the anti-novel over the novel and the anti-hero over the hero. Postmodern writers include Thomas Pynchon, Margaret Drabble, and Gabriel Garcia Marquez.

Prologue: An introductory section of a literary work. It often contains information establishing the situation of the characters or presents information about the setting, time period, or action. In drama, the prologue is spoken by a chorus or by one of the principal characters.

Prose: A literary medium that attempts to mirror the language of everyday speech. It is distinguished from poetry by its use of unmetered, unrhymed language consisting of logically related sentences. Prose is usually grouped into paragraphs that form a cohesive whole such as an essay or a novel. The term is sometimes used to mean an author's general writing.

Protagonist: The central character of a story who serves as a focus for its themes and incidents and as the principal rationale for its development. The protagonist is sometimes referred to in discussions of modern literature as the hero or anti-hero. Well-known protagonists are Hamlet in William Shakespeare's *Hamlet* and Jay Gatsby in F. Scott Fitzgerald's *The Great Gatsby.*

R

Realism: A nineteenth-century European literary movement that sought to portray familiar characters, situations, and settings in a realistic manner. This was done primarily by using an objective narrative point of view and through the buildup of accurate detail. The standard for success of any realistic work depends on how faithfully it transfers common experience into fictional forms. The realistic method may be altered or extended, as in stream of consciousness writing, to record highly subjective experience. Contemporary authors who often write in a realistic way include Nadine Gordimer and Grace Paley.

Resolution: The portion of a story following the climax, in which the conflict is resolved. The resolution of Jane Austen's *Northanger Abbey* is neatly summed up in the following sentence: "Henry and Catherine were married, the bells rang and everybody smiled."

Rising Action: The part of a drama where the plot becomes increasingly complicated. Rising action leads up to the climax, or turning point, of a drama. The final "chase scene" of an action film is generally the rising action which culminates in the film's climax.

Roman a clef: A French phrase meaning "novel with a key." It refers to a narrative in which real persons are portrayed under fictitious names. Jack Kerouac, for example, portrayed various his friends under fictitious names in the novel *On the Road.* D. H. Lawrence based "The Rocking-Horse Winner" on a family he knew.

Romanticism: This term has two widely accepted meanings. In historical criticism, it refers to a European intellectual and artistic movement of the late eighteenth and early nineteenth centuries that sought greater freedom of personal expression than that allowed by the strict rules of literary form and logic of the eighteenth-century neoclassicists. The Romantics preferred emotional and imaginative expression to rational analysis. They considered the individual to be at the center of all experience and so placed him or her at the center of their art. The Romantics believed that the creative imagination reveals nobler truths—unique feelings and attitudes—than those that could be discovered by logic or by scientific examination. "Romanticism" is also used as a general term to refer to a type of sensibility found in all periods of literary history and usually considered to be in opposition to the principles of classicism. In this sense, Romanticism signifies any work or philosophy in which the exotic or dreamlike figure strongly, or that is devoted to individualistic expression, self-analysis, or a pursuit of a higher realm of knowledge than can be discovered by human reason. Prominent Romantics include Jean-Jacques Rousseau, William Wordsworth, John Keats, Lord Byron, and Johann Wolfgang von Goethe.

S

Satire: A work that uses ridicule, humor, and wit to criticize and provoke change in human nature and institutions. Voltaire's novella *Candide* and Jonathan Swift's essay "A Modest Proposal" are both satires. Flannery O'Connor's portrayal of the family in "A Good Man Is Hard to Find" is a satire of a modern, Southern, American family.

Science Fiction: A type of narrative based upon real or imagined scientific theories and technology. Science fiction is often peopled with alien creatures and set on other planets or in different dimensions. Popular writers of science fiction are Isaac Asimov, Karel Capek, Ray Bradbury, and Ursula K. Le Guin.

Setting: The time, place, and culture in which the action of a narrative takes place. The elements of setting may include geographic location, characters's physical and mental environments, prevailing cultural attitudes, or the historical time in which the action takes place.

Short Story: A fictional prose narrative shorter and more focused than a novella. The short story usually deals with a single episode and often a single character. The "tone," the author's attitude toward his or her subject and audience, is uniform throughout. The short story frequently also lacks *denouement*, ending instead at its climax.

Signifying Monkey: A popular trickster figure in black folklore, with hundreds of tales about this character documented since the 19th century. Henry Louis Gates Jr. examines the history of the signifying monkey in *The Signifying Monkey: Towards a Theory of Afro-American Literary Criticism,* published in 1988.

Simile: A comparison, usually using "like" or "as," of two essentially dissimilar things, as in "coffee as cold as ice" or "He sounded like a broken record." The title of Ernest Hemingway's "Hills Like White Elephants" contains a simile.

Social Realism: The Socialist Realism school of literary theory was proposed by Maxim Gorky and established as a dogma by the first Soviet Congress of Writers. It demanded adherence to a communist worldview in works of literature. Its doctrines required an objective viewpoint comprehensible to the working classes and themes of social struggle featuring strong proletarian heroes. Gabriel Garcia Marquez's stories exhibit some characteristics of Socialist Realism.

Stereotype: A stereotype was originally the name for a duplication made during the printing process; this led to its modern definition as a person or thing that is (or is assumed to be) the same as all others of its type. Common stereotypical characters include the absent-minded professor, the nagging wife, the troublemaking teenager, and the kindhearted grandmother.

Stream of Consciousness: A narrative technique for rendering the inward experience of a character. This technique is designed to give the impression of an ever-changing series of thoughts, emotions, images, and memories in the spontaneous and seemingly illogical order that they occur in life. The textbook example of stream of consciousness is the last section of James Joyce's *Ulysses.*

Structure: The form taken by a piece of literature. The structure may be made obvious for ease of understanding, as in nonfiction works, or may be obscured for artistic purposes, as in some poetry or seemingly "unstructured" prose.

Style: A writer's distinctive manner of arranging words to suit his or her ideas and purpose in writing. The unique imprint of the author's personality upon his or her writing, style is the product of an author's way of arranging ideas and his or her use of diction, different sentence structures, rhythm, figures of speech, rhetorical principles, and other elements of composition.

Suspense: A literary device in which the author maintains the audience's attention through the build-up of events, the outcome of which will soon be revealed. Suspense in William Shakespeare's *Hamlet* is sustained throughout by the question of whether or not the Prince will achieve what he has been instructed to do and of what he intends to do.

Symbol: Something that suggests or stands for something else without losing its original identity. In literature, symbols combine their literal meaning with the suggestion of an abstract concept. Literary symbols are of two types: those that carry complex associations of meaning no matter what their contexts, and those that derive their suggestive meaning from their functions in specific literary works. Examples of symbols are sunshine suggesting happiness, rain suggesting sorrow, and storm clouds suggesting despair.

T

Tale: A story told by a narrator with a simple plot and little character development. Tales are usually relatively short and often carry a simple message. Examples of tales can be found in the works of Saki, Anton Chekhov, Guy de Maupassant, and O. Henry.

Tall Tale: A humorous tale told in a straightforward, credible tone but relating absolutely impossible events or feats of the characters. Such tales were commonly told of frontier adventures during the settlement of the west in the United States. Literary use of tall tales can be found in Washington Irving's *History of New York,* Mark Twain's *Life on the Mississippi,* and in the German R. F. Raspe's *Baron Munchausen's Narratives of His Marvellous Travels and Campaigns in Russia.*

Theme: The main point of a work of literature. The term is used interchangeably with thesis. Many works have multiple themes. One of the themes of Nathaniel Hawthorne's "Young Goodman Brown" is loss of faith.

Tone: The author's attitude toward his or her audience may be deduced from the tone of the work. A formal tone may create distance or convey politeness, while an informal tone may encourage a friendly, intimate, or intrusive feeling in the reader. The author's attitude toward his or her subject matter may also be deduced from the tone of the words he or she uses in discussing it. The tone of John F. Kennedy's speech which included the appeal to "ask not what your country can do for you" was intended to instill feelings of camaraderie and national pride in listeners.

Tragedy: A drama in prose or poetry about a noble, courageous hero of excellent character who, because of some tragic character flaw, brings ruin upon him- or herself. Tragedy treats its subjects in a dignified and serious manner, using poetic language to help evoke pity and fear and bring about catharsis, a purging of these emotions. The tragic form was practiced extensively by the ancient Greeks. The classical form of tragedy was revived in the sixteenth century; it flourished especially on the Elizabethan stage. In modern times, dramatists have attempted to adapt the form to the needs of modern society by drawing their heroes from the ranks of ordinary men and women and defining the nobility of these heroes in terms of spirit rather than exalted social standing. Some contemporary works that are thought of as tragedies include *The Great Gatsby* by F. Scott Fitzgerald, and *The Sound and the Fury* by William Faulkner.

Tragic Flaw: In a tragedy, the quality within the hero or heroine which leads to his or her downfall. Examples of the tragic flaw include Othello's jealousy and Hamlet's indecisiveness, although most great tragedies defy such simple interpretation.

U

Utopia: A fictional perfect place, such as "paradise" or "heaven." An early literary utopia was described in Plato's *Republic,* and in modern literature, Ursula K. Le Guin depicts a utopia in "The Ones Who Walk Away from Omelas."

V

Victorian: Refers broadly to the reign of Queen Victoria of England (1837-1901) and to anything with qualities typical of that era. For example, the qualities of smug narrow-mindedness, bourgeois materialism, faith in social progress, and priggish morality are often considered Victorian. In literature, the Victorian Period was the great age of the English novel, and the latter part of the era saw the rise of movements such as decadence and symbolism.

Cumulative
Author/Title Index

Nationality/Ethnicity Index

Subject/Theme Index

Dream on Monkey Mountain:
223, 228, 232, 234, 236, 239
Fable: 246, 248-249, 260-261
Family Ties: 288, 294
The Farming of Bones: 312, 318
Fear: 324-325
The Garden of Forking Paths:
366-368, 382, 384-387, 390
The Handsomest Drowned Man:
431, 433
*I, Rigoberta Menchú: An Indian
Woman in Guatemala:* 470
Jasmine: 511-512, 515, 518,
522, 524
Nightmare
Breath, Eyes, Memory: 184-
185, 188
The Garden of Forking Paths:
373-379
North America
The Agüero Sisters: 2-4, 7-18
Among the Volcanoes: 30
Annie John: 39, 41, 44-48
Anthills of the Savannah: 90
An Astrologer's Day: 133-
134, 137
Bad Influence: 141, 144-154
Breath, Eyes, Memory: 184-
185, 188-203
Business: 209-211
Dream on Monkey Mountain:
222-224
Fable: 251-254
The Farming of Bones: 307-308,
312-315, 319
Fear: 327-329
The Friends: 346
Girl: 394, 397-399
The House of the Spirits: 461-462
Novel
The Agüero Sisters: 1-2, 6-
8, 14-15, 18
Among the Volcanoes: 21,
26-29, 34-36
Annie John: 41, 45, 47-48, 55-56
Anthills of the Savannah: 82,
87-89, 92-99
*Aphrodite: A Memoir of the
Senses:* 102, 112, 114
An Astrologer's Day: 122, 128-
129, 135-139
Breath, Eyes, Memory: 198-203
Family Ties: 272-273
The Farming of Bones:
308, 314-315
The Friends: 337, 342-350
The Garden of Forking Paths:
359-360, 370, 390-391
The Glass of Milk: 416-418
The Handsomest Drowned Man:
432-433
The House of the Spirits: 443-
444, 450-454

Jasmine: 495-498, 504-505, 508,
510-512, 515-518, 522-552
Nurturance
Annie John: 49, 51, 53, 58
Fear: 332-333
The Glass of Milk: 421, 423

O

Oedipus Complex
The Garden of Forking Paths:
373-376
Old Age
Anowa: 67-69, 75-80
Boesman and Lena: 160-161,
165, 177-178
Dream on Monkey Mountain: 226
Old Ways and New Ways
Among the Volcanoes: 28
Order and Disorder
*The Garden of Forking
Paths:* 360
Overcoming a History of Suffering
Anthills of the Savannah: 87

P

Painting
Annie John: 53-55
Paranormal
Dream on Monkey Mountain: 240
Patriarchy
The House of the Spirits: 455-457
Perception
Dream on Monkey Mountain:
227, 229-230, 235
Fable: 259-262
Family Ties: 267, 270-271,
276-278
The Friends: 338-339, 344, 346
The Garden of Forking Paths:
382, 384-386
Permanence
Anthills of the Savannah: 87-
88, 94-95, 99
The Farming of Bones: 314-315
Jasmine: 518
Persecution
Annie John: 57
Family Ties: 288-290
*I, Rigoberta Menchú: An Indian
Woman in Guatemala:* 473,
478-480, 485-486
Jasmine: 525-526
Personal Identity
Annie John: 38, 43-45, 48
Boesman and Lena: 174-176
Breath, Eyes, Memory: 197-201
Dream on Monkey Mountain:
218-220, 226-233, 236-238
Fable: 260, 262-264
Family Ties: 270-272
The Garden of Forking Paths:
384-387

The Handsomest Drowned Man:
439-440
*I, Rigoberta Menchú: An Indian
Woman in Guatemala:*
489, 491
Jasmine: 496, 502-504, 520-
523, 526-527
Personality Traits
Dream on Monkey Mountain: 236
*The Handsomest Drowned
Man:* 430
The House of the Spirits: 451
Jasmine: 502
Personification
*I, Rigoberta Menchú: An Indian
Woman in Guatemala:* 483
The Kiss of the Spider Woman:
544, 546-547
Phenomenology
Family Ties: 271
Philosophical Ideas
Fable: 249, 251
Family Ties: 267, 270-272,
276, 278
The Garden of Forking Paths:
357, 361-363, 372, 379-381,
385, 388-392
Jasmine: 507, 510, 521, 524
Pleasure
*Aphrodite: A Memoir of the
Senses:* 101, 103-104,
110-111, 115
Plot
The Agüero Sisters: 17, 19
An Astrologer's Day: 123,
127, 130
Boesman and Lena: 158,
160, 164-165
The Friends: 344, 346
The Garden of Forking Paths:
357, 361, 365, 388-392
Girl: 403-404
The House of the Spirits: 451
The Kiss of the Spider Woman:
542, 549-550
Poetry
Anthills of the Savannah: 95-97
Business: 206-207, 210-213
Dream on Monkey Mountain:
223-224
Fable: 246-265
Family Ties: 286-290, 293-304
Fear: 322-329, 333-334
Point of View
The Agüero Sisters: 8
Family Ties: 271-272, 278
Girl: 397-398
Political Idealism
*The Kiss of the Spider
Woman:* 534
Politicians
Anowa: 73-74